# ARGUMENT AND ANALYSIS:
# AN INTRODUCTION TO PHILOSOPHY

# ARGUMENT AND ANALYSIS:
# AN INTRODUCTION TO PHILOSOPHY

## Martin Curd
*Purdue University*

**WEST PUBLISHING COMPANY**

**St. Paul    New York    San Francisco    Los Angeles**

*Composition:* Northwestern Printcrafters
*Text Design:* Pollock Design Group
*Copyedit:* Deborah Cady
*Cover design:* Pollock Design Group
*Cover image: The Snail,* by Henri Matisse (1869-1954) Tate Gallery,
   London/Bridgeman Art Library, London. Copyright 1991
   Succession H. Matisse/ARS N.Y.


COPYRIGHT ©1992   By WEST PUBLISHING COMPANY
                  50 W. Kellogg Boulevard
                  P.O. Box 64526
                  St. Paul, MN 55164-0526

Printed in the United States of America

99  98  97  96  95  94  93  92       8  7  6  5  4  3  2  1  0

**Library of Congress Cataloging-in-Publication Data**

Curd, Martin.
   Argument and analysis : an introduction to philosophy / Martin
Curd. —
      p.   cm.
   Includes bibliographical references.
   ISBN 0-314-92208-3
   1. Philosophy—Introductions.   I. Title.
BD21.C87   1992
100—dc20

                                          91-31979
                                          CIP ⬭

*For Nick*

# CONTENTS

# PREFACE

This book is designed for the introductory philosophy courses that are taught at most colleges and universities across the country. After a survey of arguments in the book's introduction, Parts I through V are devoted to issues in five central areas of philosophy: the rationality of theistic belief, the foundations of ethics, the philosophy of mind, free will and determinism, and the problem of knowledge.

The selected readings in each part are followed by written discussions that explain key aspects of the readings and guide the student through the issues. Important arguments are isolated and analyzed at some length; central ideas and theories are presented and explained. Where it seems to me to be helpful and appropriate, the discussions introduce additional ideas, arguments, and objections that go beyond the readings. While the discussions strive to be balanced and fair, I do not hesitate to take definite positions and argue for them. In this way, students are given not only a study guide but also examples of the kind of philosophical reasoning they are being encouraged to engage in for themselves.

The discussions are fairly self-contained and divided into sections so that instructors may choose among and within them as they see fit. Many of the arguments are set apart and given names so that they can be referred to easily. Special philosophical terms are defined in the glossary at the end of the book.

This is very much a book designed to be used with an instructor. The writing in the discussions is sometimes terse and the reasoning compressed. There has been no attempt to do justice to the entire spectrum of opinion on the issues raised. My preference throughout has been to isolate what seem to me to be the central problems and arguments and to focus on them in some depth. Whenever an argument is discussed, I have tried to be reasonably precise about what its premises are and what its conclusion is and to be systematic in evaluating it.

In writing this book, I have benefited from the encouragement, advice, and criticism of many people. I appreciate the help and encouragement of Robert Jucha and the staff at West Educational Publishing. My colleagues at Purdue University deserve special thanks, especially Bill Rowe, Rod Bertolet, and Patricia Kenig Curd, for their advice and detailed criticisms. I am also grateful to the following people for their reviews of the manuscript and their many helpful suggestions: Nicholas J. Dixon (Alma College), Sandra Edwards (University of Arkansas), Joseph Ellin (Western Michigan University), Joyce Henricks (Central Michigan University), H. Scott Hestevold (University of Alabama at Tuscaloosa), Leslie Huntress Hopkins (College of Lake County), Edward Johnson (University of New Orleans), Edward W. Maine (California State University at Fullerton), Marcia McKelligan (DePauw University), Marshall Missner (University of Wisconsin—Oshkosh), Jon Moran (Southwest Missouri State University), David Morgan (Northern Iowa University), Steve Sapontzis (California State University at Hayward), Frederick F. Schmitt (University of Illinois at Urbana-Champaign), Mary Sirridge (Louisiana State University), James Stephens (Hillsdale College), Paul Tidman (Illinois State University), and Robert Trundle (Northern Kentucky University).

# INTRODUCTION

On a recent visit to Chicago I browsed through the section labeled "Philosophy" in a popular bookstore. The only philosophical works in the entire section were selections from Plato and Aristotle. The rest were mystical writings by Kahlil Gibran and books on astrology, yoga, and the occult. No wonder, then, that the public thinks that philosophers are given to uttering profound-sounding verbiage that no one can understand. In fact, most philosophers are sane, level-headed men and women who try to express themselves clearly and give persuasive reasons for what they believe. Doing philosophy requires not only imagination and the ability to handle abstract concepts but also sharp thinking and clear writing.

The Cambridge philosopher G. E. Moore (1873–1958) is reported to have responded to the question, What is philosophy? by pointing to the books on the shelves of his study and saying, "It is what all these are about."[1] Moore's response was evasive but understandable. It is difficult to even begin to explain what philosophy is until one has read some philosophers and studied some philosophical problems. (Imagine trying to explain the twelve-tone system of composition to someone who has never studied music or the plays of Samuel Beckett to someone who has neither read them nor seen them performed.)

Mark Woodhouse (who teaches philosophy at Georgia State University) offers the following definition of philosophy in his *A Preface to Philosophy*: "Philosophical problems involve questions about the meaning, truth, and logical connections of fundamental ideas that resist solution by the empirical sciences."[2] In this text (*Argument and Analysis*), we explore some of these questions about fundamental concepts that have vexed and fascinated philosophers through the centuries. Studying these problems and the attempts made to solve them will take us a long way towards answering the question, What is philosophy?

Many philosophical questions fall into one or more of three main areas in philosophy: metaphysics, ethics, and epistemology. Metaphysics (or ontology) tries to answer the questions, What basic kinds of thing exist? and How are they related? Ethics (or the theory of morality) asks, What makes actions right or wrong? and Which actions should we perform? Epistemology (or the theory of knowledge) addresses the questions, What is knowledge? and What kinds of knowledge do we have? The question of God's existence (explored in Part I of this book), the mind-body problem (Part III), the relation between freedom and determinism (Part IV), and the nature of causality (Part V) are all primarily metaphysical topics. Ethics is discussed in Part II, and some issues in epistemology are the focus of Part V.

Philosophy is characterized not only by the questions it asks but also by the way philosophers try to answer them. Philosophers use arguments to persuade us of the truth of their answers, and doing philosophy consists largely of inventing, analyzing, and criticizing these arguments. When philosophers want to prove that a claim is true, and thus rationally convince others of the truth of that claim, they give an argument for it; similarly, philosophers provide arguments when they wish to show that a claim is false. Because arguments play such a crucial role in philosophy, it is important to understand their basic features. For this reason, the remainder of this introduction is devoted to a survey of arguments and their analysis. Many of the terms and ideas explained in this survey are used in the discussions that accompany the readings.

## ARGUMENTS

When two people are having an argument, it usually means that they are having a heated disagreement, whether or not it involves any reasoning. This is *not* the sense of *argument* that interests us. When philosophers talk about arguments, they mean a set of statements (or propositions), one of which is the conclusion, the rest of which are the premises. The premises are intended to support the conclusion or give good reasons for thinking that the conclusion is true.

Here is a simple example of a philosophical argument for the conclusion that no human being has free will. It is called the Hard Determinist Argument. In Part IV, we will be exploring this and related arguments in detail. For the moment, we use it merely as an illustration.

### The Hard Determinist Argument

(1) If determinism is true, then no human being has free will.
(2) Determinism is true.

(3) No human being has free will.

Notice that we have presented the Hard Determinist Argument in a special way. First we have written down the premises; then we have drawn a line indicating that the statement that follows is the conclusion. In this example, the premises are statements (1) and (2), and the conclusion is statement (3). It is a good idea to set out all philosophical arguments in this way, since the first step towards analyzing and evaluating an argument is to decide what, exactly, are its premises and conclusion.

## VALIDITY

In the Hard Determinist Argument, the conclusion follows logically from the premises. It is an example of what logicians call a valid (or deductively valid) argument. Many of the philosophical arguments in this book are valid arguments, and so it is important to understand what this means. In a valid argument, the premises logically imply (or entail) the conclusion. In other words, *if* all the premises of a valid argument are true, *then* it must be the case that the conclusion is true, too. Here is another way of making the same point: In a valid argument, it is logically impossible for all its premises to be true and its conclusion false.

The kind of possibility involved in the definition of validity is logical possibility. If something involves no logical contradiction, then it is logically possible, even though it might violate one or more scientific laws. For example, it is logically possible that pigs have wings, that George Bush is twelve feet tall, and that the world was created five minutes ago. Throughout this introduction, the concept of possibility (and impossibility) used is that of logical possibility (and impossibility).

If the conclusion of an argument can be false even though all its premises are true, the argument is invalid. In an invalid argument, the conclusion does *not* follow logically from the premises.

How do we tell whether or not an argument is valid? Often this can be done by looking at the argument's form. Consider our example of the Hard Determinist Argument, which concludes that human beings lack free will. We can write out the argument's form as follows.

If P then Q
P
_____
Q

For historical reasons, which need not concern us, this valid form of argument is called *modus ponens*; any argument that has the form *modus ponens* is valid. Here is another example of a valid argument that follows the same pattern:

(1) If Jones is in Dallas, then Jones is in Texas.
(2) Jones is in Dallas.
_____
(3) Jones is in Texas.

Valid arguments can come in a variety of forms that differ from *modus ponens*. For example, the following argument is an instance of another valid pattern of reasoning often used by philosophers.

(1) If Jones is in Dallas, then Jones is in Texas.
(4) Jones is not in Texas.
_____
(5) Jones is not in Dallas.

Premises (1) and (4) together logically imply the conclusion (5). It is not logically possible for both premises of this argument to be true and its conclusion false. The general form of this type of valid argument is called *modus tollens*.

If P then Q
Not-Q
_____
Not-P

Here is another instance of the form *modus tollens*, which we discuss in Part III.

(1)  If minds are identical with brains, then minds can be spatially divided.
(2)  Minds cannot be spatially divided.
_____
(3)  Minds are not identical with brains.

How do we determine that an argument is invalid? One simple method is to see whether it is possible for all the premises of the argument to be true while at the same time its conclusion is false. If this is possible, then the conclusion does not follow logically from the premises, and thus the argument is invalid. Consider the following example:

(1)  All humans are mammals.
(2)  All humans use language.
_____
(3)  All mammals use language.

Here our task is easy. Although both premises are true, we know that, as a matter of fact, the conclusion is false. Many species of mammal (e.g., rats, shrews, raccoons) are not language users. So, the argument is invalid.

Here are two further examples of invalid arguments, but in these cases, *all* the statements in the arguments are true:

(1)  All presidents of the United States are human beings.
(2)  All men are human beings.
_____
(3)  All presidents of the United States are men.

(1)  If the Statue of Liberty is in Dallas, then the Statue of Liberty is in Texas.
(2)  The Statue of Liberty is not in Dallas.
_____
(3)  The Statue of Liberty is not in Texas.

Both of these arguments are invalid because it is possible for their conclusions to be false even though all their premises are true. In the first example, it is possible that some future president of the United States will be a woman, while it remains true that all presidents and all men are human beings. Similarly, although the Statue of Liberty is not in Dallas, it could be in Austin or in Abilene. In this way, we can imagine possible worlds in which the premises of the argument are true and yet the conclusion false.

These examples show that it is fallacious to conclude that an argument is valid simply because, as a matter of act, all the statements in it are true. The crucial issue is whether the conclusion follows logically from those premises, regardless of what their actual truth values are. If an argument is an instance of a valid form of argument, such as *modus ponens* or *modus tollens*, then it is valid. In a valid argument, it is not possible for all the premises to be true and the conclusion false. If it *is* possible for all the premises to be true and the conclusion false, then the argument is invalid.

## SOUNDNESS

Suppose someone proposes an argument and we recognize, correctly, that it is valid. We want to know whether the conclusion of that argument is true. As we have seen, all that we can deduce from the fact that an argument is valid is that *if* all the premises are true, *then* the conclusion must also be true. Thus, before we can infer that the conclusion is true, we need an additional piece of information. We need to know whether, as a matter of fact, all the premises are true.

An argument that is both valid and has all true premises is called a sound argument. Just as all arguments are either valid or invalid, all arguments are either sound or unsound.

The difference between validity and soundness is illustrated by the following four valid arguments, all of which have the same form:

$$\begin{array}{l} \text{All X's are Y's} \\ \text{All Y's are Z's} \\ \hline \text{All X's are Z's} \end{array}$$

| | |
|---|---|
| (F)  All cats are fish. | (F)  All dogs are cats. |
| (T)  All fish have gills. | (T)  All cats are mammals. |
| (F)  All cats have gills. | (T)  All dogs are mammals. |
| | |
| (F)  All cats are fish. | (F)  All fish are cats. |
| (F)  All fish are mammals. | (F)  All cats are dogs. |
| (T)  All cats are mammals. | (F)  All fish are cats. |

Although all these arguments are valid, none of them is sound, because each has at least one false premise. Here is a sound argument of the same form:

(T)  All cats are mammals.
(T)  All mammals have lungs.
(T)  All cats have lungs.

When evaluating the arguments given by philosophers, we will be asking two questions: Is this argument valid? and Is this argument sound? If we discover that an argument is invalid, we will know immediately that it is also unsound. On the other hand, if an argument is valid, we have to investigate its premises to see if all of them are true. Remember that an argument is sound only if it is valid and all its premises are true.

## PROOFS

The point of giving an argument is to convince us rationally that the argument's conclusion is true. An ideal argument, therefore, is one that proves its conclusion. Do all sound arguments prove their conclusions? To answer this question, we have to explore what we mean by the term *proof.*

Proof is what philosophers call an epistemological concept, since it concerns what we know or can know. (Epistemology is the traditional philosophical term for the theory of knowledge.) A proof is an argument that allows us to extend our knowledge from the premises to the conclusion. First we know that the premises are true; then we come to know that the conclusion is true by deducing the conclusion from those premises.

Thus, a sound argument is a proof only when it satisfies two further conditions: (1) we actually *know* that all the premises are true, and (2) it is possible to know that all the premises are true without first having to know that the conclusion is true. If we do not know that all the premises of a valid argument are true, the argument is not a proof, even if, unbeknownst to us, it is sound. Ignorance of the truth of any premise prevents an argument from being a proof. Similarly, a sound argument will fail to be a proof if the argument is circular. The most obvious kind of circularity arises when the conclusion simply repeats one of the premises or asserts something that is logically equivalent to one of the premises.

To illustrate the difference between a proof and a sound but circular argument, consider the following examples of arguments, all of which are valid (assume that all their premises are true):

Carter was the 39th president of the U.S.
Reagan was the next president after Carter.

Reagan was the 40th president of the U.S.

Reagan was the 40th president of the U.S.

Reagan was the 40th president of the U.S.

All the people on my list own dogs.
Sarah Gray is on my list.

Sarah Gray owns a dog.

The first of these arguments is a proof of its conclusion. Uncertain of whether Reagan was the fortieth president, I consulted my dictionary, which was published in 1980. It listed James Earl Carter, Jr., whose term of office began in 1977, as the thirty-ninth president. I knew that Reagan succeeded Carter; I thus deduced that Reagan was the fortieth president.

The second argument is circular and hence not a proof, since the conclusion repeats the single premise verbatim.

The third argument requires some explanation. Suppose that I have compiled a list of people by selecting names at random from the telephone directory. I then phone each person and discover that everyone on my list owns a dog. Sarah Gray is on my list; thus she, too, is a dog owner. The conclusion of this argument is not equivalent to either of the two premises. The argument is not circular in the same blatant fashion as the second argument about Reagan.

Furthermore, I can know that the second premise is true, that Sarah Gray is on my list, without first knowing that she owns a dog. But how could anyone know the first premise, that *all* the people on my list own dogs without first knowing that Sarah Gray is a dog owner? In this example, knowledge of the first premise seems to require prior knowledge of the conclusion. So, although the argument is sound, it does not prove its conclusion.

Finally, a reminder about the significance of showing that an argument is unsound or that it is not a proof. It is perfectly possible that the conclusion of an unsound argument or a failed proof is true, just as it is possible that the argument's conclusion is false. From the mere fact that someone has failed to show that a claim is true, we cannot conclude that the claim is false.

## *REDUCTIO AD ABSURDUM* REASONING

In several parts of this book there are important philosophical arguments that employ *reductio ad absurdum* reasoning. Here is a simple example to illustrate and explain the logic that underlies these arguments.

Suppose that someone claims that the single-celled bacterium *E. Coli* feels pain when exposed to strong acids or high temperatures. To refute this claim, I offer the following argument, which I shall call the Pain Argument. The purpose of the Pain Argument is to show that it is false that *E. Coli* can feel pain by deducing from the assumption that *E. Coli* can feel pain, a conclusion that is obviously false or "absurd."

**The Pain Argument**

(1) *E. Coli* can feel pain.
(2) If a creature can feel pain, then it must have a central nervous system.
(3) If a creature has a central nervous system, then it has more than one cell.

---

(4) *E. Coli* has more than one cell.

The Pain Argument is valid. Its form is very similar to *modus ponens*.

(1) P
(2) If P then Q
(3) If Q then R

---

(4) R

Since *E. Coli* is a single-celled organism, the conclusion of the Pain Argument is false. So, we have a valid argument with a false conclusion. In any valid argument, it is impossible for the conclusion to be false and all its premises true. At least one of the premises of the Pain Argument must therefore be false. Premises (2) and (3) are true. Therefore, premise (1) must be false: it is false that *E. Coli* can feel pain.

Understood in this way, *reductio* reasoning is really an argument about an argument. To refute a claim, we deliberately construct a target argument that has the following features:

1. The claim we wish to refute appears as the first premise.
2. The conclusion of the target argument is false.

3. The target argument is valid.
4. All the other premises of the target are true statements.

If we satisfy all four of these conditions, we can validly deduce that the first premise of the target argument is false.

In many philosophical examples of *reductio* reasoning, the conclusion of the target argument is not merely false but a logical contradiction. Though it makes no difference to the underlying logic, having a contradiction as the conclusion of the target argument has the following advantage: It removes any doubt that the conclusion is indeed false.

*Reductio* reasoning is not restricted to proving negative results. It can also be used to try to prove positive claims. For example, in the first reading in Part I, St. Anselm gives a famous *reductio* argument for God's existence. Anselm adopts as the first premise of his target argument the claim that God does not exist. He then tries to show that this is false (in other words, that God does exist) by deducing a contradiction as the conclusion of the target argument.

## INDUCTIVE ARGUMENTS

Though they are rare in philosophy, inductive arguments abound in everyday life and in the empirical sciences. A physicist who infers that a theory is probably true because it successfully predicts the outcome of an experiment is using inductive reasoning. Similarly, when a statistician draws a conclusion about the entire population of Americans from information obtained from a random sample, that, too, is an inductive inference. In both cases, there is a chance that the conclusion might be false even though all the premises are true: the scientist's theory may be false even though its predictions are correct, and the entire population of Americans might differ significantly from the people examined in the sample.

A good inductive argument is one that, although it is deductively invalid (since it is possible for its conclusion to be false even when all its premises are true), confers a high probability on its conclusion when all its premises are true.[3] How do we estimate this probability? We can make some progress towards an answer by considering how a detective would go about the business of solving a crime, say a death by poisoning.

When a man dies of poison, there are three alternatives: either (1) the death was an accident (no one was responsible), or (2) the victim killed himself (suicide), or (3) the victim was killed by someone else (murder). If the victim was murdered, then one or more people killed him. The detective proceeds by collecting evidence and testing various hypotheses. When the investigation is complete and the detective has reached a definite conclusion, she presents that conclusion in the form of an inductive argument. The premises of the argument state the evidence. The conclusion identifies the murderer or murderers (if any).

We can imagine the various possible alternative solutions to the crime as competing hypotheses about the cause (accident, suicide, murder) of an observed effect (the poisoned victim). Eventually, the detective decides on the basis of the evidence that one of these hypotheses is more credible than any of the others. This decision rests on answers to two questions: How plausible is each hypothesis considered by itself? and How well does each hypothesis explain the evidence? In the conclusion of her inductive argument, the detective tries to identify the most likely cause of the observed effect, taking into account the available evidence.

Let us now consider a philosophical example of an inductive argument, namely, the design argument for God's existence given by the British theologian and philosopher William Paley (1743–1805) in his *Natural Theology* (1802).[4] Paley noted that animals and plants (and their various organs) resemble machines, since they are highly organized and adapted to perform specific functions. For example, just as a watch is an intricate arrangement of many interrelated parts for telling the time, the human eye is an intricate arrangement of many interrelated parts for seeing. We know that watches and other machines are the result of intelligent design. Thus, Paley concluded, it is likely that animals and plants are also the result of intelligent design. Watches are designed by humans; living creatures by God. We can set out Paley's reasoning as an inductive argument from analogy.

**Paley's Design Argument**
(1) Living organisms resemble machines.
(2) Machines are the result of intelligent design.

--------

(3) Living organisms are probably the result of intelligent design.

Just like the detective, Paley is reasoning from an effect (the intricate adaptation of biological systems) to what he thinks is the most likely cause that could have produced that effect (intelligent design). Before we evaluate this argument, notice that Paley's conclusion is quite modest. Paley does not conclude that the single god of traditional Christianity created the entire universe out of nothing; rather, his conclusion is merely that one important feature of some parts of the universe (the complex adaptation of living organisms) has been caused by an intelligent, supernatural designer.

During the nineteenth century, many people found Paley's argument persuasive. Why? Because it was difficult for them to imagine any other plausible explanation for the high degree of adaptation observed in living organisms. Prior to Charles Darwin (1809–1882), there were logically possible alternatives to the design hypothesis, but none of them was very plausible. For example, it is logically possible that living organisms could have arisen by natural forces acting on inanimate matter in an entirely random fashion. But it is highly improbable that such a haphazard process could ever produce an object as intricate as the human eye, even if it had several hundred million years to operate. Throw the right mix of molecules into a vat and stir, and stir, and stir. There is no real chance that anything as complicated as a mouse, or a human eye, will ever emerge from the stew. Like watches and clocks, plants and animals seems to bear within their frame the indelible stamp of an intelligent creator who designed them.

The situation changed radically in 1859 when Charles Darwin published *On the Origin of Species*, for Darwin gave a plausible hypothesis that can explain complex adaptation without requiring an intelligent designer.[5] The heart of Darwin's theory is natural selection. Random mutations occur in the genes of all organisms. If an organism survives and reproduces, it transmits its new genetic blueprint to its offspring. Some genetic changes are lethal, and very few are beneficial; but occasionally mutations arise that give an organism a small advantage over its competitors. In such cases, the favored organism is likely to be more successful at breeding and thus produce more offspring than its rivals. Over thousands and millions of years, the gradual accumulation of these small changes can give rise to intricate structures and adaptations.

I conclude by making three brief points.

1. Although the genetic variations on which natural selection works are generated at random, natural selection itself is not a random process.[6] Natural selection may be blind (because it is not directed by an intelligent mind) but it is selective. Even small variations among members of a species can make a difference to the number of offspring that a particular organism will contribute to the next generation.

2. Darwin's theory makes a large number of testable predictions, many of which have been verified by observation. Thus, natural selection is not just a logically possible mechanism, it is one that has considerable empirical support.[7] It is a plausible hypothesis.

3. In many respects, Darwin's theory is a better explainer than the design hypothesis. As Darwin himself emphasized, his theory explains many features, such as the distribution of species in time and space, anatomical similarities between present-day species, and the presence of rudimentary organs (such as the human appendix) that have no adaptive function. These features are inexplicable on the design hypothesis.

Because Darwin's theory is a plausible hypothesis that explains the evidence better than the hypothesis of intelligent design, we conclude that Paley's inductive argument from analogy is rather weak. Though plants and animals do resemble machines in certain respects, it is unlikely that their adaptations are the work of a supernatural designer.

## NOTES

1. A. Flew, *A Dictionary of Philosophy*, revised 2nd edition (New York: St. Martin's Press, 1984), Preface, p. vii. Moore gives a more traditional answer in Chapter 1 of *Some Main Problems of Philosophy* (London: George Allen & Unwin, 1953).

2. M. B. Woodhouse, *A Preface to Philosophy*, 4th edition (Belmont, CA: Wadsworth, 1990): 2.

3. Although we rely on inductive reasoning all the time, some philosophers have questioned whether belief in the premises of an inductive argument ever justifies belief in its conclusion, even when we know that all its premises are true. The eighteenth-century philosopher David Hume argued for skepticism concerning the legitimacy of induction in his books *A Treatise of Human Nature* (1739–1740) and *An Enquiry Concerning Human Understanding* (1748). Hume's arguments are presented and discussed in Part V of this text.

4. For other versions of the design argument, see R. G. Swinburne, *The Existence of God* (Oxford: Oxford University Press, 1979), Chapter 8; and J. L. Mackie, *The Miracle of Theism* (Oxford: Oxford University Press, 1982), Chapter 8. Swinburne defends, and Mackie attacks, a version of the design argument similar to Aquinas's Fifth Way.

5. The French evolutionist Jean Baptiste Lamarck (1744–1829) had also tried to solve the problem of adaptation without appealing to a supernatural designer. Lamarck hypothesized an inner force in all living things that guides them to adapt to changing external circumstances. There is no such guiding force in Darwin's theory.

6. This is emphasized in R. Dawkins, *The Blind Watchmaker* (New York: Norton, 1986). Dawkins's title is an implicit reference to Paley.

7. See, for example, M. Ruse, *Darwinism Defended* (Reading, MA: Addison-Wesley, 1982).

# PART I

# THE RATIONALITY OF
# RELIGIOUS BELIEF

The readings and discussions in Part I explore three main questions: Has the existence of God been proven? Are there any proofs that God does not exist? Is theistic belief irrational in the absence of proof?

Some important arguments for God's existence can be divided into three types: ontological, cosmological, and teleological.[1] Arguments of the first two types (ontological and cosmological) are intended to be proofs, since they are presented as being valid deductive arguments from premises all of which are known to be true. The third group (teleological arguments) do not pretend to be deductively valid arguments. Rather, they are put forward as inductive arguments from true premises. Because many teleological arguments assert that living things, or the universe as a whole, are the result of intelligent design, they are often called design arguments. One historically important teleological argument—Paley's design argument—was discussed in the general introduction to this book.

The major difference between ontological and cosmological arguments lies in the epistemological status of the premises of these arguments. Proponents of the ontological argument claim that all its premises are known to be true *a priori,* and for that reason, the ontological argument is often said to be an *a priori* argument.

A statement is knowable *a priori* if it can be known to be true (or false) independently of experience, simply by understanding it, reflecting on it, and

1

using one's reason. The clearest examples of *a priori* statements are the ones that philosophers call analytic. Analytic statements include tautologies and contradictions. A tautology is any statement that is true solely by virtue of its logical form. For example, if someone asserts "Either God exists or God does not exist," the assertion must be true, regardless of whether God exists or not. In fact, any statement of the form "Either P or not-P" is a tautology: it is logically impossible for any statement of that form to be false. Similarly, any statement of the form "P and not-P" is a contradiction: it must be false no matter what proposition we substitute for "P".

Tautologies are not the only analytic truths. There are also statements such as "All husbands are married" and "Parallel lines never intersect." Unlike tautologies, these statements are not true solely by virtue of their logical form. But, like tautologies, they cannot be false. What guarantees their truth is the meaning of the words used to express them. They are true by definition. Given that "husband" means "married male," all husbands must be married. Similarly, given that "parallel" means "never intersecting," parallel lines cannot intersect.

Statements that are not analytic are called synthetic. For example, "Ninety percent of all men are married" is a synthetic statement. Even though we understand perfectly what it means, that alone does not tell us if it is true.

Statements that cannot be known *a priori* are called *a posteriori*, or empirical. To know that these statements are true, some experience is necessary: either one's own experience, such as seeing for oneself, or information about the world obtained from someone else's experience.[2] Unlike the ontological argument, all versions of the cosmological and design arguments include at least one empirical premise.

One of the most ingenious attempts to prove God's existence without appealing to any empirical statements is the ontological argument invented by Saint Anselm (Reading 1). In his *Proslogium*, Anselm argues that once we understand what kind of thing God is, we cannot deny God's existence without contradicting ourselves. According to Anselm, God should be understood as "that (thing) than which nothing greater can be conceived." Anselm claims that from this definition and other premises, all of which are known to be true *a priori*, we can deduce that God exists.

Important versions of the cosmological argument are given in the selections from Saint Thomas Aquinas (Reading 2) and Samuel Clarke (Reading 3). Among the premises of their arguments, both Aquinas and Clarke include a statement about the universe that is empirical. For example, in his first argument (called "The First Way"), Aquinas makes the empirical assertion that things are in motion. Similarly, Clarke relies on the empirical premise that something (rather than nothing) now exists. Aquinas and Clarke then argue to God's existence as the ultimate cause or reason that the universe is as we find it.

The Scottish philosopher David Hume was a famous critic of attempts to prove God's existence. In Part IX of his *Dialogues Concerning Natural Religion* (Reading 4), Hume attacks Clarke's version of the cosmological argument. While Hume agrees with Clarke that everything has an explanation, Hume denies that this principle allows us to deduce the existence of God from the existence of the universe.[3]

Showing that an argument fails to prove its conclusion does not, by itself, establish that its conclusion is false. Revealing the flaws in an argument for the existence of black holes, for example, does not prove that black holes do *not* exist. Even if none of the arguments for God's existence succeeds as a proof, that does not show that there is no God. If philosophers want to support atheism, they have to provide arguments for the conclusion that God does not exist.

In his paper "Evil and Omnipotence" (Reading 5), John Mackie gives a version of the most popular argument for atheism, namely, the argument from evil. Mackie argues that if we accept the traditional concept of God as being omnipotent (all-powerful), omniscient (all-knowing), and omnibenevolent (wholly good), then it is logically impossible that God would permit the existence of evil in the world. Since the world clearly does contain evil, Mackie concludes that God does not exist. Mackie discusses various ways in which theists have tried to avoid this conclusion and argues that all of them are unsuccessful.

Many people believe that God's existence can be neither proven or disproven. If this is so, can religious belief be rational in the absence of proof? In "The Wager" (Reading 6), Blaise Pascal argues that in the absence of any proofs either for theism or for atheism, rationality requires that one believe that God exists. Pascal reasons that because religion offers an infinite reward, it would be irrational not to accept the wager that God exists.

In the nineteenth century, William Clifford and William James took opposite sides on the issue of the ethics of belief. Clifford (Reading 7) insisted that when there is no evidence either for or against a proposition, we have a moral obligation to suspend our belief. In other words, Clifford maintained that in the absence of evidence, agnosticism is a moral duty. William James disagreed. In his influential paper, "The Will to Believe" (Reading 8), James argues that even when evidence is entirely lacking it is not wrong to believe as long as certain conditions are satisfied. According to James, the religious hypothesis satisfies those conditions, and thus it is legitimate for us to believe in God despite the lack of evidence.

Perhaps the most common reason given by nonphilosophers for believing in God involves an appeal to religious experience. People in many different religious traditions have reported mystic states in which they seem to be aware of God's presence. C. D. Broad (Reading 9) argues that such religious experiences can provide a rational basis for theistic belief, not only for the persons who have the experiences but also for those who hear reports of them. In "Visions" (Reading 10), Alasdair MacIntyre takes a more skeptical view. MacIntyre insists that we should judge religious experiences by the same standards that we use to evaluate other kinds of perceptual experience. But, he argues, if someone seems to see or hear X, that experience is evidence for the existence of X only if we have positive reasons for thinking that the experience was caused by X. MacIntyre concludes that religious experiences fail to meet this condition.

---

## NOTES

1. This classification was first given by the eighteenth-century German philosopher, Immanuel Kant, in his *Critique of Pure Reason* (1771). (See Chapter III, Section 3, of the Transcendental Dialectic; p. 500 in Kemp Smith's translation of the *Critique*.) Kant's term for teleological arguments was *physico-theological*. Unlike most modern authors, Kant included in this category all arguments beginning from some specific feature of the world (such as motion,

change, adaptation of plants and animals), reserving the term *cosmological* exclusively for those arguments that, like those of Clarke and Leibniz, start from the existence of the world in general. Contrary to the approach taken in this book, Kant would thus have regarded all five of the Five Ways of Aquinas as physico-theological arguments.

2. Everyone agrees that all analytic statements are *a priori*. But philosophers disagree about whether some synthetic truths can also be known *a priori*. In part, the debate depends on how broadly one construes the notion of an analytic statement. If analytic truths are restricted solely to statements that either are tautologies or can be reduced to tautologies by explicit definitions, there do seem to be statements that are not analytic but that can be known to be true simply by understanding them and reflecting on them. For example, most people who understand the statement "Nothing can be red all over and green all over at the same time" see that the statement must be true even though it is not reducible to a tautology.

3. Although Clarke's cosmological argument relies on at least one empirical premise, Hume calls it *a priori*. This is because Clarke believed that his other main premise—the principle of sufficient reason, the principle that everything has a reason or cause—is an *a priori* truth. Hume argued that Clarke was mistaken about this and that the principle of sufficient reason is based solely on experience.

**READING 1**

# The Ontological Argument
*Saint Anselm*

*Born in Italy, Saint Anselm (1033–1109) was the leading religious intellectual of his day. Anselm belonged to the Benedictine order and for fifteen years was abbot of the monastery of Bec in Normandy which, at that time, was one of the foremost centers of learning in Europe. In 1093 he was appointed Archbishop of Canterbury. Anselm's writings include works on truth, free will, and universals, but he is best known for his contributions to theology and philosophy of religion. In his* Monologium *(1076), Anselm gives several cosmological arguments for God's existence. In the preface to his* Proslogium *(1077–1078), Anselm reports that after much strenuous thinking, he has discovered a single, self-contained argument that demonstrates the existence of God.*

## CHAPTER II.
Truly there is a God, although the fool hath said in his heart, There is no God.

And so, Lord, do thou, who dost give understanding to faith, give me, so far as thou knowest it to be profitable, to understand that thou art as we believe; and that thou art that which we believe. And, indeed, we believe that thou art a being than which nothing greater can be conceived. Or is there no such nature, since the fool hath said in his heart, there is no God? (Psalms xiv. 1). But, at any rate, this very fool, when he hears of this being of which I speak—a being than which nothing greater can be conceived—understands what he hears, and what he understands is in his understanding; although he does not understand it to exist.

For, it is one thing for an object to be in the understanding, and another to understand that the object exists. When a painter first conceives of what he will afterwards perform, he has it in his understand-

**SOURCE:** From *Proslogium* (1077–1078), Chapters II–V. Reprinted from *Saint Anselm: Basic Writings*, trans. S. N. Deane (La Salle, IL: Open Court, 1962): 7–11.

ing, but he does not yet understand it to be, because he has not yet performed it. But after he has made the painting, he both has it in his understanding, and he understands that it exists, because he has made it.

Hence, even the fool is convinced that something exists in the understanding, at least, than which nothing greater can be conceived. For, when he hears of this, he understands it. And whatever is understood, exists in the understanding. And assuredly that, than which nothing greater can be conceived, cannot exist in the understanding alone: then it can be conceived to exist in reality; which is greater.

Therefore, if that, than which nothing greater can be conceived, exists in the understanding alone, the very being, than which nothing greater can be conceived, is one, than which a greater can be conceived. But obviously this is impossible. Hence, there is no doubt that there exists a being, than which nothing greater can be conceived, and it exists both in the understanding and in reality.

## CHAPTER III.
God cannot be conceived not to exist.—God is that, than which nothing greater can be conceived.—That which can be conceived not to exist is not God.

And it assuredly exists so truly, that it cannot be conceived not to exist. For, it is possible to conceive of a being which cannot be conceived not to exist; and this is greater than one which can be conceived not to exist. Hence, if that, than which nothing greater can be conceived, can be conceived not to exist, it is not that, than which nothing greater can be conceived. But this is an irreconcilable contradiction. There is, then, so truly a being than which nothing greater can be conceived to exist, that it cannot even be conceived not to exist; and this being thou art, O Lord, our God.

So truly, therefore, dost thou exist, O Lord, my God, that thou canst not be conceived not to exist; and rightly. For, if a mind could conceive of a being better than thee, the creature would rise above the Creator; and this is most absurd. And, indeed, whatever else there is, except thee alone, can be conceived not to exist. To thee alone, therefore, it belongs to exist more truly than all other beings, and hence in a higher degree than all others. For, whatever else exists does not exist so truly, and hence in a less degree it belongs to it to exist. Why, then, has the fool said in his heart, there is no God (Psalms xiv. 1), since it is so evident, to a rational mind, that thou dost exist in the highest degree of all? Why, except that he is dull and a fool?

### CHAPTER IV.
How the fool has said in his heart what cannot be conceived—A thing may be conceived in two ways: (1) when the word signifying it is conceived; (2) when the thing itself is understood. As far as the word goes, God can be conceived not to exist; in reality he cannot.

But how has the fool said in his heart what he could not conceive; or how is it that he could not conceive what he said in his heart? since it is the same to say in the heart, and to conceive.

But, if really, nay, since really, he both conceived, because he said in his heart; and did not say in his heart, because he could not conceive; there is more than one way in which a thing is said in the heart or conceived. For, in one sense, an object is conceived, when the word signifying it is conceived; and in another, when the very entity, which the object is, is understood.

In the former sense, then, God can be conceived not to exist; but in the latter, not at all. For no one who understands what fire and water are can conceive fire to be water, in accordance with the nature of the facts themselves, although this is possible according to the words. So, then, no one who understands what God is can conceive that God does not exist; although he says these words in his heart, either without any, or with some foreign, signification. For, God is that than which a greater cannot be conceived. And he who thoroughly understands this, assuredly understands that this being so truly exists, that not even in concept can it be non-existent. Therefore, he who understands that God so exists, cannot conceive that he does not exist.

I thank thee, gracious Lord, I thank thee; because what I formerly believed by thy bounty, I now so understand by thine illumination, that if I were unwilling to believe that thou dost exist, I should not be able not to understand this to be true.

### CHAPTER V.
God is whatever it is better to be than not to be; and he, as the only self-existent being, creates all things from nothing.

What art thou, then, Lord God, than whom nothing greater can be conceived? But what art thou, except that which, as the highest of all beings, alone exists through itself, and creates all other things from nothing? For, whatever is not this is less than a thing which can be conceived of. But this cannot be conceived of thee. What good, therefore, does the supreme Good lack, through which every good is? Therefore, thou art just, truthful, blessed, and whatever it is better to be than not to be. For it is better to be just than not just; better to be blessed than not blessed.

# READING 2

---

# The Five Ways
*Saint Thomas Aquinas*

*Saint Thomas Aquinas (1225–1274) is widely regarded as the greatest philosopher and theologian of the medieval period. Born in Italy, Aquinas joined the Dominican order and studied at the universities of Naples, Paris, and Rome. Aquinas wrote many works attempting to reconcile Aristotelian philosophy with Christian theology. In his influential masterpiece, the* Summa Theologica *(c. 1265–1273), Aquinas gives five ways for proving that God exists based on Aristotelian principles. In 1879, Pope Leo XIII recognized Thomism (the philosophical system of Aquinas) as the official doctrine of the Roman Catholic Church.*

The existence of God can be proved in five ways.

The first and more manifest way is the argument from motion. It is certain, and evident to our senses, that in the world some things are in motion. Now whatever is moved is moved by another, for nothing can be moved except it is in potentiality to that towards which it is moved; whereas a thing moves inasmuch as it is in act. For motion is nothing else than the reduction of something from potentiality to actuality. But nothing can be reduced from potentiality to actuality, except by something in a state of actuality. Thus that which is actually hot, as fire, makes wood, which is potentially hot, to be actually hot, and thereby moves and changes it. Now it is not possible that the same thing should be at once in actuality and potentiality in the same respect, but only in different respects. For what is actually hot cannot simultaneously be potentially hot; but it is simultaneously potentially cold. It is therefore impossible that in the same respect and in the same way a thing should be both mover and moved, *i.e.*, that it

**SOURCE:** From *Summa Theologica* (c. 1265–1273), Part I, Question 2, Article 3. "Whether God Exists?" Reprinted from *The Basic Writings of Saint Thomas Aquinas*, ed. A. C. Pegis (New York: Random House, 1945): 22–23.

should move itself. Therefore, whatever is moved must be moved by another. If that by which it is moved be itself moved, then this also must needs be moved by another, and that by another again. But this cannot go on to infinity, because then there would be no first mover, and, consequently, no other mover, seeing that subsequent movers move only inasmuch as they are moved by the first mover; as the staff moves only because it is moved by the hand. Therefore it is necessary to arrive at a first mover, moved by no other; and this everyone understands to be God.

The second way is from the nature of efficient cause. In the world of sensible things we find there is an order of efficient causes. There is no case known (neither is it, indeed, possible) in which a thing is found to be the efficient cause of itself; for so it would be prior to itself, which is impossible. Now in efficient causes it is not possible to go on to infinity, because in all efficient causes following in order, the first is the cause of the intermediate cause, and the intermediate is the cause of the ultimate cause, whether the intermediate cause be several, or one only. Now to take away the cause is to take away the effect. Therefore, if there be no first cause among efficient causes, there will be no ultimate, nor any intermediate, cause. But if in efficient causes it is possible to go on to infinity, there will be no first efficient cause, neither will there be an ultimate effect, nor any intermediate efficient causes; all of which is plainly false. Therefore it is necessary to admit a first efficient cause, to which everyone gives the name of God.

The third way is taken from possibility and necessity, and runs thus. We find in nature things that are possible to be and not to be, since they are found to be generated, and to be corrupted, and consequently, it is possible for them to be and not to be.

But it is impossible for these always to exist, for that which can not-be at some time is not. Therefore, if everything can not-be, then at one time there was nothing in existence. Now if this were true, even now there would be nothing in existence, because that which does not exist begins to exist only through something already existing. Therefore, if at one time nothing was in existence, it would have been impossible for anything to have begun to exist; and thus even now nothing would be in existence—which is absurd. Therefore, not all beings are merely possible, but there must exist something the existence of which is necessary. But every necessary thing either has it necessity caused by another, or not. Now it is impossible to go on to infinity in necessary things which have their necessity caused by another, as has been already proved in regard to efficient causes. Therefore we cannot but admit the existence of some being having of itself its own necessity, and not receiving it from another, but rather causing in others their necessity. This all men speak of as God.

The fourth way is taken from the gradation to be found in things. Among beings there are some more and some less good, true, noble, and the like. But *more* and *less* are predicated of different things according as they resemble in their different ways something which is the maximum, as a thing is said to be hotter according as it more nearly resembles that which is hottest; so that there is something which is truest, something best, something noblest, and, consequently, something which is most being, for those things that are greatest in truth are greatest in being, as it is written in *Metaph.* ii.[1] Now the maximum in any genus is the cause of all in that genus, as fire, which is the maximum of heat, is the cause of all hot things, as is said in the same book.[2] Therefore there must also be something which is to all beings the cause of their being, goodness, and every other perfection; and this we call God.

The fifth way is taken from the governance of the world. We see that things which lack knowledge, such as natural bodies, act for an end, and this is evident from their acting always, or nearly always, in the same way, so as to obtain the best result. Hence it is plain that they achieve their end, nor fortuitously, but designedly. Now whatever lacks knowledge cannot move towards an end, unless it be directed by some being endowed with knowledge and intelligence; as the arrow is directed by the archer. Therefore some intelligent being exists by whom all natural things are directed to their end; and this being we call God.

## NOTES

1. [Ed. This is a reference to Aristotle's *Metaphysics* Book II (a) 993$^b$ 30.]

2. [*Metaphysics* Book II (a) 993$^b$ 25.]

# READING 3

# A Modern Version of the Cosmological Argument

*Samuel Clarke*

*Samuel Clarke (1675–1729) was an English theologian, philosopher, and close friend of Isaac Newton. Clarke's version of the cosmological argument is taken from his Boyle lectures,* A Demonstration of the Being and Attributes of God, *delivered at St. Paul's Cathedral in London in 1704. The Boyle lectures were an annual series of eight sermons endowed by the chemist Robert Boyle for the purpose of proving the truth of the Christian religion.*

## SECTIONS I AND II.

I. First then, it is absolutely and undeniably certain that *something has existed from all eternity.* This is so evident and undeniable a proposition that no atheist in any age has ever presumed to assert the contrary; and therefore there is little need of being particular in the proof of it. For since something now is, 'tis evident that something always was: otherwise the things that now are must have risen out of nothing, absolutely and without cause: which is a flat contradiction in terms. For to say a thing is *produced* and yet that there is no *cause* at all of the production, is to say that something is *effected* when it is *effected by nothing;* that is, at the same time when it is *not effected at all.* Whatever exists has a cause of its existence, either in the necessity of its own nature, and then it must have been eternal: or in the will of some other being; and then that other being must, at least in the order of nature and causality, have existed before it. . . .

II. *There has existed from eternity some one unchangeable and independent being.* For since something must needs have been from eternity; as has been already proved, and is granted on all hands: either there has always existed some one unchangeable and *independent* being, from which all other beings that are or

**SOURCE:** From *A Demonstration of the Being and Attributes of God* (London, 1705). Propositions I and II: 18–19, 23–26. Edited.

ever were in the universe have received their original; or else there has been an infinite succession of changeable and *dependent* beings, produced one from another in an endless progression, without any original cause at all: which latter supposition is so very absurd, that tho' all atheism must in its account of most things (as shall be shown hereafter) terminate in it, yet I think very few atheists ever were so weak as openly and directly to defend it. For it is plainly impossible and contradictory to itself. I shall not argue against it from the supposed impossibility of infinite succession, *barely and absolutely considered in itself;* for a reason which shall be mentioned hereafter: but, if we consider such an infinite progression as *one* entire endless *series* of *dependent* beings; 'tis plain this whole *series* of beings can have no cause *from without* of its existence; because in it are supposed to be included *all things* that are or ever were in the universe: and 'tis plain it can have no reason *within itself* of its existence; because no one being in this infinite succession is supposed to be self-existent or *necessary* (which is the only ground or reason of existence of any thing that can be imagined *within the thing itself,* as will presently more fully appear), but every one *dependent* on the foregoing: and where *no part* is necessary, 'tis manifest *the whole* cannot be necessary: absolute necessity of existence not being an outward, relative, and accidental denomination; but an inward and essential property of the nature of the thing which so exists. An infinite succession therefore of merely *dependent* beings without any original independent cause; is a *series* of beings that has neither necessity nor cause, nor any reason *at all* of its existence, neither *within itself* nor *from without:* that is, 'tis an express contradiction and impossibility; 'tis a supposing *something* to be *caused,* (because it's granted in every one of its stages of succession not to be necessarily and from itself); and yet that in the whole it is caused *absolutely by nothing*: which every man knows is a contradiction to be done *in time;* and because duration in this case makes no difference, 'tis equally a contradiction to suppose it done from eter-

nity: and consequently there must *on the contrary* of necessity have existed from eternity some *one* immutable and *independent* being: which, what it is, remains in the next place to be inquired.

# READING 4

# A Critique of Clarke's Cosmological Argument
*David Hume*

*David Hume (1711–1776) was a philosopher, historian, and leading man of letters during the Scottish Enlightenment. He lived most of his life in Edinburgh and was a close friend of the economist Adam Smith. Although his first book,* A Treatise of Human Nature *(1739–1740), composed when Hume was in his early twenties, was not a popular success, Hume's essays and his multivolume* History of England *established his literary reputation. Hume reworked the ideas of the* Treatise *in his* An Enquiry Concerning Human Understanding *(1748) and* An Enquiry Concerning the Principles of Morals *(1751), and he is now regarded as the most important empiricist philosopher of the eighteenth century. Twice refused academic employment because of his criticisms of religion, Hume left instructions that his* Dialogues Concerning Natural Religion *be published after his death. The first edition of Hume's* Dialogues *appeared in 1779. The text in the following selection is adapted from the version in* The Philosophical Works of David Hume *(Edinburgh: A. Black and W. Tait, 1854). (For Hume's views on free will, induction, and causation, see Readings 30, 39, and 42.)*

But if so many difficulties attend the argument *a posteriori*, said DEMEA, had we not better adhere to

SOURCE: From *Dialogues Concerning Natural Religion* (1779), Part IX. Edited.

that simple and sublime argument *a priori* which, by offering to us infallible demonstration, cuts off at once all doubt and difficulty? By this argument, too, we may prove the *infinity* of the divine attributes which, I am afraid, can never be ascertained with certainty from any other topic. For how can an effect which either is finite or, for aught we know, may be so; how can such an effect, I say, prove an infinite cause? The unity too of the divine nature, it is very difficult, if not absolutely impossible, to deduce merely from contemplating the works of nature; nor will the uniformity alone of the plan, even were it allowed, give us any assurance of that attribute. Whereas the argument *a priori* . . .

You seem to reason, DEMEA, interposed CLEANTHES, as if those advantages and conveniences in the abstract argument were full proofs of its solidity. But it is first proper, in my opinion, to determine what argument of this nature you choose to insist on; and we shall afterwards, from itself, better than from its *useful* consequences, endeavour to determine what value we ought to put upon it.

The argument, replied DEMEA, which I would insist on, is the common one. Whatever exists must have a cause or reason of its existence; it being absolutely impossible for any thing to produce itself, or be the cause of its own existence. In mounting up, therefore, from effects to causes, we must either go on in tracing an infinite succession, without any ultimate cause at all; or must at last have recourse to some ultimate cause that is *necessarily* existent: now, that the first supposition is absurd, may be thus proved. In the infinite chain or succession of causes and effects, each single effect is determined to exist by the power and efficacy of that cause which immediately preceded; but the whole external chain or succession, taken together, is not determined or caused by any thing; and yet it is evident that it requires a cause or reason, as much as any particular object which begins to exist in time. The question is still reasonable, why this particular succession of causes existed from eternity, and not any other succession, or no succession at all. If there be no necessarily existent being, any supposition which can be formed is equally possible; nor is there any more absurdity in nothing's having existed from eternity than there is in that succession of causes which constitutes the universe. What was it, then, which determined something to exist rather than nothing, and bestowed being on a particular possibility, exclusive of the rest? *External causes,* there are supposed to be none. *Chance* is a word without a meaning. Was it *nothing*? But that can never produce any thing. We must, therefore, have recourse to a necessarily existent being who carries the *reason* of his existence in himself, and who cannot be supposed not to exist without an express contradiction. There is, consequently, such a being; that is, there is a Deity.

I shall not leave it to PHILO, said CLEANTHES, though I know that the starting objections is his chief delight, to point out the weakness of this metaphysical reasoning. It seems to be so obviously ill-grounded, and at the same time of so little consequence to the cause of true piety and religion, that I shall myself venture to show the fallacy of it.

I shall begin with observing that there is an evident absurdity in pretending to demonstrate a matter of fact or to prove it by any arguments *a priori.* Nothing is demonstrable unless the contrary implies a contradiction. Nothing that is distinctly conceivable implies a contradiction. Whatever we conceive as existent, we can also conceive as non-existent. There is no being, therefore, whose non-existence implies a contradiction. Consequently there is no being whose existence is demonstrable. I propose this argument as entirely decisive, and am willing to rest the whole controversy upon it.

It is pretended that the Deity is a necessarily existent being; and this necessity of his existence is at-

tempted to be explained by asserting that, if we knew his whole essence or nature, we should perceive it to be as impossible for him not to exist, as for twice two not to be four. But it is evident that this can never happen, while our faculties remain the same as at present. It will still be possible for us, at any time, to conceive the non-existence of what we formerly conceived to exist; nor can the mind ever lie under a necessity of supposing any object to remain always in being; in the same manner as we lie under a necessity of always conceiving twice two to be four. The words, therefore, *necessary existence* have no meaning; or, which is the same thing, none that is consistent.

But further, why may not the material universe be the necessarily existent being, according to this pretended explication of necessity? We dare not affirm that we know all the qualities of matter; and for aught we can determine, it may contain some qualities which, were they known, would make its non-existence appear as great a contradiction as that twice two is five. I find only one argument employed to prove that the material world is not the necessarily existent being: and this argument is derived from the contingency both of the matter and the form of the world. "Any particle of matter," it is said, "may be *conceived* to be annihilated; and any form may be *conceived* to be altered. Such an annihilation or alteration, therefore, is not impossible."[1] But it seems a great partiality not to perceive that the same argument extends equally to the Deity, so far as we have any conception of him; and that the mind can at least imagine him to be non-existent or his attributes to be altered. It must be some unknown, inconceivable qualities, which can make his non-existence appear impossible or his attributes unalterable: and no reason can be assigned why these qualities may not belong to matter. As they are altogether unknown and inconceivable, they can never be proved incompatible with it.

Add to this that in tracing an eternal succession of objects it seems absurd to enquire for a general cause or first author. How can any thing that exists from eternity have a cause, since that relation implies a priority in time and a beginning of existence?

In such a chain, too, or succession of objects, each part is caused by that which preceded it, and causes that which succeeds it. Where then is the difficulty? But the *whole*, you say, wants a cause. I answer that the uniting of these parts into a whole, like the uniting of several distinct countries into one kingdom, or several distinct members into one body, is performed merely by an arbitrary act of the mind, and has no influence on the nature of things. Did I show you the particular causes of each individual in a collection of twenty particles of matter, I should think it very unreasonable should you afterwards ask me what was the cause of the whole twenty. This is sufficiently explained in explaining the cause of the parts.

Though the reasonings which you have urged, CLEANTHES, may well excuse me, said PHILO, from starting any further difficulties, yet I cannot forbear insisting still upon another topic. It is observed by arithmeticians that the products of 9 compose always either 9 or some lesser product of 9 if you add together all the characters of which any of the former products is composed. Thus, of 18, 27, 36, which are products of 9, you make 9 by adding 1 to 8, 2 to 7, 3 to 6. Thus, 369 is a product also of 9; and if you add 3, 6, and 9, you make 18, a lesser product of 9.[2] To a superficial observer, so wonderful a regularity may be admired as the effect either of chance or design: but a skilful algebraist immediately concludes it to be the work of necessity, and demonstrates that it must forever result from the nature of these numbers. Is it not probable, I ask, that the whole economy of the universe is conducted by a like necessity, though no human algebra can furnish a key which solves the difficulty? And instead of admiring the order of natural beings, may it not happen that, could we penetrate into the intimate nature of bodies, we should clearly see why it was absolutely impossible they could ever admit of any other disposition? So dangerous is it to introduce this idea of necessity into the present question! And so naturally does it afford an inference directly opposite to the religious hypothesis!

But dropping all these abstractions, continued PHILO, and confining ourselves to more familiar topics, I shall venture to add an observation that the argument *a priori* has seldom been found very convincing, except to people of a metaphysical head who have accustomed themselves to abstract reasoning, and who, finding from mathematics that the understanding frequently leads to truth through obscurity, and contrary to first appearances, have transferred the same habit of thinking to subjects where it ought not to have place. Other people, even of good sense and the best inclined to religion, feel always some deficiency in such arguments, though they are not perhaps able to explain distinctly where it lies; a certain proof that men ever did and ever will derive their religion from other sources than from this species of reasoning.

## NOTES

1. [Ed. Hume is here paraphrasing a passage from Clarke's Boyle lectures: "For whether we consider the *form* of the world, with the *disposition* and *motion* of its parts; or whether we consider the *matter* of it, as such, without respect to its present form; every thing in it, both the *whole* and every one of its *parts*, their *situation* and *motion*, the *form* and also the *matter*, are the most arbitrary and dependent things, and the farthest removed from necessity that can possibly be imagined." *A Demonstration of the Being and Attributes of God*, Section III, pp. 43–44.]

2. [Ed. Hume refers here to the periodical *Nouvelles de la République des Lettres*, September 1685, Article II, pp. 944–945.]

## READING 5

# Evil and Omnipotence
*J. L. Mackie*

*John Leslie Mackie (1917–1981) was Reader in Philosophy at Oxford University. He is the author of many books and articles dealing with topics in epistemology, philosophy of religion, and ethics, including* The Cement of the Universe *(1974),* Problems from Locke *(1976),* Ethics: Inventing Right and Wrong *(1977), and* Hume's Moral Theory *(1980). His major work in philosophy of religion, completed shortly before his death, is* The Miracle of Theism *(1982). (For Mackie's views on causation, see Reading 44.)*

The traditional arguments for the existence of God have been fairly thoroughly criticised by philosophers. But the theologian can, if he wishes, accept this criticism. He can admit that no rational proof of God's existence is possible. And he can still retain all that is essential to his position, by holding that God's existence is known in some other, non-rational way. I think, however, that a more telling criticism can be made by way of the traditional problem of evil. Here it can be shown, not that religious beliefs lack rational support, but that they are positively irrational, that the several parts of the essential theological doctrine are inconsistent with one another, so that the theologian can maintain his position as a whole only by a much more extreme rejection of reason than in the former case. He must now be prepared to believe, not merely what cannot be proved, but what can be *disproved* from other beliefs that he also holds.

The problem of evil, in the sense in which I shall be using the phrase, is a problem only for someone who believes that there is a God who is both omnipotent and wholly good. And it is a logical problem, the problem of clarifying and reconciling a number of beliefs: it is not a scientific problem that might be solved by further observations, or a practical problem that might be solved by a decision or an action. These points are obvious; I mention them only because they are sometimes ignored by theologians, who sometimes parry a statement of the problem with such remarks as "Well, can you solve the problem yourself?" or "This is a mystery which may be revealed to us later" or "Evil is something to be faced and overcome, not to be merely discussed".

In its simplest form the problem is this: God is omnipotent; God is wholly good; and yet evil exists. There seems to be some contradiction between these three propositions, so that if any two of them were true the third would be false. But at the same time all three are essential parts of most theological positions: the theologian, it seems, at once *must* adhere and *cannot consistently* adhere to all three. (The problem does not arise only for theists, but I shall discuss it in the form in which it presents itself for ordinary theism.)

However, the contradiction does not arise immediately; to show it we need some additional premises, or perhaps some quasi-logical rules connecting the terms 'good', 'evil', and 'omnipotent'. These additional principles are that good is opposed to evil, in such a way that a good thing always eliminates evil as far as it can, and that there are no limits to what an omnipotent thing can do. From these it follows that a good omnipotent thing eliminates evil completely, and then the propositions that a good omnipotent thing exists, and that evil exists, are incompatible.

## A. ADEQUATE SOLUTIONS

Now once the problem is fully stated it is clear that it can be solved, in the sense that the problem will not arise if one gives up at least one of the propositions that constitute it. If you are prepared to say that God is not wholly good, or not quite omnipotent, or that evil does not exist, or that good is not opposed to the

**SOURCE:** From *Mind* 64 (1955): 200–212.

kind of evil that exists, or that there are limits to what an omnipotent thing can do, then the problem of evil will not arise for you.

There are, then, quite a number of adequate solutions of the problem of evil, and some of these have been adopted, or almost adopted, by various thinkers. For example, a few have been prepared to deny God's omnipotence, and rather more have been prepared to keep the term 'omnipotence' but severely to restrict its meaning, recording quite a number of things that an omnipotent being cannot do. Some have said that evil is an illusion, perhaps because they held that the whole world of temporal, changing things is an illusion, and that what we call evil belongs only to this world, or perhaps because they held that although temporal things *are* much as we see them, those that we call evil are not really evil. Some have said that what we call evil is merely the privation of good, that evil in a positive sense, evil that would really be opposed to good, does not exist. Many have agreed with Pope that disorder is harmony not understood, and that partial evil is universal good. Whether any of these views is *true* is, of course, another question. But each of them gives an adequate solution of the problem of evil in the sense that if you accept it this problem does not arise for you, though you may, of course, have *other* problems to face.

But often enough these adequate solutions are only *almost* adopted. The thinkers who restrict God's power, but keep the term 'omnipotence', may reasonably be suspected of thinking, in other contexts, that his power is really unlimited. Those who say that evil is an illusion may also be thinking, inconsistently, that this illusion is itself an evil. Those who say that "evil" is merely privation of good may also be thinking, inconsistently, that privation of good is an evil. (The fallacy here is akin to some forms of the "naturalistic fallacy" in ethics, where some think, for example, that "good" is just what contributes to evolutionary progress, and that evolutionary progress is itself good.) If Pope meant what he said in the first line of his couplet, that "disorder" is only harmony not understood, the "partial evil" of the second line must, for consistency, mean "that which, taken in isolation, falsely appears to be evil", but it would more naturally mean "that which, in isolation, really is evil". The second line, in fact, hesitates between two views, that "partial evil" isn't really evil, since only the universal quality is real, and that "partial evil" is really an evil, but only a little one.

In addition, therefore, to adequate solutions, we must recognise unsatisfactory inconsistent solutions, in which there is only a half-hearted or temporary rejection of one of the propositions which together constitute the problem. In these, one of the constituent propositions is explicitly rejected, but it is covertly re-asserted or assumed elsewhere in the system.

## B. FALLACIOUS SOLUTIONS

Besides these half-hearted solutions, which explicitly reject but implicitly assert one of the constituent propositions, there are definitely fallacious solutions which explicitly maintain all the constituent propositions, but implicitly reject at least one of them in the course of the argument that explains away the problem of evil.

There are, in fact, many so-called solutions which purport to remove the contradiction without abandoning any of its constituent propositions. These must be fallacious, as we can see from the very statement of the problem, but it is not so easy to see in each case precisely where the fallacy lies. I suggest that in all cases the fallacy has the general form suggested above: in order to solve the problem one (or perhaps more) of its constituent propositions is given up, but in such a way that it appears to have been retained, and can therefore be asserted without qualification in other contexts. Sometimes there is a further complication: the supposed solution moves to and fro between, say, two of the constituent propositions, at one point asserting the first of these but covertly abandoning the second, at another point asserting the second but covertly abandoning the first. These fallacious solutions often turn upon some equivocation with the words 'good' and 'evil', or upon some vagueness about the way in which good and evil are opposed to one another, or about how much is meant by 'omnipotence'. I propose to examine some of these so-called solutions, and to exhibit their fallacies in detail. Incidentally, I shall also be considering whether an adequate solution could be reached by a minor modification of one or more of the constituent propositions, which would, however, still satisfy all the essential requirements of ordinary theism.

(1) "Good cannot exist without evil" or "Evil is necessary as a counterpart to good."

It is sometimes suggested that evil is necessary as a counterpart to good, that if there were no evil there could be no good either, and that this solves the problem of evil. It is true that it points to an answer to the question "Why should there be evil?" But it does so only by qualifying some of the propositions that constitute the problem.

First, it sets a limit to what God can do, saying that God *cannot* create good without simultaneously creating evil, and this means either that God is not omnipotent or that there are *some* limits to what an omnipotent thing can do. It may be replied that these limits are always presupposed, that omnipotence has never meant the power to do what is logically impossible, and on the present view the existence of good without evil would be a logical impossibility. This interpretation of omnipotence may, indeed, be accepted as a modification of our original account which does not reject anything that is essential to theism, and I shall in general assume it in the subsequent discussion. It is, perhaps, the most common theistic view, but I think that some theists at least have maintained that God can do what is logically impossible. Many theists, at any rate, have held that logic itself is created or laid down by God, that logic is the way in which God arbitrarily chooses to think. (This is, of course, parallel to the ethical view that morally right actions are those which God arbitrarily chooses to command, and the two views encounter similar difficulties.) And *this* account of logic is clearly inconsistent with the view that God is bound by logical necessities—unless it is possible for an omnipotent being to bind himself, an issue which we shall consider later, when we come to the Paradox of Omnipotence. This solution of the problem of evil cannot, therefore, be consistently adopted along with the view that logic is itself created by God.

But, secondly, this solution denies that evil is opposed to good in our original sense. If good and evil are counterparts, a good thing will not "eliminate evil as far as it can". Indeed, this view suggests that good and evil are not strictly qualities of things at all. Perhaps the suggestion is that good and evil are related in much the same way as great and small. Certainly, when the term 'great' is used relatively as a condensation of 'greater than so-and-so', and 'small' is used correspondingly, greatness and smallness are counterparts and cannot exist without each other. But in this sense greatness is not a quality, not an intrinsic feature of anything; and it would be absurd to

think of a movement in favour of greatness and against smallness in this sense. Such a movement would be self-defeating, since relative greatness can be promoted only by a simultaneous promotion of relative smallness. I feel sure that no theists would be content to regard God's goodness as analogous to this—as if what he supports were not the *good* but the *better*, and as if he had the paradoxical aim that all things should be better than other things.

This point is obscured by the fact that 'great' and 'small' seem to have an absolute as well as a relative sense. I cannot discuss here whether there is absolute magnitude or not, but if there is, there could be an absolute sense for 'great', it could mean of at least a certain size, and it would make sense to speak of all things getting bigger, of a universe that was expanding all over, and therefore it would make sense to speak of promoting greatness. But in *this* sense great and small are not logically necessary counterparts: either quality could exist without the other. There would be no logical impossibility in everything's being small or in everything's being great.

Neither in the absolute nor in the relative sense, then, of 'great' and 'small' do these terms provide an analogy of the sort that would be needed to support this solution of the problem of evil. In neither case are greatness and smallness *both* necessary counterparts *and* mutually opposed forces or possible objects for support and attack.

It may be replied that good and evil are necessary counterparts in the same way as any quality and its logical opposite: redness can occur, it is suggested, only if non-redness also occurs. But unless evil is merely the privation of good, they are not logical opposites, and some further argument would be needed to show that they are counterparts in the same way as genuine logical opposites. Let us assume that this could be given. There is still doubt of the correctness of the metaphysical principle that a quality must have a real opposite: I suggest that it is not really impossible that everything should be, say, red, that the truth is merely that if everything were red we should not notice redness, and so we should have no word 'red'; we observe and give names to qualities only if they have real opposites. If so, the principle that a term must have an opposite would belong only to our language or to our thought, and would not be an ontological principle, and correspondingly, the rule that good cannot exist without evil would not state a logical necessity of a sort that God would just have to put up with. God might have made everything good, though *we* should not have noticed it if he had.

But, finally, even if we concede that this *is* an ontological principle, it will provide a solution for the problem of evil only if one is prepared to say, "Evil exists, but only just enough evil to serve as the counterpart of good". I doubt whether any theist will accept this. After all, the *ontological* requirement that non-redness should occur would be satisfied even if all the universe, except for a minute speck, were red, and, if there were a corresponding requirement for evil as a counterpart to good, a minute dose of evil would presumably do. But theists are not usually willing to say, in all contexts, that all the evil that occurs is a minute and necessary dose.

(2) "Evil is necessary as a means to good."

It is sometimes suggested that evil is necessary for good not as a counterpart but as a means. In its simple form this has little plausibility as a solution of the problem of evil, since it obviously implies a severe restriction of God's power. It would be a *causal* law that you cannot have a certain end without a certain means, so that if God has to introduce evil as a means to good, he must be subject to at least some causal laws. This certainly conflicts with what a theist normally means by omnipotence. This view of God as limited by causal laws also conflicts with the view that causal laws are themselves made by God, which is more widely held than the corresponding view about the laws of logic. This conflict would, indeed, be resolved if it were possible for an omnipotent being to bind himself, and this possibility has still to be considered. Unless a favourable answer can be given to this question, the suggestion that evil is necessary as a means to good solves the problem of evil only by denying one of its constituent propositions, either that God is omnipotent or that 'omnipotent' means what it says.

(3) "The universe is better with some evil in it than it could be if there were no evil."

Much more important is a solution which at first seems to be a mere variant of the previous one, that evil may contribute to the goodness of a whole in which it is found, so that the universe as a whole is better as it is, with some evil in it, than it would be if

there were no evil. This solution may be developed in either of two ways. It may be supported by an aesthetic analogy, by the fact that contrasts heighten beauty, that in a musical work, for example, there may occur discords which somehow add to the beauty of the work as a whole. Alternatively, it may be worked out in connexion with the notion of progress, that the best possible organisation of the universe will not be static, but progressive, that the gradual overcoming of evil by good is really a finer thing than would be the eternal unchallenged supremacy of good.

In either case, this solution usually starts from the assumption that the evil whose existence gives rise to the problem of evil is primarily what is called physical evil, that is to say, pain. In Hume's rather half-hearted presentation of the problem of evil, the evils that he stresses are pain and disease, and those who reply to him argue that the existence of pain and disease makes possible the existence of sympathy, benevolence, heroism, and the gradually successful struggle of doctors and reformers to overcome these evils. In fact, theists often seize the opportunity to accuse those who stress the problem of evil of taking a low, materialistic view of good and evil, equating these with pleasure and pain, and of ignoring the more spiritual goods which can arise in the struggle against evils.

But let us see exactly what is being done here. Let us call pain and misery 'first order evil' or 'evil (1)'. What contrasts with this, namely, pleasure and happiness, will be called 'first order good' or 'good (1)'. Distinct from this is 'second order good' or 'good (2)' which somehow emerges in a complex situation in which evil (1) is a necessary component—logically, not merely causally, necessary. (Exactly *how* it emerges does not matter: in the crudest version of this solution good (2) is simply the heightening of happiness by the contrast with misery, in other versions it includes sympathy with suffering, heroism in facing danger, and the gradual decrease of first order evil and increase of first order good.) It is also being assumed that second order good is more important than first order good or evil, in particular that it more than outweighs the first order evil it involves.

Now this is a particularly subtle attempt to solve the problem of evil. It defends God's goodness and omnipotence on the ground that (on a sufficiently long view) this is the best of all logically possible worlds, because it includes the important second order goods, and yet it admits that real evils, namely first order evils, exist. But does it still hold that good and evil are opposed? Not, clearly, in the sense that we set out originally: good does not tend to eliminate evil in general. Instead, we have a modified, a more complex pattern. First order good (*e.g.* happiness) *contrasts with* first order evil (*e.g.* misery): these two are opposed in a fairly mechanical way; some second order goods (*e.g.* benevolence) try to maximise first order good and minimise first order evil; but God's goodness is not this, it is rather the will to maximise *second* order good. We might, therefore, call God's goodness an example of a third order goodness, or good (3). While this account is different from our original one, it might well be held to be an improvement on it, to give a more accurate description of the way in which good is opposed to evil, and to be consistent with the essential theist position.

There might, however, be several objections to this solution.

First, some might argue that such qualities as benevolence—and *a fortiori* the third order goodness which promotes benevolence—have a merely derivative value, that they are not higher sorts of good, but merely means to good (1), that is, to happiness, so that it would be absurd for God to keep misery in existence in order to make possible the virtues of benevolence, heroism, etc. The theist who adopts the present solution must, of course, deny this, but he can do so with some plausibility, so I should not press this objection.

Secondly, it follows from this solution that God is not in our sense benevolent or sympathetic: he is not concerned to minimise evil (1), but only to promote good (2); and this might be a disturbing conclusion for some theists.

But, thirdly, the fatal objection is this. Our analysis shows clearly the possibility of the existence of a *second* order evil, an evil (2) contrasting with good (2) as evil (1) contrasts with good (1). This would include malevolence, cruelty, callousness, cowardice, and states in which good (1) is decreasing and evil (1) increasing. And just as good (2) is held to be the important kind of good, the kind that God is concerned to promote, so evil (2) will, by analogy, be the important kind of evil, the kind which God, if he were wholly good and omnipotent, would eliminate. And yet evil (2) plainly exists, and indeed most theists (in other contexts) stress its existence more than that of

evil (1). We should, therefore, state the problem of evil in terms of second order evil, and against this form of the problem the present solution is useless.

An attempt might be made to use this solution again, at a higher level, to explain the occurrence of evil (2): indeed the next main solution that we shall examine does just this, with the help of some new notions. Without any fresh notions, such a solution would have little plausibility: for example, we could hardly say that the really important good was a good (3), such as the increase of benevolence in proportion to cruelty, which logically required for its occurrence the occurrence of some second order evil. But even if evil (2) could be explained in this way, it is fairly clear that there would be third order evils contrasting with this third order good: and we should be well on the way to an infinite regress, where the solution of a problem of evil, stated in terms of evil ($n$), indicated the existence of an evil ($n + 1$), and a further problem to be solved.

(4) "Evil is due to human free will."

Perhaps the most important proposed solution of the problem of evil is that evil is not to be ascribed to God at all, but to the independent actions of human beings, supposed to have been endowed by God with freedom of the will. This solution may be combined with the preceding one: first order evil (*e.g.* pain) may be justified as a logically necessary component in second order good (*e.g.* sympathy) while second order evil (*e.g.* cruelty) is not *justified,* but is so ascribed to human beings that God cannot be held responsible for it. This combination evades my third criticism of the preceding solution.

The free-will solution also involves the preceding solution at a higher level. To explain why a wholly good God gave men free will although it would lead to some important evils, it must be argued that it is better on the whole that men should act freely, and sometimes err, than that they should be innocent automata, acting rightly in a wholly determined way. Freedom, that is to say, is now treated as a third order good, and as being more valuable than second order goods (such as sympathy and heroism) would be if they were deterministically produced, and it is being assumed that second order evils, such as cruelty, are logically necessary accompaniments of freedom, just as pain is a logically necessary pre-condition of sympathy.

I think that this solution is unsatisfactory primarily because of the incoherence of the notion of freedom of the will: but I cannot discuss this topic adequately here, although some of my criticisms will touch upon it.

First I should query the assumption that second order evils are logically necessary accompaniments of freedom. I should ask this: if God has made men such that in their free choices they sometimes prefer what is good and sometimes what is evil, why could he not have made men such that they always freely choose the good? If there is no logical impossibility in a man's freely choosing the good on one, or on several, occasions, there cannot be a logical impossibility in his freely choosing the good on every occasion. God was not, then, faced with a choice between making innocent automata and making beings who, in acting freely, would sometimes go wrong: there was open to him the obviously better possibility of making beings who would act freely but always go right. Clearly, his failure to avail himself of this possibility is inconsistent with his being both omnipotent and wholly good.

If it is replied that this objection is absurd, that the making of some wrong choices is logically necessary for freedom, it would seem that 'freedom' must here mean complete randomness or indeterminacy, including randomness with regard to the alternatives good and evil, in other words that men's choices and consequent actions can be "free" only if they are not determined by their characters. Only on this assumption can God escape the responsibility for men's actions; for if he made them as they are, but did not determine their wrong choices, this can only be because the wrong choices are not determined by men as they are. But then if freedom is randomness, how can it be a characteristic of *will*? And, still more, how can it be the most important good? What value or merit would there be in free choices if these were random actions which were not determined by the nature of the agent?

I conclude that to make this solution plausible two different senses of 'freedom' must be confused, one sense which will justify the view that freedom is a third order good, more valuable than other goods would be without it, and another sense, sheer randomness, to prevent us from ascribing to God a decision to make men such that they sometimes go wrong when he might have made them such that they would always freely go right.

This criticism is sufficient to dispose of this solution. But besides this there is a fundamental difficulty in the notion of an omnipotent God creating men with free will, for if men's wills are really free this must mean that even God cannot control them, that is, that God is no longer omnipotent. It may be objected that God's gift of freedom to men does not mean that he *cannot* control their wills, but that he always *refrains* from controlling their wills. But why, we may ask, should God refrain from controlling evil wills? Why should he not leave men free to will rightly, but intervene when he sees them beginning to will wrongly? If God could do this, but does not, and if he is wholly good, the only explanation could be that even a wrong free act of will is not really evil, that its freedom is a value which outweighs its wrongness, so that there would be a loss of value if God took away the wrongness and the freedom together. But this is utterly opposed to what theists say about sin in other contexts. The present solution of the problem of evil, then, can be maintained only in the form that God has made men so free that he *cannot* control their wills.

This leads us to what I call the Paradox of Omnipotence: can an omnipotent being make things which he cannot subsequently control? Or, what is practically equivalent to this, can an omnipotent being make rules which then bind himself? (These are practically equivalent because any such rules could be regarded as setting certain things beyond his control, and *vice versa*.) The second of these formulations is relevant to the suggestions that we have already met, that an omnipotent God creates the rules of logic or causal laws, and is then bound by them.

It is clear that this is a paradox: the questions cannot be answered satisfactorily either in the affirmative or in the negative. If we answer "Yes", it follows that if God actually makes things which he cannot control, or makes rules which bind himself, he is not omnipotent once he has made them; there are *then* things which he cannot do. But if we answer "No", we are immediately asserting that there are things which he cannot do, that is to say that he is already not omnipotent.

It cannot be replied that the question which sets this paradox is not a proper question. It would make perfectly good sense to say that a human mechanic has made a machine which he cannot control: if there is any difficulty about the question it lies in the notion of omnipotence itself.

This, incidentally, shows that although we have approached this paradox from the free-will theory, it is equally a problem for a theological determinist. No one thinks that machines have free will, yet they may well be beyond the control of their makers. The determinist might reply that anyone who makes anything determines its ways of acting, and so determines its subsequent behaviour: even the human mechanic does this by his *choice* of materials and structure for his machine, though he does not know all about either of these: the mechanic thus determines, though he may not foresee, his machine's actions. And since God is omniscient, and since his creation of things is total, he both determines and foresees the ways in which his creatures will act. We may grant this, but it is beside the point. The question is not whether God *originally* determined the future actions of his creatures, but whether he can *subsequently* control their actions, or whether he was able in his original creation to put things beyond his subsequent control. Even on determinist principles the answers "Yes" and "No" are equally irreconcilable with God's omnipotence.

Before suggesting a solution of this paradox, I would point out that there is a parallel Paradox of Sovereignty. Can a legal sovereign make a law restricting its own future legislative power? For example, could the British parliament make a law forbidding any future parliament to socialise banking, and also forbidding the future repeal of this law itself? Or could the British parliament, which was legally sovereign in Australia in, say, 1899, pass a valid law, or series of laws, which made it no longer sovereign in 1933? Again, neither the affirmative nor the negative answer is really satisfactory. If we were to answer "Yes", we should be admitting the validity of a law which, if it were actually made, would mean that parliament was no longer sovereign. If we were to answer "No", we should be admitting that there is a law, not logically absurd, which parliament cannot validly make, that is, that parliament is not now a legal sovereign. This paradox can be solved in the following way. We should distinguish between first order laws, that is laws governing the actions of individuals and bodies other than the legislature, and second order laws, that is laws about laws, laws governing the actions of the legislature itself. Correspondingly, we should distinguish two orders of sovereignty, first order sovereignty (sovereignty (1)) which is unlimited authority to make first order laws,

and second order sovereignty (sovereignty (2)) which is unlimited authority to make second order laws. If we say that parliament is sovereign we might mean that any parliament at any time has sovereignty (1), or we might mean that parliament has both sovereignty (1) and sovereignty (2) at present, but we cannot without contradiction mean both that the present parliament has sovereignty (2) and that every parliament at every time has sovereignty (1), for if the present parliament has sovereignty (2) it may use it to take away the sovereignty (1) of later parliaments. What the paradox shows is that we cannot ascribe to any continuing institution legal sovereignty in an inclusive sense.

The analogy between omnipotence and sovereignty shows that the paradox of omnipotence can be solved in a similar way. We must distinguish between first order omnipotence (omnipotence (1)), that is unlimited power to act, and second order omnipotence (omnipotence (2)), that is unlimited power to determine what powers to act things shall have. Then we could consistently say that God all the time has omnipotence (1), but if so no beings at any time have powers to act independently of God. Or we could say that God at one time had omnipotence (2), and used it to assign independent powers to act to certain things, so that God thereafter did not have omnipotence (1). But what the paradox shows is that we cannot consistently ascribe to any continuing being omnipotence in an inclusive sense.

An alternative solution of this paradox would be simply to deny that God is a continuing being, that any times can be assigned to his actions at all. But on this assumption (which also has difficulties of its own) no meaning can be given to the assertion that God made men with wills so free that he could not control them. The paradox of omnipotence can be avoided by putting God outside time, but the free-will solution of the problem of evil cannot be saved in this way, and equally it remains impossible to hold that an omnipotent God *binds himself* by causal or logical laws.

## CONCLUSION

Of the proposed solutions of the problem of evil which we have examined, none has stood up to criticism. There may be other solutions which require examination, but this study strongly suggests that there is no valid solution of the problem which does not modify at least one of the constituent propositions in a way which would seriously affect the essential core of the theistic position.

Quite apart from the problem of evil, the paradox of omnipotence has shown that God's omnipotence must in any case be restricted in one way or another, that unqualified omnipotence cannot be ascribed to any being that continues through time. And if God and his actions are not in time, can omnipotence, or power of any sort, be meaningfully ascribed to him?

# READING 6

# The Wager
*Blaise Pascal*

*Blaise Pascal (1623–1662) was a French mathematician, physicist, inventor, and religious thinker. He did original work in geometry and probability theory, he performed experiments with barometers that helped prove the existence of the vacuum, and he designed and built the first calculating machine. Throughout his life, Pascal suffered from terrible headaches caused by a malformed skull. He died in agony at the age of 39. Pascal's wager argument is contained in his* Pensées *(Thoughts), published in 1670 from the notes left at his death.*

Let us now speak according to our natural lights.

If there is a God, he is infinitely beyond our comprehension, since, being indivisible and without limits, he bears no relation to us. We are therefore incapable of knowing either what he is or whether he is. That being so, who would dare to attempt an answer to the question? Certainly not we, who bear no relation to him.

Who then will condemn Christians for being unable to give rational grounds for their belief, professing as they do a religion for which they cannot give rational grounds? They declare that it is a folly, *stultitiam,* in expounding it to the world, and then you

SOURCE: From *Pensées* (1670). Reprinted from *Pascal's Pensées,* trans. A. J. Krailsheimer (London: Penguin, 1966): 150–152.

complain that they do not prove it. If they did prove it they would not be keeping their word. It is by being without proof that they show they are not without sense. 'Yes, but although that excuses those who offer their religion as such, and absolves them from the criticism of producing it without rational grounds, it does not absolve those who accept it.' Let us then examine this point, and let us say: 'Either God is or he is not.' But to which view shall we be inclined? Reason cannot decide this question. Infinite chaos separates us. At the far end of this infinite distance a coin is being spun which will come down heads or tails. How will you wager? Reason cannot make you choose either, reason cannot prove either wrong.

Do not then condemn as wrong those who have made a choice, for you know nothing about it. 'No, but I will condemn them not for having made this particular choice, but any choice, for, although the one who calls heads and the other one are equally at fault, the fact is that they are both at fault: the right thing is not to wager at all.'

Yes, but you must wager. There is no choice, you are already committed. Which will you choose then? Let us see: since a choice must be made, let us see which offers you the least interest. You have two things to lose: the true and the good; and two things to stake: your reason and your will, your knowledge and your happiness; and your nature has two things to avoid: error and wretchedness. Since you must necessarily choose, your reason is no more affronted by choosing one rather than the other. That is one point cleared up. But your happiness? Let us weigh up the gain and the loss involved in calling heads that God exists. Let us assess the two cases: if you win you win everything, if you lose you lose nothing. Do not hesitate then; wager that he does exist. 'That is wonderful. Yes, I must wager, but perhaps I am wagering too much.' Let us see: since there is an equal chance of gain and loss, if you stood to win only two lives for one you could still wager, but supposing you stood to win three?

You would have to play (since you must necessarily play) and it would be unwise of you, once you are obliged to play, not to risk your life in order to win three lives at a game in which there is an equal chance of losing and winning. But there is an eternity of life and happiness. That being so, even though there were an infinite number of chances, of which only one were in your favour, you would still be right to wager one in order to win two; and you would be acting wrongly, being obliged to play, in refusing to stake one life against three in a game, where out of an infinite number of chances there is one in your favour, if there were an infinity of infinitely happy life to be won. But here there is an infinity of infinitely happy life to be won, one chance of winning against a finite number of chances of losing, and what you are staking is finite. That leaves no choice; wherever there is infinity, and where there are not infinite chances of losing against that of winning, there is no room for hesitation, you must give everything. And thus, since you are obliged to play, you must be renouncing reason if you hoard your life rather than risk it for an infinite gain, just as likely to occur as a loss amounting to nothing.

For it is no good saying that it is uncertain whether you will win, that it is certain that you are taking a risk, and that the infinite distance between the certainty of what you are risking and the uncertainty of what you may gain makes the finite good you are certainly risking equal to the infinite good that you are not certain to gain. This is not the case. Every gambler takes a certain risk for an uncertain gain, and yet he is taking a certain finite risk for an uncertain finite gain without sinning against reason. Here there is no infinite distance between the certain risk and the uncertain gain: that is not true. There is,

indeed, an infinite distance between the certainty of winning and the certainty of losing, but the proportion between the uncertainty of winning and the certainty of what is being risked is in proportion to the chances of winning or losing. And hence if there are as many chances on one side as on the other you are playing for even odds. And in that case the certainty of what you are risking is equal to the uncertainty of what you may win; it is by no means infinitely distant from it. Thus our argument carries infinite weight, when the stakes are finite in a game where there are even chances of winning and losing and an infinite prize to be won.

This is conclusive and if men are capable of any truth this is it.

'I confess, I admit it, but is there really no way of seeing what the cards are?'—'Yes. Scripture and the rest, etc.'—'Yes, but my hands are tied and my lips are sealed; I am being forced to wager and I am not free; I am being held fast and I am so made that I cannot believe. What do you want me to do then?'—'That is true, but at least get it into your head that, if you are unable to believe, it is because of your passions, since reason impels you to believe and yet you cannot do so. Concentrate then not on convincing yourself by multiplying proofs of God's existence but by diminishing your passions. You want to find faith and you do not know the road. You want to be cured of unbelief and you ask for the remedy: learn from those who were once bound like you and who now wager all they have. These people who know the road you wish to follow, who have been cured of the affliction of which you wish to be cured: follow the way by which they began. They behaved just as if they did believe, taking holy water, having masses said, and so on. That will make you believe quite naturally, and will make you more docile.'[1]—'But that is what I am afraid of.'—'But why? What have you to lose? But to show you that this is the way, the fact is that this diminishes the passions which are your great obstacles. . . .'

*End of this address.*
'Now what harm will come to you from choosing this course? You will be faithful, honest, humble, grateful, full of good works, a sincere, true friend.

---

[1]*abêtira.* That is, the unbeliever will act unthinkingly and mechanically, and in this become more like the beasts, from whom man was differentiated, according to contemporary philosophy, by his faculty of reason.

. . . It is true you will not enjoy noxious pleasures, glory and good living, but will you not have others?

'I tell you that you will gain even in this life, and that at every step you take along this road you will see that your gain is so certain and your risk so negligible that in the end you will realize that you have wagered on something certain and infinite for which you have paid nothing.'

'How these words fill me with rapture and delight!—'

'If my words please you and seem cogent, you must know that they come from a man who went down upon his knees before and after to pray this infinite and indivisible being, to whom he submits his own, that he might bring your being also to submit to him for your own good and for his glory: and that strength might thus be reconciled with lowliness.'

# READING 7

# The Ethics of Belief
*William Clifford*

*Best known for his work in non-Euclidean geometry, William Kingdon Clifford (1845–1879) was Professor of Applied Mathematics and Mechanics at University College, London. Though he studied Aquinas in his youth, as an adult, Clifford was an agnostic, judging that there is neither proof nor disproof that God exists and that the evidence is insufficient to justify belief in either theism or atheism. Clifford's philosophical writings, based mainly on his public lectures, are collected in* Lectures and Essays *(1879) and* The Common Sense of the Exact Sciences *(1885). Clifford died from tuberculosis at age 34.*

## THE ETHICS OF BELIEF[1]

### I. THE DUTY OF INQUIRY.

A shipowner was about to send to sea an emigrant-ship. He knew that she was old, and not over-

[1]*Contemporary Review,* January 1877.

**SOURCE:** From *Lectures and Essays: Volume II, Essays and Reviews* (London: Macmillan, 1879): 163–176. Edited.

well built at the first; that she had seen many seas and climes, and often had needed repairs. Doubts had been suggested to him that possibly she was not seaworthy. These doubts preyed upon his mind and made him unhappy; he thought that perhaps he ought to have her thoroughly overhauled and refitted, even though this should put him to great expense. Before the ship sailed, however, he succeeded in overcoming these melancholy reflections. He said to himself that she had gone safely through so many voyages and weathered so many storms that it was idle to suppose she would not come safely home from this trip also. He would put his trust in Providence, which could hardly fail to protect all these unhappy families that were leaving their fatherland to seek better times elsewhere. He would dismiss from his mind all ungenerous suspicions about the honesty of builders and contractors. In such ways he acquired a sincere and comfortable conviction that his vessel was thoroughly safe and seaworthy; he watched her departure with a light heart, and benevolent wishes for the success of the exiles in their strange new home that was to be; and he got his insurance-money when she went down in mid-ocean and told no tales.

What shall we say of him? Surely this, that he was verily guilty of the death of those men. It is admitted that he did sincerely believe in the soundness of his ship; but the sincerity of his conviction can in no wise help him, because *he had no right to believe on such evidence as was before him.* He had acquired his belief not by honestly earning it in patient investigation, but by stifling his doubts. And although in the end he may have felt so sure about it that he could not think otherwise, yet inasmuch as he had knowingly and willingly worked himself into that frame of mind, he must be held responsible for it.

Let us alter the case a little, and suppose that the ship was not unsound after all; that she made her voyage safely, and many others after it. Will that diminish the guilt of her owner? Not one jot. When an action is once done, it is right or wrong for ever; no accidental failure of its good or evil fruits can possibly alter that. The man would not have been innocent, he would only have been not found out. The question of right or wrong has to do with the origin of his belief, not the matter of it; not what it was, but how he got it; not whether it turned out to be true or false, but whether he had a right to believe on such evidence as was before him.

There was once an island in which some of the inhabitants professed a religion teaching neither the doctrine of original sin nor that of eternal punishment. A suspicion got abroad that the professors of this religion had made use of unfair means to get their doctrines taught to children. They were accused of wresting the laws of their county in such a way as to remove children from the care of their natural and legal guardians; and even of stealing them away and keeping them concealed from their friends and relations. A certain number of men formed themselves into a society for the purpose of agitating the public about this matter. They published grave accusations against individual citizens of the highest position and character, and did all in their power to injure these citizens in the exercise of their professions. So great was the noise they made, that a Commission was appointed to investigate the facts; but after the Commission had carefully inquired into all the evidence that could be got, it appeared that the accused were innocent. Not only had they been accused on insufficient evidence, but the evidence of their innocence was such as the agitators might easily

have obtained, if they had attempted a fair inquiry. After these disclosures the inhabitants of that country looked upon the members of the agitating society, not only as persons whose judgment was to be distrusted, but also as no longer to be counted honourable men. For although they had sincerely and conscientiously believed in the charges they had made, *yet they had no right to believe on such evidence as was before them.* Their sincere convictions, instead of being honestly earned by patient inquiring, were stolen by listening to the voice of prejudice and passion.

Let us vary this case also, and suppose, other things remaining as before, that a still more accurate investigation proved the accused to have been really guilty. Would this make any difference in the guilt of the accusers? Clearly not; the question is not whether their belief was true or false, but whether they entertained it on wrong grounds. They would no doubt say, "Now you see that we were right after all; next time perhaps you will believe us." And they might be believed, but they would not thereby become honourable men. They would not be innocent, they would only be not found out. Every one of them, if he chose to examine himself *in foro conscientiæ*, would know that he had acquired and nourished a belief, when he had no right to believe on such evidence as was before him; and therein he would know that he had done a wrong thing.

It may be said, however, that in both of these supposed cases it is not the belief which is judged to be wrong, but the action following upon it. The shipowner might say, "I am perfectly certain that my ship is sound, but still I feel it my duty to have her examined, before trusting the lives of so many people to her." And it might be said to the agitator, "However convinced you were of the justice of your cause and the truth of your convictions, you ought not to have made a public attack upon any man's character until you had examined the evidence on both sides with the utmost patience and care."

In the first place, let us admit that, so far as it goes, this view of the case is right and necessary; right, because even when a man's belief is so fixed that he cannot think otherwise, he still has a choice in regard to the action suggested by it, and so cannot escape the duty of investigating on the ground of the strength of his convictions; and necessary, because those who are not yet capable of controlling their feelings and thoughts must have a plain rule dealing with overt acts.

But this being premised as necessary, it becomes clear that it is not sufficient, and that our previous judgment is required to supplement it. For it is not possible so to sever the belief from the action it suggests as to condemn the one without condemning the other. No man holding a strong belief on one side of a question, or even wishing to hold a belief on one side, can investigate it with such fairness and completeness as if he were really in doubt and unbiassed; so that the existence of a belief not founded on fair inquiry unfits a man for the performance of this necessary duty.

Nor is that truly a belief at all which has not some influence upon the actions of him who holds it. He who truly believes that which prompts him to an action has looked upon the action to lust after it, he has committed it already in his heart. If a belief is not realised immediately in open deeds, it is stored up for the guidance of the future. It goes to make a part of that aggregate of beliefs which is the link between sensation and action at every moment of all our lives, and which is so organised and compacted together that no part of it can be isolated from the rest, but every new addition modifies the structure of the whole. No real belief, however trifling and fragmentary it may seem, is ever truly insignificant; it prepares us to receive more of its like, confirms those which resembled it before, and weakens others; and so gradually it lays a stealthy train in our inmost thoughts, which may some day explode into overt action, and leave its stamp upon our character for ever.

And no one man's belief is in any case a private matter which concerns himself alone. Our lives are guided by that general conception of the course of things which has been created by society for social purposes. Our words, our phrases, our forms and processes and modes of thought, are common property, fashioned and perfected from age to age; an heirloom which every succeeding generation inherits as a precious deposit and a sacred trust to be handed on to the next one, not unchanged but enlarged and purified, with some clear marks of its proper handiwork. Into this, for good or ill, is woven every belief of every man who has speech of his fellows. An awful privilege, and an awful responsibility, that we should help to create the world in which posterity will live.

In the two supposed cases which have been considered, it has been judged wrong to believe on insufficient evidence, or to nourish belief by suppressing doubts and avoiding investigation. The reason of this judgment is not far to seek: it is that in both these cases the belief held by one man was of great importance to other men. But forasmuch as no belief held by one man, however seemingly trivial the belief, and however obscure the believer, is ever actually insignificant or without its effect on the fate of mankind, we have no choice but to extend our judgment to all cases of belief whatever. Belief, that sacred faculty which prompts the decisions of our will, and knits into harmonious working all the compacted energies of our being, is ours not for ourselves, but for humanity. It is rightly used on truths which have been established by long experience and waiting toil, and which have stood in the fierce light of free and fearless questioning. Then it helps to bind men together, and to strengthen and direct their common action. It is desecrated when given to unproved and unquestioned statements, for the solace and private pleasure of the believer; to add a tinsel splendour to the plain straight road of our life and display a bright mirage beyond it; or even to drown the common sorrows of our kind by a self-deception which allows them not only to cast down, but also to degrade us. Whoso would deserve well of his fellows in this matter will guard the purity of his belief with a very fanaticism of jealous care, lest at any time it should rest on an unworthy object, and catch a stain which can never be wiped away.

It is not only the leader of men, statesman, philosopher, or poet, that owes this bounden duty to mankind. Every rustic who delivers in the village alehouse his slow, infrequent sentences, may help to kill or keep alive the fatal superstitions which clog his race. Every hard-worked wife of an artisan may transmit to her children beliefs which shall knit society together, or rend it in pieces. No simplicity of mind, no obscurity of station, can escape the universal duty of questioning all that we believe.

It is true that this duty is a hard one, and the doubt which comes out of it is often a very bitter thing. It leaves us bare and powerless where we thought that we were safe and strong. To know all about anything is to know how to deal with it under all circumstances. We feel much happier and more secure when we think we know precisely what to do, no matter what happens, than when we have lost our way and do not know where to turn. And if we have supposed ourselves to know all about anything, and to be capable of doing what is fit in regard to it, we naturally do not like to find that we are really ignorant and powerless, that we have to begin again at the beginning, and try to learn what the thing is and how it is to be dealt with—if indeed anything can be learnt about it. It is the sense of power attached to a sense of knowledge that makes men desirous of believing, and afraid of doubting.

This sense of power is the highest and best of pleasures when the belief on which it is founded is a true belief, and has been fairly earned by investigation. For then we may justly feel that it is common property, and holds good for others as well as for ourselves. Then we may be glad, not that *I* have learned secrets by which I am safer and stronger, but that *we men* have got mastery over more of the world; and we shall be strong, not for ourselves, but in the name of Man and in his strength. But if the belief has been accepted on insufficient evidence, the pleasure is a stolen one. Not only does it deceive ourselves by giving us a sense of power which we do not really possess, but it is sinful, because it is stolen in defiance of our duty to mankind. That duty is to guard ourselves from such beliefs as from a pestilence, which may shortly master our own body and then spread to the rest of the town. What would be thought of one who, for the sake of a sweet fruit, should deliberately run the risk of bringing a plague upon his family and his neighbours?

And, as in other such cases, it is not the risk only which has to be considered; for a bad action is always bad at the time when it is done, no matter what happens afterwards. Every time we let ourselves believe for unworthy reasons, we weaken our powers of self-control, of doubting, of judicially and fairly weighing evidence. We all suffer severely enough from the maintenance and support of false beliefs and the fatally wrong actions which they lead to, and the evil born when one such belief is entertained is great and wide. But a greater and wider evil arises when the credulous character is maintained and supported, when a habit of believing for unworthy reasons is fostered and made permanent. If I steal money from any person, there may be no harm done by the mere transfer of possession; he may not feel the loss, or it may prevent him from using the money badly. But I cannot help doing this great wrong towards Man, that I make myself dishonest. What hurts society is not that it should lose its property, but that it should become a den of thieves; for then it must cease to be society. This is why we ought not to do evil that good may come; for at any rate this great evil has come,

that we have done evil and are made wicked thereby. In like manner, if I let myself believe anything on insufficient evidence, there may be no great harm done by the mere belief; it may be true after all, or I may never have occasion to exhibit it in outward acts. But I cannot help doing this great wrong towards Man, that I make myself credulous. The danger to society is not merely that it should believe wrong things, though that is great enough; but that it should become credulous, and lose the habit of testing things and inquiring into them; for then it must sink back into savagery.

The harm which is done by credulity in a man is not confined to the fostering of a credulous character in others, and consequent support of false beliefs. Habitual want of care about what I believe leads to habitual want of care in others about the truth of what is told to me. Men speak the truth to one another when each reveres the truth in his own mind and in the other's mind; but how shall my friend revere the truth in my mind when I myself am careless about it, when I believe things because I want to believe them, and because they are comforting and pleasant? Will he not learn to cry, "Peace," to me, when there is no peace? By such a course I shall surround myself with a thick atmosphere of falsehood and fraud, and in that I must live. It may matter little to me, in my cloud-castle of sweet illusions and darling lies; but it matters much to Man that I have made my neighbours ready to deceive. The credulous man is father to the liar and the cheat; he lives in the bosom of this his family, and it is no marvel if he should become even as they are. So closely are our duties knit together, that whoso shall keep the whole law, and yet offend in one point, he is guilty of all.

To sum up: it is wrong always, everywhere, and for any one, to believe anything upon insufficient evidence.

If a man, holding a belief which he was taught in childhood or persuaded of afterwards, keeps down and pushes away any doubts which arise about it in his mind, purposely avoids the reading of books and the company of men that call in question or discuss it, and regards as impious those questions which cannot easily be asked without disturbing it—the life of that man is one long sin against mankind.

If this judgment seems harsh when applied to those simple souls who have never known better, who have been brought up from the cradle with a horror of doubt, and taught that their eternal welfare depends on *what* they believe, then it leads to the very serious question, *Who hath made Israel to sin?*

It may be permitted me to fortify this judgment with the sentence of Milton[2]—

"A man may be a heretic in the truth; and if he believe things only because his pastor says so, or the assembly so determine, without knowing other reason, though his belief be true, yet the very truth he holds becomes his heresy."

And with this famous aphorism of Coleridge[3]—

"He who begins by loving Christianity better than Truth, will proceed by loving his own sect or Church better than Christianity, and end in loving himself better than all."

Inquiry into the evidence of a doctrine is not to be made once for all, and then taken as finally settled. It is never lawful to stifle a doubt; for either it can be honestly answered by means of the inquiry already made, or else it proves that the inquiry was not complete.

"But," says one, "I am a busy man; I have no time for the long course of study which would be necessary to make me in any degree a competent judge of certain questions, or even able to understand the nature of the arguments." Then he should have no time to believe.

[2]*Areopagitica.*
[3]*Aids to Reflection.*

# READING 8

# The Will to Believe
*William James*

*The American philosopher and psychologist William James (1842–1910) taught at Harvard University for over thirty years. He was the brother of Henry James, the novelist, and a founding member of the philosophical movement known as Pragmatism. Many of James's books and articles originated as lectures and are written in a lively personal style. James's best-known books are his* Principles of Psychology *(1890) and* The Varieties of Religious Experience *(1902).*

## THE WILL TO BELIEVE[1]

In the recently published Life by Leslie Stephen of his brother, Fitz-James, there is an account of a school to which the latter went when he was a boy.

[1]An Address to the Philosophical Clubs of Yale and Brown Universities. Published in the *New World*, June, 1896.

SOURCE: From *The Will to Believe and Other Essays in Popular Philosophy* (New York: Longmans, Green & Co., 1897): 1–31. Edited.

The teacher, a certain Mr. Guest, used to converse with his pupils in this wise: "Gurney, what is the difference between justification and sanctification?—Stephen, prove the omnipotence of God!" etc. In the midst of our Harvard freethinking and indifference we are prone to imagine that here at your good old orthodox College conversation continues to be somewhat upon this order; and to show you that we at Harvard have not lost all interest in these vital subjects, I have brought with me to-night something like a sermon on justification by faith to read to you,—I mean an essay in justification *of* faith, a defence of our right to adopt a believing attitude in religious matters, in spite of the fact that our merely logical intellect may not have been coerced. 'The Will to Believe,' accordingly, is the title of my paper.

I have long defended to my own students the lawfulness of voluntarily adopted faith; but as soon as they have got well imbued with the logical spirit, they have as a rule refused to admit my contention to be lawful philosophically, even though in point of fact they were personally all the time chock-full of some faith or other themselves. I am all the while, however, so profoundly convinced that my own position is correct, that your invitation has seemed to me a good occasion to make my statements more clear. Perhaps your minds will be more open than those with which I have hitherto had to deal. I will be as little technical as I can, though I must begin by setting up some technical distinctions that will help us in the end.

## I.

Let us give the name of *hypothesis* to anything that may be proposed to our belief; and just as the electricians speak of live and dead wires, let us speak of any hypothesis as either *live* or *dead*. A live hypothesis is one which appeals as a real possibility to him to whom it is proposed. If I ask you to believe in the Mahdi, the notion makes no electric connection with your nature,—it refuses to scintillate with any credibility at all. As an hypothesis it is completely dead. To an Arab, however (even if he be not one of the Mahdi's followers), the hypothesis is among the mind's possibilities: it is alive. This shows that deadness and liveness in an hypothesis are not intrinsic properties, but relations to the individual thinker. They are measured by his willingness to act. The maximum of liveness in an hypothesis means willingness to act irrevocably. Practically, that means belief; but there is some believing tendency wherever there is willingness to act at all.

Next, let us call the decision between two hypotheses an *option*. Options may be of several kinds. They may be—1, *living* or *dead;* 2, *forced* or *avoidable;* 3, *momentous* or *trivial;* and for our purposes we may call an option a *genuine* option when it is of the forced, living, and momentous kind.

(1) A living option is one in which both hypotheses are live ones. If I say to you: "Be a theosophist or be a Mohammedan," it is probably a dead option, because for you neither hypothesis is likely to be alive. But if I say: "Be an agnostic or be a Christian," it is otherwise: trained as you are, each hypothesis makes some appeal, however small, to your belief.

(2) Next, if I say to you: "Choose between going out with your umbrella or without it," I do not offer you a genuine option, for it is not forced. You can easily avoid it by not going out at all. Similarly, if I say, "Either love me or hate me," "Either call my theory true or call it false," your option is avoidable. You may remain indifferent to me, neither loving nor hating, and you may decline to offer any judgment as to my theory. But if I say, "Either accept this truth or go without it," I put on you a forced option, for there is no standing place outside of the alternative. Every dilemma based on a complete logical disjunction, with no possibility of not choosing, is an option of this forced kind.

(3) Finally, if I were Dr. Nansen and proposed to you to join my North Pole expedition, your option would be momentous; for this would probably be your only similar opportunity, and your choice now would either exclude you from the North Pole sort of immortality altogether or put at least the chance of it into your hands. He who refuses to embrace a unique opportunity loses the prize as surely as if he tried and failed. *Per contra,* the option is trivial when the opportunity is not unique, when the stake is insignificant, or when the decision is reversible if it later prove unwise. Such trivial options abound in the scientific life. A chemist finds an hypothesis live enough to spend a year in its verification: he believes in it to that extent. But if his experiments prove inconclusive either way, he is quit for his loss of time, no vital harm being done.

It will facilitate our discussion if we keep all these distinctions well in mind.

## II.

The next matter to consider is the actual psychology of human opinion. When we look at certain facts, it seems as if our passional and volitional nature lay at the root of all our convictions. When we look at others, it seems as if they could do nothing when the intellect had once said its say. Let us take the latter facts up first.

Does it not seem preposterous on the very face of it to talk of our opinions being modifiable at will? Can our will either help or hinder our intellect in its perceptions of truth? Can we, by just willing it, believe that Abraham Lincoln's existence is a myth, and that the portraits of him in McClure's Magazine are all of some one else? Can we, by any effort of our will, or by any strength of wish that it were true, believe ourselves well and about when we are roaring with rheumatism in bed, or feel certain that the sum of the two one-dollar bills in our pocket must be a hundred dollars? We can *say* any of these things, but we are absolutely impotent to believe them; and of just such things is the whole fabric of the truths that we do believe in made up,—matters of fact, immediate or remote, as Hume said, and relations between ideas, which are either there or not there for us if we see them so, and which if not there cannot be put there by any action of our own.

In Pascal's Thoughts there is a celebrated passage known in literature as Pascal's wager. In it he tries to force us into Christianity by reasoning as if our concern with truth resembled our concern with the stakes in a game of chance. Translated freely his words are these: You must either believe or not believe that God is—which will you do? Your human reason cannot say. A game is going on between you and the nature of things which at the day of judgment will bring out either heads or tails. Weigh what your gains and your losses would be if you should stake all you have on heads, or God's existence: if you win in such case, you gain eternal beatitude; if you lose, you lose nothing at all. If there were an infinity of chances, and only one for God in this wager, still you ought to stake your all on God; for though you surely risk a finite loss by this procedure, any finite loss is reasonable, even a certain one is reasonable, if there is but the possibility of infinite gain. Go, then, and take holy water, and have masses said; belief will come and stupefy your scruples,—*Cela vous fera croire et vous abêtira.* [Ed. that will make you believe and make you more docile.] Why should you not? At bottom, what have you to lose?

You probably feel that when religious faith expresses itself thus, in the language of the gaming-table, it is put to its last trumps. Surely Pascal's own personal belief in masses and holy water had far other springs; and this celebrated page of his is but an argument for others, a last desperate snatch at a weapon against the hardness of the unbelieving heart. We feel that a faith in masses and holy water adopted wilfully after such a mechanical calculation would lack the inner soul of faith's reality; and if we were ourselves in the place of the Deity, we should probably take particular pleasure in cutting off believers of this pattern from their infinite reward. It is

evident that unless there be some pre-existing tendency to believe in masses and holy water, the option offered to the will by Pascal is not a living option. Certainly no Turk ever took to masses and holy water on its account; and even to us Protestants these means of salvation seem such foregone impossibilities that Pascal's logic, invoked for them specifically, leaves us unmoved. As well might the Mahdi write to us, saying, "I am the Expected One whom God has created in his effulgence. You shall be infinitely happy if you confess me; otherwise you shall be cut off from the light of the sun. Weigh, then, your infinite gain if I am genuine against your finite sacrifice if I am not!" His logic would be that of Pascal; but he would vainly use it on us, for the hypothesis he offers us is dead. No tendency to act on it exists in us to any degree.

The talk of believing by our volition seems, then, from one point of view, simply silly. From another point of view it is worse than silly, it is vile. When one turns to the magnificent edifice of the physical sciences, and sees how it was reared; what thousands of disinterested moral lives of men lie buried in its mere foundations; what patience and postponement, what choking down of preference, what submission to the icy laws of outer fact are wrought into its very stones and mortar; how absolutely impersonal it stands in its vast augustness,—then how besotted and contemptible seems every little sentimentalist who comes blowing his voluntary smoke-wreaths, and pretending to decide things from out of his private dream! Can we wonder if those bred in the rugged and manly school of science should feel like spewing such subjectivism out of their mouths? The whole system of loyalties which grow up in the schools of science go dead against its toleration; so that it is only natural that those who have caught the scientific fever should pass over to the opposite extreme, and write sometimes as if the incorruptibly truthful intellect ought positively to prefer bitterness and unacceptableness to the heart in its cup.

> It fortifies my soul to know
> That, though I perish, Truth is so—

sings Clough, while Huxley exclaims: "My only consolation lies in the reflection that, however bad our posterity may become, so far as they hold by the plain rule of not pretending to believe what they have no reason to believe, because it may be to their advantage so to pretend [the word 'pretend' is surely here redundant], they will not have reached the lowest depth of immortality." And that delicious *enfant terrible* Clifford writes: "Belief is desecrated when given to unproved and unquestioned statements for the solace and private pleasure of the believer. . . . Whoso would deserve well of his fellows in this matter will guard the purity of his belief with a very fanaticism of jealous care, lest at any time it should rest on an unworthy object, and catch a stain which can never be wiped away. . . . If [a] belief has been accepted on insufficient evidence [even though the belief be true, as Clifford on the same page explains] the pleasure is a stolen one. . . . It is sinful because it is stolen in defiance of our duty to mankind. That duty is to guard ourselves from such beliefs as from a pestilence which may shortly master our own body and then spread to the rest of the town. . . . It is wrong always, everywhere, and for every one, to believe anything upon insufficient evidence."

## III.

All this strikes one as healthy, even when expressed, as by Clifford, with somewhat too much of robustious pathos in the voice. Free will and simple wishing do seem, in the matter of our credences, to be only fifth wheels to the coach. Yet if any one should thereupon assume that intellectual insight is what remains after wish and will and sentimental preference have taken wing, or that pure reason is what then settles our opinions, he would fly quite as directly in the teeth of the facts.

It is only our already dead hypotheses that our willing nature is unable to bring to life again. But what has made them dead for us is for the most part a previous action of our willing nature of an antagonistic kind. When I say 'willing nature,' I do not mean only such deliberate volitions as may have set up habits of belief that we cannot now escape from,—I mean all such factors of belief as fear and hope, prejudice and passion, imitation and partisanship, the circumpressure of our caste and set. As a matter of fact we find ourselves believing, we hardly know how or why. Mr. Balfour gives the name of 'authority' to all those influences, born of the intellectual climate, that make hypotheses possible or impossible for us, alive or dead. Here in this room, we all of us believe in molecules and the conservation of energy, in democracy and necessary progress, in

Protestant Christianity and the duty of fighting for 'the doctrine of the immortal Monroe,' all for no reasons worthy of the name. We see into these matters with no more inner clearness, and probably with much less, than any disbeliever in them might possess. His unconventionality would probably have some grounds to show for its conclusions; but for us, not insight, but the *prestige* of the opinions, is what makes the spark shoot from them and light up our sleeping magazines of faith. Our reason is quite satisfied, in nine hundred and ninety-nine cases out of every thousand of us, if it can find a few arguments that will do to recite in case our credulity is criticised by some one else. Our faith is faith in some one else's faith, and in the greatest matters this is most the case. . . .

As a rule we disbelieve all facts and theories for which we have no use. Clifford's cosmic emotions find no use for Christian feelings. Huxley belabors the bishops because there is no use for sacerdotalism in his scheme of life. Newman, on the contrary, goes over to Romanism, and finds all sorts of reasons good for staying there, because a priestly system is for him an organic need and delight. Why do so few 'scientists' even look at the evidence for telepathy, so called? Because they think as a leading biologist, now dead, once said to me, that even if such a thing were true, scientists ought to band together to keep it suppressed and concealed. It would undo the uniformity of Nature and all sorts of other things without which scientists cannot carry on their pursuits. But if this very man had been shown something which as a scientist he might *do* with telepathy, he might not only have examined the evidence, but even have found it good enough. This very law which the logicians would impose upon us—if I may give the name of logicians to those who would rule out our willing nature here—is based on nothing but their own natural wish to exclude all elements for which they, in their professional quality of logicians, can find no use.

Evidently, then, our non-intellectual nature does influence our convictions. There are passional tendencies and volitions which run before and others which come after belief, and it is only the latter that are too late for the fair; and they are not too late when the previous passional work has been already in their own direction. Pascal's argument, instead of being powerless, then seems a regular clincher, and is the last stroke needed to make our faith in masses and holy water complete. The state of things is evidently far from simple; and pure insight and logic, whatever they might do ideally, are not the only things that really do produce our creeds.

### IV.

Our next duty, having recognized this mixed-up state of affairs, is to ask whether it be simply reprehensible and pathological, or whether, on the contrary, we must treat it as a normal element in making up our minds. The thesis I defend is, briefly stated, this: *Our passional nature not only lawfully may, but must, decide an option between propositions, whenever it is a genuine option that cannot by its nature be decided on intellectual grounds; for to say, under such circumstances, "Do not decide, but leave the question open," is itself a passional decision,—just like deciding yes or no,—and is attended with the same risk of losing the truth. . . .*

### VII.

One more point, small but important, and our preliminaries are done. There are two ways of looking at our duty in the matter of opinion,—ways entirely different, and yet ways about whose difference the theory of knowledge seems hitherto to have shown very little concern. *We must know the truth; and we must avoid error,*—these are our first and great commandments as would-be knowers; but they are not two ways of stating an identical commandment, they are two separable laws. Although it may indeed happen that when we believe the truth *A,* we escape as an incidental consequence from believing the falsehood *B,* it hardly ever happens that by merely disbelieving *B* we necessarily believe *A.* We may in escaping *B* fall into believing other falsehoods, *C* or *D,* just as bad as *B;* or we may escape *B* by not believing anything at all, not even *A.*

Believe truth! Shun error!—these, we see, are two materially different laws; and by choosing between them we may end by coloring differently our whole intellectual life. We may regard the chase for truth as paramount, and the avoidance of error as secondary; or we may, on the other hand, treat the avoidance of error as more imperative, and let truth take its chance. Clifford, in the instructive passage which I have quoted, exhorts us to the latter course. Believe nothing, he tells us, keep your mind in suspense forever, rather than by closing it on insufficient evidence incur the awful risk of believing lies. You, on

the other hand, may think that the risk of being in error is a very small matter when compared with the blessings of real knowledge, and be ready to be duped many times in your investigation rather than postpone indefinitely the chance of guessing true. I myself find it impossible to go with Clifford. We must remember that these feelings of our duty about either truth or error are in any case only expressions of our passional life. Biologically considered, our minds are as ready to grind out falsehood as veracity, and he who says, "Better go without belief forever than believe a lie!" merely shows his own preponderant private horror of becoming a dupe. He may be critical of many of his desires and fears, but this fear he slavishly obeys. He cannot imagine any one questioning its binding force. For my own part, I have also a horror of being duped; but I can believe that worse things than being duped may happen to a man in this world: so Clifford's exhortation has to my ears a thoroughly fantastic sound. It is like a general informing his soldiers that it is better to keep out of battle forever than to risk a single wound. Not so are victories either over enemies or over nature gained. Our errors are surely not such awfully solemn things. In a world where we are so certain to incur them in spite of all our caution, a certain lightness of heart seems healthier than this excessive nervousness on their behalf. At any rate, it seems the fittest thing for the empiricist philosopher.

### VIII.

And now, after all this introduction, let us go straight at our question. I have said, and now repeat it, that not only as a matter of fact do we find our passional nature influencing us in our opinions, but that there are some options between opinions in which this influence must be regarded both as an inevitable and as a lawful determinant of our choice.

I fear here that some of you my hearers will begin to scent danger, and lend an inhospitable ear. Two first steps of passion you have indeed had to admit as necessary,—we must think so as to avoid dupery, and we must think so as to gain truth; but the surest path to those ideal consummations, you will probably consider, is from now onwards to take no further passional step.

Well, of course, I agree as far as the facts will allow. Wherever the option between losing truth and gaining it is not momentous, we can throw the chance of *gaining truth* away, and at any rate save ourselves from any chance of *believing falsehood*, by not making up our minds at all till objective evidence has come. In scientific questions, this is almost always the case; and even in human affairs in general, the need of acting is seldom so urgent that a false belief to act on is better than no belief at all. Law courts, indeed, have to decide on the best evidence attainable for the moment, because a judge's duty is to make law as well as to ascertain it, and (as a learned judge once said to me) few cases are worth spending much time over: the great thing is to have them decided on *any* acceptable principle, and got out of the way. But in our dealings with objective nature we obviously are recorders, not makers, of the truth; and decisions for the mere sake of deciding promptly and getting on to the next business would be wholly out of place. Throughout the breadth of physical nature facts are what they are quite independently of us, and seldom is there any such hurry about them that the risks of being duped by believing a premature theory need be faced. The questions here are always trivial options, the hypotheses are hardly living (at any rate not living for us spectators), the choice between believing truth or falsehood is seldom forced. The attitude of sceptical balance is therefore the absolutely wise one if we would escape mistakes. What difference, indeed, does it make to most of us whether we have or have not a theory of the Röntgen rays [Ed. X-rays], whether we believe or not in mind-stuff, or have a conviction about the causality of conscious states? It makes no difference. Such options are not forced on us. On every account it is better not to make them, but still keep weighing reasons *pro et contra* with an indifferent hand.

I speak, of course, here of the purely judging mind. For purposes of discovery such indifference is to be less highly recommended, and science would be far less advanced than she is if the passionate desires of individuals to get their own faiths confirmed had been kept out of the game. See for example the sagacity which Spencer and Weismann now display. On the other hand, if you want an absolute duffer in an investigation, you must, after all, take the man who has no interest whatever in its results: he is the warranted incapable, the positive fool. The most useful investigator, because the most sensitive observer, is always he whose eager interest in one side of the question is balanced by an equally keen nervousness lest he become deceived.[2] Science has organized this nervousness into a regular *technique*, her so-called method of verification; and she has fallen so deeply in love with the method that one may even say she has ceased to care for truth by itself at all. It is only truth as technically verified that interests her. The truth of truths might come in merely affirmative form, and she would decline to touch it. Such truth as that, she might repeat with Clifford, would be stolen in defiance of her duty to mankind. Human passions, however, are stronger than technical rules. "Le cœur a ses raisons," as Pascal says, "que la raison ne connaît pas;" [Ed. the heart has its reasons of which reason is ignorant] and however indifferent to all but the bare rules of the game the umpire, the abstract intellect, may be, the concrete players who furnish him the materials to judge of are usually, each one of them, in love with some pet 'live hypothesis' of his own. Let us agree, however, that wherever there is no forced option, the dispassionately judicial intellect with no pet hypothesis, saving us, as it does, from dupery at any rate, ought to be our ideal.

The question next arises: Are there not somewhere forced options in our speculative questions, and can we (as men who may be interested at least as much in positively gaining truth as in merely escaping dupery) always wait with impunity till the coercive evidence shall have arrived? It seems *a priori* improbable that the truth should be so nicely adjusted to our needs and powers as that. In the great boarding-house of nature, the cakes and the butter and the syrup seldom come out so even and leave the plates so clean. Indeed, we should view them with scientific suspicion if they did.

## IX.

*Moral questions* immediately present themselves as questions whose solution cannot wait for sensible proof. A moral question is a question not of what sensibly exists, but of what is good, or would be good if it did exist. Science can tell us what exists; but to compare the *worths*, both of what exists and what does not exist, we must consult not science, but what Pascal calls our heart. . . .

Turn now from these wide questions of good to a certain class of questions of fact, questions concern-

[2]Compare Wilfrid Ward's essay, "The Wish to Believe," in his *Witnesses to the Unseen*, Macmillan & Co., 1893.

ing personal relations, states of mind between one man and another. *Do you like me or not?*—for example. Whether you do or not depends, in countless instances, on whether I meet you half-way, am willing to assume that you must like me, and show you trust and expectation. The previous faith on my part in your liking's existence is in such cases what makes your liking come. But if I stand aloof, and refuse to budge an inch until I have objective evidence, until you shall have done something apt, as the absolutists say, *ad extorquendum assensum meum,* [Ed. to compel my assent] ten to one your liking never comes. How many women's hearts are vanquished by the mere sanguine insistence of some man that they *must* love him! he will not consent to the hypothesis that they cannot. The desire for a certain kind of truth here brings about that special truth's existence; and so it is in innumerable cases of other sorts. Who gains promotions, boons, appointments, but the man in whose life they are seen to play the part of live hypotheses, who discounts them, sacrifices other things for their sake before they have come, and takes risks for them in advance? His faith acts on the powers above him as a claim, and creates its own verification.

A social organism of any sort whatever, large or small, is what it is because each member proceeds to his own duty with a trust that the other members will simultaneously do theirs. Wherever a desired result is achieved by the co-operation of many independent persons, its existence as a fact is a pure consequence of the precursive faith in one another of those immediately concerned. A government, an army, a commercial system, a ship, a college, an athletic team, all exist on this condition, without which not only is nothing achieved, but nothing is even attempted. A whole train of passengers (individually brave enough) will be looted by a few highwaymen, simply because the latter can count on one another, while each passenger fears that if he makes a movement of resistance, he will be shot before any one else backs him up. If we believed that the whole car-full would rise at once with us, we should each severally rise, and train-robbing would never even be attempted. There are, then, cases where a fact cannot come at all unless a preliminary faith exists in its coming. *And where faith in a fact can help create the fact,* that would be an insane logic which should say that faith running ahead of scientific evidence is the 'lowest kind of immorality' into which a thinking being can fall. Yet such is the logic by which our scientific absolutists pretend to regulate our lives!

### X.

In truths dependent on our personal action, then, faith based on desire is certainly a lawful and possibly an indispensable thing.

But now, it will be said, these are all childish human cases, and have nothing to do with great cosmical matters, like the question of religious faith. Let us then pass on to that. Religions differ so much in their accidents that in discussing the religious question we must make it very generic and broad. What then do we now mean by the religious hypothesis? Science says things are; morality says some things are better than other things; and religion says essentially two things.

First, she says that the best things are the more eternal things, the overlapping things, the things in the universe that throw the last stone, so to speak, and say the final word. "Perfection is eternal,"—this phrase of Charles Secrétan seems a good way of putting this first affirmation of religion, an affirmation which obviously cannot yet be verified scientifically at all.

The second affirmation of religion is that we are better off even now if we believe her first affirmation to be true.

Now, let us consider what the logical elements of this situation are *in case the religious hypothesis in both its branches be really true.* (Of course, we must admit that possibility at the outset. If we are to discuss the question at all, it must involve a living option. If for any of you religion be a hypothesis that cannot, by any living possibility be true, then you need go no farther. I speak to the 'saving remnant' alone.) So proceeding, we see, first, that religion offers itself as a *momentous* option. We are supposed to gain, even now, by our belief, and to lose by our nonbelief, a certain vital good. Secondly, religion is a *forced* option, so far as that good goes. We cannot escape the issue by remaining sceptical and waiting for more light, because, although we do avoid error in that way *if religion be untrue,* we lose the good, *if it be true,* just as certainly as if we positively chose to disbelieve. It is as if a man should hesitate indefinitely to ask a certain woman to marry him because he was not perfectly sure that she would prove an angel after he brought her home. Would he not cut himself off from that particular angel-possibility as decisively as if he went and married some one else? Scepticism, then, is not avoidance of option; it is option of a certain particular kind of risk. *Better risk loss of truth than chance of error,*—that is your faith-vetoer's exact position. He is actively playing his stake as much as the believer is; he is backing the field against the religious hypothesis, just as the believer is backing the religious hypothesis against the field. To preach scepticism to us as a duty until 'sufficient evidence' for religion be found, is tantamount therefore to telling us, when in presence of the religious hypothesis, that to yield to our fear of its being error is wiser and better than to yield to our hope that it may be true. It is not intellect against all passions, then; it is only intellect with one passion laying down its law. And by what, forsooth, is the supreme wisdom of this passion warranted? Dupery for dupery, what proof is there that dupery through hope is so much worse than dupery through fear? I, for one, can see no proof; and I simply refuse obedience to the scientist's command to imitate his kind of option, in a case where my own stake is important enough to give me the right to choose my own form of risk. If religion be true and the evidence for it be still insufficient, I do not wish, by putting your extinguisher upon my nature (which feels to me as if it had after all some business in this matter), to forfeit my sole chance in life of getting upon the winning side,—that chance depending, of course, on my willingness to run the risk of acting as if my passional need of taking the world religiously might be prophetic and right.

All this is on the supposition that it really may be prophetic and right, and that, even to us who are discussing the matter, religion is a live hypothesis which may be true. Now, to most of us religion comes in a still further way that makes a veto on our active faith even more illogical. The more perfect and more eternal aspect of the universe is represented in our religions as having personal form. The universe is no longer a mere *It* to us, but a *Thou,* if we are religious; and any relation that may be possible from person to person might be possible here. For instance, although in one sense we are passive portions of the universe, in another we show a curious autonomy, as if we were small active centres on our own account. We feel, too, as if the appeal of religion to us were made to our own active good-will, as if evidence might be forever withheld from us unless we met the hypothesis half-way. To take a trivial illustration: just as a man who in a company of gentlemen made no advances, asked a warrant for every concession, and believed no one's word without proof, would cut himself off by such churlishness from all the social rewards that a more trusting spirit would earn,—so here, one who should shut himself up in snarling logicality and try to make the gods extort his recognition willy-nilly, or not get it at all, might cut himself off forever from his only opportunity of making the gods' acquaintance. This feeling, forced on us we know not whence, that by obstinately believing that there are gods (although not to do so would be so easy both for our logic and our life) we are doing the universe the deepest service we can, seems part of the living essence of the religious hypothesis. If the hypothesis *were* true in all its parts, including this one, then pure intellectualism, with its veto on our making willing advances, would be an absurdity; and some participation of our sympathetic nature would be logically required. I, therefore, for one, cannot see my way to accepting the agnostic rules for truth-seeking, or wilfully agree to keep my willing nature out of the game. I cannot do so for this plain reason, that *a rule of thinking which would absolutely prevent me from acknowledging certain kinds of truth if those kinds of truth were really there, would be an irrational rule.* That for me is the long and short of the formal logic of the situation, no matter what the kinds of truth might materially be.

I confess I do not see how this logic can be escaped. But sad experience makes me fear that some of you may still shrink from radically saying with me, *in abstracto,* that we have the right to believe at our own risk any hypothesis that is live enough to tempt our will. I suspect, however, that if this is so, it is because you have got away from the abstract logical point of view altogether, and are thinking (perhaps without realizing it) of some particular religious hypothesis which for you is dead. The freedom to 'believe what we will' you apply to the case of some patent superstition; and the faith you think of is the faith defined by the schoolboy when he said, "Faith is when you believe something that you know ain't true." I can only repeat that this is misapprehension. *In concreto,* the freedom to believe can only cover living options which the intellect of the individual cannot by itself resolve; and living options never seem absurdities to him who has them to consider. When I look at the religious question as it really puts itself to concrete men, and when I think of all the possibilities which both practically and theoretically it involves, then this command that we shall put a stopper on our heart, instincts, and courage, and *wait*—acting of course meanwhile more or less as if religion were *not* true[3]—till doomsday, or till such time as our intellect and senses working together may have raked in evidence enough,—this command, I say, seems to me the queerest idol ever manufactured in the philosophic cave. Were we scholastic absolutists, there might be more excuse. If we had an infallible intellect with its objective certitudes, we might feel ourselves disloyal to such a perfect organ of knowledge in not trusting to it exclusively, in not waiting for its releasing word. But if we are empiricists, if we believe that no bell in us tolls to let us know for certain when truth is in our grasp, then it seems a piece of idle fantasticality to preach so solemnly our duty of waiting for the bell. Indeed we *may* wait if we will,—I hope you do not think that I am denying that,—but if we do so, we do so at our peril as much as if we believed. In either case we *act*, taking our life in our hands. No one of us ought to issue vetoes to the other, nor should we bandy words of abuse. We ought, on the contrary, delicately and profoundly to respect one another's mental free-

dom: then only shall we bring about the intellectual republic; then only shall we have that spirit of inner tolerance without which all our outer tolerance is soulless, and which is empiricism's glory; then only shall we live and let live, in speculative as well as in practical things.

I began by a reference to Fitz James Stephen; let me end by a quotation from him. "What do you think of yourself? What do you think of the world? . . . These are questions with which all must deal as it seems good to them. They are riddles of the Sphinx, and in some way or other we must deal with them. . . . In all important transactions of life we have to take a leap in the dark. . . . If we decide to leave the riddles unanswered, that is a choice; if we waver in our answer, that, too, is a choice: but whatever choice we make, we make it at our peril. If a man chooses to turn his back altogether on God and the future, no one can prevent him; no one can show beyond reasonable doubt that he is mistaken. If a man thinks otherwise and acts as he thinks, I do not see that any one can prove that *he* is mistaken. Each must act as he thinks best; and if he is wrong, so much the worse for him. We stand on a mountain pass in the midst of whirling snow and blinding mist, through which we get glimpses now and then of paths which may be deceptive. If we stand still we shall be frozen to death. If we take the wrong road we shall be dashed to pieces. We do not certainly know whether there is any right one. What must we do? 'Be strong and of a good courage.' Act for the best, hope for the best, and take what comes. . . . If death ends all, we cannot meet death better.[4]

---

[3]Since belief is measured by action, he who forbids us to believe religion to be true, necessarily also forbids us to act as we should if we did believe it to be true. The whole defence of religious faith hinges upon action. If the action required or inspired by the religious hypothesis is in no way different from that dictated by the naturalistic hypothesis, then religious faith is a pure superfluity, better pruned away, and controversy about its legitimacy is a piece of idle trifling, unworthy of serious minds. I myself believe, of course, that the religious hypothesis gives to the world an expression which specifically determines our reactions, and makes them in a large part unlike what they might be on a purely naturalistic scheme of belief.

[4]*Liberty, Equality, Fraternity*, p. 353, 2d edition. London, 1874.

## READING 9

# The Argument from Religious Experience

*C. D. Broad*

*The English philosopher Charlie Dunbar Broad (1887–1972) was Knightbridge Professor of Moral Philosophy at the University of Cambridge. He wrote widely on issues in epistemology, philosophy of science, ethics, and philosophy of mind. Broad was also keenly interested in parapsychology and psychical research. His books include* Scientific Thought *(1923);* The Mind and Its Place in Nature *(1925); and* Religion, Philosophy, and Scientific Research *(1953). See Reading 21 for Broad's views on the mind-body problem.*

. . . Some people seem to be almost wholly devoid of any specifically religious experience; and among those who have it the differences of kind and degree are enormous. Founders of religions and saints, e.g., often claim to have been in direct contact with God, to have seen and spoken with Him, and so on. An ordinary religious man would certainly not make any such claim, though he might say that he had had experiences which assured him of the existence and presence of God. So the first thing that we have to notice is that capacity for religious experience is in certain respects like an ear for music. There are a few people who are unable to recognize and distinguish the simplest tune. But they are in a minority, like the people who have absolutely no kind of religious experience. Most people have some slight appreciation of music. But the differences of degree in this respect are enormous, and those who have not much gift for music have to take the statements of accomplished musicians very largely on trust. Let us, then, compare tone-deaf persons to those who have no recognizable religious experience at all; the ordinary followers of a religion to men who have some taste for music but can neither appreciate the more difficult kinds nor compose; highly religious men and saints to persons with an exceptionally fine ear for music who may yet be unable to compose it; and the founders of religions to great musical composers, such as Bach and Beethoven.

This analogy is, of course, incomplete in certain important respects. Religious experience raises three problems, which are different though closely interconnected. (i) What is the *psychological analysis* of religious experience? Does it contain factors which are present also in certain experiences which are not religious? Does it contain any factor which never occurs in any other kind of experience? If it contains no such factor, but is a blend of elements each of which can occur separately or in non-religious experiences, its psychological peculiarity must consist in the characteristic way in which these elements are blended in it. Can this peculiar structural feature of religious experience be indicated and described? (ii) What are the *genetic and causal conditions* of the existence of religious experience? Can we trace the origin and development of the disposition to have religious experiences (*a*) in the human race, and (*b*) in each individual? Granted that the disposition is present in nearly all individuals at the present time, can we discover and state the variable conditions which call it into activity on certain occasions and leave it in abeyance on others? (iii) Part of the content of religious experience is alleged knowledge or well-founded belief about the nature of reality, e.g., that we are dependent on a being who loves us and whom we ought to worship, that values are somehow conserved in spite of the chances and changes of the material world at the mercy of which they seem *prima facie* to be, and so on. Therefore there is a third problem. Granted that religious experience exists, that it

SOURCE: From "Arguments for the Existence of God. II," *Journal of Theological Studies* 40 (1939); 157-167. Reprinted in C. D. Broad, *Religion, Philosophy, and Psychical Research* (London: Routledge & Kegan Paul, 1953): 190–201.

has such-and-such a history and conditions, that it seems vitally important to those who have it, and that it produces all kinds of effects which would not otherwise happen, is it *veridical*? Are the claims to knowledge or well-founded belief about the nature of reality, which are an integral part of the experience, *true or probable*? Now, in the case of musical experience, there are analogies to the psychological problem and to the genetic or causal problem, but there is no analogy to the epistemological problem of validity. For, so far as I am aware, no part of the content of musical experience is alleged knowledge about the nature of reality; and therefore no question of its being veridical or delusive can arise.

Since both musical experience and religious experience certainly exist, any theory of the universe which was incompatible with their existence would be false, and any theory which failed to show the connexion between their existence and the other facts about reality would be inadequate. So far the two kinds of experience are in exactly the same position. But a theory which answers to the condition that it allows of the *existence* of religious experience and indicates the *connexion* between its existence and other facts about reality may leave the question as to its *validity* quite unanswered. Or, alternatively, it may throw grave doubt on its cognitive claims, or else it may tend to support them. Suppose, e.g., that it could be shown that religious experience contains no elements which are not factors in other kinds of experience. Suppose further it could be shown that this particular combination of factors tends to originate and to be activated only under certain conditions which are known to be very commonly productive of false beliefs held with strong conviction. Then a satisfactory answer to the questions of psychological analysis and causal antecedents would have tended to answer the epistemological question of validity in the negative. On the other hand, it might be that the only theory which would satisfactorily account for the origin of the religious disposition and for the occurrence of actual religious experiences under certain conditions was a theory which allowed some of the cognitive claims made by religious experience to be true or probable. Thus the three problems, though entirely distinct from each other, may be very closely connected; and it is the existence of the third problem in connexion with religious experience which puts it, for the present purpose, in a different category from musical experience.

In spite of this essential difference the analogy is not to be despised, for it brings out at least one important point. If a man who had no ear for music were to give himself airs on that account, and were to talk *de haut en bas* about those who can appreciate music and think it highly important, we should regard him, not as an advanced thinker, but as a self-satisfied Philistine. And, even if he did not do this but only propounded theories about the nature and causation of musical experience, we might think it reasonable to feel very doubtful whether his theories would be adequate or correct. In the same way, when persons without religious experience regard themselves as being *on that ground* superior to those who have it, their attitude must be treated as merely silly and offensive. Similarly, any theories about religious experience constructed by persons who have little or none of their own should be regarded with grave suspicion. (For that reason it would be unwise to attach very much weight to anything that the present writer may say on this subject.)

On the other hand, we must remember that the possession of a great capacity for religious experience, like the possession of a great capacity for musical appreciation and composition, is no guarantee of high general intelligence. A man may be a saint or a magnificent musician and yet have very little common sense, very little power of accurate introspection or of seeing causal connexions, and scarcely any capacity for logical criticism. He may also be almost as ignorant about other aspects of reality as the non-musical or non-religious man is about musical or religious experience. If such a man starts to theorize about music or religion, his theories may be quite as absurd, though in a different way, as those made by persons who are devoid of musical or religious experience. Fortunately it happens that some religious mystics of a high order have been extremely good at introspecting and describing their own experiences. And some highly religious persons have had very great critical and philosophical abilities. St. Teresa is an example of the first, and St. Thomas Aquinas of the second.

Now I think it must be admitted that, if we compare and contrast the statements made by religious mystics of various times, races, and religions, we find a common nucleus combined with very great differences of detail. Of course the interpretations which they have put on their experiences are much more varied than the experiences themselves. It is obvious that the interpretations will depend in a large measure on the traditional religious beliefs in which various mystics have been brought up. I think that such traditions probably act in two different ways.

(i) The tradition no doubt affects the theoretical interpretation of experiences which would have taken place even if the mystic had been brought up in a different tradition. A feeling of unity with the rest of the universe will be interpreted very differently by a Christian who has been brought up to believe in a personal God and by a Hindu mystic who has been trained in a quite different metaphysical tradition.

(ii) The traditional beliefs, on the other hand, probably determine many of the details of the experience itself. A Roman Catholic mystic may have visions of the Virgin and the saints, whilst a Protestant mystic pretty certainly will not.

Thus the relations between the experiences and the traditional beliefs are highly complex. Presumably the outlines of the belief are determined by the experience. Then the details of the belief are fixed for a certain place and period by the special peculiarities of the experiences had by the founder of a certain religion. These beliefs then become traditional in that religion. Thenceforth they in part determine the details of the experiences had by subsequent mystics of that religion, and still more do they determine the interpretations which these mystics will put upon their experiences. Therefore, when a set of religious beliefs has once been established, it no doubt tends to produce experiences which can plausibly be taken as evidence for it. If it is a tradition in a certain religion that one can communicate with saints, mystics of that religion will seem to see and to talk with saints in their mystical visions; and this fact will be taken as further evidence for the belief that one can communicate with saints.

Much the same double process of causation takes place in sense-perception. On the one hand, the beliefs and expectations which we have at any moment largely determine what *interpretation* we shall put on a certain sensation which we should in any case have had then. On the other hand, our beliefs and expectations do to some extent determine and modify some of the sensible characteristics of the *sensa themselves*. When I am thinking only of diagrams a certain visual stimulus may produce a sensation of a

sensibly flat sensum; but a precisely similar stimulus may produce a sensation of a sensibly solid sensum when I am thinking of solid objects.

Such explanations, however, plainly do not account for the first origin of religious beliefs, or for the features which are common to the religious experiences of persons of widely different times, races, and traditions.

Now, when we find that there are certain experiences which, though never very frequent in a high degree of intensity, have happened in a high degree among a few men at all times and places; and when we find that, in spite of differences in detail which we can explain, they involve certain fundamental conditions which are common and peculiar to them; two alternatives are open to us. (i) We may suppose that these men are in contact with an aspect of reality which is not revealed to ordinary persons in their everyday experience. And we may suppose that the characteristics which they agree in ascribing to reality on the basis of these experiences probably do belong to it. Or (ii) we may suppose that they are all subject to a delusion from which other men are free. In order to illustrate these alternatives it will be useful to consider three partly analogous cases, two of which are real and the third imaginary.

(*a*) Most of the detailed facts which biologists tell us about the minute structure and changes in cells can be perceived only by persons who have had a long training in the use of the microscope. In this case we believe that the agreement among trained microscopists really does correspond to the facts which untrained persons cannot perceive. (*b*) Persons of all races who habitually drink alcohol to excess eventually have perceptual experiences in which they seem to themselves to see snakes or rats crawling about their rooms or beds. In this case we believe that this agreement among drunkards is merely a uniform hallucination. (c) Let us now imagine a race of beings who can walk about and touch things but cannot see. Suppose that eventually a few of them developed the power of sight. All that they might tell their still blind friends about colour would be wholly unintelligible to and unverifiable by the latter. But they would also be able to tell their blind friends a great deal about what the latter would feel if they were to walk in certain directions. These statements would be verified. This would not, of course, *prove* to the blind ones that the unintelligible statements about colour correspond to certain aspects of the world which they cannot perceive. But it would show that the seeing persons had a source of additional information about matters which the blind ones could understand and test for themselves. It would not be unreasonable then for the blind ones to believe that probably the seeing ones are also able to perceive other aspects of reality which they are describing correctly when they make their unintelligible statements containing colour-names. The question then is whether it is reasonable to regard the agreement between the experiences of religious mystics as more like the agreement among trained microscopists about the minute structure of cells, or as more like the agreement among habitual drunkards about the infestation of their rooms by pink rats or snakes, or as more like the agreement about colours which the seeing men would express in their statements to the blind men.

Why do we commonly believe that habitual excess of alcohol is a cause of a uniform delusion and not a source of additional information? The main reason is as follows. The things which drunkards claim to perceive are not fundamentally different in kind from the things that other people perceive. We have all seen rats and snakes, though the rats have generally been grey or brown and not pink. Moreover the drunkard claims that the rats and snakes which he sees are literally present in his room and on his bed, in the same sense in which his bed is in his room and his quilt is on his bed. Now we may fairly argue as follows. Since these are the sort of things which we could see if they were there, the fact that we cannot see them makes it highly probable that they are not there. Again, we know what kinds of perceptible effect would generally follow from the presence in a room of such things as rats or snakes. We should expect fox-terriers or mongooses to show traces of excitement, cheese to be nibbled, corn to disappear from bins, and so on. We find that no such effects are observed in the bedrooms of persons suffering from *delirium tremens*. It therefore seems reasonable to conclude that the agreement among drunkards is a sign, not of a revelation, but of a delusion.

Now the assertions in which religious mystics agree are not such that they conflict with what we can perceive with our senses. They are about the structure and organization of the world as a whole and about the relations of men to the rest of it. And they have so little in common with the facts of daily life that there is not much chance of direct collision.

I think that there is only one important point on which there is conflict. Nearly all mystics seem to be agreed that time and change and unchanging duration are unreal or extremely superficial, whilst these seem to plain men to be the most fundamental features of the world. But we must admit, on the one hand, that these temporal characteristics present very great philosophical difficulties and puzzles when we reflect upon them. On the other hand, we may well suppose that the mystic finds it impossible to state clearly in ordinary language what it is that he experiences about the facts which underlie the appearance of time and change and duration. Therefore it is not difficult to allow that what we experience as the temporal aspect of reality corresponds in some sense to certain facts, and yet that these facts appear to us in so distorted a form in our ordinary experience that a person who sees them more accurately and directly might refuse to apply temporal names to them.

Let us next consider why we feel fairly certain that the agreement among trained microscopists about the minute structure of cells expresses an objective fact, although we cannot get similar experiences. One reason is that we have learned enough, from simpler cases of visual perception, about the laws of optics to know that the arrangement of lenses in a microscope is such that it will reveal minute structure, which is otherwise invisible, and will not simply create optical delusions. Another reason is that we know of other cases in which trained persons can detect things which untrained people will overlook, and that in many cases the existence of these things can be verified by indirect methods. Probably most of us have experienced such results of training in our own lives.

Now religious experience is not in nearly such a strong position as this. We do not know much about the laws which govern its occurrence and determine its variations. No doubt there are certain standard methods of training and meditation which tend to produce mystical experiences. These have been elaborated to some extent by certain Western mystics and to a very much greater extent by Eastern Yogis. But I do not think that we can see here, as we can in the case of microscopes and the training which is required to make the best use of them, any conclusive reason why these methods should produce veridical rather than delusive experiences. Uniform methods of training and meditation would be likely to produce more or less similar experiences, whether these experiences were largely veridical or wholly delusive.

Is there any analogy between the facts about religious experience and the fable about the blind men some of whom gained the power of sight? It might be said that many ideals of conduct and ways of life, which we can all recognize now to be good and useful, have been introduced into human history by the founders of religions. These persons have made actual ethical discoveries which others can afterwards recognize to be true. It might be said that this is at least roughly analogous to the case of the seeing men telling the still blind men of facts which the latter could and did verify for themselves. And it might be said that this makes it reasonable for us to attach some weight to what founders of religions tell us about things which we cannot understand or verify for ourselves; just as it would have been reasonable for the blind men to attach some weight to the unintelligible statements which the seeing men made to them about colours.

I think that this argument deserves a certain amount of respect, though I should find it hard to estimate how much weight to attach to it. I should be inclined to sum up as follows. When there is a nucleus of agreement between the experiences of men in different places, times, and traditions, and when they all tend to put much the same kind of interpretation on the cognitive content of these experiences, it is reasonable to ascribe this agreement to their all being in contact with a certain objective aspect of reality *unless* there be some positive reason to think otherwise. The practical postulate which we go upon everywhere else is to treat cognitive claims as veridical unless there be some positive reason to think them delusive. This, after all, is our only guarantee for believing that ordinary sense-perception is veridical. We cannot *prove* that what people agree in perceiving really exists independently of them; but we do always assume that ordinary waking sense-perception is veridical unless we can produce some positive ground for thinking that it is delusive in any given case. I think it would be inconsistent to treat the experiences of religious mystics on different principles. So far as they agree they should be provisionally accepted as veridical unless there be some positive ground for thinking that they are not. So the next question is whether there is any positive ground for holding that they are delusive.

There are two circumstances which have been commonly held to cast doubt on the cognitive claims of religious and mystical experience. (i) It is alleged that founders of religions and saints have nearly always had certain neuropathic symptoms or certain bodily weaknesses, and that these would be likely to produce delusions. Even if we accept the premisses, I do not think that this is a very strong argument. (*a*) It is equally true that many founders of religions and saints have exhibited great endurance and great power of organization and business capacity which would have made them extremely successful and competent in secular affairs. There are very few offices in the cabinet or in the highest branches of the civil service which St. Thomas Aquinas could not have held with conspicuous success. I do not, of course, regard this as a positive reason *for* accepting the metaphysical doctrines which saints and founders of religions have based on their experiences; but it is relevant as a *rebuttal* of the argument which we are considering. (*b*) Probably very few people of extreme genius in science or art are perfectly normal mentally or physically, and some of them are very crazy and eccentric indeed. Therefore it would be rather surprising if persons of religious genius were completely normal, whether their experiences be veridical or delusive. (*c*) Suppose, for the sake of argument, that there is an aspect of the world which remains altogether outside the ken of ordinary persons in their daily life. Then it seems very likely that some degree of mental and physical abnormality would be a necessary condition for getting sufficiently loosened from the objects of ordinary sense-perception to come into cognitive contact with this aspect of reality. Therefore the fact that those persons who claim to have this peculiar kind of cognition generally exhibit certain mental and physical abnormalities is rather what might be anticipated if their claims were true. One might need to be slightly 'cracked' in order to have some peep-holes into the super-sensible world. (*d*) If mystical experience were veridical, it seems quite likely that it would *produce* abnormalities of behaviour in those who had it strongly. Let us suppose, for the sake of argument, that those who have religious experience are in frequent contact with an aspect of reality of which most men get only rare and faint glimpses. Then such persons are, as it were, living in two worlds, while the ordinary man is living in only one of them. Or, again, they might be compared to a man who has to conduct his life with one ordinary eye and another of a telescopic kind. Their behaviour may be appropriate to the aspect of reality which they alone perceive and think all-important; but, for that very reason, it may be inappropriate to those other aspects of reality which are all that most men perceive or judge to be important and on which all our social institutions and conventions are built.

(ii) A second reason which is commonly alleged for doubt about the claims of religious experience is the following. It is said that such experience always originates from and remains mixed with certain other factors, e.g., sexual emotion, which are such that experiences and beliefs that arise from them are very likely to be delusive. I think that there are a good many confusions on this point, and it will be worth while to begin by indicating some of them.

When people say that B 'originated from' A, they are liable to confuse at least three different kinds of connexion between A and B. (i) It might be that A is a necessary but insufficient condition of the existence of B. (ii) It might be that A is a necessary and sufficient condition of the existence of B. Or (iii) it might be that B simply *is* A in a more complex and disguised form. Now, when there is in fact evidence only for the first kind of connexion, people are very liable to jump to the conclusion that there is the third kind of connexion. It may well be the case, e.g., that no one who was incapable of strong sexual desires and emotions could have anything worth calling religious experience. But it is plain that the possession of a strong capacity for sexual experience is not a *sufficient* condition of having religious experience; for we know that the former quite often exists in persons who show hardly any trace of the latter. But, even if it could be shown that a strong capacity for sexual desire and emotion is *both* necessary and sufficient to produce religious experience, it would not follow that the latter is just the former in disguise. In the first place, it is not at all easy to discover the exact meaning of this metaphorical phrase when it is applied to psychological topics. And, if we made use of physical analogies, we are not much helped. A mixture of oxygen and hydrogen in the presence of a spark is necessary and sufficient to produce water accompanied by an explosion. But water accompanied by an explosion is not a mixture of oxygen and hydrogen and a spark 'in a disguised form', whatever that may mean.

Now I think that the present rather vaguely formulated objection to the validity of the claims of religious experience might be stated somewhat as follows. 'In the individual religious experience originates from, and always remains mixed with, sexual desires and emotions. The other generative factor of it is the religious tradition of the society in which he lives, the teachings of his parents, nurses, schoolmasters, etc. In the race religious experience originated from a mixture of false beliefs about nature and man, irrational fears, sexual and other impulses, and so on. Thus the religious tradition arose from beliefs which we now recognize to have been false and from emotions which we now recognize to have been irrelevant and misleading. It is now drilled into children by those who are in authority over them at a time of life when they are intellectually and emotionally at much the same stage as the primitive savages among whom it originated. It is, therefore, readily accepted, and it determines beliefs and emotional dispositions which persist long after the child has grown up and acquired more adequate knowledge of nature and of himself.'

Persons who use this argument might admit that it does not definitely *prove* that religious beliefs are false and groundless. False beliefs and irrational fears in our remote ancestors *might* conceivably be the origin of true beliefs and of an appropriate feeling of awe and reverence in ourselves. And, if sexual desires and emotions be an essential condition and constituent of religious experience, the experience *may* nevertheless be veridical in important respects. We might merely have to rewrite one of the beatitudes and say "Blessed are the *im*pure in heart, for they shall see God'. But, although it is logically possible that such causes should produce such effects, it would be said that they are most unlikely to do so. They seem much more likely to produce false beliefs and misplaced emotions.

It is plain that this argument has considerable plausibility. But it is worth while to remember that modern science has almost as humble an ancestry as contemporary religion. If the primitive witch-smeller is the spiritual progenitor of the Archbishop of Canterbury, the primitive rain-maker is equally the spiritual progenitor of the Cavendish Professor of Physics. There has obviously been a gradual refinement and purification of religious beliefs and concepts in the course of history, just as there has been in the beliefs and concepts of science. Certain persons of religious genius, such as some of the Hebrew prophets and the founders of Christianity and of Buddhism, do seem to have introduced new ethico-religious concepts and beliefs which have won wide acceptance, just as certain men of scientific genius, such as Galileo, Newton, and Einstein, have done in the sphere of science. It seems somewhat arbitrary to count this process as a continual approximation to true knowledge of the material aspect of the world in the case of science, and to refuse to regard it as at all similar in the case of religion. Lastly, we must remember that all of us have accepted the current common-sense and scientific view of the material world on the authority of our parents, nurses, masters, and companions at a time when we had neither the power nor the inclination to criticize it. And most of us accept, without even understanding, the more recondite doctrines of contemporary physics simply on the authority of those whom we have been taught to regard as experts.

On the whole, then, I do not think that what we know of the conditions under which religious beliefs and emotions have arisen in the life of the individual and the race makes it reasonable to think that they are *specially* likely to be delusive or misdirected. At any rate any argument which starts from that basis and claims to reach such a conclusion will need to be very carefully handled if its destructive effects are to be confined within the range contemplated by its users. It is reasonable to think that the concepts and beliefs of even the most perfect religions known to us are extremely inadequate to the facts which they express; that they are highly confused and are mixed up with a great deal of positive error and sheer nonsense; and that, if the human race goes on and continues to have religious experiences and to reflect on them, they will be altered and improved almost out of recognition. But all this could be said, *mutatis mutandis,* of scientific concepts and theories. The claim of any particular religion or sect to have complete or final truth on these subjects seems to me to be too ridiculous to be worth a moment's consideration. But the opposite extreme of holding that the whole religious experience of mankind is a gigantic system of pure delusion seems to me to be almost (though not quite) as far-fetched.

## READING 10

---

# Visions
*Alasdair MacIntyre*

*Alasdair MacIntyre (1929–    ) is McMahon/Hank Professor of Philosophy at the University of Notre Dame. His books include* A Short History of Ethics *(1966),* After Virtue *(1981), and* Whose Justice? Which Rationality? *(1988).*

(1) The attempt to found religious belief upon the evidence of religious experience has traditionally taken two main forms. Among Protestants the appeal has usually been to the evidence of certain feeling-states. Among Catholic contemplatives and also among the more eccentric Protestant sects religious experience has been understood to include the seeing of visions and the hearing of voices. I want in this paper to defend three theses: *first,* that no experience less explicit than visions and voices could provide evidence for religious beliefs; *second,* that visions and voices could not in principle provide evidence of the existence of invisible and supernatural beings; and *third,* that, even if this were not so, over the claims made in connection with any particular vision or voice insuperable difficulties must arise. The logical issues that arise in the discussion can be treated for the most part in terms of visions and therefore I shall not often refer explicitly to voices.

(2) Contemplative theologians customarily distinguish three classes of visions, the external, the imaginary or the imaginal, and the intellectual. An external vision is one in which what appears appears as part of the environment and may be confused with the ordinary world of things and people. An imaginal vision is one in which what appears appears as an object of vision in some sense, but can be distinguished sharply from material objects. An intel-

lectual vision is not a vision at all but a feeling of presence. For our purposes these can be reduced to two classes: first, those visions which can properly be called such, that is, those where something is *seen;* and second, those where the experience is of a feeling-state or of a mental image, which are only called visions by an honorific extension of the term. It is worth making two observations initially. The first is that the classic contemplatives such as St. Theresa value intellectual visions the most highly and external visions the least so, whereas their ostensible evidential value is, it will be argued, if anything, the reverse, and from this it would seem to follow, as the argument will in fact entail, that whatever value visions may have, they possess it not because they are evidence. The second point to be made is that those experiences to which visions are customarily assimilated, namely hallucinations, are inappropriately chosen for the comparison. For we call an apparition of an elephant in a public house hallucinatory because we can compare its behaviour with the behaviour of the non-hallucinatory, normal elephants in the zoo, and it is the discrepancy with normal experience that justifies us in applying the term 'hallucination'. Whenever we apply the term there is an implicit comparison with the normal behaviour of what is ostensibly experienced and therefore, if we want to say, 'This *x* is hallucinatory', we must always be able to say what a normal case of *x* would be like. Now clearly we cannot do this with visions of, for example, the Blessed Virgin or the Archangel Gabriel. All experience of archangels is visionary and there is no normal non-visionary experience of them. Hence there can be no comparison with a normal case and lacking this we cannot call the vision hallucinatory. Indeed when we speak of 'a vision' we imply a visitant of an abnormal kind, rather than a normal being (an elephant or a rat) behaving abnormally.

**SOURCE:** From A. Flew and A. MacIntyre, Eds., *New Essays in Philosophical Theology* (New York: Macmillan, 1955): 254–260.

(3) We can now return to our twofold classification of visions, and I want to argue that neither feeling-states nor mental images could provide evidence for religious belief even on the assumptions of the protagonists of religious experience. To uphold their case nothing less than visions (and voices) will do. The reason for this is that the point of the experience is allegedly that it conveys information about something other than the experience, namely about the ways of God. Now an experience of a distinctly 'mental' kind, a feeling-state or an image cannot 'of itself yield us any information about anything other than the experience. We could never know from such experiences that they had the character of messages from the divine, unless we already possessed a prior knowledge of the divine and of the way in which messages from it were to be identified. The decisive evidence for the divine would then be anterior to the experience and not derived from it, whereas what we are concerned with here is how far the experience itself can provide such evidence.

We can approach this same difficulty from the question of the meaning of religious expressions. Either the believer who founds his faith upon religious experience learns the meaning of the religious expressions which he employs in his assertions from his experiences or he does not. If he defines their meaning ostensively by referring to his experiences, then we can inquire what there is in common between the word 'God' as he uses it and the word 'God' as it is used, for example, in the creeds. If he uses the word with the meaning that it possesses in traditional contexts such as the creeds, we are entitled to ask how he knows that it was the maker of heaven and earth who was manifested in his feeling-state. Surely nothing that occurs as a constituent of a feeling-state could provide us with satisfactory evidence on the basis of which either of these questions could be answered.

Behind these difficulties which arise from the claim that the divine is revealed in certain inner *Bewusstseinslage* lies one of the simplest and crudest difficulties of orthodox theism. If God is infinite, how can he be manifest in any particular finite object or experience? The definition of God as infinite is intended precisely to distinguish between God and everything finite, but to take the divine out of the finite is to remove it from the entire world of human experience. The inexorable demands of religiously adequate language seem to make of experience of God a notion that is a contradiction in terms.

The appeal to visions and voices is not, however, in quite the same difficulty here. For here there is no claim to an immediate experience of the infinite creator. There may be all sorts of difficulties about the relation between God and his messengers, but the primary claim that in a vision we confront a messenger and not God enables us to answer the question of how the information is conveyed by the experience. For here there is no esoteric interpretation of feelings, but information conveyed by a speaking figure in an ordinary language, Latin or Portuguese or whatever it is. The problem of the meaning of the religious expressions used by the apparition is not complicated by any attempt to define them ostensively in terms of the experience. Hence if we are to have an appeal to religious experience, it must be to visions rather than to feelings.

(4) There is, however, a further difficulty in the notion of religious experience which is peculiarly applicable to the claims made on the basis of visions. It may be thought that to treat a vision as a sign of the invisible is to accept in the realm of religious belief a procedure which we are accustomed to employ elsewhere. For certainly we do constantly infer the as yet unseen or the no longer seen from what we now see. If we infer fires from smoke, approaching trains from signals, why not gods from apparitions? The answer is that we can only infer the unseen from the seen when we have a rule of inference which entitles us to do so. The justification of any such rule can only be that we have grounds for believing in a correlation between the occurrence of the sign (the seen) and the thing signified (the unseen). So that in order to infer the divine from an apparition we should have to have experience of a connection between them in the way in which we do have experience of the connection between smoke and fires.[1] But what we experience and all that we experience is the vision, and if indeed we had the additional experience of the divine which we should need in order to assert that it was indeed the author of the vision, we should presumably not require the vision to tell us of the divine.

Could not the vision, however, be self-authenticating? If an angel appeared and announced himself as a messenger from God, would we not have grounds

---

[1] Compare Hume's *Dialogues Concerning Natural Religion, passim.*, and *An Enquiry Concerning Human Understanding*, §§ X and XI.

for believing him if we could find grounds for believing in his general reliability? And could we not find such grounds if the angel gave us verifiable information which invariably turned out to be correct? The fallacy in this argument is as follows. Suppose that the angel successfully predicted the winner of every classic race, appearing a week before the race in order to do so. This would justify us in inferring 'x will win the Derby' from 'the angel says that x will win the Derby', but the fact that the angel's predictions were invariably accurate would not justify us in any inference whatsoever as to the source of the angel's knowledge. We would not even be justified in saying that the angel *knew* the Derby winner, unless the angel told us the grounds for his prediction, and if those grounds were to be intelligible to us they would have to include no unverifiable assertions and hence no reference to invisible realities. Thus the angel's accuracy would be no warrant for accepting any distinctively religious utterance which he might make. Here we can restate Hume's point when he argues that from past traces of design in the Universe we can perhaps infer future traces of design but not an unseen designer.[2] From past phenomena we can infer future phenomena but not what belongs to a realm beyond phenomena. Visions are but one set of phenomena which may or may not be correlated with other phenomena, but they no more than any other occurrence lead us beyond the world of experience.

(5) The difficulties that we have so far encountered could be adduced against any vision whatever. Let us now pass on to consider some of the difficulties that inevitably arise over particular visions. Let us consider, for instance, visions of the Blessed Virgin Mary, such as that which William James[3] cites in the case of M. Alphonse Ratisbonne, a free-thinker who became a Roman Catholic in response to a vision. How did he know that it was the Virgin? Presumably only because she appeared in a Roman Catholic church and she looked like the religious paintings he had seen. But surely such an identification is inadequate? And yet what further identification could there be? These questions are not merely the doubts of the sceptic. They are raised also, for example, by the religious admission that such visions may well be wiles of the devil rather than messages from God. This rules out any assurance that M. Ratisbonne might have gained from the apparition announcing herself as the Virgin. What criteria does the believer invoke to distinguish true visions from false? The only criterion possible is presumably the congruence of the messages delivered in the vision with such theological doctrines as are already believed. If this be admitted it might be argued that visions could never be the original ground of a belief but yet might afford it confirmation. This will not do. Since we should only accept as genuine those experiences which did in fact afford confirmation to belief, the statement that genuine religious experience affords confirmation of belief would be an empty tautology.

Or consider the question as one of personal identity. Someone who appeared again after an absence of five years would have to be very much changed before we had real doubts as to his identity; but after two thousand years even Rip van Winkle would find it hard to gain credence of his identity. In the example of the Blessed Virgin, however, the case is worse. No one has authentic evidence as to what she looked like. So to identify her from religious paintings is to have no warrant that she who appeared to M. Ratisbonne is she who lived in Galilee as the mother of Jesus. The ordinary difficulties that arise in specifying the criteria of personal identity are intensified, for we normally judge of personal identity by standard tests. Is this the Tichborne heir? Does he resemble him sufficiently? Does he understand Latin? Does he remember his school days with the Jesuits? Only a correct answer to these three and other relevant questions would justify us in saying that this is indeed none other than the lost heir. Is this the Blessed Virgin? Does she look like her? We do not know what the Blessed Virgin looked like. Does she speak Aramaic? Appearances of the Blessed Virgin would be remarkably impressive if she did, but, to the best of my knowledge, in the classic apparitions of modern Mariolatry the messages delivered are always in the tongue of the recipient. Does the Blessed Virgin remember Galilee? What would be the appropriate criteria for testing her memory? We would have to have an independent source of information about matters on which she could be presumed to have special knowledge and we lack any such source. In so far as what the figure in the apparition said merely agreed with the Gospel narrative, we could have no guarantee that the source of the informa-

[2]*loc. cit.*
[3]*The Varieties of Religious Experience*, Ch. X.

tion was not the Gospel. It is clear that the difficulty is to find a ground for asserting that any given vision is indeed a vision of the Blessed Virgin.

There remains a final difficulty in the use of visions as evidence. If from premisses reporting a vision we could infer ontological conclusions, the occurrence of rival visions would validate mutually exclusive ontologies. On visions of the Blessed Virgin some Roman Catholics have based beliefs about her present status and works. From visions of Krishna Hindus construct a theology which, if true, invalidates Roman Catholicism. We may note in passing that it is almost always Roman Catholics who have visions of the Virgin and almost always Hindus who have visions of Krishna and extraordinarily rarely, if ever, *vice versa*.

This completes the case against vindicating religious beliefs by referring to visions. If valid ground for religious belief is to be found, it must be found elsewhere. Equally, if there is to be a valid place in religion for visionary experience, it must be understood other than as evidence for belief.

# DISCUSSION: The Ontological Argument

The ontological argument was first proposed as a proof of God's existence in the eleventh century by St. Anselm and has been controversial ever since. It was rejected as unsound by St. Thomas Aquinas in the thirteenth century. A very simple version of the argument was then resurrected in the seventeenth century by Descartes, in his *Fifth Meditation*. Kant criticized the Cartesian version in his *Critique of Pure Reason* in the eighteenth century, and until quite recently, most philosophers regarded the ontological argument as having been refuted by Kant.[1]

## ANSELM'S ARGUMENT

In analyzing the ontological argument, we shall concentrate solely on the version presented by Anselm in Chapter II of his *Proslogium*. We can break down Anselm's reasoning into three steps.

Step 1. Even someone who denies that God exists must understand what the word *God* means if the denial is to make sense. If someone understands the meaning of a term referring to a thing, Anselm says that the thing referred to by that term exists in the person's understanding. Of course, there are many things that exist *only* in the understanding because, like unicorns and the Easter Bunny, they are fictitious entities. Unicorns and the Easter Bunny exist in the understanding (since we have an idea of them in our minds); but unlike tigers and the White House, they do not also exist in reality. Anyone who denies God's existence must therefore believe that God (like unicorns and the Easter Bunny) exists *only* in the understanding.

Step 2. What is the concept of God that we have in our minds when we affirm or deny God's existence? Anselm proposes that we should regard God as "that than which nothing greater can be conceived." This is a very abstract way of thinking about God, but many philosophers and theologians have agreed with Anselm that this definition captures the essence of God in the Western monotheistic tradition. The God of Judaism, Christianity, and Islam is not merely the greatest thing in the universe, as Everest is the Earth's tallest mountain and the Amazon its longest river; rather, God is the greatest thing that can *possibly* exist. According to Anselm's definition, God is a thing so great that it is logically impossible for there to be anything greater. So, God is not merely the greatest thing; God is the greatest thing that can possibly exist.

Step 3. Anselm then concludes that it is false that God exists only in the understanding. Why? Because God might have existed in reality; and if God exists only in the understanding but might have existed in reality, then a thing greater than God is conceivable. But this conclusion is a contradiction, since

God is a thing than which nothing greater can be conceived; and it is logically impossible to conceive of a thing greater than God if God is that than which nothing greater can be conceived. So, God cannot exist in the understanding alone but must also exist in reality.

Anselm's argument is an extremely terse example of *reductio ad absurdum* reasoning. The first premise of the target argument is the claim that God exists in the understanding but not also in reality. Anselm then uses reductio reasoning to show that this premise is false.

To complete the target argument, Anselm needs two further premises. First, Anselm needs the premise that God might have existed. This seems uncontroversial, since both the theist and the atheist agree that it is logically possible that God exists in reality. Even if God does not exist, God might have existed. Second, Anselm needs the premise that real existence is one of the properties that makes a thing greater than it would have been otherwise. This greatness principle, which serves as the third premise of Anselm's target argument, is difficult to understand, but we can illustrate Anselm's idea with the following example. Suppose that we compare the Santa Claus who exists solely in our imagination with the real living, breathing person who would have existed if Santa Claus had been real. Who is greater: the fictitious Santa or the person who would have existed had Santa been real? It seems that the Santa who exists in reality must be the greater of the two. If Santa really existed, he would give *real* presents to *real* children and perform all kinds of good actions. The Santa who exists solely in the understanding can do none of these things. More generally, only beings that exist in reality have the power to perform actions in the real world. Thus, if real existence were to be added to a thing that exists only in the understanding, then that thing would thereby be made greater than it is.[2]

We can write out Anselm's target argument as follows.

### Anselm's Ontological Argument, *Proslogium*, Chapter II
(1) God, the greatest thing possible, exists only in the understanding.
(2) God might have existed in reality.
(3) If something exists only in the understanding and might have existed in reality, then it might have been greater than it is.

_____

(4) God might have been greater than he is.

This a valid argument—the conclusion follows logically from the premises—but the conclusion (statement 4) is a contradiction. Because God is the greatest thing possible, it is logically impossible that God might have been greater than he is. So, we have a valid argument with a false conclusion. Premises (2) and (3) are true. Therefore, premise (1) is false. It is false that God exists only in the understanding.

Step 4. We complete the argument for God's existence by adopting statement (5) (which is the negation of statement 1) as a premise.

(5) It is false that God exists only in the understanding.
(6) God exists in the understanding.

_____

(7) God exists in reality as well as in the understanding.

Anselm's entire argument for the conclusion (statement 7) that God actually exists is valid. So, if we are to reject it as a proof of God's existence, then we can do so only on one or more of the following three grounds: (i) at least one of the premises (2), (3), or (6) is false, and hence the argument is unsound; (ii) we do not know (and perhaps cannot know) that statements (2), (3), and (6) are true; (iii) we cannot know that statements (2), (3), and (6) are true without first knowing that the conclusion is true.

When they first confront Anselm's argument, many people are convinced that it must be unsound. They reason that the existence of any thing, even the supreme being, God, is an empirical matter. In other words, existence claims can be known only *a posteriori*, through experience. No *a posteriori* statement can be validly deduced from true premises, all of which are *a priori*, or knowable independently of experience. So, they conclude, the ontological argument is valid but unsound.

The argument I have just given is a common all-purpose objection to Anselm's argument or to any other attempt to prove God's existence *a priori*. It rests on two premises: all existence claims are empirical or *a posteriori*, and no *a posteriori* statement can be deduced from *a priori* ones. There is much that could be said about both of these premises, but I will focus on the first. Is it true that all existence claims are empirical? Consider the statements, "There exists a prime number between 11 and 17" and "There is exactly one even prime number." These are existence claims, but they are not empirical, and no experience is required to verify their truth. The nugget of truth in the assertion that all existence claims are empirical seems to be that all existence claims *about physical objects* are empirical. But numbers are not physical objects, and neither is God. So, I conclude that we cannot dismiss Anselm's argument on the basis of the common all-purpose objection. We have to look at a more specific diagnosis of what, if anything, is wrong with it.

## GAUNILO'S "LOST ISLAND" OBJECTION

One of the earliest criticisms of Anselm's argument came from a monk named Gaunilo. Like Anselm, Gaunilo was convinced that God exists; but Gaunilo doubted that Anselm's argument *proved* that God exists. In his *On Behalf of the Fool*, Gaunilo advanced several criticisms of Anselm, but the most famous is his "Lost Island" objection.[3]

Gaunilo imagines that somewhere in the ocean is an island, called *Lost Island*, which is more excellent than any other country or island inhabited by human beings. If Anselm's ontological argument for God's existence were a proof, then we could also prove, by parallel reasoning, that the Lost Island exists. But, Gaunilo objects, that is absurd. Just because he can imagine such an island, that is no guarantee that such an island exists. So, Anselm's reasoning must be flawed.

Gaunilo did not say what, exactly, is wrong with Anselm's original argument, and Anselm in his reply was very brief. Anselm simply denied that his reasoning could be used to prove the existence of anything other than God (that than which nothing greater can be conceived.

We can make some progress by considering more carefully what Gaunilo's Lost Island is supposed to be. All that Gaunilo says is that the Lost Island is more excellent than all other lands. In other words, Gaunilo is not imagining an island than which none better is possible but merely an island that in respect of climate, fertility, and so on is superior to any other on Earth. Certainly we have *that* Lost Island in our understanding, and it is possible that it could exist in reality. If it did exist in reality then, according to Anselm's greatness principle, the Lost Island would be greater than if it were merely fictitious. So, it is possible that there could exist an island that is greater or more excellent than the Lost Island.

But how does this generate a contradiction that would parallel Anselm's reasoning? Surely, what Gaunilo needs is not just an island that is better than any other (existing) land but an island that is so excellent that no other land could possibly be better. In other words, to generate an exact parallel with Anselm's reasoning, we need to define the Lost Island not as "the best island" but as "the island than which none better is possible." And now we have serious doubts about whether we have clear idea in our understanding of what this might mean.

Anselm's remark that his argument can be used only to prove God's existence, but not to prove the existence of anything else, suggests that Anselm may have thought that while we understand what it means for a thing to be the best possible in all respects (the wisest, the most powerful, the most worthy of respect, and so on), we do not understand what it means for a thing of a particular type (such as an island or a bus driver) to be the best possible thing of its type. That *thing* than which no greater *thing* is possible is a coherent, intelligible concept. That *island* (or bus driver) than which no greater *island* (or bus driver) is possible is not a coherent, intelligible concept. One thing (namely God) can be better than any other thing can possibly be, but an island or a bus driver can only be better (or worse) than another. It makes no sense to talk about the best possible bus driver or the best possible island.

So, one way that Anselm can block Gaunilo's objection is by arguing that "the X than which none greater is possible" makes sense only when we substitute "thing" for "X". When X is an island, the phrase does not make sense, and hence "the island than which none greater is possible" does not exist in the understanding.

## KANT'S "EXISTENCE IS NOT A REAL PREDICATE" OBJECTION

Kant's objection to the ontological argument was directed against the version of it given in Descartes' *Fifth Meditation*. Descartes assumes explicitly that existence is a property that belongs necessarily to God, just as having an angle sum of 180 degrees belongs necessarily to a triangle. Descartes argued thus: by definition, God has all the properties that make anything perfect; existence is one of the properties that makes anything perfect; therefore, God exists.

When Kant objected that "*Being* is obviously not a real predicate," he was denying that existence is a property.[4] Kant was writing at a time when it was thought that all propositions have subject-predicate form; that is, the form, "S is P," where "S" is the subject term and "P" the predicate term. For example, "All men are mortal" predicates mortality of men. Kant did not actually deny that "exists" is a predicate term, but he did insist that it did not name a real property; it is not a "*real* predicate."

Kant was advancing a philosophical thesis about what existence claims mean, regardless of how they are expressed in sentences. For example, when comparing the sentence "Tigers are fierce" with "Tigers exist," the word *exists* does not appear on the surface to be a predicate term. But the sentence

"Tigers exist" can be rephrased as "Tigers are real" or, as Anselm would express it, "Tigers exist in reality." Kant is not denying that existence claims can often be rephrased so that the words *real* or *exist in reality* function as predicate terms. But he insists that even when we do this, these words do not stand for any real property the way that *red* stands for the color red or *tall* for the property of being tall.

Imagine that you are asked to describe a butler. Let us call him Jeeves. You list his attributes: he has impeccable manners, he is the soul of discretion, he mixes an exquisitely dry martini, and so on. It would be odd for someone to complain that your list is incomplete if it did not also include the property of existence. You might well agree with Kant that to say that Jeeves exists is not to attribute yet another property to him or to add another descriptive predicate to the list that defines your concept of "Jeeves"; rather, the sentence "Jeeves exists" is true if there is a real existing person to whom your concept of Jeeves applies. To put the point another way: Jeeves exists if and only if your description of him is satisfied by a living person.

If successful, Kant's thesis that existence is not a property refutes Descartes' version of the ontological argument. For, if existence is not a property, then it cannot be one of the properties that makes anything perfect. Similarly, if Kant is correct, then Anselm's greatness principle is false. To see why, consider our concept of Santa Claus. Either Santa Claus exists or he does not. If he does not exist, then our concept of Santa Claus fails to apply to any existing man. If he does exist, then our concept of Santa Claus does apply to a real person. But, in both cases, our concept of Santa Claus is exactly the same. Now consider Anselm's greatness principle: "If something exists only in the understanding and might have existed in reality, then *it* might have been greater than *it* is." What does the word *it* refer to? It cannot refer to a real person, since when Santa Claus exists only in the understanding, there is no real person who satisfies our concept of him. So, "it" must refer to our concept of Santa Claus. But, whether or not Santa Claus exists, there is only one concept of him, not two. So, the one cannot be greater than the other. Therefore, Anselm's greatness principle is false.

Not everyone agrees with Kant that existence is not a real property.[5] If we allow that existence is a property and that Anselm's greatness principle is true, does Anselm's argument prove that God actually exists? According to the American philosopher William Rowe, the answer to this question is "No."

## ROWE'S CIRCULARITY OBJECTION

Most of the traditional criticisms of Anselm's argument have tried to show that premise (3), Anselm's greatness principle, is false. By contrast, Rowe argues that Anselm's reasoning fails as a proof because the argument is circular. Rowe claims that if Anselm's greatness principle is true, then we cannot know that premise (2) is true (that God might have existed in reality) without first knowing Anselm's conclusion, that God actually exists. So, if Rowe was correct, we cannot know that all the premises of Anselm's argument are true without first knowing that its conclusion is true.[6]

On the face of it, Rowe's assertion seems false. Normally we judge that a thing that does not actually exist (such as a unicorn, a dragon, or Santa Claus) might have existed simply by examining our concept of the thing and seeing whether it is free from logical contradiction. However bizarre the concept, if it involves no logical contradiction, then the concept could be satisfied and a thing of that sort might have existed in reality. So, why can we not perform the same procedure on Anselm's concept of God? Anselm's concept of God does not involve any logical contradiction. So, the concept could be satisfied, and thus we know that Anselm's God might have existed in reality.

In response to this criticism, Rowe makes two points. First, there is a crucial difference between *normal concepts,* which do not include actual existence as one of their defining properties, and what I shall call *existential concepts.* Unlike normal concepts, existential concepts include the property of actual existence as part of their definition. For example, we can contrast the normal and existential concepts of Jeeves as follows.

**Jeeves$_1$: A Normal Concept**
(1)  impeccable manners
(2)  soul of discretion
(3)  mixes a great martini

**Jeeves$_2$: An Existential Concept**
(1)  impeccable manners
(2)  soul of discretion
(3)  mixes a great martini
(4)  actually exists

Since we are now treating existence (actual existence, existence in reality) as a genuine property, Jeeves$_1$ and Jeeves$_2$ are two different concepts: Jeeves$_1$ is defined by three properties; Jeeves$_2$ is defined by four properties. Jeeves$_1$ is a normal concept, and properties (1), (2), and (3) involve no logical contradiction; thus we know that Jeeves$_1$ might have existed in reality. But what about Jeeves$_2$? By definition, Jeeves$_2$ is something that actually exists. Thus, nothing satisfies the concept of Jeeves$_2$ unless there is a *real* butler with properties (1), (2), and (3); that is, unless Jeeves$_1$ actually exists. For something to satisfy the concept of Jeeves$_2$, Jeeves$_1$ must actually exist. I can imagine a possible world in which a butler exists with properties (1), (2), and (3); but unless that butler actually exists, unless he also exists in the actual world with those properties, I have imagined Jeeves$_1$, not Jeeves$_2$. It is very difficult to see how a human being could know that an existential concept (such as Jeeves$_2$) is satisfied in a possible world (and hence that Jeeves$_2$ might have existed in reality) without first knowing that its corresponding normal concept (Jeeves$_1$) is satisfied in the actual world (and hence that both Jeeves$_1$ and Jeeves$_2$ actually exist).

Rowe's second point is that Anselm's concept of God is an existential concept, not a normal one. Since actual existence is a great-making property and Anselm defines God as the greatest thing that can possibly exist, Anselm's concept of God, like Descartes', includes actual existence as one of its defining properties. Given the greatness principle, Anselm's concept of God is an existential concept, not a normal one. So, if both Rowe's points are correct, Anselm's ontological argument is circular and hence fails to prove that God actually exists.

## NOTES

1. Since 1960, some philosophers (Charles Hartshorne, Normal Malcolm, Alvin Plantinga) have revived versions of the ontological argument based on Anselm's reasoning in Chapter III of the *Proslogium.* Because of their technical nature, we do not discuss these versions in this book. For an introduction to these modern developments and a useful anthology of the historical materials, see A. Plantinga, Ed., *The Ontological Argument* (Garden City, NY: Doubleday, 1965); and J. Hick and A. C. McGill, Eds., *The Many-faced Argument* (New York: Macmillan, 1967).

2. On this reading of the concept of greatness, Anselm would also have to regard an *evil* person (such as Adolf Hitler) as greater if he existed in reality than if he were merely fictitious. There is no indication in the *Proslogium* that Anselm believed existence in reality is a great-making property only for things that are morally good.

3. Gaunilo's criticism and Anselm's reply can be found in *St. Anselm: Basic Writings*, trans. by S. N. Deane (La Salle, IL: Open Court, 1961).

4. I. Kant, *Critique of Pure Reason* (1781), trans. by N. Kemp Smith (New York: St. Martin's, 1965): 504–505.

5. For a penetrating criticism of Kant's argument, see J. Shaffer, "Existence, Predication and the Ontological Argument," *Mind* 71 (1962): 307–325.

6. See W. L. Rowe, "The Ontological Argument and Question-Begging," *International Journal for Philosophy of Religion* 7 (1976): 425–432; and W. L. Rowe, *Philosophy of Religion* (Encino, CA: Dickenson, 1978), Chapter 3.

# DISCUSSION: The Cosmological Argument

Cosmological arguments can be found in the writings of Plato and Aristotle and in the works of many philosophers and theologians up to the present day. They have been defended by Anselm, Aquinas, Descartes, Samuel Clarke, Leibniz, and the contemporary philosopher, Richard Taylor.[1] They have also been attacked by Hume, Kant, Bertrand Russell, and Paul Edwards.[2] This group of arguments is probably the most popular and common of all the philosophical attempts to prove God's existence.

All cosmological arguments have at least one *a posteriori* premise asserting some general empirical fact about the world, for example, that things are in motion, that there are causal chains, that there are objects in the world that are contingent and depend on other things for their existence. From this empirical premise, together with other premises, different versions of the cosmological argument deduce that there is an unmoved mover, or an uncaused "first" cause, or a necessary being. The arguments are then completed by identifying that entity with God. We shall not discuss the final stage of these arguments in detail except to point out that it requires that the entity mentioned in the conclusion of the preceding step be unique. For example, if an unmoved mover is identified with the traditional God of Judaism, Islam, and Christianity, then there cannot be more than one unmoved mover.

We begin by examining the first three of the "Five Ways" from the *Summa Theologica* of Saint Thomas Aquinas. The first four of these five ways are cosmological arguments; the fifth is teleological. We shall ignore the fourth and fifth ways entirely.[3] Later we will analyze Samuel Clarke's version of the cosmological argument.

## AQUINAS'S FIRST AND SECOND WAYS

To a modern reader, Aquinas's language may seem strange and difficult to understand. There are good reasons for this strangeness. First, Aquinas wrote in Latin that has been translated into fairly literal English. Second, Aquinas was an Aristotelian, a follower of the doctrines of Aristotle (384–322 B.C.). Thus, for example, in the first way, Aquinas follows Aristotle in defining motion as "the reduction of something from potentiality to actuality." For Aristotle and Aquinas, motion included not only the movement of an object from one place to another but also any qualitative change that a body could experience while remaining in the same place. Thus, an apple falling to the ground and a stationary poker being heated by a fire are both examples of what Aquinas understands by "motion." For the sake of simplicity, we will treat motion as locomotion or change of place and ignore its wider Aristotelian meaning.

In his second way, Aquinas talks of "efficient" causes. This is a technical term from Aristotle for things that produce a change in another thing or cause a new thing to come into existence: one's fist pounding on a piece of putty causes the putty to change its shape; a fire beneath a kettle of water causes the water to become hot; parents are the cause of the children whom they produce. Basically, efficient causes are what we would now call causes, and we need not worry about what other sorts of cause (material, formal, final) Aristotle and Aquinas thought existed.

The first two ways are arguments with a parallel form.

### Aquinas's First Way

(1) Some things move.
(2) If anything moves, then its motion is caused by something other than itself.
(3) It is impossible for the chain of movers to go back infinitely far.

(4) There is a first mover that is not moved by anything else.

### Aquinas's Second Way

(1) Some things are caused.
(2) If anything is caused, then it is caused by something other than itself.
(3) It is impossible for the chain of causes to go back infinitely far.

(4) There is a first cause that is not caused by anything else.

Notice that I have phrased the first premise of each argument using "some" not "all": if *all* things were in motion, or if *all* things were caused, these statements would contradict the conclusions, and the arguments would be unsound.

Several criticisms have been made of the second and third premises of the two arguments. It has been pointed out, for example, that in the world as described by Newtonian (not Aristotelian!) mechanics, no external force or cause of any kind is required to maintain uniform motion in a straight line. Also, it is claimed, there is no logical impossibility involved in the idea of an infinite causal chain. I shall discuss Aquinas's argument against infinite causal chains later. For the moment I wish to focus on the validity of the two arguments. Consider the following argument about the inheritance of property:

### The Inheritance Argument

(1) Some people inherit property.
(2) If anyone inherits property, then it is inherited from another person.
(3) It is impossible for the chain of inheritance to go back infinitely far.

(4) There is a first person who bequeathed property but who did not inherit property from anyone else.

The Inheritance Argument has exactly the same form as Aquinas's first two ways. Clearly, the argument is invalid if the conclusion means that there is *a single person* from whom all property has been inherited. What follows logically from the premises is merely that there is at least one "first bequeather." Similarly, the most that Aquinas's first two ways can establish, even if their premises are true, is that there is at least one unmoved mover or uncaused cause. To complete the argument for God's existence, Aquinas would have to show that there is at most one such entity.

Was Aquinas correct in believing that an infinite chain of efficient causes is logically impossible? His argument runs as follows:[4]

### Aquinas's Causal Chain Argument
(1)  If the first step of a causal chain is missing, then all the later steps are missing, too.
(2)  The first step of an infinite causal chain is missing.

_____

(3)  All the later steps of an infinite causal chain are missing, too.

The infinite causal chains that concern us extend indefinitely far into the past, even though they may terminate in the future. Thus, these infinite chains have no first step. But in what sense is the first step of an infinite chain "missing"? A step can be missing only if it was there originally and then has been removed, or "taken away," as Aquinas puts it. An infinite chain has no first step to take away. So, it is false that the first step of an infinite chain is missing.

We can gain further insight into the problem with Aquinas's Causal Chain Argument if we change it slightly so that its second premise is now true.

### Revised Version of the Causal Chain Argument
(1*)  If a causal chain has no first step, then it has no later steps.
(2*)  An infinite causal chain has no first step.

_____

(3)   An infinite causal chain has no later steps.

The difficulty now lies with premises (1*), which asserts that a causal chain must have a first step. We agree that it is true of *finite* causal chains, where the later steps depend on the earlier steps for their very existence; that is, chains in which step (n) exists only if step (n − 1) exists. For then it follows logically that if step (1) does not exist, neither does step (2) nor step (3), and so on. In a chain of dependent causes, if any step lacks the preceding step necessary for its existence, then all the subsequent steps will fail to exist. But *in an infinite chain, for any step (n), the preceding step (n − 1) always exists.* So, in an infinite chain, there is no step that lacks the preceding step necessary for its existence. Thus, we have no reason to think that premise (1*) is true of infinite chains.

At this point, I think we need a fresh approach. Why not allow that an infinite chain of dependent causes is logically possible and then see whether we can argue that even in this case there must exist a being that is not dependent on any other as a cause of its existence? This was the approach taken by Samuel Clarke.

## AQUINAS'S THIRD WAY

Aquinas divides his third way "taken from possibility and necessity" into two stages. He begins the first stage by noting that many of the things that we find in the world around us are perishable. Like animals and plants, they exist only because they were brought into existence by something else: they were born or "generated." And they exist for only a finite amount of time and then pass out of existence: they die or are "corrupted." Aquinas describes this feature by saying that these are things "that are possible to be and not to be." He then gives a *reductio ad absurdum* argument to show that it is not possible that everything is perishable.

Aquinas reasons that if everything were perishable, then at some time in the past nothing would have existed; and if at some time in the past nothing existed, then nothing would exist now. Since the conclusion of this target argument is obviously false, it follows that the initial premise—that everything is perishable—is false. So, Aquinas concludes that there must be at least one thing that is *im*perishable, or what he calls "necessary." A necessary thing, for Aquinas, is one that exists forever because it contains no tendency to decay and cannot be created or destroyed by natural means.[5] Aquinas then uses his conclusion—that there is at least one necessary thing—as a premise in the second stage of the third way.

### The First Stage of Aquinas's Third Way

(1) Everything is perishable.
(2) If everything were perishable, then at some time in the past nothing would have existed.
(3) If at some time in the past nothing existed, then nothing would exist now.

(4) Nothing exists now.

This is a valid argument with a false conclusion. Premises (2) and (3) are true. Therefore, premise (1) is false. So, there must be at least one thing that is not perishable, but what Aquinas calls "necessary."

Since the first stage is a valid argument, our evaluation must focus on premises (2) and (3).

Premise (3) asserts that if at any time in the past nothing existed, then nothing would exist now. This is based in turn on the causal principle that something can begin to exist only if it is caused to begin existing by something else that already exists. The principle that "nothing can come from nothing" seems a plausible assumption. We shall discuss some possible objections to it when we analyze Samuel Clarke's version of the cosmological argument.

Many critics of Aquinas's third way have attacked premise (2). There are two main objections to the claim that if everything were perishable, then at some time in the past nothing would have existed. First, just because something, X, *can* fail to exist, that does not guarantee that X has not always existed in the past or that X will cease to exist in the future. It is logically possible that a thing that can be destroyed just happens to last forever. Perhaps some neutrinos are like this: they could be annihilated in a rare collision, but as a matter of brute fact, they never collide with anything else during the entire history of the universe.

Second, even if we allow that for every perishable thing there is a time in the past when it did not exist, this does not logically imply that there was ever a time when *none* of them existed: their finite lifespans could overlap so that at all times at least one of them exists. Consider, for example, the lifespans of human beings. Every human being lives for only a finite amount of time, but it does not follow from this that there must have been a day when everyone died and no one was born. Similarly, an unbroken rope can consist of many overlapping strands, none of which stretches from one end of the rope to the other. So, premise (2) is false.

Let us now complete our discussion of Aquinas by considering the second stage of the third way. Aquinas takes his conclusion from the first stage—that there is at least one necessary thing—and argues that it is impossible that every necessary thing have its necessity caused by another. Thus, Aquinas concludes that there must be one necessary thing (God) that does not have its necessity caused by anything else. Here is an outline of Aquinas's argument:

### The Second Stage of Aquinas's Third Way
(5) There is at least one necessary thing.
(6) For each necessary thing, either its necessity is caused by another necessary thing or it has of itself its own necessity.
(7) It is impossible for there to be an infinite series of necessary things, each the cause of the necessity of another.

---

(8) There is a necessary thing that has of itself its own necessity and that causes the necessity of all other necessary things.

What does Aquinas mean when he talks of one necessary thing having its necessity caused by another? One suggestion is that a necessary thing, X, causes the necessity of another, Y, when Y depends on X for its continued existence. In other words, X explains why Y has always existed. Examples are not easy to think of, but at least we can imagine one eternal object, Y, depending on another eternal object, X, for its continued existence; perhaps an everlasting fish bowl resting on an everlasting table. If the table were not there, the bowl would fall, break, and hence cease to exist. On this interpretation, a thing would "have of itself its own necessity" if it were not causally dependent on anything else but contained within itself the entire reason for its existence. Understood in this way, premise (6) seems to rest on the principle that for everything that exists there is a reason or explanation of its existence. This principle, the Principle of Sufficient Reason, is discussed in the next section.

As Aquinas himself points out, premise (7) rests on the claim that it is impossible for there to be an infinite chain of causes. We have already criticized Aquinas's argument for this claim in our discussion of the second way. Given our criticisms of both stages of the third way, it seems reasonable to conclude that Aquinas's argument fails to prove the existence of God.

Despite its failure as a proof, Aquinas's third way contains some valuable suggestions that have been used in more modern versions of the cosmological argument. We now consider one such version—that given by the eighteenth-century philosopher Samuel Clarke.

## CLARKE'S VERSION OF THE COSMOLOGICAL ARGUMENT
Clarke's version of the cosmological argument is contained in his Boyle lectures, *A Demonstration of the Being and Attributes of God*, delivered in 1704.[6] Like

Aquinas's third way, Clarke's argument can be divided into two stages. In the first stage (contained in Section I of Reading 3), Clarke defends the proposition that "something has existed from all eternity." Clarke then uses that conclusion as a premise in the second stage (contained in Section II) to deduce that there has always existed what Clarke calls an independent being. By an independent being, Clarke means a being that does not depend causally on the existence of any other being for its own existence but is the ultimate cause of everything else that exists. Eventually, Clarke will identify this independent being, this uncreated creator, with God.

### The First Stage of Clarke's Argument

(1) If at any time in the past nothing existed, then nothing would exist now.
(2) Something does exist now.

---

(3) Something has always existed.

It is important not to misconstrue Clarke's conclusion. What it means, literally, is that there was no time in the infinite past when nothing at all existed. It would be a misuse of the term *thing* to conclude that "some *thing*" has always existed, since the "thing" in question might be a *series* of dependent beings, each producing its successor in an infinite causal series with no beginning. A series or set of individual objects (whether finite or infinite) is not itself an individual object, no more than a set of knives is itself a knife or a group of human beings is itself a human being. Clarke is clearly aware that he has not established that *one and the same individual thing* has always existed.[7] So, the conclusion of the first stage is merely that at any time throughout the infinite past there has existed at least one thing at that time.

Everyone agrees that premise (2)—the fact that the world now contains objects and things—is an empirical statement known *a posteriori*, by experience. But what about premise(1)? Clarke claimed that it was a necessary truth known *a priori*. For this he was criticized by David Hume in Part IX of his *Dialogues Concerning Natural Religion* (Reading 4). (This is why Hume refers to Clarke's cosmological argument as an argument that purports to be *a priori*.) Both Hume and Clarke agree that a statement is a necessary truth only if its negation is a logical contradiction. Clarke argued that if X is an object that begins to exist at a given time, then the statement "X is not caused to exist by anything" is a contradiction. Clarke's error was to equate the statement "X is not caused to exist by anything" with "X is caused to exist by nothing" and then argue that this implies that X was caused after all, which contradicts the claim that X has no cause. The reasoning is atrocious. The statement "X is caused to exist by nothing" says simply that X has no cause; it does not attribute a shadowy "nothing" as its cause.

Thus, Clarke has not shown that premise (1) is a necessary truth, and it seems likely that Hume was correct in judging that it is logically possible for it to be false. Of course, this is not the same as judging that it is false. Indeed, Hume himself thought that it was true, not because it was a necessary truth, but because it was an extremely well confirmed generalization from experience. Things and objects do not just pop into existence out of the blue. Invariably, when something, X, begins to exist, there is always some other object, Y, that already exists and that causes X to begin existing.

The principle that anything that begins to exist is caused to exist by some-thing else was regarded by Clarke and many of his contemporaries as an in-stance of a more general principle, the Principle of Sufficient Reason.[8] When Y causes X to begin existing, Y is the explanation or reason why X exists. The Principle of Sufficient Reason states that for every thing that exists there must be an explanation or a reason why that thing exists. The Principle of Sufficient Reason also plays a major role in the second stage of Clarke's argument, to which we now turn.[9]

### The Second Stage of Clarke's Argument

(3) Something always existed.

(4) If something has always existed, then either the whole of reality has been an infinite succession of dependent beings or there has always existed an independent being.

(5) It is impossible for the whole of reality to have been an infinite succession of dependent beings.

(6) There has always existed an independent being.

This is not the end of Clarke's argument. In further lectures he goes on to argue that (a) an independent (or self-existing) being (that is, a being that does not depend on anything else for its existence) is a necessary being (that is, for Clarke, a being whose nonexistence is logically impossible), (b) this necessary and self-existing being is unique (that is, there can be only one such being), and (c) this necessary being has all the traditional attributes of God: omnipo-tence, omniscience, omnibenevolence. We shall not discuss Clarke's reasoning for these further steps.

## THE PRINCIPLE OF SUFFICIENT REASON

Clarke bases premise (4) of his argument on the Principle of Sufficient Reason.

**The Principle of Sufficient Reason:** For every thing that exists, there must be an explanation or a reason why that thing exists.

If the Principle of Sufficient Reason is true, then for every thing, X, that exists, either the explanation of X's existence is some other object, Y, which causes X to exist, in which case X is a dependent being, or the explanation of X's existence lies within X itself, in which case X is an independent or self-ex-istent being. Thus, if throughout the infinite past there was never a time when nothing existed, either the whole of reality has been an unending succession of dependent beings, each caused by its predecessor, stretching back to infinity, or there is an independent being (plus either a finite or an infinite number of dependent beings.)[10]

Let us now examine Clarke's premise (5). Unlike Aquinas, Clarke allows that, considered by itself, an infinite series of dependent beings is logically possible. But, he thinks, such a series cannot constitute the whole of reality, since it would violate the Principle of Sufficient Reason. He reasons that if the whole of reality consisted of nothing but a series of dependent beings, then there would be some "thing" that would remain unexplained, namely, why there is any such series at all.

Strictly speaking, a series or set of things is not itself a thing. So, to do justice to Clarke's reasoning, we need to amend slightly our formulation of the Principle of Sufficient Reason. The simplest way to do this is to add a further clause that states that there is an explanation, not just of every thing, but also of every positive fact.

**The Principle of Sufficient Reason:** (P1) For every thing that exists, there must be an explanation or a reason why that thing exists; and (P2) for every positive fact, there must be an explanation or a reason why that fact is the case.[11]

A positive fact is a fact about any thing that actually exists or any series of such things, or about any event that actually happens or any series of such events. If there are and always have been dependent beings, then according to (P2), there must be an explanation of that positive fact. But if *everything* that exists were a dependent being, such an explanation would be impossible. Thus, premise (5) follows from (P2).

It is important to realize that Clarke bases premise (5) on the Principle of Sufficient Reason, not on the argument that Bertrand Russell criticized in his debate with Father Copleston.[12] Russell accused proponents of the cosmological argument of reasoning thus: There is an explanation of why each member of the set of dependent beings exists; therefore, there must be an explanation of why the set as a whole exists. This kind of argument is often described as committing the fallacy of composition; that is, the fallacy of thinking that just because every member of a set has a certain property, the set as a whole must have that property, too. Russell's counterexample shows immediately why this kind of reasoning is invalid. It is true that every person has a mother, but it is false that the human race has a mother.

(P2) of the Principle of Sufficient Reason implies premise (5) only if explaining the positive fact of the existence of each member of a collection of dependent beings does not automatically explain the positive fact of the existence of the collection as a whole. Some critics (e.g., David Hume, Paul Edwards) argue that if (C1) is satisfied, then so too is (C2):

(C1)  There is an explanation of the existence of each of the members of the collection of dependent beings.

(C2)  There is an explanation of why there are *any* dependent beings at all.

Hume's example of "twenty particles of matter" shows that once we have explained why each of the twenty particles exist, we have shown why the entire collection of all twenty exist. In a more recent example, Paul Edwards invites us to imagine that there are five Eskimos standing on the corner of Sixth Avenue and 50th Street in New York.[13] Once we have explained why each of them came to New York, we have explained why the group as a whole came to New York.

Let us allow that Hume and Edwards have shown that the following principle is true of all *finite* sets: An explanation of why *every* member of the set exists is the explanation of why the set as a whole exists (or, of why the set has any members at all). But we cannot infer that this principle which is true of finite sets will also hold true of infinite sets, because there are some principles that are true of all finite sets but false of all infinite ones. For example, it is a principle true of all finite sets that the whole is greater than any of its parts; or, more technically, that the members of a finite set cannot be put into one-to-one correspondence with the members of any of its proper subsets. But this principle does not hold true of any infinite set. For example, the set of even numbers is a proper subset of the set of positive integers; but the members of the set of integers can be put into one-to-one correspondence with the set of even numbers.[14]

William Rowe has argued that Hume and Edwards are mistaken. Rowe allows that for some sets (both finite and infinite), if (C1) is true, then so too is (C2), but this does not *have* to be the case for all infinite sets. Imagine that there exists both a series of dependent beings (finite or infinite) and a self-existent being, G, and that each dependent being is produced *directly* by G. Rowe thinks that in *this* case, to explain why each dependent being exists (C1) *is* to explain why there are dependent beings at all (C2), but only because we have gone outside the series of dependent beings and included a self-existent being in our explanation. Rowe's point is that if we remain within a set of dependent beings, then a positive fact remains unexplained, namely, why there are dependent beings at all.

## EXPLANATION AND THE CONCEPT OF A NECESSARY BEING

Let us allow that Rowe is correct and that if the Principle of Sufficient Reason is true, then to explain why there is an infinite series of dependent beings requires the existence of an independent being. Let us also assume that Clarke was correct in asserting that an independent being must be a necessary being. I now wish to question whether the existence of a necessary being would explain why there exists an infinite succession of dependent beings.

Up until now we have accepted the notion that we can we can explain one thing, X, by another, Y, that causes it to exist. For example, we might say that the explanation of my existence lies with my parents. But the mere existence of my parents does not explain why I exist, since many married couples are childless. Perhaps what explains my existence is the copulation of my parents; but even this is not a satisfactory explanation, since relatively few copulations result in conception. Giving an adequate explanation of why X exists involves more than simply mentioning another object or set of objects, Y, that caused X to exist. We need to specify the properties and activities of Y such that, given those properties and activities of Y, the existence of X had to follow. This suggests that an explanation is a set of true statements about the objects that caused X's existence, from which we can logically deduce the conclusion "X exists." The explanatory argument, the explanation proper, must be deductively valid, since unless the statement "X exists" follows from the premises logically, we do not have an adequate explanation of why the conclusion "X exists" is true. Thus, an auto mechanic may point her oily finger at a damaged carburetor and say "That explains why your car won't start," but the explanation proper is an argument from which we can deduce that the car will not start.

Samuel Clarke's notion of a necessary being is that of a being that must exist, a thing whose existence is logically necessary. If G is a necessary being, then the statement "G exists" is necessarily true. According to the view of explanation sketched in the previous paragraph, explanations are a special type of deductively valid argument. If a group of statements, P, is a complete and adequate explanation of some statement, Q, then Q must be deducible from P, because only then will the truth of P explain why Q has to be true. On this view of explanation, it follows that if G is a necessary being and it explains the existence of a contingent being, X, then the statement "X exists" is deducible from the statement "G exists" plus other statements about G. But "G exists" is a necessary truth. So, unless some of the other statements about G are contingent, the statement "X exists" would have to be necessarily true also. But X is a contingent being, and therefore the statement "X exists" is also contingent. Thus, if a necessary being is to explain the existence of a contingent being, there have to be some contingent statements about the necessary being.

There is no problem, in principle, in there being contingent statements about necessary beings. Consider numbers. They exist in all possible worlds and are thus necessary beings. And, there are many true statements about numbers that are contingent. For example, "the number 139 is being thought of by me at this moment." Similarly, if the necessary existence of God explains the contingent fact that matter exists, then it must be a contingent fact that God wills matter to exist. But if the Principle of Sufficient Reason is true, there must be an explanation of the fact that God wills matter to exist. What is this explanation? It, too, must have at least one contingent premise; and so we generate an infinite regress of explanations. It is hard to see why an infinite regress of explanations that refer to God is any more satisfactory than an infinite regress of explanations that refer to physical things.

## IS THE PRINCIPLE OF SUFFICIENT REASON KNOWN TO BE TRUE?

If the Principle of Sufficient Reason is the only ground for believing that premises (4) and (5) of Clarke's cosmological argument are true, then the argument is a proof only if we know that the Principle of Sufficient Reason is true. Rowe criticizes Clarke and others for claiming either that it is a necessary truth (it is not, since it can be denied without contradiction) or that it is known intuitively to be true (it is not, since of those people who understand it, not all are convinced of its truth, and some are convinced that it is false). Similarly, even if people and scientists always look for and often find explanations, this does not imply that explanations always exist for every thing and every fact. Rowe's final verdict is that Clarke's argument is not a proof, because we do not know that the Principle of Sufficient Reason is true.

I wish to conclude by suggesting that the truth of Principle of Sufficient Reason is, ultimately, an empirical question and that it can be decided only by looking at all the relevant evidence. Part of the relevant evidence includes the excellent grounds we now have for thinking that quantum mechanics is true. If quantum mechanics is true, then there are some facts that have no explanation. For example, the truth of quantum mechanics implies that there is no explanation for the fact that a particular tritium nucleus disintegrates when it does. Since we have good grounds for thinking that quantum mechanics is true, we have good grounds for thinking that the Principle of Sufficient Reason is false.[15]

## NOTES

1. See R. Descartes, *Third Meditation;* R. Taylor, *Metaphysics* (Englewood Cliffs, NJ: Prentice-Hall, 1983), 3rd edition, Chapter 10; D. R. Burrill, Ed., *The Cosmological Arguments* (Garden City, NY: Doubleday, 1967); And W. L. Craig, *The Cosmological Argument from Plato to Leibniz* (London: Macmillan, 1980).

2. See "The Argument from Contingency" in B. Russell and F. C. Copleston, "A Debate on the Existence of God," a transcript of the BBC radio discussion broadcast in 1948, reprinted in J. Hicks, Ed., *The Existence of God* (New York: Macmillan, 1964): 168–178; and P. Edwards, "The Cosmological Argument," *The Rationalist Annual* (London: 1959), reprinted in B. Brody, Ed., *Readings in the Philosophy of Religion* Englewood Cliffs, NJ: Prentice-Hall, 1974): 71–83.

3. For a careful analysis of all five arguments, see A. Kenny, *The Five Ways: St. Thomas Aquinas' Proofs of God's Existence* (Notre Dame, IN: University of Notre Dame Press, 1980).

4. For a more sophisticated analysis that takes into account the Aristotelian distinction between an *essentially* ordered and an *accidentally* ordered series of causes, see Patterson Brown, "Infinite Causal Regression," *The Philosophical Review* 75 (1966): 510–525.

5. Necessary things for Aquinas would include immaterial entities such as human souls and angels. They can be created and destroyed only by God.

6. In his will, Robert Boyle left money to pay a minister to preach eight sermons a year "for proving the Christian religion against notorious infidels, *viz.,* atheists, theists [*i.e.,* deists who rejected all revealed religion], pagans, Jews, and Mohammedans, not descending lower to any controversies that are among Christians themselves." Anthony Collins, a friend of John Locke, joked that no one doubted God's existence until the Boyle lecturers endeavored to prove it.

7. John Locke makes this mistake in *An Essay Concerning Human Understanding* (1689), Book IV, Chapter 10.

8. The Principle of Sufficient Reason is a central metaphysical principle in the writings of Leibniz, who was a contemporary of both Clarke and Newton. Newton waged a bitter priority dispute with Leibniz over who invented the calculus; also, Clarke entered into a lengthy correspondence with Leibniz, defending Newton's theory of absolute space and time against Leibniz's criticisms.

9. The account of the role of the Principle of Sufficient Reason in Clarke's reasoning and the outline of Clarke's argument is indebted to W. L. Rowe, *Philosophy of Religion* (Encino, CA: Dickenson, 1978), Chapter 2. My reconstruction of the second stage of Clarke's cosmological argument differs slightly from Rowe's. I have used the term *independent* where Rowe uses *self-existent,* and I have added an extra premise to emphasize the connection between the first stage and the second stage.

10. In many respects, Clarke's concept of an independent being resembles Aquinas's concept of a being that has of itself its own necessity. Both authors have the idea of a being that is not dependent on anything else for its existence but which contains the reason or explanation for its existence within itself. Such a being cannot be caused to begin existing, nor can it be destroyed. Thus, if an independent being exists at all, it must be eternal. Where Clarke differs from Aquinas is that Clarke insists that it is logically necessary that an independent being exist. In other words, Clarke's view was that, given a proper understanding of what the term *independent being* means, it follows logically that the assertion "an independent being (God) does not exist" is a logical contradiction. This matter receives a thorough discussion in W. L. Rowe, *The Cosmological Argument* (Princeton: University of Princeton Press, 1975), Chapter IV.

11. This formulation is based on W. L. Rowe, *Philosophy of Religion* (Encino, CA: Dickenson, 1978), Chapter 2. Strictly speaking (P1) is redundant, since if any being exists, it is a positive fact that it exists. In other words, (P2) entails (P1). But it is helpful to consider them separately, since Clarke bases premise (4) on (P1) and premise (5) on (P2).

12. See "The Argument from Contingency" from "A Debate on the Existence of God," a transcript of the BBC radio discussion broadcast in 1948, reprinted in J. Hicks, Ed., *The Existence of God* (New York: Macmillan, 1964): 168–178.

13. P. Edwards, "The Cosmological Argument," *op. cit.*

14. W. L. Rowe, *The Cosmological Argument, op. cit.,* Chapter III.

15. See J. Leslie, *Physical Cosmology and Philosophy* (New York: Macmillan, 1990) for readable accounts of modern "big bang" theories of the origin of the universe. In these theories, the universe began about 13 billion years ago as an *uncaused* quantum fluctuation in a vacuum initially devoid of matter and radiation.

# **DISCUSSION:** The Problem of Evil

Laugh where we must, be candid where we can;
But vindicate the ways of God to man.

All Nature is but Art, unknown to thee;
All Chance, Direction, which thou canst not see;
All Discord, Harmony not understood;
All partial Evil, universal Good.

Alexander Pope, *An Essay on Man* (1733–1734).

Philosophers and theologians who discuss the problem of evil usually divide evils into two classes: moral and natural. Moral evils are those evils caused by the free choices and actions of human beings. They include such things as murder, rape, torture, and genocide. Moral evils often result from desires and attitudes that are themselves evil, such as greed, the lust for power, indifference to the suffering of others, or the desire to cause humiliation, suffering and death.

Natural (or physical) evils are those intrinsically bad states of affairs that are not brought about deliberately by human beings. Either human beings cause them without knowing or intending that they will occur, or they are caused by natural forces that lie outside of human control. They include the pain, suffering, and premature death caused by natural disasters (such as earthquakes, droughts, and floods) and the diseases that afflict millions of humans and animals each year. An infant writhing in pain as she dies of meningitis in a Cairo slum, the degradation and suffering of cancer victims, and a fawn burning to death in a forest fire are graphic examples of natural evil.[1]

The problem of evil is the problem of explaining how moral and natural evil can be reconciled with the traditional conception of God as the omnipotent (all-powerful), omniscient (all-knowing), and omnibenevolent (wholly good) creator of the world. For, it is argued, an omnipotent being can do anything and thus can prevent any evil it chooses; and a wholly good being must want to eliminate suffering. Why, then, does God permit evil things to occur when it is in God's power to prevent them?

Some philosophers, such as John Mackie and Antony Flew, have argued that the problem of evil is insoluble.[2] Thus, they regard the logical problem of evil as a convincing argument for atheism.

## **THE LOGICAL PROBLEM OF EVIL**

Mackie (in Reading 5) claims that the existence of evil in the world makes theistic belief irrational because statements (G) and (E) are logically inconsistent.[3]

  (G)  God created the world and is omnipotent, omniscient, and
       omnibenevolent.
  (E)  The world contains evil.

Mackie argues that because (E) is obviously true and because inconsistent statements cannot both be true, (G) must be false. Hence, God does not exist.

Proving that (G) and (E) are logically inconsistent is not as easy as it might seem. A pair of propositions is logically inconsistent when it is logically impossible that they both be true. Propositions (G) and (E) are not obviously inconsistent, since (G) does not explicitly assert what (E) denies. So, Mackie has to *prove* that they are inconsistent.

The general strategy for proving inconsistency can be illustrated by propositions (a) and (b).

(a) My sweater is red.
(b) My sweater is not colored.

Just like (G) and (E), (a) and (b) do not contradict each other explicitly. But if we add to proposition (a), proposition (c), which is a necessary truth, then we can deduce the negation of (b).

(c) All red things are colored.

It is important that (c) be a necessary truth, because only then does it follow that (a) and (b) are logically inconsistent. Remember, in a valid argument it is logically impossible for all the premises to be true and the conclusion false. So, in the valid argument "(a), (c); therefore, not-(b)," if the conjunction [(a) and (c)] is true, then the conclusion not-(b) must be true, too. In other words, if [(a) and (c)] is true, (b) must be false. But if (c) is a necessary truth, it is always true and cannot be false. Consequently, whenever (a) is true, it must be the case that [(a) and (c)] is true, too. It thus follows that if (a) is true, (b) must be false, and if (b) is true, (a) must be false.

Thus, the relevant question for the problem of evil is this: Are there necessarily true propositions that, when conjoined with (G), will enable us to deduce that (E) is false? In other words, is there a valid argument having (G) as its first premise, in which all the other premises are necessary truths and whose conclusion is that the world does not contain any evil at all?

Mackie proposes the following propositions, (M1) and (M2), as plausible candidates:

(M1) A good thing always eliminates evil as far as it can.
(M2) There are no limits to what an omnipotent thing can do.

Mackie's position is that (M1) and (M2) are necessary truths which, when conjoined with (G), logically imply that (E) is false. Another way of understanding Mackie's position is to note that (M1) and (M2) together imply (M).

(M) If God created the world and is omnipotent, omniscient, and omnibenevolent, then the world would contain no evil.

Clearly, if Mackie were correct in thinking that (M) is a necessary truth, then God's existence would be logically inconsistent with the world's evil.

Much of Mackie's article is taken up with defending (M) against objections. Many of these objection can be regarded as attacks on either (M1) or (M2). Either there are some things (superficially regarded as evil) that even a wholly good being would not want to eliminate: hence (M1) is false; or there are limits on what even an omnipotent being can do: hence (M2) is false. But before looking at these objections and Mackie's response to them, there are some important methodological issues that we need to clarify.

First, it is Mackie who is using (M) (via M1 and M2) to argue for atheism. Hence, the burden of proof is on Mackie to show that (M) is a necessary truth. Even if Mackie is able to refute all the objections to (M), that by itself does not show that (M) *must* be true.

Second, when theists raise objections to (M), they do not have to give convincing reasons for thinking that (M) is actually false in order to defend theism against Mackie's attack. A *defense* to the logical problem of evil is adequate if it can show that it is logically possible for (M) to be false; for, if it is logically possible for God to create a world containing evil, then the logical problem of evil is solved. Thus, theists do not have to "justify God's ways to man" or construct a full-blown *theodicy* to answer Mackie.[4] It suffices if they can show, without logical contradiction, why God *might* permit some kinds of evil or how it *could* be that God is unable to prevent them, even though God is both omnibenevolent and omnipotent.

Third, some philosophers believe not only that Mackie has failed to show that (G) and (E) are inconsistent but also that it can be proved that (G) *is* logically consistent with (E), that it *is* logically possible for both propositions to be true. The American philosopher Alvin Plantinga offers such a proof in his version of the Free Will Defense.[5] We shall examine Plantinga's argument later. For the moment, I want to point out that even if the logical problem of evil can be solved along the lines suggested by Plantinga and others, there would still remain the evidential problem of evil, which arises from considering the quantity and types of evil that we find in the world. Many natural evils, for example, are instances of suffering that seem to have no moral justification at all. Surely, it is argued, this kind of seemingly superfluous evil makes it highly unlikely that the world was created by an omnipotent, omnibenevolent god. In this way, the evidential problem of evil can be used as an inductive argument for atheism, even if the logical problem of evil has been solved. We shall return to it at the end of this discussion.

Mackie considers four important responses to the logical problem of evil which he identifies by means of the following slogans:

(1) "Good cannot exist without evil," or "Evil is necessary as a counterpart to good."
(2) "Evil is necessary as a means to good."
(3) "The universe is better with some evil in it than it could be if there were no evil."
(4) "Evil is due to human free will."

For obvious reasons, the last of these responses is often called the Free Will Defense. For convenience I shall refer to the third response as the Greater Goods Defense.

Mackie dismisses the first two responses fairly quickly. He agrees that the only obvious constraints on an omnipotent being are logical ones, but he sees no reason to think that evil is a logically necessary counterpart to good. Surely, he insists, many kinds of good can exist without logically requiring the existence of any evil at all. Good and evil are not like the opposite sides of the same curve, concave and convex, respectively. Many good things and good actions can exist in the absence of evil without any logical contradiction.

The second response is based on the observation that many good things are such that to bring them about it is necessary to inflict or undergo some pain and suffering. For example, it is sometimes impossible to treat serious diseases such as cancer without causing the patient considerable discomfort and pain. Similarly, it is impossible to achieve many goals in life without experiencing some degree of sacrifice and hardship. But, of course, these are limitations placed on human beings by their bodies, their incomplete knowledge, and the laws of nature. God has no body, and God's knowledge is perfect. Moreover, if God is genuinely omnipotent, then God is not constrained by the causal laws of nature. On the traditional view, God not only is the author of the laws of nature but also retains the power to act contrary to them by performing miracles.

## THE GREATER GOODS DEFENSE

The target of the greater goods defense is (M1), the claim that a good thing always eliminates evil as far as it can. The greater goods defense argues that, far from (M1) being a necessary truth, (M1) is false. This is because there are certain kinds of goods that *logically* require their associated evils. Mackie calls these 2nd order goods. They include moral virtues, such as facing danger with courage, bearing pain with fortitude, and being charitable to the needy. As Mackie rightly stresses, if the greater goods defense is to work, the connection between 2nd order goods and 1st order evils must be a logical one, not merely a causal one, since an omnipotent God is constrained only by logical possibility, not mere physical or causal impossibility. So, for example, in a world without famine, not even God can make it true that Mother Theresa gives bread to the starving. Similarly, if no one ever faced danger or hardship, it would be impossible to display courage.

Several important questions need to be answered about this formulation of the greater goods defense. First, does the 2nd order good lie in the mere possession of a virtuous character trait or in its active exercise (or in both)? Presumably, for the defense to succeed, the answer has to be the latter. While some 1st order evils may be logically necessary for the active exercise of virtues such as courage and charity, it seems logically possible for these virtues to exist even though they are never exercised. Virtues are dispositions to act in certain ways in certain circumstances. Just as a cube of sugar can be soluble even though it is never dissolved in water, a person can be brave even though she is never in danger. The defense thus requires not merely that moral virtues exist but also that people exercise them, since only the latter seems to logically imply the existence of 1st order evils.

Second, *is* it logically necessary for the active exercise of virtues such as courage, compassion, and charity, that animals and humans actually suffer? Would it not be sufficient for the exercise of compassion, for example, if the compassionate person merely believed that another person was in pain? One answer to this question is that the compassionate person herself must have experienced pain at least once in her life in order to understand what someone else might be suffering now.

Third, are moral virtues intrinsically good, or are they good only because, when successfully exercised, they reduce the amount of pain and suffering in the world? The view that moral virtues have value only as a means to eliminating 1st order evil makes the greater goods defense self-defeating. For, on this view, pain exists to make possible a virtuous human response, but that response has value only because it diminishes the pain. The very act of behaving virtuously would thus diminish the value of one's action (by reducing to some degree the opportunities for further virtuous actions). If everyone acted virtuously, and all pain were eliminated, then virtue would lose all its value. For these reasons, most proponents of the greater goods defense regard moral virtue as intrinsically good, as something that ennobles the character of virtuous persons and makes them and the world they inhabit better as a result.

The main point of the greater goods defense is that a world with some 1st order evils in it can be better than a world with none, since only a world with some 1st order evils can contain 2nd order goods, and the 2nd order goods can outweigh the 1st order evils required for their existence. Thus, while it is true that there are evils that God could have prevented, it is false that the world would thereby have been made better.

Since the greater goods defense maintains, quite plausibly, that at least some evils are logically necessary for the occurrence of goods that outweigh them, it follows that it is possible that an omnibenevolent thing would not want to eliminate all evil from the world. But, as Mackie points out, a world that allows for the possible exercise of virtue is also a world that permits vice to flourish. The very same conditions that enable people to be charitable, if they choose, also permit people to be indifferent to suffering, or even to take a malevolent delight in the misfortunes of others. The possibility of courage, benevolence, and love brings with it the possibility of cowardice, malevolence, and hatred. And, as a matter of fact, the actual world we live in has a generous supply of these 2nd order evils.

Mackie thinks that this objection is fatal for the greater goods defense. He reasons that any attempt to justify 2nd order evil by appealing to 3rd order good (and so on) must generate an objectionable form of infinite regress. For, at each stage, nth order evil is justified by appeal to the $(n + 1)$th order good it makes possible; but if $(n + 1)$th order good is possible, then so too is $(n + 1)$th order evil, and so on. Thus, at no level do we have a justification of the evil that exists *at that level*. It is this difficulty with the greater goods defense that leads us to consider the free will defense. The aim of the free will defense is to stop the regress at level 2, not by insisting that moral vice is justified by any higher order goods it makes possible, but by arguing that God, even though omnipotent, may be unable to prevent it.

## THE FREE WILL DEFENSE

The free will defense claims that for virtuous actions to have moral value, for them to be *goods* of the 2nd order variety, those actions must be performed freely. It is crucial to the free will defense that it be a logically necessary truth that no person who performs a genuinely free act is *caused* to perform it. In other words, the free will defense relies on the metaphysical thesis called *incompatibilism*: if person P does X freely, then P is not caused or causally determined to do X; acting freely is logically incompatible with causal determinism.[6] According to incompatibilism and the free will defense, persons must be able to choose of their own free will whether to resist or succumb to temptation. It must be up to them alone whether to be naughty or nice. Thus, not even God can bring it about that human beings freely do nothing but good, because a genuinely free action lies outside the control of everyone except the person who chooses either to perform it or to refrain from performing it.

If incompatibilism is true, then (M2) is false, since there are limits to what an omnipotent thing can do. Even though a world in which persons do nothing wrong is logically possible, it may be that God cannot *create* such a world. When God decides to create the world, he decides which people will exist in it, which possible persons will be actualized. But once these people appear in the world, it is then up to them whether or not they will refrain from evil. It is logically possible that the world God creates and populates with persons will turn out to be a world in which no one freely does anything wrong. But God cannot guarantee this result merely by actualizing possible persons in the first place.

Before pursuing the free will defense further, it is helpful to consider what the concept of omnipotence really means. Up to this point we have assumed that the only limitations on the power of an omnipotent thing are logical ones. That is, we have assumed that as long as a state of affairs or a possible world involves no logical contradiction, an omnipotent thing could bring about that state of affairs or create that world if it chooses to do so. But it is pretty clear that this concept of omnipotence, as the power to bring about anything that is logically possible, is defective. For example, it is not the case that an omnipotent being can create any world that is logically possible. Though it is true that no one, not even God, can bring about a state of affairs that is logically impossible, it is not true that God can create any logically possible world. For example, it is logically possible that there exist a world containing things that are not created by God. But it is logically impossible for *God* to create that world. With this in mind, we must amend our understanding of omnipotence from $(O_1)$ to $(O_2)$.

(O₁)  An omnipotent being can create any world that is logically possible.

(O₂)  An omnipotent being can create any world that is logically possible for it to create.

With these changes, we see that the free will defense is really an attack on $(O_2)$. Though it may sound paradoxical, if incompatibilism is true, then God cannot create any world that it is logically possible for God to create. To see this, consider the following illustration. If Raoul freely performs some action, such as going to the movies this evening, then, since he acts freely, Raoul could have refrained from going to the movies. No one, not even God, can determine Raoul's action; it is entirely up to Raoul himself. Let $W_1$ be the world in which Raoul freely goes to the movies, and let $W_2$ be the world in which Raoul freely refrains from going to the movies. Whether the world God has created turns out to be $W_1$ or $W_2$ depends on how Raoul acts. It is logically possible that the world created by God is $W_1$; it is also logically possible that the world created by God is $W_2$. But if Raoul freely goes to the movies, then as a matter of contingent fact, God cannot create $W_2$. Similarly, if Raoul freely refrains from going the the movies, then God cannot create $W_1$.

The problem with the free will defense as described thus far is that it seems incompatible with God's omniscience.[7] God knows everything that is going to happen in any possible world that he chooses to create. Thus, if God knows that if he creates a world, W, in which Harriet exists, Harriet will freely perform at least one wrong action, given the temptations that exist in W, why does God actualize that world (W) which contains temptations to which Harriet will succumb; or, if Harriet will perform at least one wrong action in all the worlds in which she could be actualized, why does God actualize Harriet at all?

The answer to this question depends, in part, on accepting the claim that human freedom is a good of such overwhelming value that God must create a world that contains at least some persons who are free to decide how they will act. The second part of the answer depends on accepting that it is logically possible that the hypothesis of transworld depravity is true.

**The Hypothesis of Transworld Depravity (D):** In every possible world that God can create that contains persons who act freely, at least one of those persons performs at least one wrong action.

The core of the free will defense as developed by Plantinga is the claim that it is logically possible that the hypothesis of transworld depravity is true. If it is true, then God is incapable of creating a possible world in which no freely acting person ever does anything wrong. Plantinga is not claiming that (D) is true, or even plausible; merely that it is possible that is true, that the truth of (D) is a contingent matter.

From premise (G) conjoined with (D), we can deduce that any world created by God will contain at least some (moral) evil, which makes statement (E) true. Since (D) is a contingent statement, this shows that (G) and (E) are logically consistent. Why? Because it is logically possible that both (G) and (D) are true; (G) and (D) together entail (E); thus, it is logically possible that both (G) and (E) are true.

Let us assume that between them, the greater goods defense and the free will defense provide persuasive grounds for rejecting the logical problem of evil as a proof of atheism. God's existence is not logically inconsistent with the presence of at least some evil in the world. Let us also assume that the greater goods defense and the free will defense work as partial theodicies; that is, they explain why God permits moral evil and as much physical evil as is logically necessary for the 2nd order goods that outweigh it.[8] Even if these assumptions were correct, there would still remain the evidential problem of evil based on those 1st order, physical evils that do not appear to serve any purpose that would explain why a perfectly good and omnipotent God permits them to exist.

## THE EVIDENTIAL PROBLEM OF EVIL

We can present the evidential problem of evil as an argument for atheism in the following manner:

(A) There exist superfluous evils.
(B) If God exists, then there are no superfluous evils.

(C) God does not exist.

Superfluous evils are evils such that God could have prevented them, and if God had prevented them, then the world as a whole would have been better (or, at least, no worse) than it is.

The argument for atheism from superfluous evil is valid, and premise (B) seems to be a necessary truth about a perfectly good God. Thus, if we have sufficient evidence to make (A) more probable than not, it follows that God's nonexistence is more probable than his existence. More generally, the stronger the evidence in favor of (A), the stronger the case against God's existence.[9]

Premise (A) is supported by the numerous cases of intense suffering, such as the fawn burning to death in a forest fire, for which there is no apparent justification. There seem to be many cases of animal and human suffering such that (a) they do not contribute to a higher good, (b) God could have prevented them, and (c) if God had prevented them, then the world would have been better than it is. In other words, there are many examples of suffering that are not the result of the exercise of free will and that do not appear to be logically necessary for the existence of any higher order good that outweighs them. Admittedly, the case for premise (A) is not conclusive, since it is based on the way things seem to be, and it is possible that we are mistaken in believing that that is the way things actually are. But until we are given grounds for doubting our judgments (grounds that are more than the mere logical possibility of error), we should believe that the way things seem to be to the best of our ability to judge is in fact the way things are.

I will conclude by commenting on just one of the responses that theists have made to the evidential problem of evil. Many theists accept the truth of (B), but they are also convinced that God exists. They turn the reasoning around and argue: (C) is false, and (B) is true; thus, (A) is false. Their argument is valid. If there is a proof of God's existence, then they are home and dry. But if, as seems likely, there is no such proof, we have to consider what evidence, if any, makes God's existence probable. The evidence that is often appealed to includes miracles (either witnessed at first hand or, more usually, testified about by others) and personal religious experiences. There are many interesting epistemological problems raised by these appeals to miracles and religious experiences that we cannot pursue here.[10] But we can say this: In evaluating the evidential problem of evil, we must consider all the relevant evidence; that is, not just the evidence for superfluous evil, but also the evidence for God's existence. Only when we have weighed all the evidence, when we have considered its quantity, quality, and reliability, can we reach a reasoned judgment about the probability of God's existence in light of the world's evil.

---

## NOTES

1. William Rowe uses the fawn example in his paper "The Problem of Evil and Some Varieties of Atheism," *American Philosophical Quarterly* 16 (1979); 335–341. Many questions can be raised about the proper use of the term *evil* and about the classification of evils as either natural or moral according to their origin. For example, is it the diseases themselves that are natural evils or only the suffering they produce in sentient creatures? If someone is justly punished for wrongdoing, is the suffering caused by the punishment an instance of moral evil? If X knows that he can prevent Y from experiencing a terrible pain from some natural cause but deliberately refrains from intervening, is Y's pain both a natural evil and a moral evil?

2. Flew, "Divine Omnipotence and Human Freedom," in A. Flew and A. C. MacIntyre, Eds., *New Essays in Philosophical Theology* (New York: Macmillan, 1955): 144–169; A. Flew, *The Presumption of Atheism* (New York: Barnes & Noble, 1976), Chapter 7, "The Free Will Defense," pp. 81–99; and J. L. Mackie, *The Miracle of Theism* (Oxford: Clarendon Press, 1982), Chapter 9.

3. Though it plays no explicit role in Mackie's discussion, it is important that God be omniscient; otherwise God might fail to prevent some evils out of sheer ignorance. Also, Mackie is assuming the traditional view that if God exists, God created the world.

4. A theodicy (from the Greek words for "god" and "justice") is an attempt to explain what God's reasons actually are for allowing evil to exist in the world. A defense aims to show

merely that God's existence is not logically inconsistent with evil. Thus, a theodicy is more ambitious than a defense.

5. A. Plantinga, *God, Freedom, and Evil* (New York: Harper & Row, 1974): 29–59.

6. Advocates of the free will defense are libertarians, since they defend both incompatibilism *and* the claim that many human actions are free. See the introduction to Part IV, "Determinism and Free Will," later in this volume.

7. For a challenging discussion of whether God's omniscience is compatible with human beings acting freely, see N. Pike, "Divine Omniscience and Voluntary Action," *The Philosophical Review* 74 (1965): 27–46.

8. For criticisms of these theodicies, see H. J. McCloskey, "God and Evil," *The Philosophical Quarterly* 10 (1960): 97–114; and N. Pike, "Over-Power and God's Responsibility for Sin," in A. J. Freddoso, Ed., *The Existence and Nature of God* (Notre Dame, IN: University of Notre Dame Press, 1983): 11–35.

9. For a more sophisticated treatment of the evidential problem of evil, see W. L. Rowe, "The Problem of Evil and Some Varieties of Atheism," *American Philosophical Quarterly* 16 (1979): 335–341; and W. L. Rowe, "Evil and the Theistic Hypothesis: A Response to Wykstra," *International Journal of Philosophy of Religion* 16 (1984): 95–100.

10. See the discussion, "The Argument from Religious Experience," later in Part I of this book.

# DISCUSSION: Pascal's Wager

On the night of 23 November 1654, Blaise Pascal had a mystical religious experience that changed his life.[1] As a result, he became a devout Christian and joined the Jansenists, a rather Puritanical sect of the Roman Catholic Church to which other members of his family already belonged.

Until his conversion, Pascal had run with a fast crowd of freethinkers who enjoyed gambling, drinking, and womanizing. In his *Pensées,* published from the notes left at his death, Pascal gave his famous wager argument. It was designed to persuade his libertine friends, most of whom were lapsed Catholics, to give up their pleasure-loving way of life and become sober, pious believers in God.

## PASCAL'S ARGUMENT

Pascal's wager is address to those who, like Pascal's worldly friends, believe both (A) and (B).

(A) The only religious hypothesis that has even a chance of being true is H, according to which there exists a god who grants eternal happiness to all and only sincere believers in him. The probability of H, Pr(H), is greater than zero; the probability of all rival religions is zero.

(B) There are no rational grounds for deciding whether or not H is true: there are no arguments that prove H is true; there are no arguments that prove H is false; there is not even any evidence to confirm H (or if there is, it is counterbalanced by equally strong evidence for atheism). Epistemic rationality cannot settle the question of God's existence.

Pascal himself does not include as part of H that God will condemn all non-believers to eternal damnation. I shall consider later what difference this might make to the argument.

Pascal then argues that if anyone believes that (A) and (B) are true, then (C) is also true of that person.

(C) Prudential rationality requires that one immediately start living piously, going to mass, taking holy water; in short, doing anything that will maximize one's chances of coming to believe that H is true. Let us refer to these actions, collectively, as P. Anyone who does not start doing P is acting irrationally.

Thus, Pascal's argument runs as follows: If you believe both (A) and (B), then prudential rationality requires that you do P. Interpreted in this way, Pascal's wager is an *ad hominem* argument: it is addressed solely to those people who believe that (A) and (B) are true.[2] Though Pascal himself thinks that (A) and (B) are true, I shall not address the question of whether we should agree with him. I shall be concerned solely with the question, Has Pascal shown that rationality requires doing P if one believes (A) and (B)?

## EPISTEMIC AND PRUDENTIAL RATIONALITY

It is sometimes said that Pascal concluded that it is rational to believe that God exists, or that H is true. This cannot be correct for two reasons. First, if the conclusion of Pascal's argument were really that it is epistemically rational to believe that H is true, this would contradict (B), which states that reason and evidence are incapable of deciding whether or not H is true. Second, as the text of the wager makes clear (and as Pascal stresses elsewhere in the *Pensées*), the kind of belief required for salvation is a passionate, emotional conviction that God exists, not a cold intellectual judgment. For Pascal, believing in God is more like loving a friend than simply believing that one's friend exists. Loving a friend implies that one believes that the friend exists, but it also involves an extra emotional ingredient.

Pascal thinks that intellectual reason alone cannot yield a sincere, passionate belief in God's existence, but it can be caused by the type of overwhelming mystical experience responsible for his own conversion, or it can arise gradually through doing P. Doing P is prudentially rational because it has a good chance of leading to, of causing, that passionate, emotional belief in God required for salvation. Presumably, if there were a belief pill or a completely safe and effective brain operation that would induce the requisite state of belief, Pascal would argue that one should swallow the pill or have the operation. As it is, there is no quick fix. The best one can do is live piously and hope that faith follows. Thus, the conclusion of Pascal's wager is about the prudential rationality of action, not the epistemic rationality of belief.

One reason that it is easy to conflate the rationality of doing P with the rationality of believing H is that anyone who does sincerely believe H will automatically perform P as the natural expression of that belief. Of course, for such a person, giving up sin and adopting a pious lifestyle would not involve any "cost" at all, since the person will enjoy doing P, unlike the libertines whom Pascal is addressing who would regard doing P as a sacrifice (until their conversion). Also, the persons who are persuaded by

Pascal's wager will genuinely want to believe H; they will not simply be going through the motions like actors genuflecting to a cardboard altar. Such persons would pray to a God in whom they do not, as yet, fully believe to grant them genuine faith.

## PASCAL'S THREE VERSIONS OF HIS ARGUMENT

Pascal's presentation of his argument is difficult to follow because he gives three different versions, each successively more refined.[3] In each version, the person who believes (A) and (B) faces a choice: Either start doing P, or continue doing not-P. We will describe this as the choice between accepting the wager (that is, wagering that God exists by doing P) and rejecting the wager (by continuing to do not-P).

### Version I

Either God (as described by H) exists or he does not. If God exists, then the consequences of accepting the wager are much better than the consequences of rejecting it. If God does not exist, then accepting and rejecting the wager are on a par, since you lose nothing. Since you are never worse off by accepting the wager, and you could be enormously better off by accepting it, you should accept it. In this first version, there is no appeal to probabilities, but the argument assumes that the lottery ticket costs nothing.

The flaw with Version I is that "perhaps I am wagering too much." That is, if I accept the wager and God does not exist, I will have paid an unnecessary price, namely, foregoing the pleasures of the flesh for the rest of my one and only life and wasting my time with boring and unpleasant rituals. The lottery ticket does cost me something; it costs me my life, or at least that remaining portion of it that I devote to the church. Is accepting the wager worth this investment of my life? Notice that just as with a lottery ticket (and unlike betting at the racetrack), the price of making the bet is not refunded. If you buy a lottery ticket for $1 and win the grand prize of $1,000, what you receive is just $1,000; thus, your net gain is $999.

### Version II

Assume that "there is equal chance of gain and loss" or, in other words, that $Pr(H) = Pr(not\text{-}H) = \frac{1}{2}$ . Since the price of the lottery ticket is a single life, as long as I receive at least three lives if I win, it is prudent to accept the wager. (I am assuming here that the gambler who rejects the wager enjoys her one life and that's that; she who accepts the wager gives up her one life and so needs to win back more than two to do more than break even.)

In fact, of course, the reward promised by H is not just a few extra lives, but an infinity of lives (eternal life) that will be perfectly happy. In the final version of the argument, Pascal describes this as "an infinity of infinitely happy life to be won."

In this and the following version of his argument, Pascal assumes that (P1) is a correct principle of prudential rationallity.

(P1)  If the expected utility of doing X (e.g., buying a lottery ticket, accepting the wager) exceeds the price of doing X, then not to do X is irrational.

To understand the notion of expected utility, consider buying a ticket in a lottery that offers only a single prize worth \$Y. The probability that you will win \$Y is P, and the probability that you will win nothing is (1 – P). The expected utility of buying the ticket is calculated by multiplying the probability of each of the two possible outcomes by the value (in dollars) that you will receive if that outcome is realized. The expected utility of buying the ticket is thus \$PY + \$ (1 – P) (0) = \$PY. Principle (P1) says that it is irrational not to buy a ticket if it costs less than \$PY. In the case of the religious hypothesis, H, the value you receive if God exists is infinite, and if God does not exist you receive nothing. So, since Pr(H) = ½, the expected utility of accepting Pascal's wager is infinite.

The flaw with Version II is that we do not know that Pr(H) = ½ ; in fact, the probability may be much lower. (This sounds like objective probability, but, of course, Pascal must be referring to subjective probabilities: your personal degree of confidence in the truth of H may be much lower than one half.) This leads Pascal to the third, and final, version of his wager argument.

### Version III

It does not matter how low Pr(H) is, because if H is true, then accepting the wager yields a reward of infinite value. Thus, as long as the probability of winning is not zero, the expected utility of acceptance has infinite value, compared with the finite value of rejecting it. Thus, principle (P1) dictates that you should accept the wager.

### SOME CRITICISMS OF PASCAL'S WAGER

There have been many criticisms of Pascal's wager. The most often discussed is the Many-Gods Objection.[4] I shall ignore it, since it challenges the truth of (A). If one assigns a nonzero probability both to H and to some rival religion, J, that also promises infinite rewards, then Pascal might argue that it is prudentially rational to wager on one or the other of them. But if J threatens damnation to the followers of H, and vice versa, then the expected utility of wagering on either of them is zero, since in each case there is a nonzero probability of getting an infinitely pleasant reward and a nonzero probability of getting an infinitely nasty punishment.

Similarly, though it is true that not everyone would assign a positive value to the eternal afterlife promised by H, this again amounts to denying (A), which promises eternal happiness. (Milton's Satan would rather rule in hell than serve in heaven; he would be eternally unhappy in heaven.)

But what about principle (P1)? Imagine that I offer you a chance to play a simple game with me. You have to pay \$100,000 for the privilege of playing, and that amount is nonrefundable. The game is this. I toss a fair coin exactly once. If it comes up heads, you get nothing. If it comes up tails, I give you \$1 million. If (P1) is true, then you are irrational not to play, since the expected utility of playing is \$500,000, which exceeds the \$100,000 it costs to enter the game. I think we can all agree that you would not be irrational if you declined to participate. Therefore, (P1) is false.

Of course, if you played this same game over and over again, then, in the long run, you will probably win a tremendous amount of money. But, as with Pascal's wager, you play only once, and that's it. The libertine who rejects Pascal's wager is not obviously irrational if he prefers the certainty of a life led the way he wants to lead it to a small chance of everlasting bliss.

Now, it has been argued that when the potential winnings are infinite and the price of wagering is finite, it would be irrational not to accept the wager. Thus, the proposal is that (P2) is true.

(P2) If the expected utility of doing X is infinite and the price of doing X is finite, then not to do X is irrational.

To evaluate (P2), consider the St. Petersburg game invented by the mathematician Nicolaus Bernouilli in the eighteenth century. In this game, there are two players. Let us call them Al and Bob. First, Al pays Bob a finite amount of money, say a hundred dollars, for the privilege of playing the game. Then, Bob takes a fair coin and keeps tossing it until the coin comes up heads for the first time. When Bob throws his first head, the game is over and he pays Al his winnings. If the coin comes up heads on the first toss, Al wins two dollars; if it comes up tails on the first toss and then heads on the second, Al wins four dollars; if it first comes up heads on the third toss, Al wins eight dollars; and so on. The probability of winning two dollars is $\frac{1}{2}$; the probability of winning four dollars is $\frac{1}{4}$; the probability of winning eight dollars is $\frac{1}{8}$; and so on. So, the expected utility of playing the St. Petersburg game is $\$ (2) \times (\frac{1}{2}) + (4) \times (\frac{1}{4}) + (8) \times (\frac{1}{8}) \ldots = \$ 1 + 1 + 1 \ldots$, which is infinite. But few of us would think it rational to pay even twenty dollars to participate. This shows that (P2) is false: even though the game offers an infinite expected utility for a finite price, refusing to play at that price is not irrational.

There is a third criticism of Pascal's argument.[5] Though it is unlikely, it is not impossible that I should eventually become a sincere believer even though I continue my decadent lifestyle. Some of the most debauched characters in history have experienced sudden conversions to the church. So, if I reject the wager, there is a nonzero probability that I will convert and, if God exists, I will get an infinite reward. Thus, rejecting the wager has the same infinite expected utility as accepting it. (Perhaps what we need is a further principle of rationality: When choosing between several actions that each have infinite expected utility, choose the one with the highest probability of yielding the infinite reward.[6])

## DAMNATION

Finally, I want to address the question of damnation. Let us amend H so that it now threatens eternal misery to all nonbelievers. Here, of course, the lottery analogy breaks down (which may be why Pascal did not include hell as a possible outcome of not accepting the wager). We do not normally imagine that failing to buy a lottery ticket might lead to dreadful consequences. But we do make decisions in everyday life between alternative courses of action, some of which carry with them the nonzero probability of personal disaster. Suppose that the worst thing that could possibly happen to you, even worse than death, is to be hideously mutilated and spend the rest of your life in unrelenting agony. There is a nonzero probability that this fate will befall anyone who rides in a car. But no one thinks that it is irrational to ride in a car. This disposes, I think, of the negative analogue of (P1).

It will be objected that unlike a finite lifetime of unbearable agony, eternal damnation has an infinite negative utility and that when the expected utility of rejecting the wager is infinitely negative, it would be irrational not to accept it.

We could evade the problem of eternal damnation by denying that it is logically possible for a perfectly good God to condemn anyone, however wicked, to eternal punishment, since it would violate the fundamental principle of justice that the severity of the punishment should match the seriousness of the crime. All human wickedness is finite; thus, no one deserves eternal punishment.

But I think we can construct a counterexample to the negative analogue of (P2) using the St. Petersburg game. Imagine someone, call him Waldo, who regards the thrill of gambling as one of the finer things in life. Waldo offers another gambler one play of the St. Petersburg game for 10 dollars, hoping for some pleasant diversion. From our previous discussion, it should be clear that Waldo has chosen an action that has an infinite negative utility. But I submit that Waldo's action is not irrational. In all likelihood, Waldo will not even be out of pocket, and he will consider his time to have been well spent.

In conclusion, I would like to repeat the qualification I made earlier. I have not addressed the question of whether (A) and (B) are true, merely the issue of whether Pascal's conclusion (C) must apply to anyone who believes that (A) and (B) are true. My main criticism of Pascal's argument is that it relies on principles of prudential rationality that seem to be false. It is not always irrational to pass up a slender chance of an infinite gain, nor is it always irrational to choose an action that carries with it a slender chance of an infinite loss.

---

## NOTES

1. Pascal summarized this experience on a piece of parchment which he carried with him for the remaining eight years of his life. See "The Memorial" in *Pascal's Pensées*, trans. by A. J. Krailsheimer (London: Penguin, 1966): 309–310.

2. An *ad hominem* argument is literally an argument "directed at a man." It can mean either (1) the fallacy of trying to refute a view by attacking the character of the person who holds it or (2) an attempt to persuade someone to accept a conclusion by deducing it from premises that she already accepts. There is nothing fallacious or dishonest about the second kind of *ad hominem* argument. For example, suppose that Joan is not a vegetarian but opposes hunting on the grounds that killing animals is wrong. One could offer Joan an *ad hominem* argument for the conclusion that she should stop eating meat because it, too, involves killing animals.

3. See I. Hacking, "The Logic of Pascal's Wager," *American Philosophical Quarterly* 9 (1972): 186–192.

4. See J. Cargile, "Pascal's Wager," *Philosophy* 41 (1966): 229-236; A. Flew, "Is Pascal's Wager the Only Safe Bet?" in *God, Freedom and Immortality* (Buffalo, NY: Prometheus, 1984): 61–68; and W. G. Lycan and G. N. Schlesinger, "You Bet Your Life: Pascal's Wager Defended," in J. Feinberg, Ed., *Reason and Responsibility*, 7th ed. (Belmont, CA: Wadsworth, 1989): 82–90.

5. See A. Duff, "Pascal's Wager and Infinite Utilities," *Analysis* 46 (1986): 107–109.

6. G. Schlesinger, *New Perspectives on Old-Time Religion* (Oxford: Clarendon Press, 1988): 154.

# DISCUSSION: The Will to Believe

In his introductory remarks to *The Will to Believe,* William James describes his lecture as "something like a sermon on justification by faith . . . an essay in justification *of* faith, a defense of our right to adopt a believing attitude in religious matters, in spite of the fact that our merely logical intellect may not have been coerced." James was responding mainly to "that delicious *enfant terrible* Clifford," and the disagreement between them is captured in their slogans.

*Clifford:* It is wrong always, everywhere, and for anyone, to believe anything upon insufficient evidence.

*James:* Our passional nature not only lawfully may, but must, decide an option between propositions, whenever it is a genuine option that cannot by its nature be decided on intellectual grounds.

We can emphasize the disagreement by adopting the following formulations. With regard to any proposition, P, we have three choices: Either believe that P is true, or believe that P is false, or remain agnostic about P.

*Clifford:* If the decision between believing P and believing not-P cannot be made on the basis of evidence, then one ought to remain agnostic about P.

*James:* If the decision between believing P and believing not-P cannot be made on the basis of evidence and the option is a genuine one, then it is not wrong to believe P (or to believe not-P) as one wishes.[1]

Clifford's position in *The Ethics of Belief*—that it is always wrong to adopt a belief on insufficient evidence—is not confined to religion; it covers any belief whatever. Similarly, in his reply, James argues that Clifford's general position is incorrect, not just its application to matters of religion. For convenience, I shall use the term *agnosticism* so that it can apply to any belief whatever, not just to beliefs about God. Thus understood, Clifford is claiming that agnosticism is a moral duty when we are faced with insufficient evidence.

I shall not discuss whether or not Clifford and James were correct in assuming that neither theism nor atheism is warranted by the available evidence. Instead, I shall focus solely on Clifford's arguments for his general position on the ethics of belief. Later, I will judge whether James has refuted Clifford, and, separately, whether religious belief is actually licensed by James's theory.

## CLIFFORD'S FOUR ARGUMENTS

Clifford argues that in every single case, adopting a belief on insufficient evidence is wrong, even if in a particular case it does not lead to any immediate harm, and even when the belief in question turns out to be true. Here are his four main arguments followed by my brief comments on each.

(1) The Duty to Question Argument. We have a "universal duty of questioning all that we believe." Believing without sufficient evidence violates that duty. Thus, it is immoral.

This first argument is incomplete. Let us grant to Clifford that we have a duty to doubt and question all our beliefs. But why does this duty imply that it is wrong to adopt beliefs on insufficient evidence in the first place? Clifford's own formulation of our "universal duty" presupposes that we can question and raise doubts about beliefs we already have. Why can't we just believe willy-nilly without being overly concerned about the evidence and then, later, subject our beliefs to critical scrutiny?

Clifford may have reasoned as follows. If we allow ourselves to believe promiscuously at the outset, then many of our beliefs will in fact be false. And, if we have already accepted many false beliefs, then our ability to evaluate any one of them will be undermined. For example, if someone already believes (falsely) that anecdotal testimony is reliable evidence for the effectiveness of medical treatments, then that person will be a poor judge of his belief in a new cancer therapy. Too much promiscuity in belief acquisition compromises our subsequent attempts at belief evaluation.

> (2)  The Duty Not to Harm Others Argument. Believing without sufficient evidence often leads to believing what is false. Beliefs, either individually or in conjunction with others, influence action. Actions are more likely to prove harmful when based on false beliefs than when based on true ones. Thus, in the long run, believing without sufficient evidence increases the probability that people will be harmed by our actions. It is wrong to expose people to avoidable harm. So, it is wrong to believe without sufficient evidence.

This is Clifford's best argument. Especially interesting is the first premise that believing without sufficient evidence often leads to having false beliefs. Clifford's reasons for this premise are similar to those expressed by Sigmund Freud in his *The Future of an Illusion* (1927).[2] For example, Clifford speaks of such beliefs being adopted "for the solace and private pleasure of the believer; to add a tinsel splendour to the plain straight road of our life and display a bright mirage beyond it." The idea is not that unfounded beliefs are just as likely to be false as true, but that they are more likely to be false because they result from wish fulfillment, because they satisfy our desire for comfort and reassurance rather than stemming solely from a passion for the truth, however disquieting it may turn out to be.

> (3)  The Bad Habits Argument. Even if the belief should turn out to be true, believing without sufficient evidence reinforces bad habits, it weakens "our powers of self-control, of doubting, of judicially and fairly weighing evidence"; in short, it makes us mentally flabby. Thus, it damages our mind and character, and it diminishes our ability to discharge the universal duty of questioning. Hence, it is wrong.

The frequent performance of any type of action can inculcate a habit. People who believe in such things as fairies, ghosts, channelling, and the power of prayer to heal illness on the merest shreds of evidence are likely to turn into gullible fools who are far too ready to believe anything simply because they want to believe it. Such people would be failing to develop their mental powers to their fullest extent; they would be guilty of mental laziness. On some moral theories, this failure to develop one's talents and to exercise them when appropriate is morally wrong. But Clifford's argument has little force against someone who, like James, would exercise the "will to believe" only after meticulously and scrupulously investigating all the relevant evidence and finding it inconclusive. For, in such a person, the capacity and appetite for rigorous investigation would survive undiminished.

(4) The Self-Interest Argument. If we are credulous, then people are less likely to believe what we say. We will lose their respect, and other people will be more likely to lie to us and deceive us. Thus, it is against our self-interest to believe on insufficient evidence.

This is not a convincing argument. A gullible person will lose the respect of a tough-minded intellectual like Clifford; but not everyone has such high standards, and in a society rife with superstition, a gullible person might fare better than a critical inquirer. Even if, in some societies, gullible people do elicit contempt and are vulnerable to liars and cheats, they are more to be pitied than condemned. Clifford is too quick to excoriate the weak-minded.

## JAMES'S RESPONSE TO CLIFFORD

One of James's criticisms is directed at both Clifford and Pascal. James charges that both men falsely assume that for any proposition whatever we can voluntarily choose whether we believe it, disbelieve it, or reserve our judgment. According to James, this assumption contradicts the facts of human psychology, since we cannot believe any proposition that seems to us patently false or any hypothesis which for us is dead. Which propositions and hypotheses we are capable of believing depends on our desires and emotions, not on our intellect alone. James insists that "as a rule we disbelieve all facts and theories for which we have no use." James also dismisses all appeals to authority as unjustified and asserts that even when we find arguments for our beliefs, they are often empty rationalizations, the intellectual tail pretending to wag the emotional dog.

James misrepresents Pascal, but does he have a telling point against Clifford?[3] Let me respond on Clifford's behalf. Most people, regrettably, do not have as their sole and ruling passion the desire to believe only what is true. But if a person has any intellectual standards at all, she will not complacently tolerate false beliefs. Thus, most people are psychologically able to ask the questions, Are my present beliefs adequately supported by evidence? and Do I have good reasons for thinking that my beliefs are true? The desire for truth and the desire to avoid error may be only a part—but they *are* a part—of our passional nature.

However uncritical I may have been in adopting my beliefs in the first place, and whatever the emotional satisfaction they now give me, I am capable of critically assessing the beliefs I have. If I realize that my evidence for P is insufficient, I should withhold my intellectual assent from P. Granted, I may not be able to control my strong emotional attachment to P, and that feeling may persist for a long time, but I should resist the temptation to act as if I knew that P is true. Thus, in one sense of the term *belief,* I may still believe P; but I also now believe, strongly and passionately, that I have no right to act on P as if I knew it were true. In this way, we attempt to suppress and eventually eliminate many of the superstitious, racist, sexist, and other unfounded beliefs that we have absorbed uncritically from our parents, friends, and society.

This response does rebut James's objection to Clifford. It acknowledges that many of our beliefs, particularly those formed in childhood, and especially those about religion, politics, and morality, were not examined critically before they were first acquired. But this does not prevent those beliefs from being rigorously examined now, nor does it imply that as skeptical adults we cannot try to be more discriminating about what we come to believe in the future.

James assumes, falsely, that most if not all of our beliefs are caused by passions, prejudices, hopes, fears, and social pressures, over which we have little control. For example, James suggests that Clifford's policy of agnosticism stems from Clifford's passionate fear of error. But this is unfair to Clifford, who gives arguments for his position. Unfortunately, James fails to give those arguments the attention they deserve, though, as indicated earlier in the discussion of the Bad Habits Argument, James could respond plausibly to some of them.

## DOES THE RELIGIOUS HYPOTHESIS PRESENT US WITH A GENUINE OPTION?

James agrees with Clifford that (a) we ought to believe that P is true if there is sufficient evidence in P's favor and (b) we ought to believe that P is false if there is sufficient evidence against P. To that extent, both men are evidentialists: both insist sufficient evidence for P morally requires that we believe P.[4] But when there is no decisive evidence for P or against it, James rejects Clifford's contention that it is always our moral duty to suspend judgment. Instead, James proposes that in the absence of evidence it is permissible to follow our emotional inclination to believe P if that hypothesis presents us with a genuine option.

James describes a genuine option as a decision between two hypotheses that is living, momentous, and forced.

An option is *living* (not dead) for a person when both hypotheses make some appeal to the person's belief, and thus for each hypothesis there is a real chance, however small, that the person could believe it. When an option is living for us, we are not indifferent between the two alternatives; we care which is true.

An option is *momentous* (not trivial) when there is something important that hangs on our making the right choice, when the opportunity of choosing may not recur, and when the choice cannot easily be reversed.

An option is *forced* (not avoidable) if the consequences of refusing to decide for one or the other of the two hypotheses are the same as actually deciding for one of them.

The choice between believing that P is true and believing that P is false is never forced with respect to truth and error, since one can always suspend one's judgment, thus avoiding both truth and error. The choice is forced only when some other benefit (or harm) is at stake and when refusing to decide will have the same outcome as deciding positively one way or the other.

When James applies his doctrine of the will to believe to religious belief, he defines the religious hypothesis, H, in a rather strange way. H has two parts: (a) the best things are eternal, and (b) we are better off even now if we believe that the best things are eternal.

The strangeness of the first part results from James's desire to be ecumenical. James wants to characterize the religious hypothesis in terms so general that it can apply to most, if not all, religions, theistic or otherwise. We shall be more direct and confine our attention to standard theism.

**The Religious Hypothesis, H:** (a) God exists, and (b) we are better off even now if we believe that God exists.

Let us grant that the choice between believing that H is true and believing that H is false is a live option that is intellectually undecidable. Is the option momentous, and is it forced, as James assumes? The option is a genuine one only if the answer to both these questions is "Yes" and only then, according to James, may we believe as our nature inclines us, either to theism or to atheism.

The benefits from theistic belief fall into two general categories: (1) the benefits one can receive only from God both during one's life and after one's death and (2) the benefits one can receive during one's lifetime even if God does not exist. Let us call these the *divine* and *natural* benefits, respectively. Divine benefits would include the granting of prayers, supernatural assistance in facing life's trials and dangers, spiritual companionship, and salvation after death. Natural benefits might include the feeling of comfort and assurance that comes from believing that God exists and cares for one, the fellowship and support of fellow believers, an ordered plan for living one's life, and a lack of anxiety about death.

With regard to the divine benefits, James is mistaken in thinking that the religious option is momentous. For, if there is no God, the divine benefits of belief and nonbelief are the same—namely, none at all. Thus, the option is not momentous. All we can say is that *if H is true*, then the option is momentous. James seems aware of the problem, since he invites us to "consider what the logical elements are *in case the religious hypothesis in both its branches be really true.*" But he fails to note the difference between this and the option being momentous *un*conditionally.

Similarly, with respect to divine benefits, James is mistaken in asserting that "religion is a forced option, so far as that good goes." For, with respect to divine benefits, the option is force *in the intended sense* only if God exists. I say "in the intended sense" because if God does not exist, there is a trivial sense in which the option is forced, namely that the divine benefits of theism, atheism, and agnosticism are the same. Thus, if we focus solely on the consequences of theistic belief that depend on God for their existence, James's theory of the will to believe does not legitimate religious belief.[5]

## JAMES AND THE PRAGMATIC THEORY OF BELIEF

How does James's doctrine fare if we consider the natural benefits of religious belief? James was a proponent of the pragmatic theory of belief, which asserts that there is an intimate connection between what one believes and how one acts.[6] According to James's version of the pragmatic theory, beliefs that are truly different must make a difference to the way we act. If two beliefs have the same consequences for action, then they are the same belief; if the consequences are different, then the beliefs are different. In a footnote to Section X of *The Will to Believe,* James applies this theory to the religious option:

> Since belief is measured by action, he who forbids us to believe religion to be true, necessarily also forbids us to act as we should if we did believe it to be true. The whole defence of religious faith hinges upon action. If the action required or inspired by the religious hypothesis is in no way different from that dictated by the naturalistic hypothesis, then religious faith is a

pure superfluity, better pruned away, and controversy about its legitimacy is a piece of idle trifling, unworthy of serious minds. I myself believe, of course, that the religious hypothesis gives to the world an expression which specifically determines our reactions, and makes them in a large part unlike what they might be on a purely naturalistic scheme of belief.

In the first sentence of this quotation, James infers from "belief is measured by action" that "he who forbids us to believe religion to be true, necessarily also forbids us to act as we should if we did believe it to be true." What James seems to be assuming is that for each distinct belief, P, there is a distinct range of actions that can be produced by that belief and by no other. Let us call that range of actions "acting as if we believed that P is true." Thus, someone who does not believe that P is true cannot perform exactly that range of actions associated with believing that P is true; or, as James puts it, the person cannot act as if he or she believed that P is true.

James's version of the pragmatic theory of belief has the startling consequence that *all* belief options are forced.[7] For any proposition, P, believing P will have consequences (namely, acting as if one believed that P is true) that cannot be realized by believing not-P, reserving judgment about P, or believing some other proposition, Q. Thus, James's pragmatic theory of belief guarantees that the religious option is forced: we have to choose whether or not to act as if the religious hypothesis is true, and, according to James, the only way to act as if theism is true is to actually believe it.

Let us assume that James is correct in judging that the theist's pattern of life will inevitably be different from that of either the atheist or the agnostic. It is unlikely that nontheists will regularly attend the synagogue, mosque, or church or engage in the worship of God. But James has to show further that the ways in which the life patterns of theists and nontheists differ will confer natural benefits on the theist that cannot be enjoyed by the nontheist. James says very little about this matter, which is, essentially, an empirical question. It is not obvious that theistic belief confers natural benefits which, in kind and degree, are unobtainable in any secular system for conducting one's life. Certainly, an optimistic attitude to life, moral integrity, a compassionate concern for the welfare of others, equanimity in the face of danger and death, leading a purposeful life, and enjoying the companionship of like-minded people are not features exclusive to the lives of religious believers.

## JAMES'S PRINCIPLE OF INQUIRY

Apart from James's official doctrine of the will to believe, there is another argument sketched in his essay that merits consideration. In Section X, for instance, there is a paragraph in which James suggests that we might have to meet the religious hypothesis halfway in order to stand any chance at all of "making the gods' acquaintance" (as he puts it). In other words, although the religious hypothesis is undecidable on the basis of our present evidence, we might be able to acquire evidence in its favor only if we first adopt a believing attitude. Though James's argument is not entirely clear, it seems to rest on the following general principle, which I shall call James's Principle of Inquiry:

**James's Principle of Inquiry:** If one's only chance to acquire evidence for a live hypothesis, H, is first to believe that H is true, then it is irrational to suppress one's inclination to believe H.

The kinds of evidence that James had in mind are religious experiences. I consider in the next discussion whether or not such experiences should be regarded as evidence for theism. For the moment, I wish to focus on James's Principle of Inquiry and its application to religious belief.

Elsewhere in his essay and in his other writings, James discusses self-verifying beliefs. One famous example is the alpine climber.

> Suppose, for example, that I am climbing in the Alps, and have had the ill-luck to work myself into a position from which the only escape is by a terrible leap. Being without similar experience, I have no evidence of my ability to perform it successfully; but hope and confidence in myself make me sure I shall not miss my aim, and nerve my feet to execute what without those subjective emotions would perhaps have been impossible. But suppose that, on the contrary, the emotions of fear and mistrust preponderate; or suppose that, having just read the Ethics of Belief, I feel it would be sinful to act upon an assumption unverified by previous experience,—why, then I shall hesitate so long that at last, exhausted and trembling, and launching myself in a moment of despair, I miss my foothold and roll into the abyss. In this case (and it is one of an immense class) the part of wisdom clearly is to believe what one desires; for the belief is one of the indispensable preliminary conditions of the realization of its object. *There are then cases where faith creates its own verification.* Believe, and you shall be right, for you shall save yourself; doubt, and you shall again be right, for you shall perish. The only difference is that to believe is greatly to your advantage.[8]

Undoubtedly, there are cases of self-verifying beliefs such as James describes where a belief cannot become true unless one first believes it and where believing something (having faith) helps to make it true. Usually in these cases, one's present belief about the outcome of a future action has a crucial influence on one's ability to perform that action successfully. But there is a crucial disanalogy between these cases and religious belief: believing the religious hypothesis will not make it true that God (or the gods) exist. At best, believing the religious hypothesis might enable us to acquire evidence that would otherwise elude us. Thus, the situation with respect to theism is not like that of the alpine climber, but more like that of the scientist trying to find evidence for a hypothesis.

There is reason to doubt that the religious hypothesis satisfies the conditions laid down in James's Principle of Inquiry. Well-documented cases of religious conversion suggest that having a prior religious faith is not a necessary condition of having a religious experience. Some atheists and agnostics have been converted to theism because they had such experiences, but they were not believers before their experiences.

Even if James's Principle of Inquiry is true, and even if the religious hypothesis satisfies it, the kind of belief that it permits is a cautious, tentative acceptance of theism as a provisional hypothesis. John Mackie aptly names this "an experimental faith."[9] While it might be difficult psychologically, there is no logical inconsistency between being a Cliffordian agnostic while at the same time adopting theism "on trial," so to speak, to see whether any evidence then reveals itself. But, of course, this is a far cry from having a full-blooded, passionate commitment to theism prior to the appearance of any such evidence. Also, as Mackie points out, if an experiment is to be a genuine test of a hypothesis capable of providing evidence in its support, there must also be some chance that the experiment could turn out negatively and thus *disconfirm* the hypothesis. In the case of the religious hypothesis, having a religious experience is regarded as confirming evidence; but what would count as disconfirming evidence?

---

## NOTES

1. I have deliberately omitted James's claim that in such cases our passional nature *must* decide the option.

2. In chapter 6 of *The Future of an Illusion* (1927), Sigmund Freud (1865–1939) distinguishes between illusions and delusions. Both types of belief stem from wish fulfillment, and both involve ignoring reality; but unlike delusions (which are always false), illusions might turn out to be true. Freud gives as an example of an illusion that turned out to be true the belief of alchemists that some metals can be turned into gold. Such cases are rare, in Freud's view, because ignoring reality is a poor guide to truth. Thus, while Freud's characterization of religion as an illusion does not imply that religious beliefs are false, it is also his view that any belief derived primarily from wish fulfillment is unlikely to be true.

3. As we have seen, Pascal's wager was addressed to those for whom Roman Catholicism was the only religious hypothesis worth considering. Also, contrary to James's assertion, Pascal does not assume that we can simply decide to believe that God exists.

4. Some philosophers have argued against the "evidentialism" which Clifford and James share. See J. W. Meiland, "What Ought We to Believe? or The Ethics of Belief Revisited," *American Philosophical Quarterly* 17 (1980): 15–24; and G. Nakhnikian, *An Introduction to Philosophy* (New York: Knopf, 1967), Part IV. Both authors argue against the thesis that we ought to believe P whenever there is sufficient evidence for P. Meiland defends the view that it is sometimes permissible to believe P even when the evidence is clearly against P. Nakhnikian defends the stronger thesis that there are times when we ought to believe P even though there is almost conclusive evidence against it. If either view were correct, then James's more restricted position on believing in the absence of evidence would follow without further ado.

5. The theory could be amended. For example, we might say: (J*) If the decision between believing P and believing not-P is a living option that cannot be made on the basis of evidence and either the option is momentous and forced or it would be momentous and forced if P were true, then one may believe (and must believe) as one wishes.

The main problem with this new formulation is that it seems far too liberal. (J*) would legitimate accepting any undecidable hypothesis that promised substantial benefits to those who believed it.

6. James was also an advocate of the pragmatic theory of truth, which says, roughly, that a proposition is true if it has good consequences for the person who believes it. There are devastating criticisms of this theory in B. Russell, *A History of Western Philosophy* (New York: Simon and Schuster, 1945), Chapter 29; and in G. Nakhnikian, *An Introduction to Philosophy* (New York: Knopf, 1967), Part IV.

7. This is pointed out in G. Mavrodes, "James and Clifford on 'The Will to Believe'," *The Personalist* 44 (1963): 191–198. Mavrodes concludes that on James's theory of belief there is no difference between atheism and agnosticism, since their practical consequences are the same. Hence, James has no need of his "will to believe" doctrine to eliminate Clifford's agnosticism.

8. James, "The Sentiment of Rationality," reprinted in *The Will to Believe and Other Essays in Popular Philosophy* (New York: Dover, 1956): 96–97.

9. J. L. Mackie, *The Miracle of Theism* (Oxford: Clarendon Press, 1982): 210.

# DISCUSSION: The Argument from Religious Experience

The ontological and cosmological arguments are not the only ways in which people have attempted to justify their religious beliefs. Instead of giving arguments that purport to prove that God exists, some theists have settled for the more modest goal of showing that their belief in God is rational or reasonable. In general, a person is rational in holding some belief that p if the belief is held on the basis of evidence, e, that supports it or confirms it.[1] The evidence, e, by itself, does not logically imply that p is true, but it lends to p some degree of probability. In this way, we often reason in everyday life from the available evidence to conclusions about such matters as the guilt or innocence of suspects, the prospects of rain, and the likelihood of the Chicago Cubs reaching the World Series. Our conclusions are established with probability, not certainty; and the greater the degree of probability, the greater our confidence.

## TYPES OF EVIDENCE FOR THEISM

There are three different kinds of facts and phenomena that have been proposed as evidence to support theism. In the first group are facts about the physical universe revealed by observation and scientific investigation. Before the Darwinian revolution in biology, it was common to argue that a very intelligent designer (God) must be responsible for the exquisite organization and adaptation of plants and animals. Similarly, appeal was made to the particular arrangement of planets and stars in the universe that permits life to flourish on Earth. Others have referred to universal physical laws, such as those of gravitational attraction and energy conservation, as evidence for a single, supernatural designer. Of these design arguments, only the last has not been completely undermined by the progress of science.

A second kind of evidence for theism is miracles. Many different religions, Christian and non-Christian, monotheistic and polytheistic, have records of historical events which, it is claimed, were miraculous. These events were not merely improbable or unlikely, but involved the violation of laws of nature by the direct action of God or some other supernatural agent. In this category fall accounts of healing the sick, restoring sight to the blind, and resurrecting the dead.

Much of the discussion of whether or not these accounts of purported miracles are evidence for theism has been influenced by the skeptical arguments of David Hume. In Section X of *An Enquiry Concerning Human Understanding* (1748), Hume argued that one would never be justified in believing that a genuine miracle had occurred on the basis of someone else's testimony. Because miracles are violations of laws of nature, if they occur at all, they would have the lowest degree of probability that any event can possess. Hume argued that this improbability, coupled with known instances of religious fraud, deception, and gullibility, implies that one would never be justified in believing that a miracle had occurred. It would always be more rational to believe either that the account was fictitious or that a surprising but nonmiraculous event had occurred which we cannot explain, given the present state of our science, but which we might be able to explain scientifically in the future.

Hume's conclusion that accounts of miracles are worthless as evidence for theism was contested by his contemporaries, and the debate over the soundness of Hume's argument continues to the present day. We cannot pursue here the many interesting issues raised by this controversy.[2]

The third kind of evidence for theism is religious experience. As suggested by the title of Williams James's pioneering study, *The Varieties of Religious Experience: A Study in Human Nature* (1902), religious experiences not only are a feature of many different cultures and religious traditions but also are highly varied in their manifestations.[3] They range from mystical states of feeling at one with God (or with an impersonal nondivine universe) to an overwhelming sense of melancholy, fear, and dread; from states of rapturous ecstasy (such as those recorded by St. Theresa of Avila) to having visions of saints and angels or hearing the voice of God, as did Saul of Tarsus, we are told, on the road to Damascus.

## RELIGIOUS EXPERIENCES

In his article "Visions," (Reading 10) Alasdair MacIntyre divides religious experiences into two main classes: external visions and all the rest. External visions are experiences in which the subject seems to see (or hear) an external object whose appearance is much the same as that of ordinary objects and people and could be mistaken for them. The remainder of religious experiences comprise (a) states of consciousness ("Bewusstseinslage"), mystical states, which are accompanied by a feeling of a divine or supernatural presence, but which involve no visual imagery; and (b) states that do involve some form of image but which, unlike external visions, are not accompanied by a tendency to interpret the image as a real, external object that is causing the experience. MacIntyre calls these *feeling-states* and *mental images,* respectively, to distinguish them from external visions.

Not all mystical feeling-states are religious experiences: some atheists have had them and have even been confirmed in their atheism by them; and many devout religious people never have any intense mystical experience of any kind.[4] Moreover, a variety of experiences have been produced under the influence of psychoactive drugs (e.g., psilocybin, mescalin, LSD, nitrous oxide) that in many respects are indistinguishable from those of religious mystics who had not taken such drugs.[5]

It will facilitate the discussion if we use the term *religious experience* in the following way: Whether or not a person has taken psychoactive drugs, if person S has an experience *which she takes to be* of God or of some other divine reality, however vaguely described, then S's experience is a religious one; and if S does not interpret her experience in this way, then it is not a religious experience. Defining religious experiences in terms of the subject's own interpretation has two advantages. First, it acknowledges that the subject herself is the best judge of what she *seems* to be experiencing. A mystical experience, for example, will qualify as being religious if and only if it seems so to the person who has it. Given the variety and controversial nature of such experiences, this seems better than trying to decide at the outset which experiences are genuinely religious and which are not. Second, it leaves open the question as to whether the subject's experience was actually caused by God or by something else.

## EVIDENCE, TESTIMONY, AND JUSTIFICATION

Given this characterization of religious experiences, there are two major questions of philosophical interest about them. (1) Does S's religious experience *justify* her in believing that her experience was veridical. In other words, is S justified in believing that God (or whatever divine reality that her experience seemed to be an experience of) really exists? (2) Should persons other than S who have not had the same kind of experience as S take S's report of her experience as evidence of God's existence or the existence of some kind of divine reality?

Posing the two questions in this way acknowledges a fundamental difference between the position of the person who has a vivid experience and that of some other person who hears an account of the experience at secondhand. Consider the following example. Person S sees what seems to her to be a glowing ball of fire that flies in through an open window and then explodes at her feet. Normally, we would judge that a person is justified in believing that what she seems to experience really happened. With respect to our senses of sight, hearing, touch, smell, and taste, there is a presumption of reliability: we are justified in believing that things are the way they appear to be unless and until we have positive reasons to think that our senses are deluding us. Since it concerns what the subject of an experience is justified in believing, let us call this the Principle of Credulity.[6]

**The Principle of Credulity:** If S has an experience that she takes to be an experience of X, then S is justified in believing that X exists unless and until she has positive reasons for thinking otherwise.

A principle similar to the Principle of Credulity is often applied to cases that involve accepting the testimony of others about their experiences. Continuing with the fireball example, imagine that person R is in a different position from S. R did not see the fireball; she merely heard about it from S. R accepts S's testimony as evidence that the fireball actually existed, but given the unusual character of the apparent phenomenon, R might not be justified in believing that S's account is literally true solely on the basis of S's testimony. While having an experience can justify a belief for the subject of the experience, a report of that experience might merely be evidence that falls short of justification for someone else.

**The Principle of Testimony:** If S reports an experience that she takes to be an experience of X, then R should accept S's report as evidence for the existence of X unless R has some positive reason to think that S's experience was delusive or that S was lying.

We can easily imagine circumstances in which R would cease to regard S's testimony as evidence, even of the weakest sort, for the existence of fireballs. If R should find out that S is a chronic liar or that S had ingested hallucinogenic drugs prior to the alleged episode, then S's testimony would be discounted entirely. On the other hand, if R were to discover that other people were present when S seemed to see the fireball, then their testimony might confirm and support the fireball hypothesis.

We often use the Principle of Agreement to evaluate reports of unusual physical events. In the fireball example, if several people give similar accounts that agree with S's, then, in the absence of any evidence of collusion and fraud, this raises the probability that S's account is true. If, on the other hand, many people who were in a position to see what, if anything, actually happened, report seeing nothing at all, then this discredits S's testimony. In the intermediate sort of case, several witnesses may attest to having seen something more or less similar to the fireball as described by S. The various accounts may differ with respect to the apparent color of the object, its estimated velocity and size, whether there was one or several objects, and so on. In cases like this, the rule is to regard only the common content of the differing accounts as having been corroborated. In other words, in those respects in which S's report differs from others, it is undermined by conflicting testimony; in those respects in which it agrees with other accounts, it is supported. As with the Principle of Testimony, the Principle of Agreement holds only in the absence of positive reasons to suspect fraud and collusion among the witnesses.

## BROAD'S ARGUMENT FROM RELIGIOUS EXPERIENCE

Let us now return to consider the argument from religious experience. I shall first summarize the argument as presented by C. D. Broad; then I shall consider some of the criticisms raised by MacIntyre and by Broad himself.

Broad's version of the argument from religious experience rests squarely on the Principle of Testimony.[7] I will follow Broad and MacIntyre in focusing on what it is rational for people to believe on the basis of reports of the religious experiences of others. In other words, the issue is not whether the subject, S, derives justification from her own experience but whether another person, R, should accept reports of such experiences as evidence of God's existence.

### Broad's Argument From Religious Experience

(1) Some people report experiences that they take to be experiences of God or some other supernatural reality.

(2) If S reports an experience that she takes to be an experience of X, then R should accept S's report as evidence for the existence of X unless R has some positive reason to think that S's experience was delusive or that S was lying.

(3) We have no positive reason for thinking that religious experiences are delusive or that people who report such experiences are lying.

(4) We should accept reports of religious experiences as evidence for the existence of God or some other supernatural reality.

This argument is valid, and there is no dispute about the truth of its first premise. Thus, the issue is the truth of premises (2) and (3).

Let us begin with premise (3) and accept, for the sake of argument, that the vast majority of persons who report religious experiences are sincere. So, the question is, Are there positive reasons for thinking that all these experiences are delusive? Notice that if there are such positive reasons and they were known to someone who had a religious experience, then this would also undermine that person's justification for believing in God on the basis of the experience.

The two reasons most commonly given for thinking that religious experiences are delusive are (1) the lack of intersubjective agreement about the content of those experiences and (2) the abnormal physical and psychological state of the experiencing subjects. Both are discussed at length by Broad.

As MacIntyre points out, the content of visions seems to depend on a person's prior religious beliefs and expectations. Very few (if any) Hindus have visions of the Virgin Mary, and very few (if any) Roman Catholics see apparitions of Krishna, Siva, and Vishnu. If Roman Catholicism is true, then Hinduism is false, and if Hinduism is true, then Roman Catholicism is false. Thus, the diversity of content among visions counts against basing a specific set of religious doctrines on a particular vision.[8] But does it also show that the experiences themselves are delusive? I think the answer is "Yes." Though the figures that appear in visions rarely say outright, "I am (or represent) the one true god," nonetheless their identification as the figures they are has certain religious implications. If it is literally true that one saw Jesus, then this implies that the Christian deity exists and there are no other gods. If it is literally true that one saw Vishnu, then this implies that the Christian deity is not the only god. These implications cannot both be true. Therefore, their associated visions cannot both be veridical.

Broad's response to the conflicting content objection is to argue as William James did in the *Varieties of Religious Experience* that, at least with respect to mystical religious experiences, there seems to be a vague general similarity in the experiences that can be separated from the particular sectarian interpretations which often vary from person to person. In the same way, we might respond to conflicting accounts of a fireball by arguing that at least all the witnesses saw some sort of localized atmospheric phenomenon. Even if this move is legitimate in the case of religious experience, it results in extreme vagueness: at best, the entire range of religious experiences becomes evidence for some sort of supernatural (?) reality that is neither identifiably personal nor identifiably impersonal.[9]

The abnormality objection is raised with great gusto by Bertrand Russell. Some religious mystics starve themselves, undergo severe sensory deprivation, or take psychoactive drugs to achieve states of spiritual revelation. Others suffer from well-defined psychotic disorders. In both cases, we know that being in such abnormal states results in delusory perceptions of the physical world. Thus, we have reason to believe that the religious experiences achieved when in these states are also delusory. As Russell put it: "From a scientific point of view, we can make no distinction between the man who eats little and sees heaven and the man who drinks much and sees snakes. Each is in an abnormal physical condition and therefore has abnormal perceptions."[10]

Broad's reply is that the "scientific standpoint" tells us only about perception of the physical world, not supernatural revelation. In the case of drunkards, we are able to compare their (fairly uniform) experiences of seeming to see rats and snakes with the contrary perceptions of the sober. It is on these grounds that we judge the drunkards' experiences to be delusory. No such comparison can be made in the case of religious mystics. Nothing the mystic seemingly experiences of the *nonphysical* world contradicts what the nonmystic perceives of the *physical* world. Perhaps, Broad says, "one might need to be slightly 'cracked' in order to have some peep-holes into the super-sensible world."

Perhaps Broad's conjecture is correct. Perhaps psychological derangement and hallucinogenic drugs facilitate and enhance our glimpses of a world beyond the physical. Even if we discovered that certain drugs and procedures inevitably produce certain kinds of religious experience, one could still argue that this does not show that the religious experiences thus produced are delusory, since we have no veridical experiences with which to compare them.[11] But replying in this way to the abnormality objection involves paying a large price. It involves admitting that apart from agreement at a vague and general level (which can also characterize delusory experiences produced by drugs and mental disorders), we have no way whatever of judging the veridicality of any religious experience. This may well lead us to doubt that appropriate use has been made of the Principle of Testimony in the second premise of Broad's argument.[12]

Premise (2) states what we have called the Principle of Testimony. The issue is not *how much* evidence for X is provided by an experiential report, but whether or not a report counts at all as evidence for X if it satisfies the stated conditions. The relevant condition in this case is that we have no reason to think that the reported experience is delusive. In normal cases of perception of the physical world, the Principle of Testimony seems reasonable. But it is also true in these cases that we know how to find out whether a perception is veridical or not. We can check up and investigate whether the X really exists that someone claims to have experienced. No such procedures exist for investigating the veridicality of religious experiences. With respect to our experiences of the natural world, the Principle of Testimony interacts with the other epistemic principles that guide our evaluation of beliefs. In the case of religious experiences, the Principle of Testimony is isolated. It stands alone, unable to be corrected or confirmed in its specific applications. This suggests that it is illegitimate to apply the Principle of Testimony to religious experiences, where its reliability cannot be monitored by other epistemic principles. In brief, the claim is that the Principle of Testimony is not true as stated. It requires an additional clause specifying that we know how to discover when positive reasons exist for thinking that experiences are delusive. In the case of religious experiences, no such means exist. Therefore, Broad's argument from religious experience is unsound.

## IS BELIEF IN GOD PROPERLY BASIC?

It is now time to return to the issue of whether religious belief can be rational when it is based not on the testimony of others but on personal experience. Some people do not *infer* that God exists as the conclusion of an argument but acquire a direct and immediate conviction of God's existence as the result of various experiences. These experiences can range from dramatic visions of saints and angels to a feeling of God's presence upon reading the Bible or surveying the heavens. Other people believe in God without having any of these experiences; they believe simply because that is the way they have been brought up. The general issue is: Can theistic belief be rational when it is not inferred from any other beliefs but *caused* by certain kinds of experience or by one's upbringing?

As explained later in this book (in the introduction to Part V and Reading 38), if "evidence" means "another belief," then it cannot be the case that all our beliefs are based on evidence. Some beliefs are basic and not inferred from other beliefs. Many of our basic beliefs about the external world, for example, are grounded in (caused by) certain kinds of perceptual experience. Similarly, my conviction that I had breakfast this morning is not derived from other beliefs but is grounded in memory. Moreover, these beliefs are not only basic but also justified. They are what the American philosopher Alvin Plantinga has called *properly basic beliefs,* that is, beliefs we are entitled to hold without inferring them from anything else.

As a matter of psychological fact, theistic belief is basic for many religious believers. Many theists accept God's existence without inferring it from other propositions. Recently, Alvin Plantinga has claimed that such theistic beliefs are not only basic but also properly basic (rational, justified) for the people who hold them.[13]

Plantinga rests his case on two contentions. First, he claims that no one has given a plausible criterion of proper basicality that can rule out basic theistic beliefs as *un*justified. Second, he argues that in the absence of a defensible criterion of proper basicality, it is reasonable to put theistic belief in the same class as other beliefs that we all unhesitatingly accept as properly basic. Plantinga offers three propositions as paradigms of properly basic beliefs.

(1) I see a tree.
(2) I had breakfast this morning.
(3) That person is angry.

For the sake of argument, let us concede Plantinga's first point and agree that we lack an adequate criterion of rationality for basic beliefs. Should we also agree that belief in God is relevantly similar to examples (1), (2), and (3)? As several critics have pointed out, there are important differences between theistic belief and the propositions on Plantinga's list.[14]

One difference concerns the possibility of gathering evidence that can either confirm or disconfirm the belief. I can check the refrigerator and the dishwasher to see whether I really did have breakfast this morning; I can walk up to the tree and touch it; I can interrogate the person who seems to be angry. The belief that God exists is not amenable to the same kind of investigation through the use of one's senses.

Another disparity concerns the universality of basic perceptual beliefs. Any normal person who stands where I am standing during the daytime and opens her eyes will come to believe that she sees a tree. But two people can survey the same heavens, read the same Bible, or enjoy the same performance of Bach's St. Matthew Passion without spontaneously acquiring the same theistic belief. Plantinga's reply is that if a person does not spontaneously form theistic beliefs in the right kind of circumstances, then there is something wrong with her faculties. But we cannot check Plantinga's conjecture as we can test hypotheses about a defect in someone's hearing or vision. Indeed, the wide variation in experiences and spontaneous beliefs formed in the same circumstances—even among followers of the same religion—makes Plantinga's conjecture seems arbitrary and implausible.

Lastly, for beliefs such as (1), (2), and (3), which are grounded in memory and perception, we have a good understanding of how and why those basic beliefs are usually acquired. Someone comes to believe that she sees a tree because there is a tree in front of her that causes the belief; the reason I seem to remember eating breakfast is that I really did eat breakfast. In these explanations, the objects (or events) that the beliefs are about play a crucial *causal* role, and the explanations have no serious competitor. When we turn to theistic beliefs caused by religious experiences or by one's upbringing, there are two kinds of explanation: one psychological and sociological, the other theistic. Only the latter requires the existence of God as the cause of the belief, and the former has empirical support. For example, the best explanation of why children become Hindus, Zoroastrians, or Mormons makes no reference to the truth of the religion in question.

In conclusion, there are good reasons to agree with Plantinga that theistic belief is often basic, not inferred, and that basic beliefs can be rational or properly basic. But there are also good reasons to disagree with Plantinga about whether basic theistic beliefs are sufficiently similar to the other beliefs on his list to warrant being included among them as properly basic.

## NOTES

1. See the final section of this discussion for more on whether all beliefs can be based on evidence.

2. See, for example, C. D. Broad, "Hume's Theory of the Credibility of Miracles," *Proceedings of the Aristotelian Society* 17 (1916–1917): 77–94; R. Swinburne, *The Concept of Miracle* (London: Macmillan, 1970); and M. P. Levine, *Hume and the Problem of Miracles: A Solution* (Dordrecht, Holland: Kluwer, 1989).

3. W. James, *The Varieties of Religious Experience* (New York: New American Library, 1957). James's book is based on his Gifford lectures in natural religion, delivered at the University of Edinburgh, 1901–1902. In *The Varieties of Religious Experience,* William James gives a disguised account of an episode of intense melancholia and horrible dread from his own youth and compares it with an experience described by John Bunyan. See *The Varieties of Religious Experience,* Lectures 6 and 7, "The Sick Soul," pp. 135–136; and B. W. Wilshire, Ed., *William James: The Essential Writings* (New York: Harper, 1971): 232–233. In his lectures, James pretended that the account came from a French correspondent. It probably occurred in 1870 when James was close to nervous collapse.

4. Both Virginia Woolf and her husband Leonard reported having had mystical experiences during childhood. Both were atheists. See V. Woolf, *Moments of Being* (New York: Harcourt Brace Jovanovich, 1976): 71–73; and L. Woolf, *Sowing* (New York: Harcourt Brace Jovanovich, 1960): 39–42.

5. See the accounts in H. Smith, "Do Drugs Have Religious Import?" *Journal of Philosophy* 61 (1964): 517–530.

6. The phrase "Principle of Credulity" was coined by Richard Swinburne as an appropriate name for the principle on which C. D. Broad's argument relies. See R. Swinburne, *The Existence of God* (Oxford: Oxford University Press, 1979), Chapter 13. Not all philosophers accept the Principle of Credulity as a general epistemological principle. Hume rejected it, and so does MacIntyre (in section 4 of his article).

7. The following reconstruction is based on W. L. Rowe, "Religious Experience and the Principle of Credulity," *International Journal of Philosophy of Religion* 13 (1982): 85–92.

8. David Hume made a similar point about the miracles claimed by competing religious sects. It cannot be the case that each miracle validates its associated religion if the religions themselves are mutually inconsistent.

9. MacIntyre questions the legitimacy of the move by arguing that only external visions have sufficient content to possibly convey information about a supernatural cause of the experience. Mere feeling-states and mental images by themselves tell us nothing about what the causes of these experiences might be.

10. B. Russell, *Religion and Science* (Oxford: Oxford University Press, 1935): 188.

11. On the issue of whether giving a natural explanation of a religious experience implies that the experience is delusory (because it is not caused by supernatural agents), see W. J. Wainwright, "Natural Explanations and Religious Experience," *Ratio* 16 (1974): 98–101.

12. The following criticism is borrowed from W. L. Rowe, "Religious Experience and the Principle of Credulity," *International Journal of Philosophy of Religion* 13 (1982): 85–92.

13. See A. Plantinga, "Is Belief in God Properly Basic?" *Noûs* 15 (1981): 41–51; and "Is Belief in God Rational?" in C. F. Delaney, Ed., *Rationality and Religious Belief* (Notre Dame, IN: University of Notre Dame Press, 1979): 7–27. As Plantinga himself points out, for many theists it is not the belief that God exists that is basic, but propositions such as "God loves me" and "God created the universe" that self-evidently entail that God exists.

14. See R. Grigg, "Theism and Proper Basicality: A Response to Plantinga," *International Journal of Philosophy of Religion* 14 (1983): 123–127; S. J. Wykstra, "Toward a Sensible Evidentialism: On the Notion of 'Needing Evidence'," in W. L. Rowe and W. J. Wainwright, Eds., *Philosophy of Religion: Selected Readings,* 2nd Edition (New York: Harcourt Brace Jovanovich, 1989): 426–437; R. Audi, "Direct Justification, Evidential Dependence, and Theistic Belief," in R. Audi and W. J. Wainwright, Eds., *Rationality, Religious Belief, and Moral Commitment* (Ithaca, NY: Cornell University Press, 1986): 139–166; and G. Gutting, *Religious Belief and Religious Skepticism* (Notre Dame, IN: University of Notre Dame Press, 1982), Chapter 3.

# PART II

## THE FOUNDATIONS OF MORALITY

Before beginning our discussion of the foundations of morality, it is important to appreciate the distinction between descriptive and theoretical ethics.

Descriptive ethics is the empirical study of people's practices and moral beliefs. It describes what people do and the codes of behavior people accept. For example, the Ancient Greeks practiced infanticide on defective newborns, believing that this was the morally right thing to do; in nearly all countries today, racial discrimination is regarded as morally wrong; and, in the United States, abortion and capital punishment are morally controversial: some people think these practices are right under some circumstances, while others think they are always wrong. All these claims fall within the province of the historian, the sociologist, and the anthropologist.

Philosophers want to know what people *ought* to do and which moral beliefs are *true*. These are questions of theoretical ethics and cannot be answered merely by describing what people do and believe. For example, it does not follow from the fact that people actually behave in a certain way that that is the way they ought to behave. Indeed, on the practical side, philosophers often try to give people good reasons to change their behavior and moral beliefs.

Normative ethics is the branch of theoretical ethics that attempts to provide theories that tell us which actions are right and which are wrong. Examples of such theories are ethical egoism (examined in the discussion entitled "Egoism"), John Stuart Mill's utilitarianism (see Readings 13, 14, and 15), and the deontological theories of Immanuel Kant (Reading 16) and W. D. Ross (Reading 17). With the exception of Ross's theory, each of these theories consists of one or two fundamental moral generalizations or basic ethical principles from which, in conjunction with empirical information about the world, we can deduce what we morally ought to do. For example, Mill's utilitarianism is based on the Principle of Utility, or the Greatest Happiness Principle; and Kant's theory is based on the Categorical Imperative, or the Principle of Universalizability.

Since a normative theory of ethics aims to tell us what we morally ought to do or refrain from doing, it is reasonable to expect that for any action, the theory will say whether that action is forbidden, obligatory, or (merely) permissible.

To say that an action is forbidden means that it is morally wrong, that one has a moral obligation to refrain from performing it. If an action is obligatory, one must perform it, and it would be wrong not to do it. Clearly, if an action is obligatory, it must also be permissible, but there are many permissible actions that are not obligatory. Examples are trivial actions, such as deciding to wear red socks in the morning or reading a page of *Paradise Lost* before going to sleep at night. We shall call such morally insignificant actions that are not obligatory "merely permissible." A merely permissible act is morally indifferent: it is neither forbidden nor obligatory; it is not wrong to do it, and it is not wrong to refrain from doing it. Some theories also recognize a fourth category—the supererogatory—which is the class of actions (sometimes described as being saintly or heroic) that are exceptionally good to perform but are not morally required.[1]

The main function of theories of normative ethics is to tell us which actions are right and which are wrong; and there are several rival theories from which we must try to make a rational choice.[2]

Metaethics is the philosophical study of morality at a higher level of abstraction than normative ethics. Metaethics investigates the meaning of moral terms and the nature and justification of moral statements. For example, all of the following are metaethical questions: What does the word *good* mean? Is morality subjective or objective? Why should I be moral? What justifies us in accepting the fundamental principles on which a normative theory is based? Attempts can be made to answer many metaethical questions without first having to decide which, if any, of the rival normative theories of ethics is true.

One of the most fundamental metaethical questions is whether moral judgments can be objectively true. In "Moral Skepticism" (Reading 11), James Rachels examines three popular arguments for moral skepticism. According to the subjectivist and relativist varieties of moral skepticism, there is no objective truth in matters of morality; moral judgments are merely matters of opinion that vary from person to person and from culture to culture. Rachels concludes that none of the three arguments he examines proves that moral skepticism is true. The failure of these arguments does not show that moral skepticism is false, but it does undermine the reasons most often given for thinking that moral subjectivism and relativism are true.

An even more radical variety of moral skepticism is emotivism. Emotivists agree with moral subjectivists and relativists that moral judgments are not objective, but they go further and insist that moral judgments are incapable of being true or false at all. According to the emotivist, moral utterances are not statements but merely expressions of feelings, attitudes, and emotions (and thus neither true nor false). Gilbert Harman takes up this issue in his "Emotivism as Moderate Nihilism" (Reading 12). Emotivism, subjectivism, and relativism are also explored in the discussion entitled "Moral Skepticism."

Egoism is a recurring theme in the history of ethics. It comes in two main varieties: psychological and ethical. As its name implies, psychological egoism is about the psychology of human beings. It asserts that as a matter of empirical fact, people are incapable of desiring anything but their own self-interest. By contrast, ethical egoism is a normative theory of ethics that tries to base morality on self-interest. According to ethical egoism, what a person morally ought to do depends entirely on what would benefit that person the most. Both varieties of egoism and the relation between them are analyzed in the discussion entitled "Egoism."

One of the major disputes within normative ethics is about the relevance of consequences to the morality of action. According to John Stuart Mill's utilitarianism (Reading 13), whether an action is right or wrong depends entirely on the consequences that result from it. For this reason, utilitarianism is often referred to as a consequentialist theory of ethics. Mill proposes that we have a moral obligation to perform those actions that have the highest utility, that is, the actions that would result in the best consequences when summed over everyone affected by them.

In his paper "Extreme and Restricted Utilitarianism" (Reading 14), J.J.C. Smart draws an important distinction between what he calls the extreme and the restricted versions of the utilitarian theory. Extreme utilitarianism (often called act utilitarianism) looks at the consequences of each individual act; restricted utilitarianism (often called rule utilitarianism) refers each act to general rules and then looks at the consequences of following those rules. Smart vigorously defends extreme (act) utilitarianism.

Incisive criticisms of utilitarianism, and of consequentialism in general, are offered by Bernard Williams (Reading 15). Williams argues that utilitarianism's exclusive focus on consequences undermines our personal integrity, since it would prevent us from acting on those deeply held principles that define our character. Also, because the consequences of our actions often depend on the actions of other people, utilitarianism makes incorrect judgments of responsibility. In a similar vein, W. D. Ross (in the first few pages of Reading 17) criticizes utilitarianism for requiring us always to produce the greatest amount of good regardless of the relations in which we stand to other people.

One of the most dramatic alternatives to utilitarianism is the deontological theory of Immanuel Kant (Reading 16), who thinks that consequences are irrelevant to ethics. At the heart of Kant's theory is the idea that morality depends on general principles of action and whether those principles can be appropriately universalized. Kant calls the requirement of universalizability "the Categorical Imperative" and illustrates its operation with four examples. According to Kant, all correct moral judgments can be deduced from applying the Categorical Imperative.

W. D. Ross (in Reading 17) shares Kant's rejection of utilitarianism, but he doubts that all correct moral judgments can be deduced from the Categorical Imperative. Ross proposes instead a pluralistic theory involving several different principles, none of which can be reduced to anything more simple or general. To support these principles, such as the general duty to keep promises,

Ross appeals to intuition and tries to defend intuition as a reliable guide to the fundamental elements of morality.

The final two readings concern the metaethical question, Why be moral? Why should we strive to be moral, especially when this conflicts with our self-interest? In a famous passage from Plato's dialogue the *Republic* (Reading 18), Glaucon and Adeimantus put this question to Socrates in a particularly dramatic way. In "The Ultimate Question" (Reading 19), Paul Taylor criticizes those who reject the question as absurd and examines the connection between morality, rationality, and self-interest. Taylor concludes that committing oneself to moral principles can be informed by reason, but it is ultimately a matter of one's will, a question of deciding what kind of person one wants to be.

---

## NOTES

1. For a defense of this category as a test of the adequacy of normative theories of ethics, see J. O. Urmson, "Saints and Heroes," in *Essays in Moral Philosophy*, Ed., A. I. Melden (Seattle: University of Washington Press, 1958): 198–216.

2. Notice the ambiguity of the word *right*: usually it means merely permissible, but occasionally it means obligatory. For example, to say that abortion is right presumably means that it is permissible, not obligatory; but to say that you should support your parents because it's the right thing to do implies that it is duty, something that you ought to do.

## READING 11

---

# Moral Skepticism
*James Rachels*

*James Rachels (1941–   ) is University Professor of Philosophy at the University of Alabama at Birmingham. He has written widely on contemporary ethical issues such as euthanasia, reverse discrimination, and the treatment of animals. His books include* The Elements of Moral Philosophy *(1986),* The End of Life: Euthanasia and Morality *(1986),* The Right Thing to Do: Basic Readings in Moral Philosophy *(1989), and* Created from Animals: The Moral Implications of Darwinism *(1990).*

Let us consider the idea that *there is no such thing as objective moral truth.* We may call this idea Moral Skepticism. It is not merely the idea that we cannot *know* the truth about right and wrong. It is the more radical idea that such "truth" does not *exist.* The essential point may be put in several different ways. At one time or another, you have probably heard these remarks, or remarks like them:

> Morality is subjective; it is a matter of how we feel about things, not a matter of how things *are.*
> Morality is only a matter of opinion, and one person's opinion is just as good as another's.
> Values exist only in our minds, not in the world outside us.

However the point is put, the underlying thought is the same: the idea of "objective moral truth" is only a fiction; in reality, no such thing exists.

Is Moral Skepticism *correct*? Is the idea of moral "truth" only an illusion? What arguments can be given in favor of this idea? To determine whether it

SOURCE: From *The Right Thing to Do* (New York: Random House, 1989), Chapter 2, pp. 35–46. Edited.

is correct, we need to ask what arguments can be given for it, and whether those arguments are sound.

## THE CULTURAL DIFFERENCES ARGUMENT

One argument for Moral Skepticism can be based on the observation that in different cultures people have different ideas concerning right and wrong. For example, in traditional Eskimo society, infanticide is thought to be morally acceptable: if a family already has too many children, a new baby might be placed in the snow and allowed to die. (This is more likely to happen to girl than to boy babies.) In our own society, however, this would be considered wrong. There are many other examples of the same kind; different cultures have different moral codes.

Reflecting on such facts, many people have concluded that there is no such thing as objective right and wrong. Thus they advance the following argument:

(4) In some societies, such as among the Eskimos, infanticide is thought to be morally acceptable.

In other societies, such as our own, infanticide is thought to be morally odious.

Therefore, infanticide is neither objectively right nor objectively wrong. It is merely a matter of opinion, which varies from culture to culture.

We may call this the "Cultural Differences Argument." This kind of argument has been tremendously influential; it has persuaded many people to be skeptical of the whole idea of moral "truth." (This argument is the primary thought behind Cultural Relativism, discussed in the first introductory essay in this book.) But is it a sound argument? We can ask two questions about it: first, Are the premises true? and second, Does the conclusion really follow from them? If the answer to either question is "No," then the argument must be rejected as unsound. In this case, the premises seem to be correct—there have been many cultures in which infanticide was accepted. Therefore, our attention must focus on the second question, Is the argument valid?

. . . To figure this out, we begin by noting that the premises concern *what people believe*. In some societies, people think infanticide is all right. In others, people believe it is immoral. The conclusion, however, concerns not what people believe, but whether infanticide *really is* immoral. Now the problem is that this sort of conclusion does not follow from this sort of premise. It does not follow, from the mere fact that people have different beliefs about something, that there is no "truth" in the matter. Therefore, the Cultural Differences Argument is not valid.

To make the point clearer, consider this parallel argument:

(5) In some societies, the world is thought to be flat.

In other societies, the world is thought to be round.

Therefore, objectively speaking, the world is neither flat nor round. It is merely a matter of opinion, which varies from culture to culture.

Clearly *this* argument is not valid. We cannot conclude that the world is shapeless simply because not everyone agrees what shape it has. But exactly the same can be said about the Cultural Differences Argument: we cannot validly move from premises about what people *believe* to be the case to a conclusion about what *is* the case, because people—even whole societies—can be wrong. The world has a definite shape, and those who think it is flat are mistaken. Similarly, infanticide might be objectively wrong (or not wrong), and those who think differently might be mistaken. Therefore, the Cultural Differences Argument is not valid, and so it provides no legitimate support for the idea that moral "truth" is only an illusion. There are two common reactions to this analysis. These reactions illustrate traps that people often fall into.

The first misguided reaction goes like this. Many people find the conclusion of the Cultural Differences Argument very appealing. This makes it hard for them to believe that the argument is invalid; when it is pointed out that the argument is fallacious, they tend to respond: "But right and wrong really *are* only matters of opinion!" They make the mistake of thinking that if we reject an argument, we are somehow impugning the truth of its conclusion. But that, as we have seen, is not so. An argument can have a true conclusion and still be a bad argument. . . . If an argument is unsound, then it fails to provide any reason for thinking the conclusion is true. The conclusion may still be true—that remains an open question—the point is just that the unsound argument gives it no support.

Second, some might object that it is unfair to compare morality with an obviously objective matter like the shape of the earth. We *know* what shape the earth has—it is provable by scientific methods—and so we know that the flat-earthers are simply wrong. But, this objection continues, morality is different: there is no way to prove a moral opinion true or false. Thus morality might be a subjective matter even though the shape of the earth is perfectly objective.

This objection misses the point. The Cultural Differences Argument tries to derive the skeptical conclusion about morality *from a certain set of facts*, namely, the facts about cultural disagreements. The objection suggests that the conclusion might be validly derived from a *different* set of facts, namely, facts about what is and what is not provable. It suggests, in effect, a different argument, which might be formulated like this:

(6) If infanticide (or anything else, for that matter) is objectively right or wrong, then it should be possible to *prove* it right or wrong.

But it is not possible to prove infanticide right or wrong.

Therefore, infanticide is neither objectively right nor objectively wrong. It is merely a matter of opinion, which varies from culture to culture.

This argument is fundamentally different from the Cultural Differences Argument, even though the two arguments have the same conclusion. They are different because they appeal to entirely different considerations in trying to prove that conclusion—in other words, they have different premises. Therefore, the question of whether argument (6) is sound is separate from the question of whether the Cultural Differences Argument is sound. The Cultural Differences Argument is not valid, for the reason given previously.

We should emphasize the importance of *keeping arguments separate*. It is easy to slide from one argument to another without realizing what one is doing. It is easy to think that if moral judgments are "unprovable," then the Cultural Differences Argument is strengthened. But it is not. Argument (6) merely introduces a different set of issues. It is important to pin down an argument, and evaluate *it* as carefully as possible, before moving on to different considerations.

## THE PROVABILITY ARGUMENT

Let us now consider in more detail the question of whether it is possible to prove a moral judgment true or false. The following argument, which we might call the *Provability Argument,* is a more general form of argument (6):

(7) If there were any such thing as objective truth in ethics, we should be able to *prove* that some moral opinions are true and others false.

But in fact we cannot prove which moral opinions are true and which are false.

Therefore, there is no such thing as objective truth in ethics.

Once again, we have an argument with a certain superficial appeal. But are the premises true? And does the conclusion really follow from them? It seems that the conclusion does follow. Therefore, the crucial question will be whether the premises are in fact true.

The general claim that moral judgments cannot be proven *sounds* right: anyone who has ever argued about a matter like abortion knows how frustrating it can be to try to "prove" that one's point of view is correct. However, if we inspect this claim more closely, it turns out to be dubious.

Let's begin with a matter that is simpler than abortion. Suppose a student says that a test given by a teacher was unfair. This is clearly a moral judgment—fairness is a basic moral value. Can this judgment be proven? The student might point out that the test was so long that not even the best students could complete it in the time allowed (and the test was to be graded on the assumption that it *should* be completed). Moreover, the test covered in detail matters that were quite trivial, while ignoring matters the teacher had stressed as very important. Finally, the test included questions about some matters that were not covered in either the assigned readings or the class discussions.

Suppose all this is true. And further suppose that the teacher, when asked to explain, has no defense to offer. (In fact, the teacher, who is rather inexperienced, seems muddled about the whole thing and doesn't seem to have had any very clear idea of what he was doing.) Now, hasn't the student proved the test was unfair? What more in the way of proof could we possibly want?

It is easy to think of other examples that make the same point:

> *Jones is a bad man.* To prove this, one might point out that Jones is a habitual liar; he manipulates people; he cheats when he thinks he can get away with it; he is cruel to other people; and so on.
>
> *Dr. Smith is irresponsible.* She bases her diagnoses on superficial considerations; she drinks before performing delicate surgery; she refuses to listen to other doctors' advice; and so on.
>
> *A certain used-car salesman is unethical.* He conceals defects in his cars; he takes advantage of poor people by high-pressuring them into paying exorbitant prices for cars he knows to be defective; he runs false advertisements in any newspaper that will carry them; and so on.

The point is that we can, and often do, back up our ethical judgments with good reasons. Thus it does not seem right to say that they are all unprovable, as though they were nothing more than "mere opinions." If a person has good reasons for his judgments, then he is not *merely* giving "his opinion." On the contrary, he may be making a judgment with which any reasonable person would have to agree.

If we can sometimes give good reasons for our moral judgments, what accounts for the persistent impression that they are "unprovable"? Why is the Provability Argument so persuasive? There are two reasons why the argument appears to be more potent than it actually is.

First, there is a tendency to focus attention only on the most difficult moral issues. The question of abortion, for example, is an enormously complicated and troublesome matter. No one, to my knowledge, has yet produced a perfectly convincing analysis that would show once and for all where the truth lies. If we think of questions like *this,* it is easy to believe that "proof" in ethics is impossible. The same could be said of the sciences. There are many complicated matters that physicists cannot agree on; and if we focused our attention entirely on *them* we might conclude that there is no "proof" in physics. But of course, many simpler matters in physics *can* be proven, and about those all competent physicists agree. Similarly, in ethics there are many matters far simpler than abortion, about which all reasonable people must agree. The examples given above are examples of this type.

Second, it is easy to confuse the following two matters, which are really very different:

(1) Proving an opinion to be correct.
(2) Persuading someone to accept your proof.

Suppose you are having an argument with someone about some moral issue, and you have perfectly cogent reasons in support of your position, while they have no good reasons on their side—or, if they do have some reasons, you can refute them convincingly. Still, they refuse to accept your logic and continue to insist they are right. This is a common, if frustrating, experience. You may be tempted to conclude that it is impossible to prove you are right. But this would be a mistake. Your proof may be impeccable; the trouble may be that the other person is being bull-headed. (Of course, that is not the *only* possible explanation of what is going on; but it is one possible explanation that cannot be dismissed out of hand.) The same thing can happen in any sort of discussion. You may be arguing about creationism versus evolution, and the other person may be unreasonable. But that does not necessarily mean something is wrong with your arguments. Something may be wrong with him.

## THE PSYCHOLOGICAL ARGUMENT

Now we turn to a third argument that has often been advanced in support of Moral Skepticism. This argument undermines confidence in the objectivity of ethics by making us aware of the nonrational ways in which moral beliefs are formed in the individual. Among psychologists, there is considerable agreement about how this happens; the picture remains remarkably constant, even when we consider radically different psychological theories.

Sigmund Freud (1856–1939) was, of course, the "father of psychoanalysis" and was one of the most influential figures in the history of psychology. Among other things, Freud formulated an account of how we acquire our moral beliefs. Young children, he said, have no conception of right and wrong.

However, they *are* capable of experiencing pleasure and pain, and they naturally strive to maximize one and minimize the other. The child therefore adapts its behavior in whatever ways are necessary to increase pleasure and avoid suffering.

Freud emphasized that children are almost totally dependent on their parents; without the parents' constant attention and help the child cannot satisfy its most basic needs (the need for food, for example). Thus retaining the parents' love becomes the most important thing in the child's life; without it, the child cannot survive. For their part, parents have definite ideas about how children should behave. They are ready to reward children when they behave in desired ways and to punish them when they behave in unwanted ways. The rewards and punishments may be very subtle; they may consist of nothing more than smiles, frowns, and harsh words. This is enough because, as Freud notes, the parent's disapproval is the thing the child fears most.

This little drama is played out over and over again as children grow up. As a result, children learn to behave in "accepted" ways. Children also learn how to *talk* about their behavior: they learn to call the approved ways "right" and the disapproved ways "wrong." This is the origin of our moral concepts. "Moral" and "immoral" are simply names for approved and disapproved conduct.

To this, Freud adds one other distinctively "Freudian" idea. He says that there exists within us a psychic mechanism for internalizing the role of the parent. After a while, we no longer need parents to punish us for acting "badly"—we come to punish ourselves, through feelings of guilt. This mechanism he calls the "superego." It is, Freud says, the same thing that is commonly called the conscience. But in reality it is nothing more than the internalized voice of the parent.

Other psychologists tell much the same story. The behaviorists regard psychology as the study of human *behavior,* and have little patience with Freudian speculations. Nevertheless, their fundamental ideas concerning moral development are quite similar. Where Freud speaks of "the pleasure principle" and of parental approval, the behaviorists speak of "positive reinforcements." Children are positively reinforced (rewarded) when they behave in certain ways; and so they tend to repeat those behaviors. They are negatively reinforced (punished) for other actions, which they subsequently tend not to repeat. Thus patterns of behavior are established: some types of conduct come to be accepted, others come to be rejected. A child whose vocabulary has become sufficiently rich learns to speak of the former behavior as right and the latter as wrong. Indeed, the leading theorist of behaviorism, B. F. Skinner, goes so far as to suggest that the word "good" may be defined as "positively reinforcing."

All this suggests a certain conclusion. Our values are simply the result of our having been conditioned to behave in a certain way. We may feel that certain actions are good and others are evil, but that is only because we have been trained to have those feelings, starting when we were babies. If we had been trained differently, we would have different values, and we would feel just as strongly about them. The obvious conclusion is that the belief that one's values are anything more than the result of this conditioning is simply naive.

We may, therefore, call this the "Psychological Argument":

(8) We acquire our moral beliefs by a process of psychological conditioning. If we had been conditioned differently, we would have different moral beliefs.

Therefore, our moral beliefs are neither true nor false; there is no such thing as objective truth in ethics.

The Psychological Argument is, without doubt, impressive. And if it is sound, it provides powerful evidence that Moral Skepticism is true. However, it contains a serious flaw. The argument begins with a premise concerning *how we acquire* our moral beliefs, and ends with a conclusion about the *status* of those beliefs. Now, for our purposes at least, we may grant that the premise is true—as far as we know, we do acquire our moral beliefs by a process like the one the psychologists describe. But, even granting the truth of the premise, we may still ask: *does the conclusion follow logically from it?*

Consider this. Virtually every kind of belief is acquired, in the beginning, through a process of rewards and punishments (or, as the behaviorists would say, through a system of positive and negative reinforcements). The facts of American history are certainly learned in this way. A teacher asks a first-grade student "Who was the first president of the United States?" If the student responds "George Washington," the teacher smiles approval. If some

other answer is given, the teacher frowns and the student is upset. In this way the student is conditioned to believe that Washington was the first president.

Now suppose the following argument were proposed:

(9) Our beliefs about American history are the result of our having been conditioned to have certain beliefs rather than others.

We may be very confident of our beliefs—we may feel strongly that George Washington *really was* the first president.

However, if we had been conditioned differently, we would have different beliefs, and we would feel just as confident about *them*. (For example, if our teachers had smiled approval when we answered "Abraham Lincoln," we might now firmly believe that Lincoln was the first president.)

Therefore, it is naive to think there are any "objective facts" in American history. There are no facts. No one was "really" the first president.

This argument, of course, is transparently fallacious. But why? It is not because the premises are false. The premises are true: we do acquire many of our early beliefs about American history through a system of positive and negative reinforcements. The argument is fallacious because, *even if the premises are true, the skeptical conclusion does not follow from them.* The question of how we acquire our beliefs is logically independent of, and separate from, the question of whether there are any objective facts to which those beliefs correspond.

But exactly the same thing can be said of the Psychological Argument. The Psychological Argument commits the same mistake—it tries to reach a conclusion about the status of our beliefs ("There is no objective truth in ethics") from a premise about how we acquire those beliefs ("We acquire them through a process of conditioning"). The conclusion simply does not follow.

Now you may feel uneasy about this, because you think learning American history is not comparable to learning about right and wrong. Nevertheless, the logical point is the same in both cases: the conclusion of the argument does not follow from the premises. In fact, the analogy is instructive in other ways as well. Let us take it one step further.

Why do we think that the facts of American history are objectively true? Consider this. A student goes through two stages of development. In the first stage, he learns by rote. He learns to say things like "George Washington was the first president" even though he has no idea *why* we think this is so. He has no conception of historical evidence, no understanding of records or the methods historians use to verify such things. Later, however, he may learn about evidence, records, and historical method. Then he not only believes Washington was the first president; he has *good reasons* for that belief. Thus he can be confident that this belief is not "merely a matter of opinion."

Something very much like this is true of a child's instruction in how to behave. When a child is very young, he will respond to the parent's instructions even though he has no idea *why* the parent gives those instructions. The mother may say "Don't play in the street" and the child may obey, even though he does not understand why playing in the street is undesirable. He may obey simply because he fears a spanking. Later, however, he will become capable of understanding the reason: he will see that if he plays in the street, he may be seriously hurt or even killed.

Again, when the child is very young, the mother may say "Don't kick your brother" and the child may obey because she will be spanked. But later, when the child is older and more mature, the mother may say something very different. She may say "When you kick your brother, it *hurts* him," or "How would you like it if someone went around kicking *you*?" In saying these things, and others like them, the mother is bringing the child to understand the most elementary reasons why little brother should not be abused.

At one stage of development, children learn to behave in certain ways simply because they will be re-warded if they do and punished if they don't. At a later, more mature stage they learn that there are good reasons for behaving in those ways. At which stage is a child learning morality? In one sense, of course, children are learning to behave morally even at the earliest stage: they are learning to do things that it is morally good to do. But in a deeper sense, real moral instruction begins only at the later stage. There is a difference between *being made to do what's right* and *acting as a moral agent*. Only at the later stage do children begin to learn how to reason and act as moral agents. Spanking children just keeps them in line until they are old enough to understand reasons.

This suggests that the Psychological Argument makes another subtle mistake. It represents the process of acquiring moral beliefs as though it were only a matter of being conditioned to behave in certain ways. But morality is more than that. Functioning as a moral agent means making choices based on reasons; it means deliberating, weighing alternatives, and deciding for oneself what is best. It may very well be that we learn all this by being taught by our parents, and rewards and punishments may fit somewhere into the picture even at this level of learning. But it is important, if we are going to speculate about the sources of morality, first to be clear about what morality *is*.

## CONCLUSION

We have examined three of the most important arguments in support of Moral Skepticism, and seen that these arguments are no good. Moral Skepticism might still turn out to be true, but if so, then other and better arguments will have to be found. Provisionally, at least, we have to conclude that Moral Skepticism is not nearly as plausible as we might have thought. . . .

# READING 12

---

# Emotivism as Moderate Nihilism
*Gilbert Harman*

*Gilbert Harman (1926– ) is Professor of Philosophy at Princeton University. He has written widely on topics in epistemology and philosophy of language. His books include* Thought *(1973),* The Nature of Morality *(1977),* Change in View: Principles of Reasoned Revision *(1986), and two volumes co-edited with Donald Davidson,* Semantics of Natural Language *(1971) and* The Logic of Grammar *(1975).*

## (1) Emotivism: The basic idea

Nihilism is the doctrine that there are no moral facts, no moral truths, no moral knowledge. Moderate nihilism says that nihilism is no reason to abandon morality, since morality does not describe facts but does something else. One often made suggestion is that moral judgments express the feelings or attitudes of people making those judgments.

When you look at a moral disagreement you can see what suggests that moral judgments are merely expressions of attitudes. If I say that the Oregon Taxpayers Union was right to kidnap Sally Jones and you say that it was wrong, you and I are disagreeing. Among other things, we disagree in our attitude toward the kidnapping. I favor it and you are against it. I have a pro-attitude toward the kidnapping and you have a con-attitude. We may or may not differ in our beliefs about the Oregon Taxpayers Union, what they did, who Sally Jones is, who her father, Austin P. Jones, is, and so forth. But whether or not we differ in belief, we also disagree in attitude, and our moral disagreement, concerning whether it was right or wrong for the Oregon Taxpayers Union to kidnap Sally Jones, is this disagreement in attitude. No matter what beliefs about the facts we come to agree on, as long as we disagree in attitude our moral disagree-

**SOURCE:** From *The Nature of Morality: An Introduction to Ethics* (New York: Oxford University Press, 1977), Chapter 3, pp. 27–40.

ment persists. And, as soon as we agree in attitude, our moral disagreement has ended, no matter what difference in belief remains.

You might say then that "X is wrong" means "I disapprove of X." But that would not be a correct formulation. My moral judgment is not *about* my approval or disapproval; rather it *expresses* my approval or disapproval. My moral judgment is to my moral approval as my factual judgment is to my belief. If I say that Sally Jones was a sophomore in college at the time that she was kidnapped and you say that she was a junior, our disagreement is a disagreement in belief—but we are not talking *about* our beliefs, we are expressing them. The remark, "Sally Jones was a sophomore" is not equivalent to the remark, "One of my beliefs is that Sally Jones was a sophomore." But the remark, "Sally Jones was a sophomore" expresses the belief that Sally Jones was a sophomore. Similarly, if I remark that the Oregon Taxpayers Union was right to have kidnapped Sally Jones, what I say is not equivalent to *saying that* I approve of the Union having done that, but it does express my approval of the kidnapping.

The view we have been discussing is often called "emotivism"—moral judgments express the speaker's emotions, feelings, attitudes, intentions, or more generally, norms and values. For to value something is not just to have a belief about something; it is to have an attitude toward something. It is to be in favor of something. To value something is to be in an emotional state, not a cognitive state.

Emotivism may at first appear to be a radical and controversial theory. But when it has been fully elaborated and when objections have been disposed of, we shall see that it has become a tamer view than it seemed at the beginning.

Notice, for one thing, that emotivism is a version of what we earlier called moderate nihilism. It holds that there are no moral facts; but it does not conclude that moral terminology is confused and dispensible in the way that religious terminology is, according to an atheist. People are in favor of some things and against other things and what they are in favor of and against has a bearing on what they decide to do. A practical decision requires a kind of practical reasoning that is not simply reasoning about what to believe but is concerned with what to do. Moral terminology is needed to express the considerations that are relevant to practical reasoning and argument.

## (2) Emotivism and the open question argument

Emotivists often invoke the open question argument against ethical naturalists. The emotivist is inclined to suppose that it will always be an open question whether something that has any given natural characteristic is wrong, because the emotivist believes that the word "wrong" carries an emotive force that a descriptive expression like "causes human suffering" must lack. No matter what natural characteristic C is, the emotivist is inclined to argue, to believe that something is C is not yet to have an attitude of disapproval, whereas to think that something is wrong is already to be against it. To agree that something is C is, so far, to leave it open whether you think that it is wrong, the emotivist argues.

Although emotivists often use the open question argument in this way, they rely on something that goes beyond the basic principles of emotivism. There is also a hidden assumption here that must be brought into the open, namely the assumption that values are not universal. For suppose that values are universal. In particular, suppose that whenever anyone believes that an action causes human suffering, he immediately disapproves of it. Then the open question argument fails. For then, to believe that an action causes human suffering is automatically to disapprove of it and therefore, given emotivism, to believe that it is wrong. The question whether an action that causes human suffering is wrong is no longer an open question. The gap between "causes human suffering" and "is wrong" is closed.

It is compatible with emotivism to say that there are universal values. Such values might be innate, "wired in" genetically by virtue of evolution. People born without built-in values of sociability and self-preservation may have lost out in the evolutionary

competition to others who were born with such values. The Scottish philosopher David Hume (1711–1776) argues that people are so constructed that they feel a certain weak sympathy for other people. According to Hume, as long as your own interests are not at stake, you will automatically be in favor of what is for the good of other people. If Hume is right, it cannot be an open question whether or not you favor doing something that will benefit some people and harm no one. For to think that something would accomplish this is to be in favor of it, according to Hume, and that would be to think that it was a good thing, according to emotivism.

If emotivism is accepted, the extent to which there is a gap between is and ought becomes the psychological question, "What values are part of human nature?" It is conceivable that, given human nature as it is, moral thinking always relies upon certain basic universal values. If this is true, emotivism can be conjoined with a highly nonskeptical and nonrelativistic ethical theory. On the other hand, it is also possible that human nature is more variable and that different people have different values and principles and this variation does not have to involve irrationality. If so, emotivism becomes a more skeptical, more relativistic ethical theory.

Emotivism says that moral judgments express attitudes for and against things. This can be part of a nonrelativistic theory if it is combined with the view that there is a uniformity in basic human attitudes. If emotivism is combined with the view that there is no such uniformity, it becomes part of a more relativistic theory. But the relativism derives not so much from the emotivism as from the view taken of human nature.

This means that emotivism is not, by itself, a version of nihilism. It is compatible with emotivism to assume that there are moral facts, if you also assume that there is enough uniformity in human nature. An emotivist can even be an ethical naturalist. For example, if an emotivist believes that moral approval and disapproval derives from a universal sympathy we feel for others, then he might adopt a naturalistic definition of moral wrongness—X is wrong to the extent that X causes human suffering. The open question argument would present no obstacle to this definition, since such an emotivist will hold that, because of universal sympathy, it cannot be an open question whether something that causes human suffering is to that extent wrong. Hume has been interpreted, in this way, as both an emotivist and an ethical naturalist.

A difference between emotivism and ethical naturalism emerges only if a different view is taken of human nature. For example, suppose that human nature imposes no real constraints on basic values and that practical reasoning creates no new values but only enables you to pursue your values in the light of whatever information you have. Suppose, then, that there are no universal values it is irrational not to have. In other words, suppose that practical reason always is and ought to be the slave of the passions. This would be to accept the sort of conception of practical reasoning we find in Aristotle (384–322 B.C.) or Hume.

This idea is that you start out with certain ends—things that you favor or want. Then theoretical reasoning tells you that, in order to get one of these ends, you need something else. This might be something you can do or something that might happen. Then practical reasoning leads you to take this other thing as an intermediate end—something that you favor or want because it will lead to your original end. Practical reasoning is always means-ends reasoning of this sort, according to Hume and Aristotle; you can come to want something as a means to something else you already want. But such reasoning can have no effect on your ultimate ends. You cannot reason yourself into having something as a new ultimate end, since you always reason from your ends to things that are means to those ends.

It is not obvious that this account of practical reasoning is correct; as we shall see there are those who reject it. But it is a plausible account and, if that account of practical reasoning is accepted and if there are no interesting constraints on ultimate ends, then emotivism has to be a relativistic and skeptical theory. Emotivism cannot in that case involve ethical naturalism; indeed, emotivists will then say that the open question argument shows that there is a naturalistic fallacy.

The ethical naturalist identifies an action's being wrong with its having some natural characteristic. He may say, for example, that for an act to be wrong is for it to cause human suffering. Now, it is true that if someone's ultimate ends are such that he is against any act that causes human suffering, he will not think that it is an open question whether an act that causes human suffering is thereby wrong. But we are now assuming for the moment that there will also be

people with different ultimate ends who do not care whether acts cause human suffering. Such people will think that it is (at least) an open question whether an act that causes human suffering is thereby wrong. These people will be able to think that an act causes human suffering without disapproving of it and, since we are supposing that it is not irrational of them to fail in this way to disapprove of acts that cause human suffering, it will in fact be for them an open question whether or not an act that causes human suffering is thereby wrong. So, the ethical naturalist in question will not have captured the way in which these people use the term "wrong."

The ethical naturalist might reply that he is not trying to capture everyone's usage, only his own. He defines his terms as he does because he disapproves of acts that cause human suffering, even if there are other people who do not similarly disapprove of acts that cause human suffering. But this is unsatisfactory. The ethical naturalist's definition will not work even when he applies it to his own usage. For suppose he gets into an argument with someone who does not disapprove of acts that cause human suffering. This other person says that these things are *not wrong*. "Ah!" replies the ethical naturalist, "As I am using words, these things are wrong, since I define 'wrong' to mean 'causes human suffering.' " And of course, the ethical naturalist can use words any way he wishes. But that will not end the disagreement between him and the other person; and the ethical naturalist will want to be able to express what is at issue in their disagreement. But how? If his terminology is purely descriptive and factual, there may be no way to express the disagreement, for the two of them may agree about all relevant facts. It will not do to say that in such a case there is no real disagreement, because there is still a disagreement in attitude. Of course, the ethical naturalist can allow this disagreement in attitude to be *described*. He can say that he is against something that the other person is not against. But he cannot allow this disagreement to be *expressed* unless he allows into his language not only ways of talking *about* attitudes but ways of expressing attitudes. And once he allows himself a way of expressing attitudes, he is using terminology that cannot be defined in purely descriptive terms, given our present assumption that human nature is not so uniform that we all have the same basic values (and given that reason is the slave of the passions). Given this assumption, emotivism is therefore much more plausible than ethical naturalism.

## (3) Advantages of emotivism

Let me now briefly review what I have been saying. Emotivism is the theory that your moral judgments express your attitudes. In other words, your moral beliefs (if it is proper to speak of "beliefs" in this connection) are not cognitive but are themselves attitudes for or against something. According to emotivism, "I believe that this act is wrong" means roughly "I disapprove of this act." But "This act is wrong," by itself, cannot be equated with any purely naturalistic expression like "this act causes human suffering" unless there is a law of nature that to think that an act causes human suffering is to be against it—to disapprove of it.

Emotivism has a number of things in its favor. First, it gives a plausible account of moral disagreement. Such disagreement is a kind of disagreement in attitude, one person favors something, another is against it. Furthermore, certain moral disagreements are irresolvable; the parties to the disagreement can argue and argue—quite rationally and even calmly—without reaching agreement. The emotivist can explain this by assuming that the parties to the dispute have different basic values. Ultimately, they want different things and neither need be irrational or confused in wanting what he wants.

Second, emotivism accounts for the importance of moral questions in our lives and for the way in which our moral beliefs are tied to our acts. To be in favor of something is to want it to happen. To be against something is to want it not to happen. And what you want influences what you do.

To think that you ought to do something is to be motivated to do it. To think that it would be wrong to do something is to be motivated not to do it. Emotivism can explain this. Naturalism could explain it, too, but only by supposing a law of nature that, say, everyone disapproves of acts that cause human suffering. The naturalistic explanation is less secure, ad hoc, and not as fundamental as the emotivist explanation, which does not assume any such law of nature.

These are the advantages of emotivism: its account of moral disagreement and its emphasis on the connection between moral beliefs and passions and acts. Now let us turn to possible objections and problems.

## (4) Truth in ethics

I mentioned one objection in the previous chapter. How can emotivism account for the fact that we sometimes call moral judgments true or false? Feelings and passions cannot be true or false; and, if certain remarks simply express feelings or passions, it is not easy to see how these remarks are true or false. It may be true that I like something, that I am in favor of it; but can my liking be true? If you say that political kidnapping is wrong, I can quite intelligibly agree with you by saying, "That's true." But suppose you simply express your feelings. You say, "Wow!" or "Oh boy!" or "Ugh!" Then, for me to agree by saying, "That's true!" would be inappropriate. Similarly, if you were to utter the command, "Catch those kidnappers!" it would be odd for me to express my agreement with your sentiments by saying, "That's true!"

An emotivist *might* reply that for me to agree with your moral judgment by saying, "That's true!" is for me to misuse the term "true." Strictly speaking, he might say, moral judgments are neither true nor false, since they express attitudes that can be neither true nor false. Although this is one possible reply, it does run afoul of a maxim or rule of thumb for philosophers, namely that, if a philosophical theory conflicts with ordinary ways of thinking and speaking, examine the argument for that theory very closely, since something has probably gone wrong.

This is not an absolutely conclusive point. An atheist may arrive at conclusions that are in conflict with ordinary ways of thinking and speaking and nevertheless may feel, perhaps correctly, that it is the ordinary ways of thinking and speaking that are wrong rather than his theory. The same thing *might* be true of an emotivism that denies that moral judgments are ever true or false. Nevertheless, a conflict with ordinary ways of thinking and speaking may indicate that something has gone wrong so it is useful to consider an alternative line an emotivist might take.

The emotivist might agree that moral judgments can be properly said to be true or false. What this shows, he might go on to say, is that certain attitudes and feelings can be properly said to be true or false. This initially seems odd, he might continue, because we misconstrue what is involved in saying that something is true or false. We suppose that to say that something is true is to say that it corresponds to the facts. Since we do not see how feelings and attitudes can correspond to the facts, we do not see how they can be properly said to be either true or false. But that is because we have a misleading picture of truth as correspondence with the facts.

Consider a truth of arithmetic: "2 + 2 = 4." Does that correspond to the facts? Perhaps. But what facts? If it can be said to correspond to any fact at all, it must be the fact that 2 + 2 = 4, if that is properly called a fact.

"Snow is white" is true if and only if that remark corresponds to the facts. In other words, that remark is true if and only if it is a fact that snow is white. "Snow is white" is true if and only if snow is white. Similarly, "2 + 2 = 4" is true if and only if 2 + 2 = 4. "S" is true if and only if S. What it means to say that truth is correspondence with the facts is that all such principles hold, no matter what indicative sentence replaces S. To see this is to see what "true" means. The principle in question holds whether or not the sentence replacing "S" is used to express a factual or an arithmetical belief—it holds even if this sentence expresses a moral attitude. "Incest is wrong" is true if and only if incest is wrong.

If you say that incest is wrong and I say "That's true!" I am simply agreeing with you. I am not saying that your remark corresponds to the facts in some strong sense of "fact." I am only saying this in the weaker sense in which, when I say that it is a fact that incest is wrong, I am saying only that incest is wrong.

In other words, the emotivist can account for our tendency to use the words "true" or "false" of moral judgments by invoking a theory of truth according to which "it is true that S" means no more than "S." So perhaps there is a good reply to the first objection to emotivism.

In taking this line, the emotivist may appear to have abandoned nihilism. Nihilism, you will recall, is the doctrine that there are no moral facts, no moral truths, and no moral knowledge. What we have seen is that the emotivist can argue that, in the ordinary senses of "fact" and "true," there are moral facts and there are moral truths. But he cannot in any similar way argue that there is moral knowledge, since these "moral facts" and "moral truths" are neither of any apparent help in explaining why anyone observes what he observes nor in any obvious way reducible to facts and truths that are of help in explaining why anyone observes what he observes. He can agree that there are moral facts and moral truths, in a manner

of speaking, even in the ordinary manner of speaking—he will not, however, suppose that these facts and truths are part of the order of nature in the sense that a scientific account of nature is incomplete if it leaves them out, nor will he suppose that there can be knowledge of facts of this sort. So there is a sense in which an emotivist who takes this line retains his nihilism.

But according to this the first objection to emotivism has not been completely met, since we do ordinarily think and talk as if we occasionally knew that we ought or ought not to do various things. Here, perhaps, the emotivist may have to say that our ordinary ways of talking and thinking are simply mistaken.

## (5) Moral reasoning

Now let us consider a second objection, one that asks whether emotivism can account for moral reasoning. There is, evidently, such a thing as moral reasoning; and we sometimes adopt a particular moral opinion—if "opinion" is the right word—in consequence of such reasoning. Furthermore, it strikes us as appropriate to ask for someone's reasons for his moral opinion. If someone says that it is a good thing that the Oregon Taxpayers Union kidnapped Sally Jones, we will ask him why he supposes that it is. It would strike us as odd if he said that he had no reasons—that's just the way he feels about it. That would strike us as odd because his saying that the kidnapping was a good thing suggests or even implies that (he thinks that) there are reasons for supposing that the kidnapping is a good thing.

Reasoning is not relevant in the same way to feelings. You do not reason yourself into liking or disliking something. It is often true that you simply like something, or dislike it, without having a reason. Of course, you may like something in certain respects and not in others. But this is not the same thing as liking it for certain reasons or as the result of argument.

There is a difference between ethics and aesthetics in this respect. There is moral reasoning in a sense in which there is not aesthetic reasoning. Not that there is nothing that might be called aesthetic reasoning, but the situation in aesthetics is different from the situation in ethics. What might be called aesthetic reasoning is really not reasoning at all, strictly speaking. It amounts to pointing to certain aspects of a work of art in order to have someone appreciate those aspects.

Something like that can go on in ethics too. You point out aspects of a situation to get someone to appreciate them more fully; in arguing for vegetarianism, for example, you might describe in detail how animals are treated before slaughter. But there is also something else in ethics—appeal to principle. There are moral principles and these play a role in moral argument. If someone makes a moral judgment, it strikes us as appropriate to ask him what the relevant principles are in a way that seems less appropriate when someone makes an aesthetic judgment. It is not appropriate to ask someone who admires a painting what his principle is. And it is not clear that the emotivist can account for the relevance of reasoning and appeal to principle for moral judgment.

The emotivist holds that moral judgments are expressions of feeling. But expressions of feeling do not depend on reasoning from general principles, nor do they require defense by appeal to principle, whereas moral judgments do depend on reasoning from general principles and do require defense by appeal to principle. Therefore, the emotivist would seem to be mistaken in treating moral judgments as expressions of feeling.

The emotivist might reply that "there are feelings and feelings." Some feelings, he might agree, are simple reactions, such as likes and dislikes. Other feelings, more properly called attitudes, he might continue, are more complex and involve principles and one's basic values. Moral beliefs cannot be identified with any feelings whatsoever—only with these more complex feelings and attitudes.

But, unless the emotivist says more than this, his view takes on an ad hoc character. For nothing has so far been said as to why certain feelings should differ from others in this way. It is obscure why a feeling or attitude is the sort of thing to which reasoning from principles could be relevant. But before we consider what more an emotivist might say about this, let us consider a third objection that reinforces the second.

You sometimes make a moral judgment that you later decide was mistaken. If your moral beliefs were simply feelings, it is not clear how they could be mistaken in this way. At one time you felt one way; now you feel another way. In what sense can you suppose that your first feeling was mistaken? Years ago you used to like sugar in your coffee; now you do not. But you would not say that you were mistaken to have once liked sugar. On the other hand, if you

once thought that incest was wrong and now think that it is right, you do suppose you were mistaken before. How can this change in moral belief be simply a change in your feelings?

## (6) Hume's way out

Now Hume, who may or may not be an emotivist, suggests a way round both these objections. Hume points out that many feelings and passions depend on your having beliefs about the objects of the feelings. If these beliefs are seriously mistaken, you will also say that the feeling is mistaken. In other words, you transfer the word "mistaken" from the beliefs to the feelings that depend on them.

For example, you may be mistaken in having trusted someone. Your beliefs about the reliability and sentiments of that person may be mistaken. You trusted him because you had certain beliefs about him. Since those beliefs were mistaken—and since you would not have trusted him had you known the truth—you say that your trust is mistaken.

A revolutionary might be happy that the Oregon Taxpayers Union kidnapped Sally Jones because he believes that the kidnapping will eventually lead to a revitalization of the revolutionary left. If his belief is mistaken and the kidnapping revitalizes the revolutionary right, he will say that he was mistaken to be happy.

In other words, feelings are said to be or not to be mistaken with reference to beliefs, which may or may not be mistaken, on which the feelings depend. If moral feelings are the sorts of feelings, like trust and happiness, that depend on your beliefs, it will be appropriate to say that moral feelings are mistaken when the relevant beliefs are mistaken. For example, if the revolutionary had initially judged that the Jones kidnapping was a good thing, because of his beliefs about its consequences, and then came to believe that the consequences were going to be the exact opposite, he would then suppose that his initial moral judgment had been mistaken, because the beliefs on which it had been based had been mistaken.

This shows that the emotivist can account for our willingness to say that our own past moral judgments were mistaken and can therefore answer the third objection. Hume would also say that a similar answer can be given to the second objection, concerning moral principles and moral reasoning. For, if moral judgments express attitudes that depend on beliefs about facts of a certain sort, and if these beliefs involve assumptions of a general sort, then the reasoning relevant to these factual assumptions may involve general principles. And, just as we are willing to say that moral judgments are mistaken if the corresponding beliefs are—thus transferring the word "mistaken" from beliefs to the feelings that depend on them—so too we are willing to say that reasoning from general principles is relevant to morality if it is relevant to the corresponding beliefs—in this case we transfer the relevance of principled reasoning from certain beliefs to the associated feelings that depend on those beliefs.

The difference between ethics and aesthetics, according to Hume, is a difference in the relevant passions or feelings. Hume thinks that our moral feelings involve, among other things, a general sympathy for others and, consequently, our moral feelings are often based on beliefs about the general tendencies of acts to affect people's interests. We morally approve a course of action if we believe that course of action falls under principles that, if generally followed, would promote human happiness and diminish misery. This is not the only moral concern that we have, according to Hume, but it is one of them; and it is because of this concern that we suppose that moral judgment involves an appeal to general principles. The general principles in question are, in the first instance, principles about the tendency of certain courses of action, if generally adhered to, to promote happiness and diminish misery. The relevant reasoning really concerns the facts—the issue is whether or not these courses of action will in fact improve well-being. By a principle of courtesy we call this *moral* reasoning and say that the relevant principles are *moral* principles. This, then, is the way emotivism might answer the second objection.

## (7) The triviality of emotivism

So far we have considered three related objections to emotivism and we have seen how an emotivist might answer them. The first objection was that moral judgments are often said to be true or false; the second was that reasoning from general principles is relevant to moral judgments; the third was that we sometimes think that our moral judgments are mistaken. The emotivist might answer the first objection by appealing to a redundancy theory of truth. He might answer the second and third objections by proposing the theory that we transfer to moral judgments talk that strictly speaking applies to the factual beliefs on which the moral judgments depend.

But when emotivism is defended in this way it appears less radical than it seemed at first. For one thing, emotivism is not, even by itself, a version of ethical nihilism, since, by itself, it is compatible with ethical naturalism. It diverges from ethical naturalism only when certain assumptions are made. Furthermore, even given those assumptions, the emotivist can allow that there are moral facts and moral truths, in the ordinary sense of these terms; he can even allow that there is something properly called moral reasoning and he can agree that people can sometimes quite correctly be said to be mistaken in their moral opinions. We may begin to wonder how emotivism differs from simple common sense.

## READING 13

# Utilitarianism
*John Stuart Mill*

*John Stuart Mill (1806–1873) was an eminent Victorian liberal. Renowned as an economist, as a philosopher of science and ethics, and as a political and social theorist, he was an outspoken advocate of freedom of speech and the emancipation of women. Mill served for three years in the British parliament as the Member for Westminster. His works include* A System of Logic *(1843),* On Liberty *(1859), and* Utilitarianism *(1861). A short account of Mill's life can be found in his* Autobiography *(1873).*

### CHAPTER I

#### GENERAL REMARKS

There are few circumstances among those which make up the present condition of human knowledge more unlike what might have been expected, or more significant of the backward state in which speculation on the most important subjects still lingers, than the little progress which has been made in the decision of the controversy respecting the criterion of right and wrong. From the dawn of philosophy, the question concerning the *summum bonum,* or, what is the same thing, concerning the foundation of morality, has been accounted the main problem in speculative thought, has occupied the most gifted intellects and divided them into sects and schools carrying on a vigorous warfare against one another. And after more than two thousand years the same discussions continue, philosophers are still ranged under the same contending banners, and neither thinkers nor mankind at large seem nearer to being unanimous on the subject than when the youth Socrates listened to the old Protagoras and asserted (if Plato's dialogue be grounded on a real conversation)

SOURCE: First published in *Fraser's Magazine,* October 1861. Reprinted from *Utilitarianism* (1864), Chapters I and II. Edited.

the theory of utilitarianism against the popular morality of the so-called sophist.

It is true that similar confusion and uncertainty and, in some cases, similar discordance exist respecting the first principles of all the sciences, not excepting that which is deemed the most certain of them—mathematics—without much impairing, generally indeed without impairing at all, the trustworthiness of the conclusions of those sciences. An apparent anomaly, the explanation of which is that the detailed doctrines of a science are not usually deduced from, nor depend for their evidence upon, what are called its first principles. Were it not so, there would be no science more precarious, or whose conclusions were more insufficiently made out, than algebra, which derives none of its certainty from what are commonly taught to learners as its elements, since these, as laid down by some of its most eminent teachers, are as full of fictions as English law, and of mysteries as theology. The truths which are ultimately accepted as the first principles of a science are really the last results of metaphysical analysis practiced on the elementary notions with which the science is conversant; and their relation to the science is not that of foundations to an edifice, but of roots to a tree, which may perform their office equally well though they be never dug down to and exposed to light. But though in science the particular truths precede the general theory, the contrary might be expected to be the case with a practical art, such as morals or legislation. All action is for the sake of some end, and rules of action, it seems natural to suppose, must take their whole character and color from the end to which they are subservient. When we engage in a pursuit, a clear and precise conception of what we are pursuing would seem to be the first thing we need, instead of the last we are to look forward to. A test of right and wrong must be the means, one would think, of ascertaining what is right or wrong, and not a consequence of having already ascertained it.

The difficulty is not avoided by having recourse to the popular theory of a natural faculty, a sense of instinct, informing us of right and wrong. For—besides that the existence of such a moral instinct is itself one of the matters in dispute—those believers in it who have any pretensions to philosophy have been obliged to abandon the idea that it discerns what is right or wrong in the particular case in hand, as our other senses discern the sight or sound actually present. Our moral faculty, according to all those of its interpreters who are entitled to the name of thinkers, supplies us only with the general principles of moral judgments; it is a branch of our reason, not of our sensitive faculty, and must be looked to for the abstract doctrines of morality, not for perception of it in the concrete. The intuitive, no less than what may be termed the inductive, school of ethics insists on the necessity of general laws. They both agree that the morality of an individual action is not a question of direct perception, but of the application of a law to an individual case. They recognize also, to a great extent, the same moral laws, but differ as to their evidence and the source from which they derive their authority. According to the one opinion, the principles of morals are evident *a priori*, requiring nothing to command assent except that the meaning of the terms be understood. According to the other doctrine, right and wrong, as well as truth and falsehood, are questions of observation and experience. But both hold equally that morality must be deduced from principles, and the intuitive school affirm as strongly as the inductive that there is a science of morals. Yet they seldom attempt to make out a list of the *a priori* principles which are to serve as the premises of the science; still more rarely do they make any effort to reduce those various principles to one first principle or common ground of obligation. They either assume the ordinary precepts of morals as of *a priori* authority, or they lay down as the common groundwork of those maxims some generality much less obviously authoritative than the maxims themselves, and which has never succeeded in gaining popular acceptance. Yet to support their pretensions there ought either to be some one fundamental principle or law at the root of all morality, or, if there be several, there should be a determinate order of precedence among them; and the one principle, or the rule for deciding between the various principles when they conflict, ought to be self-evident.

To inquire how far the bad effects of this deficiency have been mitigated in practice, or to what extent the moral beliefs of mankind have been vitiated or made uncertain by the absence of any distinct recognition of an ultimate standard, would imply a complete survey and criticism of past and present ethical doctrine. It would, however, be easy to show that whatever steadiness or consistency these moral beliefs have attained has been mainly due to the tacit influence of a standard not recognized. Although the nonexistence of an acknowledged first principle has made ethics not so much a guide as a consecration of men's actual sentiments, still, as men's sentiments, both of favor and of aversion, are greatly influenced by what they suppose to be the effects of things upon their happiness, the principle of utility, or, as Bentham latterly called it, the greatest happiness principle, has had a large share in forming the moral doctrines even of those who most scornfully reject its authority. Nor is there any school of thought which refuses to admit that the influence of actions on happiness is a most material and even predominant consideration in many of the details of morals, however unwilling to acknowledge it as the fundamental principle of morality and the source of moral obligation. I might go much further and say that to all those *a priori* moralists who deem it necessary to argue at all, utilitarian arguments are indispensable. It is not my present purpose to criticize these thinkers; but I cannot help referring, for illustration, to a systematic treatise by one of the most illustrious of them, the *Metaphysics of Ethics* by Kant. This remarkable man, whose system of thought will long remain one of the landmarks in the history of philosophical speculation, does, in the treatise in question, lay down a universal first principle as the origin and ground of moral obligation; it is this: "So act that the rule on which thou actest would admit of being adopted as a law by all rational beings." But when he begins to deduce from this precept any of the actual duties of morality, he fails, almost grotesquely, to show that there would be any contradiction, any logical (not to say physical) impossibility, in the adoption by all rational beings of the most outrageously immoral rules of conduct. All he shows is that the *consequences* of their universal adoption would be such as no one would choose to incur.

On the present occasion, I shall, without further discussion of the other theories, attempt to contribute something toward the understanding and appreciation of the "utilitarian" or "happiness" theory, and toward such proof as it is susceptible of. It is evident that this cannot be proof in the ordinary and popular meaning of the term. Questions of ultimate ends are not amenable to direct proof. Whatever can be proved to be good must be so by being shown to be a means to something admitted to be good without proof. The medical art is proved to be good by its conducing to health; but how is it possible to prove that health is good? The art of music is good, for the reason, among others, that it produces pleasure; but what proof is it possible to give that pleasure is good? If, then, it is asserted that there is a comprehensive formula, including all things which are in themselves good, and that whatever else is good is not so as an end but as a means, the formula may be accepted or rejected, but is not a subject of what is commonly understood by proof. We are not, however, to infer that its acceptance or rejection must depend on blind impulse or arbitrary choice. There is a larger meaning of the word "proof," in which this question is as amenable to it as any other of the disputed questions of philosophy. The subject is within the cognizance of the rational faculty; and neither does that faculty deal with it solely in the way of intuition. Considerations may be presented capable of determining the intellect either to give or withhold its assent to the doctrine; and this is equivalent to proof.

We shall examine presently of what nature are these considerations, in what manner they apply to the case, and what rational grounds, therefore, can be given for accepting or rejecting the utilitarian formula. But it is a preliminary condition of rational acceptance or rejection that the formula should be correctly understood. I believe that the very imperfect notion ordinarily formed of its meaning is the chief obstacle which impedes its reception, and that, could it be cleared even from only the grosser misconceptions, the question would be greatly simplified and a large proportion of its difficulties removed. Before, therefore, I attempt to enter into the philosophical grounds which can be given for assenting to the utilitarian standard, I shall offer some illustrations of the doctrine itself, with the view of showing more clearly what it is, distinguishing it from what it is not, and disposing of such of the practical objections to it as either originate in, or are

closely connected with, mistaken interpretations of its meaning. Having thus prepared the ground, I shall afterwards endeavor to throw such light as I can call upon the question considered as one of philosophical theory.

## CHAPTER II

## WHAT UTILITARIANISM IS

. . . The creed which accepts as the foundation of morals "utility" or the "greatest happiness principle" holds that actions are right in proportion as they tend to promote happiness; wrong as they tend to produce the reverse of happiness. By happiness is intended pleasure and the absence of pain; by unhappiness, pain and the privation of pleasure. To give a clear view of the moral standard set up by the theory, much more requires to be said; in particular, what things it includes in the ideas of pain and pleasure, and to what extent this is left an open question. But these supplementary explanations do not affect the theory of life on which this theory of morality is grounded—namely, that pleasure and freedom from pain are the only things desirable as ends, and that all desirable things (which are as numerous in the utilitarian as in any other scheme) are desirable either for pleasure inherent in themselves or as means to the promotion of pleasure and the prevention of pain.

Now such a theory of life excites in many minds, and among them in some of the most estimable in feeling and purpose, inveterate dislike. To suppose that life has (as they express it) no higher end than pleasure—no better and nobler object of desire and pursuit—they designate as utterly mean and groveling, as a doctrine worthy only of swine, to whom the followers of Epicurus were, at a very early period, contemptuously likened; and modern holders of the doctrine are occasionally made the subject of equally polite comparisons by its German, French, and English assailants.

When thus attacked, the Epicureans have always answered that it is not they, but their accusers, who represent human nature in a degrading light, since the accusation supposes human beings to be capable of no pleasures except those of which swine are capable. If this supposition were true, the charge could not be gainsaid, but would then be no longer an imputation; for if the sources of pleasure were precisely the same to human beings and to swine, the rule of life which is good enough for the one would be good enough for the other. The comparison of the Epicurean life to that of beasts is felt as degrading, precisely because a beast's pleasures do not satisfy a human being's conceptions of happiness. Human beings have faculties more elevated than the animal appetites and, when once made conscious of them, do not regard anything as happiness which does not include their gratification. I do not, indeed, consider the Epicureans to have been by any means faultless in drawing out their scheme of consequences from the utilitarian principle. To do this in any sufficient manner, many Stoic, as well as Christian, elements require to be included. But there is no known Epicurean theory of life which does not assign to the pleasures of the intellect, of the feelings and imagination, and of the moral sentiments, a much higher value as pleasures than to those of mere sensation. It must be admitted, however, that utilitarian writers in general have placed the superiority of mental over bodily pleasures chiefly in the greater permanency, safety, uncostliness, etc., of the former—that is, in their circumstantial advantages rather than in their intrinsic nature. And on all these points utilitarians have fully proved their case; but they might have taken the other and, as it may be called, higher ground, with entire consistency. It is quite compatible with the principle of utility to recognize the fact that some kinds of pleasure are more desirable and more valuable than others. It would be absurd that, while in estimating all other things quality is considered as well as quantity, the estimation of pleasure should be supposed to depend on quantity alone.

If I am asked what I mean by difference of quality in pleasures, or what makes one pleasure more valuable than another, merely as a pleasure, except its being greater in amount, there is but one possible answer. Of two pleasures, if there be one to which all or almost all who have experience of both give a decided preference, irrespective of any feeling of moral obligation to prefer it, that is the more desirable pleasure. If one of the two is, by those who are competently acquainted with both, placed so far above the other that they prefer it, even though knowing it to be attended with a greater amount of discontent, and would not resign it for any quantity of the other pleasure which their nature is capable of, we are justified in ascribing to the preferred enjoyment a superiority in quality so far outweighing quantity as to render it, in comparison, of small account.

Now it is an unquestionable fact that those who are equally acquainted with and equally capable of appreciating and enjoying both do give a most marked preference to the manner of existence which employs their higher faculties. Few human creatures would consent to be changed into any of the lower animals for a promise of the fullest allowance of a beast's pleasures; no intelligent human being would consent to be a fool, no instructed person would be an ignoramus, no person of feeling and conscience would be selfish and base, even though they should be persuaded that the fool, the dunce, or the rascal is better satisfied with his lot than they are with theirs. They would not resign what they possess more than he for the most complete satisfaction of all the desires which they have in common with him. If they ever fancy they would, it is only in cases of unhappiness so extreme that to escape from it they would exchange their lot for almost any other, however undesirable in their own eyes. A being of higher faculties requires more to make him happy, is capable probably of more acute suffering, and is certainly accessible to it at more points, than one of an inferior type; but in spite of these liabilities, he can never really wish to sink into what he feels to be a lower grade of existence. We may give what explanation we please of this unwillingness: we may attribute it to pride, a name which is given indiscriminately to some of the most and to some of the least estimable feelings of which mankind are capable; we may refer it to the love of liberty and personal independence, an appeal to which was with the Stoics one of the most effective means for the inculcation of it; to the love of power or to the love of excitement, both of which do really enter into and contribute to it; but its most appropriate appellation is a sense of dignity, which all human beings possess in one form or other, and in some, though by no means in exact, proportion to their higher faculties, and which is so essential a part of the happiness of those in whom it is strong that nothing which conflicts with it could be otherwise than momentarily an object of desire to them. Whoever supposes that this preference takes place at a sacrifice of happiness—that the superior being, in anything like equal circumstances, is not happier than the inferior—confounds the two very different ideas of happiness and content. It is indisputable that the being whose capacities of enjoyment are low has the greatest chance of having them fully satisfied; and a highly endowed being will always feel that any happiness which he can look for, as the world is constituted, is imperfect. But he can learn to bear its imperfections, if they are at all bearable; and they will not make him envy the being who is indeed unconscious of the imperfections, but only because he feels not at all the good which those imperfections qualify. It is better to be a human being dissatisfied than a pig satisfied; better to be Socrates dissatisfied than a fool satisfied. And if the fool, or the pig, are of a different opinion, it is because they only know their own side of the question. The other party to the comparison knows both sides.

It may be objected that many who are capable of the higher pleasures occasionally, under the influence of temptation, postpone them to the lower. But this is quite compatible with a full appreciation of the intrinsic superiority of the higher. Men often, from infirmity of character, make their election for the nearer good, though they know it to be the less valuable; and this no less when the choice is between two bodily pleasures than when it is between bodily and mental. They pursue sensual indulgences to the injury of health, though perfectly aware that health is the greater good. It may be further objected that many who begin with youthful enthusiasm for everything noble, as they advance in years, sink into indolence and selfishness. But I do not believe that those who undergo this very common change voluntarily choose the lower description of pleasures in preference to the higher. I believe that, before they devote themselves exclusively to the one, they have already become incapable of the other. Capacity for the nobler feelings is in most natures a very tender plant, easily killed, not only by hostile influences, but by mere want of sustenance; and in the majority of young persons it speedily dies away if the occupations to which their position in life has devoted them, and the society into which it has thrown them, are not favorable to keeping that higher capacity in exercise. Men lose their high aspirations as they lose their intellectual tastes, because they have not time or opportunity for indulging them; and they addict themselves to inferior pleasures, not because they deliberately prefer them, but because they are either the only ones to which they have access or the only ones which they are any longer capable of enjoying. It may be questioned whether anyone who has remained equally susceptible to both classes of pleasures ever knowingly and calmly preferred the lower, though many, in all ages, have broken down in an ineffectual attempt to combine both.

From this verdict of the only competent judges, I apprehend there can be no appeal. On a question which is the best worth having of two pleasures, or which of two modes of existence is the most grateful to the feelings, apart from its moral attributes and from its consequences, the judgment of those who are qualified by knowledge of both, or, if they differ, that of the majority among them, must be admitted as final. And there needs be the less hesitation to accept this judgment respecting the quality of pleasures, since there is no other tribunal to be referred to even on the question of quantity. What means are there of determining which is the acutest of two pains, or the intensest of two pleasurable sensations, except the general suffrage of those who are familiar with both? Neither pains nor pleasures are homogeneous, and pain is always heterogeneous with pleasure. What is there to decide whether a particular pleasure is worth purchasing at the cost of a particular pain, except the feelings and judgment of the experienced? When, therefore, those feelings and judgment declare the pleasures derived from the higher faculties to be preferable *in kind*, apart from the question of intensity, to those of which the animal nature, disjoined from the higher faculties, is susceptible, they are entitled on this subject to the same regard.

I have dwelt on this point as being a necessary part of a perfectly just conception of utility or happiness considered as the directive rule of human conduct. But it is by no means an indispensable condition to the acceptance of the utilitarian standard, for that standard is not the agent's own greatest happiness, but the greatest amount of happiness altogether; and if it may possibly be doubted whether a noble character is always the happier for its nobleness, there can be no doubt that it makes other people happier, and that the world in general is immensely a gainer by it. Utilitarianism, therefore, could only attain its end by the general cultivation of nobleness of character, even if each individual were only benefited by the nobleness of others, and his own, so far as happiness is concerned, were a sheer deduction from the benefit. But the bare enunciation of such an absurdity as this last renders refutation superfluous.

According to the greatest happiness principle, as above explained, the ultimate end with reference to and for the sake of which all other things are desirable—whether we are considering our own good or that of other people—is an existence exempt as far as possible from pain, and as rich as possible in enjoyments, both in point of quantity and quality; the test of quality and the rule for measuring it against quantity being the preference felt by those who, in their opportunities of experience, to which must be added their habits of self-consciousness and self-observation, are best furnished with the means of comparison. This, being according to the utilitarian opinion the end of human action, is necessarily also the standard of morality, which may accordingly be defined "the rules and precepts for human conduct," by the observance of which an existence such as has been described might be, to the greatest extent possible, secured to all mankind; and not to them only, but, so far as the nature of things admits, to the whole sentient creation.

Against this doctrine, however, arises another class of objectors who say that happiness, in any form, cannot be the rational purpose of human life and action, because, in the first place, it is unattainable; and they contemptuously ask, What right hast thou to be happy?—a question which Mr. Carlyle clinches by the addition, What right, a short time ago, hadst thou even *to be*? Next they say that men can do w*ithout* happiness; that all noble human beings have felt this, and could not have become noble but by learning the lesson of *Entsagen,* or renunciation; which lesson, thoroughly learned and submitted to, they affirm to be the beginning and necessary condition of all virtue.

The first of these objections would go to the root of the matter were it well founded; for if no happiness is to be had at all by human beings, the attainment of it cannot be the end of morality or of any rational conduct. Though, even in that case, something might still be said for the utilitarian theory, since utility includes not solely the pursuit of happiness, but the prevention or mitigation of unhappiness; and if the former aim be chimerical, there will be all the greater scope and more imperative need for the latter, so long at least as mankind think fit to live and do not take refuge in the simultaneous act of suicide recommended under certain conditions by Novalis. When, however, it is thus positively asserted to be impossible that human life should be happy, the assertion, if not something like a verbal quibble, is at least an exaggeration. If by happiness be meant a continuity of highly pleasurable excitement, it is evident enough that this is impossible. A state of exalted pleasure lasts only moments or in some cases, and with some intermissions, hours or days, and is the occasional brilliant flash of enjoyment, not its permanent and steady flame. Of this the philosophers who have taught that happiness is the end of life were as fully aware as those who taunt them. The happiness which they meant was not a life of rapture, but moments of such, in an existence made up of few and transitory pains, many and various pleasures, with a decided predominance of the active over the passive, and having as the foundation of the whole not to expect more from life than it is capable of bestowing. A life thus composed, to those who have been fortunate enough to obtain it, has always appeared worthy of the name of happiness. And such an existence is even now the lot of many during some considerable portion of their lives. The present wretched education and wretched social arrangements are the only real hindrance to its being attainable by almost all.

The objectors perhaps may doubt whether human beings, if taught to consider happiness as the end of life, would be satisfied with such a moderate share of it. But great numbers of mankind have been satisfied with much less. The main constituents of a satisfied life appear to be two, either of which by itself is often found sufficient for the purpose: tranquillity and excitement. With much tranquillity, many find that they can be content with very little pleasure; with much excitement, many can reconcile themselves to a considerable quantity of pain. There is assuredly no inherent impossibility of enabling even the mass of mankind to unite both, since the two are so far from being incompatible that they are in natural alliance, the prolongation of either being a preparation for, and exciting a wish for, the other. It is only those in whom indolence amounts to a vice that do not desire excitement after an interval of repose; it is only those in whom the need of excitement is a disease that feel the tranquillity which follows excitement dull and insipid, instead of pleasurable in direct proportion to the excitement which preceded it. When people who are tolerably fortunate in their outward lot do not find in life sufficient enjoyment to make it valuable to them, the cause generally is caring for nobody but themselves. To those who have neither public nor private affections, the excitements of life are much curtailed, and in any case dwindle in value as the time approaches when all selfish interests must be terminated by death; while those who leave after them objects of personal affection, and especially those who have also cultivated a fellow-feeling with the collective interests of mankind, retain as lively an interest in life on the eve of death as in the vigor of youth and health. Next to selfishness, the principal cause which makes life unsatisfactory is want of mental cultivation. A cultivated mind—I do not mean that of a philosopher, but any mind to which the fountains of knowledge have been opened, and which has been taught, in any tolerable degree, to exercise its faculties—finds sources of inexhaustible interest in all that surrounds it: in the objects of nature, the achievements of art, the imaginations of poetry, the incidents of history, the ways of mankind, past and present, and their prospects in the future. It is possible, indeed, to become indifferent to all this, and that too without having exhausted a thousandth part of it, but only when one has had from the beginning no moral or human interest in these things and has sought in them only the gratification of curiosity.

Now there is absolutely no reason in the nature of things why an amount of mental culture sufficient to give an intelligent interest in these objects of contemplation should not be the inheritance of everyone born in a civilized country. As little is there an inherent necessity that any human being should be a selfish egotist, devoid of every feeling or care but those which center in his own miserable individuality. Something far superior to this is sufficiently common even now, to give ample earnest of what the human species may be made. Genuine private affections and a sincere interest in the public good are possible, though in unequal degrees, to every rightly brought up human being. In a world in which there is so much to interest, so much to enjoy, and so much also to correct and improve, everyone who has this moderate amount of moral and intellectual requisites is capable of an existence which may be called enviable; and unless such a person, through bad laws or subjection to the will of others, is denied the liberty to use the sources of happiness within his reach, he will not fail to find this enviable existence, if he escape the positive evils of life, the great sources of physical and mental suffering—such as indigence, disease, and the unkindness, worthlessness, or premature loss of objects of affection. The main stress of the problem lies, therefore, in the contest with

these calamities from which it is a rare good fortune entirely to escape; which, as things now are, cannot be obviated, and often cannot be in any material degree mitigated. Yet no one whose opinion deserves a moment's consideration can doubt that most of the great positive evils of the world are in themselves removable, and will, if human affairs continue to improve, be in the end reduced within narrow limits. Poverty, in any sense implying suffering, may be completely extinguished by the wisdom of society combined with the good sense and providence of individuals. Even that most intractable of enemies, disease, may be indefinitely reduced in dimensions of good physical and moral education and proper control of noxious influences, while the progress of science holds out a promise for the future of still more direct conquests over this detestable foe. And every advance in that direction relieves us from some, not only of the chances which cut short our own lives, but, what concerns us still more, which deprive us of those in whom our happiness is wrapt up. As for vicissitudes of fortune and other disappointments connected with worldly circumstances, these are principally the effect either of gross imprudence, of ill-regulated desires, or of bad or imperfect social institutions. All the grand sources, in short, of human suffering are in a great degree, many of them almost entirely, conquerable by human care and effort; and though their removal is grievously slow—though a long succession of generations will perish in the breach before the conquest is completed, and this world becomes all that, if will and knowledge were not wanting, it might easily be made—yet every mind sufficiently intelligent and generous to bear a part, however small and inconspicuous, in the endeavor will draw a noble enjoyment from the contest itself, which he would not for any bribe in the form of selfish indulgence consent to be without.

And this leads to the true estimation of what is said by the objectors concerning the possibility and the obligation of learning to do without happiness. Unquestionably it is possible to do without happiness; it is done involuntarily by nineteen-twentieths of mankind, even in those parts of our present world which are least deep in barbarism; and it often has to be done voluntarily by the hero or the martyr, for the sake of something which he prizes more than his individual happiness. But this something, what is it, unless the happiness of others or some of the requisites of happiness? It is noble to be capable of resigning entirely one's own portion of happiness, or chances of it; but, after all, this self-sacrifice must be for some end; it is not its own end; and if we are told that its end is not happiness but virtue, which is better than happiness, I ask, Would the sacrifice be made if the hero or martyr did not believe that it would earn for others immunity from similar sacrifices? Would it be made if he thought that his renunciation of happiness for himself would produce no fruit for any of his fellow creatures, but to make their lot like his and place them also in the condition of persons who have renounced happiness? All honor to those who can abnegate for themselves the personal enjoyment of life when by such renunciation they contribute worthily to increase the amount of happiness in the world; but he who does it or professes to do it for any other purpose is no more deserving of admiration than the ascetic mounted on his pillar. He may be an inspiriting proof of what men *can* do, but assuredly not an example of what they *should*.

Though it is only in a very imperfect state of the world's arrangements that anyone can best serve the happiness of others by the absolute sacrifice of his own, yet, so long as the world is in that imperfect state, I fully acknowledge that the readiness to make such a sacrifice is the highest virtue which can be found in man. I will add that in this condition of the world, paradoxical as the assertion may be, the conscious ability to do without happiness gives the best prospect of realizing such happiness as is attainable. For nothing except that consciousness can raise a person above the chances of life by making him feel that, let fate and fortune do their worst, they have not power to subdue him; which, once felt, frees him from excess of anxiety concerning the evils of life and enables him, like many a Stoic in the worst times of the Roman Empire, to cultivate in tranquillity the sources of satisfaction accessible to him, without concerning himself about the uncertainty of their duration any more than about their inevitable end.

Meanwhile, let utilitarians never cease to claim the morality of self-devotion as a possession which belongs by as good a right to them as either to the Stoic or to the Transcendentalist. The utilitarian morality does recognize in human beings the power of sacrificing their own greatest good for the good of others. It only refuses to admit that the sacrifice is itself a good. A sacrifice which does not increase or tend to increase the sum total of happiness, it considers as wasted. The only self-renunciation which it applauds is devotion to the happiness, or to some of the means of happiness, of others, either of mankind collectively or of individuals within the limits imposed by the collective interests of mankind.

I must again repeat what the assailants of utilitarianism seldom have the justice to acknowledge, that the happiness which forms the utilitarian standard of what is right in conduct is not the agent's own happiness but that of all concerned. As between his own happiness and that of others, utilitarianism requires him to be as strictly impartial as a disinterested and benevolent spectator. In the golden rule of Jesus of Nazareth, we read the complete spirit of the ethics of utility. "To do as you would be done by," and "to love your neighbor as yourself," constitute the ideal perfection of utilitarian morality. As the means of making the nearest approach to this ideal, utility would enjoin, first, that laws and social arrangements should place the happiness or (as, speaking practically, it may be called) the interest of every individual as nearly as possible in harmony with the interest of the whole; and, secondly, that education and opinion, which have so vast a power over human character, should so use that power as to establish in the mind of every individual an indissoluble association between his own happiness and the good of the whole, especially between his own happiness and the practice of such modes of conduct, negative and positive, as regard for the universal happiness prescribes; so that not only he may be unable to conceive the possibility of happiness to himself, consistently with conduct opposed to the general good, but also that a direct impulse to promote the general good may be in every individual one of the habitual motives of action, and the sentiments connected therewith may fill a large and prominent place in every human being's sentient existence. If the impugners of the utilitarian morality represented it to their own minds in this its true character, I know not what recommendation possessed by any other morality they could possibly affirm to be wanting to it, what more beautiful or more exalted developments of human nature any other ethical system can be supposed to foster, or what springs of action, not accessible to the utilitarian, such systems rely on for giving effect to their mandates.

The objectors to utilitarianism cannot always be charged with representing it in a discreditable light.

On the contrary, those among them who entertain anything like a just idea of its disinterested character sometimes find fault with its standard as being too high for humanity. They say it is exacting too much to require that people shall always act from the inducement of promoting the general interests of society. But this is to mistake the very meaning of a standard of morals and confound the rule of action with the motive of it. It is the business of ethics to tell us what are our duties, or by what test we may know them; but no system of ethics requires that the sole motive of all we do shall be a feeling of duty; on the contrary, ninety-nine hundredths of all our actions are done from other motives, and rightly so done if the rule of duty does not condemn them. It is the more unjust to utilitarianism that this particular misapprehension should be made a ground of objection to it, inasmuch as utilitarian moralists have gone beyond almost all others in affirming that the motive has nothing to do with the morality of the action, though much with the worth of the agent. He who saves a fellow creature from drowning does what is morally right, whether his motive be duty or the hope of being paid for his trouble; he who betrays the friend that trusts him is guilty of a crime, even if his object be to serve another friend to whom he is under greater obligations.[1] But to speak only of actions done from the motive of duty, and in direct obedience to principle: it is a misapprehension of the utilitarian mode of thought to conceive it as implying that people should fix their minds upon so wide a generality as the world, or society at large. The great majority of good actions are intended not for the benefit of the world, but for that of individuals, of which the good of the world is made up; and the thoughts of the most virtuous man need not on these occasions travel beyond the particular persons concerned, except so far as is necessary to assure himself that in benefiting them he is not violating the rights, that is, the legitimate and authorized expectations, of anyone else. The multiplication of happiness is, according to the utilitarian ethics, the object of virtue: the occasions on which any person (except one in a thousand) has it in his power to do this on an extended scale—in other words, to be a public benefactor—are but exceptional; and on these occasions alone is he called on to consider public utility; in every other case, private utility, the interest or happiness of some few persons, is all he has to attend to. Those alone, the influence of whose actions extends to society in general, need concern themselves habitually about so large an object. In the case of abstinences indeed—of things which people forbear to do from moral considerations, though the consequences in the particular case might be beneficial—it would be unworthy of an intelligent agent not to be consciously aware that the action is of a class which, if practiced generally, would be generally injurious, and that this is the ground of the obligation to abstain from it. The amount of regard for the public interest implied in this recognition is no greater than is demanded by every system of morals, for they all enjoin to abstain from whatever is manifestly pernicious to society.

The same considerations dispose of another reproach against the doctrine of utility, founded on a

---

[1]An opponent, whose intellectual and moral fairness it is a pleasure to acknowledge (the Rev. J. Llewellyn Davies), has objected to this passage, saying, "Surely the rightness or wrongness of saving a man from drowning does depend very much upon the motive with which it is done. Suppose that a tyrant, when his enemy jumped into the sea to escape from him, saved him from drowning simply in order that he might inflict upon him more exquisite tortures, would it tend to clearness to speak of that rescue as 'a morally right action'? Or suppose again, according to one of the stock illustrations of ethical inquiries, that a man betrayed a trust received from a friend because the discharge of it would fatally injure that friend himself or someone belonging to him, would utilitarianism compel one to call the betrayal 'a crime' as much as if it had been done from the meanest motive?"

I submit that he who saves another from drowning in order to kill him by torture afterwards does not differ only in motive from him who does the same thing from duty or benevolence; the act itself is different. The rescue of the man is, in the case supposed, only the necessary first step of an act far more atrocious than leaving him to drown would have been. Had Mr. Davies said, "The rightness or wrongness of saving a man from drowning does depend very much"—not upon the motive, but—"upon the *intention*," no utilitarian would have differed from him. Mr. Davies, by an oversight too common not to be quite venial, has in this case confounded the very different ideas of Motive and Intention. There is no point which utilitarian thinkers (and Bentham pre-eminently) have taken more pains to illustrate than this. The morality of the action depends entirely upon the intention—that is, upon what the agent *wills to do*. But the motive, that is, the feeling which makes him will so to do, if it makes no difference in the act, makes none in the morality: though it makes a great difference in our moral estimation of the agent, especially if it indicates a good or a bad habitual *disposition*—a bent of character from which useful, or from which hurtful actions are likely to arise. [This footnote appeared only in the edition of 1864.]

still grosser misconception of the purpose of a standard of morality and of the very meaning of the words "right" and "wrong." It is often affirmed that utilitarianism renders men cold and unsympathizing; that it chills their moral feelings toward individuals; that it makes them regard only the dry and hard consideration of the consequences of actions, not taking into their moral estimate the qualities from which those actions emanate. If the assertion means that they do not allow their judgment respecting the rightness or wrongness of an action to be influenced by their opinion of the qualities of the person who does it, this is a complaint not against utilitarianism, but against any standard of morality at all; for certainly no known ethical standard decides an action to be good or bad because it is done by a good or a bad man, still less because done by an amiable, a brave, or a benevolent man, or the contrary. These considerations are relevant, not to the estimation of actions, but of persons; and there is nothing in the utilitarian theory inconsistent with the fact that there are other things which interest us in persons besides the rightness and wrongness of their actions. The Stoics, indeed, with the paradoxical misuse of language which was part of their system, and by which they strove to raise themselves above all concern about anything but virtue, were fond of saying that he who has that has everything; that he, and only he, is rich, is beautiful, is a king. But no claim of this description is made for the virtuous man by the utilitarian doctrine. Utilitarians are quite aware that there are other desirable possessions and qualities besides virtue, and are perfectly willing to allow to all of them their full worth. They are also aware that a right action does not necessarily indicate a virtuous character, and that actions which are blamable often proceed from qualities entitled to praise. When this is apparent in any particular case, it modifies their estimation, not certainly of the act, but of the agent. I grant that they are, notwithstanding, of opinion that in the long run the best proof of a good character is good actions; and resolutely refuse to consider any mental disposition as good of which the predominant tendency is to produce bad conduct. This makes them unpopular with many people, but it is an unpopularity which they must share with everyone who regards the distinction between right and wrong in a serious light; and the reproach is not one which a conscientious utilitarian need be anxious to repel.

If no more be meant by the objection than that many utilitarians look on the morality of actions, as measured by the utilitarian standards, with too exclusive a regard, and do not lay sufficient stress upon the other beauties of character which go toward making a human being lovable or admirable, this may be admitted. Utilitarians who have cultivated their moral feelings, but not their sympathies, nor their artistic perceptions, do fall into this mistake; and so do all other moralists under the same conditions. What can be said in excuse for other moralists is equally available for them, namely, that, if there is to be any error, it is better that it should be on that side. As a matter of fact, we may affirm that among utilitarians, as among adherents of other systems, there is every imaginable degree of rigidity and of laxity in the application of their standard; some are even puritanically rigorous, while others are as indulgent as can possibly be desired by sinner or by sentimentalist. But on the whole, a doctrine which brings prominently forward the interest that mankind have in the repression and prevention of conduct which violates the moral law is likely to be inferior to no other in turning the sanctions of opinion against such violations. It is true, the question "What does violate the moral law?" is one on which those who recognize different standards of morality are likely now and then to differ. But difference of opinion on moral questions was not first introduced into the world by utilitarianism, while that doctrine does supply, if not always an easy, at all events a tangible and intelligible mode of deciding such differences.

It may not be superfluous to notice a few more of the common misapprehensions of utilitarian ethics, even those which are so obvious and gross that it might appear impossible for any person of candor and intelligence to fall into them; since persons, even of considerable mental endowment, often give themselves so little trouble to understand the bearings of any opinion against which they entertain a prejudice, and men are in general so little conscious of this voluntary ignorance as a defect that the vulgarest misunderstandings of ethical doctrines are continually met with in the deliberate writings of persons of the greatest pretensions both to high principle and to philosophy. We not uncommonly hear the doctrine of utility inveighed against as a *godless* doctrine. If it be necessary to say anything at all against so mere an assumption, we may say that the question depends upon what idea we have formed of the moral character of the Deity. If it be a true belief that God desires, above all things, the happiness of his creatures, and that this was his purpose in their creation, utility is not only not a godless doctrine, but more profoundly religious than any other. If it be meant that utilitarianism does not recognize the revealed will of God as the supreme law of morals, I answer that a utilitarian who believes in the perfect goodness and wisdom of *God* necessarily believes that whatever God has thought fit to reveal on the subject of morals must fulfill the requirements of utility in a supreme degree. But others besides utilitarians have been of opinion that the Christian revelation was intended, and is fitted, to inform the hearts and minds of mankind with a spirit which should enable them to find for themselves what is right, and incline them to do it when found, rather than to tell them, except in a very general way, what it is; and that we need a doctrine of ethics, carefully followed out, to *interpret* to us the will of God. Whether this opinion is correct or not, it is superfluous here to discuss, since whatever aid religion, either natural or revealed, can afford to ethical investigation is as open to the utilitarian moralist as to any other. He can use it as the testimony of God to the usefulness or hurtfulness of any given course of action by as good a right as others can use it for the indication of a transcendental law having no connection with usefulness or with happiness.

Again, utility is often summarily stigmatized as an immoral doctrine by giving it the name of "expediency," and taking advantage of the popular use of that term to contrast it with principle. But the expedient, in the sense in which it is opposed to the right, generally means that which is expedient for the particular interest of the agent himself, as when a minister sacrifices the interest of his country to keep himself in place. When it means anything better than this, it means that which is expedient for some immediate object, some temporary purpose, but which violates a rule whose observance is expedient in a much higher degree. The expedient, in this sense, instead of being the same thing with the useful, is a branch of the hurtful. Thus it would often be expedient, for the purpose of getting over some momentary embarrassment, or attaining some object immediately useful to ourselves or others, to tell a lie. But inasmuch as the cultivation in ourselves of a sensitive feeling on the subject of veracity is one of the most useful, and the enfeeblement of that feeling one of the most hurtful, things to which our conduct can be instrumental; and inasmuch as any, even unintentional, deviation from truth does that much toward weakening the trustworthiness of human assertion, which is not only the principal support of all present social well-being, but the insufficiency of which does more than any one thing that can be named to keep back civilization, virtue, everything on which human happiness on the largest scale depends—we feel that the violation, for a present advantage, of a rule of such transcendent expediency is not expedient, and that he who, for the sake of convenience to himself or to some other individual, does what depends on him to deprive mankind of the good, and inflict upon them the evil, involved in the greater or less reliance which they can place in each other's word, acts the part of one of their worst enemies. Yet that even this rule, sacred as it is, admits of possible exceptions is acknowledged by all moralists; the chief of which is when the withholding of some fact (as of information from a malefactor, or of bad news from a person dangerously ill) would save an individual (especially an individual other than oneself) from great and unmerited evil, and when the withholding can only be effected by denial. But in order that the exception may not extend itself beyond the need, and may have the least possible effect in weakening reliance on veracity, it ought to be recognized and, if possible, its limits defined; and, if the principle of utility is good for anything, it must be good for weighing these conflicting utilities against one another and marking out the region within which one or the other preponderates.

Again, defenders of utility often find themselves called upon to reply to such objections as this—that there is not time, previous to action, for calculating and weighing the effects of any line of conduct on the general happiness. This is exactly as if anyone were to say that it is impossible to guide our conduct by Christianity because there is not time, on every occasion on which anything has to be done, to read through the Old and New Testaments. The answer to the objection is that there has been ample time, namely, the whole past duration of the human species. During all that time mankind have been learning by experience the tendencies of actions, on which experience all the prudence as well as all the morality of life are dependent. People talk as if the commencement of this course of experience had hitherto been put off, and as if, at the moment when some man feels tempted to meddle with the property or life of another, he had to begin considering for the first time whether murder and theft are injurious to human happiness. Even then I do not think that he would find the question very puzzling; but, at all events, the matter is now done to his hand. It is truly a whimsical supposition that, if mankind were agreed in considering utility to be the test of morality, they would remain without any agreement as to what *is* useful, and would take no measures for having their notions on the subject taught to the young and enforced by law and opinion. There is no difficulty in proving any ethical standard whatever to work ill if we suppose universal idiocy to be conjoined with it; but on any hypothesis short of that, mankind must by this time have acquired positive beliefs as to the effects of some actions on their happiness; and the beliefs which have thus come down are the rules of morality for the multitude, and for the philosopher, until he has succeeded in finding better. That philosophers might easily do this, even now, on many subjects, that the received code of ethics is by no means of divine right, and that mankind have still much to learn as to the effects of actions on the general happiness, I admit or rather earnestly maintain. The corollaries from the principle of utility, like the precepts of every practical art, admit of indefinite improvement, and, in a progressive state of the human mind, their improvement is perpetually going on. But to consider the rules of morality as improvable is one thing; to pass over the intermediate generalization entirely and endeavor to test each individual action directly by the first principle is another. It is a strange notion that the acknowledgment of a first principle is inconsistent with the admission of secondary ones. To inform a traveler respecting the place of his ultimate destination is not to forbid the use of landmarks and direction-posts on the way. The proposition that happiness is the end and aim of morality does not mean that no road ought to be laid down to that goal, or that persons going thither should not be advised to take one direction rather than another. Men really ought to leave off talking a kind of nonsense on this subject, which they would neither talk nor listen to on other matters of practical concernment. Nobody argues that the art of navigation is not founded on astronomy because sailors cannot wait to calculate the Nautical Almanac. Being rational creatures, they go to sea with it ready calculated; and all rational creatures go out upon the sea of life with their minds made up on the common questions of right and wrong, as well as on many of the far more difficult questions of wise and foolish. And this, as long as foresight is a human quality, it is to be presumed they will continue to do. Whatever we adopt as the fundamental principle of morality, we require subordinate principles to apply it by; the impossibility of doing without them, being common to all systems, can afford no argument against any one in particular; but gravely to argue as if no such secondary principles could be had, and as if mankind had remained till now, and always must remain, without drawing any general conclusions from the experience of human life is as high a pitch, I think, as absurdity has ever reached in philosophical controversy.

The remainder of the stock arguments against utilitarianism mostly consist in laying to its charge the common infirmities of human nature, and the general difficulties which embarrass conscientious persons in shaping their course through life. We are told that a utilitarian will be apt to make his own particular case an exception to moral rules, and, when under temptation, will see a utility in the breach of a rule, greater than he will see in its observance. But is utility the only creed which is able to furnish us with excuses for evil-doing and means of cheating our own conscience? They are afforded in abundance by all doctrines which recognize as a fact in morals the existence of conflicting considerations, which all doctrines do that have been believed by sane persons. It is not the fault of any creed, but of the complicated nature of human affairs, that rules of conduct cannot be so framed as to require no exceptions, and that hardly any kind of action can safely be laid down as either always obligatory or always condemnable. There is no ethical creed which does not temper the rigidity of its laws by giving a certain latitude, under the moral responsibility of the agent, for accommodation to peculiarities of circumstances; and under every creed, at the opening thus made, self-deception and dishonest casuistry get in. There exists no moral system under which there do not arise unequivocal cases of conflicting obligation. These are the real difficulties, the knotty points both in the theory of ethics and in the conscientious guidance of personal conduct. They are overcome practically, with greater or with less success, according to the intellect and virtue of the individual; but it can hardly be pretended that anyone will be the less qualified for dealing with them, from possessing an ultimate standard to which conflicting rights and duties can be referred. If utility is the ultimate source of moral obligations, utility may be invoked to decide between them when their demands are incompatible. Though the application of the standard may be difficult, it is better than none at all; while in other systems, the moral laws all claiming independent authority, there is no common umpire entitled to interfere between them; their claims to precedence one over another rest on little better than sophistry, and,

unless determined, as they generally are, by the unacknowledged influence of consideration of utility, afford a free scope for the action of personal desires and partialities. We must remember that only in these cases of conflict between secondary principles is it requisite that first principles should be appealed to. There is no case of moral obligation in which some secondary principle is not involved; and if only one, there can seldom be any real doubt which one it is, in the mind of any person by whom the principle itself is recognized.

## READING 14

# Extreme and Restricted Utilitarianism
*J.J.C. Smart*

*Before his retirement in 1985, J.J.C. Smart (1920–  ) was Professor of Philosophy at the Research School of Social Sciences, Australian National University. He has taught at the University of Oxford and the University of Adelaide and has been Visiting Professor of Philosophy at Harvard, Princeton, and Yale. He is the author of many articles on topics ranging from utilitarianism and materialism to the philosophy of time. His books include* An Outline of a System of Utilitarian Ethics *(1961),* Philosophy and Scientific Realism *(1963),* Utilitarianism: For and Against *(1973) (co-authored with B. Williams),* Ethics, Persuasion and Truth *(1984),* Essays Metaphysical and Moral *(1987), and* Our Place in the Universe *(1989).*

I

Utilitarianism is the doctrine that the rightness of actions is to be judged by their consequences. What

SOURCE: From *Philosophical Quarterly* 6 (1956): 344–354, as reprinted with slight revisions in P. Foot, Ed., *Theories of Ethics* (Oxford: Oxford University Press, 1967).

do we mean by 'actions' here? Do we mean particular actions or do we mean classes of actions? According to which way we interpret the word 'actions' we get two different theories, both of which merit the appellation 'utilitarian'.

(1) If by 'actions' we mean particular individual actions we get the sort of doctrine held by Bentham, Sidgwick, and Moore. According to this doctrine we test individual actions by their consequences, and general rules, like 'keep promises', are mere rules of thumb which we use only to avoid the necessity of estimating the probable consequences of our actions at every step. The rightness or wrongness of keeping a promise on a particular occasion depends only on the goodness or badness of the consequences of keeping or of breaking the promise on that particular occasion. Of course part of the consequences of breaking the promise, and a part to which we will normally ascribe decisive importance, will be the weakening of faith in the institution of promising. However, if the goodness of the consequences of breaking the rule is *in toto* greater than the goodness

of the consequences of keeping it, then we must break the rule, irrespective of whether the goodness of the consequences of *everybody's* obeying the rule is or is not greater than the consequences of *everybody's* breaking it. To put it shortly, rules do not matter, save *per accidens* as rules of thumb and as *de facto* social institutions with which the utilitarian has to reckon when estimating consequences. I shall call this doctrine 'extreme utilitarianism'.

(2) A more modest form of utilitarianism has recently become fashionable. The doctrine is to be found in Toulmin's book *The Place of Reason in Ethics*, in Nowell-Smith's *Ethics* (though I think Nowell-Smith has qualms), in John Austin's *Lectures on Jurisprudence* (Lecture II), and even in J. S. Mill, if Urmson's interpretation of him is correct (*Philosophical Quarterly*, Vol. 3, pp. 33–39, 1953). Part of its charm is that it appears to resolve the dispute in moral philosophy between intuitionists and utilitarians in a way which is very neat. The above philosophers hold, or seem to hold, that moral rules are more than rules of thumb. In general the rightness of an action is *not* to be tested by evaluating its consequences but only by considering whether or not it falls under a certain rule. Whether the rule is to be considered an acceptable moral rule, is, however, to be decided by considering the consequences of adopting the rule. Broadly, then, actions are to be tested by rules and rules by consequences. The only cases in which we must test an individual action directly by its consequences are *(a)* when the action comes under two different rules, one of which enjoins it and one of which forbids it, and *(b)* when there is no rule whatever that governs the given case. I shall call this doctrine 'restricted utilitarianism'.

It should be noticed that the distinction I am making cuts across, and is quite different from, the distinction commonly made between hedonistic and ideal utilitarianism. Bentham was an extreme hedonistic utilitarian and Moore an extreme ideal utilitarian, and Toulmin (perhaps) could be classified as a restricted ideal utilitarian. A hedonistic utilitarian holds that the goodness of the consequences of an action is a function only of their pleasurableness and an ideal utilitarian, like Moore, holds that pleasurableness is not even a necessary condition of goodness. Mill seems, if we are to take his remarks about higher and lower pleasures seriously, to be neither a pure hedonistic nor a pure ideal utilitarian. He seems to hold that pleasurableness is a necessary

condition for goodness, but that goodness is a function of other qualities of mind as well. Perhaps we can call him a quasi-ideal utilitarian. When we say that a state of mind is good I take it that we are expressing some sort of *rational preference*. When we say that it is pleasurable I take it that we are saying that it is enjoyable, and when we say that something is a higher pleasure I take it that we are saying that it is more truly, or more deeply, enjoyable. I am doubtful whether 'more deeply enjoyable' does not just mean 'more enjoyable, even though not more enjoyable on a first look', and so I am doubtful whether quasi-ideal utilitarianism, and possibly ideal utilitarianism too, would not collapse into hedonistic utilitarianism on a closer scrutiny of the logic of words like 'preference', 'pleasure,' 'enjoy', 'deeply enjoy', and so on. However, it is beside the point of the present paper to go into these questions. I am here concerned only with the issue between extreme and restricted utilitarianism and am ready to concede that both forms of utilitarianism can be either hedonistic or non-hedonistic.

The issue between extreme and restricted utilitarianism can be illustrated by considering the remark 'But suppose everyone did the same'. (Cf. A. K. Stout's article in *The Australasian Journal of Philosophy*, Vol. 32, pp. 1–29) Stout distinguishes two forms of the universalization principle, the causal forms and the hypothetical form. To say that you ought not to do an action A because it would have bad results if everyone (or many people) did action A may be merely to point out that while the action A would otherwise be the optimific one, nevertheless when you take into account that doing A will probably cause other people to do A too, you can see that A is not, on a broad view, really optimific. If this causal influence could be avoided (as may happen in the case of a secret desert island promise) then we would disregard the universalization principle. This is the causal form of the principle. A person who accepted the universalization principle in its hypothetical form would be one who was concerned only with what would happen *if* everyone did the action A: he would be totally unconcerned with the question of whether in fact everyone would do the action A. That is, he might say that it would be wrong not to vote because it would have bad results if everyone took this attitude, and he would be totally unmoved by arguments purporting to show that my refusing to vote has no effect whatever on other people's propensity to vote. Making use of Stout's distinction, we can say that an extreme utilitarian would apply the universalization principle in the causal form, while a restricted utilitarian would apply it in the hypothetical form.

How are we to decide the issue between extreme and restricted utilitarianism? I wish to repudiate at the outset that milk and water approach which describes itself sometimes as 'investigating what is implicit in the common moral consciousness' and sometimes as 'investigating how people ordinarily talk about morality'. We have only to read the newspaper correspondence about capital punishment or about what should be done with Formosa to realize that the common moral consciousness is in part made up of superstitious elements, of morally bad elements, and of logically confused elements. I address myself to good hearted and benevolent people and so I hope that if we rid ourselves of the logical confusion the superstitious and morally bad elements will largely fall away. For even among good hearted and benevolent people it is possible to find superstitious and morally bad reasons for moral beliefs. These superstitious and morally bad reasons hide behind the protective screen of logical confusion. With people who are not logically confused but who are openly superstitious or morally bad I can of course do nothing. That is, our ultimate pro-attitudes may be different. Nevertheless I propose to rely on *my own* moral consciousness and to appeal to *your* moral consciousness and to forget about what people ordinarily say. 'The obligation to obey a rule', says Nowell-Smith (*Ethics*, p. 239), 'does not, *in the opinion of ordinary men*', (my italics), 'rest on the beneficial consequences of obeying it in a particular case'. What does this prove? Surely it is more than likely that ordinary men are confused here. Philosophers should be able to examine the question more rationally.

## II

For an extreme utilitarian moral rules are rules of thumb. In practice the extreme utilitarian will mostly guide his conduct by appealing to the rules ('do not lie', 'do not break promises', etc.) of common sense morality. This is not because there is anything sacrosanct in the rules themselves but because he can argue that probably he will most often act in an extreme utilitarian way if he does not think as a utilitarian. For one thing, actions have frequently to be done in a hurry. Imagine a man seeing a person drowning. He jumps in and rescues him. There is no time to reason the matter out, but usually this will be the course of action which an extreme utilitarian would recommend if he did reason the matter out. If, however, the man drowning had been drowning in a river near Berchtesgaden in 1938, and if he had had the well known black forelock and moustache of Adolf Hitler, an extreme utilitarian would, if he had time, work out the probability of the man's being the villainous dictator, and if the probability were high enough he would, on extreme utilitarian grounds, leave him to drown. The rescuer, however, has not time. He trusts to his instincts and dives in and rescues the man. And this trusting to instincts and to moral rules can be justified on extreme utilitarian grounds. Futhermore, an extreme utilitarian who knew that the drowning man was Hitler would nevertheless praise the rescuer, not condemn him. For by praising the man he is strengthening a courageous and benevolent disposition of mind, and in general this disposition has great positive utility. (Next time, perhaps, it will be Winston Churchill that the man saves!) We must never forget that an extreme utilitarian may praise actions which he knows to be wrong. Saving Hitler was wrong, but it was a member of a class of actions which are generally right, and the motive to do actions of this class is in general an optimific one. In considering questions of praise and blame it is not the expediency of the praised or blamed action that is at issue, but the expediency of the praise. It can be expedient to praise an inexpedient action and inexpedient to praise an expedient one.

Lack of time is not the only reason why an extreme utilitarian may, on extreme utilitarian principles, trust to rules of common sense morality. He knows that in particular cases where his own interests are involved his calculations are likely to be biased in his own favour. Suppose that he is unhappily married and is deciding whether to get divorced. He will in all probability greatly exaggerate his own unhappiness (and possibly his wife's) and greatly underestimate the harm done to his children by the break up of the family. He will probably also underestimate the likely harm done by the weakening of the general faith in marriage vows. So probably he will come to the correct extreme utilitarian conclusion if he does not in this instance think as an extreme utilitarian but trusts to common sense morality.

There are many more and subtle points that could be made in connexion with the relation between extreme utilitarianism and the morality of common sense. All those that I have just made and many more will be found in Book IV Chapters 3–5 of Sidgwick's *Methods of Ethics*. I think that this book is the best book ever written on ethics, and that these chapters are the best chapters of the book. As they occur so near the end of a very long book they are unduly neglected. I refer the reader, then, to Sidgwick for the classical exposition of the relation between (extreme) utilitarianism and the morality of common sense. One further point raised by Sidgwick in this connexion is whether an (extreme) utilitarian ought on (extreme) utilitarian principles to propagate (extreme) utilitarianism among the public. As most people are not very philosophical and not good at empirical calculations, it is probable that they will most often act in an extreme utilitarian way if they do not try to think as extreme utilitarians. We have seen how easy it would be to misapply the extreme utilitarian criterion in the case of divorce. Sidgwick seems to think it quite probable that an extreme utilitarian should not propagate his doctrine too widely. However, the great danger to humanity comes nowadays on the plane of public morality—not private morality. There is a greater danger to humanity from the hydrogen bomb than from an increase of the divorce rate, regrettable though that might be, and there seems no doubt that extreme utilitarianism makes for good sense in international relations. When France walked out of the United Nations because she did not wish Morocco discussed, she said that she was within her rights because Morocco and Algiers are part of her metropolitan territory and nothing to do with U.N. This was clearly a legalistic if not superstitious argument. We should not be concerned with the so-called 'rights' of France or any other country but with whether the cause of humanity would best be served by discussing Morocco in U.N. (I am not saying that the answer to this is 'Yes'. There are good grounds for supposing that more harm than good would come by such a discussion.) I myself have no hesitation in saying that on extreme utilitarian principles we ought to propagate extreme utilitarianism as widely as possible. But Sidgwick had respectable reasons for suspecting the opposite.

The extreme utilitarian, then, regards moral rules as rules of thumb and as sociological facts that have to be taken into account when deciding what to do, just as facts of any other sort have to be taken into account. But in themselves they do not justify any action.

III

The restricted utilitarian regards moral rules as more than rules of thumb for short-circuiting calculations of consequences. Generally, he argues, consequences are not relevant at all when we are deciding what to do in a particular case. In general, they are relevant only to deciding what rules are good reasons for acting in a certain way in particular cases. This doctrine is possibly a good account of how the modern unreflective twentieth-century Englishman often thinks about morality, but surely it is monstrous as an account of how it is most rational to think about morality. Suppose that there is a rule $R$ and that in 99% of cases the best possible results are obtained by acting in accordance with $R$. Then clearly $R$ is a useful rule of thumb; if we have not time or are not impartial enough to assess the consequences of an action it is an extremely good bet that the thing to do is to act in accordance with $R$. But is it not monstrous to suppose that if we *have* worked out the consequences and if we have perfect faith in the impartiality of our calculations, and if we *know* that in this instance to break $R$ will have better results than to keep it, we should nevertheless obey the rule? Is it not to erect $R$ into a sort of idol if we keep it when breaking it will prevent, say, some avoidable misery? Is not this a form of superstitious rule-worship (easily explicable psychologically) and not the rational thought of a philosopher?

The point may be made more clearly it we consider Mill's comparison of moral rules to the tables in the nautical almanack. (*Utilitarianism*, Everyman Edition, pp. 22–23). This comparison of Mill's is adduced by Urmson as evidence that Mill was a restricted utilitarian, but I do not think that it will bear this interpretation at all. (Though I quite agree with Urmson that many other things said by Mill are in harmony with restricted rather than extreme utilitarianism. Probably Mill had never thought very much about the distinction and was arguing for utilitarianism, restricted or extreme, against other and quite non-utilitarian forms of moral argument.) Mill says: 'Nobody argues that the art of navigation is not founded on astronomy, because sailors cannot wait to calculate the Nautical Almanack. Being rational creatures, they go to sea with it ready calculated; and all rational creatures go out upon the sea of life with their minds made up on the common questions of right and wrong, as well as on many of the far more difficult questions of wise and foolish. . . . Whatever we adopt as the fundamental principle of morality, we require subordinate principles to apply it by'. Notice that this is, as it stands, only an argument for subordinate principles as rules of thumb. The example of the nautical almanack is misleading because the information given in the almanack is in all cases the same as the information one would get if one made a long and laborious calculation from the original astronomical data on which the almanack is founded. Suppose, however, that astronomy were different. Suppose that the behaviour of the sun, moon and planets was very nearly as it is now, but that on rare occasions there were peculiar irregularities and discontinuities, so that the almanack gave us rules of the form 'in 99% of cases where the observations are such and such you can deduce that your position is so and so'. Furthermore, let us suppose that there were methods which enabled us, by direct and laborious calculation from the original astronomical data, not using the rough and ready tables of the almanack, to get our correct position in 100% of cases. Seafarers might use the almanack because they never had time for the long calculations and they were content with a 99% chance of success in calculating their positions. Would it not be absurd, however, if they *did* make the direct calculation, and finding that it disagreed with the almanack calculation, nevertheless they ignored it and stuck to the almanack conclusion? Of course the case would be altered if there were a high enough probability of making slips in the direct calculation: then we might stick to the almanack result, liable to error though we knew it to be, simply because the direct calculation would be open to error for a different reason, the fallibility of the computer. This would be analogous to the case of the extreme utilitarian who abides by the conventional rule against the dictates of his utilitarian calculations simply because he thinks that his calculations are probably affected by personal bias. But if the navigator were sure of his direct calculations would he not be foolish to abide by his almanack? I conclude, then, that if we change our suppositions about astronomy and the almanack (to which there are no exceptions) to bring the case into line with that of morality (to whose rules there are exceptions), Mill's example loses its appearance of supporting the restricted form of utilitarianism. Let me

say once more that I am not here concerned with how ordinary men think about morality but with how they ought to think. We could quite well imagine a race of sailors who acquired a superstitious reverence for their almanack, even though it was only right in 99% of cases, and who indignantly threw overboard any man who mentioned the possibility of a direct calculation. But would this behaviour of the sailors be rational?

Let us consider a much discussed sort of case in which the extreme utilitarian might go against the conventional moral rule. I have promised to a friend, dying on a desert island from which I am subsequently rescued, that I will see that his fortune (over which I have control) is given to a jockey club. However, when I am rescued I decide that it would be better to give the money to a hospital, which can do more good with it. It may be argued that I am wrong to give the money to the hospital. But why? (a) The hospital can do more good with the money than the jockey club can. (b) The present case is unlike most cases of promising in that no one except me knows about the promise. In breaking the promise I am doing so with complete secrecy and am doing nothing to weaken the general faith in promises. That is, a factor, which would normally keep the extreme utilitarian from promise breaking even in otherwise unoptimific cases, does not at present operate. (c) There is no doubt a slight weakening in my own character as an habitual promise keeper, and moreover psychological tensions will be set up in me every time I am asked what the man made me promise him to do. For clearly I shall have to say that he made me promise to give the money to the hospital, and, since I am an habitual truth teller, this will go very much against the grain with me. Indeed I am pretty sure that in practice I myself would keep the promise. But we are not discussing what my moral habits would probably make me do; we are discussing what I ought to do. Moreover, we must not forget that even if it would be most rational of me to give the money to the hospital it would also be most rational of you to punish or condemn me if you did, most improbably, find out the truth (e.g. by finding a note washed ashore in a bottle). Furthermore, I would agree that though it was most rational of me to give the money to the hospital it would be most rational of you to condemn me for it. We revert again to Sidgwick's distinction between the utility of the action and the utility of the praise of it.

Many such issues are discussed by A. K. Stout in the article to which I have already referred. I do not wish to go over the same ground again, especially as I think that Stout's arguments support my own point of view. It will be useful, however, to consider one other example that he gives. Suppose that during hot weather there is an edict that no water must be used for watering gardens. I have a garden and I reason that most people are sure to obey the edict, and that as the amount of water that I use will be by itself negligible no harm will be done if I use the water secretly. So I do use the water, thus producing some lovely flowers which give happiness to various people. Still, you may say, though the action was perhaps optimific, it was unfair and wrong.

There are several matters to consider. Certainly my action should be condemned. We revert once more to Sidgwick's distinction. A right action may be rationally condemned. Furthermore, this sort of offence is normally found out. If I have a wonderful garden when everybody else's is dry and brown there is only one explanation. So if I water my garden I am weakening my respect for law and order, and as this leads to bad results an extreme utilitarian would agree that I was wrong to water the garden. Suppose now that the case is altered and that I can keep the thing secret: there is a secluded part of the garden where I grow flowers which I give away anonymously to a home for old ladies. Are you still so sure that I did the wrong thing by watering my garden? However, this is still a weaker case than that of the hospital and the jockey club. There will be tensions set up within myself: my secret knowledge that I have broken the rule will make it hard for me to exhort others to keep the rule. These psychological ill effects in myself may be not inconsiderable: directly and indirecty they may lead to harm which is at least of the same order as the happiness that the old ladies get from the flowers. You can see that on an extreme utilitarian view there are two sides to the question.

So far I have been considering the duty of an extreme utilitarian in a predominantly non-utilitarian society. The case is altered if we consider the extreme utilitarian who lives in a society every member, or most members, of which can be expected to reason as he does. Should he water his flowers now? (Granting, what is doubtful, that in the case already considered he would have been right to water his flowers.) As a first approximation, the answer is that he should not do so. For since the situation is a com-

pletely symmetrical one, what is rational for him is rational for others. Hence, by a *reductio ad absurdum* argument, it would seem that watering his garden would be rational for none. Nevertheless, a more refined analysis shows that the above argument is not quite correct, though it is correct enough for practical purposes. The argument considers each person as confronted with the choice either of watering his garden or of not watering it. However there is a third possibility, which is that each person should, with the aid of a suitable randomizing device, such as throwing dice, give himself a certain probability of watering his garden. This would be to adopt what in the theory of games is called 'a mixed strategy'. If we could give numerical values to the private benefit of garden watering and to the public harm done by 1, 2, 3, etc., persons using the water in this way, we could work out a value of the probability of watering his garden that each extreme utilitarian should give himself. Let $a$ be the value which each extreme utilitarian gets from watering his garden, and let $f(1), f(2), f(3)$, etc., be the public harm done by exactly 1, 2, 3, etc., persons respectively watering their gardens. Suppose that $p$ is the probability that each person gives himself of watering his garden. Then we can easily calculate, as functions of $p$, the probabilities that exactly 1, 2, 3, etc., persons will water their gardens. Let these probabilities be $p_1, p_2, \ldots p_n$. Then the total net probable benefit can be expressed as

$$V = p_1 (a - f(1)) + p_2 (2a - f(2)) + \ldots p_n (na - f(n))$$

Then if we know the function $f(x)$ we can calculate the value of $p$ for which $(dV/dp) = 0$. This gives the value of $p$ which it would be rational for each extreme utilitarian to adopt. The present argument does not of course depend on a perhaps unjustified assumption that the values in question are measurable, and in a practical case such as that of the garden watering we can doubtless assume that $p$ will be so small that we can take it near enough as equal to zero. However the argument is of interest for the theoretical underpinning of extreme utilitarianism, since the possibility of a mixed strategy is usually neglected by critics of utilitarianism, who wrongly assume that the only relevant and symmetrical alternatives are of the form 'everybody does $X$' and 'nobody does $X$.'

I now pass on to a type of case which may be thought to be the trump card of restricted utilitarianism. Consider the rule of the road. It may be said that since all that matters is that everyone should do the same it is indifferent which rule we have, 'go on the left hand side' or 'go on the right hand side'. Hence the only *reason* for going on the left hand side in British countries is that this is the rule. Here the rule does seem to be a reason, in itself, for acting in a certain way. I wish to argue against this. The rule in itself is not a reason for our actions. We would be perfectly justified in going on the right hand side if *(a)* we knew that the rule was to go on the left hand side, and *(b)* we were in a country peopled by super-anarchists who always on principle did the opposite of what they were told. This shows that the rule does not give us a reason for acting so much as an indication of the probable actions of others, which helps us to find out what would be our own most rational course of action. If we are in a country not peopled by anarchists, but by non-anarchist extreme Utilitarians, we expect, other things being equal, that they will keep rules laid down for them. Knowledge of the rule enables us to predict their behaviour and to harmonize our own actions with theirs. The rule 'keep to the left hand side', then, is not a logical *reason* for action but an anthropological *datum* for planning actions.

I conclude that in every case if there is a rule *R* the keeping of which is in general optimific, but such that in a special sort of circumstances the optimific behaviour is to break *R*, then in these circumstances we should break *R*. Of course we must consider all the less obvious effects of breaking *R*, such as reducing people's faith in the moral order, before coming to the conclusion that to break *R* is right: in fact we shall rarely come to such a conclusion. Moral rules, on the extreme utilitarian view, are rules of thumb only, but they are not bad rules of thumb. But if we *do* come to the conclusion that we should break the rule and if we have weighed in the balance our own fallibility and liability to personal bias, what good reason remains for keeping the rule? I can understand 'it is optimific' as a reason for action, but why should 'it is a member of a class of actions which are usually optimific' or 'it is a member of a class of actions which as a class are more optimific than any alternative general class' be a good reason? You might as well say that a person ought to be picked to play for Australia just because all his brothers have been, or that the Australian team should be composed entirely of the Harvey family because this would be better than composing it entirely of any other family.

The extreme utilitarian does not appeal to artificial feelings, but only to our feelings of benevolence, and what better feelings can there be to appeal to? Admittedly we can have a pro-attitude to anything, even to rules, but such artificially begotten pro-attitudes smack of superstition. Let us get down to realities, human happiness and misery, and make these the objects of our pro-attitudes and anti-attitudes.

The restricted utilitarian might say that he is talking only of *morality*, not of such things as rules of the road. I am not sure how far this objection, if valid, would affect my argument, but in any case I would reply that as a philosopher I conceive of ethics as the study of how it would be *most rational* to act. If my opponent wishes to restrict the word 'morality' to a narrower use he can have the word. The fundamental question is the question of rationality of action *in general*. Similarly if the restricted utilitarian were to appeal to ordinary usage and say 'it might be most rational to leave Hitler to drown but it would surely not be *wrong* to rescue him', I should again let him have the words 'right' and 'wrong' and should stick to 'rational' and 'irrational'. We already say that it would be rational to praise Hitler's rescuer, even though it would have been most rational not to have rescued Hitler. In ordinary language, no doubt, 'right' and 'wrong' have not only the meaning 'most rational to do' and 'not most rational to do' but also have the meaning 'praiseworthy' and 'not praiseworthy'. Usually to the utility of an action corresponds utility of praise of it, but as we saw, this is not always so. Moral language could thus do with tidying up, for example by reserving 'right' for 'most rational' and 'good' as an epithet of praise for the motive from which the action sprang. It would be more becoming in a philosopher to try to iron out illogicalities in moral language and to make suggestions for its reform than to use it as a court of appeal whereby to perpetuate confusions. One last defence of restricted utilitarianism might be as follows. 'Act optimifically' might be regarded as itself one of the rules of our system (though it would be odd to say that this rule was justified by its optimificality). According to Toulmin (*The Place of Reason in Ethics*, pp. 146–8) if 'keep promises', say, conflicts with another rule we are allowed to argue the case on its merits, as if we were extreme utilitarians. If 'act optimifically' is itself one of our rules then there will always be a conflict of rules whenever to keep a rule is not itself optimific. If this is so, restricted utilitarianism collapses into extreme utilitarianism. And no one could read Toulmin's book or Urmson's article on Mill without thinking that Toulmin and Urmson are of the opinion that they have thought of a doctrine which does *not* collapse into extreme utilitarianism, but which is, on the contrary, an improvement on it.

# READING 15

# A Critique of Utilitarianism
*Bernard Williams*

*The English-born philosopher Bernard Williams (1929– ) has taught at the universities of Oxford, London, and Cambridge and has held visiting appointments in Ghana and Australia and in the United States at Princeton and Harvard. He was Provost of King's College and Knightbridge Professor of Philosophy at the University of Cambridge before becoming Professor of Philosophy at the University of California at Berkeley. His books include* Morality: An Introduction to Ethics *(1972),* Problems of the Self *(1973),* Descartes: The Project of Pure Enquiry *(1978), and* Ethics and the Limits of Philosophy *(1985).*

## NEGATIVE RESPONSIBILITY: AND TWO EXAMPLES

Consequentialism is basically indifferent to whether a state of affairs consists in what I do, or is produced by what I do, where that notion is itself wide enough to include, for instance, situations in which other people do things which I have made them do, or allowed them to do, or encouraged them to do, or given them a chance to do. All that consequentialism is interested in is the idea of these doings being *consequences* of what I do, and that is a relation broad enough to include the relations just mentioned, and many others.

SOURCE: From J.J.C. Smart and B.Williams, *Utilitarianism: For and Against* (Cambridge: Cambridge University Press, 1973): 96–117. Edited.

Just what the relation is, is a different question, and at least as obscure as the nature of its relative, cause and effect. It is not a question I shall try to pursue; I will rely on cases where I suppose that any consequentialist would be bound to regard the situations in question as consequences of what the agent does. There are cases where the supposed consequences stand in a rather remote relation to the action, which are sometimes difficult to assess from a practical point of view, but which raise no very interesting question for the present enquiry. The more interesting points about consequentialism lie rather elsewhere. There are certain situations in which the causation of the situation, the relation it has to what I do, is in no way remote or problematic in itself, and entirely justifies the claim that the situation is a consequence of what I do: for instance, it is quite clear, or reasonably clear, that if I do a certain thing, this situation will come about, and if I do not, it will not. So from a consequentialist point of view it goes into the calculation of consequences along with any other state of affairs accessible to me. Yet from some, at least, non-consequentialist points of view, there is a vital difference between some such situations and others: namely, that in some a vital link in the production of the eventual outcome is provided by *someone else's* doing something. But for consequentialism, all causal connexions are on the same level, and it makes no difference, so far as that goes, whether the causation of a given state of affairs lies through another agent, or not.

Correspondingly, there is no relevant difference which consists *just* in one state of affairs being brought about by me, without intervention of other agents, and another being brought about through the intervention of other agents; although some genuinely causal differences involving a difference of value may correspond to that (as when, for instance, the other agents derive pleasure or pain from the transaction), that kind of difference will already be included in the specification of the state of affairs to be produced. Granted that the states of affairs have been adequately described in causally and evaluatively relevant terms, it makes no further comprehensible difference who produces them. It is because consequentialism attaches value ultimately to states of affairs, and its concern is with what states of affairs the world contains, that it essentially involves the notion of *negative responsibility:* that if I am ever responsible for anything, then I must be just as much responsible for things that I allow or fail to prevent, as I am for things that I myself, in the more everyday restricted sense, bring about. Those things also must enter my deliberations, as a responsible moral agent, on the same footing. What matters is what states of affairs the world contains, and so what matters with respect to a given action is what comes about if it is done, and what comes about if it is not done, and those are questions not intrinsically affected by the nature of the causal linkage, in particular by whether the outcome is partly produced by other agents.

The strong doctrine of negative responsibility flows directly from consequentialism's assignment of ultimate value to states of affairs. Looked at from another point of view, it can be seen also as a special application of something that is favoured in many moral outlooks not themselves consequentialist—something which, indeed, some thinkers have been disposed to regard as the essence of morality itself: a principle of impartiality. Such a principle will claim that there can be no relevant difference from a moral point of view which consists just in the fact, not further explicable in general terms, that benefits or harms accrue to one person rather than to another—'it's me' can never in itself be a morally comprehensible reason.[1] This principle, familiar with regard to

the reception of harms and benefits, we can see consequentialism as extending to their production: from the moral point of view, there is no comprehensible difference which consists just in my bringing about a certain outcome rather than someone else's producing it. That the doctrine of negative responsibility represents in this way the extreme of impartiality, and abstracts from the identity of the agent, leaving just a locus of causal intervention in the world—that fact is not merely a surface paradox. It helps to explain why consequentialism can seem to some to express a more serious attitude than non-consequentialist views, why part of its appeal is to a certain kind of high-mindedness. Indeed, that is part of what is wrong with it.

For a lot of the time so far we have been operating at an exceedingly abstract level. This has been necessary in order to get clearer in general terms about the differences between consequentialist and other outlooks, an aim which is important if we want to know what features of them lead to what results for our thought. Now, however, let us look more concretely at two examples, to see what utilitarianism might say about them, what we might say about utilitarianism and, most importantly of all, what would be implied by certain ways of thinking about the situations. The examples are inevitably schematized, and they are open to the objection that they beg as many questions as they illuminate. There are two ways in particular in which examples in moral philosophy tend to beg important questions. One is that, as presented, they arbitrarily cut off and restrict the range of alternative courses of action—this objection might particularly be made against the first of my two examples. The second is that they inevitably present one with the situation as a going concern, and cut off questions about how the agent got into it, and correspondingly about moral considerations which might flow from that: this objection might perhaps specially arise with regard to the second of my two situations. These difficulties, however, just have to be accepted, and if anyone finds these examples cripplingly defective in this sort of respect, then he must in his own thought rework them in richer and less question-begging form. If he feels that no presentation of any imagined situation can ever be other than misleading in morality, and that there can never be any substitute for the concrete experienced complexity of actual moral situations, then this discussion, with him, must certainly grind

[1]There is a tendency in some writers to suggest that it is not a comprehensible reason at all. But this, I suspect, is due to the overwhelming importance those writers ascribe to the moral point of view.

to a halt: but then one may legitimately wonder whether every discussion with him about conduct will not grind to a halt, including any discussion about the actual situations, since discussion about how one would think and feel about situations somewhat different from the actual (that is to say, situations to that extent imaginary) plays an important role in discussion of the actual.

(1) George, who has just taken his Ph.D. in chemistry, finds it extremely difficult to get a job. He is not very robust in health, which cuts down the number of jobs he might be able to do satisfactorily. His wife has to go out to work to keep them, which itself causes a great deal of strain, since they have small children and there are severe problems about looking after them. The results of all this, especially on the children, are damaging. An older chemist, who knows about this situation, says that he can get George a decently paid job in a certain laboratory, which pursues research into chemical and biological warfare. George says that he cannot accept this, since he is opposed to chemical and biological warfare. The older man replies that he is not too keen on it himself, come to that, but after all George's refusal is not going to make the job or the laboratory go away; what is more, he happens to know that if George refuses the job, it will certainly go to a contemporary of George's who is not inhibited by any such scruples and is likely if appointed to push along the research with greater zeal than George would. Indeed, it is not merely concern for George and his family, but (to speak frankly and in confidence) some alarm about this other man's excess of zeal, which has led the older man to offer to use his influence to get George the job ... George's wife, to whom he is deeply attached, has views (the details of which need not concern us) from which it follows that at least there is nothing particularly wrong with research into CBW. What should he do?

(2) Jim finds himself in the central square of a small South American town. Tied up against the wall are a row of twenty Indians, most terrified, a few defiant, in front of them several armed men in uniform. A heavy man in a sweat-stained khaki shirt turns out to be the captain in charge and, after a good deal of questioning of Jim which establishes that he got there by accident while on a botanical expedition, explains that the Indians are a random group of the inhabitants who, after recent acts of protest against the government, are just about to be killed to remind other possible protestors of the advantages of not protesting. However, since Jim is an honoured visitor from another land, the captain is happy to offer him a guest's privilege of killing one of the Indians himself. If Jim accepts, then as a special mark of the occasion, the other Indians will be let off. Of course, if Jim refuses, then there is no special occasion, and Pedro here will do what he was about to do when Jim arrived, and kill them all. Jim, with some desperate recollection of schoolboy fiction, wonders whether if he got hold of a gun, he could hold the captain, Pedro and the rest of the soldiers to threat, but it is quite clear from the set-up that nothing of that kind is going to work: any attempt at that sort of thing will mean that all the Indians will be killed, and himself. The men against the wall, and the other villagers, understand the situation, and are obviously begging him to accept. What should he do?

To these dilemmas, it seems to me that utilitarianism replies, in the first case, that George should accept the job, and in the second, that Jim should kill the Indian. Not only does utilitarianism give these answers but, if the situations are essentially as described and there are no further special factors, it regards them, it seems to me, as *obviously* the right answers. But many of us would certainly wonder whether, in (1), that could possibly be the right answer at all; and in the case of (2), even one who came to think that perhaps that was the answer, might well wonder whether it was obviously the answer. Nor is it just a question of the rightness or obviousness of these answers. It is also a question of what sort of considerations come into finding the answer. A feature of utilitarianism is that it cuts out a kind of consideration which for some others makes a difference to what they feel about such cases: a consideration involving the idea, as we might first and very simply put it, that each of us is specially responsible for what *he* does, rather than for what other people do. This is an idea closely connected with the value of integrity. It is often suspected that utilitarianism, at least in its direct forms, makes integrity as a value more or less unintelligible. I shall try to show that this suspicion is correct. Of course, even if that is correct, it would not necessarily follow that we should reject utilitarianism; perhaps, as utilitarians sometimes suggest, we should just forget about integrity, in favour of such things as a concern for the general good. However, if I am right, we cannot merely do that, since the reason why utilitarianism cannot understand integrity is that it cannot coherently describe the relations between a man's projects and his actions.

## TWO KINDS OF REMOTER EFFECT

A lot of what we have to say about this question will be about the relations between my projects and other people's projects. But before we get on to that, we should first ask whether we are assuming too hastily what the utilitarian answers to the dilemmas will be. In terms of more direct effects of the possible decisions, there does not indeed seem much doubt about the answer in either case; but it might be said that in terms of more remote or less evident effects counterweights might be found to enter the utilitarian scales. Thus the effect on George of a decision to take the job might be invoked, or its effect on others who might know of his decision. The possibility of there being more beneficent labours in the future from which he might be barred or disqualified, might be mentioned; and so forth. Such effects—in particular, possible effects on the agent's character, and effects on the public at large—are often invoked by utilitarian writers dealing with problems about lying or promise-breaking, and some similar considerations might be invoked here.

There is one very general remark that is worth making about arguments of this sort. The certainty that attaches to these hypotheses about possible effects is usually pretty low; in some cases, indeed, the hypothesis invoked is so implausible that it would scarcely pass if it were not being used to deliver the respectable moral answer, as in the standard fantasy that one of the effects of one's telling a particular lie is to weaken the disposition of the world at large to tell the truth. The demands on the certainty or probability of these beliefs as beliefs about particular actions are much milder than they would be on beliefs favouring the unconventional course. It may be said that this is as it should be, since the presumption must be in favour of the conventional course: but that scarcely seems a *utilitarian* answer, unless utilitarianism has already taken off in the direction of not applying the consequences to the particular act at all.

Leaving aside that very general point, I want to consider now two types of effect that are often invoked by utilitarians, and which might be invoked in connexion with these imaginary cases. The attitude or tone involved in invoking these effects may some-

times seem peculiar; but that sort of peculiarity soon becomes familiar in utilitarian discussions, and indeed it can be something of an achievement to retain a sense of it.

First, there is the psychological effect on the agent. Our descriptions of these situations have not so far taken account of how George or Jim will be after they have taken the one course or the other; and it might be said that if they take the course which seemed at first the utilitarian one, the effects on them will be in fact bad enough and extensive enough to cancel out the initial utilitarian advantages of that course. Now there is one version of this effect in which, for a utilitarian, some confusion must be involved, namely that in which the agent feels bad, his subsequent conduct and relations are crippled and so on, *because he thinks that he has done the wrong thing*—for if the balance of outcomes was as it appeared to be *before* invoking this effect, then he has not (from the utilitarian point of view) done the wrong thing. So that version of the effect, for a rational and utilitarian agent, could not possibly make any difference to the assessment of right and wrong. However, perhaps he is not a thoroughly rational agent, and is disposed to have bad feelings, whichever he decided to do. Now such feelings, which are from a strictly utilitarian point of view irrational—nothing, a utilitarian can point out, is advanced by having them—cannot, consistently, have any great weight in a utilitarian calculation. I shall consider in a moment an argument to suggest that they should have no weight at all in it. But short of that, the utilitarian could reasonably say that such feelings should not be encouraged, even if we accept their existence, and that to give them a lot of weight is to encourage them. Or, at the very best, even if they are straightforwardly and without any discount to be put into the calculation, their weight must be small: they are after all (and at best) one man's feelings.

That consideration might seem to have particular force in Jim's case. In George's case, his feelings represent a larger proportion of what is to be weighed, and are more commensurate in character with other items in the calculation. In Jim's case, however, his feelings might seem to be of very little weight compared with other things that are at stake. There is a powerful and recognizable appeal that can be made on this point: as that a refusal by Jim to do what he has been invited to do would be a kind of self-indulgent squeamishness. That is an appeal which can be made by other than utilitarians—indeed, there are some uses of it which cannot be consistently made by utilitarians, as when it essentially involves the idea that there is something dishonourable about such self-indulgence. But in some versions it is a familiar, and it must be said a powerful, weapon of utilitarianism. One must be clear, though, about what it can and cannot accomplish. The most it can do, so far as I can see, is to invite one to consider how seriously, and for what reasons, one feels that what one is invited to do is (in these circumstances) wrong, and in particular, to consider that question from the utilitarian point of view. When the agent is not seeing the situation from a utilitarian point of view, the appeal cannot force him to do so; and if he does come round to seeing it from a utilitarian point of view, there is virtually nothing left for the appeal to do. If he does not see it from a utilitarian point of view, he will not see his resistance to the invitation, and the unpleasant feelings he associates with accepting it, *just* as disagreeable experiences of his; they figure rather as emotional expressions of a thought that to accept would be wrong. He may be asked, as by the appeal, to consider whether he is right, and indeed whether he is fully serious, in thinking that. But the assertion of the appeal, that he is being self-indulgently squeamish, will not itself answer that question, or even help to answer it, since it essentially tells him to regard his feelings just as unpleasant experiences of his, and he cannot, by doing that, answer the question they pose when they are precisely not so regarded, but are regarded as indications[2] of what he thinks is right and wrong. If he does come round fully to the utilitarian point of view then of course he will regard these feelings just as unpleasant experiences of his. And once Jim—at least—has come to see them in that light, there is nothing left for the appeal to do, since *of course* his feelings, so regarded, are of virtually no weight at all in relation to the other things at stake. The 'squeamishness' appeal is not an argument which adds in a hitherto neglected consideration. Rather, it is an invitation to consider the situation, and one's own feelings, from a utilitarian point of view.

[2]On the non-cognitivist meta-ethic in terms of which Smart presents his utilitarianism, the term 'indications' here would represent an understatement.

The reason why the squeamishness appeal can be very unsettling, and one can be unnerved by the suggestion of self-indulgence in going against utilitarian considerations, is not that we are utilitarians who are uncertain what utilitarian value to attach to our moral feelings, but that we are partially at least not utilitarians, and cannot regard our moral feelings merely as objects of utilitarian value. Because our moral relation to the world is partly given by such feelings, and by a sense of what we can or cannot 'live with', to come to regard those feelings from a purely utilitarian point of view, that is to say, as happenings outside one's moral self, is to lose a sense of one's moral identity; to lose, in the most literal way, one's integrity. At this point utilitarianism alienates one from one's moral feelings; we shall see a little later how, more basically, it alienates one from one's actions as well.

If, then, one is really going to regard one's feelings from a strictly utilitarian point of view, Jim should give very little weight at all to his; it seems almost indecent, in fact, once one has taken that point of view, to suppose that he should give any at all. In George's case one might feel that things were slightly different. It is interesting, though, that one reason why one might think that—namely that one person principally affected is his wife—is very dubiously available to a utilitarian. George's wife has some reason to be interested in George's integrity and his sense of it; the Indians, quite properly, have no interest in Jim's. But it is not at all clear how utilitarianism would describe that difference.

There is an argument, and a strong one, that a strict utilitarian should give not merely small extra weight, in calculations of right and wrong, to feelings of this kind, but that he should give absolutely no weight to them at all. This is based on the point, which we have already seen, that if a course of action is, before taking these sorts of feelings into account, utilitarianly preferable, then bad feelings about that kind of action will be from a utilitarian point of view irrational. Now it might be thought that even if that is so, it would not mean that in a utilitarian calculation such feelings should not be taken into account; it is after all a well-known boast of utilitarianism that it is a realistic outlook which seeks the best in the world as it is, and takes any form of happiness or unhappiness into account. While a utilitarian will no doubt seek to diminish the incidence of feelings which are utilitarianly irrational—or at least of disagreeable feelings which are so—he might be expected to take them into account while they exist. This is without doubt classical utilitarian doctrine, but there is good reason to think that utilitarianism cannot stick to it without embracing results which are startlingly unacceptable and perhaps self-defeating.

Suppose that there is in a certain society a racial minority. Considering merely the ordinary interests of the other citizens, as opposed to their sentiments, this minority does no particular harm; we may suppose that it does not confer any very great benefits either. Its presence is in those terms neutral or mildly beneficial. However, the other citizens have such prejudices that they find the sight of this group, even the knowledge of its presence, very disagreeable. Proposals are made for removing in some way this minority. If we assume various quite plausible things (as that programmes to change the majority sentiment are likely to be protracted and ineffective) then even if the removal would be unpleasant for the minority, a utilitarian calculation might well end up favouring this step, especially if the minority were a rather small minority and the majority were very severely prejudiced, that is to say, were made very severely uncomfortable by the presence of the minority.

A utilitarian might find that conclusion embarrassing; and not merely because of its nature, but because of the grounds on which it is reached. While a utilitarian might be expected to take into account certain other sorts of consequences of the prejudice, as that a majority prejudice is likely to be displayed in conduct disagreeable to the minority, and so forth, he might be made to wonder whether the unpleasant experiences of the prejudiced people should be allowed, *merely as such,* to count. If he does count them, merely as such, then he has once more separated himself from a body of ordinary moral thought which he might have hoped to accommodate; he may also have started on the path of defeating his own view of things. For one feature of these sentiments is that they are from the utilitarian point of view itself irrational, and a thoroughly utilitarian person would either not have them, or if he found that he did tend to have them, would himself seek to discount them. Since the sentiments in question are such that a rational utilitarian would discount them in himself, it is reasonable to suppose that he should discount them in his calculations about society; it does seem quite unreasonable for him to give just as

much weight to feelings—considered just in themselves, one must recall, as experiences of those that have them—which are essentially based on views which are from a utilitarian point of view irrational, as to those which accord with utilitarian principles. Granted this idea, it seems reasonable for him to rejoin a body of moral thought in other respects congenial to him, and discount those sentiments, just considered in themselves, totally, on the principle that no pains or discomforts are to count in the utilitarian sum which their subjects have just because they hold views which are by utilitarian standards irrational. But if he accepts that, then in the cases we are at present considering no extra weight at all can be put in for bad feelings of George or Jim about their choices, if those choices are, leaving out those feelings, on the first round utilitarianly rational.

The psychological effect on the agent was the first of two general effects considered by utilitarians, which had to be discussed. The second is in general a more substantial item, but it need not take so long, since it is both clearer and has little application to the present cases. This is the *precedent effect.* As Burke rightly emphasized, this effect can be important: that one morally *can* do what someone has actually done, is a psychologically effective principle, if not a deontically valid one. For the effect to operate, obviously some conditions must hold on the publicity of the act and on such things as the status of the agent (such considerations weighed importantly with Sir Thomas More); what these may be will vary evidently with circumstances.

In order for the precedent effect to make a difference to a utilitarian calculation, it must be based upon a confusion. For suppose that there is an act which would be the best in the circumstances, except that doing it will encourage by precedent other people to do things which will not be the best things to do. Then the situation of those other people must be relevantly different from that of the original agent; if it were not, then in doing the same as what would be the best course for the original agent, they would necessarily do the best thing themselves. But if the situations are in this way relevantly different, it must be a confused perception which takes the first situation, and the agent's course in it, as an adequate precedent for the second.

However, the fact that the precedent effect, if it really makes a difference, is in this sense based on a confusion, does not mean that it is not perfectly real, nor that it is to be discounted: social effects are by their nature confused in this sort of way. What it does emphasize is that calculations of the precedent effect have got to be realistic, involving considerations of how people are actually likely to be influenced. In the present examples, however, it is very implausible to think that the precedent effect could be invoked to make any difference to the calculation. Jim's case is extraordinary enough, and it is hard to imagine who the recipients of the effect might be supposed to be; while George is not in a sufficiently public situation or role for the question to arise in that form, and in any case one might suppose that the motivations of others on such an issue were quite likely to be fixed one way or another already.

No appeal, then, to these other effects is going to make a difference to what the utilitarian will decide about our examples. Let us now look more closely at the structure of those decisions.

## INTEGRITY

The situations have in common that if the agent does not do a certain disagreeable thing, someone else will, and in Jim's situation at least the result, the state of affairs after the other man has acted, if he does, will be worse than after Jim has acted, if Jim does. The same, on a smaller scale, is true of George's case. I have already suggested that it is inherent in consequentialism that it offers a strong doctrine of negative responsibility: if I know that if I do $X$, $O_1$ will eventuate, and if I refrain from doing $X$, $O_2$ will, and that $O_2$ is worse than $O_1$, then I am responsible for $O_2$ if I refrain voluntarily from doing $X$. 'You could have prevented it', as will be said, and truly, to Jim, if he refuses, by the relatives of the other Indians. (I shall leave the important question, which is to the side of the present issue, of the obligations, if any, that nest round the word 'know': how far does one, under utilitarianism, have to research into the possibilities of maximally beneficent action, including prevention?)

In the present cases, the situation of $O_2$ includes another agent bringing about results worse than $O_1$. So far as $O_2$ has been identified up to this point—merely as the worse outcome which will eventuate if I refrain from doing $X$—we might equally have said that what that other brings about is $O_2$; but that would be to underdescribe the situation. For what occurs if Jim refrains from action is not solely twenty Indians dead, but *Pedro's killing twenty Indians,* and

that is not a result which Pedro brings about, though the death of the Indians is. We can say; what one does is not included in the outcome of what one does, while what another does can be included in the outcome of what one does. For that to be so, as the terms are now being used, only a very weak condition has to be satisfied: for Pedro's killing the Indians to be the outcome of Jim's refusal, it only has to be causally true that if Jim had not refused, Pedro would not have done it.

That may be enough for us to speak, in some sense, of Jim's responsibility for that outcome, if it occurs; but it is certainly not enough, it is worth noticing, for us to speak of Jim's *making* those things happen. For granted this way of their coming about, he could have made them happen only by making Pedro shoot, and there is no acceptable sense in which his refusal makes Pedro shoot. If the captain had said on Jim's refusal, 'you leave me with no alternative', he would have been lying, like most who use that phrase. While the deaths, and the killing, may be the outcome of Jim's refusal, it is misleading to think, in such a case, of Jim having an *effect* on the world through the medium (as it happens) of Pedro's acts; for this is to leave Pedro out of the picture in his essential role of one who has intentions and projects, projects for realizing which Jim's refusal would leave an opportunity. Instead of thinking in terms of supposed effects of Jim's projects on Pedro, it is more revealing to think in terms of the effects of Pedro's projects on Jim's decision. This is the direction from which I want to criticize the notion of negative responsibility.

There are of course other ways in which this notion can be criticized. Many have hoped to discredit it by insisting on the basic moral relevance of the distinction between action and inaction, between intervening and letting things take their course. The distinction is certainly of great moral significance, and indeed it is not easy to think of any moral outlook which could get along without making some use of it. But it is unclear, both in itself and in its moral applications, and the unclarities are of a kind which precisely cause it to give way when, in very difficult cases, weight has to be put on it. There is much to be said in this area, but I doubt whether the sort of dilemma we are considering is going to be resolved by a simple use of this distinction. Again, the issue of negative responsibility can be pressed on the question of how limits are to be placed on one's apparently boundless obligation, implied by utilitarianism, to improve the world. Some answers are needed to that, too—and answers which stop short of relapsing into the bad faith of supposing that one's responsibilities could be adequately characterized just by appeal to one's roles.[3] But, once again, while that is a real question, it cannot be brought to bear directly on the present kind of case, since it is hard to think of anyone supposing that in Jim's case it would be an adequate response for him to say that it was none of his business.

What projects does a utilitarian agent have? As a utilitarian, he has the general project of bringing about maximally desirable outcomes; how he is to do this at any given moment is a question of what causal levers, so to speak, are at that moment within reach. The desirable outcomes, however, do not just consist of agents carrying out *that* project; there must be other more basic or lower-order projects which he and other agents have, and the desirable outcomes are going to consist, in part, of the maximally harmonious realization of those projects ('in part', because one component of a utilitarianly desirable outcome may be the occurrence of agreeable experiences which are not the satisfaction of anybody's projects). Unless there were first-order projects, the general utilitarian project would have nothing to work on, and would be vacuous. What do the more basic or lower-order projects comprise? Many will be the obvious kinds of desires for things for oneself, one's family, one's friends, including basic necessities of life, and in more relaxed circumstances, objects of taste. Or there may be pursuits and interests of an intellectual, cultural or creative character. I introduce those as a separate class not because the objects of them lie in a separate class, and provide—as some utilitarians, in their churchy way, are fond of saying—'higher' pleasures. I introduce them separately because the agent's identification with them may be of a different order. It does not have to be: cultural and aesthetic interests just belong, for many, along with any other taste; but some people's commitment to these kinds of interests just is at once more thoroughgoing and serious than their pursuit of various objects of taste, while it is more individual

and permeated with character than the desire for the necessities of life.

Beyond these, someone may have projects connected with his support of some cause: Zionism, for instance, or the abolition of chemical and biological warfare. Or there may be projects which flow from some more general disposition towards human conduct and character, such as a hatred of injustice, or of cruelty, or of killing.

It may be said that this last sort of disposition and its associated project do not count as (logically) 'lower-order' relative to the higher-order project of maximizing desirable outcomes; rather, it may be said, it is itself a 'higher-order' project. The vital question is not, however, how it is to be classified, but whether it and similar projects are to count among the projects whose satisfaction is to be included in the maximizing sum, and, correspondingly, as contributing to the agent's happiness. If the utilitarian says 'no' to that, then he is almost certainly committed to a version of utilitarianism as absurdly superficial and shallow as Benthamite versions have often been accused of being. For this project will be discounted, presumably, on the ground that it involves, in the specification of its object, the mention of other people's happiness or interests: thus it is the kind of project which (unlike the pursuit of food for myself) presupposes a reference to other people's projects. But that criterion would eliminate any desire at all which was not blankly and in the most straightforward sense egoistic.[4] Thus we should be reduced to frankly egoistic first-order projects, and—for all essential purposes—the one second-order utilitarian project of maximally satisfying first-order projects. Utilitarianism has a tendency to slide in this direction, and to leave a vast hole in the range of human desires, between egoistic inclinations and necessities at one end, and impersonally benevolent happiness-management at the other. But the utilitarianism which has to leave this hole is the most primitive form, which offers a quite rudimentary account of desire. Modern versions of the theory are supposed to be neutral with regard to what sorts of things make people happy or what their projects are. Utilitarianism would do well then to acknowledge the ev-

---

[3]For some remarks bearing on this, see *Morality*, the section on 'Goodness and roles', and Cohen's article there cited.

[4]On the subject of egoistic and non-egoistic desires, see 'Egoism and altruism', in *Problems of the Self* (Cambridge University Press, London, 1973).

ident fact that among the things that make people happy is not only making other people happy, but being taken up or involved in any of a vast range of projects, or—if we waive the evangelical and moralizing associations of the word—commitments. One can be committed to such things as a person, a cause, an institution, a career, one's own genius, or the pursuit of danger.

Now none of these is itself the *pursuit of happiness:* by an exceedingly ancient platitude, it is not at all clear that there could be anything which was just that, or at least anything that had the slightest chance of being successful. Happiness, rather, requires being involved in, or at least content with, something else.[5] It is not impossible for utilitarianism to accept that point: it does not have to be saddled with a naïve and absurd philosophy of mind about the relation between desire and happiness. What it does have to say is that if such commitments are worth while, then pursuing the projects that flow from them, and realizing some of those projects, will make the person for whom they are worth while, happy. It may be that to claim that is still wrong: it may well be that a commitment can make sense to a man (can make sense of his life) without his supposing that it will make him *happy*.[6] But that is not the present point; let us grant to utilitarianism that all worthwhile human projects must conduce, one way or another, to happiness. The point is that even if that is true, it does not follow, nor could it possibly be true, that those projects are themselves projects of pursuing happiness. One has to believe in, or at least want, or quite minimally, be content with, other things, for there to be anywhere that happiness can come from.

Utilitarianism, then, should be willing to agree that its general aim of maximizing happiness does not imply that what everyone is doing is just pursuing happiness. On the contrary, people have to be pursuing other things. What those other things may be, utilitarianism, sticking to its professed empirical stance, should be prepared just to find out. No doubt some possible projects it will want to discourage, on the grounds that their being pursued involves a negative balance of happiness to others: though even there, the unblinking accountant's eye of the strict utilitarian will have something to put in the positive column, the satisfactions of the destructive agent. Beyond that, there will be a vast variety of generally beneficent or at least harmless projects; and some no doubt, will take the form not just of tastes or fancies, but of what I have called 'commitments'. It may even be that the utilitarian researcher will find that many of those with commitments, who have really identified themselves with objects outside themselves, who are thoroughly involved with other persons, or institutions, or activities or causes, are actually happier than those whose projects and wants are not like that. If so, that is an important piece of utilitarian empirical lore.

When I say 'happier' here, I have in mind the sort of consideration which any utilitarian would be committed to accepting: as for instance that such people are less likely to have a break-down or commit suicide. Of course that is not all that is actually involved, but the point in this argument is to use to the maximum degree utilitarian notions, in order to locate a breaking point in utilitarian thought. In appealing to this strictly utilitarian notion, I am being more consistent with utilitarianism than Smart is. In his struggles with the problem of the brain-electrode man, Smart (p. 22) commends the idea that 'happy' is a partly evaluative term, in the sense that we call 'happiness' those kinds of satisfaction which, as things are, we approve of. But *by what standard* is this surplus element of approval supposed, from a utilitarian point of view, to be allocated? There is no source for it, on a strictly utilitarian view, except further degrees of satisfaction, but there are none of those available, or the problem would not arise. Nor does it help to appeal to the fact that we dislike in prospect things which we like when we get there, for from a utilitarian point of view it would seem that the original dislike was merely irrational or based on an error. Smart's argument at this point seems to be embarrassed by a well-known utilitarian uneasiness, which comes from a feeling that it is not respectable

---

[5]This does not imply that there is no such thing as the project of pursuing pleasure. Some writers who have correctly resisted the view that all desires are desires for pleasure, have given an account of pleasure so thoroughly adverbial as to leave it quite unclear how there could be a distinctively hedonist way of life at all. Some room has to be left for that, though there are important difficulties both in defining it and living it. Thus (particularly in the case of the very rich) it often has highly ritual aspects, apparently part of a strategy to counter boredom.

[6]For some remarks on this possibility, see *Morality*, section on 'What is morality about?'

to ignore the 'deep', while not having anywhere left in human life to locate it.[7]

Let us now go back to the agent as utilitarian, and his higher-order project of maximizing desirable outcomes. At this level, he is committed only to that: what the outcome will actually consist of will depend entirely on the facts, on what persons with what projects and what potential satisfactions there are within calculable reach of the causal levers near which he finds himself. His own substantial projects and commitments come into it, but only as one lot among others—they potentially provide one set of satisfactions among those which he may be able to assist from where he happens to be. He is the agent of the satisfaction system who happens to be at a particular point at a particular time: in Jim's case, our man in South America. His own decisions as a utilitarian agent are a function of all the satisfactions which he can affect from where he is: and this means that the projects of others, to an indeterminately great extent, determine his decision.

This may be so either positively or negatively. It will be so positively if agents within the causal field of his decision have projects which are at any rate harmless, and so should be assisted. It will equally be so, but negatively, if there is an agent within the causal field whose projects are harmful, and have to be frustrated to maximize desirable outcomes. So it is with Jim and the soldier Pedro. On the utilitarian view, the undesirable projects of other people as much determine, in this negative way, one's decisions as the desirable ones do positively: if those people were not there, or had different projects, the causal nexus would be different, and it is the actual state of the causal nexus which determines the decision. The determination to an indefinite degree of my decisions by other people's projects is just another aspect of my unlimited responsibility to act for the best in a causal framework formed to a considerable extent by their projects.

The decision so determined is, for utilitarianism, the right decision. But what if it conflicts with some project of mine? This, the utilitarian will say, has already been dealt with: the satisfaction to you of fulfilling your project, and any satisfactions to others of your so doing, have already been through the calcu-

lating device and have been found inadequate. Now in the case of many sorts of projects, that is a perfectly reasonable sort of answer. But in the case of projects of the sort I have called 'commitments', those with which one is more deeply and extensively involved and identified, this cannot just by itself be an adequate answer, and there may be no adequate answer at all. For, to take the extreme sort of case, how can a man, as a utilitarian agent, come to regard as one satisfaction among others, and a dispensable one, a project or attitude round which he has built his life, just because someone else's projects have so structured the causal scene that that is how the utilitarian sum comes out?

The point here is not, as utilitarians may hasten to say, that if the project or attitude is that central to his life, then to abandon it will be very disagreeable to him and great loss of utility will be involved. I have already argued in section 4 that it is not like that; on the contrary, once he is prepared to look at it like that, the argument in any serious case is over anyway. The point is that he is identified with his actions as flowing from projects and attitudes which in some cases he takes seriously at the deepest level, as what his life is about (or, in some cases, this section of his life—seriousness is not necessarily the same as persistence). It is absurd to demand of such a man, when the sums come in from the utility network which the projects of others have in part determined, that he should just step aside from his own project and decision and acknowledge the decision which utilitarian calculation requires. It is to alienate him in a real sense from his actions and the source of his action in his own convictions. It is to make him into a channel between the input of everyone's projects, including his own, and an output of optimific decision; but this is to neglect the extent to which *his* actions and *his* decisions have to be seen as the actions and decisions which flow from the projects and attitudes with which he is most closely identified. It is thus, in the most literal sense, an attack on his integrity.[8]

---

[7]One of many resemblances in spirit between utilitarianism and high-minded evangelical Christianity.

[8]Interestingly related to these notions is the Socratic idea that courage is a virtue particularly connected with keeping a clear sense of what one regards as most important. They also centrally raise questions about the value of pride. Humility, as something beyond the real demand of correct self-appraisal, was specially a Christian virtue because it involved subservience to God. In a secular context it can only represent subservience to other men and their projects.

These sorts of considerations do not in themselves give solutions to practical dilemmas such as those provided by our examples; but I hope they help to provide other ways of thinking about them. In fact, it is not hard to see that in George's case, viewed from this perspective, the utilitarian solution would be wrong. Jim's case is different, and harder. But if (as I suppose) the utilitarian is probably right in this case, that is not to be found out just by asking the utilitarian's questions. Discussions of it—and I am not going to try to carry it further here—will have to take seriously the distinction between my killing someone, and its coming about because of what I do that someone else kills them: a distinction based, not so much on the distinction between action and inaction, as on the distinction between my projects and someone else's projects. At least it will have to start by taking that seriously, as utilitarianism does not; but then it will have to build out from there by asking why that distinction seems to have less, or a different, force in this case than it has in George's. One question here would be how far one's powerful objection to killing people just is, in fact, an application of a powerful objection to their being killed. Another dimension of that is the issue of how much it matters that the people at risk are actual, and there, as opposed to hypothetical, or future, or merely elsewhere.[9]

There are many other considerations that could come into such a question, but the immediate point of all this is to draw one particular contrast with utilitarianism: that to reach a grounded decision in such a case should not be regarded as a matter of just discounting one's reactions, impulses and deeply held projects in the face of the pattern of utilities, nor yet merely adding them in—but in the first instance of trying to understand them.

Of course, time and circumstances are unlikely to make a grounded decision, in Jim's case at least, possible. It might not even be decent. Instead of thinking in a rational and systematic way either about utilities or about the value of human life, the relevance of the people at risk being present, and so forth, the presence of the people at risk may just have its effect. The significance of the immediate should not be underestimated. Philosophers, not only utilitarian ones, repeatedly urge one to view the world *sub specie aeternitatis*,[10] but for most human purposes that is not a good *species* to view it under. If we are not agents of the universal satisfaction system, we are not primarily janitors of any system of values, even our own: very often, we just act, as a possibly confused result of the situation in which we are engaged. That, I suspect, is very often an exceedingly good thing.

---

[9]For a more general discussion of this issue see Charles Fried, *An Anatomy of Values* (Harvard University Press, Cambridge, Mass., 1970), Part Three.

[10]Cf. Smart, *Utilitarianism: For and Against*, p. 63.

**READING 16**

---

# The Categorical Imperative
*Immanuel Kant*

*The Prussian philosopher Immanuel Kant (1724–1804) spent his entire academic life lecturing and writing in Königsberg, a city now called Kaliningrad that lies within the Soviet Union. Kant wrote widely on subjects ranging from epistemology and philosophy of science to philosophy of religion, ethics, and aesthetics. His most famous work, the* Critique of Pure Reason *(1781), has had a tremendous influence on the development of philosophy. Among Kant's works on ethics, the best-known and most widely read is his* Groundwork of the Metaphysic of Morals *(1785), often referred to simply as the* Groundwork. *This book is short: just three chapters, of which our anthology includes an excerpt from Chapter 2, dealing with the core of Kant's theory. The translation is by the distinguished Kant scholar, H. J. Paton.*

All *imperatives* command either *hypothetically* or *categorically*. Hypothetical imperatives declare a possible action to be practically necessary as a means to the attainment of something else that one wills (or that one may will). A categorical imperative would be one which represented an action as objectively necessary in itself apart from its relation to a further end.

Every practical law represents a possible action as good and therefore as necessary for a subject whose actions are determined by reason. Hence all imperatives are formulae for determining an action which is necessary in accordance with the principle of a will in some sense good. If the action would be good solely as a means *to something else*, the imperative is *hypothetical;* if the action is represented as good *in itself* and therefore as necessary, in virtue of its princi-

**SOURCE:** From *Groundwork of the Metaphysic of Morals* (1785). Reprinted from *The Moral Law*, trans. H. J. Paton (New York: Harper & Row, 1948): 82–92. Edited.

ple, for a will which of itself accords with reason, then the imperative is *categorical*.

An imperative therefore tells me which of my possible actions would be good; and it formulates a practical rule for a will that does not perform an action straight away because the action is good—whether because the subject does not always know that it is good or because, even if he did know this, he might still act on maxims contrary to the objective principles of practical reason.

A hypothetical imperative thus says only that an action is good for some purpose or other, either *possible* or *actual*. In the first case it is a *problematic* practical principle; in the second case an *assertoric* practical principle. A categorical imperative, which declares an action to be objectively necessary in itself without reference to some purpose—that is, even without any further end—ranks as an *apodeictic* practical principle.

Everything that is possible only through the efforts of some rational being can be conceived as a possible purpose of some will; and consequently there are in fact innumerable principles of action so far as action is thought necessary in order to achieve some possible purpose which can be effected by it. All sciences have a practical part consisting of problems which suppose that some end is possible for us and of imperatives which tell us how it is to be attained. Hence the latter can in general be called imperatives of *skill*. Here there is absolutely no question about the rationality or goodness of the end, but only about what must be done to attain it. A prescription required by a doctor in order to cure his man completely and one required by a poisoner in order to make sure of killing him are of equal value so far as each serves to effect its purpose perfectly. Since in early youth we do not know what ends may present themselves to us in the course of life, parents seek above all to make their children learn things *of many kinds;* they provide carefully for *skill* in the use of means to all sorts of *arbitrary* ends, of none of which can they be certain that it could not in the future become an actual purpose of their ward, while it is always *possible* that he might adopt it. Their care in this matter is so great that they commonly neglect on this account to form and correct the judgment of their children about the worth of the things which they might possibly adopt as ends.

There is, however, *one* end that can be presupposed as actual in all rational beings (so far as they are dependent beings to whom imperatives apply); and thus there is one purpose which they not only *can* have, but which we can assume with certainty that they all *do* have by a natural necessity—the purpose, namely, of *happiness.* A hypothetical imperative which affirms the practical necessity of an action as a means to the furtherance of happiness is *assertoric.* We may represent it, not simply as necessary to an uncertain, merely possible purpose, but as necessary to a purpose which we can presuppose *a priori* and with certainty to be present in every man because it belongs to his very being. Now skill in the choice of means to one's own greatest well-being can be called *prudence*[1] in the narrowest sense. Thus an imperative concerned with the choice of means to one's own happiness—that is, a precept of prudence—still remains *hypothetical*: an action is commanded, not absolutely, but only as a means to a further purpose.

Finally, there is an imperative which, without being based on, and conditioned by, any further purpose to be attained by a certain line of conduct, enjoins this conduct immediately. This imperative is *categorical.* It is concerned, not with the matter of the action and its presumed results, but with its form and with the principle from which it follows; and what is essentially good in the action consists in the mental disposition, let the consequences be what

they may. This imperative may be called the imperative of *morality.*

Willing in accordance with these three kinds of principle is also sharply distinguished by a *dissimilarity* in the necessitation of the will. To make this dissimilarity obvious we should, I think, name these kinds of principle most appropriately in their order if we said they were either *rules* of skill or *counsels* of prudence or *commands (laws)* of morality. For only *law* carries with it the concept of an *unconditioned,* and yet objective and so universally valid, *necessity;* and commands are laws which must be obeyed—that is, must be followed even against inclination. *Counsel* does indeed involve necessity, but necessity valid only under a subjective and contingent condition—namely, if this or that man counts this or that as belonging to his happiness. As against this, a categorical imperative is limited by no condition and can quite precisely be called a command, as being absolutely, although practically necessary. We could also call imperatives of the first kind *technical* (concerned with art); of the second kind *pragmatic*[2] (concerned with well-being); of the third kind *moral* (concerned with free conduct as such—that is, with morals).

The question now arises 'How are all these imperatives possible?' This question does not ask how we can conceive the execution of an action commanded by the imperative, but merely how we can conceive the necessitation of the will expressed by the imperative in setting us a task. How an imperative of skill is possible requires no special discussion. Who wills the end, wills (so far as reason has decisive influence on his actions) also the means which are indispensably necessary and in his power. So far as willing is concerned, this proposition is analytic: for in my willing of an object as an effect there is already conceived the causality of myself as an acting cause—that is, the use of means; and from the concept of willing an end the imperative merely extracts the concept of ac-

---

[1] The word 'prudence' (*Klugheit*) is used in a double sense: in one sense it can have the name of 'worldly wisdom' (*Weltklugheit*); in a second sense that of 'personal wisdom' (*Privatklugheit*). The first is the skill of a man in influencing others in order to use them for his own ends. The second is sagacity in combining all these ends to his own lasting advantage. The latter is properly that to which the value of the former can itself be traced; and of him who is prudent in the first sense, but not in the second, we might better say that he is clever and astute, but on the whole imprudent.

[2] It seems to me that the proper meaning of the word '*pragmatic*' can be defined most accurately in this way. For those *Sanctions* are called Pragmatic which, properly speaking, do not spring as necessary laws from the Natural Right of States, but from *forethought* in regard to the general welfare. A *history* is written pragmatically when it teaches *prudence*—that is, when it instructs the world of to-day how to provide for its own advantage better than, or at least as well as, the world of other times.

tions necessary to this end. (Synthetic propositions are required in order to determine the means to a proposed end, but these are concerned, not with the reason for performing the act of will, but with the cause which produces the object.) That in order to divide a line into two equal parts on a sure principle I must from its ends describe two intersecting arcs—this is admittedly taught by mathematics only in synthetic propositions; but when I know that the aforesaid effect can be produced only by such an action, the proposition 'If I fully will the effect, I also will the action required for it' is analytic; for it is one and the same thing to conceive something as an effect possible in a certain way through me and to conceive myself as acting in the same way with respect to it.

If it were only as easy to find a determinate concept of happiness, the imperatives of prudence would agree entirely with those of skill and would be equally analytic. For here as there it could alike be said 'Who wills the end, wills also (necessarily, if he accords with reason) the sole means which are in his power'. Unfortunately, however, the concept of happiness is so indeterminate a concept that although every man wants to attain happiness, he can never say definitely and in unison with himself what it really is that he wants and wills. The reason for this is that all the elements which belong to the concept of happiness are without exception empirical—that is, they must be borrowed from experience; but that none the less there is required for the Idea of happiness an absolute whole, a maximum of well-being in my present, and in every future, state. Now it is impossible for the most intelligent, and at the same time most powerful, but nevertheless finite, being to form here a determinate concept of what he really wills. Is it riches that he wants? How much anxiety, envy, and pestering might he not bring in this way on his own head! Is it knowledge and insight? This might perhaps merely give him an eye so sharp that it would make evils at present hidden from him and yet unavoidable seem all the more frightful, or would add a load of still further needs to the desires which already give him trouble enough. Is it long life? Who will guarantee that it would not be a long misery? Is it at least health? How often has infirmity of body kept a man from excesses into which perfect health would have let him fall!—and so on. In short, he has no principle by which he is able to decide with complete certainty what will make him truly happy,

since for this he would require omniscience. Thus we cannot act on determinate principles in order to be happy, but only on empirical counsels, for example, of diet, frugality, politeness, reserve, and so on—things which experience shows contribute most to well-being on the average. From this it follows that imperatives of prudence, speaking strictly, do not command at all—that is, cannot exhibit actions objectively as practically *necessary*; that they are rather to be taken as recommendations (*consilia*), than as commands (*praecepta*), of reason; that the problem of determining certainly and universally what action will promote the happiness of a rational being is completely insoluble; and consequently that in regard to this there is no imperative possible which in the strictest sense could command us to do what will make us happy, since happiness is an Ideal, not of reason, but of imagination—an Ideal resting merely on empirical grounds, of which it is vain to expect that they should determine an action by which we could attain the totality of a series of consequences which is in fact infinite. Nevertheless, if we assume that the means to happiness could be discovered with certainty, this imperative of prudence would be an analytic practical proposition; for it differs from the imperative of skill only in this—that in the latter the end is merely possible, while in the former the end is given. In spite of this difference, since both command solely the means to something assumed to be willed as an end, the imperative which commands him who wills the end to will the means is in both cases analytic. Thus there is likewise no difficulty in regard to the possibility of an imperative of prudence.

Beyond all doubt, the question 'How is the imperative of *morality* possible?' is the only one in need of a solution; for it is in no way hypothetical, and consequently we cannot base the objective necessity which it affirms on any presupposition, as we can with hypothetical imperatives. Only we must never forget here that it is impossible to settle *by an example*, and so empirically, whether there is any imperative of this kind at all: we must rather suspect that all imperatives which seem to be categorical may none the less be covertly hypothetical. Take, for example, the saying 'Thou shalt make no false promises'. Let us assume that the necessity for this abstention is no mere advice for the avoidance of some further evil—as it might be said 'You ought not to make a lying promise lest, when this comes to light, you destroy your credit'. Let us hold, on the contrary, that an action of this kind must be considered as bad in itself, and that the imperative of prohibition is therefore categorical. Even so, we cannot with any certainty show by an example that the will is determined here solely by the law without any further motive, although it may appear to be so; for it is always possible that fear of disgrace, perhaps also hidden dread of other risks, may unconsciously influence the will. Who can prove by experience that a cause is not present? Experience shows only that it is not perceived. In such a case, however, the so-called moral imperative, which as such appears to be categorical and unconditioned, would in fact be only a pragmatic prescription calling attention to our advantage and merely bidding us take this into account.

We shall thus have to investigate the possibility of a *categorical* imperative entirely *a priori*, since here we do not enjoy the advantage of having its reality given in experience and so of being obliged merely to explain, and not to establish, its possibility. So much, however, can be seen provisionally—that the categorical imperative alone purports to be a practical *law*, while all the rest may be called *principles* of the will but not laws; for an action necessary merely in order to achieve an arbitrary purpose can be considered as in itself contingent, and we can always escape from the precept if we abandon the purpose; whereas an unconditioned command does not leave it open to the will to do the opposite at its discretion and therefore alone carries with it that necessity which we demand from a law.

In the second place, with this categorical imperative or law of morality the reason for our difficulty (in comprehending its possibility) is a very serious one. We have here a synthetic *a priori* practical proposition;[3] and since in theoretical knowledge there is so much difficulty in comprehending the possibility of propositions of this kind, it may readily be gath-

ered that in practical knowledge the difficulty will be no less.

In this task we wish first to enquire whether perhaps the mere concept of a categorical imperative may not also provide us with the formula containing the only proposition that can be a categorical imperative; for even when we know the purport of such an absolute command, the question of its possibility will still require a special and troublesome effort, which we postpone to the final chapter.

When I conceive a *hypothetical* imperative in general, I do not know beforehand what it will contain—until its condition is given. But if I conceive a *categorical* imperative, I know at once what it contains. For since besides the law this imperative contains only the necessity that our maxim[4] should conform to this law, while the law, as we have seen, contains no condition to limit it, there remains nothing over to which the maxim has to conform except the universality of a law as such; and it is this conformity alone that the imperative properly asserts to be necessary.

There is therefore only a single categorical imperative and it is this: *'Act only on that maxim through which you can at the same time will that it should become a universal law'.*

Now if all imperatives of duty can be derived from this one imperative as their principle, then even although we leave it unsettled whether what we call duty may not be an empty concept, we shall still be able to show at least what we understand by it and what the concept means.

Since the universality of the law governing the production of effects constitutes what is properly called *nature* in its most general sense (nature as regards its form)—that is, the existence of things so far as determined by universal laws—the universal imperative of duty may also run as follows: *'Act as if the maxim of your action were to become through your will a universal law of nature.'*

---

[3]Without presupposing a condition taken from some inclination I connect an action with the will *a priori* and therefore necessarily (although only objectively so—that is, only subject to the Idea of a reason having full power over all subjective impulses to action). Here we have a practical proposition in which the willing of an action is not derived analytically from some other willing already presupposed (for we do not possess any such perfect will), but is on the contrary connected immediately with the concept of the will of a rational being as something which is not contained in this concept.

[4]A *maxim* is a subjective principle of action and must be distinguished from an *objective principle*—namely, a practical law. The former contains a practical rule determined by reason in accordance with the conditions of the subject (often his ignorance or again his inclinations): it is thus a principle on which the subject *acts*. A law, on the other hand, is an objective principle valid for every rational being; and it is a principle on which he *ought to act*—that is, an imperative.

We will now enumerate a few duties, following their customary division into duties towards self and duties towards others and into perfect and imperfect duties.[5]

(1) A man feels sick of life as the result of a series of misfortunes that has mounted to the point of despair, but he is still so far in possession of his reason as to ask himself whether taking his own life may not be contrary to his duty to himself. He now applies the test 'Can the maxim of my action really become a universal law of nature?' His maxim is 'From self-love I make it my principle to shorten my life if its continuance threatens more evil than it promises pleasure'. The only further question to ask is whether this principle of self-love can become a universal law of nature. It is then seen at once that a system of nature by whose law the very same feeling whose function (*Bestimmung*) is to stimulate the furtherance of life should actually destroy life would contradict itself and consequently could not subsist as a system of nature. Hence this maxim cannot possibly hold as a universal law of nature and is therefore entirely opposed to the supreme principle of all duty.

(2) Another finds himself driven to borrowing money because of need. He well knows that he will not be able to pay it back; but he sees too that he will get no loan unless he gives a firm promise to pay it back within a fixed time. He is inclined to make such a promise; but he has still enough conscience to ask 'Is it not unlawful and contrary to duty to get out of difficulties in this way?' Supposing, however, he did resolve to do so, the maxim of his action would run thus: 'Whenever I believe myself short of money, I will borrow money and promise to pay it back, though I know that this will never be done'. Now this principle of self-love or personal advantage is perhaps quite compatible with my own entire future welfare; only there remains the question 'Is it right?' I therefore transform the demand of self-love into a universal law and frame my question thus 'How would things stand if my maxim became a universal law?' I then see straight away that this maxim can never rank as a universal law of nature and be self-consistent, but must necessarily contradict itself. For the universality of a law that every one believing himself to be in need can make any promise he pleases with the intention not to keep it would make promising, and the very purpose of promising, itself impossible, since no one would believe he was being promised anything, but would laugh at utterances of this kind as empty shams.

(3) A third finds in himself a talent whose cultivation would make him a useful man for all sorts of purposes. But he sees himself in comfortable circumstances, and he prefers to give himself up to pleasure rather than to bother about increasing and improving his fortunate natural aptitudes. Yet he asks himself further 'Does my maxim of neglecting my natural gifts, besides agreeing in itself with my tendency to indulgence, agree also with what is called duty?' He then sees that a system of nature could indeed always subsist under such a universal law, although (like the South Sea Islanders) every man should let his talents rust and should be bent on devoting his life solely to idleness, indulgence, procreation, and, in a word, to enjoyment. Only he cannot possibly *will* that this should become a universal law of nature or should be implanted in us as such a law by a natural instinct. For as a rational being he necessarily wills that all his powers should be developed, since they serve him, and are given him, for all sorts of possible ends.

(4) Yet a *fourth* is himself flourishing, but he sees others who have to struggle with great hardships (and whom he could easily help); and he thinks 'What does it matter to me? Let every one be as happy as Heaven wills or as he can make himself; I won't deprive him of anything; I won't even envy him; only I have no wish to contribute anything to his well-being or to his support in distress!' Now admittedly if such an attitude were a universal law of nature, mankind could get on perfectly well—better no doubt than if everybody prates about sympathy and goodwill, and even takes pains, on occasion, to practise them, but on the other hand cheats where he can, traffics in human rights, or violates them in other ways. But although it is possible that a universal law of nature could subsist in harmony with this maxim, yet it is impossible to *will* that such a princi-

---

[5]It should be noted that I reserve my division of duties entirely for a future *Metaphysic of Morals* and that my present division is therefore put forward as arbitrary (merely for the purpose of arranging my examples). Further, I understand here by a perfect duty one which allows no exception in the interests of inclination, and so I recognize among *perfect duties*, not only outer ones, but also inner. This is contrary to the accepted usage of the schools, but I do not intend to justify it here, since for my purpose it is all one whether this point is conceded or not.

ple should hold everywhere as a law of nature. For a will which decided in this way would be in conflict with itself, since many a situation might arise in which the man needed love and sympathy from others, and in which, by such a law of nature sprung from his own will, he would rob himself of all hope of the help he wants for himself.

These are some of the many actual duties—or at least of what we take to be such—whose derivation from the single principle cited above leaps to the eye. We must *be able to will* that a maxim of our action should become a universal law—this is the general canon for all moral judgement of action. Some actions are so constituted that their maxim cannot even be *conceived* as a universal law of nature without contradiction, let alone be *willed* as what *ought* to become one. In the case of others we do not find this inner impossibility, but it is still impossible to *will* that their maxim should be raised to the universality of a law of nature, because such a will would contradict itself. It is easily seen that the first kind of action is opposed to strict or narrow (rigorous) duty, the second only to wider (meritorious) duty, and thus that by these examples all duties—so far as the type of obligation is concerned (not the object of dutiful action)—are fully set out in their dependence on our single principle.

If we now attend to ourselves whenever we transgress a duty, we find that we in fact do not will that our maxim should become a universal law—since this is impossible for us—but rather that its opposite should remain a law universally: we only take the liberty of making an *exception* to it for ourselves (or even just for this once) to the advantage of our inclination. Consequently if we weighed it all up from one and the same point of view—that of reason—we should find a contradiction in our own will, the contradiction that a certain principle should be objectively necessary as a universal law and yet subjectively should not hold universally but should admit of exceptions. Since, however, we first consider our action from the point of view of a will wholly in accord with reason, and then consider precisely the same action from the point of view of a will affected by inclination, there is here actually no contradiction, but rather an opposition of inclination to the precept of reason (*antagonismus*), whereby the universality of the principle (*universalitas*) is turned into a mere generality (*generalitas*) so that the practical principle of reason may meet our maxim half-way. This procedure, though in our own impartial judgement it cannot be justified, proves none the less that we in fact recognize the validity of the categorical imperative and (with all respect for it) merely permit ourselves a few exceptions which are, as we pretend, inconsiderable and apparently forced upon us.

We have thus at least shown this much—that if duty is a concept which is to have meaning and real legislative authority for our actions, this can be expressed only in categorical imperatives and by no means in hypothetical ones. At the same time—and this is already a great deal—we have set forth distinctly, and determinately for every type of application, the content of the categorical imperative, which must contain the principle of all duty (if there is to be such a thing at all). . . .

## READING 17

---

# What Makes Right Acts Right?
*W. D. Ross*

*William David Ross (1877–1967) had a distinguished career at Oxford University both as a classical scholar and as a moral philosopher. Ross translated and edited many works by Aristotle and was the leading defender of ethical intuitionism in England during the 1930s. His books include* Aristotle *(1923),* The Right and the Good *(1930),* Foundations of Ethics *(1939), and* Kant's Ethical Theory *(1954). Knighted in 1938, Ross served on the British tribunal for conscientious objectors during the Second World War.*

The real point at issue between hedonism and utilitarianism on the one hand and their opponents on the other is not whether 'right' means 'productive of so and so'; for it cannot with any plausibility be maintained that it does. The point at issue is that to which we now pass, viz. whether there is any general character which makes right acts right, and if so, what it is. Among the main historical attempts to state a single characteristic of all right actions which is the foundation of their rightness are those made by egoism and utilitarianism. But I do not propose to discuss these, not because the subject is unimportant, but because it has been dealt with so often and so well already, and because there has come to be so much agreement among moral philosophers that neither of these theories is satisfactory. A much more attractive theory has been put forward by Professor Moore: that what makes actions right is that they are productive of more *good* than could have been produced by any other action open to the agent.

This theory is in fact the culmination of all the attempts to base rightness on productivity of some sort of result. The first form this attempt takes is the attempt to base rightness on conduciveness to the ad-

**SOURCE:** From *The Right and the Good* (Oxford: Clarendon Press, 1930): 16–42. Edited.

vantage or pleasure of the agent. This theory comes to grief over the fact, which stares us in the face, that a great part of duty consists in an observance of the rights and a furtherance of the interests of others, whatever the cost to ourselves may be. Plato and others may be right in holding that a regard for the rights of others never in the long run involves a loss of happiness for the agent, that 'the just life profits a man'. But this, even if true, is irrelevant to the rightness of the act. As soon as a man does an action *because* he thinks he will promote his own interests thereby, he is acting not from a sense of its rightness but from self-interest.

To the egoistic theory hedonistic utilitarianism supplies a much-needed amendment. It points out correctly that the fact that a certain pleasure will be enjoyed by the agent is no reason why he *ought* to bring it into being rather than an equal or greater pleasure to be enjoyed by another, though, human nature being what it is, it makes it not unlikely that he *will* try to bring it into being. But hedonistic utilitarianism in its turn needs a correction. On reflection it seems clear that pleasure is not the only thing in life that we think good in itself, that for instance we think the possession of a good character, or an intelligent understanding of the world, as good or better. A great advance is made by the substitution of 'productive of the greatest good' for 'productive of the greatest pleasure'.

Not only is this theory more attractive than hedonistic utilitarianism, but its logical relation to that theory is such that the latter could not be true unless *it* were true, while it might be true though hedonistic utilitarianism were not. It is in fact one of the logical bases of hedonistic utilitarianism. For the view that what produces the maximum pleasure is right has for its bases the views (1) that what produces the maximum good is right, and (2) that pleasure is the only thing good in itself. If they were not assuming that what produces the maximum *good* is right, the utilitarians' attempt to show that pleasure is the only thing good in itself, which is in fact the point they take most pains to establish, would have been quite irrelevant to their attempt to prove that only what produces the maximum *pleasure* is right. If, therefore, it can be shown that productivity of the maximum good is not what makes all right actions right, we shall *a fortiori* have refuted hedonistic utilitarianism.

When a plain man fulfils a promise because he thinks he ought to do so, it seems clear that he does so with no thought of its total consequences, still less with any opinion that these are likely to be the best possible. He thinks in fact much more of the past than of the future. What makes him think it right to act in a certain way is the fact that he has promised to do so—that and, usually, nothing more. That his act will produce the best possible consequences is not his reason for calling it right. What lends colour to the theory we are examining, then, is not the actions (which form probably a great majority of our actions) in which some such reflection as 'I have promised' is the only reason we give ourselves for thinking a certain action right, but the exceptional cases in which the consequences of fulfilling a promise (for instance) would be so disastrous to others that we judge it right not to do so. It must of course be admitted that such cases exist. If I have promised to meet a friend at a particular time for some trivial purpose, I should certainly think myself justified in breaking my engagement if by doing so I could prevent a serious accident or bring relief to the victims of one. And the supporters of the view we are examining hold that my thinking so is due to my thinking that I shall bring more good into existence by the one action than by the other. A different account may, however, be given of the matter, an account which will, I believe, show itself to be the true one. It may be said that besides the duty of fulfilling promises I have and recognize a duty of relieving distress,[1] and that when I think it right to do the latter at the cost of not doing the former, it is not because I think I shall produce more good thereby but because I think it the duty which is in the circumstances more

of a duty. This account surely corresponds much more closely with what we really think in such a situation. If, so far as I can see, I could bring equal amounts of good into being by fulfilling my promise and by helping some one to whom I had made no promise, I should not hesitate to regard the former as my duty. Yet on the view that what is right is right because it is productive of the most good I should not so regard it.

There are two theories, each in its way simple, that offer a solution of such cases of conscience. One is the view of Kant, that there are certain duties of perfect obligation, such as those of fulfilling promises, of paying debts, of telling the truth, which admit of no exception whatever in favour of duties of imperfect obligation, such as that of relieving distress. The other is the view of, for instance, Professor Moore and Dr. Rashdall, that there is only the duty of producing good, and that all 'conflicts of duties' should be resolved by asking 'by which action will most good be produced?' But it is more important that our theory fit the facts than that it be simple, and the account we have given above corresponds (it seems to me) better than either of the simpler theories with what we really think, viz. that normally promise-keeping, for example, should come before benevolence, but that when and only when the good to be produced by the benevolent act is very great and the promise comparatively trivial, the act of benevolence becomes our duty.

In fact the theory of 'ideal utilitarianism', if I may for brevity refer so to the theory of Professor Moore, seems to simplify unduly our relations to our fellows. It say, in effect, that the only morally significant relation in which my neighbours stand to me is that of being possible beneficiaries by my action.[2] They do stand in this relation to me, and this relation is morally significant. But they may also stand to me in the relation of promisee to promiser, of creditor to debtor, of wife to husband, of child to parent, of friend to friend, of fellow countryman to fellow countryman, and the like; and each of these relations is the foundation of a *prima facie* duty, which is more or less incumbent on me according to the circumstances of the case. When I am in a situation, as per-

---

[1] These are not strictly speaking duties, but things that tend to be our duty, or *prima facie* duties.

[2] Some will think it, apart from other considerations, a sufficient refutation of this view to point out that I also stand in that relation to myself, so that for this view the distinction of oneself from others is morally insignificant.

haps I always am, in which more than one of these *prima facie* duties is incumbent on me, what I have to do is to study the situation as fully as I can until I form the considered opinion (it is never more) that in the circumstances one of them is more incumbent than any other; then I am bound to think that to do this *prima facie* duty is my duty *sans phrase* in the situation.

I suggest '*prima facie* duty' or 'conditional duty' as a brief way of referring to the characteristic (quite distinct from that of being a duty proper) which an act has, in virtue of being of a certain kind (e.g. the keeping of a promise), of being an act which would be a duty proper if it were not at the same time of another kind which is morally significant. Whether an act is a duty proper or actual duty depends on all the morally significant kinds it is an instance of. The phrase '*prima facie* duty' must be apologized for, since (1) it suggests that what we are speaking of is a certain kind of duty, whereas it is in fact not a duty, but something related in a special way to duty. Strictly speaking, we want not a phrase in which duty is qualified by an adjective, but a separate noun. (2) '*Prima*' *facie* suggests that one is speaking only of an appearance which a moral situation presents at first sight, and which may turn out to be illusory; whereas what I am speaking of is an objective fact involved in the nature of the situation, or more strictly in an element of its nature, though not, as duty proper does, arising from its *whole* nature. . . .

There is nothing arbitrary about these *prima facie* duties. Each rests on a definite circumstance which cannot seriously be held to be without moral significance. Of *prima facie* duties I suggest, without claiming completeness or finality for it, the following division.[3]

(1) Some duties rest on previous acts of my own. These duties seem to include two kinds, (a) those resting on a promise or what may fairly be called an implicit promise, such as the implicit undertaking not to tell lies which seems to be implied in the act of entering into conversation (at any rate by civilized men), or of writing books that purport to be history and not fiction. These may be called the duties of fidelity. (b) Those resting on a previous wrongful act. These may be called the duties of reparation. (2) Some rest on previous acts of other men, i.e. services done by them to me. These may be loosely described as the duties of gratitude. (3) Some rest on the fact or possibility of a distribution of pleasure or happiness (or of the means thereto) which is not in accordance with the merit of the persons concerned; in such cases there arises a duty to upset or prevent such a distribution. These are the duties of justice. (4) Some rest on the mere fact that there are other beings in the world whose condition we can make better in respect of virtue, or of intelligence, or of pleasure. These are the duties of beneficence. (5) Some rest on the fact that we can improve our own condition in respect of virtue or of intelligence. These are the duties of self-improvement. (6) I think that we should distinguish from (4) the duties that may be summed up under the title of 'not injuring others'. No doubt to injure others is incidentally to fail to do them good; but it seems to me clear that non-maleficence is apprehended as a duty distinct from that of beneficence, and as a duty of a more stringent character. It will be noticed that this alone among the types of duty has been stated in a negative way. An attempt might no doubt be made to state this duty, like the others, in a positive way. It might be said that it is really the duty to prevent ourselves from acting either from an inclination to harm others or from an inclination to seek our own pleasure, in doing which we should incidentally harm them. But on reflection it seems clear that the primary duty here is the duty not to harm others, this being a duty whether or not we have an inclination that if followed would lead to our harming them; and that when we have such an inclination the primary duty not to harm others gives rise to a consequential duty to resist the inclination. The recognition of this duty of non-maleficence is the first step on the way to the recognition of the duty of beneficence; and that accounts for the prominence of the commands 'thou shalt not kill', 'thou shalt not commit adultery', 'thou shalt not

[3]I should make it plain at this stage that I am *assuming* the correctness of some of our main convictions as to *prima facie* duties, or, more strictly, am claiming that we *know* them to be true. To me it seems as self-evident as anything could be, that to make a promise, for instance, is to create a moral claim on us in someone else. Many readers will perhaps say that they do *not* know this to be true. If so, I certainly cannot prove it to them; I can only ask them to reflect again, in the hope that they will ultimately agree that they also know it to be true. The main moral convictions of the plain man seem to me to be, not opinions which it is for philosophy to prove or disprove, but knowledge from the start; and in my own case I seem to find little difficulty in distinguishing these essential convictions from other moral convictions which I also have, which are merely fallible opinions based on an imperfect study of the working for good or evil of certain institutions or types of action.

steal', 'thou shalt not bear false witness', in so early a code as the Decalogue. But even when we have come to recognize the duty of beneficence, it appears to me that the duty of non-maleficence is recognized as a distinct one, and as *prima facie* more binding. We should not in general consider it justifiable to kill one person in order to keep another alive, or to steal from one in order to give alms to another.

The essential defect of the 'ideal utilitarian' theory is that it ignores or at least does not do full justice to, the highly personal character of duty. If the only duty is to produce the maximum of good, the question who is to have the good—whether it is myself, or my benefactor, or a person to whom I have made a promise to confer that good on him, or a mere fellow man to whom I stand in no such special relation—should make no difference to my having a duty to produce that good. But we are all in fact sure that it makes a vast difference. . . .

If the objection be made, that this catalogue of the main types of duty is an unsystematic one resting on no logical principle, it may be replied, first, that it makes no claim to being ultimate. It is a *prima facie* classification of the duties which reflection on our moral convictions seems actually to reveal. And if these convictions are, as I would claim that they are, of the nature of knowledge, and if I have not misstated them, the list will be a list of authentic conditional duties, correct as far as it goes though not necessarily complete. The list of *goods* put forward by the rival theory is reached by exactly the same method—the only sound one in the circumstances—viz. that of direct reflection on what we really think. Loyalty to the facts is worth more than a symmetrical architectonic or a hastily reached simplicity. If further reflection discovers a perfect logical basis for this or for a better classification, so much the better.

It may, again, be objected that our theory that there are these various and often conflicting types of *prima facie* duty leaves us with no principle upon which to discern what is our actual duty in particular circumstances. But this objection is not one which the rival theory is in a position to bring forward. For when we have to choose between the production of two heterogeneous goods, say knowledge and pleasure, the 'ideal utilitarian' theory can only fall back on an opinion, for which no logical basis can be offered, that one of the goods is the greater; and this is no better than a similar opinion that one of two duties is the more urgent. And again, when we consider

the infinite variety of the effects of our actions in the way of pleasure, it must surely be admitted that the claim which *hedonism* sometimes makes, that it offers a readily applicable criterion of right conduct, is quite illusory.

I am unwilling, however, to content myself with an *argumentum ad hominem*, and I would contend that in principle there is no reason to anticipate that every act that is our duty is so for one and the same reason. Why should two sets of circumstances, or one set of circumstances, *not* possess different characteristics, any one of which makes a certain act our *prima facie* duty? When I ask what it is that makes me in certain cases sure that I have a *prima facie* duty to do so and so, I find that it lies in the fact that I have made a promise; when I ask the same question in another case, I find the answer lies in the fact that I have done a wrong. And if on reflection I find (as I think I do) that neither of these reasons is reducible to the other I must not on any *a priori* ground assume that such a reduction is possible. . . .

It is necessary to say something by way of clearing up the relation between *prima facie* duties and the actual or absolute duty to do one particular act in particular circumstances. If as almost all moralists except Kant are agreed, and as most plain men think, it is sometimes right to tell a lie or to break a promise, it must be maintained that there is a difference between *prima facie* duty and actual or absolute duty. When we think ourselves justified in breaking, and indeed morally obliged to break, a promise in order to relieve some one's distress, we do not for a moment cease to recognize a *prima facie* duty to keep our promise, and this leads us to feel, not indeed shame or repentance, but certainly compunction, for behaving as we do; we recognize, further, that it is our duty to make up somehow to the promisee for the breaking of the promise. We have to distinguish from the characteristic of being our duty that of tending to be our duty. Any act that we do contains various elements in virtue of which it falls under various categories. In virtue of being the breaking of a promise, for instance, it tends to be wrong; in virtue of being an instance of relieving distress it tends to be right. Tendency to be one's duty may be called a parti-resultant attribute, i.e. one which belongs to an act in virtue of some one component in its nature. *Being* one's duty is a toti-resultant attribute, one which belongs to an act in virtue of its whole nature and of nothing less than this. . . .

Another instance of the same distinction may be found in the operation of natural laws. *Qua* subject to the force of gravitation towards some other body, each body tends to move in a particular direction with a particular velocity; but its actual movement depends on *all* the forces to which it is subject. It is only by recognizing this distinction that we can preserve the absoluteness of laws of nature, and only by recognizing a corresponding distinction that we can preserve the absoluteness of the general principles of morality. But an important difference between the two cases must be pointed out. When we say that in virtue of gravitation a body tends to move in a certain way, we are referring to a causal influence actually exercised on it by another body or other bodies. When we say that in virtue of being deliberately untrue a certain remark tends to be wrong, we are referring to no causal relation, to no relation that involves succession in time, but to such a relation as connects the various attributes of a mathematical figure. And if the word 'tendency' is thought to suggest too much a causal relation, it is better to talk of certain types of act as being *prima facie* right or wrong (or of different persons as having different and possibly conflicting claims upon us), than of their tending to be right or wrong.

Something should be said of the relation between our apprehension of the *prima facie* rightness of certain types of act and our mental attitude towards particular acts. It is proper to use the word 'apprehension' in the former case and not in the latter. That an act, *qua* fulfilling a promise, or *qua* effecting a just distribution of good, or *qua* returning services rendered, or *qua* promoting the good of others, or *qua* promoting the virtue or insight of the agent, is *prima facie* right, is self-evident; not in the sense that it is evident from the beginning of our lives, or as soon as we attend to the proposition for the first time, but in the sense that when we have reached sufficient mental maturity and have given sufficient attention to the proposition it is evident without any need of proof, or of evidence beyond itself. It is self-evident just as a mathematical axiom, or the validity of a form of inference, is evident. The moral order expressed in these propositions is just as much part of the fundamental nature of the universe (and, we may add, of any possible universe in which there were moral agents at all) as is the spatial or numerical structure expressed in the axioms of geometry or arithmetic. In our confidence that these propositions are true there is involved the same trust in our reason that is involved in our confidence in mathematics; and we should have no justification for trusting it in the latter sphere and distrusting it in the former. In both cases we are dealing with propositions that cannot be proved, but that just as certainly need no proof. . . .

Our judgements about our actual duty in concrete situations have none of the certainty that attaches to our recognition of the general principles of duty. A statement is certain, i.e. is an expression of knowledge, only in one or other of two cases: when it is either self-evident, or a valid conclusion from self-evident premises. And our judgements about our particular duties have neither of these characters. (1) They are not self-evident. Where a possible act is seen to have two characteristics, in virtue of one of which it is *prima facie* right, and in virtue of the other *prima facie* wrong, we are (I think) well aware that we are not certain whether we ought or ought not to do it; that whether we do it or not, we are taking a moral risk. We come in the long run, after consideration, to think one duty more pressing than the other, but we do not feel certain that it is so. And though we do not always recognize that a possible act has two such characteristics, and though there *may* be cases in which it has not, we are never certain that any particular possible act has not, and therefore never certain that it is right, nor certain that it is wrong. For, to go no further in the analysis, it is enough to point out that any particular act will in all probability in the course of time contribute to the bringing about of good or of evil for many human beings, and thus have a *prima facie* rightness or wrongness of which we know nothing. (2) Again, our judgements about our particular duties are not logical conclusions from self-evident premises. The only possible premises would be the general principles stating their *prima facie* rightness or wrongness *qua* having the different characteristics they do have; and even if we could (as we cannot) apprehend the extent to which an act will tend on the one hand, for example, to bring about advantages for our benefactors, and on the other hand to bring about disadvantages for fellow men who are not our benefactors, there is no principle by which we can draw the conclusion that it is on the whole right or on the whole wrong. In this respect the judgement as to the rightness of a particular act is just like the judgement as to the beauty of a particular natural object or work of art. A poem is, for instance, in respect of certain qualities beautiful and in respect of certain others not beautiful; and our judgement as to the degree of beauty it possesses on the whole is never reached by logical reasoning from the apprehension of its particular beauties or particular defects. Both in this and in the moral case we have more or less probable opinions which are not logically justified conclusions from the general principles that are recognized as self-evident.

There is therefore much truth in the description of the right act as a fortunate act. If we cannot be certain that it is right, it is our good fortune if the act we do is the right act. This consideration does not, however, make the doing of our duty a mere matter of chance. There is a parallel here between the doing of duty and the doing of what will be to our personal advantage. We never *know* what act will in the long run be to our advantage. Yet it is certain that we are more likely in general to secure our advantage if we estimate to the best of our ability the probable tendencies of our actions in this respect, than if we act on caprice. And similarly we are more likely to do our duty if we reflect to the best of our ability on the *prima facie* rightness or wrongness of various possible acts in virtue of the characteristics we perceive them to have, than if we act without reflection. With this greater likelihood we must be content.

Many people would be inclined to say that the right act for me is not that whose general nature I have been describing, viz. that which if I were omniscient I should see to be my duty, but that which on all the evidence available to me I should think to be my duty. But suppose that from the state of partial knowledge in which I think act *A* to be my duty, I could pass to a state of perfect knowledge in which I saw act *B* to be my duty, should I not say 'act *B* was the right act for me to do'? I should no doubt add 'though I am not to be blamed for doing act *A*'. . . .

The general principles of duty are obviously not self-evident from the beginning of our lives. How do they come to be so? The answer is, that they come to be self-evident to us just as mathematical axioms do. We find by experience that this couple of matches and that couple make four matches, that this couple of balls on a wire and that couple make four balls: and by reflection on these and similar discoveries we come to see that it is of the nature of two and two to make four. In a precisely similar way, we see the *prima facie* rightness of an act which would be the fulfilment of a particular promise, and of another which would be the fulfilment of another promise, and when we have reached sufficient maturity to think in general terms, we apprehend *prima facie* rightness to belong to the nature of any fulfilment of promise. What comes first in time is the apprehension of the self-evident *prima facie* rightness of an individual act of a particular type. From this we come by reflection to apprehend the self-evident general principle of *prima facie* duty. From this, too, perhaps along with the apprehension of the self-evident *prima facie* rightness of the same act in virtue of its having another characteristic as well, and perhaps in spite of the apprehension of its *prima facie* wrongness in virtue of its having some third characteristic, we come to believe something not self-evident at all, but an object of probable opinion, viz. that this particular act is (not *prima facie* but) actually right.

In this respect there is an important difference between rightness and mathematical properties. A triangle which is isosceles necessarily has two of its angles equal, whatever other characteristics the triangle may have—whatever, for instance, be its area, or the size of its third angle. The equality of the two angles is a parti-resultant attribute. And the same is true of all mathematical attributes. It is true, I may add, of *prima facie* rightness. But no act is ever, in virtue of falling under some general description, necessarily actually right; its rightness depends on its whole nature[4] and not on any element in it. The reason is that no mathematical object (no figure, for instance, or angle) ever has two characteristics that tend to give it opposite resultant characteristics, while moral acts often (as every one knows) and indeed always (as on reflection we must admit) have different characteristics that tend to make them at the same time *prima facie* right and *prima facie* wrong; there is probably no act, for instance, which does good to any one without doing harm to some one else, and *vice versa*.

Supposing it to be agreed, as I think on reflection it must, that no one *means* by 'right' just 'productive of the best possible consequences', or 'optimific', the

---

[4]To avoid complicating unduly the statement of the general view I am putting forward, I have here rather overstated it. Any act is the origination of a great variety of things many of which make no difference to its rightness or wrongness. But there are always many elements in its nature (i.e. in what it is the origination of) that make a difference to its rightness or wrongness, and no element in its nature can be dismissed without consideration as indifferent.

attributes 'right' and 'optimific' might stand in either of two kinds of relation to each other. (1) They might be so related that we could apprehend a *priori*, either immediately or deductively, that any act that is optimific is right and any act that is right is optimific, as we can apprehend that any triangle that is equilateral is equiangular and *vice versa*. Professor Moore's view is, I think, that the coextensiveness of 'right' and 'optimific' is apprehended immediately.[5] He rejects the possibility of any proof of it. Or (2) the two attributes might be such that the question whether they are invariably connected had to be answered by means of an inductive inquiry. Now at first sight it might seem as if the constant connexion of the two attributes could be immediately apprehended. It might seem absurd to suggest that it could be right for any one to do an act which would produce consequences less good than those which would be produced by some other act in his power. Yet a little thought will convince us that this is not absurd. The type of case in which it is easiest to see that this is so is, perhaps, that in which one has made a promise. In such a case we all think that *prima facie* it is our duty to fulfil the promise irrespective of the precise goodness of the total consequences. And though we do not think it is necessarily our actual or absolute duty to do so, we are far from thinking that any, even the slightest, gain in the value of the total consequences will necessarily justify us in doing something else instead. Suppose, to simplify the case by abstraction, that the fulfilment of a promise to *A* would produce 1,000 units of good[6] for him, but that by doing some other act I could produce 1,001 units of good for *B*, to whom I have made no promise, the other consequences of the two acts being of equal value; should we really think it self-evident that it was our duty to do the second act and not the first? I think not. We should, I fancy, hold that only a much greater disparity of value between the total consequences would justify us in failing to discharge our *prima facie* duty to *A*. After all, a promise is a promise, and is not to be treated so lightly as the theory we are examining would imply. What, exactly, a

promise is, is not so easy to determine, but we are surely agreed that it constitutes a serious moral limitation to our freedom of action. To produce the 1,001 units of good for *B* rather than fulfil our promise to *A* would be to take, not perhaps our duty as philanthropists too seriously, but certainly our duty as makers of promises too lightly.

Or consider another phase of the same problem. If I have promised to confer on *A* a particular benefit containing 1,000 units of good, is it self-evident that if by doing some different act I could produce 1,001 units of good for *A* himself (the other consequences of the two acts being supposed equal in value), it would be right for me to do so? Again, I think not. Apart from my general *prima facie* duty to do *A* what good I can, I have another *prima facie* duty to do him the particular service I have promised to do him, and this is not to be set aside in consequence of a disparity of good of the order of 1,001 to 1,000 though a much greater disparity might justify me in so doing.

Or again, suppose that *A* is a very good and *B* a very bad man, should I then, even when I have made no promise, think it self-evidently right to produce 1,001 units of good for *B* rather than 1,000 for *A*? Surely not. I should be sensible of a *prima facie* duty of justice, i.e. of producing a distribution of goods in proportion to merit, which is not outweighed by such a slight disparity in the total goods to be produced.

Such instances—and they might easily be added to—make it clear that there is no self-evident connexion between the attributes 'right' and 'optimific'. The theory we are examining has a certain attractiveness when applied to our decision that a particular act is our duty (though I have tried to show that it does not agree with our actual moral judgements even here). But it is not even plausible when applied to our recognition of *prima facie* duty. For if it were self-evident that the right coincides with the optimific, it should be self-evident that what is *prima facie* right is *prima facie* optimific. But whereas we are certain that keeping a promise is *prima facie* right, we are not certain that it is *prima facie* optimific (though we are perhaps certain that it is *prima facie* bonific). Our certainty that it is *prima facie* right depends not on its consequences but on its being the fulfilment of a promise. The theory we are examining involves too much difference between the evident ground of our conviction about *prima facie* duty and the alleged ground of our conviction about actual duty. . . .

[5]*Ethics*, 181.
[6]I am assuming that good is objectively quantitative, but not that we can accurately assign an exact quantitative measure to it. Since it is of definite amount, we can make the *supposition* that its amount is so-and-so, though we cannot with any confidence *assert* that it is.

I conclude that the attributes 'right' and 'optimific' are not identical, and that we do not know either by intuition, by deduction, or by induction that they coincide in their application, still less that the latter is the foundation of the former. It must be added, however, that if we are ever under no special obligation such as that of fidelity to a promisee or of gratitude to a benefactor, we ought to do what will produce most good; and that even when we are under a special obligation the tendency of acts to promote general good is one of the main factors in determining whether they are right.

In what has preceded, a good deal of use has been made of 'what we really think' about moral questions; a certain theory has been rejected because it does not agree with what we really think. It might be said that this is in principle wrong; that we should not be content to expound what our present moral consciousness tells us but should aim at a criticism of our existing moral consciousness in the light of theory. Now I do not doubt that the moral consciousness of men has in detail undergone a good deal of modification as regards the things we think right, at the hands of moral theory. But if we are told, for instance, that we should give up our view that there is a special obligatoriness attaching to the keeping of promises because it is self-evident that the only duty is to produce as much good as possible, we have to ask ourselves whether we really, when we reflect, *are* convinced that this is self-evident, and whether we really *can* get rid of our view that promise-keeping has a bindingness independent of productiveness of maximum good. In my own experience I find that I cannot, in spite of a very genuine attempt to do so; and I venture to think that most people will find the same, and that just because they cannot lose the sense of special obligation, they cannot accept as self-evident, or even as true, the theory which would require them to do so. In fact it seems, on reflection, self-evident that a promise, simply as such, is something that *prima facie* ought to be kept, and it does *not*, on reflection, seem self-evident that production of maximum good is the only thing that makes an act obligatory. And to ask us to give up at the bidding of a theory our actual apprehension of what is right and what is wrong seems like asking people to repudiate their actual experience of beauty, at the bidding of a theory which says 'only that which satisfies such and such conditions can be beautiful'. If what I have called our actual apprehension is (as I would maintain that it is) truly an apprehension, i.e. an instance of knowledge, the request is nothing less than absurd.

I would maintain, in fact, that what we are apt to describe as 'what we think' about moral questions contains a considerable amount that we do not think but know, and that this forms the standard by reference to which the truth of any moral theory has to be tested, instead of having itself to be tested by reference to any theory. I hope that I have in what precedes indicated what in my view these elements of knowledge are that are involved in our ordinary moral consciousness.

It would be a mistake to found a natural science on 'what we really think', i.e. on what reasonably thoughtful and well-educated people think about the subjects of the science before they have studied them scientifically. For such opinions are interpretations, and often misinterpretations, of sense-experience; and the man of science must appeal from these to sense-experience itself, which furnishes his real data. In ethics no such appeal is possible. We have no more direct way of access to the facts about rightness and goodness and about what things are right or good, than by thinking about them; the moral convictions of thoughtful and well-educated people are the data of ethics just as sense-perceptions are the data of a natural science. Just as some of the latter have to be rejected as illusory, so have some of the former; but as the latter are rejected only when they are in conflict with other more accurate sense-perceptions, the former are rejected only when they are in conflict with other convictions which stand better the test of reflection. The existing body of moral convictions of the best people is the cumulative product of the moral reflection of many generations, which has developed an extremely delicate power of appreciation of moral distinctions; and this the theorist cannot afford to treat with anything other than the greatest respect. The verdicts of the moral consciousness of the best people are the foundation on which he must build; though he must first compare them with one another and eliminate any contradictions they may contain.

## READING 18

# The Ring of Gyges
*Plato*

*Universally recognized as one of the world's greatest philosophers, Plato (427–348 B.C.) was the pupil of Socrates (c. 470–399 B.C.) and the teacher of Aristotle (384–322 B.C.). Plato spent most of his life in Athens, where he founded the school known as the Academy. His works are in the form of dialogues, and Socrates is often the principal character. Plato portrays Socrates as seeking to understand the true nature of concepts such as piety and courage by questioning the other characters and then refuting their assertions by skillful arguments. The* Republic *is one of Plato's longest and best-known works. In Book II, from which our excerpt is taken, the focus is on the definition and nature of justice.*

### BOOK II

With these words I was thinking that I had made an end of the discussion; but the end, in truth, proved to be only a beginning. For Glaucon, who is always the most pugnacious of men, was dissatisfied at Thrasymachus' retirement; he wanted to have the battle out. So he said to me: Socrates, do you wish really to persuade us, or only to seem to have persuaded us, that to be just is always better than to be unjust?

I should wish really to persuade you, I replied, if I could.

Then you certainly have not succeeded. Let me ask you now:—How would you arrange goods—are there not some which we welcome for their own sakes, and independently of their consequences, as, for example, harmless pleasures and enjoyments, which delight us at the time, although nothing follows from them?

I agree in thinking that there is such a class, I replied.

SOURCE: From the *Republic* (c. 374 B.C.), Book II, 357A–367E. Reprinted from *The Dialogues of Plato*, trans. B. Jowett (1871).

Is there not also a second class of goods, such as knowledge, sight, health, which are desirable not only in themselves, but also for their results?

Certainly, I said.

And would you not recognize a third class, such as gymnastic, and the care of the sick, and the physician's art; also the various ways of money-making—these do us good but we regard them as disagreeable; and no one would choose them for their own sakes, but only for the sake of some reward or result which flows from them?

There is, I said, this third class also. But why do you ask?

Because I want to know in which of the three classes you would place justice?

In the highest class, I replied,—among those goods which he who would be happy desires both for their own sake and for the sake of their results.

Then the many are of another mind; they think that justice is to be reckoned in the troublesome class, among goods which are to be pursued for the sake of rewards and of reputation, but in themselves are disagreeable and rather to be avoided.

I know, I said, that this is their manner of thinking, and that this was the thesis which Thrasymachus was maintaining just now, when he censured justice and praised injustice. But I am too stupid to be convinced by him.

I wish, he said, that you would hear me as well as him, and then I shall see whether you and I agree. For Thrasymachus seems to me, like a snake, to have been charmed by your voice sooner than he ought to have been; but to my mind the nature of justice and injustice have not yet been made clear. Setting aside their rewards and results, I want to know what they are in themselves, and how they inwardly work in the soul. If you please, then, I will revive the argument of Thrasymachus. And first I will speak of the nature and origin of justice according to the common view of them. Secondly, I will show that all men who practise justice do so against their will, of necessity, but not as a good. And thirdly, I will argue that there is reason in this view, for the life of the unjust is after all better far than the life of the just—if what they say is true, Socrates, since I myself am not of their opinion. But still I acknowledge that I am perplexed when I hear the voices of Thrasymachus and myriads of others dinning in my ears; and, on the other hand, I have never yet heard the superiority of justice to injustice maintained by any one in a satisfactory way. I want to hear justice praised in respect of itself; then I shall be satisfied, and you are the person from whom I think that I am most likely to hear this; and therefore I will praise the unjust life to the utmost of my power, and my manner of speaking will indicate the manner in which I desire to hear you too praising justice and censuring injustice. Will you say whether you approve of my proposal?

Indeed I do; nor can I imagine any theme about which a man of sense would oftener wish to converse.

I am delighted, he replied, to hear you say so, and shall begin by speaking, as I proposed, of the nature and origin of justice.

They say that to do injustice is by nature, good; to suffer injustice, evil; but that the evil is greater than the good. And so when men have both done and suffered injustice and have had experience of both, not being able to avoid the one and obtain the other, they think that they had better agree among themselves to have neither; hence there arise laws and mutual covenants; and that which is ordained by law is termed by them lawful and just. This they affirm to be the origin and nature of justice;—it is a mean or compromise between the best of all, which is to do injustice and not be punished, and the worst of all, which is to suffer injustice without the power of retaliation; and justice, being at a middle point between the two, is tolerated not as a good, but as the lesser evil, and honoured by reason of the inability of men to do injustice. For no man who is worthy to be called a man would ever submit to such an agreement if he were able to resist; he would be mad if he did. Such is the received account, Socrates, of the nature and origin of justice.

Now that those who practise justice do so involuntarily and because they have not the power to be unjust will best appear if we imagine something of this kind: having given both to the just and the unjust power to do what they will, let us watch and see whither desire will lead them; then we shall discover in the very act the just and unjust man to be proceeding along the same road, following their interest, which all natures deem to be their good, and are only diverted into the path of justice by the force of law. The liberty which we are supposing may be most completely given to them in the form of such a power as is said to have been possessed by Gyges the ancestor of Croesus the Lydian. According to the tradition, Gyges was a shepherd in the service of the king of Lydia; there was a great storm, and an earthquake made an opening in the earth at the place where he was feeding his flock. Amazed at the sight, he descended into the opening, where, among other marvels, he beheld a hollow brazen horse, having doors, at which he stooping and looking in saw a dead body of stature, as appeared to him, more than human, and having nothing on but a gold ring; this he took from the finger of the dead and reascended. Now the shepherds met together, according to custom, that they might send their monthly report about the flocks to the king; into their assembly he came having the ring on his finger, and as he was sitting among them he chanced to turn the collet of the ring inside his hand, when instantly he became invisible to the rest of the company and they began to speak of him as if he were no longer present. He was astonished at this, and again touching the ring he turned the collet outwards and reappeared; he made several trials of the ring, and always with the same result—when he turned the collet inwards he became invisible, when outwards he reappeared. Whereupon he contrived to be chosen one of the messengers who were sent to the court; where as soon as he arrived he seduced the queen, and with her help conspired against the king and slew him, and took the kingdom. Suppose now that there were two such magic rings, and the just put on one of them and the unjust the other; no man can be imagined to be of such an iron nature that he would stand fast in justice. No man would keep his hands off what was not his own when he could safely take what he liked out of the market, or go into houses and lie with any one at his pleasure, or kill or release from prison whom he would, and in all respects be like a God among men. Then the actions of the just would be as the actions of the unjust; they would both come at last to the same point. And this we may truly affirm to be a great proof that a man is just, not willingly or because he thinks that justice is any good to him individually, but of necessity, for wherever any one thinks that he can safely be unjust, there he is unjust. For all men believe in their hearts that injustice is far more profitable to the individual than justice, and he who argues as I have been supposing, will say that they are right. If you could imagine any one obtaining this power of becoming invisible, and never doing any wrong or touching what was another's, he would be thought by the lookers-on to be a most wretched idiot, although they would praise him to one another's faces, and keep up appearances with one another from a fear that they too might suffer injustice. Enough of this.

Now, if we are to form a real judgment of the life of the just and unjust, we must isolate them; there is no other way; and how is the isolation to be effected? I answer: Let the unjust man be entirely unjust, and the just man entirely just; nothing is to be taken away from either of them, and both are to be perfectly furnished for the work of their respective lives. First, let the unjust be like other distinguished masters of craft; like the skilful pilot or physician, who knows intuitively his own powers and keeps within their limits, and who, if he fails at any point, is able to recover himself. So let the unjust make his unjust attempts in the right way, and lie hidden if he means to be great in his injustice (he who is found out is nobody): for the highest reach of injustice is, to be deemed just when you are not. Therefore I say that in the perfectly unjust man we must assume the most perfect injustice; there is to be no deduction, but we must allow him, while doing the most unjust acts, to have acquired the greatest reputation for justice. If he have taken a false step he must be able to recover himself; he must be one who can speak with effect, if any of his deeds come to light, and who can force his way where force is required by his courage and strength, and command of money and friends. And at his side let us place the just man in his nobleness and simplicity, wishing, as Aeschylus says, to be and not to seem good. There must be no seeming, for if he seem to be just he will be honoured and rewarded, and then we shall not know whether he is just for the sake of justice or for the sake of honours and rewards; therefore, let him be clothed in justice only, and have no other covering; and he must be imagined in a state of life the opposite of the former. Let him be the best of men, and let him be thought the worst; then he will have been put to the proof; and we shall see whether he will be affected by the fear of infamy and its consequences. And let him continue thus to the hour of death; being just and seeming to be unjust. When both have reached the uttermost extreme, the one of justice and the other of injustice, let judgment be given which of them is the happier of the two.

Heavens! my dear Glaucon, I said, how energetically you polish them up for the decision, first one and then the other, as if they were two statues.

I do my best, he said. And now that we know what they are like there is no difficulty in tracing out the sort of life which awaits either of them. This I will proceed to describe; but as you may think the description a little too coarse, I ask you to suppose, Socrates, that the words which follow are not mine— Let me put them into the mouths of the eulogists of injustice: They will tell you that the just man who is thought unjust will be scourged, racked, bound—will have his eyes burnt out; and, at last, after suffering every kind of evil, he will be impaled: Then he will understand that he ought to seem only, and not to be, just; the words of Aeschylus may be more truly spoken of the unjust than of the just. For the unjust is pursuing a reality; he does not live with a view to appearances—he wants to be really unjust and not to seem only:—

'His mind has a soil deep and fertile.
Out of which spring his prudent counsel.'[1]

In the first place, he is thought just, and therefore bears rule in the city; he can marry whom he will, and give in marriage to whom he will; also he can trade and deal where he likes, and always to his own advantage, because he has no misgivings about injustice; and at every contest, whether in public or private, he gets the better of his antagonists, and gains at their expense, and is rich, and out of his gains he can benefit his friends, and harm his enemies; moreover, he can offer sacrifices, and dedicate gifts to the gods abundantly and magnificently, and can honour the gods or any man whom he wants to honour in a far better style than the just, and therefore he is likely to be dearer than they are to the gods. And thus, Socrates, gods and men are said to

[1] *Seven against Thebes*, 574.

unite in making the life of the unjust better than the life of the just.

I was going to say something in answer to Glaucon, when Adeimantus, his brother, interposed: Socrates, he said, you do not suppose that there is nothing more to be urged?

Why, what else is there? I answered.

The strongest point of all has not been even mentioned, he replied.

Well, then, according to the proverb, 'Let brother help brother'—if he fails in any part do you assist him; although I must confess that Glaucon has already said quite enough to lay me in the dust, and take from me the power of helping justice.

Nonsense, he replied. But let me add something more: There is another side to Glaucon's argument about the praise and censure of justice and injustice, which is equally required in order to bring out what I believe to be his meaning. Parents and tutors are always telling their sons and their wards that they are to be just; but why? not for the sake of justice, but for the sake of character and reputation; in the hope of obtaining for him who is reputed just some of those offices, marriages, and the like which Glaucon has enumerated among the advantages accruing to the unjust from the reputation of justice. More, however, is made of appearances by this class of persons than by the others; for they throw in the good opinion of the gods, and will tell you of a shower of benefits which the heavens, as they say, rain upon the pious; and this accords with the testimony of the noble Hesiod and Homer, the first of whom says, that the gods make the oaks of the just—

> 'To bear acorns at their summit, and bees in the middle;
>   And the sheep are bowed down with the weight of their fleeces,[2]'

and many other blessings of a like kind are provided for them. And Homer has a very similar strain; for he speaks of one whose fame is—

> 'As the fame of some blameless king who, like a god,
>   Maintains justice; to whom the black earth brings forth
>   Wheat and barley, whose trees are bowed with fruit,

> And his sheep never fail to bear, and the sea gives him fish.[3]'

Still grander are the gifts of heaven which Musaeus and his son[4] vouchsafe to the just; they take them down into the world below, where they have the saints lying on couches at a feast, everlastingly drunk, crowned with garlands; their idea seems to be that an immortality of drunkenness is the highest meed of virtue. Some extend their rewards yet further; the posterity, as they say, of the faithful and just shall survive to the third and fourth generation. This is the style in which they praise justice. But about the wicked there is another strain; they bury them in a slough in Hades, and make them carry water in a sieve; also while they are yet living they bring them to infamy, and inflict upon them the punishments which Glaucon described as the portion of the just who are reputed to be unjust; nothing else does their invention supply. Such is their manner of praising the one and censuring the other.

Once more, Socrates, I will ask you to consider another way of speaking about justice and injustice, which is not confined to the poets, but is found in prose writers. The universal voice of mankind is always declaring that justice and virtue are honourable, but grievous and toilsome; and that the pleasures of vice and injustice are easy of attainment, and are only censured by law and opinion. They say also that honesty is for the most part less profitable than dishonesty; and they are quite ready to call wicked men happy, and to honour them both in public and private when they are rich or in any other way influential, while they despise and overlook those who may be weak and poor, even though acknowledging them to be better than the others. But most extraordinary of all is their mode of speaking about virtue and the gods: they say that the gods apportion calamity and misery to many good men, and good and happiness to the wicked. And mendicant prophets go to rich men's doors and persuade them that they have a power committed to them by the gods of making an atonement for a man's own or his ancestor's sins by sacrifices or charms, with rejoicings and feasts; and they promise to harm an enemy, whether just or unjust, at a small cost; with magic arts and incantations binding heaven, as they say, to

---

[2]Hesiod, *Works and Days*, 230.

[3]Homer, *Odyssey*, xix. 109.
[4]Eumolpus.

execute their will. And the poets are the authorities to whom they appeal, now smoothing the path of vice with the words of Hesiod:—

> 'Vice may be had in abundance without trouble; the way is smooth and her dwelling-place is near. But before virtue the gods have set toil[5],'

and a tedious and uphill road: then citing Homer as a witness that the gods may be influenced by men; for he also says:—

> 'The gods, too, may be turned from their purpose; and men pray to them and avert their wrath by sacrifices and soothing entreaties, and by libations and the odour of fat, when they have sinned and transgressed[6].'

And they produce a host of books written by Musaeus and Orpheus, who were children of the Moon and the Muses—that is what they say—according to which they perform their ritual, and persuade not only individuals, but whole cities, that expiations and atonements for sin may be made by sacrifices and amusements which fill a vacant hour, and are equally at the service of the living and the dead; the latter sort they call mysteries, and they redeem us from the pains of hell, but if we neglect them no one knows what awaits us.

He proceeded: And now when the young hear all this said about virtue and vice, and the way in which gods and men regard them, how are their minds likely to be affected, my dear Socrates,—those of them, I mean, who are quickwitted, and, like bees on the wing, light on every flower, and from all that they hear are prone to draw conclusions as to what manner of persons they should be and in what way they should walk if they would make the best of life? Probably the youth will say to himself in the words of Pindar—

> 'Can I by justice or by crooked ways of deceit ascend a loftier tower which may be a fortress to me all my days?'

For what men say is that, if I am really just and am not also thought just, profit there is none, but the pain and loss on the other hand are unmistakeable. But if, though unjust, I acquire the reputation of justice, a heavenly life is promised to me. Since then, as

---

[5]Hesiod, *Works and Days*, 287.
[6]Homer, *Iliad*, ix. 493.

philosophers prove, appearance tyrannizes over truth and is lord of happiness, to appearance I must devote myself. I will describe around me a picture and shadow of virtue to be the vestibule and exterior of my house; behind I will trail the subtle and crafty fox, as Archilochus, greatest of sages, recommends. But I hear some one exclaiming that the concealment of wickedness is often difficult; to which I answer, Nothing great is easy. Nevertheless, the argument indicates this, if we would be happy, to be the path along which we should proceed. With a view to concealment we will establish secret brotherhoods and political clubs. And there are professors of rhetoric who teach the art of persuading courts and assemblies; and so, partly by persuasion and partly by force, I shall make unlawful gains and not be punished. Still I hear a voice saying that the gods cannot be deceived, neither can they be compelled. But what if there are no gods? or, suppose them to have no care of human things—why in either case should we mind about concealment? And even if there are gods, and they do care about us, yet we know of them only from tradition and the genealogies of the poets; and these are the very persons who say that they may be influenced and turned by 'sacrifices and soothing entreaties and by offerings.' Let us be consistent then, and believe both or neither. If the poets speak truly, why then we had better be unjust, and offer of the fruits of injustice; for if we are just, although we may escape the vengeance of heaven, we shall lose the gains of injustice; but, if we are unjust, we shall keep the gains, and by our sinning and praying, and praying and sinning, the gods will be propitiated, and we shall not be punished. 'But there is a world below in which either we or our posterity will suffer for our unjust deeds.' Yes, my friend, will be the reflection, but there are mysteries and atoning deities, and these have great power. That is what mighty cities declare; and the children of the gods, who were their poets and prophets, bear a like testimony.

On what principle, then, shall we any longer choose justice rather than the worst injustice? when, if we only unite the latter with a deceitful regard to appearances, we shall fare to our mind both with gods and men, in life and after death, as the most numerous and the highest authorities tell us. Knowing all this, Socrates, how can a man who has any superiority of mind or person or rank or wealth, be willing to honour justice; or indeed to refrain from laughing when he hears justice praised? And even if there should be some one who is able to disprove the truth of my words, and who is satisfied that justice is best, still he is not angry with the unjust, but is very ready to forgive them, because he also knows that men are not just of their own free will; unless, peradventure, there be some one whom the divinity within him may have inspired with a hatred of injustice, or who has attained knowledge of the truth—but no other man. He only blames injustice who, owing to cowardice or age or some weakness, has not the power of being unjust. And this is proved by the fact that when he obtains the power, he immediately becomes unjust as far as he can be.

The cause of all this, Socrates, was indicated by us at the beginning of the argument, when my brother and I told you how astonished we were to find that of all the professing panegyrists of justice—beginning with the ancient heroes of whom any memorial has been preserved to us, and ending with the men of our own time—no one has ever blamed injustice or praised justice except with a view to the glories, honours, and benefits which flow from them. No one has ever adequately described either in verse or prose the true essential nature of either of them abiding in the soul, and invisible to any human or divine eye; or shown that of all the things of a man's soul which he has within him, justice is the greatest good, and injustice the greatest evil. Had this been the universal strain, had you sought to persuade us of this from our youth upwards, we should not have been on the watch to keep one another from doing wrong, but every one would have been his own watchman, because afraid, if he did wrong, of harbouring in himself the greatest of evils. I dare say that Thrasymachus and others would seriously hold the language which I have been merely repeating, and words even stronger than these about justice

and injustice, grossly, as I conceive, perverting their true nature. But I speak in this vehement manner, as I must frankly confess to you, because I want to hear from you the opposite side; and I would ask you to show not only the superiority which justice has over injustice, but what effect they have on the possessor of them which makes the one to be a good and the other an evil to him. And please, as Glaucon requested of you, to exclude reputations; for unless you take away from each of them his true reputation and add on the false, we shall say that you do not praise justice, but the appearance of it; we shall think that you are only exhorting us to keep injustice dark, and that you really agree with Thrasymachus in thinking that justice is another's good and the interest of the stronger, and that injustice is a man's own profit and interest, though injurious to the weaker. Now as you have admitted that justice is one of that highest class of goods which are desired indeed for their results, but in a far greater degree for their own sakes—like sight or hearing or knowledge or health, or any other real and natural and not merely conventional good—I would ask you in your praise of justice to regard one point only: I mean the essential good and evil which justice and injustice work in the possessors of them. Let others praise justice and censure injustice, magnifying the rewards and honours of the one and abusing the other; that is a manner of arguing which, coming from them, I am ready to tolerate, but from you who have spent your whole life in the consideration of this question, unless I hear the contrary from your own lips, I expect something better. And therefore, I say, not only prove to us that justice is better than injustice, but show what they either of them do to the possessor of them, which makes the one to be a good and the other an evil, whether seen or unseen by gods and men.

**READING 19**

# The Ultimate Question
*Paul W. Taylor*

*Paul Warren Taylor (1923–   ) is Professor of Philosophy at Brooklyn College. His books include* Problems of Moral Philosophy *(1967),* Principles of Ethics *(1975), and* Respect for Nature: A Theory of Environmental Ethics *(1986).*

## THE DEMAND FOR A JUSTIFICATION OF MORALITY

There is one problem of ethics that perhaps deserves, more than any other, to be called the Ultimate Question. It is the question of the rationality of the moral life itself. It may be expressed thus: Is the commitment to live by moral principles a commitment grounded on reason or is it, in the final analysis, an arbitrary decision?

The Ultimate Question is not itself a moral question. That is to say it does not ask what we morally ought to do or even how we can discover our moral duty. It is, instead, a question about the justification of morality as a whole. Why, it asks, should we be concerned with morality at all? If living by moral principles can at times be so difficult, if our moral integrity may, in some circumstances, require the sacrifice of our happiness or even of our life, why not simply reject the whole moral "game" and live amorally? In short, why be moral?

It is important to see exactly why this is not a moral question or a question about what actions are morally right. When a person asks why he should be moral, he assumes he already knows what "being moral" means. He could not understand his own question when he asked, "Why should I do what is morally right, especially when it conflicts with my self-interest?" unless he understood the meaning of doing what is morally right. Moreover, if his question

concerns a *particular* case of conflict between moral duty and self-interest, then it is assumed that the questioner accepts the fact that, in the specific circumstances referred to, a certain action *is* his duty. He recognizes it as an action which, from the moral point of view, he ought to perform. But he also recognizes it as conduct which, from the standpoint of his self-interest, would be irrational. He then asks, Why, after all, should I do it? In effect he is asking, Why should moral duty *outweigh* or *override* self-interest when there is a conflict between them?

The Ultimate Question, then, is not a moral question but rather a demand for reasons that would show why anyone should live by moral principles instead of some other principles, such as self-interest. The final justifiability of the moral life itself thus becomes a subject of ethical inquiry. The issue is a fundamental one: Is a person's commitment to live the moral life ultimately an arbitrary choice on his part, a preferring of the moral to the amoral life with no reason whatever for such a preference? If it were, then it seems that a person would be quite justified in ignoring the demands of morality whenever he could thereby gain some advantage or benefit for himself. Assuming that a person's commitment to being moral may involve, at least in some situations, the frustration of his own interests, it would seem that the most sensible thing for anyone to do would be simply to ignore moral principles and live amorally.

The demand for an ultimate justification of morality was first stated in its classic form in Plato's *Republic.* Glaucon and Adeimantus, two of the figures participating in the dialogue, challenge Socrates, the protagonist, to justify the living of a morally upright life. . . .

Socrates' . . . reply . . ., which forms the main argument of Plato's *Republic*, consists in trying to show

SOURCE: From *Principles of Ethics: An Introduction* (Belmont, CA: Wadsworth, 1975), Chapter 9, pp. 208–227. Edited.

that moral virtue is its own reward and that only the just (morally upright) man is truly happy. Thus, in effect, Socrates claims that in the long run there is no real conflict between duty and self-interest. Philosophers have been disputing about this ever since.

In order to see exactly what is at stake in trying to answer the question, Why be moral? we must recognize how it differs from a question about the nature of moral reasoning. For the question, Why be moral? arises the moment when someone realizes that, if he commits himself to the principles of moral reasoning, he may find himself in circumstances where his reasoning leads to the conclusion that he ought to do an act which entails some inconvenience, unpleasantness, or frustration for himself. It might even lead to the conclusion that in the given situation confronting him he must give up his life. He then wants to know why he should follow the rules of moral reasoning.

It should be noted that this problem does not arise for the ethical egoist, who *identifies* moral reasoning with prudential reasoning. . . . Ethical egoism is the view that each person ought to do whatever will most further his self-interest in the long run. If this is taken as an ultimate moral principle then the question, Why be moral? becomes the question, Why seek the furtherance of my self-interest in the long run? Such a question would only be asked by someone who did not want to give up his pleasures or who was satisfied with pursuing short-range goals in life, and who realized at the same time that his long-range interests might not be furthered by his continuing to live in the way he had been living. The answer to his question, of course, would be that, if he is not willing to put up with inconveniences and discomforts and if he is not able to discipline himself to sacrifice his short-range goals when his pursuit of them prevents him from achieving lasting satisfactions in life, then he will not in fact be happy. But for the ethical egoist, no sacrifice of his self-interest *as a whole* would ever be justified and no such sacrifice would ever be morally required of him.

Since the Ultimate Question arises only when it is logically possible for there to be a conflict between the demands of morality and the pursuit of self-interest, we shall be concerned from this point on with nonegoist moral principles only. We are not assuming that morality is superior to self-interest, but only that it is possible for them to be in conflict. Under this assumption, then, the next point to realize is that the Ultimate Question lies outside the framework of the logic of moral reasoning itself. For the logic of moral reasoning tells us what a good reason in ethics is. It defines the method of reasoning a person should use *if* he were to commit himself to trying to find out what he morally ought to do. In asking, Why be moral? on the other hand, one is challenging the reasonableness of being committed to trying to find out what one morally ought to do. It is a challenge to the whole enterprise of moral reasoning and moral conduct. The challenge can be put this way: Suppose there is a valid method of moral reasoning and suppose, by following it, I do find out what I morally ought to do. Why should I bother to act in accordance with this knowledge? Why shouldn't I follow my self-interest instead? In other words, granted that there is a logic of moral reasoning, why should I choose to let this logic outweigh the logic of self-interest or prudence when there is a conflict between them? In making this challenge the person is not questioning the validity of moral reasoning. Rather, he is asking why such reasoning should guide his conduct when he could just as well choose to have his conduct guided by another set of rules of reasoning, namely, the furtherance of his own self-interest. Thus, he is demanding a justification for morality (the commitment to use moral reasoning as a guide to conduct) *as a whole.* . . .

## IS THE ULTIMATE QUESTION AN ABSURDITY?

One view that has been taken by philosophers regarding the Ultimate Question is that it cannot be answered because it is absurd. It has been seen that a person who asks why he should do what is morally right already presupposes that he knows, or at least believes, that certain acts *are* right. In asking his question, therefore, he is not asking what he morally ought to do. He already has an answer to this. What, then, does he want to know? It seems that he wants to know why he should do what he knows to be right. It is as if he is saying, "I know what my moral duty is—now tell me why I ought to act in accordance with this knowledge." This, however, is absurd. For if the person knows that something is his duty, then he already knows why he ought to do it, namely, *just because it is his duty.*

When it is understood in this way, the Ultimate Question cannot be answered. But the reason it cannot is that no real question is being asked. For suppose we try to answer it by showing the person why he ought to do a certain action. We are then giving him moral reasons for doing that particular action. This, however, will not be accepted by him as an answer to the question he is asking. *His* question is, Why should I do what is right?, not, Why is this action the right thing to do? So if we show him that it is the right thing to do, he will not be satisfied. He will still ask for reasons for being *committed to doing* what he *acknowledges* to be something he ethically ought to do. Therefore it is no answer to give him moral reasons for doing the action in question. One cannot cite moral reasons for being moral (that is, for being committed to do what one believes to be right). Someone who wants to justify being moral is asking why he ought to use moral reasons as actual guides in his practical life. To give him such reasons is to assume that he will accept them as reasons for action. But this is the very thing he is questioning.

Once we become aware of this, however, we can see that there is a deep confusion behind the question Why be moral? when it is interpreted as a demand for reasons for doing what one acknowledges to be morally right. A moral reason is, by its very nature, a *"reason for acting."* It is not merely a "reason for believing," that is, a reason for accepting or acknowledging the truth of a proposition such as, Act X is morally right. To show why act X is morally right is to give moral reasons why a person should actually perform it. At the same time, it justifies accepting the statement "Act X is morally right" as true. It has been pointed out that the person who asks, Why be moral? is asking (under the present interpretation), Why should I *do* what I *believe* to be morally right? It can now be seen that he is confused in asking this. For he is assuming a separation between moral belief and moral action that isn't possible. To *believe* that an action is morally right is to have a reason for *doing* it, namely, that it is morally right. It is this confusion that explains why his question cannot be answered by giving him moral reasons for being moral. The point is that, once a person accepts moral reasons for *believing* that some action ought to be done, he has all the basis he needs for *doing* it, to wit, those very reasons for believing it ought to be done.

Given this interpretation of the Ultimate Question, it can be dismissed as resting on a mistake. It is not worth trying to answer, since a clear-thinking person would never ask it.

## THE MEANING OF THE ULTIMATE QUESTION

Does the foregoing argument successfully dispose of the Ultimate Question? Some philosophers are convinced that it does not. They claim that there is a genuine question behind the apparent oddity of asking why one ought to do something while acknowledging that a moral person would have good reason to do it. The true significance of the question, they say, has to do with a choice or decision to be made between two sorts of reasons: moral reasons and reasons of self-interest. To hold that a person who asks why he ought to do what is morally right already knows why (namely, because it *is* morally right), is to miss the real point of the Ultimate Question. It is true that one cannot give moral arguments for being moral, just as one cannot give prudential arguments for being prudent. Nevertheless there may be moral reasons *for*, and prudential reasons *against*, a certain action, and there may be moral reasons *against* and prudential reasons *for* another action. In situations of that sort, one must act either morally or in one's self-interest; one cannot do both. How is one to decide?

It is here that the question, Why be moral? does not seem at all absurd. This was why Socrates took seriously the challenge to morality expressed in the Myth of Gyges. He realized that, in normal circumstances of life, we do not ask for a justification of morality because society sees to it that it is generally in a person's self-interest to be moral. It pays to avoid social disapproval and to maintain a good reputation. But the philosopher cannot be satisfied with this, since it is possible to imagine a case where a person has the power (as described in the Myth of Gyges) to act immorally and escape social sanctions. Why, then, should he not act immorally? Unless there is a *reason* for his not doing so, morality reduces to the self-interested avoidance of social disapproval. Conformity to the actual moral code of one's own society would then be one's highest duty. This entails, of course, normative ethical relativism. The norms of each society would determine what is right and wrong in it, and no society's code as a whole could be shown to be unjust or evil. But to take the Ultimate Question seriously is to seek a reason for being moral even when it doesn't pay, and even when being moral involves a clash with what is socially approved.

So let us now interpret the Ultimate Question as asking, When moral reasons and reasons of self-interest are in conflict, why should one follow the first rather than the second (assuming that one had the power to do either)?

One possible response to the question so understood might be to try to strengthen in the questioner the desire to be moral, so that he will in fact act morally even when it is contrary to his self-interest. The Ultimate Question is then being taken as a demand for *motivating* reasons (reasons that will actually move a person to act) rather than as a demand for *justifying* reasons (reasons that show why an act ought to be done). Now it may sometimes be true that a person who asks, Why be moral? in real life does want to be motivated to such conduct. We then answer him, not by presenting him with a sound philosophical argument, but by trying to persuade or influence him so that he will feel inspired to do what is right. We try to reinforce his moral motives and strengthen his sense of duty. If he is a child we give him a moral upbringing. We not only try to instill in him a desire to abide by moral rules (of honesty, fairness, nonmaleficence, et cetera), we also try to develop his capacity and inclination to reason morally for himself. If we are successful in this, he will not feel the need to ask the question, Why be moral? in later life. He will have been motivated to be moral and thus not find it psychologically necessary to ask to be motivated.

The philosopher, however, is not interested in engaging in this kind of response. For him the Ultimate Question is a demand for a justification for being moral, not a request to be motivated to be moral. The difference is not always easy to grasp. (Indeed, there is a whole theory in psychology—the behaviorism of Professor B. F. Skinner—which overlooks the difference!) A person's motivation, we have seen, has to do with his desires, his actual tendencies to aim at certain ends or goals. Here the relevant questions are, Does this individual have a desire to be moral, and if so, how strong is that desire? In particular, is it strong enough to overcome the motive to pursue his self-interest in cases of conflict between what he believes to be morally right and what he believes will serve his own interests? Justification, on the other hand, has to do with reasons, not with desires. To justify being moral is to vindicate the belief that moral reasons outweigh or override reasons of self-interest when they conflict. It is to show why moral reasons take priority over, and hence are superior to, prudential reasons. Now the idea of one sort of rea-

sons taking priority over, or being superior to, another sort is not to be confused with the idea of one sort of reasons having greater motivational strength than another sort. A person's believing that moral reasons are better or weightier grounds for an action than prudential ones does not imply that he will always be more strongly motivated to do what is moral than what is prudent. If there is such a discrepancy in a person between justifying reasons and their motivational effectiveness, the person is said to have "weakness of will," and he may even recognize this in himself as a flaw in his character. It is then possible for him to consider an action *unjustified* (because it is morally wrong though prudentially expedient) and still actually do it. In that case his desires and actions are simply not consistent with his moral beliefs.

To justify anyone's being moral, as distinct from motivating some particular individual to be moral, is to give a sound argument in support of the claim that moral reasons take priority over reasons of self-interest whenever they conflict. If we were able to discover, or construct, such an argument, it would follow that everyone ought to be motivated by moral reasons for acting rather than by prudential reasons for acting in cases of conflict. Whether any given individual will in fact be so motivated depends on the strength of his desires, not on the soundness of an argument. Even if a person's desire to be moral were indeed strengthened by his reading or hearing such an argument, thus motivating him to be moral, this is irrelevant to the question of whether the argument actually showed the moral reasons to be superior to those of self-interest. Similarly, the argument might not convince someone intellectually, nor persuade him to act morally, nor reinforce his moral motivation. But the failure of the argument to bring about such results in any given individual is strictly irrelevant to the philosophical acceptability of the argument's content.

Suppose, then, that the Ultimate Question is understood to mean, Why do moral reasons outweigh prudential reasons in cases of conflict, rather than the other way around? Now it will not do to reply, Because morality *by definition* is that set of principles which outweigh all other principles that might conflict with them. This is not an acceptable answer because a person might decide to make reasons of self-interest *his* highest overriding principles. Then, by the given definition, self-interest would become morality in his case, and there could be no conflict between moral reasons and prudential reasons. In short, he would be an ethical egoist, and we saw earlier that the Ultimate Question presupposes that ethical egoism is false. (If ethical egoism were true, the whole issue would cease to be a meaningful problem.)

It has now become clear where the crux of the matter lies. The Ultimate Question places before us a challenge that concerns our *ultimate normative commitments*. It asks: Are there any reasons that would justify our commitment to moral principles as being the supreme overriding norms of our practical life (where "moral principles" are not by definition supreme and where it is logically possible for them to be in conflict with prudential principles)? We shall take this as our final formulation of the Ultimate Question. What answers might be proposed for it when it is understood this way?

## TWO PROPOSED ANSWERS TO THE ULTIMATE QUESTION

(1) The first answer is that there are reasons that justify *everyone's* commitment to the priority of moral principles over self-interest. For suppose *everyone* took the opposite position and made a commitment such that, whenever self-interest and morality conflict, considerations of self-interest are to override moral considerations. The consequence would be the total collapse of any social order. Each person would be out for himself and would know that every other person was out for himself. Thus, each could have no confidence that others would refrain from harming him. Everyone would live in continual fear of everyone else, since all would realize that no constraints upon self-interest would be operative (even when such constraints were required by moral principles of fairness and respect for life). A world where the priority rule, "Self-interest is to take precedence over morality," was generally accepted would be a world where no one could attain his goals. Each would lack the basic security of being able to count on others not to interfere with his pursuit of his own ends.

The conclusion is evident. The whole point of any individual's committing himself to the supremacy of self-interest over morality is to promote his own welfare. But if this commitment were made by everyone, each would be unable to promote his self-interest to as great a degree as he would when everyone made the opposite commitment. This is the paradox of universal selfishness. No one would be as well off as he would be under universal conformity to moral rules. The very purpose of universal selfishness, in other words, is undermined by its practice. The priority of self-interest over morality is therefore a self-defeating commitment. It frustrates its own purpose and is consequently irrational. Commitment to the priority of morality over self-interest, on the contrary, is self-fulfilling. Its purpose is to create a social order where everyone benefits from mutual trust. This trust is only possible under the condition that everyone makes a firm commitment to the supremacy of such moral principles as justice and nonmaleficence. For only under that condition can each person count on others not to harm him or interfere with his pursuit of his own goals.

Is this an acceptable answer to the Ultimate Question? Does it provide a sound argument to justify being moral? It seems not, for it is open to the following objection. The answer that has been proposed overlooks an important distinction, which can be brought out by comparing these two questions: (a) Why should I be moral? (b) Why should people in general be moral? The argument given above is an adequate answer to (b), but not to (a). And it is (a) that is the Ultimate Question. The person who asks, Why be moral? is asking why he, *as an individual*, should commit himself to the priority of moral principles over his self-interest. If such a person were given the argument stated above, he would reply, Yes, I agree that if *everyone* were to commit himself to the supremacy of self-interest, it would lead to the frustration of my own as well as everyone else's self-interest. So I agree that it would be irrational for everyone to do this. However, this does not show that it would be irrational for *me* to make such a commitment. For in the world as it is (where others are at least sometimes committed to being moral), by making the commitment to self-interest over morality I would thereby gain a major advantage for myself. This would be especially true if I kept my commitment a secret from others. My self-interest would be promoted by such a commitment on my part, and hence it would not be self-defeating, but quite the contrary. So how can it be shown to be irrational?

When the person who asks the Ultimate Question takes this stand, it is true that the answer to (b) will not provide him with an answer to *his* question, which is (a). But a new aspect of the situation has now come to light; we see that such a person is assuming that his case is an exception to a general rule. The argument against everyone's making a commitment to self-interest, he claims, does not hold for him. Why not? Because his commitment to self-interest can be self-fulfilling only when others do not make a similar commitment. We can then ask him, Why should your case be considered an exception? What is so special about you that makes your commitment justifiable when those of others, in circumstances similar to yours, are not? Indeed, by your own argument you can be justified in making your commitment only on the condition that others do *not* make the same commitment. Now unless you can show that you deserve to be treated as a special case, you have provided no justification for considering yourself an exception.

There is, however, a reply that can be made to this objection—a reply available to the person who asks question (a). He can say, Since I am asking for reasons that support an *ultimate* normative commitment, I am seeking to justify commitment to *any* principle as a supreme one, including the principle that I am not to make my case an exception to a general rule. After all, I can always point to some property that I have and that no one else has as the basis for claiming that my own case is to be treated differently from theirs. That is, I can commit myself to the *principle* (as a supreme one) that having the attribute in question is a relevant difference between one person and another, as far as the promotion of self-interest is concerned. The Ultimate Question can now simply be restated to include this principle, thus: Why ought a person—*any* person—having that property not be considered an exception to the general rule that moral reasons override reasons of self-interest?

To see how such a position is perfectly consistent, consider the property of having six toes on each foot with a wart on each toe. Suppose someone endowed by nature with that property states that he adopts, as an ultimate normative commitment, the principle that *anyone* with such feet is to be permitted to further his interests whenever they conflict with the interest of others. It is not possible, then, to claim that he is making an unjustifiable exception in his own favor (knowing that he alone has the property in question). For he is quite willing to universalize that principle, letting *everyone* commit himself to it and letting it be applied to *all* cases where the property in question is exemplified. Thus he is not claiming that

his own case is to be treated differently from others' *merely because it is his own*. Instead, he is committing himself to the principle (as a supreme one) that having the property in question is a relevant difference between persons.

Given this commitment, the Ultimate Question can be rephrased as follows. Instead of asking "Why should I be moral?" the individual now can ask, "Why should I not adopt the principle that anyone having six toes on each foot with a wart on each toe is an exception to the general rule that moral reasons override reasons of self-interest?" This question cannot be answered by asserting that there is no relevant difference between the questioner's case and that of others, for this would simply mean that the one who asserts this does not subscribe to the principle adopted by the questioner. To make such a statement is not to show why the questioner is mistaken, illogical, or unjustified in adopting his principle. It is merely to indicate that one has not made the same ultimate normative commitment that the questioner has. So an adequate answer has not yet been given to question (a): Why should I (as an individual) be moral?

(2) A second way to respond to the Ultimate Question can be seen as emerging from the foregoing considerations. When the Ultimate Question is interpreted as question (a),—Why should I be moral?—what is being asked for are reasons that would justify an individual's making an ultimate choice of the priority of morality over self-interest. But an *ultimate* choice, by its very nature, cannot be based on reasons, since any arguments given to justify it will themselves presuppose a principle that has already been chosen, from which it follows that the choice being justified is not an ultimate one. Let us set out this argument fully and explicitly.

To give "reasons for choosing" is to show that a person is justified in choosing one thing rather than another when he can do one or the other but not both. Giving such reasons is possible only within the framework of some principle according to which the reasons given do indeed warrant the choice based on them. (That doing X will satisfy a desire is a reason for choosing to do X only because one accepts the *principle*, What satisfies a desire is a good thing to do.) Thus giving reasons for choosing already presupposes commitment to a principle. Now suppose one were to give reasons for choosing one principle rather than another—that is, justification for a commitment to follow one as a guide to conduct rather than another. Then to give reasons for choosing *that* principle would presuppose commitment to some higher principle. And if reasons for choosing this higher principle were offered, commitment to still another at a higher level would be presupposed. And so on, for any higher principle. Therefore, with regard to any choice, if reasons for choosing are given to justify it, it cannot be an *ultimate* choice—the choice of a *highest* principle. Now the Ultimate Question is precisely the demand for reasons for making an ultimate choice. Such a demand is incoherent, as can be seen from the fact that it asks for what is impossible. No reasons can be given for an ultimate choice, for an ultimate choice rules out the possibility of reasons for choosing.

We are now in a position to understand how the challenge expressed in the Ultimate Question is to be met. We simply say to the person who poses the question, "We cannot give you reasons that will show what choice you must make. You must decide for yourself. You cannot avoid this final responsibility. The choice of how you are to live, of the supreme normative axioms of your conduct, is a choice that no one can make but yourself. Even your own reason cannot do this job for you. As we have seen, your acceptance of any reasons for choosing will presuppose some principle that has already been chosen by you. Thus it is a matter, not of your reason, but of your will. You must *decide* what shall be your ultimate commitment, and this requires an exercise of your capacity to make an autonomous, self-directed choice about the kind of life you are to live. In this sort of situation to ask for reasons is actually an unconscious attempt to evade the burden of an ultimate choice. Such an attempt is futile, however, for it is an attempt to deny what cannot be denied: that each individual must finally answer for himself the question of what principles he is to live by."

This line of thought has led some philosophers to the following conclusion. To make an ultimate commitment is nothing less than *to define oneself.* It is to decide to be a certain kind of person. There is no way to escape this choice, the reason being that we *are* at every moment what we choose to *make* ourselves, and we can always choose to create a different self and so define our nature in a new way. Most of our decisions and choices, it is true, are not consciously directed to alternatives of this ultimate kind. But that is because we make most decisions and choices within the framework of a way of life. Our way of life is our mode or "style" of carrying on human existence. It is the expression of our own conception of what it means to be human, and it includes our commitment to the very principles that determine what we accept as reasons for acting and reasons for choosing. Hence, though we make decisions and choices in daily life that are not themselves ultimate, we do so only in terms of the conceptual system embodied in the ultimate principles of our way of life.

Since our way of life is our way of defining ourselves, it is not imposed on us from the outside. Nor is it merely a reflection of the kind of person we already are. For our being a certain kind of person is due to our having chosen to live in a certain way, not the other way around. (This is a logical point about the concepts of a way of life and of personhood, not a psychological account of the origins of our "personality." To exist as a person by choosing to define oneself in a certain way is logically prior to having a "personality" as that is empirically explained and described by the science of psychology.) At every moment, whether we realize it or not, we are choosing our way of life, since at each instant there is some way of life that may be correctly ascribed to us. The fact that we do not change our mode of living from one moment to the next does not show that no choice is being made. For if we do not change, we are choosing to continue to be what we have been. And so we are still creating ourselves, making ourselves in a certain image of man, defining our own nature by living as we do. Thus, whether our way of life is one in which morality outweighs self-interest (in cases of conflict between them) or one in which self-interest overrides morality, it is our way of life because we have *made* it so. It is we who determine which shall be supreme, ethics or ego. As an ultimate choice, it is a matter of how we decide to live and to define ourselves. And whether our past decisions continue to mold our way of life in the present is something only we have the power to determine. The decision to change or not to change is forever inescapable. We cannot free ourselves from the responsibility to define our selfhood at every moment. At the same time, at every moment we have the "existential" freedom to define our selfhood as we will.

## THE COMMITMENT TO BE MORAL

Do these considerations necessarily imply that a person's commitment to the supremacy of moral principles over self-interest is an *arbitrary* decision, like the tossing of a coin? As an ultimate choice it can be called extrarational, beyond reason, neither rational nor irrational. But one can say the same of the contrary choice, by which a person commits himself to the priority of self-interest over morality. Is this all there is to be said?

Something further can indeed be said, but this something further is not the giving of a reason that would justify the choice of one alternative rather than the other. It is, instead, a matter of bringing clearly before one's mind a full recognition of the *nature* of the choice, an ultimate one. Now if it is true that in some sense ultimate choices cannot be avoided—that everyone must make them, and at every moment of life—then making such choices is simply a necessary aspect of one's autonomy as an individual. Thus suppose someone said, "I refuse to make an ultimate choice between morality and self-interest." He would actually be making an ultimate choice, namely, not to commit himself in advance but to wait until he finds himself in a situation of conflict between morality and self-interest and then commit himself on the spur of the moment. His supreme commitment is to whatever principles he chooses to follow as an immediate reaction to particular situations confronting him with the necessity to choose. This is the way he is defining *his* nature. And his decision to refuse to commit himself in advance is itself an exercise of his autonomy as an individual! It seems, then, that there can be no genuine counterinstance to the generalizations that ultimate choices must be made at every moment by each person, and that such choices realize or express the autonomy of each individual.

Now this is of great significance. For if every person, as a person, must bear the responsibility of making his own ultimate choices at every moment of his life, anything that took away or diminished the possibility of someone's exercise of this autonomy would be a violation of the very foundation of rational action and choice in that person's life. In not allowing the person to define himself, it would deny him existence as a person. What is more, to interfere with or destroy someone's capacity for making ultimate choices would be to negate that person's responsibility to answer the Ultimate Question for himself. So if the Ultimate Question is not an absurdity and if one individual can never answer if for another but each must find his own answer, then, as far as solving the

Ultimate Question is concerned, each person must be unhindered in the exercise of his autonomy as a maker of ultimate choices.

The necessary conditions for each person's asking and answering the Ultimate Question are now seen to impose a restriction upon human conduct: that no one shall deprive another of his capacity to make ultimate choices, nor interfere with his exercise of that capacity. To put it another way, each person must respect every other person's autonomy. If, in any particular set of circumstances, one person's acting from self-interest would transgress this primary rule of respect for everyone's autonomy, then his action must not be permitted. To allow him to do it would be to deny the principle which lies at the very foundation of all rational action and choice. For the freedom to make ultimate choices is necessarily presupposed by anyone's having *any* reasons for acting and reasons for choosing, whether they be moral or prudential reasons.

It seems plausible to hold that respect for the autonomy of persons is itself a moral principle. If this is so, then the choice between *this* principle and the pursuit of self-interest, even when it is an ultimate choice, is not arbitrary. Although one cannot give reasons for choosing this moral principle, one can examine fully the true nature of the choice and recognize that commitment to the principle in question is a precondition for all ultimate choices made by anyone, and hence a precondition for anyone's being able to carry on practical reasoning.

Let us then suppose, as our final consideration, that a person who has followed the foregoing argument still wants to know why he should be moral to the extent of respecting the autonomy of others. He admits that he can meaningfully ask this question only because others are respecting *his* autonomy and that, if he were not to respect *their* autonomy, they would be unable to find an answer, or even seek an answer, to the Ultimate Question. But he says, "Why should I care whether they seek an answer, or find one?"

There are no reasons that can be given which provide an answer to his question. He must decide for himself what he is to care about in his life. The only thing that can be done is to point out to him that this is a decision of a fundamental kind. It is the decision to be a certain sort of person. Can he face himself openly and unevasively and still decide not to respect the autonomy of others, having clearly before his mind the full meaning of such a choice? If he can, then he has determined what conception of being human shall be exemplified in his life and this is all one can say about his decision. No argument can be given to show that his decision is irrational or that it is based on false assumptions.

This, after all, is in keeping with the idea emphasized above: that each person must take upon himself the responsibility for his ultimate normative commitment. In subscribing to the basic principles of his way of life, a person chooses to define himself in a certain way. If he decides to be the kind of person who deprives another of the capacity for an autonomous choice of a way of life, he cannot be said to be inconsistent. One can only ask, Can he make such a decision *authentically,* that is, sincerely acknowledging it as his own and at the same time making the decision, as it were, with his whole being? If he can, he knows what sort of conception of man he chooses to exemplify. And if he is willing to choose to be that sort of person—one who denies the personhood of another in the very act of defining his own personhood—nothing more can be said.

Commitment to moral principles, then, is finally a matter of one's will, not of one's reason. Reason can make clear to us the nature of the commitment and can lead us to a full awareness of the alternatives among which we must choose. But reason alone cannot tell us what choice to make. We must not expect, therefore, that someone might provide us with an argument showing which alternative *ought* to be chosen. There is simply no way to evade the responsibility—a responsibility that rests upon each of us alone—for defining our own selves. It is up to us to answer, each in his own way, that haunting question, Who am I? We give our answer to it by deciding whether our lives shall exemplify, to whatever extent is in our power, the principles of morality, or some other principles. Even to say, "Let each one decide for himself," is to express a doctrine that imposes a restraint upon action. And it is possible for a person to commit himself to some other principle contrary to this one, without being inconsistent. As long as he understands and acknowledges the nature of his choice and does not try to evade the fact that it is *his* choice, such a person cannot be shown to have chosen against the dictates of reason.

It is simply that he decides to be a certain kind of human being. Whether we also decide to be that kind of human being ourselves is a question only we can answer. For no one can escape the necessity to determine for himself what the answer, in his own life, shall be.

# DISCUSSION: Moral Skepticism

In his book, *The Nature of Morality* (from which Reading 12, "Emotivism as Moderate Nihilism," is taken), Gilbert Harman distinguishes between two forms of moral skepticism: extreme and moderate nihilism. Both forms of nihilism assert that there are no moral facts, no moral truths, and no moral knowledge. Extreme nihilists insist that morality is a delusion and we should abandon it, just as atheists abandon religion once they have decided that there is no God. As Harman notes, this is not an easy view to accept, since it entails that there is nothing wrong with murdering one's father, torturing children, or keeping slaves.[1]

Moderate nihilists agree that there are no moral truths, but they do not think that it follows from this that we should stop using moral language to criticize and approve human behavior. Many moderate nihilists are emotivists. According to emotivism, moral utterances are neither true nor false, but they still have a valuable function, namely, to express our feelings and to influence the feelings of others.

Though not as radical as extreme nihilism, emotivism is widely at odds with our ordinary ways of thinking about morality. For example, when Nelson Mandela says that apartheid is morally wrong, he says something that he believes to be true. If emotivism is correct, then Mandela is mistaken. Because moral utterances cannot be true or false, saying "Apartheid is morally wrong" is merely a way of expressing his opposition to racial discrimination and trying to produce a similar attitude in his audience.

Moral subjectivism is a less radical form of moral skepticism than emotivism. Moral subjectivists admit that moral utterances are genuine statements that are either true or false, but they deny that the truth or falsity of these statements depends on anything objective. In this discussion, we explore moral subjectivism and emotivism, two skeptical metaethical theses about the nature of morality.

## MORAL SUBJECTIVISM

Throughout history many societies have held beliefs about morality that are strikingly different from our own. Some societies have approved of behavior and institutions that we now condemn as immoral. Good examples are slavery, the subjugation of women, and infanticide. Some present-day cultures are appalled at our behavior, and we at theirs. And even within our own culture, there are violent disagreements about the morality of such practices as abortion, homosexuality, and the use of animals in biomedical research.

That human beings disagree with one another on fundamental issues is hardly news. But unlike, say, the disputes between scientists over the existence of magnetic monopoles or the age of the universe, which are resolvable in principle by experiment and observation, ethical disputes often seem to be irresolvable. On the face of it, there does not seem to be in morality that steady progress and widespread consensus that we find in the natural sciences.

One possible explanation for this difference is that morality lacks the kind of objective basis the sciences have. For example, if Fred believes that the sun revolves around the earth and Samantha believes that the earth revolves around the sun, then what makes Samantha's belief true and Fred's belief false is the objective physical fact that, independently of what anyone believes, the earth does indeed go round the sun. Perhaps the reason for the persistence of ethical disagreements lies in the absence of any "ethical facts" that would make ethical beliefs true in the same way that physical facts make beliefs about the physical world true.

One way of trying to capture this notion that morality lacks an objective basis is through the metaethical thesis of moral subjectivism. The basic idea is that what makes a moral statement true or false is not anything objective, but something subjective, namely the subjective states of one or more individuals.[2] Subjective states are such things as beliefs, attitudes, and feelings; they are, literally, states of subjects, states of human beings.

**Moral Subjectivism:** The truth or falsity of moral statements is determined by the subjective states of one or more human beings.

Moral subjectivism comes in two main varieties: personal and cultural. According to personal subjectivism, when I say "Action X is morally wrong," all that my statement really means is that I disapprove of that action. Similarly, when I say that an action is right, this means I approve of it and nothing more. Thus understood, personal subjectivism is a metaethical thesis about what moral statements mean and what makes them true. For each person, what makes that person's moral statements true (or false) are the beliefs, attitudes, and feelings of that person.

**Personal Subjectivism:** When a person says "X is right (wrong)," this means that the person approves (disapproves) of X, and if the person approves (disapproves) of X, then X *is* right (wrong).

The other common form of moral subjectivism is cultural subjectivism, according to which the beliefs and attitudes that determine morality must be shared by most of the people in a given culture or society.

**Cultural Subjectivism:** An action X is right (wrong, or permissible) for people in a given culture if and only if all (most, the majority of) the people in that culture believe that it is right (wrong, or permissible).

One advantage that is claimed for subjectivism is that it explains the persistence of moral disagreements both within a given culture and among different cultures by removing any objective ethical facts that could be used to settle moral disputes. Also, it is claimed, subjectivism encourages us to be tolerant of the moral beliefs of others. For example, if cultural subjectivism is true, then the moral beliefs of all societies are created equal and deserve equal respect. Just as it was true for some Ancient Greeks that pederasty is morally permissible, so it is true for us that having sex with young boys is morally wrong. Thus, while critics such as James Rachels (in Reading 11) are correct to emphasize that the usual arguments presented in favor of moral skepticism and subjectivism are unsound, there might still be good reasons for thinking that these doctrines are true.

## MORAL RELATIVISM

There are several compelling objections to moral subjectivism as a correct account of the nature of morality.

First, there is the problem for the cultural subjectivist of identifying the relevant culture or society and fixing in some nonarbitrary way the percentage of people in that group whose shared beliefs make moral statements true. Inevitably, because of the moral disagreements that exist in even the most homogeneous societies, cultural subjectivism has a tendency to collapse into personal subjectivism.[3]

Second, it is important to realize that both personal and cultural subjectivism are vulnerable to a devastatingly simple form of *reductio ad absurdum* argument. Take any two people, or any two cultures, that hold diametrically opposed moral beliefs about the same action. From the statement of personal (or cultural) subjectivism as a premise, we can then deduce that one and the same action is both morally wrong and morally permissible. But this conclusion is a logical contradiction; hence it is false. So, moral subjectivism in either of its two forms is false.[4]

The only way for moral subjectivism to avoid immediate refutation by this *reductio* argument is to change the meaning of the moral terms *right, wrong, permissible,* and so on, and regard them all as being implicitly relational. I shall call this thesis about the meaning of moral terms, moral relativism.[5]

**Moral Relativism:** All moral terms such as *right, wrong,* and *permissible* are implicitly relational.

According to moral relativism, the assertion "killing children is wrong" means "killing children is wrong for . . ." and needs to be completed by adding the name of a person or a group before it can be either true or false. The word *wrong* no longer stands for a simple property of actions. Rather, it is a relation between an action and a person (or group of people) just as "taller than" is a relation between two people. Another analogy is with the meaning of the words *up* and *down*. These words carry with them an implicit reference to the direction of a line joining the earth's center to a point on its surface.

What is this relation in the case of moral terms? A plausible candidate is something like "is approved (disapproved) of by." So, when we combine moral subjectivism with moral relativism, what we end up with is this: When Jack says "Prostitution is morally wrong," this means "Jack disapproves of prostitution"; when Jill says "Prostitution is morally right," this means "Jill approves of prostitution."

Notice that if moral relativism is true, moral statements made by different people can never conflict. Moral relativism rules out even the possibility of moral disagreement. Thus, either moral subjectivism is false (because of the *reductio* argument) or moral relativism is true. But if moral relativism is true, moral disagreement is impossible. But moral disagreement is possible. So, both moral relativism and moral subjectivism are false.

The third and final point against moral subjectivism combined with moral relativism is that it makes everyone an infallible judge of morality. As long as I know what my true feelings are about an action, when I say "X is wrong" I must be correct, since all I am really saying is "I morally disapprove of X." Thus, if this view were correct, all moral judgments would be infallible. But moral judgments are not infallible. So, moral subjectivism combined with moral relativism is false.

## EMOTIVISM

A noteworthy feature of many moral beliefs is the passionate intensity with which the beliefs are held. Because they feel so strongly, people are sometimes prompted to act on their moral convictions at considerable cost to themselves. This suggests that perhaps morality is more a matter of feeling than of reason, more a matter of passionate reaction than cool reflection. Certainly no abstract argument is needed to persuade us that when we see a gang of hoodlums pour gasoline on a cat and then light it, what we are witnessing is morally wrong.[6] Our visceral, emotional reactions are often a direct and immediate source of our moral judgments.

Closely related to the observation that feelings are a source of moral beliefs is the idea that moral utterances are an expression of those feelings rather than being descriptions of facts. On this view, uttering the sentence "Capital punishment is morally wrong" would be analogous to exclaiming "Yuk!" to the idea of eating raw caterpillars or shouting "Go Tigers!" at a football game since, in all three cases, the speaker would be giving vent to personal feelings rather than making any sort of claim that could be true or false. This metaethical thesis about moral discourse is called emotivism. A less reverent name for it is "the boo-hooray theory" of moral utterances.

**Emotivism:** Moral utterances are neither true nor false. They are not statements at all, but rather expressions of feelings and attitudes.

A. J. Ayer defends a version of emotivism in Chapter 6 of his book *Language, Truth and Logic* (1936). Ayer writes:

> If I . . . say "Stealing is wrong," I produce a sentence which has no factual meaning—that is, expresses no proposition which can be either true or false. It is as if I had written "Stealing money!!"— where the shape and thickness of the exclamation marks show, by a suitable convention, that a special sort of moral disapproval is the feeling which is being expressed. It is clear that there is nothing said here which can be true or false. Another man may disagree with me about the wrongness of stealing, in the sense that he may not have the same feelings about stealing as I have, and he may quarrel with me on account of my moral sentiments. But he cannot, strictly speaking, contradict me. For in saying that a certain type of action is right or wrong, I am not making any factual statement, not even a statement about my own state of mind. I am merely expressing certain moral sentiments.[7]

Emotivism is far more radical than moral subjectivism. Unlike moral subjectivism, which says that what makes moral statements true or false is people's attitudes and beliefs, emotivism denies that moral utterances are statements that can be true or false at all. For the emotivist, moral discourse has the same noncognitive function as squeals of disgust, whoops of admiration, and cries of pain.

None of the arguments that defeat moral subjectivism works against emotivism. According to emotivism, moral judgments are neither true nor false. Hence, they cannot be fallible or infallible. Since they are not statements, they cannot lead to contradiction. And since we can have conflicting attitudes, just as we can have conflicting desires, emotivism is consistent with the possibility of moral conflict. In this way, the emotivist can block all the arguments we made against moral subjectivism.

## REASON AND EMOTION IN ETHICS

One important objection to emotivism is based on the role of reasoning in ethics. When a man is asked to explain why he holds the moral beliefs he does, or when we attempt to understand the moral code of a foreign culture, we inevitably find people giving reasons for their ethical judgments. Usually they appeal both to factual beliefs and to higher level moral generalizations from which their moral beliefs are deducible. Often what we find is that people who may seem so different from us at first sight actually share with us many of the same moral principles, but are applying them to radically different situations and relying on beliefs about the world that differ from ours. Some of their beliefs may be false, some of their inferences may be faulty, and there may be some residual conflict between their higher level moral principles and ours, but the significant point is that *the logic of their moral reasoning is the same as ours.*

If emotivism is true, then all such reasoning is a sham since only statements (that have truth-values) can be logically deduced from other statements. Emotivism asserts that moral judgments are merely expressions of feeling, not statements at all. Therefore, if emotivism is true, moral judgments cannot be the conclusions of arguments, and reasoning is irrelevant to morality. Thus, if emotivism were true, reasoning would be irrelevant to morality. But reasoning *is* relevant to morality. Therefore, emotivism is false.

The emotivist could respond to these criticisms by pointing out that our moral feelings often depend causally on our factual beliefs. For example, Hermione is an emotivist who feels that it is morally permissible to cook lobsters by plunging them alive into boiling water because she believes that lobsters are incapable of feeling pain. If Hermione should then be convinced by neurophysiological experiments that lobsters do experience pain when they are boiled alive, she might then say that she had a reason for thinking that her moral attitude was mistaken. In this way, moral sentiments could be said to be "false" if based on false beliefs; and reasoning would be relevant to moral feelings because it is relevant to the beliefs that cause those feelings.

Gilbert Harman discusses this and other emotivist responses to criticism in "Emotivism as Moderate Nihilism" (Reading 12). Harman concludes that the measures taken to defend it make emotivism far less exciting and radical than it appears to be at first sight.

Even if emotivism is false, this does not imply that feeling is irrelevant to morality. Emotions can be both a moral indicator and a spur to action. They can provide both evidence and incentive; but when asked to justify their moral practices and beliefs, people rarely appeal to mere feeling alone, and when they do, there is a strong presumption that their moral beliefs are ill-founded.

## NOTES

1. See G. Harman, *The Nature of Morality: An Introduction to Ethics* (New York: Oxford University Press, 1977), Chapter 2.

2. A moral statement is any statement that asserts of an action (or class of actions) that it is right, wrong, or permissible. For example: cannibalism is wrong; helping the needy is a moral duty; studying philosophy is morally permissible.

3. There is also the problem, noted by Marcus Singer, that it would be difficult, if not impossible, for a society of people who accepted cultural subjectivism to decide which actions are right. Each person would have to wait for the others to make up their minds before deciding what view to adopt. See M. G. Singer, "Moral Skepticism," in *Skepticism and Moral Principles*, ed. C. L. Carter (Evanston, IL: New University Press, 1973): 89.

4. This refutation of moral subjectivism and the criticisms that follow can be found in many places. See, for example, G. E. Moore, *Ethics* (London: Oxford University Press, 1912), Chapters 3 and 4; W. T. Stace, *The Concept of Morals* (New York: Macmillan, 1962), Chapters 1 and 2; J. Rachels, *The Elements of Moral Philosophy* (New York: Random House, 1986), Chapter 3. Moore notes that there is another *reductio* of personal subjectivism based on the possibility that someone might change his mind about a particular action performed in the past. This would lead the subjectivist to the absurd conclusion that the very same action could be right at one time and wrong at another.

5. This argument is borrowed from P. Montague, "Are There Objective and Absolute Moral Standards?" in *Reason and Responsibility*, 4th edition, ed. J. Feinberg (Belmont, CA: Dickenson, 1978): 580–591. Montague uses the term *subjective relativism* for what I call moral relativism.

6. The example is from G. Harman, *The Nature of Morality*, p. 4.

7. A. J. Ayer, *Language, Truth and Logic* (London: Penguin, 1971): 107.

# DISCUSSION: Egoism

Can I honestly say that I believe Gandhi was acting selfishly when he "sacrificed" himself for the freedom of the Indian people? No, I can't say that I believe it. It would be more proper to say that I know it for a fact. . . . Whatever Gandhi did, out of rational or irrational choice, he did because he chose to do it. . . . Martyrs are selfish people—the same as you and me—but with insatiable egos.

Robert Ringer, *Looking Out for #1* (New York: Fawcett Crest, 1977), page 50.

There are two different sorts of egoism: psychological egoism and ethical egoism. Psychological egoism is a descriptive, empirical thesis about the motives and desires people have and are capable of having; ethical egoism is a theory of normative ethics that purports to tell us which acts are morally right and which are not. The exact formulation of each of them is controversial, but for the moment, these crude formulations will suffice.

**Psychological Egoism:** All human beings are, at bottom, self-interested. People are incapable of desiring or pursuing anything unless they believe that thing is in their self-interest, either directly or indirectly.

**Ethical Egoism:** Each person morally ought to do only what is in his or her self-interest. For each person, moral duty coincides with doing what is best for that person.

## PSYCHOLOGICAL EGOISM

Since psychological egoism is an empirical thesis, you might wonder why philosophers should bother to discuss it at all. Why not leave to psychologists the task of either confirming or refuting it on the basis of experiment and observation?

In principle, this objection to philosophers doing armchair psychology is sound; but psychological egoism is too vague and sweeping a generalization about human nature to be of much interest to contemporary scientists; and it is philosophical insight, not scientific evidence, that is needed to expose the bad arguments often proposed in its defense. Most of the debate over psychological egoism occurred during the history of philosophy before psychology became a separate science. The evidence relevant to its evaluation consists of simple, everyday observations about human motivation and behavior.

The main philosophical significance of psychological egoism is the role it has played in the history of ethics. Thinkers such as the British philosopher Thomas Hobbes (1588–1679) used psychological egoism as an argument for ethical egoism. The connecting link between them is the plausible principle that "ought" implies "can." More precisely, the principle is that if some person, P, is incapable of performing some action, X, then it is false that P has a moral duty to do X. For example, it cannot be my moral duty to rescue a child from the path of a speeding train if I am unable to rise from my wheelchair. We can reconstruct the argument from psychological egoism to ethical egoism as follows. For the sake of brevity, we will use the term *disinterested* to mean "not in one's own self-interest."

### The Argument from Psychological Egoism to "Ethical Egoism"

(1) Psychological egoism is true.
(2) If psychological egoism is true, then no one can perform any disinterested action.
(3) If no one can perform any disinterested action, then no one has a moral duty to perform any disinterested action.

(4) No one has a moral duty to perform any disinterested action.

Notice, first, that the conclusion of this argument, statement (4), is not actually the full thesis of ethical egoism that we were led to expect. For (4) merely says that if it is not the case that doing X is in P's self-interest, then it is not the case that P has a moral duty to do X. But if ethical egoism is a normative ethical theory, it must tell us not merely what we are *not* morally obligated to do but also what we *are* morally obligated to do. So, even if the argument were sound, it would not establish the truth of ethical egoism (though it would rule out many rival theories of ethics).

Second, even if, as seems likely, psychological egoism is false, this does not prove that the conclusion of the argument is false. This is important to bear in mind since, while statement (4) is not equivalent to the full statement of ethical egoism, it still has profound implications for ethics. We need an independent argument to show that (4)—and, more generally, ethical egoism—is false. Thus, even after demolishing psychological egoism, we still have to explain why ethical egoism is false.

## BUTLER'S ATTACK ON PSYCHOLOGICAL EGOISM

In evaluating the Argument from Psychological Egoism to "Ethical Egoism," we have to decide whether premise (2) should be interpreted subjectively or objectively.[1]

> (2)  If psychological egoism is true, then no one can perform any disinterested action.

If psychological egoism asserts that people always act in ways that are *objectively* in their self-interest, then the theory is clearly false. As Bishop Butler (1692–1752) wryly remarked, the world would be a much better place than it is if more people acted out of cool and reasonable self-love, rather than responding impulsively to the passions and desires of the moment.[2] So, we must interpret psychological egoism *subjectively.* In other words, the issue is not whether an action is actually in my own self-interest, but whether I *believe* that it is so. This yields

> (2a)  If psychological egoism is true, then no one can perform any action that she believes is not in her self-interest.

But even with this change, statement (2a) is clearly false, since people do perform actions that benefit (or harm) others or harm themselves while believing (correctly) that these actions jeopardize their own self-interest. The most vivid examples are drug addicts who continue using nicotine, ethanol, or opiates while being fully aware that their health and lives are being ruined; soldiers who knowingly sacrifice their lives in battle for the sake of their comrades; and people who are so consumed with hatred that they destroy themselves in order to bring harm to an enemy.

To appreciate fully why the usual arguments for psychological egoism fail, we need to distinguish between (a) the ownership of a desire (whose desire it is) and (b) the object of the desire (what the desire is a desire for). It is a tautology—a necessary truth—that all my desires are *my* desires, that they belong to me; but it certainly does not follow from this that my desires always have my own self-interest as their object.

As Butler pointed out, an action is an interested one if it is done with the purpose of benefiting the agent (the person performing it). Any action that is not interested is disinterested; and just as many benevolent actions are disinterested, so too are many that are malevolent or impulsive.

The desires that we actually have are usually desires for particular things: the desire for food, drink, companionship, warmth. Many, but not all, of these desires refer to ourselves. For example, I want it to be the case that I eat food, that I am the one who drinks and enjoys the company of friends. But I also want my children to be clothed and fed, my friends to be happy, and my parents to be healthy. Now, when I get what I want, I feel a characteristic glow of accomplishment, I experience a feeling of pleasure. Does not this show that psychological egoism is correct after all, since it is really my own pleasure that is the end and purpose of each of my actions, even those that are directed towards others?

Before responding to this argument, notice that it involves a crucial shift in the definition of psychological egoism; for the claim is no longer that I act always in pursuit of my own self-interest, but rather that all my actions are motivated by a desire to experience pleasure. Thus, what we are now considering is the hedonistic version of psychological egoism which says that ultimately all of one's desires are for one's own pleasure and the avoidance of pain. The pleasure need not be restricted to simple sensory states but could include the feeling of accomplishment on finishing a philosophy paper or the satisfaction that comes from helping people one cares about.

Again, the theory is not supported by the evidence. Even if it were true that achieving my desires always brings me pleasure, it does not follow that all my actions are prompted by the expectation of that pleasure. When I drive to school, I know that some rubber will be worn from my tires, but it is certainly not true that I drive to school in order to wear down my tires.

Butler observed that the very fact that one is able to feel pleasure upon the successful completion of an action presupposes that one already has a desire for something other than that pleasure.[3] For example, to enjoy a good day's fishing, one must want to fish, or to be with friends, or to enjoy the solitude of the river bank, and so on. Butler never denied that many benevolent actions bring us contentment, satisfaction, and pleasure; but he did insist, correctly, that unless we had an original desire to promote the good of others in the first place, we would be incapable of experiencing that feeling of personal satisfaction.[4]

I think enough has been said (and said much better by Butler himself) to show that the usual arguments for psychological egoism are worthless and that an impartial survey of human behavior clearly establishes that psychological egoism is false. It is false that all actions are performed out of self-interest, and it is false that all actions are selfish.[5] Let us now consider ethical egoism.

## ETHICAL EGOISM

The first thing to note about ethical egoism is that it is a consequentialist theory of normative ethics, since it insists that the sole determinant of the morality of an action is the consequences that follow from it. What kind of consequences are relevant? For ethical egoists, the only morally relevant consequences are the welfare, happiness, and general self-interest of the agent (the person performing the action).

To qualify as a complete theory of normative ethics, ethical egoism needs to tell us with respect to every action whether the action is obligatory, forbidden, or merely permissible. Since ethical egoism identifies the interest of the agent as the ultimate good, this suggests the following formulation:

**Ethical Egoism:** An action is morally obligatory if and only if it maximizes the self-interest of the agent.

This definition of ethical egoism has a number of interesting features. First, it is a universal or "impersonal" version of the egoist theory, since it does not single out any particular person whose interests are to be furthered. Though it is logically possible, I am assuming that no one would consider seriously as a normative theory of ethics, a version that said that everyone is morally obligated to perform all and only those actions that bring maximum advantage to David Letterman. While it may not be a requirement of rationality, it does seem to a requirement of morality that a theory that tells us what we should do does not arbitrarily single out one individual as the center around which everyone else's life should revolve.

Second, though it is not made explicit in my formulation, I am assuming that the self-interest in question is objective, not subjective. In other words, however we identify what is the genuine self-interest of a human being, whether it be mere pleasure and gratification or the fulfillment of genuinely desirable wishes, the relevant issue is not what the agent *believes* to be in his or her self-interest, but what actually *is* in his or her self-interest, whether the agent realizes it or not. Unless we make this stipulation, it is difficult to see how the theory could explain how anyone could do anything that is wrong. Presumably, the ethical egoist wants to acknowledge that sometimes people end up doing what is morally wrong, either through miscalculation, stupidity, ignorance, or indoctrination by some rival theory of normative ethics. Thus, we take an objective view of what is in the self-interest of the agent, not a subjective one.

Third, why should ethical egoism require the maximization of the self-interest of the agent? The simple and straightforward answer is that if, as ethical egoism insists, the only morally good thing in the world is the self-interest of the agent, then anything less than the highest possible degree of that quantity is morally undesirable. It is hard to see why a committed ethical egoist should tolerate as morally permissible an action that failed to realize the maximum possible benefit that the agent could have enjoyed had the agent acted with greater prudence. This may sound harsh, but the reader is invited to formulate an alternative version of ethical egoism that is not simply arbitrary. (Remember that we are sometimes forced to act in situations such that no matter what we do, we will enjoy no positive benefit whatever. The way to read the formula is that an act is obligatory for an agent if and only if there is no other act that the agent is capable of performing that will bring him or her greater advantage.)

## OBJECTIONS TO ETHICAL EGOISM

The objections to ethical egoism as the correct theory of normative ethics fall into three camps: (l) claims that the theory implies a logical contradiction, (2) accusations that it has consequences that violate fundamental principles of metaethics, and (3) charges that the theory leads to moral conclusions that we know to be false. Let me deal with these accusations in order.

First, is ethical egoism false because it entails a logical contradiction? The usual cases brought against it are examples of competition where one person's gain is another's loss and vice versa. Suppose that George and Martha are implacable enemies cast adrift in a small lifeboat surrounded by hungry sharks.[6] Unless one of them is cast overboard, the boat will capsize and both will be eaten. The action that would maximize George's self-interest is to throw Martha overboard, thus ensuring that he is the sole survivor. Similarly, the best action for Martha is for her to jettison George and for her to be the sole survivor. Now, according to ethical egoism, George morally ought to throw Martha overboard to the sharks and be the lone survivor. Similarly, if ethical egoism is true, then Martha morally ought to throw George to the sharks, thus making her the sole survivor. Clearly, it is logically impossible for both George and Martha to be the sole survivor. So, ethical egoism implies a contradiction and is thus false.

This argument is unsound. What ethical egoism implies is that both George and Martha have a moral obligation to be the sole survivor and there is no explicit contradiction involved in that. But if we accept the following metaethical principles, then we can deduce a falsehood from ethical egoism:

(A) If P morally ought to do X, then it morally ought to be the case that P does X.

(B) If it morally ought to be the case that X and it morally ought to be the case that Y, then it morally ought to be the case that (X and Y).

(C) If it morally ought to be the case that Z, then Z must be logically possible.

It is logically impossible for both George and Martha to be the sole survivor, and ethical egoism implies that each of them morally ought to be the sole survivor. So, if we accept principles (A), (B), and (C), then we can validly deduce a false conclusion from an argument in which the statement of ethical egoism is the first premise and all the other premises are true. Therefore, ethical egoism is false.[7]

The usual response to this *reductio* is for the ethical egoist to deny (A). But it is hard to see how the ethical egoist can do this without lapsing into subjective relativism. For if morality is truly objective, then an action such as P's doing X is not merely "obligatory for P" but morally desirable, period. In other words, if ethical egoism is really an objective theory of normative ethics, then it entails not merely that P should do X but that it morally ought to be the case that P does X.

Perhaps the most compelling theoretical objection to ethical egoism is the charge of arbitrariness. This objection to ethical egoism rests on the fundamental moral principle that treating people differently is justified only if there is some relevant difference between the people that can justify the difference in treatment. We appeal to this principle in many different contexts to explain what is wrong with racism, anti-Semitism, and sexism. We have every reason to believe that this fundamental moral principle is true, since it captures the essence of why it is morally wrong to discriminate solely on the basis of race, religion, or sex. Yet, ethical egoism violates that principle because it says of any moral agent that she ought to put her interests above those of any other person simply because she is the one performing the action. But this factual difference is not relevant to justifying the difference in treatment. So, ethical egoism is false.

The specific moral conclusions that refute ethical egoism depend on exactly how one interprets the notion of self-interest. If one is a hedonistic ethical egoist, then the objection is that it is simply false that the sadist is doing what he morally ought to do when he tortures people. If one understands self-interest to include *everything* that is in a particular person's best interest *regardless of its effect on others*, then ethical egoism seems to make a moral requirement out of expediency, cruelty, and selfishness. It would, for example, have been not simply foolish, but morally wrong, for the plantation owners of South Carolina and Georgia in the 1840s to have freed their slaves or even to have treated their slaves as fellow human beings.

The basic flaw with ethical egoism as a moral theory is its failure to universalize in the right way; it does not treat people as moral equals deserving the same respect and consideration (unless there are justifiable grounds for differential treatment). The ethical egoist does universalize but does so inadequately; he allows every person the moral right to discriminate against his fellow human beings on irrelevant grounds.

## NOTES

1. This and the following criticisms of psychological egoism can be found in Joseph Butler's *Fifteen Sermons Preached at the Rolls Chapel* (1726). Butler became Bishop of Bristol in 1738 and was made Bishop of Durham in 1751; he declined the offer to become Archbishop of Canterbury. Butler's *Sermons* are widely recognized as containing the definitive critique of psychological egoism.

2. "The thing to be lamented is not that men have so great regard to their own good or interest in the present world, for they have not enough; but that they have so little to the good of others. And this seems plainly owing to their being so much engaged in the gratification of particular passions unfriendly to benevolence, and which happen to be most prevalent in them, much more than to self-love." Joseph Butler, *Five Sermons*, Ed. S. M. Brown, Jr., (Indianapolis: Bobbs-Merrill, 1950) the Preface: 16.

3. "Besides, the very idea of an interested pursuit necessarily presupposes particular passions or appetites, since the very idea of happiness consists in this that an appetite or affection enjoys its objects. It is not because we love ourselves that we find delight in such and such objects, but because we have particular affections toward them." Butler, *Five Sermons*, the Preface: 14.

4. Butler insisted, correctly, that benevolence is no more inconsistent with self-love than is any other particular affection. But he also realized that "benevolence toward particular persons may be to a degree of weakness, and so be blamable; and disinterestedness is so far from being in itself commendable that the utmost possible depravity which we can in imagination conceive is that of disinterested cruelty." Butler, *Five Sermons*, the Preface: 15.

5. What is the difference between a selfish action and one that is self-interested? An action is selfish when it serves the self-interest of the agent at the expense of the welfare of others in a morally criticizable way. Thus, to call an action selfish is to evaluate it morally and to condemn it. Flossing my teeth regularly is a self-interested action on my part, but it is not selfish. Similarly, to call an action altruistic is to give it a positive moral evaluation. Many self-destructive actions are not self-interested, but neither are they altruistic, since they do not benefit others. An altruistic action is one that is morally good, benefits the intended subject, and is done at the expense of the agent. A benevolent action is one that benefits the intended subject but may not involve any self-sacrifice and may not even be morally good.

6. See Andrew G. Oldenquist, *Moral Philosophy* (Boston: Houghton Mifflin, 1978), Chapter 5.

7. Kurt Baier's *reductio* against ethical egoism (in his book *The Moral Point of View*) is defective, since it relies on the principle that no one ought to thwart anyone's efforts to do what he or she ought to do. But, as Jesse Kalin points out in "Baier's Refutation of Ethical Egoism," *Philosophical Studies* 22 (1971): 74–78, if Brown and Green have both promised to buy a certain toy for their children and there is only one such toy left in the store, then Brown must thwart Green's efforts to do her duty in order for Brown to do his duty, and vice versa. What seems analytically true is that no one ought *wrongly* to prevent someone from doing what he or she ought to do. But then, if ethical egoism (rather than some rival moral theory) is used to determine which acts of prevention are wrong, no logical contradiction will result.

# DISCUSSION: Utilitarianism

Though he did not invent utilitarianism, the British philosopher John Stuart Mill (1806–1873) wrote the most influential work expounding and defending it. The complete text of *Utilitarianism* (1861) is short, just five chapters, of which Chapters I and II are reprinted in Reading 13.

John Stuart Mill was profoundly influenced by the writings of Jeremy Bentham (1748-1832), who, together with Mill's father, James Mill, was the leader of the Radicals, the major party for legal and political reform in nineteenth-century England. James Mill and Jeremy Bentham were ardent utilitarians; it was the intellectual source of their reforming zeal. Although John Stuart Mill later modified some aspects of Bentham's theory, he remained a committed utilitarian for the rest of his life.[1]

## BENTHAM AND MILL ON RIVAL THEORIES

Like many reformers, Bentham was more interested in advocating improvements in human life and society than in providing a carefully worked out theory from which the moral desirability of those changes could be deduced. In the first five chapters of his *Introduction to the Principles of Morals and Legislation* (1789), Bentham contemptuously dismisses all alternative normative theories of ethics, especially those that appeal to intuition or to religion as a foundation. Part of the reason for Bentham's offhand repudiation of rival theories was undoubtedly his psychological egoism: any theory that requires us to act in ways that are painful and unpleasant must be false, since we are incapable of so acting. Bentham was convinced that of all normative theories of ethics, utilitarianism alone is compatible with the facts of human nature.

Bentham makes three significant points about the justification of the Principle of Utility or the fundamental principles of any normative theory of ethics, and these points are repeated by Mill in Chapter I of *Utilitarianism.*

First, Bentham charges that those who claim that the first principles of morality are known *a priori* or by intuition rarely tell us what those principles are; when they do, there is often disagreement about their truth; and when there are several such principles that can come into conflict, no means for resolving the competition between them is provided. This casts doubt on the claim that these principles can be seen to be self-evidently true simply by reflecting on them. The utilitarian theory of Bentham and Mill is based on a single principle—the Principle of Utility—and so conflicts between principles cannot arise. Moreover, both Bentham and Mill claimed that although their theory is not known to be true *a priori,* it is confirmed and supported by empirical evidence, in the same way that empirical theories in the sciences are confirmed by observations and experiment.

Second, both Bentham and Mill argue that in the strict sense of proof (what Mill calls "proof in the ordinary and popular meaning of the term"), the first principles of any theory of ethics cannot be proven to be true. Anything that is good is either good in itself (an intrinsic good) or as a means to some other good (an instrumental good). Thus, if something (such as the utilitarian's happiness or pleasure) really is an ultimate and intrinsic good, we cannot prove it to be so by showing that it is a means to any other good. By their very nature, ultimate goods are insusceptible of proof.[2]

Third, both Bentham and Mill charge that even their critics make implicit use of utilitarianism when they attempt to do any moral reasoning at all. Mill accuses Kant of doing this when he attempts to deduce actual moral duties from his Categorical Imperative. We examine whether this accusation is warranted in the discussion "Kant's Theory of Ethics." For the moment we simply note that people often do, as matter of fact, make appeal to the consequences of actions, good and bad, when trying to justify or condemn them. The point Bentham and Mill are making is that if we consider consequences as morally relevant at all, then we are utilitarians, whether we admit it or not.

## ACT UTILITARIANISM AND THE PRINCIPLE OF UTILITY

Though the Principle of Utility is central to the utilitarian theory of ethics, neither Bentham nor Mill gives the principle a clear and acceptable formulation. Here are their exact words.

**Bentham's Version of the Principle of Utility:** "By the principle of utility is meant that principle which approves or disapproves of every action whatsoever, according to the tendency which it appears to have to augment or diminish the happiness of the party whose interest is in question. . . . The interest of the community then is, what?—the sum of the interests of the several members who compose it. . . . An action then may be said to be conformable to the principle of utility . . . when the tendency it has to augment the happiness of the community is greater than any it has to diminish it." (*Introduction to the Principles of Morals and Legislation,* Chapter l)

**Mill's Version of the Principle of Utility:** "The creed which accepts as the foundation of morals 'utility' or the 'greatest happiness principle' holds that actions are right in proportion as they tend to promote happiness; wrong as they tend to produce the reverse of happiness. By happiness is intended pleasure and the absence of pain; by unhappiness, pain and the privation of pleasure." (*Utilitarianism,* Chapter II)

The standard interpretation of Bentham and Mill is that they are both act utilitarians. Act utilitarianism (what J.J.C. Smart, in Reading 14, calls extreme utilitarianism) regards each individual action, each unique event of a human being doing something, as the fundamental unit of moral evaluation. The major alternative to act utilitarianism is rule utilitarianism, which Smart calls restricted utilitarianism. Rule utilitarianism applies the Principle of Utility not to individual actions but to general rules under which those actions fall. Later we shall consider rule utilitarianism in detail. For the moment, we will proceed as if Bentham and Mill are espousing act utilitarianism unequivocally.[3]

Unlike ethical egoism, act utilitarianism is a thoroughly universalized theory of normative ethics, since it considers not merely the interests of the agent, but all the effects, both good and bad, on *everyone* affected by an action.[4] There is a strong democratic streak in Bentham and Mill. In Chapter V of *Utilitarianism,* Mill quotes with approval Bentham's dictum of impartiality: ". . . everyone to count for one, nobody for more than one"; and in Chapter II, Mill reminds us that ". . . the happiness which forms the utilitarian standard of what is right in conduct is not the agent's own happiness but that of all concerned. As between his own happiness and that of others, utilitarianism requires him to be as strictly impartial as a disinterested and benevolent spectator."

To discuss how act utilitarianism should formulate the Principle of Utility, it is helpful to define first what we mean by the utility of an action.

**The Utility of an Action:** The utility of an action is the result of summing up over all persons the total amount of all the nonmoral good produced by the action and subtracting from it the total amount of all the nonmoral evil produced by the action.

This is the most general definition of utility within the consequentialist framework. It captures the basic idea that the moral quality of an action depends entirely on the amount of nonmoral good and evil that causally results from the action. It leaves open the question as to whether there is only one basic kind of nonmoral good or many. Notice, too, that our definition of utility is entirely objective concerning causal consequences: the utility of an action depends on the action's actual consequences, not the consequences intended by the agent nor the consequences that a reasonable person would expect to result from the action.

Bentham and Mill were both hedonists. They believed that happiness or pleasure is the only intrinsic nonmoral good and that unhappiness or pain is the only intrinsic nonmoral evil. Thus, the utility of an action is the total amount of pleasure minus the total amount of pain caused by the action. As we noted earlier, in forming this sum, each person receives the same weighting: the sufferings and enjoyments of a duchess are no more or less important than those of a beggar; all that matters is the total amount of the pleasure and pain produced, not the identities of the persons in whom the experiences occur. We will consider shortly how amounts of pleasure and pain should be calculated. For the moment, I wish to concentrate on how the morality of action is connected with its utility.

In their quoted statements, both Bentham and Mill agree that the more happiness or pleasure an action produces, the better it is, and the more unhappiness or pain it causes, the worse it is. But how are these comparative notions of morally better and worse to be connected with the moral categories: obligatory, forbidden, and permissible? One suggestion, made by Bentham, is that any action that detracts from the general happiness is morally wrong and any action that adds to it is morally permissible, but not obligatory. But this does not tell us which actions we have a moral duty to perform. Perhaps Bentham's idea was that when there are several alternatives, each of which would augment the general happiness, we have a moral obligation to perform one of them, but not any particular one. The problem with this is that it is perfectly possible that we be faced with situations in which all of our alternatives diminish the general happiness to some extent. Surely, in such a case it would not be wrong to perform the least harmful action, since there is no other action available to us that has greater utility.

These reflections suggest that act utilitarians should adopt the following version of a principle of utility. Imagine that we can enumerate all the actions that an agent could possibly perform in a given situation. Calculate the utility of each alternative. Either there is one action that has the highest utility or there are several that are tied for first place. If there is a single action that maximizes utility, the agent is morally required to perform it. If there are several actions that are tied for first place, it is permissible for the agent to choose one rather than another, but the agent must perform one of them. It is always morally wrong for a person to perform an action that has lower utility than some other action that she could have performed instead. This proposal is somewhat startling, since it significantly reduces the class of actions that are merely permissible. In most cases, whether we know it or not, one action will have higher utility than any other. In such cases, we are morally obliged to perform that action, and we are morally obliged to refrain from performing any other.

Before turning to Mill's replies to the critics of utilitarianism in Chapter II, there is one further point I wish to make about the Principle of Utility. Utilitarians are often described as advocating the principle of "the greatest happiness of the greatest number." Unfortunately, this is not acceptable as a formulation of the Principle of Utility, even when we interpret "happiness" as "utility," because it does not give a unique verdict about the morality of every action. Its basic flaw is that it requires us to maximize simultaneously two independent variables: the total amount of utility and the total number of people who are benefited by an action. It is all too easy to envisage situations in which we can produce more utility overall only by making some people much better off than others, or even by making some people worse off than they would have been otherwise. It is very difficult for the act utilitarian to devise any acceptable principle of utility other than the straight maximization of utility formula that I have suggested. By its very nature, act utilitarianism is insensitive to the distribution of the nonmoral good.

Thus, we have arrived at the following version of act utilitarianism that we shall attribute to Mill and Bentham:

**The Hedonist Definition of the Utility of an Action:** The utility of an action is the total amount of happiness (pleasure) minus the total amount of unhappiness (pain) caused by the action.

**The Principle of Utility:** An action is morally permissible if and only if there is no other action that the agent could have done instead that has higher utility. If only one action is permissible, then it is obligatory.

## MILL'S RESPONSE TO OBJECTIONS

I now wish to explore three of the objections to act utilitarianism that Mill responds to in Chapter II: the Doctrine of Swine Objection, the Too High for Humanity Objection, and the Lack of Time Objection.[5]

### The Doctrine of Swine Objection

> Now, such a theory of life excites in many minds, and among them in some of the most estimable in feeling and purpose, inveterate dislike. To suppose that life has (as they express it) no higher end than pleasure—no better and nobler object of desire and pursuit—they designate as utterly mean and groveling, as a doctrine worthy only of swine. . . .

The Doctrine of Swine Objection—the accusation that utilitarianism is a theory fit only for pigs—is leveled against versions of act utilitarianism that, like Bentham's, define the utility of an act solely in terms of the quantity of pleasure and pain the act produces. Bentham went into some detail about how to measure amounts of pleasure and pain, considering a variety of factors beyond mere intensity and duration of sensations.[6] But he steadfastly refused to recognize as morally relevant any judgments about the intrinsic value of the activities that produce pleasure and pain. Bentham wrote: "Prejudice apart, the game of push-pin is of equal value with the arts and sciences of music and poetry."[7]

Mill's response to the Doctrine of Swine Objection is to amend utilitarianism by allowing that "some *kinds* of pleasure are more desirable and more valuable than others." While Mill seems to recognize a *qualitative* dimension to pleasure and happiness distinct from its quantity, it is doubtful whether he can do this without changing his theory radically. For, if two activities give exactly the same quantity of pleasure, but one is better than the other, then pleasure by itself is not the only nonmoral good. On this view, some activities are intrinsically better than others regardless of how much pleasure they produce. We need to know what this other nonmoral good is and how to adjudicate conflicts between it and quantity of pleasure.

Mill's answer to this problem is to let informed persons judge which of two activities is better by seeing which they prefer when they have experienced both. This is problematic, since it is not clear that the preference—say, a stronger desire for A than for B—is not really just a quantitative estimate that A would be more pleasant than B. Those who would prefer reading philosophy to watching dirty movies believe, correctly, that they are the sort of people who will derive more pleasure from philosophy than from pornography. To rate intellectual activities higher than merely sensual ones, as Mill does, is thus to regard them as more pleasurable.

In other words, when Mill says, "it is better to be a human being dissatisfied than a pig satisfied; better to be Socrates dissatisfied than a fool satisfied," either he is introducing into the definition of utility a nonmoral value other than pleasure with all its attendant difficulties or, despite his assertions to the contrary, this new qualitative aspect reduces, ultimately, to sheer quantity of pleasure after all.

### The Too High for Humanity Objection

> The objectors to utilitarianism cannot always be charged with representing it in a discreditable light. On the contrary, those among them who entertain anything like a just idea of its disinterested character sometimes find fault with its standard as being too high for humanity. They say it is exacting too much to require that people shall always act from the inducement of promoting the general interests of society.

Mill's response to this objection is to distinguish between the morality of an action and the evaluation of the person who performs it. The rightness or wrongness of an action depends solely on the action's consequences; motives are relevant only to the second issue. Thus, someone with bad motives can perform an action that is objectively right, just as someone can do the wrong thing though she acts with the best of intentions. The further issue of whether someone should be praised or blamed, punished or rewarded, for her action can be decided only by a further application of the utilitarian theory. The Principle of Utility does not imply that we have an obligation to perform each of our actions from the sole motive of doing our moral duty, or maximizing utility. Thus, the objection is overturned.

### The Lack of Time Objection

> Again, defenders of utility often find themselves called upon to reply to such objections as this—that there is no time, previous to action, for calculating and weighing the effects of any line of conduct on the general happiness.

Mill's response to this objection is to deny that the Principle of Utility requires that we perform a utilitarian calculation prior to each action. In fact, given the length of time needed for such calculations, the Principle of Utility tells us that it would be wrong to perform the calculations if doing so would prevent us from acting swiftly to avert a disaster. Mill points out that we already possess reliable maxims and rules based on the collective experience of mankind about which kinds of actions are generally conducive to human happiness and which are not.

We can appreciate Mill's point by distinguishing between theoretical ethics and practical ethics. The difference between them is analogous to the difference between practical tables such as the Nautical Almanac and the theory of astronomy used to calculate them. It would be absurd for sailors to recalculate the tables every time before setting sail. Similarly, we are not required to recalculate the utility of actions such as theft, rape, and torture. Our common everyday convictions that theft, rape, and torture are morally wrong are reliable guides to what a detailed utilitarian calculation would tell us if only we had time to perform it.

If Mill was an act utilitarian, as I have been supposing, then "the rules of morality for the multitude" are rules of thumb, practical guides for action—not rules that actually determine in any final and authoritative way what we ought to do. But if the analogy with the Nautical Almanac is to hold, then at some time or other the utilitarian calculation has to be performed to make sure that the rules are indeed a reliable guide. This raises three further objections against act utilitarianism that are widely thought to be damaging.

## FURTHER OBJECTIONS TO ACT UTILITARIANISM

Act utilitarianism is a pure consequentialist theory. Future consequences alone determine the morality of action, and all the consequences that will affect human beings have to be included in the utilitarian calculation. While these calculations need not be prior to every action, it is crucial to the theory that the calculations can be performed in principle and that they give the correct answer.

### The Ripple Objection

It is difficult to see how the calculations required by act utilitarianism could ever be performed, even in principle. The causal consequences of any action spread out in time and space like the expanding ripples caused by a stone flung into a pond. But unlike the ripples, which diminish in intensity as they spread, there is no guarantee that the more distant consequences of an action will be less important than those closer to it. This problem is especially difficult when our actions affect which persons might exist in the future. At the very least, the conscientious utilitarian has to decide whether utility is to be summed over all and only those persons who exist at present or whether it should also include all those who might exist, depending on what we do now.[8]

### The Responsibility Objection

Bernard Williams voices an important objection to act utilitarianism in "A Critique of Utilitarianism" (Reading 15). Williams charges that act utilitarianism (and indeed any consequentialist theory that attaches value ultimately to states of affairs rather than to persons) cannot do justice to the notion of personal integrity, since it makes us just as responsible for actions that we allow to occur or fail to prevent as we are for those that we bring about in the normal sense of that phrase. Since *all* the causal consequences of an action determine the action's morality for the utilitarian, it is irrelevant that some of those consequences occur because other people act in response to what we do or fail to do. But this seems mistaken, since it would make us responsible for the evil committed by others. Williams uses a graphic example to illustrate the objection.

> Jim finds himself in the central square of a small South American town. Tied up against the wall are a row of twenty Indians, most terrified, a few defiant, in front of them several armed men in uniform. A heavy man in a sweat-stained khaki shirt turns out to be the captain in charge and, after a good deal of questioning of Jim which establishes that he got there by accident while on a botanical expedition, explains that the Indians are a random group of the inhabitants who, after recent acts of protest against the government, are just about to be killed to remind other possible protestors of the advantages of not protesting. However, since Jim is an honoured visitor from another land, the captain is happy to offer him a guest's privilege of killing one of the Indians himself. If Jim accepts, then as a special mark of the occasion, the other Indians will be let off. Of course, if Jim refuses, then there is no special occasion, and Pedro here will do what he was about to do when Jim arrived, and kill them all. Jim, with some desperate recollection of schoolboy fiction, wonders whether if he got hold of a gun, he could hold the captain, Pedro and the rest of the soldiers to threat, but it is quite clear from the set-up that nothing of that kind is going to work: any attempt at that sort of thing will mean that all the Indians will be killed, and himself. The men against the wall, and the other villagers, understand the situation, and are obviously begging him to accept. What should he do?

Let us assume that it is true that Pedro will kill all twenty Indians if Jim refuses to kill one of them and that if Jim does not refuse, the remaining nineteen will be spared. Thus, it is true that the killing of the twenty is one of the very bad things that will be caused to happen if Jim refuses; but Williams insists that it is a mistake to regard the death of the twenty as something for which Jim is responsible, since the killing is an act of another human being. Because act utilitarianism considers all the consequences of our actions without regard to the role played by other human agents with their own intentions and projects, it fails to recognize the crucial element of integrity in our moral life.[9]

### The Wrong Answer Objection

A common objection to act utilitarianism is that it simply gives the wrong answers when applied to situations such as promise keeping, truth telling, punishment, and the distribution of resources. Part of the problem stems from the fact that act utilitarianism is exclusively forward looking in its evaluation of actions. It is of no relevance to act utilitarianism that someone has already made a promise. All that matters is whether the future consequences of keeping the promise will maximize utility.

While few people would insist that it is always wrong to break a promise, most think that the fact that one has made a promise is in itself a morally relevant consideration. Similarly, it is possible that under special circumstances, utility would be maximized by punishing a man for a crime that we know he did not commit. It might be the only way to quell civil unrest. Yet the fact that the man is innocent, that he did not actually break the law, is thought to be a decisive reason for not punishing him.[10] It is a widely accepted principle of justice that it is always wrong to punish the innocent. Act utilitarianism implies that it is sometimes our moral obligation to punish the innocent. Therefore, act utilitarianism is false.

Finally, given the formulation of the Principle of Utility that requires the maximization of utility, many social arrangements ranging from slavery to economic discrimination would be morally permissible if act utilitarianism were correct.[11] For example, act utilitarians should be willing to kill an innocent, healthy person if the organs from that victim could be used to save the lives of several people needing transplants. But, the objection runs, it is always wrong to benefit some people by exploiting others, even though such exploitation might produce more utility than a fairer system. So, act utilitarianism is false.[12] This objection, that act utilitarianism is inconsistent with fundamental principles of justice, is a potent criticism of the theory.

## RULE UTILITARIANISM

Many philosophers who are attracted to utilitarianism as a normative theory of ethics believe that the most important objections to act utilitarianism can be avoided by applying the Principle of Utility to moral rules rather than to each individual act. The basic idea behind rule utilitarianism (what Smart calls restricted utilitarianism) is this: We decide whether an action is forbidden, obligatory, or permissible by consulting a list of correct moral rules; we decide which moral rules are the correct ones by applying the Principle of Utility to them, not to individual acts. In this way, it is claimed, we can make room for a significant class of permissible acts, and even supererogatory ones, and also avoid many of the counterintuitive consequences of act utilitarianism.

Before we can decide whether rule utilitarianism successfully avoids the problems with act utilitarianism, we need to answer some key questions. First, what is a moral rule? Second, how should we define the utility of a moral rule? Third, how exactly do we apply the Principle of Utility to candidate rules to determine which ones are correct?

Familiar examples of moral rules are the imperatives—some affirmative, some prohibitive—of the Ten Commandments and similar codes: e.g., Do not bear false witness. Honor thy father and thy mother. For the sake of generality and to facilitate comparisons between rival rules, we shall regard a moral rule as having the form: If one is in a situation of type S, then do (or do not do) action X. Thus, moral rules can conflict if they tell us to do different things in the same situation. With respect to any group of rules, an action is obligatory if the rules require it, forbidden if the rules require that it not be done, and merely permissible if there is no rule that forbids it or requires it.

Thus, unlike act utilitarianism, rule utilitarianism can easily acknowledge a wide range of actions that are merely permissible simply by not mentioning them at all. For example, my act of eating granola rather than cold pizza for breakfast this morning was, presumably, neither obligatory nor forbidden, since there is no rule that says that I ought to eat granola and there is no rule that says that I ought not to eat granola. But, according to the maximization version of the Principle of Utility for *act* utilitarianism, my eating granola for breakfast would have been morally wrong had it brought me less pleasure than anything else I could have done at that time in the morning. Similarly, rule utilitarianism is consistent with a class of supererogatory actions which, though extremely good, are not required by any moral rule.

The problem of defining the utility of a rule arises because, unlike actions, rules are not events, and so they do not have causal consequences. Perhaps the simplest way of assigning utility to a rule is in terms of the utility that would result if everyone's behavior conformed with it rather than with any other rules with which it competes. Two rules compete if they prescribe or proscribe different kinds of action in the same type of situation. This definition of competition does not imply that people who conform with different rules will always behave differently, since if one rule forbids X in situation S, and another, rival, rule forbids Y in the same type of situation, then one could obey both by doing neither X nor Y. Similarly, if rival rules prescribe different action types in the same type of situation, then, unless it is impossible for the agent to do both, she might be able to satisfy the demands of each.

At this point, it is helpful to draw a distinction between not violating a rule and conforming one's behavior to the rule. Since moral rules are conditional statements of the form, "If one is in a situation of type S, then do (or do not do) X," this means that one does not violate a particular rule if either one is not in situation S or one is in situation S and does (or does not do) X. In just the same way, one avoids violating the law that requires the purchase of a dog license either by not owning a dog at all or by owning a dog and purchasing a license.

One conforms to a moral rule of the form "Do X in situation S" if and only if one does X whenever one is in a situation of type S. It is important to realize that conforming to a moral rule does not require that one recognize that it is a rule and approve of it or even that one is aware of it. As long as one behaves as the rule requires, one is conforming with it regardless of one's intentions and beliefs.

We can now define the conformance utility of a moral rule, the notion of a moral rule being correct, and the new version of the Principle of Utility for rule utilitarianism as follows. The conformance utility of a rule is the sum of the utilities of all the actions that would be performed if everyone always behaved in conformity with that rule. We then compare competing rules such as "Do X in situation S" and "Do Y in situation S" to see which one has the highest conformance utility. The rule that would produce the most utility if everyone conformed to it in situations of type S is the correct one for that situation. We then repeat this process to discover which rules are correct in other types of situation. Finally, we judge the morality of individual actions by looking at the complete set of correct moral rules. Our new version of the Principle of Utility says that an action is morally obligatory if a correct moral rule requires doing it, forbidden if a correct moral rule requires not doing it, and merely permissible if there is no moral rule that either forbids or requires doing it.

As it stands, this proposal will not work, for, as many utilitarians themselves have pointed out, this simple version of rule utilitarianism collapses into act utilitarianism. In other words, the theory gives exactly the same verdict about every particular action that act utilitarianism does. Thus, if act utilitarianism is unsatisfactory, so too is this simple version of rule utilitarianism.

To see why our simple version of rule utilitarianism collapses into act utilitarianism, consider the following two rules, R1 and R2:

R1: In situations of type S, do X.
R2: In situations of type S, either do X or whatever else will maximize utility.

Clearly, R2 will never have less utility than R1, and so R2, and not R1, is the correct moral rule governing situations of type S. But the consequences of following R2 are exactly the same as the ones that result from act utilitarianism. Moreover, even in situations that are not governed by any explicit rule that has actually been formulated, following a degenerate rule such as R2 will maximize utility, and so the class of merely permissible actions is eroded.

The most popular solution to this difficulty involves changing the definition of a rule's utility and considering a complete integrated code of moral rules rather than evaluating them individually. Richard Brandt and J. O. Urmson are two twentieth-century proponents of what is called ideal moral code utilitarianism.[13]

## IDEAL MORAL CODE UTILITARIANISM

Most versions of ideal moral code utilitarianism are sophisticated and complicated, and their details vary from author to author. All we can do here is to sketch their most important common features. We will show how they avoid the collapse of rule utilitarianism into act utilitarianism and indicate some of their problems.

According to proponents of ideal moral code utilitarianism, conformance utility is not the appropriate measure of a rule's utility, since it fails to take into account what would actually happen if that rule were adopted by a society. It is reasonable to believe that if people deliberately and conscientiously tried to act on the degenerate rule R2, the overall results would be worse than if they just tried to follow simple rules like R1. This is because R2 requires the same kind of mind-boggling calculation as act utilitarianism and people have an inevitable tendency to exaggerate their own interests when trying to calculate the utility of a particular action that affects them. Similarly, though a vast array of very complicated rules might, in principle, yield the greatest possible utility *if everyone acted on them infallibly,* a relatively small set of simple rules that people can understand and apply easily is far more likely to have the greater utility in practice. As Urmson points out, we cannot expect 100 percent compliance from everyone all the time, but people are more likely to make a sincere and successful effort to do what morality requires of them if its demands are not too excessive. Again, a moral code that does not attempt to legislate every detail of one's life will probably have more beneficial consequences in the long run than a code that is intrusive and complex.

This suggests that in evaluating a particular action we refer it to a correct moral rule, but now, instead of applying the Principle of Utility to rules to see which is correct, we ask whether the rule is a member of the ideal moral code for that society. What makes a code ideal? A code is ideal when it would produce at least as much net utility per person as would any other code if it were current in that society.[14] But what does it mean to say that a code is current for a given society? The rough idea is that a code is current when the majority of adults, say 90 percent, subscribe to it and believe that most other members of the society subscribe to it, too.

The code that is ideal for a society is not necessarily the code that is actually current in that society, and it might be markedly different from it. Thus, ideal moral code utilitarianism is not committed to endorsing the moral status quo in societies that condone bribery, child prostitution, or cruelty to animals.

Two general problems faced by ideal moral code utilitarianism are these: How are we to determine the boundaries of the society to which our moral code applies? To what extent should possible moral codes be constrained by or presuppose existing social institutions?

It is usually assumed that the society to which a moral code applies is a political unit, a country, or a nation. But one could argue that many people belong to several different societies: to families, tribes, religious orders, trade unions. If each of these societies has a different ideal moral code, what are the moral obligations of an individual who belongs to more than one society? One answer is to extend the boundaries of one society so that it includes the others as subgroups and specify rules that take into account family relationships and tribal and political affiliations. This leads to the second problem.

Many moral rules presuppose existing social institutions such as families, monogamous marriages, a capitalist economic system, and a democratic political organization. When devising possible moral codes so as to compare their respective utilities, should we exercise free license to imagine radically different social institutions? And if we do this, should we estimate the utility that would result if the codes were current, or should we consider the utility that would result from trying to adopt the codes, given our present social and political arrangements?

Brandt's answer is rather conservative: We are to consider only what is the best moral code, given the present institutional setting, rather than consider what the best set of rules would require in a more ideal setting. Here is one of Brandt's examples. Among the Hopi Indians, a boy is expected to care for all his relatives on his mother's side, all of whom, unlike his father, belong to the same clan. This arrangement is not perfect, since there is little natural affection between a boy and an elderly maternal uncle. Does the boy nonetheless have a moral obligation to care for his aged uncle? Brandt answers "Yes," partly because, given the present arrangement, if the child does not care for his uncle, the uncle's needs will go unmet. Thus the boy will be obliged to act by a general rule of humane treatment that will be part of the ideal code for that society. Brandt also thinks that a boy who failed to fulfill his institutional obligation towards his uncle would be acting unfairly by freeloading on a system from which he has already derived substantial benefits.

---

## NOTES

1. Except, perhaps, in *On Liberty* (1859).

2. In Chapter IV of *Utilitarianism,* entitled "Of What Sort of Proof the Principle of Utility Is Susceptible," Mill gives an argument for the Principle of Utility that has been widely criticized. What Mill actually says is that the only reason that can be given for thinking that each person's happiness is desirable is the fact that everyone desires his own happiness. He

then argues that since each person's happiness is a good, the sum of all these goods or, in other words, the happiness of society, must also be a good.

3. Neither Bentham nor Mill made a clear distinction between act utilitarianism and rule utilitarianism, and so some of their remarks favor act utilitarianism (e.g., they both talk of *actions*) and some favor rule utilitarianism (e.g., they both talk of *tendencies* of actions). As J. O. Urmson notes: ". . . strictly one can say that a certain action tends to produce a certain result only if one is speaking of type- rather than token-actions. Drinking alcohol may tend to promote exhilaration, but my drinking this particular glass either does or does not produce it." Also, Mill talks explicitly about moral rules in Chapter V of *Utilitarianism* on justice. The strongest case for reading Mill as a consistent rule utilitarian in both *Utilitarianism* and in *On Liberty* is made in J. 0. Urmson, "The Interpretation of the Moral Philosophy of J. S. Mill," *The Philosophical Quarterly* 3 (1953): 33–39. Urmson's interpretation is contested in J. D. Mabbott, "Interpretations of Mill's *Utilitarianism*," *The Philosophical Quarterly* 6 (1956): 115–120.

4. Some utilitarians, such as Bentham and Peter Singer, would insist that we also consider the effects on animals just as long as they are able to feel pleasure and pain. Utilitarians have traditionally defended the inclusion of animals within the scope of morality. As Bentham put it, "The question is not, Can they reason? nor Can they *talk?* but, *Can they suffer?*" Quoted by Peter Singer, *Practical Ethics* (Cambridge: Cambridge University Press, 1979): 50.

5. See Fred Feldman, *Introductory Ethics* (Englewood Cliffs, NJ: Prentice-Hall, 1978), Chapter 3.

6. See J. Bentham, *An Introduction to the Principles of Morals and Legislation* (1789), Chapter IV, "Value of a Lot of Pleasure or Pain, How to Be Measured."

7. See the entry "Push-pin" in the *Oxford English Dictionary.* Push-pin was a trivial game played by children. Many authors paraphrase Bentham's aphorism as: "Quantity of pleasure being equal, push-pin is as good as poetry."

8. For a searching discussion of the ethics of producing future generations, see D. Parfit, *Reasons and Persons* (Oxford: Clarendon Press, 1984), Part IV, and, by the same author, "Overpopulation and the Quality of Life," in P. Singer, Ed., *Applied Ethics* (New York: Oxford University Press, 1986): 145–164. See also J. Narveson, "Utilitarianism and New Generations, " *Mind* 76 (1967): 262–272.

9. If the situation really is as Williams describes it, then Smart thinks that Jim should overcome his "squeamishness" and shoot the one Indian in order to save the lives of the other nineteen. Utilitarian principles sometimes require us to sacrifice our own inner harmony for the greater good. See J.J C. Smart, "Utilitarianism and Justice," *Journal of Chinese Philosophy* (1978). Excerpt reprinted as "Integrity and Squeamishness," in J. Glover, Ed., *Utilitarianism and Its Critics* (New York: Macmillan, 1990): 170–174. Williams's example is also discussed in D. W. Brock, "Moral Prohibitions and Consent," *Action and Responsibility,* ed. M. Bradie and M. Brand (Bowling Green, OH: Bowling Green State University, 1980): 111–121. Brock argues that Jim would be justified in killing one of the innocent Indians because all of them have consented to Jim's acceptance of the captain's offer. (In Williams's version of the story, they "are obviously begging him to accept.")

10. In his influential article, "Two Concepts of Rules," *Philosophical Review* 64 (1955): 3–32, John Rawls coins the term *telishment* for the institution of arranging for the trial and condemnation of an innocent man when officials believe that this will serve the best interests of society. Rawls defends utilitarianism against the punish-the-innocent objection by arguing that the enormous risks of adding telishment to our penal system make it unlikely that adopting telishment as an official *practice* would maximize utility. But accepting what Rawls calls the practice conception of rules requires giving up act utilitarianism in favor of a version of rule utilitarianism.

11. For a utilitarian reply to the slavery objection, see R. M. Hare, "What Is Wrong with Slavery?" *Philosophy & Public Affairs* 8 (Winter 1979). Reprinted in P. Singer, Ed., *Applied Ethics,* pp. 165–183.

12. See J. Harris, "The Survival Lottery," *Philosophy* 50 (1975): 81–87, for a defense of the utilitarian view that under carefully specified circumstances there is nothing wrong with killing one innocent person in order to save two. This article is reprinted in P. Singer, Ed., *Applied Ethics* pp. 87–95, and in J. Glover, Ed., *Utilitarianism and Its Critics,* pp. 123–130.

13. See J. O. Urmson, "Saints and Heroes," in *Essays in Moral Philosophy,* ed. A. I. Melden (Seattle: University of Washington Press, 1958): 198–216; and R. B. Brandt, "Some Merits of One Form of Rule-Utilitarianism," *University of Colorado Series in Philosophy* 3 (1967): 39–65. Brandt's paper is reprinted in *Utilitarianism with Critical Essays,* ed. S. Gorovitz (Indianapolis:

Bobbs-Merrill, 1971). Brandt claims that his theory is very similar to Mill's, when understood correctly.

14. Brandt prefers to maximize average utility (per person) rather than the total amount of utility in order to avoid problems with population control.

# DISCUSSION: Kant's Theory of Ethics

In spite of its horrifying title Kant's *Groundwork of the Metaphysic of Morals* is one of the small books which are truly great: it has exercised on human thought an influence almost ludicrously disproportionate to its size.

> H. J. Paton, Translator's Preface to the *Groundwork of the Metaphysic of Morals* (New York: Harper & Row, 1964).

Many philosophers agree that consequentialist theories of ethics in general, and specific versions of utilitarianism in particular, are incorrect. It is false that the morality of each individual action depends entirely on the action's consequences; false that the correctness of moral rules is determined solely by the rules' utility; and false that happiness or pleasure is the *summum bonum,* the ultimate good at which all moral action should aim.

Even when we take a broad view of human happiness as including not merely sensory pleasure but also the satisfaction of a wide range of interests and desires, it is hard to see why maximizing happiness is *morally* good if the persons in question do not *deserve* to be happy. Surely a world in which wrongdoers who commit evil and are happy is a worse world, from a moral point of view, than a world in which wrongdoers are punished and suffer their just deserts, even though the first world may contain more happiness than the second.

Similarly, there seems to be an important moral difference between people who conscientiously strive to do what they believe, correctly, to be their moral duty (e.g., to tell the truth or to keep a promise), regardless of the consequences and their natural inclinations, and people who perform the same action but only because they realize that it serves their self-interest or because it is a kind of action that they feel like doing, regardless of any considerations of morality.

The most influential nonconsequentialist theory of normative ethics proposed in modern times is the deontological theory of Immanuel Kant (1724–1804). As with other great philosophers who have made contributions to wide areas of human thought, it is difficult to talk about just a few of Kant's ideas without simplifying them and ignoring some of their subtleties. In presenting Kant's deontological theory, I shall concentrate on the excerpt from his *Groundwork of the Metaphysic of Morals* in Reading 16.

## HYPOTHETICAL AND CATEGORICAL IMPERATIVES

Kant begins by distinguishing between hypothetical and assertoric imperatives on the one hand and categorical imperatives on the other. Later, he argues that only categorical imperatives express moral duties and that all these duties can be derived from a single principle of universalizability which he calls the Categorical Imperative.

As their name suggests, hypothetical imperatives have the form, "If you want X, then do Y." For example, "If you want to attend law school, then study hard in college," or "If your end is to intimidate people, then be ruthless and aggressive." These imperatives are "hypothetical" or "conditional" because the imperative part, "Do X!" is conditional upon one's having a particular desire or end that one wants to achieve. If you do not have that end or goal, then the imperative does not apply to you. Kant refers to these hypothetical imperatives as rules of skill.

Assertoric imperatives are a special case of hypothetical imperatives, namely hypothetical imperatives that have the achievement of happiness as their goal. Kant assumes that every human being naturally desires her own happiness. It is an essential part of human nature to will to be happy. So, because everyone has her own happiness as a goal, if X is a means to happiness, we can simply assert that someone should "do X," without mentioning happiness explicitly. Kant's point is that such assertoric imperatives, expressing what he calls counsels of prudence, are implicitly hypothetical. It is still the case that an action is being rationally recommended only because it is a means to an end.

When we turn to the categorical imperatives that express the laws of morality, we find that they have no hypothetical or conditional element whatsoever. They command absolutely and unconditionally; they tell us what we must do, period, regardless of our particular goals, regardless of their possible effect on our happiness. Unlike hypothetical and assertoric imperatives, the imperatives of morality are universal in scope. They dictate what every single rational being should do, not just those persons who happen to have goals of a particular sort, not just human beings. The laws of morality are binding on *all* intelligent beings, whether they be humans, Martians, angels, or gods. In this respect, the laws of morality are like the fundamental laws of physics: the laws of physics describe how every object must behave; the laws of morality stipulate how every rational agent should behave.[1]

Kant next raises the question, How are all these imperatives possible? I think we can understand what Kant is driving at if we paraphrase his question as: Why would a rational being recognize the imperative as a true statement of what it should do, and thus strive to will what the imperative commands? In the case of hypothetical imperatives, the answer is simple, since "whoever wills the end . . . wills also the indispensably necessary means to it that lie in his power." Or, in other words, "whoever wills the end, wills the means." Kant regards this as an analytic truth, a proposition whose truth is determined solely by what terms like *will* mean.

It is important to realize that for Kant, willing—unlike mere wishing— is an activity constrained by the laws of logic. Kant often emphasizes this feature of willing by talking about *consistent* willing. Thus, for example, no one can consistently will that a contradiction be true. Similarly, while I may wish that I win the state lottery, if I never buy a ticket, then I cannot properly be said to *will* that I win, since buying a ticket is indispensably necessary (though not sufficient) to winning. So, if one genuinely has X as one's goal, and if one cannot attain X without doing Y, then anyone who wills to achieve X must also will to do Y. This is just a special case of the more general principle that if it is impossible that both X and Y be true, then one cannot will X *and* will Y, even though each can be willed separately.

Assertoric imperatives, which tell us what we should do to achieve happiness, are just special cases of hypothetical imperatives. The only problem with them is our ignorance about which actions will make us happy. Kant thought that we would have to be omniscient to know for sure which counsels of prudence are true.

## THE CATEGORICAL IMPERATIVE

When we turn to categorical imperatives that express moral laws, it is more difficult to see why they are true (since they aim at no object or goal) and to understand why all rational beings should will actions that conform to them. Kant's argument at this point in the text is very obscure. Its conclusion is that there is only one fundamental categorical imperative, the principle of universalizability, or *the* Categorical Imperative. He gives two very similar versions of it.[2]

**The Categorical Imperative:** "Act only on that maxim through which you can at the same time will that it should become a universal law." "Act as if the maxim of your action were to become through your will a universal law of nature."

Kant claims that all our specific moral duties can be derived from the Categorical Imperative. We shall look at this claim and Kant's illustrations of it shortly. For the moment, I suggest the following crude interpretation of Kant's answer to his question, How are categorical imperatives possible? Specific categorical imperatives are possible because they are all derivable from *the* Categorical Imperative. The Categorical Imperative is possible because it is the only general formula that captures in the right way the essential characteristics of morality: its unconditional nature and its unrestricted universality. It is as if Kant were saying to us: Look, I cannot prove that my theory of normative ethics is true; but once you properly understand the nature of morality, and if you agree that there really are such things as moral duties and moral laws that every rational being must obey, then you must admit that my theory of ethics is the correct one.[3]

To evaluate Kant's Categorical Imperative, we must first understand what Kant means by maxims and universal laws of nature. Maxims are what Kant calls subjective principles of action, to distinguish them from the objective principles or laws of morality. Kant assumes that whenever a person performs an action, there is always a general principle that expresses what that person takes himself to be doing in that situation. For example, if Nigel drives past a woman covered in blood standing at the edge of the interstate highway waving her arms, Nigel might be acting on the maxim that he will never stop on the interstate even if someone appears to be in distress. Now, let us suppose that Nigel's beliefs about the situation were entirely mistaken. The woman was an actress, filming an outdoor scene with a camera crew hidden from his sight. But the fact remains that his subjective principle about never stopping on the interstate correctly captures his maxim—the general policy on which he is acting on this occasion.

Thus, when someone performs an action, the question, What is the maxim on which the person is acting? is an empirical, psychological question that can only be answered properly by the person himself. It depends on what the person *believes* is the situation in which he finds himself and what the person's general policy is in this kind of situation. We cannot infer infallibly someone's maxim simply by observing his external behavior. Two people can behave in identical ways while an acting on different maxims; and two people can behave differently in the same situation and yet be acting on the same maxim (because their beliefs about the nature of the situation may differ).

Universal laws of nature are generalizations, like the laws of physics and chemistry, that describe how things must behave. The "must" here is not logical or moral necessity, but physical necessity. Thus, while it is logically possible for a body on which no forces are acting to move in a circle, such behavior is not physically possible, since it would violate a universal law of nature. Likewise, it is not physically possible to produce gold simply by muttering an incantation over a piece of lead. So, when Kant talks of "willing that your maxim become a universal law," he means willing that the generalized form of one's maxim be a law of nature that every rational being would obey with the same inevitability that a falling stone obeys the law of mechanics. The generalized form of Nigel's interstate maxim expressed as a universal law would be, therefore: No one ever stops for any other person on the interstate, regardless of whether that person appears to be in distress.

At this point, we must address a key deficiency in Kant's explicit formulation of the Categorical Imperative. Which of the following, (A) or (B) or both, is Kant's considered view?

(A)  If it is morally permissible for you to act on maxim M, then you can consistently will that M become a universal law.
(B)  If you can consistently will that maxim M become a universal law, then it is morally permissible for you to act on M.

(A) makes universalizability a necessary condition for the morality of action; (B) makes it a sufficient condition. Statement (A) is the thesis that comes closest to capturing Kant's explicit wording of the Categorical Imperative. It is also the premise that Kant uses in each of his four examples, for, in each case, his argument has the following form:

(A)  If it is morally permissible for you to act on maxim M, then you can consistently will that M become a universal law.
(2)  You cannot consistently will that M become a universal law.

(3)  It is morally wrong for you to act on maxim M.

There is no inconsistency between (A) and (B), and it is evident from what Kant says elsewhere in the *Groundwork* and in his *Metaphysics of Morals* that he regarded the Categorical Imperative as telling us not merely what is morally forbidden but also what is morally permitted. Adding (B) to (A) is important, since we need (B) to judge which actions are morally obligatory. For example, when we apply (B) to a maxim such as "Always tell the truth under all circumstances," we can deduce that acting on the maxim is permissible; and since the maxim itself tells us what we should always do, it follows that we have a moral obligation to tell the truth under all circumstances.

In what follows, we shall treat Kant's Categorical Imperative as the conjunction of (A) and (B). Let us state it that way.

**The Categorical Imperative (CI):** It is morally permissible for you to act on maxim M if and only if you can consistently will that M become a universal law.

Before discussing Kant's four applications of the Categorical Imperative, we should note that the principle of universalizability embodied in (CI) is not identical with the golden rule found in the Christian New Testament and elsewhere. The golden rule can be given a number of formulations (e.g., do unto others as you would have them do unto you), but the most plausible is this:

**The Golden Rule:** It is morally permissible for you to perform an act if and only if, in performing it, you refrain from treating others in ways that you would not want others to treat you.

As Kant himself points out in the *Groundwork,* the Categorical Imperative and the golden rule are not equivalent. The golden rule permits suicide and any other self-regarding act that does not involve the "treatment" of anyone other than oneself; the Categorical Imperative might not yield this result, depending on whether or not the maxim involved is universalizable. Similarly, someone who is self-sufficient or a masochist might not object to being ignored or even mistreated by others; hence, according to the golden rule, it is permissible for such a person to ignore or mistreat others; but according to the Categorical Imperative, such behavior would be immoral if the relevant maxim cannot be consistently willed as a universal law for all rational agents.

## KANT'S FOUR EXAMPLES

Kant applies his theory to four examples, each of which is supposed to illustrate a different type of moral duty.

> *The Suicide Example:*  A perfect duty to oneself.
> *The Lying Promise Example:*  A perfect duty to others.
> *The Rusting Talents Example:*  An imperfect duty to oneself.
> *The Helping the Needy Example:*  An imperfect duty to others.

Kant gives a brief explanation of his distinction between perfect and imperfect duties in a footnote. A perfect duty is "one which allows no exception in the interests of inclination." Thus, for example, if telling the truth is a perfect duty (as Kant believes it is), then one must tell the truth on all occasions when one has the opportunity to lie, no matter what one's inclination might be or how it might affect one's self-interest or the welfare of others. Usually, perfect duties consist in an obligation to refrain from treating other people in certain ways: for example, not lying to them, not stealing from them, not killing them. Imperfect duties, such as the duty to be charitable, involve an optional element; they do not require that we always perform a certain type of action on every occasion when the opportunity arises, merely that we sometimes do.

Kant's discussion of his four examples is not easy to follow and has elicited a good deal of criticism. I shall begin by making three general points before commenting on each example in turn.

First, in each of the four examples, Kant aims to show that the Categorical Imperative gives the correct verdict that actions of certain kinds are morally wrong. Now it may be that you disagree with Kant, but that disagreement can take two forms: (1) You might disagree with Kant that we have a moral duty to refrain from suicide or a moral duty to ourselves to develop our talents. (2) You might disagree with Kant that it follows from the Categorical Imperative that these kinds of action are morally wrong. It is important not to confuse these two different kinds of criticism. For example, if Kant was mistaken in believing that suicide is wrong, it is a good thing for his theory if this result is *not* actually deducible from it. One has a compelling criticism of Kant's theory only if there is a moral judgment that both follows from the Categorical Imperative and is obviously incorrect.

Second, though it is tempting to portray Kant's theory as delivering verdicts about all actions of a given type, our earlier discussion of maxims reveals that this is a misleading simplification. The issue is not whether suicide is always wrong, or whether one has a perfect duty to refrain from lying, but rather whether instances of these action-types would be permissible when done from a particular type of maxim. Thus, for example, one should not conclude from Kant's discussion that his theory entails that all acts of suicide are wrong, regardless of the maxim that is being followed.[4]

This last point about the maxim-relative nature of the conclusions generated by Kant's theory is easy to forget, especially since Kant himself often overlooked it. For example, in his essay, "On a Supposed Right to Lie from Altruistic Motives," Kant argues that one must always tell the truth, even to a murderer who is looking for his victim.[5] Apparently, Kant never considered that on this sort of occasion one might be acting on the basis of a complex maxim that has appropriate exceptions built into it.

Third, Kant's strategy in examples (1) and (2) differs from his strategy in examples (3) and (4). In (l) and (2), Kant argues that it is not possible for a rational person to will that maxim M be a universal law of nature, because it is not possible for that maxim to be a universal law of nature. Thus, one cannot will X, because X is impossible. In (3) and (4), Kant admits that M could be a universal law of nature, but he argues that this would be inconsistent with something else that a rational person must necessarily will to be the case. Thus, one cannot will X, because although X is self-consistent, it is inconsistent with Y, and everyone must will that Y.

### The Suicide Example

The maxim here is, "From self-love I make it my principle to shorten my life if its continuance threatens more evil then it promises pleasure." Kant argues that the generalized form of this maxim cannot be a law of nature, because the natural function of self-love is "to stimulate the furtherance of life." It would be a contradiction for the same faculty to have, as a matter of natural or physical necessity, functions that are opposed to one another. Kant thought that this would be like a stone's obeying two different laws of mechanics at the same time.

Kant's insistence that self-love can have only one natural function is not convincing. Why should we conceive of self-love in this way? Why not argue that self-love has two consistent functions: to promote life when its continuation is beneficial and to end it when it is not?

### The Lying Promise Example

This is Kant's most convincing argument. Kant is not indulging in the utilitarian reasoning that Mill accused him of; he is concerned, not with causal consequences, but with the logical implications of trying to make the lying-promises maxim a law of nature. Thus, his point is not that making lying promises would have bad consequences because it would lead to an erosion of trust. Rather, Kant is reminding us that to make a promise in the correct sense of that term is not just to utter a certain form of words but to say those words with the *intention* of fulfilling what the speaker has committed himself to doing. If making the lying-promises maxim were a law of nature, promises thus understood could not exist. Thus, there is an implicit contradiction involved in trying to will the maxim as a universal law.

Another way of putting Kant's point is to claim that promising is dependent on a set of institutional rules in much the same way as the game of baseball depends for its existence on the rules that define it. Admittedly, it is possible for people to play baseball even though the rules are sometimes violated; but what is not possible is to still be playing the original game of baseball when the rules themselves have been changed.

### The Rusting Talents Example

Let us take the relevant maxim to be, "If at any particular time, pleasure is more agreeable to me than developing a particular natural talent, I will not develop that talent at that time." Kant admits that it is possible that everyone emulate "the South Sea Islanders" in living a life of "idleness, indulgence, [and] procreation." Thus, he admits that it is possible for the generalized form of the maxim (extending over all talents and all times) to be a universal law. But, he argues, this conflicts with something that every rational agent must also will, namely, that those talents be developed that are necessary for achieving the agent's purposes and goals. Thus, it is morally wrong for someone to let *all* of her talents go to waste.

Kant's reasoning concerns whether developing one's natural talents is an imperfect duty. He is not arguing that one has a moral duty to develop all of one's talents all the time, merely that it would be wrong to never develop any of one's natural talents. He seems to assume that any rational agent must have at least some projects, aims, and goals and that some of them require the development of at least some natural talents for their successful realization.

One strange feature of this example is that it is not inconsistent with the imperfect duty of self-improvement that there be a particular talent that I never develop at all, just as long as I spend some time developing some of the others. Kant seems to have assumed, perhaps incorrectly, that the appropriately generalized form of the maxim would apply to all talents at all times.

### The Helping the Needy Example

The issue here is the imperfect duty to be charitable towards some of the needy at least some of the time. Kant does not say what the maxim is here. Let us assume that the maxim is, "If at any time I am doing well, then I will not help those who are in distress at that time." The generalized version then becomes, "No one who is doing well ever helps anyone who is in distress" (generalizing over all persons and all times). Kant claims that this is possible as a law of nature but that a rational agent cannot consistently will it to be a law, because it conflicts with something else that each person must of necessity will, namely, that others come to her aid when she is in distress.

Kant has uncovered an explicit contradiction in willing only if he is correct in assuming that a rational agent must will to be helped when she is in distress herself. Let us call the generalized form of the maxim, G. If I will G to be a law of nature, then I will that as matter of physical necessity, no one ever helps anyone else. It is possible, both logically and physically, that a time will come when I am in distress. If Kant is correct, then, in such a situation, a rational agent necessarily wills to be helped by others. At that time, if it should ever arise, I would be guilty of inconsistent willing, since I would be attempting to will something that is contrary to a law of nature.[6]

## SOME CRITICISMS OF KANT'S THEORY

Quite apart from the obscurity of Kant's presentation of his theory of ethics based on the Categorical Imperative, it is widely thought that Kant's theory fails for a number of theoretical reasons. We can divide these criticisms into four groups.

(1) Contrary to what Kant claims, some important moral duties cannot be derived from the Categorical Imperative alone.

(2) Some maxims cannot be universally willed, and yet it does not seem wrong to act on them.

(3) Some maxims can be universally willed, but it would be morally wrong to act on them.

(4) When perfect and imperfect duties conflict, Kant's theory sometimes gives the wrong answer.

We will discuss each of these criticisms in turn.

(1) As we have already seen in the discussion of Kant's four examples, the derivation of specific moral duties does not proceed from the Categorical Imperative alone. Kant has to rely on additional assumptions about what rational agents must necessarily will and about the natural function of principles such as self-love. These assumptions are not obviously true and might well be false. For example, it is not clear why a rational man could not be a conscientious "rugged individualist," who would not only refrain from helping others but also scrupulously refuse help when he needed it himself. Similarly, there might be fanatics who, as a matter of principle, treat others in abominable ways and would also be willing to be so treated themselves. It is logically possible that a seemingly rational "conscientious Nazi" would agree that *he* should be put to death if it should turn out that *his* parents were Jewish.[7]

(2) Given the way that Kant reaches his verdicts in his four examples, it would seem that the same kind of reasoning leads to false conclusions about the morality of actions. Consider Samantha, who acts on the maxim, "Whenever I have sexual intercourse, I shall practice a completely effective form of contraception." Presumably, the generalized form of this maxim cannot be willed as a universal law, since it would be inconsistent with the existence of the human race; but, surely, it is not wrong for a particular person to refrain from reproducing. We do not, for example, condemn monks and other celibates as immoral because they deliberately avoid having children. Similarly, consider the woman who acts on the maxim of withdrawing all her money from the bank and buying gold whenever interest rates fall below 9 percent. If everyone were to act on this maxim, the results would be disastrous; no rational person

would will the collapse of the economic system. Thus, there are many sorts of actions that are morally permissible and yet, given Kant's conception of willing, could not be willed as a universal law by a rational being. So, Kant's theory is false, since it gives incorrect answers in these cases: being unable to will that everyone behave as we do, does not, by itself, make our actions wrong.

(3) While Kant seems correct in judging that immorality often results from an unwillingness to allow others to behave on the same principles that one follows oneself, his official theory of the Categorical Imperative does not capture this insight successfully. For, imagine an egoist called Humphrey who wills that everyone refrain from stealing except himself. Thus, one of Humphrey's maxims is, "Whenever I, Humphrey, need money and the only way to obtain it is by theft, then I, Humphrey, will steal." Assume that Kant is right and that, as it stands, this maxim cannot be universalized. But suppose that there is a description of Humphrey that applies to him and to no one else. Perhaps Humphrey is the only person in the world with a diamond-shaped birthmark on his left buttock. The revised formulation of the maxim now reads, "Whenever anyone with a diamond-shaped birthmark on his left buttock needs money and the only way to obtain it is by theft, then that person will steal." There is no obvious reason why Humphrey cannot will that this maxim be a universal law. So, Kant's theory again gives an incorrect answer, since it would be just as wrong for Humphrey to act on the maxim in its revised form as it would have been for him to act on it in its original form.

(4) The objection that is raised most often against Kant's theory is that it gives the wrong answer in some cases in which a perfect duty comes into conflict with an imperfect one. The criticism can be used as an argument to show that Kant's theory is false.

(1) If Kant's theory is true, then all conflicts between a perfect and an imperfect duty should be resolved in favor of the perfect duty.
(2) Some conflicts between a perfect and an imperfect duty should be resolved in favor of the imperfect duty.

(3) Kant's theory is false.

Conflicts between perfect and imperfect moral duties arise in the kind of situation described by W. D. Ross in Reading 17. You have promised to meet a friend at a particular time for some trivial purpose, but on the way to the meeting you encounter the victim of a serious accident. If you stop and give aid, then you fail to fulfill the perfect duty to keep promises. If you do not stop and give aid, then you fail to act in accordance with the imperfect duty to help those in distress. Ross thinks, correctly, that in this situation the right thing to do is to break your engagement and give aid to the accident victim. Thus, he concludes that Kant was mistaken in claiming that perfect duties always take precedence over imperfect ones.

The problem with Kant's theory, or at least, the problem with Kant's theory as interpreted by Ross and others, is that it implies that there are absolute moral duties to tell the truth, to keep promises, to pay one's debts, that never admit of any exception.[8] As mentioned earlier, Kant himself emphasized this interpretation of his theory by insisting that one must always tell the truth, even to a murderer inquiring into the whereabouts of his intended victim. Thus, while one may choose when to fulfill one's imperfect duties, such as the duty to be charitable or the duty to help those in distress, one has no choice at all about when to fulfill one's perfect duties.

In his own deontological theory (examined in the next discussion), Ross abandons the attempt to derive all moral judgments from a single fundamental principle such as the Categorical Imperative and accepts conflicts of duty as a fact of moral life. In this way, Ross tries to avoid the major objections to Kant's theory while sharing Kant's rejection of utilitarianism.

---

## NOTES

1. Kant's point is not about the grammatical form of these imperatives, but about their fundamental nature, regardless of how they are expressed in language. Thus, it is possible for a categorical imperative expressing a moral law to have a hypothetical form (e.g., if you have made a promise, then keep it), just as a hypothetical imperative can lack the form of a conditional statement (e.g., either work harder or give up your plans to have a career in biochemistry).

2. Kant later gives an entirely different formulation of the fundamental principle of morality: Act in such a way that you always treat humanity, whether in your own person or in the person of any other, never simply as a means, but always at the same time as an end. The relationship between this and the Categorical Imperative is controversial.

3. Kant's problem was that he believed that we cannot decide empirically "whether what we call duty may not be an empty concept." Psychological investigation cannot answer the question, because at best it might reveal that an action was not performed from any *discernible* motive or inclination; but Kant thought that an action has moral value only if it is done solely out of respect for the moral law and thus has no empirical motive whatever.

4. In *The Metaphysics of Morals, Part II,* "The Metaphysical Principle of Virtue" (1797), Kant asks several "casuistical questions" about suicide. These questions suggest that Kant may have had an open mind about the morality of acts of altruistic suicide, that is, self-destructive actions performed with the noble aim of benefiting others or protecting them from harm. See I. Kant, *Ethical Philosophy,* trans. J. W. Ellington (Indianapolis: Hackett, 1983):84–85.

5. I. Kant, "On a Supposed Right to Lie from Altruistic Motives," in I. Kant, *Critique of Practical Reason and Other Writings in Moral Philosophy,* trans. L. W. Beck (Chicago: University of Chicago Press, 1949): 346–350.

6. Moreover, the inconsistency in willing exists even at the earlier time, since I would be willing that a violation of a law of nature be physically possible. I know at time $t_1$ that situation S is physically possible at time $t_2$; if S is actual at time $t_2$, then I know that I shall necessarily will that I be helped at $t_2$; thus, at time $t_1$, I will that it be physically possible that I am helped at $t_2$. But I also will at $t_1$ that G is a law of nature and hence that it is not physically possible that I be helped at $t_2$. So, at time $t_1$, I am willing two propositions about $t_2$ that cannot both be true. Hence, I am willing inconsistently at time $t_1$.

7. See R. M. Hare, *Freedom and Reason* (Oxford: Oxford University Press, 1963), Chapter 9. Hare calls such people fanatics.

8. Earlier I argued that in Kant's theory the morality of each action depends on the subjective maxim of the agent who performs it. Thus, when properly understood, Kant's theory does not imply that certain kinds of action are always wrong; rather, the theory implies that actions *performed on the basis of certain maxims* are always wrong.

# DISCUSSION: Ross's Intuitionism

In Reading 17, excerpted from his book *The Right and the Good,* W. D. Ross offers a normative theory of ethics that differs from Kant's in at least two important respects.

## ROSS AND KANT

First, Ross is a pluralist. Unlike Kant, he does not believe that all moral duties can be deduced from a single general principle such as Kant's Categorical Imperative. Rather, Ross thinks that there are several right-making (and wrong-making) properties of actions and these characteristics cannot be reduced to anything more fundamental.

Second, Ross criticizes Kant's theory for its faulty psychology. According to Ross, Kant maintains that an action can have moral value (and hence be morally right) only if it is performed from a good motive (which, for Kant, is the desire to obey the moral law, the desire to perform the action solely because we recognize that it is our moral duty). But, Ross objects, we cannot just decide at a given moment to act from one motive rather than another, since which motives we have is not under the control of our will. Hence, by applying the general principle that "ought implies can," it cannot be our moral duty to act from a good motive.[1]

Ross insists we distinguish between someone's act (what is done) and someone's motive for performing that act. An act may be morally right even though the motive behind it was morally bad; and an act may be morally wrong despite the good motives of the person performing it. Proceeding from a good motive is not what makes a right act right.[2]

Despite his criticisms of Kant, it is important to stress that Ross, just like Kant, is a deontologist. He is not a utilitarian. In his example of helping someone injured in an accident, Ross does not think that the reason one should give aid to the accident victim is that the act would produce more good than any other alternative act one could perform in such a situation. Rather, he says that providing aid is one's actual duty (or one's duty proper) in such a situation, regardless of how much good is produced as a consequence. While promise keeping (fidelity) is usually a more stringent *prima facie* duty than benevolence (beneficence), occasionally it is more important to display benevolence than it is to keep a promise, and so one's actual duty, or one's duty proper, is to render aid at the expense of breaking a promise.

## *PRIMA FACIE* DUTIES AND ACTUAL DUTY

Ross admits that his phrase "*prima facie* duty" is misleading for two reasons: (1) it might suggest, wrongly, that the term refers to a mere appearance rather than an objective fact, and (2) *prima facie* duties are not really duties at all but objective components of an act that make a partial contribution to the act's moral status. Perhaps a better term than "*prima facie* duty" would be "a property of an act that is relevant to whether or not that act is our actual duty." Ross writes:

> We have to distinguish from the characteristic of being our duty that of tending to be our duty. Any act that we do contains various elements in vir-

tue of which it falls under various categories. In virtue of being the breaking of a promise, for instance, it tends to be wrong; in virtue of being an
instance of relieving distress it tends to be right. Tendency to be one's duty
may be called a parti-resultant attribute, i.e. one which belongs to an act in
virtue of some one component in its nature. *Being* one's duty is a toti-resultant attribute, one which belongs to an act in virtue of its whole nature
and of nothing less than this.

On this account, each *prima facie* duty (such as telling the truth, paying one's
debts, refraining from injuring others) is a right-making property. Violations
of those duties are wrong-making properties. Any particular act will have some
(or possibly none) of these right-making characteristics and will have some (or
possibly none) of these wrong-making characteristics. Insofar as a particular
act has any one of the right-making properties (i.e., insofar as an act is an instance of a *prima facie* duty), the act acquires a tendency to be morally right.
Similarly, its wrong-making properties (i.e., those respects in which the act violates a *prima facie* duty) confer on the act a tendency to be wrong. Whether or
not it is our actual duty to perform the act depends on all of its right- and
wrong-making properties considered together.

Ross sometimes calls *prima facie* duties conditional duties. What I think he
means by this is that an act that is an instance of a *prima facie* duty would be our
actual duty on the condition that the act had no wrong-making properties. Or,
in other words, the act would be our actual duty if there were no other *prima
facie* duties that the act would violate.

Among the most important *prima facie* duties, Ross lists the following:

(1) Fidelity and reparation
(2) Gratitude
(3) Justice
(4) Beneficence
(5) Self-improvement
(6) Nonmaleficence

Ross does not claim that this is a complete list of all the *prima facie* duties,
and he makes no attempt to derive them from a more fundamental principle
such as Kant's Categorical Imperative. Instead, he claims that it is self-evident
that, say, promise keeping or promoting the good of others is a right-making
property of an act. Once we understand what making a promise is, we apprehend with certainty that promise keeping is a *prima facie* moral duty, just as we
apprehend the truth of the axioms of geometry or arithmetic. In other words,
Ross is an intuitionist about the right-making properties of acts.[3]

## ETHICAL INTUITIONISM: ROSS AND MOORE

In *The Right and the Good*, Ross offers some criticisms of the utilitarian theory of
ethics presented by G. E. Moore (1873–1958) in his *Principia Ethica* (1903) and
then modified slightly in *Ethics* (1912). The contrast between Moore and Ross
is instructive, since both men are intuitionists: Moore is an intuitionist about
the good; Ross is an intuitionist about the right.

Though Moore agreed with Bentham and Mill that the rightness of an act
should be judged solely by the goodness of the act's consequences, Moore argued that the term *good* does not mean "pleasure" or "happiness." According

to Moore, goodness is an unanalyzable, nonnatural property, and the term *good* is indefinable. Just as many things in the world are yellow even though *yellow* itself is indefinable, so too, Moore argued, many things in the world are good even though *good* cannot be defined or goodness analyzed into anything simpler.

If goodness is a nonnatural property as Moore claims, then (unlike the property of being yellow) it cannot be seen or experienced by any of our senses. And since it is unanalyzable, it cannot be decomposed into simpler elements that can be experienced. How then do we know which things are good? Moore's answer is *intuition*. When we imagine what it would be like for X to exist in the universe without anything else existing, we can judge directly whether X is intrinsically good by seeing whether it is better that X exist or does not. Following this procedure, Moore claimed that we know intuitively that several different kinds of things are good (e.g., the love of friends, the enjoyment of beauty) and some things are intrinsically evil (e.g., the consciousness of pain).[4] Thus, Moore was an intuitionist about goodness and a pluralist, since he believed that we know by intuition that more than one kind of thing is good.

Moore's account of the connection between the right and the good rests on the Principle of Utility adopted by many other act utilitarians: An act is right if and only if it produces the best possible consequences.[5] Since Moore doubted that we ever know with any degree of certainty what all the consequences of any action will be, he was not an intuitionist about which acts are morally right. Which things are good in themselves is self-evident; which particular acts we are morally obliged to perform is not self-evident.

Ross argues that Moore's Principle of Utility is not self-evidently true, since it conflicts with self-evident moral truths. There is, as Ross puts it, "no self-evident connexion between the attributes 'right' and 'optimific'." Ross claims that we know with intuitive certainty that features such as promise keeping and honoring the demands of justice are right-making properties, regardless of the net amount of good any particular act of those types might produce. Certainly, he thinks, our obligation to keep promises and to be just cannot be outweighed by small differences in utility.

Appeals to intuition are often regarded with suspicion in philosophy. Rather like appeals to patriotism in politics, they can indicate that someone lacks a good argument where one is needed. What Ross says in his defense is that morally reflective people (the "best people") agree that promise keeping is one of the features of an act that make the act a morally right thing to do. Surely, we seem more certain of the *prima facie* rightness of promise keeping than we do of the Principle of Utility or any other fundamental principle of normative ethics that has been proposed over the centuries. What further justification could we have for an ethical theory, Ross asks, than agreement with "the moral convictions of thoughtful and well-educated people"?

By its nature, intuitionism is a difficult theory to defend, since genuinely self-evident truths cannot be proven by any argument. The analogy with mathematics is worth exploring. Consider the claim that the axioms of Euclidean geometry are known to be true with self-evident certainty. The idea is that once we fully understand what the concepts *straight line, point,* and *parallel* mean, it is self-evident that one and only one straight line can connect two points and that one and only one straight line can be drawn parallel to another line through a point that lies outside it. This is not the same as claiming that the Euclidean axioms are the only ones that are logically possible. Indeed, there are logically consistent geometries in which more than one "straight line" connects any two points and in which there are many (or no) "straight lines" parallel to another through a point outside it. But the intuitionist will say in these cases that while these alternative geometries are logically consistent, they use terms such as *straight line* with meanings different from those employed in Euclidean geometry. Thus, they are not counterexamples to the thesis that the axioms of *Euclidean* geometry are self-evident truths. Similarly, if a woman complains that she cannot see why we have a *prima facie* obligation to keep promises, the intuitionist response is to question whether she really understands what promise keeping is.[6]

## WHAT IS OUR ACTUAL DUTY WHEN *PRIMA FACIE* DUTIES CONFLICT?

When an act has at least one right-making property and at least one wrong-making property (or, in other words, when *prima facie* duties conflict), what determines whether or not the act is our actual duty? To this vital question Ross gives no definite answer. Thus, while Ross is an intuitionist about *prima facie* duties, he does not maintain that we have the same kind of intuitive certainty about our actual duty. He honestly admits that his theory does not always yield a definite conclusion about our actual duty. At best, his theory tells us which *prima facie* duties, under normal circumstances, are more stringent than others; but which is our actual duty in a given situation cannot be predicted infallibly in advance. As Ross himself points out, there is a significant disanalogy here with mathematics. Once we know the axioms of arithmetic or geometry, we can logically deduce theorems from them with certainty, but in Ross's theory, there is no deductive relation between his (supposedly self-evident) *axioms* (the *prima facie* duties) and the *theorems* (our actual duties). For example, when we know that a triangle has two equal sides, we can deduce with certainty that the triangle has two equal angles. All further information about the triangle (such as its size and the length of its third side) are irrelevant. But when we are told that an act is an instance of promise keeping (and hence a *prima facie* duty), we cannot deduce from that information alone that it is our actual duty to perform it. If we add the information that the promise was an undertaking to do an extremely vicious and cruel act, then it would be our actual duty to refrain from performing it.

Ross claims that any pluralistic utilitarian theory such as Moore's will be similarly unable to deductively imply what one should actually do when there are incommensurable goods, such as knowledge and the appreciation of beauty, to be considered. Ross also makes an interesting comparison between ethical and aesthetic judgments. He writes:

> A poem is, for instance, in respect of certain qualities beautiful and in respect of certain others not beautiful; and our judgment as to the degree of beauty it possesses on the whole is never reached by logical reasoning from the apprehension of its particular beauties or particular defects. Both in this and in the moral case we have more or less probable opinions which are not logically justified conclusions from the general principles that are recognized as self-evident.

When duties conflict, all we can do is examine the situation carefully, conscientiously weigh the competing *prima facie* duties, and then decide what to do, recognizing that we might be mistaken. According to Ross, this is as much as we can expect from any theory of normative ethics that is true to the realities of our moral life: we should not expect an ethical theory to do all our moral thinking for us.

## NOTES

1. Ross also offers a *reductio ad absurdum* of the claim that "it is my duty to do A from a sense of duty" always means "it is my duty [to do A from the sense that it is my duty to do A]." He argues that the phrase in brackets implies that I think that it is my duty to do A *simpliciter,* not to do A from a certain motive. (See *The Right and the Good*, page 5.)

2. Ross suggests (on page 7 of *The Right and the Good*) that clarity might be served if we distinguish between acts and actions in the following way: An act is what is done; an action is the doing of it from a certain motive. Acts (but not actions) can be right or wrong; actions (but not acts) can be morally good or bad. An action is morally good if it proceeds from a good motive; but proceeding from a good motive (and thus being morally good) is not what makes a right act right.

3. As Ross acknowledges, his ethical intuitionism was influenced heavily by H. A. Prichard, especially Prichard's "Does Moral Philosophy Rest on a Mistake?" *Mind* 21 (1912): 21–37. Reprinted in the Gorovitz edition of Mill's *Utilitarianism.*

4. For Moore it is the enjoyment of beauty that is good, not the mere existence of beautiful objects. Also, while the consciousness of pain is intrinsically evil, the experience of pleasure is not good in itself. Because he denied that goodness itself can be identified with any of the things that are good, Moore is sometimes described as an "ideal" utilitarian.

5. As Ross notes, there is a subtle shift between *Principia Ethica* and *Ethics.* Moore originally claimed that *right* means "optimific." He later claimed that it is self-evident that all right acts are optimific. (Compare "all grapefruit are yellow" with "the terms *grapefruit* and *yellow* mean the same thing.")

6. Intuitionism is more plausible in ethics than it is in geometry. We have a fairly good understanding of what a promise is that does not depend on already accepting the truth of a particular moral theory. But when challenged to explain the meaning of *Euclidean straight line,* it is hard to give any characterization of the concept other than "whatever makes the Euclidean axioms and theorems about straight lines come out true." If we say that a Euclidean straight line is either (1) the path of a light ray or (2) the shortest distance between two points or (3) the path taken by a body on which no external forces are acting, then there is a chance that the resulting geometrical statements will turn out to be false. According to modern physics, neither the paths of light rays nor those of freely falling bodies are Euclidean straight lines; nor is a Euclidean straight line the shortest distance between any two points in the universe.

# **DISCUSSION:** Why Should I Be Moral?

> . . . what theory of morals can serve any useful purpose unless it can show, by a particular detail, that all the duties which it recommends are also the true interest of each individual?
>
> David Hume, *An Enquiry Concerning the Principles of Morals*
> (1752), Section IX, Part II.

The question, Why should I be moral? (which Paul Taylor, in Reading 19, calls the Ultimate Question) has been asked and attempts made to answer it since the time of Plato and Aristotle. In Plato's *Republic* (Reading 18), the question is posed by Plato's elder brothers, Glaucon and Adeimantus, as the demand for Socrates to show that being just and acting justly are *intrinsically* good.

## **THE CHALLENGE OF GLAUCON AND ADEIMANTUS**

Glaucon begins by distinguishing between three kinds of goods: those that are valued for their own sake regardless of their consequences (intrinsic goods); those that are desirable in themselves and for their consequences (goods that are both intrinsic and instrumental); those that are not valued for their own sake at all but only for the good things they lead to and the bad things they enable us to avoid (instrumental goods that are intrinsically bad).

According to Glaucon, the popular view of justice is that it is an instrumental good that is intrinsically bad. Keeping promises, telling the truth, refraining from killing, adultery, and theft are intrinsically disagreeable constraints on our natural desire to benefit ourselves at the expense of others. These activities are valued only for the external rewards and benefits associated with them in a well-regulated society. In a civilized city-state such as Athens, a person who acts justly acquires a reputation for honesty and integrity and is honored and praised; the more harmful kinds of immorality, such as killing and theft, are punished by the law. Thus, given the way society is arranged, being just is in one's self-interest, even though it requires a self-imposed limitation on one's natural desires and impulses.

Glaucon then sketches a social contract theory of the nature and origins of justice and morality. On this theory, morality is a human convention, invented and adopted by tacit consent as a compromise. It avoids the worst of all possible worlds: to suffer injustice without the power of retaliation. But it requires giving up the best of all possible worlds: to commit injustice oneself without fear of punishment.

The point is reinforced by the mythical story of the ring of Gyges. Even the most respectable citizen would become a thief, seducer, and murderer if he could commit these crimes under the cloak of invisibility. Anyone who refrained from unjust behavior when he was safe from detection would be thought "a most wretched idiot."

What is valuable about acting justly under normal circumstances is the reputation and honors that attend it. But imagine that a just person acquires an undeserved reputation for injustice and is tortured, blinded, and disemboweled while, at the same time, an unjust villain acquires an undeserved reputation for justice and is showered with honors and rewards and lives in comfort and luxury. Surely the life of the successful rogue is better than the sufferings of a martyr. So, when divorced from its usual accompaniments, justice by itself is worthless.

Adeimantus completes Glaucon's case against the intrinsic value of justice by emphasizing that children are taught to honor justice for the sake of the rewards they will receive not only from other people but also from the gods. Even if the gods cannot be bribed with sacrifices to confer benefits on the unjust (as some Greek mystery religions maintained), it is still the case that justice is being commended not for its own sake but for the advantages that accompany it.

## SOCRATES' ANSWER

No one can accuse Plato of having made his task easy. Through the character of Socrates, Plato aims to show that being just is always in one's self-interest, regardless of the vicissitudes of fortune, and regardless of any benefits or punishments conferred by men or gods.

We can summarize the relevant part of Socrates' answer as follows. If you commit injustice, then you damage your soul, your true inner self, since deliberately doing what you know to be wrong corrupts your personality and character. Thus, if you act unjustly, then your true self, your soul, will be in a worse state than if you act justly. Since the state of one's soul is far more important than any physical and material benefits that might result from wrongdoing, committing injustice always does one more harm than good. Moreover, someone with a corrupted soul is incapable of leading a happy life. Thus, doing what is right is always, ultimately, in one's true self-interest.

Socrates' attempt to show that being moral always benefits a person rests on the assumptions that (1) only a just person can have a harmonious soul, (2) having a harmonious soul is intrinsically good, and (3) having a harmonious soul is necessary and sufficient for leading a happy life.

Some philosophers object to one or more of the premises in Socrates' argument and conclude that his reasoning is unsound. For example, it is doubted whether deliberate wrongdoing is always psychologically damaging. A hardened criminal such as Bill Sikes (the vicious burglar in Charles Dickens's *Oliver Twist*) is hardly likely to spend sleepless nights racked by the pangs of conscience. Admittedly Bill Sikes's soul is in worse shape than the Pope's, but, given Sikes's depravity and his indifference to the demands of morality, he simply does not care. Given the sort of person that he is, Sikes's continuing with his criminal career will not make him worse than he already is. Socrates' premise about the harmful psychic effects of wrongdoing seems to be true only of those people who recognize the claims of morality in the first place.

Plato might respond to this objection by pointing out that it is still true that Sikes would have been better off had he never embarked on a life of crime. Though he is now beyond redemption, there was a time when Sikes could have strived to be virtuous. So, let us allow that Sikes is not a psychopath and could have become an upright citizen if he had chosen to act justly.[1] Still, it is not obvious why Sikes will have a disordered soul if he acts on his desire to steal. Why does Plato believe that only persons who act justly can have harmonious souls? In the preceding paragraph, I suggested that disharmony results from psychic conflict: a person wants to do X and considers X desirable but, through weakness of will or failure of courage, she fails to do X. But there are other reasons why someone might fail to do X: the person might simply decide that it is more desirable to do Y instead. Why, in the case of morality, should we think that wanting to be moral must be rationally overriding? In other words, I am suggesting that Plato's account assumes the very point at issue. The fundamental question, Why is it rational to put being moral above all other considerations? has not yet been answered.

One could also question whether the good of one's soul must always outweigh any amount of pain or pleasure. Plato is sometimes accused of having redefined the very notion of *self-interest* as the good of "the self" (identified with the soul), so that all physical, sensory, and material considerations become irrelevant simply as a matter of definition. It is thus argued that Plato has not really answered the original challenge of showing why it is always in one's self-interest to be moral, given the ordinary, everyday meaning of *self-interest* which includes things like freedom from pain and hunger and the enjoyment of the good things in life. Experience amply confirms that being moral does not always result in happiness.[2]

## MORALITY AND RATIONALITY

Some philosophers have criticized Socrates' answer because they think that the whole idea of trying to give a prudential justification for morality is unnecessary or inappropriate. Paul Taylor discusses this objection under the heading "Is the Ultimate Question an Absurdity?" On this view, one ought to do whatever it is one's moral duty to do simply because it is one's moral duty. No further justification is necessary. Once you have recognized that it is your moral duty to tell the truth, keep a promise, or sacrifice your life, then that is what you ought to do, period. Your reasons for thinking that an act is morally obligatory simply are your reasons for thinking that you ought to do it. To demand a further reason for doing what you admit that you morally ought to do is to betray your lack of understanding of the nature of morality.[3]

Taylor's response to this objection is to emphasize the distinction between moral reasons and prudential ones. Once this is done, the objection collapses. For, while it may be absurd and unnecessary to ask for *moral* reasons to do what morality requires, it is not obviously a mistake to ask for *prudential* reasons for being moral.

The Ultimate Question is usually presented as a demand to show why it is rational for me to be moral on those occasions when behaving morally conflicts with my self-interest. Lurking behind the question is the presumption that such behavior would be irrational. We can make this presumption explicit by proposing the following argument for analysis:

### The Rationality Argument
(1)  If it is rational for me to do X, then doing X is in my self-interest.
(2)  Doing what morality requires is sometimes contrary to my self-interest.

---

(3)  Doing what morality requires is not always rational for me.

This argument is valid. So, if we wish to reject its conclusion, we have to reject one or both of its premises as false. Thus, on our interpretation of Socrates' answer, Plato attacked premise (2) by arguing that one is always better off by acting morally (being just), when self-interest is understood correctly. But, as we have seen, Plato can be accused of changing the meaning of the term *self-interest*.

Another way of attacking premise (2), while retaining the ordinary meaning of *self-interest*, is to argue for the truth of ethical egoism.

**Ethical Egoism:** Each person morally ought to do only what is in his or her self-interest. For each person, moral duty coincides with doing what is best for that person.

Obviously, if ethical egoism were true, morality and self-interest could never conflict. But it was argued in the discussion entitled "Egoism" that ethical egoism is *not* a correct theory of normative ethics. So, it seems more promising to focus our attention on premise (1).

Premise (1) asserts that if it is rational for me to do X, then doing X is in my self-interest. What does the term *rational* mean here? Obviously, it cannot mean simply "is in my self-interest," since that would reduce premise (1) to a trivial tautology. In general, being rational is a matter of acting on the basis of reasons rather than acting on impulse or acting for no reason at all. Reasons are closely linked with desires: a woman who wants to be a surgeon has a reason for attending medical school; someone who wants to harm an enemy has a reason for setting a trap; a person who wants to alleviate human suffering has a reason for joining a charity. Thus, we have:

(R)  If it is rational for me to do X, then I have a reason to do X.
(D)  If I have a reason to do X, then either I desire X as an end in itself or I desire X as a means to an end.

But why should we think that premise (1) in the Rationality Argument follows from (R) and (D)? The usual answer is that premise (1) follows from (R) and (D) because psychological egoism is true.

**Psychological Egoism:** All human beings are, at bottom, self-interested. No one is capable of desiring or pursuing anything unless that thing is in the person's *own* self-interest, either directly or indirectly.

Psychological egoism is an empirical thesis about the motives and desires that human beings actually have and are capable of having. If it were true, then premise (1) would be established; but, as we saw in the discussion entitled "Egoism," the usual arguments for psychological egoism are unsound and the evidence against it is compelling.

Let us assume that psychological egoism is false and people are capable of desiring things other than their own self-interest. We might still argue for premise (1) by insisting that whenever these other desires are not reducible to self-interest, they are always subordinate to the pursuit of personal gain. Thus, we concede that someone can have moral reasons for performing actions and that these reasons do not reduce to the single-minded pursuit of self-interest; but when moral reasons conflict with reasons of self-interest, rationality requires that self-interest should always take precedence over morality. So, while I can have a reason for behaving altruistically or benevolently, I can never have a *conclusive* reason for so acting. A reason is conclusive when it overrides all others that may conflict with it.

> (S) If doing X is in my self-interest, then I have a conclusive reason to do X. (Self-interest always overrides morality when they conflict.)

Statement (S) is closely related to Taylor's final formulation of the Ultimate Question in Reading 19. It allows that people can and do have moral reasons for their actions, reasons that can compete with self-interest; but it insists that when moral reasons and prudential reasons do conflict, rationality requires that self-interest win out over morality.

It is important to stress that (S) is a normative principle, not a descriptive one. The idea is not to rehash psychological egoism by describing how people actually make decisions but to stipulate how they ought to make them. The norm here is one of the rationality of action, not morality. (S) is about what we should do *all things considered*, where the claims of morality are just one consideration among others.

## TAYLOR'S RESPONSE TO THE ULTIMATE QUESTION

Taylor himself does not endorse (S). He puts the Ultimate Question as a question, not as a defense of immorality. According to Taylor's final position, no rational justification of (S) is possible, since (S) purports to state an ultimate principle of rationality. We can present Taylor's reasoning as a *reductio* argument. Assume that (S) is an ultimate principle of rationality and that it can be justified. If (S) can be rationally justified, then it can be deduced from a principle of rationality that is even more fundamental. Thus, if (S) can be justified, it is not an ultimate principle. Conclusion: If (S) is an ultimate principle of rationality, then it cannot be rationally justified.

We can gain further insight into Taylor's position by comparing (S) with (M).

> (M) If doing X is morally obligatory, then I have a conclusive reason for doing X. (Morality always overrides self-interest when they conflict.)

If Taylor is correct, the choice between (S) and (M) cannot be made on rational grounds. Neither of these ultimate principles can be shown to be true by any argument without contradicting the claim that they are indeed ultimate principles. We have reached an intellectual impasse.

Let me illustrate what Taylor is driving at. We cannot refute (S) simply by interpreting *conclusive reasons* to mean "morally conclusive reasons," since the normative principle it expresses is not intended to be a moral one. Similarly, it will not do to argue for (M) simply on the grounds that if I morally ought to do something, then I have a *morally* conclusive reason for doing it. In both (M) and (S), the issue is what I should do *all things considered* in a sense of *should* that is *not* a moral sense.

On Taylor's analysis, choosing between (S) and (M) is a matter not of reasoning but of commitment, a matter of deciding to be the sort of person who always subordinates the claims of morality to his self-interest rather than someone who always puts morality first, even when it conflicts with self-interest. In the final analysis, one answers the Ultimate Question by deciding to make (or by deciding not to make) "moral principles . . . the supreme overriding norms of our practical life." The decision is neither rational nor irrational; it is extrarational—beyond reason. At best, we can make clear to ourselves the nature of the choice we confront and the kind of people we will become as a consequence of choosing one way or the other.

One virtue of Taylor's account is that it does enable us to reject the Rationality Argument; for if Taylor is correct, no reason can be given for thinking that premise (1) is true once this is understood as (S). The drawback is that we cannot answer the Ultimate Question by showing that a commitment to morality is rational. In other words, we avoid the accusation that being moral is irrational, but the price we pay is to give up being able to show that it is rational. Is this really the best we can do?

One thing that we should stress is that Taylor is using the term *rational* in a very strict and limited sense to mean "derivable from a principle of rationality." But a choice can be nonrational (or "extrarational" in Taylor's sense) and yet still be an informed decision, taken in the light of our preferences, our beliefs about human nature, and the likely consequences of deciding one way or the other, given the way the world works. The decision also depends on which theory of normative ethics determines the nature and scope of our moral obligations.

When we take all these factors into account, there is a case to be made for allowing morality to override self-interest, except in the most dire circumstances; for in the world that most of us actually inhabit, we gain more than we lose by being moral. True, morality does require us to perform some acts that are genuinely disadvantageous; but we are more than compensated by the acts that others perform that are disadvantageous to them but that benefit us.

A good example of morality yielding advantages that mere prudence cannot is the keeping of contracts, agreements, and promises. The following illustration is from the American philosopher David Gauthier.[4]

Imagine that there are two countries, A and B, who sign a disarmament pact and are considering which strategy to pursue—whether to adhere to the agreement or to violate it. Suppose that their preference rankings range from (1) (= most preferable) to (4) (= least preferable).

|  |  | <B> | |
|  |  | adheres | violates |
| [A] | adheres | [2], <2> | [4], <1> |
|  | violates | [1], <4> | [3], <3> |

If A looks simply at which action is in A's self-interest, regardless of what B does, then A is always better off by violating no matter what B does; similarly for B. And if both nations reason in the same way, then both end up violating, which is not the optimal outcome. But as long as both nations rank mutual adherence above mutual violation, each gains less from its own violations (one unit) than it loses from the other's (two units); and this is true despite the fact that mutual adherence is not the best possible outcome for either.

What this example shows is that being trustworthy (adhering to agreements) can yield advantages that mere prudence cannot if there is a pre-existing tendency to be trustworthy and if duplicitous behavior is detectable.[5] All this, of course, is very similar to the picture presented by Glaucon and Adeimantus. If either nation has a "ring of Gyges" to conceal its activities from the prying eyes of its neighbor, then self-interest dictates violating in private and lying in public. And if there is no reason to expect any tendency towards trustworthiness in one's rival, then violation is the only rational course. But if there is reason to expect some commitment to morality on the part of others, then a wary commitment to morality on one's own part is rational, since it permits, through cooperation, the attainment of mutually advantageous goals that are not otherwise achievable.

## NOTES

1. For the relevance of psychopathy to the question, Why act morally?, see P. Singer, *Practical Ethics* (Cambridge: University of Cambridge Press, 1979), Chapter 10.

2. John Hospers criticizes Plato's claim that morality is necessary and sufficient for happiness in his *Human Conduct: Problems of Ethics*, 2nd. edition (New York: Harcourt Brace Jovanovich, 1982): 22–26.

3. This position is defended in H. A. Prichard, "Does Moral Philosophy Rest on a Mistake?" *Mind* 21 (1912): 21–37, echoing the Kantian view that unless virtue is valued for its own sake, it has no moral value at all.

4. D. Gauthier, "Morality and Advantage," *The Philosophical Review* 76 (1967): 460–475. The disarmament pact example is a special case of the Prisoner's Dilemma. For further details, see R. Nozick, *Philosophical Explanations* (Cambridge, MA: Harvard University Press, 1981): 539–545; and D. Parfit, *Reasons and Persons* (Oxford: Clarendon Press, 1984), Chaper 2.

5. It has become common for people to argue that reciprocal altruism has a biological basis. See P. Singer, *The Expanding Circle* (New York: Farrar, Strauss & Giroux, 1981); and J. L. Mackie, "The Law of the Jungle: Moral Alternatives and Principles of Evolution," *Philosophy* 53 (1978) 455–464.

# PART III

# THE NATURE OF MIND

The readings in Part III deal with issues in the philosophy of mind. Though it also involves topics in epistemology, philosophy of language, and philosophy of science, philosophy of mind is first and foremost a branch of metaphysics, since it concerns the nature and properties of a fundamental entity, namely, the mind. Among the questions addressed are, What are minds? How are minds related to brains and bodies? Can computers think? Can persons survive death? The second question—How are minds related to brains and bodies?—is often referred to as "the mind-body problem."

Before embarking on this project, a few words about terminology are in order. Not all languages contain the rich diversity of terms that we find in English for talking about the subject of mental phenomena: mind, spirit, soul, self, person, consciousness, intellect, psyche, and so on. Descartes originally wrote and published his *Meditations* (1641) in Latin, using the terms *mens* and *anima*. These have been translated as "mind" and "soul." But, as Descartes himself emphasized, he made no distinction between them.[1]

Like Descartes, Locke, Hume, and other writers, we will treat the terms *mind* and *soul* as synonyms. Thus, while it is more idiomatic to speak of "the immortality of the soul" rather than the "immortality of the mind," and while it is true that English lacks an adjective that stands in the same relation to the noun *soul* as does *mental* to *mind*, we will not regard these differences as having any philosophical significance. In common with the vast majority of philosophers

217

who have offered theories of mind—atheists and theists alike—we make no distinction between souls and minds. A disordered mind is a disordered soul; if minds cannot survive bodily death, neither can souls. To the extent that theories of personal identity are theories about the identity of individual minds, they are, to the same extent, theories about the identity of individual souls. To deny that nonhuman animals have souls is to deny that they have minds such as humans possess.

Wherever possible, I shall use the term *mind* rather than *soul* or *spirit* to refer to the subject of mental phenomena, whatever that subject may be. In other words, the term *mind* is intended to be a neutral way of referring to whatever it is that believes, thinks, perceives, feels; it presupposes neither that the subject of mental phenomena is an immaterial substance nor that it is purely material.

Mental phenomena include both states (persisting conditions) and events (things that happen at a particular time) of the following sorts: cognitive states and events (e.g., believing that Canberra is the capital of Australia; coming to doubt that interest rates will decrease); emotional states and events (e.g., feeling sad about the plight of the African elephant; being shocked by the sight of a dismembered elephant carcass); perceptual states and events (e.g., having a persistent green afterimage after staring at a red star; seeing that smoke is billowing from the toaster); sensory feelings of pain, dizziness, warmth, intoxication (e.g., being aware of a dull ache in one's lower back; feeling a sharp twinge of pain in an amputated limb); volitions (e.g., making a determined effort of will to move an injured limb). In short, minds are the things in which occur events and states such as believing, hoping, sensing, imagining, dreaming, remembering, willing, and doubting.

Mental phenomena have a number of distinctive properties that any adequate theory of minds has to take account of. The following is a list of the most important of these properties:

*(a) Qualitative Content.* Sensations, emotions, and other mental states have a qualitative "feel" to them that is difficult to describe in words and perhaps can be known only by personal experience: e.g., the taste of a pineapple, the sensation of seeing the color purple, the agony of toothache, the fear of drowning. Philosophers sometimes refer to the qualitative aspect of sensations as *qualia*: the distinctive taste experienced when one bites into a fresh pineapple is the *quale* of that sensory experience.

*(b) Intentional Content.* Cognitive states such as believing that Santa Claus has a white beard or hoping that it will snow at Thanksgiving are intentional; they are about the objects and states of affairs indicated by the "that" clauses. Philosophers call this "aboutness" of mental states intentionality. It has no connection with the ordinary sense of *intention* in sentences such as "It was no accident that Foster crashed his car; he steered into the tree intentionally."

*(c) Privileged Access.* We are immediately and directly aware of what is in our own minds. This seems especially true of sensory and perceptual states. We do not, for example, *infer* that we are in pain, we just know it; nor do we *deduce* that we seem to be seeing a rabbit or that we are thinking of Rome. Introspection tells us immediately, without inference, what we are thinking or imagining or seem to be seeing, and so on. We do not have the same kind of direct, noninferential access to anyone else's mind.

*(d) Incorrigibility.* Many philosophers insist that when we introspect the contents of our own minds, we cannot be mistaken about what we find there.

First-person statements such as "I am in pain," "I am conscious," and "It looks to me as if there is a rabbit on the lawn" are, it is claimed, incorrigible; they are immune from error.

*(e) Causal Relation to One's Own Body.*    Minds are able to causally affect the bodies they animate and to be causally affected by them. Stabbing my leg with a pin causes the occurrence of a mental event—pain. Also, I can cause my limbs to move by an act of willing or volition. These causal relations hold only between *my* mind and *my* body, not between my mind and anyone else's body or between my body and anyone else's mind.

*(f) Unity.*    The visual and auditory sensations I have at a concert are unified; they are *my* sensations, the sensations of a single perceiver. There is a difference between my experiences and the sensations of two other persons, one blind, the other deaf, who attend the same concert.

The traditional way of thinking about mind-body theories is to divide them into two classes: dualistic theories and monistic theories. Dualistic theories postulate the existence of two distinct and utterly different kinds of substance (physical matter and immaterial minds); in monistic theories, there is just one kind of substance: either just regular matter (the identity theory, eliminative materialism, behaviorism, functionalism) or just minds (reductive idealism) or just some third sort of stuff (double aspect theories).[2] The following is a list of the main alternatives.[3]

## DUALISTIC MIND-BODY THEORIES

**Cartesian Dualism:** There is a two-way causal interaction between immaterial minds and physical bodies. (Plato, R. Descartes, C. D. Broad, C. J. Ducasse, J. Eccles)

**Epiphenomenalism:** The causal connection between bodies and minds is strictly one-way, from bodies to minds, but not vice versa; physical events cause mental events, but mental events do not cause physical events or other mental events. (T. H. Huxley, J. Lachs, J. W. Cornman, K. Campbell)

**Parallelism:** There is no causal connection between minds and bodies; God arranges the correlation between physical events and mental events. (N. Malebranche; G. W. Leibniz)

## MONISTIC MIND-BODY THEORIES

**Reductive Materialism, The Identity Theory, Physicalism:** Everything that exists is physical; mental states are identical with brain states; minds are nothing but brains. (T. Hobbes, J.J.C. Smart, D. Armstrong)

**Eliminative Materialism:** Talk about minds and mental states is literally false; there are no such things. Folk psychology is a false theory that will be replaced by neuroscience. (R. Rorty, S. Stich, P. S. Churchland, P. M. Churchland)

**Reductive Idealism:** Brains and all other physical objects are nothing but mental perceptions; minds and their perceptions are the only things that exist. (G. Berkeley)

**Double Aspect Theories:** There is just one type of substance that has both physical and mental attributes (B. Spinoza); some individual substances—persons—have both physical and mental attributes. (P. F. Strawson)

**Philosophical Behaviorism, Logical Behaviorism:** Mental statements describe nothing but behavior and dispositions to behave; statements about minds and mental contents are just confused ways of talking about observable behavior. (L. Wittgenstein, N. Malcolm, G. Ryle, B. F. Skinner)

**Functionalism:** Mental states are defined functionally by their causal relations to other mental states, stimuli, and behavior; minds are suitably programmed machines. (H. Putnam, J. Fodor, D. C. Dennett)

In his *Sixth Meditation* (Reading 20), Descartes argues that his body (made up of extended matter) and his mind (whose essence is thought and consciousness) are distinct substances, capable of separate existence. C. D. Broad also defends Cartesian dualism in "The Traditional Problem of Body and Mind" (Reading 21). Broad is particularly concerned to defend what he calls Two-sided Interaction (the two-way causal interaction between minds and bodies) from critics who charge that such an interaction would violate scientific laws such as the principle of energy conservation. Both Descartes' arguments and Broad's defense are examined in the discussion entitled "Dualism."

One of the most influential attacks on Cartesian dualism in the twentieth century came in Gilbert Ryle's book *The Concept of Mind* (1949). In the book's first chapter, "Descartes' Myth" (Reading 22), Ryle accuses dualism of being based on the misuse and misunderstanding of ordinary language. Ryle's own position—philosophical (or logical) behaviorism—maintains that all our talk about beliefs, desires, motives, volitions, ideas, thoughts, and the like really refers to actual and possible behavior (including verbal behavior), not to mysterious episodes in a ghostly, nonmaterial mind. The link between mental states and behavior is not causal but logical. Some of the difficulties with Ryle's position are explored in the discussion entitled "Behaviorism."

One popular alternative to both dualism and behaviorism is materialism. The materialist regards human beings as nothing more than complicated physico-chemical mechanisms, amenable to the same kind of scientific investigation as other physical objects. On the reductive (or identity theory) version of materialism, consciousness, pains, and sensations are not fictions or oblique ways of talking about behavior; nor are they states of an immaterial mind. Rather, they are real inner states of one's physical body that cause characteristic types of behavior. Just as lightning is identical with a discharge of electricity and heat is identical with the motions of molecules, mental phenomena are identical with states, events, and processes in the brain and central nervous system. In "Sensations and Brain Processes" (Reading 23), J.J.C. Smart defends the identity version of materialism against a variety of objections.

Some philosophers who reject both reductive materialism and behaviorism concede that each contains important insights into the nature of the mind. In "The Mind-Body Problem" (Reading 24), Jerry Fodor explains how functionalism recognizes the causal link between mental states and behavior (thus siding with the materialist) while acknowledging that each type of mental state has to stand in certain characteristic relations to other mental states and behavior (thus agreeing with the behaviorist). Fodor argues that mental states must be defined functionally in terms of their causal relations to stimuli, behavior, and other mental states. For example, consider three people—Adam, Betty, and Clarissa—each of whom believes that Einstein is dead. It may well be true that in each of these three people, his or her belief that Einstein is dead is identical with a particular physical state of that person's brain. But though each believes the same thing, the *physical* states of the brains of Adam, Betty, and Clarissa might be quite different. What makes each of these brain states the same *mental* state of believing that Einstein is dead is its place in a causal network. Believing that Einstein is dead is the sort of state that is typically *caused* by hearing or reading that Einstein has died; it tends to *cause* other mental states, such as the belief that the founder of relativity theory is no longer alive; it is likely to *cause* behavior such as writing or uttering "Einstein is dead" in appropriate contexts. Functionalism, the identity theory, and other varieties of materialism are examined in the discussion entitled "Materialism."

As Fodor himself points out, functionalism as a theory of mind has been heavily influenced by the distinction between hardware and software drawn by computer scientists. The same computer program (software, mental states) can be run on many different machines (hardware, brains). This suggests that if functionalism is true, it should be possible for things other than brains to have mental states. In particular, functionalism suggests that computers might be able to think, believe, perhaps even suffer pain, simply by running the right kind of program.

In "Minds, Brains, and Programs" (Reading 25), John Searle aims to refute the thesis of "strong AI" (artificial intelligence) that computers can have beliefs and other cognitive mental states simply by being suitably programmed. Searle's attempt to disprove strong AI rests on a thought experiment (*Gedankenexperiment*) that has become known as the Chinese Room Argument. Though Searle anticipates many objections and responds to them in his paper, the Chinese Room Argument has generated considerable controversy among philosophers of mind and cognitive scientists. In "Artificial Intelligence and Personal Identity" (Reading 26), David Cole reviews some recent criticisms of Searle and proposes a new diagnosis of why the Chinese Room Argument fails to prove its conclusion.

Much of Cole's analysis rests on a view of personal identity and the individuation of minds that originated with the seventeenth-century British philosopher John Locke. In "Of Identity and Diversity" (Reading 27), Locke addresses the question, "What makes a set of mental states over time the states of one and the same mind or person?" Locke's answer is that regardless of the substance in which they are realized, mental states belong to the same person if they are connected by consciousness or memory. For example, I am the same person as my teenage self because I can remember, now, having done some of the things that I did as a teenager.

In response to criticism from Butler, Reid, and others, Locke's memory theory of personal identity has been refined and altered by its proponents. In its modern guise as the psychological continuity theory, it is essentially a functionalist theory of personal identity. At a single time, mental states are unified (they have synchronic unity) because of what they cause or are capable of causing. Mental states are unified over a period of time (they have diachronic unity) because of the causal relations among them. In this way, Locke's theory has been generalized to include not only memory but also the entire range of mental states, personality and character traits, skills, and preferences that can interact to produce other mental states and behavior. On this view, personal identity consists in a causal network of functionally defined states. Two mental states are states of the same person if they belong to the same network.

Sydney Shoemaker is a modern defender of the psychological continuity theory of personal identity. In "Personal Identity: A Materialist's Account"

(Reading 28), Shoemaker explores how the theory can handle hypothetical cases of brain duplication without running into contradiction. Because he is a materialist, Shoemaker believes that the causal network of mental states that constitutes a person's identity is realized in the physical mechanism of the brain. If a new brain is created in exactly the same physical state as the old, then it has the same mental states associated with it. So, Shoemaker concludes that a brain-state transfer is simply a case of a person switching bodies. But what if the old brain is not destroyed but continues to exist unimpaired alongside the new one? We now have two brains, each containing states that are psychologically continuous with the states of the brain that existed prior to the duplication procedure. Which brain belongs to the person who underwent the procedure? Shoemaker argues that our preference for psychological continuity that is brought about in the normal way (simply by the same brain growing older) over psychological continuity brought about by an exotic brain-state transfer device ultimately rests on what he calls a "parochial" intuition.

Jim Stone launches an attack on the psychological continuity theory in his "Parfit and the Buddha: Why There Are No People" (Reading 29). Stone takes as his point of departure Derek Parfit's version of the theory—called Reductionism—that there is nothing more to personal identity than (non-branching) psychological connectedness and continuity. Stone gives a version of Parfit's Spectrum Argument to show that personal identity can be indeterminate. In some cases, there is no right answer to the question, Is this person identical with someone who existed earlier? But, Stone argues, while the Spectrum Argument refutes Realism—the doctrine that persons are something over and above their physical bodies and psychological states—it does not prove that Reductionism is true, since the indeterminacy of personal identity is also consistent with Eliminativism—the doctrine that there are no persons at all. In the remainder of his article, Stone argues that what we really care about in survival is *our* survival as identically the same person, not just the continuation of someone who happens to resemble us closely. Reductionism denies that there is anything more to personal identity than resemblance. Thus, Reductionism entails that there are no persons. That leaves Realism and Eliminativism. Realism—the doctrine that persons are nonmaterial Cartesian minds—has all the problems of dualism and is discredited by the Spectrum Argument. So, Stone concludes that we are left with the view of Hume and the Buddha: it is merely an illusion that we are persons persisting through time.

## NOTES

1. See, for example, the final sentence of Descartes' discussion of the *Second Meditation* in the *Synopsis*, *The Philosophical Works of Descartes*, Volume I, trans. E. S. Haldane and G. R. T. Ross (Cambridge University Press, 1931): 141.

2. The traditional division of mind-body theories into the dualistic and the monistic is not entirely satisfactory for several reasons. (1) Epiphenomenalism is often presented as a theory about the relation between brain events and mental events, without any commitment to an immaterial mental substance. In fact, many epiphenomenalists deny the existence of an immaterial substance and regard minds as logical constructions from mental events. (2) Functionalism is not really a substance theory at all, since it is consistent with the possibility that minds might be realized not only in human brains and electronic computers but also in immaterial substances, if they should exist and permit of causal relations. (3) While Spinoza's panpsychism is monistic (since, for Spinoza, everything has both mental and physical

properties), Strawson's version of the double aspect theory is dualistic, since there are two kinds of substances: purely physical bodies and persons.

3. Some philosophers on this list may be wrongly classified. For example, at the end of his *The Mind and Its Place in Nature* (1951), Broad says that epiphenomenalism is to be preferred to dualism in the light of the scientific evidence; though he was one of its pioneers, Putnam has now disavowed Turing machine functionalism (see H. Putnam, *Representation and Reality* (Cambridge, MA: MIT Press, 1988), Chapters 5–7); and in his book *Brainstorms* (Cambridge, MA: MIT Press, 1981), Dennett distinguishes his position from type functionalism.

**READING 20**

# Sixth Meditation

*René Descartes*

*The French philosopher and mathematician René Descartes (1596–1650) was one of the key figures in the scientific revolution of the seventeenth century and one of the founders of modern philosophy. After serving in several European armies, Descartes retired to the Dutch country-side in 1628 and began writing. Even though Holland had a reputation for freedom of expression and publication, Descartes suppressed his first major work,* Le Monde (The World), *in 1634 upon hearing that Galileo had been condemned by the Roman Catholic Church for defending the Copernican theory. In his later works,* Discourse on Method *(1637) and* Principles of Philosophy *(1644), Descartes made important contributions to optics and cosmology and invented analytical geometry. In 1649, Descartes left Holland for Stockholm, having accepted the post of tutor to Queen Christina of Sweden. He died of pneumonia during the severe Swedish winter of 1649–1650. Descartes' philosophical masterpiece, his six* Meditations on First Philosophy, *were published in Latin in 1641, followed by a French translation which Descartes considered excellent. The English translators Haldane and Ross have followed the original Latin, indicating in brackets some alternative readings from the French.*

Of the Existence of Material Things, and of the
real distinction between the Soul and Body of Man.

Nothing further now remains but to inquire whether material things exist. And certainly I at least know that these may exist in so far as they are considered as the objects of pure mathematics, since in this aspect I perceive them clearly and distinctly. For there is no doubt that God possesses the power to

SOURCE: From *Meditations on First Philosophy* (1641). Reprinted from *The Philosophical Works of Descartes*, Volume 1, trans. and ed. E. S. Haldane and G. R. T. Ross (Cambridge: Cambridge University Press, 1931): 185–199.

produce everything that I am capable of perceiving with distinctness, and I have never deemed that anything was impossible for Him, unless I found a contradiction in attempting to conceive it clearly. Further, the faculty of imagination which I possess, and of which, experience tells me, I make use when I apply myself to the consideration of material things, is capable of persuading me of their existence; for when I attentively consider what imagination is, I find that it is nothing but a certain application of the faculty of knowledge to the body which is immediately present to it, and which therefore exists.

And to render this quite clear, I remark in the first place the difference that exists between the imagination and pure intellection [or conception]. For example, when I imagine a triangle, I do not conceive it only as a figure comprehended by three lines, but I also apprehend these three lines as present by the power and inward vision of my mind, and this is what I call imagining. But if I desire to think of a chiliagon, I certainly conceive truly that it is a figure composed of a thousand sides, just as easily as I conceive of a triangle that it is a figure of three sides only; but I cannot in any way imagine the thousand sides of a chiliagon [as I do the three sides of a triangle], nor do I, so to speak, regard them as present [with the eyes of my mind]. And although in accordance with the habit I have formed of always employing the aid of my imagination when I think of corporeal things, it may happen that in imagining a chiliagon I confusedly represent to myself some figure, yet it is very evident that this figure is not a chiliagon, since it in no way differs from that which I represent to myself when I think of a myriagon or any other many-sided figure; nor does it serve my purpose in discovering the properties which go to form the distinction between a chiliagon and other polygons. But if the question turns upon a pentagon, it is quite true that I can conceive its figure as well as that of a chiliagon without the help of my imagination; but I can also imagine it by applying the attention of my mind to each of its five sides, and at the same time to the space which they enclose. And thus I clearly recognise that I have need of a particular effort of mind in order to effect the act of imagination, such as I do not require in order to understand, and this particular effort of mind clearly manifests the difference which exists between imagination and pure intellection.

I remark besides that this power of imagination which is in one, inasmuch as it differs from the power of understanding, is in no wise a necessary element in my nature, or in [my essence, that is to say, in] the essence of my mind; for although I did not possess it I should doubtless ever remain the same as I now am, from which it appears that we might conclude that it depends on something which differs from me. And I easily conceive that if some body exists with which my mind is conjoined and united in such a way that it can apply itself to consider it when it pleases, it may be that by this means it can imagine corporeal objects; so that this mode of thinking differs from pure intellection only inasmuch as mind in its intellectual activity in some manner turns on itself, and considers some of the ideas which it possesses in itself; while in imagining it turns towards the body, and there beholds in it something conformable to the idea which it has either conceived of itself or perceived by the senses. I easily understand, I say, that the imagination could be thus constituted if it is true that body exists; and because I can discover no other convenient mode of explaining it, I conjecture with probability that body does exist; but this is only with probability, and although I examine all things with care, I nevertheless do not find that from this distinct idea of corporeal nature, which I have in my imagination, I can derive any argument from which there will necessarily be deduced the existence of body.

But I am in the habit of imagining many other things besides this corporeal nature which is the object of pure mathematics, to wit, the colours, sounds, scents, pain, and other such things, although less distinctly. And inasmuch as I perceive these things much better through the senses, by the medium of which, and by the memory, they seem to have reached my imagination, I believe that, in order to examine them more conveniently, it is right that I should at the same time investigate the nature of sense perception, and that I should see if from the ideas which I apprehend by this mode of thought, which I call feeling, I cannot derive some certain proof of the existence of corporeal objects.

And first of all I shall recall to my memory those matters which I hitherto held to be true, as having perceived them through the senses, and the foundations on which my belief has rested; in the next place I shall examine the reasons which have since obliged me to place them in doubt; in the last place I shall consider which of them I must now believe.

First of all, then, I perceived that I had a head, hands, feet, and all other members of which this body—which I considered as a part, or possibly even as the whole, of myself—is composed. Further I was sensible that this body was placed amidst many others, from which it was capable of being affected in many different ways, beneficial and hurtful, and I remarked that a certain feeling of pleasure accompanied those that were beneficial, and pain those which were harmful. And in addition to this pleasure and pain, I also experienced hunger, thirst, and other similar appetites, as also certain corporeal inclinations towards joy, sadness, anger, and other similar passions. And outside myself, in addition to extension, figure, and motions of bodies, I remarked in them hardness, heat, and all other tactile qualities, and, further, light and colour, and scents and sounds, the variety of which gave me the means of distinguishing the sky, the earth, the sea, and generally all the other bodies, one from the other. And certainly, considering the ideas of all these qualities which presented themselves to my mind, and which alone I perceived properly or immediately, it was not without reason that I believed myself to perceive objects quite different from my thought, to wit, bodies from which those ideas proceeded; for I found by experience that these ideas presented themselves to me without my consent being requisite, so that I could not perceive any object, however desirous I might be, unless it were present to the organs of sense; and it was not in my power not to perceive it, when it was present. And because the ideas which I received through the senses were much more lively, more clear, and even, in their own way, more distinct than any of those which I could of myself frame in meditation, or than those I found impressed on my memory, it appeared as though they could not have proceeded from my mind, so that they must necessarily have been produced in me by some other things. And having no knowledge of those objects excepting the knowledge which the ideas themselves gave me, nothing was more likely to occur to my mind than that the objects were similar to the ideas which were caused. And because I likewise remembered that I had formerly made use of my senses rather than my reason, and recognised that the ideas which I formed of myself were not so distinct as those which I perceived through the senses, and that they were most frequently even composed of portions of these last, I persuaded myself easily that I had no idea in my mind which had not formerly come to me through the senses. Nor was it without some reason that I believed that this body (which by a certain special right I call my own) belonged to me more properly and more strictly than any other; for in fact I could never be separated from it as from other bodies; I experienced in it and on account of it all my appetites and affections, and finally I was touched by the feeling of pain and the titillation of pleasure in its parts, and not in the parts of other bodies which were separated from it. But when I inquired, why, from some, I know not what, painful sensation, there follows sadness of mind, and from the pleasurable sensation there arises joy, or why this mysterious pinching of the stomach which I call hunger causes me to desire to eat, and dryness of throat causes a desire to drink, and so on, I could give no reason excepting that nature taught me so; for there is certainly no affinity (that I at least can understand) between the craving of the stomach and the desire to eat, any more than between the perception of whatever causes pain and the thought of sadness which arises from this perception. And in the same way it appeared to me that I had learned from nature all the other judgments which I formed regarding the objects of my senses, since I remarked that these judgments were formed in me before I had the leisure to weigh and consider any reasons which might oblige me to make them.

But afterwards many experiences little by little destroyed all the faith which I had rested in my senses; for I from time to time observed that those towers which from afar appeared to me to be round, more closely observed seemed square, and that colossal statues raised on the summit of these towers, appeared as quite tiny statues when viewed from the bottom; and so in an infinitude of other cases I found error in judgments founded on the external senses. And not only in those founded on the external senses, but even in those founded on the internal as well; for is there anything more intimate or more internal than pain? And yet I have learned from some persons whose arms or legs have been cut off, that they sometimes seemed to feel pain in the part which had been amputated, which made me think that I could not be quite certain that it was a certain member which pained me, even although I felt pain in it. And to those grounds of doubt I have lately added two others, which are very general; the first is that I never have believed myself to feel anything in waking moments which I cannot also sometimes believe myself to feel when I sleep, and as I do not think that these things which I seem to feel in sleep, proceed from objects outside of me, I do not see any reason why I should have this belief regarding objects which I seem to perceive while awake. The other was that being still ignorant, or rather supposing myself to be ignorant, of the author of my being, I saw nothing to prevent me from having been so constituted by nature that I might be deceived even in matters which seemed to me to be most certain. And as to the grounds on which I was formerly persuaded of the truth of sensible objects, I had not much trouble in replying to them. For since nature seemed to cause me to lean towards many things from which reason repelled me, I did not believe that I should trust much to the teachings of nature. And although the ideas which I receive by the senses do not depend on my will, I did not think that one should for that reason conclude that they proceeded from things different from myself, since possibly some faculty might be discovered in me—though hitherto unknown to me—which produced them.

But now that I begin to know myself better, and to discover more clearly the author of my being, I do not in truth think that I should rashly admit all the matters which the senses seem to teach us, but, on the other hand, I do not think that I should doubt them all universally.

And first of all, because I know that all things which I apprehend clearly and distinctly can be created by God as I apprehend them, it suffices that I am able to apprehend one thing apart from another clearly and distinctly in order to be certain that the one is different from the other, since they may be made to exist in separation at least by the omnipotence of God; and it does not signify by what power this separation is made in order to compel me to judge them to be different: and, therefore, just because I know certainly that I exist, and that meanwhile I do not remark that any other thing necessarily pertains to my nature or essence, excepting that I am a thinking thing, I rightly conclude that my essence consists solely in the fact that I am a thinking thing [or a substance whose whole essence or nature is to think]. And although possibly (or rather certainly, as I shall say in a moment) I possess a body with which I am very intimately conjoined, yet because, on the one side, I have a clear and distinct idea of myself inasmuch as I am only a thinking and unextended thing, and as, on the other, I possess a distinct idea of body, inasmuch as it is only an extended and unthinking thing, it is certain that this I [that is to say, my soul by which I am what I am], is entirely and absolutely distinct from my body, and can exist without it.

I further find in myself faculties employing modes of thinking peculiar to themselves, to wit, the faculties of imagination and feeling, without which I can easily conceive myself clearly and distinctly as a complete being; while, on the other hand, they cannot be so conceived apart from me, that is without an intelligent substance in which they reside, for [in the notion we have of these faculties, or, to use the language of the Schools] in their formal concept, some kind of intellection is comprised, from which I infer that they are distinct from me as its modes are from a thing. I observe also in me some other faculties such as that of change of position, the assumption of different figures and such like, which cannot be conceived, any more than can the preceding, apart from some substance to which they are attached, and consequently cannot exist without it; but it is very clear that these faculties, if it be true that they exist, must be attached to some corporeal or extended substance, and not to an intelligent substance, since in the clear and distinct conception of these there is some sort of extension found to be present, but no intellection at all. There is certainly further in me a certain passive faculty of perception, that is, of receiving and recognising the ideas of sensible things, but this would be useless to me [and I could in no way avail myself of it], if there were not either in me or in some other thing another active faculty capable of forming and producing these ideas. But this active faculty cannot exist in me [inasmuch as I am a thing that thinks] seeing that it does not presuppose thought, and also that those

ideas are often produced in me without my contributing in any way to the same, and often even against my will; it is thus necessarily the case that the faculty resides in some substance different from me in which all the reality which is objectively in the ideas that are produced by this faculty is formally or eminently contained, as I remarked before. And this substance is either a body, that is, a corporeal nature in which there is contained formally [and really] all that which is objectively [and by representation] in those ideas, or it is God Himself, or some other creature more noble than body in which that same is contained eminently. But, since God is no deceiver, it is very manifest that He does not communicate to me these ideas immediately and by Himself, nor yet by the intervention of some creature in which their reality is not formally, but only eminently, contained. For since He has given me no faculty to recognise that this is the case, but, on the other hand, a very great inclination to believe [that they are sent to me or] that they are conveyed to me by corporeal objects, I do not see how He could be defended from the accusation of deceit if these ideas were produced by causes other than corporeal objects. Hence we must allow that corporeal things exist. However, they are perhaps not exactly what we perceive by the senses, since this comprehension by the senses is in many instances very obscure and confused; but we must at least admit that all things which I conceive in them clearly and distinctly, that is to say, all things which, speaking generally, are comprehended in the object of pure mathematics, are truly to be recognised as external objects.

As to other things, however, which are either particular only, as, for example, that the sun is of such and such a figure, etc., or which are less clearly and distinctly conceived, such as light, sound, pain and the like, it is certain that although they are very dubious and uncertain, yet on the sole ground that God is not a deceiver, and that consequently He has not permitted any falsity to exist in my opinion which He has not likewise given me the faculty of correcting, I may assuredly hope to conclude that I have within me the means of arriving at the truth even here. And first of all there is no doubt that in all things which nature teaches me there is some truth contained; for by nature, considered in general, I now understand no other thing than either God Himself or else the order and disposition which God has established in created things; and by my nature in particular I understand no other thing than the complexus of all the things which God has given me.

But there is nothing which this nature teaches me more expressly [nor more sensibly] than that I have a body which is adversely affected when I feel pain, which has need of food or drink when I experience the feelings of hunger and thirst, and so on; nor can I doubt there being some truth in all this.

Nature also teaches me by these sensations of pain, hunger, thirst, etc., that I am not only lodged in my body as a pilot in a vessel, but that I am very closely united to it, and so to speak so intermingled with it that I seem to compose with it one whole. For if that were not the case, when my body is hurt, I, who am merely a thinking thing, should not feel pain, for I should perceive this wound by the understanding only, just as the sailor perceives by sight when something is damaged in his vessel; and when my body has need of drink or food, I should clearly understand the fact without being warned of it by confused feelings of hunger and thirst. For all these sensations of hunger, thirst, pain, etc. are in truth none other than certain confused modes of thought which are produced by the union and apparent intermingling of mind and body.

Moreover, nature teaches me that many other bodies exist around mine, of which some are to be avoided, and others sought after. And certainly from the fact that I am sensible of different sorts of colours, sounds, scents, tastes, heat, hardness, etc., I very easily conclude that there are in the bodies from which all these diverse sense-perceptions proceed certain variations which answer to them, although possibly these are not really at all similar to them. And also from the fact that amongst these different sense-perceptions some are very agreeable to me and others disagreeable, it is quite certain that my body (or rather myself in my entirety, inasmuch as I am formed of body and soul) may receive different impressions agreeable and disagreeable from the other bodies which surround it.

But there are many other things which nature seems to have taught me, but which at the same time I have never really received from her, but which have been brought about in my mind by a certain habit which I have of forming inconsiderate judgments on things; and thus it may easily happen that these judgments contain some error. Take, for example, the opinion which I hold that all space in which there is nothing that affects [or makes an impression on] my senses is void; that in a body which is warm there is something entirely similar to the idea of heat which is in me; that in a white or green body there is the same whiteness or greenness that I perceive; that in a bitter or sweet body there is the same taste, and so on in other instances; that the stars, the towers, and all other distant bodies are of the same figure and size as they appear from far off to our eyes, etc. But in order that in this there should be nothing which I do not conceive distinctly, I should define exactly what I really understand when I say that I am taught somewhat by nature. For here I take nature in a more limited signification than when I term it the sum of all the things given me by God, since in this sum many things are comprehended which only pertain to mind (and to these I do not refer in speaking of nature) such as the notion which I have of the fact that what has once been done cannot ever be undone and an infinitude of such things which I know by the light of nature [without the help of the body]; and seeing that it comprehends many other matters besides which only pertain to body, and are no longer here contained under the name of nature, such as the quality of weight which it possesses and the like, with which I also do not deal; for in talking of nature I only treat of those things given by God to me as a being composed of mind and body. But the nature here described truly teaches me to flee from things which cause the sensation of pain, and seek after the things which communicate to me the sentiment of pleasure and so forth; but I do not see that beyond this it teaches me that from those diverse sense-perceptions we should ever form any conclusion regarding things outside of us, without having [carefully and maturely] mentally examined them beforehand. For it seems to me that it is mind alone, and not mind and body in conjunction, that is requisite to a knowledge of the truth in regard to such things. Thus, although a star makes no larger an impression on my eye than the flame of a little candle there is yet in me no real or positive propensity impelling me to believe that it is not greater than that flame; but I have judged it to be so from my earliest years, without any rational foundation. And although in approaching fire I feel heat, and in approaching it a little too near I even feel pain, there is at the same time no reason in this which could persuade me that there is in the fire something resembling this heat any more than there is in it something resembling the pain; all that I have any reason to believe from this is, that there is something in it, whatever it may be, which excites in me these sensations of heat or of pain. So also, although there are spaces in which I find nothing which excites my senses, I must not from that conclude that these spaces contain no body; for I see in this, as in other similar things, that I have been in the habit of perverting the order of nature, because these perceptions of sense having been placed within me by nature merely for the purpose of signifying to my mind what things are beneficial or hurtful to the composite whole of which it forms a part, and being up to that point sufficiently clear and distinct, I yet avail myself of them as though they were absolute rules by which I might immediately determine the essence of the bodies which are outside me, as to which, in fact, they can teach me nothing but what is most obscure and confused.

But I have already sufficiently considered how, notwithstanding the supreme goodness of God, falsity enters into the judgments I make. Only here a new difficulty is presented—one respecting those things the pursuit or avoidance of which is taught me by nature, and also respecting the internal sensation which I possess, and in which I seem to have sometimes detected error [and thus to be directly deceived by my own nature]. To take an example, the agreeable taste of some food in which poison has been intermingled may induce me to partake of the poison, and thus deceive me. It is true, at the same time, that in this case nature may be excused, for it only induces me to desire food in which I find a pleasant taste, and not to desire the poison which is unknown to it; and thus I can infer nothing from this fact, except that my nature is not omniscient, at which there is certainly no reason to be astonished, since man, being finite in nature, can only have knowledge the perfectness of which is limited.

But we not unfrequently deceive ourselves even in those things to which we are directly impelled by nature, as happens with those who when they are sick desire to drink or eat things hurtful to them. It will perhaps be said here that the cause of their deceptiveness is that their nature is corrupt, but that does not remove the difficulty, because a sick man is none the less truly God's creature than he who is in health; and it is therefore as repugnant to God's goodness for the one to have a deceitful nature as it is for the other. And as a clock composed of wheels and counter-weights no less exactly observes the laws of nature when it is badly made, and does not show the time properly, than when it entirely satisfies the wishes of its maker, and as, if I consider the body of a man as being a sort of machine so built up and composed of nerves, muscles, veins, blood and skin, that though there were no mind in it at all, it would not cease to have the same motions as at present, exception being made of those movements which are due to the direction of the will, and in consequence depend upon the mind [as opposed to those which operate by the disposition of its organs], I easily recognise that it would be as natural to this body, supposing it to be, for example, dropsical, to suffer the parchedness of the throat which usually signifies to the mind the feeling of thirst, and to be disposed by this parched feeling to move the nerves and other parts in the way requisite for drinking, and thus to augment its malady and do harm to itself, as it is natural to it, when it has no indisposition, to be impelled to drink for its good by a similar cause. And although, considering the use to which the clock has been destined by its maker, I may say that it deflects from the order of its nature when it does not indicate the hours correctly; and as, in the same way, considering the machine of the human body as having been formed by God in order to have in itself all the movements usually manifested there, I have reason for thinking that it does not follow the order of nature when, if the throat is dry, drinking does harm to the conservation of health, nevertheless I recognise at the same time that this last mode of explaining nature is very different from the other. For this is but a purely verbal characterisation depending entirely on my thought, which compares a sick man and a badly constructed clock with the idea which I have of a healthy man and a well made clock, and it is hence extrinsic to the things to which it is applied; but according to the other interpretation of the term nature I understand something which is truly found in things and which is therefore not without some truth.

But certainly although in regard to the dropsical body it is only so to speak to apply an extrinsic term when we say that its nature is corrupted, inasmuch as apart from the need to drink, the throat is parched; yet in regard to the composite whole, that is to say, to the mind or soul united to this body, it is not a purely verbal predicate, but a real error of nature, for it to have thirst when drinking would be hurtful to it. And thus it still remains to inquire how the goodness of God does not prevent the nature of man so regarded from being fallacious.

In order to begin this examination, then, I here say, in the first place, that there is a great difference between mind and body, inasmuch as body is by nature always divisible, and the mind is entirely indivisible. For, as a matter of fact, when I consider the mind, that is to say, myself inasmuch as I am only a thinking thing, I cannot distinguish in myself any parts, but apprehend myself to be clearly one and entire; and although the whole mind seems to be united to the whole body, yet if a foot, or an arm, or some other part, is separated from my body, I am aware that nothing has been taken away from my mind. And the faculties of willing, feeling, conceiving, etc. cannot be properly speaking said to be its parts, for it is one and the same mind which employs itself in willing and in feeling and understanding. But it is quite otherwise with corporeal or extended objects, for there is not one of these imaginable by me which my mind cannot easily divide into parts, and which consequently I do not recognize as being divisible; this would be sufficient to teach me that the mind or soul of man is entirely different from the body, if I had not already learned it from other sources.

I further notice that the mind does not receive the impressions from all parts of the body immediately, but only from the brain, or perhaps even from one of its smallest parts, to wit, from that in which the common sense is said to reside, which, whenever it is disposed in the same particular way, conveys the same thing to the mind, although meanwhile the other portions of the body may be differently disposed, as is testified by innumerable experiments which it is unnecessary here to recount.

I notice, also, that the nature of body is such that none of its parts can be moved by another part a little way off which cannot also be moved in the same way by each one of the parts which are between the two, although this more remote part does not act at all. As, for example, in the cord *ABCD* [which is in tension] if we pull the last part *D*, the first part *A* will not be moved in any way differently from what would be the case if one of the intervening parts *B* or *C* were pulled, and the last part *D* were to remain unmoved. And in the same way, when I feel pain in my foot, my knowledge of physics teaches me that this sensation is communicated by means of nerves dispersed through the foot, which, being extended like

cords from there to the brain, when they are contracted in the foot, at the same time contract the inmost portions of the brain which is their extremity and place of origin, and then excite a certain movement which nature has established in order to cause the mind to be affected by a sensation of pain represented as existing in the foot. But because these nerves must pass through the tibia, the thigh, the loins, the back and the neck, in order to reach from the leg to the brain, it may happen that although their extremities which are in the foot are not affected, but only certain ones of their intervening parts [which pass by the loins or the neck], this action will excite the same movement in the brain that might have been excited there by a hurt received in the foot, in consequence of which the mind will necessarily feel in the foot the same pain as if it had received a hurt. And the same holds good of all the other perceptions of our senses.

I notice finally that since each of the movements which are in the portion of the brain by which the mind is immediately affected brings about one particular sensation only, we cannot under the circumstances imagine anything more likely than that this movement, amongst all the sensations which it is capable of impressing on it, causes mind to be affected by that one which is best fitted and most generally useful for the conservation of the human body when it is in health. But experience makes us aware that all the feelings with which nature inspires us are such as I have just spoken of; and there is therefore nothing in them which does not give testimony to the power and goodness of the God [who has produced them]. Thus, for example, when the nerves which are in the feet are violently or more than usually moved, their movement, passing through the medulla of the spine to the inmost parts of the brain, gives a sign to the mind which makes it feel somewhat, to wit, pain, as though in the foot, by which the mind is excited to do its utmost to remove the cause of the evil as dangerous and hurtful to the foot. It is true that God could have constituted the nature of man in such a way that this same movement in the brain would have conveyed something quite different to the mind; for example, it might have produced consciousness of itself either in so far as it is in the brain, or as it is in the foot, or as it is in some other place between the foot and the brain, or it might finally have produced consciousness of anything else whatsoever; but none of all this would have contributed so well to the conservation of the body. Similarly, when we desire to drink, a certain dryness of the throat is produced which moves its nerves, and by their means the internal portions of the brain; and this movement causes in the mind the sensation of thirst, because in this case there is nothing more useful to us than to become aware that we have need to drink for the conservation of our health; and the same holds good in other instances.

From this it is quite clear that, notwithstanding the supreme goodness of God, the nature of man, inasmuch as it is composed of mind and body, cannot be otherwise than sometimes a sourse of deception. For if there is any cause which excites, not in the foot but in some part of the nerves which are extended between the foot and the brain, or even in the brain itself, the same movement which usually is produced when the foot is detrimentally affected, pain will be experienced as though it were in the foot, and the sense will thus naturally be deceived; for since the same movement in the brain is capable of causing but one sensation in the mind, and this sensation is much more frequently excited by a cause which hurts the foot than by another existing in some other quarter, it is reasonable that it should convey to the mind pain in the foot rather than in any other part of the body. And although the parchedness of the throat does not always proceed, as it usually does, from the fact that drinking is necessary for the health of the body, but sometimes comes from quite a different cause, as is the case with dropsical patients, it is yet much better that it should mislead on this occasion that if, on the other hand, it were always to deceive us when the body is in good health; and so on in similar cases.

And certainly this consideration is of great service to me, not only in enabling me to recognise all the errors to which my nature is subject, but also in enabling me to avoid them or to correct them more easily. For knowing that all my senses more frequently indicate to me truth than falsehood respecting the things which concern that which is beneficial to the body, and being able almost always to avail myself of many of them in order to examine one particular thing, and, besides that, being able to make use of my memory in order to connect the present with the past, and of my understanding which already has discovered all the causes of my errors, I ought no longer to fear that falsity may be found in matters every day presented to me by my senses. And I ought to set aside all the doubts of these past days as hyperbolical and ridiculous, particularly that very common uncertainty respecting sleep, which I could not distinguish from the waking state; for at present I find a very notable difference between the two, inasmuch as our memory can never connect our dreams one with the other, or with the whole course of our lives, as it unites events which happen to us while we are awake. And, as a matter of fact, if someone, while I was awake, quite suddenly appeared to me and disappeared as fast as do the images which I see in sleep, so that I could not know from whence the form came nor whither it went, it would not be without reason that I should deem it a spectre or a phantom formed by my brain [and similar to those which I form in sleep], rather than a real man. But when I perceive things as to which I know distinctly both the place from which they proceed, and that in which they are, and the time at which they appeared to me; and when, without any interruption, I can connect the perceptions which I have of them with the whole course of my life, I am perfectly assured that these perceptions occur while I am waking and not during sleep. And I ought in no wise to doubt the truth of such matters, if, after having called up all my senses, my memory, and my understanding, to examine them, nothing is brought to evidence by any one of them which is repugnant to what is set forth by the others. For because God is in no wise a deceiver, it follows that I am not deceived in this. But because the exigencies of action often oblige us to make up our minds before having leisure to examine matters carefully, we must confess that the life of man is very frequently subject to error in respect to individual objects, and we must in the end acknowledge the infirmity of our nature.

**READING 21**

# The Traditional Problem of Body and Mind
*C. D. Broad*

*For biographical details, see Reading 9.*

In the last chapter we considered organisms simply as complicated material systems which behave in certain characteristic ways. We did not consider the fact that some organisms are animated by minds, and that all the minds of whose existence we are certain animate organisms. And we did not deal with those features in the behaviour of certain organisms which are commonly supposed to be due to the mind which animates the organism. It is such facts as these, and certain problems to which they have given rise, which I mean to discuss in the present chapter. There is a question which has been argued about for some centuries now under the name of "Interaction"; this is the question whether minds really do act on the organisms which they animate, and whether organisms really do act on the minds which animate them. (I must point out at once that I imply no particular theory of mind or body by the word "to animate". I use it as a perfectly neutral name to express the fact that a certain mind is connected in some peculiarly intimate way with a certain body, and, under normal conditions with no other body. This is a fact even on a purely behaviouristic theory of mind; on such a view to say that the mind M animates the body B would mean that the body B, in so far as it behaves in certain ways, *is* the mind M. A body which did not act in these ways would be said not to be animated by a mind. And a different Body B′, which acted in the same general way as B, would be said to be animated by a different mind M′.)

The problem of Interaction is generally discussed at the level of enlightened common-sense; where it is

SOURCE: From *The Mind and Its Place in Nature* (Atlantic Highlands, NJ: Humanities Press, 1925): 95–97, 103–121.

assumed that we know pretty well what we mean by "mind", by "matter" and by "causation". Obviously no solution which is reached at that level can claim to be ultimate. If what we call "matter" should turn out to be a collection of spirits of low intelligence, as Leibniz thought, the argument that mind and body are so unlike that their interaction is impossible would become irrelevant. Again, if causation be nothing but regular sequence and concomitance, as some philosophers have held, it is ridiculous to regard psychoneural parallelism and interaction as mutually exclusive alternatives. For interaction will mean no more than parallelism, and parallelism will mean no less than interaction. Nevertheless I am going to discuss the arguments here at the common-sense level, because they are so incredibly bad and yet have imposed upon so many learned men.

We start then by assuming a developed mind and a developed organism as two distinct things, and by admitting that the two are now intimately connected in some way or other which I express by saying that "this mind *animates* this organism". We assume that bodies are very much as enlightened common-sense believes them to be; and that, even if we cannot define "causation", we have some means of recognising when it is present and when it is absent. The question then is: "Does a mind ever act on the body which it animates, and does a body ever act on the mind which animates it?" The answer which common-sense would give to both questions is: "Yes, certainly." On the face of it my body acts on my mind whenever a pin is stuck into the former and a painful sensation thereupon arises in the latter. And, on the face of it, my mind acts on my body whenever a desire to move my arm arises in the former and is followed by this movement in the latter. Let us call this common-sense view "Two-sided Interaction". Although it seems so obvious it has been denied by probably a majority of philosophers and a majority of physiologists. So the question is: "Why should so many distinguished men, who have studied the subject, have denied the apparently obvious fact of Two-sided Interaction?"....

## SCIENTIFIC ARGUMENTS AGAINST TWO-SIDED INTERACTION

There are, so far as I know, two of these. One is supposed to be based on the physical principle of the Conservation of Energy, and on certain experiments which have been made on human bodies. The other is based on the close analogy which is said to exist between the structures of the physiological mechanism of reflex action and that of voluntary action. I will take them in turn.

(1) *The Argument from Energy.* It will first be needful to state clearly what is asserted by the principle of the Conservation of Energy. It is found that, if we take certain material systems, *e.g.,* a gun, a cartridge, and a bullet, there is a certain magnitude which keeps approximately constant throughout all their changes. This is called "Energy". When the gun has not been fired it and the bullet have no motion, but the explosive in the cartridge has great chemical energy. When it has been fired the bullet is moving very fast and has great energy of movement. The gun, though not moving fast in its recoil, has also great energy of movement because it is very massive. The gases produced by the explosion have some energy of movement and some heat-energy, but much less chemical energy than the unexploded charge had. These various kinds of energy can be measured in common units according to certain conventions. To an innocent mind there seems to be a good deal of "cooking" at this stage, *i.e.,* the conventions seem to be chosen and various kinds and amounts of concealed energy seem to be postulated in order to make the principle come out right at the end. I do not propose to go into this in detail, for two reasons. In the first place, I think that the conventions adopted and the postulates made, though somewhat suggestive of the fraudulent company-promoter, can be justified by their coherence with certain experimental facts, and that they are not simply made *ad hoc.* Secondly, I shall show that the Conservation of Energy is absolutely irrelevant to the question at issue, so that it would be waste of time to treat it too seriously in the present connexion. Now it is found that the total energy of all kinds in this system, when

measured according to these conventions, is approximately the same in amount though very differently distributed after the explosion and before it. If we had confined our attention to a part of this system and *its* energy this would not have been true. The bullet, *e.g.,* had no energy at all before the explosion and a great deal afterwards. A system like the bullet, the gun, and the charge, is called a "Conservative System"; the bullet alone, or the gun and the charge, would be called "Non-conservative Systems". A conservative system might therefore be defined as one whose total energy is redistributed, but not altered in amount, by changes that happen within it. Of course a given system might be conservative for some kinds of change and not for others.

So far we have merely defined a "Conservative System", and admitted that there are systems which, for some kinds of change at any rate, answer approximately to our definition. We can now state the principle of the Conservation of Energy in terms of the conceptions just defined. The principle asserts that every material system is either itself conservative, or, if not, is part of a larger material system which is conservative. We may take it that there is good inductive evidence for this proposition.

The next thing to consider is the experiments on the human body. These tend to prove that a living body, with the air that it breathes and the food that it eats, forms a conservative system to a high degree of approximation. We can measure the chemical energy of the food given to a man, and that which enters his body in the form of oxygen breathed in. We can also, with suitable apparatus, collect, measure and analyse the air breathed out, and thus find its chemical energy. Similarly, we can find the energy given out in bodily movement, in heat, and in excretion. It is alleged that, on the average, whatever the man may do, the energy of his bodily movements is exactly accounted for by the energy given to him in the form of food and of oxygen. If you take the energy put in in food and oxygen, and subtract the energy given out in waste-products, the balance is almost exactly equal to the energy put out in bodily movements. Such slight differences as are found are as often on one side as on the other, and are therefore probably due to unavoidable experimental errors. I do not propose to criticise the intepretation of these experiments in detail, because, as I shall show soon, they are completely irrelevant to the problem of whether mind and body interact. But there is just one point that I will make before passing on. It is perfectly clear that such experiments can tell us only what happens on the average over a long time. To know whether the balance was accurately kept at every moment we should have to kill the patient at each moment and analyse his body so as to find out the energy present then in the form of stored-up products. Obviously we cannot keep on killing the patient in order to analyse him, and then reviving him in order to go on with the experiment. Thus it would seem that the results of the experiment are perfectly compatible with the presence of quite large excesses or defects in the total bodily energy at certain moments, provided that these average out over longer periods. However, I do not want to press this criticism; I am quite ready to accept for our present purpose the traditional interpretation which has been put on the experiments.

We now understand the physical principle and the experimental facts. The two together are generally supposed to prove that mind and body cannot interact. What precisely is the argument, and is it valid? Imagine that the argument, when fully stated, would run somewhat as follows: "I will to move my arm, and it moves. If the volition has anything to do with causing the movement we might expect energy to flow from my mind to my body. Thus the energy of my body ought to receive a measurable increase, not accounted for by the food that I eat and the oxygen that I breathe. But no such physically unaccountable increases of bodily energy are found. Again, I tread on a tin-tack, and a painful sensation arises in my mind. If treading on the tack has anything to do with causing the sensation we might expect energy to flow from my body to my mind. Such energy would cease to be measurable. Thus there ought to be a noticeable decrease in my bodily energy, not balanced by increases anywhere in the physical system. But such unbalanced decreases of bodily energy are not found." So it is concluded that the volition has nothing to do with causing my arm to move, and that treading on the tack has nothing to do with causing the painful sensation.

Is this argument valid? In the first place it is important to notice that the conclusion does not follow from the Conservation of Energy and the experimental facts alone. The real premise is a tacitly assumed proposition about causation; viz., that, if a change in A has anything to do with causing a change in B, energy must leave A and flow into B.

This is neither asserted nor entailed by the Conservation of Energy. What *it* says is that, *if* energy leaves A, it must appear in something else, say B; so that A and B together form a conservative system. Since the Conservation of Energy is not itself the premise for the argument against Interaction, and since it does not entail that premise, the evidence for the Conservation of Energy is not evidence against Interaction. Is there any independent evidence for the premise? We may admit that it *is* true of many, though not of all, transactions within the physical realm. But there are cases where it is not true even of purely physical transactions; and, even if it were always true in the physical realm, it would not follow that it must also be true of transphysical causation. Take the case of a weight swinging at the end of a string hung from a fixed point. The total energy of the weight is the same at all positions in its course. It is thus a conservative system. But at every moment the direction and velocity of the weight's motion are different, and the proportion between its kinetic and its potential energy is constantly changing. These changes are caused by the pull of the string, which acts in a different direction at each different moment. The string makes no difference to the total energy of the weight; but it makes all the difference in the world to the particular way in which the weight moves and the particular way in which the energy is distributed between the potential and the kinetic forms. This is evident when we remember that the weight would begin to move in an utterly different course if at any moment the string were cut.

Here, then, we have a clear case even in the physical realm where a system is conservative but is continually acted on by something which affects its movement and the distribution of its total energy. Why should not the mind act on the body in this way? If you say that you can see how a string can affect the movement of a weight, but cannot see how a volition could affect the movement of a material particle, you have deserted the scientific argument and have gone back to one of the philosophical arguments. Your real difficulty is either that volitions are so very unlike movements, or that the volition is in your mind whilst the movement belongs to the physical realm. And we have seen how little weight can be attached to these objections.

The fact is that, even in purely physical systems, the Conservation of Energy does not explain what changes will happen or when they will happen. It merely imposes a very general limiting condition on the changes that are possible. The fact that the system composed of bullet, charge, and gun, in our earlier example, is conservative does not tell us that the gun ever will be fired, or when it will be fired if at all, or what will cause it to go off, or what forms of energy will appear if and when it does go off. The change in this case is determined by pulling the trigger. Likewise the mere fact that the human body and its neighbourhood form a conservative system does not explain any particular bodily movement; it does not explain why I ever move at all, or why I sometimes write, sometimes walk, and sometimes swim. To explain the happening of these particular movements at certain times it seems to be essential to take into account the volitions which happen from time to time in my mind; just as it is essential to take the string into account to explain the particular behaviour of the weight, and to take the trigger into account to explain the going off of the gun at a certain moment. The difference between the gun-system and the body-system is that a little energy does flow into the former when the trigger is pulled, whilst it is alleged that none does so when a volition starts a bodily movement. But there is not even this amount of difference between the body-system and the swinging weight.

Thus the argument from energy has no tendency to disprove Two-sided Interaction. It has gained a spurious authority from the august name of the Conservation of Energy. But this impressive principle proves to have nothing to do with the case. And the real premise of the argument is not self-evident, and is not universally true even in purely intra-physical transactions. In the end this scientific argument has to lean on the old philosophic arguments; and we have seen that these are but bruised reeds. Nevertheless, the facts brought forward by the argument from energy do throw some light on the *nature* of the interaction between mind and body, assuming this to happen. They do suggest that all the energy of our bodily actions comes out of and goes back into the physical world, and that minds neither add energy to nor abstract it from the latter. What they do, if they do anything, is to determine that at a given moment so much energy shall change from the chemical form to the form of bodily movement; and they determine this, so far as we can see, without altering the total amount of energy in the physical world.

(2) *The Argument from the Structure of the Nervous System.* There are purely reflex actions, like sneezing and blinking, in which there is no reason to suppose that the mind plays any essential part. Now we know the nervous structure which is used in such acts as these. A stimulus is given to the outer end of an afferent nerve; some change or other runs up this nerve, crosses a synapse between this and an efferent nerve, travels down the latter to a muscle, causes the muscle to contract, and so produces a bodily movement. There seems no reason to believe that the mind plays any essential part in this process. The process may be irreducibly vital, and not merely physico-chemical; but there seems no need to assume anything more than this. Now it is said that the whole nervous system is simply an immense complication of interconnected nervous arcs. The result is that a change which travels inwards has an immense number of alternative paths by which it may travel outwards. Thus the reaction to a given stimulus is no longer one definite movement, as in the simple reflex. Almost any movement may follow any stimulus according to the path which the efferent disturbance happens to take. This path will depend on the relative resistance of the various synapses at the time. Now a variable response to the same stimulus is characteristic of deliberate as opposed to reflex action.

These are the facts. The argument based on them runs as follows. It is admitted that the mind has nothing to do with the causation of purely reflex actions. But the nervous structure and the nervous processes involved in deliberate action do not differ in kind from those involved in reflex action; they differ only in degree of complexity. The variability which characterises deliberate action is fully explained by the variety of alternative paths and the variable resistances of the synapses. So it is unreasonable to suppose that the mind has any more to do with causing deliberate actions than it has to do with causing reflex actions.

I think that this argument is invalid. In the first place I am pretty sure that the persons who use it have before their imagination a kind of picture of how mind and body must interact if they interact at all. They find that the facts do not answer to this picture, and so they conclude that there is no interaction. The picture is of the following kind. They think of the mind as sitting somewhere in a hole in the brain, surrounded by telephones. And they think of the afferent disturbance as coming to an end at one of these telephones and there affecting the mind. The mind is then supposed to respond by sending an efferent impulse down another of these telephones. As no such hole, with afferent nerves stopping at its walls and efferent nerves starting from them can be found, they conclude that the mind can play no part in the transaction. But another alternative is that this picture of how the mind must act if it acts at all is wrong. To put it shortly, the mistake is to confuse a gap in an explanation with a spatio-temporal gap, and to argue from the absence of the latter to the absence of the former.

The Interactionist's contention is simply that there is a gap in any purely physiological explanation of deliberate action; *i.e.*, that all such explanations fail to account completely for the facts because they leave out one necessary condition. It does not follow in the least that there must be a spatio-temporal breach of continuity in the physiological conditions, and that the missing condition must fill this gap in the way in which the movement of a wire fills the spatio-temporal interval between the pulling of a bell-handle and the ringing of a distant bell. To assume this is to make the mind a kind of physical object, and to make its action a kind of mechanical action. Really, the mind and its actions are not literally in space at all, and the time which is occupied by the mental event is no doubt *also* occupied by some part of the physiological process. Thus I am inclined to think that much of the force which this argument actually exercises on many people is simply due to the presupposition about the *modus operandi* of interaction, and that it is greatly weakened when this presupposition is shown to be a mere prejudice due to our limited power of envisaging unfamiliar alternative possibilities.

We can, however, make more detailed objections to the argument than this. There is a clear introspective difference between the mental accompaniment of voluntary action and that of reflex action. What goes on in our minds when we decide with difficulty to get out of a hot bath on a cold morning is obviously extremely different from what goes on in our minds when we sniff pepper and sneeze. And the difference is qualitative; it is not a mere difference of complexity. This difference has to be explained somehow; and the theory under discussion gives no plausible explanation of it. The ordinary view that, in the latter case, the mind is not acting on the body at all; whilst, in the former, it is acting on the body in a specific way, does at least make the introspective difference between the two intelligible.

Again, whilst it is true that deliberate action differs from reflex action in its greater variability of response to the same stimulus, this is certainly not the whole or the most important part of the difference between them. The really important difference is that, in deliberate action, the response is varied *appropriately* to meet the special circumstances which are supposed to exist at the time or are expected to arise later; whilst reflex action is not varied in this way, but is blind and almost mechanical. The complexity of the nervous system explains the *possibility* of variation; it does not in the least explain why the alternative which actually takes place should as a rule be appropriate and not merely haphazard. And so again it seems as if some factor were in operation in deliberate action which is not present in reflex action; and it is reasonable to suppose that this factor is the volition in the mind.

It seems to me that this second scientific argument has no tendency to disprove interaction; but that the facts which it brings forward do tend to suggest the particular form which interaction probably takes if it happens at all. They suggest that what the mind does to the body in voluntary action, if it does anything, is to lower the resistance of certain synapses and to raise that of others. The result is that the nervous current follows such a course as to produce the particular movement which the mind judges to be appropriate at the time. On such a view the difference between reflex, habitual, and deliberate actions for the present purpose becomes fairly plain. In pure reflexes the mind cannot voluntarily affect the resistance of the synapses concerned, and so the action takes place in spite of it. In habitual action it deliberately refrains from interfering with the resistance of the synapses, and so the action goes on like a complicated reflex. But it *can* affect these resistances if it wishes, though often only with difficulty; and it is ready to do so if it judges this to be expedient. Finally, it may lose the power altogether. This would be what happens when a person becomes a slave to some habit, such as drug-taking.

I conclude that, at the level of enlightened common-sense at which the ordinary discussion of Interaction moves, no good reason has been produced for doubting that the mind acts on the body in volition, and that the body acts on the mind in sensation. The philosophic arguments are quite inconclusive; and the scientific arguments, when properly understood, are quite compatible with Two-sided Interaction. At most they suggest certain conclusions as to the form which interaction probably takes if it happens at all.

## DIFFICULTIES IN THE DENIAL OF INTERACTION

I propose now to consider some of the difficulties which would attend the denial of Interaction, still keeping the discussion at the same common-sense level. If a man denies the action of body on mind he is at once in trouble over the causation of new sensations. Suppose that I suddenly tread on an unsuspected tin-tack. A new sensation suddenly comes into my mind. This is an event, and it presumably has some cause. Now, however carefully I introspect and retrospect, I can find no other mental event which is adequate to account for the fact that just that sensation has arisen at just that moment. If I reject the common-sense view that treading on the tack is an essential part of the cause of the sensation, I must suppose either that it is uncaused, or that it is caused by other events in my mind which I cannot discover by introspection or retrospection, or that it is caused telepathically by other finite minds or by God. Now enquiry of my neighbours would show that it is not caused telepathically by any event in their minds which they can introspect or remember. Thus anyone who denies the action of body on mind, and admits that sensations have causes, must postulate either (*a*) immense numbers of unobservable states in his own mind; or (*b*) as many unobservable states in his neighbours' minds, together with telepathic action; or (*c*) some non-human spirit together with telepathic action. I must confess that the difficulties which have been alleged against the action of body on mind seem to be mild compared with those of the alternative hypotheses which are involved in the denial of such action.

The difficulties which are involved in the denial of the action of mind on body are at first sight equally great; but I do not think that they turn out to be so serious as those which are involved in denying the action of body on mind. The *prima facie* difficulty is this. The world contains many obviously artificial objects, such as books, bridges, clothes, etc. We know that, if we go far enough back in the history of their production, we always do in fact come on the actions of some human body. And the minds connected with these bodies did design the objects in question, did will to produce them, and did believe that they were initiating and guiding the physical process by means of these designs and volitions. If it be true that the mind does not act on the body, it follows that the designs and volitions in the agents' minds did not in fact play any part in the production of books, bridges, clothes, etc. This appears highly paradoxical. And it is an easy step from it to say that anyone who denies the action of mind on body must admit that books, bridges, and other such objects *could* have been produced even though there had been no minds, no thought of these objects and no desire for them. This consequence seems manifestly absurd to common-sense, and it might be argued that it reflects its absurdity back on the theory which entails it.

The man who denies that mind can act on body might deal with this difficulty in two ways: (1) He might deny that the conclusion *is* intrinsically absurd. He might say that human bodies are extraordinarily complex physical objects, which probably obey irreducible laws of their own, and that we really do not know enough about them to set limits to what their unaided powers could accomplish. This is the line which Spinoza took. The conclusion, it would be argued, *seems* absurd only because the state of affairs which it contemplates is so very unfamiliar. We find it difficult to imagine a body like ours without a mind like ours; but, if we could get over this defect in our powers of imagination, we might have no difficulty in admitting that such a body could do all the things which our bodies do. I think it must be admitted that the difficulty is not so great as that which is involved in denying the action of body on mind. There we had to postulate *ad hoc* utterly unfamiliar entities and modes of action; here it is not certain that we should have to do this.

(2) The other line of argument would be to say that the alleged consequence does not necessarily follow from denying the action of mind on body. I assume that both parties admit that causation is something more than mere *de facto* regularity of sequence and concomitance. If they do not, of course the whole controversy between them becomes futile; for there will certainly be causation between mind and body and between body and mind, in the only sense in which there is causation anywhere. This being presupposed, the following kind of answer is logically possible. When I say that B could not have happened unless A had happened, there are two alternative possibilities. (*a*) A may itself be an indis-

pensable link in any chain of causes which ends up with B. (b) A may not itself be a link in any chain of causation which ends up with B. But there may be an indispensable link α in any such chain of causation, and A may be a necessary accompaniment or sequent of α. These two possibilities may be illustrated by diagrams. (a) is represented by the figure below:—

$$A_0 \qquad A \qquad A_1 \qquad A_2 \qquad B$$
$$. \longrightarrow . \longrightarrow . \longrightarrow . \longrightarrow .$$

The two forms of (b) are represented by the two figures below:—

$$A_0 \qquad \overset{A}{\underset{\alpha}{\uparrow}} \qquad A_1 \qquad A_2 \qquad B$$

and

$$A_0 \qquad \overset{A}{\nearrow} \quad A_1 \qquad A_2 \qquad B$$

Evidently, if B cannot happen unless α precedes, and if α cannot happen without A accompanying or immediately following it, B will not be able to happen unless A precedes it. And yet A will have had no part in causing B. It will be noticed that, on this view, α has a complex effect AA$_1$, of which a certain part, viz., A$_1$ is sufficient by itself to produce A$_2$ and ultimately B. Let us apply this abstract possibility to our present problem. Suppose that B is some artificial object, like a book or a bridge. If we admit that this could not have come into existence unless a certain design and volition had existed in a certain mind, we could interpret the facts in two ways. (a) We could hold that the design and volition are themselves an indispensable link in the chain of causation which ends in the production of a bridge or a book. This is the common view, and it requires us to admit the action of mind on body. (b) We might hold that the design and the volition are not themselves a link in the chain of causation which ends in the production of the artificial object; but that they are a necessary accompaniment or sequent of something which is an indispensable link in this chain of causation. On this view the chain consists wholly of physical events; but one of these physical events (viz., some event in the brain) has a complex consequent. One part of this consequent is purely physical, and leads by purely physical causation to the ultimate production of a bridge or a book. The other is purely mental, and

consists of a certain design and volition in the mind which animates the human body concerned. If this has any consequences they are purely mental. Each part of this complex consequent follows with equal necessity; this particular brain-state could no more have existed without such and such a mental state accompanying or following it than it could have existed without such and such a bodily movement following it. If we are willing to take some such view as this, we can admit that certain objects could not have existed unless there had been designs of them and desires for them; and yet we could consistently deny that these desires and designs have any effect on the movements of our bodies.

It seems to me then that the doctrine which I will call "One-sided Action of Body on Mind" is logically possible; i.e., a theory which accepts the action of body on mind but denies the action of mind on body. But I do not see the least reason to accept it, since I see no reason to deny that mind acts on body in volition. One-sided Action has, I think, generally been held in the special form called "Epiphenomenalism." I take this doctrine to consist of the following four propositions: (1) Certain bodily events cause certain mental events. (2) No mental event plays any part in the causation of any bodily event. (3) No mental event plays any part in the causation of any other mental event. Consequently (4) all mental events are caused by bodily events and by them only. Thus Epiphenomenalism is just One-sided Action of Body on Mind, together with a special theory about the nature and structure of mind. This special theory does not call for discussion here, where I am dealing only with the relations between minds and bodies, and am not concerned with a detailed analysis of mind. . . .

## ARGUMENTS IN FAVOUR OF INTERACTION

The only arguments for One-sided Action of Body on Mind or for Parallelism are the arguments against Two-sided Interaction; and these, as we have seen, are worthless. Are there any arguments in favour of Two-sided Interaction? I have incidentally given two which seem to me to have considerable weight. In favour of the action of mind on body is the fact that we seem to be immediately aware of a causal relation when we voluntarily try to produce a bodily movement, and that the arguments to show that this cannot be true are invalid. In favour of the action of body on mind are the insuperable difficulties which I have pointed out in accounting for the happening of new sensations on any other hypothesis. There are, however, two other arguments which have often been thought to prove the action of mind on body. These are (1) an evolutionary argument, first used, I believe, by William James; and (2) the famous "telegram argument." They both seem to me to be quite obviously invalid.

(1) The evolutionary argument runs as follows: It is a fact, which is admitted by persons who deny Two-sided Interaction, that minds increase in complexity and power with the growth in complexity of the brain and nervous system. Now, if the mind makes no difference to the actions of the body, this development on the mental side is quite unintelligible from the point of view of natural selection. Let us imagine two animals whose brains and nervous systems were of the same degree of complexity; and suppose, if possible, that one had a mind and the other had none. If the mind makes no difference to the behaviour of the body the chance of survival and of leaving descendants will clearly be the same for the two animals. Therefore natural selection will have no tendency to favour the evolution of mind which has actually taken place. I do not think that there is anything in this argument. Natural selection is a purely negative process; it simply tends to eliminate individuals and species which have variations unfavourable to survival. Now, by hypothesis, the possession of a mind is not *unfavourable* to survival; it simply makes no difference. Now it may be that the existence of a mind of such and such a kind is the inevitable consequence of the existence of a brain and nervous system of such and such a degree of complexity. Indeed we have seen that some such view is essential if the opponent of Two-sided Interaction is to answer the common-sense objection that artificial objects could not have existed unless there had been a mind which designed and desired them. On this hypothesis there is no need to invoke natural selection twice over, once to explain the evolution of the brain and nervous system, and once to explain the evolution of the mind. If natural selection will account for the evolution of the brain and nervous system, the evolution of the mind will follow inevitably, even though it adds nothing to the survival-value of the organism. The plain fact is that natural selection does not account for the origin or for the growth in complexity of anything whatever; and therefore it is no objection to any particular theory of the relations of mind and body that, if it were true, natural selection would not explain the origin and development of mind.

(2) The "telegram argument" is as follows: Suppose there were two telegrams, one saying "Our son has been killed", and the other saying: "Your son has been killed". And suppose that one or other of them was delivered to a parent whose son was away from home. As physical stimuli they are obviously extremely alike, since they differ only in the fact that the letter "*Y*" is present in one and absent in the other. Yet we know that the reaction of the person who received the telegram might be very different according to which one he received. This is supposed to show that the reactions of the body cannot be wholly accounted for by bodily causes, and that the mind must intervene causally in some cases. Now I have very little doubt that the mind does play a part in determining the action of the recipient of the telegram; but I do not see why this argument should prove it to a person who doubted or denied it. If two very similar stimuli are followed by two very different results, we are no doubt justified in concluding that these stimuli are not the complete causes of the reactions which follow them. But of course it would be admitted by every one that the receipt of the telegram is not the complete cause of the recipient's reaction. We all know that his brain and nervous system play an essential part in any reaction that he may make to the stimulus. The question then is whether the minute structure of his brain and nervous system, including in this the supposed traces left by past stimuli and past reactions, is not enough to account for the great difference in his behaviour on receiving two very similar stimuli. Two keys may be very much alike, but one may fit a certain lock and the other may not. And, if the lock be connected with the trigger of a loaded gun, the results of "stimulating" the system with one or other of the two keys will be extremely different. We know that the brain and nervous system are very complex, and we commonly suppose that they contain more or less permanent traces and linkages due to past stimuli and reactions. If this be granted, it is obvious that two very similar stimuli may produce very different results, simply because one fits in with the internal structure of the brain and nervous system whilst the other does not. And I do not see how we can be sure that anything more is needed to account for the mere difference of reaction adduced by the "telegram argument."

**READING 22**

# Descartes' Myth

*Gilbert Ryle*

*Gilbert Ryle (1900–1976) was Waynflete Professor of Metaphysical Philosophy at Oxford University, where he was a leading advocate of the philosophical movement known as linguistic philosophy. Ryle believed that many apparent problems and absurdities in philosophy arose from the misuse of language and could be removed by paying close attention to what words and expressions mean. In* The Concept of Mind *(1949), Ryle launched an all-out attack on Cartesian dualism by defending logical behaviorism—the view that mental terms refer to observable behavior, not to immaterial minds. Ryle's other books include* Dilemmas *(1953) and* Plato's Progress *(1966).*

## (1) THE OFFICIAL DOCTRINE

There is a doctrine about the nature and place of minds which is so prevalent among theorists and even among laymen that it deserves to be described as the official theory. Most philosophers, psychologists and religious teachers subscribe, with minor reservations, to its main articles and, although they admit certain theoretical difficulties in it, they tend to assume that these can be overcome without serious modifications being made to the architecture of the theory. It will be argued here that the central principles of the doctrine are unsound and conflict with the whole body of what we know about minds when we are not speculating about them.

The official doctrine, which hails chiefly from Descartes, is something like this. With the doubtful exceptions of idiots and infants in arms every human being has both a body and a mind. Some would prefer to say that every human being is both a body and a mind. His body and his mind are ordinarily harnessed together, but after the death of the body his mind may continue to exist and function.

SOURCE: From *The Concept of Mind* (London: Hutchinson and Co., 1949), Chapter 1, pp. 11–24.

Human bodies are in space and are subject to the mechanical laws which govern all other bodies in space. Bodily processes and states can be inspected by external observers. So a man's bodily life is as much a public affair as are the lives of animals and reptiles and even as the careers of trees, crystals and planets.

But minds are not in space, nor are their operations subject to mechanical laws. The workings of one mind are not witnessable by other observers; its career is private. Only I can take direct cognisance of the states and processes of my own mind. A person therefore lives through two collateral histories, one consisting of what happens in and to his body, the other consisting of what happens in and to his mind. The first is public, the second private. The events in the first history are events in the physical world, those in the second are events in the mental world.

It has been disputed whether a person does or can directly monitor all or only some of the episodes of his own private history; but, according to the official doctrine, of at least some of these episodes he has direct and unchallengeable cognisance. In consciousness, self-consciousness and introspection he is directly and authentically apprised of the present states and operations of his mind. He may have great or small uncertainties about concurrent and adjacent episodes in the physical world, but he can have none about at least part of what is momentarily occupying his mind.

It is customary to express this bifurcation of his two lives and of his two worlds by saying that the things and events which belong to the physical world, including his own body, are external, while the workings of his own mind are internal. This antithesis of outer and inner is of course meant to be construed as a metaphor, since minds, not being in space, could not be described as being spatially inside anything else, or as having things going on spatially inside themselves. But relapses from this good intention are common and theorists are found speculating how stimuli, the physical sources of which are yards or miles outside a person's skin, can generate mental responses inside his skull, or how decisions framed inside his cranium can set going movements of his extremities.

Even when 'inner' and 'outer' are construed as metaphors, the problem how a person's mind and body influence one another is notoriously charged with theoretical difficulties. What the mind wills, the legs, arms and the tongue execute; what affects the ear and the eye has something to do with what the mind perceives; grimaces and smiles betray the mind's moods and bodily castigations lead, it is hoped, to moral improvement. But the actual transactions between the episodes of the private history and those of the public history remain mysterious, since by definition they can belong to neither series. They could not be reported among the happenings described in a person's autobiography of his inner life, but nor could they be reported among those described in some one else's biography of that person's overt career. They can be inspected neither by introspection nor by laboratory experiment. They are theoretical shuttlecocks which are forever being bandied from the physiologist back to the psychologist and from the psychologist back to the physiologist.

Underlying this partly metaphorical representation of the bifurcation of a person's two lives there is a seemingly more profound and philosophical assumption. It is assumed that there are two different kinds of existence or status. What exists or happens may have the status of physical existence, or it may have the status of mental existence. Somewhat as the faces of coins are either heads or tails, or somewhat as living creatures are either male or female, so, it is supposed, some existing is physical existing, other existing is mental existing. It is a necessary feature of what has physical existence that it is in space and time; it is a necessary feature of what has mental existence that it is in time but not in space. What has physical existence is composed of matter, or else is a function of matter; what has mental existence consists of consciousness, or else is a function of consciousness.

There is thus a polar opposition between mind and matter, an opposition which is often brought out as follows. Material objects are situated in a common field, known as 'space', and what happens to one body in one part of space is mechanically connected with what happens to other bodies in other parts of space. But mental happenings occur in insulated fields, known as 'minds', and there is, apart maybe from telepathy, no direct causal connection between what happens in one mind and what happens in another. Only through the medium of the public physical world can the mind of one person make a difference to the mind of another. The mind is its own place and in his inner life each of us lives the life of a ghostly Robinson Crusoe. People can see, hear and jolt one another's bodies, but they are irremediably blind and deaf to the workings of one another's minds and inoperative upon them.

What sort of knowledge can be secured of the workings of a mind? On the one side, according to the official theory, a person has direct knowledge of the best imaginable kind of the workings of his own mind. Mental states and processes are (or are normally) conscious states and processes, and the consciousness which irradiates them can engender no illusions and leaves the door open for no doubts. A person's present thinkings, feelings and willings, his perceivings, rememberings and imaginings are intrinsically 'phosphorescent'; their existence and their nature are inevitably betrayed to their owner. The inner life is a stream of consciousness of such a sort that it would be absurd to suggest that the mind whose life is that stream might be unaware of what is passing down it.

True, the evidence adduced recently by Freud seems to show that there exist channels tributary to this stream, which run hidden from their owner. People are actuated by impulses the existence of which they vigorously disavow; some of their thoughts differ from the thoughts which they acknowledge; and some of the actions which they think they will to perform they do not really will. They are thoroughly gulled by some of their own hypocrisies and they successfully ignore facts about their mental lives which on the official theory ought to be patent to them. Holders of the official theory tend, however, to maintain that anyhow in normal circumstances a person must be directly and authentically seized of the present state and workings of his own mind.

Besides being currently supplied with these alleged immediate data of consciousness, a person is also generally supposed to be able to exercise from time to time a special kind of perception, namely inner perception, or introspection. He can take a (non-optical) 'look' at what is passing in his mind. Not only can he view and scrutinize a flower through his sense of sight and listen to and discriminate the notes of a bell through his sense of hearing; he can also reflectively or introspectively watch, without any bodily organ of sense, the current episodes of his inner life. This self-observation is also commonly supposed to be immune from illusion, confusion or doubt. A mind's reports of its own affairs have a certainty superior to the best that is possessed by its reports of matters in the physical world. Sense-perceptions can, but consciousness and introspection cannot, be mistaken or confused.

On the other side, one person has no direct access of any sort to the events of the inner life of another. He cannot do better than make problematic inferences from the observed behaviour of the other person's body to the states of mind which, by analogy from his own conduct, he supposes to be signalised by that behaviour. Direct access to the workings of a mind is the privilege of that mind itself; in default of such privileged access, the workings of one mind are inevitably occult to everyone else. For the supposed arguments from bodily movements similar to their own to mental workings similar to their own would lack any possibility of observational corroboration. Not unnaturally, therefore, an adherent of the official theory finds it difficult to resist this consequence of his premises, that he has no good reason to believe that there do exist minds other than his own. Even if he prefers to believe that to other human bodies there are harnessed minds not unlike his own, he cannot claim to be able to discover their individual characteristics, or the particular things that they undergo and do. Absolute solitude is on this showing the ineluctable destiny of the soul. Only our bodies can meet.

As a necessary corollary of this general scheme there is implicitly prescribed a special way of construing our ordinary concepts of mental powers and operations. The verbs, nouns and adjectives, with which in ordinary life we describe the wits, characters and higher-grade performances of the people with whom we have to do, are required to be construed as signifying special episodes in their secret histories, or else as signifying tendencies for such episodes to occur. When someone is described as knowing, believing or guessing something, as hoping, dreading,

intending or shirking something, as designing this or being amused at that, these verbs are supposed to denote the occurrence of specific modifications in his (to us) occult stream of consciousness. Only his own privileged access to this stream in direct awareness and introspection could provide authentic testimony that these mental-conduct verbs were correctly or incorrectly applied. The onlooker, be he teacher, critic, biographer or friend, can never assure himself that his comments have any vestige of truth. Yet it was just because we do in fact all know how to make such comments, make them with general correctness and correct them when they turn out to be confused or mistaken, that philosophers found it necessary to construct their theories of the nature and place of minds. Finding mental-conduct concepts being regularly and effectively used, they properly sought to fix their logical geography. But the logical geography officially recommended would entail that there could be no regular or effective use of these mental-conduct concepts in our descriptions of, and prescriptions for, other people's minds.

## (2) THE ABSURDITY OF THE OFFICIAL DOCTRINE

Such in outline is the official theory. I shall often speak of it, with deliberate abusiveness, as 'the dogma of the Ghost in the Machine'. I hope to prove that it is entirely false, and false not in detail but in principle. It is not merely an assemblage of particular mistakes. It is one big mistake and a mistake of a special kind. It is, namely, a category-mistake. It represents the facts of mental life as if they belonged to one logical type or category (or range of types or categories), when they actually belong to another. The dogma is therefore a philosopher's myth. In attempting to explode the myth I shall probably be taken to be denying well-known facts about the mental life of human beings, and my plea that I aim at doing nothing more than rectify the logic of mental-conduct concepts will probably be disallowed as mere subterfuge.

I must first indicate what is meant by the phrase 'Category-mistake'. This I do in a series of illustrations.

A foreigner visiting Oxford or Cambridge for the first time is shown a number of colleges, libraries, playing fields, museums, scientific departments and administrative offices. He then asks 'But where is the University? I have seen where the members of the

Colleges live, where the Registrar works, where the scientists experiment and the rest. But I have not yet seen the University in which reside and work the members of your University.' It has then to be explained to him that the University is not another collateral institution, some ulterior counterpart to the colleges, laboratories and offices which he has seen. The University is just the way in which all that he has already seen is organized. When they are seen and when their co-ordination is understood, the University has been seen. His mistake lay in his innocent assumption that it was correct to speak of Christ Church, the Bodleian Library, the Ashmolean Museum *and* the University, to speak, that is, as if 'the University' stood for an extra member of the class of which these other units are members. He was mistakenly allocating the University to the same category as that to which the other institutions belong.

The same mistake would be made by a child witnessing the march-past of a division, who, having had pointed out to him such and such battalions, batteries, squadrons, etc., asked when the division was going to appear. He would be supposing that a division was a counterpart to the units already seen, partly similar to them and partly unlike them. He would be shown his mistake by being told that in watching the battalions, batteries and squadrons marching past he had been watching the division marching past. The march-past was not a parade of battalions, batteries, squadrons *and* a division; it was a parade of the battalions, batteries and squadrons *of* a division.

One more illustration. A foreigner watching his first game of cricket learns what are the functions of the bowlers, the batsmen, the fielders, the umpires and the scorers. He then says 'But there is no one left on the field to contribute the famous element of team-spirit. I see who does the bowling, the batting and the wicket-keeping; but I do not see whose role it is to exercise *esprit de corps.*' Once more, it would have to be explained that he was looking for the wrong type of thing. Team-spirit is not another cricketing-operation supplementary to all of the other special tasks. It is, roughly, the keenness with which each of the special tasks is performed, and performing a task keenly is not performing two tasks. Certainly exhibiting team-spirit is not the same thing as bowling or catching, but nor is it a third thing such that we can say that the bowler first bowls *and* then exhibits team-spirit or that a fielder is at a given moment *either* catching *or* displaying *esprit de corps.*

These illustrations of category-mistakes have a common feature which must be noticed. The mistakes were made by people who did not know how to wield the concepts *University, division* and *team-spirit.* Their puzzles arose from inability to use certain items in the English vocabulary.

The theoretically interesting category-mistakes are those made by people who are perfectly competent to apply concepts, at least in the situations with which they are familiar, but are still liable in their abstract thinking to allocate those concepts to logical types to which they do not belong. An instance of a mistake of this sort would be the following story. A student of politics has learned the main differences between the British, the French and the American Constitutions, and has learned also the differences and connections between the Cabinet, Parliament, the various Ministries, the Judicature and the Church of England. But he still becomes embarrassed when asked questions about the connections between the Church of England, the Home Office and the British Constitution. For while the Church and the Home Office are institutions, the British Constitution is not another institution in the same sense of that noun. So inter-institutional relations which can be asserted or denied to hold between the Church and the Home Office cannot be asserted or denied to hold between either of them and the British Constitution. 'The British Constitution' is not a term of the same logical type as 'the Home Office' and 'the Church of England'. In a partially similar way, John Doe may be a relative, a friend, an enemy or a stranger to Richard Roe; but he cannot be any of these things to the Average Taxpayer. He knows how to talk sense in certain sorts of discussions about the Average Taxpayer, but he is baffled to say why he could not come across him in the street as he can come across Richard Roe.

It is pertinent to our main subject to notice that, so long as the student of politics continues to think of the British Constitution as a counterpart to the other institutions, he will tend to describe it as a mysteriously occult institution; and so long as John Doe continues to think of the Average Taxpayer as a fellow-citizen, he will tend to think of him as an elusive insubstantial man, a ghost who is everywhere yet nowhere.

My destructive purpose is to show that a family of radical category-mistakes is the source of the double-life theory. The representation of a person as a ghost mysteriously ensconced in a machine derives from this argument. Because, as is true, a person's thinking, feeling and purposive doing cannot be described solely in the idioms of physics, chemistry and physiology, therefore they must be described in counterpart idioms. As the human body is a complex organised unit, so the human mind must be another complex organised unit, though one made of a different sort of stuff and with a different sort of structure. Or, again, as the human body, like any other parcel of matter, is a field of causes and effects, so the mind must be another field of causes and effects, though not (Heaven be praised) mechanical causes and effects.

## (3) THE ORIGIN OF THE CATEGORY-MISTAKE

One of the chief intellectual origins of what I have yet to prove to be the Cartesian category-mistake seems to be this. When Galileo showed that his methods of scientific discovery were competent to provide a mechanical theory which should cover every occupant of space, Descartes found in himself two conflicting motives. As a man of scientific genius he could not but endorse the claims of mechanics, yet as a religious and moral man he could not accept, as Hobbes accepted, the discouraging rider to those claims, namely that human nature differs only in degree of complexity from clockwork. The mental could not be just a variety of the mechanical.

He and subsequent philosophers naturally but erroneously availed themselves of the following escape-route. Since mental-conduct words are not to be construed as signifying the occurrence of mechanical processes, they must be construed as signifying the occurrence of non-mechanical processes; since mechanical laws explain movements in space as the effects of other movements in space, other laws must explain some of the non-spatial workings of minds as the effects of other non-spatial workings of minds. The difference between the human behaviours which we describe as intelligent and those which we describe as unintelligent must be a difference in their causation; so, while some movements of human tongues and limbs are the effects of mechanical causes, others must be the effects of non-mechanical causes, i.e. some issue from movements of particles of matter, others from workings of the mind.

The differences between the physical and the mental were thus represented as differences inside the common framework of the categories of 'thing', 'stuff', 'attribute', 'state', 'process', 'change', 'cause' and 'effect'. Minds are things, but different sorts of things from bodies; mental processes are causes and effects, but different sorts of causes and effects from bodily movements. And so on. Somewhat as the foreigner expected the University to be an extra edifice, rather like a college but also considerably different, so the repudiators of mechanism represented minds as extra centres of causal processes, rather like machines but also considerably different from them. Their theory was a para-mechanical hypothesis.

That this assumption was at the heart of the doctrine is shown by the fact that there was from the beginning felt to be a major theoretical difficulty in explaining how minds can influence and be influenced by bodies. How can a mental process, such as willing, cause spatial movements like the movements of the tongue? How can a physical change in the optic nerve have among its effects a mind's perception of a flash of light? This notorious crux by itself shows the logical mould into which Descartes pressed his theory of the mind. It was the self-same mould into which he and Galileo set their mechanics. Still unwittingly adhering to the grammar of mechanics, he tried to avert disaster by describing minds in what was merely an obverse vocabulary. The workings of minds had to be described by the mere negatives of the specific descriptions given to bodies; they are not in space, they are not motions, they are not modifications of matter, they are not accessible to public observation. Minds are not bits of clockwork, they are just bits of not-clockwork.

As thus represented, minds are not merely ghosts harnessed to machines, they are themselves just spectral machines. Though the human body is an engine, it is not quite an ordinary engine, since some of its workings are governed by another engine inside it—this interior governor-engine being one of a very special sort. It is invisible, inaudible and it has no size or weight. It cannot be taken to bits and the laws it obeys are not those known to ordinary engineers. Nothing is known of how it governs the bodily engine.

A second major crux points the same moral. Since, according to the doctrine, minds belong to the same category as bodies and since bodies are rigidly governed by mechanical laws, it seemed to many theorists to follow that minds must be similarly governed by rigid non-mechanical laws. The physical world is a deterministic system, so the mental world must be a deterministic system. Bodies cannot help the modifications that they undergo, so minds cannot help pursuing the careers fixed for them. *Responsibility, choice, merit* and *demerit* are therefore inapplicable concepts—unless the compromise solution is adopted of saying that the laws governing mental processes, unlike those governing physical processes, have the congenial attribute of being only rather rigid. The problem of the Freedom of the Will was the problem how to reconcile the hypothesis that minds are to be described in terms drawn from the categories of mechanics with the knowledge that higher-grade human conduct is not of a piece with the behaviour of machines.

It is an historical curiosity that it was not noticed that the entire argument was broken-backed. Theorists correctly assumed that any sane man could already recognise the differences between, say, rational and non-rational utterances or between purposive and automatic behaviour. Else there would have been nothing requiring to be salved from mechanism. Yet the explanation given presupposed that one person could in principle never recognise the difference between the rational and the irrational utterances issuing from other human bodies, since he could never get access to the postulated immaterial causes of some of their utterances. Save for the doubtful exception of himself, he could never tell the difference between a man and a robot. It would have to be conceded, for example, that, for all that we can tell, the inner lives of persons who are classed as idiots or lunatics are as rational as those of anyone else. Perhaps only their overt behaviour is disappointing; that is to say, perhaps 'idiots' are not really idiotic, or 'lunatics' lunatic. Perhaps, too, some of those who are classed as sane are really idiots. According to the theory, external observers could never know how the overt behaviour of others is correlated with their mental powers and processes and so they could never know or even plausibly conjecture whether their applications of mental-conduct concepts to these other people were correct or incorrect. It would then be hazardous or impossible for a man to claim sanity or logical consistency even for himself, since he would be debarred from comparing his own performances with those of others. In short, our characterisations of persons and their performances

as intelligent, prudent and virtuous or as stupid, hypocritical and cowardly could never have been made, so the problem of providing a special causal hypothesis to serve as the basis of such diagnoses would never have arisen. The question, 'How do persons differ from machines?' arose just because everyone already knew how to apply mental-conduct concepts before the new causal hypothesis was introduced. This causal hypothesis could not therefore be the source of the criteria used in the applications. Nor, of course, has the causal hypothesis in any degree improved our handling of those criteria. We still distinguish good from bad arithmetic, politic from impolitic conduct and fertile from infertile imaginations in the ways in which Descartes himself distinguished them before and after he speculated how the applicability of these criteria was compatible with the principle of mechanical causation.

He had mistaken the logic of his problem. Instead of asking by what criteria intelligent behaviour is actually distinguished from non-intelligent behaviour, he asked 'Given that the principle of mechanical causation does not tell us the difference, what other causal principle will tell it us?' He realised that the problem was not one of mechanics and assumed that it must therefore be one of some counterpart to mechanics. Not unnaturally psychology is often cast for just this role.

When two terms belong to the same category, it is proper to construct conjunctive propositions embodying them. Thus a purchaser may say that he bought a left-hand glove and a right-hand glove, but not that he bought a left-hand glove, a right-hand glove and a pair of gloves. 'She came home in a flood of tears and a sedan-chair' is a well-known joke based on the absurdity of conjoining terms of different types. It would have been equally ridiculous to construct the disjunction 'She came home either in a flood of tears or else in a sedan-chair'. Now the dogma of the Ghost in the Machine does just this. It maintains that there exist both bodies and minds; that there occur physical processes and mental processes; that there are mechanical causes of corporeal movements and mental causes of corporeal movements. I shall argue that these and other analogous conjunctions are absurd; but, it must be noticed, the argument will not show that either of the illegitimately conjoined propositions is absurd in itself. I am not, for example, denying that there occur mental processes. Doing long division is a mental process and so is making a joke.

But I am saying that the phrase 'there occur mental processes' does not mean the same sort of thing as 'there occur physical processes', and, therefore, that it makes no sense to conjoin or disjoin the two.

If my argument is successful, there will follow some interesting consequences. First, the hallowed contrast between Mind and Matter will be dissipated, but dissipated not by either of the equally hallowed absorptions of Mind by Matter or of Matter by Mind, but in quite a different way. For the seeming contrast of the two will be shown to be as illegitimate as would be the contrast of 'she came home in a flood of tears' and 'she came home in a sedan-chair'. The belief that there is a polar opposition between Mind and Matter is the belief that they are terms of the same logical type.

It will also follow that both Idealism and Materialism are answers to an improper question. The 'reduction' of the material world to mental states and processes, as well as the 'reduction' of mental states and processes to physical states and processes, presuppose the legitimacy of the disjunction 'Either there exist minds or there exist bodies (but not both)'. It would be like saying, 'Either she bought a left-hand and a right-hand glove or she bought a pair of gloves (but not both)'.

It is perfectly proper to say, in one logical tone of voice, that there exist minds and to say, in another logical tone of voice, that there exist bodies. But these expressions do not indicate two different species of existence, for 'existence' is not a generic word like 'coloured' or 'sexed'. They indicate two different senses of 'exist', somewhat as 'rising' has different senses in 'the tide is rising', 'hopes are rising', and 'the average age of death is rising'. A man would be thought to be making a poor joke who said that three things are now rising, namely the tide, hopes and the average age of death. It would be just as good or bad a joke to say that there exist prime numbers and Wednesdays and public opinions and navies; or that there exist both minds and bodies. In the succeeding

chapters I try to prove that the official theory does rest on a batch of category-mistakes by showing that logically absurd corollaries follow from it. The exhibition of these absurdities will have the constructive effect of bringing out part of the correct logic of mental-conduct concepts.

## (4) HISTORICAL NOTE

It would not be true to say that the official theory derives solely from Descartes' theories, or even from a more widespread anxiety about the implications of seventeenth century mechanics. Scholastic and Reformation theology had schooled the intellects of the scientists as well as of the laymen, philosophers and clerics of that age. Stoic-Augustinian theories of the will were embedded in the Calvinist doctrines of sin and grace; Platonic and Aristotelian theories of the intellect shaped the orthodox doctrines of the immortality of the soul. Descartes was reformulating already prevalent theological doctrines of the soul in the new syntax of Galileo. The theologian's privacy of conscience became the philosopher's privacy of consciousness, and what had been the bogy of Predestination reappeared as the bogy of Determinism.

It would also not be true to say that the two-worlds myth did no theoretical good. Myths often do a lot of theoretical good, while they are still new. One benefit bestowed by the para-mechanical myth was that it partly superannuated the then prevalent para-political myth. Minds and their Faculties had previously been described by analogies with political superiors and political subordinates. The idioms used were those of ruling, obeying, collaborating and rebelling. They survived and still survive in many ethical and some epistemological discussions. As, in physics, the new myth of occult Forces was a scientific improvement on the old myth of Final Causes, so, in anthropological and psychological theory, the new myth of hidden operations, impulses and agencies was an improvement on the old myth of dictations, deferences and disobediences.

**READING 23**

---

# Sensations and Brain Processes

## J.J.C. Smart

*For biographical details see Reading 14.*

This paper[1] takes its departure from arguments to be found in U. T. Place's "Is Consciousness a Brain Process?"[2] I have had the benefit of discussing Place's thesis in a good many universities in the United States and Australia, and I hope that the present paper answers objections to his thesis which Place has not considered and that it presents his thesis in a more nearly unobjectionable form. This paper is meant also to supplement the paper "The 'Mental' and the 'Physical,'" by H. Feigl,[3] which in part argues for a similar thesis to Place's.

Suppose that I report that I have at this moment a roundish, blurry-edged after-image which is yellowish towards its edge and is orange towards its center. What is it that I am reporting? One answer to this question might be that I am not reporting anything, that when I say that it looks to me as though there is a roundish yellowy-orange patch of light on the wall I am expressing some sort of *temptation*, the temptation to say that there *is* a roundish yellowy-orange patch on the wall (though I may know that there is not such a patch on the wall). This is perhaps Wittgenstein's view in the *Philosophical Investigations* (see §§ 367, 370). Similarly, when I "report" a pain, I am not really reporting anything (or, if you like, I am reporting in a queer sense of "reporting"), but am doing a sophisticated sort of wince. (See § 244: "The verbal expression of pain replaces crying and does not describe it." Nor does it describe anything else?)[4] I prefer most of the time to discuss an after-image rather than a pain, because the word "pain" brings in something which is irrelevant to my purpose: the notion of "distress." I think that "he is in pain" entails "he is in distress," that is, that he is in a certain agitation-condition.[5] Similarly, to say "I am in pain" may be to do more than "replace pain behavior": it may be partly to report something, though this something is quite nonmysterious, being an agitation-condition, and so susceptible of behavioristic analysis. The suggestion I wish if possible to avoid is a different one, namely that "I am in pain" is a genuine report, and that what it reports is an irreducibly psychical something. And similarly the suggestion I wish to resist is also that to say "I have a yellowish-orange after-image" is to report something irreducibly psychical.

---

[1] This is a very slightly revised version of a paper which was first published in the *Philosophical Review,* LXVIII (1959), 141–56. Since that date there have been criticisms of my paper by J. T. Stevenson, *Philosophical Review,* LXIX (1960), 505–10, to which I have replied in *Philosophical Review,* LXX (1961), 406–7, and by G. Pitcher and by W. D. Joske, *Australasian Journal of Philosophy,* XXXVIII (1960), 150–60, to which I have replied in the same volume of that journal, pp. 252–54.

[2] *British Journal of Psychology,* XLVII (1956), 44–50. Reprinted in *The Philosophy of Mind,* ed. V. C. Chappell (Englewood Cliffs, NJ: Prentice-Hall, 1962), pp. 101–109. (Page references are to the reprint in that volume.)

[3] *Minnesota Studies in the Philosophy of Science,* Vol. II (Minneapolis: University of Minnesota Press, 1958), pp. 370–497.

**SOURCE:** From *Philosophical Review* 68 (1959): 141–156. As reprinted with slight revisions in V. C. Chappell, Ed., *The Philosophy of Mind* (Englewood Cliffs, NJ: Prentice-Hall, 1962): 160–172.

[4] Some philosophers of my acquaintance, who have the advantage over me in having known Wittgenstein, would say that this interpretation of him is too behavioristic. However, it seems to me a very natural interpretation of his printed words, and whether or not it is Wittgenstein's real view it is certainly an interesting and important one. I wish to consider it here as a possible rival both to the "brain-process" thesis and to straight-out old-fashioned dualism.

[5] See Ryle, *The Concept of Mind* (London: Hutchinson's University Library, 1949), p. 93.

Why do I wish to resist this suggestion? Mainly because of Occam's razor. It seems to me that science is increasingly giving us a viewpoint whereby organisms are able to be seen as physicochemical mechanisms:[6] it seems that even the behavior of man himself will one day be explicable in mechanistic terms. There does seem to be, so far as science is concerned, nothing in the world but increasingly complex arrangements of physical constituents. All except for one place: in consciousness. That is, for a full description of what is going on in a man you would have to mention not only the physical processes in his tissues, glands, nervous system, and so forth, but also his states of consciousness: his visual, auditory, and tactual sensations, his aches and pains. That these should be *correlated* with brain processes does not help, for to say that they are *correlated* is to say that they are something "over and above." You cannot correlate something with itself. You correlate footprints with burglars, but not Bill Sikes the burglar with Bill Sikes the burglar. So sensations, states of consciousness, do seem to be the one sort of thing left outside the physicalist picture, and for various reasons I just cannot believe that this can be so. That everything should be explicable in terms of physics (together of course with descriptions of the ways in which the parts are put together—roughly, biology is to physics as radio-engineering is to electromagnetism) except the occurrence of sensations seems to me to be frankly unbelievable. Such sensations would be "nomological danglers," to use Feigl's expression.[7] It is not often realized how odd would be the laws whereby these nomological danglers would dangle. It is sometimes asked, "Why can't there be psychophysical laws which are of a novel sort, just as the laws of electricity and magnetism were novelties from the standpoint of Newtonian mechanics?" Certainly we are pretty sure in the future to come across new ultimate laws of a novel type, but I expect them to relate simple constituents: for example, whatever ultimate particles are then in vogue, I cannot believe that ultimate laws of nature could relate simple constituents to configurations consisting of perhaps billions of neurons (and goodness knows how many billion billions of ultimate particles) all put together for all the world as though their main purpose in life was to be a negative feedback mechanism of a complicated sort. Such ultimate laws would be like nothing so far known in science. They have a queer "smell" to them. I am just unable to believe in the nomological danglers themselves, or in the laws whereby they would dangle. If any philosophical argument seemed to compel us to believe in such things, I would suspect a catch in the argument. In any case it is the object of this paper to show that there are no philosophical arguments which compel us to be dualists.

The above is largely a confession of faith, but it explains why I find Wittgenstein's position (as I construe it) so congenial. For on this view there are, in a sense, no sensations. A man is a vast arrangement of physical particles, but there are not, over and above this, sensations or states of consciousness. There are just behavioral facts about this vast mechanism, such as that it expresses a temptation (behavior disposition) to say "there is a yellowish-red patch on the wall" or that it goes through a sophisticated sort of wince, that is, says "I am in pain." Admittedly Wittgenstein says that though the sensation "is not a something," it is nevertheless "not a nothing either" (§ 304), but this need only mean that the word "ache" has a use. An ache is a thing, but only in the innocuous sense in which the plain man, in the first paragraph of Frege's *Foundations of Arithmetic*, answers the question "What is the number one?" by "a thing." It should be noted that when I assert that to say "I have a yellowish-orange after-image" is to express a temptation to assert the physical-object statement "There is a yellowish-orange patch on the wall," I mean that saying "I have a yellowish-orange after-image" is (partly) the exercise of the disposition[8] which is the temptation. It is not to *report* that I have the temptation, any more than is "I love you" normally a report that I love someone. Saying "I love

[6]On this point see Paul Oppenheim and Hilary Putnam, "Unity of Science as a Working Hypothesis," in *Minnesota Studies in the Philosophy of Science*, Vol. II (Minneapolis: University of Minnesota Press, 1958), pp. 3–36.

[7]Feigl, *op. cit.*, p. 428. Feigl uses the expression "nomological danglers" for the laws whereby the entities dangle: I have used the expression to refer to the dangling entities themselves.

[8]Wittgenstein did not like the word "disposition." I am using it to put in a nutshell (and perhaps inaccurately) the view which I am attributing to Wittgenstein. I should like to repeat that I do not wish to claim that my interpretation of Wittgenstein is correct. Some of those who knew him do not interpret him in this way. It is merely a view which I find myself extracting from his printed words and which I think is important and worth discussing for its own sake.

you" is just part of the behavior which is the exercise of the disposition of loving someone.

Though for the reasons given above, I am very receptive to the above "expressive" account of sensation statements, I do not feel that it will quite do the trick. Maybe this is because I have not thought it out sufficiently, but it does seem to me as though, when a person says "I have an after-image," he *is* making a genuine report, and that when he says "I have a pain," he *is* doing more than "replace pain behavior," and that "this more" is not just to say that he is in distress. I am not so sure, however, that to admit this is to admit that there are nonphysical correlates of brain processes. Why should not sensations just be brain processes of a certain sort? There are, of course, well-known (as well as lesser-known) philosophical objections to the view that reports of sensations are reports of brain processes, but I shall try to argue that these arguments are by no means as cogent as is commonly thought to be the case.

Let me first try to state more accurately the thesis that sensations are brain processes. It is not the thesis that, for example, "after-image" or "ache" means the same as "brain process of sort X" (where "X" is replaced by a description of a certain sort of brain process). It is that, in so far as "after-image" or "ache" is a report of a process, it is a report of a process that *happens to be* a brain process. It follows that the thesis does not claim that sensation statements can be *translated* into statements about brain processes.[9] Nor does it claim that the logic of a sensation statement is the same as that of a brain-process statement. All it claims is that in so far as a sensation statement is a report of something, that something is in fact a brain process. Sensations are nothing over and above brain processes. Nations are nothing "over and above" citizens, but this does not prevent the logic of nation statements being very different from the logic of citizen statements, nor does it insure the translatability of nation statements into citizen statements. (I do not, however, wish to assert that the relation of sensation statements to brain-process statements is very like that of nation statements to citizen statements. Nations do not just *happen to be* nothing over and above citizens, for example. I bring in the "nations" example merely to make a negative point: that the fact that the logic of A-statements is different from

that of B-statements does not insure that A's are anything over and above B's.)

## REMARKS ON IDENTITY

When I say that a sensation is a brain process or that lightning is an electric discharge, I am using "is" in the sense of strict identity. (Just as in the—in this case necessary—proposition "7 is identical with the smallest prime number greater than 5.") When I say that a sensation is a brain process or that lightning is an electric discharge I do not mean just that the sensation is somehow spatially or temporally continuous with the brain process or that the lightning is just spatially or temporally continuous with the discharge. When on the other hand I say that the successful general is the same person as the small boy who stole the apples I mean only that the successful general I see before me is a time slice[10] of the same four-dimensional object of which the small boy stealing apples is an earlier time slice. However, the four-dimensional object which has the general-I-see-before-me for its late time slice is identical in the strict sense with the four-dimensional object which has the small-boy-stealing-apples for an early time slice. I distinguish these two senses of "is identical with" because I wish to make it clear that the brain-process doctrine asserts identity in the *strict* sense.

I shall now discuss various possible objections to the view that the processes reported in sensation statements are in fact processes in the brain. Most of us have met some of these objections in our first year as philosophy students. All the more reason to take a good look at them. Others of the objections will be more recondite and subtle.

*Objection 1.* Any illiterate peasant can talk perfectly well about his after-images, or how things look or feel to him, or about his aches and pains, and yet he may know nothing whatever about neurophysiology. A man may, like Aristotle, believe that the brain is an organ for cooling the body without any impairment of his ability to make true statements about his sensations. Hence the things we are talking about

---

[9]See Place, *op. cit.*, p. 102, and Feigl, *op. cit.*, p. 390, near top.

[10]See J. H. Woodger, *Theory Construction*, International Encyclopedia of Unified Science, II, No. 5 (Chicago: University of Chicago Press, 1939), 38. I here permit myself to speak loosely. For warnings against possible ways of going wrong with this sort of talk, see my note "Spatialising Time," *Mind*, LXIV (1955), 239–41.

when we describe our sensations cannot be processes in the brain.

*Reply.* You might as well say that a nation of sluga-beds, who never saw the Morning Star or knew of its existence, or who had never thought of the expression "the Morning Star," but who used the expression "the Evening Star" perfectly well, could not use this expression to refer to the same entity as we refer to (and describe as) "the Morning Star."[11]

You may object that the Morning Star is in a sense not the very same thing as the Evening Star, but only something spatiotemporally continuous with it. That is, you may say that the Morning Star is not the Evening Star in the strict sense of "identity" that I distinguished earlier.

There is, however, a more plausible example. Consider lightning.[12] Modern physical science tells us that lightning is a certain kind of electrical discharge due to ionization of clouds of water vapor in the atmosphere. This, it is now believed, is what the true nature of lightning is. Note that there are not two things: a flash of lightning and an electrical discharge. There is one thing, a flash of lightning, which is described scientifically as an electrical discharge to the earth from a cloud of ionized water molecules. The case is not at all like that of explaining a footprint by reference to a burglar. We say that what lightning really is, what its true nature as revealed by science is, is an electrical discharge. (It is not the true nature of a footprint to be a burglar.)

To forestall irrelevant objections, I should like to make it clear that by "lightning" I mean the publicly observable physical object, lightning, not a visual sense-datum of lightning. I say that the publicly observable physical object lightning is in fact the electrical discharge, not just a correlate of it. The sense-datum, or rather the having of the sense-datum, the "look" of lightning, may well in my view be a correlate of the electrical discharge. For in my view it is a brain state *caused* by the lightning. But we should no more confuse sensations of lightning with lightning than we confuse sensations of a table with the table.

In short, the reply to Objection 1 is that there can be contingent statements of the form "A is identical with B," and a person may well know that something is an A without knowing that it is a B. An illiterate peasant might well be able to talk about his sensations without knowing about his brain processes, just as he can talk about lightning though he knows nothing of electricity.

*Objection 2.* It is only a contingent fact (if it is a fact) that when we have a certain kind of sensation there is a certain kind of process in our brain. Indeed it is possible, though perhaps in the highest degree unlikely, that our present physiological theories will be as out of date as the ancient theory connecting mental processes with goings on in the heart. It follows that when we report a sensation we are not reporting a brain process.

*Reply.* The objection certainly proves that when we say "I have an after-image" we cannot *mean* something of the form "I have such and such a brain process." But this does not show that what we report (having an after-image) is not *in fact* a brain process. "I see lightning" does not *mean* "I see an electrical discharge." Indeed, it is logically possible (though highly unlikely) that the electrical discharge account of lightning might one day be given up. Again, "I see the Evening Star" does not *mean* the same as "I see the Morning Star," and yet "The Evening Star and the Morning Star are one and the same thing" is a contingent proposition. Possibly Objection 2 derives some of its apparent strength from a "Fido"–Fido theory of meaning. If the meaning of an expression were what the expression named, then of course it *would* follow from the fact that "sensation" and "brain process" have different meanings that they cannot name one and the same thing.

*Objection 3.*[13] Even if Objections 1 and 2 do not prove that sensations are something over and above brain processes, they do prove that the qualities of sensations are something over and above the qualities of brain processes. That is, it may be possible to

---

[11]Cf. Feigl, *op. cit.,* p. 439.
[12]See Place, *op. cit.,* p. 106; also Feigl, *op. cit.,* p. 438.

[13]I think this objection was first put to me by Professor Max Black. I think it is the most subtle of any of those I have considered, and the one which I am least confident of having satisfactorily met.

get out of asserting the existence of irreducibly psychic processes, but not out of asserting the existence of irreducibly psychic *properties*. For suppose we identify the Morning Star with the Evening Star. Then there must be some properties which logically imply that of being the Morning Star, and quite distinct properties which entail that of being the Evening Star. Again, there must be some properties (for example, that of being a yellow flash) which are logically distinct from those in the physicalist story.

Indeed, it might be thought that the objection succeeds at one jump. For consider the property of "being a yellow flash." It might seem that this property lies inevitably outside the physicalist framework within which I am trying to work (either by "yellow" being an objective emergent property of physical objects, or else by being a power to produce yellow sense-data, where "yellow," in this second instantiation of the word, refers to a purely phenomenal or introspectible quality). I must therefore digress for a moment and indicate how I deal with secondary qualities. I shall concentrate on color.

First of all, let me introduce the concept of a normal percipient. One person is more a normal percipient than another if he can make color discriminations that the other cannot. For example, if A can pick a lettuce leaf out of a heap of cabbage leaves, whereas B cannot though he can pick a lettuce leaf out of a heap of beetroot leaves, then A is more normal than B. (I am assuming that A and B are not given time to distinguish the leaves by their slight difference in shape, and so forth.) From the concept of "more normal than" it is easy to see how we can introduce the concept of "normal." Of course, Eskimos may make the finest discriminations at the blue end of the spectrum, Hottentots at the red end. In this case the concept of a normal percipient is a slightly idealized one, rather like that of "the mean sun" in astronomical chronology. There is no need to go into such subtleties now. I say that "This is red" means something roughly like "A normal percipient would not easily pick this out of a clump of geranium petals though he would pick it out of a clump of lettuce leaves." Of course it does not exactly mean this: a person might know the meaning of "red" without knowing anything about geraniums, or even about normal percipients. But the point is that a person can be *trained* to say "This is red" of objects which would not easily be picked out of geranium petals by

a normal percipient, and so on. (Note that even a color-blind person can reasonably assert that something is red, though of course he needs to use another human being, not just himself, as his "color meter.") This account of secondary qualities explains their unimportance in physics. For obviously the discriminations and lack of discriminations made by a very complex neurophysiological mechanism are hardly likely to correspond to simple and nonarbitrary distinctions in nature.

I therefore elucidate colors as powers, in Locke's sense, to evoke certain sorts of discriminatory responses in human beings. They are also, of course, powers to cause sensations in human beings (an account still nearer Locke's). But these sensations, I am arguing, are identifiable with brain processes.

Now how do I get over the objection that a sensation can be identified with a brain process only if it has some phenomenal property, not possessed by brain processes, whereby one-half of the identification may be, so to speak, pinned down?

*Reply.* My suggestion is as follows. When a person says, "I see a yellowish-orange after-image," he is saying something like this: "*There is something going on which is like what is going on when* I have my eyes open, am awake, and there is an orange illuminated in good light in front of me, that is, when I really see an orange." (And there is no reason why a person should not say the same thing when he is having a veridical sense-datum, so long as we construe "like" in the last sentence in such a sense that something can be like itself.) Notice that the italicized words, namely "there is something going on which is like what is going on when," are all quasilogical or topic-neutral words. This explains why the ancient Greek peasant's reports about his sensations can be neutral between dualistic metaphysics or my materialistic metaphysics. It explains how sensations can be brain processes and yet how a man who reports them need know nothing about brain processes. For he reports them only very abstractly as "something going on which is like what is going on when. . . ." Similarly, a person may say "someone is in the room," thus reporting truly that the doctor is in the room, even though he has never heard of doctors. (There are not two people in the room: "someone" *and* the doctor.) This account of sensation statements also explains the singular elusiveness of "raw feels"—why no one seems to be able to pin any properties on them.[14] Raw feels, in my view, are colorless for the very same reason that *something* is colorless. This does not mean that sensations do not have plenty of properties, for if they are brain processes they certainly have lots of neurological properties. It only means that in speaking of them as being like or unlike one another we need not know or mention these properties.

This, then, is how I would reply to Objection 3. The strength of my reply depends on the possibility of our being able to report that one thing is like another without being able to state the respect in which it is like. I do not see why this should not be so. If we think cybernetically about the nervous system we can envisage it as able to respond to certain likenesses of its internal processes without being able to do more. It would be easier to build a machine which would tell us, say on a punched tape, whether or not two objects were similar, than it would be to build a machine which would report wherein the similarities consisted.

*Objection 4.* The after-image is not in physical space. The brain process is. So the after-image is not a brain process.

*Reply.* This is an *ignoratio elenchi.* I am not arguing that the after-image is a brain process, but that the experience of having an after-image is a brain process. It is the *experience* which is reported in the introspective report. Similarly, if it is objected that the after-image is yellowy-orange, my reply is that it is the experience of seeing yellowy-orange that is being described, and this experience is not a yellowy-orange something. So to say that a brain process cannot be yellowy-orange is not to say that a brain-process cannot in fact be the experience of having a yellowy-orange after-image. There is, in a sense, no such thing as an after-image or a sense-datum, though there is such a thing as the experience of having an image, and this experience is described indirectly in material object language, not in phenomenal language, for there is no such thing.[15] We describe the experience by saying, in effect, that it is like the experience we have when, for example, we really see a yellowy-orange patch on the wall. Trees

and wallpaper can be green, but not the experience of seeing or imagining a tree or wallpaper. (Or if they are described as green or yellow this can only be in a derived sense.)

*Objection 5.* It would make sense to say of a molecular movement in the brain that it is swift or slow, straight or circular, but it makes no sense to say this of the experience of seeing something yellow.

*Reply.* So far we have not given sense to talk of experiences as swift or slow, straight or circular. But I am not claiming that "experience" and "brain process" mean the same or even that they have the same logic. "Somebody" and "the doctor" do not have the same logic, but this does not lead us to suppose that talking about somebody telephoning is talking about someone over and above, say, the doctor. The ordinary man when he reports an experience is reporting that something is going on, but he leaves it open as to what sort of thing is going on, whether in a material solid medium or perhaps in some sort of gaseous medium, or even perhaps in some sort of nonspatial medium (if this makes sense). All that I am saying is that "experience" and "brain process" may in fact refer to the same thing, and if so we may easily adopt a convention (which is not a change in our present rules for the use of experience words but an addition to them) whereby it would make sense to talk of an experience in terms appropriate to physical processes.

*Objection 6.* Sensations are private, brain processes are *public.* If I sincerely say, "I see a yellowish-orange after-image," and I am not making a verbal mistake, then I cannot be wrong. But I can be wrong about a brain process. The scientist looking into my brain might be having an illusion. Moreover, it makes sense to say that two or more people are observing the same brain process but not that two or more people are reporting the same inner experience.

---

[14]See B. A. Farrell, "Experience," *Mind,* LIX (1950), 170-98. Reprinted in *The Philosophy of Mind,* ed. V. C. Chappell (Englewood Cliffs, NJ: Prentice-Hall, 1962), pp. 23–48; see especially p. 27 of that volume.

[15]Dr. J. R. Smythies claims that a sense-datum language could be taught independently of the material object language ("A Note on the Fallacy of the 'Phenomenological Fallacy,' " *British Journal of Psychology,* XLVII [1957], 141–44). I am not so sure of this: there must be some public criteria for a person having got a rule wrong before we can teach him the rule. I suppose someone might *accidentally* learn color words by Dr. Smythies' procedure. I am not, of course, denying that we can learn a sense-datum language in the sense that we can learn to report our experience. Nor would Place deny it.

*Reply.* This shows that the language of introspective reports has a different logic from the language of material processes. It is obvious that until the brain-process theory is much improved and widely accepted there will be no *criteria* for saying "Smith has an experience of such-and-such a sort" *except* Smith's introspective reports. So we have adopted a rule of language that (normally) what Smith says goes.

*Objection 7.* I can imagine myself turned to stone and yet having images, aches, pains, and so on.

*Reply.* I can imagine that the electrical theory of lightning is false, that lightning is some sort of purely optical phenomenon. I can imagine that lightning is not an electrical discharge. I can imagine that the Evening Star is not the Morning Star. But it is. All the objection shows is that "experience" and "brain process" do not have the same meaning. It does not show that an experience is not in fact a brain process.

This objection is perhaps much the same as one which can be summed up by the slogan: "What can be composed of nothing cannot be composed of anything."[16] The argument goes as follow: on the brain-process thesis the identity between the brain process and the experience is a contingent one. So it is logically possible that there should be no brain process, and no process of any other sort either (no heart process, no kidney process, no liver process). There would be the experience but no "corresponding" physiological process with which we might be able to identify it empirically.

I suspect that the objector is thinking of the experience as a ghostly entity. So it is composed of something, not of nothing, after all. On his view it is composed of ghost stuff, and on mine it is composed of brain stuff. Perhaps the counter-reply will be[17] that the experience is simple and uncompounded, and so it is not composed of anything after all. This seems to be a quibble, for, if it were taken seriously, the remark "What can be composed of nothing cannot be composed of anything" could be recast as an a priori argument against Democritus and atomism and for Descartes and infinite divisibility. And it seems odd that a question of this sort could be set-

tled a priori. We must therefore construe the word "composed" in a very weak sense, which would allow us to say that even an indivisible atom is composed of something (namely, itself). The dualist cannot really say that an experience can be composed of nothing. For he holds that experiences are something over and above material processes, that is, that they are a sort of ghost stuff. (Or perhaps ripples in an underlying ghost stuff.) I say that the dualist's hypothesis is a perfectly intelligible one. But I say that experiences are not to be identified with ghost stuff but with brain stuff. This is another hypothesis, and in my view a very plausible one. The present argument cannot knock it down a priori.

*Objection 8.* The "beetle in the box" objection (see Wittgenstein, *Philosophical Investigations*, § 293). How could descriptions of experiences, if these are genuine reports, get a foothold in language? For any rule of language must have public criteria for its correct application.

*Reply.* The change from describing how things are to describing how we feel is just a change from uninhibitedly saying "this is so" to saying "this looks so." That is, when the naïve person might be tempted to say, "There is a patch of light on the wall which moves whenever I move my eyes" or "A pin is being stuck into me," we have learned how to resist this temptation and say "It *looks as though* there is a patch of light on the wallpaper" or "It *feels as though* someone were sticking a pin into me." The introspective account tells us about the individual's state of consciousness in the same way as does "I see a patch of light" or "I feel a pin being stuck into me": it differs from the corresponding perception statement in so far as it withdraws any claim about what is actually going on in the external world. From the point of view of the psychologist, the change from talking about the environment to talking about one's perceptual sensations is simply a matter of disinhibiting certain reactions. These are reactions which one normally suppresses because one has learned that in the prevailing circumstances they are unlikely to provide a good indication of the state of the environment.[18] To say that something looks green to me is simply to say that my experience is like the experience I get when I see something that really is green. In my re-

---

[16]I owe this objection to Dr. C. B. Martin. I gather that he no longer wishes to maintain this objection, at any rate in its present form.

[17]Martin did not make this reply, but one of his students did.

[18]I owe this point to Place, in correspondence.

ply to Objection 3, I pointed out the extreme openness or generality of statements which report experiences. This explains why there is no language of private qualities. (Just as "someone," unlike "the doctor," is a colorless word.)[19]

If it is asked what is the difference between those brain processes which, in my view, are experiences and those brain processes which are not, I can only reply that it is at present unknown. I have been tempted to conjecture that the difference may in part be that between perception and reception (in D. M. MacKay's terminology) and that the type of brain process which is an experience might be identifiable with MacKay's active "matching response."[20] This, however, cannot be the whole story, because sometimes I can perceive something unconsciously, as when I take a handkerchief out of a drawer without being aware that I am doing so. But at the very least, we can classify the brain processes which are experiences as those brain processes which are, or might have been, causal conditions of those pieces of verbal behavior which we call reports of immediate experience.

I have now considered a number of objections to the brain-process thesis. I wish now to conclude with some remarks on the logical status of the thesis itself. U. T. Place seems to hold that it is a straight-out scientific hypothesis.[21] If so, he is partly right and partly wrong. If the issue is between (say) a brain-process thesis and a heart thesis, or a liver thesis, or a kidney thesis, then the issue is a purely empirical one, and the verdict is overwhelmingly in favor of the brain. The right sorts of things don't go on in the heart, liver, or kidney, nor do these organs possess the right sort of complexity of structure. On the other hand, if the issue is between a brain-or-liver-or-kidney thesis (that is, some form of materialism) on the one hand and epiphenomenalism on the other hand, then the issue is not an empirical one. For there is no conceivable experiment which could decide between materialism and epiphenomenalism.

This latter issue is not like the average straight-out empirical issue in science, but like the issue between the nineteenth-century English naturalist Philip Gosse[22] and the orthodox geologists and paleontologists of his day. According to Gosse, the earth was created about 4000 B.C. exactly as described in *Genesis,* with twisted rock strata, "evidence" of erosion, and so forth, and all sorts of fossils, all in their appropriate strata, just as if the usual evolutionist story had been true. Clearly this theory is in a sense irrefutable: no evidence can possibly tell against it. Let us ignore the theological setting in which Philip Gosse's hypothesis had been placed, thus ruling out objections of a theological kind, such as "what a queer God who would go to such elaborate lengths to deceive us." Let us suppose that it is held that the universe just *began* in 4004 B.C. with the initial conditions just everywhere as they were in 4004 B.C., and in particular that our own planet began with sediment in the rivers, eroded cliffs, fossils in the rocks, and so on. No scientist would ever entertain this as a serious hypothesis, consistent though it is with all possible evidence. The hypothesis offends against the principles of parsimony and simplicity. There would be far too many brute and inexplicable facts. Why are pterodactyl bones just as they are? No explanation in terms of the evolution of pterodactyls from earlier forms of life would any longer be possible. We would have millions of facts about the world as it was in 4004 B.C. that just have to be *accepted.*

The issue between the brain-process theory and epiphenomenalism seems to be of the above sort. (Assuming that a behavioristic reduction of introspective reports is not possible.) If it be agreed that there are no cogent philosophical arguments which force us into accepting dualism, and if the brain-process theory and dualism are equally consistent with the facts, then the principles of parsimony and simplicity seem to me to decide overwhelmingly in favor of the brain-process theory. As I pointed out earlier, dualism involves a large number of irreducible psychophysical laws (whereby the "nomological danglers" dangle) of a queer sort, that just have to be taken on trust, and are just as difficult to swallow as the irreducible facts about the paleontology of the earth with which we are faced on Philip Gosse's theory.

---

[19]The "beetle in the box" objection is, *if it is sound,* an objection to *any* view, and in particular the Cartesian one, that introspective reports are genuine reports. So it is no objection to a weaker thesis that I would be concerned to uphold, namely, that if introspective reports of "experiences" are genuinely reports, then the things they are reports of are in fact brain processes.

[20]See his article "Towards an Information-Flow Model of Human Behaviour," *British Journal of Psychology,* XLVII (1956), 30–43.

[21]*Op. cit.* For a further discussion of this, in reply to the original version of the present paper, see Place's note "Materialism as a Scientific Hypothesis," *Philosophical Review,* LXIX (1960), 101–4.

[22]See the entertaining account of Gosse's book *Omphalos* by Martin Gardner in *Fads and Fallacies in the Name of Science,* 2nd ed. (New York: Dover, 1957), pp. 124–27.

**READING  24**

# The Mind-Body Problem

*Jerry A. Fodor*

*Jerry Fodor (1935–   ) is a leading advocate of function-alism in the philosophy of mind and has written widely on issues in cognitive science and semantics. His books include* Psychological  Explanation *(1968),* Representations *(1981), and* Psychosemantics *(1987). Fodor is Professor of Philosophy at Rutgers University and at the City University of New York Graduate Center.*

> Could calculating machines have pains, Martians have expectations and disembodied spirits have thoughts? The modern functionalist approach to psychology raises the logical possibility that they could.

Modern philosophy of science has been devoted largely to the formal and systematic description of the successful practices of working scientists. The philosopher does not try to dictate how scientific inquiry and argument ought to be conducted. Instead he tries to enumerate the principles and practices that have contributed to good science. The philosopher has devoted the most attention to analyzing the methodological peculiarities of the physical sciences. The analysis has helped to clarify the nature of confirmation, the logical structure of scientific theories, the formal properties of statements that express laws and the question of whether theoretical entities actually exist.

It is only rather recently that philosophers have become seriously interested in the methodological tenets of psychology. Psychological explanations of behavior refer liberally to the mind and to states, operations and processes of the mind. The philosophical difficulty comes in stating in unambiguous language what such references imply.

Traditional philosophies of mind can be divided into two broad categories: dualist theories and materialist theories. In the dualist approach the mind is a nonphysical substance. In materialist theories the mental is not distinct from the physical; indeed, all mental states, properties, processes and operations are in principle identical with physical states, properties, processes and operations. Some materialists, known as behaviorists, maintain that all talk of mental causes can be eliminated from the language of psychology in favor of talk of environmental stimuli and behavioral responses. Other materialists, the identity theorists, contend that there are mental causes and that they are identical with neurophysiological events in the brain.

In the past 15 years a philosophy of mind called functionalism that is neither dualist nor materialist has emerged from philosophical reflection on developments in artificial intelligence, computational theory, linguistics, cybernetics and psychology. All these fields, which are collectively known as the cognitive sciences, have in common a certain level of abstraction and a concern with systems that process information. Functionalism, which seeks to provide a philosophical account of this level of abstraction, recognizes the possibility that systems as diverse as human beings, calculating machines and disembodied spirits could all have mental states. In the functionalist view the psychology of a system depends not on the stuff it is made of (living cells, metal or spiritual energy) but on how the stuff is put together. Functionalism is a difficult concept, and one way of coming to grips with it is to review the deficiencies of the dualist and materialist philosophies of mind it aims to displace.

The chief drawback of dualism is its failure to account adequately for mental causation. If the mind is nonphysical, it has no position in physical space.

How, then, can a mental cause give rise to a behavioral effect that has a position in space? To put it another way, how can the nonphysical give rise to the physical without violating the laws of the conservation of mass, of energy and of momentum?

The dualist might respond that the problem of how an immaterial substance can cause physical events is not much obscurer than the problem of how one physical event can cause another. Yet there is an important difference: there are many clear cases of physical causation but not one clear case of nonphysical causation. Physical interaction is something philosophers, like all other people, have to live with. Nonphysical interaction, however, may be no more than an artifact of the immaterialist construal of the mental. Most philosophers now agree that no argument has successfully demonstrated why mind-body causation should not be regarded as a species of physical causation.

Dualism is also incompatible with the practices of working psychologists. The psychologist frequently applies the experimental methods of the physical sciences to the study of the mind. If mental processes were different in kind from physical processes, there would be no reason to expect these methods to work in the realm of the mental. In order to justify their experimental methods many psychologists urgently sought an alternative to dualism.

In the 1920's John B. Watson of Johns Hopkins University made the radical suggestion that behavior does not have mental causes. He regarded the behavior of an organism as its observable responses to stimuli, which he took to be the causes of its behavior. Over the next 30 years psychologists such as B. F. Skinner of Harvard University developed Watson's ideas into an elaborate world view in which the role of psychology was to catalogue the laws that determine causal relations between stimuli and responses. In this "radical behaviorist" view the problem of explaining the nature of the mind-body interaction vanishes; there is no such interaction.

Radical behaviorism has always worn an air of paradox. For better or worse, the idea of mental causation is deeply ingrained in our everyday language and in our ways of understanding our fellow men and ourselves. For example, people commonly attribute behavior to beliefs, to knowledge and to expectations. Brown puts gas in his tank because he believes the car will not run without it. Jones writes not "acheive" but "achieve" because he knows the rule about putting *i* before *e*. Even when a behavioral response is closely tied to an environmental stimulus, mental processes often intervene. Smith carries an umbrella because the sky is cloudy, but the weather is only part of the story. There are apparently also mental links in the causal chain: observation and expectation. The clouds affect Smith's behavior only because he observes them and because they induce in him an expectation of rain.

The radical behaviorist is unmoved by appeals to such cases. He is prepared to dismiss references to mental causes, however plausible they may seem, as the residue of outworn creeds. The radical behaviorist predicts that as psychologists come to understand more about the relations between stimuli and responses they will find it increasingly possible to explain behavior without postulating mental causes.

The strongest argument against behaviorism is that psychology has not turned out this way; the opposite has happened. As psychology has matured, the framework of mental states and processes that is apparently needed to account for experimental observations has grown all the more elaborate. Particularly in the case of human behavior psychological theories satisfying the methodological tenets of radical behaviorism have proved largely sterile, as would be expected if the postulated mental processes are real and causally effective.

Nevertheless, many philosophers were initially drawn to radical behaviorism because, paradoxes and all, it seemed better than dualism. Since a psychology committed to immaterial substances was unacceptable, philosophers turned to radical behaviorism because it seemed to be the only alternative materialist philosophy of mind. The choice, as they saw it, was between radical behaviorism and ghosts.

By the early 1960's philosophers began to have doubts that dualism and radical behaviorism exhausted the possible approaches to the philosophy of mind. Since the two theories seemed unattractive, the right strategy might be to develop a materialist philosophy of mind that nonetheless allowed for mental causes. Two such philosophies emerged, one called logical behaviorism and the other called the central-state identity theory.

Logical behaviorism is a semantic theory about what mental terms mean. The basic idea is that attributing a mental state (say thirst) to an organism is the same as saying that the organism is disposed to behave in a particular way (for example to drink if there is water available). On this view every mental ascription is equivalent in meaning to an if-then statement (called a behavioral hypothetical) that expresses a behavioral disposition. For example, "Smith is thirsty" might be taken to be equivalent to the dispositional statement "If there were water available, then Smith would drink some." By definition a behavioral hypothetical includes no mental terms. The if-clause of the hypothetical speaks only of stimuli and the then-clause speaks only of behavioral responses. Since stimuli and responses are physical events, logical behaviorism is a species of materialism.

The strength of logical behaviorism is that by translating mental language into the language of stimuli and responses it provides an interpretation of psychological explanations in which behavioral effects are attributed to mental causes. Mental causation is simply the manifestation of a behavioral disposition. More precisely, mental causation is what happens when an organism has a behavioral disposition and the if-clause of the behavioral hypotheical expressing the disposition happens to be true. For example, the causal statement "Smith drank some water because he was thirsty" might be taken to mean "If there were water available, then Smith would drink some, and there was water available."

I have somewhat oversimplified logical behaviorism by assuming that each mental ascription can be translated by a unique behavioral hypothetical. Actually the logical behaviorist often maintains that it takes an open-ended set (perhaps an infinite set) of behavioral hypotheticals to spell out the behavioral disposition expressed by a mental term. The mental ascription "Smith is thirsty" might also be satisfied by the hypothetical "If there were orange juice available, then Smith would drink some" and by a host of other hypotheticals. In any event the logical behaviorist does not usually maintain he can actually enumerate all the hypotheticals that correspond to a behavioral disposition expressing a given mental term. He only insists that in principle the meaning of any mental term can be conveyed by behavioral hypotheticals.

The way the logical behaviorist has interpreted a mental term such as thirsty is modeled after the way many philosophers have interpreted a physical disposition such as fragility. The physical disposition "The glass is fragile" is often taken to mean something like "If the glass were struck, then it would

break." By the same token the logical behaviorist's analysis of mental causation is similar to the received analysis of one kind of physical causation. The causal statement "The glass broke because it was fragile" is taken to mean something like "If the glass were struck, then it would break, and the glass was struck."

By equating mental terms with behavioral dispositions the logical behaviorist has put mental terms on a par with the nonbehavioral dispositions of the physical sciences. That is a promising move, because the analysis of nonbehavioral dispositions is on relatively solid philosophical ground. An explanation attributing the breaking of a glass to its fragility is surely something even the staunchest materialist can accept. By arguing that mental terms are synonymous with dispositional terms, the logical behaviorist has provided something the radical behaviorist could not: a materialist account of mental causation.

Nevertheless, the analogy beween mental causation as construed by the logical behaviorist and physical causation goes only so far. The logical behaviorist treats the manifestation of a disposition as the sole form of mental causation, whereas the physical sciences recognize additional kinds of causation. There is the kind of causation where one physical event causes another, as when the breaking of a glass is attributed to its having been struck. In fact, explanations that involve event-event causation are presumably more basic than dispositional explanations, because the manifestation of a disposition (the breaking of a fragile glass) always involves event-event causation and not vice versa. In the realm of the mental many examples of event-event causation involve one mental state's causing another, and for this kind of causation logical behaviorism provides no analysis. As a result the logical behaviorist is committed to the tacit and implausible assumption that psychology requires a less robust notion of causation than the physical sciences require.

Event-event causation actually seems to be quite common in the realm of the mental. Mental causes typically give rise to behavioral effects by virtue of their interaction with other mental causes. For example, having a headache causes a disposition to take aspirin only if one also has the desire to get rid of the headache, the belief that aspirin exists, the belief that taking aspirin reduces headaches and so on. Since mental states interact in generating behavior, it will be necessary to find a construal of psychological explanations that posits mental processes: causal sequences of mental events. It is this construal that logical behaviorism fails to provide.

Such considerations bring out a fundamental way in which logical behaviorism is quite similar to radical behaviorism. It is true that the logical behaviorist, unlike the radical behaviorist, acknowledges the existence of mental states. Yet since the underlying tenet of logical behaviorism is that references to mental states can be translated out of psychological explanations by employing behavioral hypotheticals, all talk of mental states and processes is in a sense heuristic. The only facts to which the behaviorist is actually committed are facts about relations between stimuli and responses. In this respect logical behaviorism is just radical behaviorism in a semantic form. Although the former theory offers a construal of mental causation, the construal is Pickwickian. What does not really exist cannot cause anything, and the logical behaviorist, like the radical behaviorist, believes deep down that mental causes do not exist.

An alternative materialist theory of the mind to logical behaviorism is the central-state identity theory. According to this theory, mental events, states and processes are identical with neurophysiological events in the brain, and the property of being in a certain mental state (such as having a headache or believing it will rain) is identical with the property of being in a certain neurophysiological state. On this basis it is easy to make sense of the idea that a behavioral effect might sometimes have a chain of mental causes; that will be the case whenever a behavioral effect is contingent on the appropriate sequence of neurophysiological events.

The central-state identity theory acknowledges that it is possible for mental causes to interact causally without ever giving rise to any behavioral effect, as when a person thinks for a while about what he ought to do and then decides to do nothing. If mental processes are neurophysiological, they must have the causal properties of neurophysiological processes. Since neurophysiological processes are presumably physical processes, the central-state identity theory ensures that the concept of mental causation is as rich as the concept of physical causation.

The central-state identity theory provides a satisfactory account of what the mental terms in psychological explanations refer to, and so it is favored by psychologists who are dissatisfied with behaviorism. The behaviorist maintains that mental terms refer to nothing or that they refer to the parameters of stimulus-response relations. Either way the existence of mental entities is only illusory. The identity theorist, on the other hand, argues that mental terms refer to neurophysiological states. Thus he can take seriously the project of explaining behavior by appealing to its mental causes.

The chief advantage of the identity theory is that it takes the explanatory constructs of psychology at face value, which is surely something a philosophy of mind ought to do if it can. The identity theory shows how the mentalistic explanations of psychology could be not mere heuristics but literal accounts of the causal history of behavior. Moreover, since the identity theory is not a semantic thesis, it is immune to many arguments that cast in doubt logical behaviorism. A drawback of logical behaviorism is that the observation "John has a headache" does not seem to mean the same thing as a statement of the form "John is disposed to behave in such and such a way." The identity theorist, however, can live with the fact that "John has a headache" and "John is in such and such a brain state" are not synonymous. The assertion of the identity theorist is not that these sentences mean the same thing but only that they are rendered true (or false) by the same neurophysiological phenomena.

The identity theory can be held either as a doctrine about mental particulars (John's current pain or Bill's fear of animals) or as a doctrine about mental universals, or properties (having a pain or being afraid of animals). The two doctrines, called respectively token physicalism and type physicalism, differ in strength and plausibility. Token physicalism maintains only that all the mental particulars that happen to exist are neurophysiological, whereas type physicalism makes the more sweeping assertion that all the mental particulars there could possibly be are neurophysiological. Token physicalism does not rule out the logical possibility of machines and disembodied spirits having mental properties. Type physicalism dismisses this possibility because neither machines nor disembodied spirits have neurons.

Type physicalism is not a plausible doctrine about mental properties even if token physicalism is right about mental particulars. The problem with type physicalism is that the psychological constitution of a system seems to depend not on its hardware, or physical composition, but on its software, or program. Why should the philosopher dismiss the possibility that silicon-based Martians have pains, assuming that the silicon is properly organized? And why should the philosopher rule out the possibility of machines having beliefs, assuming that the machines are correctly programmed? If it is logically possible that Martians and machines could have mental properties, then mental properties and neurophysiological processes cannot be identical, however much they may prove to be coextensive.

What it all comes down to is that there seems to be a level of abstraction at which the generalizations of psychology are most naturally pitched. This level of abstraction cuts across differences in the physical composition of the systems to which psychological generalizations apply. In the cognitive sciences, at least, the natural domain for psychological theorizing seems to be all systems that process information. The problem with type physicalism is that there are possible information-processing systems with the same psychological constitution as human beings but not the same physical organization. In principle all kinds of physically different things could have human software.

This situation calls for a relational account of mental properties that abstracts them from the physical structure of their bearers. In spite of the objections to logical behaviorism that I presented above, logical behaviorism was at least on the right track in offering a relational interpretation of mental properties: to have a headache is to be disposed to exhibit a certain pattern of relations between the stimuli one encounters and the responses one exhibits. If that is what having a headache is, however, there is no reason in principle why only heads that are physically similar to ours can ache. Indeed, according to logical behaviorism, it is a necessary truth that any system that has our stimulus-response contingencies also has our headaches.

All of this emerged 10 or 15 years ago as a nasty dilemma for the materialist program in the philosophy of mind. On the one hand the identity theorist (and not the logical behaviorist) had got right the causal character of the interactions of mind and body. On the other the logical behaviorist (and not the identity theorist) had got right the relational character of mental properties. Functionalism has apparently been able to resolve the dilemma. By stressing the distinction computer science draws between hardware and software the functionalist can make sense of both the causal and the relational character of the mental.

The intuition underlying functionalism is that what determines the psychological type to which a mental particular belongs is the causal role of the particular in the mental life of the organism. Functional individuation is differentiation with respect to causal role. A headache, for example, is identified with the type of mental state that among other things causes a disposition for taking aspirin in people who believe aspirin relieves a headache, causes a desire to rid oneself of the pain one is feeling, often causes someone who speaks English to say such things as "I have a headache" and is brought on by overwork, eyestrain and tension. This list is presumably not complete. More will be known about the nature of a headache as psychological and physiological research discovers more about its causal role.

Functionalism construes the concept of causal role in such a way that a mental state can be defined by its causal relations to other mental states. In this respect functionalism is completely different from logical behaviorism. Another major difference is that functionalism is not a reductionist thesis. It does not foresee, even in principle, the elimination of mentalistic concepts from the explanatory apparatus of psychological theories.

The difference between functionalism and logical behaviorism is brought out by the fact that functionalism is fully compatible with token physicalism. The functionalist would not be disturbed if brain events turn out to be the only things with the functional properties that define mental states. Indeed, most functionalists fully expect it will turn out that way.

Since functionalism recognizes that mental particulars may be physical, it is compatible with the idea that mental causation is a species of physical causation. In other words, functionalism tolerates the materialist solution to the mind-body problem provided by the central-state identity theory. It is possible for the functionalist to assert both that mental properties are typically defined in terms of their relations and that interactions of mind and body are typically causal in however robust a notion of causality is required by psychological explanations. The logical behaviorist can endorse only the first assertion and the type physicalist only the second. As a result functionalism seems to capture the best features of the materialist alternatives to dualism. It is no wonder that functionalism has become increasingly popular.

Machines provide good examples of two concepts that are central to functionalism: the concept that mental states are interdefined and the concept that they can be realized by many systems. The illustration on the next page contrasts a behavioristic Coke machine with a mentalistic one. Both machines dispense a Coke for 10 cents. (The price has not been affected by inflation.) The states of the machines are defined by reference to their causal roles, but only the machine on the left would satisfy the behaviorist. Its single state (S0) is completely specified in terms of stimuli and responses. S0 is the state a machine is in if, and only if, given a dime as the input, it dispenses a Coke as the output.

The machine on the right in the illustration has interdefined states (S1 and S2), which are characteristic of functionalism. S1 is the state a machine is in if, and only if, (1) given a nickel, it dispenses nothing and proceeds to S2, and (2) given a dime, it dispenses a Coke and stays in S1. S2 is the state a machine is in if, and only if, (1) given a nickel, it dispenses a Coke and proceeds to S1, and (2) given a dime, it dispenses a Coke and a nickel and proceeds to S1. What S1 and S2 jointly amount to is the machine's dispensing a Coke if it is given a dime, dispensing a Coke and a nickel if it is given a dime and a nickel and waiting to be given a second nickel if it has been given a first one.

Since S1 and S2 are each defined by hypothetical statements, they can be viewed as dispositions. Nevertheless, they are not behavioral dispositions because the consequences an input has for a machine in S1 or S2 are not specified solely in terms of the output of the machine. Rather, the consequences also involve the machine's internal states.

Nothing about the way I have described the behavioristic and mentalistic Coke machines puts constraints on what they could be made of. Any system whose states bore the proper relations to inputs, outputs and other states could be one of these machines. No doubt it is reasonable to expect such a system to be constructed out of such things as wheels, levers and diodes (token physicalism for Coke machines). Similarly, it is reasonable to expect that our minds may prove to be neurophysiological (token physicalism for human beings).

Nevertheless, the software description of a Coke machine does not logically require wheels, levers and diodes for its concrete realization. By the same token, the software description of the mind does not logically require neurons. As far as functionalism is concerned a Coke machine with states S1 and S2

could be made of ectoplasm, if there is such stuff and if its states have the right causal properties. Functionalism allows for the possibility of disembodied Coke machines in exactly the same way and to the same exent that it allows for the possibility of disembodied minds.

To say that S1 and S2 are interdefined and realizable by different kinds of hardware is not, of course, to say that a Coke machine has a mind. Although interdefinition and functional specification are typical features of mental states, they are clearly not sufficient for mentality. What more is required is a question to which I shall return below.

Some philosophers are suspicious of functionalism because it seems too easy. Since functionalism licenses the individuation of states by reference to their causal role, it appears to allow a trivial explanation of any observed event E, that is, it appears to postulate an E-causer. For example, what makes the valves in a machine open? Why, the operation of a valve opener. And what is a valve opener? Why, anything that has the functionally defined property of causing valves to open.

In psychology this kind of question-begging often takes the form of theories that in effect postulate homunculi with the selfsame intellectual capacities the theorist set out to explain. Such is the case when visual perception is explained by simply postulating psychological mechanisms that process visual information. The behaviorist has often charged the mentalist, sometimes justifiably, of mongering this kind of question-begging pseudo explanation. The charge will have to be met if functionally defined mental states are to have a serious role in psychological theories.

The burden of the accusation is not untruth but triviality. There can be no doubt that it is a valve opener that opens valves, and it is likely that visual perception is mediated by the processing of visual information. The charge is that such putative functional explanations are mere platitudes. The functionalist can meet this objection by allowing functionally defined theoretical constructs only where mechanisms exist that can carry out the function and only where he has some notion of what such mechanisms might be like. One way of imposing this requirement is to identify the mental processes that psychology postulates with the operations of the restricted class of possible computers called Turing machines.

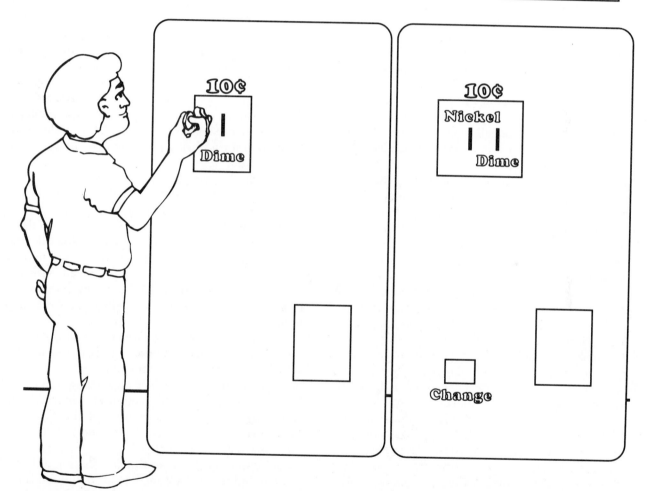

| | STATE S0 |
|---|---|
| DIME INPUT | DISPENSES A COKE |

| | STATE S1 | STATE S2 |
|---|---|---|
| NICKEL INPUT | GIVES NO OUTPUT AND GOES TO S2 | DISPENSES A COKE AND GOES TO S1 |
| DIME INPUT | DISPENSES A COKE AND STAYS IN S1 | DISPENSES A COKE AND A NICKEL AND GOES TO S1 |

TWO COKE MACHINES bring out the difference between behaviorism (the doctrine that there are no mental causes) and mentalism (the doctrine that there are mental causes). Both machines dispense a Coke for 10 cents and have states that are defined by reference to their causal role. The machine at the left is a behavioristic one: its single state (S0) is defined solely in terms of the input and the output. The machine at the right is a mentalistic one: its two states (S1, S2) must be defined not only in terms of the input and the output but also in terms of each other. To put it another way, the output of the Coke machine depends on the state the machine is in as well as on the input. The functionalist philosopher maintains that mental states are interdefined, like the internal states of the mentalistic Coke machine.

A Turing machine can be informally characterized as a mechanism with a finite number of program states. The inputs and outputs of the machine are written on a tape that is divided into squares each of which includes a symbol from a finite alphabet. The machine scans the tape one square at a time. It can erase the symbol on a scanned square and print a new one in its place. The machine can execute only the elementary mechanical operations of scanning, erasing, printing, moving the tape and changing state.

The program states of the Turing machine are defined solely in terms of the input symbols on the tape, the output symbols on the tape, the elementary operations and the other states of the program. Each program state is therefore functionally defined by the part it plays in the overall operation of the machine. Since the functional role of a state depends on the relation of the state to other states as well as to inputs and outputs, the relational character of the mental state is captured by the Turing-machine version of functionalism. Since the definition of a program state never refers to the physical structure of the system running the program, the Turing-machine version of functionalism also captures the idea that the character of a mental state is independent of its physical realization. A human being, a roomful of people, a computer and a disembodied spirit would all be a Turing machine if they operated according to a Turing-machine program.

The proposal is to restrict the functional definition of psychological states to those that can be expressed in terms of the program states of Turing machines. If this restriction can be enforced, it provides a guarantee that psychological theories will be compatible with the demands of mechanisms. Since Turing machines are very simple devices, they are in principle quite easy to build. Consequently by formulating a psychological explanation as a Turing-machine program the psychologist ensures that the explanation is mechanistic, even though the hardware realizing the mechanism is left open.

There are many kinds of computational mechanisms other than Turing machines, and so the formulation of a functionalist psychological theory in Turing-machine notation provides only a sufficient condition for the theory's being mechanically realizable. What makes the condition interesting, however, is that the simple Turing machine can perform many complex tasks. Although the elementary operations of the Turing machine are restricted, iterations of the operations enable the machine to carry out any well-defined computation on discrete symbols.

An important tendency in the cognitive sciences is to treat the mind chiefly as a device that manipulates symbols. If a mental process can be functionally defined as an operation on symbols, there is a Turing machine capable of carrying out the computation and a variety of mechanisms for realizing the Turing machine. Where the manipulation of symbols is important the Turing machine provides a connection between functional explanation and mechanistic explanation.

The reduction of a psychological theory to a program for a Turing machine is a way of exorcising the homunculi. The reduction ensures that no operations have been postulated except those that could be performed by a familiar mechanism. Of course, the working psychologist usually cannot specify the reduction for each functionally individuated process in every theory he is prepared to take seriously. In practice the argument usually goes in the opposite direction; if the postulation of a mental operation is essential to some cherished psychological explanation, the theorist tends to assume that there must be a program for a Turing machine that will carry out that operation.

The "black boxes" that are common in flow charts drawn by psychologists often serve to indicate postulated mental processes for which Turing reductions are wanting. Even so, the possibility in principle of such reductions serves as a methodological constraint on psychological theorizing by determining what functional definitions are to be allowed and what it would be like to know that everything has been explained that could possibly need explanation.

Such is the origin, the provenance and the promise of contemporary functionalism. How much has it actually paid off? This question is not easy to answer because much of what is now happening in the philosophy of mind and the cognitive sciences is directed at exploring the scope and limits of the functionalist explanations of behavior. I shall, however, give a brief overview.

An obvious objection to functionalism as a theory of the mind is that the functionalist definition is not limited to mental states and processes. Catalysts, Coke machines, valve openers, pencil sharpeners, mousetraps and ministers of finance are all in one way or another concepts that are functionally defined, but none is a mental concept such as pain, belief and desire. What, then, characterizes the mental? And can it be captured in a functionalist framework?

The traditional view in the philosophy of mind has it that mental states are distinguished by their having what are called either qualitative content or intentional content. I shall discuss qualitative content first.

It is not easy to say what qualitative content is; indeed, according to some theories, it is not even possible to say what it is because it can be known not by description but only by direct experience. I shall nonetheless attempt to describe it. Try to imagine looking at a blank wall through a red filter. Now change the filter to a green one and leave everything else exactly the way it was. Something about the character of your experience changes when the filter does, and it is this kind of thing that philosophers call qualitative content. I am not entirely comfortable about introducing qualitative content in this way, but it is a subject with which many philosophers are not comfortable.

The reason qualitative content is a problem for functionalism is straightforward. Functionalism is committed to defining mental states in terms of their causes and effects. It seems, however, as if two mental states could have all the same causal relations and yet could differ in their qualitative content. Let me illustrate this with the classic puzzle of the inverted spectrum.

It seems possible to imagine two observers who are alike in all relevant psychological respects except that experiences having the qualitative content of red for one observer would have the qualitative content of green for the other. Nothing about their behavior need reveal the difference because both of them see ripe tomatoes and flaming sunsets as being similar in color and both of them call that color "red." Moreover, the causal connection between their (qualitatively distinct) experiences and their other mental states could also be identical. Perhaps they both think of Little Red Riding Hood when they see ripe tomatoes, feel depressed when they see the color green and so on. It seems as if anything that could be packed into the notion of the causal role of their experiences could be shared by them, and yet the qualitative content of the experiences could be as different as you like. If this is possible, then the functionalist account does not work for mental states that have qualitative content. If one person is having a green experience while another person is having a red one, then surely they must be in different mental states.

The example of the inverted spectrum is more than a verbal puzzle. Having qualitative content is supposed to be a chief factor in what makes a mental

state conscious. Many psychologists who are inclined to accept the functionalist framework are nonetheless worried about the failure of functionalism to reveal much about the nature of consciousness. Functionalists have made a few ingenious attempts to talk themselves and their colleagues out of this worry, but they have not, in my view, done so with much success. (For example, perhaps one is wrong in thinking one can imagine what an inverted spectrum would be like.) As matters stand, the problem of qualitative content poses a serious threat to the assertion that functionalism can provide a general theory of the mental.

Functionalism has fared much better with the intentional content of mental states. Indeed, it is here that the major achievements of recent cognitive science are found. To say that a mental state has intentional content is to say that it has certain semantic properties. For example, for Enrico to believe Galileo was Italian apparently involves a three-way relation between Enrico, a belief and a proposition that is the content of the belief (namely the proposition that Galileo was Italian). In particular it is an essential property of Enrico's belief that it is about Galileo (and not about, say, Newton) and that it is true if, and only if, Galileo was indeed Italian. Philosophers are divided on how these considerations fit together, but it is widely agreed that beliefs involve semantic properties such as expressing a proposition, being true or false and being about one thing rather than another.

It is important to understand the semantic properties of beliefs because theories in the cognitive sciences are largely about the beliefs organisms have. Theories of learning and perception, for example, are chiefly accounts of how the host of beliefs an organism has are determined by the character of its experiences and its genetic endowment. The functionalist account of mental states does not by itself provide the required insights. Mousetraps are functionally defined, yet mousetraps do not express propositions, and they are not true or false.

There is at least one kind of thing other than a mental state that has intentional content: a symbol. Like thoughts, symbols seem to be about things. If someone says "Galileo was Italian," his utterance, like Enrico's belief, expresses a proposition about Galileo that is true or false depending on Galileo's homeland. This parallel between the symbolic and the mental underlies the traditional quest for a unified treatment of language and mind. Cognitive science is now trying to provide such a treatment.

The basic concept is simple but striking. Assume that there are such things as mental symbols (mental representations) and that mental symbols have semantic properties. On this view having a belief involves being related to a mental symbol, and the belief inherits its semantic properties from the mental symbol that figures in the relation. Mental processes (thinking, perceiving, learning and so on) involve causal interactions among relational states such as having a belief. The semantic properties of the words and sentences we utter are in turn inherited from the semantic properties of the mental states that language expresses.

Associating the semantic properties of mental states with those of mental symbols is fully compatible with the computer metaphor, because it is natural to think of the computer as a mechanism that manipulates symbols. A computation is a causal chain of computer states, and the links in the chain are operations on semantically interpreted formulas in a machine code. To think of a system (such as the nervous system) as a computer is to raise questions about the nature of the code in which it computes and the semantic properties of the symbols in the code. In fact, the analogy between minds and computers actually implies the postulation of mental symbols. There is no computation without representation.

The representational account of the mind, however, predates considerably the invention of the computing machine. It is a throwback to classical epistemology, which is a tradition that includes philosophers as diverse as John Locke, David Hume, George Berkeley, René Descartes, Immanuel Kant, John Stuart Mill and William James.

Hume, for one, developed a representational theory of the mind that included five points. First, there exist "Ideas," which are a species of mental symbol. Second, having a belief involves entertaining an Idea. Third, mental processes are causal associations of Ideas. Fourth, Ideas are like pictures. And fifth, Ideas have their semantic properties by virtue of what they resemble: the Idea of John is about John because it looks like him.

Contemporary cognitive psychologists do not accept the details of Hume's theory, although they endorse much of its spirit. Theories of compu-

tation provide a far richer account of mental processes than the mere association of Ideas. And only a few psychologists still think that imagery is the chief vehicle of mental representation. Nevertheless, the most significant break with Hume's theory lies in the abandoning of resemblance as an explanation of the semantic properties of mental representations.

Many philosophers, starting with Berkeley, have argued that there is something seriously wrong with the suggestion that the semantic relation between a thought and what the thought is about could be one of resemblance. Consider the thought that John is tall. Clearly the thought is true only of the state of affairs consisting of John's being tall. A theory of the semantic properties of a thought should therefore explain how this particular thought is related to this particular state of affairs. According to the resemblance theory, entertaining the thought involves having a mental image that shows John to be tall. To put it another way, the relation between the thought that John is tall and his being tall is like the relation between a tall man and his portrait.

The difficulty with the resemblance theory is that any portrait showing John to be tall must also show him to be many other things: clothed or naked, lying, standing or sitting, having a head or not having one, and so on. A portrait of a tall man who is sitting down resembles a man's being seated as much as it resembles a man's being tall. On the resemblance theory it is not clear what distinguishes thoughts about John's height from thoughts about his posture.

The resemblance theory turns out to encounter paradoxes at every turn. The possibility of construing beliefs as involving relations to semantically interpreted mental representations clearly depends on having an acceptable account of where the semantic properties of the mental representations come from. If resemblance will not provide this account, what will?

The current idea is that the semantic properties of a mental representation are determined by aspects of its functional role. In other words, a sufficient condition for having semantic properties can be specified in causal terms. This is the connection between functionalism and the representational theory of the mind. Modern cognitive psychology rests largely on the hope that these two doctrines can be made to support each other.

No philosopher is now prepared to say exactly how the functional role of a mental representation determines its semantic properties. Nevertheless, the functionalist recognizes three types of causal relation among psychological states involving mental representations, and they might serve to fix the semantic properties of mental representations. The three types are causal relations among mental states and stimuli, mental states and responses and some mental states and other ones.

Consider the belief that John is tall. Presumably the following facts, which correspond respectively to the three types of causal relation, are relevant to determining the semantic properties of the mental representation involved in the belief. First, the belief is a normal effect of certain stimulations, such as seeing John in circumstances that reveal his height. Second, the belief is the normal cause of certain behavioral effects, such as uttering "John is tall." Third, the belief is a normal cause of certain other beliefs and a normal effect of certain other beliefs. For example, anyone who believes John is tall is very likely also to believe someone is tall. Having the first belief is normally causally sufficient for having the second belief. And anyone who believes everyone in the room is tall and also believes John is in the room will very likely believe John is tall. The third belief is a normal effect of the first two. In short, the functionalist maintains that the proposition expressed by a given mental representation depends on the causal properties of the mental states in which the mental representation figures.

The concept that the semantic properties of mental representations are determined by aspects of their functional role is at the center of current work in the cognitive sciences. Nevertheless, the concept may not be true. Many philosophers who are unsympathetic to the cognitive turn in modern psychology doubt its truth, and many psychologists would probably reject it in the bald and unelaborated way that I have sketched it. Yet even in its skeletal form, there is this much to be said in its favor: It legitimizes the notion of mental representation, which has become increasingly important to theorizing in every branch of the cognitive sciences. Recent advances in formulating and testing hypotheses about the character of mental representations in fields ranging from phonetics to computer vision suggest that the concept of mental representation is fundamental to empirical theories of the mind.

The behaviorist has rejected the appeal to mental representation because it runs counter to his view of the explanatory mechanisms that can figure in psychological theories. Nevertheless, the science of mental representation is now flourishing. The history of science reveals that when a successful theory comes into conflict with a methodological scruple, it is generally the scruple that gives way. Accordingly the functionalist has relaxed the behaviorist constraints on psychological explanations. There is probably no better way to decide what is methodologically permissible in science than by investigating what successful science requires.

**READING 25**

# Minds, Brains, and Programs

*John R. Searle*

*John R. Searle (1932–   ) is Professor of Philosophy at the University of California at Berkeley. He is the author of many articles in philosophy of language and philosophy of mind. A prominent critic of the thesis of strong AI, his books include* Speech Acts *(1969),* Expression and Meaning *(1979),* Intentionality: An Essay in the Philosophy of Mind *(1983), and* Minds, Brains and Science *(1984).*

**ABSTRACT:** This article can be viewed as an attempt to explore the consequences of two propositions. (1) Intentionality in human beings (and animals) is a product of causal features of the brain. I assume this is an empirical fact about the actual causal relations between mental processes and brains. It says simply that certain brain processes are sufficient for intentionality. (2) Instantiating a computer program is never by itself a sufficient condition of intentionality. The main argument of this paper is directed at establishing this claim. The form of the argument is to show how a human agent could instantiate the program and still not have the relevant intentionality. These two propositions have the following consequences: (3) The explanation of how the brain produces intentionality cannot be that it does it by instantiating a computer program. This is a strict logical consequence of 1 and 2. (4) Any mechanism capable of producing intentionality must have causal powers equal to those of the brain. This is meant to be a trivial consequence of 1. (5) Any attempt literally to create intentionality artificially (strong AI) could not succeed just by designing programs but would have to duplicate the causal powers of the human brain. This follows from 2 and 4.

"Could a machine think?" On the argument advanced here *only* a machine could think, and only very special kinds of machines, namely brains and machines with internal causal powers equivalent to those of brains. And that is why strong AI has little to tell us about thinking, since it is not about machines but about programs, and no program by itself is sufficient for thinking.

**SOURCE:** From *The Behavioral and Brain Sciences* 3 (1980): 417–424.

What psychological and philosophical significance should we attach to recent efforts at computer simulations of human cognitive capacities? In answering this question, I find it useful to distinguish what I will call "strong" AI from "weak" or "cautious" AI (Artificial Intelligence). According to weak AI, the principal value of the computer in the study of the mind is that it gives us a very powerful tool. For example, it enables us to formulate and test hypotheses in a more rigorous and precise fashion. But according to strong AI, the computer is not merely a tool in the study of the mind; rather, the appropriately programmed computer really *is* a mind, in the sense that computers given the right programs can be literally said to *understand* and have other cognitive states. In strong AI, because the programmed computer has cognitive states, the programs are not mere tools that enable us to test psychological explanations; rather, the programs are themselves the explanations.

I have no objection to the claims of weak AI, at least as far as this article is concerned. My discussion here will be directed at the claims I have defined as those of strong AI, specifically the claim that the appropriately programmed computer literally has cognitive states and that the programs thereby explain human cognition. When I hereafter refer to AI, I have in mind the strong version, as expressed by these two claims.

I will consider the work of Roger Schank and his colleagues at Yale (Schank & Abelson 1977), because I am more familiar with it than I am with any other similar claims, and because it provides a very clear example of the sort of work I wish to examine. But nothing that follows depends upon the details of Schank's programs. The same arguments would apply to Winograd's SHRDLU (Winograd 1973), Weizenbaum's ELIZA (Weizenbaum 1965), and indeed any Turing machine simulation of human mental phenomena.

Very briefly, and leaving out the various details, one can describe Schank's program as follows: the aim of the program is to simulate the human ability to understand stories. It is characteristic of human beings' story-understanding capacity that they can answer questions about the story even though the information that they give was never explicitly stated in the story. Thus, for example, suppose you are given the following story: "A man went into a restaurant and ordered a hamburger. When the hamburger arrived it was burned to a crisp, and the man stormed out of the restaurant angrily, without paying for the hamburger or leaving a tip." Now, if you are asked "Did the man eat the hamburger?" you will presumably answer, "No, he did not." Similarly, if you are given the following story: "A man went into a restaurant and ordered a hamburger; when the hamburger came he was very pleased with it; and as he left the restaurant he gave the waitress a large tip before paying his bill," and you are asked the question, "Did the man eat the hamburger?," you will presumably answer, "Yes, he ate the hamburger." Now Schank's machines can similarly answer questions about restaurants in this fashion. To do this, they have a "representation" of the sort of information that human beings have about restaurants, which enables them to answer such questions as those above, given these sorts of stories. When the machine is given the story and then asked the question, the machine will print out answers of the sort that we would expect human beings to give if told similar stories. Partisans of strong AI claim that in this question and answer sequence the machine is not only simulating a human ability but also

(1) that the machine can literally be said to *understand* the story and provide the answers to questions, and

(2) that what the machine and its program do *explains* the human ability to understand the story and answer questions about it.

Both claims seem to me to be totally unsupported by Schank's[1] work, as I will attempt to show in what follows.

One way to test any theory of the mind is to ask oneself what it would be like if my mind actually worked on the principles that the theory says all minds work on. Let us apply this test to the Schank program with the following *Gedankenexperiment*. Suppose that I'm locked in a room and given a large batch of Chinese writing. Suppose furthermore (as is indeed the case) that I know no Chinese, either written or spoken, and that I'm not even confident that I could recognize Chinese writing as Chinese writing distinct from, say, Japanese writing or meaningless squiggles. To me, Chinese writing is just so many meaningless squiggles. Now suppose further that after this first batch of Chinese writing I am given a second batch of Chinese script together with a set of rules for correlating the second batch with the first batch. The rules are in English, and I understand these rules as well as any other native speaker of English. They enable me to correlate one set of formal symbols with another set of formal symbols, and all that "formal" means here is that I can identify the symbols entirely by their shapes. Now suppose also that I am given a third batch of Chinese symbols together with some instructions, again in English, that enable me to correlate elements of this third batch with the first two batches, and these rules instruct me how to give back certain Chinese symbols with certain sorts of shapes in response to certain sorts of shapes given me in the third batch. Unknown to me, the people who are giving me all of these symbols call the first batch "a script," they call the second batch a "story," and they call the third batch "questions." Furthermore, they call the symbols I give them back in response to the third batch "answers to the questions," and the set of rules in English that they gave me, they call "the program." Now just to complicate the story a little, imagine that these people also give me stories in English, which I understand, and they then ask me questions in English about these stories, and I give them back answers in English. Suppose also that after a while I get so good at following the instructions for manipulating the Chinese symbols and the programmers get so good at writing the programs that from the external point of view—that is, from the point of view of somebody outside the room in which I am locked—my answers to the questions are absolutely indistinguishable from those of native Chinese speakers. Nobody just looking at my answers can tell that I don't speak a word of Chinese. Let us also suppose that my answers to the English questions are, as they no doubt would be, indistinguishable from those of other native English speakers, for the simple reason that I am a native English speaker. From the external point of view—from the point of view of someone reading my "answers"—the answers to the Chinese questions and the English questions are equally good. But in the Chinese case, unlike the English case, I produce the answers by manipulating uninterpreted formal symbols. As far as the Chinese is concerned, I simply behave like a computer; I perform computational operations on formally specified elements. For the purposes of the Chinese, I am simply an instantiation of the computer program.

Now the claims made by strong AI are that the programmed computer understands the stories and that the program in some sense explains human understanding. But we are now in a position to examine these claims in light of our thought experiment.

1. As regards the first claim, it seems to me quite obvious in the example that I do not understand a word of the Chinese stories. I have inputs and outputs that are indistinguishable from those of the native Chinese speaker, and I can have any formal program you like, but I still understand nothing. For the same reasons, Schank's computer understands nothing of any stories, whether in Chinese, English, or whatever, since in the Chinese case the computer is me, and in cases where the computer is not me, the computer has nothing more than I have in the case where I understand nothing.

2. As regards the second claim, that the program explains human understanding, we can see that the computer and its program do not provide sufficient conditions of understanding since the computer and the program are functioning, and there is no understanding. But does it even provide a necessary condition or a significant contribution to understanding? One of the claims made by the supporters of strong AI is that when I understand a story in English, what I am doing is exactly the same—or perhaps more of the same—as what I was doing in manipulating the Chinese symbols. It is simply more formal symbol manipulation that distinguishes the case in English, where I do understand, from the case in Chinese, where I don't. I have not demonstrated that this claim is false, but it would certainly appear an incredible claim in the example. Such plausibility as the claim has derives from the supposition that we can construct a program that will have the same inputs and outputs as native speakers, and in addition we assume that speakers have some level of description where they are also instantiations of a program. On the basis of these two assumptions we assume that even if Schank's program isn't the whole story about understanding, it may be part of the story. Well, I suppose that is an empirical possibility, but not the slightest reason has so far been given to believe that it is true, since what is suggested—though certainly not demonstrated—by the example is that the computer program is simply irrelevant to my understanding of the story. In the Chinese case I have everything that artificial intelligence can put into me by way of a program, and I understand nothing; in the English case I understand everything, and there is so far no reason at all to suppose that my understanding has anything to do with computer programs, that is, with computational operations on purely formally specified elements. As long as the program is defined in terms of computational operations on purely formally defined elements, what the example suggests is that these by themselves have no interesting connection with understanding. They are certainly not sufficient conditions, and not the slightest reason has been given to suppose that they are necessary conditions or even that they make a significant contribution to understanding. Notice that the force of the argument is not simply that different machines can have the same input and output while operating on different formal principles—that is not the point at all. Rather, whatever purely formal principles you put into the computer, they will not be sufficient for understanding, since a human will be able to follow the formal principles without understanding anything. No reason whatever has been offered to suppose that such principles are necessary or even contributory, since no reason has been given to suppose that when I understand English I am operating with any formal program at all.

Well, then, what is it that I have in the case of the English sentences that I do not have in the case of the Chinese sentences? The obvious answer is that I know what the former mean, while I haven't the faintest idea what the latter mean. But in what does this consist and why couldn't we give it to a machine, whatever it is? I will return to this question later, but first I want to continue with the example.

I have had the occasions to present this example to several workers in artificial intelligence, and, interestingly, they do not seem to agree on what the proper reply to it is. I get a surprising variety of replies, and in what follows I will consider the most common of these (specified along with their geographic origins).

But first I want to block some common misunderstandings about "understanding": in many of these discussions one finds a lot of fancy footwork about the word "understanding." My critics point out that there are many different degrees of understanding; that "understanding" is not a simple two-place predicate; that there are even different kinds and levels of understanding, and often the law of excluded middle doesn't even apply in a straightforward way to statements of the form "x understands y"; that in many cases it is a matter for decision and not a simple matter of fact whether x understands y; and so on. To all of these points I want to say: of course, of course. But they have nothing to do with the points at issue. There are clear cases in which "understanding" literally applies and clear cases in which it does not apply; and these two sorts of cases are all I need for this argument.[2] I understand stories in English; to a lesser degree I can understand stories in French; to a still lesser degree, stories in German; and in Chinese, not at all. My car and my adding machine, on the other hand, understand nothing: they are not in that line of business. We often attribute "understanding" and other cognitive predicates by metaphor and analogy to cars, adding machines, and other artifacts but nothing is proved by such attributions. We say, "The door *knows* when to open because of its photoelectric cell," "The adding machine *knows how* (*understands how,* is *able*) to do addition and subtraction but not division," and "The thermostat *perceives* changes in the temperature." The reason we make these attributions is quite interesting, and it has to do with the fact that in artifacts we extend our own intentionality;[3] our tools are extensions of our purposes, and so we find it natural to make metaphorical attributions of intentionality to them; but I take it no philosophical ice is cut by such examples. The sense in which an automatic door "understands instructions" from its photoelectric cell is not at all the sense in which I understand English. If the sense in which Schank's programmed computers understand stories is supposed to be the metaphorical sense in which the door understands, and not the sense in which I understand English, the issue would not be worth discussing. But Newell and Simon (1963) write that the kind of cognition they claim for computers is exactly the same as for human beings. I like the straightforwardness of this claim, and it is the sort of

claim I will be considering. I will argue that in the literal sense the programmed computer understands what the car and the adding machine understand, namely, exactly nothing. The computer understanding is not just (like my understanding of German) partial or incomplete; it is zero.

Now to the replies:

I.

## THE SYSTEMS REPLY (BERKELEY)

"While it is true that the individual person who is locked in the room does not understand the story, the fact is that he is merely part of a whole system, and the system does understand the story. The person has a large ledger in front of him in which are written the rules, he has a lot of scratch paper and pencils for doing calculations, he has 'data banks' of sets of Chinese symbols. Now, understanding is not being ascribed to the mere individual; rather it is being ascribed to this whole system of which he is a part."

My response to the systems theory is quite simple: let the individual internalize all of these elements of the system. He memorizes the rules in the ledger and the data banks of Chinese symbols, and he does all the calculations in his head. The individual then incorporates the entire system. There isn't anything at all to the system that he does not encompass. We can even get rid of the room and suppose he works outdoors. All the same, he understands nothing of the Chinese, and a fortiori neither does the system, because there isn't anything in the system that isn't in him. If he doesn't understand, then there is no way the system could understand because the system is just a part of him.

Actually I feel somewhat embarrassed to give even this answer to the systems theory because the theory seems to me so unplausible to start with. The idea is that while a person doesn't understand Chinese, somehow the *conjunction* of that person and bits of paper might understand Chinese. It is not easy for me to imagine how someone who was not in the grip of an ideology would find the idea at all plausible. Still, I think many people who are committed to the ideology of strong AI will in the end be inclined to say something very much like this; so let us pursue it a bit further. According to one version of this view, while the man in the internalized systems example doesn't understand Chinese in the sense that a native

Chinese speaker does (because, for example, he doesn't know that the story refers to restaurants and hamburgers, etc.), still "the man as a formal symbol manipulation system" *really does understand Chinese.* The subsystem of the man that is the formal symbol manipulation system for Chinese should not be confused with the subsystem for English.

So there are really two subsystems in the man; one understands English, the other Chinese, and "it's just that the two systems have little to do with each other." But, I want to reply, not only do they have little to do with each other, they are not even remotely alike. The subsystem that understands English (assuming we allow ourselves to talk in this jargon of "subsystems" for a moment) knows that the stories are about restaurants and eating hamburgers, he knows that he is being asked questions about restaurants and that he is answering questions as best he can by making various inferences from the content of the story, and so on. But the Chinese system knows none of this. Whereas the English subsystem knows that "hamburgers" refers to hamburgers, the Chinese subsystem knows only that "squiggle squiggle" is followed by "squoggle squoggle." All he knows is that various formal symbols are being introduced at one end and manipulated according to rules written in English, and other symbols are going out at the other end. The whole point of the original example was to argue that such symbol manipulation by itself couldn't be sufficient for understanding Chinese in any literal sense because the man could write "squoggle squoggle" after "squiggle squiggle" without understanding anything in Chinese. And it doesn't meet that argument to postulate subsystems within the man, because the subsystems are no better off than the man was in the first place; they still don't have anything even remotely like what the English-speaking man (or subsystem) has. Indeed, in the case as described, the Chinese subsystem is simply a part of the English subsystem, a part that engages in meaningless symbol manipulation according to rules in English.

Let us ask ourselves what is supposed to motivate the systems reply in the first place; that is, what *independent* grounds are there supposed to be for saying that the agent must have a subsystem within him that literally understands stories in Chinese? As far as I can tell the only grounds are that in the example I have the same input and output as native Chinese speakers and a program that goes from one to the

other. But the whole point of the examples has been to try to show that that couldn't be sufficient for understanding, in the sense in which I understand stories in English, because a person, and hence the set of systems that go to make up a person, could have the right combination of input, output, and program and still not understand anything in the relevant literal sense in which I understand English. The only motivation for saying there *must* be a subsystem in me that understands Chinese is that I have a program and I can pass the Turing test; I can fool native Chinese speakers. But precisely one of the points at issue is the adequacy of the Turing test. The example shows that there could be two "systems," both of which pass the Turing test, but only one of which understands; and it is no argument against this point to say that since they both pass the Turing test they must both understand, since this claim fails to meet the argument that the system in me that understands English has a great deal more than the system that merely processes Chinese. In short, the systems reply simply begs the question by insisting without argument that the system must understand Chinese.

Furthermore, the systems reply would appear to lead to consequences that are independently absurd. If we are to conclude that there must be cognition in me on the grounds that I have a certain sort of input and output and a program in between, then it looks like all sorts of noncognitive subsystems are going to turn out to be cognitive. For example, there is a level of description at which my stomach does information processing, and it instantiates any number of computer programs, but I take it we do not want to say that it has any understanding [cf. Pylyshyn: "Computation and Cognition" *BBS* 3(1) 1980]. But if we accept the systems reply, then it is hard to see how we avoid saying that stomach, heart, liver, and so on, are all understanding subsystems, since there is no principled way to distinguish the motivation for saying the Chinese subsystem understands from saying that the stomach understands. It is, by the way, not an answer to this point to say that the Chinese system has information as input and output and the stomach has food and food products as input and output, since from the point of view of the agent, from my point of view, there is no information in either the food or the Chinese—the Chinese is just so many meaningless squiggles. The information in the Chinese case is solely in the eyes of the programmers and the interpreters, and there is nothing to prevent them from treating the input and output of my digestive organs as information if they so desire.

This last point bears on some independent problems in strong AI, and it is worth digressing for a moment to explain it. If strong AI is to be a branch of psychology, then it must be able to distinguish those systems that are genuinely mental from those that are not. It must be able to distinguish the principles on which the mind works from those on which nonmental systems work; otherwise it will offer us no explanations of what is specifically mental about the mental. And the mental-nonmental distinction cannot be just in the eye of the beholder but it must be intrinsic to the systems; otherwise it would be up to any beholder to treat people as nonmental and, for example, hurricanes as mental if he likes. But quite often in the AI literature the distinction is blurred in ways that would in the long run prove disastrous to the claim that AI is a cognitive inquiry. McCarthy, for example, writes, "Machines as simple as thermostats can be said to have beliefs, and having beliefs seems to be a characteristic of most machines capable of problem solving performance" (McCarthy 1979). Anyone who thinks strong AI has a chance as a theory of the mind ought to ponder the implications of that remark. We are asked to accept it as a discovery of strong AI that the hunk of metal on the wall that we use to regulate the temperature has beliefs in exactly the same sense that we, our spouses, and our children have beliefs, and furthermore that "most" of the other machines in the room—telephone, tape recorder, adding machine, electric light switch,—also have beliefs in this literal sense. It is not the aim of this article to argue against McCarthy's point, so I will simply assert the following without argument. The study of the mind starts with such facts as that humans have beliefs, while thermostats, telephones, and adding machines don't. If you get a theory that denies this point you have produced a counterexample to the theory and the theory is false. One gets the impression that people in AI who write this sort of thing think they can get away with it because they don't really take it seriously, and they don't think anyone else will either. I propose for a moment at least, to take it seriously. Think hard for one minute about what would be necessary to establish that that hunk of metal on the wall over there had real beliefs, beliefs with direction of fit, propositional content, and conditions of satisfaction; beliefs that had the possibility of being strong beliefs or weak beliefs;

nervous, anxious, or secure beliefs; dogmatic, rational, or superstitious beliefs; blind faiths or hesitant cogitations; any kind of beliefs. The thermostat is not a candidate. Neither is stomach, liver, adding machine, or telephone. However, since we are taking the idea seriously, notice that its truth would be fatal to strong AI's claim to be a science of the mind. For now the mind is everywhere. What we wanted to know is what distinguishes the mind from thermostats and livers. And if McCarthy were right, strong AI wouldn't have a hope of telling us that.

II.

## THE ROBOT REPLY (YALE)

"Suppose we wrote a different kind of program from Schank's program. Suppose we put a computer inside a robot, and this computer would not just take in formal symbols as input and give out formal symbols as output, but rather would actually operate the robot in such a way that the robot does something very much like perceiving, walking, moving about, hammering nails, eating, drinking—anything you like. The robot would, for example, have a television camera attached to it that enabled it to 'see,' it would have arms and legs that enabled it to 'act,' and all of this would be controlled by its computer 'brain.' Such a robot would, unlike Schank's computer, have genuine understanding and other mental states."

The first thing to notice about the robot reply is that it tacitly concedes that cognition is not solely a matter of formal symbol manipulation, since this reply adds a set of causal relation with the outside world [cf. Fodor: "Methodological Solipsism" *BBS* 3(1)1980]. But the answer to the robot reply is that the addition of such "perceptual" and "motor" capacities adds nothing by way of understanding, in particular, or intentionality, in general, to Schank's original program. To see this, notice that the same thought experiment applies to the robot case. Suppose that instead of the computer inside the robot, you put me inside the room and, as in the original Chinese case, you give me more Chinese symbols with more instructions in English for matching Chinese symbols to Chinese symbols and feeding back Chinese symbols to the outside. Suppose, unknown to me, some of the Chinese symbols that come to me come from a television camera attached to the robot and other Chinese symbols that I am giving out serve to make the motors inside the robot move the robot's legs or arms. It is important to emphasize that all I am doing is manipulating formal symbols: I know none of these other facts. I am receiving "information" from the robot's "perceptual" apparatus, and I am giving out "instructions" to its motor apparatus without knowing either of these facts. I am the robot's homunculus, but unlike the traditional homunculus, I don't know what's going on. I don't understand anything except the rules for symbol manipulation. Now in this case I want to say that the robot has no intentional states at all; it is simply moving about as a result of its electrical wiring and its program. And furthermore, by instantiating the program I have no intentional states of the relevant type. All I do is follow formal instructions about manipulating formal symbols.

III.

## THE BRAIN SIMULATOR REPLY (BERKELEY AND M.I.T.)

"Suppose we design a program that doesn't represent information that we have about the world, such as the information in Schank's scripts, but simulates the actual sequence of neuron firings at the synapses of the brain of a native Chinese speaker when he understands stories in Chinese and gives answers to them. The machine takes in Chinese stories and questions about them as input, it simulates the formal structure of actual Chinese brains in processing these stories, and it gives out Chinese answers as outputs. We can even imagine that the machine operates, not with a single serial program, but with a whole set of programs operating in parallel, in the manner that actual human brains presumably operate when they process natural language. Now surely in such a case we would have to say that the machine understood the stories; and if we refuse to say that, wouldn't we also have to deny that native Chinese speakers understood the stories? At the level of the synapses, what would or could be different about the program of the computer and the program of the Chinese brain?"

Before countering this reply I want to digress to note that it is an odd reply for any partisan of artificial intelligence (or functionalism, etc.) to make: I thought the whole idea of strong AI is that we don't need to know how the brain works to know how the mind works. The basic hypothesis, or so I had supposed, was that there is a level of mental operations consisting of computational processes over formal elements that constitute the essence of the mental and can be realized in all sorts of different brain processes, in the same way that any computer program can be realized in different computer hardwares: on the assumptions of strong AI, the mind is to the brain as the program is to the hardware, and thus we can understand the mind without doing neurophysiology. If we had to know how the brain worked to do AI, we wouldn't bother with AI. However, even getting this close to the operation of the brain is still not sufficient to produce understanding. To see this, imagine that instead of a monolingual man in a room shuffling symbols we have the man operate an elaborate set of water pipes with valves connecting them. When the man receives the Chinese symbols, he looks up in the program, written in English, which valves he has to turn on and off. Each water connection corresponds to a synapse in the Chinese brain, and the whole system is rigged up so that after doing all the right firings, that is after turning on all the right faucets, the Chinese answers pop out at the output end of the series of pipes.

Now where is the understanding in this system? It takes Chinese as input, it simulates the formal structure of the synapses of the Chinese brain, and it gives Chinese as output. But the man certainly doesn't understand Chinese, and neither do the water pipes, and if we are tempted to adopt what I think is the absurd view that somehow the *conjunction* of man *and* water pipes understands, remember that in principle the man can internalize the formal structure of the water pipes and do all the "neuron firings" in his imagination. The problem with the brain simulator is that it is simulating the wrong things about the brain. As long as it simulates only the formal structure of the sequence of neuron firings at the synapses, it won't have simulated what matters about the brain, namely its causal properties, its ability to produce intentional states. And that the formal properties are not sufficient for the causal properties is shown by the water pipe example: we can have all the formal properties carved off from relevant neurobiological causal properties.

IV.

## THE COMBINATION REPLY (BERKELEY AND STANFORD)

"While each of the previous three replies might not be completely convincing by itself as a refutation of the Chinese room counterexample, if you take all three together they are collectively much more convincing and even decisive. Imagine a robot with a brain-shaped computer lodged in its cranial cavity, imagine the computer programmed with all the synapses of a human brain, imagine the whole behavior of the robot is indistinguishable from human behavior, and now think of the whole thing as a unified system and not just as a computer with inputs and outputs. Surely in such a case we would have to ascribe intentionality to the system."

I entirely agree that in such a case we would find it rational and indeed irresistible to accept the hypothesis that the robot had intentionality, as long as we knew nothing more about it. Indeed, besides appearance and behavior, the other elements of the combination are really irrelevant. If we could build a robot whose behavior was indistinguishable over a large range from human behavior, we would attribute intentionality to it, pending some reason not to. We wouldn't need to know in advance that its computer brain was a formal analogue of the human brain.

But I really don't see that this is any help to the claims of strong AI; and here's why: According to strong AI instantiating a formal program with the right input and output is a sufficient condition of, indeed is constitutive of, intentionality. As Newell (1979) puts it, the essence of the mental is the operation of a physical symbol system. But the attributions of intentionality that we make to the robot in this example have nothing to do with formal programs. They are simply based on the assumption that if the robot looks and behaves sufficiently like us, then we would suppose, until proven otherwise, that it must have mental states like ours that cause and are expressed by its behavior and it must have an inner mechanism capable of producing such mental states. If we knew independently how to account for its behavior without such assumptions we would not attribute intentionality to it, especially if we knew it had a formal program. And this is precisely the point of my earlier reply to objection II.

Suppose we knew that the robot's behavior was entirely accounted for by the fact that a man inside it was receiving uninterpreted formal symbols from the robot's sensory receptors and sending out uninterpreted formal symbols to its motor mechanisms, and the man was doing this symbol manipulation in accordance with a bunch of rules. Furthermore, suppose the man knows none of these facts about the ro-

bot, all he knows is which operations to perform on which meaningless symbols. In such a case we would regard the robot as an ingenious mechanical dummy. The hypothesis that the dummy has a mind would now be unwarranted and unnecessary, for there is now no longer any reason to ascribe intentionality to the robot or to the system of which it is a part (except of course for the man's intentionality in manipulating the symbols). The formal symbol manipulations go on, the input and output are correctly matched, but the only real locus of intentionality is the man, and he doesn't know any of the relevant intentional states; he doesn't, for example, *see* what comes into the robot's eyes, he doesn't *intend* to move the robot's arm, and he doesn't *understand* any of the remarks made to or by the robot. Nor, for the reasons stated earlier, does the system of which man and robot are a part.

To see this point, contrast this case with cases in which we find it completely natural to ascribe intentionality to members of certain other primate species such as apes and monkeys and to domestic animals such as dogs. The reasons we find it natural are, roughly, two: we can't make sense of the animal's behavior without the ascription of intentionality, and we can see that the beasts are made of similar stuff to ourselves—that is an eye, that a nose, this is its skin, and so on. Given the coherence of the animal's behavior and the assumption of the same causal stuff underlying it, we assume both that the animal must have mental states underlying its behavior, and that the mental states must be produced by mechanisms made out of the stuff that is like our stuff. We would certainly make similar assumptions about the robot unless we had some reason not to, but as soon as we knew that the behavior was the result of a formal program, and that the actual causal properties of the physical substance were irrelevant we would abandon the assumption of intentionality. [See "Cognition and Consciousness in Nonhuman Species" *BBS* I(4) 1978.]

There are two other responses to my example that come up frequently (and so are worth discussing) but really miss the point.

V.

## THE OTHER MINDS REPLY (YALE)

"How do you know that other people understand Chinese or anything else? Only by their behavior.

Now the computer can pass the behavioral tests as well as they can (in principle), so if you are going to attribute cognition to other people you must in principle also attribute it to computers."

This objection really is only worth a short reply. The problem in this discussion is not about how I know that other people have cognitive states, but rather what it is that I am attributing to them when I attribute cognitive states to them. The thrust of the argument is that it couldn't be just computational processes and their output because the computational processes and their output can exist without the cognitive state. It is no answer to this argument to feign anesthesia. In "cognitive sciences" one presupposes the reality and knowability of the mental in the same way that in physical sciences one has to presuppose the reality and knowability of physical objects.

## VI.

## THE MANY MANSIONS REPLY (BERKELEY)

"Your whole argument presupposes that AI is only about analogue and digital computers. But that just happens to be the present state of technology. Whatever these causal processes are that you say are essential for intentionality (assuming you are right), eventually we will be able to build devices that have these causal processes, and that will be artificial intelligence. So your arguments are in no way directed at the ability of artificial intelligence to produce and explain cognition."

I really have no objection to this reply save to say that it in effect trivializes the project of strong AI by redefining it as whatever artificially produces and explains cognition. The interest of the original claim made on behalf of artificial intelligence is that it was a precise, well defined thesis: mental processes are computational processes over formally defined elements. I have been concerned to challenge that thesis. If the claim is redefined so that it is no longer that thesis, my objections no longer apply because there is no longer a testable hypothesis for them to apply to.

Let us now return to the question I promised I would try to answer: granted that in my original example I understand the English and I do not understand the Chinese, and granted therefore that the machine doesn't understand either English or Chinese, still there must be something about me that makes it the case that I understand English and a

corresponding something lacking in me that makes it the case that I fail to understand Chinese. Now why couldn't we give those somethings, whatever they are, to a machine?

I see no reason in principle why we couldn't give a machine the capacity to understand English or Chinese, since in an important sense our bodies with our brains are precisely such machines. But I do see very strong arguments for saying that we could not give such a thing to a machine where the operation of the machine is defined solely in terms of computational processes over formally defined elements; that is, where the operation of the machine is defined as an instantiation of a computer program. It is not because I am the instantiation of a computer program that I am able to understand English and have other forms of intentionality (I am, I suppose, the instantiation of any number of computer programs), but as far as we know it is because I am a certain sort of organism with a certain biological (i.e. chemical and physical) structure, and this structure, under certain conditions, is causally capable of producing perception, action, understanding, learning, and other intentional phenomena. And part of the point of the present argument is that only something that had those causal powers could have that intentionality. Perhaps other physical and chemical processes could produce exactly these effects; perhaps, for example, Martians also have intentionality but their brains are made of different stuff. That is an empirical question, rather like the question whether photosynthesis can be done by something with a chemistry different from that of chlorophyll.

But the main point of the present argument is that no purely formal model will ever be sufficient by itself for intentionality because the formal properties are not by themselves constitutive of intentionality, and they have by themselves no causal powers except the power, when instantiated, to produce the next stage of the formalism when the machine is running, and any other causal properties that particular realizations of the formal model have, are irrelevant to the formal model because we can always put the same formal model in a different realization where those causal properties are obviously absent. Even if, by some miracle, Chinese speakers exactly realize Schank's program, we can put the same program in English speakers, water pipes, or computers, none of which understand Chinese, the program notwithstanding.

What matters about brain operations is not the formal shadow cast by the sequence of synapses but rather the actual properties of the sequences. All the arguments for the strong version of artificial intelligence that I have seen insist on drawing an outline around the shadows cast by cognition and then claiming that the shadows are the real thing.

By way of concluding I want to try to state some of the general philosophical points implicit in the argument. For clarity I will try to do it in a question and answer fashion, and I begin with that old chestnut of a question:

"Could a machine think?"

The answer is, obviously, yes. We are precisely such machines.

"Yes, but could an artifact, a man-made machine, think?"

Assuming it is possible to produce artificially a machine with a nervous system, neurons with axons and dendrites, and all the rest of it, sufficiently like ours, again the answer to the question seems to be obviously, yes. If you can exactly duplicate the causes, you could duplicate the effects. And indeed it might be possible to produce consciousness, intentionality, and all the rest of it using some other sorts of chemical principles than those that human beings use. It is, as I said, an empirical question.

"OK, but could a digital computer think?"

If by "digital computer" we mean anything at all that has a level of description where it can correctly be described as the instantiation of a computer program, then again the answer is, of course, yes, since we are the instantiations of any number of computer programs, and we can think.

"But could something think, understand, and so on *solely* in virtue of being a computer with the right sort of program? Could instantiating a program, the right program of course, by itself be a sufficient condition of understanding?"

This I think is the right question to ask, though it is usually confused with one or more of the earlier questions, and the answer to it is no.

"Why not?"

Because the formal symbol manipulations by themselves don't have any intentionality; they are quite meaningless; they aren't even *symbol* manipulations, since the symbols don't symbolize anything. In the linguistic jargon, they have only a syntax but no semantics. Such intentionality as computers appear to have is solely in the minds of those who program them and those who use them, those who send in the input and those who interpret the output.

The aim of the Chinese room example was to try to show this by showing that as soon as we put something into the system that really does have intentionality (a man), and we program him with the formal program, you can see that the formal program carries no additional intentionality. It adds nothing, for example, to a man's ability to understand Chinese.

Precisely that feature of AI that seemed so appealing—the distinction between the program and the realization—proves fatal to the claim that simulation could be duplication. The distinction between the program and its realization in the hardware seems to be parallel to the distinction between the level of mental operations and the level of brain operations. And if we could describe the level of mental operations as a formal program, then it seems we could describe what was essential about the mind without doing either introspective psychology or neurophysiology of the brain. But the equation, "mind is to brain as program is to hardware" breaks down at several points, among them the following three:

First, the distinction between program and realization has the consequence that the same program could have all sorts of crazy realizations that had no form of intentionality. Weizenbaum (1976, Ch. 2), for example, shows in detail how to construct a computer using a roll of toilet paper and a pile of small stones. Similarly, the Chinese story understanding program can be programmed into a sequence of water pipes, a set of wind machines, or a monolingual English speaker, none of which thereby acquires an understanding of Chinese. Stones, toilet paper, wind, and water pipes are the wrong kind of stuff to have intentionality in the first place—only something that has the same causal powers as brains can have intentionality—and though the English speaker has the right kind of stuff for intentionality you can easily see that he doesn't get any extra intentionality by memorizing the program, since memorizing it won't teach him Chinese.

Second, the program is purely formal, but the intentional states are not in that way formal. They are defined in terms of their content, not their form. The belief that it is raining, for example, is not defined as a certain formal shape, but as a certain mental content with conditions of satisfaction, a direction of fit (see Searle 1979), and the like. Indeed the belief as such hasn't even got a formal shape in this syntactic sense, since one and the same belief can be given an indefinite number of different syntactic expressions in different linguistic systems.

Third, as I mentioned before, mental states and events are literally a product of the operation of the brain, but the program is not in that way a product of the computer.

"Well if programs are in no way constitutive of mental processes, why have so many people believed the converse? That at least needs some explanation."

I don't really know the answer to that one. The idea that computer simulations could be the real thing ought to have seemed suspicious in the first place because the computer isn't confined to simulating mental operations, by any means. No one supposes that computer simulations of a five-alarm fire will burn the neighborhood down or that a computer simulation of a rainstorm will leave us all drenched. Why on earth would anyone suppose that a computer simulation of understanding actually understood anything? It is sometimes said that it would be frightfully hard to get computers to feel pain or fall in love, but love and pain are neither harder nor easier than cognition or anything else. For simulation, all you need is the right input and output and a program in the middle that transforms the former into the latter. That is all the computer has for anything it does. To confuse simulation with duplication is the same mistake, whether it is pain, love, cognition, fires, or rainstorms.

Still, there are several reasons why AI must have seemed—and to many people perhaps still does seem—in some way to reproduce and thereby explain mental phenomena, and I believe we will not succeed in removing these illusions until we have fully exposed the reasons that give rise to them.

First, and perhaps most important, is a confusion about the notion of "information processing": many people in cognitive science believe that the human brain, with its mind, does something called "information processing," and analogously the computer with its program does information processing; but fires and rainstorms, on the other hand, don't do information processing at all. Thus, though the computer can simulate the formal features of any process whatever, it stands in a special relation to the mind and brain because when the computer is properly programmed, ideally with the same program as the brain, the information processing is identical in the two cases, and this information processing is really the essence of the mental. But the trouble with this argument is that it rests on an ambiguity in the notion of "information." In the sense in which people "process information" when they reflect, say, on problems in arithmetic or when they read and answer questions about stories, the programmed computer does not do "information processing." Rather, what it does is manipulate formal symbols. The fact that the programmer and the interpreter of the computer output use the symbols to stand for objects in the world is totally beyond the scope of the computer. The computer, to repeat, has a syntax but no semantics. Thus, if you type into the computer "2 plus 2 equals?" it will type out "4." But it has no idea that "4" means 4 or that it means anything at all. And the point is not that it lacks some second-order information about the interpretation of its first-order symbols, but rather that its first-order symbols don't have any interpretations as far as the computer is concerned. All the computer has is more symbols. The introduction of the notion of "information processing" therefore produces a dilemma: either we construe the notion of "information processing" in such a way that it implies intentionality as part of the process or we don't. If the former, then the programmed computer does not do information processing, it only manipulates formal symbols. If the latter, then, though the computer does information processing, it is only doing so in the sense in which adding machines, typewriters, stomachs, thermostats, rainstorms, and hurricanes do information processing; namely, they have a level of description at which we can describe them as taking information in at one end, transforming it, and producing information as output. But in this case it is up to outside observers to interpret the input and output as information in the ordinary sense. And no similarity is established between the computer and the brain in terms of any similarity of information processing.

Second, in much of AI there is a residual behaviorism or operationalism. Since appropriately programmed computers can have input-output patterns similar to those of human beings, we are tempted to postulate mental states in the computer similar to human mental states. But once we see that it is both conceptually and empirically possible for a system to have human capacities in some realm without having any intentionality at all, we should be able to overcome this impulse. My desk adding machine has calculating capacities, but no intentionality, and in this paper I have tried to show that a system could have input and output capabilities that duplicated those of a native Chinese speaker and still not understand Chinese, regardless of how it was programmed. The Turing test is typical of the tradition in being unashamedly behavioristic and operationalistic, and I believe that if AI workers totally repudiated behaviorism and operationalism much of the confusion between simulation and duplication would be eliminated.

Third, this residual operationalism is joined to a residual form of dualism; indeed strong AI only makes sense given the dualistic assumption that, where the mind is concerned, the brain doesn't matter. In strong AI (and in functionalism, as well) what matters are programs, and programs are independent of their realization in machines; indeed, as far as AI is concerned, the same program could be realized by an electronic machine, a Cartesian mental substance, or a Hegelian world spirit. The single most surprising discovery that I have made in discussing these issues is that many AI workers are quite shocked by my idea that actual human mental phenomena might be dependent on actual physical-chemical properties of actual human brains. But if you think about it a minute you can see that I should not have been surprised; for unless you accept some form of dualism, the strong AI project hasn't got a chance. The project is to reproduce and explain the mental by designing programs, but unless the mind is not only conceptually but empirically independent of the brain you couldn't carry out the project, for the program is completely independent of any realization. Unless you believe that the mind is separable from the brain both conceptually and empirically—dualism in a strong form—you cannot hope to reproduce the mental by writing and running programs since programs must be independent of brains or any other particular forms of instantiation. If mental operations consist in computational operations on formal symbols, then it follows that they have no interesting connection with the brain; the only connection would be that the brain just happens to be one of the indefinitely many types of machines capable of instantiating the program. This form of dualism is not the traditional Cartesian variety that claims there are two sorts of *substances*, but it is Cartesian in the sense that it insists that what is specifically mental about the mind has no intrinsic connection with the actual properties of the brain. This underlying dualism is masked from us by the fact that AI literature contains frequent fulminations against "dualism"; what the authors seem to be unaware of is that their position presupposes a strong version of dualism.

"Could a machine think?" My own view is that *only* a machine could think, and indeed only very special kinds of machines, namely brains and machines that had the same causal powers as brains. And that is the main reason strong AI has had little to tell us about thinking, since it has nothing to tell us about machines. By its own definition, it is about programs, and programs are not machines. Whatever else intentionality is, it is a biological phenomenon, and it is as likely to be as causally dependent on the specific biocheminstry of its origins as lactation, photosynthesis, or any other biological phenomena. No one would suppose that we could produce milk and sugar by running a computer simulation of the formal sequences in lactation and photosynthesis, but where the mind is concerned many people are willing to believe in such a miracle because of a deep and abiding dualism: the mind they suppose is a matter of formal processes and is independent of quite specific material causes in the way that milk and sugar are not.

In defense of this dualism the hope is often expressed that the brain is a digital computer (early computers, by the way, were often called "electronic brains"). But that is no help. Of course the brain is a digital computer. Since everything is a digital compuer, brains are too. The point is that the brain's causal capacity to produce intentionality cannot consist in its instantiating a computer program, since for any program you like it is possible for something to instantiate that program and still not have any mental states. Whatever it is that the brain does to produce intentionality, it cannot consist in instantiating a program since no program, by itself, is sufficient for intentionality.

## ACKNOWLEDGMENTS

I am indebted to a rather large number of people for discussion of these matters and for their patient attempts to overcome my ignorance of artificial intelligence. I would especially like to thank Ned Block, Hubert Dreyfus, John Haugeland, Roger Schank, Robert Wilensky, and Terry Winograd.

## NOTES

1. I am not, of course, saying that Schank himself is committed to these claims.

2. Also, "understanding" implies both the possession of mental (intentional) states and the truth (validity, success) of these states. For the purposes of this discussion we are concerned only with the possession of the states.

3. Intentionality is by definition that feature of certain mental states by which they are directed at or about objects and states of affairs in the world. Thus, beliefs, desires, and intentions are intentional states; undirected forms of anxiety and depression are not. For further discussion see Searle (1979c).

## REFERENCES

Fodor, J. A. 1968. The appeal to tacit knowledge in psychological explanation. *Journal of Philosophy* 65: 627–40.

Fodor, J. A. 1980. Methodological solipsism considered as a research strategy in cognitive psychology. *Behavioral and Brain Sciences* 3:1.

McCarthy, J. 1979. Ascribing mental qualities to machines. In: *Philosophical perceptives in artifical intelligence*, ed. M. Ringle. Atlantic Highlands, NJ: Humanities Press.

Newell, A. 1973. Physical symbol systems. Lecture at the La Jolla Conference on Cognitive Science.

Newell, A., and Simon, H. A. 1963. GPS, a program that simulates human thought. In: *Computers and thought*, ed. A. Feigenbaum & V. Feldman, pp. 279-93. New York: McGraw-Hill.

Pylyshyn, Z. W. 1980. Computation and cognition: issues in the foundations of cognitive science. *Behavioral and Brain Sciences* 3.

Schank, R. C., and Abelson, R. P. 1977. *Scripts, plans, goals, and understanding*. Hillsdale, NJ: Lawrence Erlbaum Press.

Searle, J. R. 1979. The intentionality of intention and action. *Inquiry* 22: 253–80.

Weizenbaum, J. 1965. Eliza—a computer program for the study of natural language communication between man and machine. *Communication of the Association for Computing Machinery* 9:36–45.

Weizenbaum, J. 1976. *Computer power and human reason*. San Francisco: W. H. Freeman.

Winograd, T. 1973. A procedural model of language understanding. In: *Computer models of thought and language*, ed. R. Schank & K. Colby. San Francisco: W. H. Freeman.

# READING 26

---

# Artificial Intelligence and Personal Identity
*David Cole*

*David Cole (1948–    ) teaches philosophy at the University of Minnesota at Duluth and has published a number of papers on issues in the cognitive sciences and philosophy of mind. He is the co-editor with James Fetzer and Terry Rankin of* Philosophy, Mind, and Cognitive Inquiry *(1990).*

**ABSTRACT:** Considerations of personal identity bear on John Searle's Chinese Room argument, and on the opposed position that a computer itself could really understand a natural language. In this paper I develop the notion of a *virtual person*, modelled on the concept of virtual machines familiar in computer science. I show how Searle's argument, and J. Maloney's attempt to defend it, fail. I conclude that Searle is correct in holding that no digital machine could understand language, but wrong in holding that artificial minds are impossible: minds and persons are not the same as the machines, biological or electronic, that realize them.

**SOURCE:** From *Synthese* 88 (1991). Kluwer Academic Publishers. Printed in the Netherlands.

Many workers in cognitive science believe that computers can potentially have genuine mental abilities. John Searle has been a prominent critic of this optimism about the abilities of computers. Searle argues that computers can at best simulate, but not possess, intelligence. If Searle is correct, even though a computer might eventually pass the Turing Test, no computer will ever actually understand natural language or have genuine propositional attitudes, such as beliefs. Searle's argument is interesting both because of its import and because it appears to some to be valid (e.g., Maloney 1987), and to others to be invalid (e.g., many of the "peer" commentators following Searle 1980, Sharvy 1983, Carleton 1984, Rey 1986, Anderson 1987).

The following is a defense of the potential mental abilities of digital computers against Searle's criticism. I shall clarify precisely why his argument is logically invalid. The missing premise that would render the argument valid reflects a form of personal identity theory that Searle may accept but which is widely, and I believe rightly, regarded as false.

However, Searle has indeed, I believe, succeeded in proving that no computer will ever understand English or any other natural language.[1] And he is correct in rejecting the "system reply".[2] But, I shall show how this is consistent with the computer's causing a new entity to exist (a) that is not identical with the computer, but (b) that exists solely in virtue of the machine's computational activity, and (c) that does understand English. That is, showing that the machine itself does not understand does not show that nothing does. We can introduce the concept of a *Virtual Person* (or *Virtual Mind*), an entity that may be realized by the activity of something that is not a person (or mind). Thus, I believe, Searle's argument fails in establishing any limitations on Artificial Intelligence (AI).

Thus, one can show, by a line of reasoning independent of Searle's, that it would always be a mistake to attribute understanding to a computer. The line of argument is inspired by considerations raised by John Locke and his successors (Grice, Quinton, Parfit, Perry and Lewis) in the development of theories of personal identity, a branch of analytical metaphysics perhaps not obviously related to AI. This line of reasoning reveals the abstractness of the entity that understands, and so the irrelevance of the fact that hardware (including the system) itself does not understand. Searle was both right and wrong on this assessment; he wins a battle, but loses the war.

## SEARLE'S ARGUMENT

Searle's argument is straightforward. It is possible to write computer programs that produce responses in natural language to questions about some subject domain. Some believe that through such clever programming actual understanding is produced. Others believe that genuine understanding is not *yet* achieved, but it may be in the future with improved programming techniques, larger databases and faster machines. But, as Searle argues, consider that no matter how clever and complex the program, a human could do exactly what the computer does: follow instructions for generating strings of symbols in response to incoming strings.

Suppose, for example, a person (Searle, in the original statement of the argument) who does not know Chinese sits in a room with instructions written *in English* (a "program") that tell one in detail how to manipulate *Chinese* symbols, producing strings in response to the strings given to one. We are to suppose that the instructions are such that they permit successful passage of this variation on a Turing Test: even with trials of indefinite duration those outside the room cannot tell the difference between the room as described and a room that contains a human native speaker of Chinese. Since the instructions tell one what to do entirely on the basis of formal or syntactic features of the strings, without ever mentioning (or revealing) meaning, one can generate Chinese sentences without any understanding of what they mean—indeed without even knowing that they are Chinese sentences. That is, doing exactly what a computer does would not give one the ability to understand Chinese. Therefore, the computer does not understand Chinese either. Thus, mere programming cannot produce understanding of a natural language.

I wish now to consider three claims made in the course of this argument:

(1) the claim that the person following the English instructions would not understand Chinese;

(2) the inferred claim that a computer following a program would not understand Chinese; and

(3) the inferred final claim in the preceding summary that programming cannot produce understanding of a natural language.

There is some reason to be critical of claim (1). Searle's self-report of incomprehension of Chinese in his scenario conflicts with other evidence, notably the response in Chinese to Chinese questions. One might hold that the person in the room understands Chinese albeit with certain odd deficiencies not characteristic of polyglots: most notably, an inability to translate.[3] One may also be critical of the inference to (2). There are important disanalogies between a human following understood English instructions and a computer running a program—the computer does not literally understand its program "instructions"; the computer would not be conscious of its program; the explicitly syntactic character of the "instructions" in the program is a red herring in that whatever is produced by programming a programmable computer could have been hardwired in a dedicated computer (Cole 1984).[4]

But let us suppose that the crucial premise (1) is true: Searle would not understand Chinese merely by following the instructions in English for syntactic manipulation. Let us also concede (2) for the sake of argument. Nevertheless, (3) does not follow.

Clearly from the fact that *someone* does not understand Chinese it does not follow that *no one* understands Chinese. And from Searle's linguistic disabilities in the Chinese Room scenario, it does not follow that no one *in the room* understands Chinese, unless Searle is *alone* in the room. And, finally and this is the main point here, it does not *follow* logically from the premise, that Searle is initially alone in the room and that no one else *enters* the room from outside, that Searle remains alone in the room.

## THE KORNESE ROOM

The Chinese Room argument as it stands is logically invalid. The question then is whether it is legitimate to assume that if anyone understands Chinese, it must be Searle (who does not). It might be thought, since the question-answering performance suggests that there is someone who understands Chinese and that the only one around is Searle, that the only one who could possibly be the one who understands Chinese is just Searle. But it is not necessary that it be the case that the performance of the room suggests that there is any *one* who understands Oriental languages in the room.

To show that, let us consider a variation on Searle's thought experiment. Once again we are to imagine Searle in a room, following instructions for

dealing with strings of alien characters slipped under the door. The room is a bit more crowded than before: the size of the set of instruction manuals is almost doubled from before. And the pace is more hectic. Searle flips vigorously through manuals as a steady stream of squiggles and squoggles is slipped under the door. He generates reams of marks in return, as instructed by the manuals. As before, many of those outside believe that someone in the room understands Chinese, for they are receiving replies to questions submitted in Chinese.

But unlike before, those outside *also* believe someone in the room speaks Korean, for they are receiving replies in Korean to questions submitted in Korean. Furthermore, they also believe that the room is more crowded than before: there appear to be at least two people in the room, one who understands Chinese (call him Pc) but not Korean, and another who understands Korean but not Chinese (call him Pk). The evidence seems quite clear that Pc is not Pk. In fact let us suppose that the response abilities and dispositions embodied in the Pc database were derived from an elderly Chinese woman, whereas those in the Pk database were from a young Korean male who was a victim of a truck-bicycle collision.[5] The person, if any, who understands Chinese, is not the person, if any, who understands Korean. The answers to the questions in Chinese appear to reveal a clever, witty, jocular mind, knowledgeable about things in China, but quite ignorant of both the Korean language and events in Korea. Pc reports being seventy-two years old and is both wise and full of interesting observations on what it has been like to be a woman in China for the tumultuous past half-century. By contrast, the replies to Korean questions reveal quite a dull young man. Pk is misogynous. Pk has a vitriolic hatred of China, but is largely ignorant of events there. Pk is very avaricious, and soon discovers that he can demand money for answering the questions slipped under the door. Pk reports that he works in a television factory and gives accurate descriptions of television assembly. The only other subject about which Pk exhibits much interest or knowledge are the Olympic Games held in Korea.

Thus, suppose that the behavioral evidence is as clear as can be in such a case that there are two *distinct* individuals in the room. Try as they might, interlocutors outside the room can find no hint that there might be but a single person pretending to be two. Information provided in Chinese is unavailable to Pk, even when offers of substantial rewards are made to him in Korean for answers based on the information provided in Chinese.

But behavioral evidence is certainly not decisive here. Indeed behavioral evidence is the very category of evidence called into question in rejecting the adequacy of the Turing Test as a test of mental abilities. Fortunately, a stronger case can be made by considering information not available to the interlocutors outside the room. There is in fact no individual inside the room who understands both Chinese and Korean. Searle understands neither. And the instructions for generating replies to Chinese input and those for dealing with Korean input are distinct, with no exchange of information between the databases consulted (although this is not known by Searle.) If there were a single person duplicitously feigning being two, the person would, on the one hand, realize that something was being asked about events that he/she knew about and then would pretend not to know about them. That never happens in the room. And the histories of the representations in the Pc and Pk databases are completely independent, involving individuals in China and Korea respectively. Thus *if* Pc and Pk are persons, they are distinct.

At this point considerations emerge familiar from arguments in other contexts concerning personal identity (c.f., for example, Perry 1978, pp. 32-36). Pc cannot be identical with Pk. The grounds for saying that Pc is Searle are just the same as those for holding that Pk is identical with Searle. We cannot hold that both are identical with Searle, for this would violate the transitivity of identity. Therefore, we must hold that neither is Searle. Thus, by a line of reasoning quite independent of that used by Searle, we arrive at the conclusion that the person, if any, who understands Chinese is not Searle.

## COMPUTERS AND PERSONS

Consider now a computer system. Suppose that a program has been written for this machine which embodies the very algorithm for replying to questions that was used in the English instructions imagined in the Kornese room scenario. Again, there is no interchange of world-information between the Korean and the Chinese databases. Let us suppose then that the computer system responds to questions asked in Chinese and to questions asked in Korean, with performance indistinguishable from the Kornese room. Now let us suppose that someone wished to say that the computer itself understands Chinese, say, and can answer questions about China. But when the system is asked in *Korean* if it understands *Chinese,* the reply comes back that it does not. Does anyone *lie?* Does *the computer* lie? The behavioral evidence is, *ex hypothesi,* just what it was in the Kornese Room scenario. When asked in Korean about China, the replies do not demonstrate knowledge of China, only a vitriolic prejudice against China. When asked similar questions in Chinese, the replies exhibit knowledge and love of China. Does *the computer* like China or not?

These considerations suggest that it would be a mistake to attribute these properties to the computer itself. One would have equally good grounds for attributing incompatible properties to the computer. For the same reason it would be equally incorrect to attribute knowledge or ignorance of China to the *program.* Again, one cannot attribute inconsistent properties to a single entity. The solution is to hold that no single entity understands both Chinese and Korean; there are two subjects, two virtual persons: one who understands Chinese and one who understands Korean.[6] These two virtual subjects are realized by a single substratum, the computer.

The concept of a *virtual machine* is familiar in computer science. And some computer scientists, such as Paul Smolensky, have viewed consciousness as a virtual machine.[7] Each computer has an intrinsic instruction set: the capacity to perform a certain set of operations is wired into the central processor. And in virtue of the construction of the machine, a certain syntactic string will cause one of the intrinsic operations to be performed. But it is possible to write a program which will cause one machine to behave as a different machine, one with a different intrinsic instruction set. Thus, such emulation software may make a computer built using an Intel 8088 processor behave as though it were a Z80. Then, there is said to be a virtual machine. The virtual machine can run software written for a Z80, using the Z80 instruction set. The 8088 realizes a virtual Z80. Of interest, some newer processors (for example, the Intel 80386) can realize multiple virtual processors concurrently, and this capacity is wired in as an intrinsic capability of the computer.

Now it might be thought that a virtual machine is not a real machine. But there is no reason for this reservation. One machine can very literally realize, or make real, another or several other machines. In fact, a manufacturer could decide to sell very real computers in which the nominal processor was realized by another. For example, a Reduced Instruction Set Computer (RISC) processor might be used, because of its great speed, instead of a normal full instruction set 80386. The user might be quite unaware that his 80386 was in fact a virtual machine, realized on a RISC that was not intrinsically an 80386. And there are physical LISP machines as well as virtual LISP language processing machines.[8] The only difference between the physical and the virtual machine has to do with intrinsic instruction sets, with consequences for speed and volatility. When the emulation software is not running, the virtual machine does not exist.

Note that the physical and the virtual machines differ in properties. They run different programs. At a given time, the physical machine will be running the emulation program, whereas the virtual machine may be running an application. The two machines have different instruction sets. And the speeds at which the two machines perform basic operations will differ. Thus, the physical machine and the virtual machine(s) it realizes are not identical. And the virtual machine is not identical with the emulation program that realizes it when the program is run on the physical machine. The emulation program may be long or short, may be written in a language, may contain comments, may be copyrighted, but the virtual machine has none of these properties.

There are additional considerations that count against holding that the *program* incorporating the Chinese or Kornese Room algorithm understands language or likes China. The program itself is entirely inert until it runs. In Aristotelian terms, a program could be but the form of some matter—without an underlying substance, it does nothing. The program exists before and after it is run, but understanding, if any, exists only while the program is running.

In the light of this result and consideration of the Kornese room, let us reconsider Searle's original scenario. It is clear that the knowledge, personality, beliefs and desires apparently revealed in the Chinese answers to questions submitted to the room might be quite unlike Searle's own. Indeed, Searle himself

could receive no knowledge through information provided in Chinese—and he can reveal none that he has. He cannot express *himself* or anything about himself in the Chinese answers. Similarly, the answers in Chinese reflect no access to Searle's knowledge, preferences, or personality. If there is a person who understands Chinese, it is clearly *not* Searle.

Thus, what follows from the fact that Searle does not understand Chinese is just that the person, if any, who does understand Chinese is *not* Searle. A tacit premise, needed for the inference from 2) to 3), is that there is no *other* mind. But Searle gives us no reason for believing that this premise is true. There may well be a mind *realized* by Searle's activity, a virtual person. But the *same* mind could have been realized by the activity of someone other than Searle—Searle could even resign his job in the Room and be replaced by another—while the Chinese conversation continues. This is additional evidence that the Chinese understanding person is not Searle. Searle is not essential to the existence of the Chinese understanding person.

## FUNCTIONALISM AND MULTIPLE MINDS

Georges Rey (1986) advocates a version of the system reply incorporating the robot reply. Rey holds that

> Searle's example burdens [AI] with a quite extreme view about the 'autonomy' of language, a view that would allow that understanding a language need involve *only intra-linguistic symbol manipulations.* (p. 171)

Clearly functionalism will require more integration than that. Rey goes on to consider a robot (a system with sense organs) and argues that, on a sketched in causal theory of meaning, the system would understand language. But Searle is quite clear and correct in pointing out, in his discussion of the robot reply, that his argument is not affected in its essentials by extension to include extra-linguistic capabilities. Therefore, Searle is not (merely) attacking a strawman. Sharvy (1983, p. 128) also seems too cavalier in saying that Searle's argument against the system reply is just an "intuition pump".

Maloney (1987) disagrees with Rey's rejection of the extreme view of autonomy of language, citing severely handicapped individuals as support for the autonomy. The counterexamples are not conclusive, I believe, because they focus on overt behavior—even the handicapped have the neuronal subsystems that in normal individuals serve motor and perceptual skills. In any case, we can sidestep this issue by simply considering a robot system, for Searle claims that his argument applies equally to the robot system as to the original person confined to the room and to exclusively linguistic input and output.

Cole (1984) and Rey (1986, p. 174–75) hold that Searle, despite protests, understands Chinese in the room. Maloney (1987, p. 355–59) and Cole point to Searle's failure to translate; Cole finds it only odd, but Maloney finds it decisive for denying language comprehension. But then Maloney goes on to consider a view similar to the one advocated here, which agrees that the English-speaking occupant of the room (Maloney calls him "Marco") is not the person who understands Chinese. The view Maloney considers is that "there must be another agent, Polo, who does realize the program and thereby understands Chinese" (p. 359).

But, says Maloney, "there is an overwhelming difficulty with postulating Polo that emerges upon closely examining him" (p. 360). Polo shares Marco's sensory and motor systems and goes wherever Marco goes; thus *how* can Polo be distinct from Marco?

> Marco learned how to manipulate the cards in much the same way in which he has previously learned lots of different things, including poker. According to Strong AI, understanding how to play poker involves mastering the proper program, just as understanding Chinese amounts to running the right program. Now, since Marco both learned how to play poker and also plays poker, i.e. understands poker, why is it Polo rather than Marco who understands Chinese, since it was Marco, not Polo, who mastered the program for Chinese? (p. 362)

Maloney does not wait for an answer:

> . . . all that Marco did in order to understand poker was learn a program. . . . If anyone here understands Chinese, it must be Marco, not Polo. And so, since we have already established that, despite realizing the formal program for Chinese, Marco is ignorant of Chinese, Strong AI is finally and thoroughly false. (p. 362)

This conclusion is premature. Maloney's argument seems most forceful as a critique of Sharvy (1983). Sharvy says:

> First, consider a man who is locked in a room receiving symbolic inputs and calculating symbolic outputs according to a purely formal algorithm, but who does all this completely blind to any interpretation of those symbols. That man cannot truly be said to be playing chess. This is so even if men outside the room interpret the symbols as representing moves in a chess game. But a computer running that very same program is playing chess and is doing so *by* running that program.
>
> So playing chess is an example of something that computers come to do by instantiating a program, but which a man in a room does not come to do by instantiating that same program. (p. 127)

This position is odd, and surely Sharvy needs an explanation of the sort Maloney demands for the difference. In any case, Sharvy's position is incompatible with functionalist approaches to mentality. My task here is to develop an assessment of the relation of machines to minds which is compatible with functionalism and to show why a functionalist ought to view Searle's argument as unsound.

Maloney's argument does not show, as he seems to think, that there is not a difference between learning to play poker and learning to run the Chinese Room program. For one thing, Maloney appears not to appreciate the possible relations between Marco and Polo. Accordingly, he offers us a false dichotomy in the following passage:

> . . . Strong AI must accept one of two alternatives. Either Marco and Polo are cognitive system sharing time in the same nervous system, now one using it, now the other, or they must be genuine parallel processors, different programs simultaneously realized in different sections of the central nervous system . . . (p. 361)

This is not true. When one system realizes another, it is not the same thing as either parallel processing, with both programs running independently and simultaneously, nor time sharing, with now one program using the central processor and then the other, sequentially. The virtual system is realized *now* by the operations *now* of a single implementing system. Both parallel processing and sequential time sharing imply complete independence between the operations of the two systems (except for time delays). For example, if programs A and B are running on parallel processors, the operations performed by A (say, a statistical analysis program) make no difference to the operations of B, which might be a game. The same is true of time sharing. The two programs are logically independent and this is an essential feature of their relation. If they interacted, it would defeat the whole purpose of the system.

The case of a virtual system is quite different. Here the activity of the virtual system A occurs solely in virtue of the activity of the realizing system B. Changes in operations performed in B directly affect the operations in A. And a certain group of B's operations is the same as one of A's operations, hence, the direct effect.

This misunderstanding of the relation between the physical and the virtual system affects Maloney's (and Searle's) failure to see the difference between learning to play poker, for example, and realizing a distinct personality which might understand a foreign language unknown to the physical system itself. The failure is striking in Maloney's case, for in arguing that the physical system ('Marco') does not itself understand Chinese, he presents the considerations relevant to answering the question of how to distinguish learning to play poker from realizing Polo, a Chinese understander.

Not surprisingly, the key difference is psychological integration, that is, access and control. This is not surprising for these are just the characteristics that arise in assessments of multiple personality. When one learns to play poker, one understands the objectives of the game and how the rules constrain the players' pursuit of those objectives. All aspects of play can be affected by other psychological aspects of the player. If one is a risk taker, it will be reflected in one's poker play. And one can explicitly relate poker playing to other games, or to life in general. But this level of psychological integration is precisely what is missing in Marco's activity that produces strings of Chinese characters. None of Marco's psychology is reflected in Polo's performance because Marco has no access to the semantic content of the Chinese characters.

This suggests that we consider two ways of learning to play poker. One would be the usual method, whereby one is told the rules and objectives of the game, as well as various informal strategies for success, and allowed to watch a game or run through a couple of hands. The second would be where someone who did not know how to play poker was given a formal program for manipulating strings of ones and zeros which, unbeknown to one, represented in binary code various combinations of cards and information about the betting behavior of poker players. One could then sit in a "Poker Room", having strings of digits fed to one and, in accord with the program, issue strings in response. Persons outside the room might interpret these strings as poker play, having been told that they were playing with an eccentric computer scientist recluse.

Would one thereby have learned to play poker? One would deny knowing how to play if asked if one could play. And the actual "play" would in no way reflect one's personality, aversion to risk, flamboyance, memory skills, cunning, or skill in the assessment of the psychology of others. One would derive no more pleasure from 'winning' than from 'losing'—one would not know that one had done any of these things. The same considerations of lack of integration which count against saying that Searle or Marco understands Chinese in the Chinese room count against saying that the physical Poker Room occupant plays poker. Thus, the alleged problematic difference between learning poker and learning to respond to Chinese turns out not to be a difference at all, and so certainly is not a demonstration that Strong AI is "thoroughly and finally false".

## FUNCTIONALISM, PERSONS AND BODIES

I do not believe it can be proven that there is a person who understands Chinese in the scenario. But this difficulty is a completely general difficulty familiar as The Problem of Other Minds. My argument so far has been to show that even those who do believe that there might be one who understands Chinese in the scenario should resist any temptation to think, as Searle would have them, that it would have to be Searle. Now I wish to argue that support for the view that it is possible for there to be other than a one-to-one correspondence between living bodies and minds comes from plausible accounts of the relation of mind to body. Then, if the actual replies to questions demonstrate understanding and a personality, it would be an inference to the best explanation that there is a person who understands the questions.

Psychiatry has long recognized cases of multiple personality. The condition is rare (under two hundred total reported cases), but is more frequently diagnosed now than in the past. The American Psychiatric Association (*Diagnostic and Statistical Manual of Mental Disorders*, Vol. III) characterizes this disorder as follows:

> The essential feature is the existence within the individual of two or more distinct personalities, each of which is dominant at a particular time. Each personality is a fully integrated and complete unit with unique memories, behavior patterns, and social relationships that determine the nature of the individual's acts when that personality is dominant. (p. 257).

It is of philosophic interest that the diagnostic indication emphasizes the functionalist feature of integration. The disorder is a subtype of "Dissociative Disorders", a variety that includes retrograde amnesia. The DSM reports that usually the 'original' person has no knowledge of any of the "subpersonalities", but that the latter may be aware of one another. Recently the law has had occasion to take note of the phenomenon: William Mulligan was found not guilty by reason of insanity of four rapes. Mulligan displayed ten personalities; "the Lesbian Adelena is thought to be the 'personality' who committed the rapes" (Sarason and Sarason 1987, p. 138-39). Apparently, some evidence suggests that different areas of the brain are responsible for different personalities (Braun 1984).

In any case, the considerations raised by the Chinese and Kornese Room scenarios mirror familiar metaphysical problems and positions in the philosophy of mind. There appear to be good reasons for holding that it is false to say that I am identical with my body. But this is not to say, with the dualist, that I am identical with some substance other than my body, or identical with a whole composed of two substances. And yet the dualist is correct in holding that I might exist while my (present) body did not.

These, I believe, are metaphysical consequences of functionalism. Functionalists have not generally been concerned with how functionalism bears on traditional metaphysical questions, such as the possibility of immortality, but I believe it has interesting implications for these questions (cf. Cole and Foelber 1984). I shall not defend functionalism here, but shall indicate how it bears on the nature of persons and how this is relevant to Artificial Intelligence and Searle's argument.

Functionalism rejects a type-type identity between psychological states and physical states. Some instances of being in pain, say, may be physiologically different from others. There could even be alien life-forms with psychological states that were of the *same* type as psychological states had by humans, but that

had quite a different underlying physical system (for example, based on silicon rather than carbon).

Furthermore, although this has received less attention, these considerations apply to a single individual across time. My psychological states in 1989 need not be realized by the same physical states as were my type-identical psychological states in 1979. For example, a portion of my brain may have sustained injury in the interim and its function may have been assumed by a physiologically distinct structure. Or, it may become possible to replace damaged portions of my brain with cultured neonatal tissue that grows to assume functions temporarily lost. Finally, it might even become possible to replace entire damaged neurons by functionally equivalent silicon-based electronic devices.

Contemporary discussions of holistic models of cognitive function also underscore that identity of realizations is not essential for type identity of psychological states over time. If Connectionist or Parallel Distributed Processing models of psychological function are correct, the underlying system that realizes the cognitive states of persons is continually changing as learning takes place. The system is radically dynamic, as each bit of new information slightly changes weightings and probabilities of a given global response.

Functionalism thus takes the underlying substance type to be nonessential to the psychological states. This is not to suppose that there can be psychological states without *any* underlying substratum—the inference from the nonessentiality of any *given* substratum to the nonessentiality of the existence of *some* substratum or other would be a modal scope fallacy. Given that the most reasonable supposition is that dualists are wrong in holding that there is any other than physical substance, and in fact only organic neural substance is capable at present of realizing mental states, the result is clear: no brain, no pain. But this is not to say that in order for *me* to experience pain it must be with *this* brain with each of its *current* constituent cells and molecules.

## WHY THE "SYSTEM REPLY" TO SEARLE'S ARGUMENT IS WRONG

The functionalist diachronic perspective on persons suggests that persons or minds are more abstract than a simple identity of a person with a body (or a Cartesian soul or individual *res cogitans*) would suppose. This position is not new in this century; it was an implication of Locke's theory of personal identity which invoked a functional connection, memory, as the glue of the mind. Locke says:

> . . . it must be allowed, that, if the same consciousness . . . can be transferred from one thinking substance to another, it will be possible that two thinking substances may make but one person. For the same consciousness being preserved, whether in the same or different substances, the personal identity is preserved. [*Essay*, Bk. ii, chap. 27]

Locke goes on to indicate that a single substance might be the seat of more than one person (if there is not psychological continuity over time).

This view rejects a simple identity of person with underlying substance, whether that substance is or is not material. Presumably Searle would say that I am identical with my body and could not exist without it, or at least not without the brain. But Locke's view suggests that I could. Another body and brain exactly like his one, with the same "causal powers", could, in principle, replace this one. (Indeed, for all I know this may have happened!)

Note that even in the case of bodies, a simple identification with the physical constituents fails to do justice to the identity conditions we in fact employ: Is my body identical with this particular collection of molecules that now constitutes it? No, my body can change, acquiring and losing constituents. A person is an attribute of a body. A single body might realize more than one person, and a single person might be realized by more than one body.

Thus, the "system reply", as Searle represents it, is not quite right either. The Chinese understanding person is not identical with a whole system composed of Searle, the instruction manuals, and the scraps of paper on which he makes notes. As Searle rightly notes, he could in principle commit the contents of all the instruction manuals to memory and follow the instructions completely in his head. That is, he could sit in an otherwise bare room with only a pen and the pieces of paper upon which he writes the outgoing strings of symbols. Still, he would no more understand Chinese than he did when he consulted the manuals for instruction each step of the way. So, the entity that understands Chinese is not Searle nor Searle and paper and manuals.

It will not do to hold (with Cole 1984 and Rapaport 1990) that Searle understands Chinese but does not understand that he understands Chinese; for the Kornese room scenario shows that contradictory psychological attributes can be had by the (virtual) persons manifested by the system. While a single individual might conceivably understand Chinese but not know this, a single individual cannot plausibly be held in any straightforward sense to both find Chinese music always restful and conducive to thought and also to find this music always to be cacophonous and disturbing. Nor could one believe that Malraux's novels misportrayed events in China and also believe that one had never heard of Malraux. There is no reason to suppose that persons realized in the Chinese room would have psychological properties compatible with one another nor that the realized would have the properties of the realizer. Thus, in the original Chinese Room situation, there is no reason to attribute the psychological properties of the virtual person to Searle himself nor to the system consisting of Searle and inanimate paraphernalia.

So who or what *does* understand Chinese in the Chinese room? An unnamed Chinese person. This person is not Searle, but this person cannot exist unless someone—Searle or any competent other—brings to life the Chinese mind by following the instructions in the room.

## CONCLUSION

In the rejection by functionalists of type-type identities of psychological events or states with physical events or states, the way is opened for different persons to have quite different underlying physical realizations of their mental states. Functionalism takes certain of the causal properties of an event to be determinants of the psychological properties. One of the psychological properties thus determined is just which mind the event belongs to. Causality may or may not be the cement of the universe but it is what holds bundles of psychological states and events together to form a single mind over time.

Functionalism does not require a one-to-one correspondence between persons and bodies. Contingently, there generally is such a correspondence, which is exactly what functionalism would lead one to expect. The causal properties of psychological states are just those of the system literally embodying them. And in the ordinary course of events, the physiological characteristics of brains permit psychological integration and continuity for the entire duration of the operating life of the brain. But it *could* be otherwise, and may in fact be. There may be multiple persons embodied by a single brain in cases of "multiple personality". Whether there are or not, I believe, turns on the extent of causal connection (and, hence, access) between the personalities. My impression is that actual cases reported to be of multiple personality typically involve a degree of shared access to information which is not characteristic of distinct persons; the multiple personalities typically speak the same language and (this is not independent of the shared linguistic abilities) have shared knowledge of general facts. Experience with severed corpus callosum and with various memory deficits, as in Alzheimer's disease, suggests that there may be no well-defined threshold of integration (causal interconnectivity) at which one can say that above this threshold there is a single mind and below it there are two or none. Experience specifically with the split brains demonstrates the contingency of the character and count of minds upon causal features of the underlying system.

From the fact that there is a single physical system, then, nothing follows about the number of minds which the system might realize. Depending on the causal character of the system, it might realize no minds, one mind, or more than one mind. This is the case whether the system employs neurons, as in humans, entire humans, as in the Chinese Room, or programmed computers, as in AI. As a result, Searle's Chinese Room argument shows nothing about the possibilities of artificial intelligence.

## NOTES

1. This represents a rejection of the position I took several years ago in Cole (1984).

2. I defend Searle against several other criticisms, advanced by Philip Cam, in a paper in the *Australasian Journal of Philosophy* (September 1991).

3. See Cole 1984.

4. A similar point is made in the Searle-Churchlands debate in *Scientific American*. (See Churchland and Churchland 1990 and Searle 1990.)

5. The derivation should be by whatever causal process that can preserve the representational properties of the brain states of the original biological persons. Xeroxing preserves the representational properties of written information; so does conversion to electronic media. The analogous process for brains might be as detailed as a digitized functional equivalent of the entire brain—a neural net—or (more plausibly) a functional equivalent at a higher level of analysis, such as would be provided by an exhaustive intellectual and personality

inventory. However, the former might well be technically simpler and more expeditious, just as xerographic copies are more easily obtained than paraphrases or translations.

6. As some readers have suggested, one could avoid the incompatible properties problem by attributing understanding to *parts* of the program, with Chinese understanding and Korean understanding attributed to different parts. This tack raises problematic issues concerning the identity conditions of programs, some of which are currently being explored by the courts. In a nutshell, my response is that programs are abstract, but not as abstract as persons. Since it is a person who understands, and the same person can be realized by distinct programs, the understanding person is not identical with the program. This reasoning parallels the standard functionalist objections to identifying a person with his/her body. These considerations are set out in this paper in the section below on the 'systems reply'. I believe the reasoning was interestingly anticipated by Descartes in his argument for The Real Difference between mind and body, but that topic is beyond the scope of this paper.

7. See, for example, Smolensky: "We can view the top-level conscious processor of individual people as a *virtual machine— the conscious rule interpreter*—and we can view cultural knowledge as a program that runs on that machine" (1988, p. 4). While I treat distinct persons realized by a single body as virtual persons, Smolensky views a single person as a collection of virtual machines.

8. My thanks to an anonymous referee for this point. The referee goes on to remark, in support of my main point about the locus of understanding, that "nobody ever suggests that the LISP interpreter 'understands' the application the LISP program encodes."

## REFERENCES

American Psychiatric Association: 1987, *Diagnostic and Statistical Manual of Mental Disorders,* Vol. III, American Psychiatric Association, Washington D.C.

Anderson, David: 1987, 'Is the Chinese Room the Real Thing?', *Philosophy* 62, 389–93.

Braun, B. G.: 1984, 'Toward a Theory of Multiple Personality and Other Dissociative Phenomena', *Symposium on Multiple Personality, Psychiatric Clinics of North America* Saunders, Philadelphia, Vol. 7, pp. 171–93.

Cam, Philip: 1990, 'Searle on Strong AI', *Australasian Journal of Philosophy* 68, 103–08.

Churchland, Paul M. and Patricia Smith Churchland: 1990, 'Could a Machine Think?', *Scientific American* January, 32–37.

Carleton, Lawrence: 1984, 'Programs, Language Understanding and Searle', *Synthese* 59, 219–30.

Cole, David: 1984, 'Thought and Thought Experiments', *Philosophical Studies* 45, 431–44.

Cole, David: 1990, 'Cognitive Inquiry and the Philosophy of Mind', in Cole, Fetzer and Rankin (eds.).

Cole, David: 1991, 'Artificial Minds: Cam on Searle', *Australasian Journal of Philosophy* 69(3).

Cole, David, James Fetzer, and Terry Rankin (eds.): 1990, *Philosophy, Mind, and Cognitive Inquiry*, Kluwer Academic Publishers, Dordrecht.

Cole, David and Robert Foelber: 1984, 'Contingent Materialism', *Pacific Philosophical Quarterly* 65, 74–85.

Double, Richard: 1983, 'Searle, Programs and Functionalism', *Nature and System* 5, 107–14.

Dretske, Fred: 1985, 'Machines and the Mental', Presidential Address delivered before the Central Division of the American Philosophical Association (reprinted in Cole, Fetzer & Rankin (eds.)).

Fields, C. A.: 1984, 'Double on Searle's Chinese Room', *Nature and System* 6, 51–54.

Grice, H. Paul: 1941, 'Personal Identity', *Mind* 50, 330–50.

Lewis, David: 1976, 'Survival and Identity', in A. E. Rorty (ed.), *The Identities of Persons*, University of California Press, Berkeley.

Maloney, J. Christopher: 1987, 'The Right Stuff', *Synthese* 70, 349–72.

Perry, John (ed.): 1975, *Personal Identity*, University of California Press, Berkeley.

Perry, John: 1978, *A Dialogue on Personal Identity and Immortality*, Hackett Publishing Company, Indianapolis.

Quinton, A. M.: 1962, 'The Soul', *Journal of Philosophy* 59, 393–409 (reprinted in Perry 1975).

Rapaport, William J.: 1986, 'Searle's Experiments with Thought', *Philosophy of Science* 53, 271–79.

Rapaport, William J.: 1988, 'Syntactic Semantics', in James Fetzer (ed.), *Aspects of Artificial Intelligence*, Kluwer Academic Publishers, Dordrecht.

Rapaport, William J.: 1988, 'Review of John Searle's *Minds, Brains and Science*', *Nous* XXII, 585–609.

Rapaport, William J.: 1990, 'Computer Processes and Virtual Persons: Comments on Cole's 'Artificial Intelligence and Personal Identity', Technical Report 90–13, Department of Computer Science, State University of New York at Buffalo.

Rey, Georges: 1986, 'What's Really Going on in Searle's "Chinese Room" ', *Philosophical Studies* 50, 169–85.

Sarason, Irwin G. and Barbara R. Sarason: 1987, *Abnormal Psychology*, Prentice-Hall, Englewood Cliffs, NJ.

Searle, John: 1980, 'Minds, Brains and Programs', *Behavioral and Brain Sciences* 3, 417–57.

Searle, John: 1982, 'The Myth of the Computer', *New York Review of Books*, 29 April 1982, pp. 3–6.

Searle, John: 1984, *Minds, Brains and Science*, Harvard University Press, Cambridge MA.

Searle, John: 1990, 'Is the Brain's Mind a Computer Program?', *Scientific American* January, 26–31.

Sharvy, Richard: 1983, 'It Ain't the Meat, It's the Motion', *Inquiry* 26, 125–31.

Smolensky, Paul: 1988, 'On the Proper Treatment of Connectionism', *Behavioral and Brain Sciences* 11(1), 1–74 (reprinted in Cole, Fetzer and Rankin (eds.)).

Whitmer, Jeffrey: 1983, 'Intentionality, Artificial Intelligence and the Causal Powers of the Brain', *Auslegung* 10, 194–210, 214–17.

**READING 27**

# Of Identity and Diversity

*John Locke*

*John Locke (1632–1704) was one of England's most in-fluential philosophers. He was the first major figure in the philosophical school known as British empiricism and a persuasive advocate of liberal democracy. Locke was a friend of Robert Boyle and Isaac Newton and served as personal physician to the first Earl of Shaftesbury. Like Shaftesbury, Locke was a Whig and opposed to the Stuart monarchy. On Shaftesbury's death, Locke moved to Hol-land, returning to England only after Charles II had been deposed by William and Mary in the Glorious Revolution of 1688. Locke's best known works,* An Essay Concern-ing Human Understanding *and* Two Treatises of Government, *were both published in 1690. "Of Identity and Diversity" first appeared in the second edition of the* Essay *published in 1694 and is here reproduced from the abridged version edited by John Yolton.*

CHAPTER XXVII. OF IDENTITY AND DI-VERSITY.

9. . . . to find wherein *personal identity* consists, we must consider what *person* stands for; which, I think, is a thinking intelligent being that has reason and re-flection and can consider itself as itself, the same thinking thing in different times and places; which it does only by that consciousness which is inseparable from thinking and, as it seems to me, essential to it: it being impossible for anyone to perceive without per-ceiving that he does perceive. When we see, hear, smell, taste, feel, meditate, or will anything, we know that we do so. Thus it is always as to our present sen-sations and perceptions, and by this everyone is to himself that which he calls *self:* it not being consid-ered in this case whether the same *self* be continued in the same or divers substances. For since conscious-

ness always accompanies thinking, and it is that which makes everyone to be what he calls *self*, and thereby distinguishes himself from all other thinking things: in this alone consists *personal identity*, i.e. the sameness of a rational being. And as far as this con-sciousness can be extended backwards to any past ac-tion or thought, so far reaches the identity of that *person:* it is the same *self* now it was then, and it is by the same *self* with this present one that now reflects on it, that that action was done.

10. But it is further inquired whether it be the same identical substance? This, few would think they had reason to doubt of, if these perceptions, with their consciousness, always remained present in the mind whereby the same thinking thing would be al-ways consciously present and, as would be thought, evidently the same to itself. But that which seems to make the difficulty is this: that this consciousness be-ing interrupted always by forgetfulness, there being no moment of our lives wherein we have the whole train of all our past actions before our eyes in one view, but even the best memories losing the sight of one part whilst they are viewing another; and we sometimes, and that the greatest part of our lives, not reflecting on our past selves, being intent on our present thoughts, and in sound sleep having no thoughts at all, or at least none with that conscious-ness which remarks our waking thoughts; I say, in all these cases, our consciousness being interrupted, and we losing the sight of our past *selves*, doubts are raised whether we are the same thinking thing, i.e. the same substance, or no. Which, however reason-able or unreasonable, concerns not *personal identity* at all: the question being what makes the same *person*, and not whether it be the same identical substance, which always thinks in the same person; which, in this case, matters not at all: different substances, by the same consciousness (where they do partake in it)

SOURCE: From *An Essay Concerning Human Understanding*, 2nd edition (1694), Book II, Chapter 27. From the abridged edition by John W. Yolton (London: Everyman's Library, 1976): 162–171.

being united into one person, as well as different bodies by the same life are united into one animal, whose *identity* is preserved in that change of substances by the unity of one continued life. For, it being the same consciousness that makes a man be himself to himself, *personal identity* depends on that only, whether it be annexed solely to one individual substance, or can be continued in a succession of several substances. For as far as any intelligent being can repeat the *idea* of any past action with the same consciousness it had of it at first, and with the same consciousness it has of any present action, so far it is the same *personal self.* For it is by the consciousness it has of its present thoughts and actions that it is *self* to *itself* now, and so will be the same *self* as far as the same consciousness can extend to actions past or to come, and would be by distance of time or change of substance no more two *persons* than a man be two men by wearing other clothes today than he did yesterday, with a long or a short sleep between: the same consciousness uniting those distant actions into the same *person,* whatever substances contributed to their production.

11. That this is so, we have some kind of evidence in our very bodies, all whose particles, whilst vitally united to this same thinking conscious self so that we feel when they are touched and are affected by and conscious of good or harm that happens to them, are a part of our *selves;* i.e. of our thinking conscious *self.* Thus, the limbs of his body are to everyone a part of *himself;* he sympathizes and is concerned for them. Cut off a hand, and thereby separate it from that consciousness he had of its heat, cold, and other affections, and it is then no longer a part of that which is *himself,* any more than the remotest part of matter. Thus, we see the *substance* whereof *personal self* consisted at one time may be varied at another, without the change of personal *identity:* there being no question about the same person, though the limbs, which but now were a part of it, be cut off.

12. But the question is whether, if the same substance, which thinks, be changed, it can be the same person, or, remaining the same, it can be different persons.

And to this I answer, first, this can be no question at all to those who place thought in a purely material animal constitution, void of an immaterial substance. For, whether their supposition be true or no, it is plain they conceive personal identity preserved in something else than identity of substance, as animal identity is preserved in identity of life and not of substance. And therefore those who place thinking in an immaterial substance only, before they can come to deal with these men, must show why personal identity cannot be preserved in the change of immaterial substances, or variety of particular immaterial substances, as well as animal identity is preserved in the change of material substances, or variety of particular bodies: unless they will say, it is one immaterial spirit that makes the same life in brutes, as it is one immaterial spirit that makes the same person in men; which the *Cartesians* at least will not admit, for fear of making brutes thinking things too.

13. But next, as to the first part of the question, whether, if the same thinking substance (supposing immaterial substances only to think) be changed, it can be the same person, I answer: That cannot be resolved but by those who know what kind of substances they are that do think, and whether the consciousness of past actions can be transferred from one thinking substance to another. I grant, were the same consciousness the same individual action, it could not; but, it being a present representation of a past action, why it may not be possible that that may be represented to the mind to have been which really never was, will remain to be shown. And therefore how far the consciousness of past actions is annexed to any individual agent, so that another cannot possibly have it, will be hard for us to determine, till we know what kind of action it is that cannot be done without a reflex act of perception accompanying it, and how performed by thinking substances, who cannot think without being conscious of it. But that which we call the *same consciousness* not being the same individual act, why one intellectual substance may not have represented to it, as done by itself, what it never did, and was perhaps done by some other agent: why, I say, such a representation may not possibly be without reality of matter of fact, as well as several representations in dreams are, which yet whilst dreaming we take for true, will be difficult to conclude from the nature of things. And that it never is so will by us, till we have clearer views of the nature of thinking substances, be best resolved into the goodness of God, who, as far as the happiness or misery of any of his sensible creatures is concerned in it, will not, by a fatal error of theirs, transfer from one to another that consciousness which draws reward or punishment with it. How

far this may be an argument against those who would place thinking in a system of fleeting animal spirits, I leave to be considered. But yet, to return to the question before us, it must be allowed that, if the same consciousness (which, as has been shown, is quite a different thing from the same numerical figure or motion in body) can be transferred from one thinking substance to another, it will be possible that two thinking substances may make but one person. For the same consciousness being preserved, whether in the same or different substances, the personal identity is preserved.

14. As to the second part of the question, whether, the same immaterial substance remaining, there may be two distinct persons, which question seems to me to be built on this: whether the same immaterial being, being conscious of the actions of its past duration, may be wholly stripped of all the consciousness of its past existence and lose it beyond the power of ever retrieving again and so, as it were beginning a new account from a new period, have a consciousness that cannot reach beyond this new state. All those who hold pre-existence are evidently of this mind, since they allow the soul to have no remaining consciousness of what it did in that pre-existent state, either wholly separate from body, or informing any other body; and if they should not, it is plain experience would be against them. So that, personal identity reaching no further than consciousness reaches, a pre-existent spirit, not having continued so many ages in a state of silence, must needs make different persons. Suppose a *Christian Platonist,* or *Pythagorean* should, upon God's having ended all his works of creation the seventh day, think his soul hath existed ever since, and should imagine it has revolved in several human bodies, as I once met with one who was persuaded his had been the soul of *Socrates* (how reasonably I will not dispute; this I know, that in the post he filled, which was no inconsiderable one, he passed for a very rational man, and the press has shown that he wanted not parts or learning); would anyone say that he, being not conscious of any of *Socrates's* actions or thoughts, could be the same person with *Socrates*? Let anyone reflect upon himself and conclude that he has in himself an immaterial spirit, which is that which thinks in him and in the constant change of his body keeps him the same and is that which he calls himself; let him also suppose it to be the same soul that was in *Nestor* or *Thersites* at the siege of *Troy* (for souls being, as far as

we know anything of them, in their nature indifferent to any parcel of matter, the supposition has no apparent absurdity in it), which it may have been, as well as it is now the soul of any other man; but he now having no consciousness of any of the actions either of *Nestor* or *Thersites*, does or can he conceive himself the same person with either of them? Can he be concerned in either of their actions, attribute them to himself, or think them his own, more than the actions of any other men that ever existed? So that, this consciousness not reaching to any of the actions of either of those men, he is no more one *self* with either of them than if the soul or immaterial spirit that now informs him had been created and began to exist, when it began to inform his present body, though it were ever so true that the same spirit that informed *Nestor's* or *Thersites's* body were numerically the same that now informs his. For this would no more make him the same person with *Nestor* than if some of the particles of matter that were once a part of *Nestor* were now a part of this man: the same immaterial substance, without the same consciousness, no more making the same person by being united to any body than the same particle of matter, without consciousness, united to any body, makes the same person. But let him once find himself conscious of any of the actions of *Nestor,* he then finds himself the same person with *Nestor*.

15. And thus we may be able, without any difficulty, to conceive the same person at the resurrection, though in a body not exactly in make or parts the same which he had here, the same consciousness going along with the soul that inhabits it. But yet the soul alone, in the change of bodies, would scarce, to anyone but to him that makes the soul the *man,* be enough to make the same *man*. For should the soul of a prince, carrying with it the consciousness of the prince's past life, enter and inform the body of a cobbler as soon as deserted by his own soul, everyone sees he would be the same person with the prince, accountable only for the prince's actions; but who would say it was the same man? The body too goes to the making the man and would, I guess, to everybody, determine the man in this case, wherein the soul, with all its princely thoughts about it, would not make another man: but he would be the same cobbler to everyone besides himself. I know that in the ordinary way of speaking, the same person and the same man stand for one and the same thing. And indeed, everyone will always have a liberty to speak

as he pleases and to apply what articulate sounds to what *ideas* he thinks fit, and change them as often as he pleases. But yet when we will inquire what makes the same *spirit, man,* or *person,* we must fix the *ideas* of *spirit, man,* or *person* in our minds; and having resolved with ourselves what we mean by them, it will not be hard to determine in either of them or the like when it is the *same* and when not.

16. But though the same immaterial substance or soul does not alone, wherever it be, and in whatsoever state, make the same man: yet, it is plain, consciousness, as far as ever it can be extended, should it be to ages past, unites existences and actions very remote in time into the same person, as well as it does the existences and actions of the immediately preceding moment, so that whatever has the consciousness of present and past actions is the same person to whom they both belong. Had I the same consciousness that I saw the ark and *Noah's* flood as that I saw an overflowing of the *Thames* last winter, or as that I write now, I could no more doubt that I that write this now, that saw the *Thames* overflowed last winter, and that viewed the flood at the general deluge, was the same *self,* place that *self* in what substance you please, than I that write this am the same *myself* now whilst I write (whether I consist of all the same substance, material or immaterial, or no) that I was yesterday. For as to this point of being the same *self,* it matters not whether this present *self* be made up of the same or other substances, I being as much concerned and as justly accountable for any action that was done a thousand years since, appropriated to me now by this self-consciousness, as I am for what I did the last moment.

17. *Self* is that conscious thinking thing (whatever substance made up of, whether spiritual or material, simple or compounded, it matters not) which is sensible or conscious of pleasure and pain, capable of happiness or misery, and so is concerned for *itself,* as far as that consciousness extends. Thus everyone finds that, whilst comprehended under that consciousness, the little finger is as much a part of *itself* as what is most so. Upon separation of this little finger, should this consciousness go along with the little finger and leave the rest of the body, it is evident the little finger would be the *person,* the *same person;* and self then would have nothing to do with the rest of the body. As in this case it is the consciousness that goes along with the substance, when one part is separate from another, which makes the same *person* and

constitutes this inseparable *self:* so it is in reference to substance remote in time. That with which the *consciousness* of this present thinking thing can join itself makes the same *person* and is one *self* with it, and with nothing else, and so attributes to *itself* and owns all the actions of that thing as its own, as far as that consciousness reaches, and no further; as everyone who reflects will perceive.

18. In this *personal identity* is founded all the right and justice of reward and punishment: happiness and misery being that for which everyone is concerned for *himself,* and not mattering what becomes of any substance not joined to or affected with that consciousness. For, as it is evident in the instance I gave but now, if the consciousness went along with the little finger when it was cut off, that would be the same *self* which was concerned for the whole body yesterday, as making part of *itself,* whose actions then it cannot but admit as its own now. Though, if the same body should still live and immediately from the separation of the little finger have its own peculiar consciousness, whereof the little finger knew nothing, it would not at all be concerned for it as a part of *itself,* or could own any of its actions, or have any of them imputed to him.

19. This may show us wherein *personal identity* consists: not in the identity of substance but, as I have said, in the identity of *consciousness,* wherein, if *Socrates* and the present mayor of *Queenborough* agree, they are the same person; if the same *Socrates* waking and sleeping do not partake of the same *consciousness, Socrates* waking and sleeping is not the same person. And to punish *Socrates* waking for what sleeping *Socrates* thought, and waking *Socrates* was never conscious of, would be no more of right than to punish one twin for what his brother-twin did, whereof he knew nothing, because their outsides were so like that they could not be distinguished; for such twins have been seen.

20. But yet possibly it will still be objected, suppose I wholly lose the memory of some parts of my life beyond a possibility of retrieving them, so that perhaps I shall never be conscious of them again: yet am I not the same person that did those actions, had those thoughts that I once was conscious of, though I have now forgot them? To which I answer that we must here take notice what the word *I* is applied to, which, in this case, is the man only. And the same man being presumed to be the same person, *I* is easily here supposed to stand also for the same person.

But if it be possible for the same man to have distinct incommunicable consciousness at different times, it is past doubt the same man would at different times make different persons; which, we see, is the sense of mankind in the solemnest declaration of their opinions, human laws not punishing the *mad man* for the *sober man's* actions, nor the *sober man* for what the *mad man* did, thereby making them two persons: which is somewhat explained by our way of speaking in *English* when we say such an one *is not himself*, or is *beside himself*; in which phrases it is insinuated, as if those who now, or at least first used them, thought that *self* was changed, the *self*-same person was no longer in that man.

21. But yet it is hard to conceive that *Socrates*, the same individual man, should be two persons. To help us a little in this, we must consider what is meant by *Socrates* or the same individual *man*.

*First*, it must be either the same individual, immaterial, thinking substance; in short, the same numerical soul, and nothing else.

*Secondly*, or the same animal, without any regard to an immaterial soul.

*Thirdly*, or the same immaterial spirit united to the same animal.

Now, take which of these suppositions you please, it is impossible to make personal identity to consist in anything but consciousness, or reach any further than that does.

For, by the first of them, it must be allowed possible that a man born of different women, and in distant times, may be the same man. A way of speaking which, whoever admits, must allow it possible for the same man to be two distinct persons, as any two that have lived in different ages without the knowledge of one another's thoughts.

By the second and third, *Socrates*, in this life and after it, cannot be the same man any way but by the same consciousness; and so, making *human identity* to consist in the same thing wherein we place *personal identity*, there will be no difficulty to allow the same man to be the same person. But then they who place *human identity* in consciousness only, and not in something else, must consider how they will make the infant *Socrates* the same man with *Socrates* after the resurrection. But whatsoever to some men makes a *man*, and consequently the same individual man, wherein perhaps few are agreed, personal identity can by us be placed in nothing but consciousness (which is that alone which makes what we call *self*), without involving us in great absurdities.

22. But is not a man drunk and sober the same person, why else is he punished for the fact he commits when drunk, though he be never afterwards conscious of it? Just as much the same person as a man that walks and does other things in his sleep is the same person and is answerable for any mischief he shall do in it. Human laws punish both, with a justice suitable to their way of knowledge; because, in these cases, they cannot distinguish certainly what is real, what counterfeit; and so the ignorance in drunkenness or sleep is not admitted as a plea. For, though punishment be annexed to personality, and personality to consciousness, and the drunkard perhaps be not conscious of what he did, yet human judicatures justly punish him, because the fact is proved against him, but want of consciousness cannot be proved for him. But in the Great Day, wherein the secrets of all hearts shall be laid open, it may be reasonable to think no one shall be made to answer for what he knows nothing of, but shall receive his doom [ed., judgment], his conscience accusing or excusing him.

23. Nothing but consciousness can unite remote existences into the same person: the identity of substance will not do it; for whatever substance there is however framed, without consciousness there is no person; and a carcass may be a person, as well as any sort of substance be so, without consciousness.

Could we suppose two distinct incommunicable consciousnesses acting the same body, the one constantly by day, the other by night; and, on the other side, the same consciousness acting by intervals, two distinct bodies: I ask, in the first case, whether the *day-* and the *night-man* would not be two as distinct persons as *Socrates* and *Plato*? And whether, in the second case, there would not be one person in two distinct bodies, as much as one man is the same in two distinct clothings? Nor is it at all material to say that this same and this distinct *consciousness*, in the cases above mentioned, is owing to the same and distinct immaterial substances, bringing it with them to those bodies; which, whether true or no, alters not the case, since it is evident the *personal identity* would equally be determined by the consciousness, whether that consciousness were annexed to some individual immaterial substance or no. For, granting that the thinking substance in man must be necessarily supposed immaterial, it is evident that immaterial thinking thing may sometimes part with its past consciousness and be restored to it again, as appears in the forgetfulness men often have of their past actions; and the mind many times recovers the memory of a past consciousness, which it had lost for twenty years together. Make these intervals of memory and forgetfulness to take their turns regularly by day and night, and you have two persons with the same immaterial spirit, as much as in the former instance two persons with the same body. So that *self* is not determined by identity or diversity of substance, which it cannot be sure of, but only by identity of consciousness.

26. *Person,* as I take it, is the name for this *self.* Wherever a man finds what he calls *himself,* there, I think, another may say is the *same person.* It is a forensic term, appropriating actions and their merit, and so belongs only to intelligent agents, capable of a law, and happiness and misery. This personality extends *itself* beyond present existence to what is past, only by consciousness; whereby it becomes concerned and accountable, owns and imputes to *itself* past actions, just upon the same ground and for the same reason that it does the present. All which is founded in a concern for happiness, the unavoidable concomitant of consciousness: that which is conscious of pleasure and pain desiring that that self that is conscious should be happy. And therefore whatever past actions it cannot reconcile or appropriate to that present *self* by consciousness, it can be no more concerned in than if they had never been done; and to receive pleasure or pain, i.e. reward or punishment, on the account of any such action, is all one as to be made happy or miserable in its first being, without any demerit at all. For supposing a man punished now for what he had done in another life, whereof he could be made to have no consciousness at all, what difference is there between that punishment and being created miserable? And therefore conformable to this, the Apostle tells us, that at the Great Day, when everyone shall *receive according to his doings, the secrets of all hearts shall be laid open.* The sentence shall be justified by the consciousness all persons shall have that they *themselves,* in what bodies soever they appear, or what substances soever that consciousness adheres to, are the *same* that committed those actions and deserve that punishment for them.

## READING 28

# Personal Identity: A Materialist's Account

*Sydney Shoemaker*

*Sydney Shoemaker (1931–   ) is Susan Linn Sage Professor of Philosophy at Cornell University. He has written many articles dealing with the problem of personal identity and other issues in metaphysics and philosophy of mind. He is the author of* Self-Knowledge and Self-Identity *(1963) and* Identity, Cause, and Mind *(1984) and joint author, with Richard Swinburne, of* Personal Identity *(1984), from which this reading is taken.*

### 10. THE BRAIN-STATE TRANSFER DEVICE

. . . A number of philosophers have envisaged the possibility of a device which records the state of one brain and imposes that state on a second brain by restructuring it so that it has exactly the state the first brain had at the beginning of the operation.[1] We will suppose that this process obliterates the first brain, or at any rate obliterates its current state. Discussions of this example usually proceed on the assumption that mental states are at least 'supervenient' on brain states, which means that creatures cannot differ in their mental states without differing in their brain states, and therefore that the 'recipient' of a total brain-state transfer would have exactly the same mental states the 'donor' had immediately before. Philosophers who have discussed this sort of case have differed in their intuitions as to whether the brain-state transfer would amount to a person's changing bodies—whether, as I shall put it, the procedure would be 'person-preserving'. Some think it would. Others think that it would amount to killing the original person and at the same time creating (or converting someone into) a psychological duplicate of him.

Initially, I think, most people are inclined to take the latter view. But one can tell a story which enhances the plausibility of the former view. Imagine a society living in an environment in which an increase in some sort of radiation has made it impossible for a human body to remain healthy for more than a few years. Being highly advanced technologically, the society has developed the following procedure for dealing with this. For each person there is a stock of duplicate bodies, cloned from cells taken from that person and grown by an accelerated process in a radiation-proof vault, where they are then stored. Periodically a person goes into the hospital for a 'body-change'. This consists in his total brain-state being transferred to the brain of one of his duplicate bodies. At the end of the procedure the original body is incinerated. We are to imagine that in this society going in for a body-change is as routine an occurrence as going to have one's teeth cleaned is in ours. It is taken for granted by everyone that the procedure is person-preserving. One frequently hears remarks like 'I can't meet you for lunch on Tuesday, because that is the day for my body-change; let's make it Wednesday instead'. All of the social practices of the society presuppose that the procedure is person-preserving. The brain-state recipient is regarded as owning the property of the brain-state donor, as being married to the donor's spouse, and as holding whatever offices, responsibilities, rights, obligations, etc. the brain-state donor held. If it is found that the brain-state donor had committed a crime, everyone regards it as just that the brain-state recipient should be punished for it.

Let us suppose, for now, that materialism is true; the world does not contain any non-material substances, and all of the entities in it are composed exclusively of the entities recognized by physics. The members of my hypothetical society know this, and

[1]See Williams 1970, p. 162, and Nozick 1981, p. 39.

SOURCE: From S. Shoemaker and R. Swinburne, *Personal Identity* (Oxford: Basil Blackwell, 1984). Edited. Sections 10 (108–111), 12 (115–118), 13 (119–121), and 16 (130–132).

they know precisely what happens, physically speaking, in the brain-state transfer procedure (for short, the BST-procedure). There is no clear sense in which they can be said to be mistaken about a matter of fact in regarding the procedure as person-preserving. If we confronted such a society, there would, I think, be a very strong case for saying that what *they* mean by 'person' is such that the BST-procedure *is* person-preserving (using 'person' in *their* sense). And, what goes with this, it would be very hard to maintain that they are being irrational when, being under no misconception concerning matters of fact, they willingly submit themselves to the BST-procedure. But there would also be a strong reason for saying that what they mean by 'person' is what we mean by it; they call the same things persons, offer the same sorts of characterizations of what sorts of things persons are, and attach the same kinds of social consequences to judgements of personal identity—i.e., personal identity has with them the same connections with moral responsibility, ownership of property, etc. as it does with us. But if they are right in thinking that the BST-procedure is person-preserving, and if they mean the same by 'person' as we do, then it seems that *we* ought to regard the BST-procedure as person-preserving.

A variety of objections have been raised against the view that anything like the BST-procedure could be person-preserving, and some of these would also apply, if valid, to the view that the brain-transplant procedure . . . could be person-preserving. Some of these will be discussed in the following sections. Here I want to consider the bearing of this example on the question of whether a materialist view of mind requires personal identity to be realized in the identity of some sort of physical body.

On the face of it, if one allows that the BST-procedure is person-preserving, one must hold that the answer to this question is 'no'. For the BST-procedure does not involve the transfer of any bodily organ, or of any matter at all, from the one body to the other. All that is transferred, it is natural to say, is 'information'. If we have personal identity here, it is apparently not carried by the identity of any body. Yet it seems clear that one is not committed to dualism, or the rejection of materialism, in holding that the procedure is person-preserving; on the contrary, the plausibility of holding the latter seems to depend on the materialist assumption that mental states are re-

alized in, or at least supervenient on, states of the brain.

But how can this be reconciled with my claim in section 9 that the physical realization of a mental state requires the existence of a physical 'mechanism' whereby it stands, or is capable of standing, in the functionally appropriate causal relations to other mental states of the same person, including its successor states? I think that what one must say, if one allows that the BST-procedure would be person-preserving, is that in the circumstances I have imagined the mechanism in which the mental states of a person are realized does not include just the person's body or brain; it also includes the BST-device, and perhaps the social institutions that govern its use. For it is in virtue of the existence of all this that mental states existing immediately before a body-change produce the functionally appropriate successor states. What one has here is a nonstandard (relative to us) way of realizing mental states and the relation of copersonality, one that relies for the most part on the mechanism in which these are realized in us, but which supplements these with an additional mechanism. The mechanism as a whole does not consist in any *single* physical body, or even depend on any single one (for the BST-device could wear out and be replaced several times during a person's lifetime). Thus it is that we have personal identity without the identity of any body, even though nothing non-physical is involved.

## 12. THE DUPLICATION OBJECTION

A common objection to the view that something like the BST-procedure could be person-preserving goes along the following lines. It might happen that the BST-device misfunctions, and produces the states of brain A in brain B without obliterating those states in brain A, or produces these states not only in brain B but also in brain C. If this happened the post-transfer possessor of brain B could not be identical to the pre-transfer possessor of brain A—or at any rate, he could not be so simply in virtue of his psychological continuity with that person. But surely (it is said), whether a person X at time $t_2$ is identical to person Y existing at an earlier time $t_1$ cannot depend on whether there happens to be another person Z whose state at $t_2$ is related to Y's state at $t_1$ in the same way that X's state at $t_2$ is related to it. So even if the machine functions properly, and there is no duplication, the post-transfer possessor of brain B cannot be identical to the pre-transfer possessor of brain A in virtue of his psychological continuity with him.[2]

One could meet this objection just by stipulating that the BST-procedure is such as to make such duplication nomologically impossible—it essentially depends on the states of the original brain being obliterated, and is such that the states can be transferred to only one brain. But I shall not rely on such a stipulation. Let us suppose that duplication of the sort envisaged is nomologically possible, and that only the vigilance of the operators of the BST-device prevents it from happening.

The duplication objection cannot be that the psychological continuity account of personal identity (which is presupposed by the view that the BST-procedure is person-preserving) has the absurd consequence that both post-transfer duplicates (the A-brain person and the B-brain person, or the A-brain person and the C-brain person) are identical to the original A-brain person. We guarded the account against that objection by having it say, not that personal identity consists in psychological continuity *simpliciter*, but that it consists in *non-branching* psychological continuity. The objection is rather that this way of guarding against that absurd consequence makes the identity depend on something it cannot depend on. Later on (in section 16) I will concede something (not much) to the duplication objection. Here I want to reveal the extent to which it rests on confusion.

Suppose that the BST-device functions correctly, and that after the transfer only brain B has the states that brain A had immediately before the transfer. Let 'Smith' name the pre-transfer A-brain person, and let 'George' name the post-transfer B-brain person. It might appear that my version of the psychological continuity account, with its 'non-branching' provision, commits us to saying the following: since there was no branching in the psychologically continuous series of person-stages connecting Smith before the transfer and George after the transfer, George and Smith are the same person; but the BST-device could have misfunctioned and left brain A unaffected, in which case Smith and George would have been different persons. Now this would be an absurd

consequence. If Smith and George are in fact one and the same person, they are necessarily the same, and there is no possible circumstance in which they are different persons.[3] But it is a confusion to think that this absurd consequence follows from the non-branching psychological continuity view (together with the assumption that the BST-device in fact functioned correctly, but could have misfunctioned in the way envisaged).

What does follow is this: in fact the post-transfer B-brain person is identical to the pre-transfer A-brain person, but if the BST-device had misfunctioned in the way envisaged, the post-transfer B-brain person would not have been the pre-transfer A-brain person. This does not offend against the principle that identity holds necessarily if at all, and it is analogous to the following observation (which is true on one natural reading of it): in fact the president of the US in 1982 is the only former governor of California who began his career as a movie actor, but if Carter had received a lot more votes then the president of the US in 1982 would not have been that former governor. The crucial difference here is that whereas names like 'George' and 'Smith' are what Saul Kripke has called 'rigid designators', and have the same reference in talk about hypothetical or counterfactual situations ('other possible worlds') as they do in talk about the actual situation, definite descriptions like 'the post-transfer B-body person' and 'the president of the US in 1982' are not rigid designators.[4] It is only identity statements whose terms are rigid designators that have to be necessarily true if true at all, and so cannot be such that they are true but might have been false. It is not possible that George should have failed to be Smith; what is possible (on the non-branching psychological continuity view) is that George (i.e., Smith) should not have been the post-transfer B-brain person, either because he failed to survive the transfer or because he survived it as the post-transfer A-brain person. If either of the latter possibilities had been realized, the post-transfer B-brain person would have been somebody else—perhaps somebody who was created (with a set of memories corresponding to George's past) by the BST-procedure.

[2]For this general sort of objection, see Williams 1957–58. For a recent formulation, see Wiggins 1980, pp. 95–6.

[3]Here I assume the truth of Saul Kripke's view that identity propositions having names as terms are necessarily true if true at all. See Kripke 1980.
[4]See Kripke 1980.

In part, I think, the duplication objection is the result of a failure to distinguish rigid and non-rigid designators and their roles in identity statements. But it has other sources as well. One of these, which comes out in a version of the duplication objection raised by Richard Swinburne, is connected with one of the central issues about personal identity.[5]

Recall the 'fission' example of section 4 which involves the transplantation of the two hemispheres of someone's brain into two different bodies. Swinburne envisages a theory of personal identity which holds (as indeed our psychological continuity theory seems to do) that whether the post-operative owner of one hemisphere is identical to the original person depends on whether the transplantation of the other hemisphere 'takes'. One of his objections to this is the one we have already answered. He thinks that such a view has the absurd consequence that 'Who I am depends on whether you exist' (1973–74, p. 236). Now there is a perfectly good sense in which 'who I am' *can* depend on whether you exist; e.g., whether I am the heir to someone's fortune may depend on this (if his will stipulates that I inherit only if you no longer exist). What cannot depend on whether you exist is whether I am identical to some particular person. But the theory in question does not imply that there could be such a dependence. To be sure, if I am the post-operative possessor of the left brain hemisphere, then in order to establish whether I am identical to the original person I might have to establish whether the transplantation of the right hemisphere was successful. But suppose that it was in fact successful (and the post-operative possessor of the right hemisphere is you). In that case neither of us is identical to the original person. And it would be wrong to say that if the other half-brain transplantation had failed, then I would have been the original person; one should say instead that if it had failed *I* would not exist (although there would exist someone with this body and these memories). If we suppose instead that the actual situation is that in which the other transplant failed, and in which I am identical to the original person (according to our theory), then the true counterfactual is not that if the other transplant had succeeded I would not have been the original person, but that in that case I (= the original person) would no longer exist.

[5]See Swinburne 1973–74.

But Swinburne says that the view in question has a second absurd consequence, namely that

> The way for a man to ensure his own survival is to ensure the non-existence of future persons too similar to himself. Suppose the mad surgeon had told $P_1$ before the operation what he was intending to do . . . $P_1$ is unable to escape the clutches of the mad surgeon, but is nevertheless very anxious to survive the operation. If the empiricist theory in question is correct there is an obvious policy which will guarantee his survival. He can bribe one of the nurses to ensure that the right half-brain does *not* survive successfully. (1973–74, p. 237)

I think that it can be agreed that it does seem absurd for $P_1$ to try to guarantee his survival by bribing the nurse. But I think that it is not absurd for the reason Swinburne thinks it is.

## 13. SURVIVAL AND THE IMPORTANCE OF IDENTITY

What is at stake here is what it is that we really care about when we care about our own survival and our own future well-being. Swinburne makes the natural assumption that when I want to survive it is essential to the satisfaction of my want that I, the very person who is now wanting this, should exist in the future. But this can be questioned.

Consider another variant of our half-brain transplant case. Suppose that half of my brain and all of the rest of my body are ridden with cancer, and that my only hope for survival is for my healthy half-brain to be transplanted to another body. There are two transplantation procedures available. The first, which is inexpensive and safe (so far as the prospects of the recipient are concerned) involves first transplanting the healthy hemisphere and then destroying (or allowing to die) the diseased hemisphere that remains. The other, which is expensive and risky (the transplant may not take, or it may produce a psychologically damaged person) involves first destroying the diseased hemisphere and then transplanting the other. Which shall I choose? Notice that if I choose the first procedure there will be, for a short while, two persons psychologically continuous with the original person (me), and therefore that on the non-branching psychological continuity theory the recipient of the healthy hemisphere cannot count as me. If I choose the second procedure, on the other hand, then at no point will the recipient (the post-operative possessor of the healthy hemisphere) have any 'competitor' for the status of being me, so it seems that he can count as me (if the transplantation takes). Should I therefore choose the expensive and risky procedure? This seems absurd. The thing to do is to choose the first procedure, even though (I think) it guarantees that the transplant recipient will not be me.

How can this be? Am I relying on some moral principle that requires one to so act as to maximize the number and well-being of future persons, independently of who those persons are, even if this involves sacrificing oneself? No. The reason is that whether the future person will be me is *in a case like this* of no importance to me. This is why I find it absurd for $P_1$ in Swinburne's example to bribe the nurse with the object of ensuring that the left half-brain recipient is himself; I see that if I were in $P_1$'s position, bribing the nurse would contribute nothing to giving me what I really want in wanting to survive.

Consider again our original fission case, in which both half-brain transplantations take and there are two later persons who are psychologically continuous with the owner of the original brain. How should the original person view the prospect of this? Let us suppose that he accepts the analysis according to which neither offshoot will be him (where 'be him' means 'be identical to him'). Does this mean that he must view the impending fission as his death and replacement by duplicates? Remember that the offshoots will be (and we can suppose him to know that they will be) psychologically continuous with him in all of the ways in which a person at one time is continuous with himself at other times. Not only will they remember his past; they will also be influenced by his intentions and motivated by his desires (or by desires which are 'successor states' of his pre-operative desires). For him now to deliberate about and plan their future careers would be just as efficacious as it is for a person to deliberate about and plan his own future career. Their future sufferings and delights, their prospects of success and failure, could not be a matter of indifference to him. Indeed, if his attitude towards these were not essentially like those a person normally has towards his own future sufferings, delights, successes and failures, then we would not have full psychological continuity between the original person and the offshoots.

Since cases of this sort do not occur, we are ill-equipped with language for talking about them. One

way of doing so, adopted by Derek Parfit, is to sever the connection between our current notion of survival and the concept of identity, and to speak of the original person as 'surviving as' both offshoots.[6] The rationale for doing this is that the attitudes that are appropriate in a case in which one believes that one will survive as a person of a certain description (fear of that person's suffering, hope for that person's success, etc.) are ones which a man could appropriately have towards the future states of both of his offshoots in a case of impending fission. But even if one does not want to call this survival, one can allow that it could be just as good (or, as the case might be, just as bad) as survival.

Considerations like these have led some philosophers to maintain that what matters in survival is not identity, *per se*, but the psychological continuity or connectedness which normally accompany and constitute it, namely when there is no branching.[7] This is not, certainly, the view that recommends itself to pre-analytic intuition. One's initial inclination is to say that if one cares especially about the future person who will be psychologically continuous with one, this is because one believes that that person will be oneself. What reflection on the fission case suggests is that it is just the other way around; one cares about the future person who will be oneself because (normally) it is that person who is psychologically continuous with one.[8]

To the extent that our having this concern is a contingent fact about us, the explanation of it no doubt lies in part in evolutionary considerations. But there is something ludicrous about the idea of a competition for survival between creatures having such a concern and otherwise similar creatures who totally lack it. For the latter are, I think, inconceivable. If a creature is enough like us to be capable of pleasure and pain, and be able to envisage future states of affairs at all, it will have some degree of future directed concern. Special circumstances aside, it is inconceivable that a creature should be indifferent to

---

[6]See Parfit 1971b.

[7]See Shoemaker 1970a, and Parfit 1971b. See also Perry 1976a.

[8]Several philosophers have proposed ways—which I have not the space to discuss here—of reconciling the claim that what we care about in survival is identity, with the intuition that if faced with the prospect of fission one would (or reasonably could) care about each offshoot as if it were oneself. See Perry 1972, Lewis 1976, and Nozick 1981, pp. 62–8.

its *present* pleasures and pains. But the future is continuous with the present; it is inconceivable that a creature should want its present pain to cease, or its present pleasure to continue, and yet be indifferent as to whether it has a qualitatively identical pain or pleasant experience a moment hence. It seems implicit in knowing what pain and pleasure are that (other things being equal, of course) one wants one's immediate future to be free of the one and to contain the other. To a certain extent, then, this special concern for one's own future well-being is built into the nature of human mental states.

## 16. THE DUPLICATION ARGUMENT REVISITED

. . . I think that we must acknowledge that our ordinary conception of personal identity, as reflected in our intuitions about possible cases, has a parochial element in it. This comes out in something I temporarily suppressed in my discussion of the duplication argument in section 12.

Consider again the case in which the BST-device misfunctions, and fails to erase the states of brain A when it records them and imposes identical states on brain B. In this case we are (I think) strongly inclined to say that Smith, the pre-transfer A-brain person, continues to exist with the same body and brain, and that the post-transfer B-brain person is simply a newly created duplicate of Smith. But this seems to conflict with the non-branching psychological continuity view; a proponent of that view seems to be obliged to say that since there has been a branching, neither the post-transfer A-brain person nor the post-transfer B-brain person is identical to Smith. What causes trouble here is the 'parochial' intuition that psychological continuity which is carried in the ordinary way by the brain takes precedence over psychological continuity mediated by the BST-procedure.

A way out of the difficulty would be to adopt the still more parochial view that the causal connections between earlier and later stages brought about by the BST-procedure are not causal connections 'of the appropriate kind' to yield memory and other sorts of psychological connectedness, and so do not give us psychological continuity of the relevant sort. This would amount to denying that this case counts as a case of 'branching'. But one cannot say this if one holds, as I am inclined to, that when the BST-device functions properly, and erases the states

of the 'donor' brain before imposing them on the 'recipient' brain, the procedure is person-preserving.

What is needed here is a refinement of the non-branching psychological continuity view. Let us distinguish between 'equal' and 'unequal' branching. There are at least two ways in which branching could be unequal. One, which is not what we have in our present example, involves a person-stage at one time having psychological connections with two different person-stages at another time, but (to put it crudely) having many more psychological connections with one than with the other (e.g., a bit of my brain matter is put in your brain, giving you a few memories from the inside of my past life; but you have a much greater memory access to your own past life than you have to mine, and I have a much greater memory access to my past life than you have to mine). In the case of the misfunctioning BST-device we have a different sort of inequality; the inequality stems, not from the amount of psychological connectedness, but from the different sorts of causal mechanisms involved in it. This difference constitutes inequality if we think, as we apparently do, that personal identity, or psychological unity, is somehow better realized in the continued normal functioning of the brain than it is in the operations of the BST-device.

The recognition that our conception of personal identity has this parochial element—that the way personal identity is in fact realized in us is given a privileged status—is compatible with the claim that where the BST-device functions properly its operation is person-preserving. But to reconcile these we need to modify the non-branching provision of the psychological continuity theory into something like Robert Nozick's 'closest continuer theory'.[9] In cases of equal branching we can say, as I said earlier about branching in general, that neither 'offshoot' counts as identical to the original person. In cases of unequal branching, the offshoot that is the 'closest continuer' of the original person counts as identical to him. There will be various dimensions of 'closeness'. The one that concerns us here might be called the dimension of 'aptness of causal mechanism'. In our example, one can hold that if the BST-device functions properly then the closest continuer of Smith is the post-transfer B-brain person, while allowing that if it misfunctions in the way imagined the closest continuer is the post-transfer A-brain person.

[9]See Nozick 1981.

If I am asked why I regard the continued normal functioning of the brain as a better realization of psychological unity than the operation of the BST-device, I can give no reason. And I can give no reason why I would prefer (as I now can't help feeling that I would) to survive in the ordinary way, with my present brain and body, rather than to have my brain-states transferred to a healthy clone of my body (even assuming that the transfer procedure is sure-fire). I also am not sure that these are attitudes I would continue to have if I lived in the society imagined in section 10, where the BST-device plays a central role in people's lives. And I cannot see that I would be in any way irrational if I changed these attitudes and became like the people in that society. What I feel quite confident of is that there is no *metaphysical* consideration which provides a valid reason for having attitudes towards personal identity and survival which are 'parochial' to the extent these attitudes are.

## REFERENCES

Kripke, Saul 1980: *Naming and Necessity*, Oxford, and Cambridge, Mass.

Lewis, David 1976: "Survival and Identity," in Amélie Rorty, (ed.), *The Identities of Persons*, Berkeley, Los Angeles, and London.

Nozick, Robert 1981: *Philosophical Explanations*, chapter 1, Cambridge, Mass.

Parfit, Derek 1971b: "Personal Identity," *The Philosophical Review*, 80, pp. 3–27. Reprinted in Perry 1975a.

Perry, John 1972: "Can the Self Divide?" *Journal of Philosophy*, 69, p. 463–88.

Perry, John, (ed.) 1975a: *Personal Identity*, Berkeley, Los Angeles, and London.

Perry, John 1976a: "The Importance of Being Identical," in Amelie Rorty (ed.), *The Identities of Persons*, Berkeley, Los Angeles, and London.

Shoemaker, Sydney 1970a: "Persons and their Pasts," *American Philosophical Quarterly*, 7, pp. 269–85.

Swinburne, Richard 1973–74: "Personal Identity," *Proceedings of the Aristotelian Society*, 74, pp. 231–48.

Wiggins, David 1980: *Sameness and Substance*, Oxford.

Williams, Bernard 1956–57: "Personal Identity and Individuation," *Proceedings of the Aristotelian Society*, 57 pp. 229–52. Reprinted in Williams 1973.

Williams, Bernard 1970: "The Self and the Future," *The Philosophical Review* 79, pp. 161–80. Reprinted in Williams 1973 and Perry 1975a.

Williams, Bernard 1973: *Problems of the Self*, Cambridge.

## READING 29

# Parfit and the Buddha: Why There Are No People
*Jim Stone*

*Jim Stone (1942–   ) teaches philosophy at the University of New Orleans and has published papers on a variety of topics in ethics, metaphysics, and epistemology. In 1986–1987 he was a Fulbright Teaching Fellow in India.*

What are we really? A *person*, Locke tells us, is "a thinking intelligent being, that has reason and reflection and can consider itself as itself, the same thinking thing, in different times and places."[1] This is illuminating: I am a person if I am anything. But what is the ontological status of persons? Derek Parfit maintains that a person just consists in the existence of a brain and body, and the occurrence of a series of interrelated physical and mental states. Persons aren't something extra. Further, the fact of a person's identity through time isn't a deep further fact: it just consists in the holding of certain more particular facts, facts which can be fully described in a completely impersonal way. Because a person just consists in the existence of other impersonal things, though persons exist, we could give a complete description of reality without claiming they do.[2]

Parfit's Reductionism appears to provide a handy middle ground between the view that persons are extra and the view that they don't exist at all. The Realist assures us the status of ultimate substances, at the price of making us queer entities. If persons are extra to bodies, brains, and psychophysical events, what are we and in what relation do we stand to these things? The Eliminativist ejects us with the on-tological bathwater, alarming those of us who are convinced that we exist and depriving deontological ethics of a subject matter. Parfit combines persons and a recognizable (though altered) morality with a comfortable Eliminativist ontology of bodies, brains, and psychophysical events; and he gives ingenious arguments for the Reductionist position.

I will argue for Eliminativism. My strategy will be to demolish Reductionism, so that we must choose between Realism and Eliminativism; then I will show that Realism verges on absurdity and Eliminativism is the reasonable choice. In the parts I and II of this paper, I consider two of Parfit's most forceful arguments for Reductionism. Modified so that it works, the spectrum argument supports Eliminativism as much as Reductionism. The argument from fissioning purports to show that identity isn't what matters in survival—psychological connectedness and/or continuity is what matters—but the argument is circular and a counterargument shows that if identity isn't what matters, nothing matters. I exploit this conclusion in part III to show that Reductionism is incoherent: either persons are extra or there aren't any. There is no middle ground. In part IV, I argue that Eliminativism is the consequence of a consistent naturalism. To put the matter paradoxically, either we must embrace an extremely dubious ontology, or we must face the fact that we don't exist.

### I.

If we accept a Reductionist view about some kind of thing, Parfit writes, "there may be cases where we believe the identity of such a thing to be, in a quite unpuzzling way, *indeterminate*."[3] The question "Is this the same?" is empty. Some of the members of a club which hasn't met for years form a club with the

---

[1] John Locke, *Essay Concerning Human Understanding*, chapter 27, in *Personal Identity*, ed. John Perry (Berkeley: University of California Press, 1975), p. 39.

[2] Derek Parfit, *Reasons and Persons* (Oxford: Clarendon Press, 1984) pp. 209–17.

SOURCE: From *Philosophy and Phenomenological Research* 48 (March 1988): 519–532.

[3] Parfit, p. 213. All italics in original.

same name and rules. "Is this the same club or a similar club?" may be an empty question. When we know all the facts about how people held meetings and about club rules, we know everything there is to know. We could stipulate an answer if we wanted, for the sake of neatness. As there is no fact of the matter, we cannot be making a mistake.

Parfit's spectrum argument for Reductionism purports to prove that personal identity can be indeterminate. He considers a range of cases which involves "all of the possible variations in the degrees of *both* physical *and* psychological connectedness.[4]"

> In the first case in this spectrum, at the near end, nothing would be done. In the second case, a few of the cells in my brain and body would be replaced. The new cells would *not* be exact duplicates. As a result, there would be somewhat less psychological connectedness between me and the person who wakes up. This person would not have all of my memories, and his character would be in one way unlike mine. He would have some apparent memories of Greta Garbo's life, and have one of Garbo's characteristics . . . . Further along the spectrum, a larger percentage of my cells would be replaced, again with dissimilar cells. The resulting person would be in fewer ways psychologically connected with me, and in more ways connected with Garbo . . .[5]

At the far end of the spectrum the scientists simply destroy my brain and body and create a replica of Garbo out of new materials.

Here we cannot conclude that the resulting person would in every case be me: the person at the far end of the spectrum has no connection with me at all. If we insist that personal identity must be determinate, we are forced to conclude that somewhere in this spectrum there is a sharp borderline, even though we can never know where it is.

> There must be some critical set of the cells replaced, and some critical degree of psychological change, which would make all the difference. If the surgeons replace slightly fewer than these cells, and produce one fewer psychological change, it will be me who wakes up. If they replace the few extra cells, and produce one more psychological change, I shall cease to exist. . .[6]

[4]Parfit, p. 236.
[5]Parfit, p. 237.
[6]Parfit, pp. 238–39.

It is far more plausible to concede that there is no sharp borderline, that there are cases in the spectrum where there is no real difference between the resulting person being me or someone else. It is an empty question whether the resulting person is me. This is the Reductionist view—when I know the degree of psychological continuity in these cases I know everything there is to know. So we ought to conclude that the Reductionist view is true.

Parfit has neglected to consider the difference between heaps and structures: one feature of a heap is that there are no causal relations between the entities which make it up. Remove one grain of sand and the rest remain; pull one hair from my head and the others are unaffected. Contrast a heap of bricks with a building made of bricks. Here the bricks support each other. The loss of a single brick can turn a building into a non-building; this is one of the differences between structures and heaps. Of course we can look at a structure *as if* it is a heap. The loss of a single brick considered in and of itself, aside from all causal relations, cannot change a bridge to a non-bridge. But this rather abstract point hardly entails that as long as we take away bricks one at a time we will always have a bridge. At a certain point the bridge will collapse.

Parfit's argument depends upon the assumption that people are heaps of psychological continuities. Erase continuities and replace them and the other continuities are unaffected, like the hairs on my head when one is removed. I think it is more likely that people are structures of psychological continuities; we are more like bridges than sandpiles. The different continuities and dispositions that make up my personality support one another. Memories, personality traits, skills, beliefs, values are causally intertwined; memories support other memories, skills depend on other skills, personality traits depend on beliefs, memories, and other personality traits, and so on. Psychological features are suspended in a web of causation. Remove enough of them and replace them with different features and my personality will collapse. At some point on the spectrum, the man who has undergone the surgery will wake up psychotic: there will be a general collapse of personality and psychological continuity. This provides a natural (and confirmable) place for the subscriber to the Psychological Criterion of personal identity to draw a line as to where on the continuum the original person ceases to exist. Analogously, people aren't heaps of cells: a brain half mine, half Garbo's will go into convulsions, a heart half mine, half Garbo's will stop beating. At some point along the spectrum, the man who has undergone the surgery will die. This provides a natural and confirmable place for the subscriber to the Physical Criterion of personal identity to draw a line. Parfit's argument loses its force once we count the fact that people are psychophysical structures, not heaps.

However the argument can be modified to avoid this difficulty. Surely it is physically possible that there is a different man, causally unrelated to Parfit, whose brain and body are identically similar to Parfit's, cell for cell. Perhaps there is a planet very much like Earth where this double lives. Suppose we substitute the double for Garbo in the thought experiment. As we move along the spectrum, there is less psychological connectedness between Parfit and the person who wakes up. Increasingly this man's psychological features are causally unrelated to Parfit's; he would have fewer of Parfit's memories, say, and more of the double's. But as these memories are identically similar to Parfit's (though they are *of* numerically different people and places), the man who wakes will not notice the discontinuity: he will resemble Parfit just as much as if these psychological states were causally related to Parfit's life. And his body will function just as if no cells had been replaced. He will be just like Parfit. At the end of the spectrum Parfit's brain and body are destroyed and the double is simply left alone. He has no connection with Parfit at all. If personal identity must be determinate, there must be a critical set of cells replaced and a critical degree of psychological discontinuity, which decisively ends Parfit's life and produces someone else who is identically similar. It is far more plausible to concede that there is no sharp borderline; there are cases on the spectrum where it is an empty question whether the resulting person is Parfit or the double.

The modified spectrum argument avoids another problem for the original. Geoffrey Madell observes that it hardly follows from the fact that psychological features depend upon states of the brain that "it is in principle possible to take out a chunk from one person's mind and replace it by a chunk from someone else's mind."[7] That is, there is no reason to suppose

the brain is composed of organic modules, each determining a particular psychological feature, which could replace those of other people as we replace Parfit's with Garbo's. The brain may not work that way for all psychological features; indeed, it may not work that way for any. Suppose it doesn't. Still, all along the modified spectrum the resulting brain is identically similar to Parfit's brain, so it realizes similar thoughts and psychological states even though it is physically impossible to transpose chunks of people's minds. But if identity is determinate, there must be a sharp borderline on the spectrum after which the psychological states belong to the double, not Parfit, though the states on either side of the line are identically similar. There must be some critical set of cells replaced which makes all the difference, which suddenly shifts the reference of thoughts and memories from earth to the double's world. It is far more plausible to concede that there is no sharp borderline; there are cases in which the question "Do these mental states belong to Parfit or the double?" is empty.

The modified spectrum provides a forceful argument against Realism, but not for Reductionism. For the conclusion that personal identity is indeterminate supports Eliminativism as much as Reductionism. If there are no people, the question "Is this person the same as that?" is always empty: the affirmative answer is false and the negative answer implies that *this* and *that* are persons who happen to be non-identical. The fact that questions of personal identity are sometimes empty suggests the possibility that they are always empty. Of course, the Eliminativist admits that there are cases in which we *treat* such questions as non-empty; it hardly follows that persons exist. Questions about the identity of dybbuks were once treated as non-empty and sometimes answered with confidence. At the least, the modified spectrum raises the possibility that we too are talking about fictions; personhood may be another sort of demonic possession. Indeed, it is arguable that determinacy is a *defining* feature of personhood: necessarily, if x is a person then for any future being y "Is x identical to y?" has an answer. For it seems inconceivable that some future person could neither be me nor not be me. Parfit writes "We cannot make sense of any third alternative, such as that the person . . . will be *partly* me."[8] Personhood is conceived as all or nothing. The modified spectrum shows that there

[7]Geoffrey Madell, "Derek Parfit and Greta Garbo," *Analysis* 45 (1985): 105–9.

[8]Parfit, p. 233.

is a possible future being for each of us such that the question "Am I identical to him" will be empty. It follows that we are not persons. But I am a person if I am anything. It follows that I don't exist.

## II.

According to Parfit, the fact of personal identity just consists in the holding of psychological connectedness and/or continuity, when it takes a non-branching form. If survival matters it must be on account of psychological connectedness and/or continuity; there is nothing more to identity than that. A consequence of Parfit's view, therefore, is that psychological connectedness and/or continuity is what matters in survival. Identity matters, not for its own sake, but because it accompanies what matters.[9]

Parfit attempts to prove this is true. He supposes he is one of three identical triplets.

> My body is fatally injured, as are the brains of my two brothers. My brain is divided, and each half is successfully transplanted into the body of one of my brothers. Each of the resulting people believes that he is me, seems to remember living my life, has my character, and is in every other way psychologically continuous with me. And he has a body that is very like mine.[10]

Parfit believes it is an empty question whether or not he survives the transplant, though he admits that one answer is best. "Since I cannot be identical with two different people, and it would be arbitrary to call one of these people me, we can best describe the case by saying neither of these people will be me.[11] But it would be "irrational" to regard division as being as bad as ordinary death.

> Consider my relation to each of these people. Does this relation fail to contain some vital element that is contained in ordinary survival? It seems clear that it does not. I would survive if I stood in this very same relation to only one of the resulting people. It is a fact that someone can survive even if half his brain is destroyed. And on reflection it was clear that I would survive if my whole brain was successfully transplanted into my brother's body. It was therefore clear that I would survive if half my brain was destroyed, and the other half was successfully transplanted into my brother's body. In the case that we are now considering, my relation to each of the resulting people thus contains everything that would be needed for me to survive as that person. It cannot be the *nature* of my relation to each of the resulting people that, in this case, causes it to fail to be survival. Nothing is *missing*. What is wrong can only be the duplication.[12]

If I accept this but still regard division as being as bad as death my reaction is "indefensible."

> I would be like someone who, when told of a drug that could double his years of life, regarded the taking of this drug as death. The only difference in the case of division is that the extra years are to run concurrently. This is an interesting difference. But it cannot mean that there are *no* years to run.[13]

Here we have what matters in survival without identity, so it cannot be that identity is what matters.

An argument with a false conclusion cannot be sound; therefore, if we can show the conclusion of the argument is false, we will know the argument is fallacious, though we may not have uncovered the fallacy. Suppose, then, that identity is not what matters in survival; psychological connectedness is what matters. But there are two components to psychological connectedness: resemblance plus a cause which produces it. If psychological connectedness is what matters in an ordinary case of survival it must be because these components matter; there is nothing

---

[9]According to Parfit "*Psychological connectedness* is the holding of particular direct psychological connections" for example, when a belief, or a desire, or any other psychological feature continues to be had. "*Psychological continuity* is the holding of overlapping chains of *strong* connectedness"; chains are strong when they contain enough direct connections for personal identity. Parfit writes "Of these two relations connectedness is more important both in theory and in practice" (see Parfit, p. 206). For instance, "When some convict is now less closely connected to himself at the time of his crime, he deserves less punishment"; indeed, "if the connections are very weak, he may deserve none" (p. 326). Also, I can rationally care less about my further future because connectedness holds to a lesser degree (p. 313). Yet Parfit *also* claims that there is no reason to believe that connectedness matters more in survival than continuity: "I know of no argument for such a belief" (p. 301). This verges on self-contradiction; and it is very implausible. If identity isn't what matters, why care about some fellow in the distant future who is *utterly* unlike me, *solely* because he happens to be related to me by overlapping claims of connectedness? If identity isn't what matters, connectedness does the work.

[10]Parfit, p. 255.

[11]Parfit, p. 262.

[12]Parfit, p. 261.

[13]Parfit, p. 262.

more to psychological connectedness. But why do these components matter? If we can ask what matters in survival we can ask what matters in psychological connectedness.[14]

We can easily see why resemblance matters: resemblance is one of the features I most want in an ordinary case of survival. If the future person who will be me is nothing like me, he will lack the attributes which endear me to myself, he will not enjoy the fruits of my labors, take pride in my achievements, or even deserve praise for them. But why should the causal component matter? The natural and obvious answer—the causal component matters because, added to resemblance, it makes the future person who resembles me *me*—won't do. For we are supposing that identity *doesn't* matter; so the causal component cannot matter because it makes for identity. If identity doesn't matter, why should I want a future person to be related to me by a cause which produces resemblance? I submit that the remaining natural and obvious answer is that the causal component matters because it produces resemblance. Mapped onto my present characteristics the causal component produces duplicates in a future person; this is why I want it to obtain. If identity matters because it accompanies continuity, the causal component matters because it produces resemblance. It follows that resemblance is what matters in psychological connectedness.

This cannot be right. If a future person will merely resemble me coincidentally, it cannot be that my relation to him contains what matters in an ordinary case of survival. Suppose that scientists on Mars are mass-producing bio-programmed people to populate other planets. They are able to imprint various information on the brains of these creatures, including personalities, apparent memories, interests, and so on. Suppose that by purely random coincidence

they program a man to have a personality, memories, skill, interests, and so on just like mine, so that they unwittingly create a coincidental replica, who would be just as he is if I had never been born. I am about to die. If identity isn't what matters the fact that this coincidental replica will continue ought to be just as good as survival. If I am *not* about to die, but one of us will be tortured or shot at dawn, I have no selfish reason to hope it won't be me. My relationship to my future self and the replica contains everything that matters in an ordinary case of survival. This is plainly mistaken.

We can make this implausibility still more obvious. According to Parfit, when my relation to a future person is as good as if it were identity it carries all of the ordinary implications of identity including desert for punishment. "As Wiggins writes: 'a malefactor could scarcely evade responsibility by contriving his own fissioning.' "[15] Surely this is right: if my relation cannot provide a ground for punishment and reward, how can it contain everything that matters? Suppose then that I commit a crime, then, mistakenly believing that amnesia will excuse me of responsibility, take a pill which selectively makes me forget just that act. But the pill kills me, and my coincidental replica (who is just as I would have been if the pill had worked) is activated by the scientists on Mars. If resemblance is what matters in survival, then the coincidental replica ought to be punished for my crime. Suppose the pill doesn't kill me. Then my relation to both my future self and the replica contains everything that matters. The fact that I am identical with my future self, not the replica, has no force as identity doesn't matter. It follows that both my future self and the replica are responsible for my crime; we both deserve punishment. The punishment ought to be divided between us. But this is preposterous.

If psychological connectedness is what matters in survival, then resemblance is what really matters. Perhaps we can turn the wheel of the reductio still further. Suppose that resemblance is what matters in survival. Why does resemblance matter? Someone resembles me just in case he has the characteristics which characterize me now. If resemblance matters it must be because *these* characteristics matter; otherwise I wouldn't care whether or not they were dupli-

---

[14]I have left out psychological continuity. First I have argued that connectedness is what matters if identity isn't what matters. Second, the fact that the *immediately ensuing* fellow who is me is continuous with me is nothing more than the fact that he is connected to me. *He* is continuous just in case he is connected. If identity isn't what matters, connectedness is what matters in *this* case anyway. So we can ask here "What is it about *connectedness* that matters? And if it turns out that what matters in connectedness is resemblance, then we can conclude that overlapping chains of resemblance are as good as overlapping chains of connectedness, for both preserve what matters in survival from moment to moment. Resemblance will be what matters in continuity too.

[15]Parfit, p. 271.

cated. Why should these characteristics matter and not others?

The natural response is that these characteristics matter because they are *mine*—they characterize the man who is *identical* to me. But identity is the same relation synchronically and diachronically. If these characteristics matter because they belong to a man who is identical to me, then identity *does* matter. Why shouldn't it matter diachronically too? If identity isn't what matters in survival, it cannot be that these features matter because they are mine. Do they matter because they are of value to society? Not at all: I can imagine other characteristics far more valuable to society. Perhaps they matter because only someone with these characteristics will complete my projects and take care of my family. But the fact is that I have neither family nor projects; and I find that I want to survive just as much as when I did. The fact is that most people do not care about surviving because they believe in the *utility* of their characteristics.

But now it appears there is no reason why *these* characteristics should matter. Any other characteristics should do as well. But then resemblance only *accompanies* what matters—a future person with *some* characteristics (or at least characteristics that aren't disgraceful). If identity isn't what matters, then I have what matters if there is a presentable future person, whether she resembles me or not. *This* is what makes ordinary survival valuable. But if what matters in ordinary survival is that it insures the existence of at least one future person, then ordinary survival doesn't matter, at least under present circumstances. Because there will be millions of future people whether or not I survive, and my relation to each of them is just as good as if he or she were me. Therefore, if identity isn't what matters in ordinary survival, ordinary survival doesn't matter. Right now I will have everything that matters whether or not I survive.

This conclusion provides a powerful argument against Reductionism. We affirm the fact that Parfit is trying to account for: ordinary survival matters. It follows that identity is what matters in ordinary survival. But if identity is nothing more than psychological connectedness and/or continuity, then identity isn't what matters. It follows that the fact of identity is a deep further fact. Therefore Reductionism is false. Our earlier conclusion provides an equally powerful argument: If identity isn't what matters,

my relation to a future person who coincidentally resembles me contains everything that matters in an ordinary case of survival. But this relation does not contain everything that matters; therefore identity matters. But if identity is nothing more than psychological connectedness and/or continuity then identity doesn't matter. It follows once again that identity is a deep further fact.

Now we can locate the fallacy in Parfit's argument. He writes:

> . . . it cannot be the *nature* of my relation to each of the resulting people that, in this case, causes it to fail to be survival. Nothing is *missing*. What is wrong can only be the duplication.[16]

If identity is a further fact that matters, my relation to each of my offshoots *does* fail to contain some element that is contained in ordinary survival— identity. Something crucial is missing. It is true that I would survive if I stood in this relation to only one offshoot, but it is false that my relation to each of the resulting people contains everything that would be needed for me to survive as that person. Something extra is needed, something that *accompanies* continuity when it obtains between me and only one offshoot and is wholly absent when continuity is duplicated. The argument depends upon the assumption that identity isn't a further fact; that when continuity isn't duplicated it *is* survival. But this begs the question against the Realist.

### III.

This brings us to the center of the debate between the Reductionist and the Realist. For we can clearly discern what it is that motivates Realism about persons. The Realist is persuaded that *essential* features of personhood require an additional ontology. Joseph Butler takes it to be a consequence of Locke's reductionism that "it is a fallacy upon ourselves, to charge our present selves with anything we did, or to imagine our present selves interested in anything which befell us yesterday, or that our present self will be interested in what befalls us tomorrow."[17] John Perry, commenting on Butler, writes

---

[16]Parfit, p. 261.

[17] Joseph Butler, first appendix, *The Analogy of Religion*, in *Personal Identity*, ed. John Perry, p. 102.

That I will be run over by a truck means, says Locke, that the person who is run over by a truck will remember thinking and doing what I am thinking and doing now. But why would I care especially about that? Why should a person who is having such memories be of any more concern to me than anyone else?[18]

Suppose someone says to me, "Several people will be shot at dawn and some of them will resemble you." I feel sadness, nothing more. He adds, "One of these people will resemble you because there is a causal connection between you and him which causes him to resemble you." This is interesting but still no cause for alarm. He says, "Further, no other person will stand in this relation to you." Still no cause for terror. But *this* is all that the fact of identity comes to, on the Reductionist account. So the fact that I will be shot at dawn no longer makes it rational to fear or even anticipate the execution.

Further, the Reductionist cannot account for the rationality of our feelings of regret and remorse for our past misdeeds. If I say that I feel remorse because I murdered my brother, you would be right to be puzzled. For all this comes to is that I happen to stand in certain causal relations to the man who killed my brother and no one else does, and why feel remorse over that? Why feel guilt? And if identity is merely psychological continuity it becomes impossible to account for the fact that people bear responsibility over time. "I am the man who did the deed," the criminal confesses, "but all this comes to is that I have the misfortune to stand in certain causal relations to the man who did it and no one else does. I'm not to blame for this situation; I find myself this way. Punishing me for his crime is no better than punishing the son for the crimes of his father." If Reductionism is true, the fact that I committed the crime is an excuse.

Parfit responds:

Desert can be held to be incompatible with Reductionism. But a different law is also defensible. We can defensibly claim that psychological continuity carries with it desert for past crimes. Perhaps there is an argument that de-

cisively resolves this disagreement. But I have not yet found this argument.[19]

And Parfit writes that it is defensible to claim that psychological continuity justifies anticipation of the future. He has not found an argument which refutes this claim either.[20]

I submit that the argument I gave in the preceding section resolves the disagreements. Psychological continuity is what matters in survival only if resemblance is what matters, hence psychological continuity carries desert only if resemblance carries desert. But resemblance does not carry desert, nor does it warrant anticipation, pride, or remorse. Therefore, psychological continuity doesn't carry desert, nor does it bear the burden of anticipation, pride, and remorse.

If identity isn't a deep further fact, there is nothing on earth which is responsible for past crimes, deserving of praise for past achievements, with rational hopes, fears, anticipations about the future or regrets about the past. There is nothing which bears commitments, obligations, and rights through time. But as Locke puts it "person is a forensic term, appropriating actions and their merit."[21] Persons are *conceived* as responsibility bearers, beings which carry rights and obligations through time, capable of rational hopes, fears, and regrets. Persons are *essentially* morally interesting. Therefore, if Reductionism is true there are no persons. Either persons are extra, or there aren't any persons and deontological ethics and prudence lack a subject matter. Reductionism, which affirms the existence of persons while denying they are something extra, is incoherent.

The Reductionist might respond that persons exist on his account, only they turn out to be very *different* from what we believed. Parfit writes, "The truth may be disturbing."[22] The Reductionist might argue that there will still be thinking intelligent beings who can consider themselves as themselves in different times and places, and this is sufficient for the existence of persons. However if the Lockean definition of person is to be satisfied there must be at least one thinking intelligent being who exists at

[18]John Perry, "The Importance of Being Identical," in *The Identities of Persons*, ed. Amélie Oksenberg Rorty (University of California Press, 1976), p. 68.

[19]Parfit. p. 325.
[20]Parfit, pp. 311–12.
[21]Locke, *Essay Concerning Human Understanding*, chapter 27, in Perry, p. 50.
[22]Parfit, p. 324.

times $t_1$ and $t_2$, and recognizes at $t_1$ that he is identical to the being that exists at $t_2$ or recognizes at $t_2$ that he is identical to the being that exists at $t_1$. But if at $t_1$ I recognize that the intelligent being at $t_2$ is identical to me, then if I know he will have experience E, then it is rational for me to anticipate experiencing E. If Reductionism is true, the consequent is always false: it is never rational for me to anticipate an experience I know a future person will have. Therefore I never recognize that the being at $t_2$ is identical to me. Further, if at $t_2$ I know that the being at $t_1$ is identical to me, then if I know that he voluntarily performed a destructive and unnecessary action then it is rational for me to regret performing that act. But if Reductionism is true, this consequent is always false: it is never rational for me to regret performing an act I know a past being performed. Therefore I never recognize that the intelligent being at $t_1$ is identical to me. Consequently if Reductionism is true, the Lockean definition is never satisfied: there are no people.

## IV.

There is no handy middle ground between Realism and Eliminativism. Either persons are something extra and the fact of their identity a deep further fact, or there are no persons at all. Are there persons? To the extent that we are honest empiricists we must admit that we are confronted, within and without, by flux and diversity. My mental states are wholly new in every moment, my brain and body radically different in myriad ways than they were just before. The idea that there is something extra underlying all of this, someone uninterrupted, invariable, whose existence is all or nothing, behind the flux, is what Hume called "a metaphysical fiction of substance."[23] There is no more reason to believe that persons underlie the diversity of human lives than there is to believe that there are underlying vegetables or artifacts.

More sympathetically, we might say that persons are theoretical entities, posits in a theory intended to make moral and social life possible. But is the theory even intelligible? Considering his perceptions, Hume asks rhetorically, "After what manner therefore do they belong to self, and how are they connected with it?"[24] Again, the person *has* the diverse stages of a human life—but what is it for this extra entity to *have* a stage? What is the nature of this relation? The persisting person lends unity to the series of diverse stages: they are part of the same life because they belong to one person. But then the underlying person is *himself* reduced to a mere diversity of stages: there is the stage of his existence in which he possesses the first stage of the human life, then the different stage in which he possesses the second stage, and so on. Is there yet another person underlying the second series of person stages, possessing them, and so on to infinity? We are confronted with the Platonic problem of the one and the many: how can the one possess the many and still be one? Further, as the identity of the underlying person is *determinate*, we must say that there is a sharp borderline somewhere on the modified spectrum at which he ceases to exist and is replaced by his double. And what exactly *is* this something extra—a Cartesian ego? Finally, as persons are ontological additions to brains, bodies, and psychophysical events, there are possible worlds in which my brain, my body, and the psychophysical events which actually comprise my life exist and I do too, and other worlds identically similar except that I do not. This seems incredible; further which world is *this* world? If persons exist they will never know it.

To put the matter paradoxically, we need to face the fact that we don't exist. There is simply nothing in nature for us to be. This is probably what Heracleitus thought, it is plainly what Hume and the Buddha thought. Neither Hume nor the Buddha could find a persisting self—perhaps this explains why both of them died so well. Hume observed that the mind, confronted with what is in fact a series of different but similar beings, slurs them together into one and creates the illusion of identity. Buddhist monks and nuns analyze walking into lifting, moving, placing and shifting, and attend to each component until they recognize that there is no one there who lifts who is also there when they move, and so on. It is because we do these actions automatically, mindlessly, many of them at the same time, that we create the delusion of a persisting agent; it is the same mental slurring that Hume had in mind.

---

[23]David Hume, *Treatise of Human Nature*, in Perry, pp. 164–65.

[24]Hume, in Perry, p. 162.

The Buddha recognized that human animals are creatures of desire: desire represents its object as possessable, hence intransient. Minds and bodies, always transient, are deeply attached to themselves, hence present themselves to themselves as containing something extra, a person, which persists. In fact there are only thoughts, desires, and behaviors "which succeed each other with an inconceivable rapidity, and are in perpetual flux and movement,"[25] a succession empty of identity, utterly impersonal, with no more substance than the waterfall or the candle flame. Thoughts and desires represent the succession that contains them as a persisting substance, somehow underlying itself, thereby creating the illusion of the personal, which is cherished and nurtured by moral and cognitive behavior designed to thicken it. The slurring of different beings into one is motivated by the craving for permanence; I suspect that Hume would have liked this view. But there is nothing in the world which satisfies this representation: the fear of age and death, the suffering of repeated loss, is all in the service of that which never was. There is only the attempt by thought and desire, by mind and body, to keep themselves, to climb out of nature.

Probably we are very transient: if we exist at all we come and go in a moment. Like all processes in nature, animal lives are comprised of empty phenomena rolling on, except in this case the momentary phenomena tend to take themselves very seriously. I suspect this is the truth about us and that it is the inevitable consequence of science and empiricism, but how one lives with the truth I don't know.

[25]Hume, in Perry, p. 162.

# DISCUSSION: Dualism

About twenty-five years ago I was present in Oxford at a small philosophical meeting which deserves to be recorded for the benefit of future historians of philosophy. It was a meeting of a club called the Philosophers' Tea, and as often happened on such occasions, the discussion was dominated by my predecessor in the White's Chair of Moral Philosophy, Professor Prichard. I cannot recall the original question, but I remember that he had caught the attention of the rest of us by asserting in a casual unemphatic way that substances were obviously ingenerable and indestructible. Pressed to give an example, he then said that he himself was a substance. At this my colleague Professor Ryle, not yet a professor but an *enfant terrible,* asked "What were you doing when Julius Caesar landed in Britain?" For a moment Prichard made no reply, and then, with the air of one who is puzzled by the asking of the question rather than by the question itself, said simply "I have forgotten." Still eager for the truth, Ryle tried again. "Is it only about yourself," he asked, "that you have such knowledge, or can you be sure that I was in existence at the time of Caesar's invasion?" For a moment Prichard paused again as though puzzled by the asking of the question. Then, pointing to Ryle's body, he said brightly, "Yes, but of course I am not talking about *this:* I mean the real Ryle."

William Kneale, *On Having a Mind*
(Cambridge: Cambridge University Press, 1962), pp. 7–8.

In Chapter 1 of his book *The Concept of Mind* (Reading 22), Gilbert Ryle satirizes Cartesian dualism by calling it the dogma of the Ghost in the Machine. While it is true that for René Descartes (1596–1650), human bodies, like everything else in the universe, are machines obeying the laws of mechanics, it is unfair to call Descartes' view a dogma or to equate mental substances with ghosts. Descartes was not being dogmatic: he gave arguments for his view; and minds, unlike ghosts and other spectral apparitions, have no size, shape, or color.

Before looking at Descartes' arguments, it is worth reminding ourselves how radical his view of the universe is. It would be entirely wrong to think of Descartes as a religious reactionary concocting a metaphysical system with the primary goal of proving the soul's immortality. On the contrary, Descartes spearheaded and created much of the modern scientific outlook that we now take for granted. One of the primary forces behind Descartes' metaphysics was not religion but science. The mechanical philosophy of the seventeenth century, led by Galileo, Huyghens, and Descartes himself took mechanics to be the universal science. Whether they be stars, solar systems, clouds, animals, plants, or the human body, all these objects are made out of the same stuff, the same matter; and as a consequence, all these objects obey the same laws of physics.

Twentieth-century scientists disagree with Descartes that the only fundamental property of matter is extension and that all physical systems can be explained solely in terms of the laws of mechanics, but they still agree with him that there is no room for mental properties in physics, chemistry, and biology. For example, we now accept that light waves enter our eyes and cause nerve impulses to be transmitted to our brains, resulting in the sensation of color; but we do not attribute the sensory quality of color to the light waves, nor to the retina, nor to the nerves leading to the brain. For us, as for Descartes, it is just as wrong to locate the mental sensation of color anywhere in the physical world as it would be to attribute the sensation of pain to the knife that cuts my thumb.

## DESCARTES' ARGUMENTS FOR DUALISM

In his *Second Meditation* (Reading 36), Descartes argues that the one proposition of which he is absolutely certain is that he exists as "a thing which thinks, that is to say a mind or soul, or an understanding, or a reason." Thus, while he can doubt that there is an external world of physical objects or even that he has a material body, Descartes is incapable of doubting that he exists. The very act of trying to doubt his own existence verifies that he exists as a doubting, thinking substance. Thinking (consciousness, awareness) is one of his essential attributes. Descartes uses the term *thinking* to mean consciousness or awareness; all particular mental states and events are modifications of this basic, principal attribute: "What is a thing which thinks? It is a thing which doubts, understands, [conceives], affirms, denies, wills, refuses, which also imagines and feels." (*Second Meditation*)

Having established the certainty of his own existence as a mind that thinks, Descartes then tries to prove that his thinking mind and his extended body are distinct substances. I shall refer to these arguments for dualism as the Doubt Argument, the Conceivability Argument, and the Divisibility Argument.

The clearest statement of the Doubt Argument occurs in Part Four of the *Discourse on Method* (1637), in which Descartes summarizes his reasoning in the *Meditations*.

> I then considered attentively what I was; and I saw that while I could feign that I had no body, that there was no world, and no place existed for me to be in, I could not feign that I was not; on the contrary, from the mere fact that I thought of doubting (*je pensais à douter*) about other truths it evidently and certainly followed that I existed. On the other hand, if I had merely ceased to be conscious, even if everything else that I had ever imagined had been true, I had no reason to believe that I should still have existed. From this I recognized that I was a substance whose whole essence and nature is to be conscious (*de penser*) and whose being requires no place and depends on no material thing. Thus this self (*moi*), that is to say the soul, by which I am what I am, is entirely distinct from the body, and is even more easily known; and even if the body were not there at all the soul would be just what it is.[1]

### The Doubt Argument

(1) I can doubt that my body exists.
(2) I cannot doubt that I exist as a thinking thing.

(3) I, a thinking thing, am not identical with my body.

As it stands, the Doubt Argument is not valid, since its conclusion does not follow logically from its premises. To turn it into a valid argument, we need to add another statement to its premises. One popular choice for this missing premise that would make the argument valid is a metaphysical principle known as Leibniz's Law. Leibniz's Law is actually a conjunction of two separate statements that are logically independent of each other. The first statement, the Principle of the Indiscernibility of Identicals, is widely acknowledged to be a necessary truth about numerically identical things; the second statement, the Principle of the Identity of Indiscernibles, is a controversial metaphysical thesis. Leibniz believed that the Principle of the Identity of Indiscernibles is true, but many philosophers disagree with him.

**The Principle of the Indiscernibility of Identicals:** If two things are identical, then they have exactly the same properties.

**The Principle of the Identity of Indiscernibles:** If two things have exactly the same properties, then they are identical.

The Doubt Argument needs only the first half of Leibniz's Law, the uncontroversial Principle of the Indiscernibility of Identicals. We can, therefore, ignore the Principle of the Identity of Indiscernibles.

Most philosophers accept the Principle of the Indiscernibility of Identicals because it follows directly from the concept of numerical identity. If two things are identical, they are one and the same thing; thus, anything that is true of the first must be true of the second, since there is really just one single thing that is being referred to in two different ways. It is important to remember that identical things are not just similar or closely alike (as are so-called identical twins), but the very same thing (e.g., George Bush and the forty-first president of the United States).

With suitable revisions, the Doubt Argument now reads as follows:

(4) My body has the property of being such that I can doubt its existence.
(5) I, a thinking thing, do not have the property of being such that I can doubt my existence.
(6) If two things are identical, then they have exactly the same properties.

---

(3) I, a thinking thing, am not identical with my body.

There seems little doubt that this kind of argument is unsound. The "properties" mentioned in premises (4) and (5) are bogus; they are not examples of the real properties that premise (6), Leibniz's Law, applies to. Being an object of doubt (or belief, desire, fear) under a certain description is not a real property of a thing, for someone may recognize an object under one description but fail to recognize it under another. For example, many people who believe that Kareem Abdul Jabaar is a great basketball player do not also believe that Lew Alcindor is equally great; but Jabaar and Alcindor are the same person. Similarly, Oedipus desired to marry Jocasta, but he did not desire to marry his mother. Thus, even though my great aunt Nancy is a spiritualist who believes that she, but not her physical body, will survive death, this does not prove that she is not identical with her body.

The Conceivability Argument for dualism is given in Descartes' *Sixth Meditation*. Like the Doubt Argument, it is subject to many interpretations. Here is one version with some missing premises added (and the references to God omitted).

### The Conceivability Argument

(7) I can conceive that I, a thinking thing, exist without my extended body existing.

(8) Anything that I can conceive is logically possible.

(9) If it is logically possible that X exist without Y, then X is not identical with Y.

_____

(3) I, a thinking thing, am not identical with my extended body.

Premise (8) is a general principle that is often appealed to by philosophers in metaphysical discussions. Because of the central role it plays in many of his arguments, I shall refer to it as Hume's Law, after the Scottish philosopher, David Hume (1711–1776).

Opinions differ about what, precisely, is wrong with the Conceivability Argument. Many philosophers judge it to be unsound because Hume's Law is false: conceivability is not sufficient for logical possibility. This seems correct, especially if one regards all statements of numerical identity as necessary truths. Assume that I can conceive that the evening star exists without the morning star also existing.[2] Since the morning star is identical with the evening star—they are just different names for the planet Venus— what I conceive is not logically possible. Similarly with mathematical hypotheses such as Goldbach's conjecture which, as yet, have been neither proven nor disproven. I can conceive that someone might find an even number that is not the sum of two primes; but if Goldbach's conjecture is true, it is necessarily true, and so I will have conceived something that is not logically possible.

Where Descartes seems to have erred is in assuming that he has a *complete* concept of minds and bodies. Thus, while we might agree that thinking is essential to minds and extension is essential to bodies, it does not follow that "my essence consists *solely* in the fact that I am a thinking thing [or a substance whose *whole* essence or nature is to think]" (*Sixth Meditation*, emphasis added) unless Descartes knows that thinking and extension cannot both be properties of the same substance. In other words, even if we allow that Descartes has shown that consciousness is an essential property of mind or thinking substance, what Descartes needs is a proof that mind or thinking substance cannot have extension as another of its essential properties. Descartes attempts to provide such a proof in his Divisibility Argument, presented in the *Sixth Meditation*.[3]

### The Divisibility Argument

(1) All extended things are divisible.

(2) No minds are divisible.

_____

(3) No minds are extended things.

The vulnerable premise here is (2). In defense of the mind's indivisible unity, Descartes writes:

> ... when I consider the mind, that is to say, myself inasmuch as I am only a thinking thing, I cannot distinguish in myself any parts, but apprehend myself to be clearly one and entire; and although the whole mind seems to be united to the whole body, yet if a foot, or an arm, or some other part, is separated from my body, I am aware that nothing has been taken away from my mind.

Unfortunately for Descartes' defense, we know that something will have been taken away from my mind if a portion of my physical brain is removed. Similarly, when the corpus callosum—the bundle of nerve fibers connecting the two hemispheres of the human brain—is completely severed in a cerebral commissurotomy, the mind divides into two separate conscious awarenesses. The simplest interpretation of the effects of this operation is that even before the surgery there is a division of mental labor between the two spatially separated hemispheres.[4]

Admittedly, Descartes is correct in asserting that thoughts, memories, beliefs, and other mental states are not the sort of things that it makes sense to regard as being spatially extended; but the issue is whether the thing (or substance) that they are states of is extended. The evidence of neurophysiology strongly suggests that thoughts, memories, beliefs and other mental states are states of the physical brain, and brains can be divided into spatial parts. So, it seems that premise (2) is defensible only if we already assume that the mind is a nonmaterial substance distinct from the body and brain. Thus, the Divisibility Argument cannot serve as independent support for dualism.

## ARGUMENTS AGAINST DUALISM

Even if Descartes' arguments for dualism fail, this does not show that dualism is false. I now wish to consider some of the common arguments against dualism. These arguments fall into two categories: objections to the notion of an immaterial substance and objections to the two-sided causal interaction between minds and bodies. In the first category are the Problem of Other Minds and the Problem of Individuating Minds; in the second category are the Problem of Understanding Mind-Body Causation, the Arguments from Energy and Momentum, and the Argument from the Structure of the Nervous System.

### The Problem of Other Minds

The Problem of Other Minds is the epistemological problem of justifying our belief that other people have minds just as we do.[5] According to the dualist, I know for certain that *I* have a mind because I experience mental properties directly, by an immediate, personal awareness; but I cannot experience the minds of others in this way, and since minds lack all physical properties, they cannot be seen, touched, or perceived directly. Thus, my belief in other minds must be based on an inference, not direct perception. Presumably, I *infer* that other people have minds from observing their behavior. Since the connection between mental states is causal not logical, the inference cannot be deductive. So, it is inductive; and it must be very weak, since it is based on a single case, namely my own, in which I observe both the effect, the behavior, and the mental states that cause it. Thus, dualism leads to skepticism about other minds.

This makes dualism implausible, since while we are sometimes skeptical about whether other people have the particular emotions, feelings, and beliefs that their behavior would normally indicate, we never doubt that they have minds.

### The Problem of Individuating Minds

This is a metaphysical problem that we explore at greater length in the discussion entitled "Personal Identity." The question at issue is, What makes *this* immaterial substance, *this* mind, a different individual from *that* one? To see why answering this question is difficult for the dualist, consider two physical objects, A and B. If A and B have different properties, then, by the Principle of the Indiscernibility of Identicals, they are different, nonidentical objects. Even if A and B are exactly similar twins—the same size, the same shape, the same color, and so on—they are still nonidentical because they have different spatial locations: A is over here, and B is over there. According to the dualist, the only properties minds can have are mental ones. So, if one mind has at least one mental state (at a particular time) that another lacks (at that time), then the minds are nonidentical; but it is logically possible that two minds be exactly similar, state for state. We can no longer appeal to spatial position to individuate them, since minds are not anywhere in space at all—they do not have spatial position as one of their properties. Thus, if minds are immaterial substances, it is difficult to explain how one mind can be a distinct individual from another exactly like it.

### The Problem of Understanding Mind-Body Causation

As C. D. Broad remarks in "The Traditional Problem of Body and Mind" (Reading 21), making a distinction between interactionism (either two-sided or one-sided) and parallelism (the denial of any mind-body interaction) presupposes an account of causation that goes beyond Hume's theory of regular succession.[6] According to Hume, if events of one type, A, are always followed by events of another type, B, then each A-event is the cause of the B-event that follows it. Thus, on this regularity theory of causation, if certain kinds of bodily events always follow (or precede) certain kinds of mental events, then they are causally connected, and parallelism collapses into interactionism.

Few people agree with Hume that there is nothing more to causality than temporal priority and regular succession. In fact Hume himself, in his first published work, *A Treatise of Human Nature* (1739), added a third condition—contiguity. Two events or objects are contiguous when they are right next to each other in space. Though we often speak of remote or distal causes, that is, cases in which one event produces a distant effect, we always assume that there is an unbroken chain of proximate or contiguous causes joining the first event to its distant effect. For example, the explosion of a fireworks factory is the remote cause of windows breaking in the next town; but the two events are linked by a chain of proximate causes involving the propagation of a pressure wave through the air.

In general, an event can have as its remote effect an event that is utterly unlike it: releasing cyanide into a river can cause thousands of deaths downstream; swallowing an aspirin can reduce a fever. But the proximate links in the connecting chain are not only contiguous but also similar in their properties: a high concentration of cyanide in one part of the river causes an almost equally high concentration nearby. Thus, if there are causal connections between mental and physical events, we expect two conditions to be satisfied. First, somewhere in the chain of proximate causes that link my decision to raise my hand with my hand going up or that connect a feather brushing my cheek with my feeling a tickle, some mental event has to be right next to some physical event in space. Second, these contiguous events, mental and physical, must have some properties in common. According to dualism, neither of these conditions can be met, since mental events have no physical properties, not even spatial location. Thus, the problem for dualism is to explain how mental events and physical events can be causally related. Mere correlation is not enough; remote unlike causes imply proximate similar ones, but dualism insists that no mental event can be proximate or similar to any physical event.

## The Argument from Energy

This and the next argument are singled out by C. D. Broad as the most important of the scientific objections to interactionism. As Broad points out, the Conservation of Energy Principle by itself does not imply that interactionism is false. What is needed is a premise that connects causal action with energy flow. Broad suggests that the relevant premise is, "If a change in A has anything to do with causing a change in B, energy must leave A and flow into B." The qualification "has anything to do with" covers cases in which changes in A may be part of the cause, but not the complete cause, of changes in B. We will use the phrase "causally affect" for this purpose. Thus, the Argument from Energy can be reconstructed as follows:

### The Argument from Energy
(1) If two-sided interactionism is true, then mental events causally affect bodily events, and bodily events causally affect mental events.
(2) If A causally affects B, then energy flows from A to B.
(3) The total energy of an isolated body is constant.

(4) Two-sided interactionism is false.

As it stands, the argument is invalid, since it is logically possible that the energy flowing into and out of the mind balance exactly at every instant, however unlikely this might seem. Let us, therefore, change premise (1) so that interactionism implies that it is physically possible that there be occasions on which there is only a one-sided causal action between minds and bodies. In other words, if interactionism is true, then it is physically possible that, say, a mental event cause a bodily event at a time when no bodily event causes a mental event. We can then amend premise (3) to assert that a change in the total energy of an isolated body is not physically possible (because it would violate a law of nature, namely, the Energy Conservation Principle.)

### The Revised Argument from Energy
(1\*) If two-sided interactionism is true, then a mental event can causally affect a bodily event without, at the same time, any bodily event causally affecting a mental event.
(2) If A causally affects B, then energy flows from A to B.
(3\*) The total energy of an isolated body cannot change.

(4) Two-sided interactionism is false.

Let us put aside any doubts we may have about the accuracy with which we know that an isolated human body conserves energy and focus on Broad's criticisms of premise (2). Broad argues that premise (2) is false by considering a simple pendulum consisting of a weight swinging on the end of an inextensible string. The string does not transfer any energy to the weight (whose total energy remains constant), but it does cause the weight to move in an arc, for without the string, the weight would move in a straight line. Thus, we have a case where A causally affects B without involving any transfer of energy from A to B.

## The Argument from Momentum

Broad is correct about the pendulum showing that premise (2) is false: one body can causally affect another without involving any transfer of energy. But the pendulum, like all other systems, obeys the Conservation of Momentum Principle. The momentum of a body is its mass multiplied by its velocity. If the velocity of a body changes in either magnitude or direction, then its momentum has changed, and the body has accelerated because of the action of some force. The Conservation of Momentum Principle asserts that in any system on which no external forces are acting, the total momentum of all the bodies inside the system remains constant. For example, when two billiard balls collide, the velocity of each ball is altered, but the *sum* of the momentum of the first ball and the momentum of the second is the same after the collision as it was before. At the moment of impact, the billiard balls exert an instantaneous force on each other that causes the change in the momentum of each.

Bodies can also exert forces that act continuously. For example, the sun exerts a continuous gravitational force on the earth, thus causing the earth to accelerate towards the sun in an elliptical orbit. If gravity were suddenly switched off, the earth would move in a straight line into deep space. Similarly, the momentum of the swinging pendulum bob is constantly changing as the direction of the bob's velocity changes. The cause of the bob's acceleration is the tension in the string.

For the Conservation of Momentum Principle to be satisfied, all forces must have their source in objects that have mass. To put it crudely, all forces that act on physical bodies have to be attached to another physical body at their other end; for only then can momentum be conserved. The gravitational force acting on the earth originates from the sun, and changes in the sun's momentum compensate exactly for the changes in the momentum of the earth. (In fact, both bodies rotate around their common center of gravity.) Similarly, the pendulum string that exerts a force on the swinging bob is anchored to a rigid support standing on the earth.

For a physical body to be causally affected by something else, some change in its momentum must be produced. Either the body as a whole or some of its parts must be moved by forces. According to two-sided interactionism, minds causally affect bodies. But dualists also maintain that minds are nonphysical substances; they have no mass and hence no momentum. So, if two-sided interactionism were true, the Conservation of Momentum Principle would be violated.

**The Argument from Momentum**

(1) If two-sided interactionism is true, then a mind can change the momentum of a body.
(2) Minds have no momentum.
(3) The momentum of an isolated mind-body system cannot change.

(4) Two-sided interactionism is false.

Even though the Argument from Energy is unsound, the Argument from Momentum seems to show that two-way interactionism is false. The burden of proof is now on the dualist to explain how a mind can causally affect a body without changing the velocity or direction of motion of any of its parts.

**The Argument from the Structure of the Nervous System**

The second scientific objection to interactionism is based on the findings of neurophysiology. There are really two arguments: one based on an analogy with reflex actions, the other based on the absence of causal gaps.

(1) The processes and nerve cells involved in deliberate actions do not differ in kind from those involved in reflex actions that lie outside of our conscious control. No mental causes are at work in reflex actions. So, no mental causes are at work in deliberate actions.

(2) In both reflex and deliberate actions, we find a sequence of physical causes that is continuous in space and time. If interactionism is true, there should be gaps in the processes that produce deliberate actions corresponding to the causal activity of nonphysical, mental causes. Since we do not find any such gaps, interactionism is false.

Broad dismisses the first argument by stressing the difference, obvious to introspection, between (a) choosing to put pepper on a salad and (b) sneezing when some of the pepper irritates one's nose. There is an element of conscious deliberation present in (a), essential to explaining it fully, that is absent from (b). According to Broad, part of what the mental event is essential for explaining is the appropriateness of a voluntary action, given the circumstances in which it was performed; but many habitual actions are appropriate to their circumstances without involving conscious choice.

Broad's response to the "no causal gaps" objection also relies on the distinction between a mental event being part of the explanation of an action and that same event being a physical part of the causal chain that produces it. The absence of gaps in the chain of physical events does not imply that a complete explanation of the action can ignore the mental.

We can appreciate what Broad is driving at by exploring his suggestion that the mind might interact with the body during voluntary action by lowering the resistance of certain synapses and raising that of others. If this were so, we would have an unbroken chain of physical events corresponding to the flow of electricity through the neural network, but a complete explanation of that flow would have to explain why the resistances, which determined the path taken by the electricity, had the values they did, and that part of the explanation would require reference to the mental.

If we think of electricity as being an incompressible fluid like water, and the resistance of synapses corresponding to the diameter of various pipes through which the fluid can flow, then Broad's suggestion does not avoid the first scientific objection, the Argument from Momentum. For, on this hypothesis, the immaterial mind would have to be able to change the position and arrangement of physical matter. However slowly these changes took place, they would involve some acceleration, some change in the velocity of pieces of matter.

## EPIPHENOMENALISM

Given the many difficulties facing interactionism, especially in explaining how minds can causally affect bodies, some dualists have settled for epiphenomenalism: events in the brain and central nervous system give rise to conscious awareness, sensations, and other mental states, but those states in turn are causally impotent.[7] Bodies causally affect minds, but minds never causally affect bodies, nor do mental states causally affect other mental states. Causal chains can terminate in mental states, but they can never continue beyond them. One of the nineteenth-century proponents of epiphenomenalism, the English biologist Thomas Henry Huxley (1825–1895), described humans and some other animals as being "conscious automata."[8] Huxley imagined consciousness emerging in the course of evolution as a by-product when the brain and nervous system of a species reaches a certain degree of complexity. In a similar way, consciousness emerges gradually in the life history of an individual human being as a single fertilized egg develops into a multicellular child.

Epiphenomenalism avoids some of the problems with two-way interactionism (explaining the action of minds on bodies), shares some of its problems (explaining how physical events can be the proximate cause of mental events that are utterly unlike them), and faces some new problems of its own.

To many people, it is manifestly absurd to deny that minds have any causal influence on bodies or to suggest that human history could have taken its actual course without human beings ever being consciously aware of what they were doing. But the epiphenomenalist can defend the first "absurdity" without embracing the second by insisting that the causal connection between brains and minds is physically necessary. Thus, given a brain of a certain type, it is not physically possible for the brain to lack consciousness; nor is it physically possible for a certain kind of brain event to occur without being accompanied by a sensation of pain. This lawlike connection between brain events and mental events is also part of Broad's response to the first charge of "absurdity."

Imagine that the following conditions are satisfied. It is physically necessary that brain state Alpha produce mental state A; Alpha is the only brain state that can produce A; Alpha is an indispensable link in the causal chain that produces brain state B. Under these conditions, the following statement is true: A is not the cause, or even part of the cause, of B, and yet, if A had not occurred, neither would have B (because if A had not occurred, neither would have Alpha, and Alpha is indispensable for B). It is in this sense that the epiphenomenalist can assent to propositions such as "Jones would not have reached for the pepper if he had not decided to season his meal" while at the same time denying that the mental event of Jones deciding to season his meal was the cause or any part of the cause of his action of reaching for the pepper. In a similar fashion, the epiphenomenalist can explain the truth of assertions such as "Sheila would not have desired to divorce John if she had not believed him to be a philanderer" without admitting that Sheila's belief caused her desire. Both mental states—the desire and the belief—are the physically necessary effects of two causally linked brain states.

The defense of epiphenomenalism from the first objection depends on there being laws of nature connecting certain types of brain state with certain types of mental state. This leads to the objection, voiced by Herbert Feigl and by J.J.C. Smart (in Reading 23), that these laws would be unique among all the laws known to science in being "nomological danglers," that is, in postulating effects that cannot also be causes; these "danglers" are useless for explaining or predicting human behavior.[9] Nowhere else in science do we find laws of nature that decree that here causal chains must stop and go no further. Thus, while Feigl agrees that epiphenomenalism is superior to interactionism because it dispenses with mental causes that are not publicly observable, epiphenomenalism is itself deficient because it relies on effects that are not publicly observable.

## NOTES

1. *Descartes: Philosophical Writings*, trans. and ed. E. Anscombe and P. T. Geach (Indianapolis: Bobbs-Merrill, 1971): 32.

2. Notice that this is not the same as my conceiving that the evening star exists without my conceiving that the morning star exists. Conceiving A without B is not the same as conceiving A without conceiving B. Some of Descartes' contemporaries accused Descartes of conflating the two in asserting premise (7).

3. Apparently, Descartes did not appreciate the need for this vital step in his reasoning. The Divisibility Argument is thrown in almost as an afterthought. As the Jansenist theologian and philosopher Antoine Arnauld (1612–1694) pointed out in his *Fourth Objections*, even if Descartes knows that thinking is the only property he has for certain, this does not imply that he knows for certain that thinking is the only property he has. See A. Kenny, *Descartes: A Study of His Philosophy* (New York: Random House, 1968), Chapter 4.

4. For accounts of split-brain experiments and other neurological abnormalities, see P. S. Churchland, *Neurophilosophy: Toward a Unified Science of the Mind-Brain* (Cambridge, MA: MIT Press, 1986), Chapter 5. The philosophical significance of commissurotomies is discussed in T. Nagel, "Brain Bisection and the Unity of Consciousness," *Synthese* 22 (1971), reprinted in T. Nagel, *Mortal Questions* (Cambridge: Cambridge University Press, 1979); and R. Puccetti, "The Case for Mental Duality: Evidence from Split-Brain Data and Other Considerations," *Behavioral and Brain Sciences* 4 ( 1981): 93–99.

5. For some contrasting views, see J. S. Mill, *An Examination of Sir William Hamilton's Philosophy* (1865), Chapter 12; A. J. Ayer, "One's Knowledge of Other Minds," *Theoria* 19 (1953), reprinted in *Philosophical Essays* (London: Macmillan, 1965), Chapter 6; N. Malcolm, "Knowledge of Other Minds," *Journal of Philosophy* 55 (1958): 969–978; N. Malcolm, *Problems of Mind* (New York: Harper & Row, 1971) 16–23; A. Plantinga, *God and Other Minds* (Ithaca, NY: Cornell University Press, 1967).

6. For more on Hume's theory and criticisms of it, see the discussion entitled "Causality" in Part V.

7. See J. Lachs, "Epiphenomenalism and the Notion of Cause," *Journal of Philosophy* 60 (1963): 141–146; J. Lachs, "The Impotent Mind," *Review of Metaphysics* 17 (1963–1964): 187–199; K. Campbell, *Body and Mind*, 2nd edition (Notre Dame, IN: University of Notre Dame, 1984), Chapter 7.

8. T. H. Huxley, "On the Hypothesis That Animals Are Automata, and Its History," (1874). Reprinted in *Essays, Volume 1: Methods and Results* (London: Macmillan, 1893).

9. H. Feigl, *The "Mental" and the "Physical"* (Minneapolis: University of Minnesota Press, 1967): 139. As the term is used by Feigl, nomological danglers are psychophysical laws, not the mental entities that dangle from them. Feigl's objection is that such laws would have to be

ultimate, not further explicable or derivable from other laws, as a matter of principle. For example, it would have to be a brute, inexplicable, lawlike fact that certain highly complex brain events are always associated with certain mental events, such as having a yellow afterimage.

# DISCUSSION: Behaviorism

The human body is the best picture of the human soul.

Ludwig Wittgenstein, *Philosophical Investigations,*
3rd edition, trans. G.E.M. Anscombe
(New York: Macmillan, 1968), page 178.

Before evaluating the merits of behaviorism as a solution to the mind-body problem, it is important to distinguish between philosophical (logical, or analytical) behaviorism on the one hand and methodological (or scientific) behaviorism on the other.

## TWO KINDS OF BEHAVIORISM

Philosophical behaviorism is a philosophical theory defended by Gilbert Ryle in *The Concept of Mind* (1949) and by Ludwig Wittgenstein in his *Philosophical Investigations* (1953).[1] It is a thesis about the meaning of everyday assertions that apparently refer to pains, beliefs, desires, dreams, sensations, fears, as the internal, mental causes of human behavior. Philosophical behaviorism is an attempt to solve the mind-body problem by clarifying the true meaning of sentences that use folk-psychological terms and removing the confusions that surround them. Thus, philosophical behaviorism tries to solve (or dissolve) the traditional mind-body problem by analyzing the meaning of ordinary, everyday talk about minds and mental phenomena and showing that this talk is really about publicly observable behavior, not about private episodes taking place in an immaterial conscious substance. In this way, we avoid the difficulties of interactionism and at the same time dispel skepticism about other minds.

Methodological behaviorism is the widely held view among practicing scientists that when new theoretical terms (e.g., schizophrenia, Oedipus complex, dyslexia) are introduced into psychology, each term should be connected with observable behavior in such a way as to permit the objective application of the term and the possibility of testing theoretical claims that use it. In its strongest form, methodological behaviorism requires that each new theoretical term be given an operational definition in terms of observable behavior.[2] Thus, methodological behaviorism is a constraint on theory-construction in the psychological sciences. Unlike philosophical behaviorism, it is not intended as a solution to the mind-body problem, nor is it a thesis about the meanings of everyday statements concerning pains, beliefs, and desires.

Strictly speaking, operational definitions are not definitions at all, since they have nothing to do with equivalences of meaning. Terms such as *manic depres-*

*sive* and *electrically charged* are operationally defined when one specifies a procedure—a set of operations in the literal sense—for determining when the term applies (a sufficient condition) and when it does not (a necessary condition) and, where appropriate, for measuring the numerical value of the quantity named by the term.

The main motivation for methodological behaviorism in the twentieth century was the desire to make psychology into a genuine science by emulating the methods of physics.[3] It was assumed that the main reason why physics, unlike psychology, had made such progress since the seventeenth century was that its concepts were closely linked to procedures that allowed hypotheses concerning them to be confirmed or refuted by experiment. The great success of special relativity theory and quantum mechanics, for example, was attributed to their operational definitions of concepts such as simultaneity and quantum state. Few of the terms used by the competing schools of psychoanalysis had the same direct connection with observation; as a result, the hypotheses that used them were vague and difficult to test.

## PHILOSOPHICAL BEHAVIORISM

A scientist can be a methodological behaviorist and yet still be a Cartesian dualist. Even though new psychological concepts are given definite behavioral criteria for their application, they might still refer to mental episodes that can be privately experienced but not publicly observed. Philosophical behaviorism is far more radical than methodological behaviorism, since it declares that dualism is both redundant and meaningless. Once one realizes that all mental talk is really about behavior alone, the Cartesian mind becomes an idle wheel that turns nothing. According to Ryle, it is a category mistake to assert that minds are separate immaterial substances that cause behavior, just as it would be a category mistake to think that "the average American" refers to a real person. Thus, throughout the rest of this discussion, I shall ignore methodological behaviorism, since it has little relevance to the traditional problems in the philosophy of mind. From now on, whenever I use the term *behaviorism* without qualification, I will be referring to philosophical behaviorism, not methodological behaviorism.

We can grasp the essential idea behind behaviorism by considering the nature of dispositional predicates such as *fragile, soluble,* and *inflammable.* When we say that a sugar cube is soluble, we mean that the cube would dissolve if it were placed in water. Similarly, gasoline is inflammable, even when it is not burning, if a spark would ignite it in the presence of oxygen. Now, suppose that at midnight on Christmas Eve, two events occur: A sugar cube is placed in water and dissolves; a spark ignites a puddle of gasoline. Why did these events—the dissolving of the sugar and the ignition of the gasoline—occur when they did? If we are seeking a *causal* explanation, it would be wrong to say that the reason the sugar cube dissolved in water was because it is soluble or that the reason the gasoline ignited is because it is inflammable. Solubility is not some internal state of sugar that causes it to dissolve; rather, being soluble is just a shorthand description of the cube's propensity to dissolve in water. The connection between solubility and dissolving is not causal but logical. From the statement, "This sugar cube is soluble," it follows logically that the cube will dissolve when placed in water; but what *caused* the cube to dissolve is not the cube's solubility but the event of the cube's being placed in water. Similarly, what caused the gasoline to ignite is the spark, not the liquid's inflammability.

Dispositional terms such as *soluble* and *inflammable* also illustrate how the behaviorist disposes of skepticism. Once we see an object dissolve or burst into flame, we know for sure that it has the property of being able to do these things. If something actually dissolves, then it follows logically that it is soluble.

The behaviorist analyzes mental terms as expressing nothing more than behavioral dispositions. To say that a woman is angry or afraid or that she believes that all sound arguments are valid, is to attribute a set of dispositions to her concerning how she would behave, act, and talk under various circumstances. On this view, anger, fear, and beliefs are not private, internal states that cause behavior; rather, they are dispositional properties that can be defined solely in behavioral terms.

## CRITICISMS OF PHILOSOPHICAL BEHAVIORISM

The most potent objection to behaviorism is its failure to provide adequate translations of mental expressions into statements about behavioral dispositions that do not themselves make essential reference to beliefs and other mental states. Some philosophers have argued that this failure is not just a temporary shortcoming that might be overcome with ingenuity and effort, but a fundamental limitation that behaviorist analyses cannot overcome as a matter of principle.

The basic difficulty can be illustrated by the statement, "Anne wants a Caribbean holiday." Unlike solubility, which is a single-tracked disposition involving only one kind of behavior (namely dissolving), wanting a Caribbean holiday is a multitracked disposition that connects with an open-ended range of different kinds of external behavior, such as saying certain things and acting in certain ways under an enormously wide variety of circumstances.[4] Not only is it impossible to say what the entire range of relevant behavior is, specifying the circumstances under which that behavior would be manifested inevitably makes reference to mental states. Thus, for example, one of the components of the behaviorist analysis of "Anne wants a Caribbean holiday" will be "If Anne is asked whether she wants a Caribbean holiday, she will assert 'Yes,' or some other equivalent utterance." This will not do as it stands, because Anne might very well want a holiday in the Caribbean yet be unwilling to reveal that information. She will answer "Yes" to a direct question only if she does not *desire* to conceal the information, only if she *wants* the questioner to know about her dream vacation. In this way, the behaviorist analysis of just one very small part of the meaning of "Anne wants a Caribbean holiday" is forced to reintroduce the same kind of mental terms that the analysis is supposed to eliminate.

The same criticism can be made of behaviorist translations of statements such as "Anne is in pain," "Anne is perceiving a red apple," and "Anne is dreaming of Hawaii." Moreover, not only will the specification of these mental states as multitracked behavioral dispositions remain open-ended and question-begging, but it will also omit the qualitative aspect of the feeling of pain or the sensation of red. Thus, leaving aside the circularity objection, even if "Anne is in pain" is translated as "Anne is acting as if she were in pain," the two expressions are not equivalent in meaning, since the second statement could be true even though Anne is not experiencing the agonizing raw feel that is an essential condition for the truth of the first statement.

Despite its falsity, there is much that is insightful and correct about behaviorism. For example, the behaviorist is right to point out that mental terms must be "logically" connected with distinctive kinds of behavior if we are to understand how infants first learn to apply them correctly; but it does not follow from this that the word *pain* refers exclusively to that behavior and to nothing else. In fact, there is no logically deductive connection between exhibiting pain behavior and actually being in pain: it is always logically possible to have the one without the other. We explain how children learn to use the word *pain* and how we can know that other people are in pain by realizing that pain behavior is the evidential criterion for the ascription of pains to other people. To believe that someone is in pain on the basis of her pain behavior is to be justified in believing that another person is in pain.[5]

Similarly, the behaviorist is correct to insist on the dispositional character of mental states such as belief and desire. Someone who claims to desire the equality of women but would never do anything to further women's rights under any possible circumstances is either insincere or deluded. The major flaw with behaviorism does not lie in its thesis that mental states such as belief are dispositional or in its insistence that the meaning of mental terms is essentially connected with behavioral criteria for their correct application. Its fault lies in an inadequate conception of the nature of dispositional terms.

Consider again the dispositional terms *fragile, soluble,* and *inflammable.* To explain the allure of behaviorism, I deliberately chose these terms because they are what I shall call superficial dispositions. Not only are they single-tracked (referring solely to breaking, dissolving, and igniting, respectively), but they are also completely free of any implications about the underlying cause or causes of the dispositions that they describe.[6] Consider another dispositional term, namely, *electrically charged.* Back in the seventeenth century when the term *electricity* was first introduced (from the Greek word for amber), a body was considered charged if it attracted little pieces of paper after being rubbed vigorously with cat's fur. Slowly, this single-tracked dispositional term became multitracked as more was learned concerning the superficial, directly observable properties of charged bodies. At the same time, the concept of something's being electrically charged deepened to include essential reference to the fluid (or fluids) thought to be the underlying cause of these dispositional traits.

In the same way, many diseases begin life as syndromes; their names are simply labels for groups of symptoms that are observed to occur together. Later, the symptoms are regarded as having a common cause, perhaps an infection or an injured organ, so that it becomes part of the meaning of the term that it refer to that cause, whatever it might turn out to be. I shall call this kind of multitracked disposition involving a putative common cause a causal disposition.

Most multitracked dispositions are not superficial but causal. Their names are supposed to refer not merely to the range of properties that are the criteria for applying the term but also to the entities, processes, or states that are the common cause of those properties. Thus, while many dispositional terms start off by being single-tracked and superficial, they soon become multitracked and causal. In the seventeenth century it would have been a category mistake to say (in response to a request for a causal explanation) that a piece of rubbed amber attracts lint because it is electrically charged; for, at that time, *electrically charged* simply meant "having a disposition to attract chaff when rubbed." A few years later, such an explanation did make sense because by then *being electrically charged* had become a causal disposition term relating a range of different phenomena to a putative common cause.

Folk psychology, our common everyday way of talking about mental phenomena, treats mental terms as causal dispositions. It is for this reason that we regard John's having a headache as an explanation of his disposition to produce headache behavior, such as groaning out loud, taking aspirin, and yelling at his kids to be quiet. Simply put, headaches are conceived as mental states, whatever they may turn out to be, that can interact with other mental states, such as desires and beliefs, to produce behavior that serves as the normal evidential criterion for deciding when another person is in that kind of state. Thus, the way is now clear to consider materialism and functionalism as philosophical accounts of the nature of mental states.

---

## NOTES

1. Wittgenstein's later views are rather subtle. For a good account of how they differ from the reductionist version of behaviorism discussed here, see A. Donagan, "Wittgenstein on Sensation," in *Wittgenstein: The Philosophical Investigations*, ed. G. Pitcher (Notre Dame, IN: University of Notre Dame Press, 1968): 324–351.

2. For a defense of operationism in the sciences, see P. W. Bridgman, *The Logic of Modern Physics* (New York: Macmillan, 1928). Carl Hempel diagnoses the inadequacies of Bridgman's operationism as an account of the meaning of scientific terms in "A Logical Appraisal of Operationism," *Scientific Monthly* 79 (1954): 215–220. Reprinted in C. G. Hempel, *Aspects of Scientific Explanation* (New York: Macmillan, 1965): 123–133.

3. See, for example, B. F. Skinner, *Science and Human Behavior* (New York: Macmillan, 1953). For an illuminating account of why Skinner rejects "inner" mental causes as scientifically illegitimate, see D. Dennett, "Skinner Skinned," in his *Brainstorms: Philosophical Essays on Mind and Psychology* (Cambridge, MA: MIT Press, 1978), Chapter 4.

4. The example and the terminology are borrowed from P. M. Churchland, *Matter and Consciousness* (Cambridge, MA: MIT Press, 1984).

5. I am assuming here that behavior is described in nonmental terms. Obviously, "Harriet is writhing *in pain*" logically implies that Harriet is in pain, but then the question would be, How do we know that the first statement is true? For better or worse, we follow the behaviorist in requiring that descriptions of behavior be certain.

6. Well, almost. They do carry with them the implication that the dispositions in question are intrinsic properties of the kinds of substances involved and not the result of external influences. What makes a wafer of glass fragile is its internal structure, not a "fragility spell" that is cast over it.

# DISCUSSION: Materialism

I have been accused of denying consciousness, but I am not conscious of having done so. Consciousness is to me a mystery, and not one to be dismissed. We know what it is like to be conscious, but not how to put it into satisfactory scientific terms. Whatever it precisely may be, consciousness is a state of the body, a state of nerves.

W. V. O. Quine, *Quiddities* (Cambridge, MA: Belknap, 1987), pp. 132–133.

There are several materialist theories of mind under active discussion by modern philosophers. I will begin by discussing the identity theory (often called reductive materialism, physicalism, or the central-state identity theory). I will then examine two other materialist theories—eliminative materialism and functionalism—which have been proposed in response to objections to the identity theory.[1]

## THE IDENTITY THEORY

The identity theory can be summarized very simply: Mental processes, states, and events are identical with brain processes, states, and events.[2] For every belief and desire that a person has, for every sensation of red and feeling of pain that she experiences, for every memory recalled, image conceived, and proposition contemplated, there is some physical state, event, or process in that person's brain and central nervous system with which it is numerically identical. Mental phenomena are identical with brain phenomena in the same way that optical phenomena are identical with electromagnetic phenomena: the former are completely reducible to the latter. Red light just *is* electromagnetic radiation of a certain frequency; an electrical current just *is* a flow of electrons; mental states just *are* brain states of a certain kind.

The identity theory has a number of persuasive reasons in its favor.

(1) It avoids the problems, both conceptual and scientific, with Cartesian dualism: no mysterious immaterial substances; no causal interactions between immaterial minds and physical matter. Since mental states are brain states, mental events are physical events. Hence, they can cause other physical events to occur (as in deliberate action) and be caused to occur by them (as in having a sensation of color or a feeling of pain) without violating any laws of physics.

(2) Since mental states are numerically identical with brain states, the question, How can mental states cause the brain states with which they are identified? cannot arise. Imagine that we give the proper name "Hurtie" to a particular pain that I experience and the proper name "Stimie" to the stimulation of certain fibers (C-fibers) in my brain.[3] According to the identity theory, Stimie does not cause Hurtie, but the perfect correlation between them is given a complete explanation: they are perfectly correlated because they are one and the same thing. It is just like explaining the remarkable coincidence in the locations of Dr. Jekyll and Mr. Hyde or the perfect match between the polarization of a light ray and the plane of oscillation of the magnetic vector of an electromagnetic wave of the same frequency. Reducing perfect correlations to iden-

tities gives an explanation that is final and complete: no further explanatory or causal questions can be asked.[4]

(3) The identity theory also avoids the principal objections to behaviorism. We can do justice to folk psychology and regard beliefs, desires, sensations, dreams, and other mental phenomena as internal states that can interact with one another and cause behavior and tendencies to act. The identity theory does not require us to translate all talk about mental states into statements about multitracked behavioral dispositions. Also, as Fodor points out in "The Mind-Body Problem" (Reading 24), it is a merit of the identity theory over behaviorism that the theory is consistent with cases in which no behavior results from deliberation because we decide *not* to act.

(4) Finally, the identity theory squares nicely with the thoroughgoing physicalism of modern biology and neurophysiology. Whether in the evolutionary origin of species or the embryological development of individual organisms, whether in studies of the normal functioning of the brain or investigations of its responses to disease and injury, we find an unbroken chain of physical and biochemical causes. This is exactly what we would expect if the identity theory were true.

## OBJECTIONS TO THE IDENTITY THEORY

The identity theory has received a number of criticisms both from dualists and from fellow materialists.

### The Privacy Objection

The first criticism, the Privacy Objection, incorporates several of the eight objections to the identity theory discussed by Smart in his "Sensations and Brain Processes" (Reading 23). As we noted in the introduction to Part III, mental states have a number of distinctive features, including qualitative content (the "raw feel" of many sensations), intentional content (the "aboutness" of beliefs, desires, hopes, and fears), and privileged access. If any of these are *real* properties of mental states but not properties of any brain state, then we can prove that the identity theory is false by invoking the Principle of the Indiscernibility of Identicals. The restriction to real properties is crucial here. As we noted during the analysis of Descartes' Doubt Argument in the discussion entitled "Dualism", there are many properties (e.g., being an object of someone's belief) that fall outside the scope of the Principle of the Indiscernibility of Identicals.

If the privileged access we have to mental states means that we know for certain that we have them, then this is not the kind of real property to which Leibniz's Law applies. (Oedipus knew for certain that he was married to Jocasta; he did not know for certain that he was married to his mother. But this does not prove that Jocasta was not his mother.) If it means that they have the property of being know*able* by introspection, then the premise that denies that we have the same introspective access to brain states begs the question against the identity theory. (Oedipus was *able* to know that he was married to his mother and did come to know it as soon as he realized that Jocasta and his mother were one and the same person.)

In assessing Cartesian objections to the identity theory, it is important to remember that the identity theorist is claiming an identity of reference, not an identity of meaning. The phrases "I am now feeling a sharp pain" and "The C-fibers are firing in such-and-such manner in such-and-such part of my brain" clearly do not mean the same thing. Thus, I can know that the first is true without having a clue about the truth of the second. But if the identity theory is true, the phrases refer to exactly the same set of neurophysiological events.

How do we discover whether the identity theory is true—whether mental states are identical with brain states? According to the reductive materialist, this is an empirical question that can be settled only by empirical research. The fate of the identity theory lies in the hands of science. Just as water was discovered to be identical with oxygen dihydride molecules, and genes to be identical with segments of DNA, so we will discover which precise neurophysiological states, events, and processes (if any) are identical with beliefs, memories, perceptions, nightmares, and afterimages of various types.[5]

## Rorty's Objection and Eliminative Materialism

Richard Rorty and other eliminative materialists have pointed out that the "scientific" and empirical character of the identity theory and reductive materialism is a two-edged sword, for in the history of science, there are many examples of successful reductions in which the predecessor theory was entirely abandoned and replaced by its successor.[6] For example, the modern chemical theory of oxidation reduced the phlogiston theory of burning by eliminating it entirely. Similarly, caloric and the aether have disappeared from physics just as surely as demons have been banished from medicine. These are examples of revolutionary takeovers—reductions by replacement—as contrasted with conservative takeovers—reductions by absorption—in which the new theory preserves the ontology of the old.

Rorty argues that if the reduction of psychology to neurophysiology posited by the identity theory succeeds, it will eliminate entirely our customary ways of talking about human minds. Beliefs, desires, and sensations will be discarded as fictions as were phlogiston, caloric, and demons. When we discovered that what we used to call unicorn horns are in fact nothing but the horns of narwhals, we ceased referring to them as unicorn horns because we no longer believed that there are any such creatures. Similarly, when the identity theory succeeds in identifying mental states with brain states, we will stop talking about pains, afterimages, and sensations because we will no longer believe that there are any such things.[7] The real causes of our behavior are neurophysiological processes, not mental events, just as the real causes of disease are germs not demons. People who thought they saw demons were hallucinating; people who thought they saw unicorn horns were misdescribing their experiences.

In response to the objection that it is absurd to suggest that pains, sensations, and other mental phenomena are nonexistent, Rorty writes:

> The absurdity of saying "Nobody has ever felt a pain" is no greater than that of saying "Nobody has ever seen a demon," *if* we have a suitable answer to the question "What *was* I reporting when I said I felt a pain?" To this question, the science of the future may reply "You were reporting the occurrence of a certain brain-process, and it would make life simpler for us if you would, in the future, *say* "My C-fibers are firing" instead of saying "I'm in pain." In so saying, he has as good a prima facie case as the scientist who answers the witch-doctor's question "What *was* I reporting when I reported a demon?" by saying "You were reporting the content of your hallucination,

and it would make life simpler if, in the future, you would describe your experiences in those terms."[8]

Not all reductions are revolutionary. Even though clouds are nothing but water droplets, and water itself nothing but $H_2O$ molecules, we do not deny that clouds and water exist. Rorty's case for eliminative materialism rests on defending the analogy between the identities posited by the identity theory and cases of revolutionary reduction, such as the replacement of the demon theory with the germ theory of disease. One relevant disanalogy concerns the explanation of error: the new theory must explain why we mistakenly believed in the existence of entities that are now regarded as fictitious. For example, the witch-doctor reported seeing demons because he had eaten hallucinogenic mushrooms; but we cannot appeal to hallucinations to explain why we believed that there are pains, since hallucinations are themselves mental entities. Similarly, it is difficult to see what false beliefs we have about pains that neurophysiology would require us to give up. Is it false that pains are painful; that they are often caused by injury and disease; that they have a tendency to cause pain-avoidance behavior?

A study of the wide range of reductions that have occurred in the sciences suggests that most reductions are located on a spectrum between the two extremes of complete replacement and complete absorption. Typically, when a new theory reduces an older one, there is partial absorption accompanied by some reinterpretation of concepts. Thus, when classical genetics is reduced to molecular biology, we see that Mendel's laws of independent assortment and segregation are only useful approximations to the truth and that, in reality, genes are not indivisible atoms of inheritance that are always transferred as whole units during reproduction, each independently of its neighbors.[9] We also realize that genes are better defined in terms of the proteins for which they code rather than in terms of observable features of an animal's body such as eye color. Of course, we could describe this reduction by saying that according to molecular biology, classical genes do not exist, but this would be an exaggeration, since modern molecular biology preserves what was true and useful in classical genetics while at the same time improving on it. In the same way, it is conceivable that neurophysiology will force us to modify the concepts of folk psychology and, perhaps, to admit that some of our beliefs about sensations, pains, desires, and the like were false. We can do this, however, without having to take the more radical step of abandoning traditional psychology as a total fiction. Given the explanatory strength of folk psychology, it is more likely that in future reductions, mental states will survive like classical genes in biology rather than being exorcised as demons were from medicine.

### The Qualia Objection

Identity theorists often describe the identity between brain states and mental states as being "strict" but also "empirical" and "contingent." Yet if the identity between the mental and the physical is as strict as that which holds between the morning star and the evening star, it is logically impossible that a world contain the one without also containing the other. Admittedly, our finding out whether the identity holds is a matter of empirical research, but the holding of the identity is not contingent. So, if we give the names "Stimie" and "Hurtie" to the brain state and the mental state that are identical, there are no logically possible worlds in which Stimie exists but Hurtie does not.

Now, the objection runs, it is logically possible that Stimie (the stimulation of the C-fibers in my brain) exist without its being painful or hurting in the slightest. This could happen if my brain were wired differently or if the laws of chemistry were different from what they actually are. There is no logical necessity that Stimie be accompanied by a feeling of pain rather than by a mildly pleasant tickle or some qualitatively neutral sensation. But, it is argued, it is an essential property of Hurtie and of pains in general that they are painful; it is logically impossible that the mental state named "Hurtie" not hurt. Thus, it is concluded that the identity theory is false, since there are possible worlds in which Stimie exists (painlessly) but Hurtie does not.

The most plausible response that the identity theorist can make to this argument is, I think, to deny that the qualitative raw feel of pain is an essential property of Hurtie or any other pain state.[10] If the identity theory is true, then mental states are individuated by the brain states with which they are identical. It is, therefore, only a contingent feature of the experiences that we call pains that they hurt. An analogy would be the orbital period of Venus. Since the morning star is identical with the evening star, both planets orbit the Sun in exactly the same period of time. In our world, this period is 225 days, but it is both logically and physically possible that it could have been longer or shorter (if either Venus were farther from the Sun or the law of gravity were different from what it actually is). Compare this with Stimie and Hurtie. Since Stimie and Hurtie are identical, they have the same properties. In some possible worlds, Stimie does not hurt; therefore, the fact that Hurtie hurts in this world is a contingent property of this pain sensation, not a property that is essential to it.

This response to the Qualia Objection can also provide an answer to the Inverted Spectrum Objection to functionalism mentioned by Fodor in his "The Mind-Body Problem" (Reading 24). The core of the objection is that it is possible that mental states that are functionally identical (and hence the same mental state according to the functionalist) might have a different qualitative raw feel. Specifically, I can imagine waking up one morning and finding that red things (e.g., stop signs, fire engines, the Soviet flag) now look blue, and blue things (e.g., the sky, the ocean, blueberries) now look red.[11] My spectrum has become inverted, perhaps because some wires have been crossed in my brain. Since I remember how things used to look, this is very disconcerting; but eventually I learn to adapt and call fire engines red (even though they look blue to me) and the sky blue (even though it produces in me a sensation of red). So, after a period of adaptation, I end up in states that are functionally identical to the old ones but qualitatively different. But if functionalism is true, this cannot happen.

The response consists of two claims.[12] First, the functionalist denies that having a specific qualitative content is essential to any mental state being the kind of mental state that it is. This step is easy for functionalists because, for them, mental states are individuated solely on the basis of their functional and causal role. The second and more difficult step is to explain how qualia get into the picture at all, since no functionalist characterization of mental states, however detailed, requires that mental states feel a certain way to the creature that has them.

At this point the functionalist appeals to the physical properties of the actual physical states and processes that each mental state is identical with. The qualitative feel—the *quale*—of a sensory state just is that set of physical properties of the physical process that its possessor is responding to when it recognizes that it is in that state. Thus, if Hurtie plays exactly the same functional role for a silicon Martian as it does for us, it could feel different for the Martian simply because the Martian's internal receptors are responding to a property of his Stimie that is different from ours. Thus, it is possible that the Martian's pains do not hurt. (Same functionally defined Hurtie, but different physical Stimie and different qualitative Feelie.) It is also logically possible that the same physical Stimie feel different to differently wired organic creatures of the same basic type if their internal discriminators are keyed to different properties of the same neural process. (Same physical Stimie and same functionally defined Hurtie, but different qualitative Feelie.)

## WHAT IS SUPPOSED TO BE IDENTICAL WITH WHAT?

The gene-DNA analogy is helpful in understanding exactly what is being identified with what in the identity theory. In classical genetics, genes are defined as the units of inheritance that causally determine phenotypic characteristics such as eye color in fruit flies and wrinkled or smooth seed coats in peas. There are three biological levels at which we can ask about the identity of classical genes: the individual plant or animal, the species, and whole groups of species. Because a species is an interbreeding population of individuals that are very similar in their physiology, it is natural to think that the gene responsible for albinism in *this* Thompson's gazelle is the same gene (that is, another instance of the same gene) as the one that causes the same trait in *that* Thompson's gazelle; and at the molecular level we expect to find the same sequence of bases in the corresponding segments of DNA.

In another species, such as the water buffalo, there is no reason to expect that the gene that causes albinism in it will be exactly the same as the gene responsible for albinism in the Thompson's gazelle. Same function only implies same DNA structure within the same species (and there are even some viruses whose genes are not made of DNA at all, but of RNA). Thus, when someone claims that genes are identical with segments of DNA or that classical genetics has been reduced to molecular biology, the identity of genes with DNA segments is supposed to hold at the level of the species, but not beyond that level. The same gene is responsible for albinism in all lions, but the gene that causes albinism in the lion is not necessarily the same as the gene that causes albinism in the leopard.

The only clear-cut cases of mental phenomena (beyond simple sensory experiences) occur in living human beings, all members of the same species and thus very similar in the physiology of their brains. There are no noncontroversial cases of minds that are not intimately associated with some biological organism (or, possibly, with some inorganic system such as a computer). If there were minds without matter, Cartesian dualism would be true and materialism false. To that extent, the identity theory, being a version of materialism, is empirically falsifiable. But can we say what testable content the identity theory has beyond the general claim that the mental is entirely dependent on the physical? For even epiphenomenalism says this much.

All materialists, including identity theorists, are token-physicalists; that is, they believe that each instance of a mental state or event is identical with some physical state or event. In human beings and other sentient terrestrial organisms, these physical states are states of brains and central nervous systems, not of the kidney, heart, or liver. Where materialists differ among themselves is with respect to type-physicalism, that is, with respect to the doctrine that the same type of mental state must always be identical to the same type of physical state as a matter of lawlike necessity.

Many philosophers have been persuaded by functionalist arguments that type-physicalism is false, since if we define mental states functionally, it is physically possible that a Martian made of silicon or a suitably programmed computer have a belief or be in pain without having a brain and central nervous system made of organic cells. A more down-to-earth example would be the pain of an octopus: both the octopus and I can be in pain, yet because of the gross anatomical differences between us, the octopus cannot be undergoing exactly the same neurophysiological processes in its nervous system that I am undergoing in mine.

Most identity theorists thus espouse only a limited form of type-physicalism at the level of species: among individuals belonging to the same species, mental states of the same type are identical with brain states of the same type. This at least allows the identity theory to be tested (in principle) by seeing whether a purported identity holds in several members of the same species (e.g., human beings); but it also makes the identity theory less interesting as a theory of the *mental*, since it is not about pains, beliefs, and desires in general but about octopodal pain, human beliefs, Martian desires, and so on. By contrast, functionalism offers a truly comprehensive theory of mental states by abstracting away from the particular biological or physical system in which they are realized.

## FUNCTIONALISM

In the decades since 1960, functionalism has emerged as a popular account of the nature of mental states. Though specific versions of functionalism differ in their details, all share the basic view that mental states are defined in terms of their causal role. What makes a mental state a belief that P, a sensation of Q, or a desire that R is its causal relations to other mental states, sensory inputs, and behavioral outputs. In this way, it is claimed, functionalism can combine the best features of both materialism and behaviorism while avoiding the drawbacks of each.

On the one hand, functionalists agree with materialists that mental states are often the inner causes of observable behavior and that mental states can interact with one another to produce a particular behavioral output. Thus, talk about beliefs, desires, sensations, and the rest cannot be translated into talk solely about behavioral responses to sensory stimuli. Reference to other mental states is essential to the explanation of behavior.

On the other hand, functionalists agree with the behaviorists that the connection between mental states and behavior is not merely accidental but logical. A mental state has to be connected with the typical behavioral expressions of pain to qualify as a sensation of pain. One difference between functionalism and behaviorism is that functionalists insist that the connection between a sensation of pain and pain behavior essentially involves other mental states, such as beliefs and desires. For example, if a man experiences a sharp, excruciating pain but *believes* that other people will be offended by his yelling "Damn!" and *desires* that other people not be offended, then he probably will not utter the expletive that he would invariably produce if he believed that no one was in earshot.

Most functionalists are token-physicalists. They believe that each mental state (characterized functionally) of a particular person corresponds to a particular physical state of that person's brain. This is minimal materialism. *My* belief that Jimmy Carter is from Georgia may not be realized by exactly the same type of brain state as *your* belief that Jimmy Carter is from Georgia. But if both brain states play exactly the same functional role, then they are instances of the same belief.

Many functionalists have been influenced by analogies from computer science. The same software program can be run on a number of physically different machines. Thus, an IBM may not be in exactly the same physical state as a Toshiba when it records the result of adding 213 to 498. Yet the answer, 711, is represented in both machines; that state is caused by the same set of states (namely all those that represent computable problems whose solution is 711); and that state will causally produce the same set of other states when instructed to do so. Thus, as far as the functionalist is concerned, the IBM and the Toshiba are in the same state, since states are characterized functionally, not physically. Similarly, Robert Redford, George Bush, and a Klingon from a distant galaxy can be in the same mental state of wishing that people were kinder and gentler to one another if and only if the functional characterization of that state is the same in all three cases. A crude analogy to this is Fodor's Coke machine. As long as a machine delivers Cokes and change in response to the insertion of dimes and nickels as specified in Fodor's machine table, then it is irrelevant what the machine is made of or what it looks like.

### The Intentionality Objection

In his article "The Mind-Body Problem" (Reading 24), Jerry Fodor considers two objections to functionalism as an account of mental states: the qualia objection and the intentionality objection. Since I have already discussed materialist responses to the qualia objection, I shall now focus on the intentionality objection.

Many philosophers have regarded the intentionality of cognitive mental states as an insuperable barrier to both materialism and the token-physicalism of functionalism. Typical examples of intentional states are Othello's belief that Desdemona loves Cassio, Hamlet's suspicion that his father was murdered by Claudius, Lady Macbeth's obsession that her hands are stained with Duncan's blood. In each case, the mental state has a specific "aboutness" captured in the "that" clause—a reference to something beyond itself that may or may not exist—that distinguishes it from other mental states of the same type. Thus, the fact that Gertrude's belief that Ophelia is mad is about Ophelia's madness is what distinguishes it from Gertrude's belief that Ophelia is the daughter of Polonius.

Dualists have often claimed that intentionality is a primitive, unanalyzable property that is uniquely mental. Materialists have countered by pointing out that symbols and sentences are physical objects, and yet they too have semantic content, a meaning that makes them about one thing rather than another. Functionalists such as Fodor have attempted to analyze the semantic content of mental representations in terms of their functional role: what causes them, what they cause, how they interact with other representations. Much of this work is sketchy and controversial, but it prompts the following observations:

(1) It is not obvious that it cannot succeed. Thus, the intentionality of the mental is not an immediate disproof of materialism and functionalism.

(2) It is not clear that dualism fares any better than materialism and functionalism in explaining what makes my thought of oranges about oranges rather than tangerines. If the dualist can legitimately claim that intentionality is an unanalyzable property of mental states, why cannot the materialist claim with equal justification that it is an unanalyzable property of the brain states with which they are identical?

(3) The analogy between the intentionality of thoughts and the meaning of linguistic symbols suggests that beliefs and other intentional states are stored in the brain as representations. Consider my belief that primroses are yellow and my belief that violets are blue. Each of these two different beliefs will have a distinct representation in my brain; each will be written in my brain, so to speak, as a different mental sentence. But if functionalism individuates beliefs and other mental states solely on the basis of causal relations between representations in the brain, sensory inputs, and behavioral outputs, then the theory seems to give the wrong answer to some questions of belief individuation. For there are convincing arguments that the full meanings of terms like *water, primrose*, and *Jimmy Carter* are not solely in the head: identity of mental representation and functional role does not guarantee identity of reference. Which objects words and thoughts refer to depends on factors outside the head, such as social context and practices.

Stephen Stich gives the following example of beliefs that, although they differ in semantic content (that is, they are about different things), a functionalist analysis appears forced to regard as instances of the same belief-type.[13]

Imagine that on a distant planet called Yon there is a replica of Fodor that reproduces the terrestrial Fodor in every detail, molecule for molecule. Furthermore, all the inhabitants of Earth have their equivalents on Yon who are qualitatively identical to the people on Earth in every physical respect. The brain of Yon-Fodor consists of exactly the same kind of matter as the brain of Earth-Fodor, and it is arranged in exactly the same way. Both Yon-Fodor and Earth-Fodor have a belief that is represented in each of their brains as "Carter comes from Georgia." Are these beliefs the same belief or different beliefs? Since, by hypothesis, the physical states of the brains of Yon-Fodor and Earth-Fodor are the same and the functional role of those states is the same in each person, the functionalist account that relies on brain representations must conclude that the two Fodors share the same belief. But the beliefs are not the same. Earth-Fodor's belief is about the terrestrial Jimmy Carter; Yon-Fodor's belief is about the Yon-Jimmy Carter. Thus, functionalism is false, since it implies that Earth-Fodor and Yon-Fodor have the same belief.[14]

Fodor's response to this problem is to bite the bullet and insist that as far as psychological science is concerned, Earth-Fodor and Yon-Fodor have the same belief when each has the same representation playing the same functional role. The only things that can possibly affect a person's behavior or help to explain it are factors that are in or that interact with that person's brain and nervous system. Semantic properties (such as reference and truth) that are not represented syntactically are not such factors. Therefore, it is no defect if an otherwise adequate psychological theory is forced to ignore those factors.[15]

Unfortunately for Fodor's reply, it seems that a psychological theory that ignores what thoughts are about is not going to provide an adequate account of human behavior. Suppose, for example, that Fodor desperately wants to shake hands with Jimmy Carter. He sees someone who looks like Carter across the room and walks up to him. How do we explain why Fodor performed this action rather than, say, hopping on the next space shuttle to Yon? It is hard to resist the conclusion that Fodor acts as he does because his belief is about *our* Jimmy Carter (the earthling) and not about Yon-Jimmy Carter.

## NOTES

1. There are many confusing disagreements among contemporary functionalists. Some functionalists claim that functionalism is consistent with but does not imply physicalism. Others claim that functionalism shows that physicalism is false. Some of this disagreement is the result of ambiguity: functionalism is consistent with token-physicalism but implies that type-physicalism is almost certainly false. See N. Block, "Introduction: What Is Functionalism?" and N. Block and J. Fodor, "What Psychological States Are Not," in N. Block, Ed., *Readings in Philosophy of Psychology* (Cambridge, MA: Harvard University Press, 1980): 171–184, 237–250. The Block and Fodor article first appeared in *Philosophical Review* 81 ( 1972 ): 159–181.

2. When first introduced by U. T. Place, H. Feigl, and J.J.C. Smart in the 1950s, the identity theory was restricted to a thesis about mental *events*, such as having a sensation or an afterimage, thinking a particular thought, imagining a scene. Only later did D. M. Armstrong and other materialists argue that both mental events *and* mental states (such as beliefs, desires, hopes, and fears) are identical with physical states of the brain and central nervous system. Place continues to regard mental states as causally dependent on the brain's microstructure but not identical with it. See U. T. Place, "Is Consciousness a Brain Process?" *British Journal of Psychology* 47 (1956): 44–50; "Thirty Years On—Is Consciousness Still a Brain Process?" *Australasian Journal of Philosophy* 66 (1988): 208–219; and D. M. Armstrong, *A Materialist Theory of Mind* (London: Routledge and Kegan Paul, 1968). I shall ignore this interesting difference between versions of the identity theory; and often, for the sake of brevity, I use the term *mental state* to refer to either mental states or mental events.

3. These names are borrowed from Michael A. Slote, *Reason and Scepticism* (New York: Humanities Press, 1970): 52. I address Slote's criticisms of the identity theory in the discussion of the Qualia Objection.

4. The thesis that if A is identical with B, then A cannot also be the cause of B is denied by John Searle in his *Minds, Brains and Science* (Cambridge, MA: Harvard University Press, 1984), Chapter 1. Searle argues both that mental phenomena are caused by brain processes and that mental phenomena just are features of the brain.

5. At the end of his article, Smart denies that the choice between the identity theory and epiphenomenalism can be made on empirical grounds because the two theories have exactly the same testable consequences. Smart argues that the identity theory is preferable to epiphenomenalism because it is simpler.

6. See R. Rorty, "Mind-Body Identity, Privacy, and Categories," *The Review of Metaphysics* 19 (1965): 24–54. Reprinted along with other papers on eliminative materialism in D. Rosenthal, Ed., *Materialism and the Mind-Body Problem* (Englewood Cliffs, NJ: Prentice-Hall, 1977), Part Five.

7. Of course, if there are no such things as beliefs, we will not *believe* that there are no beliefs, but we will no longer believe that there are.

8. R. Rorty, "Mind-Body Identity, Privacy, and Categories," in D. Rosenthal, Ed., *Materialism and the Mind-Body Problem*, 179–180.

9. For a good introduction to the complexity of the reduction of Mendelian to molecular genetics see M. Ruse, *The Philosophy of Biology* (London: Hutchinson, 1973) and D. L. Hull, *Philosophy of Biological Science* (Englewood Cliffs, NJ: Prentice-Hall, 1974).

10. For a fascinating discussion of the relation between pain and pain sensations and a defense of the claim that one can be in pain without feeling pain sensations, see N. Nelkin, "Pain and Pain Sensations," *Journal of Philosophy* 83 (1986): 129–148.

11. This version of the Inverted Spectrum Objection is borrowed from H. Putnam, *Reason, Truth and History* (Cambridge: Cambridge University Press, 1981): 80–81. Putnam's version avoids the epistemological difficulties in supposing that a person could be born with her spectrum inverted with respect to the rest of the population. For, in that case, how could the person—or anyone else—ever know it?

12. See P. M. Churchland, *Matter and Consciousness,* revised edition (Cambridge, MA: MIT Press, 1988): 38–42. For different responses, see S. Shoemaker, "Functionalism and Qualia," *Philosophical Studies* 27 (1975): 291–315; S. Shoemaker, "The Inverted Spectrum," *Journal of Philosophy* 79 (1982): 357–381; and D. Cole, "Functionalism and Inverted Spectra," *Synthese* 82 (1990): 207–222.

13. See J. Fodor, "Methodological Solipsism Considered as a Research Strategy in Cognitive Psychology," *Behavioral and Brain Sciences* 3 (1980): 63–109. Stich's commentary is on pages 97–98; Fodor's reply is on page 108.

14. This sort of argument for the conclusion that meanings are not solely in the head originated with Hilary Putnam, "The Meaning of 'Meaning'," in *Minnesota Studies in the Philosophy of Science,* Volume 7, ed. K. Gunderson (Minneapolis: University of Minnesota Press, 1975). Reprinted in H. Putnam, *Philosophical Papers,* Volume 2 (Cambridge: Cambridge University Press, 1975): 215–271. The functionalist who relies on representations to capture the content of beliefs also has problems with indexical terms such as *I, here,* and *now.* Anna's belief "I am too tired to read now" and Midori's belief "I am too tired to read now" have the same representation but different meanings.

15. For more on this issue, see L. R. Baker, *Saving Belief: A Critique of Physicalism* (Princeton, NJ: Princeton University Press, 1987).

# DISCUSSION: Minds, Brains, and Computers

. . . if there were machines resembling our bodies, and imitating our actions as far as is morally possible, we should still have two means of telling that, all the same, they were not real men. First, they could never use words or other constructed signs, as we do to declare our thoughts to others. It is quite conceivable that a machine should be so made as to utter words, and even utter them in connexion with physical events that cause a change in one of its organs . . . but not that it should be so made as to arrange words variously in response to the meaning of what is said in its presence, as even the dullest men can do. Secondly, while they might do many things as well as any of us or better, they would infallibly fail in others, revealing that they acted not from knowledge but only from the disposition of their organs. For while reason is a universal tool that may serve in all kinds of circumstances, these organs need a special arrangement for each special action; so it is morally impossible that a machine should contain so many varied arrangements as to act in all the events of life in the way reason enables us to act.

R. Descartes, *Discourse on Method,* Part V, trans. and ed.
E. Anscombe and P. T. Geach (London: Thomas Nelson and Sons, 1954).

Although the development of electronic computers has given a special interest to the question, Can machines think?, the philosophical issue has been discussed from at least the time of Descartes. I first consider the views of Descartes on whether animals, machines, and other physical systems can think. I then discuss the Turing Test for machine intelligence. I conclude this discussion with an examination of John Searle's attempt to refute the strong claims made by some researchers in the field of artificial intelligence.

## DESCARTES, MINDS, AND MACHINES

Descartes believed that all animal bodies and all human bodies are machines obeying the laws of mechanics. What distinguishes humans from animals is the additional presence in humans of an immaterial mind that, according to Descartes, is the only sort of thing that can reason and think. Thus, Descartes' answer to the question, Can machines think? would be "No" because Descartes would insist that machines are material things and only immaterial minds can think. Even in human beings that have minds, the thing that does the thinking is not any part of the material body, such as the brain, but the mind itself, which then communicates its results to the brain.

On the other hand, if you were to ask Descartes, Can machines have a mind?, his answer would be "Yes," since Descartes believes that human bodies are machines that also have minds "in" them. Finally, and most interesting of all, there is the question, Are we ever justified in believing that a machine either does or does not contain a mind? According to Descartes, the only way one could be positively, absolutely certain about whether or not a mind is present is to be that mind oneself. For only then could one prove with absolute certainty that "I, a thinking thing" exist. In all other cases, inferring the presence or absence of a mind from a creature's behavior can yield only moral certainty, that is, certainty of the sort that suffices for all practical purposes but that falls short of being a demonstration.

Descartes argues that there are two criteria that reliably indicate the presence of a mind: (1) the use of language and (2) the ability to do the entire range of things that human beings can do. Criterion (2) is not very helpful, because human beings differ markedly from one another in the sorts of things they can do. Also, there are many things that humans do that are irrelevant to the issue of whether humans have minds. Since the entire range of human activities includes the use of language, and since Descartes clearly thought that language use was the most important indicator of mentality, I shall concentrate on criterion (1).

Surely Descartes was correct to single out language use as the prime indicator of mentality. One of the best ways to find out whether someone (or something) is thinking or reasoning or has beliefs is to have the results of that inner activity communicated to us. Such communication is one of the most important uses of language. We could gather even more convincing evidence for mentality if we were able to question the subject and see how well it responded. In many situations, speaking is thinking out loud; it is thought made manifest. For Descartes, it was inconceivable that a mere mindless machine or mindless animal body could ever match the linguistic performance of even the most slow-witted human adult.

In singling out language use as the primary mental indicator, Descartes is careful to distinguish genuine speech from mere utterances in response to stimuli. Thus, Descartes would be entirely unimpressed by a device that always produced one of a small number of words or phrases when a button was pressed. Even a tape recording of a Shakespearean monologue does not count as the tape recorder producing language. Genuine language use must be flexible, capable of producing new grammatical sentences that are appropriate to the situation. Writing in the first half of the seventeenth century, Descartes could not have envisaged the advent of computers, which can, to a very limited extent, mimic some of the linguistic flexibility that comes naturally to humans. If Descartes were confronted with a machine that could converse just like a human being, then presumably he would conclude, with moral if not absolute certainty, that the machine had a thinking mind that was directing it. This idea—that linguistic ability is a reliable guide to mentality— lies at the heart of the Turing Test in modern discussions of artificial intelligence.

## THE TURING TEST

In his influential article "Computing Machinery and Intelligence,"[1] the British mathematician A. M. Turing argues that it is possible for a machine to think. Turing's strategy is two-pronged. On the negative side, Turing criticizes the main objections (nine in all) that have been raised against the claim that machines can think. On the positive side, Turing presents his own argument for the conclusion that machines are capable of thought and intelligence. It is this argument that I shall now examine.

Turing proposes what has come to be called the Turing Test for answering the question, Can machines think?[2] One is invited to imagine playing the Imitation Game, in which a human interrogator, C, converses via a teleprinter with two subjects, A and B. A is a man, and B is a woman. C is told, correctly, that one of the subjects is male and the other female, but C is not told which is which. C can put any question to either subject, and the subject to whom the question is addressed must respond. The object of the game is for C to guess correctly which subject is male and which is female. A strives to mislead C; B tries to help C. When played as described, C will guess correctly a certain percentage of the time. Now imagine that a machine (such as a digital computer appropriately programmed) replaces the man as subject A. Will the interrogator do significantly better at the Imitation Game? The Turing Test for machine intelligence is thus a test of how well a machine can imitate the verbal behavior of a human being in a structured setting such as the Imitation Game.[3]

Turing knew in 1950 (when he devised the test) that there were no machines then in existence that could play the Imitation Game. So, he proposed that we apply the Turing Test not to actual machines, but to a suitably programmed digital computer that would have enough memory and speed to compete. Thus, our original question, Can machines think? (which Turing dismissed as "too meaningless to deserve discussion") is replaced by Can a physically possible digital computer pass the Turing Test? Turing's own answer to this question was "Yes". Turing predicted that by the year 2000, the average interrogator would have no more than a 70 percent chance of making the right identification after five minutes of questioning.

We can express the core of Turing's reasoning in the following argument:

### Turing's Argument
(1) If X is a machine that passes the Turing Test, then X thinks.
(2) It is possible for a machine to pass the Turing Test.

(3) It is possible for a machine to think.

Turing might object to this reconstruction of his reasoning on the grounds that when X is a machine, the question, Can X think?—and hence the assertion that X thinks—is meaningless. His proposal is to replace (A): "X, a machine, thinks" with (B): "X, a machine, passes the Turing Test." But if this replacement is to have any warrant, the two statements must be connected in some way. If "X, a machine, thinks" is completely meaningless, then (A) and (B) cannot mean the same thing, since (B) has a clear meaning. There seem to be only two alternatives for the connection between (A) and (B) that would make sense of Turing's proposal. Either (A) is not completely meaningless and (B) captures whatever intelligible meaning (A) has, or (B) is a sufficient condition for (A), even though (B) does not capture all the intelligible content of (A). In either case, Turing should accept premise (1) which says "If B, then A."

Many philosophers have been critical of Turing's approach to answering the question, Can machines think?, especially his proposal that the original question be replaced by "Can a machine pass the Turing Test?"[4] One criticism of premise (1) runs as follows. Assume that a machine does pass the Turing Test. A machine passes the test when a human interrogator cannot tell whether he is conversing with a machine or with another human being. But it is still possible that there is nothing going on in the machine that is remotely like human thought and reasoning. In other words, a machine can pass the Turing Test without anything that can properly be called thinking or reasoning being responsible for its success. Thus, passing the Turing Test does not logically imply that a machine can think.

Notice that this criticism does not dispute that a computer might (one day) be able to mimic a significant portion of human linguistic behavior. Nor is it being argued that computers, by their very nature, are incapable of thought. Rather the objection is that passing the Turing Test is not the same as thinking, nor does it imply it. To equate the question, Can machines think? with Can a computer pass the Turing Test? is to conflate the imitation of an activity with the activity itself. Even Descartes would agree that passing the Turing Test is good evidence for machine intelligence (or, as Descartes would prefer, for believing that the machine has a mind), but passing the test is not the same as thinking, nor does it logically imply it.

Another way of putting the same criticism is to point out that to count as "thinking," not only must a machine be externally indistinguishable from a human in its (verbal) behavior, but it must also go through internal states that simulate human cognitive activity. Mimicking the output would be an impressive technological achievement, but it is not sufficient to qualify as thought without a real correspondence between the internal causal processes in human and machine that *produce* that output. This criticism is a reflection of the disagreement between behaviorists and materialists (identity theorists and functionalists) about the nature of human mentality. Contrary to the behaviorists who defend the Turing Test, belief, thinking, and understanding cannot be defined solely in terms of behavior, nor is behavior an infallible indicator of it.

## SEARLE'S CHINESE ROOM ARGUMENT

We have now reached a point at which we can appreciate the claim made by some proponents of "strong" AI (artificial intelligence). It is this claim that John Searle attacks in his article, "Minds, Brains, and Programs" (Reading 25).

As we saw in the previous discussion, "Materialism," functionalists define mental states in terms of their causal relations with each other, sensory inputs, and behavioral outputs. Thus, functionalists might accept that if a computer "merely" imitates the relations between sensory input and verbal output, that alone does not imply that the machine is thinking or that it understands the sentences emerging on its teleprinter. But if the computer program is of the right sort—that is, if it causes the computer not only to imitate human verbal behavior but also to duplicate the sequence of states that in a human mind produce that behavior—then the computer is thinking, understanding, believing, and so on. In short, if the computer runs the right kind of program, it is a mind; and any system, including the human brain, is a mind if it runs that program. Thus, while some proponents of AI might insist that any programmed computer that passes the Turing Test is a mind, functionalists require that the program be of the right sort. But all proponents of strong AI agree that the stuff the system is made out of is irrelevant; what makes a system a mind is the formal program it instantiates. Instantiating a program is what makes the brain a mind; and instantiating the same program will make anything else a mind, too.

Searle's two principal targets are the claims that (1) "the appropriately programmed computer literally has cognitive states" and (2) "the programs thereby explain human cognition." Both targets are attacked by means of the *Gedankenexperiment* (thought experiment) of the Chinese Room. Searle is locked in a room with a pile of pages written in Chinese (the "script"). Searle understands no Chinese whatsoever. To him all Chinese symbols are meaningless squiggles. He is then given a second batch of Chinese writing (the "story") and instructions, in English, about how to correlate the second batch with the first. Then he is given a third batch of Chinese writing (the "questions") plus more rules, again in English (the "program"), which tell him how to generate strings of Chinese symbols (the "answers") in response to the questions he has received. These answers are in idiomatic Chinese and appropriate to the questions asked, courtesy of the extraordinary ingenuity of the programmers who gave Searle his rules to follow. But throughout this entire process of mechanically following his program, Searle has not understood a single word of Chinese. He has simply manipulated uninterpreted formal symbols (the Chinese characters) in accordance with his instructions. Thus, Searle concludes, this refutes the claims made by strong AI. For in the Chinese Room, we have a system (Searle plus his pieces of paper) that instantiates a formal program, yet neither the system nor any of its parts understands Chinese. Moreover, no matter what program is involved, the result will be the same: no understanding at all of what Chinese symbols mean.

We can lay out Searle's criticism of strong AI explicitly in the following way. Searle points out that the following three statements, (P), (Q), and (R), form an inconsistent set.

(P)  If system X runs the right kind of program, then X acquires intentionality (e.g., can understand Chinese) in virtue of running that program.

(Q)  The Chinese room system runs the right kind of program.

(R)  The Chinese room system does not acquire any intentionality or understanding in virtue of running its program.

(P) expresses the thesis of strong AI. It is logically impossible for all three propositions (P), (Q), and (R) to be true. According to Searle, we know that both (Q) and (R) are true, and so it must be the case that (P) is false. After giving his core argument, Searle then considers six replies to his Chinese Room thought experiment and argues that none of them can save strong AI from refutation.

The persuasive power of Searle's argument lies in its simplicity. Searle does not have to consider the minute details of the programs invented by Shank, Abelson, and Winograd to convince us that (R) is true. No matter what the program is, neither Searle nor the room he is in will come to understand anything merely as a result of executing that program. Thus, it will not do to complain that (Q) is false because Searle has not considered the "right" kind of program.

Searle is not contesting that machines can think. *We* are machines, and *we* think. In fact, given Turing's abstract notion of what a machine is (roughly, a digital computer), Searle concedes that *everything* is a machine. The interesting question is, What explains the difference between machines that have intentional states and those that do not? Searle maintains that it cannot be the kind of program that they run.

Much of Searle's discussion is phrased in terms of intentionality. Intentional states are mental states that are *about* objects or states of affairs or are directed at them. The content of intentional states—what they are about—is expressed in "that" clauses. Examples are John's belief that tomorrow will be dry, Searle's understanding that the word *chien* in French means "dog," Scarlett's hope that she will never be hungry again. In some later replies to his critics, Searle distinguishes between metaphorical and literal attributions of intentionality and between intrinsic and derivative intentionality.[5] Though we often make attributions of intentionality to inanimate objects such as cars, thermostats, and computers, this is, at best, metaphorical. The thermostat does not literally *want* to keep the room at 75 degrees; the word processor does not *believe* that its file disk is full. When we attribute meanings to words and sentences, the attribution is true and literal, but the intentionality is derived, not intrinsic. For example, there is nothing metaphorical in saying that "chien" *means* "dog," but the meaning is not intrinsic to the word *chien*. "Chien" means "dog" only because we give it that interpretation; it is what *we* mean by it. Ultimately, all intentionality, all "aboutness," on Searle's view derives from the intentionality of human mental states. Since those states are causally produced by the human brain, only neuroscience, not computer science, can tell us more about them.

Even if Searle's Chinese Room criticism of strong AI and functionalism is correct, this does not show that materialism is false. Searle himself is a materialist, not a dualist. Searle believes that organic human brains have intentional states because they are made of the right stuff.[6] Based on the available evidence, mentality appears to be a biological phenomenon. Whether or not an inorganic machine could have mental states is an empirical question. All that Searle wishes to contest is the strong AI claim that if a system runs the right kind of program, then it automatically will be a mind. In fact, Searle accuses functionalists and proponents of strong AI of being "closet dualists," not because they believe that minds are immaterial substances, but because they deny that minds have any intrinsic connection with the stuff out of which they are made.

## CRITICISMS OF SEARLE'S ARGUMENT

In "Artificial Intelligence and Personal Identity" (Reading 26), David Cole identifies three steps in the reasoning Searle uses to reach his conclusion that programming alone cannot produce understanding of any language. Those steps are:

(1) The person following the English instructions would not thereby understand Chinese. Therefore,

(2) A computer following a program would not thereby understand Chinese. Therefore,

(3) Programming cannot produce understanding of Chinese or any other natural language.

For the purposes of his discussion in "Artificial Intelligence and Personal Identity," Cole is prepared to concede that both (1) and (2) are true, and he focuses his attention on denying (3).[7] Cole argues that even if (2) is true, it does not follow that there is *no one* who understands Chinese when the program is being run. Cole defends a functionalist view of persons according to which one or more persons (or minds) can be associated with the same material system. He offers two suggestive analogies: (1) the creation of one or more virtual machines by a suitably programmed computer and (2) the appearance of multiple personalities in the same human being. On Cole's view, persons are abstract entities; though they depend on appropriately organized physical systems (such as brains or computers) for their existence, they are not literally identical with those physical systems. Thus, Cole concludes, it is possible that when Searle is following the English instructions, *someone* understands Chinese, but that person is not Searle, nor is that person identical with the Chinese Room system.

As Cole notes, his criticism of Searle's argument depends on accepting a theory about the nature and identity of persons that traces back to John Locke. We examine that theory in the following discussion, "Personal Identity." In the remainder of this discussion, I wish to raise an objection to step (2) of Searle's reasoning.

Step (2) is equivalent to statement (R) in our first reconstruction of Searle's argument. It asserts that a computer (or the Chinese Room system) does not come to understand Chinese (or acquire intentionality) by following a program. Searle infers (2) from (1). He reasons that because he, Searle, does not understand Chinese when he is following instructions in English, it must be the case that no computer can understand Chinese when it runs the same program.

To some people, there seems to be a flaw in Searle's reasoning here, because even when both Searle and a computer instantiate the same formal program, they "run" that program in entirely different ways. When Searle "runs" the program, he does so by consciously following instructions (in English), which he understands and then carries out. When a computer "runs" a program, this is a completely different process. The computer does not *do* anything. The program (essentially, a sequence of electrical pulses) causes changes to occur in the computer's circuitry so that a general purpose machine can now perform a specific task. In principle, this programming could be effected by rewiring the machine and setting its switches by hand.[8] Since Searle's simulation of a computer by consciously following instructions in English is totally unlike a computer responding to a string of electrical pulses, there is no reason to expect that Searle's failure to understand Chinese guarantees a similar failure in the case of the computer.

Notice that this criticism cannot be avoided by having Searle memorize all the rules (in English) for generating appropriate answers to questions in Chinese. For it is highly unlikely that the organizational changes in Searle's brain resulting from this memorization would be anything like the functional reorganization caused by a program acting on a computer. To make running a program in a computer relevantly similar to running the same program in Searle would require wiring the appropriate reorganization into Searle's brain.

Imagine that Searle's brain is reorganized in an appropriate way. Suppose that without consciously translating from Chinese into English and back again, Searle now gives appropriate answers in flawless Mandarin to a wide range of questions put to him in the same language. Searle would probably not understand *how* he was able to achieve this kind of linguistic proficiency, but then native speakers of any language are similarly ignorant about the neurophysiological causes of *their* competence. Even if Searle is unable to translate from Chinese to English and vice versa, the same inability is not unknown among people who become fluent in a second language. In short, there seem to be no conclusive reasons for denying that if the right kind of program were hardwired into Searle's brain, Searle would understand Chinese in the same way that a native speaker of the language does.[9] Thus, there are reasons for doubting that Searle's Chinese Room argument refutes the thesis of strong AI. Searle has not proven that a computer cannot acquire intentionality and linguistic understanding by being programmed in the right way.

---

## NOTES

1. A. M. Turing, "Computing Machinery and Intelligence," *Mind* 59 (1950): 433–460. Alan Mathison Turing (1912–1954) made fundamental contributions to mathematical logic and the theory of computing. He was a pioneer in the development of the first electronic computers and played a vital role in cracking German codes during World War II. For an account of Turing's life and work, see A. Hodges, *Alan Turing: The Enigma* (New York: Simon & Schuster, 1983).

2. The Turing Test should be distinguished from a Turing machine. A Turing machine is an elementary type of machine consisting of a read-write head and an infinitely long tape, which the head scans one cell at a time. Whenever the head lands on a cell, it reads what is there. The head then writes on the present cell (replacing whatever was there previously), and it either stays put and scans the same cell again, halts completely, or moves one cell to the right or one cell to the left and scans that cell. Which action the machine performs is determined entirely by what it reads on the present cell (the input) and the internal state the machine is in. Those two factors also determine the next internal state of the machine. Each Turing machine is completely specified by its machine table, which lists the action the machine will perform in response to each possible combination of input and internal state. (Machine tables are similar to the table that defines the operation of Fodor's Coke machine in Reading 24.) Turing's conjecture, now widely accepted, is that for all deterministic, formal systems that run automatically there is an equivalent Turing machine. Turing proved there are universal Turing machines that can duplicate, move for move, all other Turing machines. For a good, informal treatment of this and related topics, see J. Haugeland, *Artificial Intelligence: The Very Idea* (Cambridge, MA: MIT Press, 1985).

3. Turing's own description of the test is rather vague and a little confusing. At the end of Section 5 of his paper, Turing uses "C" to represent a particular digital computer that takes the place of A in the Imitation Game; and for some reason, B has changed sex.

4. See K. Gunderson, *Mentality and Machines*, 2nd edition (Minneapolis: University of Minnesota Press, 1985).

5. J. Searle, "The Chinese Room Revisited," *Behavioral and Brain Sciences* 5 (1982): 345–348.

6. See J. C. Maloney, "The Right Stuff," *Synthese* 70 (1987): 349–372.

7. Cole contests both (1) and (2) in "Thought and Thought Experiments," *Philosophical Studies* 45 (1984): 431–444.

8. See D. Cole, "Thought and Thought Experiments," *Philosophical Studies* 45 (1984), Section III.

9. For a related criticism of Searle, see L. M. Russow, "Unlocking the Chinese Room," *Nature and System* 6 (1984): 221–227. See also the remarks of William Smythe in his commentary on Searle's article, *Behavioral and Brain Sciences* 3 (1980): 448–449, and Searle's reply to Smythe on page 455.

# DISCUSSION: Personal Identity

The conviction which every man has of his identity, as far back as his memory reaches, needs no aid of philosophy to strengthen it; and no philosophy can weaken it, without first producing some degree of insanity.

Thomas Reid, *Essays on the Intellectual Powers of Man* (1785),
Essay III, Ch. IV.

The concept of personal identity has two features that make questions about the identity of persons through time more than just intriguing intellectual puzzles. Those features are the responsibility we bear for our own past actions and the special concern we have for our own future welfare.

Each of us is uniquely responsible for his or her past actions. If I am the person who robbed the bank last year, I am now personally accountable for what I did in a way that no one else can be. It would be wrong to punish anyone else for something that I did. Similarly, if I am the long-lost relative who is the beneficiary in a will, then I and no one else can legitimately inherit the family estate. Locke refers to this aspect of personal identity by calling it a "forensic" notion, since it determines liability for punishment and blame, reward and praise, for past actions both in courts of law and in any divine tribunal that may await us after death.

One's personal identity extends not only into the past but also into the future. If I am told that tomorrow someone will experience an excruciating pain, this might make me sad; but if I am also told that *I* will be that person, then I become anxious and alarmed. I have a special concern for my own future, for my own future sufferings and pleasures, that I do not have for anyone else's. I *care* about what will happen to me in a way that I cannot care about what happens to anyone else. Similarly, if I speculate about the possibility of surviving death, what really interests me is surviving as *me*, the person that I am, not merging into some anonymous spiritual stew or becoming an impersonal ghost.

## SIMPLE VERSUS COMPLEX THEORIES

Theories of personal identity can be divided into two main groups. In the first group are theories that accept what Richard Swinburne calls the simple view.[1] According to this view, which Swinburne himself endorses, personal identity is a simple, indefinable, and unanalyzable feature of persons. Because the simple view holds that personal identity cannot be reduced to anything simpler or more basic, it is also called Non-Reductionist.[2]

According to the simple view, we have direct, intuitive knowledge of our own identity as persons. Unless we are mentally ill or deranged, we know who we are "from the inside," not by any inference, and our beliefs about our own identity are always correct. The simple view also agrees with common sense in insisting that (1) personal identity is a fully determinate concept and (2) questions of personal identity always have a definite answer. Thus, one person cannot be "more or less identical" with another, nor can personal identity vary in degree. Either two people existing at different times are identical or they are not; and there is always a correct answer corresponding to one of these two exclusive and exhaustive alternatives.

Many of the philosophers who hold the Non-Reductionist, simple view are dualists. They include Bishop Berkeley, Joseph Butler, Thomas Reid, and Roderick Chisholm. In his article "Parfit and the Buddha: Why There Are No People" (Reading 29), Jim Stone calls philosophers in this group Realists, since they believe that persons are real entities, over and above their bodies, their brains, and any properties that depend on them. As Stone puts it, on the Realist view, "persons are something extra and the fact of their identity a deep further fact [about them]." On the dualist version of the simple view, persons are Cartesian minds (immaterial substances, souls) that can exist without bodies and thus are capable of surviving death.[3] The simple view is the one that is imbedded in many Western religious traditions such as Christianity.

The second group of theories accept the complex view of personal identity. Here we find Reductionist theories that attempt to give a reductive analysis of personal identity in terms of such concepts as (a) having the same body, (b) having the same brain, (c) memory, (d) psychological continuity, which includes memory but is not restricted to it, or (e) some combination of the preceding factors. Some Reductionist theories are clearly inconsistent with extended personal survival beyond death. If personal identity depends on the continued existence of one's body, then no one can survive biological death. If personal identity depends solely on one's brain, then since that bodily organ is not immortal, neither are persons. Thus, strictly materialist theories based on (a) or (b) offer no hope whatever to those who fear personal extinction. Theories that regard the continued existence of psychological traits such as memory and character as sufficient for personal identity are consistent with long-term survival of biological death, but only if either (1) psychological traits can exist without any material thing existing or (2) psychological traits can be transferred from a brain (or a body) to another physical object, such as another brain (or body) or a computer.[4]

## IDENTITY THROUGH TIME

Before discussing Reductionist theories of personal identity, it is helpful to think about the identity of ordinary physical objects through time. Typically, we have an object at one time, $t_1$, such as a cup, an oak tree, or a dog, and we want to know which object of the same type, if any, at a later time, $t_2$, is identical with it. If nothing at $t_2$ is identical with the object that existed at $t_1$, then the original object has ceased to exist.

The notion of identity here is strict or numerical identity: we want to know whether anything existing at $t_2$ is one and the same object as that which existed at $t_1$. There are three important features associated with this concept of identity through time: uniqueness, transitivity, and consistency with change.

At time $t_2$ there can be at most one object that is identical with what existed earlier at $t_1$. This is because identity entails uniqueness at every instant: at any particular time, everything is identical with itself, and nothing can be identical with anything apart from itself at that time. So-called identical twins are merely very similar; they are not numerically identical; neither are two water molecules, one in the Atlantic Ocean and the other in the Pacific.

Just like "being taller than" and "being older than," numerical identity is a transitive relation: if A is identical with B, and B is identical with C, then A is identical with C. For example, if the vinyl record of Shostakovich's Piano Trio that I bought in 1985 is the one that I scratched on June 8, 1988, and if the record I scratched on June 8, 1988 is the one that I gave to the Public Library the following year, then the record I gave to the Public Library in 1989 is the same record of Shostakovich's Piano Trio that I bought in 1985.

This identity through time of the record that I bought, scratched, and then gave away remains entirely unaffected by the fact that in July of 1988 I purchased a second copy of the same recording. Even a perfect duplicate is just that, a duplicate; it is not, and cannot be, numerically identical with the original. Thus, even if we make a perfect copy of the Mona Lisa, matching Leonardo Da Vinci's masterpiece molecule for molecule, and even if we destroy Leonardo's original painting at the very moment that our perfect copy is completed, what we are left with is still a copy, not the original.

A few philosophers (such as Joseph Butler and David Hume) have insisted that numerical identity of an object through time requires that the object remain completely unaltered in every respect. Thus, Hume says that "we attribute identity, in an improper sense, to variable or interrupted objects."[5] This is false. A cup remains the same cup even though it becomes chipped; a ship remains one and the same vessel despite having its rotten boards replaced over the years; oak trees and dogs retain their numerical identity even though they grow larger and their original atoms are replaced by new ones.

The mistake of thinking that alteration is incompatible with identity through time probably arises from confusing the two similar-sounding questions, Is this X the same as it was before? and Is this the same X as it was before? For example, in response to the question, Is this the same car that you had last year?, there might be two different replies: "No, it is not the same. I have had it repainted" and "No, it is not the same. I sold the car I had last year and bought a new one that looks exactly the same." In the first answer, "it" refers to identically the same car that has changed its appearance; in the second answer, "it" refers to a new and different car that just happens to look the same.

It would be a mistake to defend the Butler-Hume view of strict identity by appealing to Leibniz's Law. For example, someone might claim that since my car last year had the property of being green and this year it has the property of being red, last year's car cannot be identical with this year's car. The correct way of describing the change, however, is to say that the same identical car has the property of being-green-in-1990 and also has the property of being-red-in-1991; or, more simply, my car was green and now is red. In the same way I can acquire a suntan, lose a finger, and have my hair cut without any threat to my identity. So, in what follows I shall apply the term *identity* to things that can change with time without calling it "fictitious" or "improper" identity, as Hume and Butler thought we should.

In defending the common view that things can remain identically the same even though they change, I am not denying that there are difficult philosophical problems in specifying necessary and sufficient conditions for the identity of manufactured objects such as ships, chairs, and automobiles. Consider, for example, the Ship of Theseus problem.[6] The vessel in which Theseus sailed to Crete to confront the Minotaur was called the *Theoris*. Over a period of ten years, every single plank in the *Theoris* has been replaced by a new one. Suppose that the original planks are not destroyed but are used to assemble a new vessel called the *Phoenix*, which has exactly the same design as the *Theoris*. Thus, at the end of ten years we have two ships: the *Phoenix*, which contains the same stuff as the original *Theoris* organized in exactly the same way, and the *Ariadne*, all of whose timbers are spanking new. Which one of these ships, the *Phoenix* or the *Ariadne*, is identical with the original *Theoris*? Continuity and gradualness of change favor the *Ariadne*; resemblance of matter and form favor the *Phoenix*. Since they are two different vessels existing at the same time, they cannot both be identical with the *Theoris*.

If the *Theoris* were a living thing—a plant or an animal—each of whose molecules were replaced one at a time (as indeed they are over the years), then I think we would unhesitatingly plump for the *Ariadne* as being identical with the *Theoris*. Why? Because that is how we judge the identity of living things when their discarded molecules are not conserved, and it seems irrelevant to a creature's identity whether or not someone uses those cast-off molecules to assemble a new organism.

## LOCKE'S MEMORY THEORY

I now wish to consider some Reductionist theories of personal identity, beginning the memory theory defended by John Locke in "Of Identity and Diversity" (Reading 27). Since the problem of personal identity is the problem of deciding which person at $t_2$ is identical with a person at $t_1$, we need to consider what we mean by the term *person*. For John Locke, a person is "a thinking intelligent being that has reason and reflection and can consider itself as itself, the same thinking thing in different times and places" (Reading 27, Section 9). Thus, a person does not have to be a human being, a "man" in Locke's phrase, a member of one particular biological species, since we can imagine a smart, articulate parrot being a person. Conversely, not all members of our species have to be persons, and Locke clearly thought that some of them are not. The important ingredients in our concept of a person are not bodily and biological attributes, but mental skills and abilities. In short, persons and selves are individual minds.

Locke was a Cartesian dualist. Though he expressed severe doubts about whether we have a clear idea of substance in general or of Cartesian immaterial substance in particular, Locke was able to imagine the soul of a prince being transported into the body of a cobbler as easily we now contemplate brain transplants. What is remarkable about Locke's treatment of soul transplants is that Locke denies that the identity of the immaterial soul substance entails the identity of persons, and he also denies that the diversity of immaterial soul substance entails personal diversity.

For Locke, the identity of the immaterial substance of the soul is as irrelevant to the issue of personal identity as is the identity of the physical substance of the body. The only relevant purpose of the soul is to act as a bearer of consciousness. It is consciousness, and consciousness alone, that unites mental states into a single individual person.

What Locke understands by consciousness is memory, for it is only by memory that I can extend my present consciousness into the past. Though it may not have been precisely Locke's own theory, we can learn a great deal about memory theories of personal identity by considering the following proposal:

> Person $P_2$ at $t_2$ is identical with person $P_1$ at $t_1$ if and only if $P_2$ at $t_2$ contains a memory of *at least one* of the mental states that $P_1$ had at $t_1$.[7]

The basic idea behind this theory is that actually remembering is both necessary and sufficient for the identity of persons. If $P_2$ and $P_1$ are the same person, then $P_2$ must remember at least one of the experiences that $P_1$ had; and if $P_2$ remembers at least one of $P_1$'s experiences, then $P_2$ and $P_1$ must be the same person.

The most common objection to this proposal is that actually remembering seems too strong to be a necessary condition for being the same person. Surely, I can be the same person as my infant self without now remembering a single thing of what I did on many a fine summer day during my childhood. For most of us, our present memories of our own pasts are extremely spotty. I can remember my fourth birthday party and my first day at school at age four and a half, but not much in between. Is Locke really suggesting that if my memory has a number of temporal gaps, then I am not one continuously existing person, but several?

One ingenious response to the gap problem is to introduce the idea of a chain of memory connections: if $P_2$ has a memory of $P_1$, and $P_3$ has a memory of $P_2$, and so on up to $P_n$, then $P_n$ and $P_1$ are memory connected. Thus, $P_n$ and $P_1$ can be memory connected, even though $P_n$ at $t_n$ has no memory of anything that $P_1$ experienced at $t_1$. Notice that the chain does not have to be continuous: it is consistent with my being often asleep and with my not being engaged in the activity of remembering for long periods of time.

The other common objection to Locke's theory is that it is too weak. Merely having an ostensible memory of a past experience is not sufficient to guarantee that it was really me who experienced it or that it was experienced by anyone at all. The phenomenon of ostensible but false memories is quite common: people claim to have witnessed the Battle of Waterloo or the building of the pyramids; their apparent memories of these events are vivid, convincing, and false. If memories are to be sufficient for personal identity, they must be real memories, not merely ostensible ones.

Many critics of the memory theory of personal identity, such as Joseph Butler, have argued that there is no noncircular way for Locke to discriminate between ostensible memories and real ones, for what makes it possible for me to really remember something (as opposed to falsely believing that I remember it) is the fact that it really happened to me, that I was the very same person who had that experience. If this is correct, then the memory theory presupposes the very thing it is trying to analyze, namely, personal identity.[8]

## THE PSYCHOLOGICAL CONTINUITY THEORY

Given the circularity objection to the memory theory and the current popularity of materialism in the philosophy of mind, why not simply identify persons with their brains and use the physical identity of that biological organ as a necessary and sufficient condition for personal identity?

One merit of this proposal is that it agrees with most people's intuitions about brain transplants. Unlike every other kind of organ transplant, brain transplants are the only kind in which most people would rather be the donor than the recipient. Nearly everyone is convinced that if the donor's brain is placed in someone's else decerebrate body, then the donor, not the recipient, will be the person who survives the operation. But this conviction rests on the presumption that when transplanted into a new skull, the donor's brain carries with it all of its psychological traits, memories, mental skills and habits. If this presumption were false—if, for example, you, the donor, were told that, as an inevitable part of the procedure, your brain will be "zapped," that is, it will be completely stripped of all its memories and other psychological traits—then the operation would no longer seem to be a means of ensuring the personal survival of you, the donor.

The brain-zap argument strongly suggests that what is important for personal identity and survival is psychological continuity and connectedness. The continued existence of one's own physical brain is valued only insofar as it is the bearer of one's own mental states. Thus, any purely materialist theory of personal identity based on brains alone is inadequate.

Let us, therefore, return to the memory theory. From now on, we will assume that the theory has been broadened to include other psychological traits and characteristics besides memory. Following Shoemaker, who defends such an account in his "Personal Identity: A Materialist's Account" (Reading 28), we will call it the Psychological Continuity Theory. Even if Butler's circularity objection can be circumvented, there are other problems with the Psychological Continuity Theory that are of considerable philosophical interest.[9]

We will begin by considering Shoemaker's brain-state transfer (BST) procedure. In this procedure, a device records the physical state of a brain down to the last molecule. It then restructures a second brain so that it is in exactly the same state as the first brain. When the device is working properly, it destroys the first brain immediately before the second brain is restructured. Let us assume that when two brains are in exactly the same physical state they are also in exactly the same mental state. Thus, when the BST device is working properly, the original brain is replaced by one exactly like it, both physically and psychologically. The BST procedure duplicates brain states, but does it preserve personal identity? Does the person associated with the first brain at the beginning of the procedure continue to exist as that very same person when the procedure is over?

Shoemaker acknowledges that the initial intuition of most people is that the BST procedure is not person preserving. Shoemaker thinks that it is. He defends his answer by inviting us to imagine a technologically advanced society in which BST devices are used regularly to effect "body-changes." The people in this society seem to use the word *person* the same way we do. Both we and they agree that materialism is true; thus, Shoemaker argues, *if* they are right in regarding the BST procedure as person preserving, we ought to agree with them. At best, this argument shows that it is possible that *we might come to believe* that the BST procedure is person preserving. I do not think it shows that the procedure *is* person preserving or even that it is logically possible that it preserves personal identity. For what it is worth, my own intuition is that the BST procedure does *not* preserve personal identity. If I were dying in a hospital bed, I would derive no comfort at all from being told that all my psychological characteristics would be preserved in a replica of my brain. Another person just like me would attend my funeral; but it would not be me.

Since intuitions differ on the BST procedure, they are not a reliable basis on which to judge that the Psychological Continuity Theory is false. Let us, therefore, turn to other grounds on which the theory has been criticized. But before discussing these other criticisms, there is an important point about the formulation of the theory that we need to understand.

All proponents of the Psychological Continuity Theory recognize that psychological continuity alone cannot be sufficient for personal identity. This is because of so-called fission cases, in which there are two separate persons, B and C, at $t_2$, both of whom are psychologically continuous with person A at $t_1$. One way in which such cases might conceivably arise is by transplanting one hemisphere of A's brain into one decerebrate body (thus generating person B) and putting the other half of A's brain into another decerebrate body (thus generating person C). Another way these cases could arise is through a malfunction of the BST device such that it produces two duplicate brains instead of one. If psychological continuity all by itself were sufficient for personal identity, then both B and C would be identical with A. But that would imply that B and C are identical, which is impossible, since they are different persons existing at the same time. So, the Psychological Continuity Theory must be amended to rule out such fission cases. This is usually done by adding the stipulation that the psychological continuity be non-branching. From now on, we shall assume that the Psychological Continuity Theory contains a "no branching" clause.

## THE DUPLICATION OBJECTION

The Duplication Objection is a criticism of the way in which the Psychological Continuity Theory with the "no branching" clause handles the possibility of fission. Suppose that brain bisection surgery is performed on A, but that only one of the hemispheres survives in a new body. Suppose it is B. In that case, B is psychologically continuous with A in a non-branching way. So, according to the Psychological Continuity Theory, B is the same person as A. But if the second hemisphere had not died, there would have been two persons, B and C, neither of whom is related to A in a non-branching way. In that case, B would not be the same person as A. But, the objection runs, whether or not B is the same person as A cannot depend on the existence or nonexistence of some third person, C. If B is identical with A, then that is a necessary truth about them; it is not logically possible that two persons who are in fact identical could have been nonidentical.

Shoemaker's response to the charge of logical incoherence is, I think, sound. He points out, correctly, that identity statements are logically necessary only when the things or persons concerned are referred to by proper names, not when they are picked out by definite descriptions. Thus, if Brian is identical with Arthur (in other words, if these are just two different names for identically the same person at different times), then that is a necessary truth that cannot be affected by the possible existence of Charles. But, the definite description "the person who inherited Arthur's left hemisphere" picks out Brian only if no one inherits Arthur's right hemisphere. In a world in which both hemispheres survive, the description "the person who inherited Arthur's left hemisphere" picks out some person other than Brian, a person who is not identical with Arthur. Let us call that person David.

The problem with Shoemaker's response is that it is difficult to see why Brian and David are different persons. Physically they are the same; psychologically they are the same; both were generated from Arthur's left hemisphere and are psychologically continuous with Arthur. It seems that only the desire to save the Psychological Continuity Theory from refutation motivates us to deny that Brian and David are the same person.

The sort of criticism sketched in the preceding paragraph becomes even more potent when one considers the malfunction of the BST device discussed by Shoemaker in the section of his article titled "The Duplication Argument Revisited." Imagine that the device fails to erase or destroy brain A when it produces the duplicate brain B. Thus, the pre-transfer A-brain is related by *branching* psychological continuity to both the post-transfer A-brain and to the post-transfer B-brain. As Shoemaker admits, we have a strong inclination to judge that the post-transfer A-brain person is identical with the pre-transfer A-brain person. After all, why should making a copy of my brain affect my continued identity as the person I am? But the Psychological Continuity Theory denies this. Since there is branching of psychological continuity, neither of the post-transfer persons is identical with the pre-transfer person. Shoemaker admits that this is an acute difficulty for the Psychological Continuity Theory that might require a modification of the theory.[10]

There is further difficulty with brain bisection cases that cuts right to the heart of the Psychological Continuity Theory. It is graphically illustrated by Shoemaker's story, which I will relate, as he does, in the first person.

Suppose that I have cancer in all of my body except for the left hemisphere of my brain. Though my right hemisphere is cancerous, it is still functioning normally. My only chance of survival is to undergo a brain transplant. The safest and least expensive procedure is to transplant the healthy left hemisphere, leaving behind the disease-ridden right hemisphere to die with the rest of my body. A much riskier and more expensive alternative is to first destroy the diseased right hemisphere and then transplant the healthy left hemisphere. Which operation should I prefer?

If I choose the first procedure, there is a good chance that someone will survive who is psychologically continuous with me. But since, for a while at least, there will be two such persons, the Psychological Continuity Theory (with the no-branching clause) entails that neither will be identical with me. If I choose the second procedure, there is only a small chance that the operation will be successful, but if it does succeed, the survivor will be me.

Shoemaker surmises that most people placed in this situation would definitely prefer the first procedure. From the point of view of the Reductionist, this preference shows that what people really care about in survival is not personal identity but psychological continuity. From the point of view of the Non-

Reductionist, it shows that the Psychological Continuity Theory is flawed, since it has failed to do justice to one of our basic intuitions about personal identity. According to the Non-Reductionist, when we choose the first procedure, we are convinced that we will survive even though we cannot predict in which body our consciousness will be located when the anesthesia wears off.

In his article "Parfit and the Buddha: Why There Are No People" (Reading 29), Jim Stone explores further some of the consequences of the Psychological Continuity Theory. For example, Stone defends a version of Parfit's *Spectrum Argument*, arguing that Reductionists are correct to insist that in some cases, personal identity is indeterminate. Stone eventually concludes that both Reductionism (the Psychological Continuity Theory) and Realism (the dualist theory) are false. This leaves only one alternative, Eliminativism: there are no persons who endure through time.

## NOTES

1. R. Swinburne, "Personal Identity: The Dualist Theory," in S. Shoemaker and R. Swinburne, *Personal Identity* (Oxford: Basil Blackwell, 1984).

2. This is the term used by Derek Parfit in his *Reasons and Persons* (Oxford: Clarendon Press, 1984).

3. One could, I suppose, hold the view that personal identity is unanalyzable without also being a dualist; but anyone who identifies persons with indivisible, immaterial substances will be a Non-Reductionist about personal identity. John Locke is an interesting example of someone who accepted dualism but did not identify persons with immaterial substances. Instead, Locke proposed a memory-based Reductionist theory of personal identity.

4. Biological death occurs when an organism ceases to exist as the biological organism that it is. Thus, a human being (what Locke calls a "man") dies when his or her body irreversibly ceases to function as a biologically integrated human organism. So, for example, John can die of a heart attack, even though some of his blood cells continue to survive in a test tube. The point of this digression is that even if personal survival can be prolonged by transplanting one's brain or a portion of it, not even brains are immortal. Thus, on Reductionist theories, *long-term* personal survival after biological death depends on the conditions mentioned in the text.

5. D. Hume, *A Treatise of Human Nature*, (1739), Book I, Part IV, Section VI; 2nd edition (Oxford: Clarendon Press, 1978), ed. P. H. Nidditch, p. 255.

6. Thomas Hobbes gives a classic analysis of this problem in his *De Corpore*, Chapter XI. See *The English Works of Thomas Hobbes* (London: John Bohn, 1839), Volume I, pp. 132–138.

7. Some people think that Locke's theory requires that $P_2$ at $t_2$ remember *everything* that $P_1$ was consciously aware of at $t_1$. But as Thomas Reid pointed out, that version of the theory (which Reid takes to be Locke's) is easily refuted. See T. Reid, *Essays on the Intellectual Powers of Man* (1785), Essay III, Chapter VI.

8. See J. Butler, "Of Personal Identity," in his *Analogy of Religion* (1736). Reprinted in J. Perry, Ed., *Personal Identity* (Berkeley: University of California Press, 1975): 99–105. Derek Parfit responds to the circularity objection in *Reasons and Persons*, Chapter 11.

9. For Shoemaker's reply to the circularity objection, see S. Shoemaker and R. Swinburne, *Personal Identity*, pp. 98–101.

10. The modification he suggests is that personal identity is non-branching psychological continuity *unless the psychological continuity of one of the branches is realized through the normal functioning of the same brain.* When a branch has the same brain, it qualifies as being identical with the original person because it is the "closest continuer" of the original. Shoemaker admits that he is hard pressed to defend the "parochial intuition" that underlies this modification. In "Shoemaker on the Duplication Argument, Survival, and What Matters," *Australasian Journal of Philosophy* 66 (1988): 234–239, L. Nathan Oaklander argues that apart from its *ad hocness*, Shoemaker's modification involves admitting that what matters in survival is personal identity, not psychological continuity. In Reading 29, Jim Stone offers a similar criticism of Parfit's reductionist theory.

# PART IV

## DETERMINISM AND FREE WILL

Assumptions about freedom of will and action permeate our attitudes towards ourselves and others. They form an integral part of our concept of ourselves as persons who choose between alternatives and are held accountable for the choices we make. Looking back at some of my past actions, I feel emotions such as pride, regret, and shame. These emotions make sense only if I believe that when I performed those actions, there was a genuine possibility that I could have refrained from doing them and could have performed some other actions instead. Similarly, when we judge the actions of others, we may feel approval, anger, or resentment. These attitudes would be irrational if people had no genuine freedom or control over their actions. It would make as little sense to blame someone for an unfree action as it would to blame a stone for falling to the earth or a virus for infecting a child.

Determinism is the view that everything that happens is determined by what happened previously. Given the state of the world in the past, what happens now *had* to happen and could not have turned out differently. Most modern proponents of determinism see it as part and parcel of the scientific outlook.[1] Science has been remarkably successful at finding theories and laws that enable us to predict what will happen in the future on the basis of what has occurred in the past. Admittedly, psychology, sociology, and economics have not had the same success as physics, but presumably this is because human beings are vastly more complex than stones and electrons. From the standpoint of scientific materialism, the behavior of human beings is the determined outcome of their genetic endowment and environmental influences.[2]

Determinism appears to threaten the existence of free will. Consider morality. It is widely held that the moral evaluation of human actions and our practice of punishing some and praising others is appropriate only if the human beings who perform them are acting freely.[3] If an action is entirely outside a person's control, if it is involuntary (like a sneeze) or caused by a brain hemorrhage, then it would be wrong to blame or punish the person for performing it. Similarly, when a person's action is partly determined by external causes, we often hold the agent only partly, but not fully, responsible for his action. For example, in his famous defense of the eighteen-year-old Chicagoans Nathan Leopold and Richard Loeb, Clarence Darrow persuaded the judge to impose life imprisonment rather than the death penalty by stressing the extent to which Leopold and Loeb's dreadful crime had been causally determined by events in their childhood and upbringing.[4] Darrow's argument relied on the seemingly plausible principle that our moral responsibility for our actions diminishes in proportion to the degree to which they are caused by factors that lie outside our control. If our actions were completely determined by such factors, our moral responsibility would be reduced to zero, and we would lack entirely the kind of freedom that is indispensable for morality.

Despite their profound implications for morality, free will and determinism are primarily topics in metaphysics rather than ethics. There are two fundamental questions, neither of which is an ethical question: (1) Are all human actions determined? and (2) If all human actions are determined, does this entail that free will is an illusion? The first question concerns the truth of determinism; the second concerns the compatibility of determinism with acting freely.

The three main positions in the free-will debate are hard determinism, libertarianism, and compatibilism.

The hard determinist argues from the truth of determinism to the absence of freedom. The argument has two premises. First, determinism is true: all events, including all human actions, are causally determined by prior events. Second, determinism is incompatible with free will. From these premises it follows that free will is a myth: no one ever acts freely.

### The Hard Determinist Argument

(1) Determinism is true.
(2) If determinism is true, then no human actions are free.

(3) No human actions are free.

Prominent hard determinists are Baruch Spinoza, Baron d'Holbach, Arthur Schopenhauer, and B. F. Skinner. It should be remembered that these authors are attacking the notion of what Hume (in Reading 30) calls the liberty of indifference—the power to do something different in exactly the same circumstances. According to hard determinists, it is this kind of freedom that is relevant to ascriptions of moral responsibility, praise, and blame and is ruled out by determinism. Hard determinists are not necessarily denying the existence of freedom in *all* of its many senses (e.g., what Hume called the liberty of spontaneity—the ability to act as one wills).

The libertarian argues in the opposite direction, from the fact of freedom to the falsity of determinism. The libertarian insists that despite its popularity among scientists, universal determinism is a controversial metaphysical thesis, not a self-evident truth. We do not know for certain that determinism is true. But we do know, from introspection, that many of our actions are free. Typically, these free actions are preceded by a period of conscious deliberation during which we weigh the various alternatives and eventually choose which action to perform. Thus, the libertarian concludes that universal determinism—the doctrine that *all* events are determined—is false. Prominent libertarians include Thomas Reid, Immanuel Kant, C. A. Campbell, and Richard Taylor.

### The Libertarian Argument

(4) Some human actions are free.
(2) If determinism is true, then no human actions are free.

(5) Determinism is false.

The hard determinist argument and the libertarian argument are both valid: they are related as *modus ponens* is to *modus tollens*. It is important to notice that both arguments share premise (2) in common. Both the hard determinist and the libertarian are incompatibilists. Both are committed to the incompatibilist thesis (I) that if determinism is true, then no human actions are free. The most common argument for incompatibilism is the following which, for the sake of clarity, is phrased in terms of an arbitrary human being, S. Since S can be anyone, the argument is perfectly general and applies to all human actions.

### The Incompatibilist Argument

(A) If determinism is true, then S could not have done otherwise.
(B) If S acts freely, then S could have done otherwise.

(I) If determinism is true, then S does not act freely.

Many philosophers (usually ones sympathetic to determinism) have said to libertarianism and hard determinism "a plague on both your houses" and have argued that the incompatibilist thesis is false. For obvious reasons, these philosophers are called compatibilists. Compatibilists who also believe that determinism is true are often referred to as soft determinists. According to soft determinism, all human actions are causally determined, but some are free and some not, depending on the kinds of causes that are involved. The mere fact that an action is caused does not, by itself, imply anything about whether the act is free or unfree. Famous soft determinists include Thomas Hobbes, John Locke, David Hume, John Stuart Mill, G. E. Moore, Moritz Schlick, and Walter T. Stace. The arguments of these writers are often based on claims about the meaning of the terms *free, acting freely,* and *voluntary* and about how these terms are used in ordinary English. Many compatibilists insist that liberty of spontaneity is sufficient for freedom. In other words, the proposal is roughly this: I act freely when I do what I want to do, when I act in accordance with my wishes free from coercion, threat, and constraints.

In "Liberty and Necessity" (Reading 30), David Hume gives a classic account of the case for soft determinism. Hume argues that the apparent conflict between liberty (freedom) and necessity (determinism) is an illusion resulting from confusions of language. Once we clarify what the terms *liberty* and *necessity* mean, Hume thinks that it will become obvious to everyone that all human actions are determined while, at the same time, many of them are performed freely. Part of Hume's case rests on an analysis of acting freely which Hume borrowed from Locke. On this analysis, a person acts freely when he is able to act or refrain from acting "according to the determinations of the will."

Paul Edwards doubts that determinism and freedom are reconciled so easily. In his "Hard and Soft Determinism" (Reading 31), Edwards quotes with approval the hard determinists Baron d'Holbach and Schopenhauer, who point out that if determinism is true, then our will also is determined. What difference can it make if we act in accordance with our will if what we will to do is inexorably determined by prior events? Similarly, if determinism is true, then our characters, which play a large role in determining how we act, are ultimately shaped by factors that lie completely outside our control. It seems as if the kind of freedom that is compatible with determinism is inconsistent with holding people morally responsible for their actions.

In "Actions, Predictions, and Books of Life" (Reading 32), Alvin Goldman carefully examines a family of objections that have been made against determinism on the basis of the unpredictability of some human actions. If determinism is true, then all human actions should be predictable. But, for a variety of reasons, some actions are not predictable. Thus, determinism is false. Without passing judgment on whether determinism is actually true, Goldman concludes that none of the unpredictability arguments shows that determinism must be false. To illustrate his contention that determinism could be true, Goldman imagines finding a book correctly describing all his future actions. Even though Goldman reads the book and tries to refute its predictions, he never succeeds.

The Locke-Hume definition of acting freely was criticized in the eighteenth century by the philosopher Thomas Reid. In "Two Concepts of Freedom" (Reading 33), William Rowe examines the debate between Locke, the compatibilist, and Reid, the incompatibilist libertarian. Rowe agrees with Reid that the Lockean conception of freedom is vulnerable to "utterly devastating objections." Rowe then examines Reid's libertarian conception of freedom as an agent's "power over the determinations of his own will" and argues that Reid's theory needs to be amended in order to avoid a fatal objection. Finally, Rowe discusses the relevance for Reid's position of some recent work by Frankfurt and Nozick, who argue that an agent can be morally responsible for an action even though she could neither act nor will otherwise. Rowe concludes that Frankfurt and Nozick are correct but that this does not undermine Reid's theory.

As Rowe emphasizes in his discussion of Reid, many libertarians are committed to the view that there are two kinds of causation operating in the world: event-causation, by which one event causes another; and agent-causation, by which persons freely cause their actions. Many people find the concept of agent-causation mysterious. It involves the idea that persons are substances that can bring about acts of will directly without being caused to do so by anything else. In "Has the Self 'Free Will'?" (Reading 34) and "Freedom and Determinism" (Reading 35), the libertarians C. A. Campbell and Richard Taylor try to clarify the notion of agent-causation. They argue that our personal experience as agents who deliberate and make moral choices gives us good grounds for thinking that agent-causation exists. Their arguments are examined in the discussion entitled "Libertarianism."

---

## NOTES

1. Some philosophers and theologians have argued for versions of determinism on logical and religious grounds. The argument from logic usually concludes with fatalism: whatever happens must happen of logical necessity. The religious argument is based on God's foreknowledge of future events. See R. Taylor, "Fate," *Metaphysics* 3rd edition (Englewood Cliffs, NJ: Prentice-Hall, 1983), Chapter 6; G. Ryle, "It Was to Be," in *Dilemmas* (New York: Cambridge University Press, 1954); N. Pike, "Divine Omniscience and Voluntary Action," *The Philosophical Review* 74 (1965): 27–46; and J. M. Fischer, Ed., *God, Foreknowledge, and Freedom* (Stanford, CA: Stanford University Press, 1989).

2. See, for example, A. Grünbaum, "Free Will and Laws of Human Behavior," *American Philosophical Quarterly* 8 (1971): 299–317; G. D. Wassermann, "Morality and Determinism," *Philosophy* 63 (1988): 211–230.

3. If someone did not act freely, we might still use punishment and condemnation as a form of behavior control, in the same way we might "punish" a dog in order to influence its future behavior. But in the absence of freedom, the recipient would not *deserve* such treatment, nor would the treatment be justified on moral grounds. For two contrasting views, see J.J.C. Smart, "Free-Will, Praise and Blame," *Mind* 70 (1961): 291–306; and P. Strawson, "Freedom and Resentment," *Proceedings of the British Academy* 48 (1962): 1–25, reprinted in G. Watson, Ed., *Free Will* (New York: Oxford University Press, 1982): 59–80.

4. See C. Darrow, "The Defense of Leopold and Loeb," in *Attorney for the Damned*, ed. A. Weinberg (New York: Simon and Schuster, 1957). Leopold and Loeb murdered a younger boy, Bobbie Franks, for the thrill of committing the "perfect crime."

# READING 30

---

# Liberty and Necessity
*David Hume*

*For biographical details, see Reading 4. The selections from Hume's* An Enquiry Concerning Human Understanding *in Readings 30, 39, and 42 are adapted from the text in* The Philosophical Works of David Hume, *ed. T. H. Green and T. H. Grose (London: Longmans, Green, and Co., 1882). Spelling and punctuation have been modernized. Reading 30 consists of Part I of Section VIII of the* Enquiry. *Part II of Section VIII has been omitted.*

## SECTION VIII: OF LIBERTY AND NECESSITY.

### PART I.

It might reasonably be expected, in questions which have been canvassed and disputed with great eagerness since the first origin of science and philosophy, that the meaning of all the terms, at least, should have been agreed upon among the disputants, and our enquiries, in the course of two thousand years, been able to pass from words to the true and real subject of the controversy. For how easy may it seem to give exact definitions of the terms employed in reasoning, and make these definitions, not the mere sound of words, the object of future scrutiny and examination? But if we consider the matter more narrowly, we shall be apt to draw a quite opposite conclusion. From this circumstance alone, that a controversy has been long kept on foot and remains still undecided, we may presume that there is some ambiguity in the expression, and that the disputants affix different ideas to the terms employed in the controversy. For as the faculties of the mind are supposed to be naturally alike in every individual—otherwise nothing could be more fruitless than to

reason or dispute together—it were impossible, if men affix the same ideas to their terms, that they could so long form different opinions of the same subject, especially when they communicate their views, and each party turn themselves on all sides in search of arguments which may give them the victory over their antagonists. It is true, if men attempt the discussion of questions which lie entirely beyond the reach of human capacity, such as those concerning the origin of worlds or the economy of the intellectual system or region of spirits, they may long beat the air in their fruitless contests and never arrive at any determinate conclusion. But if the question regard any subject of common life and experience, nothing, one would think, could preserve the dispute so long undecided, but some ambiguous expressions which keep the antagonists still at a distance and hinder them from grappling with each other.

This has been the case in the long disputed question concerning liberty and necessity, and to so remarkable a degree that, if I be not much mistaken, we shall find that all mankind, both learned and ignorant, have always been of the same opinion with regard to this subject, and that a few intelligible definitions would immediately have put an end to the whole controversy. I own that this dispute has been so much canvassed on all hands, and has led philosophers into such a labyrinth of obscure sophistry, that it is no wonder if a sensible reader indulge his ease so far as to turn a deaf ear to the proposal of such a question from which he can expect neither instruction nor entertainment. But the state of the argument here proposed may, perhaps, serve to renew his attention, as it has more novelty, promises at least some decision of the controversy, and will not much disturb his ease by any intricate or obscure reasoning.

SOURCE: From *An Enquiry Concerning Human Understanding* (1748), Section VIII, Part I.

I hope, therefore, to make it appear that all men have ever agreed in the doctrine both of necessity and of liberty, according to any reasonable sense which can be put on these terms, and that the whole controversy has hitherto turned merely upon words. We shall begin with examining the doctrine of necessity.

It is universally allowed that matter, in all its operations, is actuated by a necessary force, and that every natural effect is so precisely determined by the energy of its cause that no other effect, in such particular circumstances, could possibly have resulted from it. The degree and direction of every motion is, by the laws of nature, prescribed with such exactness that a living creature may as soon arise from the shock of two bodies, as motion, in any other degree or direction than what is actually produced by it. Would we, therefore, form a just and precise idea of *necessity,* we must consider whence that idea arises when we apply it to the operation of bodies.

It seems evident that, if all the scenes of nature were continually shifted in such a manner that no two events bore any resemblance to each other, but every object was entirely new, without any similitude to whatever had been seen before, we should never, in that case, have attained the least idea of necessity or of a connection among these objects. We might say, upon such a supposition, that one object or event has followed another, not that one was produced by the other. The relation of cause and effect must be utterly unknown to mankind. Inference and reasoning concerning the operations of nature would, from that moment, be at an end; and the memory and senses remain the only canals by which the knowledge of any real existence could possibly have access to the mind. Our idea, therefore, of necessity and causation arises entirely from the uniformity observable in the operations of nature, where similar objects are constantly conjoined together, and the mind is determined by custom to infer the one from the appearance of the other. These two circumstances form the whole of that necessity which we ascribe to matter. Beyond the constant *conjunction* of similar objects and the consequent *inference* from one to the other, we have no notion of any necessity or connection.

If it appear, therefore, that all mankind have ever allowed, without any doubt or hesitation, that these two circumstances take place in the voluntary actions of men and in the operations of mind, it must follow that all mankind have ever agreed in the doctrine of necessity, and that they have hitherto disputed merely for not understanding each other.

As to the first circumstance, the constant and regular conjunction of similar events, we may possibly satisfy ourselves by the following considerations. It is universally acknowledged that there is a great uniformity among the actions of men, in all nations and ages, and that human nature remains still the same in its principles and operations. The same motives always produce the same actions; the same events follow from the same causes. Ambition, avarice, self-love, vanity, friendship, generosity, public spirit: these passions, mixed in various degrees and distributed through society, have been, from the beginning of the world, and still are, the source of all the actions and enterprises which have ever been observed among mankind. Would you know the sentiments, inclinations, and course of life of the Greeks and Romans? Study well the temper and actions of the French and English: you cannot be much mistaken in transferring to the former *most* of the observations which you have made with regard to the latter. Mankind are so much the same, in all times and places, that history informs us of nothing new or strange in this particular. Its chief use is only to discover the constant and universal principles of human nature by showing men in all varieties of circumstances and situations, and furnishing us with materials from which we may form our observations and become acquainted with the regular springs of human action and behaviour. These records of wars, intrigues, factions, and revolutions, are so many collections of experiments by which the politician or moral philosopher fixes the principles of his science, in the same manner as the physician or natural philosopher becomes acquainted with the nature of plants, minerals, and other external objects, by the experiments which he forms concerning them. Nor are the earth, water, and other elements examined by Aristotle and Hippocrates more like to those which at present lie under our observation than the men described by Polybius and Tacitus are to those who now govern the world.

Should a traveller, returning from a far country, bring us an account of men wholly different from any with whom we were ever acquainted, men who were entirely divested of avarice, ambition, or revenge, who knew no pleasure but friendship, generosity, and public spirit, we should immediately, from these circumstances, detect the falsehood and prove him a liar with the same certainty as if he had stuffed his narration with stories of centaurs and dragons, miracles and prodigies. And if we would explode any forgery in history, we cannot make use of a more convincing argument than to prove that the actions ascribed to any person are directly contrary to the course of nature, and that no human motives, in such circumstances, could ever induce him to such a conduct. The veracity of Quintus Curtius is as much to be suspected when he describes the supernatural courage of Alexander by which he was hurried on singly to attack multitudes, as when he describes his supernatural force and activity by which he was able to resist them. So readily and universally do we acknowledge a uniformity in human motives and actions as well as in the operations of body.

Hence, likewise, the benefit of that experience acquired by long life and a variety of business and company, in order to instruct us in the principles of human nature and regulate our future conduct as well as speculation. By means of this guide we mount up to the knowledge of men's inclinations and motives from their actions, expressions, and even gestures, and again descend to the interpretation of their actions from our knowledge of their motives and inclinations. The general observations, treasured up by a course of experience, give us the clue of human nature and teach us to unravel all its intricacies. Pretexts and appearances no longer deceive us. Public declarations pass for the specious colouring of a cause. And though virtue and honour be allowed their proper weight and authority, that perfect disinterestedness, so often pretended to, is never expected in multitudes and parties, seldom in their leaders, and scarcely even in individuals of any rank or station. But were there no uniformity in human actions, and were every experiment which we could form of this kind irregular and anomalous, it were impossible to collect any general observations concerning mankind, and no experience, however accurately digested by reflection, would ever serve to any purpose. Why is the aged husbandman more skillful in his calling than the young beginner, but because there is a certain uniformity in the operation of the sun, rain, and earth towards the production of vegetables, and experience teaches the old practitioner the rules by which this operation is governed and directed?

We must not, however, expect that this uniformity of human actions should be carried to such a length as that all men, in the same circumstances, will always act precisely in the same manner, without making any allowance for the diversity of characters, prejudices, and opinions. Such a uniformity in every particular, is found in no part of nature. On the contrary, from observing the variety of conduct in different men we are enabled to form a greater variety of maxims which still suppose a degree of uniformity and regularity.

Are the manners of men different in different ages and countries? We learn thence the great force of custom and education which mould the human mind from its infancy and form it into a fixed and established character. Is the behaviour and conduct of the one sex very unlike that of the other? It is thence we become acquainted with the different characters which nature has impressed upon the sexes, and which she preserves with constancy and regularity. Are the actions of the same person much diversified in the different periods of his life from infancy to old age? This affords room for many general observations concerning the gradual change of our sentiments and inclinations, and the different maxims which prevail in the different ages of human creatures. Even the characters which are peculiar to each individual have a uniformity in their influence, otherwise our acquaintance with the persons, and our observation of their conduct, could never teach us their dispositions or serve to direct our behaviour with regard to them.

I grant it possible to find some actions which seem to have no regular connection with any known motives and are exceptions to all the measures of conduct which have ever been established for the government of men. But if we would willingly know what judgment should be formed of such irregular and extraordinary actions, we may consider the sentiments commonly entertained with regard to those irregular events which appear in the course of nature and the operations of external objects. All causes are not conjoined to their usual effects with like uniformity. An artificer who handles only dead matter may be disappointed of his aim, as well as the politician who directs the conduct of sensible and intelligent agents.

The vulgar, who take things according to their first appearance, attribute the uncertainty of events to such an uncertainty in the causes as makes the latter often fail of their usual influence, though they meet with no impediment in their operation. But philosophers, observing that almost in every part of nature there is contained a vast variety of springs and principles which are hid by reason of their minuteness or remoteness, find that it is at least possible the contrariety of events may not proceed from any contingency in the cause but from the secret operation of contrary causes. This possibility is converted into certainty by farther observation when they remark that, upon an exact scrutiny, a contrariety of effects always betrays a contrariety of causes and proceeds from their mutual opposition. A peasant can give no better reason for the stopping of any clock or watch than to say that it does not commonly go right. But an artist easily perceives that the same force in the spring or pendulum has always the same influence on the wheels, but fails of its usual effect, perhaps by reason of a grain of dust which puts a stop to the whole movement. From the observation of several parallel instances, philosophers form a maxim that the connection between all causes and effects is equally necessary, and that its seeming uncertainty in some instances proceeds from the secret opposition of contrary causes.

Thus, for instance, in the human body, when the usual symptoms of health or sickness disappoint our expectation, when medicines operate not with their wonted powers, when irregular events follow from any particular cause, the philosopher and physician are not surprised at the matter, nor are ever tempted to deny, in general, the necessity and uniformity of those principles by which the animal economy is conducted. They know that a human body is a mighty complicated machine, that many secret powers lurk in it which are altogether beyond our comprehension, that to us it must often appear very uncertain in its operations, and that, therefore, the irregular events which outwardly discover themselves can be no proof that the laws of nature are not observed with the greatest regularity in its internal operations and government.

The philosopher, if he be consistent, must apply the same reasoning to the actions and volitions of intelligent agents. The most irregular and unexpected resolutions of men may frequently be accounted for by those who know every particular circumstance of their character and situation. A person of an obliging disposition gives a peevish answer; but he has the toothache, or has not dined. A stupid fellow discov-

ers an uncommon alacrity in his carriage; but he has met with a sudden piece of good fortune. Or even when an action, as sometimes happens, cannot be particularly accounted for, either by the person himself or by others, we know, in general, that the characters of men are to a certain degree inconstant and irregular. This is, in a manner, the constant character of human nature, though it be applicable, in a more particular manner, to some persons who have no fixed rule for their conduct, but proceed in a continued course of caprice and inconstancy. The internal principles and motives may operate in a uniform manner, notwithstanding these seeming irregularities; in the same manner as the winds, rain, clouds, and other variations of the weather are supposed to be governed by steady principles, though not easily discoverable by human sagacity and enquiry.

Thus it appears not only that the conjunction between motives and voluntary actions is as regular and uniform as that between the cause and effect in any part of nature, but also that this regular conjunction has been universally acknowledged among mankind, and has never been the subject of dispute either in philosophy or common life. Now, as it is from past experience that we draw all inferences concerning the future, and as we conclude that objects will always be conjoined together which we find to have always been conjoined, it may seem superfluous to prove that this experienced uniformity in human actions is a source whence we draw *inferences* concerning them. But in order to throw the argument into a greater variety of lights, we shall also insist, though briefly, on this latter topic.

The mutual dependence of men is so great in all societies that scarce any human action is entirely complete in itself or is performed without some reference to the actions of others, which are requisite to make it answer fully the intention of the agent. The poorest artificer who labours alone expects at least the protection of the magistrate to ensure him the enjoyment of the fruits of his labour. He also expects that when he carries his goods to market and offers them at a reasonable price, he shall find purchasers and shall be able, by the money he acquires, to engage others to supply him with those commodities which are requisite for his subsistence. In proportion as men extend their dealings and render their intercourse with others more complicated, they always comprehend in their schemes of life a greater variety of voluntary actions which they expect, from the proper motives, to co-operate with their own. In all these conclusions they take their measures from past experience, in the same manner as in their reasonings concerning external objects, and firmly believe that men, as well as all the elements, are to continue in their operations the same that they have ever found them. A manufacturer reckons upon the labour of his servants for the execution of any work as much as upon the tools which he employs, and would be equally surprised were his expectations disappointed. In short, this experimental inference and reasoning concerning the actions of others enters so much into human life that no man, while awake, is ever a moment without employing it. Have we not reason, therefore, to affirm that all mankind have always agreed in the doctrine of necessity, according to the foregoing definition and explication of it?

Nor have philosophers ever entertained a different opinion from the people in this particular. For, not to mention that almost every action of their life supposes that opinion, there are even few of the speculative parts of learning to which it is not essential. What would become of *history*, had we not a dependence on the veracity of the historian according to the experience which we have had of mankind? How could *politics* be a science, if laws and forms of government had not a uniform influence upon society? Where would be the foundation of *morals*, if particular characters had no certain or determinate power to produce particular sentiments, and if these sentiments had no constant operation on actions? And with what pretence could we employ our *criticism* upon any poet or polite author, if we could not pronounce the conduct and sentiments of his actors either natural or unnatural to such characters and in such circumstances? It seems almost impossible, therefore, to engage either in science or action of any kind without acknowledging the doctrine of necessity, and this *inference* from motives to voluntary actions, from characters to conduct.

And, indeed, when we consider how aptly *natural* and *moral* evidence link together and form only one chain of argument, we shall make no scruple to allow that they are of the same nature and derived from the same principles. A prisoner who has neither money nor interest discovers the impossibility of his escape as well when he considers the obstinacy of the gaoler as the walls and bars with which he is surrounded; and, in all attempts for his freedom, chooses rather to work upon the stone and iron of the one than upon the inflexible nature of the other. The same prisoner, when conducted to the scaffold, foresees his death as certainly from the constancy and fidelity of his guards as from the operation of the ax or wheel. His mind runs along a certain train of ideas: the refusal of the soldiers to consent to his escape; the action of the executioner; the separation of the head and body; bleeding, convulsive motions, and death. Here is a connected chain of natural causes and voluntary actions, but the mind feels no difference between them in passing from one link to another, nor is less certain of the future event than if it were connected with the objects present to the memory or senses by a train of causes cemented together by what we are pleased to call a *physical* necessity. The same experienced union has the same effect on the mind, whether the united objects be motives, volition, and actions, or figure and motion. We may change the name of things, but their nature and their operation on the understanding never change.

Were a man whom I know to be honest and opulent, and with whom I live in intimate friendship, to come into my house, where I am surrounded with my servants, I rest assured that he is not to stab me before he leaves it in order to rob me of my silver standish [ed., either a stand containing writing materials or an inkpot]; and I no more suspect this event than the falling of the house itself, which is new and solidly built and founded.—*But he may have been seized with a sudden and unknown frenzy.*—So may a sudden earthquake arise, and shake and tumble my house about my ears. I shall, therefore, change the suppositions. I shall say that I know with certainty that he is not to put his hand into the fire and hold it there till it be consumed. And this event I think I can foretell with the same assurance as that, if he throw himself out at the window and meet with no obstruction, he will not remain a moment suspended in the air. No suspicion of an unknown frenzy can give the least possibility to the former event, which is so contrary to all the known principles of human nature. A man who at noon leaves his purse full of gold on the pavement at Charing Cross may as well expect that it will fly away like a feather as that he will find it untouched an hour after. Above one half of human reasonings contain inferences of a similar nature, attended with more or less degrees of certainty, proportioned to our experience of the usual conduct of mankind in such particular situations.

I have frequently considered what could possibly be the reason why all mankind, though they have ever, without hesitation, acknowledged the doctrine of necessity in their whole practice and reasoning, have yet discovered such a reluctance to acknowledge it in words, and have rather shown a propensity, in all ages, to profess the contrary opinion. The matter, I think, may be accounted for after the following manner. If we examine the operations of body and the production of effects from their causes, we shall find that all our faculties can never carry us further in our knowledge of this relation than barely to observe that particular objects are *constantly conjoined* together, and that the mind is carried, by a *customary transition,* from the appearance of one to the belief of the other. But though this conclusion concerning human ignorance be the result of the strictest scrutiny of this subject, men still entertain a strong propensity to believe that they penetrate further into the powers of nature and perceive something like a necessary connection between the cause and the effect. When, again, they turn their reflections towards the operations of their own minds and *feel* no such connection of the motive and the action, they are thence apt to suppose that there is a difference between the effects which result from material force and those which arise from thought and intelligence. But being once convinced that we know nothing further of causation of any kind than merely the *constant conjunction* of objects and the consequent *inference* of the mind from one to another, and finding that these two circumstances are universally allowed to have place in voluntary actions, we may be more easily led to own the same necessity common to all causes. And though this reasoning may contradict the systems of many philosophers in ascribing necessity to the determinations of the will, we shall find, upon reflection, that they dissent from it in words only, not in their real sentiment. Necessity, according to the sense in which it is here taken, has never yet been rejected, nor can ever, I think, be rejected by any philosopher. It may only, perhaps, be pretended that the mind can perceive in the operations of matter some further connection between the cause and effect, and a connection that has not place in the voluntary actions of intelligent beings. Now, whether it be so or not can only appear upon examination, and it is incumbent on these philosophers to make good their assertion by defining or describing that necessity, and pointing it out to us in the operations of material causes.

It would seem, indeed, that men may begin at the wrong end of this question concerning liberty and necessity when they enter upon it by examining the faculties of the soul, the influence of the understanding, and the operations of the will. Let them first discuss a more simple question, namely, the operations of body and of brute unintelligent matter, and try whether they can there form any idea of causation and necessity, except that of a constant conjunction of objects and subsequent inference of the mind from one to another. If these circumstances form, in reality, the whole of that necessity which we conceive in matter, and if these circumstances be also universally acknowledged to take place in the operations of the mind, the dispute is at an end; at least, must be owned to be thenceforth merely verbal. But as long as we will rashly suppose that we have some further idea of necessity and causation in the operations of external objects, at the same time that we can find nothing further in the voluntary actions of the mind, there is no possibility of bringing the question to any determinate issue while we proceed upon so erroneous a supposition. The only method of undeceiving us is to mount up higher, to examine the narrow extent of science when applied to material causes, and to convince ourselves that all we know of them is the constant conjunction and inference above mentioned. We may, perhaps, find that it is with difficulty we are induced to fix such narrow limits to human understanding, but we can afterwards find no difficulty when we come to apply this doctrine to the actions of the will. For as it is evident that these have a regular conjunction with motives and circumstances and characters, and as we always draw inferences from one to the other, we must be obliged to acknowledge in words that necessity which we have already avowed in every deliberation of our lives, and in every step of our conduct and behavior.[1]

But to proceed in this reconciling project with regard to the question of liberty and necessity—the most contentious question of metaphysics, the most contentious science—it will not require many words to prove that all mankind have ever agreed in the doctrine of liberty as well as in that of necessity, and that the whole dispute, in this respect also, has been hitherto merely verbal. For what is meant by liberty when applied to voluntary actions? We cannot surely mean that actions have so little connection with motives, inclinations, and circumstances that one does not follow with a certain degree of uniformity from the other, and that one affords no inference by which we can conclude the existence of the other. For these are plain and acknowledged matters of fact. By liberty, then, we can only mean *a power of acting or not acting, according to the determinations of the will;* that is, if we choose to remain at rest, we may; if we choose to move, we also may. Now this hypothetical liberty is universally allowed to belong to everyone who is not a prisoner and in chains. Here, then, is no subject of dispute.

Whatever definition we may give of liberty, we should be careful to observe two requisite circumstances; *first,* that it be consistent with plain matter of fact; *secondly,* that it be consistent with itself. If we observe these circumstances and render our definition intelligible, I am persuaded that all mankind will be found of one opinion with regard to it.

It is universally allowed that nothing exists without a cause of its existence, and that chance, when strictly examined, is a mere negative word and means not any real power which has anywhere a being in nature. But it is pretended that some causes are necessary, some not necessary. Here then is the advantage of definitions. Let anyone *define* a cause without comprehending, as a part of the definition, a *necessary connection* with its effect, and let him show distinctly the origin of the idea, expressed by the definition, and I shall readily give up the whole controversy. But if the foregoing explication of the matter be received, this must be absolutely impracticable. Had not objects a regular conjunction with each other, we should never have entertained any notion of cause and effect; and this regular conjunction produces that inference of the understanding which is the only connection that we can have any comprehension of. Whoever attempts a definition of cause exclusive of these circumstances will be obliged either to employ unintelligible terms or such as are synonymous to the term which he endeavours to define.[2] And if the definition above mentioned be admitted, liberty, when opposed to necessity, not to constraint, is the same thing with chance, which is universally allowed to have no existence.

## NOTES

1. The prevalence of the doctrine of liberty may be accounted for from another cause, viz., a false sensation or seeming experience which we have, or may have, of liberty or indifference in many of our actions. The necessity of any action, whether of matter or of mind, is not, properly speaking, a quality in the agent but in any thinking or intelligent being who may consider the action; and it consists chiefly in the determination of his thoughts to infer the existence of that action from some preceding objects; as liberty, when opposed to necessity, is nothing but the want of that determination, and a certain looseness or indifference, which we feel in passing, or not passing, from the idea of one object to that of any succeeding one. Now we may observe that though, in *reflecting* on human actions, we seldom feel such a looseness or indifference, but are commonly able to infer them with considerable certainty from their motives, and from the dispositions of the agent; yet it frequently happens that, in *performing* the actions themselves, we are sensible of something like it; and as all resembling objects are readily taken for each other, this has been employed as a demonstrative and even intuitive proof of human liberty. We feel that our actions are subject to our will on most occasions, and imagine we feel that the will itself is subject to nothing, because, when by a denial of it we are provoked to try, we feel that it moves easily every way, and produces an image of itself, (or a *Velleity,* as it is called in the schools), even on that side on which it did not settle. This image, or faint motion, we persuade ourselves, could at that time have been completed into the thing itself, because, should that be denied, we find upon a second trial that, at present, it can. We consider not that the fantastical desire of showing liberty is here the motive of our actions. And it seems certain that however we may imagine we feel a liberty within ourselves, a spectator can commonly infer our actions from our motives and character; and even where he cannot, he concludes in general that he might, were he perfectly acquainted with every circumstance of our situation and temper, and the most secret springs of our complexion and disposition. Now this is the very essence of necessity, according to the foregoing doctrine.

2. Thus, if a cause be defined, *that which produces anything,* it is easy to observe that *producing* is synonymous to *causing.* In like manner, if a cause be defined, *that by which anything exists,* this is liable to the same objection. For what is meant by these words, *by which?* Had it been said that a cause is *that* after which *anything constantly exists,* we should have understood the terms. For this is, indeed, all we know of the matter. And this constancy forms the very essence of necessity, nor have we any other idea of it.

# READING 31

# Hard and Soft Determinism
*Paul Edwards*

*Paul Edwards (1923–   ) is Professor of Philosophy at Brooklyn College of City University of New York. Editor-in-chief of the* Encyclopedia of Philosophy *(1967), Edwards has written on causation, induction, and arguments for God's existence and is well-known for his criticisms of religious and metaphysical philosophies of the twentieth century. His books include* The Logic of Moral Discourse *(1955),* Buber and Buberism: A Critical Evaluation *(1969), and* Heidegger and Death: A Deflationary Critique *(1979), and he is the editor with Arthur Pap of* A Modern Introduction to Philosophy. *"Hard and Soft Determinism" was delivered as a talk at the first annual New York Institute of Philosophy in 1957, hence, the reference to "the philosophers present in this room."*

In his essay "The Dilemma of Determinism," William James makes a distinction that will serve as a point of departure for my remarks. He there distinguishes between the philosophers he calls "hard" determinists and those he labels "soft" determinists. The former, the hard determinists, James tells us, "did not shrink from such words as fatality, bondage of the will, necessitation and the like." He quotes a famous stanza from Omar Khayyám as representing this kind of determinism:

> With earth's first clay they did the last man knead,
> And there of the last harvest sowed the seed.
> And the first morning of creation wrote
> What the last dawn of reckoning shall read.

Another of Omar's verses expresses perhaps even better the kind of theory that James has here in mind:

> 'Tis all a checker-board of nights and days,
> Where destiny with men for pieces plays;

SOURCE: From S. Hook, Ed., *Determinism and Freedom in the Age of Modern Science* (New York: Macmillan, 1961): 117–125.

> Thither and thither moves, and metes, and slays,
> And one by one back to the closet lays.

James mentioned no names other than Omar Khayyám. But there is little doubt that among the hard determinists he would have included Jonathan Edwards, Anthony Collins, Holbach, Priestley, Robert Owen, Schopenhauer, Freud, and also, if he had come a little earlier, Clarence Darrow.

James of course rejected both hard and soft determinism, but for hard determinism he had a certain respect: the kind of respect one sometimes has for an honest, straightforward adversary. For soft determinism, on the other hand, he had nothing but contempt, calling it a "quagmire of evasion." "Nowadays," he writes, "we have a *soft* determinism which abhors harsh words, and repudiating fatality, necessity, and even predetermination, says that its real name is 'freedom.'" From his subsequent observations it is clear that he would include among the evasionists not only neo-Hegelians like Green and Bradley but also Hobbes and Hume and Mill; and if he were alive today James would undoubtedly include Schlick and Ayer and Stevenson and Noel-Smith, not to mention some of the philosophers present in this room.

The theory James calls soft determinism, especially the Hume-Mill-Schlick variety of it, has been extremely fashionable during the last twenty-five years, while hardly anybody can be found today who has anything good to say for hard determinism. In opposition to this contemporary trend, I should like to strike a blow on behalf of hard determinism in my talk today. I shall also try to bring out exactly what is really at issue between hard and soft determinism. I think the nature of this dispute has frequently been misconceived chiefly because many writers, including James, have a very inaccurate notion of what is maintained by actual hard determinists, as distinct from the bogey men they set up in order to score an easy victory.

To begin with, it is necessary to spell out more fully the main contentions of the soft determinists. Since it is the dominant form of soft determinism at the present time, I shall confine myself to the Hume-Mill-Schlick theory. According to this theory there is in the first place no contradiction whatsoever between determinism and the proposition that human beings are sometimes free agents. When we call an action "free" we never in any ordinary situation mean that it was uncaused; and this emphatically includes the kind of action about which we pass moral judgments. By calling an action "free" we mean that the agent was not compelled or constrained to perform it. Sometimes people act in a certain way because of threats or because they have been drugged or because of a posthypnotic suggestion or because of an irrational overpowering urge such as the one that makes a kleptomaniac steal something he does not really need. On such occasions human beings are not free agents. But on other occasions they act in certain ways because of their own rational desires, because of their own unimpeded efforts, because they have chosen to act in these ways. On these occasions they are free agents although their actions are just as much caused as actions that are not deemed free. In distinguishing between free and unfree actions we do not try to mark the presence and absence of causes but attempt to indicate the *kind* of causes that are present.

Secondly there is no antithesis between determinism and moral responsibility. When we judge a person morally responsible for a certain action, we do indeed presuppose that he was a free agent at the time of the action. But the freedom presupposed is not the contracausal freedom about which indeterminists go into such ecstatic raptures. It is nothing more than the freedom already mentioned—the ability to act according to one's choices or desires. Since determinism is compatible with freedom in this sense, it is also compatible with moral responsibility. In other words, the world is after all wonderful: we can be determinists and yet go on punishing our enemies and our children, and we can go on blaming ourselves, all without a bad intellectual conscience.

Mill, who was probably the greatest moralizer among the soft determinists, recognized with particular satisfaction the influence or alleged influence of one class of human desires. Not only, for example,

does such a lowly desire as my desire to get a new car influence my conduct. It is equally true, or so at least Mill believed, that my desire to become a more virtuous person does on occasion influence my actions. By suitable training and efforts my desire to change my character may in fact bring about the desired changes. If Mill were alive today he might point to contemporary psychiatry as an illustration of his point. Let us suppose that I have an intense desire to become famous, but that I also have an intense desire to become a happier and more lovable person who, among other things, does not greatly care about fame. Let us suppose, furthermore, that I know of a therapy that can transform fame-seeking and unlovable into lovable and fame-indifferent character structures. If, now, I have enough money, energy, and courage, and if a few other conditions are fulfilled, my desire may actually lead to a major change in my character. Since we can, therefore, at least to some extent, form our own character, determinism according to Mill is compatible not only with judgments of moral responsibility about this or that particular *action* flowing from an unimpeded desire, but also, within limits, with moral judgments about the *character* of human beings.

I think that several of Mill's observations were well worth making and that James's verdict on his theory as a "quagmire of evasion" is far too derogatory. I think hard determinists have occasionally written in such a way as to suggest that they deny the causal efficacy of human desires and efforts. Thus Holbach wrote:

> You will say that I feel free. This is an illusion, which may be compared to that of the fly in the fable, who, lighting upon the pole of a heavy carriage, applauded himself for directing its course. Man, who thinks himself free, is a fly who imagines he has power to move the universe, while he is himself unknowingly carried along by it.

There is also the following passage in Schopenhauer:

> Every man, being what he is and placed in the circumstances which for the moment obtain, but which on their part also arise by strict necessity, can absolutely never do anything else than just what at that moment he does do. Accordingly, the whole course of a man's life, in all its incidents great and small, is as necessarily predetermined as the course of a clock.

Voltaire expresses himself in much the same way in the article on "Destiny" in the *Philosophical Dictionary*.

> Everything happens through immutable laws, . . . everything is necessary. . . . "There are," some persons say, "some events which are necessary and others which are not." It would be very comic that one part of the world was arranged, and the other were not; that one part of what happens had to happen and that another part of what happens did not have to happen. If one looks closely at it, one sees that the doctrine contrary to that of destiny is absurd; but there are many people destined to reason badly; others not to reason at all, others to persecute those who reason. . . .
>
> . . . I necessarily have the passion for writing this, and you have the passion for condemning me; both of us are equally fools, equally the toy of destiny. Your nature is to do harm, mine is to love truth, and to make it public in spite of you.

Furthermore there can be little doubt that Hume and Mill and Schlick were a great deal clearer about the relation between motives and actions than the hard determinists, who either conceived it, like Collins, as one of logical necessity or, like Priestley and Voltaire and Schopenhauer, as necessarily involving coercion or constraint.

But when all is said and done, there remains a good deal of truth in James's charge that soft determinism is an evasion. For a careful reading of their works shows that none of the hard determinists really denied that human desires, efforts, and choices make a difference in the course of events. Any remarks to the contrary are at most temporary lapses. This, then, is hardly the point at issue. If it is not the point at issue, what is? Let me at this stage imagine a hard determinist replying to a champion of the Hume-Mill theory: "You are right," he would say, "in maintaining that some of our actions are caused by our desires and choices. But you do not pursue the subject far enough. You arbitrarily stop at the desires and volitions. We must not stop there. We must go on to ask where *they* come from; and if determinism is true there can be no doubt about the answer to this question. Ultimately our desires and our whole character are derived from our inherited equipment and the environmental influences to which we were subjected at the beginning of our lives. It is clear that we had no hand in shaping either of these." A hard determinist could quote a number of eminent support-

ers. "Our volitions and our desires," wrote Holbach in his little book *Good Sense,* "are never in our power. You think yourself free, because you do what you will; but are you free to will or not to will; to desire or not to desire?" And Schopenhauer expressed the same thought in the following epigram: "A man can surely do what he wills to do, but he cannot determine what he wills."

Let me turn once more to the topic of character transformation by means of psychiatry to bring out this point with full force. Let us suppose that both *A* and *B* are compulsive and suffer intensely from their neuroses. Let us assume that there is a therapy that could help them, which could materially change their character structure, but that it takes a great deal of energy and courage to undertake the treatment. Let us suppose that *A* has the necessary energy and courage while *B* lacks it. *A* undergoes the therapy and changes in the desired way. *B* just gets more and more compulsive and more and more miserable. Now, it is true that *A* helped form his own later character. But his starting point, his desire to change, his energy and courage, were already there. They may or may not have been the result of previous efforts on his own part. But there must have been a first effort, and the effort at that time was the result of factors that were not of his making.

The fact that a person's character is ultimately the product of factors over which he had no control is not denied by the soft determinists, though many of them don't like to be reminded of it when they are in a moralizing mood. Since the hard determinists admit that our desires and choices do on occasion influence the course of our lives, there is thus no disagreement between the soft and the hard determinists about the empirical facts. However, some hard determinists infer from some of these facts that human beings are never morally responsible for their actions. The soft determinists, as already stated, do not draw any such inference. In the remainder of my paper I shall try to show just what it is that hard determinists are inferring and why, in my opinion, they are justified in their conclusion.

I shall begin by adopting for my purposes a distinction introduced by C. A. Campbell in his extremely valuable article "Is Free Will a Pseudo-Problem?"[1] in which he distinguishes between two

---

[1] *Mind,* 1951.

conceptions of moral responsibility. Different persons, he says, require different conditions to be fulfilled before holding human beings morally responsible for what they do. First, there is what Campbell calls the ordinary unreflective person, who is rather ignorant and who is not greatly concerned with the theories of science, philosophy, and religion. If the unreflective person is sure that the agent to be judged was acting under coercion or constraint, he will not hold him responsible. If, however, he is sure that the action was performed in accordance with the agent's unimpeded rational desire, if he is sure that the action would not have taken place but for the agent's decision, then the unreflective person will consider ascription of moral responsibility justified. The fact that the agent did not ultimately make his own character will either not occur to him, or else it will not be considered a sufficient ground for withholding a judgment of moral responsibility.

In addition to such unreflective persons, continues Campbell, there are others who have reached "a tolerably advanced level of reflection."

> Such a person will doubtless be acquainted with the claims advanced in some quarters that causal law operates universally; or/and with the theories of some philosophies that the universe is throughout the expression of a single supreme principle; or/and with the doctrines of some theologians that the world is created, sustained and governed by an Omniscient and Omnipotent Being.

Such a person will tend to require the fulfillment of a further condition before holding anybody morally responsible. He will require not only that the agent was not coerced or constrained but also—and this is taken to be an additional condition—that he "could have chosen otherwise than he actually did." I should prefer to put this somewhat differently, but it will not affect the main conclusion drawn by Campbell, with which I agree. The reflective person, I should prefer to express it, requires not only that the agent was not coerced; he also requires that the agent *originally chose his own character*—the character that now displays itself in his choices and desires and efforts. Campbell concludes that determinism is indeed compatible with judgments of moral responsibility in the unreflective sense, but that it is incompatible with judgments of moral responsibility in the reflective sense.

Although I do not follow Campbell in rejecting determinism, I agree basically with his analysis, with one other qualification. I do not think it is a question of the different senses in which the term is used by ignorant and unreflective people, on the one hand, and by those who are interested in science, religion, and philosophy, on the other. The very same persons, whether educated or uneducated, use it in certain contexts in the one sense and in other contexts in the other. Practically all human beings, no matter how much interested they are in science, religion, and philosophy, employ what Campbell calls the unreflective conception when they are dominated by violent emotions like anger, indignation, or hate, and especially when the conduct they are judging has been personally injurious to them. On the other hand, a great many people, whether they are educated or not, will employ what Campbell calls the reflective conception when they are not consumed with hate or anger—when they are judging a situation calmly and reflectively and when the fact that the agent did not ultimately shape his own character has been vividly brought to their attention. Clarence Darrow in his celebrated pleas repeatedly appealed to the jury on precisely this ground. If any of you, he would say, had been reared in an environment like that of the accused or had to suffer from his defective heredity, *you* would now be standing in the dock. . . . Darrow nearly always convinced the jury that the accused could not be held morally responsible for his acts; and certainly the majority of the jurors were relatively uneducated.

I have so far merely distinguished between two concepts of moral responsibility. I now wish to go a step farther and claim that only one of them can be considered, properly speaking, a moral concept. This is not an easy point to make clear, but I can at least indicate what I mean. We do not normally consider just any positive or negative feeling a "moral" emotion. Nor do we consider just any sentence containing the words "good" or "bad" expressions of "moral" judgment. For example, if a man hates a woman because she rejected him, this would not be counted as a moral emotion. If, however, he disapproves, say, of Senator McCarthy's libelous speech against Adlai Stevenson before the 1952 election because he disapproves of slander in general and not merely because he likes Stevenson and dislikes McCarthy, his feeling would be counted as moral. A feeling or judgment must in a certain sense be "impersonal" before we consider it moral. To this I would add that it must also be independent of violent emotions. Confining myself to judgments, I would say that a judgment was "moral" only if it was formulated in a calm and reflective mood, or at least if it is supported in a calm and reflective state of mind. If this is so, it follows that what Campbell calls the reflective sense of "moral responsibility" is the only one that qualifies as a properly moral use of the term.

Before I conclude I wish to avoid a certain misunderstanding of my remarks. From the fact that human beings do not ultimately shape their own character, I said, it *follows* that they are never morally responsible. I do not mean that by reminding people of the ultimate causes of their character one makes them more charitable and less vengeful. Maybe one does, but that is not what I mean. I mean "follow" or "imply" in the same sense as, or in a sense closely akin to, that in which the conclusion of a valid syllo-

gism follows from the premises. The effectiveness of Darrow's pleas does not merely show, I am arguing, how powerfully he could sway the emotions of the jurors. His pleas also brought into the open one of the conditions the jurors, like others, consider necessary on reflection before they hold an agent morally responsible. Or perhaps I should say that Darrow *committed* the jurors in their reflective nature to a certain ground for the ascription of moral responsibility.[2]

---

[2]*Author's Note.* This paper was written in the hope of stimulating discussion of a position which has not received adequate attention in recent years. The position was stated rather bluntly and without the necessary qualifications because of limitations of time. I hope to return to the subject at greater length in the near future, and on that occasion to present a more balanced treatment which will attempt to meet criticisms made in the discussion. (*December 1957.*)

# READING 32

# Actions, Predictions, and Books of Life
*Alvin I. Goldman*

*Alvin Goldman (1938–   ) is Professor of Philosophy at the University of Arizona. His books include* A Theory of Human Action *(1970) and* Epistemology and Cognition *(1986). Reading 32 is an abridged and simplified version of the paper with the same title that was first published in* American Philosophical Quarterly 5 *(1968): 135–151. A slightly different version appears as Chapter 6 of* A Theory of Human Action. *The reader should consult either of these two longer versions for a more rigorous treatment.*

**SOURCE:** From *American Philosophical Quarterly* 5 (1968): 135–151. Edited.

Are actions determined? It is difficult to tell "directly" whether or not actions are governed by universal laws, so some philosophers resort to the following "indirect" argument:

> If actions are determined, it is possible to predict them (with certainty).
> It is not possible for actions to be predicted (with certainty). Therefore, actions are not determined.

This position will be called "anti-predictionism," and a defender of it is an "anti-predictionist." The aim of this paper is to rebut anti-predictionism.

Both premises of the anti-predictionist argument will come under attack. The first premise asserts that determinism implies the possibility of prediction, or, in its contrapositive form, that the impossibility of prediction implies indeterminism. But on a reasonable definition of determinism this premise is false. One can specify events which it is logically impossible to predict, but which nonetheless may be determined. Setting such events aside, however, there is a presumptive connection between determinism and the possibility of prediction. To support the second premise the anti-predictionist may call attention to a problem concerning the possibility of writing a complete description of someone's life—including his voluntary actions—even before he is born. If actions were determined, it would be possible for such a "book of life" to be written. The anti-predictionist contends, however, that no such book of life could be written, at least not with any assurance that its predictions would come true. For a book of life might be discovered and read by the agent whose actions it predicts; but if the agent reads these predictions he can choose to falsify them. Hence nobody could write such a book of life with any certainty that his predictions would be fulfilled. Therefore, the anti-predictionist concludes, determinism does not hold. Against this position, I maintain that it may well be possible for books of life to be written, and for the author of such a book to know (with certainty) that its predictions will be fulfilled.

Anti-predictionists generally support their second premise by contrasting the predictability of human behavior with that of physical events. They allege that special difficulties of a purely conceptual sort arise for the prediction of action, difficulties that are unparalleled in the realm of purely physical phenomena. I shall argue that there are no essential differences between actions and physical events with respect to the problem of prediction. More precisely, *conceptual* reflection on the nature of human behavior (as opposed to *empirical* investigation by the special sciences) does not reveal any peculiar immunity of action to prediction.

I am not attempting to prove the thesis that actions are determined; I merely wish to show that the anti-predictionist's arguments fail to prove that actions are not determined. It is, of course, conceivable that actions are undetermined. If so, they are not perfectly predictable. My contention is just that the arguments of philosophers, based on familiar, com-mon-sense features of human action and choice, do not prove that actions are undetermined or immune to prediction. My aim, in other words, is not to establish the *truth,* but merely the *tenability,* of the thesis that actions are determined.

II.

Some writers have pointed out that certain actions (under certain descriptions, at least) cannot be predicted: i.e., it is logically impossible for them to be predicted. They have inferred from this that these actions are not determined. I am prepared to concede that it is indeed logically impossible for certain actions (under certain descriptions) to be predicted. But it does not follow from this that they are undetermined.

Before turning to these cases, let us present some relevant definitions. I shall define *determinism* as the view that every event and state of affairs is determined in every detail. An event is *determined* (in a given detail) if and only if it is *deducible from some set of antecedent conditions and laws of nature.* Roughly, a law of nature is any true non-analytic universal statement of unlimited scope which supports counterfactual conditionals. Notice that this definition makes no reference to predictability, and thereby leaves open the connection, if any, between determinism and predictability. When an event is deducible from certain laws and antecedent conditions, I shall say that these antecedent conditions *causally necessitate* this event. I assume that if human actions are determined, then among the events or conditions that causally necessitate them are desires, beliefs, and decisions of the agent.

In our discussion of predictability we need a sense of 'prediction' distinct from mere lucky guesses or precognition. We must be concerned with predictions made on the basis of laws and antecedent condition. I shall call a prediction a *scientific prediction* if and only if it is made by *deducing* the predicted event from known laws and antecedent conditions. A scientific predictor may learn of the laws and antecedent conditions in any number of ways. (On my definition, most predictions made by actual scientists are not "scientific predictions," since real scientists seldom, if ever, *deduce* subsequent events from laws and prior conditions. But scientific prediction, as defined here, may be regarded as an ideal of prediction to which scientists can aspire.)

With these definitions at hand, let us examine same cases in which actions, or action-related events, are logically impossible to predict. Let the expression 'invent *x*' mean 'think of *x* for the very first time.' Now suppose that Sam invents the corkscrew in 1625—in other words, the first thought of the corkscrew occurs in 1625, when Sam thinks of it. It logically follows from this that nobody predicts Sam's invention of the corkscrew. For in order to predict Sam's invention of the corkscrew, the predictor would himself have to think of the corkscrew, and he would have to have such a thought before 1625. But if someone did have such a thought before 1625, then Sam would not *invent* the corkscrew in 1625: Sam's thinking of the corkscrew in 1625 would not count as an inventing of the corkscrew. Thus, it is logically impossible that anyone should (correctly) predict Sam's inventing of the corkscrew.

Does it follow from this that Sam's invention of the corkscrew is undetermined? Certainly not. Although it is logically impossible for anyone to predict Sam's invention of the corkscrew, his invention of the corkscrew may be deducible from laws and antecedent conditions. Consider an analogous case in the realm of purely physical phenomena. Let the expression 'a tornado strikes *x by surprise at t*' mean 'a tornado strikes *x* at *t*, and before *t* nobody thinks of a tornado striking *x*.' Now suppose that a tornado strikes Timbuktu by surprise at *t*. It is logically impossible for this event to be predicted, for if someone did predict it, there would be a thought, prior to *t*, of a tornado striking Timbuktu, and hence there would be no event of a striking Timbuktu *by surprise* at *t*. But there is no reason to conclude that the event of a tornado striking Timbuktu by surprise is undetermined. We may well suppose that this event is deducible from laws and antecedent conditions. For surely we may suppose that a tornado's striking Timbuktu at *t* is deducible from prior meteorological conditions and physical laws. But if we simply add to these antecedent conditions the further (antecedent) condition that nobody thinks of a tornado striking Timbuktu before *t*, we obtain a set of laws and antecedent conditions which jointly entail that a tornado strikes Timbuktu *by surprise* at *t*. We see, then, that the logical impossibility of an event being predicted does not prove that this event is undetermined.

With this point in mind, consider a case involving not actions, but decisions. In his article "Can The Will Be Caused?" Carl Ginet claims that it is impossible ("conceptually impossible") for anyone to predict his own decisions. And he regards this as a reason for concluding that decisions are not caused, i.e., determined. The argument begins by defining 'deciding to do *A*' as 'passing into a state of knowledge (of a certain kind) that one will do, or try to do, *A*.' Now suppose that Sam, at *t*, decides to do *A*. If Sam had predicted that he would make this decision—and if this prediction had involved *knowledge*—then Sam could not, at *t*, decide to do *A*. For if, before *t*, he knew that he would decide to do *A*, then he knew before *t* that he would do, or, try to do, *A*. But if he knew, before *t*, that he would do, or try to do, *A*, he could not, at *t*, have *passed into* a state of knowing that he would do, or try to do, *A*. Thus, it is logically impossible for anyone to predict his own decision.

Of course, one might predict one's future decision and then forget about it. Having forgotten about this prediction—i.e., having lost this knowledge—one could later *pass into* a state of (renewed) knowledge that one would do, or try to do, an action. But if one *retains* the foreknowledge, nothing one does later can count as *deciding*.

But does it follow from this that a person's decisions are uncaused, or undetermined? As before, the answer is no. From the fact that it is logically impossible for anyone to predict his own decision (and retain the knowledge contained in this prediction) it does not follow that the decision is not deducible from laws and antecedent conditions. Once we notice that there are certain events, the occurrence of which presupposes that they have not been predicted, we readily see that it is logically impossible for some events to be predicted. But it does not follow that these events are undetermined. Determinism simply does not entail the logical possibility of prediction.

III.

Let us set aside the special class of events, including inventions, surprise tornadoes, and decisions, which logically presuppose the absence of prediction or foreknowledge. If we set these aside, it appears that determinism does imply the possibility, in principle, of prediction. For if an event is deducible from laws and antecedent conditions, then if anyone knew these laws and antecedent conditions beforehand, and if he had sufficient reasoning or calculational powers to make the relevant deduction, he could know, beforehand, that the indicated event would occur. In the actual world, of course, there may be no beings with sufficient knowledge of prior conditions and laws, or sufficient deductive powers, to make scientific predictions, especially scientific predictions of (voluntary) human actions. But if we are interested in the possibility, *in principle,* of prediction, we must not confine ourselves to the actual world. We will have to consider certain *non-actual* possible worlds in which a potential predictor is endowed with all relevant information and calculational powers.

The anti-predictionist would contend that there are *no* possible worlds in which scientific predictions are made of an agent's voluntary actions. Or, at any rate, there are no possible worlds in which scientific predictions are made of an agent's voluntary actions and in which the agent learns of these predictions prior to the actions. This is because it is always open to an agent to act contrary to the prediction; in other words, he can always choose to *refute* the prediction, no matter what has been predicted. According to the anti-predictionist, then, there are no possible worlds in which a book of someone's life is written (scientifically) before he is born, a book which he reads during his lifetime, and parts of which he reads prior to the time of the recorded (i.e., predicted) actions. I contend that this claim is mistaken. I think there may well be possible worlds in which books of life are (scientifically) written and yet read at appropriate times by the agent in question. This, then, is an appropriate test of the anti-predictionist's position.

In order to ascertain whether there are possible worlds of the indicated kind, we must try to imagine such worlds. Now we are not interested in possible worlds that are radically different from our own, for the only point of appealing to these possible worlds is to shed light on the actual one. Specifically, we shall want our possible worlds to contain all and only the physical and psychological laws that the actual world contains. Since we do not know all the laws of the actual world, however, we proceed as follows. We see whether we can coherently imagine a world in which scientific predictions of actions are made but which contains no *apparent* difference from our own world with respect to laws of nature. Since this world contains *scientific* predictions, it means that it must be deterministic (at least it must be deterministic with respect to the events being predicted). But this does not beg any questions, for the very fact that such a

world does not diverge in any obvious way from the actual world (in terms of laws or regularities) lends credence to the view that the actual world is deterministic. Of course, it does not prove the actual world to be deterministic; but it is not my purpose here to offer such a proof.

My strategy, then, is to sketch a possible world in which a book of life is scientifically written, and in which the agent reads portions of this book. What is problematic and interesting about this is that the book may have a causal effect on the actions it predicts. That is, it may have an effect on the truth or falsity of the statements contained in the book. It is obvious that the prospective author of such a book must take such "reflexivity" into account. Before sketching my possible world, let us examine the structure of prediction-making where the prediction itself has a causal effect on the predicted event.

Consider the problem of an election predictor. He may know what the precise results of the upcoming election will be, if he makes no public prediction of the election. If he publishes a prediction, however, some of the voters, having found out what the results will be, may change their votes and thereby falsify his prediction. How, then, can a pollster make a genuinely scientific and accurate prediction of an election? Can he take into account the effect of the prediction itself? Herbert Simon has shown that, under specifiable conditions, a predictor can do this. Essentially, what the predictor must know is the propensity of the voters in the community to *change* their voting intention in accordance with their expectations of the outcome. If persons are more likely to vote for a candidate when they expect him to win than when they expect him to lose, we have a "bandwagon" effect; if the opposite holds, we have an "underdog" effect.

Let us suppose that a given pollster has ascertained that, two days before the election, 60 percent of the electorate plans to vote for candidate *A* and 40 percent for *B*. He also knows that, unless he publishes a prediction, the percentages will be the same on election day. Further suppose he knows that there is a certain "bandwagon" effect obtaining in the voting community. (That this bandwagon effect holds in the community could be discovered either by studying previous elections or by deducing it from "higher-level" generalizations found to be true of the community.) When the original intention of the electorate is to vote 60 percent for *A*, this bandwagon effect can be expressed by the equation $V = 60 + .2(P - 50)$, where $P$ is the percentage vote for $A$ publicly predicted by a pollster, and $V$ is the actual resultant vote for $A$. Clearly, if the pollster publicly predicts that $A$ will receive 60 percent of the vote, his prediction will be falsified. Putting $P = 60$, the equation tells us that $V = 62$. In other words, the effect of the prediction, combined with the original voting intention of the electorate, would result in a 62 percent vote for $A$. However, the pollster can easily calculate a value for $P$ which will make $P = V$. He need only solve the two equations, $P = V$ and $V = 60 + .2(P - 50)$. Such a solution yields $P = 62.5$. Thus, the pollster can publish a prediction saying that 62.5 percent of the electorate will vote for $A$, knowing that his own prediction will bring an additional 2.5 percent of the electorate into the $A$ column, and thereby make his prediction come true.

If someone wishes to predict a single person's behavior and yet let him learn of the prediction, the predictor must employ the same sort of strategy as the pollster. He must take into account the agent's reaction to the prediction. There are several kinds of circumstances in which, having made the appropriate calculations, he will be able to make a correct prediction: (1) The agent learns of the prediction but does not want to falsify it. (2) Upon hearing the prediction, the agent decides to falsify it, but later, when the time of the action approaches, he acquires preponderant reasons for doing what was predicted after all. (3) Having decided to refute the prediction, the agent performs the action conforming with it because he doesn't realize that he is conforming with it. (4) At the time of the action the agent lacks either the ability or the opportunity to do anything but conform with the prediction, though he may have believed that he would be able to falsify it. In any of these four kinds of cases, a predictor would be able to calculate that his prediction, together with numerous other antecedent conditions, would causally necessitate that the agent perform the predicted action. In a case of type (2), for example, the predictor may be able to foresee that the agent will first read his prediction and decide to falsify it. But other factors will crop up—ones which the agent did not originally count on—that will make him change his mind and perform the predicted action after all. And the predictor also foresees this.

In the first three types of cases, (1), (2), and (3), the agent performs the predicted action *voluntarily*

(though in (3) he does not realize that what he is doing falls under the description "what was predicted"). In other words, in each of these three kinds of cases, the agent *could have* acted otherwise. Thus, the possibility of a scientific prediction does not require that the agent be *unable* to act in any way different from the prediction. All that is required is that the agent will not *in fact* act in any way different from the prediction. A predictor might know that an agent will in fact act in a certain way, not because he knows the agent will be incapable of doing otherwise, but because he knows that the agent will *choose* or *decide* to act as predicted.

IV.

I shall now sketch a possible world in which scientific predictions are made of an agent's life and inscribed in a "book of life," (parts of) which the agent subsequently reads. Obviously I cannot describe the whole of this world, but I shall describe some of its most important and problematic features, namely the interaction between the agent and the book. Unfortunately, I shall have to omit a description of another important part of the world, the part in which the predictor (or predictors) gathers his data and makes his calculations. I am unable to describe this part of the world, first, because I do not know all the laws which the predictor would have at his disposal, and secondly, because I am not able to say just what the structure of this being would be. However, the main features of the predictor's *modus operandi* should be clear from our discussion of the pollster, whose technique is at the heart of such predicting.

While browsing around the library one day, I notice an old dusty tome, quite large, entitled "Alvin I. Goldman." I take it from the shelf and start reading. In great detail, it describes my life as a little boy. It always gibes with my memory and frequently revives my memory of forgotten events. I realize that this purports to be a book of my life and I resolve to test it. Turning to the section with today's date on it, I find the following entry for 2:36 P.M. "He discovers me on the shelf. He takes me down and starts reading me. . . ." I look at the clock and see that it is 3:03. It is quite plausible, I say to myself, that I found the book about half an hour ago. I turn now to the entry for 3:03. It reads: "He is reading me. He is reading me. He is reading me." I continue looking at the book in this place, meanwhile thinking how remarkable the book is. The entry reads: "He continues to look at me, meanwhile thinking how remarkable I am."

I decide to defeat the book by looking at a future entry. I turn to an entry eighteen minutes hence. It says, "He is reading this sentence." Aha, I say to myself, all I need do is refrain from reading that sentence eighteen minutes from now. I check the clock. To ensure that I won't read that sentence, I close the book. My mind wanders; the book has revived a buried memory and I reminisce about it. I decide to re-read the book there and relive the experience. That's safe, I tell myself, because it is an earlier part of the book. I read that passage and become lost in reverie and rekindled emotion. Time passes. Suddenly I start. Oh yes, I intended to refute the book. But what was the time of the listed action?, I ask myself. It was 3:19, wasn't it? But it's 3:21 now, which means I have already refuted the book. Let me check and make sure. I inspect the book at the entry for 3:17. Hmm, that seems to be the wrong place for there it says I'm in a reverie. I skip a couple of pages and suddenly my eyes alight on the sentence: "He is reading this sentence." But it's an entry for 3:21, I notice! So I made a mistake. The action I had intended to refute was to occur at 3:21, not 3:19. I look at the clock, and it is still 3:21. I have not refuted the book after all.

I now turn to the entry for 3:28. It reads, "He is leaving the library, on his way to the President's office." Good heavens, I say to myself, I had completely forgotten my appointment with the President of the University at 3:30. I suppose I could falsify the book by not going, but it is much more important for me not to be late for that appointment. I'll refute the book some other time! Since I do have a few minutes, however, I turn back to the entry for 3:22. Sure enough, it says that my reading the 3:28 entry has reminded me about the appointment. Before putting the book back on the shelf, and leaving, I turn to an entry for tomorrow at 3:30 P.M. "He's still riding the bus bound for Chicago," it reads. Well, I say to myself, *that* prediction will be easy to refute. I have absolutely no intention of going to Chicago tomorrow.

Despite by decision to refute the book, events later induce me to change my mind and to conform to it, for stronger reasons arise for not refuting it. When I get home that evening I find a note from my wife saying that her father (in Chicago) is ill and that she had to take the car and drive to Chicago. I call her there and she explains what has happened. I tell her

about the book. Next morning she calls again with news that her father's condition is deteriorating and that I must come to Chicago immediately. As I hang up I realize that the book may turn out right after all, but the situation nevertheless demands that I go to Chicago. I might still refute it by going by plane or train. However, I call the airlines and am told that the fog is delaying all flights. The railroad says that there are no trains for Chicago till later in the day. So, acquiescing, I take a bus to Chicago, and find myself on it at 3:30.

V.

I have given several cases in which the book is not refuted, and the reader should be convinced that I could easily continue this way. But it is important now to reply to several objections which the anti-predictionist is anxious to make against my procedure.

1. "*Your story clearly presupposes determinism. But whether or not determinism is true is the central matter of dispute. Hence, you are begging the question.*" Admittedly, my story does presuppose determinism. Unless determinism were true, the imagined predictor could not have figured out what actions the agent would perform and then have written them in the book. However, this does not beg the question. For I am not trying to prove that determinism *is* true. I am merely trying to show that the thesis of determinism is quite compatible with the world as we know it and with human nature as we know it. The world depicted in my story is very much like the real world, except that it contains different antecedent conditions. The fact that this imagined world is determined and contains predictions of actions, and yet resembles the real world so closely, suggests that the real world may also be determined. At any rate, this supposition seems quite tenable, and its tenability is what I seek to establish.

2. "*The story you told was fixed. Events might have been different from the way you described them. For example, the fog might not have curtailed all air traffic.*" No, events could not be different *in the world I am imagining.* That is, in my world all the events I described were causally necessitated by prior antecedent conditions. I did not describe all the antecedent conditions, so perhaps the reader cannot see that each event I did describe was causally necessitated by them. But, since it is a deterministic world, that is so. No one can imagine *my* world and also substitute the negation of one of the events I described.

I'm not "fixing" the story by saying that the fog curtailed air traffic; that just is the way my imagined world goes.

3. "*But I can imagine a world in which some putative predictions of actions are refuted.*" I have no doubt that you can; that is very easy. You could even imagine a world *somewhat* like the one I have just described, but in which putative predictions are falsified. But this proves nothing at all. I would never deny that one can construct some possible worlds in which putative scientific predictions of actions are not successful. I have only claimed that one can (also) construct *some* possible worlds in which genuine scientific predictions of actions are made (and are successful). The situation with predictions of actions is no different from the one with predictions of physical events. We can construct possible worlds in which predictions of physical phenomena are correct. But we can also construct worlds in which putative scientific predictions of physical phenomena are incorrect. If our ability to construct worlds in which predictions are unsuccessful proves the inherent unpredictableness of the kind of phenomena unsuccessfully predicted, then we can prove the unpredictableness of physical phenomena as easily as the unpredictableness of human action.

4. "*The world you have described, though possible, is a highly improbable world. Worlds in which putative predictions of actions are falsified are much more probable.*" The notion of one possible world being "more probable" than another seems to me unintelligible. Surely the statistical sense of probability cannot be intended. There is no way of "sampling" from possible worlds to discover that features most of them have. Perhaps the anti-predictionist means that we can *imagine* more worlds in which putative predictions of actions are falsified. But this too is questionable. I can imagine indefinitely many worlds in which successful predictions of actions are made.

Perhaps the anti-predictionist means that it is improbable that any such sequence of events as I described would occur in the *real* world. He may well be right on this point. However, to talk about what is probable (in the evidential sense) in the real world is just to talk about what has happened, is happening, and will happen *as a matter of fact*. But the dispute between predictionists and anti-predictionists is, presumably, not about what *will* happen, but about what *could* happen *in principle*. This "in principle" goes beyond the particular facts of the actual world.

5. "*The difference between physical phenomena and action is that predictions of actions can defeat themselves; but predictions of physical events cannot.*" This is not so. One can construct worlds in which the causal effect of a putative prediction of a physical event falsifies that prediction. Jones calculates the position of a speck of dust three inches from his nose and the direction and velocity of wind currents in the room. He then announces his prediction that five seconds thence the speck will be in a certain position. He neglects to account for the wind expelled from his mouth when he makes the prediction, however, and this factor changes the expected position of the speck of dust. Perhaps one can imagine a wider variety of cases in which predictions affect human action more than physical phenomena. But this is only a difference of *degree*, not of kind.

6. "*Predictions of physical events can refute themselves because the predictor may fail to account for the effect of his own prediction. But were he to take this effect into account, he would make a correct prediction. On the other hand, there are conditions connected with the prediction of action in which, no matter what prediction the predictor makes, his prediction will be falsified. Here there is no question of inaccurate calculation or insufficient information. Whatever he predicts will be incorrect. Yet this situation arises only in connection with human action, not physical events.*"

This is an important objection and warrants detailed discussion.

VI.

Suppose I wish to predict what action you will perform thirty seconds from now, but that I shall not try to change or affect your behavior except by making my prediction. (Thus, I shall not, for example, predict that you will perform no action at all and then make that prediction come true by killing you.) Further suppose that the following conditions obtain. At this moment you want to falsify any prediction that I shall make of your action. Moreover, you will still have this desire thirty seconds from now, and it will be stronger than any conflicting desire you will have at that time. Right now you intend to do action A, but you are prepared to perform $-A$ (not A) if I predict that you will perform A. Thirty seconds hence you will have the ability and opportunity to do A and the ability and opportunity to do $-A$. Finally, conditions are such that, if I make a prediction in English in your presence, you will understand it, will remember it for thirty seconds, and will be able to tell whether any of your actions will conform to it or not. Given all these conditions, whatever I predict—at least, if I make the prediction by saying it aloud, in your presence, in English, etc.—will be falsified. If I predict you will do $A$, then you will do $-A$, while if I predict that you will do $-A$, you will proceed to do $A$. In other words, in these conditions any prediction of mine will causally necessitate the non-occurrence of the event I predict.

Notice that this example does not prove that it is impossible "simpliciter" for me to make a scientific prediction of your action. All that it proves is that I cannot make such a prediction *in a certain manner*, viz., by announcing it to you in English. If I predict your action in some other manner, by thinking it to myself or by saying it aloud in Hindustani, for example, the effect on your action would not be the same as if I say it aloud in English. Assume that, if you do not hear me make any prediction or if you hear me say something you fail to understand, you will proceed to perform action $A$. Then it is possible for me to predict your action correctly by announcing the prediction in Hindustani.

In determining whether or not a certain set of events, including (1) a prediction, (2) the event predicted, and (3) certain other assumed conditions, is a "causally compossible" set, it is essential to specify the manner of the prediction. This is true *in general*, not just in the case of predictions of action. A prediction which is "embodied" or expressed in one way will not have the same causal effects as the same prediction expressed in another way. We can see this in the case of the speck of dust. Jones predicted the position of the dust by announcing it orally, and this resulted in the falsification of the prediction. But had he made the same prediction in another fashion— say by moving his toes in a certain conventional pattern—his prediction would not have been falsified, for the position of the dust would not have been affected.

What is the significance of the fact that it is impossible, in some circumstances, for a (correct) prediction of an action to be made in a specified manner? First, this unpredictability does not prove that these actions are undetermined. Indeed, the very construction of the case in which no prediction is possible *presupposed* the existence of laws of nature which, together with a given prediction, would result in a certain action. In short, the case under discussion should, if anything, support rather than defeat the

thesis that actions are determined. The only reason one might have for thinking the contrary is the assumption—which should by now appear very dubious—that determinism entails predictability. What our present case shows, I think, is that under some circumstances, even a determined event may not be susceptible of being correctly predicted in a specified manner. This fact can be further supported by adducing a similar case connected with purely physical events. And this brings me to my second point: the case produced above does not reflect a peculiarity of human action, since parallel examples can be found among physical phenomena.

Imagine a certain physical apparatus placed in front of a piano keyboard. A bar extends from the apparatus and is positioned above a certain key. (Only white keys will be considered.) If the apparatus is not disturbed, the bar will strike that key at a certain time. Now let us suppose that the apparatus is sensitive to sound, and, in particular, can discriminate between sounds of varying pitches. If the apparatus picks up a certain sound, the position of the bar will move to the right and proceed to strike the key immediately to the right of the original one (if there is one). Specifically, if the sound has the same pitch as that of the key over which the bar is poised, the bar will move. If the monitored sound has any other pitch, the bar will remain in its position and proceed to strike that key.

Now suppose that someone (or something) wishes to make predictions of the behavior of the apparatus. He wishes to predict what key the bar will strike. But the following restriction is made on the *manner* in which the prediction is to be made. The prediction must be expressed according to a specific set of conventions or symbols. To predict that the bar will strike middle C, for example, the predictor must emit a sound with the pitch of middle C. To predict that the bar will strike D, he must emit a sound with the pitch of that key, etc. All sound emissions are to be made in the neighborhood of the apparatus. Given this restriction on the manner of prediction, it will be causally incompossible for the predictor to make a correct prediction. Suppose that the bar is poised above middle C. If he predicts that it will strike middle C—that is, if he emits a sound of that pitch—the bar will move and proceed to strike D. But if he predicts any other behavior of the bar, for example, that it will strike D, the bar will remain in its original position and strike middle C.

Admittedly, the manner of prediction I have allowed to the predictor of this physical phenomenon is much more narrowly restricted than the manner of prediction allowed to the predictor of human action. But we could imagine physical apparatuses with a greater degree of complexity, able to "refute" predictions made in any of a wider variety of manners. In any case, the principle of the situation is the same for both physical phenomena and human actions, though the manners of prediction which affect one phenomenon may be different from the manners of prediction which affect the other. The latter difference simply reflects that fact that physical objects and human beings do not respond in precisely the same ways to the same causes. But this is equally true of different kinds of physical objects and of different pairs of human beings.

## VII.

I have shown that there are possible worlds in which voluntary actions are scientifically predicted. Are there possible worlds in which a person predicts one of his *own* actions? I think that there are such worlds, which I shall illustrate by continuing the sketch of the world described earlier.

Having tested my book of life on a very large number of occasions during many months and having failed to refute it, I become convinced that whatever it says is true. I have about as good inductive evidence for this proposition as I do for many another proposition I could be said to know. Finally, I get up enough courage to look at the very end of the book and, as expected, it tells when and how I shall die. Dated five years hence, it describes my committing suicide by jumping off the eighty-sixth floor observation deck of the Empire State Building. From a description of the thoughts which will flash through my mind before jumping, it is clear that the intervening five years will have been terrible. As the result of those experiences, I shall have emotions and desires (and beliefs) which will induce me to jump. Since I trust the book completely, I now conclude that I *shall* commit suicide five years hence. Moreover, I can be said to *know* that I shall commit suicide.

This example shows, contrary to the view of some authors, that we can have knowledge of our own future actions, knowledge which is not based on having already made a decision or formed an intention to perform the future action. In this case, there is a time at which I have certain knowledge of what I

shall do (at any rate, about as "certain" as one can be with inductive evidence) and yet I have formed no intention nor made any decision to perform that action. At the time I read the book's prediction, I do not intend to commit suicide. But although I do not intend to commit suicide, I fully believe and know that, five years later, I shall intend to commit suicide. I firmly believe that, at that later time, I shall feel certain emotions and have certain desires which will induce me to jump off the Empire State Building. At the time of my reading the book I do not feel those things, but I commiserate with my future self, much as I commiserate with and understand another person's desires, beliefs, feelings, intentions, etc. Still, my understanding of these states of mind and of the action in which they will issue is the understanding of a spectator; my knowledge of these states and of my future action is purely inductive. Moreover, this knowledge is of a particular *voluntary* act to be performed at a specified time. Though the suicide will be a "desperate" action, it will in no sense be "coerced" or done unknowingly; it will flow from a firm intention, an intention formed very deliberately. But that intention will not be formed until after I have had certain experiences, experiences which, at the time I am reading the book, I have not yet had.

We can imagine two alternative series of events to occur between my reading the book and my suicide. First, I might *forget* what I have learned from the book, and later decide to commit suicide. Secondly, while never forgetting the prediction, the knowledge of my future suicide may gradually change from mere inductive knowledge to knowledge based on intention. In this second alternative, there is never any "moment" of decision. I never pass from a state of complete doubt about committing suicide into a sudden intention of committing suicide. Rather, there is a gradual change, over the five-year period, from mere inductive knowledge that I shall commit suicide to an intention to commit suicide. When I first read the book I am fully prepared to assent to the proposition that I shall commit suicide. But I am saddened by the thought; my heart isn't in it. Later, as a result of various tragic experiences, my *will* acquiesces in the idea. I begin to welcome the thought of suicide, to entertain the thought of committing suicide with pleasure and relief. When the appointed time comes around, I am *bent* on suicide. This gradual change in attitude constitutes the difference between the kinds of knowledge of my future suicide, the difference between mere inductive knowledge and knowledge based on intention.

Many philosophers are very uncomfortable with the idea of a book of life. They believe that the existence of such books—or of foreknowledge of actions in any form—would deprive us of all the essential characteristics of voluntary behavior: choice, decision, deliberation, etc. I do not think this fear is warranted. I have just shown that even if a person reads what a book of life predicts, and believes this prediction, he can still perform the indicated action voluntarily. Moreover, the existence of predictions which the agent does *not* read leaves ample opportunity for deliberation and decision. An agent may know that a book of his life exists and yet proceed to make decisions and to deliberate as all of us do now. The agent's belief that there is such a book, and his belief that the book's existence implies that his actions are causally necessitated, is compatible with his deliberating whether to do one action or another. Although his future action is causally necessitated, one of the antecedent conditions which necessitate it is his deliberation. Indeed, the prediction in the book of life was made precisely because its writer knew that the agent would deliberate and then decide to do the predicted action. Thus, the book of life can hardly be said to preclude deliberation. Nor does the book of life imply that the agent's deliberation is "for naught," or "irrelevant." On the contrary, his deliberation is a crucial antecedent condition: were he not to deliberate, he probably would not perform the action he eventually does perform. Deliberation and decision are perfectly compatible with the existence of books of life; and they are perfectly compatible with the thesis that they, and the actions in which they issue, are determined.

# READING 33

# Two Concepts of Freedom
*William L. Rowe*

*William L. Rowe (1931–   ) is Professor of Philosophy at Purdue University. He is the author of* Religious Symbols and God: A Study of Tillich's Theology *(1968),* The Cosmological Argument *(1975),* Philosophy of Religion *(1978), and* Thomas Reid on Freedom and Morality *(1991) and co-editor, with William J. Wainwright, of* Philosophy of Religion: Selected Readings *(1973; 2nd ed., 1989).*

SOURCE: From *Proceedings and Addresses of the APA* (September 1987), Supplement to Volume 61, no. 1, pp. 43–64.

*Presidential Address delivered before the Eighty-fifth Annual Meeting of the Central (formerly Western) Division of the American Philosophical Association in Chicago, Illinois, May 1, 1987.

In his life of Samuel Johnson, Boswell reports Johnson as saying: "All theory is against freedom of the will; all experience for it." The first part of this remark would be agreeable to many 18th-century philosophers: those believing that certain theoretical principles concerning explanation or causality support the doctrine of necessity. But the second part, that experience is on the side of free will, would be somewhat puzzling to those 18th-century philosophers who hold that free will is a power and that a power, as opposed to an activity, is not something we can directly experience or be conscious of.[1] In his journal, however, which presumably was written shortly after the actual conversation with Johnson, Boswell reports Johnson's remark differently. There he has Johnson saying: "All theory against freedom of will, all practice for it."[2] Here the second part makes better philosophical sense, for that our practice of moral praise and blame is on the side of free will was a standard theme among 18th-century advocates of free will, and it is perfectly understandable, therefore, that Johnson would have cited practice as on the side of freedom. But what is the *concept* of freedom that lies behind this remark by Johnson? And more generally, what *conceptual issues* were at the center of the controversy over freedom and necessity that occupied the last half of the 17th and most of the 18th century, a controversy bringing forward as its champions, on one side or another, such formidable figures as Hobbes, Locke, Samuel Clarke, Leibniz, Hume and Thomas Reid? I want to answer these questions, not simply in order to deepen our understanding of this historical episode in the controversy over freedom and necessity, as important as that may be, but because I believe a clear understanding of this episode in the controversy can help us in our current thinking about the problem of freedom and necessity.

My belief is that when all is said and done there are two fundamentally different conceptions of freedom that occupy center stage in the controversy that we may arbitrarily date as beginning with Thomas Hobbes and Bishop Bramhall (in the second half of the 17th century) and ending with Thomas Reid and Joseph Priestley (in the late 18th century). Vestiges of these two conceptions are very much alive in the 20th century. I intend, however, to examine these two conceptions in their earlier setting, analyzing and evaluating them in the light of criticisms advanced against them, both then and now. The first of these conceptions, of which John Locke is a major advocate, I will call *Lockean freedom*. The other conception, of which Thomas Reid is the leading advocate, I will call *Reidian freedom*. The history of the controversy in the period we are considering is fundamentally a dispute over which of these two concepts of freedom is more adequate to our commonsense beliefs about freedom and our general metaphysical and scientific principles.

Before we begin with Locke's conception of freedom, it is best to note that all participants in the controversy embraced what has come to be known as the volitional theory of action. Since this theory is common to the controversy we are examining, it plays no significant role in the controversy itself. Neverthe-less, some brief description of it will help us understand certain points that emerge in the controversy. According to this theory, actions are of two sorts: those that involve thoughts and those that involve motions of the body. What makes the occurrence of a certain thought or bodily motion an *action* is its being preceded by a certain act of will (a volition) which brings about the thought or motion. Volitions, then, are "action starters." On the other hand, they are also themselves referred to as "actions." Of course, if we do classify volitions as actions, we cannot say that *every* action must be preceded by a volition. For then no action could occur unless it were preceded by an absolutely infinite number of volitions. But we still can say that thoughts and bodily motions are action only if *they* are preceded by volitions that cause them. It is not clear whether volitions that start actions are viewed as distinct from the actions started, or as a part of the actions. It is also unclear just what the agent wills when his volition starts (or is part of) a certain action. These uncertainties, however, will have little bearing on our examination of the two conceptions of freedom that dominated 18th century thought.

## I. LOCKEAN FREEDOM

Locke distinguished between a free action and a voluntary action. For your action to be voluntary all that is required is that you will to do that action and perform it, presumably as a result of your willing to do it. Suppose you are sitting in your chair and someone invites you to go for a walk. You reject the idea, choosing instead to remain just where you are. Your so remaining, Locke would say, is a voluntary act. But was it a free act? This is a further question for Locke, and it depends on whether you could have done otherwise had you so willed. If I had injected you with a powerful drug, so that at the time—perhaps without your being aware of it—your legs were paralyzed, then your act of remaining in the chair was voluntary but not free, for you could not have got up and walked had you willed to do so. A free act, says Locke, is not just a voluntary act.[3] An act is free if it is voluntary *and* it is true that had you willed to do otherwise you would have been able to do otherwise. For Locke, then, we can say that you are free with respect to a certain action provided it is in your power to do it if you will to do it *and* in your power to refrain from doing it if you should will to refrain. Locke tells us that a man who is chained in prison does not stay in prison freely—even if that is what he wants to do—because it is not in his power to leave if he should will to leave. But if the prison doors are thrown open, and his chains are removed, he is free to leave and free to stay—for he can do either, depending on his will.

So far, of course, little or nothing has been said about the question of whether the will is free. And this was what Locke preferred, thinking on the whole that the question of freedom is the question of whether you are free *to do* what you will; much confusion, he thought, results from asking whether you are free *to will* what you will. But the chief merit of Locke's conception of freedom, or so it seemed to many, is that it fits nicely with the belief that our acts of will are causally necessitated by prior events and circumstances. Anthony Collins, Locke's friend and follower, took up this topic in his book, *A Philosophical Inquiry Concerning Human Liberty*, published in London in 1717. Collins argued that all our actions are subject to causal necessity; he argued, that is, that our actions are so determined by the causes preceding them that, given the causes and circumstances, no other actions were possible. What are the causes of our actions? Well, the immediate cause of the action is you decision or act of will to perform that action. What is the cause of your making that decision? According to Locke and Collins, the cause of that act of will is your desires, judgments, and the circumstances that prevailed just prior to that decision. Given your desires and judgments at the time, and given the circumstances that prevailed, it was impossible for you not to will as you did. And given the desires, judgments, circumstances and the act of will, it was impossible for you not to act as you did. Now this impossibility of willing and acting otherwise does not conflict with Lockean freedom. For Lockean freedom does not require that *given the causes*, we somehow could have acted differently. All it requires is that *if* we had decided or willed differently *then* we could have acted differently. Indeed, Locke is careful to note that the absolute determination of the will or preference of the mind does not preclude freedom so far as the action flowing from the will or preference of the mind is concerned. He remarks:

> But though the preference of the Mind be always determined . . . ; yet the Person who has the Power, in which alone consists liberty to act, or not to act according to such preference, is nevertheless free, such determination abridges not that Power. He that has his Chains knocked off, and the Prison-doors set open to him, is perfectly at liberty, because he may either go or stay as he best likes; though his preference be determined to stay by the darkness of the Night, or illness of the Weather, or want of other Lodging. He ceases not to be free; though that which at that time appears to him the greater Good absolutely determines his preference, and makes him stay in his Prison.[4]

Let us call those who believe both that we have Lockean freedom and that our actions and acts of will are subject to causal necessity, 'necessitarians.' It is likely that Locke was a necessitarian; Hobbes and Collins most certainly were. Those who, like Clarke and Reid, hold that necessity and freedom are really inconsistent with one another do not disagree with the necessitarians concerning the consistency of *Lockean freedom* with the causal necessity of our actions and acts of will. What they reject is the whole notion of Lockean freedom. Before we state their conception of freedom, however, we had best consider what their objections are to the Lockean idea of freedom.[5]

Lockean freedom, as we saw, exists solely at the level of *action*: you are free with respect to some action provided that you have the power to do the act if you will to do it, and have the power not to do it if you will not to do it. But what about the *will*? What if you don't have the power to will the action, or don't have the power not to will it? To see the difficulty here, let's return to our example where you are sitting down, someone asks you to get up and walk over to the window to see what is happening outside, but you are quite satisfied where you are and choose to remain sitting. We earlier supposed that I had injected you with a powerful drug so that you can't move your legs. Here Locke would say that you don't sit freely, since it was not in your power to do otherwise if you had willed otherwise—say, to get up and walk to the window. But let's now suppose that instead of paralyzing your legs I had hooked up a machine to your brain so that I can and do cause you to will to sit, thus depriving you of the *capacity* to will to do otherwise. It's still true that you have the power to get up and walk *if* you should will to do so—I haven't taken away your physical capacity to walk, as I did when I paralyzed your legs. Here the problem is that you can't *will* to do anything other than sit. In this case, it seems clear that you sit of necessity, not freely. You can't do otherwise than sit, not because you lack the power to get up and walk if you should manage to choose to do that, but because you lack the power to *choose* to get up and walk. On Locke's account of freedom, however, it remains true that you sit freely and not of necessity. And this being so, we must conclude that Locke's account of freedom is simply inadequate. It is not sufficient that you have the power to do otherwise *if* you so will; it must also be true that you have the power to will to do otherwise. Freedom that is worth the name, therefore, must include power *to will*, not simply power *to do if we will*.

There is a second objection to Lockean freedom, an objection based on the fact that Lockean freedom is consistent with the causal necessity of our actions and decisions. According to the necessitarians, you are totally determined to will and act as you do by your motives and circumstances. Indeed, Leibniz quotes with favor Bayle's comparison of the influence of motives on an agent to the influence of weights on a balance. Referring to Bayle, Leibniz remarks: "According to him, one can explain what passes in our resolutions by the hypothesis that the will of man is like a balance which is at rest when the weights of its two pans are equal, and which always inclines either to one side or the other according to which of the pans is the more heavily laden."[6] Bayle's idea is that just as the heavier weight determines the movement of the balance, so does the strong motive determine the movement of your will. If your motive to get up and walk to the window is stronger than whatever motive you have to remain sitting, then it determines you to will to get up and walk to the window. Given the respective strength of these motives, it is no more possible for you to will to remain sitting than it is possible for a balance to stay even when a heavier weight is placed in one of its pans than in the other. Motives, on this view, are determining causes of the decisions of our will in precisely the way in which weights are the determining causes of the movements of the balance. But if all this is so, claim the opponents of the necessitarians, then no one acts freely, no one has power over his will. For it was generally agreed that our motives are determined by factors largely beyond our control, and if these motives determine our acts of will as weights determine the movement of a balance, then we can no more control our will than the balance can control its movements. Just as a balance has no freedom of movement, so

the person would have no freedom of will. Freedom would be an illusion if our will is subjected to causal necessity by motives and circumstances. Since Lockean freedom is consistent with such causal necessity, Lockean freedom is really not freedom at all.[7]

We've looked at two major objections to Lockean freedom. According to Locke, freedom to do a certain thing is (roughly) the power to do that thing if we will to do it. Our first objection is that we might have the power to do something if we willed to do it and yet lack the power to will to do it. Surely, freedom must include the power to will, and not just the power to do *if* we will. Our second objection is against the necessitarian view that our acts of will are causally necessitated by prior events and circumstances. If that is so then we *now* have no more control over what we will to do than a balance has over how it moves once the weights are placed in its pans. Causal necessitation of our acts of will denies to us any real power over the determinations of our will. And without such power we do not act freely. To be told, as Locke would tell us, that we could have done something else if we had so willed, is of course interesting, and perhaps not unimportant. But if we are totally determined to will as we do and cannot will otherwise, then it is absurd to say we act freely simply because had we willed otherwise—which we could not do—we could have acted otherwise.

I believe these objections to Lockean freedom are in the end totally convincing. Indeed, it puzzles me that the notion of Lockean freedom continues to survive in the face of such utterly devastating objections. But before passing on to the second concept of freedom, *Reidian freedom,* we should note an attempt or two to defend or amend Lockean freedom so that it will appear less implausible.

At the level of action we are free, for Locke, provided we could have done otherwise if we had chosen or willed to do otherwise. Basically, our objections to Lockean freedom point out the need to supplement freedom at the level of action with freedom at the level of the will. The problem for the necessitarian is how to do this without abandoning the causal necessitation of the will by our motives and circumstances. Now one might be tempted to suggest that at the level of the will we are free provided we could have willed to do otherwise *if* we had been in different circumstances or had different motives—a thesis that in no way conflicts with the act of will being causally necessitated by our actual motives and circumstances.

Such a suggestion of what it means to have free will fully merits, I believe, the contempt and ridicule that Kant meant when he spoke of a "wretched subterfuge" and William James meant when he spoke of "a quagmire of evasion."[8] If Lockean freedom is to be saved, we need a better account of free will than this suggestion provides.

In his discussion of Locke's account of freedom, Leibniz generally endorses Locke's view but points out its failure to provide any account of free will. He suggests two accounts of free will, one in contrast to the bondage of the passions, an account drawn from the Stoics; a second in contrast to necessity, an account that is Leibniz's own.[9] Although neither account removes the causal necessitation of the will, the first account does appear to soften the blow. Leibniz remarks: "the Stoics said that only the wise man is free; and one's mind is indeed not free when it is possessed by a great passion, for then one cannot will as one should, i.e. with proper deliberation. It is in that way that God alone is perfectly free, and that created minds are free only in proportion as they are above passion; . . . "[10] Here we have a nice amendment to Lockean freedom. For an action to be free it must not only be willed and such that we could have done otherwise if we had willed otherwise, but also the act of will must have been free in the sense of resulting at least partially from the proper exercise of reason. If the passions totally determine the act of will and the consequent action, we need not say that the person acts freely. However, if the judgments of reason and our circumstances totally determine our will so that given those judgments and circumstances no other act of will was possible, we can still say that we act freely, provided we could have done otherwise had we chosen or willed to do otherwise, for as rational beings we are willing as we should. This amendment, I believe, softens the necessitarian view; but it fails to solve the basic problem. For to will as we should is one thing, and to will freely is another. The problem with Lockean freedom is not that it fails to rule out necessitation of the will *by the passions*; the problem is that it fails to rule out the necessitation of the will *period*. It is time to turn to our second concept of freedom.

## II. REIDIAN FREEDOM

The clearest statement of our second concept of freedom is by the Scottish philosopher, Thomas Reid. Here is what Reid says.

> By the *liberty* of a moral agent, I understand, a power over the determinations of his own will.
>
> If, in any action, he had power to will what he did, or not to will it, in that action he is free. But if, in every voluntary action, the determination of his will be the necessary consequence of something involuntary in the state of his mind, or of something in his external circumstances, he is not free; he has not what I call the liberty of a moral agent, but is subject to necessity.[11]

It is helpful, I believe, to divide Reid's view of freedom into two theses: a negative thesis and a positive thesis. The negative thesis is this: if some action of ours is free then our decision or act of will to do that action cannot have been causally necessitated by any prior events, whether they be internal or external. If I have a machine hooked up to your brain in such a manner that my flip of a switch causally necessitates your decision to get up and walk across the room, it follows that you are not free in your action of getting up and walking across the room. In this case your decision to do that action is causally necessitated by some prior *external* event, the flipping of the switch. On the other hand, if your decision to do the act was causally necessitated by your motives and circumstances, then the causally necessitating event is *internal,* and the action again is not free. You are free in some action only if your decision to do that act is not causally necessitated by any involuntary event, whether internal or external. This is the negative thesis.

All too often, it is assumed that this second concept of freedom, which I have called *Reidian freedom,* consists in nothing more than this negative thesis. And the major objection of the necessitarians to Reidian freedom is based on this assumption. According to Reid, our free acts of will are not caused by any prior events, whether external or internal. And the difficulty with this, so the objection goes, is that it conflicts with the view that every event has a cause, a view that most 18th-century philosophers, including Reid, accepted. What this objection reveals, however, is that the necessitarians hold to only one sort of causation, causation by prior events. Thus once it was denied that our free acts of will are caused by any prior events, the necessitarians concluded that the advocates of Reidian freedom were committed to the view that our free acts of will are totally uncaused events. But Reid, following Samuel Clarke, Edmund

Law, and others, believed in another sort of causation, causation by persons or agents. And what they affirmed in their positive thesis is that free acts of will are caused by the agent whose acts they are. Reid, then, no less than the necessitarians affirmed that all events, including our free acts of will, are caused. As he remarks: "I grant, then, that an effect uncaused is a contradiction, and that an event uncaused is an absurdity. The question that remains is whether a volition, undetermined by motives, is an event uncaused. This I deny. The cause of the volition is the man that willed it."[12]

What we've just seen is that the advocates of Reidian freedom agree with the necessitarians in holding that every event has a cause. What they deny is that every event has an event-cause. In the case of our free acts of will the cause is not some prior event but the agent whose acts they are. To understand Reidian freedom, therefore, we need to look at the foundation on which it rests, the idea of agent causation.

Reid believed that the original notion of 'cause' is that of an agent who brings about changes in the world by *acting*. To be such a cause, Reid held that a thing or substance must satisfy three conditions: first, it must have the power to bring about the change in the world; second, it must exert its power to bring about the change; and third, it must have the power not to bring about that change. It will help us to understand and appreciate his view if we contrast two examples. Suppose a piece of zinc is dropped into some acid, and the acid dissolves the zinc. In this example, we might say that the acid has the power to bring about a certain change in the zinc. We might also be willing to say that in this instance the acid *exerted* its power to bring about this change, it *exerted* its power to dissolve the zinc. But can we reasonably say that the acid had the power not to bring about this change? Clearly we cannot. The acid has no power to refrain from dissolving the zinc. When the conditions are right, the acid must dissolve the zinc. So Reid's third condition is not satisfied. The acid, therefore, is not an agent-cause of the zinc's dissolving. Turning to our second example, suppose I invite you to write down the word 'cause.' Let's suppose that you have the power to do so and that you exert that power with the result that a change in the world occurs, and the word 'cause' is written on a piece of paper. Here, when we look at Reid's third condition, we believe that it does obtain.

We believe that you had the power to refrain from initiating your action of writing down the word 'cause.' The acid had no power to refrain from dissolving the zinc, but you had the power not to bring about your action of writing down the word 'cause.' If these things are so, then in this instance you are a true agent-cause of a certain change in the world, for you had the power to bring about that change, you exerted that power by acting, and finally, you had the power not to bring about that change.

There is one very important point to note concerning Reid's idea of agent causation. We sometimes speak of causing someone to cause something else. But if we fully understand Reid's notion of agent causation we can see, I think, that no event or agent can cause someone to agent-cause some change. And this, again, is because of Reid's third condition of agent causation, the condition that requires that you have the power to refrain from bringing about the change. Suppose an event occurs that causes you to cause something to happen—some boiling water spills on your hand, say, causing you to drop the pot of boiling water. Now if the spilling of the boiling water on your hand really does cause you to bring about your dropping the pot, if it causally necessitates you to cause your dropping of the pot, then given the spilling of the boiling water on your hand it wasn't in your power not to bring about your dropping the pot. But you are the agent-cause of some change only if it was in your power at the time not to cause that change. This being so, it is quite impossible that anything should ever cause you to agent-cause some change. Since having the power not to cause a change is required for you to be the agent-cause of some change, and since being caused to cause some change implies that you cannot refrain from causing that change, it follows that no one can be caused to agent-cause a change. If you are the agent-cause of some change, it follows that you were not caused to agent-cause that change.

Having taken a brief look at Reid's notion of agent causation, we can return to what I have been calling Reidian freedom. According to Reidian freedom, any action we perform as a result of our act of will to do that action is a free action, provided that we were the agent-cause of the act of will to perform that action. And since to agent-cause an act of will includes the power not to cause it, we can say that every act of will resulting in a *free* action is an act of will we had power to produce and power not to produce. As

Reid says: "If, in any action, he had power to will what he did, or not to will it, in that action he is free."

Suppose someone wills to perform a certain action, say revealing a secret of great importance that he has been entrusted with. Since his act of will must have a cause, either it is caused by the agent himself—in which case he is the agent-cause of that act of will and his action is free—or something else causes his act of will and his action, although voluntary, is not free. In some cases, it will not be difficult to decide the matter. Suppose our person has been offered a small bribe and, as a result, reveals the important secret. Here, we would judge that the person does act freely, believing that the desire for the bribe is not sufficient of itself to cause the agent to will as he did. On the other hand, if our agent is placed on the rack and made to suffer intensely over a period of time and finally, after much pain, divulges the secret, we would all judge that the intense pain was such as to cause directly the volition to reveal the important secret. The volition was not agent-caused and the action of revealing the secret was not *free*. But these are the easy cases. Clearly, between these two extremes there is a continuum of cases in which we would find the judgment between agent-cause and other cause extraordinarily difficult to make with any assurance. To help us here, we need to note another important element in Reid's theory of human freedom.

Reid believes that freedom is a *power*, a power over the determinations of our will. Now power is something that can come in degrees—you may have more or less of it. Presumably, under torture on the rack, your power over your will may be reduced to zero and your freedom thereby destroyed. On the other hand, your desire for a small bribe is unlikely to diminish significantly your power not to will to reveal the secret. Between these two extremes the mounting strength of your desires and passions will make it increasingly difficult for you to refrain from willing to reveal the secret. But so long as their strength is not irresistible, if you do will to reveal it, you will be at least a *partial agent-cause* of your act of will, and, therefore, will act with a certain degree of freedom and a corresponding degree of responsibility. Of course, people may differ considerably in terms of the power they possess over their wills. So a desire of a given strength may overwhelm one person while only slightly diminishing another person's power over his will. Therefore, in order to determine whether a person acted freely and with what degree of freedom, we need to judge two things: we need to judge the degree of power over the will that the person possesses *apart* from the influence of his desires and passions; and we need to judge the strength of his desires and passions. Clearly these are matters about which at best only reasonable or probable judgments can be made.

Leibniz once remarked concerning a version of the free will doctrine: "What is asserted is impossible, but if it came to pass it would be harmful."[13] This remark nicely captures most of the objections to the view of Reid and other free will advocates. For these objections divide into those that argue that the view is impossible because it is internally inconsistent or inconsistent with some well-established principle of causality or explanation, and those that argue that the possession of free will would be harmful because the agent's actions would then be capricious, uninfluenced by motives, rewards or punishment. I want here to look at two different objections that fall into the first category. The first of these, and by far the most popular, is, I believe, a spurious objection. Since it is spurious, I will bury it in a footnote.[14] The second, however, is a very serious objection, revealing, I believe, a real difficulty in Reid's agent-cause account of freedom.

The second objection (the serious one), like the first, arrives at the absurd conclusion that any action requires an infinite series of antecedent events, each produced by the agent who produces the action. This absurd conclusion, I believe, does follow from Reid's view of agent-causation in conjunction with the principle that every event has a cause. I propose here to explain how this absurdity is embedded in Reid's theory and what can be done to remove it.

On Reid's theory, when an agent wills some action, the act of will is itself an event and, as such, requires a cause. If the act of will is free, its cause is not some event, it is the agent whose act of will it is. Being the cause of the act of will, the agent must satisfy Reid's three conditions of agent-causation. Thus the agent must have had the power to bring about the act of will as well as the power to refrain from bringing about the act of will, and she must have *exerted* her power to bring about the act of will. It is the last of these conditions that generates an infinite regress of events that an agent must cause if she is to cause her act of will. For what it tells us is that to produce the act of will the agent must *exert* her power to bring about the act of will. Now an exertion of power is itself an event. As such, it too must have a cause. On Reid's view the cause must again be the agent herself. But to have caused this exertion the agent must have had the power to bring it about and must have *exerted* that power. Each exertion of power is itself an event which the agent can cause only by having the power to cause it and by *exerting* that power. As Reid reminds us, "In order to the production of any effect, there must be in the cause, not only power, but the exertion of that power: for power that is not exerted produces no effect."[15] The result of this principle, however, is that in order to produce any act of will whatever, the agent must cause an infinite number of exertions. Reid's theory of agent-causation, when conjoined with the principle that every event has a cause, leads to the absurdity of an infinite regress of agent-produced exertions for every act of will the agent produces.

It is remarkable that Reid appears never to have seen this difficulty in his theory. Occasionally he joins the causal principle and his view of agent-causation into a single remark, with the result that the difficulty fairly leaps up from the page. For example, in discussing Leibniz's view that every action has a sufficient reason, Reid remarks: "If the meaning of the question be, was there a cause of the action? Undoubtedly there was: of every event there must be a cause, that had power sufficient to produce it, and that exerted that power for the purpose."[16] If exertions of power are events—and what else could they be?—the infinite regress of exertions produced by the agent who performs any action is abundantly apparent in this remark. Perhaps Reid didn't see the problem because he always had in mind the basic distinction between the *effects* agents produce by their actions and the *actions* of the agents by which they produce those effects. With this distinction in mind, it is natural to suppose that *everything* an agent causes (the effects) she causes not simply by virtue of having a certain power but by acting, by exerting that power. Put this way, Reid's notion that an agent can cause something only by acting, by *exerting* her power, is intuitively attractive—so attractive, perhaps, that one may be blind to the difficulty that appears when actions themselves are held to be among the things that an agent causes.

One solution to the difficulty requires that we view some acts of the agent as caused by the agent, but not caused by some *exertion* of the agent's power to produce them. Perhaps we should think of the act of will as in some way a special sort of action, a *basic act*. A basic act of an agent is one that she causes but not by any exertion of power or any other act. Short of some such view, it seems that we must either accept the absurdity of the infinite regress, view some act of the agent as itself uncaused (thus abandoning the causal principle), or take the view that an act of will is not itself an event and, therefore, does not fall under the causal principle. This last move, however, would leave the act of will as a surd in Reid's theory and plainly conflicts with his stated position that acts of will are effects. "I consider the determination of the will as an effect."[17]

The solution I've proposed requires a significant change in Reid's view of agent-causation. Not every act of the agent can be produced by the agent only by the agent's *exerting* her power to produce it. Acts of will that are produced by the agent whose acts they are, we shall say, are such that the agent causes them but not by another other act or any exertion of the power she has to produce the acts of will. We thus can halt the regress of acts of exertions that is implied by the conjunction of the causal principle and Reid's analysis of what it is to be a cause 'in the strict and proper sense.' The price, of course, is a significant modification of Reid's account of agent-causation.

Can we afford this price? Many philosophers would agree with Jonathan Edwards in holding that it is simply impossible that the agent should *cause* his act of will without an *exertion* of his power to produce that act of will, an exertion that is *distinct* from the act of will that is produced.[18]

The answer to Edwards is that although some actions (moving one's arm, e.g.) can be caused by the agent only by the agent exerting his power to produce his action of moving his arm, other actions such as acts of will are produced directly by the agent and not by means of exertions that are distinct from the acts of will produced. To deny the possibility of the latter is simply to claim that ultimately only events can be causes of events—thus if there is no exertion of power by the agent (and no other event causes the volition), no act of will can be produced. But the whole idea of agent-causation is that agents are causes of events, that in addition to event-causes there are causes of a wholly different kind—agents. If we take the view that persons really are active, rather than passive, in the production of their acts, then the modification I've suggested is precisely what one might expect the theory of agency embraced by Reid ultimately to imply. For, on the one hand, it is Reid's view that events and circumstances and other agents do not cause the person to agent-cause his acts of will. If other agents or prior events cause the person to do something, then the person lacks power to refrain and, therefore, is not the agent-cause of those doings: he is in fact passive with respect to his actions. And, on the other hand, if the person is the agent-cause of some act of his then on pain of infinite regress there must be some exertion or act he brings about without engaging in some other exertion or act in order to bring it about. In short, once we fully grasp the idea of agent-causation we can see, I believe, that it implies that when an agent causes his action there is some event (an act of will, perhaps) that the agent causes without bringing about any other event as a means to producing it.[19]

## III. REIDIAN FREEDOM AND RESPONSIBILITY

We started with Johnson's remark that although all theory is against free will, all experience or practice is for it. Among the several arguments Reid advanced in favor of free will, his argument from our *practice* of holding persons morally responsible for their actions and decisions is undoubtedly the strongest. I believe that Reid's argument from the fact of moral responsibility to the existence of Reidian freedom merits careful examination. But I have no time here to do that. Instead, I want to sharpen our grasp of Reidian freedom by considering just what it implies with respect to the vexing question of whether the agent could have done or willed otherwise. For there are, I believe, good reasons to doubt the traditional claim that an agent is morally responsible for doing A only if she could have avoided doing A. And there appear to be good reasons to doubt the claim that an agent is morally responsible for doing A only if she could have refrained from willing to do A. Now if this should be so, then if Reidian freedom implies either of these claims, it will *not* be true that an agent is morally responsible only if she possesses Reidian freedom—Reid's strongest argument for Reidian freedom will stand refuted.

According to Locke, the agent freely does A only if she could have refrained from doing A had she so willed. Reid says that freedom must include power over the determinations of our will. Perhaps then,

Reidian freedom is simply Lockean freedom with the addition of the power to will to do A and the power to will to refrain from doing A.[20] If so, I'm afraid that moral responsibility does not entail Reidian freedom. For moral responsibility does not entail Lockean freedom. One of Locke's examples is of a man who wills to stay in a room, not knowing that he is locked in. We may hold such a person responsible even though he would not have been able to avoid staying in the room had he willed not to stay in the room. For the agent who willingly does what he does, believing it to be in his power to do otherwise, must be distinguished from the person who stays in the room unwillingly because he is unable to leave. And if such a person is morally accountable for what he does, moral responsibility does not entail Reidian freedom *if* Reidian freedom is correctly understood as Lockean freedom with the addition of power over the will. But a careful look at Reid's account of a free action shows that it is a mistake so to understand Reidian freedom. What he says is this: "If, in any action, he had power to will what he did, or not to will it, in that action he is free." There is nothing in Reid's account to suggest that the agent must have had the power to do otherwise had he so willed. What Reid says is that if a person wills to perform some action and does so, then he performs that action freely provided he had the power not to will to do that action.

An interesting challenge to the idea that we are morally responsible for our action only if we could have refrained from willing it has been advanced by Frankfurt and Nozick.[21] To see the challenge, consider the following example. Suppose a mad scientist has gained access to your volitional capacity and not only can tell what act of will you are about to bring about but, worse yet, can send electrical currents into your brain that will cause a particular act of will to occur even though it is not the act of will that you would have brought about if left to your own devices. We will suppose that you are deliberating on a matter of great concern: killing Jones. Our mad scientist happens to be interested in Jones's going on to his reward, but he want Jones to die by your hand. His complicated machinery tells him that you are about to conclude your deliberations by willing *not* to kill Jones. Quickly, he pushes the buttons sending certain currents into your brain with the result that the volition to kill Jones occurs in you and results, let us say, in your actually killing Jones. Clearly you are not here morally accountable for your act of will and subsequent action of killing Jones. Were matters left to you, you would have willed not to kill Jones and would not have killed him. Although on Reid's account of this case it would be true that you willed to kill Jones, it is also true that you were not the agent-cause of your act of will and are therefore not morally accountable for your willing and your action.

Our second case is similar to, but also crucially different from, the first case. The mad scientist is intent on seeing to it that Jones is killed by your hand. But rather than activate the machine to cause your act of will to kill Jones, he would prefer that you bring about that act of will and the subsequent action of killing Jones. This time, however, your deliberations result in your act of will to kill Jones. The mad scientist could and would have caused that act of will in you had you been going to will not to kill Jones. But no such action on his part was necessary. There is a process in place (the machine, etc.) that assures that you shall will to kill Jones. But the process is activated *only if* you are not going to initiate your act of will to kill Jones. Given the machine, it was not in your power to avoid willing to kill Jones. But this fact *played no role* in what actually led to your willing to kill Jones and the actual killing that resulted. In this case, we do wish to hold you morally responsible for your act of will and the resulting action. And this is so even though it was not in your power to prevent your willing to kill Jones and not in your power to refrain from killing Jones.

Frankfurt argues that the fact that there are circumstances that make it impossible for an agent to avoid performing a certain action diminishes or extinguishes moral accountability for the action only if those circumstances in some way *bring it about* that the agent performs the action in question. This is true in our first case, where the mad scientist pushes the buttons that send the current causing your volition to kill Jones. Here the circumstances that prevent you from *not* willing to kill Jones *brings about* your volition to kill Jones. But in the second case, the circumstances that make it impossible for you not to will to kill Jones *play no role* in bringing it about that you willed to kill Jones. As Frankfurt remarks: "For those circumstances, by hypothesis, actually had nothing to do with his having done what he did. He would have done precisely the same thing, . . . , even if they had not prevailed."[22] It is because these circumstances play no role in what the agent willed and did that the agent bears moral responsibility for his

volition and act, even though it was not in his power to refrain from doing what he did. I believe Frankfurt is right about this matter. What remains to be seen, however, is whether Reid's basic intuition of a necessary connection between moral accountability and power over the will is unable to accommodate the case in which the agent is morally accountable but cannot prevent willing to kill Jones.

The second mad scientist example shows that an agent may be morally accountable for an act of will to do A even though it is not in the agent's power not to will that action. This certainly *appears* to conflict with Reid's theory. But we need to recall here that what is *crucial* for Reid's view of moral accountability is that the person be the *agent-cause* of her volition to do A. His view is that the agent is morally accountable for her voluntary action only if she is the agent-cause of her volition to do A. Now we already have seen that she may be the agent-cause of her volition to do A and not have it in her power not to will that action. This is what we learned, in part, from our second mad scientist case. But here, I believe, we need to distinguish between

(1) It was in the agent's power not to will doing A.

and

(2) It was in the agent's power *not* to cause her volition to do A.

In our second mad scientist case, (1) is false. But (2) is not false. The agent does have the power not to cause her volition to do A. The mad scientist has so arranged matters that the machine automatically causes the volition to do A in our agent if, but only if, the agent is about not to will to do A. This being so, (1) is clearly false. The agent cannot prevent her willing to do A; for if she does not cause her willing to do A the machine will cause her act of will to do A. But it still may be up to the agent whether *she* shall be the cause of her volition to do A. This power, Reid would argue, depends on a number of factors: the will of God, the continued existence of the agent, the absence of prior internal events and circumstances determining the occurrence of the volition to do A, etc. It also depends on the mad scientist's decision to activate the machine *only if* the agent is about not to will to do A. The scientist can cause our agent to will to do A. He does this by causing that act of will in the agent.[23] But if he does so then the agent does not agent-cause her volition to do A. The real agent-cause is the scientist. So if the agent has the power to cause her volition to do A she also has the power *not to cause* that volition. If she does not cause the volition and the machine activates, she, nevertheless, wills to do A—but *she* is not the cause of that act of will. I propose, therefore, the following as representing Reid's basic intuition concerning the connection between moral accountability and power:

(P)  A person is morally accountable for his
     action A only if he causes the volition
     to do A and it was in his power not to
     cause his volition to do A.[24]

(I believe this principle expresses Reid's view of our moral accountability for volitions as well. Simply replace 'action A' with 'volition to do A'.)

Principle P accords with our intuitions concerning both of the mad scientist cases. In the first case, when the machinery causes the volition to kill Jones, we do not wish to hold the agent morally accountable for the volition and its causal products. After all, if left to himself he would have willed to refrain from killing Jones. In the second case, where the machinery is not activated, we do hold the agent responsible for the volition and the action of killing Jones. And this is just what principle P will support. For the agent caused his volition to kill Jones and had it in his power not to cause that volition. I suggest, therefore, that the Frankfurt-Nozick examples do not refute the thesis that moral responsibility for a voluntary action implies Reidian freedom with respect to that action.[25]

## CONCLUSION

Some philosophical questions eventually yield to fairly definitive answers, answers which succeeding generations of philosophers accept, thereby contributing to our sense of progress in the discipline. Other philosophical questions seem to defy progress in the sense of definitive answers that are commonly accepted. Progress regarding them consists largely in deeper understanding and clarity concerning the questions and their possible answers. These are the deep philosophical questions. My conviction is that the question of human freedom is of the latter sort. I know that by setting forth the two concepts of freedom that were at the center of the 18th-century con-

troversy over freedom and necessity, and by criticizing the one, Lockean freedom, and recommending the other, Reidian freedom, I have not contributed to philosophical progress in the first sense. I haven't given any definitive answer. And in these compatibilist days, I certainly haven't given any answer that would be commonly accepted in my own department, let alone the discipline. My hope is that I have made some of these issues clearer and more understandable and have thereby contributed to philosophical progress in the second sense, helping us to grasp more clearly the philosophical question of human freedom and its relation both to causality and to moral responsibility.

## NOTES

1.  Thus Thomas Reid remarks: "Power is not an object of any of our external senses, nor even an object of consciousness." *Essays on the Active Powers of Man*, IV, Ch. I, p. 512. References are to the 1983 printing by Georg Olms Verlag of *The Works of Thomas Reid, D.D.*, 8th edition, edited by Sir William Hamilton (James Thin, 1895).

2.  I am grateful to the distinguished Johnson scholar, Donald Green, for pointing this out to me.

3.  Don Locke in "Three Concepts of Free Action" fails to see that John Locke distinguishes between a voluntary and a free act. Thus he wrongly interprets Locke as holding "that to act freely is to act as you want to: the man who wants to get out of a locked room does not remain there freely but, Locke insists, a man who wants to stay there, to speak to a friend, does stay freely, even if the door is locked." *Proceedings of the Aristotelian Society*, supplementary volume, 1975, p. 96.

4.  *An Essay Concerning Human Understanding*, edited by Peter H. Nidditch (Oxford University Press, 1975), Bk. II, Ch. 21, Section 33 (first edition).

5.  There is an objection due to J. L. Austin that also should be considered, since it attacks a point that is assumed by the other objections. Locke and Collins, as we just saw, took the view that *given* the causes of your action A, you could not have done anything other than A. Yet this does not preclude it being true that you could have done something else *if* you had willed to do something else. For with a difference in the causes, we might expect a difference in our powers. Now this nice harmony of causal necessity and freedom of action presupposes that the 'if' in statements of the form 'S could have done X if S had chosen or willed to do X' is an 'if' of causal condition. And Austin had an apparently devastating argument to show that the 'if' in 'S could have done X if S had chosen or willed to do X' is not the 'if' of causal condition. (See "Ifs and Cans," *Proceedings of the British Academy*, Vol. XLII, 1956, pp. 107–132.) The argument is this: if we consider an 'if' of causal condition, as in the statement 'This zinc will dissolve if placed in that acid', we can note two points. First, it will follow that if this zinc does not dissolve then it has not been placed in that acid. Second, it will not follow simpliciter that this zinc will dissolve. Just the opposite holds, however, of statements of the form 'S could

have done X if S had chosen or willed to do X.' First it will *not* follow that if S could not have done X then S has not chosen or willed to do X. And second it *will* follow simpliciter that S could have done X. From these premises Austin concludes that the 'if' in 'S could have done X if S had chosen or willed to do X' is not the 'if' of causal condition. But all that really follows from these premises is that the 'if' in 'S could have done X if S had chosen or willed to do X' does not present a condition of the *main clause*, 'S could have done X.' It may still be, for all Austin has shown, an 'if' of causal condition of something else. What else? Clearly, as Kurt Baier has argued, it would have to be of S's doing X. ("Could and Would," *Analysis*, XIII [1963], supplement, 20–29.). The 'if' in 'S could have done X if S had chosen or willed to do X' is an 'if' of causal condition of the doing of X by S. What statements of this form tell us is that a set of conditions necessary for S's doing X obtained at the time in question, and had S chosen or willed to do X there would then have been a set of conditions sufficient for S's doing X. On this account, 'S could have done X if S had chosen or willed to do X' implies the genuinely conditional statement form, 'S would have done X if S had chosen or willed to do X.' So Austin's argument fails to establish that Locke and Collins were wrong to suppose that the 'if' in 'S could have done X if S had chosen or willed to do X' is an 'if' of causal condition.

6. *Theodicy*, paragraph 324.

7. These two objections, and others, are expressed by Reid, Clarke, and Edmund Law. Perhaps their most forceful presentation is contained in Clarke's stinging attack on Collins's work. See *Remarks upon a Book, entitled, A Philosophical Enquiry Concerning Human Liberty*, 1717, in Samuel Clarke, *The Works*, 1738, Vol. 4. The 1738 edition has been reprinted by Garland Publishing Inc., 1978.

8. See Kant's *Critique of Practical Reason*, tr. by Lewis W. Beck (Bobbs-Merrill Co., Inc., 1956), p. 99. Also see W. James's "The Dilemma of Determinism" in *The Writings of William James*, ed. by John J. McDermott (The University of Chicago Press, 1977), p. 590.

9. In his second account of free will Leibniz insists that the act of will must be free in the sense of not being necessitated by the motives and circumstances that give rise to it. His often repeated dictum on this matter is that motives "incline without necessitating." This remark has the appearance of giving the free will advocate just what he wants, the power to have willed otherwise even though the motives and circumstances be unchanged. But Leibniz meant no such thing. The motive that inclines most determines the will and the action, just as the weight that is heaviest determines the movement of the balance. Motives and circumstances necessitate the act of will in the sense that it is logically or causally impossible that those motives and circumstances should obtain and the act of will not obtain. Leibniz's claim that they don't necessitate the act of will means only that the act of will *itself* is not thereby rendered an absolute or logical necessity. Since Spinoza, Hobbes, and Collins held that the act of will is itself absolutely necessary, Leibniz's point is well taken. But, as we noted, it does nothing to remove the causal necessity of the act of will.

10. *New Essays on Human Understanding*, tr. & ed. by P. Remnant and J. Bennett (Cambridge: Cambridge University Press, 1982), Bk. II, Ch. XXI, Section 8.

11. *Active Powers*, IV, Ch. I, p. 599.

12. Letter to Dr. James Gregory, 1793, *Works*, p. 87.

13. "Observations on the book concerning 'The Origin of Evil,'" *Theodicy*, ed. by Austin Farrer, tr. by E. M. Huggard (La Salle: Open Court, 1985), p. 406.

14. The spurious objection is that the doctrine of the freedom of the will implies that each act of will that is free is itself the result of a prior act of will, *ad infinitum*. According to the free will position, an action is free provided it is willed and the agent freely determined or brought about that act of will. But, so the spurious objection goes, to determine freely an act of will is to will freely that act of will. So an act of will is freely determined only if it is freely chosen. But an agent freely chooses an act of will only if his choice of that act of will is itself freely determined by the agent, in which case the choice of the act of will is itself the result of a prior free choice by the agent. And so we are off to the races, each determination of the will by the agent being preceded by an infinites series of determinations of the will by the agent. This objection fails, however, because it supposes that what it is for the agent to determine his will (that is, bring it about that he wills X, rather than something else) is for the agent to *will* that his will be determined in a certain manner. [See, for example, Jonathan Edwards, *Freedom of the Will*, ed. by Paul Ramsey (New Haven, Yale University Press, 1957), p. 172]. But it is very doubtful that any free will advocate held this view. Many free will advocates attributed to the agent a power of self-determination, a self-moving principle. But by this they meant only that when the volitional act is produced by the self-moving principle, it is produced by the agent himself and not by any other thing or agent. [See "Unpublished Letters of Thomas Reid to Lord Kames,' 1762–1782," collected by Ian Simpson Ross, *Texas Studies in Literature and Language* 7 (1965), p. 51.] They did not mean that in causing his volition the agent first chose or willed to produce that volition. To attribute such a view to them is to misunderstand what they claimed. According to the free will advocates, the soul or mind determines the will but does not do so by choosing or willing that the mind will X, rather than some other act. This objection, therefore, fails.

15. *Active Powers*, IV, Ch. II, p. 603.

16. *Ibid.*, Ch. IX, p. 625.

17. *Ibid.*, Ch. I, p. 602.

18. See *Freedom of the Will*, pp. 175–176.

19. The solution I present in the text requires a major modification of Reid's theory of agent causation: dropping the requirement that the agent must *exercise* his power to bring about an act of will if the agent is to *cause* that act of will. There is, however, a way of solving the problem of the infinite regress that leaves Reid's theory intact. For the whole problem vanishes if we take the view that the *exercise* of the agent's power (in order to produce his volition) is not itself an *event*. Not being an event, we require no cause of it, thus preventing the regress from starting. Is there any basis for such a view? Perhaps so. First, we must note that on Reid's view an event is a *change* in a substance. (Actually, Reid also includes the coming into existence of a substance as an event.) The occurrence of a volition in the agent is an event. The agent causes that event by exercising his power to cause it. What then of the agent's *exercise of power*? Here we may turn to Aristotle and his view of a *self-mover*. A self-mover is distinguished from a moved-mover. The latter (for example, a stick moving a stone) has a capacity

to bring about movement in something else (the stone), but the exercise of that capacity is itself a movement. The *exercise* of the moved-mover's capacity to bring about motion in another is, therefore, an event. But the agent who causes the stick to move must be an unmoved mover—the exercise of its capacity to cause movement in another is *not itself a movement*. Not being a movement, it is not a change in a substance and is, therefore, not an event. Thus Aristotle holds that a *self-mover* has a part that is moved (undergoes a change) and a part that moves but is not itself in motion (does not undergo a change). The part that moves but is not itself in motion must, of course, *exercise* its capacity to produce motion in the part that is moved. But this *exercise* of the unmoved part's capacity to produce motion is not itself a change in the part that is not itself in motion (not itself a change in the part that is an unmoved mover). (See Aristotle's *Physics*, Bk. VIII, Sections 4 and 5.) Following Aristotle we might take Reid to hold that the exercise of the agent's power to produce the volition to do A is *not itself* a change in the agent, it is not a change the agent undergoes. Now the causal principle, as Reid interprets it, holds that every event (every change in a substance) has a cause. The exertion of power to produce a *basic* change (e.g., an act of will), however, is not itself a change the substance undergoes. Therefore, it is not an event, and, therefore, does not require a cause. It would be an interesting and important addition to historical scholarship to see if Reid's theory can bear this interpretation.

20. For such an account of Reid see Timothy Duggan's essay, "Active Power and the Liberty of Moral Agents," in *Thomas Reid: Critical Interpretations,* ed. Stephen F. Barker and Tom L. Beauchamp (Philadelphia: Philosophical Monographs, 1976), p. 106.

21. See Harry G. Frankfurt's "Alternate Possibilities and Moral Responsibility," *Journal of Philosophy* (1969), pp. 829–839.

22. Frankfurt, p. 837.

23. I take Reid to hold (rightly) that causing a volition to do A in an agent is to cause *the agent's willing to do A.* Thus when an agent wills to do A we can raise the question of whether the cause of his so willing is the agent himself or something else.

24. Of course, we hold persons accountable for actions that they do not will. If I will to open my car door and do so, with the result that I knock you off your bicycle, I may be accountable for what I did through culpable ignorance—knocking you off your bicycle—even though I did not will to do it. But we may take Reid's account of freedom as what is entailed by those *voluntary* actions for which we are morally responsible.

25. Could not a super-sophisticated scientist so arrange his machine that if the agent were about not to cause his volition to do A the machine would activate, causing him to *cause* his volition to do A? If so, and if our agent does cause his volition, with the result that the machine is not activated, isn't our agent responsible even though it is not in his power *not to cause* his volition? The Reidian reply to this is that it is *conceptually impossible* to cause an *agent* to cause (in Reid's sense) his volition. For an agent has active power to cause only if he has power not to cause. This last is a conceptual truth for Reid. "Power to produce any effect, implies power not to produce it." *Active Powers,* p. 523.

# READING 34

# Has the Self "Free Will"?

*C. A. Campbell*

*C. A. Campbell (1897–1974) was Professor of Logic and Rhetoric at Glasgow University. Campbell defended libertarian indeterminism in his Gifford lectures,* On Selfhood and Godhood *(1957), and in a number of papers collected in* In Defence of Free Will *(1967).*

1. . . . It is something of a truism that in philosophic enquiry the exact formulation of a problem often takes one a long way on the road to its solution. In the case of the Free Will problem I think there is a rather special need of careful formulation. For there are many sorts of human freedom; and it can easily happen that one wastes a great deal of labour in proving or disproving a freedom which has almost nothing to do with the freedom which is at issue in the traditional problem of Free Will. The abortiveness of so much of the argument for and against Free Will in contemporary philosophical literature seems to me due in the main to insufficient pains being taken over the preliminary definition of the problem. There is, indeed, one outstanding exception, Professor Broad's brilliant inaugural lecture entitled, 'Determinism, Indeterminism, and Libertarianism',[1] in which forty-three pages are devoted to setting out the problem, as against seven to its solution! I confess that the solution does not seem to myself to follow upon the formulation quite as easily as all that:[2] but Professor Broad's eminent example fortifies me in my decision to give here what may seem at first sight a disproportionate amount of time to the business of determining the essential characteristics of the kind of freedom with which the traditional problem is concerned.

Fortunately we can at least make a beginning with a certain amount of confidence. It is not seriously disputable that the kind of freedom in question is the freedom which is commonly recognized to be in some sense a precondition of moral responsibility. Clearly, it is on account of this integral connection with moral responsibility that such exceptional importance has always been felt to attach to the Free Will problem. But in what precise sense is free will a precondition of moral responsibility, and thus a postulate of the moral life in general? This is an exceedingly troublesome question; but until we have satisfied ourselves about the answer to it, we are not in a position to state, let alone decide, the question of whether 'Free Will' in its traditional, ethical, significance is a reality.

Our first business, then, is to ask, exactly what kind of freedom is it which is required for moral responsibility? And as to method of procedure in this inquiry, there seems to me to be no real choice. I know of only one method that carries with it any hope of success; viz. the critical comparison of those acts for which, on due reflection, we deem it proper to attribute moral praise or blame to the agents, with those acts for which, on due reflection, we deem such judgments to be improper. The ultimate touchstone, as I see it, can only be our moral consciousness as it manifests itself in our more critical and considered moral judgments. The 'linguistic' approach by way of the analysis of moral *sentences* seems to me, despite its present popularity, to be an almost infallible method for reaching wrong results in the moral field; . . .

2. The first point to note is that the freedom at issue (as indeed the very name 'Free *Will* Problem' in-

---

[1]Reprinted in *Ethics and the History of Philosophy, Selected Essays.*
[2]I have explained the grounds for my dissent from Broad's final conclusions on pp. 27 ff. of *In Defence of Free Will* (Jackson Son & Co., 1938).

SOURCE: From *On Selfhood and Godhood* (London: George Allen & Unwin, 1957): 158–179.

dicates) pertains primarily not to overt acts but to inner acts. The nature of things has decreed that, save in the case of one's self, it is only overt acts which one can directly observe. But a very little reflection serves to show that in our moral judgments upon others their overt acts are regarded as significant only in so far as they are the expression of inner acts. We do not consider the acts of a robot to be morally responsible acts; nor do we consider the acts of a man to be so save in so far as they are distinguishable from those of a robot by reflecting an inner life of choice. Similarly, from the other side, if we are satisfied (as we may on occasion be, at least in the case of ourselves) that a person has definitely elected to follow a course which he believes to be wrong, but has been prevented by external circumstances from translating his inner choice into an overt act, we still regard him as morally blameworthy. Moral freedom, then, pertains to *inner* acts.

The next point seems at first sight equally obvious and uncontroversial; but, as we shall see, it has awkward implications if we are in real earnest with it (as almost nobody is). It is the simple point that the act must be one of which the person judged can be regarded as the *sole* author. It seems plain enough that if there are any *other* determinants of the act, external to the self, to that extent the act is not an act which the *self* determines, and to that extent not an act for which the self can be held morally responsible. The self is only part-author of the act, and his moral responsibility can logically extend only to those elements within the act (assuming for the moment that these can be isolated) of which he is the *sole* author.

The awkward implications of this apparent truism will be readily appreciated. For, if we are mindful of the influences exerted by heredity and environment, we may well feel some doubt whether there is any act of will at all of which one can truly say that the self is sole author, sole determinant. No man has a voice in determining the raw material of impulses and capacities that constitute his hereditary endowment, and no man has more than a very partial control of the material and social environment in which he is destined to live his life. Yet it would be manifestly absurd to deny that these two factors do constantly and profoundly affect the nature of a man's choices. That this is so we all of us recognise in our moral judgments when we "make allowances', as we say, for a bad heredity or a vicious environment, and acknowl-

edge in the victim of them a diminished moral responsibility for evil courses. Evidently we do *try*, in our moral judgments, however crudely, to praise or blame a man only in respect of that of which we can regard him as *wholly* the author. And evidently we do recognise that, for a man to be the author of an act in the full sense required for moral responsibility, it is not enough merely that he 'wills' or 'chooses' the act: since even the most unfortunate victim of heredity or environment does, as a rule, 'will' what he does. It is significant, however, that the ordinary man, though well enough aware of the influence upon choices of heredity and environment, does not feel obliged thereby to give up his assumption that moral predicates *are* somehow applicable. Plainly he still believes that there is *something* for which a man is morally responsible, something of which we can fairly say that he is the sole author. *What is this something?* To that question common-sense is not ready with an explicit answer—though an answer is, I think, implicit in the line which its moral judgments take. I shall do what I can to give an explicit answer later in this lecture. Meantime, it must suffice to observe that, if we are to be true to the deliverances of our moral consciousness, it is very difficult to deny that *sole* authorship is a necessary condition of the morally responsible act.

Thirdly we come to a point over which much recent controversy has raged. We may approach it by raising the following question. Granted an act of which the agent is sole author, does this 'sole authorship' suffice to make the act a morally free act? We may be inclined to think that it does, until we contemplate the possibility that an act of which the agent is sole author might conceivably occur as a necessary expression of the agent's nature; the way in which, e.g. some philosophers have supposed the Divine act of creation to occur. This consideration excites a legitimate doubt; for it is far from easy to see how a person can be regarded as a proper subject for moral praise or blame in respect of an act which he *cannot help* performing—even if it be his own 'nature' which necessitates it. Must we not recognise it as a condition of the morally free act that the agent 'could have acted otherwise' than he in fact did? It is true, indeed, that we sometimes praise or blame a man for an act about which we are prepared to say, in the light of our knowledge of his established character, that he 'could no other'. But I think that a little reflection shows that in such cases we are not praising or blaming the man strictly for what he does *now* (or at any rate we ought not to be), but rather for those past acts of his which have generated the firm habit of mind from which his *present* act follows 'necessarily'. In other words, our praise and blame, so far as justified, are really retrospective, being directed not to the agent *qua* performing *this* act, but to the agent *qua* performing those past acts which have built up his present character, and in respect to which we presume that he *could* have acted otherwise, that there really *were* open possibilities before him. These cases, therefore, seem to me to constitute no valid exception to what I must take to be the rule, viz. that a man can be morally praised or blamed for an act only if he could have acted otherwise.

Now philosophers today are fairly well agreed that it is a postulate of the morally responsible act that the agent 'could have acted otherwise' in *some* sense of that phrase. But sharp differences of opinion have arisen over the way in which the phrase ought to be interpreted. There is a strong disposition to water down its apparent meaning by insisting that it is not (as a postulate of moral responsibility) to be understood as a straightforward categorical proposition, but rather as a disguised hypothetical proposition. All that we really require to be assured of, in order to justify our holding X morally responsible for an act, is, we are told, that X could have acted otherwise *if* he had *chosen* otherwise (Moore, Stevenson); or perhaps that X could have acted otherwise *if* he had had a different character, or *if* he had been placed in different circumstances.

I think it is easy to understand, and even, in a measure, to sympathise with, the motives which induce philosophers to offer these counter-interpretations. it is not just the fact that 'X could have acted otherwise', as a bald categorical statement, is incompatible with the universal sway of causal law—though this is, to some philosophers, a serious stone of stumbling. The more widespread objection is that it at least looks as though it were incompatible with that causal continuity of an agent's character with his conduct which is implied when we believe (surely with justice) that we can often tell the sort of thing a man will do from our knowledge of the sort of man he is.

We shall have to make our accounts with that particular difficulty later. At this stage I wish merely to show that neither of the hypothetical propositions suggested—and I think the same could be shown for *any* hypothetical alternative—is an acceptable substi-

tute for the categorical proposition 'X could have acted otherwise' as the presupposition of moral responsibility.

Let us look first at the earlier suggestion—'X could have acted otherwise *if* he had chosen otherwise.' Now clearly there are a great many acts with regard to which we are entirely satisfied that the agent is thus situated. We are often perfectly sure that—for this is all it amounts to—if X had chosen otherwise, the circumstances presented no external obstacle to the translation of that choice into action. For example, we often have no doubt at all that X, who in point of fact told a lie, could have told the truth *if* he had so chosen. But does our confidence on this score allay all legitimate doubts about whether X is really blameworthy? Does it entail that X is free in the sense required for moral responsibility? Surely not. The obvious question immediately arises: 'But *could* X have *chosen* otherwise than he did?' It is doubt about the true answer to *that* question which leads most people to doubt the reality of moral responsibility. Yet on this crucial question the hypothetical proposition which is offered as a sufficient statement of the condition justifying the ascription of moral responsibility gives us no information whatsoever.

Indeed this hypothetical substitute for the categorical 'X could have acted otherwise' seems to me to lack all plausibility unless one contrives to forget why it is, after all, that we ever come to feel fundamental doubts about man's moral responsibility. Such doubts are born, surely, when one becomes aware of certain reputable world-views in religion or philosophy, or of certain reputable scientific beliefs, which in their several ways imply that man's actions are necessitated, and thus could not be otherwise than they in fact are. But clearly a doubt so based is not even touched by the recognition that a man could very often act otherwise *if* he so chose. That proposition is entirely compatible with the necessitarian theories which generate our doubt: indeed it is this very compatibility that has recommended it to some philosophers, who are reluctant to give up either moral responsibility or Determinism. The proposition which we *must* be able to affirm if moral praise or blame of X is to be justified is the categorical proposition that X could have acted otherwise because—not if—he could have chosen otherwise; or, since it is essentially the inner side of the act that matters, the proposition simply that X could have chosen otherwise.

For the second of the alternative formulae suggested we cannot spare more than a few moments. But its inability to meet the demands it is required to meet is almost transparent. 'X could have acted otherwise', as a statement of a precondition of X's moral responsibility, really means (we are told) 'X could have acted otherwise *if* he were differently constituted, or *if* he had been placed in different circumstances'. It seems a sufficient reply to this to point out that the person whose moral responsibility is at issue is *X*; a specific individual, in a specific set of circumstances. It is totally irrelevant to *X*'s moral responsibility that we should be able to say that some person differently constituted from X, or X in a different set of circumstances, could have done something different from what X did.

3. Let me, then, briefly sum up the answer at which we have arrived to our question about the kind of freedom required to justify moral responsibility. It is that a man can be said to exercise free will in a morally significant sense only in so far as his chosen act is one of which he is the sole cause or author, and only if—in the straightforward, categorical sense of the phrase—he 'could have chosen otherwise'.

I confess that this answer is in some ways a disconcerting one; disconcerting, because most of us, however objective we are in the actual conduct of our thinking, would *like* to be able to believe that moral responsibility is real: whereas the freedom required for moral responsibility, on the analysis we have given, is certainly far more difficult to establish than the freedom required on the analyses we found ourselves obliged to reject. If, e.g. moral freedom entails only that I could have acted otherwise *if* I had chosen otherwise, there is no real 'problem' about it at all. I am 'free' in the normal case where there is no external obstacle to prevent my translating the alternative choice into action, and not free in other cases. Still less is there a problem if all that moral freedom entails is that I could have acted otherwise *if* I had been a differently constituted person, or been in different circumstances. Clearly I am *always* free in *this* sense of freedom. But, as I have argued, these so-called 'freedoms' fail to give us the pre-conditions of moral responsibility, and hence leave the freedom of the traditional free-will problem, the freedom that people are really concerned about, precisely where it was.

4. Another interpretation of freedom which I am bound to reject on the same general ground, i.e. that it just not the kind of freedom that is relevant to moral responsibility, is the old idealist view which identifies the *free* will with the *rational* will; the rational will in its turn being identified with the will which wills the moral law in whole-hearted, single-minded obedience to it. This view is still worth at least a passing mention, if only because it has recently been resurrected in an interesting work by Professor A. E. Teale.[3] Moreover, I cannot but feel a certain nostalgic tenderness for a view in which I myself was (so to speak) philosophically cradled. The almost apostolic fervour with which my revered nursing-mother, the late Sir Henry Jones, was wont to impart it to his charges, and, hardly less, his ill-concealed scorn for ignoble natures (like my own) which still hankered after a free will in the old 'vulgar' sense, are vividly recalled for me in Professor Teale's stirring pages.

The true interpretation of free will, according to Professor Teale, the interpretation to which Kant, despite occasional back-slidings, adhered in his better moments, is that 'the will is free in the degree that it is informed and disciplined by the moral principle'.[4]

Now this is a perfectly intelligible sense of the word 'free'—or at any rate it can be made so with a little explanatory comment which Professor Teale well supplies but for which there is here no space. But clearly it is a very different sort of freedom from that which is at issue in the traditional problem of free will. This idealist 'freedom' sponsored by Teale belongs, on his own showing, only to the self in respect of its *good* willing. The freedom with which the traditional problem is concerned, inasmuch as it is the freedom presupposed by moral responsibility, must belong to the self in respect of its *bad*, no less than its *good*, willing. It is, in fact, the freedom to decide between genuinely open alternatives of good and bad willing.

Professor Teale, of course, is not unaware that the freedom he favours differs from freedom as traditionally understood. He recognises the traditional concept under its Kantian title of 'elective' freedom. But he leaves the reader in no kind of doubt about his disbelief in both the reality and the value of this elective freedom to do, or forbear from doing, one's duty.

[3]*Kantian Ethics.*
[4]*Op. cit.* p. 261.

The question of the reality of elective freedom I shall be dealing with shortly; and it will occupy us to the end of the lecture. At the moment I am concerned only with its value, and with the rival view that all that matters for the moral life is the 'rational' freedom which a man has in the degree that his will is 'informed and disciplined by the moral principle'. I confess that to myself the verdict on the rival view seems plain and inescapable. No amount of verbal ingenuity or argumentative convolutions can obscure the fact that it is in flat contradiction to the implications of moral responsibility. The point at issue is really perfectly straightforward. If, as this idealist theory maintains, my acting in defiance of what I deem to be my duty is not a 'free' act in *any* sense, let alone in the sense that 'I could have acted otherwise', then I cannot be morally blameworthy, and that is all there is to it. Nor, for that matter, is the idealist entitled to say that I am morally praiseworthy if I act dutifully; for although that act *is* a 'free' act in the idealist sense, it is on his own avowal not free in the sense that 'I could have acted otherwise'.

It seems to me idle, therefore, to pretend that if one has to give up freedom in the traditional elective sense one is not giving up anything important. What we are giving up is, quite simply, the reality of the moral life. I recognise that to a certain type of religious nature (as well as, by an odd meeting of extremes, to a certain type of secular nature) that does not appear to matter so very much; but, for myself, I still think it sufficiently important to make it well worth while enquiring seriously into the possibility that the elective freedom upon which it rests may be real after all.

5. That brings me to the second, and more constructive, part of this lecture. From now on I shall be considering whether it is reasonable to believe that man does in fact possess a free will of the kind specified in the first part of the lecture. If so, just how and where within the complex fabric of the volitional life are we to locate it?—for although free will must presumably belong (if anywhere) to the volitional side of human experience, it is pretty clear from the way in which we have been forced to define it that it does not pertain simply to volition as such; not even to all volitions that are commonly dignified with the name of 'choices'. It has been, I think, one of the more serious impediments to profitable discussion of the Free Will problem that Libertarians and Deter-

minists alike have so often failed to appreciate the comparatively narrow area within which the free will that is necessary to 'save' morality is required to operate. It goes without saying that this failure has been gravely prejudicial to the case for Libertarianism. I attach a good deal of importance, therefore, to the problem of locating free will correctly within the volitional orbit. Its solution forestalls and annuls, I believe, some of the more tiresome clichés of Determinist criticism.

We saw earlier that Common Sense's practice of 'making allowances' in its moral judgments for the influence of heredity and environment indicates Common Sense's conviction, both that a just moral judgment must discount determinants of choice over which the agent has no control, and also (since it still accepts moral judgments as legitimate) that *something* of moral relevance survives which can be regarded as genuinely self-originated. We are now to try to discover what this 'something' is. And I think we may still usefully take Common Sense as our guide. Suppose one asks the ordinary intelligent citizen *why* he deems it proper to make allowances for X, whose heredity and/or environment are unfortunate. He will tend to reply, I think, in some such terms as these: that X has more and stronger temptations to deviate from what is right than Y or Z, who are normally circumstanced, so that he must put forth a *stronger moral effort* if he is to achieve the same level of external conduct. The intended implication seems to be that X is just as morally praiseworthy as Y or Z *if* he exerts an equivalent moral effort, even though he may not thereby achieve an equal success in conforming his will to the 'concrete' demands of duty. And this implies, again, Common Sense's belief that *in moral effort* we have something for which a man is responsible *without qualification*, something that is *not* affected by heredity and environment but depends *solely* upon the self itself.

Now in my opinion Common Sense has here, in principle, hit upon the one and only defensible answer. Here, and here alone, so far as I can see, in the act of deciding whether to put forth or withhold the moral effort required to resist temptation and rise to duty, is to be found an act which is free in the sense required for moral responsibility; an act of which the self is sole author, and of which it is true to say that 'it could be' (or, after the event, 'could have been') 'otherwise'. Such is the thesis which we shall now try to establish.

6. The species of argument appropriate to the establishment of a thesis of this sort should fall, I think, into two phases. First, there should be a consideration of the evidence of the moral agent's own inner experience. What *is* the act of moral decision, and what does it imply, from the standpoint of the actual participant? Since there is no way of knowing the act of moral decision—or for that matter any other form of activity—except by actual participation in it, the evidence of the subject, or agent, is on an issue of this kind of palmary importance. It can hardly, however, be taken as in itself conclusive. For even if that evidence should be overwhelmingly to the effect that moral decision does have the characteristics required by moral freedom, the question is bound to be raised—and in view of considerations from other quarters pointing in a contrary direction is *rightly* raised—Can we *trust* the evidence of inner experience? That brings us to what will be the second phase of the argument. We shall have to go on to show, if we are to make good our case, that the extraneous considerations so often supposed to be fatal to the belief in moral freedom are in fact innocuous to it.

In the light of what was said in the last lecture about the self's experience of moral decision as a *creative* activity, we may perhaps be absolved from developing the first phase of the argument at any great length. The appeal is throughout to one's own experience in the actual taking of the moral decision in the situation of moral temptation. 'Is it possible', we must ask, 'for anyone so circumstanced to *dis*believe that he could be deciding otherwise?' The answer is surely not in doubt. When we decide to exert moral effort to resist a temptation, we feel quite certain that we *could* withhold the effort; just as, if we decide to withhold the effort and yield to our desires, we feel quite certain that we *could* exert it—otherwise we should not blame ourselves afterwards for having succumbed. It may be, indeed, that this conviction is mere self-delusion. But that is not at the moment our concern. It is enough at present to establish that the act of deciding to exert or to withhold moral effort, as we know it from the inside in actual moral living, belongs to the category of acts which 'could have been otherwise'.

*Mutatis mutandis*, the same reply is forthcoming if we ask, 'Is it possible for the moral agent in the taking of his decision to *dis*believe that he is the *sole* author of that decision?' Clearly he cannot disbelieve that it is *he* who takes the decision. That, however, is

not in itself sufficient to enable him, on reflection, to regard himself as *solely* responsible for the act. For his 'character' as so far formed might conceivably be a factor in determining it, and no one can suppose that the constitution of his 'character' is uninfluenced by circumstances of heredity and environment with which *he* has nothing to do. But as we pointed out in the last lecture, the very essence of the moral decision as it is experienced is that it is a decision whether or not to *combat* our strongest desire, and our strongest desire *is* the expression in the situation of our character as so far formed. Now clearly our character cannot be a factor in determining the decision whether or not to *oppose* our character. I think we are entitled to say, therefore, that the act of moral decision is one in which the self is for itself not merely 'author' but 'sole author'.

7. We may pass on, then, to the second phase of our constructive argument; and this will demand more elaborate treatment. Even if a moral agent *qua* making a moral decision in the situation of 'temptation' cannot help believing that he has free will in the sense at issue—a moral freedom between real alternatives, between genuinely open possibilities—are there, nevertheless, objections to a freedom of this kind so cogent that we are bound to distrust the evidence of 'inner experience'?

I begin by drawing attention to a simple point whose significance tends, I think, to be under-estimated. If the phenomenological analysis we have offered is substantially correct, no one while functioning as a moral agent can help believing that he enjoys free will. Theoretically he may be completely convinced by Determinist arguments, but when actually confronted with a personal situation of conflict between duty and desire he is quite certain that it lies with him here and now whether or not he will rise to duty. It follows that if Determinists could produce convincing theoretical arguments against a free will of this kind, the awkward predicament would ensue that man has to deny as a theoretical being what he has to assert as a practical being. Now I think the Determinist ought to be a good deal more worried about this than he usually is. He seems to imagine that a strong case on general theoretical grounds is enough to prove that the 'practical' belief in free will, even if inescapable for us as practical beings, is mere illusion. But in fact it proves nothing of the sort. There is no reason whatever why a belief that we find ourselves obliged to hold *qua* practical beings should be required to give way before a belief which we find ourselves obliged to hold *qua* theoretical beings; or for that matter, *vice versa*. All that the theoretical arguments of Determinism can prove, unless they are reinforced by a refutation of the phenomenological analysis that supports Libertarianism, is that there is a radical conflict between the theoretical and the practical sides of man's nature, an antimony at the very heart of the self. And this is a state of affairs with which no one can easily rest satisfied. I think therefore that the Determinist ought to concern himself a great deal more than he does with phenomenological analysis, in order to show, if he can, that the assurance of free will is not really an inexpugnable element in man's practical consciousness. There is just as much obligation upon him, convinced though he may be of the soundness of his theoretical arguments, to expose the errors of the Libertarian's phenomenological analysis, as there is upon us, convinced though we may be of the soundness of the Libertarian's phenomenological analysis, to expose the errors of the Determinist's theoretical arguments.

8. However, we must at once begin the discharge of our own obligation. The rest of this lecture will be devoted to trying to show that the arguments which seem to carry most weight with Determinists are, to say the least of it, very far from compulsive.

Fortunately a good many of the arguments which at an earlier time in the history of philosophy would have been strongly urged against us make almost no appeal to the bulk of philosophers today, and we may here pass them by. That applies to any criticism of 'open possibilities' based on a metaphysical theory about the nature of the universe as a whole. Nobody today *has* a metaphysical theory about the nature of the universe as a whole! It applies also, with almost equal force, to criticisms based upon the universality of causal law as a supposed postulate of science. There have always been, in my opinion, sound philosophic reasons for doubting the validity, as distinct from the convenience, of the causal postulate in its universal form, but at the present time, when scientists themselves are deeply divided about the need for postulating causality even within their own special field, we shall do better to concentrate our attention upon criticisms which are more confidently advanced. I propose to ignore also, on different

grounds, the type of criticism of free will that is sometimes advanced from the side of religion, based upon religious postulates of Divine Omnipotence and Omniscience. So far as I can see, a postulate of human freedom is every bit as necessary to meet certain religious demands (e.g. to make sense of the 'conviction of sin'), as postulates of Divine Omniscience and Omnipotence are to meet certain other religious demands. If so, then it can hardly be argued that religious experience as such tells more strongly against than for the position we are defending; and we may be satisfied, in the present context, to leave the matter there. It will be more profitable to discuss certain arguments which contemporary philosophers do think important, and which recur with a somewhat monotonous regularity in the literature of anti-Libertarianism.

These arguments can, I think, be reduced in principle to no more than two: first, the argument from 'predictability'; second, the argument from the alleged meaninglessness of an act supposed to be the self's act and yet not an expression of the self's character. Contemporary criticism of free will seems to me to consist almost exclusively of variations on these two themes. I shall deal with each in turn.

9. On the first we touched in passing at an earlier stage. Surely it is beyond question (the critic urges) that when we know a person intimately we can foretell with a high degree of accuracy how he will respond to at least a large number of practical situations. One feels safe in predicting that one's dog-loving friend will not use his boot to repel the little mongrel that comes yapping at his heels; or again that one's wife will not pass with incurious eyes (or indeed pass at all) the new hat-shop in the city. So to behave would not be (as we say) 'in character.' But, so the criticism runs, you with your doctrine of 'genuinely open possibilities', of a free will by which the self can diverse from its own character, remove all rational basis from such prediction. You require us to make the absurd supposition that the success of countless predictions of the sort in the past has been mere matter of chance. If you *really* believed in your theory, you would not be surprised if tomorrow your friend with the notorious horror of strong drink should suddenly exhibit a passion for whisky and soda, or if your friend whose taste for reading has hitherto been satisfied with the sporting columns of the newspapers should be discovered on a fine Sat-

urday afternoon poring over the works of Hegel. But of course you *would* be surprised. Social life would be sheer chaos if there were not well-grounded social expectations; and social life is not sheer chaos. Your theory is hopelessly wrecked upon obvious facts.

Now whether or not this criticism holds good against some versions of Libertarian theory I need not here discuss. It is sufficient if I can make it clear that against the version advanced in this lecture, according to which free will is localised in a relatively narrow field of operation, the criticism has no relevance whatsoever.

Let us remind ourselves briefly of the setting within which, on our view, free will functions. There is X, the course which we believe we ought to follow, and Y, the course towards which we feel our desire is strongest. The freedom which we ascribe to the agent is the freedom to put forth or refrain from putting forth the moral effort required to resist the pressure of desire and do what he thinks he ought to do.

But then there is surely an immense range of practical situations—covering by far the greater part of life—in which there is no question of a conflict within the self between what he most desires to do and what he thinks he ought to do? Indeed such conflict is a comparatively rare phenomenon for the majority of men. Yet over that whole vast range there is nothing whatever in our version of Libertarianism to prevent our agreeing that character determines conduct. In the absence, real or supposed, of any 'moral' issue, what a man chooses will be simply that course which, after such reflection as seems called for, he deems most likely to bring him what he most strongly desires; and that is the same as to say the course to which his present character inclines him.

Over by far the greater area of human choices, then, our theory offers no more barrier to successful prediction on the basis of character than any other theory. For where there is no clash of strongest desire with duty, the free will we are defending has no business. There is just nothing for it to do.

But what about the situations—rare enough though they may be—in which there *is* this clash and in which free will does therefore operate? Does our theory entail that there at any rate, as the critic seems to suppose, 'anything may happen'?

Not by any manner of means. In the first place, and by the very nature of the case, the range of the agent's possible choices is bounded by what he thinks he ought to do on the one hand, and what he most

strongly desires on the other. The freedom claimed for him is a freedom of decision to make or withhold the effort required to do what he thinks he ought to do. There is no question of a freedom to act in some 'wild' fashion, out of all relation to his characteristic beliefs and desires. This so-called 'freedom of caprice', so often charged against the Libertarian, is, to put it bluntly, a sheer figment of the critic's imagination, with no *habitat* in serious Libertarian theory. Even in situations where free will does come into play it is perfectly possible, on a view like ours, given the appropriate knowledge of a man's character, to predict within certain limits how he will respond.

But 'probable' prediction in such situations can, I think, go further than this. It is obvious that where desire and duty are at odds, the felt 'gap' (as it were) between the two may vary enormously in breadth in different cases. The moderate drinker and the chronic tippler may each want another glass, and each deem it his duty to abstain, but the felt gap between desire and duty in the case of the former is trivial beside the great gulf which is felt to separate them in the case of the latter. Hence it will take a far harder moral effort for the tippler than for the moderate drinker to achieve the same external result of abstention. So much is matter of common agreement. And we are entitled, I think, to take it into account in prediction, on the simple principle that the harder the moral effort required to resist desire the less likely it is to occur. Thus in the example taken, most people would predict that the tippler will very probably succumb to his desires, whereas there is a reasonable likelihood that the moderate drinker will make the comparatively slight effort needed to resist them. So long as the prediction does not pretend to more than a measure of probability, there is nothing in our theory which would disallow it.

I claim, therefore, that the view of free will I have been putting forward is consistent with predictability of conduct on the basis of character over a very wide field indeed. And I make the further claim that the field will cover all the situations in life concerning which there is any empirical evidence that successful prediction is possible.

10. Let us pass on to consider the second main line of criticism. This is, I think, much the more illuminating of the two, if only because it compels the Libertarian to make explicit certain concepts which are indispensable to him, but which, being desper-

ately hard to state clearly, are apt not to be stated at all. The critic's fundamental point might be stated somewhat as follows:

'Free will as you describe it is completely unintelligible. On your own showing no *reason* can be given, because there just *is* no reason, why a man decides to exert rather than to withhold moral effort, or *vice versa*. But such an act—or more properly, such an "occurrence"—it is nonsense to speak of as an act of a *self*. If there is nothing in the self's character to which it is, even in principle, in any way traceable, the self has nothing to do with it. Your so-called "freedom", therefore, so far from supporting the self's moral responsibility, destroys it as surely as the crudest Determinism could do.'

If we are to discuss this criticism usefully, it is important, I think, to begin by getting clear about two different senses of the word 'intelligible'.

If, in the first place, we mean by an 'intelligible' act one whose occurrence is in principle capable of being inferred, since it follows necessarily from something (though we may not know in fact from what), then it is certainly true that the Libertarian's free will is unintelligible. But that is only saying, is it not, that the Libertarian's 'free' act is not an act which follows necessarily from something! This can hardly rank as a *criticism* of Libertarianism. It is just a description of it. That there can be nothing unintelligible in *this* sense is precisely what the Determinist has got to *prove*.

Yet it is surprising how often the critic of Libertarianism involves himself in this circular mode of argument. Repeatedly it is urged against the Libertarian, with a great air of triumph, that on his view he can't say *why* I now decide to rise to duty, or now decide to follow my strongest desire in defiance of duty. Of course he can't. If he could he wouldn't *be* a Libertarian. To 'account for' a 'free' act is a contradiction in terms. A free will is *ex hypothesi* the sort of thing of which the request for an *explanation* is absurd. The assumption that an explanation must be in principle possible for the act of moral decision deserves to rank as a classic example of the ancient fallacy of 'begging the question'.

But the critic usually has in mind another sense of the word 'unintelligible'. He is apt to take it for granted that an act which is unintelligible in the *above* sense (as the morally free act of the Libertarian undoubtedly is) is unintelligible in the *further* sense that we can attach no meaning to it. And this is an

altogether more serious matter. If it could really be shown that the Libertarian's 'free will' were unintelligible in this sense of being meaningless, that, for myself at any rate, would be the end of the affair. Libertarianism would have been conclusively refuted.

But it seems to me manifest that this can *not* be shown. The critic has allowed himself, I submit, to become the victim of a widely accepted but fundamentally vicious assumption. He has assumed that whatever is meaningful must exhibit its meaningfulness to those who view it from the standpoint of external observation. Now if one chooses thus to limit one's self to the rôle of external observer, it is, I think, perfectly true that one can attach no meaning to an act which is the act of something we call a 'self' and yet follows from nothing in that self's character. But then *why should we* so limit ourselves, when what is under consideration is a subjective activity? For the apprehension of subjective acts there is *another* standpoint available, that of *inner experience*, of the practical consciousness in its actual functioning. If our free will should turn out to be something to which we can attach a meaning from *this* standpoint, no more is required. And no more ought to be expected. For I must repeat that only from the inner standpoint of living experience *could* anything of the nature of 'activity' be directly grasped. Observation from without is in the nature of the case impotent to apprehend the active *qua* active. We can from without observe sequences of states. If into these we read activity (as we sometimes do), this can only be on the basis of what we discern in ourselves from the inner standpoint. It follows that if anyone insists upon taking his criterion of the meaningful simply from the standpoint of external observation, he is really deciding in advance of the evidence that the notion of activity, and *a fortiori* the notion of a free will, is 'meaningless'. He looks for the free act through a medium which is in the nature of the case incapable of revealing it, and then, because inevitably he doesn't find it, he declares that it doesn't exist!

But if, as we surely ought in this context, we adopt the inner standpoint, then (I am suggesting) things appear in a totally different light. From the inner standpoint, it seems to me plain, there is no difficulty whatever in attaching meaning to an act which is the self's act and which nevertheless does not follow from the self's character. So much I claim has been established by the phenomenological analysis, in this and the previous lecture, of the act of moral decision in face of moral temptation. It is thrown into particularly clear relief where the moral issue is to make the moral effort required to rise to duty. For the very function of moral effort, as it appears to the agent engaged in the act, is to enable the self to act against the line of least resistance, against the line to which his character as so far formed most strongly inclines him. But if the self is thus conscious here of *combating* his formed character, he surely cannot possibly suppose that the act, although his own act, *issues from* his formed character? I submit, therefore, that the self knows very well indeed—from the inner standpoint—what is meant by an act which is the *self's* act and which nevertheless does not follow from the self's *character*.

What this implies—and it seems to me to be an implication of cardinal importance for any theory of the self that aims at being more than superficial—is that the nature of the self is for itself something more than just its character as so far formed. The 'nature' of the self and what we commonly call the 'character' of the self are by no means the same thing, and it is utterly vital that they should not be confused. The 'nature' of the self comprehends, but is not without remainder reducible to, its 'character'; it must, if we are to be true to the testimony of our experience of it, be taken as including *also* the authentic creative power of fashioning and re-fashioning 'character'.

The misguided, and as a rule quite uncritical, belittlement, of the evidence offered by inner experience has, I am convinced, been responsible for more bad argument by the opponents of Free Will than has any other single factor. How often, for example, do we find the Determinist critic saying, in effect, '*Either* the act follows necessarily upon precedent states, *or* it is a mere matter of chance and accordingly of no moral significance'. The disjunction is invalid, for it does not exhaust the possible alternatives. It seems to the critic to do so only because he *will* limit himself to the standpoint which is proper, and indeed alone possible, in dealing with the physical world, the standpoint of the external observer. If only he would allow himself to assume the standpoint which is not merely proper for, but necessary to, the apprehension of subjective activity, the inner standpoint of the practical consciousness in its actual functioning, he would find himself obliged to recognise the falsity of his disjunction. Reflection upon the act of moral decision as apprehended from the inner standpoint would force him to recognise a *third* possibility, as remote from chance as from necessity, that, namely, of *creative activity*, in which (as I have ventured to express it) nothing determines the act save the agent's doing of it.

11. There we must leave the matter. But as this lecture has been, I know, somewhat densely packed, it may be helpful if I conclude by reminding you, in bald summary, of the main things I have been trying to say. Let me set them out in so many successive theses.

(1) The freedom which is at issue in the traditional Free Will problem is the freedom which is presupposed in moral responsibility.

(2) Critical reflection upon carefully considered attributions of moral responsibility reveals that the only freedom that will do is a freedom which pertains to inner acts of choice, and that these acts must be acts (a) of which the self is *sole* author, and (b) which the self could have performed otherwise.

(3) From phenomenological analysis of the situation of moral temptation we find that the self as engaged in this situation is inescapably convinced that it possesses a freedom of precisely the specified kind, located in the decision to exert or withhold the moral effort needed to rise to duty where the pressure of its desiring nature is felt to urge it in a contrary direction.

Passing to the question of the *reality* of this moral freedom which the moral agent believes himself to possess, we argued:

(4) Of the two types of Determinist criticism which seem to have most influence today, that based on the predictability of much human behaviour fails to touch a Libertarianism which confines the area of free will as above indicated. Libertarianism so understood is compatible with all the predictability that the empirical facts warrant. And:

(5) The second main type of criticism, which alleges the 'meaninglessness' of an act which is the self's act and which is yet not determined by the self's character, is based on a failure to appreciate that the standpoint of inner experience is not only legitimate but indispensable where what is at issue is the reality and nature of a subjective activity. The creative act of moral decision is inevitably meaningless to the mere external observer; but from the inner standpoint it is as real, and as significant, as anything in human experience.[5]

----

[5]An earlier, but not in substance dissimilar, version of my views on the Free Will problem has been criticised at length in Mr. Nowell-Smith's *Ethics*. A detailed reply to these criticisms will be found in Appendix B of *On Selfhood and Godhood*.

**READING 35**

# Freedom and Determinism

*Richard Taylor*

*Richard Taylor (1919– ) has taught philosophy at Brown University, Columbia University, and the University of Rochester. His books include* Metaphysics *(1963; 3rd ed., 1983),* Action and Purpose *(1966),* Good and Evil: A New Direction *(1970), and* Freedom, Anarchy, and the Law *(1973).*

## FREEDOM

To say that it is, in a given instance, up to me what I do is to say that I am in that instance *free* with respect to what I then do. Thus, I am sometimes free to move my finger this way and that, but not, certainly, to bend it backward or into a knot. But what does this mean?

It means, first, that there is no *obstacle* or *impediment* to my activity. Thus, there is sometimes no obstacle to my moving my finger this way and that, though there are obvious obstacles to my moving it backward or into a knot. Those things, accordingly, that pose obstacles to my motions limit my freedom. If my hand were strapped in such a way as to permit only a leftward motion of my finger, I would not then be free to move it to the right. If it were encased in a tight cast that permitted no motion, I would not be free to move it at all. Freedom of motion, then, is limited by obstacles.

Further, to say that it is, in a given instance, up to me what I do, means that nothing *constrains* or *forces* me to do one thing rather than another. Constraints are like obstacles, except that while the latter prevent, the former enforce. Thus, if my finger is being forcibly bent to the left—by a machine, for instance, or by another person, or by any force that I cannot overcome—then I am not free to move it this way and that. I cannot, in fact, move it at all; I can only

SOURCE: From Richard Taylor, *Metaphysics*, 3e, © 1983, pp. 41–50. Reprinted by permission of Prentice-Hall, Inc., Englewood Cliffs, New Jersey.

watch to see how it is moved, and perhaps vainly resist: Its motions are not up to me, or within my control, but in the control of some other thing or person.

Obstacles and constraints, then, both obviously limit my freedom. To say that I am free to perform some action thus means at least that there is no obstacle to my doing it, and that nothing constrains me to do otherwise.

Now if we rest content with this observation, as many have, and construe free activity simply as activity that is unimpeded and unconstrained, there is evidently no inconsistency between affirming both the thesis of determination and the claim that I am sometimes free. For to say that some action of mine is neither impeded nor constrained does not by itself imply that it is not causally determined. The absence of obstacles and constraints is a mere negative condition, and does not by itself rule out the presence of positive causes. It might seem, then, that we can say of some of my actions that there are conditions antecedent to their performance so that no other actions were possible, and also that these actions were unobstructed and unconstrained. And to say that would logically entail that such actions were both causally determined, and free.

## SOFT DETERMINISM

It is this kind of consideration that has led many philosophers to embrace what is sometimes called "soft determinism." All versions of this theory have in common three claims, by means of which, it is naïvely supposed, a reconciliation is achieved between determinism and freedom. Freedom being, furthermore, a condition of moral responsibility and the only condition that metaphysics seriously questions, it is supposed by the partisans of this view that determinism is perfectly compatible with such responsibility. This, no doubt, accounts for its great appeal and wide acceptance, even by some people of considerable learning.

The three claims of soft determinism are (1) that the thesis of determinism is true, and that accordingly all human behavior, voluntary or other, like the behavior of all other things, arises from antecedent conditions, given which no other behavior is possible—in short, that all human behavior is caused and determined; (2) that voluntary behavior is nonetheless free to the extent that it is not externally constrained or impeded; and (3) that, in the absence of such obstacles and constraints, the causes of voluntary behavior are certain states, events, or conditions within the agent himself; namely, his own acts of will or volitions, choices, decisions, desires, and so on.

Thus, on this view, I am free, and therefore sometimes responsible for what I do, provided nothing prevents me from acting according to my own choice, desire, or volition, or constrains me to act otherwise. There may, to be sure, be other conditions for my responsibility—such as, for example, an understanding of the probable consequences of my behavior, and that sort of thing—but absence of constraint or impediment is, at least, one such condition. And, it is claimed, it is a condition that is compatible with the supposition that my behavior is caused—for it is, by hypothesis, caused by my own inner choices, desires, and volitions.

## THE REFUTATION OF THIS

The theory of soft determinism looks good at first—so good that it has for generations been solemnly taught from innumerable philosophical chairs and implanted in the minds of students as sound philosophy—but no great acumen is needed to discover that far from solving any problem, it only camouflages it.

My free actions are those unimpeded and unconstrained motions that arise from my own inner desires, choices, and volitions; let us grant this provisionally. But now, whence arise those inner states that determine what my body shall do? Are they within my control or not? Having made my choice or decision and acted upon it, could I have chosen otherwise or not?

Here the determinist, hoping to surrender nothing and yet to avoid the problem implied in that question, bids us not to ask it; the question itself, he announces, is without meaning. For to say that I could have done otherwise, he says, means only that I *would* have done otherwise *if* those inner states that determined my action had been different; if, that is, I had decided or chosen differently. To ask, accordingly, whether I could have chosen or decided differently is only to ask whether, had I decided to decide differently or chosen to choose differently, or willed to will differently, I would have decided or chosen or willed differently. And this of course, *is* unintelligible nonsense.

But it is not nonsense to ask whether the causes of my actions—my own inner choices, decisions, and desires—are themselves caused. And of course they are, if determinism is true, for on that thesis everything is caused and determined. And if they are, then we cannot avoid concluding that, given the causal conditions of those inner states, I could not have decided, willed, chosen, or desired other than I in fact did, for this is a logical consequence of the very definition of determinism. Of course we can still say that, *if* the causes of these inner states, whatever they were, had been different, then their effects, those inner states themselves, would have been different, and that in this hypothetical sense I could have decided, chosen, willed, or desired differently—but that only pushes our problem back still another step. For we will then want to know whether the causes of those inner states were within my control, and so on *ad infinitum*. We are, at each step, permitted to say "could have been otherwise" only in a provisional sense—provided, that is, that something else had been different—but must then retract it and replace it with "could not have been otherwise" as soon as we discover, as we must at each step, that whatever would have to have been different could not have been different.

## EXAMPLES

Such is the dialectic of the problem. The easiest way to see the shadowy quality of soft determinism, however, is by means of examples.

Let us suppose that my body is moving in various ways, that these motions are not externally constrained or impeded, and that they are all exactly in accordance with my own desires, choices, or acts of will and whatnot. When I will that my arm should move in a certain way, I find it moving in that way, unobstructed and unconstrained. When I will to speak, my lips and tongue move, unobstructed and unconstrained, in a manner suitable to the formation of the words I choose to utter. Now, given that this is a correct description of my behavior, namely, that it consists of the unconstrained and unimpeded motions of my body in response to my own volitions, then it follows that my behavior is free, on the soft determinist's definition of "free." It follows further that I am responsible for that behavior; or at least, that if I am not, it is not from any lack of freedom on my part.

But if the fulfillment of these conditions renders my behavior free—that is to say, if my behavior satisfies the conditions of free action set forth in the theory of soft determinism—then my behavior will be no less free if we assume further conditions that are perfectly consistent with those already satisfied.

We suppose further, accordingly, that while my behavior is entirely in accordance with my own volitions, and thus "free" in terms of the conception of freedom we are examining, my volitions themselves are caused. To make this graphic, we can suppose that an ingenious physiologist can induce in me any volition he pleases, simply by pushing various buttons on an instrument to which, let us suppose, I am attached by numerous wires. All the volitions I have in that situation are, accordingly, precisely the ones he gives me. By pushing one button, he evokes in me the volition to raise my hand; and my hand, being unimpeded, rises in response to that volition. By pushing another, he induces the volition in me to kick, and my foot, being unimpeded, kicks in response to that volition. We can even suppose that the physiologist puts a rifle in my hands, aims it at some passerby, and then, by pushing the proper button, evokes in me the volition to squeeze my finger against the trigger, whereupon the passerby falls dead of a bullet wound.

This is the description of a man who is acting in accordance with his inner volitions, a man whose body is unimpeded and unconstrained in its motions, these motions being the effects of those inner states. It is hardly the description of a free and responsible agent. It is the perfect description of a puppet. To render someone your puppet, it is not necessary forcibly to constrain the motions of his limbs, after the fashion that real puppets are moved. A subtler but no less effective means of making a person your puppet would be to gain complete control of his inner states, and ensuring, as the theory of soft determinism does ensure, that his body will move in accordance with them.

The example is somewhat unusual, but it is no worse for that. It is perfectly intelligible, and it does appear to refute the soft determinist's conception of freedom. One might think that, in such a case, the agent should not have allowed himself to be so rigged in the first place, but this is irrelevant; we can suppose that he was not aware that he was and was hence unaware of the source of those inner states that prompted his bodily motions. The example can, moreover, be modified in perfectly realistic ways, so as to coincide with actual and familiar cases. One can, for instance, be given a compulsive desire for certain drugs, simply by having them administered over a course of time. Suppose, then, that I do, with neither my knowledge nor consent, thus become a victim of such a desire and act upon it. Do I act freely, merely by virtue of the fact that I am unimpeded in my quest for drugs? In a sense I do, surely, but I am hardly free with respect to whether or not I shall use drugs. I never chose to have the desire for them inflicted upon me.

Nor does it, of course, matter whether the inner states that allegedly prompt all my "free" activity are evoked in me by another agent or by perfectly impersonal forces. Whether a desire that causes my body to behave in a certain way is inflicted upon me by another person, for instance, or derived from hereditary factors, or indeed from anything at all, matters not the least. In any case, if it is in fact the cause of my bodily behavior, I cannot help but act in accordance with it. Wherever it came from, whether from personal or impersonal origins, it was entirely caused or determined, and not within my control. Indeed, if determinism is true, as the theory of soft determinism holds it to be, all those inner states that cause my body to behave in whatever ways it behaves must arise from circumstances that existed before I was born; for the chain of causes and effects is infinite, and none could have been the least different, given those that preceded.

## SIMPLE INDETERMINISM

We might at first now seem warranted in simply denying determinism, and saying that, insofar as they are free, my actions are not caused; or that, if they are caused by my own inner states—my own desires, impulses, choices, volitions, and whatnot—then these, in any case, are not caused. This is a perfectly clear sense in which a person's action, assuming that it was free, could have been otherwise. If it was uncaused, then, even given the conditions under which it occurred and all that preceded, some other act was nonetheless possible, and he did not have to do what he did. Or if his action was the inevitable consequence of his own inner states, and could not have been otherwise, given these, we can nevertheless say that these inner states, being uncaused, could have been otherwise, and could thereby have produced different actions.

Only the slightest consideration will show, however, that this simple denial of determinism has not the slightest plausibility. For let us suppose it is true, and that some of my bodily motions—namely, those that I regard as my free acts—are not caused at all or, if caused by my own inner states, that these are not caused. We shall thereby avoid picturing a puppet, to be sure—but only by substituting something even less like a human being; for the conception that now emerges is not that of a free person, but of an erratic and jerking phantom, without any rhyme or reason at all.

Suppose that my right arm is free, according to this conception; that is, that its motions are uncaused. It moves this way and that from time to time, but nothing causes these motions. Sometimes it moves forth vigorously, sometimes up, sometimes down, sometimes it just drifts vaguely about—these motions all being wholly free and uncaused. Manifestly I have nothing to do with them at all; they just happen, and neither I nor anyone can ever tell what this arm will be doing next. It might seize a club and lay it on the head of the nearest bystander, no less to my astonishment than his. There will never be any point in asking why these motions occur, or in seeking any explanation of them, for under the conditions assumed there is no explanation. They just happen, from no causes at all.

This is no description of free, voluntary, or responsible behavior. Indeed, so far as the motions of my body or its parts are entirely uncaused, such motions cannot even be ascribed to me as my behavior in the first place, since I have nothing to do with them. The behavior of my arm is just the random motion of a foreign object. Behavior that is mine must be behavior that is within my control, but motions that occur from no causes are beyond the control of anyone. I can have no more to do with, and no more control over, the uncaused motions of my limbs than a gambler has over the motions of an honest roulette wheel. I can only, like him, idly wait to see what happens.

Nor does it improve things to suppose that my bodily motions are caused by my own inner states, so long as we suppose these to be wholly uncaused. The result will be the same as before. My arm, for example, will move this way and that, sometimes up and sometimes down, sometimes vigorously and sometimes just drifting about, always in response to certain inner states, to be sure. But since these are supposed to be wholly uncaused, it follows that I have no control over them and hence none over their effects. If my hand lays a club forcefully on the nearest bystander, we can indeed say that this motion resulted from an inner club-wielding desire of mine; but we must add that I had nothing to do with that desire, and that it arose, to be followed by its inevitable effect, no less to my astonishment than to his. Things like this do, alas, sometimes happen. We are all sometimes seized by compulsive impulses that arise we know not whence, and we do sometimes act upon these. But because they are far from being examples of free, voluntary, and responsible behavior, we need only to learn that behavior was of this sort to conclude that it was not free, voluntary, or responsible. It was erratic, impulsive, and irresponsible.

## DETERMINISM AND SIMPLE INDETERMINISM AS THEORIES

Both determinism and simple indeterminism are loaded with difficulties, and no one who has thought much on them can affirm either of them without some embarrassment. Simple indeterminism has nothing whatever to be said for it, except that it appears to remove the grossest difficulties of determinism, only, however, to imply perfect absurdities of its own. Determinism, on the other hand, is at least initially plausible. People seem to have a natural inclination to believe in it; it is, indeed, almost required for the very exercise of practical intelligence. And beyond this, our experience appears always to confirm it, so long as we are dealing with everyday facts of common experience, as distinguished from the esoteric researches of theoretical physics. But determinism, as applied to human behavior, has implications that few can casually accept, and they appear to be implications that no modification of the theory can efface.

Both theories, moreover, appear logically irreconcilable to the two items of data that we set forth at the outset; namely, (1) that my behavior is sometimes the outcome of my deliberation, and (2) that in these and other cases it is sometimes up to me what I do. Because these were our data, it is important to see, as must already be quite clear, that these theories cannot be reconciled to them.

I can deliberate only about my own future actions, and then only if I do not already know what I am going to do. If a certain nasal tickle warns me that I am about to sneeze, for instance, then I cannot deliberate whether to sneeze or not; I can only prepare for the impending convulsion. But if determinism is true, then there are always conditions existing antecedently to everything I do, sufficient for my doing just that, and such as to render it inevitable. If I can know what those conditions are and what behavior they are sufficient to produce, then I can in every such case know what I am going to do and cannot then deliberate about it.

By itself this only shows, of course, that I can deliberate only in ignorance of the causal conditions of my behavior; it does not show that such conditions cannot exist. It is odd, however, to suppose that deliberation should be a mere substitute for clear knowledge. Ignorance is a condition of speculation, inference, and guesswork, which have nothing whatever to do with deliberation. A prisoner awaiting execution may not know when he is going to die, and he may even entertain the hope of reprieve, but he cannot deliberate about this. He can only speculate, guess—and wait.

Worse yet, however, it now becomes clear that I cannot deliberate about what I am going to do, if it is even *possible* for me to find out in advance, whether I do in fact find out in advance or not. I can deliberate only with the view to deciding what to do, to making up my mind; and this is impossible if I believe that it could be inferred what I am going to do from conditions already existing, even though I have not made that inference myself. If I believe that what I am going to do has been rendered inevitable by conditions already existing, and could be inferred by anyone having the requisite sagacity, then I cannot try to decide whether to do it or not, for there is simply nothing left to decide. I can at best only guess or try to figure it out myself or, all prognostics failing, I can wait and see; but I cannot deliberate. I deliberate in order to *decide* what *to* do, not to *discover* what it is that I am *going* to do. But if determinism is true, then there are always antecedent conditions sufficient for everything that I do, and this can always be inferred by anyone having the requisite sagacity;

that is, by anyone having a knowledge of what those conditions are and what behavior they are sufficient to produce.

This suggests what in fact seems quite clear, that determinism cannot be reconciled with our second datum either, to the effect that it is sometimes up to me what I am going to do. For if it is ever really up to me whether to do this thing or that, then, as we have seen, each alternative course of action must be such that I can do it; not that I can do it in some abstruse or hypothetical sense of "can"; not that I could do it if only something were true that is not true; but in the sense that it is then and there within my power to do it. But this is never so, if determinism is true, for on the very formulation of that theory whatever happens at any time is the only thing that can then happen, given all that precedes it. It is simply a logical consequence of this that whatever I do at any time is the only thing I can then do, given the conditions that precede my doing it. Nor does it help in the least to interpose, among the causal antecedents of my behavior, my own inner states, such as my desires, choices, acts of will, and so on. For even supposing these to be always involved in voluntary behavior—which is highly doubtful in itself—it is a consequence of determinism that these, whatever they are at any time, can never be other than what they then are. Every chain of causes and effects, if determinism is true, is infinite. This is why it is not now up to me whether I shall a moment hence be male or female. The conditions determining my sex have existed through my whole life, and even prior to my life. But if determinism is true, the same holds of anything that I ever am, ever become, or ever do. It matters not whether we are speaking of the most patent facts of my being, such as my sex; or the most subtle, such as my feelings, thoughts, desires, or choices. Nothing could be other than it is, given what was; and while we may indeed say, quite idly, that something—some inner state of mine, for instance—*could* have been different, had only something *else* been different, any consolation of this thought evaporates as soon as we add that whatever would have to have been different could not have been different.

It is even more obvious that our data cannot be reconciled to the theory of simple indeterminism. I can deliberate only about my own actions; this is obvious. But the random, uncaused motion of any body whatever, whether it be a part of my body or not, is no action of mine and nothing that is within my power. I might try to guess what these motions will be, just as I might try to guess how a roulette wheel will behave, but I cannot deliberate about them or try to decide what they shall be, simply because these things are not up to me. Whatever is not caused by anything is not caused by me, and nothing could be more plainly inconsistent with saying that it is nevertheless up to me what it shall be.

## THE THEORY OF AGENCY

The only conception of action that accords with our data is one according to which people—and perhaps some other things too—are sometimes, but of course not always, self-determining beings; that is, beings that are sometimes the causes of their own behavior. In the case of an action that is free, it must be such that it is caused by the agent who performs it, but such that no antecedent conditions were sufficient for his performing just that action. In the case of an action that is both free and rational, it must be such that the agent who performed it did so for some reason, but this reason cannot have been the cause of it.

Now, this conception fits what people take themselves to be; namely, beings who act, or who are agents, rather than things that are merely acted upon, and whose behavior is simply the causal consequence of conditions that they have not wrought. When I believe that I have done something, I do believe that it was I who caused it to be done, I who made something happen, and not merely something within me, such as one of my own subjective states, which is not identical with myself. If I believe that something not identical with myself was the cause of my behavior—some event wholly external to myself, for instance, or even one internal to myself, such as a nerve impulse, volition, or whatnot—then I cannot regard that behavior as being an act of mine, unless I further believe that I was the cause of that external or internal event. My pulse, for example, is caused and regulated by certain conditions existing within me, and not by myself. I do not, accordingly, regard this activity of my body as my action, and would be no more tempted to do so if I became suddenly conscious within myself of those conditions or impulses that produce it. This is behavior with which I have nothing to do, behavior that is not within my immediate control, behavior that is not only not free activity, but not even the activity of an agent to begin with; it is nothing but a mechanical reflex. Had I never learned that my very life depends on this pulse

beat, I would regard it with complete indifference, as something foreign to me, like the oscillations of a clock pendulum that I idly contemplate.

Now this conception of activity, and of an agent who is the cause of it, involves two rather strange metaphysical notions that are never applied elsewhere in nature. The first is that of a *self* or *person*—for example, a man—who is not merely a collection of things or events, but a self-moving being. For on this view it is a person, and not merely some part of him or something within him, that is the cause of his own activity. Now, we certainly do not know that a human being is anything more than an assemblage of physical things and processes that act in accordance with those laws that describe the behavior of all other physical things and processes. Even though he is a living being, of enormous complexity, there is nothing, apart from the requirements of this theory, to suggest that his behavior is so radically different in its origin from that of other physical objects, or that an understanding of it must be sought in some metaphysical realm wholly different from that appropriate to the understanding of nonliving things.

Second, this conception of activity involves an extraordinary conception of causation according to which an agent, which is a substance and not an event, can nevertheless be the cause of an event. Indeed, if he is a free agent then he can, on this conception, cause an event to occur—namely, some act of his own—without anything else causing him to do so. This means that an agent is sometimes a cause, without being an antecedent sufficient condition; for if I affirm that I am the cause of some act of mine, then I am plainly not saying that my very existence is sufficient for its occurrence, which would be absurd. If I say that my hand causes my pencil to move, then I am saying that the motion of my hand is, under the other conditions then prevailing, sufficient for the motion of the pencil. But if I then say that I cause my hand to move, I am not saying anything remotely like this, and surely not that the motion of my self is sufficient for the motion of my arm and hand, since these are the only things about me that are moving.

This conception of the causation of events by things that are not events is, in fact, so different from the usual philosophical conception of a cause that it should not even bear the same name, for "being a cause" ordinarily just means "being an antecedent sufficient condition or set of conditions." Instead, then, of speaking of agents as *causing* their own acts, it would perhaps be better to use another word entirely, and say, for instance, that they *originate* them, *initiate* them, or simply that they *perform* them.

Now this is, on the face of it, a dubious conception of what a person is. Yet it is consistent with our data, reflecting the presuppositions of deliberation, and appears to be the only conception that is consistent with them, as determinism and simple indeterminism are not. The theory of agency avoids the absurdities of simple indeterminism by conceding that human behavior is caused, while at the same time avoiding the difficulties of determinism by denying that every chain of causes and effects is infinite. Some such causal chains, on this view, have beginnings, and they begin with agents themselves. Moreover, if we are to suppose that it is sometimes up to me what I do, and understand this in a sense that is not consistent with determinism, we must suppose that I am an agent or a being who initiates his own actions, sometimes under conditions that do not determine what action I shall perform. Deliberation becomes, on this view, something that is not only possible but quite rational, for it does make sense to deliberate about activity that is truly my own and that depends in its outcome upon me as its author, and not merely upon something more or less esoteric that is supposed to be intimately associated with me, such as my thoughts, volitions, choices, or whatnot.

One can hardly affirm such a theory of agency with complete comfort, however, and wholly without embarrassment, for the conception of agents and their powers which is involved in it is strange indeed, if not positively mysterious. In fact, one can hardly be blamed here for simply denying our data outright, rather than embracing this theory to which they do most certainly point. Our data—to the effect that we do sometimes deliberate before acting, and that when we do, we presuppose among other things that it is up to us what we are going to do—rest upon nothing more than fairly common consent. These data might simply be illusions. It might in fact be that no one ever deliberates but only imagines that he does, that from pure conceit he supposes himself to be the master of his behavior and the author of his acts. Spinoza has suggested that if a stone, having been thrown into the air, were suddenly to become conscious, it would suppose itself to be the source of its own motion, being then conscious of what it was doing but not aware of the real cause of its behavior. Certainly we are *sometimes* mistaken in believing that we are behaving as a result of choice deliberately arrived at. A man might, for example, easily imagine that his embarking upon matrimony is the result of the most careful and rational deliberation, when in fact the causes, perfectly sufficient for that behavior, might be of an entirely physiological, unconscious origin. If it is sometimes false that we deliberate and then act as the result of a decision deliberately arrived at, even when we suppose it to be true, it might always be false. No one seems able, as we have noted, to describe deliberation without metaphors, and the conception of a thing's being "within one's power" or "up to him" seems to defy analysis or definition altogether, if taken in a sense that the theory of agency appears to require.

These are, then, dubitable conceptions, despite their being so well implanted in common sense. Indeed, when we turn to the theory of fatalism, we shall find formidable metaphysical considerations that appear to rule them out altogether. Perhaps here, as elsewhere in metaphysics, we should be content with discovering difficulties, with seeing what is and what is not consistent with such convictions as we happen to have, and then drawing such satisfaction as we can from the realization that, no matter where we begin, the world is mysterious and that we who try to understand it are even more so. This realization can, with some justification, make one feel wise, even in the full realization of his ignorance.

# DISCUSSION: Hard Determinism

> Man's life is a line that nature commands him to describe upon the surface of
> the earth, without his ever being able to swerve from it, even for an instant.
> He is born without his own consent; his organization does in nowise depend
> upon himself; his ideas come to him involuntarily; his habits are in the power
> of those who cause him to contract them; he is unceasingly modified by
> causes, whether visible or concealed, over which he has no control, which
> necessarily regulate his mode of existence, give the hue to his way of thinking,
> and determine his manner of acting.
>
> Baron d'Holbach, *The System of Nature* (1770),
> Chapter 11, trans. H. D. Robinson.

Hard determinists have a twofold task. First, they have to persuade us that
determinism is true. Second, they must argue for the incompatibilist thesis
that *if* determinism is true, then no one ever acts freely. In this second task,
they are aided and abetted by libertarians who, like the hard determinists, are
also incompatibilists. In recent years, the strongest defense of incompatibilism
has come from libertarians.

## PHYSICAL AND PSYCHOLOGICAL DETERMINISM

In the past, determinism was often understood as the proposition that all
events, including all human actions, are caused. The German philosopher
Arthur Schopenhauer (1788–1869), writing in the nineteenth century,
claimed that this is known to be true *a priori*, that is, independently of
experience.[1] According to Schopenhauer, what he calls the law of causality
is derivable from the Principle of Sufficient Reason. The American philosopher John Hospers, writing in the twentieth century, disagrees with Schopenhauer. Hospers appeals to empirical evidence, mainly from psychoanalysis,
to support his contention that determinism prevails in the psychological
realm.[2]

Whatever misgivings we may have about psychoanalysis as a legitimate science, I think we should side with Hospers in regarding the truth (or falsity) of
determinism as an empirical matter. It is important to distinguish here between "All effects have causes" and "All events have causes." On the one hand,
"All effects have causes" is a necessary truth, since the term *effect* simply means
"something that is caused." It is a tautology to assert that all effects have
causes, just as it would be to assert that all brothers have siblings. On the other
hand, "All events have causes" is not a necessary truth and might well be false,
just as is the claim that all persons have siblings. In the light of the empirical
success of quantum mechanics, it is difficult to argue that determinism must be
true or that it is impossible for an event to occur without being caused by some
prior event.

Even if the evidence from science were unanimously in favor of physical determinism, it is still possible that psychological determinism is false. As we have seen in our discussion of the mind-body problem, the truth of reductive materialism is not a foregone conclusion. We cannot simply argue that psychological determinism is true (that is, roughly, that motives, beliefs, and desires are the sufficient mental causes of human action) because physical and neurophysiological determinism is true, unless we can show that mental causes are reducible to physical and neurophysiological ones.[3]

In fact, most determinists (whether soft or hard) from Hume to Schopenhauer claim that psychological determinism is true without even attempting to reduce all mental states to physical ones. Most of their discussions take place at the level of folk psychology. Pitching the debate at the ordinary, everyday level of talk about mental causation emphasizes the empirical character of psychological determinism, which is both an advantage and a liability. It is an advantage, since it avoids complicated and unresolved issues in neurophysiology and philosophy of mind; it is a liability for determinists, since they have to argue against the apparent evidence from introspection that many of our choices are *not* completely determined by our beliefs, motives, and desires. Similarly, though Hume and other determinists stress the predictability of human behavior, they admit that our predictions are not perfect; people do occasionally surprise us by acting contrary to expectation. Thus, the evidence does not point conclusively to the truth of determinism.

It is important not to underestimate the difficulty of showing that psychological determinism is true. We cannot appeal to the presumed truth of physical determinism unless we also argue for reductive materialism. We cannot appeal to the necessary truth of determinism, since it appears to be an empirical claim, not one known to be true *a priori*. If we appeal to introspection and folk-psychological explanations of human action, then we have to deal with the apparent counterevidence. We cannot simply appeal, as Schopenhauer does, to the principle that the will is always moved by the strongest motive and compare this to the way that a body moves under the action of the greatest force exerted on it. The analogy with physical forces is imperfect and misleading. We have an exact rule for determining the vector sum of a number of different forces applied to the same object; it is not simply that the "strongest" force wins out over all the others. Forces are additive in a way that motives are not. Also, the vector sum rule for physical forces is empirical and testable: in principle each individual force can be measured. No such method exists for identifying motives and measuring their strength. In fact, the claim that the will is always moved by the strongest motive has every appearance of being a tautology. Which motive was the strongest? The one that prevailed! If the strongest motive principle is a tautology, then it is irrelevant to the empirical doctrine of psychological determinism.

## FREEDOM AND NECESSITY

Why are hard determinists convinced that determinism is logically incompatible with free will? One common argument begins with the premise that causes necessitate their effects. If determinism is true, then all events (including exertions of human will) are caused. Anything that is necessitated is unfree. Thus, it is concluded that the will is not free. We can sketch the argument as follows:

### The Necessitation Argument

(1) All human actions are caused by prior events.

(2) Causes necessitate their effects.

(3) Any action that is necessitated is not free.

---

(4) No human action is free.

The claim that causes necessitate their effects can be interpreted in at least two ways. One interpretation rests on a rather controversial theory of causation—the necessitation theory, which is examined in the discussion entitled "Causality" in Part V of this book. Another interpretation, which has been widely adopted by philosophers, analyzes the relation between causes and effects in terms of the logical derivability of statements. From the statement that C (the cause) occurs, we can logically deduce that E (the effect) will occur, given the law of nature that C's always produce E's.[4] In fact, it has become common to use this idea of deducibility from statements about prior events and laws of nature to give a more precise definition of what it means for an event to be determined.[5] The advantage of this approach is that it avoids philosophical disputes about the nature of causation while at the same time reflecting the law-governed nature of the world revealed by science. Thus, from now on we will adopt the following definition:

**Determinism:** An event (or state of affairs), E, is determined if and only if there is a set of prior events (or states of affairs), C, and laws of nature, L, such that C and L together entail E.

Because we often think of laws of nature as having a special kind of physical necessity, it is tempting to assume that this necessity automatically transfers to the events or states of affairs determined by them. Consider the following example:

(1) If a body of M kilograms experiences a net force of F newtons, then its acceleration must be A meters per second per second.

(2) X is a body of M kilograms that experiences a net force of F newtons.

---

(3) X must have an acceleration of A meters per second per second.

Here we have reached, by what appears to be a valid argument, the conclusion that the effect—the acceleration event—is physically necessary, that it must occur; but the appearance of validity here is deceptive. The physical necessity of the first premise cannot be validly transmitted to the conclusion unless the second premise is also necessary in exactly the same sense. In other words, I am claiming that the argument is really of the following, invalid, form:

(1) [Necessarily] If a body of M kilograms experiences a net force of F newtons, then its acceleration is A meters per second per second.

(2) X is a body of M kilograms that experiences a net force of F newtons.

---

(3) [Necessarily] X has an acceleration of A meters per second per second.

The general form of this argument is

(1) [Necessarily] If P then Q
(2) P
_____
(3) [Necessarily] Q

We can readily see that this is an invalid form of argument by inspecting the following instance of it:

(1) [Necessarily] If I have five coins in my pocket, then there is an odd number of coins in my pocket.
(2) I have five coins in my pocket.
_____
(3) [Necessarily] There is an odd number of coins in my pocket.

The first premise is logically necessary because it follows directly from the mathematical truth that five is an odd number. But the conclusion is false. No law of logic prevents me from removing a single coin from my pocket; it is logically possible that my pocket contain an even number of coins. So, the argument is invalid.

We thus see that for the Necessitation Argument to be valid, premise (2)— "Causes necessitate their effects"—must mean "All events that are caused are necessary." But even if we agree that laws of nature are necessary, it does not follow that the events produced in accordance with those laws are necessary.

What we would need to prove that any event, E, that is determined is physically necessary is the following kind of argument, which *is* valid:

(1) [Necessarily] If (C and L) then E
(2) [Necessarily] C
(3) [Necessarily] L
_____
(4) [Necessarily] E

Only if the prior events, C, are physically necessary in the same sense that the laws of nature, L, are can we validly conclude that the effect event, E, is physically necessary. It is sometimes claimed that all events must be physically necessary because determinism applies to *all* events stretching back into the infinite past; but this reasoning must fail. No matter how many repeated applications we make of an unsound argument, the result will be an unsound argument chain.

## FREEDOM AND CONTROL

At this point, hard determinists and other incompatibilists bring the notion of control into the debate.[6] They concede that the truth of determinism does not imply that all events are physically necessary. But, they argue, if all events are determined by prior events and laws of nature, then at any particular time, $T_2$, what happens at that time lies outside of all human control. It is conceded that event E at time $T_2$ did not *have* to happen, since the occurrence of E depends, in part, on events, C, that are themselves contingent, occurring at the prior time, $T_1$. Nonetheless, it is argued, *because $T_1$ now lies in the past,* no one has any control over the fact that C occurred. Since no one has any control over the laws of nature, L, it follows that no one has any control over E, which is entailed by C and L. When event E is a human action, to refrain from performing E now lies outside of anyone's control. If any event lies outside of our control, then we are not free with respect to it. Thus, it is concluded that determinism implies a complete lack of human freedom with respect to any action at any time.

Before proceeding further, it will be helpful to outline the logical skeleton of this type of control argument for incompatibilism.

### The Control Argument

(In the outline of this argument, [NC] stands for "No one has any control at time $T_2$ over the fact that . . . " or "No one can alter, change, prevent, or influence in any way at time $T_2$ the fact that. . . . ")

(1) [NC] C
(2) [NC] L
(3) [NC] If (C and L) then E
_____
(4) [NC] E

The Control Argument appears to be valid. Without the [NC] prefixes, it is certainly valid; and if no one has any control over the premises of a valid argument, then it would seem that no one has any control over the conclusion logically implied by those premises.[7]

Premises (2) and (3) seem unassailable. We do not usually think that it is within our power to change in any way the laws of nature. Similarly, if L and C together entail E, then this is an objective logical fact that no one can alter. But what about premise (1)? In the version of the Control Argument stated earlier, the reason given for thinking that C lies outside of anyone's control, now at $T_2$, is that C occurred in the past at $T_1$. The principle that no one can change the past is widely accepted. It is reflected in such sayings as "It's no use crying over spilt milk" that express a fundamental conviction that causal chains always run from the past to the future and never in the opposite direction. Thus, it seems that the Control Argument is sound.

We could argue that though the Control Argument is sound, it does not really establish an *interesting* version of incompatibilism. This is because even though E is outside our control at $T_2$—the time of its occurrence—we might still have had control over E at earlier times. Consider, for example, the following sequence of event: at $T_1$ I decide to jump off a chair; a split second later, at $T_2$, my legs propel me into space; a fraction of a second after that, at $T_3$, I am accelerating towards the floor in accordance with Newton's law of gravity. Let us agree that *at $T_3$* I have no control over the fact that I am falling; nothing I can do *at that time* can prevent my acceleration towards the floor. Nonetheless, I could have decided at $T_1$ not to jump, and if I had so decided, my leg muscles would not have contracted at $T_2$ and I would not be falling at $T_3$. Thus, I had control *at $T_1$* over what would happen later, and it is this sort of control that is relevant to the free-will debate.

We can summarize this criticism as follows. All that the Control Argument establishes is that we lack control over events and actions in a trivial sense; namely, we lack the power at the time that events and actions are occurring to do anything *at that time* about their prior causes. Imagine, as we did in the example of jumping off the chair, that under the right conditions, my deciding at

$T_1$ to do X inevitably determines that I do X at $T_2$ a split second later. The defender of free will can easily acknowledge that (1) at $T_2$ it lies outside my power to alter the fact that I willed at $T_1$ to do X and (2) given that I willed at $T_1$ to do X in the right conditions, my doing X at $T_2$ was determined. What the hard determinist has to show is that we also lack control in the interesting sense, namely, that we are powerless *at all times prior to $T_2$* to determine or affect our actions at $T_2$. For example, the incompatibilist has to show how determinism implies that it is not up to me prior to $T_1$ whether or not I decide at $T_1$ to do X.

Incompatibilists think that they can meet this challenge by repeated applications of the Control Argument to earlier and earlier events. E is determined by prior events, C; C in turn is determined by earlier events, B. If we trace back the causal chain sufficiently far, we will end up with some set of events, Z, all of which occurred during the age of the dinosaurs, well before human beings first appeared on the planet. Evidently, no human could ever have had any control over Z. Given the laws of nature, Z determines Y, Y determines X, and so on until we reach E, which is someone's action occurring right now. Let us call this the Dinosaur Argument.

Does the Dinosaur Argument establish the truth of incompatibilism? The correct answer to this question is "No." As stated, the Dinosaur Argument is invalid. Determinism says that every event is determined by earlier events. It does not follow logically from this definition of determinism that the chain of events must stretch back indefinitely far into the past.[8] All that determinism implies is that the chain of determined events has no first member. Every event is determined by a prior event; but it is logically possible that each member of the entire infinite set of events takes place no earlier than some designated time, say two hours prior to the present. How is this possible? Imagine that, starting with event E in the present, the time interval between E and C is one hour, the gap between C and B is one-half hour, the gap between B and A is one-quarter hour, and so on. The sum of the infinite series 1, ½, ¼, ⅛, . . . is two hours. Therefore, no event in the infinite chain that determines E takes place more than two hours before E.

There are several responses the hard determinist might make at this stage. First, the hard determinist might stipulate that the Gap Hypothesis is true. The Gap Hypothesis says that the length of time between a cause and its effect always exceeds some specified interval, say a millionth of a second. If this were true, then adding the Gap Hypothesis to the premises of the Dinosaur Argument would turn the Dinosaur Argument into a valid argument. But the hard determinist needs to give us a reason for thinking that the Gap Hypothesis is true. Why does there have to be a smallest interval of time between a cause and its effect? Notice that the hard determinist cannot argue for the Gap Hypothesis simply by requiring that events not be simultaneous with their causes, since every effect in the infinite series described in the previous paragraph occurs later than its cause. What we need is a reason for believing that the finite interval between cause and effect cannot be indefinitely small.

Second, the hard determinist might simply change her definition of determinism. Indeed, some incompatibilists begin by assuming that determinism means that given the laws of nature, the state of the world at any given time completely determines everything that happens later.[9] This type of determinism is sometimes called window shade determinism because it implies that if the history of the world were rolled back to some time in the past and then allowed to run forward, exactly the same sequence of events would unfold as before. In other words, according to window shade determinism, at all times the world has only one physically possible future.

Using window shade determinism, the hard determinist can simply let C be a complete description of the world during the age of the dinosaurs and use the Control Argument to move *directly* to the conclusion that no one has any control over any event E in the present. The hard determinist *can* do this but she then has to explain why we should believe that determinism *in this sense*— window shade determinism—is true. Granted, there are many scientific examples of events that, in a strictly controlled setting, are determined by earlier events. Putting a piece of zinc in hydrochloric acid, for example, will cause it to dissolve, giving off hydrogen. Also, there are very simple systems that are so isolated from outside influences that we can make reasonably precise predictions about their behavior. For example, we can make quite good predictions about the future positions of the planets as they orbit around the sun. But we have no examples at all of successful predictions of everything that will happen from a knowledge of the state of the entire world at an earlier time and the laws of nature.

As we noted at the beginning of this section, traditional hard determinists argue for two theses: (1) that determinism is true and (2) that determinism and freedom are incompatible. In light of the difficulties in establishing that either of these claims is true, the hard determinist might settle for something more modest. The hard determinist could say that regardless of whether determinism in either of its two senses is true, we know that everything humans do is, as a matter of empirical fact, determined by prior events that lie outside their control. The focus is thus shifted from metaphysical arguments to the credentials of scientific theories in genetics, developmental psychology, and neurophysiology. The problem with this move is that there is no currently available, well-confirmed scientific theory of the causes of human action— whether appeal is made to genetic inheritance, neuroses formed in the cradle, upbringing and environment, or hormonal changes in the brain—that actually supports the generalization that *all* human actions are caused by events beyond the control of the agent. Few theories imply such a sweeping generalization, and those that do are not well confirmed. At best, we have a limited understanding of some of the factors that partially determine some of the things that human beings do and say. Thus, the scientific support for asserting that no human actions are free is very slim.

## NOTES

1. Schopenhauer's position, which he derived from Kant, is more subtle than this summary suggests. The law of causality is supposed to be a necessary condition for the possibility of experience. See A. Schopenhauer, *Essay on the Freedom of the Will* (1841); trans. K. Kolenda (Indianapolis: Bobbs-Merrill, 1960).

2. See J. Hospers, "Free Will and Psychoanalysis," in W. Sellers and J. Hospers, Eds., *Readings in Ethical Theory* (New York: Appleton-Century-Crofts, 1952): 560–575; J. Hospers, "What Means This Freedom?" in S. Hook, Ed., *Determinism and Freedom In the Age of Modern Science* (New York: Macmillan, 1961): 126–142.

3. In his article "Freedom, Spontaneity and Indifference," in T. Honderich, Ed., *Essays on Freedom of Action* (London: Routledge & Kegan Paul, 1973): 89–104, Anthony Kenny explains why—even if human actions are identical with physical events and all physical events are

determined—it does not follow from this identity that all human actions are determined. Kenny argues that "being determined" is a property to which Leibniz's Principle of the Indiscernibility of Identicals does not apply.

4. In "Actions, Predictions, and Books of Life" (Reading 32), Alvin Goldman explores the relationship between determinism and predictability. For logical reasons, some actions (such as Sam's inventing the corkscrew in 1625) cannot be predicted prior to their occurrence. These logical exceptions aside, determinism does imply the possibility, in principle, of prediction. Goldman argues that there is no reason that a person's actions cannot be predicted, even if that person knows what the prediction is before she performs the action. Goldman is a compatibilist: he argues that determinism and predictability-in-principle are consistent with choice, deliberation, and voluntary action.

5. See Goldman's definition of determinism in Reading 32.

6. For a more sophisticated discussion of the control argument and responses to it, see P. Van Inwagen, *An Essay on Free Will* (Oxford: Clarendon Press, 1983); C. Ginet, "In Defense of Incompatibilism," *Philosophical Studies* 44 (1983): 391–400; D. Lewis, "Are We Free to Break the Laws?" *Theoria* 3 (1981): 113–121; M. Fischer, "Freedom and Miracles," *Noûs* 22 (1988): 235–252; M. Fischer, Ed., *Moral Responsibility* (Ithaca, NY: Cornell University Press, 1986); and T. Horgan, "Compatibilism and the Consequence Argument," *Philosophical Studies* 47 (1985): 339–356.

7. In "Selective Necessity and the Free-Will Problem," *Journal of Philosophy* 79 (1982): 5–24, Michael Slote argues that the Control Argument is invalid. Slote's point is that the necessity symbolized as [NC] in the premises of the Control Argument is selective because it selects factors that bring something about (or make something true) without involving any of the desires and abilities that the agent has *now* when action E is performed. The premises of the argument are true. But, Slote argues, the conclusion is false. When the agent performs action E, this event *does* depend on the desires and abilities that the agent has at that time.

8. See J. H. Sobel, "Determinism: A Small Point," *Dialogue* 14 (1975): 617–621. My discussion at this point is substantially indebted to Sobel's lucid treatment.

9. Some go even further and assume that determinism means that a complete description of the world at a given time determines everything that happens at every other time, whether future or past. This version of determinism is what the American philosopher C. S. Peirce (1839–1914) called the doctrine of necessity in his essay "The Doctrine of Necessity Examined." It was this extreme version of determinism that the French mathematician Laplace (1749–1827) endorsed in a famous passage from his *A Philosophical Essay on Probabilities* (1814): if a sufficiently powerful intelligence (God?) knew at a given time the position, velocity, and mass of every particle in the universe and the forces acting on those particles, then it could infallibly deduce the entire past and future of the universe.

# **DISCUSSION:** Compatibilism and Soft Determinism

All that is certain about the matter is: (1) that, if we have Free Will, it must be true, in *some* sense, that we sometimes *could* have done what we did not do; (2) that, if everything is caused, it must be true, in *some* sense, that we *never could* have done, what we did not do. What is very *un*certain, and what certainly needs to be investigated, is whether these two meanings of the word "could" are the same.

G. E. Moore, *Ethics* (1912)
(New York: Oxford University Press, 1978), page 90.

We can learn much about compatibilism and soft determinism by considering how compatibilists such as David Hume and Walter Stace (1886–1967) would respond to the argument for incompatibilism that I outlined in the introduction to Part IV.

### The Incompatibilist Argument

(A)  If determinism is true, then S could not have done otherwise.
(B)  If S acts freely, then S could have done otherwise.
_____
(I)   If determinism is true, then S does not act freely.

The underlying form of this argument can be written as

If D, then not-O
If F,  then O
_____
If D, then not-F

One can see that this form of argument is valid by comparing it with another argument that uses exactly the same pattern of reasoning.

If Sam is in Detroit, then Sam is not in Europe.
If Sam is in France, then Sam is in Europe.
_____
If Sam is in Detroit, then Sam is not in France.

This argument is certainly valid. Detroit lies outside of Europe, and France lies inside Europe; thus, if Sam is in Detroit, he cannot be in France. Since the Incompatibilist Argument has exactly the same form, it too is valid.

The compatibilist who wants to deny the conclusion of the Incompatibilist Argument has to show that the argument is unsound. This can be attempted in two ways: either (1) argue that the argument is unsound because, despite appearances to the contrary, it is invalid or (2) accept that it is valid but deny that both its premises are true. In Chapter 6 of his book *Ethics* (1912), G. E. Moore adopted the first strategy. Moore argued that the Incompatibilist Argument commits the fallacy of equivocation because "could" in premise (A) has a different meaning from "could" in premise (B). In other words, Moore denied that the Incompatibilist Argument has the valid underlying form written above. We will explore the second strategy, though most of the points we shall be making on behalf of the compatibilist are the same as those made by Moore.

## HUME'S DEFINITION OF LIBERTY

David Hume attempts to reconcile "liberty" (acting freely) with "necessity" (determinism) in Section VIII of his *An Enquiry Concerning Human Understanding* (Reading 30). After elaborating his reasons for thinking that psychological determinism is true, Hume gives the following definition of liberty or acting freely.

> By liberty, then, we can only mean *a power of acting or not acting, according to the determinations of the will;* that is, if we choose to remain at rest, we may; if we choose to move, we also may. Now this hypothetical liberty is universally allowed to belong to everyone who is not a prisoner and in chains.

In this passage, Hume follows John Locke in regarding two conditions to be individually necessary and jointly sufficient for acting freely.[1]

**The Locke/Hume Definition of Acting Freely:** S is free with respect to doing X if and only if (1) S can do X if he chooses and (2) S can refrain from doing X if he chooses.[2]

Locke is especially clear about there being two independent conditions here. An action can satisfy the first condition—and thus be what Locke calls a voluntary action—without satisfying the second condition. Locke gives the example of a man who is conveyed while asleep into a room which is then locked. On waking, the man finds himself in the company of friends and stays in the room willingly. According to Locke, the man remains in the room voluntarily, because he is doing what he wants to do; but he does not act freely in staying there, since if he chose to leave he would be unable to do so. Similarly, the paralyzed woman who chooses to remain seated in her wheelchair acts voluntarily but not freely. Freedom in the full sense requires the ability to do otherwise.

Some soft determinists give what appears to be a different definition of acting freely by requiring merely that the causes of the action be internal to the agent. Walter Stace, for example, in his *Religion and the Modern Mind* (1952), says the following:

> Acts freely done are those whose immediate causes are psychological states in the agent. Acts not freely done are those whose immediate causes are states of affairs external to the agent.[3]

Since internal psychological states include acts of will, Stace's definition corresponds roughly to the first condition of Locke and Hume; but Stace's discussion of free action reveals that Stace assumes that their second condition will also be satisfied by free actions. For example, Stace writes of people who act freely that "we should also say they could have acted otherwise, *if they had chosen*" (my emphasis).[4] Stace also remarks that someone who lied could have told the truth because the person could have told the truth *if he had wanted to*.[5] This suggests that Stace, like the other soft determinists, believes that acting freely implies that one could have done otherwise.

## THE CONDITIONAL ANALYSIS OF FREEDOM

Let us now return to the Incompatibilist Argument. The soft determinists we have been discussing would accept premise (B) but reject premise (A). In other words, these soft determinists agree with the libertarian and the hard determinist that S acts freely only if S could have done otherwise, but they think that it is false that determinism implies that S could not have done otherwise.[6]

The soft determinist rejection of premise (A) rests on a *conditional* analysis of what it means to say that S could have done otherwise. (This is why Hume calls his variety of compatibilist freedom *hypothetical* liberty, since *hypothetical* is just another word for *conditional* or anything involving an "if . . . then . . . " clause.)

**The Conditional Analysis of Freedom:** "S could have done otherwise" means "S could have done otherwise if S had chosen to do otherwise."

If this analysis were correct it would refute premise (A), since that premise would now read:

(A*) If determinism is true, then it is not the case that [if S had chosen to do otherwise, S could have done otherwise].

Determinism implies that S's action is the determined outcome of S's mental states. The last step in the psychological chain that produces an action is the act of choice, will, or volition, and it is that last step that determines whether the resulting action will be of one kind rather than another. Thus, (A*) is false, since if determinism is true, then if S had chosen differently, S would (and hence could) have acted differently.

Both hard determinists (such as Schopenhauer) and libertarians (such as Richard Taylor) have argued convincingly that adopting the Conditional Analysis of Freedom does not allow the soft determinist to refute incompatibilism. Paul Edwards, in "Hard and Soft Determinism" (Reading 31), quotes Schopenhauer's aphorism: "A man can surely do what he wills to do, but he cannot determine what he wills." These critics of soft determinism point out that if determinism is true, then S could not have chosen or willed otherwise, since S's act of choice or will, like every other event, is completely determined; and if S could not have chosen or willed otherwise, then S could not have done otherwise. Thus, the incompatibilist can simply replace the original premise (A) with (C) and (D), and the argument goes through as before.

(C) If determinism is true, then S could not have chosen otherwise.
(D) If S could not have chosen otherwise, then S could not have done otherwise.
(B) If S acts freely, then S could have done otherwise.

(I) If determinism is true, then S does not act freely.

The prospects for the soft determinist's being able to criticize this new version of the Incompatibilist Argument are not rosy. The soft determinist who attacks premise (C) by again invoking the Conditional Analysis of Freedom has to make sense of the notions of "choosing to choose" or "willing to will." In his "Freedom and Determinism" (Reading 35), Richard Taylor dismisses such notions as "unintelligible nonsense." Even if these notions do make sense, the incompatibilist can respond by adding yet another premise, and so on.[7]

## THE COUNTERFACTUAL INTERVENER ARGUMENT

Given the problems with trying to refute premise (A) of the Incompatibilist Argument [or premise (C) of the revised version], what about attacking premise (B)? Perhaps the soft determinists were mistaken in assuming that acting freely implies that one could have done otherwise. Perhaps something like Stace's definition might suffice. The basic intuition here is that one acts freely if and only if one's action is caused by one's own mental states in the right sort of way. If this condition is satisfied, then one freely does what one wants to do regardless of whether there is anything else that one could have done instead in that same situation. The picture to have in mind is that of a woman who gets on an elevator and presses the button for the ninth floor because that is where she wants to go. The elevator takes her to her desired destination; but unbeknownst to her, its control mechanism has been rigged so that it would have gone to the ninth floor no matter which button she pressed. As long as she gets to go where she wants, why should it matter that she could not have gone anywhere else?

A persuasive argument for the falsity of premise (B) is given by the American philosopher Harry Frankfurt in his article, "Alternate Possibilities and Moral Responsibility."[8] Imagine that Black is a powerful, intelligent scientist who is able to predict what I am going to will (and hence do) just a split second before I actually have the volition and then perform the action. Black strongly desires that I perform a certain action at a given time, say the action of snapping my fingers at noon. He waits to see if I am going to form the volition to snap my fingers. If I am going to will the action all by myself, he will stand back and do nothing; he will not intervene. If he sees that I am not going to will the action, he will cause me to have the volition in my mind just before noon, which will then result in my snapping my fingers at noon. How does Black cause this volition in me? Frankfurt suggests that Black might utter an irresistible threat or hypnotically implant in me an inner compulsion or directly manipulate my brain. The exact mechanism is not important, just as long as Black is able to make me will to snap my fingers at noon.

Under the conditions just described, I will snap my fingers at noon no matter what. Either I will choose to perform the action free from any outside intervention or I will be caused to choose that action if Black predicts that I will not choose it if left to myself. With respect to noonday finger snapping, it is false that I could have done otherwise. Admittedly, if Black does intervene and causes me to choose, then, just like the puppet man described by Richard Taylor, I will not be acting freely. But suppose that I form my volition in the usual way and act on it *without Black's intervening at all*. Surely in this case I still act freely, even though it is false that I could have done otherwise.

In everyday life, we often accept the plea "I could not have done otherwise" ("I was forced to do X," "I had no choice about doing X") as absolving someone from moral responsibility. Whether it is a bank teller who is forced to hand over money at gunpoint or the athlete struggling to overcome an addiction to painkillers, we excuse persons whose actions were compelled or coerced by forces that they are incapable of resisting.

In his article, Frankfurt tries to explain why we falsely believe that acting freely (being morally responsible for our actions) implies that we could have done otherwise. His explanation is that when we excuse someone for doing X, we often fail to distinguish (a) "He was unable to do otherwise" from (b) "He did X *only because* he was unable to do otherwise." Frankfurt argues that when we accept (a) as an excusing condition [and thus, apparently, endorse premise (B) of the Incompatibilist Argument], this is because we understand it to mean the slightly different claim (b). If X were an action that person P genuinely wished to perform and would have performed even if P had had other choices, then P is responsible for X (performs X freely), even though in P's actual situation, X was the only action P could have performed. As Frankfurt points out, accepting this analysis does not prove that compatibilism is true, but it does undermine one of the major arguments against it.

## THE HIERARCHICAL ANALYSIS OF FREEDOM

Our discussion thus far has been largely negative: on the one hand the Conditional Analysis of Freedom favored by many traditional compatibilists is unsatisfactory; on the other hand, the key incompatibilist premise—that acting freely implies the ability to have done otherwise—has been undermined by Frankfurt's Counterfactual Intervener Argument. So, the ball is back in the compatibilist's court. Can the compatibilist give a positive account of acting freely that is consistent with determinism?

Since the 1970s, some philosophers, notably Gerald Dworkin and Harry Frankfurt, have proposed what I shall call the Hierarchical (or double-decker) Analysis of Freedom.[9] One way to approach this new account is to see it as a refinement of the familiar idea that actions are free when they are uncoerced. A paradigm case of coercion is the bank teller—I shall call him Marcel—who hands over money to a robber at gunpoint. Though Marcel is threatened with death, he has a genuine choice: he can refuse and be shot, or consent and live. He chooses to hand over the money but does so unwillingly or, as we say, "against his will."[10]

Frankfurt analyzes this kind of coerced choice by introducing the notion of a second-order volition. A second-order volition is a special kind of second-order desire: it is the desire that a particular kind of first-order motive be the one that moves us to act. According to Frankfurt, it is the possession of such second-order volitions that distinguishes persons (capable of acting freely) from other sorts of creature. Young children and severely retarded adults have first-order desires, but without second-order volitions, they are merely what Frankfurt calls wantons. Wantons fail to be persons because they are incapable of caring about which of their wishes and desires are the ones that lead them to act.

The core of Frankfurt's double-decker theory is that an action is coerced—and hence unfree—when it results from a volition that conflicts with a second-order volition. This conflict with a second-order volition is intended to capture the sense in which coerced actions are performed unwillingly. A person, P, acts unfreely when a coercive threat (or offer) causes X to act from a desire that P would prefer not to have acted from.

**The Hierarchical Analysis of Acting Freely:** P performed X freely if and only if P did X because it conformed to P's second-order volition to act from the motive that resulted in P's doing X.[11]

Several objections have been raised to Frankfurt's proposal. I will focus on two questions: Is conformity with second-order volitions sufficient for someone to act freely (and hence be morally responsible for her actions)? and Is such conformity necessary?

### Is Frankfurt's Condition Sufficient for Acting Freely?

Let us explore further the case of the reluctant bank teller. When Marcel decides to cooperate with the bank robber, he is responding to a situation that he would prefer not to have been in. But now that he is forced to choose, Marcel decides to avoid injury and possible death by surrendering the money. According to Frankfurt's proposal, if Marcel was coerced, then he would have preferred not to have played it safe and, presumably, wished instead to have been prompted to act by some other desire, such as the desire to resist. But it does not seem at all plausible to attribute to Marcel the second-order volition to act from some desire other than prudence. Marcel does not regret his action in the slightest. He resents having been put in the situation, but he does not disapprove of the motive that guided his action. So, Marcel satisfies Frankfurt's condition. Frankfurt's theory thus implies that this is a case of free, uncoerced action for which Marcel is morally responsible. Yet few of us would blame Marcel for his action or hold him morally responsible for it. Our natural reaction is to regard Marcel's action as coerced and unfree. If our natural reaction is correct, then Frankfurt's condition is not sufficient for acting freely.[12]

Frankfurt's response to this kind of objection is instructive. Towards the end of his paper "Three Concepts of Free Action," Frankfurt writes:

> . . . assuming that we do regard the clerk as acting freely, the reason we refrain from blaming him is not that we think he bears no moral responsibility for his submission to the raider. It is that we judge him to act reasonably when he gives up the bank's money instead of his own life, and so we find nothing blameworthy in what he does.[13]

In this passage, Frankfurt is replying to a companion paper by Don Locke (a contemporary American philosopher) in which Locke argues that acting freely is neither necessary nor sufficient for moral responsibility.[14] Locke claims that the bank teller acts freely but is not morally responsible for handing over the cash. Frankfurt thinks this is a mistake. Frankfurt ties moral responsibility to acting freely but separates moral responsibility (accountability) from being blameworthy. The clerk is responsible (accountable) for what he did but should not be blamed for it. Had the action been genuinely unfree and coerced, the possibility of blame could not have arisen. Thus, being morally responsible (and acting freely) is necessary for being blameworthy, but not sufficient. This seems reasonable: not every free action is one for which we should be blamed. And it is conceivable that the teller might be liable for blame if the circumstances had been slightly different; if, for example, the robber had merely demanded money without threatening violence. So, Frankfurt has a plausible response to the charge that his condition is not sufficient for freedom.

There is another kind of objection to Frankfurt's theory that is more difficult to rebut. Just as it is logically possible that our first-order volitions might be implanted in us by a powerful scientist, so too might this scientist implant second-order desires and volitions. But it seems that our actions would no longer be free in this case, since they would be under the complete control of another person. We would be a mere puppet, whose strings are being pulled by someone else. Though we act as we wish and approve of our acting on the motives that move us, our actions would be unfree. This objection suggests that the hierarchical theory needs some refining, perhaps by requiring that second-order desires and volitions be capable of rational evaluation by the person who has them. It is not enough simply to have second-order desires; those reflective states must also be sensitive to reasons.[15]

## Is Frankfurt's Condition Necessary for Acting Freely?

Now consider a different case. Pierre is a petty thief leading a life with which he is entirely content.[16] Pierre has cleverly avoided arrest and has never considered anything other than larceny as a way of supporting himself. Unbeknownst to Pierre, stealing is for him a neurotic compulsion, so that if he were to try to avoid acting on his larcenous impulses, he would fail. His desire to steal is irresistible. But Pierre is unaware of this and steals because he enjoys it. He is like the willing addict who injects drugs for pleasure even though he would be unable to resist them if he tried.

On Frankfurt's account, Pierre's hierarchy of desires is thoroughly integrated; he approves of the desires that lead him to action. Thus, he is a free agent, fully responsible for his actions even though, given his nature, those actions are unavoidable for him.

One day Pierre falls into the hands of a social worker, who begins to reform him. Pierre starts to question his criminal way of life. He continues to steal but now disapproves of his acting on the impulses that he still cannot resist. Frankfurt's condition is no longer satisfied. Thus, on Frankfurt's theory, Pierre is no longer morally responsible for his acts of theft. But this seems mistaken. Surely it is incorrect to hold Pierre responsible for his actions when he was complacent about stealing and then absolve him from responsibility simply because he has begun to see the error of his ways. If we continue to hold Pierre morally responsible for his acts of theft after his encounter with the social worker, then we have a case in which Frankfurt's condition is not necessary for acting freely.

## NOTES

1. See John Locke, *An Essay Concerning Human Understanding,* Book II, Chapter XXI, Section 8: "So that the *idea* of *liberty* is the *idea* of a power in any agent to do or forbear any particular action, according to the determination or thought of the mind, whereby either of them is preferred to the other; where either of them is not in the power of agent to be produced by him according to his *volition,* there he is not at *liberty:* that agent is under *necessity.*"

2. The definition is phrased so that it applies not only to actions that S has performed but also to actions that S might perform.

3. W. T. Stace, *Religion and the Modern Mind* (New York: J. B. Lippincott, 1952): 254–255.

4. W. T. Stace, *Religion and the Modern Mind,* page 252.

5. W. T. Stace, *Religion and the Modern Mind,* page 256.

6. Of course, soft determinists are not denying Moore's point that there is another meaning of "could" which makes (A) true. The other meaning is captured by saying, "If determinism is true, then S would not do otherwise if *all* the causes of S's action were to remain exactly the same."

7. For an attempt to defend compatibilism by postulating a hierarchy of preferences, see K. Lehrer, "The Conditional Analysis of Freedom," in P. Van Inwagen, Ed., *Time and Cause* (Dordrecht, Holland: Reidel, 1980): 187–201.

8. H. G. Frankfurt, "Alternate Possibilities and Moral Responsibility," *Journal of Philosophy* 66 (1969): 829–839, Section IV. See also the discussion in Section III of W. L. Rowe, "Two Concepts of Freedom" (Reading 33). The only difference between Frankfurt's Principle of Alternate Possibilities and premise (B) is that Frankfurt talks of "being morally responsible for what one has done" instead of "acting freely." Since the kind of freedom at issue in the free-will debate is the kind necessary for moral responsibility, the difference is purely terminological.

9. The name "double-decker" is borrowed from Irving Thalberg, *Misconceptions of Mind and Freedom* (Lanham, MD: University Press of America, 1983), Chapter 5. See G. Dworkin, "Acting Freely," *Noûs* 4 (1970): 367–383, and "Autonomy and Behavior Control," *Hastings Center Report* 6 (1976): 23–28; H. Frankfurt, "Freedom of the Will and the Concept of a Person," *Journal of Philosophy* 68 (1971): 5–20; "Coercion and Moral Responsibility," in T. Honderich, Ed., *Essays on Freedom of Action* (London: Routledge & Kegan Paul, 1973): 65–86; and "Three Concepts of Free Action: II," *Proceedings of the Aristotelian Society,* Supplementary Volume 49 (1975): 113–125.

10. It is important for this discussion that Marcel is able to choose. He has not been so unnerved by the robber that he is totally incapable of resisting.

11. In his papers, Frankfurt defines four different concepts: "P acted freely in doing X," "P had freedom of action in doing X," "P did X of his own free will," and "P had freedom of will

in doing X." What I call the Hierarchical Analysis of Freedom most closely resembles Frankfurt's explication of "P did X of his own free will."

12. This objection is given in I. Thalberg, *Misconceptions of Mind and Freedom*, Chapter 5.

13. H. Frankfurt, "Three Concepts of Free Action: II," reprinted in *Moral Responsibility*, ed. J. M. Fischer (Ithaca, NY: Cornell University Press, 1986): 122.

14. D. Locke, "Three Concepts of Free Action: I," *Proceedings of the Aristotelian Society*, Supplementary Volume 49 (1975): 95–112; also reprinted in *Moral Responsibility*.

15. For further discussion of this objection and a reply to it, see R. Double, "Puppeteers, Hypnotists, and Neurosurgeons," *Philosophical Studies* 56 (1989): 163–173.

16. This example and the objection based on it are taken from B. Berofsky, "The Irrelevance of Morality to Freedom," in M. Bradie and M. Brand, Eds., *Action and Responsibility* (Bowling Green, OH: State University of Bowling Green Press, 1980): 38–47.

# DISCUSSION: Libertarianism

By the *liberty* of a moral agent, I understand, a power over the determinations of his own will. If, in any action, he had power to will what he did, or not to will it, in that action he is free. But if, in every voluntary action, the determination of his will be the necessary consequence of something involuntary in the state of his mind, or of something in his external circumstances, he is not free; he has not what I call the liberty of a moral agent, but is subject to necessity.

Thomas Reid, *Essays on the Active Powers of the Human Mind* (1788), Essay IV, Chapter 1.

Richard Taylor and C. A. Campbell are libertarians. They believe not only that some human actions are free in the sense required for moral responsibility but also that this freedom is incompatible with determinism. Let us explore what these authors understand by freedom of the will and see whether there are persuasive reasons for agreeing with them that we have a kind of freedom that is inconsistent with determinism.

As in our previous discussions of hard determinism and compatibilism, we will adopt the volitional model of human action. According to this model, when we act freely, the immediate cause of bodily motion (such as raising an arm) is a volition or an act of will. Thus, we have the following typical sequence. First, we deliberate about which action we should perform from among the alternatives open to us. Second, we decide which action we shall perform and will that particular action. Third, the action involving a bodily movement causally results from our exertion of will. So, we typically have deliberation followed by willing followed by a bodily movement.

## THE LIBERTARIAN CONCEPT OF UNCONDITIONAL FREEDOM

Like earlier libertarians, such as Thomas Reid (1710–1796) and Immanuel Kant (1724–1804), both Taylor and Campbell reject the conditional analysis of freedom proposed by many soft determinists. For Taylor and Campbell it is simply an evasion to say that "S could have done otherwise" means "S could have done otherwise if he had willed otherwise," since, if determinism is true,

S could not have willed otherwise. If psychological determinism is true, then S's willing as he did (and hence his acting as he did) is fully determined by S's character and his mental states; given S's desires, beliefs, and motives, S lacked the power to will anything other than what he in fact willed.

For many libertarians, the kind of freedom necessary for moral responsibility is unconditional and categorical. It is the freedom to will otherwise, even though all the antecedent mental circumstances (character, beliefs, desires, motives) are exactly the same. As Taylor puts it in "Freedom and Determinism" (Reading 35), when we act freely, it is genuinely "up to us" which action we will to perform, and there are *no* antecedent conditions that are sufficient to determine our will. Thus, the libertarians are undoubtedly correct in asserting that this kind of unconditional freedom is incompatible with determinism.

Up to this point, our characterization of the libertarian concept of freedom has been largely negative: freedom requires that determinism is false. But there is more to libertarianism than merely a commitment to indeterminism. As libertarians are the first to point out, indeterminism by itself does not imply freedom. If the disintegration of a plutonium nucleus is genuinely uncaused by any set of prior events, this does not mean that the nucleus acts freely when it decays. Indeterminism is necessary, but not sufficient, for freedom.

The crucial extra ingredient in the libertarian analysis of freedom is that the agent—the person willing the act (and then performing it)—be the agent-cause of that act. A person who is the agent-cause of her own acts initiates the acts, originates them, and is their author. If Black causes my volition to snap my fingers, then I am not the author of that volition, and hence I do not act freely.

In his lecture "Has the Self 'Free Will'?" (Reading 34), C. A. Campbell offers the following definition of willing (and hence acting) freely:

**Campbell's Definition of Willing Freely:** S wills X freely if and only if (1) S is the *sole* author of her volition and (2) S could have unconditionally willed otherwise.

This definition has been reworded slightly to emphasize that Campbell is really talking about "inner acts" (as he calls them) or volitions and regards conditions (1) and (2) as being not only individually necessary but also jointly sufficient for willing freely. (I have also added the adverb "unconditionally" to distinguish this account from the conditional analysis of freedom, which Campbell rejects.) When Campbell italicizes the word *sole* in condition (1), he means both that S is the agent-cause of her volition and that no set of events or any other agent is responsible for causing that volition to occur. Thus, we can begin by attributing to libertarians such as Campbell the following argument for incompatibilism:

### The Libertarian Argument for Incompatibilism
(E)  If determinism is true, S could not have willed otherwise.
(F)  If S acts freely, then S could have willed otherwise.

(I)  If determinism is true, then S does not act freely.

Premise (F) of this argument and Campbell's definition of *willing freely* both have a subtle flaw that is exposed by Frankfurt's counterfactual intervener argument discussed in Reading 33 and in the discussion entitled "Compatibilism and Soft Determinism." In my version of Frankfurt's example, Black, the supremely intelligent and powerful scientist, stands poised to intervene and make me have the volition to do X (snap my fingers at noon) if he knows that I am not going to will that action by myself. It is not only the case that I am going to perform action X come what may (and hence I lack the power to *do* otherwise), it is also true that I am going to have the *volition* to do X come what may (and hence I lack the power to *will* otherwise). Hence, when Black does not intervene and I perform X of my own free will, I perform X freely *even though I lack the power to will otherwise*. Thus, Campbell is mistaken in insisting that freedom requires the power to will otherwise.

From the standpoint of libertarians such as Thomas Reid, what is indispensable to performing X freely is not simply being able to will something other than X (though we usually do have that ability) but having both the power to cause the volition to do X and the ability to *refrain* from causing the volition to do X. When Black intervenes, it is because he has predicted, correctly, that I am going to refrain from being the agent-cause of the volition to do X. He then steps in and causes me to will X. When Black does not intervene, I do X freely, not because I have the power to will some other action, Y, but because I am the agent-cause of my volition to do X and I could have refrained from being the agent-cause of the volition to do X. Black can make me have the volition to do X, but he cannot make me be the agent-cause of that or any other volition. Thus, to take account of Frankfurt's example, the libertarian argument needs to be amended in the following way:

### The Amended Libertarian Argument
(G) If determinism is true, S cannot be the agent-cause of his volitions.
(H) If S acts freely, then S is the agent-cause of his volitions.

(I) If determinism is true, then S does not act freely.

Many people find the notion of a person or self being the author or agent-cause of a volition deeply obscure at best, and unintelligible at worst. Taylor discusses the concept of agent-causation in the section of Reading 35 entitled "The Theory of Agency," and Campbell responds to the charge of unintelligibility in Section 10 of Reading 34.

According to libertarians, there are two kinds of causation: event-causation, by which events cause other events to occur; and agent-causation, by which agents cause events such as volitions to occur. What are agents? Clearly, they cannot be events or sets of events. They are substances, selves, persons, self-moving agents, entities that can initiate changes in the physical world but which cannot themselves be caused to act by anything physical or psychological. In short, agents are Cartesian immaterial substances, and libertarians are dualists.

## ARGUMENTS FOR LIBERTARIANISM
I will now examine the three main arguments that Taylor and Campbell give for their position. These are the Argument from Deliberation, the Argument from Introspection, and the Argument from Ascriptions of Responsibility.

## The Argument from Deliberation

Both Taylor and Campbell give versions of this argument, Taylor in the section of Reading 35 entitled "Determinism and Simple Indeterminism as Theories," Campbell in Section 6 of Reading 34. Campbell's version is based on the psychological impossibility of believing that one is not free while engaged in moral reasoning. Taylor's version rests on the same kind of claim about anyone who is deliberating about what to do.

(1)  Anyone who deliberates must believe that he enjoys free will.
(2)  Everyone deliberates.
_____

(3)  Everyone must believe that he enjoys free will.

Even if it is true that *while deliberating* one must believe that what one will eventually do is not already determined, it does not follow that one must have this belief in unconditional freedom at times when one is *not* deliberating. Moreover, even if a belief is psychologically inescapable, it does not follow that the belief is true. In fact, it seems possible to believe that the outcome of one's deliberation is determined even while one is deliberating. Imagine, for example, that you never make a mistake at mental arithmetic, and you know this. Whenever you add up a column of numbers, you know that you will end up with the correct answer. Getting the right answer is determined by adding the numbers together in your head. But you still have to go through the mental process of addition to find out what that answer is. Similarly, even while deliberating, you can believe that the outcome of your deliberations is determined by the mental activity you are performing. You engage in deliberation to find out what the determined outcome of your deliberation will be. Thus, we can recognize that deliberation has a point without having to believe that we are unconditionally free while it is going on.

## The Argument from Introspection

Both Taylor and Campbell appeal to our personal inner experience for evidence that it is sometimes entirely up to us what we do or, in other words, that each of us has freedom in the libertarian's unconditional sense. Of particular interest is Campbell's claim on behalf of "Common Sense" that it is only in those comparatively rare situations when we are poised on the brink of moral temptation that we know for certain that we could exert our agent-causality in alternative ways. Campbell writes:

> Here, and here alone, so far as I can see, in the act of deciding whether to put forth or withhold the moral effort required to resist temptation and rise to duty, is to be found an act which is free in the sense required for moral responsibility; an act of which the self is sole author, and of which it is true to say that "it could be" (or, after the event, "could have been") "otherwise". (Reading 34, Section 5).

What makes Campbell's claim about this introspective evidence so interesting is that it concerns a class of cases that is much narrower than those usually appealed to by libertarians; for libertarians usually claim that we are aware of our creative self-agency in all cases of deliberation followed by decision, not just those in which the self intervenes at the very end as a tie breaker. This suggests that perhaps the evidence of introspection is not as self-evident as libertarians claim it is.

In fact, Campbell's evidence proves nothing. All that we are actually aware of when we decide to resist temptation (or, alternatively, to give in to temptation) is what we actually did. We have no direct evidence that we really could have willed otherwise under identically the same circumstances. For all we know, our strongest desire might have been the desire to follow duty despite the fact that the desire to do otherwise *felt* stronger. Certainly, cases in which we succumb to temptation after long deliberation are more likely to be described as episodes in which the stronger desire prevailed rather than ones in which the weaker desire triumphed. Why should cases in which we decide for duty over pleasure be described any differently? Campbell seems to be assuming that the actual strength of a desire as an influence on the will is always correctly indicated by the force it appears to have to the person experiencing it. People addicted to drugs refute that assumption, since drug addicts are notoriously unreliable at judging the actual strength of their desires as motivators of their will.

Lastly, the phenomenon of posthypnotic suggestion, influencing decisions that, to the person who makes them, appear to be entirely free, casts further doubt on the value of introspection as evidence for unconditional freedom.

### The Argument from Ascriptions of Responsibility

Libertarians often claim that their account of freedom is the only one that can do full justice to our actual practice of assigning to people moral responsibility for their actions. This claim is difficult to sustain when one considers the diversity and apparent inconsistencies in our assignments of responsibility. Not only in law, and not only in our present society, people are held accountable for actions in which upbringing, character, and fairly stable psychological dispositions play a major causative role. No one morally exculpates the desperate addict who kills for money or the reckless drunk who mows down pedestrians while cruising home from the bar. Conversely, even a moral saint deserves praise for doing the right thing under difficult circumstances.

It is false to assert, as Campbell does, that we always ascribe responsibility for action in direct proportion to the moral effort of will that its performance requires from the agent. Sometimes, doing the ordinary, morally decent thing may require extraordinary effort in the face of threats or inducements; but the fact that one was offered a very attractive bribe for committing a crime in no way diminishes one's responsibility for one's action. What Campbell is offering is a normative ethical theory about how we should make such judgments; he is not simply reporting our moral practice.

The topic of assigning responsibility for actions and justifying punishment is a large one. It includes difficult cases of acting in ignorance, negligent omissions, and unsuccessful attempts; acts performed by persons of diminished intellectual capacity; and acts performed by people in the grip of delusions and obsessions.[1] I am far from pretending that libertarianism is clearly inferior to soft determinism in helping us to navigate through these murky waters; but it is not obviously superior.

## OBJECTIONS TO LIBERTARIANISM

I now wish to consider some criticisms of libertarianism. Campbell responds to two objections: the Predictability Objection and the Unintelligibility Objection.

Certain aspects of the latter objection are discussed later in connection with the Second Regress Objection.

### The Predictability Objection

In Section 9 of Reading 34, Campbell answers determinist critics, such as David Hume, who stress the far-ranging extent to which human actions are predictable on the basis of a thorough knowledge of character and circumstance. Campbell concedes that insofar as actions are completely predictable, they are unfree. Thus, as we have already remarked, Campbell's theory locates genuine cases of free will in a very narrow domain: freedom of the will in Campbell's sense is exhibited only when our strongest desire conflicts with what we take to be our moral duty. Attending lectures, walking to the office, brushing one's teeth, refraining from theft: none of these actions is free according to Campbell, since each is predictable in principle, given who we are and the situations we are in.

### The First Regress Objection

In his discussion of Thomas Reid's concept of freedom in Reading 33, William Rowe distinguishes between two sorts of regress objection to libertarianism. The first, and most common, sort is based on the premise that for any act whatever, that act is free only if it is freely willed; but volitions are themselves acts—namely acts of will—and so those in turn must be freely willed. Thus, we generate an infinite series of willings that must be completed before the agent can act freely. Since it is impossible to complete an infinite series of acts, libertarianism is inconsistent with acting freely.

Rowe dismisses this first regress objection as spurious. As he points out in footnote 14, the objection is based on a misunderstanding of the libertarian theory. It is true that libertarians insist that freedom of action requires freedom of willing. But they also insist that acts of will are produced directly by the agent, not by some prior act of willing. So, there is no infinite regress of volitional acts to worry about.

### The Second Regress Objection

When my volition to snap my finger occurs at a particular time, say noon, an event of the willing-to-snap-my-fingers sort occurs at that time. According to the libertarian, that event, like all other events, is caused; but it is caused, not by another event, but by my self, an agent. Thus, the libertarian accepts that all events are caused but denies that all events are caused by other events. Some events are caused in a special way, not by other events but by agents. While my deliberations were undoubtedly influenced by my beliefs, desires, and character, the complete and sufficient cause of the volition-event is me, the person who willed and acted.

So far, so good; but my self, the agent, has been around for a long time. Why did it choose to will the volition-event at noon rather than at some other time? We shall suppose that my self had the power to produce that kind of volition over many years and so the mere possession of the power alone is not sufficient to explain why it produced it *now*. What we need, in addition to the power to will an action, is the decision to *exert* that power at a particular time. This leads us to the Second Regress Objection.

This second objection arises for those libertarians who, like Thomas Reid, explicitly commit themselves to the thesis that to produce an act of will, the agent must *exert* his power to bring about that volition, for this exertion of power is itself an event that must have the agent as its cause, and thus we would generate an infinite sequence of acts of exertion.

We cannot deny that acts of will and volitions are events, since they are things that happen at particular times. This leaves three possible responses:

(1) Admit that volitions and all other mental events require exertions of power, accept the infinite regress, and argue that it is not vicious, since agents can perform an infinite number of mental acts in a finite time.

(2) Admit that volitions require exertions of power but deny that exertions of power are caused. On this view, exertions of power by an agent are exceptions to the rule that all events are caused.

(3) Deny that volitions require any exertion of power and thus cut off the regress at the start. Volitions are events that are caused directly and immediately by an agent.

The first response is quite implausible because the kind of infinite regress that concerns us here is an infinite series of acts of exertion of power stretching back into the past. Such a series has no first member. Thus, it is difficult to see how the agent could ever *initiate* such a series to bring about, ultimately, an act of will.

Though he does not explicitly address the "exertion" problem, it seems that Campbell would adopt the second alternative. In Section 10 of Reading 34, Campbell writes:

> To "account for" a "free" act is a contradiction in terms. A free will is *ex hypothesi* the sort of thing of which the request for an *explanation* is absurd. The assumption that an explanation must be in principle possible for the act of moral decision deserves to rank as a classic example of the ancient fallacy of "begging the question".

Rowe favors the third alternative; he suggests that the self causes its volitions immediately and directly, not by exerting its power to produce them or by performing any other act at all. Acts of will are basic acts that an agent produces without any event intervening between the agent and the volition.

Neither Rowe's nor Campbell's response to the regress objection strikes me as satisfactory. To say, as Campbell does, that the self exerts its power at a particular time but that these free acts of exertion need no explanation sounds more like a statement of the problem than a key to its solution. Campbell's view—that agents exerting their power to will are acts that are both uncaused and inexplicable—seems to reduce libertarianism to the simple indeterminism criticized by Richard Taylor in Reading 35.

Rowe's response has at least one advantage over Campbell's, for Rowe allows that volitions have a cause, namely, the agent. But can Rowe, or any other libertarian, explain why a volition occurs when it does rather than at some other time? It is difficult to understand how a self-substance can be the agent-cause of a dated event such as the occurrence of a volition. In his article, "Determinism, Indeterminism, and Libertarianism," C. D. Broad put the objection in the form of two rhetorical questions: "How could an event possibly be determined to happen at a certain date if its total cause contained no factor to which the notion of date has any application? And how can the notion of date have any application to anything that is not an event?"[2] While it may not be true that libertarianism is, in Broad's phrase, "self-evidently impossible", this version of the intelligibility objection does render it problematic.[3]

---

## NOTES

1. See the papers in P. A. French, Ed., *The Spectrum of Responsibility* (New York: St. Martin's, 1991).

2. C. D. Broad, "Determinism, Indeterminism, and Libertarianism," in *Ethics and the History of Philosophy* (London: Routledge and Kegan Paul, 1952): 195–217. Reprinted in B. Berofsky, Ed., *Free Will and Determinism* (New York: Harper & Row, 1966): 135–159. See page 157.

3. For an incompatibilist theory that dispenses with the notion of agent-causation, see Robert Kane, *Free Will and Values* (Albany, NY: State University of New York Press, 1985); and "Two Kinds of Incompatibilism," *Philosophy and Phenomenological Research* 50 (1989): 219–254.

# PART V

## KNOWLEDGE, SKEPTICISM, AND CAUSATION

The readings and discussions in Part V concentrate on some issues in epistemology, or the theory of knowledge. The main focus is on whether our common-sense beliefs about the world are justified and whether they qualify as knowledge. Of particular concern are our beliefs that there is an external world of tables, chairs, and other objects, that these objects exist even when they are not being perceived, that in the future they will behave in much the same way as they have in the past, and that some of these objects are related to each other as causes and effects. We all believe these things, but do we *know* them?

Everyone agrees that belief and knowledge are different and that it is much easier to believe something than it is to know it. One difference between them is their connection with truth: if I believe something, then what I believe can be either true or false, depending on the fact of the matter; but if I know something, then it must be the case that what I know is true.

The truth requirement for knowledge asserts merely that truth is a necessary condition for knowledge. We are not saying that human beings have two special faculties—one for knowing and another for believing—and that when the first faculty is employed, the results are certain and infallible. On the contrary, the statement that "If S knows that p, then p is true" is an analytic truth about the meaning of the word *knows*. It is in the same class as "If S is married, then S is a spouse." Neither conditional statement carries any guarantee that its consequent is satisfied; each asserts only that *if* the antecedent is true, then so too is the consequent.

What is truth? The simplest answer to this question is provided by the correspondence theory of truth: A statement or proposition is true when it corresponds to the facts; otherwise it is false. I think we all understand this notion of true statements corresponding with the way things really are, even though it is difficult to give a satisfactory analysis of the concept of correspondence. My belief that the Eiffel Tower is in Paris is true if and only if the Eiffel Tower really is in Paris.[1] It is not enough that I believe it or that this belief fits in with my other beliefs (the coherence theory of truth) or that my belief "works" as a practical guide for action (the pragmatic theory of truth). To be true, my belief must correspond with the facts.

A second difference between belief and knowledge can be appreciated by asking what distinguishes things that we know from beliefs that just happen to be true. What must be added to a mere true belief to make it an instance of genuine knowledge?

The difference between a lucky guess and knowledge is justification. When someone knows something, it is no accident that her belief is true. The woman who knows that the square root of two is an irrational number or that Albany is the capital of the state of New York does not just happen to give the correct answer when questioned; she has reasons, evidence, and relevant information that justify her belief. If a person were unable to give any appropriate reasons for a belief, we would retract our judgment that the person really knew.

We can summarize our analysis of knowledge by asserting that there are three conditions necessary for knowledge.

**If S knows that p, then**

(1)  S believes that p,

(2)  p is true, and

(3)  S is justified in believing that p.

Until quite recently, these three conditions were regarded as being not only necessary but also sufficient for knowledge.[2] The view that knowledge is (at least) justified true belief is shared by most of the philosophers mentioned in the readings and discussions.

Many philosophers hold a view concerning the structure of knowledge called foundationalism. To understand the appeal of foundationalism as an account of how knowledge is organized, we must first consider how justification is transferred from one belief to another.

One way in which justification can be transmitted is by logical deduction. For example, from the axioms and definitions of Euclidean geometry we can deduce Pythagoras's theorem and thus come to have a justified belief that the square on the hypotenuse of a right triangle is equal to the sum of the squares on the other two sides. Similarly, if I know that the first husband of my friend Joan swam in the Olympic Games and if I also know that the mayor was Joan's first husband, then I can deduce that the mayor was an Olympic swimmer. *If* we already know some proposition, p, and can deduce another proposition, q, from p, then we can come to know q. Similarly, if someone, S, is justified in believing p and if S is also justified in believing that q is deducible from p, then S is justified in believing q.[3]

The transmission of justification through deduction is presupposed when we try to prove the conclusion of a valid argument by deducing it from premises, all of which we know to be true or are justified in accepting as true.

When we deduce one belief, q, from others, p, that we are already justified in believing, we have a case of inferential justification. We say that we are justified in believing q on the basis of p. Since inference is not limited to logical deduction, it is helpful to have a name for the more general principle of which transmission by deduction is an instance. We shall call this principle the Principle of Inferential Justification. If someone, S, is justified in believing that p and if S is justified in believing that q on the basis of p, then S is justified in believing that q.[4] (The discussion entitled "The Problem of Induction" explores the question raised by Hume whether there really are any justified inferences that are not deductive.)

It has seemed inescapable to most philosophers since Plato and Aristotle that if we have any knowledge at all, there must be some true beliefs that are not inferred from other beliefs but are known directly. These foundational beliefs are called basic beliefs. Basic beliefs are justified, but they are not inferentially justified, and the view that all human knowledge rests on a finite set of basic beliefs is called foundationalism. Any belief that is justified only because it rests on another justified belief we shall call nonbasic or indirect. In its strong form, foundationalism pictures knowledge as being like a tree. At the bottom are the basic beliefs, the roots, on which everything else rests. For any nonbasic belief higher up the tree, if it is justified, its justification can be traced back through an epistemic chain ending at the roots. All support, all justification, originates with the basic beliefs at the bottom.

Robert Audi summarizes a popular version of the Epistemic Regress Argument for foundationalism at the beginning of his "The Structure of Knowledge" (Reading 38). The aim of the argument is to show that some of our beliefs must be basic—that it is impossible for *all* our knowledge to be indirect.[5] The version of the Epistemic Regress Argument discussed by Audi assumes that there are only four possible types of epistemic chain:

(1) Infinite, straight or circular, and unanchored.
(2) Finite, circular, and unanchored.
(3) Finite, straight, and ending in a belief that is not knowledge.
(4) Finite, ending in knowledge.

The Epistemic Regress Argument then eliminates (1), (2), and (3) by arguing that these types of chain cannot yield the justification required for knowledge.

Infinite epistemic chains go on forever. If the chains are infinite, then there must be an absolute infinity of things that we are justified in believing. But no finite mind can have an actual infinity of beliefs. So, inferential chains cannot be infinite. Moreover, for many simple propositions that appear self-evident to us, it is unclear what the further beliefs might be from which the justification for those propositions could be derived. Also, if someone tried to "justify" an absurd belief by citing a string of other absurd beliefs *ad infinitum*, this would be merely a delaying tactic, a postponement of justification, not a demonstration that the demand for justification had been met.

Circular chains do not justify anything. It is just too easy to invent a circle of propositions that closes on itself. Besides, a circle of propositions cannot mirror the *causal* structure of someone's actual beliefs, because there cannot be a closed circle of causes.

As we have seen in the discussion of the inferential transmission of justification, one belief is justified by another only if that belief in turn is justified. Thus, straight finite chains transmit justification only if the first belief in the chain is justified.

As a result, only the fourth possibility—foundationalism—remains. If any beliefs are justified, there must be some basic beliefs that are justified noninferentially.

Descartes, Locke, Berkeley, Hume, and Russell are foundationalists. They agree that among the basic beliefs that are known directly without inferring them from anything else are those given by the contents of our own minds. These mental contents—thoughts, sensations, and mental images—are called ideas by Descartes, Locke, and Berkeley, perceptions by Hume (who divides them into impressions and ideas), and sense-data by Russell.[6] All these philosophers agree that we know with absolute certainty that we are in pain when we are feeling pain, that we seem to be seeing a brown table when we are looking at one, that we are having a sensation of green when we are experiencing a green afterimage, and so on. Where these thinkers disagree is in whether these kinds of basic experiential beliefs are sufficient all by themselves to yield knowledge of the external world. For the sake of brevity, I shall use the term realism to refer to the thesis that there is an external world of physical objects that exist independently of our perceiving them.

In his *First Meditation* (Reading 36), René Descartes poses the Problem of the External World, sometimes called the Veil of Perception Problem. Can we justify our belief that there is an external world of physical objects based solely on the evidence of our senses? Descartes assumes that when we perceive physical objects, what we are immediately aware of are ideas in our minds. By imagining circumstances (such as dreaming) in which the ideas in our minds could give us a false picture of the world, Descartes casts doubt on whether any of our beliefs about the external world are justified. In his *Second Meditation* (Reading 36), Descartes begins his attempt to answer these skeptical doubts by digging down to a bedrock of foundational beliefs that cannot be doubted. In the later *Meditations*, Descartes argues that these foundational beliefs can be used to justify many of our beliefs about the external world.

Hardly any realist philosophers are convinced that Descartes managed to solve the skeptical problem he set for himself. In "Appearance, Reality, and the Existence of Matter" (Reading 37), Bertrand Russell proposes a solution to the Problem of the External World that abandons strict foundationalism. Russell argues that very few of our beliefs are absolutely certain and indubitable but many of them are justified because of the way they fit together in an explanatory framework. Thus, Russell advocates a coherence theory of justification as an alternative to strict foundationalism.

In "The Structure of Knowledge" (Reading 38), Robert Audi explores the debate between foundationalist and coherence theories of justification. Audi shows that a holistic theory of justification is not ruled out by the Epistemic Regress Argument, since there is fifth kind of epistemic chain that foundationalists have ignored. Audi discusses the problems with and the merits of coherentism and explains how modest foundationalism can avoid the former and accommodate the latter.

Even if we can solve the Problem of the External World, there still remains the Problem of Induction. Can we justify our beliefs about future events and other matters that we are not experiencing at present? We can illustrate the difference between the Problem of the External World and the Problem of Induction by considering an apple that I seem to see before me. A skeptic about the external world challenges my claim to know that there really is an apple in front of me. How do I know that I am not just hallucinating or dreaming or being deceived by an evil genius who is manipulating my mind? Let us assume that we can answer these questions in a satisfactory manner. I know that there is an apple here in front of me right now because I am perceiving it; I know that it is sweet and juicy, because I am tasting it; and so on. What about apples that I am not perceiving at present? What about the apple that I will eat for lunch later today? How do I know that this apple will not poison me when I bite into it or taste of hot chili peppers? These skeptical doubts concerning the future behavior of objects and about objects we are not experiencing at present were raised by David Hume as the Problem of Induction.

In "Sceptical Doubts Concerning the Operations of the Understanding" (Reading 39), Hume denies that we have any rational justification for the inductive inferences we make from the past to the future or from the observed to the unobserved. A crucial step in Hume's reasoning is that all inductive arguments presuppose that the future will resemble the past and that nature is uniform. Hume argues that we cannot prove this presupposition deductively, and if we try to establish it inductively, we will simply be begging the question. According to Hume, there is nothing more to inductive inference than mental habits and expectations caused in us by prior experiences. We can give a psychological explanation of our inductive behavior, but it is impossible to justify our inductive inferences.

Few philosophers accept Hume's skepticism about inductive inference, but opinions differ widely about what is wrong with Hume's argument. Wesley Salmon discusses responses to Hume in "Unfinished Business: The Problem of Induction" (Reading 40). As his title indicates, Salmon does not think that any of these responses has yet proved successful.

One approach to induction that Salmon criticizes is the attempt by John Stuart Mill and others to justify induction inductively. Salmon, like Hume, thinks that this approach must fail because it begs the question. In "Reliability, Justification, and the Problem of Induction" (Reading 41), James Van Cleve argues that this criticism is a mistake. According to Van Cleve, not only has Hume failed to show that induction is irrational, but also inductive inference can be justified inductively without involving any vicious circularity of reasoning.

The final three readings concern the concept of causation. Inferences from causes to effects and from effects to causes are a common way of trying to extend our knowledge. Also, some philosophers have thought that a correct understanding of causation will help to solve the problem of induction. Whether or not causal inferences and the beliefs based upon them are justified depends in large part on what the concept of causation amounts to.

In "The Idea of Necessary Connection" (Reading 42), David Hume offers a controversial empiricist theory of causation called the regularity theory. By tracing the idea of cause and effect to the impressions from which it is derived,

Hume concludes that the objective content of our idea of causation is exhausted by temporal priority and constant conjunction. Hume admits that the idea of necessity is also an essential component of the concept of cause, but he argues that this idea is purely subjective, being derived from a feeling in the human mind.

In "Cause" (Reading 43), A. C. Ewing gives several important criticisms of Hume's regularity theory and champions his own entailment theory of causation. One famous objection, voiced by Reid and others, is that Hume's theory implies that because night always follows day, night is the cause of day. More generally, it is claimed that Hume cannot distinguish between sequences in which A's cause B's and those in which B's merely happen to follow A's without A's being the cause of B's. According to Ewing, causes are connected to their effects by an objective necessity. Causes entail their effects with a kind of logical necessity similar to that which connects the premises of a valid argument to the argument's conclusion. Given the occurrence of the cause, the effect *has* to follow.

Many of Ewing's criticisms of Hume are devastating, but few empiricist philosophers endorse Ewing's own entailment theory. In part this is because they agree with Hume that objective necessity is not something that we can observe in the world simply by looking. We see the cause; we see the effect; but we do not see the "necessity" that is supposed to bind them together. In "Causation in Concept, Knowledge, and Reality" (Reading 44), J. L. Mackie offers what he calls a conditional analysis of causation as an alternative to the regularity theory that can meet many of Ewing's objections. According to Mackie, it is a vital part of the meaning of "A is the cause of B" that if A *were* to occur, then B *would* follow. Mackie argues that we can acquire knowledge of these subjunctive conditionals because they can be tested, confirmed, or refuted in controlled experiments.

---

## NOTES

1. Among the difficult cases for the correspondence theory are propositions such as historical counterfactuals, which can be true even though there are no actual states of affairs for the propositions to correspond with. For example, if Japan had not bombed Pearl Harbor on December 7, 1941, the United States would not have declared war on Germany four days later; if I had swallowed ten grams of cyanide for breakfast I would now be dead.

2. For an important and influential attack on the claim that justified true belief is sufficient for knowledge, see E. Gettier, "Is Justified True Belief Knowledge?" *Analysis* 23 (1963): 121–123.

3. For brevity's sake, I have omitted the further requirements that S actually deduce q from p and that S accept q as a result of the deduction. Gettier properly insists on both in order to avoid cases in which S fails to draw the connection between p and q or in which S makes the deduction but accepts q for some other reason.

4. Again, as explained in footnote 3, we should also insist that S actually infer q from p and that S accept q as a result of the inference.

5. It should be emphasized that Audi himself does not endorse this argument. Audi thinks it is invalid because there is a fifth possible kind of epistemic chain that the foundationalist has ignored. This issue is taken up in Audi's discussion of holistic coherentism and in the discussion entitled "The Problem of the External World."

6. For Russell, sensations are mental acts of sensory awareness; sense-data are the contents of which we are immediately aware. In this respect, the term *idea* used by Descartes, Locke, and Berkeley is ambiguous, since it can mean either the act of perceiving or the content of the perception.

# READING 36

## First and Second Meditations
*René Descartes*

*For biographical details see Reading 20.*

### MEDITATION I
Of the things which may be brought within the sphere of the doubtful.

It is now some years since I detected how many were the false beliefs that I had from my earliest youth admitted as true, and how doubtful was everything I had since constructed on this basis; and from that time I was convinced that I must once for all seriously undertake to rid myself of all the opinions which I had formerly accepted, and commence to build anew from the foundation, if I wanted to establish any firm and permanent structure in the sciences. But as this enterprise appeared to be a very great one, I waited until I had attained an age so mature that I could not hope that at any later date I should be better fitted to execute my design. This reason caused me to delay so long that I should feel that I was doing wrong were I to occupy in deliberation the time that yet remains to me for action. To-day, then, since very opportunely for the plan I have in view I have delivered my mind from every care [and am happily agitated by no passions] and since I have procured for myself an assured leisure in a peaceable retirement, I shall at last seriously and freely address myself to the general upheaval of all my former opinions.

Now for this object it is not necessary that I should show that all of these are false—I shall perhaps never arrive at this end. But inasmuch as reason already persuades me that I ought no less carefully to

withhold my assent from matters which are not entirely certain and indubitable than from those which appear to me manifestly to be false, if I am able to find in each one some reason to doubt, this will suffice to justify my rejecting the whole. And for that end it will not be requisite that I should examine each in particular, which would be an endless undertaking; for owing to the fact that the destruction of the foundations of necessity brings with it the downfall of the rest of the edifice, I shall only in the first place attack those principles upon which all my former opinions rested.

All that up to the present time I have accepted as most true and certain I have learned either from the senses or through the senses; but it is sometimes proved to me that these senses are deceptive, and it is wiser not to trust entirely to any thing by which we have once been deceived.

But it may be that although the senses sometimes deceive us concerning things which are hardly perceptible, or very far away, there are yet many others to be met with as to which we cannot reasonably have any doubt, although we recognise them by their means. For example, there is the fact that I am here, seated by the fire, attired in a dressing gown, having this paper in my hands and other similar matters. And how could I deny that these hands and this body are mine, were it not perhaps that I compare myself to certain persons, devoid of sense, whose cerebella are so troubled and clouded by the violent vapours of black bile, that they constantly assure us that they think they are kings when they are really quite poor, or that they are clothed in purple when they are really without covering, or who imagine that they have an earthenware head or are nothing but pumpkins or are made of glass. But they are mad, and I should not be any the less insane were I to follow examples so extravagant.

**SOURCE:** From *Meditations on First Philosophy*. Reprinted from *The Philosophical Works of Descartes*, Volume 1, trans. and ed. E. S. Haldane and G.R.T. Ross (Cambridge: Cambridge University Press, 1931): 144–157.

At the same time I must remember that I am a man, and that consequently I am in the habit of sleeping, and in my dreams representing to myself the same things or sometimes even less probable things, than do those who are insane in their waking moments. How often has it happened to me that in the night I dreamt that I found myself in this particular place, that I was dressed and seated near the fire, whilst in reality I was lying undressed in bed! At this moment it does indeed seem to me that it is with eyes awake that I am looking at this paper; that this head which I move is not asleep, that it is deliberately and of set purpose that I extend my hand and perceive it; what happens in sleep does not appear so clear nor so distinct as does all this. But in thinking over this I remind myself that on many occasions I have in sleep been deceived by similar illusions, and in dwelling carefully on this reflection I see so manifestly that there are no certain indications by which we may clearly distinguish wakefulness from sleep that I am lost in astonishment. And my astonishment is such that it is almost capable of persuading me that I now dream.

Now let us assume that we are asleep and that all these particulars, e.g. that we open our eyes, shake our head, extend our hands, and so on, are but false delusions; and let us reflect that possibly neither our hands nor our whole body are such as they appear to us to be. At the same time we must at least confess that the things which are represented to us in sleep are like painted representations which can only have been formed as the counterparts of something real and true, and that in this way those general things at least, i.e. eyes, a head, hands, and a whole body, are not imaginary things, but things really existent. For, as a matter of fact, painters, even when they study with the greatest skill to represent sirens and satyrs by forms the most strange and extraordinary, cannot give them natures which are entirely new, but merely make a certain medley of the members of different animals; or if their imagination is extravagant enough to invent something so novel that nothing similar has ever before been seen, and that then their work represents a thing purely fictitious and absolutely false, it is certain all the same that the colours of which this is composed are necessarily real. And for the same reason, although these general things, to wit, [a body], eyes, a head, hands, and such like, may be imaginary, we are bound at the same time to confess that there are at least some other objects yet more simple and more universal, which are real and true; and of these just in the same way as with certain real colours, all these images of things which dwell in our thoughts, whether true and real or false and fantastic, are formed.

To such a class of things pertains corporeal nature in general, and its extension, the figure of extended things, their quantity or magnitude and number, as also the place in which they are, the time which measures their duration, and so on.

That is possibly why our reasoning is not unjust when we conclude from this that Physics, Astronomy, Medicine and all other sciences which have as their end the consideration of composite things, are very dubious and uncertain; but that Arithmetic, Geometry and other sciences of that kind which only treat of things that are very simple and very general, without taking great trouble to ascertain whether they are actually existent or not, contain some measure of certainty and an element of the indubitable. For whether I am awake or asleep, two and three together always form five, and the square can never have more than four sides, and it does not seem possible that truths so clear and apparent can be suspected of any falsity [or uncertainty].

Nevertheless I have long had fixed in my mind the belief that an all-powerful God existed by whom I have been created such as I am. But how do I know that He has not brought it to pass that there is no earth, no heaven, no extended body, no magnitude, no place, and that nevertheless [I possess the perceptions of all these things and that] they seem to me to exist just exactly as I now see them? And, besides, as I sometimes imagine that others deceive themselves in the things which they think they know best, how do I know that I am not deceived every time that I add two and three, or count the sides of a square, or judge of things yet simpler, if anything simpler can be imagined? But possibly God has not desired that I should be thus deceived, for He is said to be supremely good. If, however, it is contrary to His goodness to have made me such that I constantly deceive myself, it would also appear to be contrary to His goodness to permit me to be sometimes deceived, and nevertheless I cannot doubt that He does permit this.

There may indeed be those who would prefer to deny the existence of a God so powerful, rather than believe that all other things are uncertain. But let us not oppose them for the present, and grant that all that is here said of a God is a fable; nevertheless in whatever way they suppose that I have arrived at the state of being that I have reached—whether they attribute it to fate or to accident, or make out that it is by a continual succession of antecedents, or by some other method—since to err and deceive oneself is a defect, it is clear that the greater will be the probability of my being so imperfect as to deceive myself ever, as is the Author to whom they assign my origin the less powerful. To these reasons I have certainly nothing to reply, but at the end I feel constrained to confess that there is nothing in all that I formerly believed to be true, of which I cannot in some measure doubt, and that not merely through want of thought or through levity, but for reasons which are very powerful and maturely considered; so that henceforth I ought not the less carefully to refrain from giving credence to these opinions than to that which is manifestly false, if I desire to arrive at any certainty [in the sciences].

But it is not sufficient to have made these remarks, we must also be careful to keep them in mind. For these ancient and commonly held opinions still revert frequently to my mind, long and familiar custom having given them the right to occupy my mind against my inclination and rendered them almost masters of my belief; nor will I ever lose the habit of deferring to them or of placing my confidence in them, so long as I consider them as they really are, i.e. opinions in some measure doubtful, as I have just shown, and at the same time highly probable, so that there is much more reason to believe in than to deny them. That is why I consider that I shall not be acting amiss, if, taking of set purpose a contrary belief, I allow myself to be deceived, and for a certain time pretend that all these opinions are entirely false and imaginary, until at last, having thus balanced my former prejudices with my latter [so that they cannot divert my opinions more to one side than to the other], my judgment will no longer be dominated by bad usage or turned away from the right knowledge of the truth. For I am assured that there can be neither peril nor error in this course, and that I cannot at present yield too much to distrust, since I am not considering the question of action, but only of knowledge.

I shall then suppose, not that God who is supremely good and the fountain of truth, but some evil genius not less powerful than deceitful, has employed his whole energies in deceiving me; I shall consider that the heavens, the earth, colours, figures, sound, and all other external things are nought but the illusions and dreams of which this genius has availed himself in order to lay traps for my credulity; I shall consider myself as having no hands, no eyes, no flesh, no blood, nor any senses, yet falsely believing myself to possess all these things; I shall remain obstinately attached to this idea, and if by this means it is not in my power to arrive at the knowledge of any truth, I may at least do what is in my power [i.e. suspend my judgment], and with firm purpose avoid giving credence to any false thing, or being imposed upon by this arch deceiver, however powerful and deceptive he may be. But this task is a laborious one, and insensibly a certain lassitude leads me into the course of my ordinary life. And just as a captive who in sleep enjoys an imaginary liberty, when he begins to suspect that his liberty is but a dream, fears to awaken, and conspires with these agreeable illusions that the deception may be prolonged, so insensibly of my own accord I fall back into my former opinions, and I dread awakening from this slumber, lest the laborious wakefulness which would follow the tranquillity of this repose should have to be spent not in daylight, but in the excessive darkness of the difficulties which have just been discussed.

## MEDITATION II
### Of the Nature of the Human Mind; and that it is more easily known than the Body.

The Meditation of yesterday filled my mind with so many doubts that it is no longer in my power to forget them. And yet I do not see in what manner I can resolve them; and, just as if I had all of a sudden fallen into very deep water, I am so disconcerted that I can neither make certain of setting my feet on the bottom, nor can I swim and so support myself on the surface. I shall nevertheless make an effort and follow anew the same path as that on which I yesterday entered, i.e. I shall proceed by setting aside all that in which the least doubt could be supposed to exist, just as if I had discovered that it was absolutely false; and I shall ever follow in this road until I have met with something which is certain, or at least, if I can do nothing else, until I have learned for certain that there is nothing in the world that is certain. Archimedes, in order that he might draw the terrestrial globe out of its place, and transport it elsewhere, demanded only that one point should be fixed and immoveable; in the same way I shall have the right to conceive high hopes if I am happy enough to discover one thing only which is certain and indubitable.

I suppose, then, that all the things that I see are false; I persuade myself that nothing has ever existed of all that my fallacious memory represents to me. I consider that I possess no senses; I imagine that body, figure, extension, movement and place are but the fictions of my mind. What, then, can be esteemed as true? Perhaps nothing at all, unless that there is nothing in the world that is certain.

But how can I know there is not something different from those things that I have just considered, of which one cannot have the slightest doubt? Is there not some God, or some other being by whatever name we call it, who puts these reflections into my mind? That is not necessary, for is it not possible that I am capable of producing them myself? I myself, am I not at least something? But I have already denied that I had senses and body. Yet I hesitate, for what follows from that? Am I so dependent on body and senses that I cannot exist without these? But I was persuaded that there was nothing in all the world, that there was no heaven, no earth, that there were no minds, nor any bodies: was I not then likewise persuaded that I did not exist? Not at all; of a surety I myself did exist since I persuaded myself of something [or merely because I thought of something]. But there is some deceiver or other, very powerful and very cunning, who ever employs his ingenuity in deceiving me. Then without doubt I exist also if he deceives me, and let him deceive me as much as he will, he can never cause me to be nothing so long as I think that I am something. So that after having reflected well and carefully examined all things, we must come to the definite conclusion that this proposition: I am, I exist, is necessarily true each time that I pronounce it, or that I mentally conceive it.

But I do not yet know clearly enough what I am, I who am certain that I am; and hence I must be careful to see that I do not imprudently take some other object in place of myself, and thus that I do not go astray in respect of this knowledge that I hold to be the most certain and most evident of all that I have formerly learned. That is why I shall now consider anew what I believed myself to be before I embarked upon these last reflections; and of my former opinions I shall withdraw all that might even in a small degree be invalidated by the reasons which I have just brought forward, in order that there may be nothing at all left beyond what is absolutely certain and indubitable.

What then did I formerly believe myself to be? Undoubtedly I believed myself to be a man. But what is a man? Shall I say a reasonable animal? Certainly not; for then I should have to inquire what an animal is, and what is reasonable; and thus from a single question I should insensibly fall into an infinitude of others more difficult; and I should not wish to waste the little time and leisure remaining to me in trying to unravel subtleties like these. But I shall rather stop here to consider the thoughts which of themselves spring up in my mind, and which were not inspired by anything beyond my own nature alone when I applied myself to the consideration of my being. In the first place, then, I considered myself as having a face, hands, arms, and all that system of members composed of bones and flesh as seen in a corpse which I designated by the name of body. In addition to this I considered that I was nourished, that I walked, that I felt, and that I thought, and I referred all these actions to the soul: but I did not stop to consider what the soul was, or if I did stop, I imagined that it was something extremely rare and subtle like a wind, a flame, or an ether, which was spread throughout my grosser parts. As to body I had no manner of doubt about its nature, but thought I had a very clear knowledge of it; and if I had desired to explain it according to the notions that I had then formed of it, I should have described it thus: By the body I understand all that which can be defined by a certain figure: something which can be confined in a certain place, and which can fill a given space in such a way that every other body will be excluded from it; which can be perceived either by touch, or by sight, or by hearing, or by taste, or by smell: which can be moved in many ways not, in truth, by itself, but by something which is foreign to it, by which it is touched [and from which it receives impressions]: for to have the power of self-movement, as also of feeling or of thinking, I did not consider to appertain to the nature of body: on the contrary, I was rather astonished to find that faculties similar to them existed in some bodies.

But what am I, now that I suppose that there is a certain genius which is extremely powerful, and, if I may say so, malicious, who employs all his powers in deceiving me? Can I affirm that I possess the least of all those things which I have just said pertain to the nature of body? I pause to consider, I revolve all these things in my mind, and I find none of which I can say that it pertains to me. It would be tedious to stop to enumerate them. Let us pass to the attributes of soul and see if there is any one which is in me? What of nutrition or walking [the first mentioned]? But if it is so that I have no body it is also true that I can neither walk nor take nourishment. Another attribute is sensation. But one cannot feel without body, and besides I have thought I perceived many things during sleep that I recognised in my waking moments as not having been experienced at all. What of thinking? I find here that thought is an attribute that belongs to me; it alone cannot be separated from me. I am, I exist, that is certain. But how often? Just when I think; for it might possibly be the case if I ceased entirely to think, that I should likewise cease altogether to exist. I do not now admit anything which is not necessarily true: to speak accurately I am not more than a thing which thinks, that is to say a mind or a soul, or an understanding, or a reason, which are terms whose significance was formerly unknown to me. I am, however, a real thing and really exist; but what thing? I have answered: a thing which thinks.

And what more? I shall exercise my imagination [in order to see if I am not something more]. I am not a collection of members which we call the human body: I am not a subtle air distributed through these members, I am not a wind, a fire, a vapour, a breath, nor anything at all which I can imagine or conceive; because I have assumed that all these were nothing. Without changing that supposition I find that I only leave myself certain of the fact that I am somewhat. But perhaps it is true that these same things which I supposed were non-existent because they are unknown to me, are really not different from the self which I know. I am not sure about this, I shall not dispute about it now; I can only give judgment on things that are known to me. I know that I exist, and I inquire what I am, I whom I know to exist. But it is very certain that the knowledge of my existence taken in its precise significance does not depend on things whose existence is not yet known to me; consequently it does not depend on those which I can feign in imagination. And indeed the very term *feign* in imagination proves to me my error, for I really do this if I image myself a something, since to imagine is nothing else than to contemplate the figure or image of a corporeal thing. But I already know for certain that I am, and that it may be that all these images, and, speaking generally, all things that relate to the nature of body are nothing but dreams [and chimeras]. For this reason I see clearly that I have as little reason to say, 'I shall stimulate my imagination in order to know more distinctly what I am,' than if I were to say, 'I am now awake, and I perceive somewhat that is real and true: but because I do not yet perceive it distinctly enough, I shall go to sleep of express purpose, so that my dreams may represent the perception with greatest truth and evidence.' And, thus, I know for certain that nothing of all that I can understand by means of my imagination belongs to this knowledge which I have of myself, and that it is necesary to recall the mind from this mode of thought with the utmost diligence in order that it may be able to know its own nature with perfect distinctness.

But what then am I? A thing which thinks. What is a thing which thinks? It is a thing which doubts, understands, [conceives], affirms, denies, wills, refuses, which also imagines and feels.

Certainly it is no small matter if all these things pertain to my nature. But why should they not so pertain? Am I not that being who now doubts nearly everything, who nevertheless understands certain things, who affirms that one only is true, who denies all the others, who desires to know more, is averse from being deceived, who imagines many things, sometimes indeed despite his will, and who perceives many likewise, as by the intervention of the bodily organs? Is there nothing in all this which is as true as it is certain that I exist, even though I should always sleep and though he who has given me being employed all his ingenuity in deceiving me? Is there likewise any one of these attributes which can be distinguished from my thought, or which might be said to be separated from myself? For it is so evident of itself that it is I who doubts, who understands, and who desires, that there is no reason here to add anything to explain it. And I have certainly the power of imagining likewise; for although it may happen (as I formerly supposed) that none of the things which I imagine are true, nevertheless this power of imagining does not cease to be really in use, and it forms part of my thought. Finally, I am the same who feels, that is to say, who perceives certain things, as by the organs of sense, since in truth I see light, I hear noise, I feel heat. But it will be said that these phenomena are false and that I am dreaming. Let it be so; still it is at least quite certain that it seems to me that I see light, that I hear noise and that I feel heat. That cannot be false; properly speaking it is what is in me called feeling; and used in this precise sense that is no other thing than thinking.

From this time I begin to know what I am with a little more clearness and distinction than before; but nevertheless it still seems to me, and I cannot prevent myself from thinking, that corporeal things, whose images are framed by thought, which are tested by the senses, are much more distinctly known than that obscure part of me which does not come under the imagination. Although really it is very strange to say that I know and understand more distinctly these things whose existence seems to me dubious, which are unknown to me, and which do not belong to me, than others of the truth of which I am convinced, which are known to me and which pertain to my real nature, in a word, than myself. But I see clearly how the case stands: my mind loves to wander, and cannot yet suffer itself to be retained within the just limits of truth. Very good, let us once more give it the freest rein, so that, when afterwards we seize the proper occasion for pulling up, it may the more easily be regulated and controlled.

Let us begin by considering the commonest matters, those which we believe to be the most distinctly comprehended, to wit, the bodies which we touch and see; not indeed bodies in general, for these general ideas are usually a little more confused, but let us consider one body in particular. Let us take, for example, this piece of wax: it has been taken quite freshly from the hive, and it has not yet lost the sweetness of the honey which it contains; it still retains somewhat of the odour of the flowers from which it has been culled; its colour, its figure, its size are apparent; it is hard, cold, easily handled, and if you strike it with the finger, it will emit a sound. Finally all the things which are requisite to cause us distinctly to recognise a body, are met with in it. But notice that while I speak and approach the fire what remained of the taste is exhaled, the smell evaporates, the colour alters, the figure is destroyed, the size increases, it becomes liquid, it heats, scarcely can one handle it, and when one strikes it, no sound is emitted. Does the same wax remain after this change? We must confess that it remains; none would judge otherwise. What then did I know so distinctly in this piece of wax? It conld certainly be

nothing of all that the senses brought to my notice, since all these things which fall under taste, smell, sight, touch, and hearing, are found to be changed, and yet the same wax remains.

Perhaps it was what I now think, viz, that this wax was not that sweetness of honey, nor that agreeable scent of flowers, nor that particular whiteness, nor that figure, nor that sound, but simply a body which a little while before appeared to me as perceptible under these forms, and which is now perceptible under others. But what, precisely, is it that I imagine when I form such conceptions? Let us attentively consider this, and, abstracting from all that does not belong to the wax, let us see what remains. Certainly nothing remains excepting a certain extended thing which is flexible and movable. But what is the meaning of flexible and movable? Is it not that I imagine that this piece of wax being round is capable of becoming square and of passing from a square to a triangular figure? No, certainly it is not that, since I imagine it admits of an infinitude of similar changes, and I nevertheless do not know how to compass the infinitude by my imagination, and consequently this conception which I have of the wax is not brought about by the faculty of imagination. What now is this extension? Is it not also unknown? For it becomes greater when the wax is melted, greater when it is boiled, and greater still when the heat increases; and I should not conceive [clearly] according to truth what wax is, if I did not think that even this piece that we are considering is capable of receiving more variation in extension than I have ever imagined. We must then grant that I could not even understand through the imagination what this piece of wax is, and that it is my mind alone which perceives it. I say this piece of wax in particular, for as to wax in general it is yet clearer. But what is this piece of wax which cannot be understood excepting by the [understanding or] mind? It is certainly the same that I see, touch, imagine, and finally it is the same which I have always believed it to be from the beginning. But what must particularly be observed is that its perception is neither an act of vision, nor of touch, nor of imagination, and has never been such although it may have appeared formerly to be so, but only an intuition of the mind, which may be imperfect and confused as it was formerly, or clear and distinct as it is at present, according as my attention is more or less directed to the elements which are found in it, and of which it is composed.

Yet in the meantime I am greatly astonished when I consider [the great feebleness of mind] and its proneness to fall [insensibly] into error; for although without giving expression to my thoughts I consider all this in my own mind, words often impede me and I am almost deceived by the terms of ordinary language. For we say that we see the same wax, if it is present, and not that we simply judge that it is the same from its having the same colour and figure. From this I should conclude that I knew the wax by means of vision and not simply by the intuition of the mind; unless by chance I remember that, when looking from a window and saying I see men who pass in the street, I really do not see them, but infer that what I see is men, just as I say that I see wax. And yet what do I see from the window but hats and coats which may cover automatic machines? Yet I judge these to be men. And similarly solely by the faculty of judgment which rests in my mind, I comprehend that which I believed I saw with my eyes.

A man who makes it his aim to raise his knowledge above the common should be ashamed to derive the occasion for doubting from the forms of speech invented by the vulgar; I prefer to pass on and consider whether I had a more evident and perfect conception of what the wax was when I first perceived it, and when I believed I knew it by means of the external senses or at least by the common sense as it is called, that is to say by the imaginative faculty, or whether my present conception is clearer now that I have most carefully examined what it is, and in what way it can be known. It would certainly be absurd to doubt as to this. For what was there in this first perception which was distinct? What was there which might not as well have been perceived by any of the animals? But when I distinguish the wax from its external forms, and when, just as if I had taken from it its vestments, I consider it quite naked, it is certain that although some error may still be found in my judgment, I can nevertheless not perceive it thus without a human mind.

But finally what shall I say of this mind, that is, of myself, for up to this point I do not admit in myself anything but mind? What then, I who seem to perceive this piece of wax so distinctly, do I not know myself, not only with much more truth and certainty, but also with much more distinctness and clearness? For if I judge that the wax is or exists from the fact that I see it, it certainly follows much more clearly that I am or that I exist myself from the fact that I see it. For it may be that what I see is not really wax, it may also be that I do not possess eyes with which to see anything; but it cannot be that when I see, or (for I no longer take account of the distinction) when I think I see, that I myself who think am nought. So if I judge that the wax exists from the fact that I touch it, the same thing will follow, to wit, that I am; and if I judge that my imagination, or some other cause, whatever it is, persuades me that the wax exists, I shall still conclude the same. And what I have here remarked of wax may be applied to all other things which are external to me [and which are met with outside of me]. And further, if the [notion or] perception of wax has seemed to me clearer and more distinct, not only after the sight or the touch, but also after many other causes have rendered it quite manifest to me, with how much more [evidence] and distinctness must it be said that I now know myself, since all the reasons which contribute to the knowledge of wax, or any other body whatever, are yet better proofs of the nature of my mind! And there are so many other things in the mind itself which may contribute to the elucidation of its nature, that those which depend on body such as these just mentioned, hardly merit being taken into account.

But finally here I am, having insensibly reverted to the point I desired, for, since it is now manifest to me that even bodies are not properly speaking known by the senses or by the faculty of imagination, but by the understanding only, and since they are not known from the fact that they are seen or touched, but only because they are understood, I see clearly that there is nothing which is easier for me to know than my mind. But because it is difficult to rid oneself so promptly of an opinion to which one was accustomed for so long, it will be well that I should halt a little at this point, so that by the length of my meditation I may more deeply imprint on my memory this new knowledge.

# READING 37

---

# Appearance, Reality, and the Existence of Matter
*Bertrand Russell*

*Bertrand Russell (1872–1970) was one of the most important philosophers of the twentieth century. He made pioneering contributions to logic in* Principia Mathematica *(1910–1913), written with Alfred North Whitehead. A prolific author, Russell published some 20 books in philosophy, and 40 popular works defending his often controversial views on politics, morality, education, sex, and religion. He was awarded the Nobel Prize for Literature in 1950. Though not a pacifist, Russell opposed Britain's participation in the First World War. This cost him his lectureship in philosophy at Trinity College, Cambridge, and in 1918 he spent six months in prison for libelling the American army. Russell supported the fight against fascism in the Second World War. In the 1950's and 60's, Russell became a leading figure in the Campaign for Nuclear Disarmament and in 1961, at age 89, he was sentenced to a week in prison hospital for advocating civil disobedience. These and other episodes are described in the three volumes of Russell's* Autobiography *(1967–1969). Russell's philosophical works include* The Principles of Mathematics *(1903),* Our Knowledge of the External World *(1914),* Mysticism and Logic *(1916),* An Inquiry into Meaning and Truth *(1940),* A History of Western Philosophy *(1945), and* Human Knowledge: Its Scope and Limits *(1948).*

## CHAPTER I

## APPEARANCE AND REALITY

Is there any knowledge in the world which is so certain that no reasonable man could doubt it? This question, which at first sight might not seem difficult, is really one of the most difficult that can be asked. When we have realized the obstacles in the

SOURCE: From *The Problems of Philosophy* (1912). Reprinted (London: Oxford University Press, 1974), Chapters I and II, pages 7–26.

way of a straightforward and confident answer, we shall be well launched on the study of philosophy—for philosophy is merely the attempt to answer such ultimate questions, not carelessly and dogmatically, as we do in ordinary life and even in the sciences, but critically, after exploring all that makes such questions puzzling, and after realizing all the vagueness and confusion that underlie our ordinary ideas.

In daily life, we assume as certain many things which, on a closer scrutiny, are found to be so full of apparent contradictions that only a great amount of thought enables us to know what it is that we really may believe. In the search for certainty, it is natural to begin with our present experiences, and in some sense, no doubt, knowledge is to be derived from them. But any statement as to what it is that our immediate experiences make us know is very likely to be wrong. It seems to me that I am now sitting in a chair, at a table of a certain shape, on which I see sheets of paper with writing or print. By turning my head I see out of the window buildings and clouds and the sun. I believe that the sun is about ninety-three million miles from the earth; that it is a hot globe many times bigger than the earth; that, owing to the earth's rotation, it rises every morning, and will continue to do so for an indefinite time in the future. I believe that, if any other normal person comes into my room, he will see the same chairs and tables and books and papers as I see, and that the table which I see is the same as the table which I feel pressing against my arm. All this seems to be so evident as to be hardly worth stating, except in answer to a man who doubts whether I know anything. Yet all this may be reasonably doubted, and all of it requires much careful discussion before we can be sure that we have stated it in a form that is wholly true.

To make our difficulties plain, let us concentrate attention on the table. To the eye it is oblong, brown and shiny, to the touch it is smooth and cool and hard; when I tap it, it gives out a wooden sound. Any one else who sees and feels and hears the table will agree with this description, so that it might seem as if no difficulty would arise; but as soon as we try to be more precise our troubles begin. Although I believe that the table is 'really' of the same colour all over, the parts that reflect the light look much brighter than the other parts, and some parts look white because of reflected light. I know that, if I move, the parts that reflect the light will be different, so that the apparent distribution of colours on the table will change. It follows that if several people are looking at the table at the same moment, no two of them will see exactly the same distribution of colours, because no two can see it from exactly the same point of view, and any change in the point of view makes some change in the way the light is reflected.

For most practical purposes these differences are unimportant, but to the painter they are all-important: the painter has to unlearn the habit of thinking that things seem to have the colour which common sense says they 'really' have, and to learn the habit of seeing things as they appear. Here we have already the beginning of one of the distinctions that cause most trouble in philosophy—the distinction between 'appearance' and 'reality', between what things seem to be and what they are. The painter wants to know what things seem to be, the practical man and the philosopher want to know what they are; but the philosopher's wish to know this is stronger than the practical man's, and is more troubled by knowledge as to the difficulties of answering the question.

To return to the table. It is evident from what we have found, that there is no colour which preeminently appears to be *the* colour of the table, or even of any one particular part of the table—it appears to be of different colours from different points of view, and there is no reason for regarding some of these as more really its colour than others. And we know that even from a given point of view the colour will seem different by artificial light, or to a colour-blind man, or to a man wearing blue spectacles, while in the dark there will be no colour at all, though to touch and hearing the table will be unchanged. This colour is not something which is inherent in the table, but something depending upon the table and the spectator and the way the light falls on the table. When, in ordinary life, we speak of *the* colour of the table, we only mean the sort of colour which it will seem to

have to a normal spectator from an ordinary point of view under usual conditions of light. But the other colours which appear under other conditions have just as good a right to be considered real; and therefore, to avoid favouritism, we are compelled to deny that, in itself, the table has any one particular colour.

The same thing applies to the texture. With the naked eye one can see the grain, but otherwise the table looks smooth and even. If we looked at it through a microscope, we should see roughnesses and hills and valleys, and all sorts of differences that are imperceptible to the naked eye. Which of these is the 'real' table? We are naturally tempted to say that what we see through the microscope is more real, but that in turn would be changed by a still more powerful microscope. If, then, we cannot trust what we see with the naked eye, why should we trust what we see through a microscope? Thus, again, the confidence in our senses with which we began deserts us.

The *shape* of the table is no better. We are all in the habit of judging as to the 'real' shapes of things, and we do this so unreflectingly that we come to think we actually see the real shapes. But, in fact, as we all have to learn if we try to draw, a given thing looks different in shape from every different point of view. If our table is 'really' rectangular, it will look, from almost all points of view, as if it had two acute angles and two obtuse angles. If opposite sides are parallel, they will look as if they converged to a point away from the spectator; if they are of equal length, they will look as if the nearer side were longer. All these things are not commonly noticed in looking at a table, because experience has taught us to construct the 'real' shape from the apparent shape, and the 'real' shape is what interests us as practical men. But the 'real' shape is not what we see; it is something inferred from what we see. And what we see is constantly changing in shape as we move about the room; so that here again the senses seem not to give us the truth about the table itself, but only about the appearance of the table.

Similar difficulties arise when we consider the sense of touch. It is true that the table always gives us a sensation of hardness, and we feel that it resists pressure. But the sensation we obtain depends upon how hard we press the table and also upon what part of the body we press with; thus the various sensations due to various pressures or various parts of the body cannot be supposed to reveal *directly* any definite property of the table, but at most to be *signs* of some property which perhaps *causes* all the sensations, but is not actually apparent in any of them. And the same applies still more obviously to the sounds which can be elicited by rapping the table.

Thus it becomes evident that the real table if there is one, is not the same as what we immediately experience by sight or touch or hearing. The real table, if there is one, is not *immediately* known to us at all, but must be an inference from what is immediately known. Hence, two very difficult questions at once arise; namely, (1) Is there a real table at all? (2) If so, what sort of object can it be?

It will help us in considering these questions to have a few simple terms of which the meaning is definite and clear. Let us give the name of 'sense-data' to the things that are immediately known in sensation: such things as colours, sounds, smells, hardnesses, roughnesses, and so on. We shall give the name 'sensation' to the experience of being immediately aware of these things. Thus, whenever we see a colour, we have a sensation *of* the colour, but the colour itself is a sense-datum, not a sensation. The colour is that *of* which we are immediately aware, and the awareness itself is the sensation. It is plain that if we are to know anything about the table, it must be by means of the sense-data—brown colour, oblong shape, smoothness, etc.—which we associate with the table; but, for the reasons which have been given, we cannot say that the table *is* the sense-data, or even that the sense-data are directly properties of the table. Thus a problem arises as to the relation of the sense-data to the real table, supposing there is such a thing.

The real table, if it exists, we will call a 'physical object'. Thus we have to consider the relation of sense-data to physical objects. The collection of all physical objects is called 'matter'. Thus our two questions may be re-stated as follows: (1) Is there any such thing as matter? (2) If so, what is its nature?

The philosopher who first brought prominently forward the reasons for regarding the immediate objects of our senses as not existing independently of us was Bishop Berkeley (1685–1753). His *Three Dialogues between Hylas and Philonous, in Opposition to Sceptics and Atheists*, undertake to prove that there is no such thing as matter at all, and that the world consists of nothing but minds and their ideas. Hylas has hitherto believed in matter, but he is no match for Philonous, who mercilessly drives him into contradictions and paradoxes, and makes his own denial of matter seem, in the end, as if it were almost common sense. The arguments employed are of very different value: some are important and sound, others are confused or quibbling. But Berkeley retains the merit of having shown that the existence of matter is capable of being denied without absurdity, and that if there are any things that exist independently of us they cannot be the immediate objects of our sensations.

There are two different questions involved when we ask whether matter exists, and it is important to keep them clear. We commonly mean by 'matter' something which is opposed to 'mind', something which we think of as occupying space and as radically incapable of any sort of thought or consciousness. It is chiefly in this sense that Berkeley denies matter; that is to say, he does not deny that the sense-data which we commonly take as signs of the existence of the table are really signs of the existence of *something* independent of us, but he does deny that this something is nonmental, that it is neither mind nor ideas entertained by some mind. He admits that there must be something which continues to exist when we go out of the room or shut our eyes, and that what we call seeing the table does really give us reason for believing in something which persists even when we are not seeing it. But he thinks that this something cannot be radically different in nature from what we see, and cannot be independent of seeing altogether, though it must be independent of *our* seeing. He is thus led to regard the 'real' table as an idea in the mind of God. Such an idea has the required permanence and independence of ourselves, without being—as matter would otherwise be—something quite unknowable, in the sense that we can only infer it, and can never be directly and immediately aware of it.

Other philosophers since Berkeley have also held that, although the table does not depend for its existence upon being seen by me, it does depend upon being seen (or otherwise apprehended in sensation) by *some* mind—not necessarily the mind of God, but more often the whole collective mind of the universe. This they hold, as Berkeley does, chiefly because they think there can be nothing real—or at any rate nothing known to be real—except minds and their thoughts and feelings. We might state the argument by which they support their view in some such way as this: 'Whatever can be thought of is an idea in the mind of the person thinking of it; therefore nothing can be thought of except ideas in minds;

therefore anything else is inconceivable, and what is inconceivable cannot exist.'

Such an argument, in my opinion, is fallacious; and of course those who advance it do not put it so shortly or so crudely. But whether valid or not, the argument has been very widely advanced in one form or another; and very many philosophers, perhaps a majority, have held that there is nothing real except minds and their ideas. Such philosophers are called 'idealists.' When they come to explaining matter, they either say, like Berkeley, that matter is really nothing but a collection of ideas, or they say, like Leibniz (1646–1716), that what appears as matter is really a collection of more or less rudimentary minds.

But these philosophers, though they deny matter as opposed to mind, nevertheless, in another sense, admit matter. It will be remembered that we asked two questions; namely, (1) Is there a real table at all? (2) If so, what sort of object can it be? Now both Berkeley and Leibniz admit that there is a real table, but Berkeley says it is certain ideas in the mind of God, and Leibniz says it is a colony of souls. Thus both of them answer our first question in the affirmative, and only diverge from the views of ordinary mortals in their answer to our second question. In fact, almost all philosophers seem to be agreed that there is a real table: they almost all agree that, however much our sense-data—colour, shape, smoothness, etc.—may depend upon us, yet their occurrence is a sign of something existing independently of us, something differing, perhaps, completely from our sense-data, and yet to be regarded as causing those sense-data whenever we are in a suitable relation to the real table.

Now obviously this point in which the philosophers are agreed—the view that there *is* a real table, whatever its nature may be—is vitally important, and it will be worth while to consider what reasons there are for accepting this view before we go on to the further question as to the nature of the real table. Our next chapter, therefore, will be concerned with the reasons for supposing that there is a real table at all.

Before we go farther it will be well to consider for a moment what it is that we have discovered so far. It has appeared that, if we take any common object of the sort that is supposed to be known by the senses, what the senses *immediately* tell us is not the truth about the object as it is apart from us, but only the truth about certain sense-data which, so far as we can

see, depend upon the relations between us and the object. Thus what we directly see and feel is merely 'appearance', which we believe to be a sign of some 'reality' behind. But if the reality is not what appears, have we any means of knowing whether there is any reality at all? And if so, have we any means of finding out what it is like?

Such questions are bewildering, and it is difficult to know that even the strangest hypotheses may not be true. Thus our familiar table, which has roused but the slightest thoughts in us hitherto, has become a problem full of surprising possibilities. The one thing we know about it is that it is not what it seems. Beyond this modest result, so far, we have the most complete liberty of conjecture. Leibniz tells us it is a community of souls: Berkeley tells us it is an idea in the mind of God; sober science, scarcely less wonderful, tells us it is a vast collection of electric charges in violent motion.

Among these surprising possibilities, doubt suggests that perhaps there is no table at all. Philosophy, if it cannot *answer* so many questions as we could wish, has at least the power of *asking* questions which increase the interest of the world, and show the strangeness and wonder lying just below the surface even in the commonest things of daily life.

CHAPTER II

## THE EXISTENCE OF MATTER

In this chapter we have to ask ourselves whether, in any sense at all, there is such a thing as matter. Is there a table which has a certain intrinsic nature, and continues to exist when I am not looking, or is the table merely a product of my imagination, a dream-table in a very prolonged dream? This question is of the greatest importance. For if we cannot be sure of the independent existence of objects, we cannot be sure of the independent existence of other people's bodies, and therefore still less of other people's minds, since we have no grounds for believing in their minds except such as are derived from observing their bodies. Thus if we cannot be sure of the independent existence of objects, we shall be left alone in a desert—it may be that the whole outer world is nothing but a dream, and that we alone exist. This is an uncomfortable possibility; but although it cannot be strictly *proved* to be false, there is not the slightest reason to suppose that it is true. In this chapter we have to see why this is the case.

Before we embark upon doubtful matters, let us try to find some more or less fixed point from which to start. Although we are doubting the physical existence of the table, we are not doubting the existence of the sense-data which made us think there was a table; we are not doubting that, while we look, a certain colour and shape appear to us, and while we press, a certain sensation of hardness is experienced by us. All this, which is psychological, we are not calling in question. In fact, whatever else may be doubtful, some at least of our immediate experiences seem absolutely certain.

Descartes (1596–1650) the founder of modern philosophy, invented a method which may still be used with profit—the method of systematic doubt. He determined that he would believe nothing which he did not see quite clearly and distinctly to be true. Whatever he could bring himself to doubt, he would doubt, until he saw reason for not doubting it. By applying this method he gradually became convinced that the only existence of which he could be *quite* certain was his own. He imagined a deceitful demon, who presented unreal things to his senses in a perpetual phantasmagoria; it might be very improbable that such a demon existed, but still it was possible, and therefore doubt concerning things perceived by the senses was possible.

But doubt concerning his own existence was not possible, for if he did not exist, no demon could deceive him. If he doubted, he must exist; if he had any experiences whatever, he must exist. Thus his own existence was an absolute certainty to him. 'I think, therefore I am,' he said (*Cogito, ergo sum*); and on the basis of this certainty he set to work to build up again the world of knowledge which his doubt had laid in ruins. By inventing the method of doubt, and by showing that subjective things are the most certain, Descartes performed a great service to philosophy, and one which makes him still useful to all students of the subject.

But some care is needed in using Descartes' argument. '*I* think, therefore *I* am' says rather more than is strictly certain. It might seem as though we were quite sure of being the same person to-day as we were yesterday, and this is no doubt true in some sense. But the real Self is as hard to arrive at as the real table, and does not seem to have that absolute, convincing certainty that belongs to particular experiences. When I look at my table and see a certain brown colour, what is quite certain at once is not '*I* am seeing a brown colour', but rather, 'a brown colour is being seen'. This of course involves something (or somebody) which (or who) sees the brown colour; but it does not of itself involve that more or less permanent person whom we call 'I'. So far as immediate certainty goes, it might be that the something which sees the brown colour is quite momentary, and not the same as the something which has some different experience the next moment.

Thus it is our particular thoughts and feelings that have primitive certainty. And this applies to dreams and hallucinations as well as to normal perceptions: when we dream or see a ghost, we certainly do have the sensations we think we have, but for various reasons it is held that no physical object corresponds to these sensations. Thus the certainty of our knowledge of our own experiences does not have to be limited in any way to allow for exceptional cases. Here, therefore, we have, for what it is worth, a solid basis from which to begin our pursuit of knowledge.

The problem we have to consider is this: Granted that we are certain of our own sense-data, have we any reason for regarding them as signs of the existence of something else, which we can call the physical object? When we have enumerated all the sense-data which we should naturally regard as connected with the table, have we said all there is to say about the table, or is there still something else—something not a sense-datum, something which persists when we go out of the room? Common sense unhesitatingly answers that there is. What can be bought and sold and pushed about and have a cloth laid on it, and so on, cannot be a *mere* collection of sense-data. If the cloth completely hides the table, we shall derive no sense-data from the table, and therefore, if the table were merely sense-data, it would have ceased to exist, and the cloth would be suspended in empty air, resting, by a miracle, in the place where the table formerly was. This seems plainly absurd; but whoever wishes to become a philosopher must learn not to be frightened by absurdities.

One great reason why it is felt that we must secure a physical object in addition to the sense-data, is that we want the *same* object for different people. When ten people are sitting round a dinner-table, it seems preposterous to maintain that they are not seeing the same tablecloth, the same knives and forks and spoons and glasses. But the sense-data are private to each separate person; what is immediately present to the sight of one is not immediately present to the sight of another: they all see things from slightly different points of view, and therefore see them slightly differently. Thus, if there are to be public neutral objects, which can be in some sense known to many different people, there must be something over and above the private and particular sense-data which appear to various people. What reason, then, have we for believing that there are such public neutral objects?

The first answer that naturally occurs to one is that, although different people may see the table slightly differently, still they all see more or less similar things when they look at the table, and the variations in what they see follow the laws of perspective and reflection of light, so that it is easy to arrive at a permanent object underlying all the different people's sense-data. I bought my table from the former occupant of my room; I could not buy *his* sense-data, which died when he went away, but I could and did buy the confident expectation of more or less similar sense-data. Thus it is the fact that different people have similar sense-data, and that one person in a given place at different times has similar sense-data, which makes us suppose that over and above the sense-data there is a permanent public object which underlies or causes the sense-data of various people at various times.

Now in so far as the above considerations depend upon supposing that there are other people besides ourselves, they beg the very question at issue. Other people are represented to me by certain sense-data, such as the sight of them or the sound of their voices, and if I had no reason to believe that there were physical objects independent of my sense-data, I should have no reason to believe that other people exist except as part of my dream. Thus, when we are trying to show that there must be objects independent of our own sense-data, we cannot appeal to the testimony of other people, since this testimony itself consists of sense-data, and does not reveal other people's experiences unless our own sense-data are signs of things existing independently of us. We must therefore, if possible, find, in our own purely private experiences, characteristics which show, or tend to show, that there are in the world things other than ourselves and our private experiences.

In one sense it must be admitted that we can never *prove* the existence of things other than ourselves and our experiences. No logical absurdity results from the hypothesis that the world consists of myself and my thoughts and feelings and sensations, and that everything else is mere fancy. In dreams a very complicated world may seem to be present, and yet on waking we find it was a delusion; that is to say, we find that the sense-data in the dream do not appear to have corresponded with such physical objects as we should naturally infer from our sense-data. (It is true that, when the physical world is assumed, it is possible to find physical causes for the sense-data in dreams: a door banging, for instance, may cause us to dream of a naval engagement. But although, in this case, there is a physical cause for the sense-data, there is not a physical object *corresponding* to the sense-data in the way in which an actual naval battle would correspond.) There is no logical impossibility in the supposition that the whole of life is a dream, in which we ourselves create all the objects that come before us. But although this is not logically impossible, there is no reason whatever to suppose that it is true; and it is, in fact, a less simple hypothesis, viewed as a means of accounting for the facts of our own life, than the common-sense hypothesis that there really are objects independent of us, whose action on us causes our sensations.

The way in which simplicity comes in from supposing that there really are physical objects is easily seen. If the cat appears at one moment in one part of the room, and at another in another part, it is natural to suppose that it has moved from the one to the other, passing over a series of intermediate positions. But if it is merely a set of sense-data, it cannot have ever been in any place where I did not see it; thus we shall have to suppose that it did not exist at all while I was not looking, but suddenly sprang into being in a new place. If the cat exists whether I see it or not, we can understand from our own experience how it gets hungry between one meal and the next; but if it does not exist when I am not seeing it, it seems odd that appetite should grow during non-existence as fast as during existence. And if the cat consists only of sense-data, it cannot be *hungry,* since no hunger but my own can be a sense-datum to me. Thus the behaviour of the sense-data which represent the cat to me, though it seems quite natural when regarded as an expression of hunger, becomes utterly inexplicable when regarded as mere movements and changes of patches of colour, which are as incapable of hunger as a triangle is of playing football.

But the difficulty in the case of the cat is nothing compared to the difficulty in the case of human beings. When human beings speak—that is, when we hear certain noises which we associate with ideas, and simultaneously see certain motions of lips and expressions of face—it is very difficult to suppose that what we hear is not the expression of a thought, as we know it would be if we emitted the same sounds. Of course similar things happen in dreams, where we are mistaken as to the existence of other people. But dreams are more or less suggested by what we call waking life, and are capable of being more or less accounted for on scientific principles if we assume that there really is a physical world. Thus every principle of simplicity urges us to adopt the natural view, that there really are objects other than ourselves and our sense-data which have an existence not dependent upon our perceiving them.

Of course it is not by argument that we originally come by our belief in an independent external world. We find this belief ready in ourselves as soon as we begin to reflect: it is what may be called an *instinctive* belief. We should never have been led to question this belief but for the fact that, at any rate in the case of sight, it seems as if the sense-datum itself were instinctively believed to be the independent object, whereas argument shows that the object cannot be identical with the sense-datum. This discovery, however—which is not at all paradoxical in the case of taste and smell and sound, and only slightly so in the case of touch—leaves undiminished our instinctive belief that there *are* objects *corresponding* to our sense-data. Since this belief does not lead to any difficulties, but on the contrary tends to simplify and systematize our account of our experiences, there seems no good reason for rejecting it. We may therefore admit—though with a slight doubt derived from dreams—that the external world does really exist, and is not wholly dependent for its existence upon our continuing to perceive it.

The argument which has led us to this conclusion is doubtless less strong than we could wish, but it is typical of many philosophical arguments, and it is therefore worth while to consider briefly its general character and validity. All knowledge, we find, must be built up upon our instinctive beliefs, and if these are rejected, nothing is left. But among our instinctive beliefs some are much stronger than others, while many have, by habit and association, become entangled with other beliefs, not really instinctive, but falsely supposed to be part of what is believed instinctively.

Philosophy should show us the hierarchy of our instinctive beliefs, beginning with those we hold most strongly, and presenting each as much isolated and as free from irrelevant additions as possible. It should take care to show that, in the form in which they are finally set forth, our instinctive beliefs do not clash, but form a harmonious system. There can never be any reason for rejecting one instinctive belief except that it clashes with others; thus, if they are found to harmonize, the whole system becomes worthy of acceptance.

It is of course *possible* that all or any of our beliefs may be mistaken, and therefore all ought to be held with at least some slight element of doubt. But we cannot have *reason* to reject a belief except on the ground of some other belief. Hence, by organizing our instinctive beliefs and their consequences, by considering which among them is most possible, if necessary, to modify or abandon, we can arrive, on the basis of accepting as our sole data what we instinctively believe, at an orderly systematic organization of our knowledge, in which, though the *possibility* of error remains, its likelihood is diminished by the interrelation of the parts and by the critical scrutiny which has preceded acquiescence.

This function, at least, philosophy can perform. Most philosophers, rightly or wrongly, believe that philosophy can do much more than this—that it can give us knowledge, not otherwise attainable, concerning the universe as a whole, and concerning the nature of ultimate reality. Whether this be the case or not, the more modest function we have spoken of can certainly be performed by philosophy, and certainly suffices, for those who have once begun to doubt the adequacy of common sense, to justify the arduous and difficult labours that philosophical problems involve.

# READING 38

# The Structure of Knowledge
*Robert Audi*

*Robert Audi (1941–    ) is Professor of Philosophy at the
University of Nebraska-Lincoln. He has published widely
in the areas of epistemology, philosophy of mind, and ethics.
He is the coeditor with William J. Wainwright of* Rationality, Religious Belief, and Moral Commitment
*(1986) and author of* Belief, Justification, and Knowledge *(1988) from which the following reading is excerpted.*

## THE EPISTEMIC REGRESS ARGUMENT

. . . a version of what is called the *epistemic regress argument* . . . starts with the assumption that (1) if one
has any knowledge, it occurs in an epistemic chain
(possibly including the special case of a single link,
such as a perceptual or a priori belief, which constitutes knowledge by virtue of being anchored directly
in one's experience or reason). It then states that (2)
the only possible kinds of epistemic chains are the
four mutually exclusive kinds just discussed: the infinite, the circular, those terminating in beliefs that
are not knowledge, and those terminating in direct
knowledge. It affirms that (3) knowledge can occur
only in the fourth kind of chain; and it concludes
that (4) if one has any knowledge, one has some direct knowledge. Assuming knowledge requires a
knower, we may also draw the more general conclusion that if there *is* any knowledge, there is some direct knowledge. A similar argument was advanced by
Aristotle (in the *Posterior Analytics,* Books I and II),
and versions of the regress argument have been defended ever since.

As proponents of the argument normally understand (1), it implies that any given instance of indirect knowledge depends on at least one epistemic
chain for its status *as* knowledge. So understood, the
argument clearly implies the further conclusion that

any indirect knowledge a person has *epistemically depends on,* in the sense that it cannot be knowledge
apart from, an appropriate inferential connection,
via some epistemic chain, to some direct knowledge
that the person has. Thus, the argument would show
not only that if there is indirect knowledge, there *is*
direct knowledge, but also that if there is indirect
knowledge, that very knowledge is *traceable* to some
direct knowledge as its foundation.

A similar argument applies to justification. We
simply speak of *justificatory chains* and proceed in a
parallel way, substituting justification for knowledge;
and we arrive at the conclusion that if one has any
justified beliefs, one has some directly justified beliefs. Similarly, if one has any indirectly justified
belief, it exhibits *justificational dependence* on an
epistemic chain appropriately linking it to some directly justified belief one has, that is, to a foundational belief.

## FOUNDATIONALISM AND COHERENTISM

These two sets of conclusions constitute the heart of
the position called *epistemological foundationalism.* The
first set, concerning knowledge, may be intepreted
as the twofold thesis that the structure of a body of
knowledge, such as yours or mine, is foundational,
and therefore that any indirect (hence non-foundational) knowledge there is depends on direct (and
thus in a sense foundational) knowledge. The second set, regarding justification, may be interpreted
as the twofold thesis that the structure of a body of
justified beliefs is foundational, and therefore that
any indirectly (hence non-foundationally) justified
beliefs there are depend on directly (thus in a sense
foundationally) justified beliefs. In both cases different foundationalist theories may diverge in the kind
and degree of dependence they assert. A strong
foundationalist theory of justification, for instance,

SOURCE: From *Belief, Justification, and Knowledge* (Belmont, CA:
Wadsworth, 1988), Chapter 6, pages 86–95, 98–100. Edited.

might hold that indirectly justified beliefs derive *all* their justification from foundational beliefs; a moderate theory might maintain only that the former would not be justified apart from the latter, and the theory might allow other factors, such as coherence of a belief with others one holds that are *not* in the chain, to add to its justification.

None of the foundationalist theses I have stated says anything about the *content* of a body of knowledge or of justified belief, though proponents of foundationalism usually specify, as René Descartes (1596–1650) does in his *Meditations,* what sorts of content they think appropriate. Foundationalism thus leaves open what, in particular, is believed by a given person who has knowledge or justified belief and what *sorts* of propositions are suitable material for the foundational beliefs. I want to talk mainly about foundationalism regarding knowledge, but much of what I say can be readily applied to justified belief.

Foundationalism has been criticized on a number of points. I want to focus in particular on the most important objections that stem from the best alternative theory of the structure of knowledge, *coherentism.* There are many versions of coherentism, including some that seem mainly based on the idea that if an epistemic circle is large enough and sufficiently rich, it can generate justification and account for knowledge. But we have seen serious difficulties besetting circular chains. Let us therefore try to formulate a more plausible version of coherentism.

The central idea underlying coherentism is that the justification of a belief emerges from its coherence with other beliefs one holds. The unit of coherence may be as large as one's entire set of beliefs (though of course some may figure more significantly in producing the coherence than others, say because of differing degrees of closeness in their subject matter). This idea would be accepted by a proponent of the circular view, but the thesis I want to explore differs from that view in not being *linear:* it does not construe justification or knowledge as emerging from an inferential line going from premises to that conclusion, and from other premises to the first set of premises, and so on, until we return to the original proposition as a premise. On the circular view, no matter how wide the circle, there is a *line* from any one belief in a circular epistemic chain to any other. In practice one may never trace the entire line, as by inferring one thing one knows from a sec-

ond, the second from a third, and so on, until one reinfers the first. Still, on this view there is such a line for every belief that constitutes knowledge. Thus, the kinds of problems we encountered earlier regarding circular epistemic chains must be resolved if the view is to be sustained.

## HOLISTIC COHERENTISM

Coherentism need not be linear. It may be *holistic.* To see how a holistic theory of knowledge (and justification) works, consider a question that evokes a justification. John wonders how I know, as I sit reading, that the wind is blowing. I say that the leaves are rustling. He then asks how I know that Sally is not just shaking down apples. I reply that the apple trees are too far away. He now wonders whether I can distinguish rustling leaves from the sound of a quiet car on the pebbled driveway. I reply that what I hear is too much like a whisper to be the crunchy sound of pebbles. In giving this justification I apparently go only one step along the inferential line: just to my belief that the leaves are rustling. For my belief that there is a wind *is* based on this belief about the leaves. After that, I do not even mention anything that this belief, in turn, is based on; rather, I defend my beliefs as appropriate, in terms of an entire pattern of beliefs I hold. And I may cite many different parts of the pattern. For instance, I might have said that a shaken tree sounds different from a windblown one. On the coherentist view then, beliefs representing knowledge do not lie at one end of a grounded chain; they fit a coherent pattern, and their justification emerges from their fitting that pattern in an appropriate way.

Consider a different sort of example. A gift is delivered to you with its card apparently missing. The only people you can think of who send you gifts at this time of year live in Washington and virtually never leave there, but this is from Omaha. That origin does not cohere well with your hypothesis that it was sent by your Washington benefactors, the Smiths. Then you open it and discover that it is frozen steak. You realize that this can be ordered from anywhere. But it is not the sort of gift you would expect from the Smiths. A moment later you recall that you recently sent them cheese. You suppose that they probably are sending something in response. Suddenly you remember that they once asked if you had ever tried frozen gourmet steaks, and when you said you hadn't they replied that they would have to serve you some one of these days. You might now be justified in believing that they sent the package. When you at last find their card at the bottom of the box, then (normally) you would *know* that they sent the package. The crucial things to notice here are how, initially, a kind of *incoherence* prevents justification of your first hypothesis (that the box came from the Smiths) and how, as relevant pieces of the pattern developed, you became justified and (presumably) came to know that the Smiths sent it. Arriving at a justified belief, on this view, is more like answering a question in the light of a whole battery of relevant information than like deducing a theorem by successive inferential steps from a set of axioms.

It is important to see how, using examples like those just given, holistic coherentism can respond to the regress argument. It need *not* embrace the possibility of an epistemic circle (though its proponents need not reject that either). Instead, it can deny that there are only the four kinds of possible epistemic chains I specified. There is a fifth: that the chain terminates with belief that is *psychologically direct* and *epistemically indirect* (or, if we are talking of coherentism about justification, *justificationally indirect*). Hence, the last link is, as belief, direct, yet, as knowledge, *in*direct, not in the usual sense that it is inferential but in the broad sense that the belief constitutes knowledge only by virtue of receiving support from other knowledge or belief. Thus, my belief that there is a rustling sound is psychologically direct because it is simply grounded, causally, in my hearing and is not inferentially based on any other belief; yet my *knowledge* that there is such a sound is not epistemically direct. It is epistemically, but not inferentially, based on the coherence of my belief that there is a rustling with my other beliefs, presumably including many that represent knowledge themselves. It is thus knowledge *through*, but not by inference from, other knowledge—or at least through justified beliefs—and hence epistemically indirect. Hence, it is misleading to call the *knowledge* direct at all. Granted, the belief element *in* my knowledge is non-inferentially grounded in perception and is in that sense direct; but the belief constitutes knowledge only by virtue of coherence with my other beliefs.

One could insist that if a non-inferential, thus psychologically direct, belief constitutes knowledge, it *must* be direct knowledge. But the coherentist would reply that in that case there will be two kinds of di-

rect knowledge: the kind the foundationalist posits, which derives from grounding in a basic experiential or rational source, and the kind the coherentist posits, which derives from coherence with other beliefs and not from being based on those sources. This is surely a plausible response.

Is the holistic coherentist trying to have it both ways? Not necessarily. Holistic coherentism can grant that a variant of the regress argument holds for belief since the only kind of belief chain that it is psychologically realistic to attribute to us is the kind terminating in direct (non-inferential) belief. But even on the assumption that knowledge is constituted by (certain kinds of) beliefs, it does not follow that direct belief which is knowledge is also direct *knowledge*. Thus, the coherentist is granting a kind of *psychological foundationalism*, which says (in part) that if we have any beliefs at all, we have some direct ones, yet denying epistemological foundationalism, which requires that there be knowledge which is epistemically (and normally also psychologically) direct, if there is any knowledge at all. Holistic coherentism may grant experience and reason the status of psychological foundations of our entire structure of beliefs. But it gives them no place, independently of coherence, in generating justification or knowledge.

## THE NATURE OF COHERENCE

If holistic coherentism is interpreted as I have described it, it avoids some of the major problems for linear coherentism. But there remain serious difficulties for it. I want to discuss two of them in this section. First, what *is* coherence? Second, what reason is there to think that coherence *alone* counts towards the justification of a belief, or towards its truth, as it must in some way if it is to give us a good account of knowledge?

It turns out to be very difficult to explain what coherence is. It is not mere consistency, though *in*consistency is the clearest case of incoherence. Coherence is sometimes connected with explanation. Certainly, if the Smiths' sending the package explains why the card bears their names, then my belief of the first proposition coheres with my belief of the second (other things being equal). Probability is also relevant to coherence. If the probability of the proposition that they sent the steaks is raised in the light of the proposition that I sent them cheese, this at least counts in favor of my belief of the first cohering with my belief of the second. But how are we to understand the notions of explanation and of probability? Let us consider these questions.

Does one proposition (genuinely) explain another so long as, if the first is (or is assumed to be) true, then it is clear why the second is true? Apparently not; for if that were so, then the proposition that a benevolent genie delivered the box explains why it arrived. In any event, if that proposition did explain why the box arrived, would I be justified in believing it because my believing it coheres with my believing that I know not what other source the box might have come from? Surely not. Even if we can say what notion of explanation is relevant, it will remain very difficult to specify when an explanatory relation generates enough coherence to create justification. For one thing, consider cases in which a proposition, say that Jill hurt Jack's feelings, would, if true, very adequately explain something we believe, such as that Jack is upset. Believing Jill did this might cohere well with his being upset, but that would not, by itself, justify our believing it.

Similar points hold for probability. Not just any proposition I believe which raises the probability of my hypothesis that the gift is from the Smiths will strengthen my justification for believing that it is. Consider, for example, the proposition that the Smiths send such gifts to all their friends. Suppose I have no justification for believing this, say because I have accepted it only on the basis of testimony I should see to be unreliable (and would see to be unreliable if I thought carefully about it). Then, while the proposition raises the probability of my hypothesis and (let us assume) coheres with what I already believe, I am not entitled to believe it, and my believing it will not add to my justification for believing that the Smiths sent the box. It might be replied that this belief about the Smiths' habits does not cohere well with *other* things I believe, such as that people do not generally behave like that. But suppose I knew almost nothing about the Smiths' or other people's habits of gift-giving, and I happened, without grounds, to believe the Smiths to be both generous and rich. Then there might be a significant degree of coherence between my belief that the Smiths send gifts to all their friends and my other beliefs; yet my forming the belief that they give gifts to all their friends still would not strengthen my justification for my hypothesis.

These examples bring us to the second problem. So far as we do understand coherence, what reason is there to think that by itself it generates any justification or truth at all? Whatever coherence among beliefs is, it is an *internal* relation, in the sense that it is a matter of how one's beliefs are related *to one another* and not to anything outside one's system of beliefs, such as one's perceptual experience. Now why could there not be many, many equally coherent systems of beliefs that are mutually incompatible, so that no two of them can be true? This is part of what might be called the *isolation problem:* the problem of explaining why coherent systems of beliefs are not readily isolated from truth, and thus do not contain knowledge, which implies truth.

Consider a schizophrenic who thinks he is Napoléon. If he has a completely consistent story with enough detail, his belief system may be superbly coherent. Yet obviously there are coherent belief systems that conflict with his, such as those of his psychiatrists. If coherence alone generates justification, however, we must say that each system is equally well justified—assuming their belief systems are as coherent as his. We need not attribute knowledge to any of the systems, since any of them might contain falsehood. But is it plausible to say that a system of beliefs is highly justified when there is no limit to the number of radically different yet equally justified belief systems—even on the part of other people with experience of or pertaining to many of the same things the beliefs are about—that are incompatible with it in this thoroughgoing way? The question is especially striking when we realize that two equally coherent systems, even on the part of the same person at different times, might differ not just on one point but on *every* point: each belief in one might be opposed by an incompatible belief in the other.

One would think, moreover, that a well-justified belief may be reasonably considered *true*. But if the degree of justification of a belief is entirely a matter of its support by considerations of coherence, no degree of justification by itself can carry any greater presumption of truth than is created by the same degree of support from coherence on the part of a belief of the contradictory proposition. Thus, if "Napoléon" has a sufficiently coherent set of beliefs yielding justification of his belief that he won the Battle of Waterloo, this belief may be as well justified as his psychiatrists' belief that he did not. But if this is how justification is conceived, is there any reason to suppose that a belief justified solely by considerations of coherence is true? And if Napoléon's and the psychiatrists' belief systems are equally coherent, how can we justify our apparently quite reasonable tendency to regard their belief systems as more likely to represent truths, and on that count more likely to contain knowledge, than his? Granted, their belief that he did not win the Battle coheres with our beliefs; but why should our own beliefs be privileged over equally coherent conflicting sets? And why should agreement even with nearly everyone's beliefs, say about Napoléon's being dead, be a factor, unless we are assuming that some element other than coherence, such as perception or memory, confers justification independently? If coherence alone confers justification, it is not clear how perception or memory or introspection contribute to it. Moreover, even what seems the highest degree of justification, such as we might have for simple introspective beliefs and beliefs of self-evident truths, provides us with no presumption of truth or knowledge.

## COHERENCE, REASON, AND EXPERIENCE

This brings us to a third major problem for coherentism: how can it explain the role of experience and reason as sources of justification and knowledge? Certainly experience and reason *seem* to be basic sources of justification and knowledge. Coherentists themselves commonly *use* beliefs from these sources to illustrate coherent bodies of belief that are good candidates for knowledge. How can holistic coherentism explain the role of these sources in relation to justification and knowledge? Why is it that when I have a vivid experience of the kind characteristic of seeing a blue spruce, I am apparently justified, simply by that experience, in believing that there *is* a blue spruce before me? And why do I seem so very strongly justified, simply on the basis of my rational grasp of the proposition that if some dogs are pets then some pets are dogs, in believing this? One thing a coherentist might say here is that in fact many of our beliefs are *causally* and non-inferentially based on perception or on the use of reason; and given these similarities of origin, it is to be expected that they often cohere with one another. Hence, while we do not, and do not need to, infer propositions like those just cited from any others that might provide justifying evidence for them, they *do* cohere with many other things we believe, and that coherence justifies them.

This response is more plausible for perceptual belief than for belief of simple logical truths, at least if coherence is construed as more than consistency and as related to explanation, probability, and justification. For notice that the proposition that if some dogs are pets then some pets are dogs apparently need not explain, render probable, or justify anything else I believe, nor is it obvious that anything else I believe need explain, render probable, or justify it. Yet my belief of this proposition is justified to about as high a degree as any belief I have. On the other hand, the proposition that there is a blue spruce before me *does* cohere with other things I believe: that there is a conifer there, that I am in my backyard, and so forth; and there appear to be some explanatory and probability relations among them. For instance, that there is a blue spruce before me adds to the probability that I am in my backyard; and that I am in that yard partly explains why I see a blue spruce there.

A coherentist might respond to the difference just indicated by qualifying the view, applying it only to beliefs of empirical, rather than a priori, propositions. This move could be defended on the assumption that propositions known a priori are necessary and hence are not appropriately said to be made probable by other propositions, nor to be explained by them in the same way empirical propositions are explained. It might be argued that while we can explain the *basis* of a necessary truth and thereby show *that* it holds, still, since it cannot fail to hold, there is no explaining *why* it, *as opposed to something else*, holds. This is plausible but inconclusive reasoning. We may just as reasonably say that we can sometimes explain why a necessary truth holds and in doing so explain why a contrasting proposition is false. Imagine that someone mistakenly takes a certain geometrical proposition to be a theorem and cannot see why a closely similar, true principle is a theorem. If we now prove the correct one step by step, with accompanying examples, we might explain why it, as opposed to the other proposition, is true.

So far as explanation is central to coherence, then, coherentism apparently owes us an account of knowledge of at least some necessary truths. But suppose that it can account for knowledge of *some* necessary truths. There remain others, such as simple self-evident ones, for which we cannot find anything plausibly said to explain why they hold, nor any other way of accounting for knowledge of them as grounded in coherence. Consider how one might explain why, if it is true that Jane Austen wrote *Persuasion,* then it is not false that she did. If someone did not see this, it would probably not help to point out that no proposition is both true and false. For if one needs to have the truth of an instance of this general truth explained, one presumably cannot understand the general truth either. But suppose this is not so, and that one's grasp of the general truth is somehow the basis of one's seeing the particular truth that instantiates it; then the same point would apply to the general truth: there would apparently be nothing plausibly said to explain why *it* is true.

It might now be objected that the general truth that no proposition is both true and false, and the instances of it, are *mutually explanatory:* its truth explains why they hold, and their truth explains why it holds; and this is the chief basis of their coherence with one another. But is it really possible for one proposition to explain another *and* the other to explain it? If what explains why the grass is wet is that there is dew on it, then the same proposition—that there is dew on it—is not explained by the proposition that the grass is wet (instead, condensation explains that). Reflection on other examples also suggests that two propositions cannot explain each other, and there are apparently no general arguments that show this to be possible. Perhaps it is somehow possible; but until such an argument is given, we should conclude that even if an explanatory relation between propositions is sufficient for a belief of one to cohere with a belief of the other, coherentism does not in general provide a good account of knowledge of self-evident truths.

If coherentism applies only to empirical beliefs, however, it is not a general theory of justification or knowledge and leaves us in need of a different account of a priori justification (and knowledge). In any case, it would be premature to conclude that coherentism does account for empirical justification. Let us return to the perceptual case.

It might seem that we could decisively refute the coherence theory of justification by noting that one might have only a single belief, say that there is a blue spruce before one, and that this lone belief might still be justified. For then there would be a justified belief that coheres with no other beliefs one has. But could one have just a single belief? Could one, for instance, believe that there is a blue spruce before one, yet not believe, say, that it has branches?

It is not clear that one could; and foundationalism does not assume this possibility, though the theory may easily be wrongly criticized for implying it. Foundationalism is in fact consistent with *one* kind of coherentism, namely, a *coherence theory of concepts* according to which a person acquires concepts, say of colors and shapes, only in relation to one another and must acquire an entire set of related concepts in order to acquire any concept.

We must directly ask, then, whether one's justification for believing that there is a blue spruce *derives* from the coherence of the belief with others. Let us first grant an important point. Suppose this belief turns out to be *in*coherent with a second belief, such as that one is standing where one seems to see the tree yet *feels* nothing before one and can walk right across the spot. Then the first belief may *cease* to be justified. But this only shows that its justification is *defeasible*—liable to being outweighed (overridden) or undermined—should sufficiently serious incoherence *arise,* not that it is derivative from coherence in the first place. In this case the justification of one's visually grounded belief is outweighed: one's better justified beliefs, including the conviction that a tree must be touchable, make it more reasonable for one to believe that there is *not* a tree there. Two important questions arise here. First, could incoherence outweigh justification of a belief in the first place if we were not *independently* justified in believing that a proposition incoherent with certain other ones is, or probably is, false? Second, aren't the relevant others precisely the kind for which, directly or inferentially, we have some degree of justification through the basic experiential and rational sources? Foundationalists are likely to answer the first negatively and the second affirmatively.

There is also a second case, in which one's justification is simply undermined: one ceases to be justified in believing the proposition in question, though one does not become justified in believing it false. Suppose I cease to see the tree if I move twenty feet to my left. This could justify my believing that I might be hallucinating. This belief does not cohere with, and undermines the justification of, my visual belief that the tree is there, though it does not by itself justify my believing that there is *no* tree there. Again, however, I am apparently justified, independently of coherence, in believing that my seeing the tree there is incoherent with my merely hallucinating it there. It seems, then, that coherence has the role it does in justification only because *some* beliefs are justified independently of it.

Examples like these show that it is essential to distinguish *negative epistemic dependence*—which is simply a form of defeasibility—from *positive epistemic dependence*—the kind beliefs bear to the sources from which they *derive* any justification they have or, if they represent knowledge, their status as knowledge. The defeasibility of a belief's justification by incoherence does not imply that, as coherentists must hold, this justification positively depends on coherence. If my well is my source of water, I (positively) depend on it. The possibility that people could poison it does not make their non-malevolence part of my source of water, or imply a (positive) dependence on them, such as I have on the rainfall. Moreover, it is the rainfall that explains both my having the water and its level. So it is with perceptual experience as a source of justification. Foundationalists need not claim that justification does not negatively depend on anything else, for as we have seen they need not claim that justification must be indefeasible. But negative dependence does not imply positive dependence. Justification can be defeasible by incoherence, and thus outweighed or undermined should incoherence arise, without owing its existence to coherence in the first place. . . .

## MODEST FOUNDATIONALISM

There is far more to say about both foundationalism and coherentism. But if what has emerged here is on the right track, then the problems confronting coherentism are worse than those confronting foundationalism. The most serious problems for foundationalism are widely taken to be the difficulties of specifying source conditions for justification and knowledge and, secondly, of accounting, on the basis of those sources, for all that we seem to know. The first of these problems is addressed in Part One, which describes the basic sources and illustrates how they generate direct—though not indefeasible—knowledge, and direct (though again not generally indefeasible) justification. The second problem is treated in Chapter 5, which indicates many ways in which, even without actual inferences, knowledge and justification can be transmitted from beliefs which are justified, or represent knowledge, by virtue of being grounded in the basic sources, to other beliefs. Both problems are difficult, and they have not been completely solved here. But enough has

been said to make clear along what lines they may be dealt with in a foundationalist framework.

Still another problem for foundationalism is the difficulty of accounting for the place of coherence in justification. But this is not a crippling difficulty for the kind of foundationalism I have been describing, which need not restrict the role of coherence any more than is required by the regress argument. Indeed, while (pure) coherentism grants nothing to foundationalism beyond perhaps its underlying psychological picture of how our belief systems are structured, foundationalism can account for some of the insights of coherentism, for instance the point that a coherence theory of the acquisition of concepts is plausible.

More positively, foundationalism can acknowledge a significant role for coherence in relation to justification and can thereby answer one traditional coherentist objection. I have in mind a kind of *modest foundationalism*: a foundationalist view of knowledge or justification which (a) takes the justification of foundational beliefs to be at least typically defeasible, (b) is not *deductivist*, that is, does not demand that principles governing the inferential transmission of knowledge or justification be deductive, and (c) allows a significant role for coherence by requiring, not that inferentially justified beliefs derive *all* their justification from foundational ones, but only that they derive enough of it from the latter so that they would remain justified if any other justification they have were eliminated. (A slightly different formulation may be required, if, for the sorts of reasons to be given in Chapter 7, knowledge does not entail justification, but the formulation given will serve here.) Some versions are more modest than others, but the most plausible ones give coherence at least two roles.

The first role modest foundationalism may give to coherence, or at least to incoherence, is negative: *incoherence may defeat justification or knowledge*, even of a directly justified (foundational) belief, as where my justification for believing I may be hallucinating prevents me from knowing, or remaining justified in believing, that the spruce is before me. (If this is not ultimately a role for coherence itself, it *is* a role crucial for explaining points stressed by coherentism.) Second, modest foundationalism can employ a principle commonly emphasized by coherentists, though foundationalists need not grant that the truth of the principle is based on coherence. This is an *independence principle*: that the larger the number of independent mutually coherent factors one believes to support the truth of a proposition, the better one's justification for believing it (other things being equal). This principle can explain, for instance, why my justification for believing that the box of steaks is from the Smiths increases as I acquire new beliefs each of which supports that conclusion. Similar principles consistent with foundationalism can accommodate other cases in which coherence enhances justification, say those in which a proposition's explaining, and thereby cohering with, something one justifiably believes tends to confer some degree of justification on that proposition.

Modest foundationalism contrasts with *strong foundationalism,* which, in one form, is deductivist, takes foundational beliefs as indefeasibly justified, and allows coherence only a minimal role. To meet these conditions, strong foundationalists may reduce the basic sources of justification to reason and some form of introspection. Moreover, since they are committed to the indefeasibility of foundational justification, they would not grant that incoherence can defeat the justification of foundational beliefs. They would also concede to coherentism, and hence to any independence principle they recognize, only a minimal positive role, say by insisting that if a belief is supported by two or more independent cohering sources, its justification is increased only additively, that is, only by bringing together the justification transmitted separately from each relevant basic source.

By contrast, what modest foundationalism denies regarding coherence is only that it is a basic source of justification. Coherence by itself is not sufficient for justification. Thus, the independence principle does not apply to sources that have *no* justification; at most, it allows coherence to raise the level of justification originally drawn from other sources to a level *higher* than it would be if those sources were not mutually coherent. Similarly, if inference is a basic source of coherence (as some coherentists seem to have believed), it is not a basic source of justification. It may enhance justification, as where one strengthens one's justification for believing someone's testimony by inferring the same point from someone else's. But inference *alone* does not generate justification: I might infer any number of propositions from several I already believe merely through wishful thinking; yet even if I thereby arrive at a highly coherent set of beliefs, I have not thereby increased my justification for believing any of them.

If modest foundationalism is correct, however, it still tells us only what sort of structure a body of knowledge or of justified belief has. It says that if one has any knowledge or justified belief, then one has some direct knowledge or directly justified belief, and any other knowledge or justified belief one has is traceable to those foundations. A belief direct and foundational at one time may be indirect and non-foundational at another; it may gain or lose justification; and some foundational beliefs may even be false or cease to be justified at all. By leaving this much open, modest foundationalism avoids a narrow account of what it takes to have knowledge and justification and allows many routes to their acquisition. For similar reasons, it avoids *dogmatism,* in the sense of an attitude of smug certainty concerning claims that are not self-evident. For it allows alternative kinds of foundational beliefs for different people and under different circumstances; and, by acknowledging the fallibility of the experiential sources and of many inferences from the beliefs they generate, it also explains why it is so difficult to know that one has knowledge or justified belief, and hence important to be open to the possibility of mistakes. Foundationalism *is* committed to unmoved movers; it is not committed to unmovable movers. It leaves open, moreover, just what knowledge is, and even whether there actually is any. These questions must still be faced.

## READING 39

# Sceptical Doubts Concerning the Operations of the Understanding
*David Hume*

*For biographical details see Reading 4. This reading comprises Section IV of Hume's* Enquiry.

SECTION IV

PART I

All the objects of human reason or enquiry may naturally be divided into two kinds, to wit, *Relations of Ideas,* and *Matters of Fact.* Of the first kind are the sciences of Geometry, Algebra, and Arithmetic; and, in short, every affirmation which is either intuitively or demonstratively certain. *That the square of the hypotenuse is equal to the squares of the two sides* is a proposition which expresses a relation between these figures. *That three times five is equal to the half of thirty* expresses a relation between these numbers. Propositions of this kind are discoverable by the mere operation of thought, without dependence on what is anywhere existent in the universe. Though there never were a circle or triangle in nature, the truths demonstrated by Euclid would forever retain their certainty and evidence.

Matters of fact, which are the second objects of human reason, are not ascertained in the same manner; nor is our evidence of their truth, however great, of a like nature with the foregoing. The contrary of every matter of fact is still possible because it can never imply a contradiction and is conceived by the mind with the same facility and distinctness as if ever so conformable to reality. *That the sun will not rise tomorrow* is no less intelligible a proposition, and implies no more contradiction, than the affirmation *that it will rise.* We should in vain, therefore, attempt

**SOURCE:** From *An Enquiry Concerning Human Understanding* (1748), Section IV.

to demonstrate its falsehood. Were it demonstratively false, it would imply a contradiction and could never be distinctly conceived by the mind.

It may, therefore, be a subject worthy of curiosity to enquire what is the nature of that evidence which assures us of any real existence and matter of fact beyond the present testimony of our senses or the records of our memory. This part of philosophy, it is observable, has been little cultivated, either by the ancients or moderns; and, therefore, our doubts and errors in the prosecution of so important an enquiry may be the more excusable while we march through such difficult paths without any guide or direction. They may even prove useful by exciting curiosity and destroying that implicit faith and security which is the bane of all reasoning and free enquiry. The discovery of defects in the common philosophy, if any such there be, will not, I presume, be a discouragement, but rather an incitement, as is usual, to attempt something more full and satisfactory than has yet been proposed to the public.

All reasonings concerning matter of fact seem to be founded on the relation of *Cause and Effect.* By means of that relation alone we can go beyond the evidence of our memory and senses. If you were to ask a man why he believes any matter of fact which is absent, for instance, that his friend is in the country or in France, he would give you a reason, and this reason would be some other fact: as a letter received from him, or the knowledge of his former resolutions and promises. A man finding a watch or any other machine in a desert island would conclude that there had once been men in that island. All our reasonings concerning fact are of the same nature. And here it is constantly supposed that there is a connection between the present fact and that which is inferred from it. Were there nothing to bind them together, the inference would be entirely precarious. The hearing of an articulate voice and rational discourse in the dark assures us of the presence of some person. Why? Because these are the effects of the human make and fabric, and closely connected with it. If we anatomize all the other reasonings of this nature, we shall find that they are founded on the relation of cause and effect, and that this relation is either near or remote, direct or collateral. Heat and light are collateral effects of fire, and the one effect may justly be inferred from the other.

If we would satisfy ourselves, therefore, concerning the nature of that evidence which assures us of matters of fact, we must enquire how we arrive at the knowledge of cause and effect.

I shall venture to affirm, as a general proposition which admits of no exception, that the knowledge of this relation is not, in any instance, attained by reasonings a priori, but arises entirely from experience, when we find that any particular objects are constantly conjoined with each other. Let an object be presented to a man of ever so strong natural reason and abilities; if that object be entirely new to him, he will not be able, by the most accurate examination of its sensible qualities, to discover any of its causes or effects. Adam, though his rational faculties be supposed, at the very first, entirely perfect, could not have inferred from the fluidity and transparency of water that it would suffocate him, or from the light and warmth of fire that it would consume him. No object ever discovers, by the qualities which appear to the senses, either the causes which produced it or the effects which will arise from it; nor can our reason, unassisted by experience, ever draw any inference concerning real existence and matter of fact.

This proposition, *that causes and effects are discoverable, not by reason but by experience*, will readily be admitted with regard to such objects as we remember to have once been altogether unknown to us, since we must be conscious of the utter inability which we then lay under of foretelling what would arise from them. Present two smooth pieces of marble to a man who has no tincture of natural philosophy; he will never discover that they will adhere together, in such a manner as to require great force to separate them in a direct line, while they make so small a resistance to a lateral pressure. Such events as bear little analogy to the common course of nature are also readily

confessed to be known only by experience, nor does any man imagine that the explosion of gunpowder or the attraction of a loadstone could ever be discovered by arguments a priori. In like manner, when an effect is supposed to depend upon an intricate machinery or secret structure of parts, we make no difficulty in attributing all our knowledge of it to experience. Who will assert that he can give the ultimate reason, why milk or bread is proper nourishment for a man, not for a lion or a tiger?

But the same truth may not appear, at first sight, to have the same evidence with regard to events which have become familiar to us from our first appearance in the world, which bear a close analogy to the whole course of nature, and which are supposed to depend on the simple qualities of objects without any secret structure of parts. We are apt to imagine that we could discover these effects by the mere operation of our reason without experience. We fancy that, were we brought on a sudden into this world, we could at first have inferred that one billiard ball would communicate motion to another upon impulse, and that we needed not to have waited for the event in order to pronounce with certainty concerning it. Such is the influence of custom that, where it is strongest, it not only covers our natural ignorance, but even conceals itself and seems not to take place, merely because it is found in the highest degree.

But to convince us that all the laws of nature and all the operations of bodies without exception are known only by experience, the following reflections may perhaps suffice. Were any object presented to us, and were we required to pronounce concerning the effect which will result from it, without consulting past observation; after what manner, I beseech you, must the mind proceed in this operation? It must invent or imagine some event which it ascribes to the object as its effect; and it is plain that this invention must be entirely arbitrary. The mind can never possibly find the effect in the supposed cause by the most accurate scrutiny and examination. For the effect is totally different from the cause, and consequently can never be discovered in it. Motion in the second billiard ball is a quite distinct event from motion in the first, nor is there anything in the one to suggest the smallest hint of the other. A stone or piece of metal raised into the air and left without any support immediately falls. But to consider the matter a priori, is there anything we discover in this situation which can beget the idea of a downward, rather than an upward, or any other motion, in the stone or metal?

And as the first imagination or invention of a particular effect in all natural operations is arbitrary where we consult not experience, so must we also esteem the supposed tie or connection between the cause and effect which binds them together and renders it impossible that any other effect could result from the operation of that cause. When I see, for instance, a billiard ball moving in a straight line towards another; even suppose motion in the second ball should by accident be suggested to me as the result of their contact or impulse; may I not conceive that a hundred different events might as well follow from that cause? May not both these balls remain at absolute rest? May not the first ball return in a straight line, or leap off from the second in any line or direction? All these suppositions are consistent and conceivable. Why then should we give the preference to one which is no more consistent or conceivable than the rest? All our reasonings *a priori* will never be able to show us any foundation for this preference.

In a word, then, every effect is a distinct event from its cause. It could not, therefore, be discovered in the cause, and the first invention or conception of it *a priori* must be entirely arbitrary. And even after it is suggested, the conjunction of it with the cause must appear equally arbitrary, since there are always many other effects which, to reason, must seem fully as consistent and natural. In vain, therefore, should we pretend to determine any single event, or infer any cause or effect, without the assistance of observation and experience.

Hence we may discover the reason why no philosopher who is rational and modest has ever pretended to assign the ultimate cause of any natural operation, or to show distinctly the action of that power which produces any single effect in the universe. It is confessed that the utmost effort of human reason is to reduce the principles productive of natural phenomena to a greater simplicity, and to resolve the many particular effects into a few general causes, by means of reasonings from analogy, experience, and observation. But as to the causes of these general causes, we should in vain attempt their discovery, nor shall we ever be able to satisfy ourselves by any particular explication of them. These ultimate springs and principles are totally shut up from

human curiosity and enquiry. Elasticity, gravity, cohesion of parts, communication of motion by impulse: these are probably the ultimate causes and principles which we shall ever discover in nature; and we may esteem ourselves sufficiently happy, if, by accurate enquiry and reasoning, we can trace up the particular phenomena to, or near to, these general principles. The most perfect philosophy of the natural kind only staves off our ignorance a little longer, as perhaps the most perfect philosophy of the moral or metaphysical kind serves only to discover larger portions of it. Thus the observation of human blindness and weakness is the result of all philosophy, and meets us at every turn in spite of our endeavours to elude or avoid it.

Nor is geometry, when taken into the assistance of natural philosophy, ever able to remedy this defect or lead us into the knowledge of ultimate causes by all that accuracy of reasoning for which it is so justly celebrated. Every part of mixed mathematics proceeds upon the supposition that certain laws are established by nature in her operations, and abstract reasonings are employed, either to assist experience in the discovery of these laws, or to determine their influence in particular instances where it depends upon any precise degree of distance and quantity. Thus, it is a law of motion, discovered by experience, that the moment or force of any body in motion is in the compound ratio or proportion of its solid contents and its velocity; and, consequently, that a small force may remove the greatest obstacle or raise the greatest weight if, by any contrivance or machinery, we can increase the velocity of that force so as to make it an overmatch for its antagonist. Geometry assists us in the application of this law by giving us the just dimensions of all the parts and figures which can enter into any species of machine; but still the discovery of the law itself is owing merely to experience, and all the abstract reasonings in the world could never lead us one step towards the knowledge of it. When we reason *a priori* and consider merely any object or cause as it appears to the mind, independent of all observation, it never could suggest to us the notion of any distinct object, such as its effect, much less show us the inseparable and inviolable connection between them. A man must be very sagacious who could discover by reasoning that crystal is the effect of heat, and ice of cold, without being previously acquainted with the operation of these qualities.

PART II

But we have not yet attained any tolerable satisfaction with regard to the question first proposed. Each solution still gives rise to a new question as difficult as the foregoing and leads us on to farther enquiries. When it is asked, *What is the nature of all our reasonings concerning matter of fact?* the proper answer seems to be, that they are founded on the relation of cause and effect. When again it is asked, *What is the foundation of all our reasonings and conclusions concerning that relation?* it may be replied in one word, *experience.* But if we still carry on our sifting humour, and ask, *What is the foundation of all conclusions from experience?* this implies a new question which may be of more difficult solution and explication. Philosophers that give themselves airs of superior wisdom and sufficiency have a hard task when they encounter persons of inquisitive dispositions, who push them from every corner to which they retreat, and who are sure at last to bring them to some dangerous dilemma. The best expedient to prevent this confusion is to be modest in our pretensions, and even to discover the difficulty ourselves before it is objected to us. By this means we may make a kind of merit of our very ignorance.

I shall content myself in this section with an easy task, and shall pretend only to give a negative answer to the question here proposed. I say then, that, even after we have experience of the operations of cause and effect, our conclusions from that experience are *not* founded on reasoning or any process of the understanding. This answer we must endeavour both to explain and to defend.

It must certainly be allowed that nature has kept us at a great distance from all her secrets, and has afforded us only the knowledge of a few superficial qualities of objects, while she conceals from us those powers and principles on which the influence of these objects entirely depends. Our senses inform us of the colour, weight, and consistency of bread, but neither sense nor reason can ever inform us of those qualities which fit it for the nourishment and support of a human body. Sight or feeling conveys an idea of the actual motion of bodies, but as to that wonderful force or power which would carry on a moving body forever in a continued change of place, and which bodies never lose but by communicating it to others, of this we cannot form the most distant conception. But notwithstanding this ignorance of

natural powers[1] and principles, we always presume when we see like sensible qualities, that they have like secret powers, and expect that effects similar to those which we have experienced will follow from them. If a body of like colour and consistency with that bread which we have formerly eaten be presented to us, we make no scruple of repeating the experiment, and foresee with certainty like nourishment and support. Now this is a process of the mind or thought of which I would willingly know the foundation. It is allowed on all hands that there is no known connection between the sensible qualities and the secret powers, and, consequently, that the mind is not led to form such a conclusion concerning their constant and regular conjunction by anything which it knows of their nature. As to past *experience,* it can be allowed to give *direct* and *certain* information of those precise objects only, and that precise period of time which fell under its cognizance. But why this experience should be extended to future times and to other objects which, for aught we know, may be only in appearance similar, this is the main question on which I would insist. The bread which I formerly ate nourished me; that is, a body of such sensible qualities was, at that time, endued with such secret powers. But does it follow that other bread must also nourish me at another time, and that like sensible qualities must always be attended with like secret powers? The consequence seems nowise necessary. At least, it must be acknowledged that there is here a consequence drawn by the mind, that there is a certain step taken, a process of thought, and an inference which wants to be explained. These two propositions are far from being the same: *I have found that such an object has always been attended with such an effect,* and *I foresee that other objects which are in appearance similar will be attended with similar effects.* I shall allow, if you please, that the one proposition may justly be inferred from the other: I know, in fact, that it always is inferred. But if you insist that the inference is made by a chain of reasoning, I desire you to produce that reasoning. The connection between these propositions is not intuitive. There is required a medium which may enable the mind to draw such an inference, if indeed it be drawn by reasoning and argument. What that medium is I must confess passes my comprehension; and it is incumbent on those to produce it, who assert that it really exists and is the origin of all our conclusions concerning matter of fact.

This negative argument must certainly, in process of time, become altogether convincing if many penetrating and able philosophers shall turn their enquiries this way, and no one be ever able to discover any connecting proposition or intermediate step which supports the understanding in this conclusion. But as the question is yet new, every reader may not trust so far to his own penetration, as to conclude, because an argument escapes his enquiry, that therefore it does not really exist. For this reason it may be requisite to venture upon a more difficult task and, enumerating all the branches of human knowledge, endeavour to show that none of them can afford such an argument.

All reasonings may be divided into two kinds, namely demonstrative reasoning, or that concerning relations of ideas, and moral reasoning, or that concerning matter of fact and existence. That there are no demonstrative arguments in the case seems evident, since it implies no contradiction that the course of nature may change and that an object, seemingly like those which we have experienced, may be attended with different or contrary effects. May I not clearly and distinctly conceive that a body, falling from the clouds and which in all other respects resembles snow, has yet the taste of salt or feeling of fire? Is there any more intelligible proposition than to affirm that all the trees will flourish in December and January, and decay in May and June? Now, whatever is intelligible and can be distinctly conceived implies no contradiction, and can never be proved false by any demonstrative argument or abstract reasoning *a priori*.

If we be, therefore, engaged by arguments to put trust in past experience and make it the standard of our future judgment, these arguments must be probable only, or such as regard matter of fact and real existence, according to the division above mentioned. But that there is no argument of this kind must appear if our explication of that species of reasoning be admitted as solid and satisfactory. We have said that all arguments concerning existence are founded on the relation of cause and effect, that our knowledge of that relation is derived entirely from experience, and that all our experimental conclusions proceed upon the supposition that the future will be conformable to the past. To endeavour, therefore, the proof of this last supposition by probable arguments, or arguments regarding existence, must be evidently going in a circle and tak-

ing that for granted which is the very point in question.

In reality, all arguments from experience are founded on the similarity which we discover among natural objects, and by which we are induced to expect effects similar to those which we have found to follow from such objects. And though none but a fool or madman will ever pretend to dispute the authority of experience or to reject that great guide of human life, it may surely be allowed a philosopher to have so much curiosity at least as to examine the principle of human nature which gives this mighty authority to experience, and makes us draw advantage from that similarity which nature has placed among different objects. From causes which appear *similar,* we expect similar effects. This is the sum of all our experimental conclusions. Now it seems evident that, if this conclusion were formed by reason, it would be as perfect at first, and upon one instance, as after ever so long a course of experience. But the case is far otherwise. Nothing so like as eggs; yet no one, on account of this appearing similarity, expects the same taste and relish in all of them. It is only after a long course of uniform experiments in any kind that we attain a firm reliance and security with regard to a particular event. Now, where is that process of reasoning which, from one instance, draws a conclusion so different from that which it infers from a hundred instances that are nowise different from that single one? This question I propose as much for the sake of information as with an intention of raising difficulties. I cannot find, I cannot imagine any such reasoning. But I keep my mind still open to instruction, if anyone will vouchsafe to bestow it on me.

Should it be said that, from a number of uniform experiments, we *infer* a connection between the sensible qualities and the secret powers, this, I must confess, seems the same difficulty, couched in different terms. The question still recurs, on what process of argument this *inference* is founded? Where is the medium, the interposing ideas, which join propositions so very wide of each other? It is confessed that the colour, consistency, and other sensible qualities of bread appear not of themselves to have any connection with the secret powers of nourishment and support. For otherwise we could infer these secret powers from the first appearance of these sensible qualities without the aid of experience, contrary to the sentiment of all philosophers, and contrary to plain matter of fact. Here, then, is our natural state of ignorance with regard to the powers and influence of all objects. How is this remedied by experience? It only shows us a number of uniform effects resulting from certain objects, and teaches us that those particular objects, at that particular time, were endowed with such powers and forces. When a new object endowed with similar sensible qualities is produced, we expect similar powers and forces, and look for a like effect. From a body of like colour and consistency with bread, we expect like nourishment and support. But this surely is a step or progress of the mind which wants to be explained. When a man says, *I have found, in all past instances, such sensible qualities conjoined with such secret powers,* and when he says, *similar sensible qualities will always be conjoined with similar secret powers,* he is not guilty of a tautology, nor are these propositions in any respect the same. You say that the one proposition is an inference from the other. But you must confess that the inference is not intuitive, neither is it demonstrative. Of what nature is it then? To say it is experimental is begging the question. For all inferences from experience suppose, as their foundation, that the future will resemble the past and that similar powers will be conjoined with similar sensible qualities. If there be any suspicion that the course of nature may change, and that the past may be no rule for the future, all experience becomes useless and can give rise to no inference or conclusion. It is impossible, therefore, that any arguments from experience can prove this resemblance of the past to the future, since all these arguments are founded on the supposition of that resemblance. Let the course of things be allowed hitherto ever so regular; that alone, without some new argument or inference, proves not that for the future it will continue so. In vain do you pretend to have learned the nature of bodies from your past experience. Their secret nature, and consequently all their effects and influence, may change without any change in their sensible qualities. This happens sometimes, and with regard to some objects. Why may it not happen always, and with regard to all objects? What logic, what process of argument secures you against this supposition? My practice, you say, refutes my doubts. But you mistake the purport of my question. As an agent, I am quite satisfied in the point; but as a philosopher who has some share of curiosity, I will not say scepticism, I want to learn the foundation of this inference. No reading, no enquiry

has yet been able to remove my difficulty, or give me satisfaction in a matter of such importance. Can I do better than propose the difficulty to the public, even though, perhaps, I have small hopes of obtaining a solution? We shall at least, by this means, be sensible of our ignorance, if we do not augment our knowledge.

I must confess that a man is guilty of unpardonable arrogance who concludes, because an argument has escaped his own investigation, that therefore it does not really exist. I must also confess that, though all the learned, for several ages, should have employed themselves in fruitless search upon any subject, it may still, perhaps, be rash to conclude positively that the subject must therefore pass all human comprehension. Even though we examine all the sources of our knowledge and conclude them unfit for such a subject, there may still remain a suspicion that the enumeration is not complete or the examination not accurate. But with regard to the present subject, there are some considerations which seem to remove all this accusation of arrogance or suspicion of mistake.

It is certain that the most ignorant and stupid peasants, nay infants, nay even brute beasts, improve by experience and learn the qualities of natural objects by observing the effects which result from them. When a child has felt the sensation of pain from touching the flame of a candle, he will be careful not to put his hand near any candle, but will expect a similar effect from a cause which is similar in its sensible qualities and appearance. If you assert, therefore, that the understanding of the child is led into this conclusion by any process of argument or ratiocination, I may justly require you to produce that argument, nor have you any pretence to refuse so equitable a demand. You cannot say that the argument is abstruse and may possibly escape your enquiry, since you confess that it is obvious to the capacity of a mere infant. If you hesitate, therefore, a moment or if, after reflection, you produce any intricate or profound argument, you, in a manner, give up the question and confess that it is not reasoning which engages us to suppose the past resembling the future, and to expect similar effects from causes which are, to appearance, similar. This is the proposition which I intended to enforce in the present section. If I be right, I pretend not to have made any mighty discovery. And if I be wrong, I must acknowledge myself to be indeed a very backward scholar, since I cannot now discover an argument which, it seems, was perfectly familiar to me long before I was out of my cradle.

**NOTES**

1. The word *power* is here used in a loose and popular sense. The more accurate explication of it would give additional evidence to this argument. See Section VII. [Reading 42]

# READING 40

# Unfinished Business: The Problem of Induction
*Wesley C. Salmon*

*Wesley Salmon (1925– ) is University Professor of Philosophy at the University of Pittsburgh. Best known for his work on scientific explanation and inductive reasoning, his books include* The Foundations of Scientific Inference *(1967),* Space, Time, and Motion *(1975),* Scientific Explanation and the Causal Structure of the World *(1984), and* Four Decades of Scientific Explanation *(1989).*

Hume's *Enquiry Concerning Human Understanding* is widely recognized as a work admirably suited to stimulate genuine epistemological interest and perplexity on the part of beginning students.[1] Composed by a philosophical stylist of consummate skill, it presents, in simple and comprehensible terms, a problem of enormous intellectual and practical import—the problem of the justification of induction. Like most good philosophical problems, this one has proved amazingly refractory against some of the best efforts of first-rate philosophers, past and present. To be sure, many contemporary philosophers believe they possess a definitive answer to this puzzle, but expert opinion differs markedly regarding the nature of the correct answer. Under these circumstances, it seems extraordinary that no mention whatever was made of this problem at the Hume bicentennial conference. Such a lacuna should not, I feel, go unnoticed.

**SOURCE:** From *Philosophical Studies* 33 (1978): 1–19.

In view of the popularity of the *Enquiry* as an introductory reading, let me continue to pursue the issue from a pedagogic standpoint. How do we go about presenting this material to young minds? We try to challenge them to think about the question of what basis we have for making any inference from the observed to the unobserved. We try to make them grapple with a logical problem: How do we know what's going to happen in the future—in the next few years, the next few hours, the next few minutes? They think they know (partially at least) what's going to happen, and so do we, but how? Not by direct observation, for we do not have the gift of precognition. If we know at all, we know by some sort of inference. And once that is clear, we have them in Hume's grasp. ". . . as a philosopher, who has some share of curiosity", he said, "I want to learn the foundation of this inference".

As we follow out Hume's analysis for our students, we reveal his inability to find any rational foundation for such inferences. "If there be any suspicion that the course of nature may change, and that the past may be no rule for the future, all experience becomes useless, and can give rise to NO INFERENCE OR CONCLUSION". ". . . it is not REASONING which engages us to suppose the past resembling the future, and to expect similar effects from causes which are, to appearance, similar". "I am ready to reject ALL BELIEF AND REASONING and look upon *no opinion* as MORE PROBABLE OR LIKELY than another."[2]

Nature, of course, compels us—or exercises friendly persuasion at least—to expect the future to be like the past in significant respects. But psychological expectation is not the same thing as logical inference. Logic—reason—has nothing whatever to do with it. That's what David Hume said, we tell our introductory classes; if Hume is right, any belief about unobserved matters of fact is just as *reasonable* as any other. Not as vivid, or compelling, or natural perhaps—but just as *reasonable* or *probable* or *likely*.

Forgive me for rehearsing this familiar story. My purpose is to ask what response we are to offer. I realize that—if the past be any guide to the future—no vast numbers of students are going to be 'turned on' to any such abstract intellectual problem. But what about the small minority who read the assignment, pay attention to the lecture, and try to understand what is going on? What shall we say to them? Was Hume right? Shall we admit that reason has nothing to do with predicting the future? *I do not think we are quite ready for that concession—at least I fervently hope not.* We believe that there are rational methods of prediction, and that there are irrational ones. Moreover, I must confess, I am not as sanguine as Hume about nature's dependability in keeping us appropriately on course as we plan for the future and make our practical decisions. When I observe human behavior—including my own—I'm not encouraged.

Having been presented with a problem, our students would like to be told 'the answer'. It is, of course, contrary to all accepted principles of philosophic pedagogy to satisfy that desire without further ado, so we tell them that the solution (as if we had one to give them) cannot really be appreciated without going through the salient arguments. We therefore consider various alternative approaches; several immediately suggest themselves either for historical reasons or because of their strong psychological appeal.

(1) Many of the brightest students, when asked why they have confidence in the inductive method, will answer, "because it works". This formula has such compelling psychological appeal that it is easy to overlook the temporal ambiguity of the verb 'works'. What the argument amounts to, as Hume so masterfully explained, is the inference that induction *will work* because it *has worked*. This inference is itself inductive, and thus begs the question. Philoso-phers have, nevertheless, attempted to show how induction could be supported inductively. It has sometimes been suggested that circles can be 'virtuous' rather than 'vicious', or that an argument can be circular without committing the fallacy of *petitio principii*. But after all of the philosophical squirming—whether they are circular, the type of circularity, and whether it is bad for an argument to be circular—it remains possible to 'justify' the counter-inductive method by precisely the same type of argument as was used to justify induction.[3] Whatever 'justifies' everything justifies nothing.

(2) Kant's appeal to the synthetic a priori must be mentioned, and not just for reasons of historical completeness. Hume had severely challenged the status of the principle of uniformity of nature. Awakened from his dogmatic slumbers, Kant argued that this principle (in the form of a principle of universal causation) is secured as a synthetic a priori truth of pure reason. Kant had no doubts about the existence of synthetic a priori truths; he was merely formulating in rather clear and precise terms what philosophers had maintained about the status of geometry for more than two millenia. The subsequent discovery of non-Euclidean geometries, and the searching philosophical investigations of their applicability to the physical world, have thoroughly undercut any such view of the nature of geometry. With that (and other) developments, the basis for the synthetic a priori became tenuous indeed. Nevertheless, the last ditch resort to the synthetic a priori in order to get around the problem of induction is not a thing of the remote past. Two of the greatest scientific philosophers of the twentieth century have taken that refuge—how else can we regard Carnap's a priori measure functions in confirmation theory or Russell's postulates of scientific inference?[4] Although Russell's theory of non-demonstrative inference does not enjoy a great deal of popularity at present, Carnap's inductive logic does stand as the most highly developed and clearly articulated system we have seen to date.

(3) The tradition of British Empiricism—of which Hume was both the ablest champion and the most devastating challenger—lived on into the nineteenth century with John Stuart Mill. Mill was no friend of global synthetic a priori principles, or a priori principles of any sort. His idea was to assume just as much uniformity of nature (causality) as you need for the job at hand—no more. He seems to have

adopted a sort of postulational approach. Russell later provided a critique of postulational method which was both brief and apt: "The method of 'postulating' what we want has many advantages; they are the same as the advantages of theft over honest toil."[5] Mill, in anticipation, seems to have felt that many petty larcenies are more excusable than one big heist. Like all others who have resorted to postulates, Mill never really came to grips with Hume's problem.

(4) It has sometimes been maintained that Hume's critique of induction should be no cause for distress to any but those philosophers engaged in a 'quest for certainty'. Hume showed conclusively, they claim, that the inductive method is not infallible. That is a fact of life we must simply learn to live with.[6] This response, however, seriously fails to appreciate the import of Hume's conclusions and the arguments he adduces in their support. He argues, not that induction may upon occasion yield a false conclusion, but rather, that for all we can know, *it may never again yield a true one*. It is not that inductive conclusions fall short of certainty; rather, we have no reason to place *any confidence whatever in any inductive conclusion*. The ancient philosophers were fully aware that neither perception nor a posteriori reasoning yields absolute certainty. Hume did far more than merely to remind us of that banality.

These four approaches come readily to mind; no doubt there are others that could be placed in the same category. They all have one thing in common. Hume had already considered and answered each of them. If we had read carefully and understood, we could have saved ourselves the trouble of going through them. We should be telling our students, at this point, that Hume's arguments stand up remarkably well against all traditional efforts to refute or circumvent them.

The foregoing attempts to deal with the problem of induction are admittedly not among those which enjoy the greatest current popularity. Let us therefore consider the more serious contenders. Many twentieth-century philosophers have tried to dismiss the difficulty as a pseudo-problem; this seems to qualify as the most popular way to get around Hume's embarrassing problem.

The basic idea is that Hume did not formulate a real problem, but became enmeshed in a series of conceptual confusions. Once we straighten out those confusions—which may involve considerable subtlety—the problem will vanish. Here are some of the allegations:

- He confused induction with deduction.
- He tried, unsuccessfully of course, to transform induction into deduction.
- He inappropriately applied deductive standards to induction.
- He failed to recognize that induction has its own standards and criteria—that it is an autonomous type of logic, distinct from deduction.

The whole attempt to find a justification for induction was, according to this charge, a search for something that would be appropriate only in a deductive context.

There is no doubt that we should make every effort to avoid confusing induction with deduction. But will avoidance of such confusion make Hume's problem of induction vanish? The key notion in this approach is *autonomy;* let us see what it amounts to. The general idea seems to be that there are certain forms of argument which are not valid, but which we are not prepared to give up. When we find that our favorite argument turns out to be fallacious, but we want to cling to it, one way to save it is to call it 'inductive'. Recall Morris R. Cohen's famous quip to the effect that a logic text is a book divided into two parts; in the first part (on deduction) the fallacies are explained, while in the second part (on induction) they are committed.

Similar ploys have been adopted in other areas of philosophy. In a famous passage in the *Treatise*, Hume remarked pointedly upon the logical gap in arguments which purport to derive ought-statements from is-statements. Some moral philosophers who hanker after such inferences have sought ways of circumventing this difficulty. One device, suggested by Patrick Nowell-Smith, is the concept of 'contextual implication': ". . . a statement *p* contextually implies a statement *q* if anyone who knew the normal conventions of the language would be entitled to infer *q* from *p* in the *context in which they occur*".[7] Contextual implication, Nowell-Smith notes, does not share with standard logical implication (deductive entailment) the severe drawback of being bound by rigid rules. This very feature of contextual implication suits it for use in the 'anything-goes-if-you-want-it-badly-enough' approach to logic.

Unbridled use of contextual implication may, of course, give rise to some disquieting results. For example, in some places at the present time it seems that the statement, 'the victim of the homicide was homosexual', contextually implies the statement, 'the homicide was not a serious crime'. But what's wrong with that kind of logic? If moral philosophers want to derive ought-statements from is-statements, why should they deny themselves? If politicians fancy syllogisms with undistributed middle terms, why should they be subject to logical censure? If a particular sort of argument appeals to you—according to this way of thinking—the fact that it is unjustified should present no obstacle.

I am *not* saying that valid deductive arguments are the only admissible types. Valid deduction has a valuable property. The arguments in this category are truth-preserving; from true premises you cannot validly deduce a false conclusion. But other types of arguments are needed as well; that is precisely the reason we have a problem of justification of induction. I *am* saying that the characteristic of *being an invalid argument we prize* does not constitute a sufficient ground for considering an argument rationally admissible. Better grounds must be found.

Lest there be some feeling that, with the discussion of contextual implication, the is-ought fallacy, and undistributed middle, I have strayed too far from the main issue—induction—let me return forthwith. What reason is there to refuse to grant that the fallacy of affirming the consequent—known more politely as the 'hypothetico-deductive method'—is the legitimate method of science? We all know, of course, that it is not deductively valid, and no one is claiming otherwise. We can, nevertheless, signify our psychological attachment to this type of argument by calling it 'inductive' and saying that it 'confirms' conclusions rather than entailing them. Am I misrepresenting this attitude of logical tolerance? I do not think so, for I find it stated candidly by some of the most significant modern contributors to the philosophy of induction. Consider a famous statement by Nelson Goodman:

> . . . rules and particular inferences alike are justified by being brought into agreement with each other. *A rule is amended if it yields an inference we are unwilling to accept; an inference is rejected if it violates a rule we are unwilling to amend.* The process of justification is the delicate one of making mutual adjustments between rules

and accepted inferences, and in the agreement achieved lies the only justification needed for either.

> All this applies equally well to induction. An inductive inference, too, is justified by conformity to general rules, and a general rule by conformity to accepted inductive inferences. Predictions are justified if they conform to valid canons of induction; and the canons of induction are valid if they accurately codify accepted inductive practice.[8]

Thus, did Goodman dispatch Hume's problem—'the old riddle of induction'.

Rudolf Carnap used somewhat different terms, but espoused essentially the same view; "The reasons [for accepting any axiom of inductive logic] are based upon our intuitive judgments concerning inductive validity, i.e., concerning inductive rationality of practical decisions (e.g., about bets)".[9]

Two of the most influential philosophers to deal with the problem thus agree that there is nothing more that can be done in inductive logic than to codify and systematize our feelings about what is or is not legitimate. To show that the results of these efforts have any rational justification seems to be regarded as beyond the realm of possibility. Hume's problem is, according to them, utterly recalcitrant. They are extremely reluctant to come right out and say so, but as far as I can see, that's what it boils down to.

In an oft-quoted remark, C. D. Broad said that induction is the glory of science and the scandal of philosophy.[10] If, as Carnap and Goodman seem to admit, the problem is so intractable, why aren't contemporary philosophers more scandalized? How can Carnap, Goodman, and countless others accept the situation with such equanimity? For the answer to this query, let us turn to P. F. Strawson, who seems to have become the most prominent spokesman for a 'Wittgensteinian' approach.[11]

The 'ordinary language dissolution' of the problem of induction rests primarily upon the claim that the principles of induction are ultimate principles; they are not amenable to justification because there are no other principles which are more fundamental that could be invoked for the purpose of carrying out a justification of induction. The above-mentioned *autonomy* of inductive logic is a result of the *ultimacy* of its principles. To ask whether induction is justified is to ask whether it is reasonable to employ inductive canons. The demand for such a justification must, so the argument goes, be confused or misplaced, because the canons of induction are themselves constitutive of what it *means* to characterize something as reasonable.

This seductive approach has not gone unchallenged. Employing Herbert Feigl's important distinction between two types of justification—validation and vindication—I pointed out that a straightforward significance could be attached to the request for a justification of induction. While *validation* cannot be carried out without appeal to principles more fundamental than those whose justification is at issue, *vindication* is not subject to any such limitation. To vindicate a rule or principle is to show that its adoption will serve some specified end; this type of justification does not require an appeal to more fundamental inductive principles. Strawson's argument correctly shows that the demand for a justification of the basic canons of induction does take us beyond the limits of possible validation. His argument does *not*, however, show that such a demand takes us beyond the limits of possible *justification*, for vindication is a form of justification, and that type of justification is not touched by the appeal to ultimacy. Strawson suggests that the request for a justification of induction is like asking whether it is reasonable to be reasonable; this, he suggests, is a pointless question. I argued that such a question is not vacuous at all if we recognize two senses of 'reasonable' corresponding to Feigl's two senses of 'justification'.[12]

In a reply of somewhat less than a single page—totally ignoring the crucial distinction between validation and vindication—Strawson dismissed the objections with the remark, "If it is said that there is a problem of induction, and that Hume posed it, it must be added that he solved it."[13] One gets a distinct impression of Strawson's impatience with those who insist on dragging out the old philosophical chestnut.

Hume had, of course, maintained that induction is a matter of 'custom and habit'. This is what Strawson sees as Hume's solution to the problem. It might be reformulated in somewhat more modern terminology by saying that inductive behavior is a matter of psychological conditioning. Knowing what we do of Pavlov's dogs we would rephrase once again: "Verily I say unto you that induction is but a certain watering at the mouth!"[14]

What we know about conditioning, and about various other biological and physiological processes, is

known scientifically—inductively. It is not at all clear to me how the proponent of this Strawsonian line would argue against those who, on flagrantly unscientific and non-inductive grounds, simply reject that very scientific claim—namely that inductive behavior, in contrast to various other approaches to finding out about unobserved matters of fact, is enforced upon us by nature. As nearly as I can understand the ordinary language approach, one simply resorts to name-calling. The non-inductionist is smeared with such epithets as 'unscientific' and 'irrational'. On the other hand, "If you use inductive procedures you can call yourself 'reasonable'—*and isn't that nice!*"[15] This, it still seems to me, captures the kernel of the 'ordinary language dissolution' of the problem of induction.

Being reasonable, according to ordinary language theorists, involves fashioning one's beliefs in terms of the evidence—and inductive evidence is normally at least part of the evidence. Once more, we are told, the adoption of inductive procedures determines the very meaning of the concept of evidence, and hence, what it is to be reasonable. This argument, I believe, is vulnerable to the objection that there are many conceivable rules of inference in terms of which one might fashion one's beliefs. To be concrete, one could cite (1) induction by enumeration, (2) an a priori rule, and (3) a counter-inductive rule.[16] Depending upon which rule is adopted, a radically different concept of evidence emerges. A fact which constitutes positive evidence *for* a given hypothesis on the basis of rule (1) is *irrelevant* to that hypothesis on the basis of rule (2), while precisely the same fact is evidence *against* the very same hypothesis on rule (3). If the standard inductive rule, rather than one of the infinitely many pathological alternatives, is constitutive of rationality, it seems to me that we ought to be able to say on what grounds its superiority rests.

In response to these considerations, Stephen Barker rose to the defense of the dissolutionists. He made no secret of his feeling of fatigue:

> Wittgenstein, Strawson, and others have held that the traditional problem of induction is a pseudo-problem, resulting from conceptual confusion; a puzzle to be dissolved, not a problem to be solved in its own terms. Professor Salmon disagrees and tries to rescue the grand old problem from dissolution; or perhaps I ought rather to say that he tries to res-

urrect that grand old corpse of a problem
which many of us had hoped would now be allowed to molder in peace.[17]

Well, I do apologize for being so tiresome, but I fail
to see that Hume's problem of justification of induction is a pseudo-problem. Barker elaborates his
claim:

> Salmon would like us radically to question
> the practice of induction which shapes our
> whole form of life, but words fail. We cannot
> express such a question. We reach one of those
> points at which, as Wittgenstein says, one feels
> like uttering an inarticulate cry.[18]

I find Barker's remark incomprehensible. The claim
that the problem of induction cannot be formulated
seems manifestly false. Hume had formulated it
(whether he had also solved it or not). Russell had
formulated it. Reichenbach had formulated it. I had
just formulated it in the very paper on which Barker
was commenting. None of us, as far as I am aware,
had been reduced to inarticulate cries. Still, this response by Barker is the most serious and coherent
effort to answer these objections of which I am
aware.

In spite of damaging attacks—at least they strike
me as utterly devastating—and in the absence of any
serious defense against them, the 'ordinary language
dissolution' continues to be regarded by many as *the
definitive answer* to the problem of the justification of
induction. As recently as 1974, in a book whose title
declares that it is devoted to *Justification and Knowledge*, John Pollock begins his chapter on induction
with these remarks:

> The traditional problem of induction was
> that of justifying induction . . . it is almost ob-
> vious that nothing could possibly count as a
> justification. We cannot justify induction in-
> ductively, and, as Strawson remarked, to at-
> tempt to give a deductive justification of
> induction is to attempt to turn induction into
> deduction, which it is not. This, of course, is
> just what has always made the traditional
> problem of induction so puzzling. But the les-
> son to be learned from all this is that the at-
> tempt to justify induction is wrongheaded and
> must be forsaken. This is because the princi-
> ples of induction are instrumental in our mak-
> ing justified judgments about the world, and
> as such are involved in the justification condi-
> tions of our concepts. Insofar as the principles
> of induction are involved in the justification
> conditions of our concepts, they are partially

constitutive of the meanings of these concepts.
It is simply part of the meaning of these concepts that one can inductively generalize in
connection with them. To *justify* induction
would be to somehow derive the justification
conditions of these concepts from something
deeper, but there is nothing deeper. It is in
principle impossible to justify induction, and
there is no reason why things should be otherwise. The traditional problem of induction is
best regarded as a pseudo-problem.[19]

This is Pollock's *total* comment on Hume's problem
of induction; the remainder of the chapter is devoted to Goodman's 'new riddle of induction'.

Appalled at the continued popularity of this attempt to evade an unwanted philosophical problem,
I once remarked (of P. F. Strawson and A. J. Ayer),
"They seem to argue, by a kind of logic that frankly
escapes me, that induction needs no defense because
it is indefensible".[20] The logic still escapes me, but I
now believe I may have a clue to the willingness of so
many philosophers to adopt the dissolutionist approach even in the face of the most damaging arguments (which go largely unacknowledged). The
fundamental principle distilled from their approach
is one which must be admitted, even by those who do
not quite comprehend its derivation, to exhibit great
philosophic ingenuity. Once formulated, it can easily
be applied again: *The ordinary language 'dissolution' of
the problem of induction needs no defense precisely because
it is indefensible.*

The straightforward candor of Karl Popper's treatment of Hume's problem of induction makes a re-
freshing contrast to the ordinary language approach.
In the opening paragraph of his 1972 book, *Objective
Knowledge,* Popper says,

> I think that I have solved a major philo-
> sophical problem: the problem of induction. (I
> must have reached the solution in 1927 or
> thereabouts.) This solution has been ex-
> tremely fruitful, and it has enabled me to solve
> a good number of other philosophical prob-
> lems.[21]

The solution, very simply, is that Hume proved induction to be an untenable mode of inference, and it
must therefore be abandoned. It is not the business
of science to attempt to establish hypotheses as true
or as probable. The hypothetico-deductive form of
*confirmation* is illegitimate and has no place in sci-

ence. Hypotheses can, however, be refuted by the deductively valid *modus tollens,* and this is the most that science can aspire to. Popper's approach has been characterized as 'deductivism' and as 'the method of conjectures and refutations'.

This way of dealing with Hume's problem of induction would seem to give rise to an immediate difficulty. Deduction, as Popper is fully aware, is non-ampliative—that is, the conclusion of a valid deduction has no content which was not already present in the premises. If we grant the plausible assumption that all of our observations are confined to happenings in the past and present, then it follows immediately that observation *plus deduction* can yield no information whatever about the future. Indeed, the total information content of science cannot exceed the content of our observations themselves.

According to Popper's characterization, the method of science is to put forth generalizations as conjectures, and to attempt to falsify them. Let us see how this works. I could use fancier examples of scientific hypotheses, but the principle would be precisely the same. Suppose, on the one hand, that we entertain the generalization, 'All ravens are black', and we find that it is impervious to all efforts at falsification. The entire information thereby conveyed is that we have not observed a non-black raven. This says less than a simple report of our observations of birds. Suppose, on the other hand, that we advance the generalization, 'All swans are white', and find that it is falsified. In this case, the total information conveyed is that we have observed a non-white swan. Again, more would have been conveyed by a report of our observations of birds.[22]

According to Popper, bold conjectures and powerful theories are the pride of modern science, but according to the principles of his clearly articulated methodology, the content of scientific knowledge cannot extend beyond the content of our observation reports. Popper has sometimes chided the 'inductivists' for holding the view that science consists merely of observation reports and simple empirical generalizations upon them. He protests that science is not that poverty-stricken—a view with which inductivists heartily agree. But on his theory, the content of scientific knowledge does not even include the generalizations. It is ironic that in recent years Popper and his associates have placed great emphasis upon 'the problem of the growth of knowledge'.

According to his own principles, scientific knowledge grows at a rate not exceeding the rate of accumulation of observations. In fairness, I should add, the observations we make are significantly influenced by the hypotheses we are entertaining. But that doesn't change the fact that there is no ampliative form of scientific argument, and consequently, science provides no information whatever about the future. In answer to Hume's question, 'How are we to make reasonable inference from the observed to the unobserved', Popper's clear and unequivocal answer is, 'No way!'

It may be objected that I am distorting Popper's views by a failure to mention his concept of *corroboration.* Among hypotheses which have not been falsified, some—by reason of greater simplicity, more severe testing, or larger content—receive a higher corroboration rating than others. Popper clearly stresses that 'corroboration' is no synonym for 'confirmation'. If, however, degree of corroboration were some sort of index to the reliance we should place upon a hypothesis for predicting the future, or to the confidence we should have in the truth of the hypothesis, then Popper's deductivism would be polluted with *some* ampliative mode of inference. In that case, Popper would turn out to be an inductivist after all. But Popper adamantly denies that corroboration has any predictive import whatever; the degree of corroboration is an indication of the performance of the generalization *with respect to past occurrences alone.* Popper's deductivism remains pure; science has no predictive import.[23]

When we recover our composure after this shocking news, we may naturally feel impelled to ask on what basis we would make the kind of predictions upon which all of our practical decisions must be grounded. Popper reassures us that for such purposes "a *pragmatic belief in the results of science* is not irrational, because there is nothing more 'rational' than the method of critical discussion [conjectures and refutations], which is the method of science".[24] But recalling what Popper has explicitly stated about the predictive content of science, we must hasten to add that nothing could be less 'rational' either. When all methods are on an equal footing with respect to predictive content, Popper seems to draw the astonishing conclusion that belief in the results of none of them is 'irrational'. Predictions based upon the results of science are not irrational, but predictions based upon astrology would likewise not be irrational, since neither science nor astrology has any credentials at all when it comes to predictive value. Popper goes on to say that "it would be irrational to accept any of its [science's] results as certain", but we have recognized from the outset the truism that science is not infallible. Having offered that (unneeded) word of caution (which seems to suggest that those who do not agree with him are committed to an infallibility doctrine), he adds, "there is nothing 'better' [than science] when it comes to practical action: there is no alternative method which might be said to be more rational".[25]

If all methods of making inferences to the future are equally and totally incapable of being justified, then none is any *more* rational than any other, and none is any *less* rational than any other. All are on a par. The correct conclusion to draw, I should think, is that *all* methods, including the scientific method, are irrational bases for prediction. Thus, when the atomic scientists were contemplating the assembly of the first atomic pile in Chicago, it would, according to Popper's principles, have been just as rational to consult a crystal-gazing seer as to consult a scientist for a prediction as to whether a self-sustaining chain reaction would occur, and whether it would engulf the entire city of Chicago and possibly the whole earth in an uncontrolled nuclear blast.

Either science has predictive import or it does not. If it has none, it provides no rational basis for prediction. If it has predictive import, it must incorporate some form of ampliative inference. You can't have it both ways; it has to be one or the other. It is incredible to maintain that the *solution* to the problem of induction lies in the claim that science has no predictive content. *That* sounds a good deal more like a *statement* of the problem.

My own sympathies have lain with an approach by way of a pragmatic vindication of induction, along lines suggested by Herbert Feigl and Hans Reichenbach. Enormous difficulties, however, are encountered along this path. Reichenbach constructed a well-known pragmatic argument based upon the convergence properties of his 'rule of induction'. As he realized, the same argument provided the same sort of justification for an infinite class of 'asymptotic rules' which share the same convergence properties. On what basis, then, is the 'rule of induction'—the straight rule—to be singled out as the uniquely acceptable member of the class? With a patent misapplication of his principle of descriptive simplicity,

Reichenbach claimed to have provided a suitable rationale for the choice. But this answer would not do.

For some time I sought other, more satisfactory, principles on which to narrow down the class of candidates for basic inductive rules. Without boring you with tedious details, let me merely mention two suggestions: (1) a set of *normalizing conditions* and (2) a *criterion of linguistic invariance*. These did seem quite potent in disqualifying large classes of unacceptable asymptotic rules. Moreover, in countering the objection that even Reichenbach's rule of induction would fall victim to the criterion of linguistic invariance, I also offered a proposal for the resolution of Goodman's famous 'grue-bleen paradox'—his 'new riddle of induction'—which still seems fundamentally satisfactory. All of this was enormously pleasing; indeed, in a fit of over-optimism, I thought I had succeeded in providing satisfactory grounds for uniquely justifying the one rule.[26] This happy state of mind was shattered when I. Richard Savage and Ian Hacking independently constructed counterexamples to the general claim.[27]

I do not think either the normalizing conditions or the criterion of linguistic invariance are unsound; the difficulty is that they are not strong enough to do the job I had hoped they would do. Hacking has, however, proved that three principles would be necessary and sufficient to single out Reichenbach's rule of induction: consistency, invariance, and symmetry.[28] If, and only if, it could be shown that a satisfactory basic inductive rule must satisfy these conditions would the desired justification be forthcoming. The question then becomes, what grounds, if any, can be found for imposing just these requirements upon inductive rules. Skipping over some technical details, I would remark that the consistency requirement is analogous to my normalizing conditions, while my criterion of linguistic invariance can, I think, be legitimately extended to coincide with the invariance condition formulated by Hacking. These two requirements do not seem to me to pose insuperable difficulties. The remaining condition, symmetry, is something else again.

The crucial problem arising out of the symmetry condition can be illustrated by a simple puzzle. Consider the following initial section of a sequence of heads and tails:

H T T H T H T H H H T H T H H H H T H T H

The relative frequency of heads in this observed sequence is 6/10; on the basis of the rule of induction we might infer—or *posit*, to use Reichenbach's term—that the long run frequency of heads, if the sequence is continued, will be somewhere near that value. If, however, we examine the initial section carefully, we note that each toss corresponding to a prime number—the second, third, fifth, seventh, etc.—is a tail, while every other toss yields heads. If we use the rule of induction on the subsequences, we posit that each prime toss will be a tail and all others will be heads. Since it is known that the limiting frequency of primes among the natural numbers is zero, the induction on the subsequences entails that the limiting frequency of heads in the entire sequence is 1. Unless it can be shown how, and why, one of these inductions must supersede the other, adoption of Reichenbach's rule of induction will lead us into genuine paradox. At present, I do not know how to resolve this paradox—or whether it is, in principle, capable of resolution.

Inasmuch as philosophers have not done an outstanding job of providing answers to Hume's problem of induction, perhaps we might look elsewhere. It would surely make good sense to ask whether statisticians, whose business is to deal with certain kinds of inductive or probabilistic inference in scientific contexts, can offer any help. The answer, it turns out, is unequivocally negative.

There are two major schools of thought regarding foundations of statistics, the bayesian and the orthodox. According to the bayesian school, probabilities are merely subjective degrees of belief; they have no direct bearing upon objective facts in the world. To say that a particular future outcome is highly probable does not mean that it will usually turn out that way in similar circumstances, nor does it mean that we have good reason to believe in any such outcome. The probability, for each individual, is simply the amount of psychological confidence he happens to have—for whatever reason, rational or irrational—in that outcome. The most that statistics can do is to help us avoid a certain type of inconsistency—called *incoherence*—in combinations of beliefs; it cannot tell us whether a given degree of belief is a reasonable basis for predicting the future. L. J. Savage, the most prominent exponent of this viewpoint, explicitly acknowledged that he was a Humean skeptic where prediction is concerned.[29]

Orthodox statisticians regard probabilities as objective entities; if one knows the probabilities that govern certain types of events, one would have a rational basis for prediction and action. The problem, of course, is to establish the values of such objective probabilities. Orthodox statisticians have methods which are used for just such purposes. When these methods are examined carefully, however, it turns out that their application invariably requires synthetic general assumptions about matters of fact. Orthodox statisticians do not, in other words, have methods for making inductive inferences which do not depend upon the results of other, previous, inductions.[30] Their position is very close, I believe, to that of John Stuart Mill. If we assume some general statistical regularities, we can make inductive inferences. But on what basis are these assumptions— even fairly modest one—to be justified?

Where can we go from here? Every path we have tried to follow has turned into a blind alley. One feels an almost irresistible tendency to resonate to Hume's own reaction to such frustrations:

> The *intense* view of these manifold contradictions and imperfections in human reason has so wrought upon me, and heated my brain, that I am ready to reject all belief and reasoning, and can look upon no opinion even as more probable or likely than another. Where am I, or what? From what causes do I derive my existence, and to what condition shall I return? Whose favor shall I court, and whose anger must I dread? What beings surround me? and on whom have I any influence, or who have any influence on me? I am confounded with all these questions, and begin to fancy myself in the most deplorable condition imaginable, inviron'd with the deepest darkness, and utterly depriv'd of the use of every member and faculty.
>
> Most fortunately it happens, that since reason is incapable of dispelling these clouds, nature herself suffices to that purpose, and cures me of this philosophical melancholy and delirium, either by relaxing this bent of mind, or by some avocation, and lively impression of my senses, which obliterates all these chimeras. I dine, I play a game of backgammon, I converse, and am merry with my friends; and when after three or four hours' amusement, I wou'd return to these speculations, they appear so cold, and strain'd, and ridiculous, that I cannot find in my heart to enter into them any farther.[31]

Well, perhaps we should just let it rest there. Perhaps these philosophical doubts are empty and sterile. Perhaps, as Robert Ackermann suggests in the Preface of his 1970 introductory text, you have to be crazy to be bothered about such problems:

> I once knew a man who always worried that the roof of any room which he occupied was likely to fall in and injure or kill him. This worry was, in a sense, philosophical; no one could *prove* that the worry was without foundation in fact. But instead of being regarded as a philosopher, this worrier was thought of as a harmless lunatic, known among intimates as 'Crazy Phil'. There is an uncomfortable resemblance between Crazy Phil and many philosophers of science. Like Phil, these philosophers are motivated by private fears.[32]

If this is intended to apply to philosophers who, like Hume, Russell, Reichenbach, and many others, have grappled with the problem of justification of induction, it is a grotesque caricature. Hume was not the victim of neurotic dread.

> Let the course of things be allowed hitherto ever so regular; that alone, without some new argument or inference, proves not that, for the future, it will continue so . . . My practice, you say, refutes my doubts. But you mistake the purport of my question. As an agent, I am quite satisfied in the point. . . .[33]

These philosophers were confident that the roof would not fall in, if it was constructed in accord with suitable engineering principles, for they all had full confidence in the laws of physics. Phaedrus, the protagonist of *Zen and the Art of Motorcycle Maintenance,* in contrast, did end up in an institution on account of his worries about the problem of induction; however he hardly qualifies as a prominent contributor to the philosophical foundations of inductive logic. Concern about the philosophical problem of justification of induction may be pointless; it is not, however, crazy.

But can we really be *that* complacent? Can the problem of induction simply be dismissed as otiose? Much as I'd like to give an affirmative answer, I find I really cannot. Science *is* more reasonable than astrology, superstition, random guessing, divine revelation, and visions in LSD-induced psychedelic states. With scientific techniques we can predict an eclipse. It is reasonable to believe in this prediction. It is not reasonable to accept the prognostication, made by a religious fanatic, that the world will end tomorrow. It is silly to place confidence in forecasts found in fortune cookies in Chinese restaurants.

I am firmly convinced of this—we are all firmly convinced. But how can we show it? With Hume, "I want to know the foundation of this inference".

Without an answer, we open the door to *any mental aberration whatever*—to every form of irrationalism—allowing them all to be just as sound as science. *That simply won't do.* It is unacceptable on philosophical grounds, and it is intolerable on practical grounds. I was not indulging in whimsy when I remarked at the outset that this problem has significant practical ramifications. In a recent case, medical experts agreed that a child with diabetes would die if insulin were not administered. The fundamentalist parents had some sort of divine revelation that the child would not die if medication were halted. No insulin was administered and the child died. In another recent instance, at a commune in Arizona, a 'geomancer'—a person who walks around with hands outstretched, sensing the vibrations from the earth—predicted that crops would grow there in arid soil without cultivation or irrigation. The seed was scattered; nothing grew. In this case, the birds and small rodents, at least, benefitted.

It is not intellectually adequate simply to *call* those who practice non-inductive—non-scientific—methods of prediction 'irrational'. It does not solve the philosophical problem to lock them up, or even to perform lobotomies upon them. Nor is it acceptable to say—as one often hears—that science is, at bottom, a matter of faith; there are many faiths which are all on a par. You just choose the one you like best. It is equally unsatisfactory to give that approach a slight terminological twist and characterize the inductive method as part of 'a form of life'—one among many such 'forms', I suppose. And it is manifestly untenable to deny that there is any such thing as rationally grounded prediction.

What, then, should we say finally to our students who want to know 'the answer' to Hume's problem of induction? In my opinion we should frankly admit that, as yet, we have no completely satisfactory answer. None of the various attempts—many of them quite ingenious—to solve, resolve, or dissolve the problem is altogether successful. Does that mean that we have been dealing with a pointless question—a pseudo-problem? I do not believe so. The moral seems rather that we have an exceedingly difficult problem on our hands. In his attempts to provide logically adequate foundations of mathematics, Russell turned up a set-theoretical paradox which, he reports, it took him five agonizing years to resolve. We now have every reason to believe that the problems raised by Hume when he said, "I want to learn the foundation of this [inductive] inference", are, if anything, even more difficult. The work of Russell and others on the foundations of mathematics has considerably deepened our understanding of mathematical reasoning. A solution of Hume's problem of induction could plausibly be expected to deepen our understanding of scientific reasoning.

I have been taking an unpopular line—some might even consider it a breach of etiquette on the occasion, when everyone else politely refrained from mentioning this subject. It seems to me, however, that the least we can do on the bicentennial is to acknowledge candidly that part of Hume's legacy is work still to be done. The problem he left us is a tough one, but we have no excuse for pretending that it does not exist. And, I think, we had better not stop trying to solve it.

## NOTES

1. This point was brought home forcefully to me when, recently, trying to free my mind of all philosophical preconceptions, I reread Sections IV–VII of the *Enquiry.* As a result of this effort, I wrote a dialogue, "An Encounter with David Hume" (published in Joel Feinberg, Ed., *Reason and Responsibility,* 3rd edition, Dickenson Publ. Co., 1975) in which I try to show how this work can speak effectively to contemporary students.

2. The foregoing famous quotations are from the *Enquiry,* Part IV, and the *Treatise,* conclusion of Book I. I have added emphasis.

3. My critical discussion of this approach can be found in *The Foundations of Scientific Inference* (University of Pittsburgh Press, Pittsburgh, 1967): 12–17.

4. See *The Foundations of Scientific Inference,* pp. 27–48, 68–79. Russell's introduction of his postulates in *Human Knowledge: Its Scope and Limits* is strikingly similar to a Kantian 'transcendental deduction'.

5. Bertrand Russell, *Introduction to Mathematical Philosophy* (George Allen and Unwin, London, 1919): 71.

6. Such an answer has been suggested by Jerrold Katz, *The Problem of Induction and Its Solution* (University of Chicago Press, Chicago, 1962): 115.

7. Patrick Nowell-Smith, *Ethics* (Penguin, 1954): 80.

8. Nelson Goodman, *Fact, Fiction, and Forecast,* 2nd edition, (Bobbs-Merrill, 1965): 64.

9. P. A. Schilpp, Ed., *The Philosophy of Rudolf Carnap* (Open Court, 1963): 978.

10. *The Philosophy of Francis Bacon,* Cambridge, 1926.

11. P. F. Strawson, *Introduction to Logical Theory* (Methuen & Co., 1952), Chapter 9.

12. I offered these arguments in "Should We Attempt to Justify Induction?" *Philosophical Studies* 8 (1957): 38–42.

13. P. F. Strawson, "On Justifying Induction," *Philosophical Studies* 9 (1958): 20–21.

14. This is a paraphrase of a famous remark allegedly made by A. N. Whitehead in response to a lecture by Bertrand Russell (with much reference to Pavlov's experiments) on ethics: "Verily, I say unto you that the good is but a certain watering at the mouth."

15. Salmon, 'Should We Attempt to Justify Induction?" p. 42.

16. I stated these rules in "The Concept of Inductive Evidence," *American Philosophical Quarterly* 2 (1965): 1–6, where I also presented the ensuing argument. The same argument was spelled out more fully and precisely in "The Justification of Inductive Rules of Inference," in I. Lakatos, Ed., *The Problem of Inductive Logic* (North-Holland, 1968): 29–33.

17. Stephen F. Barker, "Discussion: Is There a Problem of Induction?" *American Philosophical Quarterly* 2 (1965): 7.

18. *Ibid.,* p. 9.

19. John Pollock, *Justification and Knowledge* (Princeton University Press, 1974): 204.

20. Salmon, "The Justification of Inductive Rules of Inference," p. 24.

21. Karl R. Popper, *Objective Knowledge* (Oxford University Press, 1972): 1.

22. I have discussed Popper's approach in *The Foundations of Scientific Inference,* pp. 21–27, and again in "The Justification of Inductive Rules of Inference," pp. 25–29.

23. See J. W. N. Watkins, "Non-inductive Corroboration," in I. Lakatos, Ed., *The Problem of Inductive Logic* (North-Holland, 1968): 61–66, and Popper, *Objective Knowledge,* pp. 18–19.

24. Popper, *Objective Knowledge,* p. 27.

25. *Ibid.*

26. The details are given in my article "On Vindicating Induction," *Philosophy of Science* 30 (1963): 252–261.

27. See I. Lakatos, *The Problem of Inductive Logic,* pp. 50–51 and pp. 86–87.

28. I. Hacking, "One Problem About Induction," in I. Lakatos, *The Problem of Inductive Logic,* pp. 57–59.

29. L. J. Savage, "Implications of Personal Probability for Induction," *Journal of Philosophy* LXIV (1967): 593–607. In *Foundations of Scientific Inference,* pp. 79–83, I discuss this approach in greater detail.

30. This matter was surveyed thoroughly by Ben Rogers in "Foundational Studies in Statistical Inference," Ph.D. dissertation, Indiana University, 1970.

31. Hume, *Treatise,* Conclusion of Book I.

32. Robert Ackermann, *The Philosophy of Science* (Pegasus, 1970): ix.

33. Hume, *Enquiry,* Sec. IV.

## READING 41

---

# Reliability, Justification, and the Problem of Induction

*James Van Cleve*

*James Van Cleve (1948–    ) is Professor of Philosophy at Brown University. He has published a number of papers on issues in epistemology and metaphysics and is co-editor with Robert E. Frederick of* The Philosophy of Right and Left: Incongruent Counterparts and the Nature of Space *(1990).*

According to the main tradition in epistemology, knowledge is a variety of justified true belief, justification is an undefinable normative concept, and epistemic principles (principles about what justifies what) are necessary truths. According to the leading contemporary rival of the tradition, justification may be defined or explained in terms of reliability, thus permitting one to say that knowledge is reliable true belief and that epistemic principles are contingent. My aim here is to show that either of these approaches will yield a solution to the problem of induction. In particular, either of them makes it possible to ascertain the reliability of induction through induction itself. Such a procedure is usually dismissed as circular, but I shall argue that it cannot be so dismissed if either approach is correct.[1]

As one would expect, the solution based on the traditional approach differs from the one based on the reliabilist alternative, but they have important features in common. The common elements are presented in sections I, II, and III, the elements specific to the reliabilist approach in sections IV, V, and VI, and those specific to the traditional approach in section VII.

SOURCE: From P. French, T. Uehling, Jr., and H. Wettstein, Eds., *Midwest Studies in Philosophy, IX* (Minneapolis: University of Minnesota Press, 1984): 555–567.

### I.

The problem of induction is the problem of showing that inductive inferences are justified. More precisely, it is the problem of showing that *some* inductive inferences are justified, for no one, I presume, holds that *all* inductive inferences are justified, at least not if 'inductive' is used broadly to cover everything that is not deductive. I shall be concerned here only with inductive inferences conforming at least roughly to the "straight rule" pattern,

> $x$% of the $A$'s I have examined were $B$'s.
>     Hence,
> $x$% of *all* $A$'s are $B$'s.

and especially with inferences of the form

> Most of the $A$'s I have examined were $B$'s.
>     Hence,
> The majority of *all* $A$'s are $B$'s.

I shall assume that we know how to restrict the predicates involved in these inferences so as to avoid Goodman's paradox about the grue emeralds.[2] That is, I shall assume that we have at least a partial answer to the "new riddle" of induction—which are the good inductive inferences, the ones that are justified if any are?—in order to tackle the traditional problem—are even *these* inferences justified?[3]

Before we can go further we need to answer the question, What is it for an inference to be justified? Taking the notion of justified *belief* for granted, I suggest the following as a preliminary account of justified *inference*: an inference is justified if and only if any person who drew the inference and who was justified in believing its premises would also be justified in believing its conclusion. We cannot rest content with this, however. To acquire justification by drawing an inference, it is not enough simply to be justified in believing the premises; in addition, (a) one must believe the conclusion *because* one believes the premises, and (b) one must not be in possession of further evidence that defeats the justification the inference would normally provide. These points are accommodated in the following account: an inference is justified if and only if any person justified in believing its premises who drew the inference and believed its conclusion as a result would be prima facie justified in this belief. The additional qualifications will seldom be important in the discussion that follows, however, so I shall generally omit them.

## II.

The case for inductive skepticism has not been improved upon since Hume. Paraphrasing the fifth and sixth paragraphs of Section IV, Part II, of the *Inquiry Concerning Human Understanding*, we may state it as follows:

> All justified inferences are either demonstrative or probable. But no inductive inference is demonstrative, for it is always conceivable that the conclusion of such an inference be false even though its premises be true.[4] Nor can any inductive inference be said to be probable. A probable inference, in order to establish its conclusion, presupposes the principle that the future will resemble the past (or, more accurately, that "instances, of which we have had no experience, resemble those, of which we have had experience").[5] This principle is not a necessary truth, for a change in the course of nature is easily conceivable. How, then, is it to be established? Not by demonstration, for it is not entailed by any premises that are accessible to us; and not by probable inference, since such inferences presuppose that very principle.[6] It must therefore be concluded that no inductive inference whatsoever is justified.

Part of this argument—that inductive inferences are not demonstrative—should be as undisturbing as it is incontestable. The real bite comes with the contention that inductive inferences are not even *probable*, since as such they would presuppose a principle that could itself be established only by induction, thus involving us in a circle. When we reflect on this part of the argument, however, a striking irrelevancy comes to light. In what sense can it be maintained that inductive inferences *presuppose* that the future will resemble the past, or any such general principle? Evidently, it is in this sense only: an inductive infer-

ence would not be valid—would not be *demonstrative*—unless its premises were augmented by some such principle. But so what? This is irrelevant to the position supposedly under attack. When it is claimed that some inductive inferences are probable, what is meant is this: there are inferences that, *despite being nondemonstrative*, confer justification on their conclusions for anyone who is justified in believing their premises.[7] That such inferences would require further premises to be valid is beside the point, since validity is not claimed for them. All that is claimed is that justified belief in the premises would make belief in the conclusion also justified, at least to some extent. Against the possibility that inductive arguments are in this sense probable it appears that Hume has made no case whatsoever.[8]

I think inductive skeptics would have to concede that this answer to Hume (sometimes known as "inductive probabilism") is correct in its negative points, but they might nonetheless try to save their case by making two claims. First, the existence of probable inductive arguments, though not disproved by Hume, has not been proved by his opponents either, and must remain an article of faith. Second, even if we knew that a given inductive argument was probable, this knowledge would scarcely be worth having. For to say that a conclusion is warranted (though not entailed) by a certain set of premises is one thing; to say that it is *likely to be true* in the sense that in believing such a conclusion on the strength of such premises one would usually be right—is another. What we *want* from an inductive inference is what Carnap called probability 2 (probability in the statistical sense), but all we get (or at least all we *know* we get) is probability 1 (probability in the "reasonable to believe" sense).[9]

We shall be in a better position to deal with these objections after considering another approach to the problem of induction.

## III.

Ask a layman why he believes in induction and you are likely to be told, "Because it works." Implicit in this response is the following argument:

*Argument A*
Most of the inductive inferences I have drawn in the past from true premises have had true conclusions.
    Hence,
The majority of *all* inductive inferences with true premises have true conclusions.

Since Argument A is itself an inductive inference, most philosophers would be quick to condemn it as circular. But I shall argue that the form of circularity present is not vicious, thus joining ranks with a small minority that has come to the defense of the inductive validation of induction.[10]

Under what circumstances is an argument viciously circular? I submit that it is so under one circumstance only: a necessary condition of using it to gain knowledge of (or justified belief in) its conclusion is that one *already have* knowledge of (or justified belief in) its conclusion.[11] Let us say that an argument with this trait is *epistemically circular*. The most obvious examples of epistemically circular arguments are those in which the conclusion or a mere stylistic variant of it occurs among the premises. More subtle examples are those in which the conclusion, though not occurring in any guise among the premises, is nonetheless epistemically prior to one of the premises, in the sense that one could arrive at knowledge of the premise only via an epistemic route that passed through the conclusion first. In either of these cases we may speak of *premise circularity*. Now Argument A does not appear to suffer from premise circularity, though I shall consider later the possibility that it does. The more likely charge against Argument A is that it is circular in a different way: it is sanctioned by a rule of inference that one could know to be correct only if one already knew that its conclusion was true.[12] Let us call this feature *rule circularity*. If to be correct a rule of inference must be such that most arguments sanctioned by it and having true premises also have true conclusions, then rule circularity is undeniably present in Argument A.[13] The question is whether rule circularity is a vice.

In answering this question, it is important to keep two points in mind: (i) rule circularity is not a vice unless it makes for epistemic circularity, and (ii) an argument that is rule circular is not on that account epistemically circular *unless knowing that its rule is correct is a precondition of using the argument to gain knowledge*. So what we must determine is whether knowing its rule to be correct is a precondition of using Argument A to gain knowledge. I shall argue that the answer is no.

In section II we saw that Hume's arguments do not exclude the possibility that some inductive arguments are probable. Let us suppose for the moment that this possibility is realized and that Argument A is a probable argument. In that case, persons who reason in accordance with Argument A and who are justified in believing its premise will acquire justified belief in its conclusion. Moreover, they will do so *without need of having a justified belief in the correctness of the rule of inference sanctioning Argument A*. This follows from our supposition: if Argument A is probable, justified belief in its premise is *all* that is required to produce justified belief in its conclusion. Or more accurately, since there are also the two requirements mentioned at the end of section I, justified belief in the premise is all that is required *by way of justified belief*. One need *not* have a justified belief about the rule. Thus Argument A, though rule circular, is not epistemically circular.

This is all very well, critics may say, but it only works given your supposition that inductive arguments like A are probable. How is one to know that this condition obtains? There are two things to be said in response to this question. First, our condition is an *external* condition, that is, one of which an inference-drawing subject need not be cognizant. In a world in which inductive arguments were probable, persons who used them would be able to acquire justified beliefs thereby, regardless of whether they *knew* inductive arguments to be probable. Second, from the stock of justified beliefs thus acquired there is a way to advance to the knowledge that inductive arguments are indeed probable. (This will be shown in the next section.) So the critics are doubly mistaken: the knowledge they think we need but cannot get is *not* needed and *can* be got.

IV.

We have seen how someone might come to know, by way of an inductive argument, that most inductive arguments with true premises have true conclusions, or in other words, that induction is *reliable*. The task we took on at the end of the last section was to show that induction is *probable*, and the task that has been with us since the beginning has been to show that induction is *justified*. To accomplish one of these tasks is automatically to accomplish the other, since a probable argument is simply a justified argument that is not demonstrative. So to complete our work we must cross (or close) the gap between 'Induction is reliable' and 'Induction is justified', and for this purpose there is obviously nothing better suited than the reliability theory of justification.

The tenets of the reliability theory can be set down in the following way, which is due to Goldman.[14] First, we distinguish two kinds of belief-forming process: those that do not "operate on" other beliefs (e.g., perception) and those that do (e.g., inference). Then we say that a process of the first sort is reliable if and only if it tends to produce only true beliefs and that a process of the second sort is reliable if and only if it tends to produce only true beliefs when applied to true beliefs. Finally, we say that a belief is justified if and only if it either (i) results from a reliable process of the first sort or (ii) results from justified beliefs via a reliable process of the second sort.

Now let us put 2 and 2 together. The conclusion of Argument A tells us that inductive inference is a reliable process. The reliability theory tells us that beliefs resulting from justified beliefs by a reliable process are themselves justified. It follows that beliefs arrived at by inductive inference from justified beliefs are themselves justified. But that is to say that inductive inferences are both *probable* (in the sense defined in section II) and *justified* (in the sense defined in section I).

Here, then, is one solution to the problem of induction: by means of Argument A one can come to know that induction is reliable, and by supplementing this result with the reliability theory one can advance to the further conclusion that induction is justified.[15]

It is instructive to note that by combining the two approaches to the problem of induction we have considered so far, the "inductive probabilism" of section II and the "inductive validation of induction" of section III, we manage to avoid objections that are damaging to either taken separately. The objection generally thought fatal to the second approach is that any attempt to argue for the reliability of induction by using induction itself is viciously circular. But if inductive arguments are probable in the sense maintained by the first approach, they may be used to gain knowledge about induction itself without epistemic circularity, which is the only vicious kind. The objections left unanswered above to the first approach were that to regard inductive arguments as probable can only be an act of faith, and that in any case, they cannot be known to be probable in any sense implying that their conclusions are usually true. But what is shown in the second approach is *precisely* that the conclusions of inductive arguments

(with true premises) are usually true, which answers the second objection; and when this result is coupled with the reliability theory, it follows that inductive arguments are justified, hence probable, which answers the first objection.

But there are other objections that must be addressed as well. The next section shows how they may be answered, at least within the reliabilist's framework.

## V.

*Objection 1*: You have made things too easy on yourself by characterizing justified inference as you did in section I. Being justified in believing a premise is never by itself sufficient for being justified in believing a conclusion drawn from it; in addition, one must be justified in believing that there is some appropriate relation of support (be it deductive or inductive) between the two.

*Reply*: One can go at least part way toward meeting this objection by making a point reminiscent of Lewis Carroll. Suppose that premise $P$ is justified for subject $S$, that $P$ entails $Q$, and that $S$ infers $Q$ from $P$. Shall we say that $Q$ is not justified for $S$ unless he is also justified in believing that $P$ does entail $Q$? But if so, shall we not also have to add the requirement that $S$ be justified in believing that if $P$ is true and $P$ entails $Q$, $Q$ is true, too? A regress impends, and to avoid it we must say that in some cases the mere *existence* of an appropriate relation between premise and conclusion, whether the subject has a justified belief about it or not, enables justification to be transmitted from one to the other. And if this must be true in some cases, why not inductive cases, too?

However that may be, there is something else to be noted about the objection. What it calls into question is the proposition that being justified in believing a premise can be a sufficient condition (or at any rate, the sole *epistemic* condition that is required) for being justified in believing a conclusion. But this proposition is an immediate consequence of the reliability theory, in particular of its second clause. (See section IV.) So if the theory stands, the objection falls.

*Objection 2*: How do you know that the *premise* of Argument A is true? There would be no problem here if your past inductions had all been inferences of the form 'Most $A$'s I have observed were $B$'s; hence, the *next* $A$ will be a $B$', since to verify the conclusion of such an inference one need only wait and see. But your stated concern is with inferences to conclusions of the form 'Most A's are B's', and such conclusions can only be confirmed by further use of induction. Thus, there is a kind of epistemic circularity present in Argument A after all—the kind you called premise circularity.

*Reply*: It is true that the success of past inductions with general conclusions can only have been confirmed through induction. This is not to say, however, that *justified belief in the reliability of induction* was required for this purpose. I have already argued that to produce justified belief in the conclusion of an inductive inference, all that is required by way of justified belief is justified belief in the premise. This point applies not only to Argument A itself, but also to the various arguments that contribute to justified belief in its premise. Thus the present objection really raises the same point as the previous one, and may be answered in the same way.

*Objection 3*: Your proposed justification of induction could be used with equal right by a *counterinductivist*. Counterinductivists believe that if most of the A's one has observed were B's, one should infer that the majority of all A's are *not B's*. If his habits of inference permitted him to live long enough, a counterinductivist would no doubt come to realize that counterinduction had led him mostly to false conclusions. But he would not be discouraged by these failures; he would regard them as evidence of future success. He would argue as follows:

*Argument B*
Most of the counterinductive inferences I have drawn in the past from true premises have had false conclusions.
     Hence,
The majority of all counterinductive inferences with true premises have *true* conclusions.

Now Argument B is as good by his standards as Argument A is by yours, but it is absurd to think it amounts to a justification of counterinduction.

*Reply*: Argument B may be as good in the eyes of the counterinductivist as Argument A is in mine, but it does not follow that the arguments are epistemically on a par. To think that they are is to embrace a subjectivism that rejects all external constraints on justification, admitting nothing as relevant but the subject's own beliefs. If we admit reliability as an external condition, however, and if our world is one in

which induction is in fact reliable, then Argument A will be justified and Argument B will not be—regardless of what the counterinductivist thinks about the matter.

*Objection 3 continued*: Yes, but by the same token if our world were one in which *counterinduction* were reliable, Argument B would be justified and Argument A would not be. So there is a standoff between the arguments after all, though at a higher level: although at most one of the arguments is justified, and although it may be the case that one of them is justified and the other not (if one is reliable and the other not), no one is in a position to say that it is A and not B or vice versa.

*Reply continued*: I am not sure that counterinduction *could* be reliable (in the long run, as the objection requires), but for the sake of argument I will grant that it could be.[16] To meet the objection it suffices to point out that in a world in which induction were reliable, not only would Argument A *in fact* be justified, but users of it could *know* that it was (and that Argument B was not). How this is so has already been explained in sections III and IV. If the reader asks, "But how could anyone ascertain the truth of the antecedent on which all this depends—that induction is reliable?" I remind him or her that (for the reliability theory, at any rate) this antecedent is an *external* antecedent. It makes knowledge possible not by being known, but simply by being true.[17]

### VI.

In one way or another, each of the objections just considered presupposes that the reliability theory is false; if the theory stands, the objections fall. But perhaps it is the theory that deserves to fall. In this section I wish to consider some possible misgivings about it.

The most likely point of dissatisfaction with the reliability theory can be brought out by the following example.[18] Suppose there is a man who predicts rain whenever his bunions throb and nearly always predicts correctly—not by luck, but because his bunions are sensitive to falling pressure—but whose poor memory makes him oblivious to his own record of success. His beliefs about the next day's weather are the result of a reliable process, but are they justified? There is a strong inclination to say no—they would not be justified unless he knew that predictions so based were generally correct. The general point would be that no matter how reliable a belief-forming process may be, its products are not justified unless the subject *knows* (or is justified in believing) that the process is reliable. But if this is so, justification cannot be grounded in reliability alone. Reliability is important only in so far as the subject has knowledge of it.

More broadly, it might be said that what is wrong with the reliability theory is that it makes one of the conditions of knowledge purely external. That is, it makes *S*'s knowing *p* dependent on a fact *q* that obtains outside *S*'s knowledge. If *q* obtains, *S* knows *p*; if it doesn't, he doesn't; and for all *S* knows, *q* might either obtain or not. But if one's knowing *p* depends on a certain fact, shouldn't one have to know that fact?

To this question we must answer no. Some external conditions of knowing are admitted by nearly everyone. The extra conditions of knowledge that some have proposed to circumvent the Gettier problem (e.g., the condition that the subject's justification be undefeated) have generally been proposed as external conditions; it has not been required that the subject know them to obtain. The causal conditions on knowledge that others have proposed (e.g., that a belief, to count as knowledge, must be caused by the fact that makes it true, or by the other beliefs that serve as reasons for it) have likewise been meant as external. In a way truth itself is an external condition, at least according to any but the most rigorous conception of knowledge: if truth is not entailed by justified belief, then whether someone who has justified belief also has knowledge depends on whether what he believes happens to be true. Of course, one cannot have knowledge of something without knowing the truth condition for this knowledge to obtain, but the latter piece of knowledge is one with the former and not a precondition of it.

To the last point it may be replied that although *knowledge* of the truth condition is not a precondition of knowledge, *justified belief* in it is. So why not require of the subject justified belief in the other conditions of knowledge as well? The answer is that if it were held that *every* condition of someone's knowing something must be a condition the knower is justified in believing to obtain, it would follow that no one could know *anything* unless one were justified in believing each of the propositions in the series

$$Kp, JKp, JJKp, JJJKp, \text{etc.},$$

which is absurd. Thus, it is inevitable that some conditions of knowing be external, not only to knowledge, but also to justification.

Of course, to show that knowledge must have *some* external conditions is not yet to show that reliability can be plausibly regarded as one of them, so what I have offered here in defense of the reliability theory hardly goes far enough. Rather than defending it further, however, I wish to go on and consider what becomes of our solution if we drop the reliability theory in favor of its less fashionable rival.

## VII.

The solution to the problem of induction outlined so far involves the following three steps: Hume's skeptical arguments do nothing to rule out the possibility that there are probable inductive inferences, i.e., inductive inferences that are justified despite being nondemonstrative (section II); if this possibility were realized, it would be possible to come to know by means of induction but without any vicious circularity that induction is reliable (section III); and from this in turn one could infer, with the help of the reliability theory, that induction is justified (section IV). The solution now to be advanced can retain the first two steps, but it will have to put something else in place of the third. It will also have to handle the objections of section V in a way that does not depend on the reliability theory.

How can we satisfy ourselves that induction is justified if not on the basis of its reliability? To this question some philosophers would reply that there is no need to ground the reasonableness of induction in its reliability or anything else, since its reasonableness is intuitively evident. Here is a representative quotation:

> I think that in some sense our justification of inductive rules must rest on an ineradicable element of inductive intuition—just as I would say our justification of deductive rules must ultimately rest, in part, on an element of deductive intuition: we *see* that *modus ponens* is truth-preserving—that is simply the same as to reflect on it and fail to see how it can lead us astray. In the same way, we *see* that if all we know about in all the world is that all the A's we've seen have been B's, it is *rational* to *expect* that the next A will be a B.[19]

Since things known by intuition are presumably known a priori, I shall refer to this view as apriorism.

Apriorism often calls forth the following objection: "Induction is justified only to the extent that the regularities we have noted in the past will continue to hold in the future. But that these or any other regularities should continue is at best a contingent feature of our world; it is conceivable that chaos should break out any minute. So how can induction be known to be justified a priori?"

It is clear, however, what the apriorist should say in reply: "You must distinguish the *reasonableness* of induction from its *reliability*. The latter depends on the contingencies you have mentioned, but the former does not. Induction would be reasonable (rational, justified) in any possible world, even if reliable only in some."[20]

The apriorist's approach to the problem of induction is of a piece with the larger epistemological tradition I mentioned at the beginning. According to this tradition, justification cannot be defined or even partly explained in terms of reliability; instead it must be either taken as primitive or defined in terms of other irreducibly epistemic concepts.[21] This makes it possible to hold that the ultimate principles of epistemic justification, of what confers evidence on what, are necessary truths known a priori.

Of course, if justification and reliability are thus driven apart, some will wonder why justification is worth having. What good is it to know that inductive inferences are justified if one does not thereby know that they usually lead to true conclusions?[22] But to this question section III of this paper has already given an answer. If induction is conceded to be justified in a sense *not* entailing that it is reliable, this will enable one to come to know that it is *also* reliable. For by means of Argument A one may arrive at justified belief in its reliability, and if it really *is* reliable this belief will be knowledge.

It was this part of the paper, however, that was the target of the objections in section V. I answered them before by invoking reliabilism; how shall we answer them if we embrace apriorism instead?

Objection 3 may be dealt with quickly: if it is evident a priori that induction is reasonable, it is also evident a priori that counterinduction is *unreasonable*.

Objections 1 and 2 require more attention. They both challenge, one explicitly and the other implicitly, the following vital point: to obtain justified belief in the conclusion of an inductive inference, we do not need justified belief in any rule or principle about the premise-conclusion nexus, but only in the

premise itself. I pointed out earlier that this proposition is an immediate consequence of reliabilism; I want to point out now that it is also a consequence, though in a way less likely to be noticed, of apriorism.

The way to see this is to focus on just what it is that the apriorist finds intuitively evident. It is not that induction inferences are *frequently truth-preserving*, for that could hardly be evident a priori. It is rather this: inductive inferences are *necessarily justification-extending*.[23] That is, if someone draws an inductive inference and is justified in believing its premise, he will also be justified in believing its conclusion. But this is to say that justified belief in the premise is *sufficient* to produce justified belief in the conclusion. And if justified belief in the premise is sufficient, justified belief about the premise-conclusion nexus is not necessary. Q.E.D.

Of course, if the intuited feature of inductive inference were what Peirce called its "truth-producing virtue," there would be room to insist that induction gives knowledge only to those who know that it has this virtue. But there is no room for such insistence if the intuited feature of inductive inference is its justification-extending virtue. This is what it is generally claimed to be; and if it were not this, what else could it be?

VIII.

For the apriorist, we know a priori that induction is justified, and can learn from Argument A that it has the *further* virtue of being reliable. For the reliabilist, we learn from Argument A that induction is reliable, and can infer from this that it has the *equivalent* virtue of being justified. What the two parties should agree on is this: there is no vicious circle in using Argument A to ascertain the reliability of induction.

I do not expect everyone to be convinced that Argument A is noncircular, but anyone who is *not* convinced is obliged to reject reliabilism and apriorism alike. It is worth noting what this double rejection would commit one to. What makes the reliabilist solution work is its tenet that reliability is *sufficient* for justification; what makes the apriorist solution work is its tenet that reliability is *not necessary* for justification. Hence, in order to reject both solutions, one would have to maintain that reliability is *necessary but not sufficient* for justification. And in that case the following question would become pressing: what is the x that must be added to reliability to obtain justification?[24]

## NOTES

1. This paper is something of a sequel to "Foundationalism, Epistemic Principles, and the Cartesian Circle," *Philosophical Review* 88 (1979): 55–91. There I argue that the reliability of intuition ("clear and distinct perception") can be known through intuition itself without vicious circularity; here I use some of the same strategy to make a similar point about induction. For a related result, see Francis W. Dauer "Hume's Skeptical Solution and the Causal Theory of Knowledge," *Philosophical Review* 89 (1980) 357–78.

2. Nelson Goodman, *Fact, Fiction, and Forecast*, 2nd edition (Indianapolis, 1965) 59–83. It is not clear to me that the paradox arises if the inferred frequency is anything less than 100%, but even so we do not want to project "grue."

3. Thus, as I see it, Goodman's "new riddle" is an *additional* problem; it may be prior to the old problem, but does not replace it.

4. I have tried to allay misgivings about the use of conceivability as a mark of possibility in "Conceivability and the Cartesian Argument for Dualism," *Pacific Philosophical Quarterly* 64 (1983): 35–45.

5. *A Treatise of Human Nature*, ed. L. A. Selby-Bigge (Oxford, 1888): 89.

6. "To endeavor, therefore, the proof of this last supposition by probable arguments . . . must be evidently going in a circle and taking that for granted which is the very point in question." *An Inquiry Concerning Human Understanding*, ed. Charles W. Hendel (Indianapolis, 1955): 49–50.

7. "There exist arguments which, although not valid (that is, their premises do not entail their conclusions), necessitate, for any rational being of limited knowledge who knows their premises, belief, rather than disbelief or the suspension of belief, in their conclusions—belief to which, nevertheless, a degree of assurance attaches, less than that (maximal) degree which a valid argument necessitates. In short, there are probable arguments." So writes D. Stove in "Hume, Probability, and Induction," *Philosophical Review* 74 (1965): 60–77. The late J. L. Mackie took a similar stand; see his "In Defense of Induction," in *Perception and Identity*, ed. Graham Macdonald (Cambridge, 1979): 113–30.

8. Stove, "Hume, Probability, and Induction," maintains that Hume did not even *intend* to argue that inductive arguments could not, in the sense explained, be probable. I do not wish to debate this point. What matters for my purposes is that try or no, he did not succeed.

9. This charge is made by John Cassidy in "The Nature of Hume's Inductive Scepticism: A Critical Notice," *Ratio* 19 (1977): 47–54.

10. The chief representatives of the minority are Richard Braithwaite, *Scientific Explanation* (Cambridge, 1953): 264–92, and Max Black, "Self-Supporting Inductive Arguments," *Journal of Philosophy* 55 (1958): 718–25. These pieces are reprinted in *The Justification of Induction*, ed. Richard Swinburne (Oxford, 1974). More recently Nicholas Rescher has advocated an inductive validation of induction; see *Induction* (Pittsburgh, 1980), especially Chapter VII. My strategy here differs from that of all three authors, but it is closest to that of Braithwaite.

11. Thus, an argument is not viciously circular just because the *truth* of its conclusion, or *belief* in it, or both, are necessary conditions of using the argument to gain knowledge. For more on this see Braithwaite, especially pp. 114–20, in Swinburne.

12. The rule in this case is "From *Most observed A's have been B's* you may infer *The majority of all A's are B's.*"

13. The same could not be said of Black's "self-supporting" inductive argument, since its conclusion pertains only to the *next* use of induction.

14. Alvin Goldman, "What Is Justified Belief?" in *Justification and Knowledge*, ed. George S. Pappas (Dordrecht, 1979): 1–23.

15. There is a complication I have so far ignored. For induction to be justified in the sense defined in section I, it is not sufficient that it lead from justified belief to justified belief in every *actual* instance of its use; it must also be such that it *would* lead from justified belief to justified belief in nonactual instances. To obtain this result we need the lemma that induction is reliable not just in the sense that it usually *does* lead from truth to truth, but also in the sense that it usually *would*. But this stronger lemma is presumably reachable by Argument A if the weaker one was; grounds that justify "Most A's are B's" must also justify "Most A's would be B's."

16. If he has noticed that most of the cars he has seen have not been red, the counterinductivist will infer that the majority of all cars are red; if he has also noticed that most of the cars he has seen have not been green, he will infer that the majority of all cars are green. He will thus often be led into inconsistent conclusions, but I do not see how to prove that he will be wrong more often than right. Black (pp. 133–34 in Swinburne) points out that if counterinduction (of a somewhat different variety from what I have considered) had a run of successful predictions it would predict its own future failure, and thus suffers from a kind of incoherence. But "incoherence" in this sense is compatible with reliability.

17. Cf. what Mackie says on p. 129 of the article cited in note 7: the principle of the uniformity of nature need only be *true* in order for induction to give us knowledge in the sense of "non-accidentally true belief."

18. For elaboration and discussion of similar examples, see Laurence BonJour, "Externalist Theories of Empirical Knowledge," *Midwest Studies in Philosophy* 5 (1980): 53–73.

19. Henry E. Kyburg, Jr. "Comments on Salmon's 'Inductive Evidence'," *American Philosophical Quarterly* 2 (1965): 274–76; reprinted in Swinburne, 62–66. A similar position is advocated by P. K. Sen, "An Approach to the Problem of Induction," in *Logic, Induction, and Ontology* (Calcutta, 1980): 82–90.

20. Compare P. F. Strawson, *Introduction to Logical Theory* (London, 1952): 261–62. It should be noted that the apriorist need not share Strawson's view that the rationality of induction is explicative of the concept of rationality.

21. The best exemplar of this approach is R. M. Chisholm, *Theory of Knowledge*, 2nd edition (Englewood Cliffs, N. J.,1977), Chapter 1.

22. This is Cassidy's complaint again. See also Wesley C. Salmon, "The Concept of Inductive Evidence" and "Rejoinder to Barker and Kyburg," *American Philosophical Quarterly* 2 (1965): 265–80; reprinted in Swinburne, pp. 48–57 and 66–73.

For Salmon, it seems, the more pressing question to ask those who would divorce justification from reliability is not "What *good* is justification?" but "What *is* justification?"

23. I omit the needed qualifications about prima facie justification.

24. For criticisms of an earlier draft, I am grateful to Diana Ackerman, Philip Quinn, and Ernest Sosa. My research was supported by a grant from the American Council of Learned Societies.

# READING 42

---

# The Idea of Necessary Connection
*David Hume*

*For biographical details see Reading 4. This reading comprises Sections II and VII of Hume's* Enquiry.

## SECTION II: OF THE ORIGIN OF IDEAS

Everyone will readily allow that there is a considerable difference between the perceptions of the mind when a man feels the pain of excessive heat or the pleasure of moderate warmth, and when he afterwards recalls to his memory this sensation or anticipates it by his imagination. These faculties may mimic or copy the perceptions of the senses, but they never can entirely reach the force and vivacity of the original sentiment. The utmost we say of them, even when they operate with greatest vigour, is that they represent their object in so lively a manner that we could *almost* say we feel or see it. But, except the mind be disordered by disease or madness, they never can arrive at such a pitch of vivacity as to render these perceptions altogether undistinguishable. All the colours of poetry, however splendid, can never paint natural objects in such a manner as to make the description be taken for a real landscape.

SOURCE: From *An Enquiry Concerning Human Understanding* (1748), Sections II and VII.

The most lively thought is still inferior to the dullest sensation.

We may observe a like distinction to run through all the other perceptions of the mind. A man in a fit of anger is actuated in a very different manner from one who only thinks of that emotion. If you tell me that any person is in love, I easily understand your meaning and form a just conception of his situation, but never can mistake that conception for the real disorders and agitations of the passion. When we reflect on our past sentiments and affections, our thought is a faithful mirror and copies its objects truly; but the colours which it employs are faint and dull in comparison of those in which our original perceptions were clothed. It requires no nice discernment or metaphysical head to mark the distinction between them.

Here, therefore, we may divide all the perceptions of the mind into two classes or species, which are distinguished by their different degrees of force and vivacity. The less forcible and lively are commonly denominated *Thoughts* or *Ideas*. The other species want a name in our language, and in most others; I suppose, because it was not requisite for any but philosophical purposes to rank them under a general term or appellation. Let us, therefore, use a little freedom and call them *Impressions*, employing that word in a sense somewhat different from the usual. By the term *impression,* then, I mean all our more lively perceptions, when we hear, or see, or feel, or love, or hate, or desire, or will. And impressions are distinguished from ideas, which are the less lively perceptions of which we are conscious when we reflect on any of those sensations or movements above mentioned.

Nothing, at first view, may seem more unbounded than the thought of man, which not only escapes all human power and authority, but is not even restrained within the limits of nature and reality. To form monsters and join incongruous shapes and appearances costs the imagination no more trouble than to conceive the most natural and familiar objects. And while the body is confined to one planet, along which it creeps with pain and difficulty, the thought can in an instant transport us into the most distant regions of the universe, or even beyond the universe into the unbounded chaos where nature is supposed to lie in total confusion. What never was seen or heard of, may yet be conceived, nor is anything beyond the power of thought except what implies an absolute contradiction.

But though our thought seems to possess this unbounded liberty, we shall find upon a nearer examination that it is really confined within very narrow limits, and that all this creative power of the mind amounts to no more than the faculty of compounding, transposing, augmenting, or diminishing the materials afforded us by the senses and experience. When we think of a golden mountain, we only join two consistent ideas, *gold* and *mountain,* with which we were formerly acquainted. A virtuous horse we can conceive, because, from our own feeling, we can conceive virtue; and this we may unite to the figure and shape of a horse, which is an animal familiar to us. In short, all the materials of thinking are derived either from our outward or inward sentiment; the mixture and composition of these belongs alone to the mind and will. Or, to express myself in philosophical language, all our ideas or more feeble perceptions are copies of our impressions or more lively ones.

To prove this, the two following arguments will, I hope, be sufficient. First, when we analyse our thoughts or ideas, however compounded or sublime, we always find that they resolve themselves into such simple ideas as were copied from a precedent feeling or sentiment. Even those ideas which, at first view, seem the most wide of this origin are found, upon a nearer scrutiny, to be derived from it. The idea of God, as meaning an infinitely intelligent, wise, and good Being, arises from reflecting on the operations of our own mind and augmenting, without limit, those qualities of goodness and wisdom. We may prosecute this enquiry to what length we please; where we shall always find that every idea which we examine is copied from a similar impression. Those who would assert that this position is not universally true nor without exception, have only one, and that an easy method of refuting it: by producing that idea which, in their opinion, is not derived from this source. It will then be incumbent on us, if we would maintain our doctrine, to produce the impression or lively perception which corresponds to it.

Secondly. If it happen, from a defect of the organ, that a man is not susceptible of any species of sensation, we always find that he is as little susceptible of the correspondent ideas. A blind man can form no notion of colours, a deaf man of sounds. Restore either of them that sense in which he is deficient by opening this new inlet for his sensations, you also open an inlet for the ideas, and he finds no difficulty in conceiving these objects. The case is the same if the object proper for exciting any sensation has never been applied to the organ. A Laplander or Negro has no notion of the relish of wine. And though there are few or no instances of a like deficiency in the mind, where a person has never felt or is wholly incapable of a sentiment or passion that belongs to his species, yet we find the same observation to take place in a less degree. A man of mild manners can form no idea of inveterate revenge or cruelty, nor can a selfish heart easily conceive the heights of friendship and generosity. It is readily allowed that other beings may possess many senses of which we can have no conception, because the ideas of them have never been introduced to us in the only manner by which an idea can have access to the mind, to wit, by the actual feeling and sensation.

There is, however, one contradictory phenomenon which may prove that it is not absolutely impossible for ideas to arise independent of their correspondent impressions. I believe it will readily be allowed that the several distinct ideas of colour, which enter by the eye, or those of sound, which are conveyed by the ear, are really different from each other, though at the same time resembling. Now, if this be true of different colours, it must be no less so of the different shades of the same colour; and each shade produces a distinct idea, independent of the rest. For if this should be denied, it is possible, by the continual gradation of shades, to run a colour insensibly into what is most remote from it; and if you will not allow any of the means to be different, you cannot, without absurdity, deny the extremes to be the same. Suppose, therefore, a person to have enjoyed his sight for thirty years and to have become perfectly acquainted with colours of all kinds, except one particular shade of blue, for instance, which it never has been his fortune to meet with. Let all the different shades of that colour, except that single one, be placed before him, descending gradually from the deepest to the lightest; it is plain that he will perceive a blank where that shade is wanting, and will be sensible that there is a greater distance in that place between the contiguous colours than in any other. Now I ask whether it be possible for him, from his own imagination, to supply this deficiency and raise up to himself the idea of that particular shade, though it had never been conveyed to him by his senses? I believe there are few but will be of opinion that he can; and this may serve as a proof that the simple ideas are not always, in every instance, derived from the correspondent impressions, though this instance is so singular that it is scarcely worth our observing, and does not merit that for it alone we should alter our general maxim.

Here, therefore, is a proposition which not only seems in itself simple and intelligible, but, if a proper use were made of it, might render every dispute equally intelligible, and banish all that jargon which has so long taken possession of metaphysical reasonings and drawn disgrace upon them. All ideas, especially abstract ones, are naturally faint and obscure: the mind has but a slender hold of them; they are apt to be confounded with other resembling ideas; and when we have often employed any term, though without a distinct meaning, we are apt to imagine it has a determinate idea annexed to it. On the contrary, all impressions, that is, all sensations either outward or inward, are strong and vivid: the limits between them are more exactly determined, nor is it easy to fall into any error or mistake with regard to them. When we entertain, therefore, any suspicion that a philosophical term is employed without any meaning or idea (as is but too frequent), we need but enquire, *from what impression is that supposed idea derived?* And if it be impossible to assign any, this will

serve to confirm our suspicion. By bringing ideas into so clear a light, we may reasonably hope to remove all dispute which may arise concerning their nature and reality.[1]

## SECTION VII: OF THE IDEA OF NECESSARY CONNECTION

### PART I

The great advantage of the mathematical sciences above the moral consists in this, that the ideas of the former, being sensible, are always clear and determinate, the smallest distinction between them is immediately perceptible, and the same terms are still expressive of the same ideas without ambiguity or variation. An oval is never mistaken for a circle, nor a hyperbola for an ellipse. Isosceles and scalene triangles are distinguished by boundaries more exact than vice and virtue, right and wrong. If any term be defined in geometry, the mind readily, of itself, substitutes, on all occasions, the definition for the term defined; or even when no definition is employed, the object itself may be presented to the senses and by that means be steadily and clearly apprehended. But the finer sentiments of the mind, the operations of the understanding, the various agitations of the passions, though really in themselves distinct, easily escape us when surveyed by reflection, nor is it in our power to recall the original object as often as we have occasion to contemplate it. Ambiguity, by this means, is gradually introduced into our reasonings: similar objects are readily taken to be the same, and the conclusion becomes at last very wide of the premises.

One may safely, however, affirm that if we consider these sciences in a proper light, their advantages and disadvantages nearly compensate each other and reduce both of them to a state of equality. If the mind, with greater facility, retains the ideas of geometry clear and determinate, it must carry on a much longer and more intricate chain of reasoning, and compare ideas much wider of each other, in order to reach the abstruser truths of that science. And if moral ideas are apt, without extreme care, to fall into obscurity and confusion, the inferences are always much shorter in these disquisitions, and the intermediate steps which lead to the conclusion much fewer than in the sciences which treat of quantity and number. In reality, there is scarcely a proposition in Euclid so simple as not to consist of more parts than are to be found in any moral reasoning which runs not into chimera and conceit. Where we trace the principles of the human mind through a few steps, we may be very well satisfied with our progress, considering how soon nature throws a bar to all our enquiries concerning causes and reduces us to an acknowledgment of our ignorance. The chief obstacle, therefore, to our improvement in the moral or metaphysical sciences is the obscurity of the ideas and ambiguity of the terms. The principal difficulty in the mathematics is the length of inferences and compass of thought requisite to the forming of any conclusion. And, perhaps, our progress in natural philosophy is chiefly retarded by the want of proper experiments and phenomena, which are often discovered by chance and cannot always be found when requisite, even by the most diligent and prudent enquiry. As moral philosophy seems hitherto to have received less improvement than either geometry or physics, we may conclude that if there be any difference in this respect among these sciences, the difficulties which obstruct the progress of the former require superior care and capacity to be surmounted.

There are no ideas which occur in metaphysics more obscure and uncertain than those of *power, force, energy,* or *necessary connection,* of which it is every moment necessary for us to treat in all our disquisitions. We shall, therefore, endeavour in this Section to fix, if possible, the precise meaning of these terms and thereby remove some part of that obscurity which is so much complained of in this species of philosophy.

It seems a proposition which will not admit of much dispute that all our ideas are nothing but copies of our impressions, or, in other words, that it is impossible for us to *think* of anything which we have not antecedently *felt,* either by our external or internal senses. I have endeavoured[2] to explain and prove this proposition, and have expressed my hopes that by a proper application of it men may reach a greater clearness and precision in philosophical reasonings than what they have hitherto been able to attain. Complex ideas may, perhaps, be well known by definition, which is nothing but an enumeration of those parts or simple ideas that compose them. But when we have pushed up definitions to the most simple ideas and find still some ambiguity and obscurity, what resource are we then possessed of? By what invention can we throw light upon these ideas and render them altogether precise and determinate to our intellectual view? Produce the impressions or original sentiments from which the ideas are copied. These impressions are all strong and sensible. They admit not of ambiguity. They are not only placed in a full light themselves, but may throw light on their correspondent ideas, which lie in obscurity. And by this means we may perhaps attain a new microscope or species of optics by which, in the moral sciences, the most minute and most simple ideas may be so enlarged as to fall readily under our apprehension, and be equally known with the grossest and most sensible ideas that can be the object of our enquiry.

To be fully acquainted, therefore, with the idea of power or necessary connection, let us examine its impression; and in order to find the impression with greater certainty, let us search for it in all the sources from which it may possibly be derived.

When we look about us towards external objects and consider the operation of causes, we are never able, in a single instance, to discover any power or necessary connection, any quality which binds the effect to the cause and renders the one an infallible consequence of the other. We only find that the one does actually, in fact, follow the other. The impulse of one billiard ball is attended with motion in the second. This is the whole that appears to the *outward* senses. The mind feels no sentiment or *inward* impression from this succession of objects. Consequently, there is not, in any single, particular instance of cause and effect, anything which can suggest the idea of power or necessary connection.

From the first appearance of an object we never can conjecture what effect will result from it. But were the power or energy of any cause discoverable by the mind, we could foresee the effect, even without experience, and might, at first, pronounce with certainty concerning it by the mere dint of thought and reasoning.

In reality, there is no part of matter that does ever, by its sensible qualities, discover any power or energy, or give us ground to imagine that it could produce anything, or be followed by any other object, which we could denominate its effect. Solidity, extension, motion: these qualities are all complete in themselves and never point out any other event which may result from them. The scenes of the universe are continually shifting, and one object follows another in an uninterrupted succession; but the power of force which actuates the whole machine is entirely concealed from us and never discovers itself in any of the sensible qualities of body. We know that, in fact, heat is a constant attendant of flame; but what is the connection between them, we have no room so much as to conjecture or imagine. It is impossible, therefore, that the idea of power can be derived from the contemplation of bodies in single instances of their operation, because no bodies ever discover any power which can be the original of this idea.[3]

Since, therefore, external objects as they appear to the senses give us no idea of power or necessary connection by their operation in particular instances, let us see whether this idea be derived from reflection on the operations of our own minds and be copied from any internal impression. It may be said that we are every moment conscious of internal power while we feel that, by the simple command of our will, we can move the organs of our body or direct the faculties of our mind. An act of volition produces motion in our limbs or raises a new idea in our imagination. This influence of the will we know by consciousness. Hence we acquire the idea of power or energy, and are certain that we ourselves and all other intelligent beings are possessed of power. This idea, then, is an idea of reflection, since it arises from reflecting on the operations of our own mind and on the command which is exercised by will, both over the organs of the body and faculties of the soul.

We shall proceed to examine this pretension and, first, with regard to the influence of volition over the organs of the body. This influence, we may observe, is a fact which, like all other natural events, can be known only by experience, and can never be foreseen from any apparent energy or power in the cause which connects it with the effect and renders the one an infallible consequence of the other. The motion of our body follows upon the command of our will. Of this we are every moment conscious. But the means by which this is effected; the energy by which the will performs so extraordinary an operation; of this we are so far from being immediately conscious that it must forever escape our most diligent enquiry.

For, *first*, is there any principle in all nature more mysterious than the union of soul with body, by which a supposed spiritual substance acquires such an influence over a material one that the most refined thought is able to actuate the grossest matter? Were we empowered by a secret wish to remove mountains or control the planets in their orbit, this extensive authority would not be more extraordinary, nor more beyond our comprehension. But if, by consciousness, we perceived any power or energy in the will, we must know this power; we must know its connection with the effect; we must know the secret union of soul and body, and the nature of both these substances by which the one is able to operate in so many instances upon the other.

*Secondly,* we are not able to move all the organs of the body with a like authority, though we cannot assign any reason, besides experience, for so remarkable a difference between one and the other. Why has the will an influence over the tongue and fingers, not over the heart and liver? This question would never embarrass us were we conscious of a power in the former case, not in the latter. We should then perceive, independent of experience, why the authority of will over the organs of the body is circumscribed within such particular limits. Being in that case fully acquainted with the power or force by which it operates, we should also know why its influence reaches precisely to such boundaries, and no further.

A man suddenly struck with palsy in the leg or arm, or who had newly lost those members, frequently endeavours, at first, to move them and employ them in their usual offices. Here he is as much conscious of power to command such limbs as a man in perfect health is conscious of power to actuate any member which remains in its natural state and condition. But consciousness never deceives. Consequently, neither in the one case nor in the other are we ever conscious of any power. We learn the influence of our will from experience alone. And experience only teaches us how one event constantly follows another, without instructing us in the secret connection which binds them together and renders them inseparable.

*Thirdly,* we learn from anatomy that the immediate object of power in voluntary motion is not the member itself which is moved, but certain muscles and nerves and animal spirits, and, perhaps, something still more minute and more unknown, through which the motion is successfully propagated ere it reach the member itself whose motion is the immediate object of volition. Can there be a more certain proof that the power by which this whole operation is performed, so far from being directly and fully known by an inward sentiment or consciousness, is to the last degree mysterious and unintelligible?

Here the mind wills a certain event; immediately another event, unknown to ourselves and totally different from the one intended, is produced. This event produces another, equally unknown, till, at last, through a long succession, the desired event is produced. But if the original power were felt, it must be known; were it known, its effect also must be known, since all power is relative to its effect. And *vice versa,* if the effect be not known, the power cannot be known nor felt. How indeed can we be conscious of a power to move our limbs when we have no such power, but only that to move certain animal spirits which, though they produce at last the motion of our limbs, yet operate in such a manner as is wholly beyond our comprehension?

We may, therefore, conclude from the whole, I hope, without any temerity, though with assurance, that our idea of power is not copied from any sentiment or consciousness of power within ourselves when we give rise to animal motion or apply our limbs to their proper use and office. That their motion follows the command of the will is a matter of common experience, like other natural events; but the power or energy by which this is effected, like that in other natural events, is unknown and inconceivable.[4]

Shall we then assert that we are conscious of a power or energy in our own minds when, by an act or command of our will, we raise up a new idea, fix the mind to the contemplation of it, turn it on all sides, and at last dismiss it for some other idea when we think that we have surveyed it with sufficient accuracy? I believe the same arguments will prove that even this command of the will gives us no real idea of force or energy.

*First,* it must be allowed that when we know a power, we know that very circumstance in the cause by which it is enabled to produce the effect, for these are supposed to be synonymous. We must, therefore, know both the cause and effect, and the relation between them. But do we pretend to be acquainted with the nature of the human soul and the nature of an idea, or the aptitude of the one to produce the other? This is a real creation, a production of something out of nothing, which implies a power so great that it may seem, at first sight, beyond the reach of any being less than infinite. At least it must be owned that such a power is not felt, nor known, nor even conceivable by the mind. We only feel the event, namely, the existence of an idea consequent to a command of the will; but the manner in which this operation is performed, the power by which it is produced, is entirely beyond our comprehension.

*Secondly,* the command of the mind over itself is limited, as well as its command over the body; and these limits are not known by reason or any acquaintance with the nature of cause and effect, but only by experience and observation, as in all other natural events and in the operation of external objects. Our authority over our sentiments and passions is much weaker than that over our ideas; and even the latter authority is circumscribed within very narrow boundaries. Will anyone pretend to assign the ultimate reason of these boundaries, or show why the power is deficient in one case, not in another?

*Thirdly,* this self-command is very different at different times. A man in health possesses more of it than one languishing with sickness. We are more master of our thoughts in the morning than in the evening; fasting, than after a full meal. Can we give any reason for these variations except experience? Where then is the power of which we pretend to be conscious? Is there not here, either in a spiritual or material substance, or both, some secret mechanism or structure of parts upon which the effect depends, and which, being entirely unknown to us, renders the power or energy of the will equally unknown and incomprehensible?

Volition is surely an act of the mind with which we are sufficiently acquainted. Reflect upon it. Consider it on all sides. Do you find anything in it like this creative power by which it raises from nothing a new idea and, with a kind of *fiat,* imitates the omnipotence of its Maker, if I may be allowed so to speak, who called forth into existence all the various scenes of nature? So far from being conscious of this energy in the will, it requires as certain experience as that of which we are possessed to convince us that such extraordinary effects do ever result from a simple act of volition.

The generality of mankind never find any difficulty in accounting for the more common and familiar operations of nature, such as the descent of heavy bodies, the growth of plants, the generation of animals, or the nourishment of bodies by food; but suppose that in all these cases they perceive the very force or energy of the cause by which it is connected with its effect, and is for ever infallible in its operation. They acquire, by long habit, such a turn of mind that, upon the appearance of the cause, they immediately expect with assurance its usual attendant, and hardly conceive it possible that any other event could result from it. It is only on the discovery of extraordinary phenomena, such as earthquakes, pestilence, and prodigies of any kind, that they find themselves at a loss to assign a proper cause and to explain the manner in which the effect is produced by it. It is usual for men, in such difficulties, to have recourse to some invisible intelligent principle[5] as the immediate cause of that event which surprises them, and which they think cannot be accounted for from the common powers of nature. But philosophers, who carry their scrutiny a little further, immediately perceive that, even in the most familiar events, the energy of the cause is as unintelligible as in the most unusual, and that we only learn by experience the frequent *conjunction* of objects, without being ever able to comprehend anything like *connection* between them. Here, then, many philosophers think themselves obliged by reason to have recourse, on all occasions, to the same principle which the vulgar never appeal to but in cases that appear miraculous and supernatural. They acknowledge mind and intelligence to be, not only the ultimate and original cause of all things, but the immediate and sole cause of every event which appears in nature. They pretend that those objects which are commonly denominated *causes* are in reality nothing but *occasions,* and that the true and direct principle of every effect is not any power or force in nature, but a volition of the Supreme Being, who wills that such particular objects should forever be conjoined with each other. Instead of saying that one billiard ball moves another by a force which it has derived from the author of nature, it is the Deity himself, they say, who, by a particular volition, moves the second ball, being determined to this operation by the impulse of the first ball, in consequence of those general laws which he has laid down to himself in the government of the universe. But philosophers, advancing still in their enquiries, discover that as we are totally ignorant of the power on which depends the mutual operation of bodies, we are no less ignorant of that power on which depends the operation of mind on body, or of body on mind; nor are we able, either from our senses or consciousness, to assign the ultimate principle in one case more than in the other. The same ignorance, therefore, reduces them to the same conclusion. They assert that the Deity is the immediate cause of the union between soul and body, and that

they are not the organs of sense which, being agitated by external objects, produce sensations in the mind; but that it is a particular volition of our omnipotent Maker which excites such a sensation, in consequence of such a motion in the organ. In like manner, it is not any energy in the will that produces local motion in our members; it is God himself, who is pleased to second our will, in itself impotent, and to command that motion which we erroneously attribute to our own power and efficacy. Nor do philosophers stop at this conclusion. They sometimes extend the same inference to the mind itself in its internal operations. Our mental vision or conception of ideas is nothing but a revelation made to us by our Maker. When we voluntarily turn our thoughts to any object and raise up its image in the fancy, it is not the will which creates that idea, it is the universal Creator who discovers it to the mind and renders it present to us.

Thus, according to these philosophers, everything is full of God. Not content with the principle that nothing exists but by his will, that nothing possesses any power but by his concession, they rob nature and all created beings of every power in order to render their dependence on the Deity still more sensible and immediate. They consider not that by this theory they diminish, instead of magnifying, the grandeur of those attributes which they affect so much to celebrate. It argues surely more power in the Deity to delegate a certain degree of power to inferior creatures than to produce everything by his own immediate volition. It argues more wisdom to contrive at first the fabric of the world with such perfect foresight that, of itself, and by its proper operation, it may serve all the purposes of providence, than if the great Creator were obliged every moment to adjust its parts, and animate by his breath, all the wheels of that stupendous machine.

But if we would have a more philosophical confutation of this theory, perhaps the two following reflections may suffice.

*First,* it seems to me that this theory of the universal energy and operation of the Supreme Being is too bold ever to carry conviction with it to a man sufficiently apprized of the weakness of human reason and the narrow limits to which it is confined in all its operations. Though the chain of arguments which conduct to it were ever so logical, there must arise a strong suspicion, if not an absolute assurance, that it has carried us quite beyond the reach of our faculties when it leads to conclusions so extraordinary and so remote from common life and experience. We are got into fairyland long ere we have reached the last steps of our theory; and *there* we have no reason to trust our common methods of argument, or to think that our usual analogies and probabilities have any authority. Our line is too short to fathom such immense abysses. And however we may flatter ourselves that we are guided, in every step which we take, by a kind of verisimilitude and experience, we may be assured that this fancied experience has no authority when we thus apply it to subjects that lie entirely out of the sphere of experience. But on this we shall have occasion to touch afterwards.[6]

*Secondly,* I cannot perceive any force in the arguments on which this theory is founded. We are ignorant, it is true, of the manner in which bodies operate on each other. Their force or energy is entirely incomprehensible. But are we not equally ignorant of the manner or force by which a mind, even the supreme mind, operates, either on itself or on body? Whence, I beseech you, do we acquire any idea of it? We have no sentiment or consciousness of this power in ourselves. We have no idea of the Supreme Being but what we learn from reflection on our own faculties. Were our ignorance, therefore, a good reason for rejecting anything, we should be led into that principle of denying all energy in the Supreme Being as much as in the grossest matter. We surely comprehend as little the operations of one as of the other. Is it more difficult to conceive that motion may arise from impulse than that it may arise from volition? All we know is our profound ignorance in both cases.[7]

### PART II

But to hasten to a conclusion of this argument, which is already drawn out to too great a length: We have sought in vain for an idea of power or necessary connection in all the sources from which we could suppose it to be derived. It appears that in single instances of the operation of bodies we never can, by our utmost scrutiny, discover anything but one event following another, without being able to comprehend any force or power by which the cause operates, or any connection between it and its supposed effect. The same difficulty occurs in contemplating the operations of mind on body, where we observe the motion of the latter to follow upon the volition of the former, but are not able to observe or conceive the tie which binds together the motion and volition,

or the energy by which the mind produces this effect. The authority of the will over its own faculties and ideas is not a whit more comprehensible; so that, upon the whole, there appears not, throughout all nature, any one instance of connection which is conceivable by us. All events seem entirely loose and separate. One event follows another, but we never can observe any tie between them. They seem *conjoined,* but never *connected.* And as we can have no idea of anything which never appeared to our outward sense or inward sentiment, the necessary conclusion *seems* to be that we have no idea of connection or power at all, and that these words are absolutely without any meaning when employed either in philosophical reasonings or common life.

But there still remains one method of avoiding this conclusion, and one source which we have not yet examined. When any natural object or event is presented, it is impossible for us, by any sagacity or penetration, to discover, or even conjecture, without experience, what event will result from it, or to carry our foresight beyond that object which is immediately present to the memory and senses. Even after one instance or experiment where we have observed a particular event to follow upon another, we are not entitled to form a general rule or foretell what will happen in like cases, it being justly esteemed an unpardonable temerity to judge of the whole course of nature from one single experiment, however accurate or certain. But when one particular species of event has always, in all instances, been conjoined with another, we make no longer any scruple of foretelling one upon the appearance of the other, and of employing that reasoning which can alone assure us of any matter of fact or existence. We then call the one object, *Cause;* the other, *Effect.* We suppose that there is some connection between them, some power in the one by which it infallibly produces the other and operates with the greatest certainty and, strongest necessity.

It appears, then, that this idea of a necessary connection among events arises from a number of similar instances which occur of the constant conjunction of these events; nor can that idea ever be suggested by any one of these instances, surveyed in all possible lights and positions. But there is nothing in a number of instances, different from every single instance, which is supposed to be exactly similar, except only that after a repetition of similar instances, the mind is carried by habit, upon the appearance of one event, to expect its usual attendant and to believe that it will exist. This connection, therefore, which we *feel* in the mind, this customary transition of the imagination from one object to its usual attendant, is the sentiment or impression from which we form the idea of power or necessary connection. Nothing further is in the case. Contemplate the subject on all sides, you will never find any other origin of that idea. This is the sole difference between one instance, from which we can never receive the idea of connection, and a number of similar instances by which it is suggested. The first time a man saw the communication of motion by impulse, as by the shock of two billiard balls, he could not pronounce that the one event was *connected*, but only that it was *conjoined* with the other. After he has observed several instances of this nature, he then pronounces them to be *connected*. What alteration has happened to give rise to this new idea of *connection*? Nothing but that he now *feels* these events to be *connected* in his imagination, and can readily foretell the existence of one from the appearance of the other. When we say, therefore, that one object is connected with another, we mean only that they have acquired a connection in òur thought, and give rise to this inference by which they become proofs of each other's existence; a conclusion which is somewhat extraordinary, but which seems founded on sufficient evidence. Nor will its evidence be weakened by any general diffidence of the understanding or sceptical suspicion concerning every conclusion which is new and extraordinary. No conclusions can be more agreeable to scepticism than such as make discoveries concerning the weakness and narrow limits of human reason and capacity.

And what stronger instance can be produced of the surprising ignorance and weakness of the understanding than the present? For surely, if there be any relation among objects which it imports to us to know perfectly, it is that of cause and effect. On this are founded all our reasonings concerning matter of fact or existence. By means of it alone we attain any assurance concerning objects which are removed from the present testimony of our memory and senses. The only immediate utility of all sciences is to teach us how to control and regulate future events by their causes. Our thoughts and enquiries are, therefore, every moment employed about this relation. Yet so imperfect are the ideas which we form concerning it, that it is impossible to give any just defi-

nition of cause, except what is drawn from something extraneous and foreign to it. Similar objects are always conjoined with similar. Of this we have experience. Suitably to this experience, therefore, we may define a cause to be *an object followed by another, and where all the objects similar to the first are followed by objects similar to the second.* Or, in other words, *where, if the first object had not been, the second never had existed.* The appearance of a cause always conveys the mind, by a customary transition, to the idea of the effect. Of this also we have experience. We may, therefore, suitably to this experience, form another definition of cause and call it *an object followed by another, and whose appearance always conveys the thought to that other.* But though both these definitions be drawn from circumstances foreign to the cause, we cannot remedy this inconvenience or attain any more perfect definition which may point out that circumstance in the cause which gives it a connection with its effect. We have no idea of this connection, nor even any distinct notion what it is we desire to know when we endeavour at a conception of it. We say, for instance, that the vibration of this string is the cause of this particular sound. But what do we mean by that affirmation? We either mean *that this vibration is followed by this sound, and that all similar vibrations have been followed by similar sounds;* or, *that this vibration is followed by this sound and that upon the appearance of one, the mind anticipates the senses and forms immediately an idea of the other.* We may consider the relation of cause and effect in either of these two lights; but beyond these we have no idea of it.[8]

To recapitulate, therefore, the reasonings of this Section: Every idea is copied from some preceding impression or sentiment; and where we cannot find any impression, we may be certain that there is no idea. In all single instances of the operation of bodies or minds there is nothing that produces any impression, nor consequently can suggest any idea of, power or necessary connection. But when many uniform instances appear, and the same object is always followed by the same event, we then begin to entertain the notion of cause and connection. We then *feel* a new sentiment or impression, to wit, a customary connection in the thought or imagination between one object and its usual attendant; and this sentiment is the original of that idea which we seek for. For as this idea arises from a number of similar instances, and not from any single instance, it must arise from that circumstance in which the number of instances differ from every individual instance. But this customary connection or transition of the imagination is the only circumstance in which they differ. In every other particular they are alike. The first instance which we saw of motion, communicated by the shock of two billiard balls (to return to this obvious illustration) is exactly similar to any instance that may at present occur to us, except only that we could not at first *infer* one event from the other, which we are enabled to do at present, after so long a course of uniform experience. I know not whether the reader will readily apprehend this reasoning. I am afraid that, should I multiply words about it or throw it into a greater variety of lights, it would only become more obscure and intricate. In all abstract reasonings there is one point of view which, if we can happily hit, we shall go further towards illustrating the subject than by all the eloquence and copious expression in the world. This point of view we should endeavour to reach, and reserve the flowers of rhetoric for subjects which are more adapted to them.

## NOTES

1. It is probable that no more was meant by those who denied innate ideas than that all ideas were copies of our impressions; though it must be confessed that the terms which they employed were not chosen with such caution, nor so exactly defined, as to prevent all mistakes about their doctrine. For what is meant by *innate*? If innate be equivalent to natural, then all the perceptions and ideas of the mind must be allowed to be innate or natural, in whatever sense we take the latter word, whether in opposition to what is uncommon, artificial, or miraculous. If by innate be meant contemporary to our birth, the dispute seems to be frivolous; nor is it worthwhile to enquire at what time thinking begins, whether before, at, or after our birth. Again, the word *idea* seems to be commonly taken in a very loose sense by Locke and others, as standing for any of our perceptions, our sensations and passions, as well as thoughts. Now, in this sense, I should desire to know what can be meant by asserting that self-love, or resentment of injuries, or the passion between the sexes is not innate?

But admitting these terms, *impressions* and *ideas*, in the sense above explained, and understanding by *innate* what is original or copied from no precedent perception, then may we assert that all our impressions are innate, and our ideas not innate.

To be ingenuous, I must own it to be my opinion that Locke was betrayed into this question by the schoolmen, who, making use of undefined terms, draw out their disputes to a tedious length without ever touching the point in question. A like ambiguity and circumlocution seem to run through all that great philosopher's reasonings on this as well as most other subjects.

2. Section II.

3. Mr. Locke, in his chapter *Of Power* [*Essay*, Book II, Chapter 21] says that, finding from experience that there are several new productions in matter, and concluding that there must somewhere be a power capable of producing them, we arrive at last by this reasoning at the idea of power. But no reasoning can ever give us a new, original, simple idea, as this philosopher himself confesses. This, therefore, can never be the origin of that idea.

4. It may be pretended, that the resistance which we meet with in bodies, obliging us frequently to exert our force and call up all our power, this gives us the idea of force and power. It is this *nisus* or strong endeavour of which we are conscious, that is the original impression from which this idea is copied. But, first, we attribute power to a vast number of objects where we never can suppose this resistance or exertion of force to take place: to the Supreme Being, who never meets with any resistance; to the mind in its command over its ideas and limbs, in common thinking and motion, where the effect follows immediately upon the will, without any exertion or summoning up of force; to inanimate matter, which is not capable of this sentiment. *Secondly*, this sentiment of an endeavour to overcome resistance has no known connection with any event. What follows it, we know by experience; but could not know it *a priori*. It must, however, be confessed that the animal *nisus* which we experience, though it can afford no accurate precise idea of power, enters very much into that vulgar, inaccurate idea which is formed of it.

5. [Hume gives a Greek phrase meaning "a *deus ex machina*," or "a god from the machine." In Greek and Roman plays, a god was sometimes brought in arbitrarily to resolve a complicated plot. By Hume's day, the term was applied more generally to any artificial and *ad hoc* element in a theory.]

6. Section XII. [Omitted in this book.]

7. I need not examine at length the *vis inertiae* [force of inertia] which is so much talked of in the new philosophy, and which is ascribed to matter. We find by experience that a body at rest or in motion continues forever in its present state, till put from it by some new cause; and that a body impelled takes as much motion from the impelling body as it acquires itself. These are facts. When we call this a *vis inertiae*, we only mark these facts, without pretending to have any idea of the inert power, in the same manner as, when we talk of gravity, we mean certain effects without comprehending that active power. It was never the meaning of Sir Isaac Newton to rob second causes of all force or energy, though some of his followers have endeavoured to establish that theory upon his authority. On the contrary, that great philosopher had recourse to an etherial active fluid to explain his universal attraction, though he was so cautious and modest as to allow that it was a mere hypothesis not to be insisted on without more experiments. I must confess that there is something in the fate of opinions a little extraordinary. Descartes insinuated that doctrine of the universal and sole efficacy of the Deity, without insisting on it. Malebranche and other Cartesians made it the foundation of all their philosophy. It had, however, no authority in England. Locke, Clarke, and Cudworth never so much as take notice of it, but suppose all along that matter has a real, though subordinate and derived, power. By what means has it become so prevalent among our modern metaphysicians?

8. According to these explications and definitions, the idea of *power* is relative as much as that of *cause*; and both have a

reference to an effect, or some other event constantly conjoined with the former. When we consider the *unknown* circumstance of an object by which the degree or quantity of its effect is fixed and determined, we call that its power. And accordingly, it is allowed by all philosophers that the effect is the measure of the power. But if they had any idea of power as it is in itself, why could not they measure it in itself? The dispute whether the force of a body in motion be as its velocity, or the square of its velocity; this dispute, I say, needed not be decided by comparing its effects in equal or unequal times, but by a direct mensuration and comparison.

As to the frequent use of the words, *Force, Power, Energy,* etc., which everywhere occur in common conversation as well as in philosophy, that is no proof that we are acquainted, in any instance, with the connecting principle between cause and effect, or can account ultimately for the production of one thing by another. These words, as commonly used, have very loose meanings annexed to them, and their ideas are very uncertain and confused. No animal can put external bodies in motion without the sentiment of a *nisus* or endeavour; and every animal has a sentiment or feeling from the stroke or blow of an external object that is in motion. These sensations, which are merely animal, and from which we can *a priori* draw no inference, we are apt to transfer to inanimate objects, and to suppose that they have some such feelings whenever they transfer or receive motion. With regard to energies, which are exerted without our annexing to them any idea of communicated motion, we consider only the constant experienced conjunction of the events; and as we *feel* a customary connection between the ideas, we transfer that feeling to the objects, as nothing is more usual than to apply to external bodies every internal sensation which they occasion.

# READING 43

---

# Cause
## A. C. Ewing

*A. C. Ewing (1899–1973) was Reader in Philosophy at the University of Cambridge. His books include* Idealism *(1934),* The Fundamental Questions of Philosophy *(1951),* Ethics *(1953),* Second Thoughts in Moral Philosophy *(1959), and* Non-Linguistic Philosophy *(1968).*

## IMPORTANCE OF CONCEPT

A conception which has played a very great part both in science and philosophy is that of cause. It is indeed sometimes said that science nowadays is able to dispense with cause, but what the people who say this have in view is some metaphysical conception of cause with which they do not agree. In one sense at least science cannot possibly dispense with cause,

SOURCE: From *The Fundamental Questions of Philosophy* (London: Routledge & Kegan Paul, 1951): 159–178.

neither can the practical man. It is essential both to science and to practice that we should be able to go beyond what has actually been observed and make inferences from it, whether in the form of generalizations as to what usually happens or predictions as to particular facts. Now, whatever else the concept of cause involves, it involves this, that we can pass from what has happened in observed cases to what is likely to happen in cases which have not been observed, and this is absolutely necessary if we are to have any science at all or if we are to take any sensible practical steps. This has always been a difficulty for the empiricist: it cannot possibly be a merely empirical matter to predict, as science does, for we have not empirically observed the future which we predict. Not that the topic is without difficulties for the rationalist also, as we shall see shortly. However in modern philosophy it was hardly questioned till the time of Hume that we knew *a priori* the principle that every change had a cause (with the possible exception of those involving 'free will' . . .), and that this principle was a necessary presupposition of science. Even Hume did not, as he is often supposed to have done, reject it, but merely raised philosophical difficulties which he thought made it impossible to justify or defend it. The minimum sense of the principle of causation which must be accepted if we are to have science is then that the repeated occurrence of a certain kind of event under certain conditions is generally evidence which makes it likely that similar events will repeat themselves under similar conditions. Without assuming this much we can never make any scientific predictions whatever or pass from the observed to the unobserved.

## REGULARITY THEORY

Let us now consider philosophical theories of what the nature of causation is or, if you prefer to put it that way, what is meant by the term 'cause'. The philosopher who is inclined to be an empiricist will be likely to adopt a view on this topic which identifies or approximates to identifying causation with regular sequence, since regular sequence is something that can be observed empirically. He will indeed have to assume one principle which he cannot justify empirically, namely, that what has succeeded a certain kind of event regularly in the past is also likely to do so in the future, but the regular sequence or 'regularity' view at any rate makes the minimum concessions to the non-empiricist. 'A causes B', if A and B stand for classes of events, will then mean that B usually or always follows A. This view is by no means identical with the common-sense view of cause, as is shown by the fact that, if it were true, there would be no more special connection between the striking of a match and the flame which followed it than between the striking of the match and an earthquake which might also occur just afterwards. It would merely be that the striking of a match is usually followed by a flame and not usually followed by earthquakes, and that would be all. We could not then say that the striking *made* the flame follow. All intrinsic necessary connection between cause and effect, all active power on the part of the cause is denied. On this view to give a cause is *toto genere* different from giving a reason, it does not in the least help to explain why the effect happened, it only tells us what preceded the effect. So it is clear that the regularity view stands in very sharp contrast to the common-sense

view of causation, though this does not necessarily refute the regularity view. Despite this the latter theory, or something very like it, is distinctly popular today. It agrees well with the modern empiricist trend, since it makes causation something that can be empirically observed and goes as far as one can towards eliminating the *a priori*. And it is in accord with one fact about causation. Whether causation is merely regular sequence or not, it is clear that at least in the physical world we cannot see any intelligible connection between cause and effect which explains why the latter must occur if the former does so. The chemist may bring propositions such as that wood burns under more general principles about the nature of matter from which they could be deduced, but these more general propositions themselves are not of such a kind that we can see at all why they should be true, we only find that empirically in fact they are true.

But there are other respects in which the theory is less plausible. First, it presents serious difficulties when we start talking about the causation of single events. 'I caused the flame by striking the match' might be interpreted as meaning: 'Striking a match by me was followed by a flame, and an event of the second class usually does follow an event of the first.' But what about events the causation of which is much more complex such as wars and economic depressions? Nobody has succeeded in discovering a really satisfactory formulation of statements about the causes of these in terms of the regularity view. If we say that Hitler's invasion of Poland caused the second world war to break out when it did we no doubt mean that the war followed it, but the rest of what we mean is not that wars always or usually follow invasions of Poland, it is something much more specific.

Another difficulty about the regularity view is that there are cases of regular sequence which nobody would call cases of causation. For instance, the sounding of a hooter at 8 a.m. in London is regularly followed not only by men going to work at that factory in London but by men going to work at a factory in Manchester which also opens at 8 a.m. Yet everybody would say that, while the arrivals at the factory in London were caused by the hooter in that factory, the arrivals at Manchester were not.

These difficulties might possibly be met by minor amendments of the theory, others are more serious. The theory seems particularly inapplicable in the case of psychology. For instance, when I believe something for a reason, surely my mental state is really determined by the apprehension of the reason and is not merely one of a class of mental states which usually follow the apprehension of similar reasons. If that is all, the belief is not reasonable; for it to be reasonable it must not merely follow on the apprehension of the reason but be determined by the intrinsic character of the reason. Again it is surely incredible that, when I will an action, the action is not determined by my will, or that to say it is 'determined' here merely means something like 'it is a kind of action which follows most or all states of mind like my own at the time in certain specific respects'. Again for memory to be possible one would think that my present state of consciousness must be genuinely determined by, not merely follow on, the past event remembered. There can be no trusting my memory of yesterday's events if it was not really determined by the events said to have been remembered.

## ENTAILMENT THEORY

All this should make one hesitate very much before accepting the regularity theory merely because it is the simplest and keeps closest to what is empirically observed. It seems that besides regularity we must introduce the notion of determination and necessity. There is a sense, it seems, in which the effect not merely does but must follow the cause, and this depends on the specific nature of the cause as such. Can we say anything more to make clearer what it is in which this necessity consists? There is another case of necessity, a clear one, which it is tempting and, I think reasonable, to take as at least an analogy. That is the necessity underlying valid inference. Where a conclusion follows logically from a premise, this must be because the fact expressed by the premise is so connected with the fact expressed by the conclusion that the former could not possibly occur without the latter occurring. This is logical necessity. The theory according to which the connection between cause and effect is the same as or very like that of logical necessity may be called the rationalist or the entailment theory of causation ('entailment' being the relation between the premises and the conclusion in an argument where the latter follows necessarily from the former or between the objective facts expressed by the premises and by the conclusion).

The entailment theory is a theory of philosophers, but it certainly is more closely akin to the common-sense view than is a purely regularity theory, and though one should not say that causation is just entailment, there is a good case for saying that it involves the entailment relation or else something very similar. It is also true of course that an effect does follow regularly its cause; the regularity theory is not mistaken in what it asserts but only in what it denies. The entailment theory was almost universal among philosophers till the nineteenth century (though they did not use that name). The first leading philosopher to question it was David Hume (1711–76), and at the time his views found little favour, though to-day the regularity theory is the one most commonly advocated.

However, it seems to me that there are two strong arguments for the entailment theory. These may be added to the arguments already given against the regularity theory, which did not by themselves suggest another theory to put in its place. The first is that we can after all make legitimate inferences from cause to effect. How could we do this if the cause did not in a very important sense entail the effect? The relation need not be exactly the same as the entailment which occurs in formal logical reasoning, but it must at least be analogous to it in the important respect that it justifies the conclusion. It would be a very odd kind of inference in which we were allowed to draw conclusions from premises which in no way entailed their conclusions. This argument gives the main, though usually unexpressed, reason why philosophers have so often believed in the rationalist (or entailment) theory of causation. I do not of course in using this argument mean to imply that a person must consciously assume the entailment theory before he can see that a particular induction is justified, only that the theory is logically presupposed if induction is to be justified. We do not know the ultimate logical presuppositions of our thinking, at any rate till we become philosophers.

The second argument is as follows. The occurrence of regularities is in any case a fact of experience. For instance, whenever solid objects are left unattached in mid-air they fall to the ground (with certain reservations to cover aeroplanes, etc.). Now, if it were not explained in any way, it would be an incredible coincidence that this should happen so constantly. It would be like having all the trumps in one hand at bridge several times running, or more improbable even than this. But what explanation could there be except that the nature of the bodies or the nature of the physical universe as a whole somehow entailed their moving in that way? If causation merely means regular sequence, to say that A causes B gives no explanation of the regular sequence of B on A, it merely affirms that B thus succeeds. Only if the cause is a *reason* for the effect, will it explain why this repeated regularity occurs, and the facts surely cry out for an explanation, since the alternative is to leave it as a mere coincidence which would be incredibly unlikely. But how can the cause be a reason for the effect if its nature does not somehow involve the effect? In that case the latter will logically follow from, i.e. be entailed by the former, or at least the relation will be very closely analogous to that of logical entailment.[1]

The following are the main objections brought against the entailment theory. (1) We cannot see any logical connection between cause and effect. This must be admitted as regards the physical world at least. We do not see any ultimate reason why water and not oil should put out a fire or why we should be nourished by bread and not by stones. No doubt a scientist could in a sense give reasons for these laws by explaining, e.g. that stones are too hard to digest and that bread contains nitrogenous matter in an organized form in which it is not present in stones; but the reasons of the scientist only amount either to interpolating intermediate causes so that he explains how A causes B by pointing to an intermediate link C, i.e. something which appears between A and B, or to showing that the generalization to be explained is just an instance of a wider generalization itself founded on experience, e.g. that no animals can extract nutriment direct from inorganic matter. In neither case does he tell us anything which amounts to more than a statement that events of a certain kind occur under certain circumstances; he does not explain why they occur. This is made clearer by comparing the conclusions of other sciences with those of mathematics. In the latter alone do we see not merely as an empirical fact that the conclusion is true but why it must be true. No causal law about the physical world even appears to us as logically necessary like the laws of mathematics; we cannot prove any such law *a priori*, but only establish it as an empirical generalization. However the fact that we cannot see any necessary *a priori* connection behind causal laws is no proof that there is not any. Till comparatively recently most of the logically necessary connections of mathematics had not been discovered by any human being, but they no doubt held all the same in prehistoric days as much as to-day. We cannot set limits to what is in nature by our ignorance. It would be very different if we were not only unable to see any necessary connection between cause and effect but were able to see positively that there is no such connection. Some philosophers think that they can see this, and if so they are justified in ruling out the entailment theory, but in the absence of this positive insight the negative argument is only of light weight.

(2) The relation between cause and effect is in one respect at least different from that holding in any generally recognized case of necessary connection, i.e. cause and effect are not, normally at least, simultaneous, but occur at different times. This of course again does not prove that necessary causal connection cannot occur, but only somewhat lessens the plausibility of the contention that it does. But if there are good positive reasons to suppose it occurs, the fact that it is unlike what happens in other cases is no adequate ground for rejecting the reasons in question.

(3) It is objected that in cases of *a priori* reasoning we attain certainty, but in cases of causal reasoning only probability. This may, however, be explained compatibly with the entailment theory. In the first place we never know the whole cause. What common sense calls the cause is only the most striking part of a vast complex of conditions all of which are relevant to the exact manner in which the effect occurs. But, even if the whole cause entails the whole effect, this gives no reason to suppose that a part of it, which is all we know, will do so. The best we can do is to conclude on the ground of previous experience that the factors in the cause of which we are not aware are unlikely to be of such a kind as to counteract the others and prevent the occurrence of something like the expected effect. Secondly, since we cannot see the necessary connection directly even if

---

[1] Some people prefer not to use the term 'entail' of the connection between facts but only of the connection between propositions, but we cannot avoid admitting that, if two true propositions are necessarily connected, the facts for which they stand must also be necessarily connected. Whether we are to call this necessary connection between facts 'entailment' or not seems to me only a verbal question.

it is there, we are in any case bound to proceed by employing the recognized methods of induction, which can logically only yield probability not certainty. For in the absence of direct insight into it, we can only arrive at conclusions as to when it occurs indirectly by considering what regularities normally occur and inferring from those what are most likely to be the laws underlying them, as on any other view of causation.

The entailment theory is of course incompatible with the view which we earlier rejected that all logically necessary propositions are verbal or analytic in a sense which would make what is entailed part of what entails. Since the effect is a different event from and not part of the cause, the two cannot be necessarily connected unless some propositions not analytic in this sense are *a priori*. Propositions about causation may be analytic in some cases, where something has been defined in terms of its causal properties, but this cannot always be so. If we define a species of thing in terms of one causal property, it will be a synthetic proposition that members of the species have any other causal property they may possess.

So far I have spoken as if it were common ground that we could never have insight into causal entailments, but I should not be ready to admit this. It seems to me true of the physical world, not of the world of psychology. Our insight that the death of a beloved person will tend to cause grief or that insults will tend to cause annoyance does not seem to be based merely on experience. We seem also to see *a priori* that the cause will tend to produce these effects. There is surely something in the thwarting of a desire which entails a tendency to produce pain. Even apart from experience it would not be as reasonable to expect that the death of a beloved person would cause the lover to jump from joy. We must indeed admit that we can at the best only see a causal *tendency* in these cases. If A loves B now, it is not certain that he will grieve if B dies, for by the time this has happened he may have gone mad or quarrelled with B so violently as to rejoice at his death. But we can see, it seems, that the nature of love is such as to tend strongly in the direction mentioned and not in the opposite one. That we can only say what its tendency is and not predict with certainty that this will be fulfilled on a given occasion is presumably because the situation is always very complex and we cannot know that there will not be factors which

counteract the tendency in question. It may further be argued that we can easily explain why we should not see entailments in the physical world even if they are really there. For, firstly it is generally held that the internal nature of matter is quite unknown to us, and how can we tell whether what is quite unknown to us does or does not entail something? In psychology alone are we immediately aware of the internal nature of the object with which we are dealing, namely mind, and here we can reasonably claim to see that certain causal entailments hold, as we have just noted. Secondly, we never are in a position to give the whole cause, and it would be the whole cause that entailed the effect, not a part of it. Incidentally it is not necessary to the entailment theory to suppose that there are any causal laws which by themselves would be self-evident even to God. It may be that any causal law depends for its evidence on the whole system to which it belongs, as many have argued to be the case even with the *a priori* propositions of mathematics. It may be that water would not freeze in the way it does in a universe where the chemical constitution of water was the same but the general world system different. The arguments I have used would be compatible even with any law we can discover being only statistical. It has been suggested that the laws of physics do not apply to each single particle but are only statistics about the way in which most particles move, but there still must surely, it seems, be some reason in the nature of things why so many more particles move in one way than in another way.

Whether we are to maintain or reject the entailment theory depends largely on our attitude to the problem of induction. Modern logicians generally have tried to solve the problem of the validity of induction without assuming the entailment theory of causation and generally admit that they have failed. They have not, even according to themselves, shown why we are entitled to make inductive predictions in advance of experience. The main trouble is that there is no reason why we should think that A will be followed by B in the future merely because it has been so in the past. But if we suppose that the repeated experience in the past is an indication of something in the nature of A which entails B, that will be a good reason for expecting B to follow on future occasions also, even if we do not see why the assumed entailment should hold. No detailed theory of induction has been worked out on this basis. But it is significant that modern logicians who will not admit the entailment theory of causation have (usually according to their own admission) failed to produce any rational justification of induction. Nevertheless it has seemed so odd to many philosophers that there should be a relation of logical entailment between different events that they would rather admit all our induction to be irrational than save its rationality in such a fashion. Yet we cannot really suppose it irrational to believe that if we jump from a height we shall fall; and even if we say that all induction is in some sense irrational, it will still be incumbent on us to explain the distinction between scientific inductions and those inductions which would be accepted by no sensible person. What is the difference between the two kinds if they are both irrational?

It has been said that inductive arguments, though not rational in the same way as deductive arguments, are rational in some other way. It is easy enough to say this, but difficult to grasp what this sense of 'rational' could be. Inductive arguments are after all inferences, and for an inference to be valid the conclusion must follow from the premises. But for this to be so the premises must entail the conclusion, or at the very least be connected with it by a relation closely analogous to that of logical entailment. It is difficult to escape this argument. Nor have those who try to meet the difficulty by saying that induction is rational but rational in a different sense from deduction succeeded in defining the sense in which induction is rational. They have either left it undefined or defined it in terms of practical utility. In the latter case an inductive inference is rational if it is of a kind which is practically useful. But this seems hardly to solve the problem. It is clear that in order to act in a practically useful way it is not enough to do what has proved useful in the past unless this is an indication that it is likely to be useful also in the future, and it is just as much an induction to infer that something will have good practical results in the future from the results it has had in the past as it is to infer that something will be true of future events because it has been true of past.

It seems to me therefore that there is a strong case for the entailment theory of causation. But I must admit that this is not the opinion of the majority of contemporary philosophers. It is in any case a very important issue metaphysically. One of the most fundamental differences there are in philosophy is between those who think of the world as a rationally connected system and those who regard it as a mere collection of brute facts externally related, and which side we take in this controversy will depend chiefly on whether we, consciously or unconsciously, assume the entailment view of causation or not. One of the chief issues in philosophy through the ages has been that between monism and pluralism, between those who look on the unity of things as more important and those who give a more fundamental position to their plurality; and we shall certainly regard the world as much more of a unity if we adopt than if we do not adopt the entailment view of causation. If that view is true, everything in the world will be united in a logical system, since everything is causally connected with everything else either directly or indirectly. If that view is true, everything in the world will be a unity in a very important sense, for the very nature of a thing will also involve the other things with which it is causally connected.

## ACTIVITY THEORY

There is a third view of causation which is now generally known as the *activity view*. We are certainly apt to think of cause as a kind of depersonalized will, and some philosophers have thought that the key to the philosophical conception of causation lay in the notion of will. This view was taken by Berkeley. He argued that for a cause to produce something it must be 'active' and assumed that activity involved willing. He therefore contended that the only possible cause was a being possessed of will and used this as his chief argument for the existence of God, whom he, denying the material world in a realist sense, made the direct cause of everything which could not be attributed to the causation of human minds. Other philosophers, e.g. Locke, while admitting that material things could be proximate causes, insisted that, since causation ultimately involved will, the only ultimate cause must be mind or spirit. They could argue that, though a physical object once started in motion might move and otherwise affect other physical objects, it could not itself originate motion. We cannot think of a chair as getting up and moving about the room of its own accord, and if it apparently did we should feel forced to suppose either that it was moved in an unknown way by some mind external to it or that it was itself animated by some sort of rudimentary mind. In this fashion the activity view of cause has often been used as the basis for an argument to the existence of God in order to get the motion started originally. There are however forms of the activity view which would not involve such an argument. It might be held that the activity presupposed by causation was not conscious rational volition, but some kind of semi-conscious striving such as we commonly suppose to occur in the lower animals and which we might then extend in a still more rudimentary form to what we call inanimate objects. The activity theory of causation would then involve panpsychism but not necessarily theism. Or we might go further still in the direction of attenuating the idea of activity, and say what is involved in causation is a quality which we experience consciously when we will but which can exist without being experienced in any way. It might in that case occur in objects which are in the full sense inanimate and might be supposed to constitute the essence also of their totally unconscious causality.

Again, the activity view has sometimes been combined with and sometimes given as an alternative to the entailment view. In modern times Prof. Stout[2] has first argued for the entailment view and then argued that the only instances in which we can conceive how the cause could entail the effect are instances where will or at least some sort of conation (striving or aiming at ends) is present, not necessarily in what we call the cause itself but in or behind the whole process. This then becomes an argument either for theism or panpsychism.[3] The chief difficulty about this argument is to be sure whether it is really the case that the cause can entail the effect only if conation is present or merely that we can conceive how it could only if conation is supposed present. The cases I have mentioned in which we did seem to see causal connection directly and any other instances I could have given are cases in which conation is in some way present, but the fact that we can see causal connection only in such cases does not necessarily prove that it is only present in such cases. Others would oppose the activity view to the entailment view as providing an alternative account of the causal necessity which the regularity view errs in denying. They think of the effect as following necessarily in the sense of being forced by the cause but not in the sense of being logically entailed by it. This notion of forcing is certainly involved in the usual common-sense view of causation, but the common-sense view also involves the notion of explanation or reason, which can only be interpreted in terms of the entailment view as far as I can see. That the entailment view is, however, not a complete account of the common-sense view can easily be seen in the following way. Entailment, if it occurs, works both ways: it is just as true that the cause can be inferred from the effect as that the effect can be inferred from the cause, and so if inference presupposes entailment it will be just as true that the effect entails the cause as that the cause entails the effect. But there is certainly a sense in which we think of the cause as necessitating or determining the effect but do not think of the effect as necessitating or determining the cause. Causation is regarded as a one-sided or irreversible relation. If I hit somebody in the face and gave him a black eye, the black eye would be produced by my blow in a sense in which the black eye certainly did not produce the blow, and we think of the future as necessitated by the past in a sense in which we should never think of the past as necessitated by the future. But it is impossible to give arguments to show that this element in our ordinary conception of causation applies to the real world, so the activity view must remain inadequately grounded.

It may be further asked how we form the idea of causation at all. On the regularity view the answer is simple: all that causation means is regular sequence, and it is obvious that we can observe regular sequence. On the entailment view the situation is more complex. If it can be claimed that we even occasionally see some causal entailments, we might derive our idea from those we see and then could easily apply it also in cases where we do not ourselves see an entailment but suppose there must be some cause. Or it might be held that the entailment element in our common-sense view of causation was derived from the analogy of non-causal arguments, where we do admittedly see entailments. On the activity view of causation the idea of cause is usually held to be derived from the experience of volition. It is supposed that, when we voluntarily move a part of our body, we are, at least in some cases, immediately aware of our will causing our body to move.[4] The

---

[2] *Proceedings of Aristotelian Soc.*, Supp. Vol. xiv, pp. 46 ff.

[3] V. Stout, *Mind and Matter*, Book I, Chapters 2–4.

[4] The common objection that an act of will does not always produce motion, since we may be struck with paralysis, might be met by saying that we could still be aware in some cases of our will as at least *tending* to produce motion.

chief objection to this is constituted by the circumstance that an act of will never moves a part of the body by direct causation, but only by means of a number of intermediate links in the nervous system. Now it is difficult to hold that we can see directly C to cause E where C does not cause E directly, but only causes an intermediate term D (a set of vibrations in the nervous system), which then produces E without our being aware of D in the least, for we have only learnt of D not through the experience of willing in ourselves but through the reports of physiologists. It is less difficult, however, to hold that we can be immediately aware of our will as cause not of physical motion but of changes in our mental states, as when we will to attend to something. If we reject the regularity view but cannot explain how our idea of what there is in causation beyond regularity is derived, we can still fall back on the theory that it is an innate idea, but we should avoid this if possible.

## EVIDENCE OF CAUSATION

. . . That causation, whether universal or not, occurs may, I think, be established by the same arguments as we used earlier for a particular view of what causation is like, the entailment view, and the arguments might be accepted as evidence for causation by some who would not go so far as to admit that they were evidence for the entailment view. Thus it is an argument for causation that inductive inference generally presupposes some causal connections in the world if it is ever to be justified; and it is also an argument for causation that, if we did not admit any causes to account for them, we should have to regard the observed regularities, of which experience furnishes us with many, as mere coincidences, whether or not these are also arguments for a particular view of causation. For it is immensely improbable that there should be such an extraordinary run of coincidences, and it is incredible that all science and all the inductive inferences we make in ordinary practical life should be unjustified. It has been objected to the argument from coincidence, that the notion of probability or improbability already presupposes causation so that the argument becomes a vicious circle; but this seems to be refuted by the fact that the notion of probability can be applied in mathematics, where causation does not occur. But there is in any case a certain lack of ultimacy about these arguments which does not leave one quite satisfied. One would have hoped that such a fundamental principle for our reasoning and life as causation could have been established in a different way. The argument could not of course in any case possibly prove that everything had a cause, only that there were some instances of causation in the universe.

## DIFFICULTIES ABOUT THE APPLICATION OF THE PRINCIPLE OF CAUSALITY

I have already indicated that what we usually call the cause of an event is not the cause, strictly speaking. Suppose a man killed by being shot through the head. We should ordinarily speak of the murderer as having caused his death by firing the pistol; but this event only produced death indirectly by first causing a series of intermediate events in the intervening atmosphere (stages in the bullet's motion). At any point in this intermediate process the bullet might have been arrested or deflected, and then death would not have occurred. We cannot therefore strictly speak of the firing of the pistol as the true cause. The cause would have to be the last stage in the intermediate process in question. But what would be the last stage? The stage at which the functioning of the brain (or heart) was brought to a standstill? But here we have no longer the cause of death but death itself, the effect, and since time and any process in time is indefinitely divisible we can never lay our hands on and specify the strictly immediate cause. Similarly, whatever happens depends partly on the environment as well as on the more obvious cause factors. If the air had become completely unbreathable first, the shot would not have killed the man even if the bullet had gone through his brain, because he would have been dead already; and if the condition of the atmosphere immediately before had been even slightly different, though he would have still died from being shot, the condition of his body at death and therefore the total character of the event described as his death would have been slightly different. For to describe his death as the effect of firing the shot as the cause is really to make a very vague statement. It was not merely firing the shot but firing the shot under such and such conditions which brought about the man's death, and the effect of this total event was not merely the man dying, but the man dying in such and such a precise way. Death is a general description of a very large class of different bodily events (ignoring the mental side here for the sake of simplicity) and any difference in the condition of his body, however slight, would be a difference in this event. (Strictly speaking, the total effect would also have to include a great many other much less striking factors besides his death which we ignore on account of their relative unimportance, e.g. the displacement of air produced by the shot.) Arguments of this kind have often led philosophers to say that the only true cause of any event is the whole previous state of the universe. Of course a momentary state is a mere abstraction, so what must be meant is some short section of the whole world process immediately preceding. Further it would be recognized that it was equally true that the effect of this whole section was not any isolable event or events but the whole subsequent world process. These conclusions might have to be modified in view of the time needed for the transmission of light, which prevents changes in the remoter bodies being part of the immediate cause, but at any rate far more than we can ever give account of would have to be included in the total cause of any event.

But that will be of little help to scientists. In order to predict or use causal arguments either for theoretical or for practical purposes we must be able to single out some parts in the whole universe from others and regard them as at least specially relevant to the effects predicted. It may be that everything had some causal connection with the death of the man, but at least we can pick out the firing of the pistol as more relevant than the ticking of the clock on the mantelpiece or millions of other things that one could name. It is said that every time we nod our head we shake all the stars, but this does not worry astronomers. The causal influence, though there, is so slight as to be practically negligible. Which events are likely to be specially relevant is largely determined by previous experience, but we are also influenced considerably by certain assumptions about causation which can only be regarded as *a priori* in character.

## ADDITIONAL ASSUMPTIONS

Of these *a priori* propositions about causation commonly believed or expectations as to what kinds of events are likely to be causes we may mention the following. Distinct doubt has been cast on some in recent years. (*a*) It is assumed that mere space or time as such cannot be causes. No doubt an alteration of position in space may have very important effects. It would make a great deal of difference to my comfort if I shifted my position and sat in the fire, but then

the unpleasant effects would be due not to the mere fact that I occupied a certain position in space but to my changed relation to certain objects in space, the burning coal, etc. It is assumed universally that there are no ultimate causal laws of the form—if A moves to such and such a position in absolute space so and so will happen, or the mere lapse of such and such a period of time will produce such and such effects. If a change of position in space does seem to produce effects, we always assume that there must be some physical object causing the change even if we cannot detect it; and similarly, if without any apparent physical change mere lapse of time seems to produce an effect on some thing, we assume that the effect is really due to a physical change which had remained undetected. This attitude may be defended on the ground that time and space are nothing in themselves, only the relations of things and events, or, even by somebody who held the absolute theory, on the ground that mere differences of position in space and time can never be causally relevant since every part of space and time is like every other except in so far as the objects and events present in the space and time are different. (*b*) A less moderate assumption than this is frequently made, namely, that no *part* of the cause can be separated by space or time from the effect except where there is an intermediate chain of causes between the two. Thus for A to affect B at a distance something must travel from A to B, and for a past event A to be even part of the cause of an event B occurring some time afterwards there must be an intermediate process of change caused by A and having as its immediate effect B. This proposition has less claim to self-evidence than (*a*), but has been very generally held. It has led to such unproved postulates as the ether to account for bodies at a distance in space acting on each other and the theory of brain- or mind-traces to account for memory, which would otherwise involve the direct action on a present state of a past event, i.e. the event remembered. (*c*) It has till recently generally been assumed on *a priori* grounds that causally determined change is always continuous and does not proceed by jumps. That is, for something to increase in quantity or degree from $A_1$ to $A_n$ it must pass through all the intermediate degrees or quantitative determinations, and for something to move in space from one position to another it must pass through all the intermediate spaces. But the quantum theory in physics involves the rejection of this principle.

(*d*) It is universally assumed that, other things being equal, an event is more likely to be relevant to the production of another event if it is near to that event in space and time than if it is remote. By assumption (*b*) it can indeed only be indirectly relevant if distant at all, but even indirect relevance may be very important, so (*d*) is not superfluous. The indirect causal influence of remote events is by no means wholly excluded, but in the hope of finding a cause attention is primarily directed to those events which are not remote.

(*e*) It is generally assumed that A is more likely to exercise a causal influence on B if there is some affinity in kind between A and B than if there is not. If put in the dogmatic form that the cause must be like the effect, this principle is very dubious, but it may be of greater value if put in terms of probability.

Whether these principles are strictly true or not, they have played a very important role in science and have to a large extent worked. Science depends on observation, but mere random observation would be of little use to the scientist. He must have an idea what to look for if he is to observe with effect. We are helped here by a distinction Kant drew between 'constitutive' and 'regulative' principles. The former assert that something is objectively true; the latter merely direct us to act *as if* something were true.[5] In order to find out the cause of something we need clues where to look. Then we can test by experiment or repeated observation which of the possible events suggested by the clues are likely to have been causally relevant to events of the kind we are wishing to explain. We need not assert that it is impossible that the principles I have mentioned should be violated, but it cannot be denied that they have been found very useful in suggesting where to look for causes. It is hard to see indeed why they should have worked as well as they have if there be no objective foundation for them, but this foundation might be stated in terms of probability. We should not say dogmatically that the cause always resembles the effect, but it may still well be true that in a given case, other things being equal, it is much more likely to do so than not, and that therefore it is rational to investigate first the possible causes which resemble the effect before we investigate those which do not. And similarly with the other principles, except, I think, the first, which does seem to me definitely true *a priori*. It may well be that these principles are not universally followed in nature but are much more commonly followed than not, at least with the type of events the scientist investigates and we encounter in daily life;[6] and if so it will, other things being equal, be more probable that any particular event in question will conform to them than not. Whether this is the meaning, the ground, or the consequence of their being more probable would be disputed, but at any rate the two—more frequent occurrence and greater probability—normally go together. In deciding the causes of something it is undoubtedly not strict certainty but probability on which we have to act.

---

[5]This is not the only meaning Kant attaches to 'regulative' principles. He describes the proposition that God exists as 'regulative', yet he certainly regards the proposition as objectively true and one that we are entitled to believe to be objectively true. But I think it is what he generally means by 'regulative' principles when he is talking of science.

[6]It might be objected in the case of the principle of continuity that, since according to the quantum theory, this does not hold for the electron, cases of its violation are much more numerous and indeed universal, but it is at least true that things *quâ* ordinarily observable normally act in a way like that which would follow from the principle of continuity.

## READING 44

# Causation in Concept, Knowledge, and Reality
*J. L. Mackie*

*For biographical details see Reading 5.*

### 1. PRELIMINARY DISTINCTIONS

There are three kinds of analysis—conceptual, factual, and epistemic—which should be distinguished but are often confused. 'What is our present established concept of causation, of what causes and effects are, and of the nature of the relation between them?' That is a problem of conceptual analysis. Factual analysis would answer the very different question, 'What is causation in reality, in the objective world: what actually goes on in what we take as typical cases of causation?' Half-way between these two lies epistemic analysis, seeking answers to such questions as this: 'What is causation in reality so far as we know it? What can we observe or discover or establish or reasonably believe about what we take as causes and their effects?'

The answers to these three questions may well fail to coincide. We may have a concept of causation which has no basis in reality, and which goes beyond what we can reasonably claim to know. Equally there may be actual relations between causes and effects of which we know nothing, or of which we know only in a few special cases, while our ordinary knowledge of causal connections is much more restricted.

Another preliminary distinction, cutting across this one, is highlighted by the question, 'Are causes and effects events or facts: to what category do causes and effects belong?' A simple example will illustrate this distinction. I toss a coin and it falls heads: did my tossing of it cause its falling heads? Well, presumably the concrete event which was my tossing of this coin on this occasion caused the later

SOURCE: From J. L. Mackie, *Logic and Knowledge: Selected Papers*, Volume 1, ed. Joan and Penelope Mackie (Oxford: Clarendon Press, 1985): 178–191.

concrete event which was its falling on the table, which included the feature of being a case of falling heads. But the fact that I tossed it did not cause it to fall heads (rather than tails). The cause of the fact that it fell heads would be some more complex fact, that I tossed it with just such-and-such a force, just so far above the table, and so on. Or suppose that the tossing of a coin were really an indeterministic process; if so, then nothing at all would have caused the fact that it fell heads; that would have been a product of pure chance. And yet even if the process were indeterministic, the concrete event that was the coin's falling was still caused by the concrete event that was its being tossed.

This example shows that both facts and concrete events can be both causes and effects: this clearly holds in conceptual analysis; and probably in factual and epistemic analysis too. It also shows that for an accurate treatment of particular cases we may need to be clear which category we are speaking about. But for many purposes this does not matter: much that needs to be said applies equally to events and to facts, and it would be needlessly pedantic constantly to specify one category or the other.

We might hope, having drawn these preliminary distinctions, to take up the great debate between rationalist and empiricist views about causation. Empiricists have held that causation is nothing but regularity in the succession of events, while rationalists have claimed that it is something more than this, that it includes some kind of power or necessity, some making of things to happen, which mere talk about regular sequences, or even laws, leaves out. But I shall try to show that this issue is rather misleadingly formulated, particularly because David Hume, the leading figure on the empiricist side—and indeed the greatest single contributor to philosophical thought about causation—went badly astray, not so much in the answer he gave but rather in the very questions he asked.

## 2. WHERE HUME WENT WRONG

It is ironical that despite the importance of Hume in the philosophy of causation, and of causation in his philosophy, it is not the primary subject of the sections in which he discusses it. His primary subject is inferences about matters of fact, the ways in which we can extend empirical knowledge beyond what we immediately observe; causation comes in because he thinks that causal inferences, especially ones from effect to cause, are our main and perhaps our sole means of so extending our knowledge; that is why he says that causation is 'to us, the cement of the universe'. But Hume's concern with inference is not only his reason for studying causation: it affects—and indeed distorts—his whole treatment of it.

He starts, reasonably enough, by asking what we find if we examine some individual instance of a cause and its effect. Two elements are relatively uncontroversial: succession and contiguity. The effect-event follows the cause-event in time, and in the central cases it follows immediately, with neither a spatial nor a temporal gap. Where there is a spatio-temporal interval between cause and effect, this interval is ordinarily bridged by a series of intermediate steps in each of which an effect follows its cause immediately. Admittedly, neither this contiguity nor even the temporal succession is entirely uncontroversial, in any kind of analysis, conceptual, factual, or epistemic: it is not clear that time-reversed causation is either factually or conceptually impossible, nor is this clear for action at a distance. I am saying only that these points are relatively uncontroversial, and that Hume does not bother much about them. What does matter to him is that even together contiguity and succession are not sufficient to constitute causation: we distinguish causal sequences from merely accidental sequences, *propter hoc* from merely *post hoc*. All of Hume's interest is focused on whatever may be the ground of this distinction.

But it is here that he begins to go astray. He should have enquired, in an open-minded way, what this third element in caustion is, what is the difference between causal sequences and mere sequences, considering both our concept and what we can discover in observed causal sequences. But he does not. He simply assumes that the third element in our concept of causation is the idea of a necessary connection. And what does he mean by that? He interprets it as something which, if we knew it, would constitute a firm basis for *a priori* causal inferences, something which we might discover in a cause by itself which would then tell us that just such an effect would follow, or which we might discover in an effect which would then tell us that just such a cause was responsible for it. He assumes that our idea of necessary connection, that is, of what differentiates causal sequences from non-causal sequences, is that of a licence for *a priori* inferences.

Having assumed that this is what we must look for, Hume has no difficulty in pointing out how hard it is to find any such thing. Since cause and effect are distinct events, occurring as they do at different times, though in close succession, there cannot be any analytic, logically necessary, connection between them. So far as logic is concerned, either could exist without the other: no purely intrinsic description of either will entail that the other, under a similarly intrinsic description, must occur. Nor can we find anything, either in a physical causal sequence or in that by which a bodily movement follows a voluntary decision, which would give us *a priori* knowledge of the synthetic truth that one stage would be followed by or would have been preceded by the other. Analytic connections between cause and effect are out of the question, and synthetic *a priori* connections simply cannot be found. All we can find is regular successions, that is, sets of sequences in which similar antecedents are repeatedly followed contiguously by similar successors: whenever an event of kind $C$ occurs, one of kind $E$ occurs immediately afterwards, and one of kind $E$ occurs only when one of kind $C$ has preceded it.

It is then easy for Hume to go on to argue that this idea of a necessary connection between cause and effect is a fiction. We cannot discover any licence for *a priori* causal inferences. The truth of the matter is just that when sequences of a certain kind have been observed a number of times an association of ideas is set up, so that on observing the antecedent we expect a successor like those which have commonly followed similar antecedent events. This expectation constitutes an inference which has no rational basis, but is due simply to custom and the imagination: but by projecting this expectation onto the objective sequence of events we create the fiction of a necessary connection between them. Instead of the causal inference being based on a perceived necessity, the supposed necessity is itself based on the inference.

This is an ingenious and plausible explanation. It could perhaps account for our having such an idea of necessity as Hume supposed that we have. Yet it almost completely misses the mark. The idea of necessary connection which it would explain is not in fact the idea that we ordinarily employ to distinguish causal from non-causal sequences. This idea of an *a priori* inference licence, of something that would make causal sequences rationally expectable, in advance of experience, and intelligible when fully known, is indeed a notion that many scientists and philosophers have had. It is particularly favoured by rationalists, yet Locke, who counts as an empiricist, endorsed it no less than Descartes. But it is not part of our ordinary everyday working concept of cause and effect.

What has gone wrong is very curious. In his epistemic analysis, his account of causation in reality so far as we know it, Hume was a regularity theorist, and perhaps in his factual analysis also. But not in his conceptual analysis. Far from saying that our concept of causation is that of regular succession alone, he accepted far too readily and uncritically the rationalist interpretation of this concept, and then displayed admirable but quite needless ingenuity in explaining it away as a fiction. It seems plain that it was his concentration on causal inference, to the relative neglect of causation itself, that led him astray, or at least made him over-ready to accept this erroneous view.

But it is not only this mistaken conceptual analysis that reflects his interest in inference: Hume's regularity theory, his own proposed epistemic and factual analysis, seems also to be adapted to this end. For a statement about a regular succession, a synthetic universal proposition connecting kinds of event, however we may have come to know it or believe it, is just what we should need as the major premiss for an inference from an observation to an unobserved matter of fact.

I have said that Hume went wrong, but I have not yet shown that he did. To establish this, I must start again and do what Hume failed to do, that is, enquire in an open-minded way what makes the difference between a causal and a non-causal sequence. So let us take an example. A man drinks a fair quantity of wine. At the same time he eats a fair quantity of bread. Soon after he shows some of the familiar signs of intoxication. Here we have two sequences, wine-drinking followed by intoxication and bread-eating followed by intoxication. So far as temporal succession and contiguity are concerned, the two sequences are exactly alike. But we would say that the first sequence is causal, the second non-causal. Never mind, for the moment, how we know this or why we believe this, or even whether we are right: let us concentrate first on what we mean when we say that the wine-drinking caused the man's drunkenness, but the bread-eating did not. Plainly, what we mean concerns this particular episode: we do not *mean* that wine-drinking is regularly followed by intoxication whereas bread-eating is not. This may or may not be the case, but it is not what we mean. But equally we do not *mean* that if only we knew enough, about the detailed structure of the wine on the one hand and of the man's body on the other, we could know *a priori* that the putting of one into the other would be followed by just such symptoms. That, too, may or may not be the case, but it is not what our singular causal statement means. Surely what it means is rather something like this: if the man hadn't drunk that quantity of wine, but everything else had been as it was, he wouldn't have become intoxicated. And when we deny that the second sequence was causal we are saying that if the man hadn't eaten the bread, but everything else (including the wine-drinking) had been as it was, he might still have become intoxicated. And, in general, when, speaking about some past sequence, we say that $X$ caused $Y$ we mean not only that $X$ was followed by $Y$—perhaps contiguously or with a chain of contiguous links—but also that if in the circumstances $X$ had not occurred, $Y$ would not have occurred either; or, briefly, that $X$ was necessary in the circumstances for $Y$.

This holds whether we think of the cause as this concrete event, the man's drinking of this wine, or as a fact, the fact that he drank at least so much wine. But the point comes out more clearly where we wish to distinguish different facts which are aspects of the same concrete event. I touch a red hot piece of iron and burn my finger. This concrete event, my touching of this piece of iron, caused the burn; that is, if I hadn't touched it I wouldn't have been burned. But, distinguishing various facts, here, we would say that it was not the fact that I touched this piece of iron that caused the burn—that would have been harmless if the iron had been cold. Nor was it the fact that I touched the iron when it was red—it might have been merely painted red. The fact-cause was that I touched the iron when it was above a certain temperature; for it was just that, and none of the concomitant facts, that was necessary in the circumstances for my being burned.

Such counterfactual conditionals as these, then, are the distinctive components of causal statements about the past. But when, speaking of the future, we say that *X* would cause *Y*, other conditional statements come into view. If I say that striking a match would cause an explosion, I mean that if, with things as they now are, a match were struck, an explosion would immediately follow, whereas if no match is struck—and things are not otherwise altered—no explosion will follow: striking of a match is necessary and sufficient in the circumstances for an explosion. These are open conditional statements, and not counterfactual ones, though they may be expressed in either the subjunctive or the indicative. But, like the counterfactuals, they are non-material conditionals: their meaning is not adequately captured by the formal logician's truth function which makes 'If *p* then *q*' equivalent to 'Either not-*p* or *q*' and to 'Not both *p* and not-*q*'.

There are various sorts of causal statements, and an accurate account of them would require additional detail and precision. But these are not needed for my present purpose. What matters is that the third element in the analysis of our established concept of causation—the item that Hume failed to find, or even properly to look for, and for which he wrongly substituted the rationalist notion of an *a priori* inference licence—is something expressed by certain non-material conditional statements.

And yet it is not quite fair to say that Hume failed to find it, though he did fail to look for it. For in the *Enquiry*, though not in the *Treatise*, he mentioned it, inadvertently. Repeating from the *Treatise* his definition of causation as regular sequence he adds 'or in other words *where, if the first object had not been, the second never had existed*'. This is exactly the counterfactual conditional on which I have been insisting. But it is not, as he claims, merely his previous regularity definition in other words, but a quite different analysis and, at least as conceptual analysis, a far more correct one. But Hume never realized its importance.

## 3. CONDITIONALS AND POSSIBLE WORLDS

Even if this is a correct initial analysis, however, it opens up more problems than it solves. Even if we stick to conceptual analysis, we may well ask what those non-material conditionals themselves mean. And if we try to proceed to epistemic and factual analysis they create further difficulties. How can we observe or verify or even confirm a counterfactual conditional? What reality could such a conditional describe or reflect? It seems that factual and epistemic analysis will come apart from the conceptual analysis of causation and we may have difficulty in finding any relation between them.

An illuminating and widely favoured step is to introduce the notion of possible worlds: we can replace our conditionals by appropriate categorical statements about such systems of possibilities. 'If in the circumstances *X* had not occurred, *Y* would not have occurred' means something like this: 'In the possible world that is, of all those in which *X* does not occur, the closest to the actual world, *Y* does not occur either'. Since this is a counterfactual, it also suggests that that closest world is other than the actual one. The open conditional 'If in the circumstances *X* were to occur, *Y* would occur' means something like 'In the possible world that is, of all those in which *X* occurs, the closest to the actual world, *Y* occurs also'; but it allows that this closest world may be the actual world itself. To assert non-material conditionals is, from this point of view, to speak about possibilities; but not about anything and everything that is barely logically possible, but only about possibilities that are somehow particularly closely related to the actual course of events.

This is a useful device for studying the meaning and the logic of non-material conditionals, but it is surely a mistake to take possible worlds very seriously or literally. It is only the actual world that really exists, and possible worlds must be explained in terms of it, including, perhaps, our operations in the actual world. Talk about possibilities, I would say, merely reflects the fact that human beings sometimes suppose things to be otherwise than they are, or otherwise than they are yet, or otherwise than they are known to be.

If conditionals, then, are equivalent to statements about certain sorts of possibilities, and possibilities are products of the human faculty of supposing, that is, of a variety of imagination, can they ever be true or false? Curiously enough, they can. For when it happens that the antecedent of a conditional is fulfilled, the possible world about which it speaks turns out to be the actual world. The actual world must then be, of all the possible worlds in which the antecedent is fulfilled, the one closest to the actual world—that is, to itself. Then if the consequent is fulfilled also, what the conditional says has turned out to be the case, so it is literally true; while if the consequent then remains unfulfilled, the conditional is as literally false. On the other hand, if the antecedent is not fulfilled—and a counterfactual presupposes this—then the conditional cannot be, strictly speaking, either true or false, since the possibilities of which it speaks remain mere possibilities, that is, expressions of our supposings; but such a conditional can be reasonable or acceptable, if it conforms to the rules and principles that standardly guide our supposings.

It would be natural, then, to go on to consider what observations and other considerations might justify our use of various non-material conditionals, and what the related realities might be. But before we do this, we must repair an omission. There is something vital that has been left out of our conceptual analysis of causation. To see what this is, let us consider a case in which some cause has two effects, and is, in the circumstances, both necessary and sufficient for each of them. For example, suppose that there are, on a table, a glass of water full to the brim and a pendulum clock in good order and wound up, but not going. I jerk the table; the clock starts and the water spills over. The movement of the table, we shall say, caused the starting of the clock and also the spilling of the water: that is, if the table hadn't moved, the clock would not have started and the water would not have spilt. But as well as these counterfactuals which agree with our causal judgement, there are others which do not. Can we not say that if the water had not spilt, the table would not have moved: since the movement of the table was sufficient in the circumstances for the spilling, the spilling was necessary in the circumstances for the movement. Yet we do not say that the spilling caused the movement. Again, if the water had not spilt, the clock would not have started, and if the clock had not started, the water would not have spilt; yet neither of these caused the other. Similarly, if we were speaking about such events before they occurred, we might use various open conditionals: not only 'If the table moves, the clock will start' but also 'If the clock starts, the water will be spilt'. But only some of these will correspond to causal assertions.

It seems, then, that our conditional analysis has left something out, and what it has left out is the lines and directions of causation—what we would very naturally represent on a diagram like this

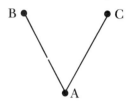

where 'A' represents the movement of the table, 'B' the spilling of the water, and 'C' the starting of the clock. But someone might protest that these features have not been left out, that they are covered by the conditional analysis, if it is handled properly. Some conditionals, it may be said, are much more natural than others: 'If the table moves, the clock will start' is more natural, more acceptable than 'If the clock starts, the water will be spilt', and similarly among the counterfactuals, 'If the table had not moved, the clock would not have started' is more acceptable than 'If the water had not spilt, the clock would not have started'. This point may be at least partially conceded. But what it shows is that there is a specially favoured sub-class of non-material conditionals, in which the antecedent and consequent correspond respectively to a cause and its effect. In terms of the possible worlds account of conditionals, this amounts to a specially favoured way of choosing the closest possible world. Of all the worlds in which the antecedent is fulfilled, the closest to the actual world is taken to be that in which something intervenes from outside the particular system under consideration (here the table and what is on and immediately around it) directly to secure the fulfilment of the antecedent, but otherwise the situation is the same, and things go on in accordance with the same regularities as in the actual world. Thus 'If the table had not moved, the clock would not have started' is acceptable, because in the possible world in which something intervenes to keep the table still, and the set-up and the laws of working are otherwise the same as in the actual world, the clock does not start. But 'If the water had not spilt, the clock would not have started' is not acceptable; for this would describe a possible world in which something intervenes directly to keep the water in the glass, but since the set-up and the laws are otherwise unchanged, the table still moves in this world and the clock still starts.

I concede that this is a specially favoured way of handling conditionals and possibilities, though I would also stress that it is not the only conceivable or even acceptable way. For some purposes we might take the closest world in which the water is not spilt to be the one in which this comes about with the least unusual sort of intervention, and hence by way of the table's not moving, not by something holding the water in, and the events in this possible world would license the conditional claim that if the water had not spilt, the clock would not have started. Since conditionals may be handled in this way, what we need for the conceptual analysis of causation is not just non-material, including counterfactual, conditionals as such, but a particular variety of these, or, what comes to the same thing, these taken along with one particular way of deciding what is to count as the closest possible world.

## 4. EXPERIMENTS AND LAWS OF WORKING

How can we justify our acceptance of conditionals of this specially favoured sort? On what sorts of observation do we rely? Now in practice our acceptance of such conditionals as those mentioned is linked with a whole complex body of information and belief and theory; but clearly the crucial question is, 'How do we get off the ground?' 'How could we begin to support beliefs of this sort starting from cold, without a body of relevant already established knowledge?' And the answer is, 'By bringing together similar cases in which we ourselves sometimes do and sometimes do not intervene'. At $t_1$ the table is still, the water remains in the glass and the clock doesn't start; at $t_2$ I jerk the table, the water spills and the clock starts. So I construct in imagination a possible world in which something intervenes to stop my moving the table at $t_2$, and I construct it on the model of the actual, observed, world at $t_1$, so as to say, 'If the table had not moved, the clock would not have started'. Having done this once, at some later time $t_3$ I have an exactly similar set-up, with everything stationary. I try to describe a possible world in which the table moves at $t_4$, and which is closer than any other such world to the actual one—it will, of course, turn out to *be* the actual one, if the table is in fact moved at $t_4$. Basing my description on what happened at $t_2$, I say that in this possible world the clock starts at $t_4$, so I endorse the open conditional, 'If the table moves at

$t_4$, the clock will start'. On the other hand, just as I start to move the table at $t_4$ I clap a cover over the glass of water and it does not spill, but the clock still starts. Constructing a possible world for $t_2$ with the $t_4$ events as my model, I reject the conditional 'If the water had not spilt at $t_2$, the clock would not have started'. And so on.

This example is highly artificial, but it shows the sorts of observation from which basic causal beliefs would in the first instance be derived. But granted that this is how we think when we come to make causal claims, what, if anything, might make it reasonable to think in this way? Since the key procedure is the transfer of features from one (observed) case to another very similar (supposed) one, we are in effect invoking regularities. But not just any regularities; what we are implicitly relying upon is regularities with respect to what Hume called 'the course of nature', the ways in which events within some system run on from something we can see as an intervention into that system. Moreover, we are acting on the assumption that these regularities are discoverable at least in part, so that some similarities that we detect can with some degree of confidence be projected so as to apply to unobserved cases. *The sort of world in which it will be reasonable to think in the ways that generate our causal assertions is one in which events take place in accordance with such laws of working.*

These regularities need not be, and indeed are not, simple. Typically, a certain result comes about only when some number of causally relevant factors are present together: the total cause is a conjunction of many contributory causes. Also, there are counteracting causes: even when we have a set of factors which is normally sufficient to produce some result, the presence of some additional item may prevent that result. Again, there may be what Mill called a plurality of causes: effects of the same sort may be produced in more than one way, so that the subject of a complete regularity statement, if it could ever be formulated, would take the form of a disjunction of conjunctions of terms. Also, the regularities are likely to involve not merely the presence and absence of features but also quantitative relationships between them: the laws will be in part at least ones of functional dependence. And some of them may be probabilistic, not strictly deterministic ones.

The laws by which the world works are thus highly complex; but we hardly ever know all or even most of their complexities. Regularities as we can claim to know them are elliptical: they have gaps where there should be terms. But, surprisingly perhaps, this is not fatal: we can test and confirm and employ for practical purposes laws of working which are very incompletely stated. Such incompletenesses are represented by the well known *ceteris paribus* clause— 'other things being equal'—and by the phrase 'in the circumstances' which I used when formulating non-material conditionals as an initial analysis of singular causal statements. In our example we certainly do not know, and do not need to know, the whole disjunction of conjunctions of factors which, in a true and complete regularity statement, would be both necessary and sufficient for such a clock as this to start. What we can reasonably believe after very little experimentation is that there is some set of relevant circumstances, instantiated here, such that this sort of movement of the table is both necessary and sufficient, along with those circumstances, for this result. But this conclusion is reasonable, in the light of our experiments, only on the assumption that there is some such, doubtless very complex, regularity or law of working covering all the cases where such a clock does or does not start.

This is just a very hasty survey of a complicated subject, which I have tried to explore in some detail in my book [*The Cement of the Universe*]. I cannot now go into any such details, rather I want to draw out some morals with respect to the factual and epistemic analysis of causation. It might seem that we have come back to one of Hume's main conclusions by another route. Regularities in the succession of events are what constitute causation in so far as it is a feature of the objective world, and incompletely known regularities constitute all that we can claim to know about this objective feature, though we commonly express this knowledge by framing what are either explicitly or implicitly non-material conditional statements, including counterfactual ones. But this is not the whole of the story. It was an essential part of our conceptual analysis that there are lines and a direction of causation. These features are reflected in the experiments by which we acquire basic causal beliefs, as illustrated in our artificial example of the table, the glass, and the clock. These turned upon what could be seen as interventions, as intrusions into some system, with continuous sequences of

events running on from those intrusions. The continuities are essential: how do I know that it is the table that I am moving directly, and hence that it is its movement that is necessary in the circumstances for the starting of the clock, rather than the other way round, except by noting that it is with the table that my hand makes contact? And this kind of thinking will be reasonable only if there are similar continuities and directedness in the objective causal processes themselves.

Of course, much more needs to be said. Exactly what constitutes the directedness or asymmetry of causation, and how this is related to the direction of time, is a very difficult problem, and I am by no means confident that I can solve it: I am, however, reasonably certain that no one else has solved it yet. Nor is it easy to describe adequately the sorts of continuity that are to be found in causal processes. However, it is plain that all three of our analyses of causation, conceptual, epistemic, and factual, diverge in varying degrees from those that Hume gave. Our conceptual analysis is radically different from his, for it centres not on the idea of an *a priori* inference licence but on that of counterfactual and other non-material conditionals, and hence on what are called possible worlds, that is, systematically related possibilities handled in a distinctive way. Our epistemic and factual analyses are closer to Hume's, since they centre, like his, on regularities in the succession of events, laws of working. But our analysis stresses the complex forms of those regularities, to which Hume paid little attention, and also the elliptical or gappy character of the regularities as known by contrast with what we reasonably suppose the objective laws to be like, and also adds what he left out, an asymmetry of cause and effect that is something other than mere temporal succession, and continuities of process that go beyond the spatio-temporal contiguity which he half-heartedly recognized. But though our account diverges thus from Hume's, it does not move at all close to the rival rationalist one. Indeed, as we have seen, Hume's primary mistake was to admit, quite gratuitously, a rationalist notion into his conceptual analysis. My main task has been to repair the damage done to the theory of causation by this false start and by Hume's excessive concern with causal *inference*.

# DISCUSSION: The Problem of the External World

> ... it still remains a scandal to philosophy and to human reason in general that the existence of things outside us ... must be accepted on *faith*, and that if anyone thinks good to doubt their existence, we are unable to counter his doubts by any satisfactory proof.
>
> I. Kant, *Critique of Pure Reason*, 2nd edition (1787); trans. N. Kemp Smith (New York: St. Martin's Press, 1965), page 34, footnote.

The classic statement of the problem of the external world is contained in Descartes' *First Meditation*. Descartes gives a number of arguments for the skeptical conclusion that our sensory experiences alone do not justify us in believing anything about the external world or even that there is such a world at all.

Before we look at these skeptical arguments, it is important to remind ourselves of Descartes' overall project. Descartes is not a skeptic. Ultimately, he aims to show that we do have knowledge of the external world and that sense experience is a reliable guide to its contents. Descartes tries to do this in the other five *Meditations*. His strategy is to find basic beliefs that are certain, indubitable, and self-justified that can serve as the foundations of knowledge. One of those foundational propositions is that he, Descartes, exists as a thinking thing. In the *Second Meditation*, Descartes argues that it is impossible for him to be mistaken about his own existence. Here, at least, is a proposition that cannot be doubted no matter how hard anyone tries to deceive him. Descartes knows with absolute certainty that he, a thinking thing, exists.

The subsequent development of Descartes' reconstruction of human knowledge is difficult and controversial. The next crucial step, in the *Third Meditation*, is an attempt to prove that a perfectly good God exists and that this God is no deceiver: it is inconsistent with God's nature that God should design and create human beings with mental faculties that would constantly mislead them into believing things that are false. Descartes' contemporaries in the seventeenth century and many philosophers since then have criticized Descartes' proof of God's existence as relying on questionable metaphysical principles. (Descartes also gives a version of the ontological argument for the existence of God in his *Fifth Meditation*.)

We shall not explore here Descartes' fascinating but intricate attempt to answer the skeptical challenge that he sets himself in the *First Meditation*.[1] Instead, we shall look at those skeptical arguments themselves to see how compelling they actually are and whether they can be answered without having to prove the existence of God. To put it bluntly, the issue is whether a nontheist (either an atheist or agnostic) can have any knowledge of the external world.

## THE SKEPTICAL ARGUMENTS IN DESCARTES' *FIRST MEDITATION*

Descartes gives three skeptical arguments in his *First Meditation:* the Sense Deception Argument, the Dream Argument, and the Evil Genius Argument.

The three arguments have skeptical conclusions that are successively more wide-ranging. The Sense Deception Argument questions some of the things that we perceive under some circumstances. The Dream Argument casts doubt on the veridicality of all our perceptions, but not on the existence of an external world of physical objects characterized in general terms. The Evil Genius Argument is the most radical. Its conclusion is that we are not justified in believing that there is any sort of physical world that exists outside of our minds.

### The Sense Deception Argument

In the *First Meditation,* Descartes admits that the senses are sometimes deceptive "concerning things which are hardly perceptible, or very far away" (Reading 36). In the *Sixth Meditation* (Reading 20), Descartes gives the following examples: large objects seen from a distance appear small; square towers seen from a distance appear round; an amputee seems to feel pain in a limb he no longer possesses.

It is a commonplace in epistemology that things are not always the way they appear to our senses: straight sticks in water look bent; cool water appears hot to a hand previously immersed in an ice bucket; pressing one's eyeball makes one see double. Thus, it seems undeniable that our senses sometimes deceive us: taking sensory appearances at their face value can sometimes lead us into error. If we always acted on the principle of believing that things are exactly the way they appear to be, some of our beliefs would turn out to be false.

From the fact the senses *sometimes* deceive him, Descartes does *not* conclude that it is possible that the senses *always* deceive him. Such an argument would be fallacious; it would be like concluding that it is possible that all bank notes are forgeries from the premise that some of them are. Rather, Descartes thinks that the unreliability of the senses can be confined to special circumstances such as viewing objects at great distances. The fact that the senses are untrustworthy in *these* situations gives him no reason to doubt that the senses are reliable when he is viewing medium-sized objects at close distances in good light. Let us call the conditions in which sense perception is reliable, C. Surely, Descartes says, I would have to be insane to doubt that I have a body, or that these are my hands, when these conditions, C, are satisfied.

### The Perception Argument

(1) If conditions C are satisfied, then I am justified in believing that I am seeing X on the basis of my sensations.
(2) Conditions C are satisfied.

(3) I am justified in believing that I am seeing X on the basis of my sensations.

As yet, Descartes has no reason to doubt that he is justified in believing, on the basis of sense experience, that he is sitting in his dressing gown by a fire with a paper in his hand. To produce radical skepticism about the external world, Descartes relies on the Dream and the Evil Genius Arguments.

## The Dream Argument

The next stage of Descartes' skeptical strategy is to cast doubt on whether we are ever justified in believing the testimony of our senses, even when we seem to be seeing medium-sized objects in good light at close distances. The precise interpretation of Descartes' argument is controversial. Here is one way of approaching it.[2]

In the Perception Argument, the conditions, C, for the reliability of sense perception are interpreted objectively, not subjectively. The reason why we readily accept premise (1) is that it says that if it really is the case that the light is good, the object X is not too far away, and so on, then my sense experiences justify my belief that I am seeing X.

Premise (2) of the Perception Argument says that these objective conditions, C, are satisfied. At this point, Descartes objects that we do not know that these conditions are satisfied unless we can rule out the possibility that we are dreaming. Though many dreams are fuzzy and indistinct, some of them are as vivid as the experiences we have while awake. With respect to any sense experiences (ideas) we have while awake, it is possible that we could have exactly the same sense experiences while dreaming. Thus, the experiences themselves give us no way of being able to distinguish between being awake and being asleep.

### The Dream Argument

(1) If I am justified in believing that P, then I am justified in believing that I am not merely dreaming that P.
(2) I am not justified in believing that I am not merely dreaming that P.

(3) I am not justified in believing that P.

We can argue for the first premise of the Dream Argument by relying on the Principle of the Transmission of Justification through Deduction. Let P be any true proposition about the external world. Let Q be the proposition that I am not merely dreaming that P. By "merely dreaming that P," I mean "dreaming that P when P is false." Since I recognize that P implies Q, I am justified in believing that P implies Q. Hence, if I am justified in believing that P, then I am justified in believing that I am not merely dreaming that P.

Descartes' reasons for asserting in the *First Meditation* that "there are no certain indications by which we may clearly distinguish wakefulness from sleep" have been widely criticized. It is interesting that when Descartes returns to the Dream Argument at the end of the *Sixth Meditation*, he notes two differences between dreams and waking experiences: (1) dreams are not connected to each other or to our waking experiences by memory, and (2) dream images are often interrupted and disconnected: in our dreams people suddenly appear and disappear in a manner that is inconsistent with our waking experiences of the world. Descartes' view seems to be that it is only after we have proved that God is not a deceiver that we can use these features as evidence to justify our belief that we are not dreaming.

Radical though the Dream Argument is, it is still not skeptical enough for Descartes' purposes. As Descartes himself points out, there are some general features that our waking experiences and dreams share in common. However fantastic our dreams may be, there are some objects "yet more simple and more universal" that appear in both. For example, both dreams and waking experiences depict a world of extended physical objects that move around in space and persist through time. The Evil Genius Argument attacks the justification for our belief in an external world having even these most basic and minimal features. If successful, the Evil Genius Argument would undermine those general beliefs about external existence that survive the Dream Argument.[3]

### The Evil Genius Argument

The Evil Genius Argument employs the same basic strategy as the Dream Argument. If some proposition, P, about the external world is true—even a proposition as general as realism itself—then it is false that there is an evil genius who is constantly deceiving me. Hence, if I am justified in believing that P, then I am justified in believing that no such demon exists. Unfortunately, the demon can produce in me all the same ideas, sensations, and beliefs that I normally acquire through my transactions with the external world. In other words, if the demon hypothesis were true, all my experiences would be exactly the same as the ones that I actually have now. Thus, sense experience alone cannot justify my belief that the demon hypothesis is false. Hence, I am not justified in believing that there is an external world.

### The Evil Genius Argument

(1)  If I am justified in believing that P, then I am justified in believing that the demon hypothesis is false.

(2)  I am not justified in believing that the demon hypothesis is false.

(3)  I am not justified in believing that P.

A modern science-fiction variant of Descartes' Evil Genius Argument employs the hypothesis that I am really a brain in a vat. According to the vat hypothesis, all my sensations and other ideas are really caused by a brilliant but demented scientist electrically stimulating my brain. If the vat hypothesis were true, then nearly all of my beliefs about the external world would be false: it would be false that I have arms and legs, that I am eating breakfast or watching TV as I seem to be doing when the scientist stimulates my brain. My experiences by themselves do not justify me in rejecting the vat hypothesis as false. Thus, even though I am not a brain in a vat, none of my beliefs about objects in the external world is justified.[4]

According to Descartes, we are justified in rejecting the demon hypothesis as false only if we can prove that God exists. Hardly anyone agrees with Descartes that theism is the only way to avoid skepticism, but opinions differ about what exactly is wrong with Descartes' argument. I shall consider several kinds of response to the Evil Genius Argument: an internalist reply, an externalist reply, and two examples of what I call dismissive replies. The two dismissive replies, provided by Bishop Berkeley (1685–1753) and the contemporary American philosopher Hilary Putnam, respectively, deny that Cartesian skepticism poses a genuine problem in the first place. Unlike the dismissers, internalists and externalists accept the problem as genuine but disagree about how it can be solved. Our example of an internalist reply is provided by Bertrand Russell, who appeals to the internal coherence between our beliefs and their explanatory power as a source of justification for realism. In sharp contrast to the internalists, externalists appeal to causal relations between our beliefs and the external world and the reliability of our perceptual systems as the proper antidote for skepticism.

## AN INTERNALIST REPLY: RUSSELL'S COHERENCE THEORY

In Chapters 1 and 2 of his *Problems of Philosophy* (Reading 37), Bertrand Russell admits that there is no conclusive proof that there is an external world of physical objects that are the causes of our sense-data; but he does regard realism as a justified belief, though not quite as certain as the sense-data themselves.

He makes two points. First, as a matter of psychological fact, realism is an *instinctive* belief, not one that was arrived at by inference or one that we can voluntarily relinquish. Second, realism provides *the best explanation* of the sense-data that we experience. Of all the possible ways of explaining the contents of our sensory experience, realism is the simplest and the most coherent.

These two points suggest that Russell would endorse the following principle:

(R)  If P is an instinctive belief, and P provides the best explanation of S's evidence, then S is justified in believing that P.

If principle (R) is true and if realism is the instinctive belief that best explains our sensory experience, then we are justified in being realists; and if realism is justified, then so too is our rejection of the demon hypothesis. Thus, the second premise of the Evil Genius Argument is false.

Russell's proposal has the merit of agreeing with common sense, but does it constitute an adequate answer to Cartesian skepticism? How, for example, could Russell defend principle (R)?

As Russell himself admits, not all our instinctive beliefs are true. He gives the example of our instinctive belief that sense-data themselves are independent objects. This is a reference to the distinction between primary and secondary qualities that plays a major role in Locke's representative theory of perception. The basic idea here is that colors and other so-called secondary qualities are not literally in physical objects the way that they seem to be. Other examples would be our instinctive belief that the objects we see exist at the moment that we see them (refuted by the discovery that the speed of light is finite) or our belief that the heavens turn daily about the stationary Earth. Thus, on Russell's view, instinctive beliefs are not immune to revision; they are simply the beliefs that are most entrenched and thus the ones that we find most difficult to give up in the face of contrary evidence and argument. What Russell needs is an argument for granting an epistemological preference to beliefs that are psychologically entrenched.

One possibility is an appeal to evolutionary theory: instinctive beliefs are probably true because they have been shaped by natural selection; creatures with false instinctive beliefs are likely to perish before they can reproduce. But such an appeal to natural selection acting on physical bodies presupposes what is at issue, namely, the truth of realism. It is also questionable in its own right, since not all false beliefs are lethal.

Most people would agree with Russell that explanatory power is an epistemological virtue. Imagine that we have two competing hypotheses, H and K, and that H explains the available evidence better than K does. If we have no reason to doubt that H is true, then we are justified in accepting H and rejecting K. This seems like a sound principle of justification similar to those employed by working scientists. Unfortunately, it will not serve to justify accepting realism as true and rejecting the demon hypothesis as false without further argument. First, the principle itself is suspect. Are we justified in believing that H is true, even when it is a lousy explanation, just because its rival is even worse? How good an explanation does realism provide of the *details* of our experience? Second, we need to justify our claim that realism is a better explanation of our experience than the demon hypothesis. While this may seem easy, remember that the demon hypothesis has been contrived so that it has exactly the same observable consequences as realism. We need an account of explanation that enables us to compare theories that are observationally equivalent; we cannot simply appeal to a vague notion of simplicity.

Russell is a good example of someone who responds to radical skepticism by articulating a theory of justification. In Russell's case, his theory resembles the modest foundationalism described by Robert Audi in "The Structure of Knowledge" (Reading 38). Russell's theory is foundationalist, since it recognizes the role of basic beliefs that are not inferred from any other beliefs. His theory is also coherentist, since an important part of what justifies a particular belief is the belief's being a member of a harmonious, coherent system. Unlike the strict foundationalist, who wants to build up human knowledge from basic beliefs that are absolutely certain, Russell begins with beliefs that are fallible but psychologically compelling. These are what Russell calls instinctive beliefs because they are held, unhesitatingly, without argument. We just find ourselves with these beliefs. Ultimately, some of these starting beliefs may have to be modified or abandoned as further beliefs are added to the system, but at no time can we guarantee that even the highest-ranked beliefs in a coherent system are true.

The problem for the coherentist—a problem that I think Russell leaves unsolved—is this: What is the connection between coherence and truth or between coherence and the *probability* of truth? After all, Descartes was interested in epistemic justification, the kind of justification that is conducive to truth. Without abandoning the correspondence theory of truth and adopting a coherence theory of truth, Russell has to show that his *coherence* notion of justification is relevant to Descartes' skeptical argument by showing that coherence increases the likelihood of truth. Merely appealing to psychological facts or to pragmatic considerations is not sufficient.[5]

## AN EXTERNALIST REPLY: THE RELIABILITY THEORY OF KNOWLEDGE

As we have seen, Russell tries to answer the Cartesian skeptic on his own terms by showing that we are indeed justified in believing a large number of common-sense propositions; for example, this is my hand, I am not dreaming, I am not being systematically deceived by an evil genius. Some philosophers have argued that this is a mistake because the traditional conception of knowledge as true belief that is (or could be) intellectually *justified* by the knowing subject is flawed from the start.

Consider the Perception Argument we discussed earlier. The second premise of that argument says that conditions C, which guarantee the reliability of perception, are satisfied. As long as that premise is in fact true, why should it matter that I cannot give an inferential justification for it? My dog Spot has only the crudest nonverbal reasoning skills. He is entirely incapable of meeting the requirement for justification. Yet, surely, Spot knows some things. He knows that his water dish is empty when it is standing empty before him, he knows that there is a squirrel in the bird feeder, he might even know that I am about to walk through the door when he recognizes the sound of my car.

The basic idea behind externalism is that what distinguishes mere true belief from knowledge is not any internal relation between beliefs (such as explanatory coherence) but an appropriate external connection between the belief and what makes the belief true. Most versions of externalism, therefore, propose that we replace the justification condition in the traditional analysis of knowledge in the following way:

**The Externalist Definition of Knowledge:** S knows that p if and only if

(1) S believes that p,
(2) p is true, and
(3) S's belief that p stands in an appropriate external relation to the fact, or state of affairs, that p.

Different externalist theories are generated by specifying the nature of the external relation mentioned in clause (3). One of the simplest proposals is the causal theory of knowledge: S knows that p if and only if S's true belief that p is *caused* by the fact that p; or, in other words, S knows that p just in case the state of affairs that makes p true is also responsible for causing S's belief.[6]

(3a) S's belief that p is caused by the fact that p.

The causal theory is motivated by considering standard cases of perception. For example, suppose that my perceptual belief that there is cup in front of me is caused by the fact that there really is a cup in front of me. Under normal circumstances, we would agree that this is sufficient for knowledge: I not only believe, but actually know, that the cup is there.

Is the causal condition (added to true belief) really sufficient for knowledge? Several philosophers have suggested that it is not. Consider a different case. I look at my watch and see that it is one o'clock. This causes me to believe that it is one o'clock, and let us assume my belief is true. But, unbeknownst to me, my watch has stopped. It reads "one o'clock" all the time, and it is just an accident that I happen to look at it at one hour past noon. In this case, I do not *know* the correct time, because there is a genuine possibility that I could have been mistaken. The process that led to my belief is not a reliable one. Our willingness to ascribe knowledge in the cup example seems to depend not only on the fact that the cup's being there caused my belief but also on the fact that if there had been *no* cup in front of me, then I would *not* have believed it. In other words, when we attribute knowledge to someone, we are making judgments about the reliability of the process that caused it. Knowledge is true belief that results from a reliable process.

The other problem with the causal theory is that it is too restrictive. Even when we focus exclusively on *empirical* knowledge, there are many things that we know about the physical world that are not caused in the way that the theory requires. For example, I know that all kangaroos have hair, that the population of Rio de Janeiro exceeds one million, and that cyanide is poisonous. But in none of these cases is my (true) belief that p caused by the fact that p. Thus, the causal condition expressed in (3a) seems to be neither necessary nor sufficient for knowledge.

Externalists have responded to the failure of the causal theory by broadening the characterization of the external relation so that it includes causation but is not restricted to it. At the same time, they have included in clause (3) an explication of the requirement that when S knows that p, S's true belief is no accident. Here are some of the main proposals:[7]

(3b) S's belief that p results from a process that has a high probability of yielding truths.

(3c) S would not believe p if p were false.

(3d) It is impossible that S believe p and p be false.

How does the externalist respond to the skeptic who urges that we do not know anything about the external world because it is possible that the demon hypothesis is true? It is important to ask what *possible* means here. Mere *logical* possibility is not enough, since any empirical claim, by definition, is such that its truth and its falsity are both logically possible. To attack a knowledge claim based on an externalist principle such as (3d), the skeptic has to show that the demon hypothesis is physically possible. In other words, the skeptic has to defend the claim that in the circumstances that actually prevail when, say, I am viewing a cup, it is *physically* possible that I would believe that the cup is there even though it is not. Clearly, the skeptic cannot do this, since this would require knowledge of the external world that the skeptic cannot appeal to.

The externalist responds to radical skepticism by shifting onto the skeptic a burden of proof that skepticism by its very nature cannot support. On the one hand, the externalist concedes that in the classical, Cartesian sense of justification, I am not justified in believing that realism is true; on the other hand, the externalist insists that that kind of justification is not necessary for knowledge.

Some of the difficult cases for externalism are those in which someone has reasons for thinking that her mechanism for acquiring beliefs is *unreliable* even though, as a matter of fact, it is fully reliable. Consider the following example. Hermione sees Samantha across the street and, on the basis of this perception, comes to believe what is in fact true, that Samantha is in town. Samantha's appearance is unmistakable: she is six feet tall, has long red hair, and always wears bright green clothes. Hermione is then told by Samantha's mother that Samantha has an identical twin sister, Cordelia, who was also in town that day dressed in Samantha's clothes. Unbeknownst to Hermione, Samantha's mother is lying: Samantha is an only child. Does Hermione still know that Samantha was in town? According to the reliabilist theory, she does, since her true belief was caused by a mechanism that is in fact reliable, given the nonexistence of Cordelia. But Hermione no longer believes that her mechanism is reliable. Hermione now believes that it could have been Cordelia across the street, and if it had been Cordelia, Hermione would have been caused to believe something that is false. There is, I think, a strong Cartesian pressure in cases like this to deny that Hermione's true belief is knowledge. It is one thing to attribute knowledge to dogs who have *no* beliefs about the reliability of their perceptual mechanisms; it is quite another to accord the status of knowledge to the true beliefs of people when those beliefs have been generated by mechanisms that they believe to be *un*reliable.[8]

## BERKELEY'S DISMISSIVE REPLY

In Chapter 1 of Reading 37, Bertrand Russell refers to Bishop Berkeley's *Three Dialogues between Hylas and Philonous* (1713). In that work, Berkeley (through the character of Philonous) sets out to prove that realism is false and that the only things that exist are minds and their ideas. I wish to focus on one remarkable passage from the First Dialogue in which Philonous persuades Hylas that realism is self-refuting.[9] In other words, Philonous claims that if Hylas or anyone else entertains the thought that physical objects exist independently of perception, then having that thought implies that its content (i.e., realism) is false. If Berkeley's argument is sound, then it is impossible for anyone to have the true belief that objects exist outside of a perceiving mind. In this way, Berkeley thinks that we can dismiss the skeptical Problem of the External World. There is no problem to be solved, because no one who understands what realism asserts can believe that realism is true.[10] Here is the relevant passage.

*Phil:* . . . If you can conceive it possible for any mixture or combination of qualities, or any sensible object whatever, to exist without the mind, then I will grant it actually to be so.

*Hyl:* If it comes to that, the point will soon be decided. What more easy than to conceive a tree or house existing by itself, independent of, and unperceived by any mind whatsoever? I do at this present time conceive them existing after that manner.

*Phil:* How say you, Hylas, can you see a thing which is at the same time unseen?

*Hyl:* No, that were a contradiction.

*Phil:* Is it not as great a contradiction to talk of *conceiving* a thing which is *unconceived*?

*Hyl:* It is.

*Phil:* The tree or house therefore which you think of, is conceived by you.

*Hyl:* How could it be otherwise?

*Phil:* And what is conceived is surely in the mind.

*Hyl:* Without question, that which is conceived is in the mind.

*Phil:* How then came you to say, you conceived a house or tree existing independent and out of all minds whatsoever?

*Hyl:* That was, I own, an oversight; but stay, let me consider what led me into it.—It is a pleasant mistake enough. As I was thinking of a tree in a solitary place, where no one was present to see it, methought that was to conceive a tree as existing unperceived or unthought of, not considering that I myself conceived it all the while. But now I plainly see that all I can do is to frame ideas in my own mind. I may indeed conceive in my own thoughts the idea of a tree, or a house, or a mountain, but that is all. And this is far from proving that I can conceive them *existing out of the minds of all spirits.*

*Phil:* You acknowledge then that you cannot possibly conceive how any one corporeal sensible thing should exist otherwise than in a mind.

*Hyl:* I do.[11]

The key premise in Berkeley's argument is that it is "a contradiction to talk of *conceiving* a thing which is *unconceived*." The deceptive plausibility of Berkeley's argument depends on Berkeley and Philonous mistakenly assuming that sentence (A) means the same thing as sentence (B).

(A)  Hylas thinks "There exists a tree about which no one is thinking."
(B)  There exists a tree about which Hylas thinks "No one is thinking about that tree."

Not only do (A) and (B) mean different things, but also it is not the case that (A) implies (B). Thus, if (B) is false, we cannot use *modus tollens* to deduce the falsity of (A). Though (B) is a peculiar statement, it is not a contradiction. If Hylas is confused or slow-witted, it is possible that he might be thinking about a particular tree and thinking to himself, "No one is thinking about that tree." But, of course, in this case, the content of Hylas's thought—the assertion that no one is thinking about that tree—will be false. Thus, (B) is not a contradiction, but if it is true, then it describes a situation in which the content of Hylas's thought is false.

Now consider the meaning of (A), which expresses the attitude of Hylas and other realists towards the external world. For realists, physical objects are not mind dependent: they can and do exist even when no one is thinking about them or perceiving them. Thus, while ideas are essentially dependent on minds, the physical objects about which we have ideas are not. Notice that for (A) to be true, Hylas does not have to be thinking of any particular tree. It suffices that Hylas entertain the thought that it is false that for every tree in the world there is at least one mind that is thinking about it. When understood correctly, (A) does not imply (B).

Berkeley was led into conflating (B) with (A) by his commitment to an excessively pictorial theory of ideas according to which any meaningful thought of trees must involve the idea or picture of a specific tree, in a particular location, with a precise number of leaves, and so on. Even if some kind of specific image must accompany thoughts such as "Many of the trees in France are deciduous," this has nothing to do with the meaning of the statement. It is no more necessary for Hylas to think of a particular tree in order to conceive of a tree existing unconceived than it is for you to think of a particular star in order to conceive of a star that has not yet been seen.

Another way of diagnosing Berkeley's error is to compare statements (C) and (D):

(C)  Hylas has an idea of [an object existing unconceived].
(D)  Hylas has [an idea of an object] existing unconceived.

(D) is a contradiction, since ideas, as mental acts, must be conceived by someone or other; ideas as mental states cannot exist without being conceived by the mind to which the ideas belong. (C) is not a contradiction in terms, since the phrase in brackets refers to the content of the idea—what the idea is about.

Demolishing Berkeley's argument in this way does not prove that realism is true, but it at least shows that realism is not self-refuting or unintelligible. I now wish to examine a more recent attempt to dismiss the Problem of the External World, this time by claiming that the skeptical alternative to realism is self-refuting.

## PUTNAM'S DISMISSIVE REPLY

In the first chapter of his book *Reason, Truth and History* (1981), the American philosopher Hilary Putnam discusses the thesis that we might be brains in a vat.[12] Putnam agrees that it is possible, logically and physically, for the following hypothesis to be true. An evil scientist removes a person's brain from his body and keeps the brain alive in a vat of nutrients. Electrical signals are fed to the brain from a super-scientific computer so that the person whose brain it is continues to believe that everything is perfectly normal. Putnam then proceeds to argue that this brain-in-a-vat hypothesis is not a skeptical possibility that we have to take seriously and that we are justified in rejecting it. His main reason is that he thinks the hypothesis is self-refuting.[13]

Much of Putnam's case rests on a thesis about how words, mental images, and concepts come to represent or refer to the objects they are about. Putnam rejects the "magical" view that there is any intrinsic or necessary connection between symbols and what they represent. He invites us to imagine that an unintelligent ant crawls across a patch of sand leaving a trail behind it. Even if the trail should end up looking like a drawing of Winston Churchill's face, that similarity does not make the ant's trail *depict* Winston Churchill. Similarly, if the ant just happens to trace out the words *Winston Churchill*, that completely accidental arrangement of sand grains does not, by itself, refer to the famous Briton. The name *Winston Churchill* has no intrinsic connection with the person Winston Churchill; its connection is contingent, conventional, and dependent on the context. And the same is true of the mental images and concepts in our heads.

Putnam is a proponent of the Causal Theory of Reference. A symbol, whether a word or a mental representation, means what it does only because it is causally connected to its referent in the right sort of way. To use another of Putnam's examples, suppose there is a planet on which human beings have evolved but which completely lacks trees. The humans on this planet have never seen trees, nor have they ever imagined them. One day, an alien spaceship drops a picture of a tree. The human beings look at the picture and store the picture's image in their minds. Even though that image is now in their heads (so to speak) they neither know nor understand what a tree is. There is a causal connection here between the mental image and trees, but it is not the right sort. The drawing depicts trees for the aliens, but not for the human beings.

Let us now return to the brain in the vat. Call the envatted person Victor and suppose that Victor's thoughts are expressed in the form of sentences. To avoid confusion, we will write those sentences using upper-case letters.[14] Victor is thinking to himself such things as "THERE IS AN ELM TREE OUTSIDE MY WINDOW" and "I WONDER IF I AM A BRAIN IN A VAT." It follows from the Causal Theory of Reference that Victor's words "ELM TREE", "BRAIN" and "VAT" do not refer to elm trees, brains, and vats at all. What they do refer to is not obvious, but perhaps they refer to patterns of electrical impulses in the computer that produced them in Victor's brain. Though he is unaware of the fact, Victor cannot speak English. His language is Vat-English. We, on the other hand, do speak English, and only we, not Victor, can entertain the question, Are we brains in a vat? So, we can imagine proposing the following argument to prove that we are not brains in a vat:

### First Vat Argument
(1) If we can ask the question, Are we brains in a vat? then we are not brains in a vat.
(2) We *can* ask the question.

(3) We are not brains in a vat.

The First Vat Argument is valid, and we have already discussed the Causal Theory of Reference, which supports the first premise. Seemingly, we can raise the question, Are we brains in a vat? Thus, the argument is sound. But does it prove its conclusion?

The problem with the second premise is that the "question" referred to is a question in English, not Vat-English. So, we have to know that we are speaking English, not Vat-English, before we can know that the second premise is true. But how can we know that, without first knowing that we are not brains in a vat? On the face of it, the argument is circular. We cannot know the second premise is true without first knowing the conclusion is true. Hence, the argument does not prove its conclusion.

We can pursue the issue further by reflecting on Putnam's contention that the vat hypothesis is self-refuting. We have already seen that this is true of the hypothesis when expressed in English, since if any English speaker believes it or asserts it, then what he believes or asserts must be false. But it is also the case that the Vat-English analogue of the vat hypothesis is similarly self-refuting. Only brains in a vat like Victor can speak Vat-English. So when Victor believes or asserts "I AM A BRAIN IN A VAT," his belief (or assertion) must also be false. Why? Because what the Vat-English version of the hypothesis means, let us suppose, is that I (Victor) am a pattern of electrical impulses in a computer. And this is false, because Victor is not a pattern of impulses; he is a brain in a vat. To avoid confusion, let us use upper-case letters to stand for Victor's VAT HYPOTHESIS.

These considerations suggest that we might try to resurrect Putnam's argument in the following way:

### Second Vat Argument
(1) Either we are speaking English or we are speaking Vat-English.
(2) If we are speaking English, then the vat hypothesis is false.
(3) If we are speaking Vat-English, then the VAT HYPOTHESIS is false.

(4) Either the vat hypothesis is false, or the VAT HYPOTHESIS is false.

The Second Vat Argument is valid and, let us allow, sound. Also, unlike its predecessor, it is not circular. But its conclusion is stunningly uninteresting, since it leaves the Problem of the External World exactly where we found it: either the vat hypothesis is false (i.e., we are not brains in a vat) or the VAT HYPOTHESIS is false (i.e., we are not patterns of electrical impulses, but brains in a vat). I conclude that Putnam, like Berkeley, has failed to give us adequate grounds for dismissing the Problem of the External World.[15]

## NOTES

1. For a very clear discussion of the traditional criticism that Descartes is guilty of arguing in a circle, see J. Van Cleve, "Foundationalism, Epistemic Principles, and the Cartesian Circle," *Philosophical Review* 88 (1979): 55–91.

2. For some different approaches, see N. Malcolm, "Dreaming and Skepticism," *Philosophical Review* 65 (1965): 14–37, reprinted in A. Sesonske and N. Fleming, Eds., *Meta-Meditations: Studies in Descartes* (Belmont, CA: Wadsworth, 1965): 5–25, and in W. Doney, Ed., *Descartes: A Collection of Critical Essays* (Notre Dame, IN: University of Notre Dame Press, 1968): 54–79; D. Blumenfeld and J. B. Blumenfeld, "Can I Know That I Am Not Dreaming," and G. Nakhnikian, "Descartes' Dream Argument," both in M. Hooker, Ed., *Descartes: Critical and Interpretative Essays* (Baltimore: The Johns Hopkins University Press, 1978): 234–255, 256–286; B. Stroud, *The Significance of Philosophical Scepticism* (Oxford: Clarendon Press, 1984), Chapter 1; and J. Heil, "Doubts about Skepticism," *Philosophical Studies* 51 (1987): 1–17.

3. There is another target of the Evil Genius Argument in the *First Meditation*, namely, our justification for believing simple truths of mathematics. Descartes remarks that even in our dreams, two and three make five and squares never have more than four sides. Since these truths do not depend on the existence of any physical objects, Descartes must have intended the Evil Genius Argument to induce a form of skepticism that goes beyond doubts about the external world. How could an evil genius make it false that $2 + 3 = 5$? Descartes believed that even mathematical truths depend on the free will of God. Thus, Descartes argued, these truths would present no logical barrier to the powers of an omnipotent being.

4. It is generally assumed in these discussions that if either the demon hypothesis or the vat hypothesis were true, I would still believe, correctly, that there is a reality outside of my consciousness, but none of my specific beliefs about tables, chairs, my body, and the like would be true. For Descartes' evil genius, this seems to be unproblematic, although O. K. Bouswma has argued otherwise in his paper, "Descartes' Evil Genius," *Philosophical Review* 58 (1949): 141–151. But if I were a brain in a vat being electrically stimulated by a mad scientist, it is more difficult to see how the scientist could ensure the falsity of all my specific beliefs about the external world. After all, wouldn't I continue to believe general propositions such as "there are tables and chairs," and wouldn't these beliefs be true if there were tables and chairs in the scientist's laboratory? For the vat hypothesis to be equivalent to the demon hypothesis, the scientist has to create in my mind a fictitious world quite unlike the one the scientist lives in. See the final section of this discussion, "Putnam's Dismissive Reply," for more on what brains in vats would believe.

5. More recent versions of coherence theory are defended in G. Harman, *Thought* (Princeton, NJ: University Press, 1973); L. BonJour, *The Structure of Empirical Knowledge* (Cambridge, MA: Harvard University Press, 1985); K. Lehrer, *Knowledge* (Oxford: Clarendon Press, 1974); and K. Lehrer, *Theory of Knowledge* (Boulder, CO: Westview, 1990).

6. Alvin Goldman proposed a version of the causal theory in his "A Causal Theory of Knowing," *Journal of Philosophy* 64 (1967): 355–372. For criticisms, see A. I. Goldman, "Discrimination and Perceptual Knowledge," *Journal of Philosophy* 73 (1976): 771–791 and F. Dretske, "Conclusive Reasons," *Australasian Journal of Philosophy* 49 (1971): 1–22. All three papers are reprinted in G. S. Pappas and M. Swain, Eds., *Essays on Knowledge and Justification* (Ithaca, NY: Cornell University Press, 1978).

7. Different versions of reliabilism are defended in D. M. Armstrong, *Belief, Truth and Knowledge* (Cambridge: Cambridge University Press, 1973); F. Dretske, *Knowledge and the Flow of Information* (Cambridge, MA: MIT Press, 1981); R. Nozick, *Philosophical Explanations* (Cambridge, MA: Harvard University Press, 1981); and A. I. Goldman, *Epistemology and Cognition* (Cambridge, MA: Harvard University Press, 1986). Goldman's version differs from the others in two main respects: (1) it endorses (3b) rather than requiring complete reliability, and (2) it accepts justification as a condition of knowledge and sees the reliability of the belief-forming process as the source of epistemic justification.

8. Goldman's theory in *Epistemology and Cognition* avoids this problem by explicitly requiring that the subject's justified beliefs (resulting from a reliable cognitive process) not be undermined by the other beliefs that the subject has. For further criticisms of reliabilism, see S. Cohen, "Justification and Truth," *Philosophical Studies* 46 (1984) 279–295; R. Feldman, "Reliability and Justification," *The Monist* 68 (1985): 159–174; L. BonJour, *The Structure of Empirical Knowledge* (Cambridge, MA: Harvard University Press, 1985),

Chapter 3; and K. Lehrer, *Theory of Knowledge* (Boulder, CO: Westview Press, 1990), Chapter 8.

9. Even though a belief or utterance is self-refuting, it is still logically possible that the content of the belief or assertion be true. Consider the following statements: "I never tell the truth," "I am not speaking," and "I do not exist." If Jones *utters* any of these statements, then what Jones says must be false. But it is logically possible that Jones always lies or stops speaking or that there will come a day when Jones no longer exists. Similarly with beliefs. Descartes was right: I cannot be wrong in thinking that I exist; but that does not prove that I must always exist. A belief or assertion can be self-refuting without also being a logical contradiction.

10. There is another possibility suggested by Berkeley's language, namely, that the doctrine of realism is unintelligible and, for that reason, cannot be believed. But if realism were meaningless, we would be incapable of believing it either truly *or falsely*. And, apparently, Berkeley does believe that realism is false. So, for the purposes of this discussion, I will assume that realism is intelligible and that we understand what it means.

11. G. Berkeley, *Three Dialogues between Hylas and Philonous*, as reprinted in *A New Theory of Vision and Other Writings* (London: J. M. Dent & Sons, 1910): 232–233.

12. Hilary Putnam, *Reason, Truth and History* (Cambridge: Cambridge University Press, 1981). For comments and criticisms, see J. MacIntyre, "Putnam's Brains," *Analysis* 44 (1984): 59–61; J. Stephens and L. Russow, "Brains in Vats and the Internalist Perspective," *Australasian Journal of Philosophy* 63 (1985): 205–212; J. Heil, "Are We Brains in a Vat? Top Philosopher Says 'No'," *Canadian Journal of Philosophy* 17 (1987): 427–436; J. Heil, "The Epistemic Route to Anti-Realism," *Australasian Journal of Philosophy* 66 (1988): 161–173; and T. Tymoczko, "In Defense of Putnam's Brains," *Philosophical Studies* 57 (1989): 281–297.

13. As several commentators have pointed out, in the first chapter of *Reason, Truth and History*, Putnam says a number of different things about the vat hypothesis: that it is "necessarily false" and "incoherent" as well as self-refuting. I shall focus solely on the last claim, since it seems to be the one that follows most naturally from Putnam's premises.

14. Here I am following the convention adopted by Russow and Stephens.

15. As several commentators point out (e.g., Heil, Russow and Stephens), Putnam thinks he has established something more interesting because he is a proponent of what he calls internalism. Elsewhere in his book (e.g., Chapter 3), Putnam characterizes internalism as the view that the question, What objects does the world consist of? can be raised only within a system of language, beliefs, and concepts, not from some "God's eye" external perspective (such as that adopted by skeptics who raise the Problem of the External World). But internalism requires an independent defense. Putnam cannot appeal to his Vat Argument as support for internalism, since without assuming that internalism is true, the Vat Argument fails to rule out the possibility that we are brains in a vat.

# DISCUSSION: The Problem of Induction

> There is a peculiarly painful chamber inhabited solely by philosophers who have refuted Hume. These philosophers, though in Hell, have not learned wisdom. They continue to be governed by their animal propensity towards induction. But every time that they have made an induction, the next instance falsifies it. This, however, happens only during the first hundred years of their damnation. After that, they learn to expect that an induction will be falsified, and therefore it is not falsified until another century of logical torment has altered their expectation. Throughout all eternity surprise continues, but each time at a higher logical level.
>
> Bertrand Russell, "The Metaphysician's Nightmare," in
> *Nightmares of Eminent Persons* (New York: Simon and Schuster, 1955).

A paradigm case of inductive reasoning is this. We investigate numerous specimens of aardvark (A's) in different parts of Africa and find that all of them are creatures that have bristles (B's). From this information, that all *observed* A's are B's, we infer inductively that probably all A's are B's (both observed *and* unobserved). When we say "all" here, we mean every single aardvark that ever has existed, does exist, or ever will exist. The conclusion of our inductive argument is a generalization about all aardvarks whatever, without geographical or temporal restriction. In a similar way, physicists draw conclusions about the charge on every electron that ever has or ever will exist from information about a relatively small, finite number of electrons whose charge has been measured in the laboratory.

Here is another paradigm case of inductive reasoning. The Gallup organization randomly selects a sample of 1,500 citizens of the United States and finds that in the year 1989, 68 percent own a VCR. Gallup concludes that probably (with a sampling error of 5 percent) 68 percent of all U.S. citizens in 1989 own a VCR.

The general form of both arguments is an inductive inference from information about a *sample* of A's that we have observed to a conclusion about the entire *population* of A's, including those as yet unobserved A's past, present, and future. Phrases such as "probably" and "it is highly likely that," which are often used to qualify the conclusions of inductive arguments, indicate that these arguments are not deductively valid: it is logically possible that their conclusions are false even though all their premises are true. We regard inductive arguments as warranted, not because their premises logically imply their conclusions, but because we believe that *most* inductive arguments with true premises also have true conclusions. The premises of good inductive arguments make their conclusions probable or likely, not certain.

### Inductive Reasoning from a Sample to a Population

(1) X% of all *observed* A's are B's.

(2) (Probably) X% of *all* A's are B's.

While it is not the only type of inductive inference, this common type of reasoning from a sample to a population can serve as a model for our discussion of induction.[1] The key epistemological question is this: If someone is justified in believing premise (1) and comes to believe conclusion (2) because she infers (2) from (1), is her belief in (2) justified as a result of this inference? Or, put more simply, is the inference from (1) to (2) a justified one?

The principle that lies behind the inference in our model argument is often called the straight rule, which says that one should extrapolate from a pattern found in a sample to the entire population from which the sample was taken. So, for example, if one observes 60 heads in 100 tosses of a coin, then according to the straight rule, one should conclude that 60 percent of all tosses of that coin will yield heads. There are many other "bent" rules that one could follow in reasoning from a sample to a population or from the present to the future. One might, for example, always follow a counterinductive rule that predicts that the future will be *unlike* the past. This is why Wesley Salmon, in his article "Unfinished Business: The Problem of Induction" (Reading 40), poses the problem of induction as the task of showing why the straight rule is superior to all its bent alternatives.

## HUME'S ATTACK ON INDUCTIVE REASONING

C. D. Broad once described inductive reasoning as "the glory of Science" and "the scandal of Philosophy."[2] The scandal to which Broad was referring was the failure of philosophers to find a convincing answer to David Hume's skeptical conclusion that inductive reasoning lacks any epistemic justification. On the one hand, we have our unquestioning reliance on induction, both in everyday life and in the sciences. Every time we drive a car, take a flight, or swallow an aspirin, we literally trust our lives to the conclusion of an inductive argument. We unhesitatingly condemn as irrational those who ignore inductive evidence in forming their beliefs; for us, inductive reasoning is the epitome of scientific and practical rationality. On the other hand, we have Hume's argument, which seems to demonstrate with devastating clarity that our commitment to inductive reasoning is just a blind, animal faith. If Hume is right, then inductive inferences can be explained psychologically but not justified intellectually.

Hume's argument is given in "Sceptical Doubts Concerning the Operations of the Understanding" (Reading 39), which is Section IV of his *An Enquiry Concerning Human Understanding* (1748). His discussion of the problem of induction differs from modern treatments in three respects. First, Hume does not use the term *induction*; instead, he talks about "moral reasoning," "probable arguments" and "experimental" inferences. Second, Hume focuses on arguments in which the premises report that *all* observed cases of A have been B, not that a certain fraction of A's have been found to be B's. Third, the conclusions of the arguments that Hume discusses often assert a *causal* connection between A and B, not merely that all A's are B's.

The second and third differences between Hume's treatment and a modern discussion stem from Hume's analysis of the causal relation. This analysis is examined in the discussion entitled "Causality." For the moment, we shall ignore Hume's treatment of causation, since it is largely irrelevant to the central epistemological point Hume is making about inductive inference.

Hume's skeptical argument about induction in Reading 39 is phrased in terms of two distinctions: (1) relations of ideas and matters of fact (which

Hume sometimes calls "matters of fact and existence") and (2) demonstrative arguments and experimental arguments.

As their name suggests, relations of ideas are propositions whose truth (or falsity) can be ascertained merely by inspecting the ideas they comprise. They are analytic propositions whose truth value can be ascertained *a priori*, independently of experience. In this category, Hume places all the truths of arithmetic, logic, algebra, and geometry. Once we understand fully what their constituent terms mean (or, as Hume would put it, once we have the requisite ideas in our minds), we can tell whether these propositions are true or false without consulting anything other than the contents of our minds.

Matters of fact are synthetic propositions, and these, Hume insists, can only be known empirically. Even when we understand them perfectly, we still need observation and experience to see whether they are true or false. In this category, Hume places all the laws of physics, the proposition that the sun will rise tomorrow, and the proposition that the sun will not rise tomorrow. No amount of introspection and analysis of ideas will tell us which of these propositions are true.

Demonstrative arguments, for Hume, are deductively valid arguments all the premises of which are relations of ideas. Hume often refers to these "demonstrations" as "reasonings *a priori*." Any other type of argument Hume calls "experimental reasoning" or "reasoning *a posteriori*." Hume points out, quite correctly, that the conclusions of demonstrations (in his sense) must be relations of ideas. Only necessary truths can be validly deduced from premises all of which are necessary truths. If the conclusion of an argument is a contingent matter of fact, the argument must be an instance of experimental reasoning *a posteriori*. It might still be a valid argument in this case, but at least one of its premises must be a matter of fact.

With this terminology in hand, we can now understand Hume's skeptical argument for his conclusion that no inductive reasoning can be rationally justified. The kind of inductive reasoning considered by Hume has a single premise asserting that all observed A's have been followed by B's and a conclusion equivalent to the assertion that all A's will be followed by B's (which, for Hume, is part of what it means to say that A is the cause of B).

Hume's argument has the form of a dilemma. If inductive reasoning is justified, then either it is a demonstrative argument (which Hume accepts as justified *a priori* without further ado) or it is an experimental argument justified *a posteriori*. In other words, either the argument is deductively valid and all its premises are relations of ideas, or it is a justified nondemonstrative argument from experience. Since the conclusion that all A's will be followed by B's is a matter of fact, not a relation of ideas, the argument cannot be a demonstration justified *a priori*. It is not a contradiction to suppose that the course of nature might change and that the regular sequence of A's followed by B's in the past be broken in the future. Thus, if the inductive reasoning is justified, it must be an experimental argument justified *a posteriori*. Hume then eliminates the second horn of the dilemma with the following words:

> To say that it is experimental is begging the question. For all inferences from experience suppose, as their foundation, that the future will resemble the past and that similar powers will be conjoined with similar sensible qualities.

Before analyzing this passage, let us outline the structure of Hume's reasoning. Hume's argument has three steps.

**Hume's Skeptical Argument**

Step 1:
  (1) All inductive inferences are either demonstrative or experimental.
  (2) No inductive inference is demonstrative.

  _____

  (3) All inductive inferences are experimental.

Step 2:
  (3) All inductive inferences are experimental.
  (4) All experimental arguments presuppose that the future will resemble the past.

  _____

  (5) All inductive inferences presuppose that the future will resemble the past.

Step 3:
  (5) All inductive inferences presuppose that the future will resemble the past.
  (6) If any inference presupposes P, then the inference is justified only if P is justified.
  (7) If any proposition P is justified, then either (a) it is a self-evident truth known *a priori* or (b) it is justified by a demonstrative argument or (c) it is justified by an experimental argument.
  (8) That the future will resemble the past is not a self-evident truth known *a priori*.
  (9) That the future will resemble the past cannot be justified demonstratively.
  (10) That the future will resemble the past cannot be justified experimentally.

  _____

  (11) No inductive inference is justified.

Though the exact interpretation of Hume's reasoning is still a matter of some controversy, I think this comes close to capturing Hume's line of thought in the *Enquiry*.[3] Let us begin by focusing on premises (5) and (6) of Step 3.

When Hume says that all inductive inferences "suppose, as their foundation, that the future will resemble the past" this is usually understood in the following way.[4] Inductive inferences are not deductively valid, since it is logically possible for their conclusions to be false even when all their premises are true. A deductively invalid argument presupposes a proposition P if the argument would be transformed into a deductively valid one by adding P to its premises. We can think of P as a missing premise that would make the argument deductively valid. The usual choice for the missing premise for inductive inferences is some version of a Principle of the Uniformity of Nature, which states that the future will resemble the past or, more precisely, that uniformities that have been observed to hold in the past (or in samples) will probably continue to hold in the future (or in the populations from which the samples were drawn).

Given what Hume understands by an inference presupposing a proposition, we can see why Hume thinks that premise (6) is true. To use an inference to reach a justified belief in its conclusion, one must first have a justified belief in its premises. If those premises include P, then one's belief in P must be justified.

Hume's reason for premise (10) is contained in the passage quoted earlier. We would be arguing in a circle, begging the question, if we tried to justify inductive reasoning inductively. Even if it were true that induction has always worked in the past, we cannot offer that as a reason for the Principle of the Uniformity of Nature, since this would presuppose the very thing we are trying to prove, namely, the legitimacy of extrapolating past regularities into the future. Thus, Hume concludes that induction cannot be justified by any experimental argument. Since he has already ruled out the possibility of knowing that the Principle of the Uniformity of Nature is true *a priori* or of justifying it by a demonstrative argument, Hume reaches his final skeptical conclusion that no inductive inference is justified.

## VAN CLEVE'S REPLY TO HUME

The problem of induction posed by Hume has met with a wide range of responses. Almost all of them defend the rationality of induction and attempt to show where Hume went wrong. (The lone exception is Karl Popper, who insists that Hume was right but that we can get along fine in science using only deduction.) Some of the most important modern approaches are discussed and criticized in Wesley Salmon's article, "Unfinished Business: The Problem of Induction" (Reading 40). These approaches include the following:

(1) Attempts to justify the Principle of the Uniformity of Nature as a synthetic truth known *a priori*. (Kant, Russell)
(2) Attempts to justify the Principle of the Uniformity of Nature inductively. (Mill, Black, Braithwaite)
(3) Attempts to dissolve the problem by linguistic and conceptual analysis of what it means to be rational. (Wittgenstein, Strawson, Ayer, Edwards)
(4) Attempts to avoid the problem by arguing that deduction is sufficient for science. (Popper)
(5) Attempts to give a pragmatic vindication of our inductive practice. (Reichenbach, Salmon)

According to Salmon, none of these approaches is an unqualified success, and some are blatant failures. Even the pragmatic vindication approach that Salmon himself favors has run into severe difficulties.[5]

Whenever we reach an impasse in dealing with a philosophical problem, it is helpful to regroup and consider whether some of the fundamental assumptions that led to the difficulty might be mistaken. This is the strategy employed by James Van Cleve in his important paper, "Reliability, Justification, and the Problem of Induction" (Reading 41). Van Cleve makes three main points that I wish to discuss.

(1) Hume has not shown that induction is unjustified.
(2) It is not necessary to show that an inductive principle of inference such as the straight rule is correct in order to be justified in believing the con-

clusion of an inductive argument on the basis of its premises. If an inference follows a correct rule, then the inference is justified whether or not one can show that the rule is correct.

(3)  One can give inductive arguments to show that the straight rule is reliable without vicious circularity.

Let us consider these points in order. First there is the question of whether or not Hume has established that induction is unjustified. In our reconstruction of Hume's skeptical argument, there were two alternatives, both of which Hume claims to have ruled out. An inductive inference is either (a) a deductively valid argument from necessary premises or (b) a deductively valid argument from premises that include some version of the Principle of the Uniformity of Nature. But there is a third alternative that Hume seems to have ignored, namely, that an inductive inference is (c) a deductively invalid argument that follows the straight rule or some other principle of inductive inference. There is, after all, a perfectly clear sense (other than Hume's) in which an argument presupposes a proposition, namely, that the proposition expresses the principle of inference which connects the argument's premises with its conclusion. For deductively valid arguments of the form *modus ponens*, the principle of inference is: From "P" and "P implies Q" infer "Q". If we expressed this inferential principle as a statement and added it to the premises, it would read: "P, and P implies Q, implies Q." For many inductive arguments, the principle of inference is: From "All observed A's are B's" infer "(Probably) all A's are B's." Expressed as a premise, this would be: "If all observed A's are B's, then probably all A's are B's."

Everyone agrees that Hume judged correctly that inductive arguments are not demonstrative. They are not deductively valid arguments from premises all of which are necessary truths (relations of ideas), nor can they be put into this form. Moreover, *if* we insist that all justified inferences are deductively valid arguments, then again Hume was correct to point out that the missing premise needed to transform inductive arguments into valid ones will be a matter of fact which itself requires justification. But why should we be deductive chauvinists? Why should we follow Hume in assuming that "arguments are deductive or defective"?[6] Nothing that Hume has said rules out alternative (c), unless we collapse (c) into (b) by insisting that for any inductive argument, the argument's principle of inference must be added to its premises so as to generate a new argument that is deductively valid. But to insist on this requirement is simply to beg the question against the inductivist, for it is tantamount to assuming that unless the premises of an argument deductively imply the argument's conclusion, they offer no reason for that conclusion. Thus, Hume has not *shown* that induction is unjustified; at best he has assumed it.

So far so good. Hume has failed to show that inductive inference is unjustified, because his argument depends on the question-begging assumption that only deductively valid arguments can be justified ones. But, as Van Cleve remarks, exposing Hume's failure does nothing to show that induction *is* justified. It is at this point that we need to draw a clear distinction between (a) an inference *being* justified and (b) *showing* that an inference is justified.[7]

An inference is a justified one if someone who has a justified belief in its premises and uses the inference to reach a belief in its conclusion thereby acquires a justified belief in that conclusion. More simply: A justified inference transmits justification from its premises to its conclusion. Notice that we do not also require that the person who uses the inference be justified in believing that its principle of inference is correct. It suffices that the principle of inference *be* correct, whether or not anyone can show it. Van Cleve alludes to a famous paper by Lewis Carroll, "What the Tortoise Said to Achilles," as an illustration of this point.[8] Carroll's own example concerns a deductively valid argument from geometry in which the premises (A) and (B) logically imply the conclusion (Z).

(A)  Things that are equal to the same are equal to each other.
(B)  The two sides of this Triangle are things that are equal to the same.

(Z)  The two sides of this Triangle are equal to each other.

The Tortoise challenges Achilles to show why he is logically forced to accept (Z) as true if he already accepts (A) and (B). In other words, can Achilles justify the inference from (A) and (B) to (Z)? After some discussion, the Tortoise agrees to accept the conditional statement (C).

(C):  If A and B are true, then Z must be true.

But when Achilles adds (C) to the premises of the original argument, the Tortoise again asks why, if he accepts (A), (B), *and* (C), should he also accept (Z). Defining a new proposition (D): If A and B and C are true, then Z must be true, and adding it as a further premise does nothing to satisfy the Tortoise, who again questions the principle of inference connecting the new set of premises to the conclusion (Z). Several months later, the argument has a thousand and one premises, and the Tortoise is still not satisfied.

Lewis Carroll's humorous story illustrates some serious points. (1) We cannot justify *every* principle of inference by giving an argument, since that must lead to an infinite regress. Every new argument we invent will itself rely on a principle of inference connecting its premises to its conclusion. (2) The fact that a justifying argument for a principle of inference uses that very same inferential principle does not, by itself, make the argument unwarranted. Each of Achilles' arguments is deductively valid; all of them are justified inferences.

So, the possibility is open that some inductive principles such as the straight rule are correct and that people who make inductive inferences are justified in the inferences they make, even though they may be unable to justify the principles on which their inferences rely. And, of course, *if* the straight rule and other inductive rules are correct, then one can use them in further inductive inferences to reach justified conclusions about the reliability of the rules themselves. Consider, for example, Van Cleve's "Argument A": Most of the inductive inferences I have drawn in the past from true premises have had true conclusions; hence, the majority of all inductive inferences with true premises have true conclusions. As Van Cleve points out, it is then but a short step for the reliabilist to argue from "induction is reliable" to "induction is justified."

There is no illicit circularity in this procedure, but it has several "ifs" attached to its results. What we have shown is:

(1) If inductive rules of inference are correct, then inductive inferences using them are justified. Nothing in Hume's argument rules out this possibility.

(2) If inductive inferences are justified, then we can use them to reach a justified belief in the proposition that induction is reliable.

(3) If the *reliability* theory of justification is correct, then our justified belief that induction is reliable shows that induction is justified.

Thus, a version of Hume's problem is soluble. We *can* justify induction *if* inductive rules of inference are correct and *if* reliabilism is true.

In Section VII of his paper, Van Cleve considers how things stand if one rejects the reliabilist account of justification and insists—against Hume and Salmon—that we have *a priori* knowledge of epistemic principles, including the principles of inductive inference. On this view, the reliability of induction is irrelevant. We know by a kind of intuitive self-evidence that we are acting reasonably in following the straight rule. Van Cleve points out that the reliability of induction can still be established without circularity; but, of course, on this *a priorist* view of epistemic principles, no argument is needed to show that induction is justified.

---

## NOTES

1. Other common types of inductive argument include argument by analogy, statistical syllogism, and induction to a particular.

2. C. D. Broad, "The Philosophy of Francis Bacon," in *Ethics and the History of Philosophy* (New York: Humanities Press, 1952): 117–143.

3. One might object to premise (4) in Step 2 on the grounds that all *experimental* means here is "nondemonstrative." Surely not every invalid argument—and every valid argument with at least one contingent premise—presupposes that the future resembles the past.

4. There is another interpretation of what it means to say that an inference presupposes a proposition that we explore below, namely, that the proposition expresses the rule of inference connecting the premises of the argument with its conclusion.

5. The basic problem is that in 1968, Ian Hacking discovered a set of three conditions that are separately necessary and jointly sufficient for singling out the straight rule from its bent competitors. The problem lies with the third condition: symmetry (what De Finetti calls exchangeability). The symmetry condition entails that in a finite sequence of coin tosses, say, one should ignore the order in which the heads are obtained and consider only their relative frequency when inferring the true probability of getting heads. De Finetti interpreted this as a purely subjective condition having to do with our indifference towards the order of the sequence. No one, to my knowledge, has explained how to give a pragmatic vindication of this condition.

6. D. C. Stove criticizes Hume's "deductivism" in *Probability and Hume's Inductive Scepticism* (Oxford: Clarendon Press, 1973).

7. In a series of important papers, William Alston describes this as the distinction between an inference *being justified* and someone *justifying* it. See his "Levels Confusions in Epistemology," *Midwest Studies in Philosophy* 5 (1980): 135–150, and "Epistemic Circularity," *Philosophy and Phenomenological Research* 47 (1986): 1–30. Both papers are reprinted in W. P. Alston, *Epistemic Justification: Essays in the Theory of Knowledge* (Ithaca, NY: Cornell University Press, 1989).

8. L. Carroll, "What the Tortoise Said to Achilles," *Mind* 14 (1895): 278–280.

# DISCUSSION: Causality

... hardly any conception could be more basic to metaphysical understanding than this one, or hardly any confusion more mischievous in its philosophical fruits. If a philosopher's analysis of causation goes wrong, then it is a good bet that most of his metaphysics will be wrong too.

Richard Taylor, *Metaphysics*, 3rd Edition
(Englewood Cliffs, NJ: Prentice-Hall, 1983), page 80.

Throughout the preceding parts of this book, causality has played a key role in many different philosophical discussions: versions of the cosmological argument posit God as the first *cause*; ethical theories such as utilitarianism judge the morality of an action according to its *causal* consequences; Cartesian dualism requires that immaterial minds *causally* interact with physical bodies; and, in the free-will debate, libertarians insist that a person who acts freely must be the *uncaused cause* of her actions.

Causality also plays a major role in epistemology. Reliabilism, for example, defines knowledge as true belief *caused* by a reliable process. More generally, most people would agree with David Hume that we acquire knowledge of the external world largely, if not exclusively, by reasoning from effects to causes and from causes to effects.

According to Hume, causal links and relations are the only way we can extend our knowledge beyond the contents of our own minds and beyond the confines of the immediate present. In Section IV of the *Enquiry* (Reading 39), Hume writes: "All reasonings concerning matter of fact seem to be founded on the relation of *Cause and Effect*. By means of that relation alone we can go beyond the evidence of our memory and sense." Thus, Hume would claim that it is only on the assumption that my idea of a red apple is caused by the fruit in front of me that the red-apple-like sensations I experience can constitute evidence for the apple's existence. Similarly, in interpreting historical documents and artifacts, whether it be a letter from a friend or a Bronze-Age axe, we rely on generalizations about physical objects and human nature to draw conclusions about the past. The reliability of carbon-dating, for example, depends on the laws of radioactive decay.

If we interpret causal laws broadly, as Hume did, so that they include all causal generalizations, then Hume was surely correct in asserting that they are one means by which we extend our knowledge from the immediate present. Where Hume was probably mistaken was in asserting that causation is the *only* way of extending our knowledge of the world, or even that it is indispensable for acquiring justified true beliefs about the external world in the first place.

Firstly, not all inductive inferences are causal inferences. For example, suppose that I draw a simple random sample of 100 balls from an urn containing many thousands and discover that 80 balls in my sample are red. My inductive inference to the conclusion that probably 80 percent of all the balls in the urn are red does not seem to depend, even implicitly, on any causal generalization. We are not, in this case, arguing from an effect to its cause. Secondly, many of the beliefs that spontaneously arise in us carry with them a presumption of epistemic warrant. Causal knowledge can undermine these beliefs, but it does not seem required to legitimate them in the first place. Memory, for example, yields justified beliefs about the past without involving explicit appeals to causation. It is true that any genuine memory trace will have been caused by the events that are recorded in it, and thus an ostensible memory can be defeated if we can show that the apparent memory was not caused in the correct way. But showing that an ostensible memory was appropriately caused does not seem necessary before we are justified in believing it initially. A number of philosophers, especially Hume's contemporary, Thomas Reid, have argued that all basic sources of belief such as perception, reasoning, relying on testimony, and memory yield justified beliefs in the absence of any reasons to doubt the reliability of the process or mechanism by which they are formed.

First in *A Treatise of Human Nature* (1739) and then in *An Enquiry Concerning Human Understanding* (1748), Hume advanced a theory about the nature of causality and causal connections that has remained controversial to the present day. Modern authors often refer to this account as the regularity theory of causation or the constant conjunction theory. Hume is the principal source of this important, empiricist analysis of the causal relation. Two rival theories to Hume's, discussed by A. C. Ewing in Reading 43, are the activity theory and the entailment theory. Ewing's entailment theory is a member of a more general class of theories that I shall call necessitarian theories of causation. What all necessitarian theories have in common is the thesis that there is an objective relation of necessary connection linking causes to their effects. In Ewing's version, the necessary connection is claimed to be logical entailment. Other versions posit the existence of a nonlogical, physical (or causal) necessity. I will first discuss the necessitarian and activity theories and Hume's criticisms of them before turning to Hume's own regularity account.

## NECESSITARIAN AND ACTIVITY THEORIES OF CAUSATION

Many of Hume's contemporaries—rationalists and empiricists alike—subscribed to the activity theory of causation. Though differing in the details of their theories, Descartes, Locke, Berkeley, and Reid all agree that causes, properly so-called, efficient causes in the true meaning of the term, produce their effects by exercising an inner active power. For these thinkers, the only substances that can possess such a power are agents, human and divine, possessed of will.[2] Thus, for example, Locke says that physical objects can transmit motion to other objects by collisions, and both agents and physical objects have the passive capacity to be affected by other objects, but only agents can move themselves and *originate* motion in other things when they themselves are at rest.[3]

In the most extreme version of the activity theory, which Hume discusses in Part I of Section VII of the *Enquiry* (Reading 42), it is denied that even human beings have the power to will their own actions. Hume is referring to the occasionalist theory of Nicholas Malebranche (1638–1715) which asserts that God is the immediate efficient cause of all physical changes, including the bodily motions that seem to be commanded by our acts of volition. Hume writes:

> Thus, according to these philosophers, everything is full of God. Not content with the principle that nothing exists but by his will, that nothing possesses any power but by his concession, they rob nature and all created

beings of every power in order to render their dependency on the Deity still more sensible and immediate.

As Hume notes, it seems to argue more wisdom on God's part to have delegated some active power to creatures rather than requiring God's continual intervention to produce everything by divine volitions. Thus, on most versions of the activity theory, human agents have active power of their own, though it originates, ultimately, from God and could be withdrawn if God chooses.[4] Many activity theorists see this qualified autonomy of human beings to produce the actions they freely will as necessary for moral responsibility.

The activity theory has consequences that are fairly surprising. If one rejects the thesis of panpsychism that all things—not just humans and God but also stones, planets, and electrons—have primitive minds capable of willing, then anything not caused by humans must have God as its efficient cause. In their various ways, Descartes, Locke, Berkeley, and Reid all embraced this conclusion. Reid, for example, says explicitly that "supposing natural philosophy [science] brought to its utmost perfection, it does not discover the efficient cause of any one phenomenon in nature."[5] Scientists discover laws of nature that describe *how* the efficient cause operates, but the efficient cause itself, God, lies always *behind* the scene. Laws of nature are not causes, since they can neither act nor be acted upon; they are only the rules according to which the efficient cause, God, operates.

Hume has some rather sarcastic things to say about the activity theory in Part I of Section VII of the *Enquiry*. He finds it incredible that our sensations are caused not by physical objects exciting our sense organs but by "a particular volition of our omnipotent Maker." When a theory leads to this sort of consequence, we should mistrust our reasoning, since "we are got into fairyland." Hume's second criticism relies on his denial that we have any idea of power derived from our experience of willing our own actions. We shall examine the grounds for Hume's denial shortly. For the present, we note that if Hume is correct, we also have no idea how God's mind operates on matter. Whether the mind be human or divine, both types of causal action from the mental to the physical would be equally mysterious and incomprehensible.

According to the entailment theory (and all other necessitarian theories), causes necessitate or determine their effects. Given the cause, the effect *has* to occur. If we had a complete and perfect understanding of a particular cause, we would see why it was necessary that its effect had to follow. The cause contains the complete explanation of and reason for the effect that it produces. On Ewing's version of the entailment theory, the connection between a cause and its effect is logical. Thus, if we had a complete knowledge of the cause, we could logically deduce the occurrence of the effect.

In one set of cases—our experience of willing our own actions—it is sometimes claimed that we actually have this complete understanding of causal necessity. Our idea of causal power is derived from our own inner mental experience of the relation between willing an action and the action that is then causally produced. Thus, while most necessitarian theorists do not limit causation to willing, many regard willing as a paradigm case in which we have special insight into the objective necessity that connects causes with their effects.

In the *Treatise* and the *Enquiry*, Hume gives several criticisms of necessitarian theories of causation. The entailment version of the necessitarian theory is criticized on the grounds that for any pair of separate events that are causally related, it is always logically possible that the first occur without the second. The only way that Ewing can avoid this objection is by denying that we ever in fact have a complete knowledge of any cause. Hume's criticism does not, however, compromise theories in which the relation of causal necessity is regarded as objective but nonlogical.

In Part I of Section VII of the *Enquiry*, Hume gives several arguments against the claim that we have a special insight into the nature of the causal relation in the case of human willing of action. Hume does not deny that in the vast majority of cases, when I will to raise my right leg, my volition is followed almost immediately by my right leg going up. But he insists we are not directly aware of any causal power by which the will produces action. His two main arguments are these.

First, if we were aware of a causal power, we would know, prior to experience, which organs we can move and which not. But we do not know this. In fact, even when we have learned which organs we can will to move, there is still the possibility that a sudden paralysis might defeat our expectation. Admittedly, individual acts of will are usually described as acts of willing to do X, where X is a description of an action. What makes two acts of volition different acts is that one is an act of willing to do X and the other is an act of willing to do Y. So, when I do will to do X, it is action X and no other that can make the volition successful. In that sense, the effect (the action X) is implied by its cause (my willing to do X). But Hume's point against the necessitarian is that even though a particular act of will must be described as my willing to do X, we cannot deduce from that description alone that action X must follow. Sometimes, willing to do X is unsuccessful.

Hume's second objection is based on the physiological process by which actions are produced. A volition to raise my right leg is not the immediate cause of a leg-raising event. The volition must first activate a chain of physical causes in my brain, nerves, and muscles. The next link in this chain after the volition is some unknown event in my brain, and it is totally different from the final link, which is the motion of my right leg. If the necessitarian theory is correct, I have a complete and direct knowledge of the causal power I exercise by willing to perform a particular action. If I know what the causal power is, then I should know what its immediate effect is. But I do not know anything about the brain event that is caused by my act of willing. So, the necessitarian theory is false.

## HUME'S REGULARITY THEORY OF CAUSATION

Hume's own view is that regardless of whether the cause is an act of will or a change in a physical object, the only objective content of the claim that "A is the cause of B" is constant conjunction or, in other words, that "A's are *always* followed by B's." In Hume's view, the element of necessity in our idea of causal connection is purely subjective; it is a feeling or impression that arises from the mind's propensity to move from the impression or idea of A to the idea of B. This propensity is a primitive, psychological tendency that is hardwired into our brains. After we have experienced a number of A's that have been followed without exception by B's, we inevitably anticipate that the next A will also be a B, rather like Pavlov's dogs salivating at the sound of a bell that has always preceded their dinners. This anticipatory tendency is experienced subjectively as the *feeling* that the next A (and all future A's) *must* be a B. As far as Hume is concerned, we come to believe that A is the cause of B when all the A's we have seen have been followed by B's, and the objective content of our causal belief is exhausted by the claim that, as a matter of fact, all A's (past, present, and future) are followed by B's.

Hume's account of causal inference is the reverse of that given by necessitarian theories. According to the latter, we infer that an effect will follow only because we already believe that it is necessarily connected with its cause. According to Hume, we feel that events are necessarily connected only after and because we habitually infer the one from the other. For the necessitarian, predictions are based on causal beliefs; for the Humean regularity theorist, causal beliefs are the outcome of our predictive habits.[6]

Hume's argument for the regularity theory is based on an analysis of our idea of causation that is part psychological and part conceptual. Hume's guiding principle in this analysis is his Copy Principle that every simple idea is copied from a corresponding simple impression.[7] Thus, in analyzing our complex idea of causation, Hume first decomposes it into its constituent simple ideas (a conceptual analysis) and then tries to trace each of those simple ideas to its corresponding simple impression (a psychological analysis).

Hume is convinced that our idea of power or necessary connection, however confused it might be, is an essential part of our idea of causation. But he is also convinced that there is no simple impression of power or necessary connection in any sensation of two physical events or in any experience of willing. In Part II of Section VII of the *Enquiry*, Hume writes: "All events seem entirely loose and separate. One event follows another, but we never can observe any tie between them. They seem *conjoined*, but never *connected*."

We have already discussed Hume's grounds for denying that we have an internal impression of causal power when we will actions, but why is Hume so sure that no impression of power can be derived from observing external events? On the face of it, Hume's claim seems false. Our normal everyday way of describing our experience of the world uses many verbs that express causal judgments. We say, for example, that we saw Jack Ruby kill Lee Harvey Oswald (that is, we saw Ruby *cause* Oswald's death) or the wind whip the roof from a building or the cue ball sink the eight ball in the corner pocket. Hume's point is that all these locutions involve an element of judgment and interpretation that goes beyond what we literally see. What we literally see is a sequence of events, each separate and distinct from one another. The fact that we often employ descriptions that imply a causal connection between events does not mean that causal necessity is itself a visible feature of the world. What we see with our eyes is what, as a matter of fact, actually *does* happen; our eyes cannot see the necessary connection that determines what *must* happen.

Given Hume's Copy Principle, we might expect Hume to deny that we have any idea of power or necessary connection, since in no single case of an A followed by a B is there any impression, either of sensation or reflection, from which the idea could be derived. But Hume is convinced that it is necessary connection that makes the crucial difference between "A is followed by B" and "A causes B." So, he traces it to its only possible remaining source, a subjective feeling of anticipation engendered in our minds by experiencing *repeated* instances of A's followed by B's. Our idea of necessary connection is a projection of a subjective feeling onto the world. We have no reason to believe that this feeling corresponds to anything objectively real.

Hume summarizes his theory in two groups of definitions near the end of Section VII. In the first group, (E1) and (E2), causation is characterized objectively, without any reference to human minds. In the second group, (E3), it is characterized subjectively in terms of Hume's analysis of necessary connection.

> Similar objects are always conjoined with similar. Of this we have experience. Suitably to this experience, therefore, we may define a cause to be (E1) *an object followed by another, and where all the objects similar to the first are followed by objects similar to the second.* Or, in other words, (E2) *where, if the first object had not been, the second never had existed.* The appearance of a cause always conveys the mind, by a customary transition, to the idea of the effect. Of this also we have experience. We may, therefore, suitably to this experience, form another definition of cause and call it (E3) *an object followed by another, and whose appearance always conveys the thought to that other.*[8]

None of these three italicized statements is a definition of the meaning of causal claims in ordinary English. But then, Hume is not writing a dictionary but presenting a philosophical theory. If (E3) were a definition in the strict sense, there could be no causes in a world without minds. This also shows that (E3) is not equivalent to the first two definitions, since both of those could be satisfied in such a world. Let us now focus on the objective definitions, beginning with (E1) which expresses the core of Hume's empiricist analysis of causation.

Hume's regularity theory summarized in (E1) says that A is the cause of B when (1) B follows A and (2) all things similar to A are followed by things similar to B. I am using "thing" here broadly to include not only Hume's "objects" but also events and states of affairs.

## CRITICISMS OF HUME'S THEORY

In Reading 43, A. C. Ewing voices five main objections to Hume's regularity theory of causation. The first two of these objections are contained in Ewing's arguments for the entailment theory.

(1) If Hume's theory is true, then no inductive inference from cause to effect is justified. Only the entailment theory can solve the problem of induction.

(2) On the regularity theory, the fact that A causes B cannot explain why A's are always followed by B's. This leaves all regularities as incredible coincidences. By regarding causes as reasons for their effects, the entailment theory can explain why regularities occur.

(3) Hume's theory is unable to give an account of the causes of unique single events, such as the outbreak of World War II.

(4) Hume's theory cannot give an adequate account of psychological phenomena, such as believing something for a reason, willing, and remembering.

(5) The regularity theory implies, falsely, that all unbroken sequences of A's followed by B's are causal sequences.

Here are a few brief comments about each of these objections.

(1) Hume would agree that his theory of causation implies that induction is unjustified but dispute Ewing's claim on behalf of the entailment theory. Suppose that Hume was wrong, and that we have direct knowledge of the inner causal power by which A produces B in a particular case. It still does not follow logically that future A's will be followed by B's unless A retains its power. What is our justification, Hume would ask, for believing that A will continue to possess the same causal power in the future?

(2) If "A causes B" means nothing but "A is always followed by B," then clearly, the former cannot explain the latter. But this does not entail that all regularities are inexplicable coincidences, for laws can be explained by more general laws. For example, Newton's laws of gravity and motion explain Galileo's law of falling bodies and Kepler's laws of planetary motion.

(3) Given a sufficiently precise specification of their characteristics and their time and place of occurrence, all events are unique. To explain an event, we subsume it under some general description that can apply to other events. In the case of the outbreak of World War II, there are, presumably, generalizations about making guarantees and resisting aggression that would explain why Hitler's invasion of Poland caused England to declare war on Germany in 1939.

(4) Neither Ewing's remark about memory requiring that one's present mental state "must be genuinely determined by, not merely follow on, the past event remembered" nor his similar remark about willing determining action seems to offer an independent argument against the regularity theory. Each merely asserts what Hume denies. The point about reasons and belief is more substantial. Imagine that I first come to believe that Q on July 4, 1991 because I realize then, for the first time, that my longstanding belief, P, entails Q. The relationship between P and Q is logical; so, it has always been true that P entails Q. Thus, the content of my longstanding belief—the proposition P—does not explain why I first come to believe Q on July 4, 1991. What is crucial is my realization on that date that P entails Q. But this event can be a Humean cause if the following generalization is true: All persons who believe P and then come to realize that P entails Q are persons who come to believe Q shortly thereafter. If this generalization were not true, it is hard to see why realizing that P entails Q would causally explain my coming to believe Q. Thus, holding beliefs on the basis of one's apprehension of reasons is not inconsistent with Hume's account.

(5) This objection cuts right to the heart of Hume's theory. Thomas Reid raised it in the eighteenth century by remarking, "It follows from this definition of a cause, that night is the cause of day, and day the cause of night. For no two things have more constantly followed each other since the beginning of the world."[9] Here are some comments on Reid's day/night objection and attempts that have been made to defend Hume against it.

First, Hume's definition of cause requires that *all* A's (past, present, and future) be followed by B's, not just all the A's we have observed up until the present. Given (1) our understanding of how day and night are produced by the earth's rotation in the light cast by the sun and (2) our best theories about the formation of the solar system and its eventual fate, night and day on the planet earth have not always alternated in the past, and they will not always alternate in the future.

Second, if A's are *always* followed by B's, then it is also true that B's are *always* followed by A's only if the alternating sequence . . . A, B, A, B, A, B, . . . has no beginning and no end. I am not aware of any such sequences. If they do exist, then Hume's definition can be amended by a clause stating that for such sequences, A is neither the cause nor the effect of B. Alternatively, we could say that A is the cause of each B that immediately follows it and B is the cause of each immediately succeeding A: chickens cause eggs, and eggs cause chickens; but no chicken lays the egg from which it itself was hatched.

Third, Ewing and Reid have a telling point against Hume if their objection is lodged against Hume's explanation of the psychological mechanism by which causal beliefs are formed. The plain fact is that (1) we often form causal beliefs after just one exposure to an A followed by a B and, more crucially (2) we often fail to believe that A is the cause of B even though we have witnessed an unbroken succession of A's that are B's. With regard to (2), we think either that the association between A and B is purely coincidental, not causal, or that A and B are joint effects of a common cause as day and night are joint effects of the earth's rotation in the light cast by the sun. Thus, Hume could respond to (2) by pointing out that since his philosophical definition (E1) deliberately excludes all factors having to do with human attitudes and beliefs, his empiricist analysis of causation can survive the defeat of his psychological explanation of how causal beliefs are formed.[10]

Fourth, many people think that there is an objective difference between uniform sequences that are causal and those that are merely accidental or the effects of a common cause. Even if every child develops a fever after the appearance of a chicken pox rash on its body, the rash is not the cause of the fever. Similarly, even if night is always followed by day, night is not the cause of day. Thus, it is concluded that the Reid/Ewing criticism proves that Hume's regularity theory is false. Hume was mistaken in thinking that invariable succession exhausts the objective content of causal claims.

When John Stuart Mill defended Hume's regularity theory against Reid's day/night objection in his *System of Logic* (1843), he agreed with Hume's critics that invariable succession alone does not yield a correct analysis of causation. Mill amended Hume's definition (E1) to require not only that B follow A invariably but also that the sequence be *unconditional*.[11] An unconditional sequence is one that is "invariable under all changes of circumstances."[12] Thus, even if A has always been followed by B in our experience, if we can imagine A occurring without being followed by B, then A is not the cause of B. Put another way, Mill is requiring that a cause be a *sufficient condition* for its effect.

The problem with Mill's definition is the threat of circularity. Since Mill, like Hume and other empiricists, insists that it is logically possible that a cause occur without being followed by its effect, Mill cannot require that causes be logically sufficient for their effects. That would lead directly to Ewing's entailment theory. So, in trying to imagine worlds where A occurs without B following, we cannot consider any logically possible world. We must restrict our imagination to worlds that are *causally possible* or *physically possible*. But this means that in defining the concept of cause as invariable and unconditional sequence, Mill has made implicit use of the concept of cause in his definition.[13]

Mill is undoubtedly correct in asserting that we use our existing knowledge of causes in order to discriminate between unbroken sequences that are causal and those that are not. He writes:

> We have an experimental knowledge of the sun which justifies us on experimental grounds in concluding, that if the sun were always above the horizon there would be day, though there had been no night, and that if the sun were always below the horizon there would be night, though there had been no day. We thus know from experience that the succession of night and day is not unconditional.[14]

But this is tantamount to saying: "Since we know, from experience, that the sun's being above the horizon is the *cause* of day, we know that night is not the cause of day, even though all nights are followed by days." How, on Mill's account, could we have acquired this causal knowledge from experience alone?

## MACKIE'S CONDITIONAL ANALYSIS OF CAUSATION

Despite the phrase "in other words" which precedes it, Hume's second definition of "cause" (E2) is not equivalent to his first definition (E1). It can be true that all A's have been followed by B's and yet false that if A had not existed, then B would not have existed. In (E2), Hume has inadvertently suggested an analysis of causation entirely different from his official regularity account. (E2) proposes that a cause is *a necessary condition* in the circumstances for its effect. Thus, even if A is followed by B on a particular occasion, if B could have occurred in those circumstances in the absence of A, then A is not necessary for B and hence not the cause of B.

In his article "Causation in Concept, Knowledge, and Reality" (Reading 44), J. L. Mackie argues that counterfactual and other subjunctive conditionals (e.g., if A had not occurred, B would not have followed; if A were to occur, B would follow) are an essential part of what causal statements mean. Mackie then explains how an empiricist might find out whether or not these conditionals are true. Mackie's account of how conditional statements—and hence, causal claims—are tested has two features that are especially interesting.

First, Mackie admits that in testing conditional statements, we sometimes need to make assumptions about what he calls "the lines and direction of causation." His example in Section 3 of his article concerns an event A (a movement of the table) that has two joint effects: B (the spilling of the water in a glass) and C (the starting of a clock). Consider the following two conditionals, X and Y:

X: If the table had not moved, the clock would not have started.
Y: If the water had not spilt, the clock would not have started.

Mackie's view is that X is true and Y is false. Thus, his problem is to explain why the possible world (and hence the experimental setup) $W_1$ supports X but does not support Y.

$W_1$: The table does not move, the water does not spill, and the clock does not start.

Mackie proposes that in choosing possible worlds (and, hence, in designing experiments) to test conditionals, we select the arrangement that fulfills the antecedent by intervening from the outside in the most direct way. The most direct way to prevent the water from spilling is to cover the glass with a lid. Thus, the relevant possible world (experimental arrangement) for testing conditional Y is not $W_1$ but $W_2$.

W$_2$: The table moves, the water does not spill (because the glass is covered), and the clock starts.

Since in $W_2$ the clock starts even though the water does not spill, conditional Y is false. One might object that Mackie is tacitly making use of causal knowledge here, specifically, that preventing the table from moving is a less direct way of (causally) preventing the water from spilling than is covering the glass with a lid. Thus, we could make the same kind of circularity charge against Mackie that we brought against Mill. Mackie himself concedes that there are other acceptable ways of analyzing conditional statements such that both X and Y would be made true by $W_1$. The moral seems to be that a conditional statement such as X is not, by itself, a complete analysis of the claim that moving the table caused the clock to start.

Second, in Section 4 of his article, Mackie admits that his account of how to test conditional statements presupposes that the world exhibits regularities—laws of working, as he often calls them—that permit us to infer from an observed case to an unobserved case that is very similar to it. Only in this way, for example, can we use the experiment of preventing A *today* and seeing that B does not follow to test the claim that *yesterday* A caused B. The inference is from "Today, in circumstances very similar to yesterday's, preventing A was not followed by B," therefore, "If A had not occurred yesterday, B also would not have occurred." Thus, Mackie's account of causation assumes that inductive inferences are justified.

---

## NOTES

1. "The faculties which nature has given us, are the only engines we can use to find out the truth. We cannot indeed prove that those faculties are not fallacious, unless God should give us new faculties to sit in judgment on the old. But we are born under a necessity of trusting them." T. Reid, *Essays on the Active Powers of the Human Mind* (1785), Essay III, Chapter VI, page 237. (All page references are to the M.I.T. Press edition of Reid's works, published in 1969.)

2. See, for example, G. Berkeley, *Principles of Human Knowledge* (1710), Sections 25–26. Even one of the staunchest defenders of Hume's regularity theory in the nineteenth century, John Stuart Mill, followed Reid and other "Scotch metaphysicians" in distinguishing "efficient causes" from "physical" (or "phenomenal") causes. See J. S. Mill, *System of Logic* (1843), Book III, Chapter 5, Section 2, page 213. (All page references are to the eighth edition of the *System of Logic* published by Longmans of London, 1874; reprinted 1967.) Though Mill officially declined to "research into the ultimate or ontological cause of anything" and thus excluded efficient causes from his study, he was highly critical of the Volition theory. On page 232 he writes: "To my apprehension, a volition is not an efficient, but simply a physical cause. Our will causes our bodily actions in the same sense, and in no other, in which cold causes ice, or a spark causes an explosion of gunpowder."

3. J. Locke, *Essay*, Book II, Chapter XXI, Section 72.

4. Thus, Reid: "This power is given by his Maker, and at his pleasure whose gift it is, it may be enlarged or diminished, continued or withdrawn. No power in the creature can be

independent of the Creator. His hook is in its nose. . . ." *Active Powers*, Essay IV, Chapter 1, page 262.

5. T. Reid, *Active Powers*, Essay 1, Chapter VI.

6. Hume's theory of causation is the historical source of the modern regularity theory of scientific laws that regards them as being simply true, universal generalizations without any additional element of physical or nomic necessity. As far as modern Humeans are concerned, there is no difference in objective status among any of the following statements: (1) no material object can travel faster than light, (2) no penguins can fly, and (3) no pieces of gold have a volume greater than one cubic mile. All are true empirical generalizations; none possesses any sort of objective physical necessity.

7. In both the *Treatise* and the *Enquiry*, Hume admits a possible exception to the Copy Principle, namely, "the missing shade of blue." See *Treatise*, Book I, Part I, Section I; *Enquiry*, Section II. For further discussion, see R. Cummins, "The Missing Shade of Blue," *Philosophical Review* 87 (1978): 548–565; and L. Russow, "Simple Ideas and Resemblance," *Philosophical Quarterly* 30 (1980): 342–350.

8. Interestingly, Hume drops the requirement that causes be spatially contiguous with their effects which he had insisted on in the *Treatise*. Perhaps this was because of the success of Newton's theory of gravitational action-at-a-distance. The other two conditions—constant conjunction and temporal priority—are the same in both works.

9. T. Reid, *Active Powers*, Essay IV, Chapter IX.

10. Hume might plausibly reply to (1) by claiming that in these cases there are broader categories, X and Y, such that the observer regards A and B as yet another case of an X followed by a Y.

11. J. S. Mill, *System of Logic*, Book III, Chapter V, Section 6.

12. *System of Logic*, page 222.

13. A related charge of circularity can be made against Hume's wording of (E1) which requires that "all objects *similar* to the first" be followed by "objects *similar* to the second." Since any two objects have some properties in common and hence are similar to some degree, the case can be made that "similar" must mean "similar in *causally* relevant respects" if Hume's definition is not to be too broad. But then, the definition is circular.

14. *System of Logic*, pages 222–223.

# GLOSSARY

### Analytic

The truth (or falsity) of an analytic statement is completely determined by the meanings of the words and symbols used to express it. All tautologies (logical truths) are analytic. Analytic statements also include propositions such as "All vixens are foxes" and "No husbands are unmarried" which are true because *vixen* means "female fox" and *husband* means "married male." All analytic statements are *a priori*.

### A posteriori

An *a posteriori* (or empirical) statement can be known to be true (or false) only through experience: either one's own experience, such as seeing for oneself, or information about the world obtained from someone else's experience. Examples: Water expands when it freezes; one of Jupiter's moons has active volcanoes; Dashiell Hammett is buried in Arlington National Cemetery.

### A priori

A statement is *a priori* if it can be known to be true (or false) independently of experience (though some experience may be necessary to understand what the statement means). The clearest examples of *a priori* statements are conceptual and logical truths. Examples: Everything is identical with itself; if some mammals are herbivores, then some herbivores are mammals; all contradictions are false.

### Basic belief

A basic belief is a belief that is not based on or inferred from any other belief. Basic beliefs are psychologically direct. Typical examples include self-evident truths (e.g., I am conscious; nothing is bigger than it is) and perceptual reports (e.g., I see my hand in front of me; there are clouds in the sky).

### Categorical imperative

Imperatives are hypothetical when they say, "If you want X, then do Y!" Imperatives are categorical when they say simply "Do X!" regardless of one's wishes and desires. In Kant's deontological theory of ethics, *the categorical imperative* is the principle that one should act on a maxim only if one can will that it become a universal law.

### Category mistake

A term coined by Gilbert Ryle for the mistake committed when an object or concept that belongs in one category is treated as if it belongs in a category of a different logical type. See Reading 22 for Ryle's own examples and his claim that dualism rests on a category mistake.

## Compatibilism

The thesis that free will is compatible with determinism.

## Conditional analysis of freedom

The view, defended by many compatibilists, that "S could have done otherwise" means "S could have done otherwise if S had chosen to do otherwise."

## Conformance utility

One way of measuring the utility of a rule in rule utilitarianism. The conformance utility of a rule is the sum of the utility of all the actions that would be performed if everyone's behavior conformed to the rule.

## Consequentialism

Any theory of normative ethics is consequentialist if it judges the morality of actions or rules solely by their consequences. Utilitarianism and ethical egoism are consequentialist theories.

## Contingent

Logically contingent propositions are true in some possible worlds but not in others. Hume calls them matters of fact and existence. Examples: Elephants exist; some horses have wings; Benjamin Franklin invented bifocals.

## Counterexample

Any case (or class of cases) that refutes a generalization. Thus, Jane Austen and George Eliot are counterexamples to the generalization that women cannot write great novels; "If John is a husband, then John is a man; John is not a husband; therefore, John is not a man" is a counterexample that shows that "If P then Q; not-P; therefore, not-Q" is not a valid form of argument.

## Cultural subjectivism

The metaethical thesis that if all (or most) of the people in a given culture believe that an action is morally right (wrong, or permissible) then that action is morally right (wrong, or permissible) for the people in that culture.

## Deontological

Deontological theories of normative ethics deny that the morality of actions or rules depends solely on their consequences. Some deontological theories (such as Kant's) insist that consequences are totally irrelevant to morality; other deontological theories (such as Ross's) allow consequences a limited and partial role (e.g., in the duty of beneficence).

## Determinism

The doctrine that the past determines a unique future. This is usually understood to mean that every event is causally determined by earlier events and thus, in principle, could have been predicted, given a sufficient knowledge of those earlier events and the laws of nature.

### Emotivism

The metaethical thesis that moral utterances are neither true nor false but merely expressions of emotion intended to express the feelings of the utterer and influence the attitudes of others.

### Epiphenomenalism

The doctrine that although mental phenomena such as consciousness, sensation, belief, and emotion are caused by the brain and central nervous system, these mental phenomena are themselves causally impotent. Mental states are epiphenomenal by-products that have no causal effect on the brain or on other mental states.

### Ethical egoism

In its "impersonal" version, ethical egoism asserts that morality requires each person to act in his or her best self-interest. In its "personal" or "individual" version, ethical egoism requires everyone to act in the best interest of some designated person.

### Externalism

A family of theories in epistemology that ground knowledge in external factors, often causal ones, that are not introspectively accessible to the subject. Example: the reliability theory of knowledge.

### Fatalism

The thesis that everything that will happen in the future is inevitable, regardless of what we do now. Unlike determinists, fatalists deny that the future depends causally on the present and the past.

### Folk psychology

The theory implicit in ordinary language that explains human behavior in terms of beliefs, desires, and intentions.

### Foundationalism

In its "strong" version, the view that all knowledge and justification rest on a bedrock of basic beliefs that are justified directly, not by being inferred from any other justified beliefs. In its "modest" version, defended by some coherentists, basic beliefs are psychologically direct but epistemically indirect, deriving their justification, at least in part, from their logical and explanatory connections to other beliefs.

### Functionalism

A family of theories in philosophy of mind that define mental states by their causal relations to other mental states, stimuli, and behavior.

### Hard determinism

The doctrine that determinism is true and hence no human actions are free.

### Hedonism

Hedonists believe that only pleasure is intrinsically good and only pain is intrinsically bad. Anything else that is good or bad is so only because it either produces or prevents pleasure and pain. Jeremy Bentham and John Stuart Mill advocated hedonist versions of utilitarianism.

### Hume's law

The view, defended by Hume, that anything that is conceivable or imaginable is possible. For example, Hume argued that the doctrine that all events are caused is not a necessary truth, because he could conceive an event's occurring without its being caused.

### Identity of indiscernibles

A controversial metaphysical principle asserting that if two things have exactly the same properties, they are numerically identical. As employed by Leibniz, for example, the principle entails that it is impossible for two different objects to have exactly the same physical properties.

### Identity theory

The thesis that because everything that exists is physical, mental states are identical with brain states and minds are nothing but brains. Sometimes called reductive materialism or physicalism.

### Impossible

A proposition is *logically* impossible if it cannot be true; it is false in all possible worlds. Examples: Alligators are reptiles and alligators are not reptiles; 2 + 3 = 4; Muriel is taller than herself; some dogs are electrons; some valid arguments with true premises have false conclusions. A proposition is *physically* impossible if it describes a state of affairs that would violate a law of nature; that is, if it is inconsistent with at least one of the natural laws that hold in the actual world. Examples: Some spacecraft can travel faster than the speed of light; Jane has designed a perpetual motion machine; some human beings have survived over ten years without oxygen. All these examples are logically possible but physically impossible.

### Incompatibilism

The thesis that determinism is incompatible with free will.

### Indiscernibility of identicals

A widely accepted principle asserting that if two things are numerically identical, they have exactly the same properties.

### Intentionality

The "aboutness" of beliefs and many other mental states, usually indicated by "that" clauses. Example: If Eve believes (hopes, fears) that it will snow tomorrow, then the intentional content of her belief (hope, fear) is "It will snow tomorrow."

### Internalism

The epistemological thesis that all justification of beliefs is grounded in factors that are internal to the mind of the subject and thus introspectively accessible.

### Intuition

Something is known by intuition when it is known directly and immediately, without being inferred from anything else. For example, ethical intuitionists typically hold either that (1) the fundamental principles of ethics are self-evident truths grasped directly by reason or (2) we are made immediately aware of the moral properties of actions and situations by a special moral sense.

### Lebniz's law

The conjunction of two distinct doctrines: the identity of indiscernibles and the indiscernibility of identicals.

### Libertarianism

The doctrine that many human actions are performed freely, thus refuting universal determinism.

### Liberty of indifference

The power to perform a different action even though all the circumstances (e.g., motives, beliefs, desires) remain the same. Sometimes this is referred to as the unconditional or categorical sense of the phrase "could have done otherwise" and is often insisted upon by libertarians as the true meaning of freedom.

### Liberty of spontaneity

The ability to act as one wills. Thus, a prisoner in a locked room has the liberty to sing but lacks the liberty to leave the room. This concept of liberty is closely associated with the conditional analysis of freedom defended by compatibilists.

### Metaethics

The study of the meaning of moral terms and the nature and justification of moral statements.

### Methodological behaviorism

Sometimes called scientific behaviorism, methodological behaviorism is the insistence that theoretical terms in psychology should be connected to observable behavior in the closest possible way.

### Modus ponens

A valid form of argument: If P then Q; P; therefore, Q.

### Modus tollens

A valid form of argument: If P then Q; not-Q; therefore, not-P.

## Moral relativism

The metaethical thesis that all moral terms such as *right*, *wrong*, and *permissible* are implicitly relational.

## Moral subjectivism

The metaethical thesis that the truth or falsity of all moral statements depends on the subjective states (e.g., beliefs, attitudes, feelings) of one or more human beings.

## Necessary

A logically necessary proposition cannot be false; it is true in all possible worlds. Examples: Either alligators are reptiles or alligators are not reptiles; 2 + 3 = 5; Muriel is not taller than herself; all valid arguments with true premises have true conclusions. Necessary truths include what Hume called relations of ideas.

## Necessary condition

If X is a necessary condition for Y, then one cannot have Y in the absence of X. Being a mammal is a necessary condition for being a dog; oxygen is a necessary condition for the rusting of iron.

## Normative ethics

The main function of theories of normative ethics is to tell us which actions (or types of action) are morally right, wrong, or permissible.

## Numerical identity

Sometimes called strict or philosophical identity. Two things are numerically identical if and only if they are one and the same thing. For example, Rabat and the capital of Morocco are numerically identical; the evening star is numerically identical with the morning star; but so-called identical twins cannot be numerically identical, no matter how similar they are in appearance.

## Personal subjectivism

The metaethical thesis that when a person says that an action is morally right (wrong), all this means is that the person approves (disapproves) of it, and if the person approves (disapproves) of it, then it *is* right (wrong).

## Philosophical behaviorism

Also called logical behaviorism, philosophical behaviorism is the doctrine that all statements about the mind and mental states are really about observable behavior and dispositions to behave.

## Physicalism

The term *physicalism* has at least two distinct meanings: (1) For some philosophers it is the thesis that all empirical statements can be translated into statements about publicly observable physical objects. (2) In this text, physicalism is used simply as another name for reductive materialism or the identity theory, which is the thesis that the mind is identical with the physical brain. Behaviorists are physicalists in the first sense but not in the second.

## Possible world

For every meaningful proposition, p, a complete description of a world contains either p or the negation of p. A (logically) possible world is a world whose complete description does not contain any logically impossible proposition. The actual world is one among many other possible worlds.

## Prima facie duty

This is a technical term in the ethical theory of W. D. Ross. For Ross, a *prima facie* duty is a right-making feature of an act. If an act has a right-making feature and no wrong-making features, then it becomes one's actual duty.

## Proof

A proof is a noncircular, deductively valid argument in which we know that all the premises are true. An argument is noncircular when it is possible to know that all the premises are true without first having to know that the conclusion is true.

## Psychological determinism

The thesis, defended by Hobbes, Hume, and other soft determinists, that every human action is causally determined by the desires, beliefs, and other mental states of the person who performs it.

## Psychological egoism

An empirical thesis about human nature that claims that all motives are, at bottom, self-interested. According to psychological egoism, people are incapable of desiring anything unless they believe that it is in their self-interest, either directly or indirectly.

## Reductio ad absurdum

A special type of valid deductive reasoning in which a claim is refuted by deducing from it a false or "absurd" conclusion. In this book, *reductio* arguments are construed as arguments about other arguments, called target arguments. The *reductio* argument says of the target argument that (1) it is valid, (2) its conclusion is false, and (3) all its premises, with one exception, are true. The *reductio* argument then validly concludes that the remaining premise of the target argument is false.

## Reliabilism

A family of externalist theories of knowledge in which knowledge is defined as true belief caused by a reliable process. A process is perfectly reliable if it yields the belief that P only when P is true.

### Semantics

The study of what signs mean and how they are related to what they signify. Theories about what words and sentences mean and theories about what makes sentences true are semantical theories.

### Sense-data

"Sense-data" is the plural of "sense-datum". The word *datum* is Latin for "given." A sense-datum is what we are immediately aware of (or "given") when we are perceiving something—or think we are perceiving something—by means of our senses. Sense-data are the appearances of things. They exist only when they are being perceived. Prior to the twentieth century, philosophers called them impressions, ideas, sensations, or perceptions.

### Soft determinism

The thesis that both determinism and compatibilism are true.

### Sound

A sound argument is valid and all its premises are true.

### Sufficient condition

If X is a sufficient condition for Y, then anything that is X must also be Y. Having atomic number 79 is sufficient for an atom to be gold; under normal circumstances, an open flame in the presence of gasoline is sufficient to produce a fire.

### Syntax

Syntax or syntactics is the study of signs independently of what the signs stand for or signify. For example, the rules governing the construction of grammatical sentences in a language are part of the language's syntax. In general, syntactics is concerned solely with the formal properties of a language, not with what the terms in the language mean. In logic, the syntax of a formal (or uninterpreted) system includes rules for the construction of well-formed formulas and rules for the derivation of theorems from the axioms of the system.

### Synthetic

A synthetic statement is not true (or false) simply by virtue of the words and symbols used to express it.

### Target argument

See *Reductio ad absurdum*.

### Tautology

A tautology is any statement that is true solely by virtue of its logical form. Examples: If pigs have wings, then pigs have wings; either cyanide is poisonous or cyanide is not poisonous.

### Theodicy

Originally the name of a work in which Leibniz tried to solve the problem of evil, it is now used to refer to any attempt to explain why God permits evil.

### Token physicalism

The thesis, accepted by all physicalists, that for every particular mental state (process, or event), there is a particular physical state (process, or event) with which it is identical. But different organisms (and, perhaps, computers) might realize the same type of mental state in physically different ways. Thus, every token of a mental type is identical with a token of a physical type, but it is not necessary that each mental type involve the *same* physical type.

### Turing machine

A simple type of deterministic machine conceived by Alan Turing. The machine consists of a read-write head and an infinitely long tape that the head scans, one cell at a time. Whenever the head lands on a cell, it reads what is there. The head then writes on the present cell (replacing whatever was there previously), and it either stays put and scans the same cell again, halts completely, or moves one cell to the right or one cell to the left and scans that cell. Which action the machine performs is determined entirely by what it reads on the present cell (the input) and the internal state the machine is in. Those two factors also determine the next internal state of the machine. Each Turing machine is completely specified by its machine table, which lists the action the machine will perform in response to each possible combination of input and internal state.

### Turing test

A behavioristic test proposed by Alan Turing for answering the question, Can machines think?

### Type physicalism

The thesis, rejected by functionalists, that mental states of the same kind must always involve the same kind of physical state. In other words, all tokens of the same mental type are identical with tokens of the same physical type.

### Utility

A technical term in utilitarianism. The utility of an action is the total amount of nonmoral good minus the total amount of nonmoral bad produced by the action when summed over everyone affected by the action. Hedonist versions of utilitarianism identify nonmoral good with pleasure (or happiness) and nonmoral bad with pain (or unhappiness).

### Valid

In a valid argument, the premises logically imply the conclusion. Hence, if all the premises of a valid argument are true, then the argument's conclusion must also be true. It is impossible for a valid argument with true premises to have a false conclusion.

### Virtual machine

A virtual machine is created when one computer is programmed to behave as a computer with different basic functions or as more than one computer (as in time sharing).

# SUGGESTIONS FOR FURTHER READING

This bibliography is restricted to books and anthologies. For further references to papers and articles, see the discussion footnotes.

## GENERAL INTRODUCTION

Cornman, James W., Keith Lehrer, and George S. Pappas. *Philosophical Problems and Arguments: An Introduction*, 3rd edition (Indianapolis: Hackett, 1987). A detailed exploration of key issues and arguments at a fairly advanced level. The book includes a comprehensive bibliography of books and articles.

Cover, J. A., and Rudy L. Garns. *Theories of Knowledge and Reality: An Introduction to the Problems and Arguments of Philosophy*, revised edition (New York: McGraw-Hill, 1990). A lively discussion of central arguments and ideas.

Edwards, Paul, Ed. *Encyclopedia of Philosophy* (New York: Macmillan, 1967), 8 volumes. An indispensable resource for all areas of philosophy and its history.

Flew, Antony. *A Dictionary of Philosophy*, revised 2nd edition (New York: St. Martin's Press, 1984). A reliable single-volume guide to the major figures and ideas in philosophy.

Hospers, John. *An Introduction to Philosophical Analysis*, 3rd edition (Englewood Cliffs, NJ: Prentice-Hall, 1988). One of the best single-author texts at an introductory level.

Russow, Lilly-Marlene, and Martin Curd, *Principles of Reasoning* (New York: St. Martin's, 1989). An introductory treatment of deductive and inductive reasoning in a variety of contexts.

Weston, Anthony. *A Rulebook for Arguments* (Indianapolis: Hackett, 1987). A concise guide to the most common types of deductive and inductive arguments.

Woodhouse, Mark B. *A Preface to Philosophy*, 4th edition (Belmont, CA: Wadsworth, 1990). A general survey of the scope and methods of philosophy. Intended for beginning students, it has chapters on how to do philosophy, read texts, and write papers.

## PART I: THE RATIONALITY OF RELIGIOUS BELIEF

Adams, Marilyn McCord, and Robert Merrihew Adams, Eds. *The Problem of Evil* (Oxford: Oxford University Press, 1990). An up-to-date collection including papers by W. L. Rowe and S. J. Wykstra on the evidential problem of evil.

Angeles, Peter, Ed. *Critiques of God* (Buffalo, NY: Prometheus Books, 1976). Arguments for atheism and attacks on theism from a variety of philosophical perspectives.

Brody, Baruch A., Ed. *Readings in the Philosophy of Religion: An Analytic Approach* (Englewood Cliffs, NJ: Prentice-Hall, 1974). A comprehensive anthology.

Burrill, Donald R., Ed. *The Cosmological Arguments* (Garden City, NY: Doubleday, 1967). This volume also includes a section on the teleological argument.

Delaney, C. F., Ed. *Rationality and Religious Belief* (Notre Dame, IN: University of Notre Dame Press, 1979). Contains A. Plantinga, "Is Belief in God Rational?", an anti-foundationalist defense of religious belief.

Helm, Paul, Ed. *Divine Commands and Morality* (New York: Oxford University Press, 1981). A collection of recent articles on the connections between religion and morality.

Hick, John, Ed. *The Existence of God* (New York: Macmillan, 1964). A useful anthology that includes the debate between Bertrand Russell and F. C. Copleston and a section on verification and falsification.

Hick, John. *Philosophy of Religion*, 4th edition (Englewood Cliffs, NJ: Prentice-Hall, 1990). A good, short introduction by an author sympathetic to theism.

Hick, John, and Arthur C. McGill, Eds. *The Many-faced Argument* (New York: Macmillan, 1967). A comprehensive collection of papers on the ontological argument.

Hume, David. *Dialogues on Natural Religion*, Ed. N. Pike (Indianapolis: Bobbs-Merrill, 1970). This edition contains a valuable essay by Pike on Hume's treatment of the design argument.

Kenny, Anthony. *The Five Ways: St. Thomas Aquinas' Proofs of God's Existence* (Notre Dame, IN: University of Notre Dame Press, 1980). One of the clearest discussions of Aquinas's arguments.

Mackie, J. L. *The Miracle of Theism* (Oxford: Clarendon Press, 1982). A provocative attack on theistic arguments by a prominent atheist philosopher.

Matson, Wallace I. *The Existence of God* (Ithaca, NY: Cornell University Press, 1965). Matson criticizes all the traditional arguments for God's existence.

Pike, Nelson, Ed. *God and Evil* (Englewood Cliffs, NJ: Prentice-Hall, 1964). Readings on the problem of evil, including H. J. McCloskey, "God and Evil" and N. Pike, "Hume on Evil."

Plantinga, Alvin, Ed. *The Ontological Argument* (Garden City, NY: Doubleday, 1965). Contains modern discussions of the ontological argument by G. E. Moore, W. P. Alston, C. Hartshorne, and N. Malcolm.

Plantinga, Alvin. *God, Freedom and Evil* (New York: Harper & Row, 1974). A good source for Plantinga's version of the free-will defense.

Plantinga, Alvin, and Nicholas Wolterstorff, Eds. *Faith and Rationality: Reason and Belief in God* (Notre Dame, IN: University of Notre Dame Press, 1983). This collection includes A. Plantinga, "Reason and Belief in God" and N. Wolterstorff, "Can Belief in God Be Rational If It Has No Foundations?"

Rowe, William L. *Philosophy of Religion* (Encino, CA: Dickenson, 1978). An exceptionally clear introductory text containing influential interpretations of the ontological and cosmological arguments.

Rowe, William L. and William J. Wainwright, Eds. *Philosophy of Religion: Selected Readings*, 2nd edition (New York: Harcourt Brace Jovanovich, 1989). A comprehensive anthology.

Swinburne, Richard. *The Existence of God* (Oxford: Clarendon Press, 1979). A defense of theism. Swinburne argues that many of the traditional attempts to prove God's existence should be regarded as inductive arguments, not deductive ones, and that these arguments show that it is probable that God exists.

Wainwright, William J. *Mysticism* (Madison, WI: University of Wisconsin Press, 1981). A thorough examination of the nature of religious experience and its philosophical significance.

Wainwright, William J. *Philosophy of Religion* (Belmont, CA: Wadsworth, 1988). In this introductory text, Wainwright discusses some recent developments in philosophy of religion and pays attention to non-Western religious traditions.

## PART II: THE FOUNDATIONS OF MORALITY

Acton, H. B. *Kant's Moral Philosophy* (London: Macmillan, 1970). A short, simple introduction to a difficult topic.

Feldman, Fred. *Introductory Ethics* (Englewood Cliffs, NJ: Prentice-Hall, 1978). An introductory text noteworthy for the clarity with which it reconstructs and evaluates arguments.

Frankena, William K. *Ethics*, 2nd edition (Englewood Cliffs, NJ: Prentice-Hall, 1973). A clear, brief introduction to ethics.

Frankena, William K. *Thinking about Morality* (Ann Arbor, MI: University of Michigan Press, 1980). Three lectures on the nature of morality, being moral, and the question, Why be moral?

Gauthier, David P., Ed. *Morality and Rational Self-Interest* (Englewood Cliffs, NJ: Prentice-Hall, 1970). Core readings on the rationality of ethical egoism and its adequacy as a normative theory of ethics.

Glover, Jonathan, Ed. *Utilitarianism and Its Critics* (New York: Macmillan, 1990). A useful collection of readings on all aspects of utilitarianism, many by contemporary philosophers.

Gorovitz, Samuel, Ed. *Mill: Utilitarianism with Critical Essays* (Indianapolis: Bobbs-Merill, 1971). This volume reprints many influential papers on utilitarianism, including R. B. Brandt, "Some Merits of One Form of Rule-Utilitarianism"; J. O. Urmson, "The Interpretation of the Philosophy of J. S. Mill"; and J. Rawls, "Two Concepts of Rules."

Harman, Gilbert. *The Nature of Morality* (New York: Oxford University Press, 1977). An introduction to ethics that focuses on metaethical issues such as relativism, conventionalism, and the relation between morality and reason. Harman rejects moral objectivism on the grounds that we can explain our moral beliefs without having to postulate the existence of objective ethical facts.

Hospers, John. *Human Conduct: Problems of Ethics*, 2nd edition (New York: Harcourt Brace Jovanovich, 1982). A lively and thorough introduction containing stimulating exercises for the reader at the end of each chapter.

Ladd, John, Ed. *Ethical Relativism* (Belmont, CA: Wadsworth, 1973). A useful collection of readings, many of them sympathetic to moral relativism and cultural subjectivism.

MacIntyre, Alasdair. *A Short History of Ethics* (New York: Macmillan, 1966). One of the best short histories of ethics.

Mackie, J. L. *Ethics: Inventing Right and Wrong* (London: Penguin, 1977). Mackie rejects moral objectivism. He argues that we can understand morality as a rational system for regulating conduct without assuming that there are any objective moral values or properties that make moral statements true.

Moore, G. E. *Ethics* (London: Oxford University Press, 1912). A classic defense of moral objectivism. This short work also contains Moore's version of act utilitarianism and his defense of compatibilism.

Paton, H. J. *The Categorical Imperative: A Study in Kant's Moral Philosophy* (New York: Harper & Row, 1967). A detailed guide to Kant's *Groundwork*.

Rachels, James. *The Elements of Moral Philosophy* (New York: Random House, 1986). A short, clear introduction.

Rachels, James, Ed. *The Right Thing To Do* (New York: Random House, 1989). An anthology of basic readings that nicely complements Rachels' *Elements*.

Ross, W. D. *Kant's Ethical Theory* (Westport, CT: Greenwood Press, 1978). A short critical commentary on Kant's *Groundwork*.

Singer, Peter. *Practical Ethics* (Cambridge: University of Cambridge Press, 1979). A provocative discussion of social issues from discrimination, civil disobedience, and animal rights to abortion and euthanasia. Singer defends a utilitarian position.

Singer, Peter, Ed. *Applied Ethics* (New York: Oxford University Press, 1986). Many of the papers in this collection either attack or defend utilitarianism. They include J. Harris, "The Survival Lottery"; D. Parfit, "Overpopulation and the Quality of Life"; and R. M. Hare, "What Is Wrong with Slavery?".

Smart, J.J.C., and Bernard Williams. *Utilitarianism: For and Against* (Cambridge: Cambridge University Press, 1973). Smart defends act utilitarianism; Williams attacks it.

Taylor, Paul W. *Principles of Ethics: An Introduction* (Belmont, CA: Wadsworth, 1975). A comprehensive introductory text.

## PART III: THE NATURE OF MIND

Anderson, Alan Ross, Ed. *Minds and Machines* (Englewood Cliffs, NJ: Prentice-Hall, 1964). A collection of classic papers including A. M. Turing, "Computing Machinery and Intelligence," and Hilary Putnam, "Minds and Machines."

Armstrong, D. M., and Norman Malcolm. *Consciousness and Causality* (Oxford: Basil Blackwell, 1984). Armstrong, a materialist, defends the functionalist thesis that mental states are brain states with certain distinctive causal powers. Malcolm, following Wittgenstein, argues that it is a mistake to think of the mind as something inside us that causes behavior.

Baker, Lynne Rudder. *Saving Belief: A Critique of Physicalism* (Princeton, NJ: Princeton University Press, 1987). A vigorous attack on both reductive and eliminative materialism. Advanced.

Campbell, Keith. *Body and Mind*, 2nd edition (Notre Dame, IN: University of Notre Dame Press, 1984). A short introduction to the mind-body problem, with a useful bibliography. In Chapter 7, Campbell defends a version of epiphenomenalism.

Churchland, Paul M. *Matter and Consciousness*, revised edition (Cambridge, MA: MIT Press, 1988). In this introductory text, Churchland argues that recent developments in neurophysiology, artificial intelligence, and cognitive science support eliminative materialism.

Flew, Antony, Ed. *Body, Mind, and Death* (New York: Macmillan, 1964). Classic writings on the possibility of surviving death.

Fodor, Jerry, A. *Psychological Explanation: An Introduction to the Philosophy of Psychology* (New York: Random House, 1968). Fodor criticizes behaviorism and defends functionalism as the best theory of mind for explaining human behavior.

Glover, Jonathan. *I: The Philosophy and Psychology of Personal Identity* (London: Penguin, 1988). A wide-ranging discussion for a general audience.

Gunderson, Keith. *Mentality and Machines*, 2nd edition (Minneapolis: University of Minnesota Press, 1985). A lively and influential critique of the Turing test as a criterion of machine intelligence.

Haugeland, John, Ed. *Mind Design* (Cambridge, MA: MIT Press, 1981). A successor to the Anderson anthology at a more advanced level.

Haugeland, John. *Artificial Intelligence: The Very Idea* (Cambridge, MA: MIT Press, 1985). An exceptionally clear introduction to the central ideas and issues in artificial intelligence.

Malcolm, Norman. *Problems of Mind: Descartes to Wittgenstein* (New York: Harper & Row, 1971). A short work attacking dualism, materialism, and behaviorism from the standpoint of the philosophy of the later Wittgenstein.

Noonan, Harold W. *Personal Identity* (London and New York: Routledge, 1989). As well as defending his own theory of personal identity, Noonan explains and criticizes the views of Locke, Hume, Williams, Shoemaker, and Parfit.

O'Connor, John, Ed. *Modern Materialism: Readings on Mind-Body Identity* (New York: Harcourt, Brace & World, 1969). A useful collection including papers by U. T. Place, R. Rorty, J. Kim, and H. Putnam.

Parfit, Derek. *Reasons and Persons* (Oxford: Clarendon Press, 1984). Parfit defends the reductionist thesis that there is nothing more to personal identity than psychological continuity and explores its implications for morality. A large book, crammed with challenging arguments. Advanced.

Perry, John, Ed. *Personal Identity* (Berkeley, CA: University of California Press, 1975). A useful collection of core readings from Locke, Hume, Butler, and Reid accompanied by some influential papers by modern philosophers, including B. Williams, "The Self and the Future", S. Shoemaker, "Personal Identity and Memory"; J. Perry, "Personal Identity, Memory, and the Problem of Circularity"; and D. Parfit, "Personal Identity."

Rosenthal, David M. *Materialism and the Mind-Body Problem* (Englewood Cliffs, NJ: Prentice-Hall, 1971). Contains papers on the identity theory, functionalism, and eliminative materialism.

Ryle, Gilbert. *The Concept of Mind* (London: Hutchinson, 1949). An influential attack on Cartesian dualism. Ryle defends logical behaviorism.

Searle, John. *Minds, Brains and Science* (Cambridge, MA: Harvard University Press, 1984). Originally given as the 1984 Reith Lectures and broadcast by BBC radio, this is a good introduction to Searle's views.

Shaffer, Jerome A. *Philosophy of Mind* (Englewood Cliffs, NJ: Prentice-Hall, 1968). A good general introduction.

Shoemaker, Sydney, and Richard Swinburne. *Personal Identity* (Oxford: Basil Blackwell, 1984). A contemporary debate between a materialist (Shoemaker) and a dualist (Swinburne).

## PART IV: DETERMINISM AND FREE WILL

Dennett, Daniel. *Elbow Room: The Varieties of Free Will Worth Wanting* (Cambridge, MA: MIT Press, 1984). A lively and iconoclastic defense of compatibilism.

Fischer, John Martin, Ed. *Moral Responsibility* (Ithaca, NY: University of Cornell Press, 1986). Some of the best recent articles on freedom, incompatibilism, and responsibility. The volume includes H. G. Frankfurt, "Alternate Possibilities and Moral Responsibility," and a very helpful introduction by the editor. The level is quite advanced.

Flew, Antony, and Godfrey Vesey. *Agency and Necessity* (Oxford: Basil Blackwell, 1987). Flew and Vesey debate the relationship between event causation and agent causation in explaining human action. Both authors reject determinism, but for different reasons.

French, Peter A., Ed. *The Spectrum of Responsibility* (New York: St. Martin's, 1991). An interesting selection of writings, mostly by twentieth-century philosophers, on many different aspects of the concept of responsibility. The volume includes discussions of blaming, collective responsibility, and ascribing responsibility for omissions.

Honderich, Ted, Ed. *Essays on Freedom of Action* (London: Routledge & Kegan Paul, 1973). This collection includes A. Kenny, "Freedom, Spontaneity, and Indifference," and H. G. Frankfurt, "Coercion and Moral Responsibility."

Hook, Sidney, Ed. *Determinism and Freedom in the Age of Modern Science* (New York: Macmillan, 1961). The proceedings of a symposium held in New York City in 1957. Most of the papers are written for a general audience.

Kenny, Anthony, *Freewill and Responsibility* (New York: Routledge & Kegan Paul, 1978). Four lectures on the concept of responsibility in criminal law. In the second lecture, Kenny summaries his defense of compatibilism.

Klein, Martha. *Determinism, Blameworthiness and Deprivation* (Oxford: Clarendon Press, 1990). Klein agrees with libertarians that genuine, ideal responsibility must satisfy the U- (or ultimacy) condition: choices for which an agent is blameworthy should not be caused by factors for which the agent is not responsible. But, Klein argues, the U-condition cannot be fulfilled. She proposes a revised, compatibilist criterion of blameworthiness as the best we can hope for. Advanced.

Lehrer, Keith, Ed. *Freedom and Determinism* (New York: Random House, 1966). An anthology of modern papers. Advanced.

O'Connor, D. J. *Free Will* (Garden City, NY: Doubleday, 1971). An introductory survey of the traditional arguments and positions.

Van Inwagen, Peter. *An Essay on Free Will* (Oxford: Clarendon Press, 1983). A rigorous and careful analysis by a leading critic of compatibilism. Advanced.

Watson, Gary, Ed. *Free Will* (Oxford: Oxford University Press, 1982). A useful collection of articles, including A. J. Ayer, "Freedom and Necessity"; P. Strawson, "Freedom and Resentment"; T. Nagel, "Moral Luck"; and D. C. Dennett, "Mechanism and Responsibility."

## PART V: KNOWLEDGE, SKEPTICISM, AND CAUSATION

Audi, Robert. *Belief, Justification, and Knowledge* (Belmont, CA: Wadsworth, 1988). An up-to-date introduction to epistemology focusing on the sources of knowledge and the justification of belief.

Ayer, A. J. *The Problem of Knowledge* (London: Penguin, 1956). A response to skepticism by a leading twentieth-century empiricist.

Ayer, A. J. *Hume* (New York: Farrar, Straus and Giroux, 1980). A concise account of Hume's life and thought in the "Past Masters" series.

Beauchamp, Tom L., and Alexander Rosenberg. *Hume and the Problem of Causation* (New York: Oxford University Press, 1981). A detailed exposition and defense of Hume's theory of causation. Advanced.

BonJour, Laurence. *The Structure of Empirical Knowledge* (Cambridge, MA: Harvard University Press, 1985). BonJour criticizes foundationalism and reliabilism and defends a coherence theory of knowledge.

Chisholm, Roderick, M. *Theory of Knowledge*, 3rd edition (Englewood Cliffs, NJ: Prentice-Hall, 1988). A rigorous introduction, foundationalist in spirit.

Doney, Willis, Ed. *Descartes: A Collection of Critical Essays* (Garden City, NY: Doubleday, 1967). Contains many seminal articles, including G. E. Moore, "Certainty"; N. Malcolm, "Dreaming and Skepticism" and "Descartes's Proof that His Essence Is Thinking."

Hamlyn, D. W. *The Theory of Knowledge* (Garden City, NY: Doubleday, 1970). A comprehensive introduction to epistemology from a Wittgensteinian perspective.

Harman, Gilbert. *Thought* (Princeton, NJ: Princeton University Press, 1973). A coherentist response to skepticism and the Gettier examples. Harman defends the view that perception involves inference to the best explanation.

Harré, R., and E. H. Madden. *Causal Powers: A Theory of Natural Necessity* (Oxford: Basil Blackwell, 1975). A sustained attack on Hume's regularity theory of causation.

Hooker, Michael, Ed. *Descartes: Critical and Interpretative Essays* (Baltimore: Johns Hopkins University Press, 1978). A sequel to the Doney anthology at a more advanced level.

Kenny, Anthony. *Descartes: A Study of His Philosophy* (New York: Random House, 1968). A valuable guide to the topics discussed in Descartes' *Meditations*.

Lehrer, Keith. *Knowledge* (Oxford: Clarendon Press, 1974). Lehrer criticizes foundationalism and externalism and defends an explanatory coherence theory of justification.

Lehrer, Keith. *Theory of Knowledge* (Boulder, CO: Westview, 1990). A sequel to *Knowledge* written as a textbook for students.

Mackie, J. L. *The Cement of the Universe: A Study of Causation* (Oxford: Clarendon Press, 1974). Extremely thorough and quite advanced.

Moser, Paul K., and Arnold vander Nat, Eds. *Human Knowledge: Classical and Contemporary Approaches* (New York: Oxford University Press, 1987). A comprehensive anthology.

Pappas, George S., and Marshall Swain, Eds. *Essays on Knowledge and Justification* (Ithaca, NY: University of Cornell Press, 1978). A collection of influential research papers in epistemology published since 1960. Some are quite advanced.

Putnam, Hilary. *Reason, Truth and History* (Cambridge: Cambridge University Press, 1981). Chapter 1 contains Putnam's dismissal of the hypothesis that we might be brains in a vat.

Roth, Michael D., and Leon Galis, Eds. *Knowing: Essays in the Analysis of Knowledge*, 2nd edition (Lanham, MD: University Press of America, 1984). Intended for undergraduate epistemology courses, this collection of papers is centered around Edmund Gettier's "Is Justified True Belief Knowledge?"

Russell, Bertrand. *The Problems of Philosophy* (New York: Oxford University Press, 1912). A modern classic, short and readable, focusing mainly on epistemological topics.

Salmon, Wesley C. *The Foundations of Scientific Inference* (Pittsburgh: University of Pittsburgh Press, 1967). A good introduction to the problem of induction and interpretations of probability.

Stroud, Barry. *The Significance of Philosophical Scepticism* (Oxford: Clarendon Press, 1984). Stroud's book is centered on the problem of the external world as posed by Descartes' dream argument. He also discusses Moore, Kant, Carnap, and Quine.

Swartz, Norman. *The Concept of Physical Law* (Cambridge: Cambridge University Press, 1985). Swartz attacks the necessitarian theory of laws and defends the regularity theory. Chapters 10 and 11 contain a remarkable defense of compatibilism: Laws do not necessitate human choice; rather, which laws are true of the world depends, in part, on what human beings choose to do.

Swartz, Robert J., Ed. *Perceiving, Sensing and Knowing* (Garden City, NY: Doubleday, 1965; reprinted by the University of California Press, 1976). A collection of writings on the philosophy of perception from the first half of the twentieth century. Advanced.

Swinburne, Richard, Ed. *The Justification of Induction* (Oxford: Oxford University Press, 1974). This volume contains several important attempts to answer Hume's skepticism about induction.

Vesey, Godfrey. *Perception* (Garden City, NY: Doubleday, 1971). A short work attacking the causal theory of perception. Vesey argues that the problem of the external world arises from a philosophical mistake and that the relation between appearance and reality is not causal but conceptual.

Wilson, Margaret Dauler. *Descartes* (London: Routledge & Kegan Paul, 1978). A lucid account of Descartes' philosophy, concentrating on the *Meditations*.

# PERMISSIONS

Reading 1. Reprinted from *St. Anselm: Basic Writings*, trans. S. N. Deane, with an Introduction by Charles Hartshorne, 2nd edition (La Salle, IL: Open Court, 1962) by permission of The Open Court Publishing Company, La Salle, Illinois. Copyright © 1962 by The Open Court Publishing Company.

Reading 2. From *The Basic Writings of Saint Thomas Aquinas*, ed. Anton C. Pegis (New York: Random House, 1945). Reprinted by permission of the A. C. Pegis Estate.

Reading 5. "Evil and Omnipotence," by J. L. Mackie from *Mind* vol 64 (1955) pp. 200–212. Reprinted by permission of Oxford University Press.

Reading 6. Reprinted from *Pensées* by Pascal translated by A. J. Krailsheimer (London: Penguin Classics, 1966) pp. 150–153. Copyright © A. J. Krailsheimer, 1966. Reproduced by permission of Penguin Books Ltd.

Reading 9. From C. D. Broad, *Religion, Philosophy and Psychical Research* (London: Routledge & Kegan Paul, 1953) pp. 190–201. Reprinted by permission of Routledge & Kegan Paul Ltd.

Reading 10. Reprinted with the permission of Macmillan Publishing Company from *New Essays in Philosophical Theology* by Anthony Flew and Alasdair MacIntyre, editors. Copyright 1955 by Anthony Flew and Alasdair MacIntyre; copyright renewed © 1963.

Reading 11. Reprinted from James Rachels, *The Right Thing To Do: Basic Readings in Moral Philosophy.* Copyright © 1989 by Random House, Inc. Reproduced by permission of McGraw Hill Publishing Company.

Reading 12. From *The Nature of Morality: An Introduction to Ethics* by Gilbert Harman. Copyright © 1977 by Oxford University Press, Inc. Reprinted by permission.

Reading 14. Reprinted from *The Philosophical Quarterly* Vol. 6 (1956) with revisions by the author. Reproduced by permission of the author and Basil Blackwell Inc.

Reading 15. From J. J. C. Smart and B. Williams, *Utilitarianism: For and Against* © Cambridge University Press 1973. Reprinted with the permission of Cambridge University Press.

Reading 29.  From *Philosophy and Phenomenological Research* 48 (March 1988) 519–532. Reprinted by permission of the author and *Philosophy and Phenomenological Research.*

Reading 31.  From *Determinism and Freedom in the Age of Modern Science*, ed. S. Hook (New York: New York University Press, 1958; reprinted by Macmillan, 1961). Reprinted by permission of New York University Press.

Reading 32.  From *American Philosophical Quarterly* 5 (1968) 135–151. Reprinted with permission of the author and the editor of *American Philosophical Quarterly.*

Reading 33.  From *Proceedings and Addresses of the APA* (September 1987) Supplement to Volume 61, #1, 43–64. Reprinted by permission of the author and the American Philosophical Association.

Reading 34.  Extract taken from C. A. Campbell *On Selfhood and Godhood* (London: George Allen & Unwin, 1957) Lecture IX, 158–179. Reproduced by kind permission of Unwin Hyman Ltd.

Reading 35.  From Richard Taylor, METAPHYSICS, 3e, © 1983, pp. 41–50. Reprinted by permission of Prentice-Hall, Inc., Englewood Cliffs, New Jersey.

Reading 36.  From *The Philosophical Works of Descartes*, Volume 1 (London: Cambridge University Press, 1931), translated and edited by Elizabeth S. Haldane and G. R. T. Ross. Reprinted with the permission of Cambridge University Press.

Reading 37.  From Bertrand Russell, *The Problems of Philosophy* (London: Oxford University Press, 1912) Chapters I and II, pp. 7–26. Reprinted by permission of Oxford University Press.

Reading 38.  From *Belief, Justification, and Knowledge: An Introduction to Epistemology* by Robert Audi © 1988 by Wadsworth, Inc. Reprinted by permission of the publisher.

Reading 40.  From *Philosophical Studies* 33 (1978) 1–19. Reprinted by permission of Kluwer Academic Publishers.

Reading 41.  James Van Cleve, "Reliability, Justification, and the Problem of Induction," *Midwest Studies in Philosophy IX 1984, Causation and Causal Theories*, edited by Peter French, Theodore Uehling, Jr., and Howard Wettstein. Copyright © 1984 by the University of Minnesota. Reprinted by permission of the University of Minnesota Press.

Reading 43.  From A. C. Ewing, *The Fundamental Questions of Philosophy* (London: Routledge & Kegan Paul, 1951), Chapter 8. Reprinted by permission of Routledge & Kegan Paul Ltd.